Dear Reader,

We are delighted to present the 2019 edition of the Michelin Main Cities of Europe guide – which for the first time includes the cities of Reykjavik in Iceland and Dubrovnik and Zagreb in Croatia.

This guide lists the best restaurants in a wide selection of European cities, so whether you're on holiday with your family or travelling with work; looking for a cosy bistro or a luxurious dining room; and fancying Italian or Thai cuisine; you'll find a restaurant within these pages that's right for you.

All the restaurants in the guide have been selected by our team of Michelin inspectors, who are the eyes and ears of our readers. Every year they search for new establishments to add to the guide – and only the best make it through. The Michelin Plate symbol highlights to our readers restaurants where you will enjoy a good meal; the 'best of the best' are recognised with Michelin Stars and Bib Gourmands.

We trust you will enjoy travelling with the 2019 edition of our Main Cities of Europe guide.

The MICHELIN Guide's Commitments

Experienced in quality!

Whether they are in Japan, the USA, China or Europe, our inspectors apply the same criteria to judge the quality of each and every restaurant that they visit. The MICHELIN guide commands a worldwide reputation thanks to the commitments we make to our readers – and we reiterate these below:

ANONYMOUS INSPECTIONS

Our inspectors make regular and anonymous visits to restaurants to gauge the quality of products and services offered to an ordinary customer. They settle their own bill and may then introduce themselves and ask for more information about the establishment. Our readers' comments are also a valuable source of information, which we can follow up with a visit of our own.

INDEPENDENCE

To remain totally objective for our readers, the selection is made with complete independence. Entry into the guide is free. All decisions are discussed with the Editor and our highest awards are considered at a European level.

SELECTION AND CHOICE

The guide offers a selection of the best restaurants in every category of comfort and price. This is only possible because all the inspectors rigorously apply the same methods.

ANNUAL UPDATES

All the practical information, classifications and awards are revised and updated every year to give the most reliable information possible.

CONSISTENCY

The criteria for the classifications are the same in every country covered by the MICHELIN guide.

The sole intention of Michelin is to make your travels safe and enjoyable.

THE MICHELIN GUIDE

2019

MAIN CITIES OF EUROPE

The MICHELIN Guide's Distinctions

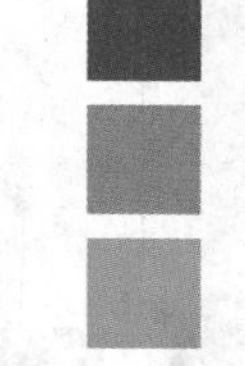

To help you select the best establishment for every occasion, we award several distinctions:

✿✿✿ **Three Stars: Exceptional cuisine, worth a special journey!**
Our highest award is given for the superlative cooking of chefs at the peak of their profession. The ingredients are exemplary, the cooking is elevated to an art form and their dishes are often destined to become classics.

✿✿ **Two Stars: Excellent cooking, worth a detour!**
The personality and talent of the chef and their team is evident in the expertly crafted dishes, which are refined, inspired and sometimes original.

✿ **One Star: High quality cooking, worth a stop!**
Using top quality ingredients, dishes with distinct flavours are carefully prepared to a consistently high standard.

Bib Gourmand: Good quality, good value cooking
'Bibs' are awarded for simple yet skilful cooking.

Plate: Good cooking
Fresh ingredients, capably prepared: simply a good meal.

Our famous one ✿, two ✿✿ and three ✿✿✿ stars identify establishments serving the highest quality cuisine – taking into account the quality of ingredients, the mastery of techniques and flavours, the levels of creativity and, of course, consistency.

Contents

Consult the MICHELIN guide at: www.ViaMichelin.com
and write to us at: themichelinguide-europe@michelin.com

Countries

How to use this Guide

RESTAURANTS

Restaurants are listed by distinction.
Within each distinction category, they are ordered by comfort.
Within each comfort category, they are then ordered alphabetically.

Distinctions:

- ✿✿✿ Three Stars: Exceptional cuisine
- ✿✿ Two Stars: Excellent cooking
- ✿ One Star: High quality cooking
- ☺ Bib Gourmand: Good quality, good value cooking
- 🍴 Plate: Good cooking

Comfort:

Level of comfort from XXXXX to X, followed by 🍷 for tapas bars and 🍺 for pubs.
Red: our most delightful places.

MONTM

MONTMARTRE – PIGALLE

✿✿ **Les Trois Maisons**
151bis r. Marcadet (18th) – Ⓜ Lamarck Ca
– ✆ 01 42 57 71 22 – www.troismaisons.fr
and August
Menu 47 € – Carte 55/85 €
• Mediterranean • Rustic • Fri
This restaurant's intimate setting highlig
sculptures on display. The fine contem
produce, including game in season. S
choice of champagnes.
→ Encornets farcis aux oignons dou
filet d'agneau des Pyrénées rôtis, jus
lante aux fruits de saison parfumés a

✿ **Caillebotte**
83 r. Lepic (18th) – Ⓜ Abbesses – ✆
– www.caillebotte.fr – closed Sun
Menu 36 € – Carte 45/55 € (dinn
• Classic • Trendy •
Two young enthusiastic food lo
viting vintage bistro with solid
nofrills dishes pay tribute to th
contrasting seasonings. Delici
→ Filet de veau, pancetta, po
colat, glace à la vanille.

☺ **Chez Camille & Pascal**
6 r. d'Orchampt (18th) – Ⓜ A
– www.chez-pascal.fr – clo
Menu 37 € – Carte 42/55 €
• Modern cuisine •
The restaurant is very mu
interior and laid-back se
according to the inspira
ravioli. Good choice of w

🍴 **Les Deux Amis**
18 r. Eugène-Sue (18th
– www.les-deux-amis
1 to 8 January, Sund
Menu 22/36€ – Cart
• Traditional cu
The façade of this p
feuilleté of calf swe
and celeriac purée
asking for more b

KEY WORDS

Each entry comes with key words, making it quick and easy to identify the type of establishment and/or the food that it serves.

PRICES

Prices are given in the currency of the country in question.

Menu 40/56	Fixed price menu - Lowest / highest price
Carte 65/78	À la carte menu - Lowest / highest price
🍷	House wine included (France)

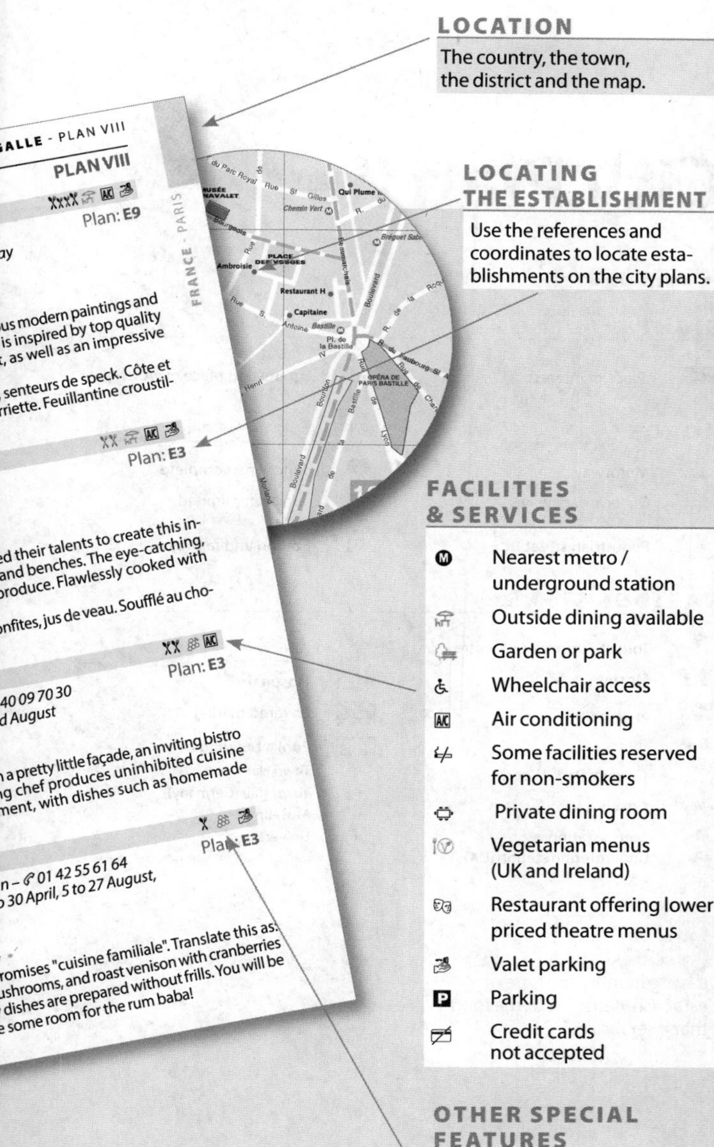

LOCATION

The country, the town, the district and the map.

LOCATING THE ESTABLISHMENT

Use the references and coordinates to locate establishments on the city plans.

FACILITIES & SERVICES

Ⓜ	Nearest metro / underground station
	Outside dining available
	Garden or park
♿	Wheelchair access
AC	Air conditioning
	Some facilities reserved for non-smokers
	Private dining room
	Vegetarian menus (UK and Ireland)
	Restaurant offering lower priced theatre menus
	Valet parking
P	Parking
	Credit cards not accepted

OTHER SPECIAL FEATURES

	Particularly interesting wine list
<	Great view

City Plan Key

- Restaurants

SIGHTS

Place of interest	Interesting place of worship

ROADS

Motorway	Junctions: complete
Dual carriageway	Junctions: limited
Pedestrian street	Station and railway

VARIOUS SIGNS

Tourist Information Centre	Airport
Mosque	Hospital
Synagogue	Covered market
Ruins	Public buildings:
Garden, Park, Wood	H Town Hall
Coach station	R Town Hall (Germany)
Metro station	M Museum
Underground station (UK)	U University

Selection by Country

VIENNA
Salzburg

AUSTRIA
ÖSTERREICH

B. Gardel/hemis.fr

VIENNA
WIEN

bluejayphoto/iStock

VIENNA IN...

→ **ONE DAY**
A tram ride round the Ringstrasse, St Stephen's Cathedral, a section of the Hofburg Palace, cakes in a café.

→ **TWO DAYS**
MuseumsQuartier, Spittelberg, Hundert-wasserhaus, Prater.

→ **THREE DAYS**
A day at the Belvedere, a night at the opera.

Beethoven, Brahms, Mozart, Haydn, Strauss...not a bad list of former residents, by any stretch of the imagination. One and all, they succumbed to the opulent aura of Vienna, a city where an appreciation of the arts is as conspicuous as its famed cakes. Sumptuous architecture and a refined air reflect the city's historic position as the seat of the powerful Habsburg dynasty and former epicentre of the Austro-Hungarian Empire.

Despite its grand image, Vienna has propelled itself into the 21C with a handful of innovative hotspots, most notably the MuseumsQuartier cultural complex, a stone's throw from the mighty Hofburg Imperial

Palace. This is not a big city, although its vivid image gives that impression. The compact centre teems with elegant shops, fashionable coffee-houses and grand avenues, and the empire's awesome 19C remnants keep visitors' eyes fixed forever upwards.

Many towns and cities are defined by their ring roads, but Vienna can boast a truly upmarket version: the Ringstrasse, a showpiece boulevard that cradles the inner city and the riches that lie therein. Just outside, to the southwest are the districts of Neubau and Spittelberg, both of which have taken on a quirky, modernistic feel. To the east lies Prater, the green lung of Vienna and further out lies the suburban area enhanced by the grandeur of the Schönbrunn palace.

EATING OUT

Vienna is the spiritual home of the café and Austrians drink nearly twice as much coffee as beer. It is also a city with a sweet tooth: cream cakes enhance the window displays of most eateries and is there a visitor to Vienna who hasn't succumbed to the sponge of the Sachertorte? Viennese food is essentially the food of Bohemia, which means that meat has a strong presence on the plate. Expect beef, veal and pork, alongside potatoes, dumplings or cabbage - be sure to try traditional boiled beef and the ubiquitous Wiener Schnitzel (deep-fried breaded veal). Also worth experiencing are the Heurigen, traditional Austrian wine taverns which are found in Grinzing, Heiligenstadt, Neustift and Nussdorf. You'll find plenty of snug cafés and bars too. If you want to snack, the place to go is Naschmarkt, Vienna's best market, where the stalls spill over into the vibrant little restaurants. When it comes to tipping, if you're in the more relaxed local pubs and wine taverns, just round up the bill, otherwise add on ten per cent.

✿✿ **Silvio Nickol Gourmet Restaurant** – Hotel Palais Coburg Residenz

Coburgbastei 4 ✉ 1010 – Ⓜ Stubentor
– ✆ (01) 51 81 81 30 – www.palais-coburg.com
– Closed 27 January-12 February, 3-11 March, 4-29 August and Sunday-Monday
Plan: **E2**

Menu 116/195 € – Carte 116/154 € – *(dinner only)*

• Modern cuisine • Elegant • Luxury •

The culinary creations served at Silvio Nickol are modern, highly elaborate, considered right down to the smallest detail, and made from nothing but the finest produce and ingredients. Whatever you do, don't forget to take a good look at the wine list as it contains some genuine rarities.

➜ Entenleber, Pilze, Fichtenwipfel, Schokolade. Reh, Fragolino Traube, Hafer, Kohlsprossen. Topinambur, Himbeer, Malz, Pistazie.

✿✿ **Steirereck im Stadtpark** (Heinz Reitbauer)

Am Heumarkt 2a ✉ 1030 – Ⓜ Stadtpark
– ✆ (01) 7 13 31 68 – www.steirereck.at
– Closed Saturday-Sunday
Plan: **F2**

Menu 98 € (lunch)/165 € – Carte 68/120 € – *(booking essential)*

• Creative • Design • Chic •

This elegant, bright and minimalist-style restaurant serves top-of-the-range Austrian cuisine. Made using only the finest ingredients, it is modern, elaborate and full of sophistication, harmonious yet full of surprises. The experience is rounded off by the professional, friendly and discreet service.

➜ Saibling im Bienenwachs mit gelber Rübe, Pollen und Rahm. Beinfleisch mit Selleriekohl, Schwarzwurzel und Semmelkren. Java Kaffee mit gelben Datteln, Zwetschken und Zimtblüten.

Meierei im Stadtpark – See below

✿✿ **Konstantin Filippou**

Dominikanerbastei 17 ✉ 1010 – Ⓜ Stubentor
– ✆ (01) 5 12 22 29 – www.konstantinfilippou.com
– Closed Saturday-Sunday and Bank Holidays
Plan: **E2**

Menu 37 € (lunch)/185 € (dinner)

• Modern cuisine • Minimalist • Romantic •

The elegant minimalist-style interior and view of the kitchen – there's even a cooking station in the restaurant itself – set the tone here at Konstantin Filippou. The food is creative and modern and comes with well-chosen wine recommendations.

➜ Langostino, Kalbszunge, Cochayuyo, Zitrus. Brandade, Amurkarpfen, Kaviar. Unagi, Ibérico, Senf, Fenchel.

O boufés – See below

✿ **Edvard** – Hotel Palais Hansen Kempinski

Schottenring 24 ✉ 1010 – Ⓜ Schottenring
– ✆ (01) 2 36 10 00 – www.kempinski.com/vienna
– Closed 14-20 January, 29 July-25 August, Sunday-Monday and Bank Holidays
Plan: **D1**

Menu 99/158 € – Carte 33/61 €

• Modern cuisine • Elegant • Luxury •

This elegant gourmet restaurant offers a successful marriage of the modern and classic, both in its sophisticated aromatic cuisine and the accomplished, pleasantly informal service. The excellent wine suggestions and good wines by the glass are also worth a mention.

➜ Flusskrebse, Butternusskürbis-Bisque, Chorizo, weiße Coco-Bohnen, Muskatgarbe. Falsches Ei "alla carbonara anno 2013", Fregola Sarda, Lardo, Flower Sprout. Saint Pierre, Salzteig-Kohlrabi, Dashi Beurre Blanc, Mönchsbart, Bronzefenchel.

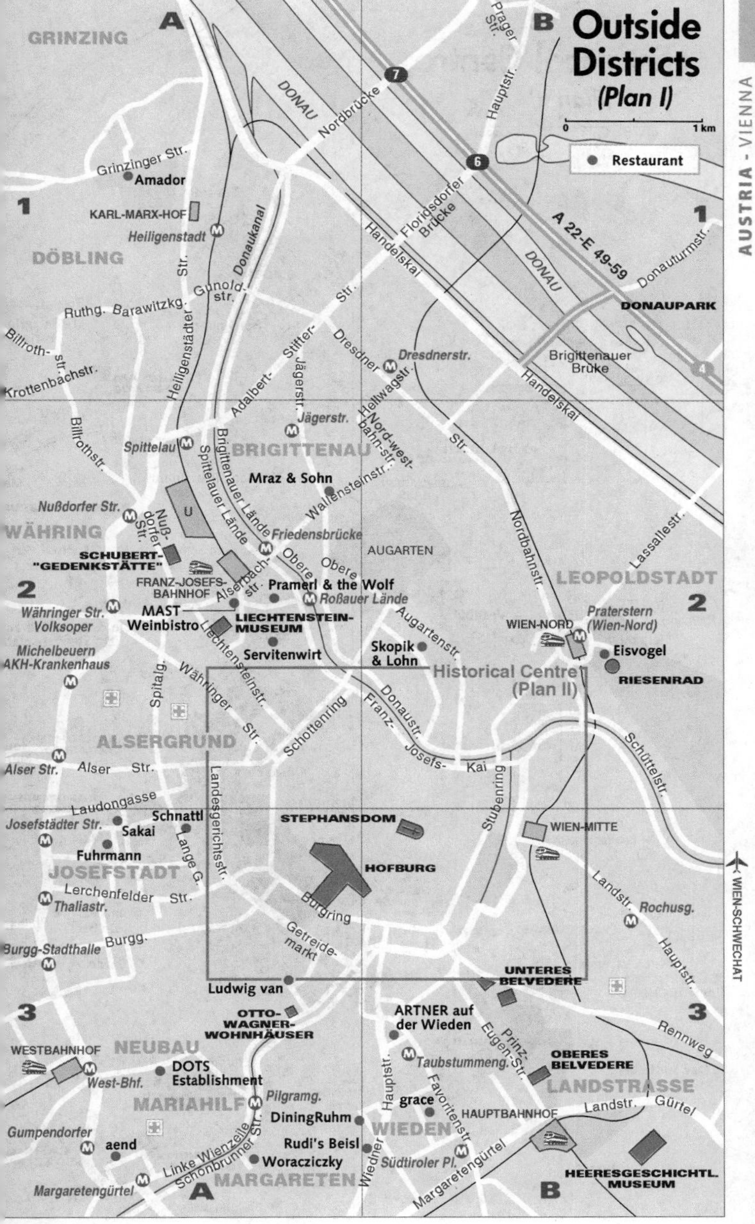
Outside Districts
(Plan I)
0
1 km
Restaurant
GRINZING
DÖBLING
WÄHRING
BRIGITTENAU
AUGARTEN
LEOPOLDSTADT
ALSERGRUND
JOSEFSTADT
NEUBAU
MARIAHILF
WIEDEN
MARGARETEN
LANDSTRASSE
DONAUPARK
Amador
KARL-MARX-HOF
Heiligenstadt
Spittelau
Nußdorfer Str.
Jägerstr.
Dresdnerstr.
Friedensbrücke
Roßauer Lände
Mraz & Sohn
Pramerl & the Wolf
SCHUBERT-"GEDENKSTÄTTE"
FRANZ-JOSEFS-BAHNHOF
MAST Weinbistro
LIECHTENSTEIN-MUSEUM
Servitenwirt
Skopik & Lohn
Währinger Str. Volksoper
Michelbeuern AKH-Krankenhaus
WIEN-NORD
Praterstern (Wien-Nord)
Eisvogel
RIESENRAD
Historical Centre (Plan II)
STEPHANSDOM
HOFBURG
WIEN-MITTE
Rochusg.
Schnattl
Sakai
Fuhrmann
Josefstädter Str.
Thaliastr.
Burgg-Stadthalle
Ludwig van
OTTO-WAGNER-WOHNHÄUSER
UNTERES BELVEDERE
ARTNER auf der Wieden
Taubstummeng.
OBERES BELVEDERE
WESTBAHNHOF
West-Bhf.
DOTS Establishment
Pilgramg.
grace
DiningRuhm
Rudi's Beisl
Woracziczky
HAUPTBAHNHOF
Gumpendorfer
aend
Südtiroler Pl.
Margaretengürtel
HEERESGESCHICHTL. MUSEUM
WIEN-SCHWECHAT
DONAU
Nordbrücke
Floridsdorfer Brücke
Brigittenauer Brüke
A 22-E 49-59
Handelskai
Donauturmstr.
Prager Str.
Hauptstr.
Grinzinger Str.
Donaukanal
Heiligenstädter Str.
Gunold-str.
Ruthg.
Barawitzkg.
Billroth-str.
Krottenbachstr.
Billrothstr.
Adalbert-Stifter-Str.
Jägerstr.
Dresdner Str.
Hellwagstr.
Nord-west-bahn-str.
Wallensteinstr.
Nordbahnstr.
Lassallestr.
Brigittenauer Lände
Spittelauer Lände
Nuß-dorfer Str.
Alserbach-str.
Obere
Augartenstr.
Liechtensteinstr.
Währinger Str.
Spitalg.
Schottenring
Franz-Josefs-Kai
Donaustr.
Schüttelstr.
Stubenring
Alser Str.
Laudongasse
Landesgerichtsstr.
Lange G.
Lerchenfelder Str.
Burgg.
Burgring
Getreide-markt
Landstr. Hauptstr.
Rennweg
Prinz-Eugen-Str.
Hauptstr.
Favoritenstr.
Landstr. Gürtel
Linke Wienzeile
Schönbrunner Str.
Wiedner
Margaretengürtel
A
B
1
2
3

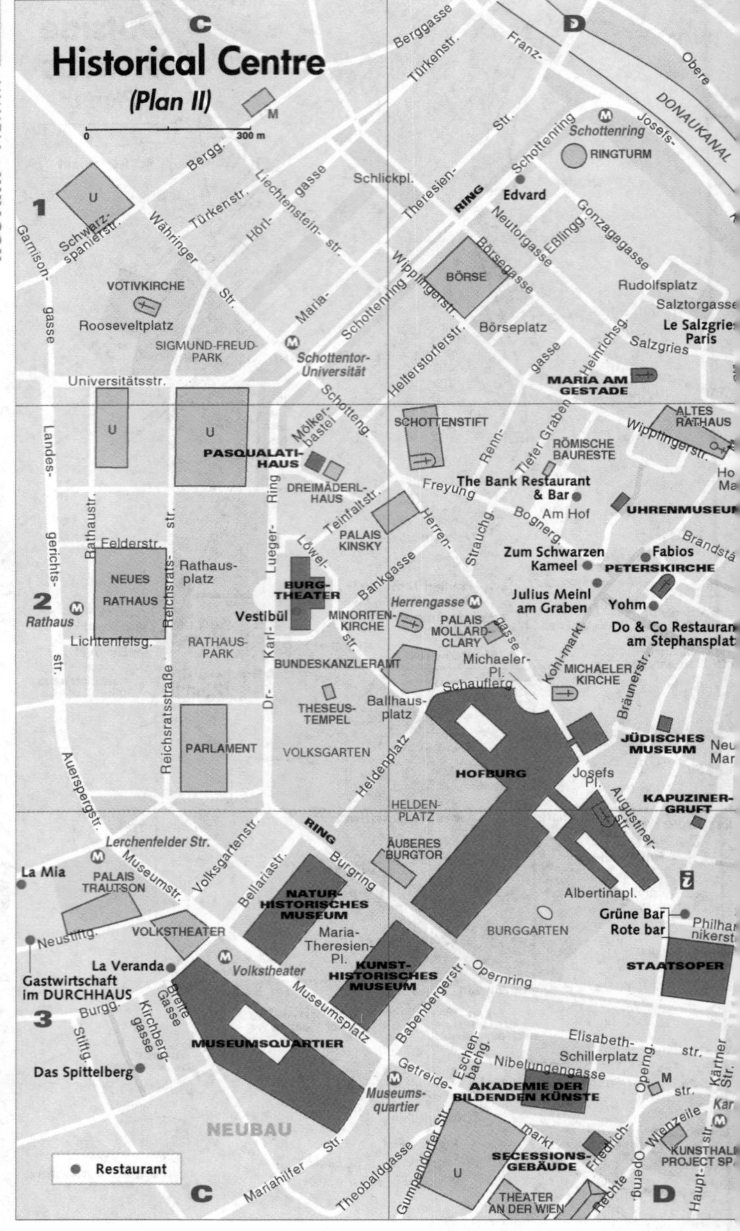
Historical Centre
(Plan II)
0
300 m
C
D
1
2
3
VOTIVKIRCHE
Rooseveltplatz
SIGMUND-FREUD-PARK
Schottentor-Universität
Universitätsstr.
BÖRSE
Börseplatz
Schottenring
RINGTURM
Edvard
DONAUKANAL
Rudolfsplatz
Salztorgasse
Le Salzgries Paris
MARIA AM GESTADE
ALTES RATHAUS
SCHOTTENSTIFT
RÖMISCHE BAURESTE
The Bank Restaurant & Bar
Am Hof
UHRENMUSEUM
PASQUALATI-HAUS
DREIMÄDERL-HAUS
PALAIS KINSKY
Freyung
Zum Schwarzen Kameel
Fabios
PETERSKIRCHE
Julius Meinl am Graben
Yohm
Do & Co Restaurant am Stephansplatz
NEUES RATHAUS
Rathausplatz
Rathaus
BURG-THEATER
Vestibül
MINORITEN-KIRCHE
Herrengasse
PALAIS MOLLARD-CLARY
Michaeler-Pl.
MICHAELER KIRCHE
RATHAUS-PARK
BUNDESKANZLERAMT
THESEUS-TEMPEL
Ballhaus-platz
PARLAMENT
VOLKSGARTEN
HOFBURG
JÜDISCHES MUSEUM
Josefs Pl.
KAPUZINER-GRUFT
HELDEN-PLATZ
ÄUßERES BURGTOR
RING
Lerchenfelder Str.
La Mia
PALAIS TRAUTSON
NATUR-HISTORISCHES MUSEUM
Albertinapl.
Grüne Bar
Rote bar
BURGGARTEN
VOLKSTHEATER
Volkstheater
Maria-Theresien-Pl.
KUNST-HISTORISCHES MUSEUM
STAATSOPER
La Veranda
Gastwirtschaft im DURCHHAUS
Opernring
MUSEUMSQUARTIER
Das Spittelberg
Museumsquartier
AKADEMIE DER BILDENDEN KÜNSTE
Schillerplatz
NEUBAU
SECESSIONS-GEBÄUDE
KUNSTHALLE PROJECT SPACE
THEATER AN DER WIEN
Restaurant

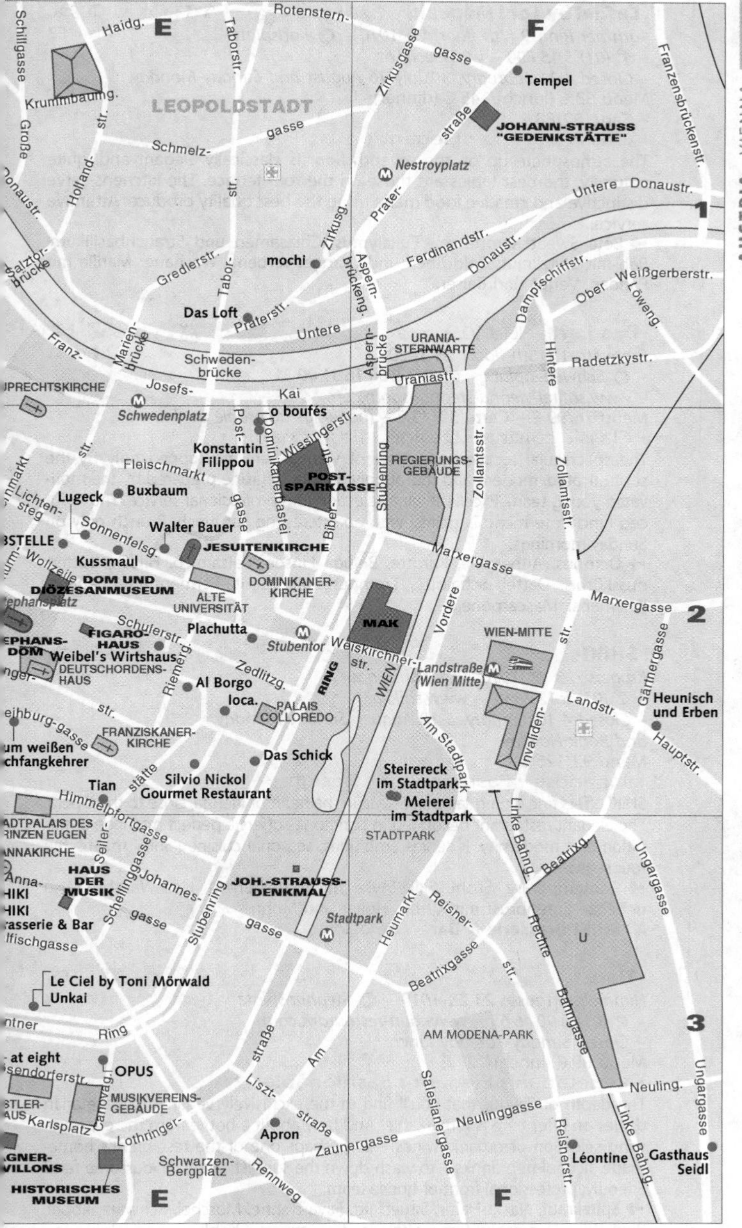
E
F
1
2
3
LEOPOLDSTADT
Tempel
JOHANN-STRAUSS "GEDENKSTÄTTE"
Nestroyplatz
mochi
Das Loft
URANIA-STERNWARTE
RUPRECHTSKIRCHE
Schwedenplatz
o boufés
Konstantin Filippou
POST-SPARKASSE
REGIERUNGS-GEBÄUDE
Lugeck
Buxbaum
Walter Bauer
JESUITENKIRCHE
Kussmaul
DOM UND DIÖZESANMUSEUM
ALTE UNIVERSITÄT
DOMINIKANER-KIRCHE
Plachutta
FIGARO-HAUS
Weibel's Wirtshaus
DEUTSCHORDENS-HAUS
Stubentor
MAK
RING
WIEN
WIEN-MITTE
Landstraße (Wien Mitte)
Heunisch und Erben
Al Borgo
loca.
PALAIS COLLOREDO
FRANZISKANER-KIRCHE
Das Schick
Steirereck im Stadtpark
Meierei im Stadtpark
Tian
Silvio Nickol Gourmet Restaurant
STADTPARK
HAUS DER MUSIK
JOH.-STRAUSS-DENKMAL
Stadtpark
Le Ciel by Toni Mörwald
Unkai
OPUS
MUSIKVEREINS-GEBÄUDE
AM MODENA-PARK
Apron
Léontine
Gasthaus Seidl
HISTORISCHES MUSEUM
Schwarzen-Bergplatz
Karlsplatz
Rennweg
Zaunergasse
Neulinggasse
Salesianergasse
Reisnerstr.
Ungargasse
Linke Bahng.
Rechte Bahngasse
Beatrixgasse
Heumarkt
Stubenring
Lothringer-
Liszt-straße
Johannesgasse
Himmelpfortgasse
Schellinggasse
Wollzeile
Fleischmarkt
Sonnenfelsg.
Schulerstr.
Zedlitzg.
Riemerg.
Biberstr.
Dominikanerbastei
Postgasse
Wiesingerstr.
Stubenring
Zollamtsstr.
Marxergasse
Vordere Zollamtsstr.
Weiskirchnerstr.
Am Stadtpark
Invalidenstr.
Landstr. Hauptstr.
Gärtnergasse
Radetzkystr.
Hintere Zollamtsstr.
Uraniastr.
Schwedenbrücke
Marienbrücke
Aspernbrücke
Aspernbrückeng.
Untere Donaustr.
Obere Donaustr.
Ferdinandstr.
Praterstr.
Taborstr.
Zirkusg.
Zirkusgasse
Rotensterngasse
Haidg.
Krummbaumg.
Große Stadtgutg.
Schmelzgasse
Hollandstr.
Gredlerstr.
Dampfschiffstr.
Weißgerberstr.
Löweng.
Franzensbrückenstr.
Josefs-Kai
Franz-Josefs-Kai
Salztorbrücke
Schiffgasse
Donaustr.
Neuling.
Canovag.
Seilerstätte
Schwarzenbergstr.

Le Ciel by Toni Mörwald – Grand Hotel

Kärntner Ring 9 (7th floor) ✉ 1010 – Ⓜ Karlsplatz Plan: **E3**
– ✆ (01) 5 15 800 – www.leciel.at
– Closed 4-11 February, 30 July-26 August and Sunday-Monday
Menu 53 € (lunch)/145 € (dinner)
– Carte 82/88 €

• Classic cuisine • Elegant •

The atmosphere up on the seventh floor is classically elegant and, quite naturally, the best tables are those on the roof terrace. The kitchens serve distinctive and creative food made using the best quality produce. Attentive service.

➜ Beta Sweet Karotte mit Eukalyptus, Chiasamen und Strauchbasilikum. Reh mit Spitzkraut, Goldrüben und Orangenverbene. Wachauer Marille mit Pandan, Verjus und Baiser.

Das Loft – Hotel SO/ Vienna

Praterstr. 1 (18th floor) ✉ 1020 Plan: **E1**
– Ⓜ Schwedenplatz – ✆ (01) 9 06 16 31 00
– www.sofitel-vienna-stephansdom.com
Menu 76/99 € – Carte 59/79 € – *(bookings advisable at dinner)*

• Classic cuisine • Design • Fashionable •

The spectacular location and view of Vienna here are topped only by the sophisticated, modern and thoroughly delicious cuisine prepared by the motivated young team. Excellent wine selection and professional service. The reduced lunchtime menu is paired with an interesting set lunch. Brunch only on Sunday mornings.

➜ Octopus, Aubergine, Karotte, Beluga Linsen, Balsamico. Hirsch, Butternusskürbis, Dattel, Schalotte, Trompetenpilz, Zimt. Fermentierte Banane, Kalamansi, Mascarpone.

SHIKI

Krugerstr. 3 ✉ 1010 – Ⓜ Karlsplatz Plan: **E3**
– ✆ (01) 5 12 73 97 – www.shiki.at
– Closed 4-10 January, 5-18 August, Sunday-Monday and Bank Holidays
Menu 92/125 €

• Japanese • Fashionable • Design •

SHIKI offers fine dining Japanese-style in the heart of Vienna, close to the Opera. The elegant restaurant decorated in dark tones offers a perfect marriage of tradition and modernity. It serves ambitious, seasonal cuisine ('Shiki' means the four seasons).

➜ Contemporary Sushi Skiki-Style mit geriebenem Hon-Wasabi. Miso gebeizte Entenbrust mit Kürbis. Holler und Mohn.

SHIKI Brasserie & Bar – See below

Tian

Himmelpfortgasse 23 ✉ 1010 – Ⓜ Stephansplatz Plan: **E2**
– ✆ (01) 8 90 46 65 – www.tian-restaurant.com
– Closed Sunday-Tuesday lunch
Menu 89 € (lunch)/127 €

• Vegetarian • Elegant • Fashionable •

The depth of flavour that you'll find in the exclusively vegan and vegetarian dishes on offer here is remarkable! And how about a bottle from the ever-growing selection of organic wines – or perhaps one of the restaurant's home-made alcohol-free drinks – to wash down the sophisticated, flavoursome fare? Friendly, professional front-of-house team.

➜ Spitzkraut, Nackt-Hafer, Sauerteig. Fava Bohne, Morchel, Schwarzpappel. Beni Wild Harvest Bitterschokolade, fermentierte Kohlsprossen, Holunderbeeren Shrub.

Walter Bauer

Sonnenfelsgasse 17 ✉ 1010 – Ⓜ Stubentor Plan: **E2**
– ✆ (01) 5 12 98 71 – Closed Saturday-Monday lunch
Menu 59/69 € – Carte 52/78 €
• Classic cuisine • Cosy • Family •

This listed building in the centre of the old town has oodles of Viennese charm, as well as a wonderful vaulted ceiling in the restaurant. The owners place great importance on providing attentive and personal service, as well as classic cuisine without frills. There is also an excellent wine list.

➜ Gänseleber mit Brioche. Rosa gebratener Tafelspitz, Semmelkren und Mark. Variation vom Spanferkel.

aend (Fabian Günzel)

Mollardgasse 76 ✉ 1010 – Ⓜ Margaretengürtel Plan I: **A3**
– ✆ (01) 5953416 – www.aend.at
– Closed 28 January-11 February, 12 August-2 September, Saturday-Sunday and Bank Holidays
Menu 39 € (lunch)/120 €
• Modern cuisine • Minimalist • Chic •

This restaurant in a residential district in the west of the city offers clean-cut design and a fashionable feel to match the modern creative cuisine prepared in the open kitchen. The result is range of punchy, pared-down dishes made using only the best, seasonal ingredients.

➜ Jakobsmuschel und Pomelo. Ente und Süßkartoffel. Kürbis und Schokolade.

Vestibül

Universitätsring 2 (at Burgtheater) ✉ 1010 Plan: **C2**
– Ⓜ Herrengasse – ✆ (01) 5 32 49 99 – www.vestibuel.at
– Closed 1-6 January, 27 July-18 August and Saturday lunch, Sunday-Monday
Menu 33/99 € (dinner) – Carte 37/87 €
• International • Classic décor • Brasserie •

Though the chef sets great store by using high quality Austrian ingredients, there is nothing that quite matches the lobster in Vestibül's highly prized Szegediner lobster with cabbage. The unusual location – in the famous and charming Burgtheater – is another selling point. Don't miss the excellent wines, some of which are available as magnums.

Eisvogel

Riesenradplatz 5 (Prater) ✉ 1020 – Ⓜ Praterstern Plan I: **B2**
– ✆ (01) 9 08 11 87 – www.stadtgasthaus-eisvogel.at
– Closed 7-20 January
Menu 45/65 € – Carte 31/54 €
• Austrian • Elegant • Friendly •

Set in the pulsating heart of Vienna next to the giant Riesenrad Ferris wheel at the entrance to the Prater, Eisvogel is a great place for an aperitif with a view (by reservation only). The excellent classic Austrian fare on offer includes Beuschel (veal lung ragout), Wiener Schnitzel and goulash. There is a small, sheltered terrace facing the Prater.

"Independence" is one of our keywords: to remain totally objective for our readers, the selection is made with complete independence. Entry into the guide is free. All decisions are discussed with the Editor and our highest awards are considered at a European level.

Meierei im Stadtpark – Restaurant Steirereck

Am Heumarkt 2a (at Stadtpark) ✉ 1030 – Ⓜ Stadtpark Plan: **F2**
– ✆ (01) 7 13 31 68 – www.steirereck.at – Closed Bank Holidays
Menu 49/60 € (dinner) – Carte 32/43 € – *(Saturday-Sunday open to 7pm)*

• Country • Friendly •

One floor below the Reitbauer's gourmet restaurant, you'll find another upmarket eatery. Alongside some 150 wonderfully matured cheeses, it boasts delicious classics like Wiener schnitzel of suckling calf. Or perhaps you'd prefer a whole Arctic char or some venison goulash? Attractive terrace facing the Stadtpark.

DiningRuhm

Lambrechtgasse 9 ✉ 1040 – Ⓜ Hauptbahnhof Plan I: **A3**
– ✆ (01) 94 52 224 – www.diningruhm.at – Closed 23 December-7 January and Sunday-Monday
Menu 49 € – Carte 28/50 €

• Fusion • Minimalist •

Set in an unassuming corner block in Vienna's 4th District, DiningRuhm surprises not only with its friendly, minimalist interior, but also with its Japanese-cum-Peruvian cuisine à la Nobu Matsuhisa. Try the kingfish sashimi with yuzu soy sauce and coriander or the Tullnerfeld belly pork with red onions, chilli and spicy miso cream.

Gasthaus Seidl

Ungargasse 63 ✉ 1030 – Ⓜ Stadtpark Plan: **F3**
– ✆ (01) 7131781 – www.gasthaus-seidl.at – Closed 24 December-6 January, Saturday-Sunday and Bank holidays
Carte 27/51 €

• Traditional cuisine • Bourgeois •

This simple, friendly restaurant in Vienna's 3rd district not far from Schloss Belvedere, the Vienna Konzerthaus and the Stadtpark serves an interesting mix of traditional and modern cuisine. Top-quality produce is transformed into pleasantly uncomplicated dishes such as fillet of salmon trout with creamy romaine lettuce and fried chicken with potato and lamb's lettuce salad. The owner is always happy to recommend his favourite wines.

Kussmaul

Bäckerstr. 5 ✉ 1010 – Ⓜ Stubentor – ✆ (01) 2861117 Plan: **E2**
– www.kussmaul-vienna.com
Carte 28/100 € – *(dinner only)*

• International • Chic • Fashionable •

Kussmaul promises a relaxed atmosphere in a fresh, stylish interior – complete with bar and vaulted cellar – in which to sample its fine international cuisine (many of the dishes come as good-value set menu servings). Alternatively try one of the "Big Cuts" – a whole fish, for example.

LABSTELLE

Lugeck 6 ✉ 1010 – Ⓜ Stephansplatz Plan: **E2**
– ✆ (01) 2 36 21 22 – www.labstelle.at – Closed Sunday and Bank Holidays
Menu 43/68 € (dinner) – Carte 37/58 €

• Country • Design • Bistro •

Labstelle offers an attractive, upmarket bistro atmosphere with a relaxed bar area. It serves ambitious seasonal, regional fare including Arctic char, Marschfeld artichoke, parsnips and parsley. There is also a reduced lunchtime menu and a pretty interior courtyard.

Lugeck

Lugeck 4 ✉ 1010 – Ⓜ Stephansplatz Plan: **E2**
– ✆ (01) 5 12 50 60 – www.lugeck.com
Carte 20/54 €

• Austrian • Contemporary décor • Rustic •

Located in Vienna's striking and history-filled Regensburger Hof building close to St Stephen's cathedral, Lugeck serves contemporary re-interpretations of traditional Viennese dishes such as Tafelspitz (boiled topside of veal) and Wiener schnitzel, alongside some appealing international cuisine.

Mochi

Praterstr. 15 ✉ 1020 – Ⓜ Nestroyplatz Plan: **E1**
– ✆ (01) 9 25 13 80 – www.mochi.at – Closed 23 December-2 January and Sunday
Carte 29/52 € – *(booking essential at dinner)*
• Japanese • Trendy • Fashionable •

This is a lively, informal restaurant serving authentic Japanese cuisine with the occasional modern twist at very moderate prices. You can watch the chefs at work as they prepare their rolls, gyoza soup and gyu tataki. At lunchtimes the food is served in simple bowls, in the evenings the presentation is a little more elaborate. Bookings start at 3pm.

Grüne Bar - Hotel Sacher

Philharmonikerstr. 4 ✉ 1010 – Ⓜ Karlsplatz Plan: **D3**
– ✆ (01) 514560 – www.sacher.com – Closed July-August
Menu 79/118 € – Carte 45/78 € – *(dinner only)*
• Classic cuisine • Luxury •

The Hotel Sacher's fine dining restaurant with its upmarket green and wood interior features a number of original paintings by Viennese impressionist Anton Faistauer. The ambitious re-interpreted classics on offer have a strong Viennese flavour, as evidenced by the Mangalitza pigs' cheeks with calf's heart and turnips.

OPUS - Hotel Imperial

Kärntner Ring 16 ✉ 1015 – Ⓜ Karlsplatz Plan: **E3**
– ✆ (01) 50 11 0 – www.imperialvienna.com – Closed mid July-mid August and Monday
Menu 96/132 € – Carte 87/107 € – *(dinner only)*
• Modern cuisine • Elegant • Luxury •

Located in an attractive, classical building, OPUS is decorated in the style of a 1930s Viennese workshop, in elegant grey tones with chandeliers and art on the walls. The ambitious cuisine is creative and regionally inspired.

Rote Bar - Hotel Sacher

Philharmonikerstr. 4 ✉ 1010 – Ⓜ Karlsplatz Plan: **D3**
– ✆ (01) 5 14 560 – www.sacher.com
Menu 60/79 € – Carte 42/92 €
• Austrian • Elegant • Traditional décor •

A mainstay of the Hotel Sacher, which epitomises the charm of this great Viennese establishment, Rote Bar is also a champion of Austrian cuisine. Treat yourself to a Wiener schnitzel or traditional rump of beef and soak up the atmosphere!

Zum Schwarzen Kameel

Bognergasse 5 ✉ 1010 – Ⓜ Herrengasse Plan: **D2**
– ✆ (01) 5 33 81 25 – www.kameel.at
Menu 69/93 € – Carte 38/78 € – *(booking essential)*
• Traditional cuisine • Friendly • Cosy •

One of Vienna's oldest restaurants (1618), fitted out in the much-admired Viennese Art Nouveau style in 1901/02. Guests are offered international and regional cuisine. The restaurant's own delicatessen and patisserie are great for buying gifts.

Al Borgo

An der Hülben 1 ✉ 1010 – Ⓜ Stubentor Plan: **E2**
– ✆ (01) 5 12 85 59 – www.alborgo.at – Closed Saturday lunch, Sunday and Bank Holidays
Carte 28/47 €
• Italian • Friendly •

Al Borgo enjoys a very central and yet secluded location in the heart of Vienna's 1st district. It serves classic Italian cuisine and a range of excellent seasonal dishes. Regular themed weeks.

Apron

XX

Am Heumarkt 35 ✉ 1030 – Ⓜ Stadtpark Plan: **E3**
– ✆ (01) 71616870 – www.restaurant-apron.at – Closed Saturday lunch, Sunday lunch
Menu 24 € (lunch)/102 € – Carte 49/71 €
• Creative • Classic décor •

You'll find this classic yet modern restaurant not far from the Stadtpark, adjoining the Sofitel Hotel. The food that comes out of the impressive open kitchen ranges from the innovative and highly ambitious Chef's Menu to a tasty Wiener schnitzel. The good-value lunch is very popular.

Buxbaum

XX

Grashofgasse 3 (at Heiligenkreuzhof) ✉ 1010 – Ⓜ Schwedenplatz – ✆ (01) 276 82 26 – www.buxbaum.restaurant – Closed Sunday and Bank Holidays Plan: **E2**
Menu 50/66 € – Carte 44/74 €
• Market cuisine • Cosy • Chic •

This comfortable, stylishly rustic restaurant lies a little out of the way in the Heiligenkreuzerhof. At midday it serves a quick business lunch, in the evenings international and regional set menus alongside the à la carte offerings. Attractive terrace.

DOTS Establishment

XX

Mariahilfer Str. 103 ✉ 1010 – Ⓜ Westbahnhof Plan I: **A3**
– ✆ (01) 920 99 80 – www.dotsgroup.eu
Menu 65/95 € – Carte 38/139 € – *(Sunday to Thursday dinner only) (booking advisable)*
• Asian • Chic • Exotic décor •

An interesting mix of bar, popular sushi joint and smart, stylish restaurant with a strong artistic touch, DOTS Establishment lies in an arcade in Vienna's Mariahilfer Straße shopping district. Alongside some excellent sushi creations you'll also find flavoursome dishes including duck breast with bitter orange and creamy jasmine rice.

Das Schick – Hotel Am Parkring

XX

Parkring 12 ✉ 1010 – Ⓜ Stubentor – ✆ (01) 51 48 00 Plan: **E2**
– www.schick-hotels.com – Closed Saturday lunch, Sunday lunch and Bank Holidays lunch
Menu 38 € (lunch)/93 € – Carte 73/88 € – *(July - August dinner only)*
• Mediterranean cuisine • Fashionable • Elegant •

Das Schick offers a friendly atmosphere, seasonal cuisine with an upmarket touch and a phenomenal view! That is the recipe that brings diners up here to the 12th floor.

Do & Co Restaurant am Stephansplatz – Do & Co Hotel Vienna

XX

Stephansplatz 12 (7th floor) ✉ 1010 – Ⓜ Stephansplatz – ✆ (01) 5 35 39 69 – www.doco.com Plan: **D2**
Carte 50/71 € – *(booking essential)*
• Asian • Trendy • Design •

An ultra-modern restaurant on the seventh floor, with a great terrace and a view of St Stephen's Cathedral. Southeast Asian dishes, including chicken kaow soy and Sushi, feature alongside Austrian classics such as braised calves' cheeks and goose liver.

Fabios

XX

Tuchlauben 6 ✉ 1010 – Ⓜ Stephansplatz Plan: **D2**
– ✆ (01) 5 32 22 22 – www.fabios.at – Closed Sunday
Carte 50/82 € – *(booking essential)*
• Italian • Trendy •

A veritable Who's Who of Vienna! The Italian cuisine served in this fashionable city restaurant is just as modern and minimalist as the interior design – two equally good reasons to give it a try! The bar also serves a range of snacks.

Julius Meinl am Graben

Graben 19 (1st floor) 1010 – Stephansplatz Plan: **D2**
– (01) 5 32 33 34 60 00 – www.meinlamgraben.at – Closed 5-25 August and Sunday
Menu 39 € (lunch)/93 € – Carte 42/77 € – *(booking essential)*
• Classic cuisine • Chic • Cosy •

This restaurant and its sister delicatessen (housed in the same building) come to life early in the morning. Ambitious food is served using the finest quality ingredients from breakfast through to dinner (make sure you try the stuffed quail with greengages) complete with a view over Vienna's pedestrian zone.

La Veranda – Hotel Sans Souci

Burggasse 2 1070 – Volkstheater Plan: **C3**
– (01) 5 22 25 20 19 4 – www.sanssouci-wien.com
Menu 38 € – Carte 40/69 €
• International • Fashionable •

The smart, fashionable and friendly restaurant at the Hotel Sans Souci serves modern Austrian fare with the occasional sally into international cuisine. Try the creamy Jerusalem artichoke soup or the Lake Neusiedl pike with parsnip, apple, spring onion and lemon. Good wine list.

Plachutta

Wollzeile 38 1010 – Stubentor – (01) 5 12 15 77 Plan: **E2**
– www.plachutta.at
Carte 31/52 €
• Austrian • Traditional décor • Inn •

For years, the Plachutta family has been committed to Viennese tradition. They serve beef in many forms in the green panelled dining room or on the large terrace.

Skopik & Lohn

Leopoldsgasse 17 1020 – Taborstrasse Plan I: **B2**
– (01) 2 19 89 77 – www.skopikundlohn.at – Closed Sunday-Monday
Menu 34 € – Carte 29/49 € – *(dinner only)*
• Austrian • Friendly • Family •

The first thing you'll notice here is the wonderful painted ceiling, the work of artist Otto Zitko. The service is friendly and attentive, the food flavoursome and the Austrian classics on the menu include Wiener schnitzel with cucumber, potato and sour cream salad and, for dessert, perhaps an île flottante?

The Bank Brasserie & Bar – Hotel Park Hyatt

Bognergasse 4 1010 – Herrengasse Plan: **D2**
– (01) 2 27 40 12 36 – www.restaurant-thebank.com
Carte 35/84 €
• International • Classic décor •

If you are looking to eat out in an unusual setting, try the period lobby in this former bank with its imposing high ceilings and marble columns. The menu offers French brasserie-style dishes that are prepared in the open show kitchen. The Am Hof café is also popular.

Unkai – Grand Hotel

Kärntner Ring 9 (7th floor) 1010 – Karlsplatz Plan: **E3**
– (01) 5 15 80 91 10 – www.grandhotelwien.com – Closed Monday lunch
Menu 35/85 € – Carte 28/70 €
• Japanese • Minimalist •

A pleasantly light and modern restaurant where you can eat either at authentic teppanyaki grill tables or more conventionally. You will also find the Unkai sushi bar on the ground floor serving a sushi brunch on Saturdays, Sundays and public holidays.

Zum weissen Rauchfangkehrer

Weihburggasse 4 ✉ 1010 – Ⓜ Stephansplatz Plan: **E2**
– ✆ (01) 5 12 34 71 – www.weisser-rauchfangkehrer.at
Menu 33/45 € – Carte 30/60 € – *(booking advisable)*
• Austrian • Traditional décor • Chic •

The Viennese cuisine includes seasonal dishes such as duo of Schneebergland duck and specials like calf's head brawn. These are served throughout the day in comfortable, traditional dining rooms. There's also a wide range of wines and digestifs.

at eight – The Ring

Kärntner Ring 8 ✉ 1010 – Ⓜ Karlsplatz Plan: **E3**
– ✆ (01) 2 21 22 – www.ateight-restaurant.com
Menu 45/55 € – Carte 38/61 €
• Traditional cuisine • Classic décor •

Simple lines set the tone here in this light and airy restaurant, where the attentive front-of-house team serve up modern cuisine alongside Viennese classics. The attractive terrace overlooks the Ring.

ARTNER auf der Wieden

Floragasse 6 ✉ 1040 – Ⓜ Taubstummengasse Plan I: **B3**
– ✆ (01) 5 03 50 33 – www.artner.co.at – Closed Saturday lunch, Sunday
Menu 45/65 € – Carte 31/62 €
• International • Fashionable • Design •

Regional and modern, the flavoursome fare on offer includes Wiener Schnitzel with parsley potatoes and Mühlbachtaler salmon trout with pan-fried citrus peel and crispy polenta, not to mention a range of grilled dishes. The interior is attractive and minimalist in style and the service is relaxed. Good value lunchtime menu.

Das Spittelberg

Spittelbergstr. 12 ✉ 1070 – Ⓜ Volkstheater Plan: **C3**
– ✆ (01) 5877628 – www.das-spittelberg.at – Closed Sunday-Monday
Menu 49/69 € – Carte 33/75 € – *(dinner only)*
• Austrian • Brasserie • Classic décor •

This friendly and welcoming restaurant located in the charming Spittelberg district revolves around the rotisserie grill in the open kitchen, where the matured Simmentaler beef is a speciality. The Austrian fare is accompanied by a range of good Austrian wines, including some magnums.

Gastwirtschaft im DURCHHAUS

Neustiftgasse 16 ✉ 1070 – Ⓜ Lerchenfelder Str. Plan: **C3**
– ✆ (01) 5 26 94 48 – www.durchhaus.at – Closed Sunday-Monday
Carte 24/49 € – *(dinner only)*
• Country • Cosy •

Though somewhat unprepossessing from the outside, this restaurant close to the Volkstheater has a pretty interior courtyard with a terrace. Couples should ask for the little alcove booth – perfect for a tête-à-tête! The regional fare includes pink roast sirloin steak with wild mushrooms and herb and mustard brioche.

Heunisch und Erben

Landstrasser Hauptstr. 17 / Seidlgasse 36 ✉ 1030 Plan: **F2**
– Ⓜ Landstraße (Wien-Mitte) – ✆ (01) 2868563 – www.heunisch.at
– Closed Sunday-Monday and Bank Holidays
Menu 37/79 € – Carte 39/52 € – *(dinner only)*
• Country • Fashionable • Neighbourhood •

In an interesting mix of modern wine bar and restaurant, Heunisch und Erben offers some 100 different wines to accompany its ambitious, market-fresh food. Menu options range from mountain trout with pumpkin, salt-baked beetroot and Uhudler wine to creamy veal goulash.

La Mia

Lerchenfelder Str. 13 ✉ 1070 – Ⓜ Lerchenfelder Str. – ✆ (01) 5 22 42 21 – www.lamia.at

Plan: **C3**

Carte 31/45 €

• Italian • Bistro • Rustic •

This lively friendly bistro with its covered interior courtyard serves pizzas and pasta dishes – try the excellent spaghetti frutti di mare – alongside grilled specialities including gamberoni alla diavola and tagliata di manzo. Just around the corner the same team offers traditional Viennese cuisine.

Ludwig van

Laimgrubengasse 22 ✉ 1060 – Ⓜ Museumsquartier – ✆ (01) 5871320 – www.ludwigvan.wien – Closed Saturday-Sunday, Monday dinner and Bank Holidays

Plan I: **A3**

Menu 47/64 € (dinner) – Carte 42/56 €

• Country • Rustic • Cosy •

The ground floor of this house where Beethoven once lived is now home to a warm and welcoming, rustic dining room with a charming front-of-house team serving contemporary takes on regional fare. Made using top-quality ingredients, the food is pleasingly simple, refined and rich in flavour.

Léontine

Reisnerstrasse 39 ✉ 1030 – Ⓜ Stadtspark – ✆ (01) 712 54 30 – www.leontine.at – Closed 1 week February, 1 week during Easter, 2 weeks August, 2 weeks end December-early January and Sunday-Monday, Tuesday dinner, Wednesday dinner

Plan: **F3**

Menu 56 € (dinner) – Carte 48/62 €

• Modern French • Bistro •

If you enjoy a bistro atmosphere, you will love this charming restaurant set in a quiet residential district close to the Stadtpark. It serves modern French cuisine with menu options including turbot with carrots, olives and macadamia nuts.

SHIKI Brasserie & Bar - Restaurant SHIKI

Krugerstr. 3 ✉ 1010 – Ⓜ Karlsplatz – ✆ (01) 5 12 73 97 – www.shiki.at – Closed 4-10 February, 5-18 August, Sunday-Monday and Bank Holidays

Plan: **E3**

Menu 58 € – Carte 50/132 €

• Japanese • Brasserie • Design •

This minimalist-style brasserie with its large terrace is SHIKI's less formal eatery. It offers a wider range of dishes from miso soup to tempura and sushi – the latter prepared before you as you sit at the sushi bar.

Sakai

Florianigasse 36 ✉ 1080 – Ⓜ Josefstädter Str. – ✆ (01) 7 29 65 41 – www.sakai.co.at – Closed 29 July-20 August and Monday-Tuesday

Plan I: **A3**

Menu 49/79 € – Carte 17/60 €

• Japanese • Minimalist •

Hiroshi Sakai, no stranger in Vienna, set up his own restaurant after 10 years at Unkai. He serves seasonally influenced, traditional Japanese cuisine. Take a seat in the authentically simple surroundings and enjoy some sushi and sashimi or better still, one of his sophisticated set Kaiseki menus.

Le Salzgries Paris

Marc-Aurel-Str. 6 ✉ 1010 – Ⓜ Schwedenplatz – ✆ (01) 5 33 40 30 – www.le-salzgries.at – Closed 1-8 January, 14-23 April and Sunday-Monday

Plan: **D1**

Menu 48/72 € (dinner) – Carte 42/72 €

• Classic French • Brasserie • Fashionable •

This exuberant, lively bistro is decorated in warm colours and has a modern b[illegible] which is a real eye-catcher. The tried and tested French cuisine offers [illegible] dishes including entrecote.

Schnattl

Lange Gasse 40 ✉ 1080 – Ⓜ Rathaus Plan I: **A3**
– ✆ (01) 4 05 34 00 – www.schnattl.com – Closed 1 week Easter, 3 weeks August, 24 December-6 January, Saturday-Sunday and Bank Holidays
Menu 22/48 € – Carte 34/56 € – *(only lunch, Friday also dinner)*
• Country • Cosy •

This friendly, personally-run restaurant is set a little out of the way but remains popular with regulars and theatregoers, who appreciate the classic cuisine and warm, friendly atmosphere.

Servitenwirt

Servitengasse 7 ✉ 1090 – Ⓜ Roßauer Lände Plan I: **A2**
– ✆ (01) 3 15 23 87 – www.servitenwirt.at
Menu 49/69 € (dinner) – Carte 28/57 €
• Austrian • Friendly • Cosy •

If you're looking for some typical, fresh Viennese fare, you'll find it in this quiet square by the church. Try the lights cooked in Riesling, the fried breaded chicken and the Topfenschmarrn, a sort of sweet quark-based pancake. Alternatively, go for the entrecote. The garden is inviting in fine weather.

Tempel

Praterstr. 56 ✉ 1020 – Ⓜ Nestroyplatz Plan: **F1**
– ✆ (01) 2 14 01 79 – www.restaurant-tempel.at – Closed 1-7 January, 6-19 August and Saturday lunch, Sunday-Monday
Menu 40/52 € – Carte 25/50 €
• Country • Bistro •

You may have to search for the slightly concealed entrance to the interior courtyard and lovely terrace that lead to this friendly restaurant. It serves flavoursome, contemporary Mediterranean cuisine and offers a good value lunchtime menu.

Weibel's Wirtshaus

Kumpfgasse 2 ✉ 1010 – Ⓜ Stubentor Plan: **E2**
– ✆ (01) 5 12 39 86 – www.weibel.at
Menu 32 € (dinner) – Carte 26/53 € – *(booking advisable)*
• Austrian • Friendly •

Just a few minutes' walk from St Stephen's Cathedral, Weibel's Wirtshaus is the archetypal Viennese restaurant – warm and friendly, rustic and snug! It also has a charming garden in the small alleyway. The food is traditional and Viennese.

Yohm

Petersplatz 3 ✉ 1010 – Ⓜ Stephansplatz Plan: **D2**
– ✆ (01) 5 33 29 00 – www.yohm.at
Carte 26/47 €
• Asian • Fashionable • Neighbourhood •

A pleasant modern restaurant with striking orange decor, occupying two floors. The open kitchen serves up contemporary twists on Southeast Asian cuisine that borrows liberally from around the globe. Good wine selection.

loca.

Stubenbastei 10 ✉ 1010 – Ⓜ Stubentor Plan: **E2**
– ✆ (01) 5 12 11 72 – www.bettereatbetter.com
Menu 38/48 € – *(dinner only) (booking advisable)*
• Country • Cosy •

"Better eat better" is the slogan of this friendly little restaurant close to the Stadtpark. The menu includes dishes such as zander served with two sorts of pumpkin and speck. Don't be afraid to ask for the special theatre menus.

O boufés

Dominikanerbastei 17 ✉ 1010 – Ⓜ Stubentor – ✆ (01) 5 12 22 29 10 – www.konstantinfilippou.com – Closed Sunday and Bank Holidays

Plan: **E2**

Carte 39/54 € – *(dinner only)*

• Mediterranean cuisine • Bistro •

Located just next door to its gourmet counterpart, this relaxed restaurant with its bare walls, high ceilings and minimalist decor, serves a varied menu. It ranges from a charcuterie plate to keftedes (meatballs) with hilopites (small green pasta squares), as well as black pudding ravioli with cuttlefish, shellfish and peas. The food is accompanied by a choice of natural wines.

OUTER DISTRICTS — PLAN I

Amador

Grinzingerstr. 86 ✉ 1190 – Ⓜ Heiligenstadt – ✆ (0660) 9070500 – www.restaurant-amador.com – Closed August and Sunday-Tuesday

Plan: **A1**

Menu 69 € (lunch)/235 € – Carte 105/135 € – *(dinner only) (booking essential)*

• Creative • Chic • Elegant •

The food on offer here is pure Juan Amador: pared down, creative, intense and full of contrasts; sophisticated, multi-layered and made using nothing but the best ingredients. The surroundings are stylish, modern and upmarket. The restaurant is located in a vaulted cellar at the Hajszan winery, a spin-off of Fritz Wieninger's wine empire.

➜ Carabineros, Karfiol, Limette, Turron. Miéral Taube, Mango, Cocos, Purple Curry. Brick in the Wall, Rote Rüben, Himbeer, Gewürzmilch.

Mraz & Sohn

Wallensteinstr. 59 ✉ 1200 – Ⓜ Friedensbrücke – ✆ (01) 3 30 45 94 – www.mrazundsohn.at – Closed 21 December-7 January, during Easter, 12 August-2 September, Saturday-Sunday and Bank Holidays

Plan: **A2**

Menu 140 € – *(dinner only)*

• Creative • Fashionable • Chic •

In the 20th district on the outskirts of Vienna, Mraz & Sohn offers some of the most creative cuisine to be found in the city, serving punchy food that is full of flavour in a distinctive, modern setting. The excellent service and first-class wine recommendations add the final touch to this culinary experience.

➜ Messermuschel, Steinpilz. Taube, Kürbis. Erdbeere, Basilikum.

Pramerl & the Wolf (Wolfgang Zankl-Sertl)

Pramergasse 21 ✉ 1090 – Ⓜ Roßauer Lände – ✆ (01) 946 41 39 – www.pramerlandthewolf.com – Closed 9-26 January, 31 July-17 August and Sunday-Monday

Plan: **A2**

Menu 65/95 € – *(dinner only) (booking essential)*

• Creative • Bistro • Neighbourhood •

This former bar in Vienna's 9th district is simple and pleasantly unpretentious, its surprise menu promising inexpensive yet sophisticated fare that is full of contrast. No unnecessary frills here, just excellent produce and great value for money! The best way to reach it is on the U4 underground line.

➜ Makrele, Kohlrabi, Salzzitrone. Steinbutt, Pilze, Vin Jaune. Alte Milchkuh, Kopfsalat, Schnittlauch.

Freyenstein

Thimiggasse 11 (by Währinger Straße) ✉ 1180 – ✆ (0664) 4 39 08 37 – www.freyenstein.at – Closed Sunday-Monday

Menu 33/58 € – *(dinner only) (booking advisable)*

• Market cuisine • Family •

This restaurant promises a warm and friendly family ambience and attentive, pleasantly informal service. However, attention focuses on the set menu, which offers two small dishes per course, and all are flavoursome and aroma[illegible] Demand for tables here is correspondingly high!

MAST Weinbistro

Porzellangasse 53 ✉ 1090 – Ⓜ Friedensbrücke Plan: **A2**
– ✆ (01) 9226679 – www.mast.wine – Closed 21 January-12 February, 5-20 August and Monday-Tuesday, Saturday lunch, Sunday lunch
Menu 59 € – Carte 35/37 €
• Austrian • Winstub • Rustic •

No wonder MAST is so popular – the atmosphere is friendly, the decor rustic yet modern and the excellent food offers great value for money! Try the braised Jerusalem artichokes, marinated fillet steak of venison and porcini.

Woracziczky

Spengergasse 52 ✉ 1050 – Ⓜ Pilgramgasse – ✆ (0699) 11 22 95 30 – www.woracziczky.at – Closed 24 December-11 January, 5-23 August, Saturday-Sunday and Bank Holidays Plan: **A3**
Carte 23/45 €
• Austrian • Neighbourhood • Family •

The chef reserves a warm personal welcome for diners in this friendly, pleasantly informal inn (pronounced 'Vorashitkzy'). It is particularly popular for its casual atmosphere and local Viennese cuisine.

57

Donau City Str. 7 (by A 22) ✉ 1220 – Ⓜ Donauinsel – ✆ (01) 9 01 04 – www.57melia.com – Closed Saturday lunch, Sunday dinner
Menu 24 € (lunch)/70 € (dinner) – Carte 45/65 €
• Mediterranean cuisine • Design •

The spectacular view from 57 – set on 57th floor of the Meliá Hotel – is completed by the smart designer interior and, of course, the menu, which contains such offerings as saddle of lamb with courgettes, mushrooms and spinach brioche.

Eckel

Sieveringer Str. 46 (by Billrothstraße) ✉ 1190 – ✆ (01) 3 20 32 18 – www.restauranteckel.at – Closed 4-19 August, 20 December-20 January and Sunday-Monday
Carte 27/71 €
• Country • Family • Traditional décor •

This family-run restaurant in the attractive 19th district attracts plenty of regulars who come to sample its fresh cuisine. Menu options include such classics as breaded veal sweetbreads with potato and lamb's lettuce salad. The cosy atmosphere and attractive dining rooms are equally appealing, as is the magnificent garden terrace.

grace

Danhausergasse 3 ✉ 1040 – Ⓜ Taubstummengasse Plan: **B3**
– ✆ (01) 503 10 22 – www.grace-restaurant.at – Closed 8-17 January, 3-14 September and Sunday-Monday
Menu 52/89 € – Carte 45/57 € – *(Tuesday - Friday dinner only)*
• Creative • Cosy •

A café in a previous incarnation, grace has been converted into a pretty, modern restaurant with a quiet, secluded terrace. You will still find the original wood panelling and tiled floor in one of the rooms. The cuisine is creative.

Fuhrmann

Fuhrmanngasse 9 ✉ 1080 – Ⓜ Rathaus Plan: **A3**
– ✆ (01) 9444324 – www.restaurantfuhrmann.com – Closed 1-6 January, Saturday-Sunday
Menu 45/59 € – Carte 34/50 €
• Austrian • Family • Friendly •

If you're after some top-of-the-range Austrian cuisine, you need look no further than this comfortable, well-run restaurant, where you might try the Donauland lamb with marinated tomatoes, puntarelle and polenta. Pretty rear courtyard terrace.

Kutschker 44

Kutschergassee 44 (by Währinger Straße) ✉ 1180 – Ⓜ Währinger Str.-Volksoper – ✆ (01) 4 70 20 47 – www.kutschker44.at – Closed Sunday-Monday and Bank Holidays

Menu 34/39 € – Carte 27/67 € – *(dinner only)*

• Traditional cuisine • Fashionable •

This relaxed and friendly, modern restaurant is very popular with locals, and no wonder given the delicious fare on offer. Menu options include chanterelle terrine with walnuts, lamb's lettuce and bresaola as well as Viennese specialities such as veal lights and Black Angus rib eye steak. Terrace onto the pedestrian zone.

Rudi's Beisl

Wiedner Hauptstr. 88 ✉ 1050 – Ⓜ Taubstummengasse Plan: **B3**
– ✆ (01) 5 44 51 02 – www.rudisbeisl.at – Closed Saturday-Sunday and Bank Holidays

Carte 16/42 €

• Country • Bourgeois • Neighbourhood •

Always busy and bustling, Rudi's Beisl is a down-to-earth eatery with lots of decoration on the walls – small, simple and snug! The friendly owner does the cooking himself: traditional fare such as schnitzel, boiled beef and pancakes.

SALZBURG
SALZBURG

oriredmouse/iStock

SALZBURG IN...

→ **ONE DAY**
Festung Hohensalzburg, Museum der Moderne, Cathedral, Residenzplatz.

→ **TWO DAYS**
Mozart's birthplace, Nonntal, Kapuzinerberg, Mirabell Gardens, concert at Mozarteum.

→ **THREE DAYS**
Mozart's residence, Hangar 7, Hellbrunn Palace, concert at Landestheater.

Small but perfectly formed, Salzburg is a chocolate-box treasure, gift-wrapped in stunning Alpine surroundings. It's immortalised as the birthplace and inspiration of one of classical music's greatest stars, and shows itself off as northern Europe's grandest exhibitor of baroque style. Little wonder that in summer its population rockets, as the sound of music wafts from hotel rooms and festival hall windows during rehearsals for the Festspiele. In quieter times of the year, Salzburgers enjoy a leisurely and relaxed pace of life. Their love of music and the arts is renowned; and they enjoy the

outdoors, too, making the most of the mountains and lakes, and the paths which run along the river Salzach and zig-zag through the woods and the grounds of Hellbrunn. The dramatic natural setting of Salzburg means you're never likely to get lost. Rising above the left bank (the Old Town) is the Mönchsberg Mountain and its fortress, the Festung Hohensalzburg, while the right bank (the New Town, this being a relative term) is guarded by the even taller Kapuzinerberg. In the New Town stands the Mozart family home, while the graceful gardens of the Schloss Mirabell draw the right bank crowds. The Altstadt (Old Town) is a UNESCO World Heritage Site and its star turn is its Cathedral. To the east is the quiet Nonntal area overlooked by the Nuns' Mountain.

EATING OUT

Salzburg's cuisine takes much of its influence from the days of the Austro-Hungarian Empire, with Bavarian elements added to the mix. Over the centuries it was characterised by substantial pastry and egg dishes to fill the stomachs of local salt mine workers; it's still hearty and meaty and is typified by dumplings and broths. In the city's top restaurants, a regional emphasis is still very important but the cooking has a lighter, more modern touch. Beyond the city are picturesque inns and tranquil beer gardens, many idyllically set by lakes. Do try the dumplings: Pinzgauer Nocken are made of potato pastry and filled with minced pork; another favourite is Gröstl, a filling meal of 'leftovers', including potatoes, dumplings, sausages and smoked meat roasted in a pan. If you want a snack, then Jausen is for you – cold meals with bread and sausage, cheese, dumplings, bacon etc, followed by an Obstler, made from distilled fruit. Salzburg's sweet tooth is evident in the Salzburger Nockerl, a rich soufflé omelette made with fruit and soft meringue.

Esszimmer (Andreas Kaiblinger)
Plan: **A1**

Müllner Hauptstr. 33 ✉ 5020 – ✆ (0662) 87 08 99 – www.esszimmer.com – Closed Sunday-Monday
Menu 45 € (lunch)/128 € – Carte 74/101 €
• Creative • Fashionable • Elegant •

Elegant but far from stiff, the Kaiblinger's restaurant is decorated with lively colour accents and the charming front-of-house team serve punchy cuisine that is modern with classical influences, always finely balanced and anything but boring! Attractive rear courtyard terrace.

→ Steinbutt mit Schmortomate, Polenta und Kräuterpaste. Kalbsbrust und Kalbsbries mit Nüssen, Zimt und Apfel. Zwetschge und Nougat mit Limettenbaiser.

The Glass Garden – Hotel Schloss Mönchstein
Plan: **A1**

Mönchsberg Park 26 ✉ 5020 – ✆ (0662) 8 48 55 50 – www.monchstein.at – Closed February-March, November and Tuesday, except festival period
Menu 58/145 € – Carte 54/116 €
• Classic cuisine • Elegant • Classic décor •

A special place serving ambitious cuisine, Schloss Mönchstein offers modern, internationally and regionally influenced fare that is prepared with skill and commitment, and includes top-quality steaks from the charcoal grill. The atmosphere is sophisticated and the setting is idyllic.

Riedenburg
Plan: **A2**

Neutorstr. 31 ✉ 5020 – ✆ (0662) 83 08 15 – www.riedenburg.at – Closed 1-9 September and Sunday-Monday, except festival period
Menu 51/72 € (dinner) – Carte 32/66 € – *(booking advisable)*
• Classic cuisine • Cosy •

Nicole and Helmut Schinwald offer classic Austrian cuisine. Wiener schnitzel, Tauern lamb and sea bass are served in comfortable yet elegant dining rooms with light wood, warm colours and modern pictures. Wonderful garden with chestnut trees.

Brunnauer
Plan: **B2**

Fürstenallee 5 ✉ 5020 – ✆ (0662) 25 10 10 – www.restaurant-brunnauer.at – Closed 3-17 February, 6-14 July and Saturday-Sunday except season
Menu 69 € – Carte 47/77 €
• French • Elegant • Friendly •

Your hosts here have created a stylish restaurant in a lovely, old Ceconi-built villa. Its high ceilings, wooden floors and well-chosen furnishings provide the atmosphere, while the upmarket menu reveals French, regional and international influences. The terrace offers a wonderful view of the fortifications.

PARADOXON
Plan: **B2**

Zugallistr. 7 ✉ 5020 – ✆ (0664) 1 61 61 91 – www.restaurant-paradoxon.com – Closed Sunday-Monday
Carte 42/64 € – *(dinner only)*
• Modern cuisine • Trendy • Friendly •

Those who like a restaurant with a difference will find both the interior and the cuisine here unpretentious, unconventional and anything but staid. The one thing you can always be sure of is the quality of the food.

Weiher Wirt

König Ludwig Str. 2 (South: 2 km by Moostr.) ✉ 5020 – ✆ (0662) 82 93 24 – www.weiherwirt.com – Closed 3 weeks January and Monday
Carte 26/62 € – *(winter: dinner only, Sunday also lunch)*
• Austrian • Inn •

This restaurant is wonderfully located on the banks of Leopoldskroner Lake. It serves regional dishes such as Szegediner pork goulash with boiled potatoes. Warm colours and modern notes provide a pleasant feel; outside is a lovely garden.

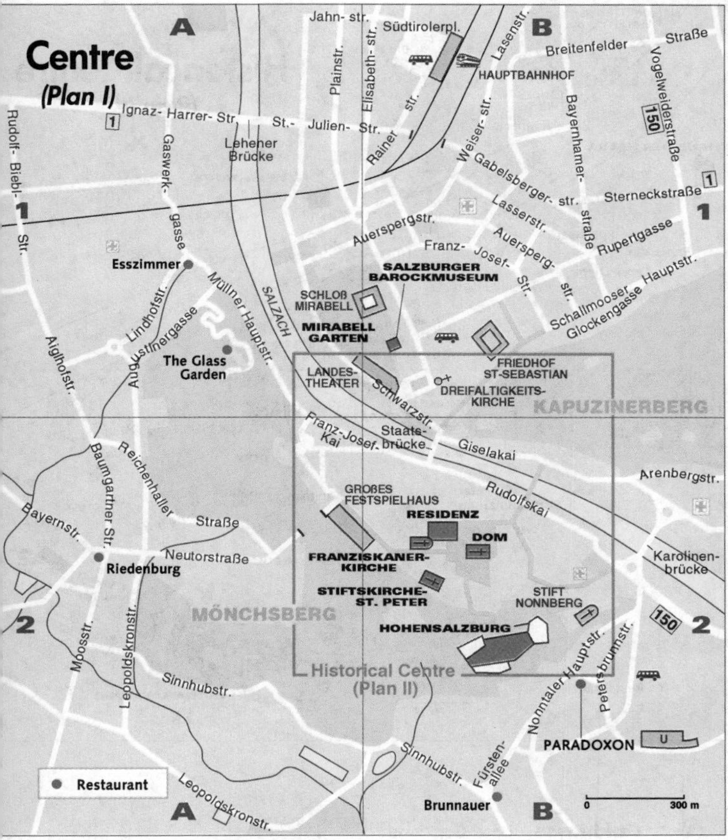

Centre
(Plan I)

A
B
Jahn- str.
Südtirolerpl.
Lasenstr.
Breitenfelder Straße
HAUPTBAHNHOF
Plainstr.
Elisabeth- str.
Rainer str.
Ignaz- Harrer- Str.
St.- Julien- Str.
Rudolf- Biebl- Str.
Gaswerk- gasse
Lehener Brücke
Weiser- str.
Bayernhamer- straße
Vogelweiderstraße
150
Gabelsberger- str.
Lasserstr.
Sterneckstraße
1
Auerspergstr.
Franz- Josef- Str.
Auersperg- str.
Rupertgasse
Esszimmer
Müllner Hauptstr.
SALZACH
SALZBURGER BAROCKMUSEUM
SCHLOß MIRABELL
Schallmooser Hauptstr.
Glockengasse
Lindhofstr.
Augustinergasse
MIRABELL GARTEN
Aiglhofstr.
The Glass Garden
LANDES-THEATER
Schwarzstr.
FRIEDHOF ST-SEBASTIAN
DREIFALTIGKEITS-KIRCHE
KAPUZINERBERG
Franz-Josef-Kai
Staatsbrücke
Giselakai
Reichenhaller Straße
Baumgartner Str.
Arenbergstr.
GROßES FESTSPIELHAUS
Rudolfskai
RESIDENZ
Bayernstr.
DOM
Neutorstraße
Riedenburg
FRANZISKANER-KIRCHE
Karolinen-brücke
STIFTSKIRCHE-ST. PETER
STIFT NONNBERG
MÖNCHSBERG
HOHENSALZBURG
2
Moosstr.
Leopoldskronstr.
Nonntaler Hauptstr.
Petersbrunnstr.
Historical Centre (Plan II)
Sinnhubstr.
PARADOXON
Restaurant
Leopoldskronstr.
Fürstenallee
Brunnauer
0
300 m

HISTORICAL CENTRE — PLAN II

Carpe Diem

XX ♿ AC

Getreidegasse 50 (1st floor) ✉ 5020 – ✆ (0662) 84 88 00 — Plan: **C1**
– www.carpediemfinestfingerfood.com – Closed 3-20 February and Sunday except Festival period, December and Bank Holidays
Menu 78/118 € – Carte 61/89 €

• Market cuisine • Fashionable • Design •

You can sample Carpe Diem's famous "cones" throughout the restaurant and its classically based cuisine with modern, international influences made using only the finest ingredients on the first floor. The service is friendly and professional. Look out for the great value lunchtime menu.

→ Kärntner Lax'n, Süßkartoffel, Zitrusfrüchte, Koriander. Heimischer Saibling, Topinambur, Quitte, Haselnuss. Limousin Lammrücken, Kichererbsen, Apfel, grünen Bohnen.

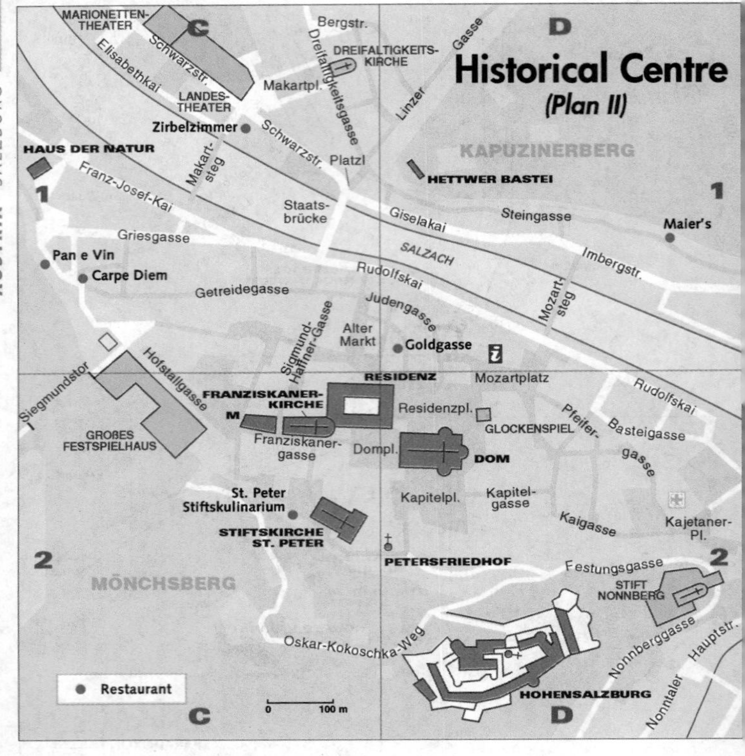

Goldgasse – Hotel Goldgasse

Goldgasse 10 ✉ 5020 – ✆ (0662) 84 56 22 – www.hotelgoldgasse.at Plan: **D1**

Carte 29/83 €

• Traditional cuisine • Cosy • Friendly •

The speciality here is new interpretations of old Salzburg recipes taken from a cookbook published in 1719! The food is a perfect match for the period setting with modern touches and the lively atmosphere – the charming service is the icing on the cake! Try the fried breaded chicken with potato and cucumber salad and cranberries and the apple strudel with vanilla sauce.

Pan e Vin

Gstättengasse 1 (1st floor) ✉ 5020 – ✆ (0662) 84 46 66 – www.panevin.at – Closed 1-10 September and Sunday, except festival period Plan: **C1**

Menu 89 € (dinner) – Carte 51/79 €

• Mediterranean cuisine • Cosy •

Pan e Vin is set in a 600 year-old building with an interior decorated in warm tones. It serves food with a distinctly Mediterranean feel alongside a well-stocked international wine list. The Azzuro on the ground floor is also a good option.

St. Peter Stiftskulinarium

St. Peter Bezirk 1/4 ✉ *5020* – ✆ *(0662) 8 41 26 80* Plan: **C2**
– *www.stpeter.at*
Carte 40/83 €
• Austrian • Traditional décor • Cosy •

Dating back to 803, this is one of the oldest restaurants in Europe! Diners sit comfortably in its lovely old interior to enjoy ambitious cuisine in the form of "connoisseur" dishes including braised Fassona beef with polenta, black salsify and truffle or traditional Austrian fare such as Wiener schnitzel. The wine list numbers some 600 different bottles and there is a lovely Baroque function room on the first floor.

Zirbelzimmer – Hotel Sacher

Schwarzstr. 5 ✉ *5020* – ✆ *(0662) 88 97 70* Plan: **C1**
– *www.sacher.com – Closed March-June*
Menu 50/90 € (dinner) – Carte 43/76 €
• Market cuisine • Elegant •

Sacher's culinary flagship offers a wide and varied menu ranging from poached langoustine to Styrian fried chicken, all served in a warm, friendly and typically Austrian setting. There is also an attractive balcony overlooking the River Salzach.

Maier's

Steingasse 61 ✉ *5020* – ✆ *(0662) 87 93 79* Plan: **D1**
– *www.maiersgastro.at – Closed Sunday-Monday*
Carte 45/75 € – *(dinner only) (booking advisable)*
• International • Friendly • Cosy •

Many regulars visit this restaurant in an old alleyway to enjoy classic fare including steaks and Szegediner goulash. The feel is welcoming, the service friendly and you can park in the multi-storey car park right opposite the restaurant.

ENVIRONS OF SALZBURG AND AIRPORT

Ikarus

Wilhelm-Spazier-Str. 7a (Hangar 7) (West: 4 km by Maxglaner Hauptstr.) ✉ *5020* – ✆ *(0662) 2 19 70 – www.hangar-7.com – closed end December-early January*
Menu 58 € (lunch)/190 € – *(Monday-Wednesday dinner only) (booking essential)*
• Creative • Fashionable • Elegant •

An unusual concept, the architecturally impressive Hangar-7 is both a Red Bull exhibition space and an ultra-modern luxury restaurant serving top quality creative cuisine. Choose from a menu devised by the international guest chef of the month or the restaurant's own Ikarus selection.

➜ Jakobsmuschel, Blumenkohl, Zitrone, Wacholder. "Rindsroulade" vom geschmorten Wagyu Beef mit Zwiebel, Senf und Kohl. Grieß, Kirsche, Pistazie, Orangenblüte.

SENNS.Restaurant

Söllheimerstr. 16 (at Gusswerk - Object 6c) (North-East: 5,5 km by Vogelweiderstraße) ✉ *5020* – ✆ *(0664) 4 54 02 32 – www.senns.restaurant – Closed 22 December-6 January and Saturday lunch, Sunday-Monday, except festival period*
Menu 99 € (lunch)/185 € – *(booking advisable)*
• Creative • Fashionable • Friendly •

There's plenty to look at in this former foundry with its stylish urban look and industrial charm, but as soon as the friendly yet discreet front-of-house team has served the first course, you'll find that Andreas Senn and Christian Geisler's creative, fully flavoured modern cuisine - made using the very best ingredients - demands your full attention.

➜ Carabinero, gelbe Karotte, Chimmichurri, Quinoa, Yuzu. Silver Hill Ente, Apfelrauch, Topinambur, Fragolino Trauben. Wagyu Short Rib, Kopfsalat, Artischocke, Physalis.

Brandstätter – Hotel Brandstätter

Münchner Bundesstr. 69 (North-West: 4,5 km by Ignaz-Harrer-Str.) ✉ 5020 – ✆ (0662) 43 45 35 – www.hotel-brandstaetter.com – Closed 23-27 December and Sunday, except festival period and Advent
Carte 35/65 € – *(booking advisable)*
• Country • Cosy •

Try the creamy veal goulash and the local venison, and don't miss the Mohr im Hemd (chocolate hazelnut pudding with an exquisite chocolate sauce)! Pretty, cosy dining rooms – the Swiss pine room with its tiled oven has its own charm.

Gasthof Auerhahn

Bahnhofstr. 15 (North: 3,5 km by Elisabeth-Str.) ✉ 5020 – ✆ (0662) 45 10 52 – www.auerhahn-salzburg.at – Closed 2 weeks January, 2 weeks June and Sunday dinner-Tuesday
Menu 28 € (Vegetarian)/88 € – Carte 29/49 €
• Country • Friendly • Cosy •

Try Topfenknödel (curd cheese dumplings) and classic dishes such as boiled beef with apple and horseradish sauce or medallions of venison with port sauce. If you like the warm and friendly dining rooms, you will love the guest-rooms, which although not huge, are pretty and well kept.

Huber's im Fischerwirt

Peter Pfenninger Str. 8 (North-West: 3,5 km by Ignaz-Harrer-Str.) ✉ 5020 – ✆ (0662) 42 40 59 – www.fischerwirt-liefering.at – Closed February and Tuesday-Wednesday
Menu 49/89 € – Carte 33/90 €
• Austrian • Cosy • Rural •

The Hubers serve regional classics and international fare in their charming restaurant. Dishes include Viennese fried chicken with lamb's lettuce and potato salad, and game stew with bread dumplings. There is also a small shop selling jams, chocolate and caviar.

Zum Buberl Gut

Gneiser Str. 31 (South: 3 km by Nonntaler Hauptstr.) ✉ 5020 – ✆ (0662) 82 68 66 – www.buberlgut.at – Closed 1 week March, 1 week June, 1 week September and Tuesday
Menu 28 € (lunch) – Carte 56/74 € – *(booking advisable)*
• Traditional cuisine • Cosy • Rustic •

This pretty 17C manor house offers more than just an attractive setting. The food served in the splendid, elegant dining rooms and lovely garden is delicious. It includes dishes such as tuna fish tartare with avocado and mango and paprika chutney, as well as ossobuco with creamed Jerusalem artichokes and gremolata.

Gasthof Schloss Aigen

Schwarzenbergpromenade 37 (South-East: 2,5 km by Karolinenbrücke) ✉ 5026 – ✆ (0662) 62 12 84 – www.schloss-aigen.at – Closed 7-17 Januar, Monday-Wednesday, except festival period
Menu 36/64 € – Carte 30/71 €
• Austrian • Inn • Friendly •

Dating back to 1402, Schloss Aigen serves traditional Austrian cuisine with modern influences. Try the boiled beef, which comes in a range of different preparations. There is also a charming interior courtyard terrace set beneath sweet chestnut trees.

AT HALLWANG North-East: 6 km by Sterneckstraße

✿ **Pfefferschiff** (Jürgen Vigné)

Söllheim 3 ✉ 5300 – ☎ (0662) 66 12 42 – www.pfefferschiff.at – Closed 2 weeks mid June-early July and Sunday-Monday, except festival period
Menu 59/120 € – Carte 64/102 € – *(Tuesday - Friday dinner only except festival period) (booking essential)*
• Classic cuisine • Elegant • Cosy •

Standing at the gates of Salzburg, this top gourmet restaurant is located in a lovely 17C former parish house. The owner Jürgen Vigné's flavoursome and distinctive cuisine is matched by the charming front-of-house team managed by his wife. The dining rooms are delightful and the terrace is wonderful.
→ Garnele, Erdnuss, Kürbis, Vulcano Schinken. Rind, Miniburger, Aubergine, Barbecue. Quitte, Holunderbeere, Zitrone, Marzipan.

AT HOF BEI SALZBURG North-East: 18 km by Wolfgangsee Straße

Schloss Restaurant – Hotel Schloss Fuschl

Schloss Str. 19 ✉ 5322 – ☎ (06229) 2 25 30 – www.schlossfuschlsalzburg.com – Closed 2 weeks November
Menu 58 € (lunch)/130 € (dinner) – Carte 64/114 € – *(winter: dinner only)*
• Classic cuisine • Romantic • Elegant •

Where else could you enjoy ambitious cuisine in such an elegant setting with a lovely lake view? The food here is a mix of classic and international, the fish comes from the restaurant's own farm and the cellar provides over 1 000 different wines to accompany the Fuschlsee whitefish, mousseline of baby leeks, porcini and beurre noisette or the Mieral pigeon with mango, purple curry and coconut.

Antwerp
BRUSSELS

BELGIUM
BELGIË - BELGIQUE

MarioGuti/iStock

Brussels
BRUXELLES/BRUSSEL

sedmak/iStock

BRUSSELS IN...

→ **ONE DAY**
Grand Place, Musées Royaux des Beaux-Arts, Place Ste-Catherine.

→ **TWO DAYS**
Marolles, Place du Grand Sablon, Musical Instrument Museum, concert at Palais des Beaux-Arts.

→ **THREE DAYS**
Parc du Cinquantenaire, Horta's house, tour St Gilles and Ixelles.

There aren't many cities where you can use a 16C century map and accurately navigate your way around; or where there are enough restaurants to dine somewhere different every day for five years; or where you'll find a museum dedicated to the comic strip – but then every city isn't Brussels. It was tagged a 'grey' capital because of its EU associations but those who've spent time here know it to be, by contrast, a buzzing town. It's the home of art nouveau, it features a wonderful maze of medieval alleys and places to eat, and it's warm and friendly, with an outgoing, cosmopolitan feel – due in no small

part to its turbulent history, which has seen it under frequent occupation. Generally speaking, the Bruxellois believe that you shouldn't take things too seriously: they have a soft spot for puppets and Tintin, street music and majorettes; and they do their laundry in communal places like the Wash Club.

The area where all visitors wend is the Lower Town and the Grand Place but the northwest and southern quarters (Ste-Catherine and The Marolles) are also of particular interest. To the east, higher up an escarpment, lies the Upper Town – this is the traditional home of the aristocracy and encircles the landmark Parc de Bruxelles. Two suburbs of interest are St Gilles, to the southwest, and Ixelles, to the southeast, where trendy bars and art nouveau are the order of the day.

EATING OUT

As long as your appetite hasn't been sated at the chocolatiers, or with a cone of frites from a street stall, you'll relish the dining experience in Brussels. As long as you stay off the main tourist drag (i.e. Rue des Bouchers), you're guaranteed somewhere good to eat within a short strolling distance. There are lots of places to enjoy Belgian dishes such as moules frites, Ostend lobster, eels with green herbs, or waterzooi (chicken or fish stew with vegetables). Wherever you're eating, at whatever price range, food is invariably well cooked and often bursting with innovative touches. As a rule of thumb, the Lower Town has the best places, with the Ste-Catherine quarter's fish and seafood establishments the pick of the bunch; you'll also find a mini Chinatown here. Because of the city's cosmopolitan character there are dozens of international restaurants - ranging from French and Italian to more unusual Moroccan, Tunisian and Congolese destinations. Belgium beers are famous the world over and are served in specially designed glasses.

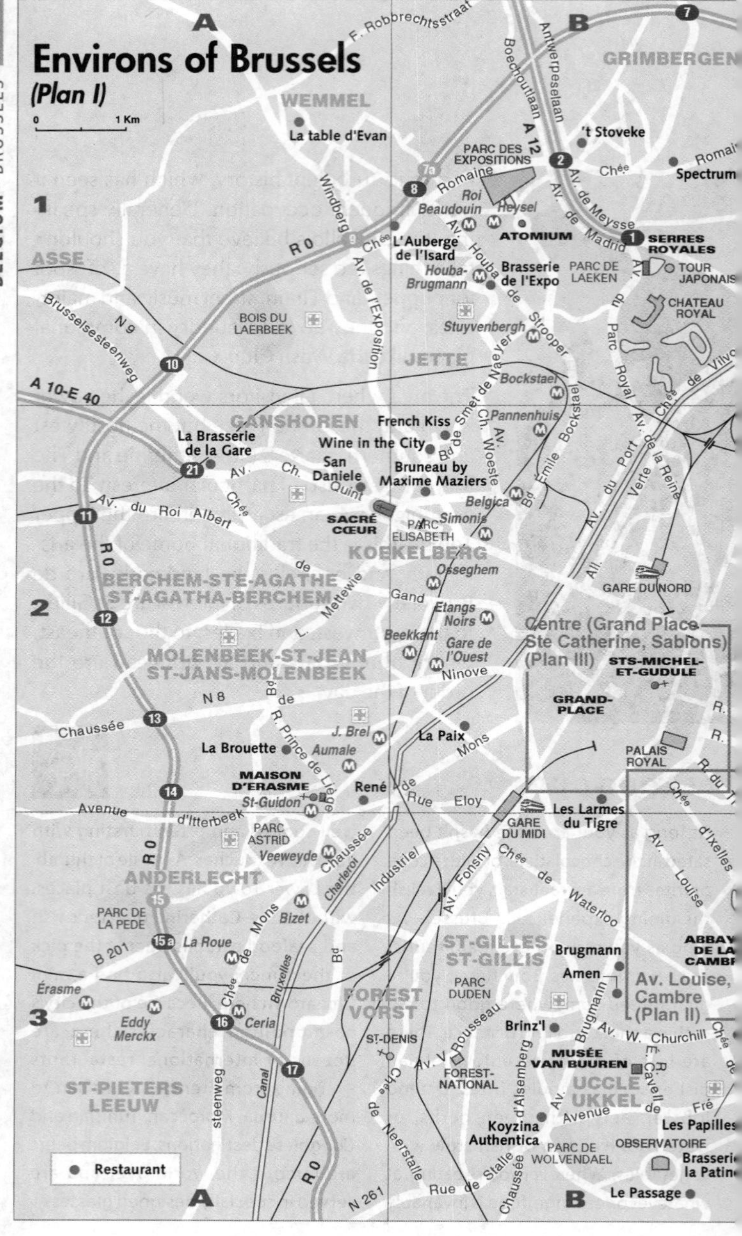
Environs of Brussels
(Plan I)
0
1 Km
A
B
1
2
3
WEMMEL
La table d'Evan
GRIMBERGEN
't Stoveke
Spectrum
PARC DES EXPOSITIONS
Heysel
ATOMIUM
SERRES ROYALES
TOUR JAPONAIS
CHATEAU ROYAL
PARC DE LAEKEN
Roi Beaudouin
L'Auberge de l'Isard
Houba-Brugmann
Brasserie de l'Expo
Stuyvenbergh
BOIS DU LAERBEEK
ASSE
JETTE
Bockstael
Pannenhuis
GANSHOREN
La Brasserie de la Gare
French Kiss
Wine in the City
San Daniele
Bruneau by Maxime Maziers
Belgica
Simonis
SACRÉ CŒUR
PARC ELISABETH
KOEKELBERG
Osseghem
GARE DU NORD
BERCHEM-STE-AGATHE
ST-AGATHA-BERCHEM
Etangs Noirs
Beekkant
Gare de l'Ouest
Centre (Grand Place Ste Catherine, Sablons) (Plan III)
STS-MICHEL-ET-GUDULE
GRAND-PLACE
PALAIS ROYAL
MOLENBEEK-ST-JEAN
ST-JANS-MOLENBEEK
J. Brel
La Paix
La Brouette
Aumale
MAISON D'ERASME
St-Guidon
René
GARE DU MIDI
Les Larmes du Tigre
PARC ASTRID
Veeweyde
ANDERLECHT
PARC DE LA PEDE
Bizet
La Roue
ST-GILLES
ST-GILLIS
Brugmann
Amen
ABBAYE DE LA CAMBRE
Av. Louise, Cambre (Plan II)
Érasme
Eddy Merckx
Ceria
FOREST
VORST
PARC DUDEN
ST-DENIS
Brinz'l
MUSÉE VAN BUUREN
FOREST-NATIONAL
UCCLE
UKKEL
ST-PIETERS LEEUW
Koyzina Authentica
PARC DE WOLVENDAEL
OBSERVATOIRE
Les Papilles
Le Passage
Restaurant
R 0
A 12
A 10-E 40
N 9
N 8
B 201
N 261
Brusselsesteenweg
F. Robbrechtsstraat
Antwerpeselaan
Boechoutlaan
Av. de l'Exposition
Windberg
Av. du Roi Albert
Chaussée de Ninove
Chaussée de Mons
Chaussée de Waterloo
Av. Louise
Av. W. Churchill
Rue Eloy
Av. Fonsny
Canal
Rue de Stalle

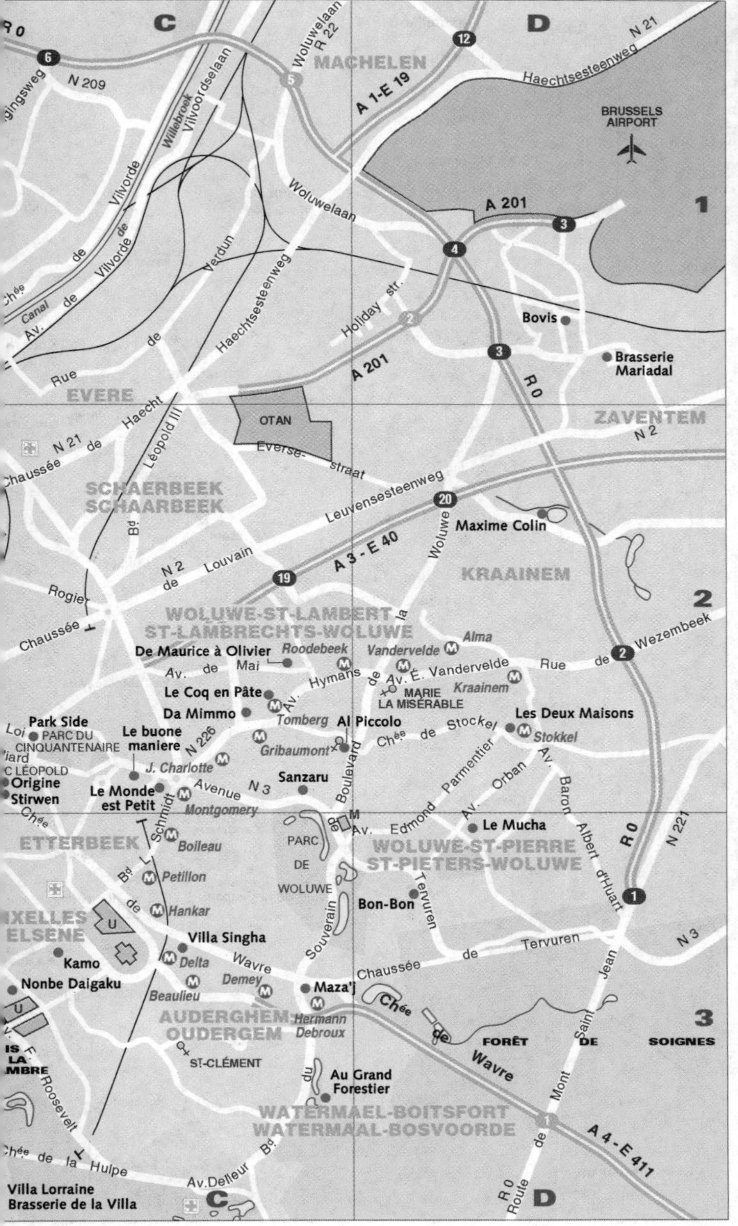
C
D
1
2
3
MACHELEN
BRUSSELS AIRPORT
EVERE
ZAVENTEM
OTAN
SCHAERBEEK
SCHAARBEEK
KRAAINEM
WOLUWE-ST-LAMBERT
ST-LAMBRECHTS-WOLUWE
ETTERBEEK
WOLUWE-ST-PIERRE
ST-PIETERS-WOLUWE
IXELLES
ELSENE
AUDERGHEM
OUDERGEM
WATERMAEL-BOITSFORT
WATERMAAL-BOSVOORDE
FORÊT DE SOIGNES
PARC DE WOLUWE
Bovis
Brasserie Mariadal
Maxime Colin
De Maurice à Olivier
Le Coq en Pâte
Da Mimmo
Al Piccolo
Les Deux Maisons
Park Side
Le buone maniere
Origine
Stirwen
Le Monde est Petit
Sanzaru
Le Mucha
Bon-Bon
Villa Singha
Kamo
Nonbe Daigaku
Maza'j
Au Grand Forestier
Villa Lorraine
Brasserie de la Villa
A 1-E 19
A 201
A 3 - E 40
A 4 - E 411
R 0
N 21
N 209
N 2
N 3
N 221
N 226
Woluwelaan
Haechtsesteenweg
Leuvensesteenweg
Chaussée de Louvain
Chaussée de Haecht
Rue de Wezembeek
Av. de Mai
Av. Hymans
Av. É. Vandervelde
Chée de Stockel
Av. Edmond Parmentier
Av. Orban
Av. Baron Albert d'Huart
Bd de la Woluwe
Bd du Souverain
Av. de Tervuren
Chaussée de Tervuren
Chée de Wavre
Chée de la Hulpe
Av. F. Roosevelt
Av. Delleur
Route de Mont Saint Jean
Holiday str.
Everse-straat
Canal de Vilvorde
Av. de Vilvorde
Vilvoordselaan
Bd Léopold III
Rue de Verdun
Rogier
Roodebeek
Vandervelde
Alma
Kraainem
Stokkel
Tomberg
Gribaumont
J. Charlotte
Montgomery
Boileau
Petillon
Hankar
Delta
Demey
Beaulieu
Hermann Debroux
MARIE LA MISÉRABLE
ST-CLÉMENT
PARC DU CINQUANTENAIRE
PARC LÉOPOLD

G
H
1
2
3
Strofilia
Selecto
Rue de Flandre
Rue
Ste-Catherine
LE BÉGUINAGE
Rue de Laeken
Bd Jacqmain
Bd Adolphe Max
Harvest
Place de Brouckère
Viva M'Boma
La Belle Maraichère
Pl. Ste-Catherine
Le Vismet
STE-CATHERINE
Rue du Houblon
Pl. du Nouveau Marché aux Grains
Antoine Dansaert
R. du Fossé aux
Samourai
THÉATRE DE LA MONNAIE
Rue N.-D. du Sommeil
Bd Anspach
R. des Fripiers
R. de l'Écuyer
De l'Ogenblik
R. des Fabriques
Rue des Chartreux
Arteveide
Pl. de la Bourse
Halles St-Géry
BOURSE
ST-NICOLAS
Scheltema
Comptoir des Galeries
HALLES ST-GÉRY
Rue T'Kint
R. des Six Jetons
RICHES CLAIRES
R. des Riches Claires
Rue Van Artevelde
GRAND-PLACE
R. Amigo
Bocconi
Cul Sec
R. du Midi
Boulevard Anspach
N.-D. DU BON SECOURS
Pl. Fontainas
MANNEKEN PIS
Lombard
Rue de Vautour
Rue de la Verdure
Rue du
R. de l'Étuve
Rue du Chêne
La Table de Mus
Anneessens
Lemonnier
Rue des Foulons
Alexandre
Rue Neuve
Rue des Alexiens
Boulevard de l'Empereur
Comme Chez Soi
Maurice
Stalingrad
Rue Terre
N.-D. DE LA CHAPELLE
Rue des Ursulines
Le Rabassier
Genco
San Sablon
Les Brigittines aux Marches de la Chapelle
Haute
Au Vieux Saint Martin
Lola
Boulevard Lemonnier
Avenue de Stalingrad
Rue Terre Neuve
Tanneurs
Rue du Miroir
Rue Blaes
Minimes
Les Petits Oignons
Bd du Poincaré
Rue du Midi
Rue Haute
R. E. Allard
CONSERVATOIRE
Pl. Poelaert
Rue des Capucins
Rue des
PALAIS DE JUSTICE
H
Restaurant

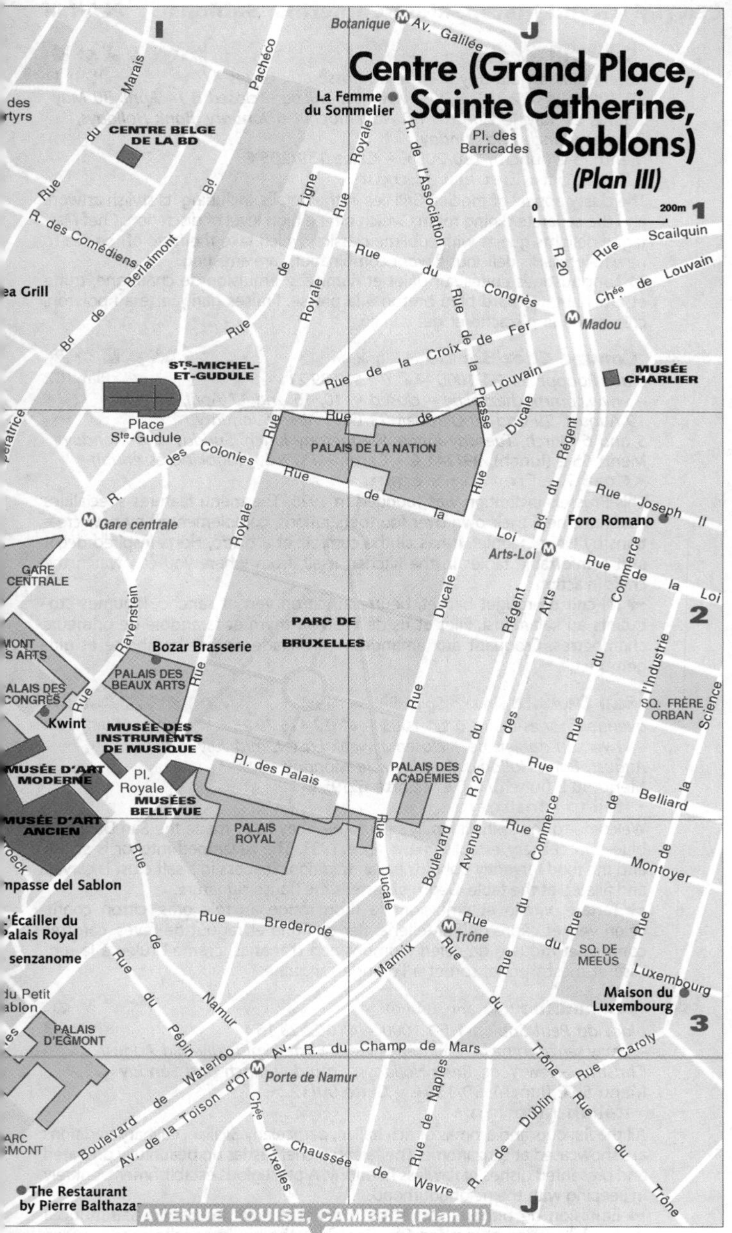
Centre (Grand Place, Sainte Catherine, Sablons)
(Plan III)
0
200m
I
J
1
2
3
Botanique
Av. Galilée
La Femme du Sommelier
Pl. des Barricades
des
rtyrs
Rue du Marais
Pacheco
CENTRE BELGE DE LA BD
R. de l'Association
Rue Royale
Rue de Ligne
Rue Royale
Bd
Rue
R. des Comédiens
Bd de Berlaimont
ea Grill
Rue du Congrès
R 20
Rue Scailquin
Chée de Louvain
Madou
Rue de la Presse
Rue de la Croix de Fer
Rue de Louvain
STS-MICHEL-ET-GUDULE
MUSÉE CHARLIER
Ducale
Place Ste-Gudule
peratrice
Rue des Colonies
PALAIS DE LA NATION
Rue de la Loi
Bd du Régent
Rue Joseph II
Foro Romano
R.
Gare centrale
Rue Royale
Arts-Loi
Rue de la Loi
Rue du Commerce
GARE CENTRALE
Ravenstein
Rue Ducale
Rue Régent
Arts
PARC DE BRUXELLES
Bozar Brasserie
MONT S ARTS
PALAIS DES BEAUX ARTS
Rue
l'Industrie
ALAIS DES CONGRÈS
Rue
Rue
SQ. FRÈRE ORBAN
Science
Kwint
MUSÉE DES INSTRUMENTS DE MUSIQUE
du
des
Rue
Pl. des Palais
PALAIS DES ACADÉMIES
Rue Belliard
la
MUSÉE D'ART MODERNE
Pl. Royale
MUSÉES BELLEVUE
R 20
de
MUSÉE D'ART ANCIEN
PALAIS ROYAL
Rue Ducale
Boulevard
Avenue
Rue du Commerce
Rue de Montoyer
roeck
Rue
mpasse del Sablon
L'Écailler du Palais Royal
Rue Brederode
Rue
Trône
Rue du
Rue
senzanome
de
Rue
Marnix
Rue
Rue
SQ. DE MEEÜS
Rue du Luxembourg
du Petit ablon
Rue du Pépin
Namur
Maison du Luxembourg
PALAIS D'EGMONT
Rue du Trône
Caroly
Av. R. du Champ de Mars
Boulevard de Waterloo
Porte de Namur
Rue de Naples
Rue
Av. de la Toison d'Or
Chée d'Ixelles
R. de Dublin
Rue du Trône
ARC MONT
Chaussée de Wavre
The Restaurant by Pierre Balthazar
AVENUE LOUISE, CAMBRE (Plan II)

✿✿ **Sea Grill** (Yves Mattagne) XXXX

Hôtel Radisson Blu Royal – rue du Fossé aux Loups 47 Plan: **I1**
✉ 1000 – ☎ 0 2 212 08 00 – www.seagrill.be – closed 8-14 April, 30 May-2 June, 21 July-15 August, 1-3 November, 1-6 January, Bank Holidays, Saturday lunch and Sunday
Menu 75 € (lunch), 150/205 € – Carte 139/205 €
• Seafood • Elegant • Luxury •

The classy appeal of the Sea Grill lies in the details, including its stylish artwork and the separate dining rooms which offer a high level of discretion. Chef Mattagne delights guests with sublime classics, which take the taste of the sea to new heights. His delicious flavour combinations are arresting.

➜ Langoustines cuites sur galet et flambées, émulsion de châtaigne, truffe et artichaut. Homard bleu breton à la presse. Fraises gariguette au poivron, crémeux à la pistache et gel vanillé.

✿✿ **Comme Chez Soi** (Lionel Rigolet) XXX

place Rouppe 23 ✉ 1000 – ☎ 0 2 512 29 21 Plan: **G2**
– www.commechezsoi.be – closed 9, 10, 16 and 17 April, 21 July-19 August, 29 and 30 October, 23 December-7 January, 5 and 6 March, Tuesday lunch, Wednesday lunch, Sunday and Monday
Menu 65 € (lunch), 99/241 € – Carte 94/377 € – *(booking essential)*
• Creative French • Elegant •

This Brussels institution was founded in 1926. The menu features specialities that have held their own over four generations, complemented by new creations by Lionel Rigolet. It has all the comfort of a bistro, Horta-inspired decor and comfortable tables in the kitchen itself, from where you can watch the chefs in action.

➜ Mi-cuit de rouget barbet, beurre au citron vert et sancho, légumes croquants au kalamansi. Filet et ris de veau au thym et farandole de primeurs champêtres. Croquant aux amandes, marmelade, sorbet framboise et gingembre.

✿ **San Daniele** (Franco Spinelli) XXX

avenue Charles-Quint 6 ✉ 1083 – ☎ 0 2 426 79 23 Plan I: **A2**
– www.san-daniele.be – closed 1 week Easter, mid July-mid August, Bank Holidays, Sunday and Monday
Menu 50 € (lunch)/110 € – Carte 62/95 €
• Italian • Intimate •

Welcome to the Spinelli family's fiefdom – they have made the San Daniele a blue-chip culinary establishment since 1983. The revamped interior is stylish and the food fervently upholds Italian tradition. Seabass in a salt crust is carved and filleted at the table. Depth of taste is the house signature.

➜ Tartare, vitello et émulsion de thon rouge au foie gras, citron confit, céleri vert et câpre de Pantelleria. Bar de ligne et ragoût de fèves, carottes confites et mousse de céleri. Composition d'ananas, crème brûlée à la réglisse et mascarpone, sorbet à l'orange sanguine.

✿ **senzanome** (Giovanni Bruno) XXX

place du Petit Sablon 1 ✉ 1000 – ☎ 0 2 223 16 17 Plan: **I3**
– www.senzanome.be – closed 1 week Easter, mid July-mid August, Christmas-New Year, Bank Holidays, Saturday lunch and Sunday
Menu 50 € (lunch), 90/120 € – Carte 90/122 €
• Italian • Design •

All the flavours and aromas of rich Italian, particularly Sicilian, culinary traditions are showcased at senzanome. The talented chef rustles up beautifully prepared and presented dishes of flawless harmony. A prestigious establishment, entirely in keeping with the neighbourhood.

➜ Émulsion de burrata, sorbet de tomate et huile au basilic. Saltimbocca de bar à la sauge et jambon San Daniele. Baba au limoncello et son caviar, crème de citron.

Bozar Restaurant (Karen Torosyan)

rue Baron Horta 3 ✉ 1000 – ✆ 0 25 03 00 00 Plan: **I2**
– www.bozarrestaurant.be – closed 1 week Easter, August, Saturday lunch, Sunday and Monday
Menu 49 € (lunch), 54/89 € – Carte 88/162 €
• Modern French • Fashionable •

Chef Torosyan's pork pie, the house speciality, is emblematic of his cuisine which subtly reinterprets traditional recipes. Do not expect pointlessly complicated dishes – the emphasis is on fine, generously served food.

➜ Rouget barbet laqué au citron confit, piment d'Espelette, fleur de courgette soufflée et jus bouillabaisse. Pigeon royal d'Anjou en croûte, foie gras d'oie et anguille fumée. Millefeuille à la vanille de Tahiti.

JB

rue du Grand Cerf 24 ✉ 1000 – ✆ 0 2 512 04 84 Plan: **H3**
– www.restaurantjb.com – closed August, 23-27 December, Bank Holidays, Monday lunch, Saturday lunch and Sunday
Menu 37/55 € – Carte 67/80 €
• Traditional cuisine • Friendly • Family •

Despite being located close to the Place Louise, this family-run restaurant remains discreet. The regulars all have their favourites, be it Flemish asparagus or grilled veal sweetbreads. Flavours are pronounced and the menu represents good value for money.

Les Petits Oignons

rue de la Régence 25 ✉ 1000 – ✆ 0 2 511 76 15 Plan: **H3**
– www.lespetitsoignons.be – closed 24 and 25 December, 1 January and 22 April
Menu 37 € – Carte 40/60 €
• Classic cuisine • Brasserie •

The visitor is of course charmed by the timeless decor and the lively atmosphere in this restaurant, but the delicious brasserie dishes are the real hit! Good quality produce, carefully prepared and simply presented dishes and an excellent wine list – you are in for VIP treatment!

Pré De Chez Nous

rue des Dominicains 19 ✉ 1000 – ✆ 0 2 833 37 37 Plan: **H1**
– www.predecheznous.be – closed Sunday and Monday
Menu 26 € (lunch), 33/51 €
• Organic • Simple •

Organic local produce takes the limelight in this urban restaurant. Vegetables are pampered by the chef and the menu always features a vegetarian dish. The chef is also a "slow food" enthusiast and cannot be faulted for his generous portions. The food is appetising and the selection of local beers is to die for!

Bocconi – Hôtel Amigo

rue de l'Amigo 1 ✉ 1000 – ✆ 0 2 547 47 15 Plan: **H2**
– www.roccofortehotels.com
Menu 20 € (lunch), 55/90 € – Carte 64/88 €
• Italian • Elegant •

This elegant Italian restaurant has taken up abode in the luxury Amigo Hotel, next-door to the Grand-Place and Manneken Pis. Appetising Italian fare (scrumptious risotto).

L'Écailler du Palais Royal

rue Bodenbroek 18 ✉ 1000 – ✆ 0 2 512 87 51 Plan: **I3**
– www.lecaillerdupalaisroyal.be – closed August and 25 December-2 January
Menu 60 € (lunch), 125/225 € 🍷 – Carte 77/180 €
• Seafood • Traditional décor •

Since 1967, this luxurious institution has been pampering its discerning clientele. The house specialty – seafood – is remarkable. The chef assembles premium produce into generous dishes that reveal the full depth and flavour of each ingredient.

El Impasse del Sablon – Hotel NH Collection Grand Sablon
r. Bodenbroek 2 – ✆ 0 2 420 48 41 Plan: I3
– www.elimpassedelsablon.com – closed August, Sunday and Monday
Menu 75 € – Carte 65/123 €
• Spanish • Elegant •
Spanish cuisine has far more to offer the discerning diner than the usual clichéd tapas and this restaurant amply proves that Spain's powerful flavours are also rich in subtlety. An intricate interplay of texture and flavour that is bound to woo your taste buds.

The Restaurant by Pierre Balthazar
The Hotel – boulevard de Waterloo 38 ✉ 1000 Plan: I3
– ✆ 0 2 504 13 33 – www.therestaurant.be – closed mid July-mid August, Bank Holidays, Monday lunch, Saturday lunch and Sunday
Menu 35 € (lunch), 59/69 € – Carte 60/68 €
• Modern cuisine • Chic • Fashionable •
Trendy bar food, made-to-measure cocktails, an inventive menu concept and a sexy lounge ambience depict The Restaurant. Chef Balthazar changes the menu weekly to allow free rein to his inspiration. The result is an enticing range of dishes with ingredients and recipes from all over the world.

Les Brigittines Aux Marches de la Chapelle
place de la Chapelle 5 ✉ 1000 – ✆ 0 2 512 68 91 Plan: H3
– www.lesbrigittines.com – closed Saturday lunch and Sunday
Menu 35 € (lunch), 55/75 € – Carte 45/67 €
• Traditional cuisine • Vintage •
This lavish Art Nouveau brasserie will, first and foremost, delight the eye! You will also find it impossible to resist the mouth-watering recipes rustled up by chef Dirk Myny. He is a genuine Brusselian, whose exuberant personality gives character to his traditional, market fresh dishes.

Alexandre
rue du Midi 164 ✉ 1000 – ✆ 0 2 502 40 55 Plan: G2
– www.restaurant-alexandre.be – closed last week August-first week September, first week January, Tuesday lunch, Saturday lunch, Sunday and Monday
Menu 45 € (lunch), 65/130 €
• Modern cuisine • Intimate •
This cosy restaurant is surprising in more than one way. From the first mouthful, diners are enchanted by the inventive recipes, rich in coherence and flavour. The lady of the house suggests excellent wine-food pairings.

La Belle Maraîchère
place Sainte-Catherine 11 ✉ 1000 – ✆ 0 2 512 97 59 Plan: G1
– www.labellemaraichere.com – closed mid July-early August, 2 weeks at Carnival, Wednesday and Thursday
Menu 44/68 € – Carte 56/115 € – (booking essential)
• Seafood • Friendly • Elegant •
This welcoming, family-run restaurant is a popular choice for locals, with its charmingly nostalgic decor. Enticing, traditional cuisine includes fish, shellfish and game depending on the season, as well as high quality sauces. Appealing set menus.

Comptoir des Galeries – Hôtel des Galeries
Galerie du Roi 6 ✉ 1000 – ✆ 0 22 13 74 74 Plan: H1
– www.comptoirdesgaleries.be – closed Sunday and Monday
Menu 26 € (lunch)/37 € – Carte 39/61 €
• Classic French • Brasserie • Friendly •
Vintage accents add character to this contemporary brasserie, in the heart of which stands a somewhat incongruous medal press! Pleasant establishment, ideal to savour brasserie classics made with good quality ingredients, or just for a glass of good wine.

Lola

place du Grand Sablon 33 ✉ 1000 – ✆ 0 2 514 24 60 Plan: **H3**
– www.restololа.be – closed 2 weeks in August and dinner 24 and 31 December
Carte 43/70 € – *(open until 11pm)*
• Mediterranean cuisine • Brasserie •
Lola is a friendly brasserie in the well-heeled Sablons district, where you can choose from a pleasant table or a seat at the bar. Appetising, varied menu, with a distinct preference for fresh ingredients. An assured choice since 1994.

Le Rabassier

rue de Rollebeek 23 ✉ 1000 – ✆ 0 2 502 04 00 Plan: **H3**
– www.lerabassier.be – closed last 2 weeks August, first 2 weeks January and Sunday
Menu 68/155 € – *(dinner only)*
• Classic cuisine • Elegant • Chic •
Whether black or white, from January to December the truffle is the star of this pocket-handkerchief restaurant. The chef is a past master in the art of extracting the full flavour of this noble ingredient. Fine French wines, attractive menus and a delightful manageress.

Au Vieux Saint Martin

place du Grand Sablon 38 ✉ 1000 – ✆ 0 2 512 64 76 Plan: **H3**
– www.auvieuxsaintmartin.be – closed 24 and 31 December
Carte 42/82 € – *(open until midnight)*
• Belgian • Brasserie • Classic décor •
The spirit of the well-heeled Sablons neighbourhood is visible in both the interior (colourful artwork) and the terrace. The brasserie is frequently packed to the seams, always proof of a good restaurant. The generous helpings of Brussels' specialties and other exquisitely prepared dishes (based on eggs) are truly mouthwatering.

Kwint

Mont des Arts 1 ✉ 1000 – ✆ 0 25 05 95 95 Plan: **I2**
– www.kwintbrussels.com
Menu 22 € (lunch), 29/46 € – Carte 36/62 € – *(open until 11pm)*
• Classic cuisine • Brasserie •
An amazing sculpture by artist Arne Quinze adds cachet to this elegant brasserie. It serves a tasty up-to-the-minute menu in which fine quality produce takes pride of place. The view of the city from the Mont des Arts is breathtaking. A great way to see another side of Brussels.

Cul Sec

rue des Chapeliers 16 ✉ 1000 – ✆ 0 2 511 06 20 Plan: **H2**
– closed 29 July-12 August and Sunday
Menu 25 € (lunch), 35/45 € – Carte 37/62 €
• French • Bistro •
While you may be tempted to knock back your wine in one go (meaning of 'cul sec'), take your time and savour the excellent French (and predominantly natural) wines served here, all the more so as the modern bistro's cuisine is a perfect pair to these fine vintages. Make a beeline for this wine bar near the Grand Place!

Genco

rue Joseph Stevens 28 ✉ 1000 – ✆ 0 2 511 34 44 Plan: **H3**
– closed 21 July-21 August, Sunday dinner and Monday
Carte 31/67 €
• Italian • Traditional décor • Bourgeois •
You will be welcomed into this Italian restaurant like a long-lost friend. Sit down to sample the chef's concoctions, whose generosity is equalled only by their flawless classicism. It is not difficult to understand why Genco has such a faithful clientele!

Harvest

place du Samedi 14 ✉ 1000 – ✆ 02 781 07 27 Plan: **H1**
– www.harvestrestaurantbruxelles.be – closed 24 December-2 January, Saturday lunch and Sunday
Menu 19 € (lunch)/39 €
• Modern French • Contemporary décor •
Harvest knows how to pamper Brussels' gourmets. It starts with a daily quest for the best produce (preferably local) and continues in the kitchen, where premium ingredients are assembled into fresh, original dishes and regularly renewed menus. A win-win recipe.

Les Larmes du Tigre

rue de Wynants 21 ✉ 1000 – ✆ 02 512 18 77 Plan I: **B2**
– www.leslarmesdutigre.be – closed Saturday lunch and Monday
Menu 17 € 🍷 (lunch), 36 € 🍷/45 € – Carte 37/48 €
• Thai • Exotic décor •
A real voyage for the taste buds! They have been serving authentic Thai food here for over 30 years, and the enjoyment for money ratio is excellent. Buffet at lunch and Sunday evenings.

De l'Ogenblik

Galerie des Princes 1 ✉ 1000 – ✆ 02 511 61 51 Plan: **H1**
– www.ogenblik.be – closed 1-15 August, lunch on Bank Holidays and Sunday
Menu 48/58 € – Carte 48/74 € – *(open until midnight)*
• Classic cuisine • Bistro • Simple •
A loyal band of regulars add a warm, friendly vibe to this former café, which has lost none of its authentic charm since it first opened its doors back in 1969. Classical repertory, bistro dishes and a fine selection of seasonal suggestions.

Samouraï

rue du Fossé aux Loups 28 ✉ 1000 – ✆ 02 217 56 39 Plan: **H1**
– www.samourai-bruxelles.be – closed 16 July-15 August, Sunday and Monday
Menu 27 € (lunch), 69/110 € – Carte 59/75 €
• Japanese • Intimate • Minimalist •
Samouraï has been brilliantly upholding Japanese culinary traditions since 1974. Characteristic, precise cuisine, in which the chef finds just the right balance between delicate, intense flavours. Note: the Samouraï has moved shop and is now next-door to the Ramen bar, opposite its original location.

San Sablon

rue Joseph Stevens 12 ✉ 1000 – ✆ 02 512 42 12 Plan: **H3**
– www.sansablon.be – closed 1 week Easter, 2 weeks in August, late December-early January, Sunday and Monday
Menu 28 € (lunch)/65 € – *(tasting menu only)*
• Creative • Bistro •
In keeping with the cosmopolitan Sablons district, the San Sablon is urbane and suave. Subtle, delicate flavours served in its hallmark bowls. The quirky, relaxed interior perfectly matches the establishment.

Scheltema

rue des Dominicains 7 ✉ 1000 – ✆ 02 512 20 84 Plan: **H1**
– www.scheltema.be – closed Sunday
Menu 18 € (lunch)/35 € – Carte 37/72 €
• Seafood • Brasserie •
As you venture inside the Scheltema, it feels like you're stepping back in time. The warm brasserie atmosphere is depicted by vintage, wooden furnishings. Classical fare with Belgian influences and seafood specialties. Its famous Brussels waffles are to die for!

Selecto

rue de Flandre 95 ✉ 1000 – ✆ 0 2 511 40 95 Plan: G1
– www.le-selecto.com – closed late December, Sunday and Monday
Menu 15 € (lunch)/42 €

• Modern French • Friendly •

In the heart of the lively Ste Catherine neighbourhood, Selecto leads Belgium's vanguard of bistronomic (bistro + gastronomic) culture. Good food, a great atmosphere and reasonable prices!

Strofilia

rue du Marché aux Porcs 11 ✉ 1000 – ✆ 0 25 12 32 93 Plan: G1
– www.strofilia.brussels – closed August, Saturday lunch and Sunday
Menu 19 € (lunch), 47/59 € – Carte 30/43 €

• Greek • Trendy •

A modern, airy interior and a relaxed ambience. Strofilia specialises in Greek and Byzantine delicacies, both in the glass and on the plate. The chef is a consummate culinary artist, whose cuisine borders on the contemporary despite his classical training.

La Table de Mus

place de la Vieille Halle aux Blés 31 ✉ 1000 Plan: H2
– ✆ 0 2 511 05 86 – www.latabledemus.be – closed 1 week Easter, last week July-first 2 weeks August, first week January, Wednesday and Sunday
Menu 31/77 €

• Modern cuisine • Friendly •

The experienced Mustafa Duran is a charismatic man – you'll notice that immediately – and he ensures that you will enjoy the chef's delicious cooking in a pleasant ambience. In every dish you'll find original touches which add fun and punch to the flavours.

Le Vismet

place Sainte-Catherine 23 ✉ 1000 – ✆ 0 2 218 85 45 Plan: H1
– www.levismet.be – closed August, Sunday and Monday
Menu 22 € (lunch)/70 € 🍷 – Carte 46/74 €

• Seafood • Traditional décor •

The Vismet (Brussels' fish market) is a stone's throw from this traditional restaurant, as quickly becomes apparent. The ambience is relaxed, the service typical of Brussels and the food scrumptious. Fish and shellfish take pride of place in dishes with an emphasis on fresh, generous portions.

Viva M'Boma

rue de Flandre 17 ✉ 1000 – ✆ 0 2 512 15 93 Plan: G1
– www.vivamboma.be – closed first week April, 22 July-6 August, first week January and Bank Holidays
Carte 32/64 €

• Country • Bistro •

This elegant canteen-style restaurant has closely packed tables and tiled walls reminiscent of a Parisian métro station. It is popular with fans of offal and old Brussels specialities (cow's udder, *choesels* (sweetbreads), marrowbone, ox cheek).

La Femme du Sommelier

rue de l'Association 9 ✉ 1000 – ✆ 0 476 45 02 10 Plan: J1
– closed Saturday and Sunday
Menu 37 € – (lunch only) (tasting menu only)

• Classic cuisine • Wine bar • Neighbourhood •

As the name suggests, this bistro is in the capable hands of a sommelier and his spouse. He advises guests on the choice of wine, while she prepares classic recipes, using only the best ingredients.

✿✿ Le Chalet de la Forêt (Pascal Devalkeneer)

drêve de Lorraine 43 ✉ 1180 – ✆ 0 2 374 54 16 – www.lechaletdelaforet.be – closed last week December-first week January, Saturday and Sunday
Menu 64 € (lunch), 145/185 € – Carte 143/178 €
• Creative • Elegant •

This chalet with its lovely terrace, set on the edge of the Sonian Forest, combines elegance and sophistication. The food has a certain cachet, with its consummate combination of classicism and creativity, finesse and generosity. Intense sensations are guaranteed.

➜ Tartare d'huîtres 'Regis Borde' au caviar oscietre et fleurs de brocoli en parmentier. Agneau de l'Aveyron sur la braise, gratin et salpicon de rognon aux amandes salées. Miel de nos ruches, yaourt fermier et gel citron-miel.

✿✿ La Villa in the Sky (Alexandre Dionisio)

avenue Louise 480 (25th floor) ✉ 1050 – ✆ 0 2 644 69 14 – www.lavillainthesky.be – closed 24 March-1 April, 28-29 May, 4-26 August, 22 December-2 January, Saturday lunch, Sunday and Monday Plan: **F3**
Menu 135 € 🍷 (lunch), 165/210 € – *(booking essential)*
• Creative • Design • Minimalist •

Taking a seat in this glass box, a full 120m/393ft high, commanding a breathtaking view of Brussels, is a once in a lifetime experience. Not only for the unusual location, but also for Alexandre Dionisio's whimsical menu. His matchless culinary craftsmanship is carefully creative and premium quality ingredients are combined into an unforgettable feast of flavours.

➜ Raviole ouverte à la joue de bœuf, foie gras et parmesan. Coquelet et pommade de pomme de terre, morilles et cromesquis de maïs, écume au vin jaune. Fraises et granité au wasabi, crémeux à la vanille.

✿ La Villa Lorraine

avenue du Vivier d'Oie 75 ✉ 1000 – ✆ 0 2 374 31 63 – www.villalorraine.be – closed 3-11 March, 4-19 August, 25 December, 1-8 January, Sunday and Monday Plan I: **C3**
Menu 56 € (lunch), 98/140 € – Carte 99/156 €
• Creative • Elegant •

Since 1953, this grande dame of the Brussels gastronomic scene has been a popular meeting place for gourmets. The grand, luxurious interior commands respect, as does the cooking. Classical dishes come with modern touches and are packed with flavour. There's also a charming terrace for warmer days.

➜ Couteaux de mer au beurre d'algues et sauce au vin jaune. Volaille de Bresse, butternut, crémeux de betterave et truffe noir. Le café : crémeux au café blanc, biscuit nougatine, dulce de leche et glace au café.

La Brasserie de la Villa – See below

✿ La Truffe Noire

boulevard de la Cambre 12 ✉ 1000 – ✆ 0 2 640 44 22 – www.truffenoire.com – closed 1 week Easter, first 2 weeks August, Christmas-New Year, Monday lunch, Saturday lunch and Sunday Plan: **F3**
Menu 85 € 🍷/225 € – Carte 84/169 €
• Italian • Elegant •

The purple colour scheme of this restaurant, rich in nostalgic appeal and decorated with art work, provides the setting for the charismatic chef to prepare beef carpaccio in front of diners. This show takes place every day, as the chef demonstrates his love of classical cuisine. Truffles, naturally, take pride of place in his mouth-watering menu.

➜ Risotto à la Piémontaise. Saint-Pierre farci aux truffes, cuit à la vapeur et son nectar truffé. Truffe au chocolat en cage de sucre filé.

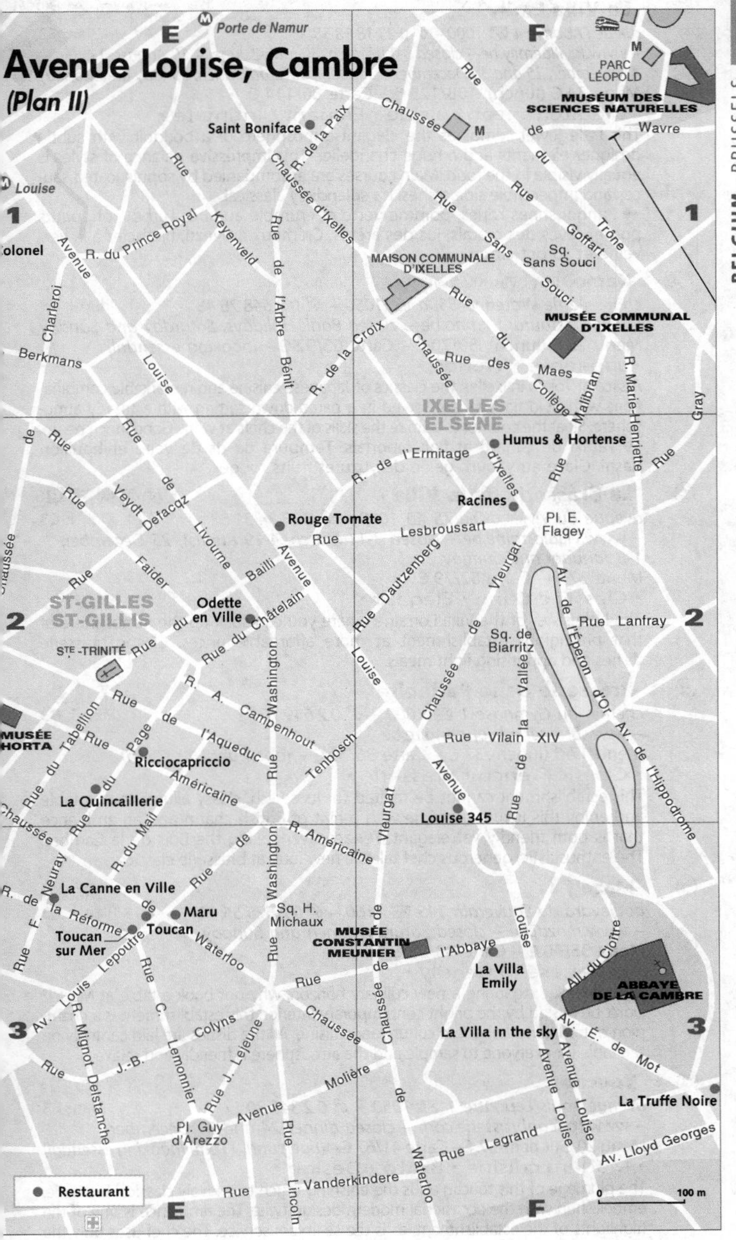
Avenue Louise, Cambre
(Plan II)
E
F
Porte de Namur
PARC LÉOPOLD
MUSÉUM DES SCIENCES NATURELLES
Saint Boniface
Chaussée de Wavre
Louise
Colonel
R. du Prince Royal
Rue Keyenveld
R. de la Paix
Chaussée d'Ixelles
Rue de l'Arbre Bénit
Rue du Trône
Rue Goffart
Rue Sans Souci
Sq. Sans Souci
MAISON COMMUNALE D'IXELLES
MUSÉE COMMUNAL D'IXELLES
Avenue Charleroi
Berkmans
Avenue Louise
R. de la Croix
Rue des Maes
Collège
Malibran
R. Marie-Henriette
Gray
IXELLES ELSENE
Humus & Hortense
R. de l'Ermitage
Rue de Veydt
Rue Defacqz
Rue de Livourne
Faider
Racines
Rouge Tomate
Rue Lesbroussart
Pl. E. Flagey
Rue Dautzenberg
Vleurgat
Bailli
Avenue
ST-GILLES ST-GILLIS
Odette en Ville
Rue du Châtelain
STE-TRINITÉ
Chaussée de Vleurgat
Sq. de Biarritz
Av. de l'Éperon d'Or
Rue Lanfray
Rue Washington
Louise
R. A. Campenhout
Rue de la Vallée
MUSÉE HORTA
Rue de l'Aqueduc
Rue du Tabellion
Rue du Page
Ricciocapriccio
Tenbosch
Rue Vilain XIV
Av. de l'Hippodrome
Américaine
La Quincaillerie
Rue du Mail
Rue de Neuray
R. Américaine
Louise 345
Chaussée
R. de la Réforme
La Canne en Ville
Maru
Toucan
Toucan sur Mer
Lepoutre
Waterloo
Sq. H. Michaux
MUSÉE CONSTANTIN MEUNIER
l'Abbaye
La Villa Emily
All. du Cloître
ABBAYE DE LA CAMBRE
Rue F.
Av. Louis
R. Mignot Delstanche
Rue C. Lemonnier
Rue J.-B. Colyns
Rue J. Lejeune
Rue de
Chaussée de Waterloo
La Villa in the sky
Av. E. de Mot
Avenue Molière
Pl. Guy d'Arezzo
Rue Lincoln
Rue Legrand
La Truffe Noire
Av. Lloyd Georges
Rue Vanderkindere
Restaurant
0
100 m
1
2
3

La Villa Emily

rue de l'Abbaye 4 ✉ 1000 – ✆ 0 23 18 18 58 Plan: **F3**
– www.lavillaemily.be – closed 3-11 March, 30 May-3 June, 4-19 August, 1-4 November, 25 and 30 December-7 January, Saturday lunch, Sunday and Monday
Menu 54 € (lunch), 108/125 € – Carte 86/114 €

• Mediterranean cuisine • Elegant • Intimate •

This little jewel combines the elegant atmosphere of a boudoir with subtle designer elements and a huge chandelier. This impressive balance of styles is equally visible in the food. Main courses are accompanied by sophisticated sauces and impeccable side dishes. It's splendidly classical.

➜ Langoustines rôties, pomme verte et crumble au lard. Turbot rôti, petits pois et fèves des marais, jus des arêtes. Crémeux au yuzu, financier à la verveine et sorbet citron.

Kamo (Tomoyasu Kamo)

chaussée de Waterloo 550a ✉ 1050 – ✆ 0 2 648 78 48 Plan I: **C3**
– www.restaurant-kamo.be – closed Bank Holidays, Saturday and Sunday
Menu 25 € (lunch), 50/70 € – Carte 68/92 € – *(booking essential)*

• Japanese • Trendy •

A slice of Tokyo in Ixelles: the classics of Japanese cuisine and remarkable combinations with bold flavours are served in a pared-down setting with a trendy atmosphere. Sit at the counter to admire the skills of the chefs at work. Good lunch bento.

➜ Tataki de canard et flan japonais. Tempura de ris de veau et bouillon dashi. Glace au yaourt, gelée de yuzu et fruits rouges.

La Brasserie de la Villa

avenue du Vivier d'Oie 75 ✉ 1000 – ✆ 0 23 74 31 63 Plan I: **C3**
– www.villalorraine.be – closed 3-11 March, 4-19 August, 25 December, 1-8 January and Sunday
Menu 37 € – Carte 52/79 €

• Classic cuisine • Elegant •

The little sister of the Villa Lorraine where you can soak up the atmosphere of that prestigious establishment at more affordable prices. Classic brasserie dishes and appetising light meals.

Brasserie de la Patinoire

chemin du Gymnase 1 ✉ 1000 – ✆ 0 2 649 70 02 Plan I: **B3**
– www.brasseriedelapatinoire.be
Menu 17 € (lunch)/37 € – Carte 36/59 € – *(open until 11.30pm)*

• Classic French • Brasserie •

This establishment cannot be faulted for its stylish, classy allure. Book a table and enjoy this luxury brasserie with a hint of British charm and an ambience that is both friendly yet elegant. Terrace overlooking the Bois de la Cambre. The enthusiastic, generous chef takes a new look at brasserie classics.

Maza'j

boulevard du Souverain 145 ✉ 1160 – ✆ 0 2 675 55 10 Plan I: **C3**
– www.mazaj.be – closed Saturday lunch and Sunday
Menu 35/60 € – Carte 33/53 €

• Lebanese • Friendly •

If you feel like exploring a new culinary horizon, why not book a table at Maza'j? Don't be misled by the bright contemporary interior, this establishment is a champion of traditional Lebanese culture and cuisine. All the dishes are laid centrally on the table for everyone to sample and the atmosphere is friendly and relaxed.

Toucan

avenue Louis Lepoutre 1 ✉ 1050 – ✆ 0 2 345 30 17 Plan: **E3**
– www.toucanbrasserie.com – closed dinner 24 and 31 December
Menu 20 € (lunch)/37 € – Carte 41/67 € – *(open until 11pm) (booking essential)*

• Modern cuisine • Bistro • Design •

The plumage of this toucan adds the finishing touch to a lovely classical brasserie, embellished with the occasional modern design twist. The ambience is one of the highlights of the establishment, as is the seamless service. The chef uses only the best quality produce and has no qualms about piling the plates high with tasty fare.

Saint Boniface

rue Saint-Boniface 9 ✉ 1050 – ✆ 0 2 511 53 66 Plan: **E1**
– www.saintboniface.be – closed first 3 weeks September, Bank Holidays, Saturday lunch, Sunday and Monday
Menu 26 € (lunch)/37 € – Carte 39/55 €

• Cuisine from South West France • Bistro •

Tightly packed tables, posters on the walls and a collection of biscuit tins characterise this extremely welcoming bistro. The locals flock here to sample its Basque, Lyonnaise and Southwestern French specialities. Cooking is generous and delicious!

Maru

chaussée de Waterloo 510 ✉ 1050 – ✆ 0 2 346 11 11 Plan: **E3**
– closed 15 July-15 August, late December-early January and Monday
Menu 18 € (lunch) – Carte 31/81 €

• Korean • Minimalist •

If your mouth is already watering at the prospect of crunchy deep-fried pancakes or sweet and sour tangsuyuk, head straight for this 'urban-style' Korean restaurant whose fresh ingredients are equalled by the authentic cooking methods. Even better, the wine list is full of pleasant surprises.

Villa Singha

rue des Trois Ponts 22 ✉ 1160 – ✆ 0 2 675 67 34 Plan I: **C3**
– www.singha.be – closed July, 24 December-5 January, Bank Holidays, Saturday lunch and Sunday
Menu 19 € (lunch), 26/37 € – Carte 29/40 €

• Thai • Exotic décor •

Singha, the mythological lion, watches over this pleasant restaurant, where fresh produce and authentic flavours enhance the traditional Thai cuisine. One such dish is Kha Nom Jeep, delicious steamed dumplings of chopped pork and Thai spices. The welcome and service are equally charming.

Brugmann

avenue Brugmann 52 ✉ 1190 – ✆ 0 2 880 55 54 Plan I: **B3**
– www.brugmann.com – closed 1-16 January, Saturday lunch and Monday
Menu 24 € (lunch), 49/85 € – Carte 66/91 €

• Modern cuisine • Elegant •

Brugmann is a picture of elegance. The interior is adorned with fine modern art and the rear terrace is superb. What is more the chef's cuisine is equally stylish, combining ingredients and techniques in dishes that are as modern as the decor. A first-class establishment.

Odette en Ville

rue du Châtelain 25 ✉ 1050 – ✆ 0 2 640 26 26 Plan: **E2**
– www.odetteenville.be – closed 28 July-20 August, 24 and 25 December, 1-7 January, Sunday and Monday
Menu 28 € (lunch)/35 € – Carte 36/76 € – *(open until 11.30pm)*

• Creative French • Trendy •

Odette is depicted by an ultra-trendy interior set in a handsome town house. Add to this a contemporary restaurant and luxurious guestrooms. The establishment is in the heart of a fashionable district, a good match for the menu of tasty, international dishes.

Stars, Bib gourmand and plate are awarded for the cooking... And keywords help you to identify the type of establishment – cuisine, decor, ambience – for an all-round culinary experience!

Rouge Tomate

avenue Louise 190 ✉ 1050 – ✆ 0 2 647 70 44 Plan: **E2**
– www.rougetomate.be – closed Bank Holidays, Saturday lunch and Sunday
Menu 35 € 🍷 (lunch), 55/75 € – Carte 49/88 €
• Creative • Trendy •
Forgo the bustle of Avenue Louise and venture into this elegant, modern mansion, and perhaps to the lovely terrace at the back or the cocktail bar on the first floor. The same harmony is present in the dishes, all of which demonstrate the young chef's desire to experiment with creative, yet balanced recipes.

Amen

rue Franz Merjay 165 ✉ 1050 – ✆ 0 2 217 10 19 Plan I: **B3**
– www.amen.restaurant – closed Sunday and Monday
Menu 27 € (lunch)/54 € – Carte 50/79 €
• Market cuisine • Friendly •
Two-star chef Pascal Devalkeneer has a knack for picking the best produce. From the contemporary dishes and intense flavours to the range of textures, his dishes are masterpieces of culinary art. Amen!

Brinz'l

rue des Carmélites 93 ✉ 1180 – ✆ 0 2 218 23 32 Plan I: **B3**
– www.brinzl.be – closed Tuesday lunch, Wednesday lunch, Saturday lunch, Sunday and Monday
Menu 49 € (lunch), 65/95 € – Carte 60/98 €
• Modern French • Contemporary décor • Bistro •
While Brinzelle (Creole for aubergine) may evoke the chef's Mauritian roots, her cuisine is nonetheless firmly French! After learning her trade in several Starred restaurants, she now excels in flavoursome, carefully assembled meals that, above all, seek to enhance the quality of the ingredients.

Colonel

rue Jean Stas 24 ✉ 1060 – ✆ 0 2 538 57 36 Plan: **E1**
– www.colonelbrussels.com – closed Sunday and Monday
Menu 24 € (lunch) – Carte 48/75 €
• Meats and grills • Brasserie • Fashionable •
Generous cuts of meat greet you as you enter this brasserie, making the house speciality blatantly clear. The quality of the charcuterie, perfectly cooked red meat, french fries and delicious sauces are quite stunning. A paradise for carnivores!

Le Passage

avenue Jean et Pierre Carsoel 17 ✉ 1180 Plan I: **B3**
– ✆ 0 2 374 66 94 – www.lepassage.be – closed 2 weeks in July, Bank Holidays, Saturday lunch and Sunday
Menu 35 € (lunch), 55/75 € – Carte 46/79 €
• Classic cuisine • Cosy •
Most diners have high expectations when they book a table here, such is the chef's reputation for creativity and flair, as he mingles tradition with modernity. You will not be disappointed by his distinctive cuisine, rich in unforgettable flavours.

La Canne en Ville

rue de la Réforme 22 ✉ 1050 – ✆ 0 2 347 29 26 Plan: **E3**
– www.lacanneenville.be – closed 8-14 April, 19 August-1 September, 24 December-13 January, Saturday lunch, Sunday and Monday
Menu 43 € (lunch), 56/66 € – Carte 64/84 €
• Market cuisine • Family • Neighbourhood •
This friendly, long-standing, neighbourhood bistro sits in a former butcher's shop, as the tiles and occasional decorative detail bear witness. Talented Kevin Lejeune, second chef at La Paix for ten years, has taken flight and is now at the helm of La Canne en Ville.

Koyzina Authentica

avenue Brugmann 519 ✉ 1180 – ✆ 0 2 346 14 38 – www.koyzinaauthentica.be – closed Sunday and Monday

Plan I: **B3**

Menu 18 € (lunch)/37 € – Carte 30/47 €

• Greek • Mediterranean décor • Neighbourhood •

Greek cuisine has far more to offer than the hackneyed *gyros* and *souvlaki*, as this friendly, if sometimes packed, restaurant proves. The traditional dishes are modern in flavour while remaining authentic.

Nonbe Daigaku

avenue Adolphe Buyl 31 ✉ 1050 – ✆ 0 2 649 21 49 – closed 1 week Easter, 21 July-15 August, 25 December-4 January, Sunday and Monday

Plan I: **C3**

Menu 20 € (lunch) – Carte 45/123 € – *(booking essential)*

• Japanese • Minimalist • Traditional décor •

If you like eating Japanese, you shouldn't miss this modest venue. The very experienced chef has mastered the subtlety and nuances that are typical of the cuisine of his home country. You can see him at work behind the sushi bar, driven and precise, creating a delicious variety of flavours and textures.

Les Papilles

chaussée de Waterloo 782 ✉ 1180 – ✆ 0 2 374 69 66 – www.lespapilles.mobi – closed Bank Holidays, Monday dinner and Sunday

Plan I: **B3**

Menu 22 € (lunch)/39 € – Carte 41/62 €

• Traditional cuisine • Wine bar •

Your taste buds will definitely start tingling when you enter this delightful establishment with a terrace to the rear. It specialises in generous French classics, using quality produce. Before sitting down for your meal, pick yourself a bottle of wine directly from the shelves. Friendly and relaxed.

La Quincaillerie

rue du Page 45 ✉ 1050 – ✆ 0 25 33 98 33 – www.quincaillerie.be – closed Sunday lunch

Plan: **E2**

Menu 18 € (lunch), 36/48 € – Carte 40/74 €

• Classic cuisine • Brasserie •

This brasserie and oyster bar is an institution in the town. Housed in a former hardware store (1903), its Art nouveau décor is worth a visit in its own right. The interior, dotted with period chests of drawers and wall shelves, is ideal to sample delicious Franco-Belgian classics.

Ricciocapriccio

rue Américaine 90 ✉ 1050 – ✆ 0 2 852 39 69 – www.ricciocapriccio.be – closed last 2 weeks August, Saturday lunch, Sunday and Monday

Plan: **E2**

Menu 18 € (lunch), 55/75 € – Carte 42/64 € – *(booking essential)*

• Italian • Bistro • Simple •

A delightful Italian-inspired ristorante tucked away in the Châtelain district. The slate menu features an enticing array of Italian delicacies, subtly reworked by the chef. The house speciality is fish and seafood (sea urchins and squid), rich in enticing Mediterranean flavours.

Toucan sur Mer

avenue Louis Lepoutre 17 ✉ 1050 – ✆ 0 2 340 07 40 – www.toucanbrasserie.com – closed dinner 24 and 31 December

Plan: **E3**

Menu 20 € (lunch) – Carte 46/62 € – *(booking essential)*

• Seafood • Bistro •

The impeccable quality and freshness of the fish and shellfish of the Toucan sur Mer are more than comparable with seafood restaurants on the coast. This pleasant bistro will certainly appeal to seafood lovers.

bon bon (Christophe Hardiquest)

avenue de Tervueren 453 ✉ 1150 – ✆ 02 346 66 15 – www.bonbon.restaurant – closed 6-22 April, 20 July-12 August, 22 December-7 January, Bank Holidays, Saturday, Sunday and Monday

Plan: **D3**

Menu 75 €, 185/240 € – Carte 146/230 €

• Creative • Elegant •

Christophe Hardiquest invites you on an adventure. A quest for culinary harmony, first-class ingredients, inventive recipes and rich flavours… this is a chef who combines flair with subtlety. Take a seat in the elegant, contemporary interior and order with complete confidence.

➜ Navet cuit en croûte de "craquelin". Pigeon à la liégeoise. Feuilletine croquante équateur, sorbet noisette et cacao whisky.

Da Mimmo

avenue du Roi Chevalier 24 ✉ 1200 – ✆ 02 771 58 60 – www.da-mimmo.be – closed 20 July-10 August, late December-early January, Saturday lunch and Sunday

Plan: **C2**

Menu 45 € (lunch), 85/145 €

• Italian • Cosy •

This elegant Italian restaurant speaks one language: that of good produce. Do not expect complex, oversophisticated dishes; they are, on the contrary, an expression of precision, bearing frank, generous flavours. This is Italian cuisine at its best... accompanied by fine wines.

➜ Cru de seriole à la violette, crème tiède de poireau. Ris de veau, langoustine et truffe en parfaite harmonie. Raviole d'ananas au fromage blanc et carvi, sorbet à la coriandre.

Les Deux Maisons

Val des Seigneurs 81 ✉ 1150 – ✆ 02 771 14 47 – www.deuxmaisons.be – closed 1 week Easter, first 3 weeks August, late December, Bank Holidays, Sunday and Monday

Plan: **D2**

Menu 21 € (lunch), 37/60 € – Carte 53/84 €

• Classic French • Classic décor • Romantic •

Two houses have merged to create this elegant restaurant, where a classically trained chef rustles up tempting dishes using excellent ingredients. The 'Tradition' menu with its luscious selection of desserts is highly recommended. There's also a fine wine cellar.

Maison du Luxembourg

rue du Luxembourg 37 ✉ 1050 – ✆ 02 511 99 95 – www.maisonduluxembourg.be – closed 31 July-26 August, 22 December-7 January, Bank Holidays, Friday dinner, Saturday and Sunday

Plan III: **J3**

Menu 26 € 🍷 (lunch)/37 € – Carte 47/72 €

• Regional cuisine • Friendly •

Country cooking from the Luxembourg region moves to Brussels. This contemporary restaurant offers well-presented classical fare, highlighting produce sourced from the French-speaking province of Luxembourg. The ingredients are superlatively fresh and the vegetable side dishes are delicious. A great advertisement for the region.

Park Side

avenue de la Joyeuse Entrée 24 ✉ 1040 – ✆ 02 238 08 08 – www.restoparkside.be – closed 3 weeks in August, Bank Holidays, Saturday and Sunday

Plan: **C2**

Menu 37/55 € – Carte 39/61 €

• Modern cuisine • Fashionable • Brasserie •

Park Side sits in a great location besides the Jubilee Park (parc du Cinquantenaire). Inside it's equally appealing, with chic decor and ultra-modern design features – the main light in particular is a talking point! Modern brasserie specialities feature on the à la carte menu.

De Maurice à Olivier

chaussée de Roodebeek 246 ✉ 1200 – ✆ 0 2 771 33 98 – www.demauriceaolivier.be – closed 8-24 April, 22 July-22 August, Monday dinner and Sunday
Plan: **C2**
Menu 22 € (lunch), 37/55 € – Carte 40/62 €
• Classic cuisine • Vintage •

Maurice, the father, has passed the business onto his son Olivier. He has also bequeathed a rich culinary heritage of French cuisine enriched in Mediterranean influences; the dishes are beautifully presented. Amusingly, the restaurant is also a newsagents.

Le Mucha

avenue Jules Du Jardin 23 ✉ 1150 – ✆ 0 2 770 24 14 – www.lemucha.be – closed last week August-first week September, Sunday dinner and Monday
Plan: **D3**
Menu 20 € (lunch)/37 € – Carte 40/63 €
• Classic cuisine • Neighbourhood • Cosy •

The interior of Le Mucha is reminiscent of Parisian brasseries in the 1900s. It's an ideal place to sample traditional French cuisine from a fine choice of classical dishes, without forgetting a few Italian favourites.

Le Buone Maniere

avenue de Tervueren 59 ✉ 1040 – ✆ 0 2 762 61 05 – www.buonemaniere.be – closed 5 August-5 September, 23 December-3 January, Saturday lunch and Sunday
Plan: **C2**
Menu 42 € (lunch), 50/95 € – Carte 65/93 €
• Italian • Traditional décor •

Maurizio Zizza's manners are impeccable! He enjoys explaining his authentic dishes in this stylish town house, which boasts a terrace. Simple, tasty dishes, which sometimes surprise, transport the diner to the Mediterranean.

Au Grand Forestier

avenue du Grand Forestier 2 ✉ 1170 – ✆ 0 2 672 57 79 – www.augrandforestier.be – closed dinner 24 and 31 December and Sunday dinner
Plan: **C3**
Carte 38/71 € – *(open until 11pm)*
• Belgian • Contemporary décor •

Pure luxury is essentially a question of detail, as this delightful brasserie so admirably illustrates! A flawless welcome and personalised service set the scene to make you feel at home. The same attention to detail can be tasted in the immaculately cooked meat, served with delicious sauces – a princely treat for your taste buds!

Le Monde est Petit

rue des Bataves 65 ✉ 1040 – ✆ 0 2 732 44 34 – www.lemondeestpetit.be – closed first week Easter, last week July-first 2 weeks August, late December-early January, Bank Holidays, Saturday and Sunday
Plan: **C2**
Menu 28 € (lunch) – Carte 55/76 €
• Creative French • Friendly • Family •

What's on offer in the market determines what will be served in this pleasant establishment, beautifully situated between Montgomery and the Parc du Cinquantenaire. The chef uses this quality produce in well-thought-through preparations which are as diverse in their influences as the international guests who like to eat here.

Sanzaru

avenue de Tervueren 292 ✉ 1150 – ✆ 0 2 773 00 80 – www.sanzaru.be – closed 22 July-7 August, Sunday and Monday
Plan: **C2**
Menu 25 € (lunch) – Carte 47/70 €
• Peruvian • Trendy •

Behind the Art nouveau façade, you will discover an engaging restaurant adorned with colourful murals, waiting to whisk you off on a journey of discovery. Japanese and Peruvian cooking, better known under the name of Nikkei cuisine. A whirlwind of fascinating flavours not to be missed, like the cocktail bar upstairs.

Stirwen

chaussée Saint-Pierre 15 ✉ 1040 – ✆ 0 2 640 85 41 Plan: **C2**
– www.stirwen.be – closed 1 June, August, 24-26 December, 1-4 January, Bank Holidays, Saturday and Sunday
Menu 40 € (lunch), 60/85 € – Carte 62/97 €
• Modern French • Bourgeois •

This renowned restaurant is today in the capable hands of an ambitious duo. David is in charge of the service, while François-Xavier takes a new look at French classics. First-class ingredients are used such as Noirmoutier sole, Lozère lamb and Corrèze veal.

Al Piccolo

rue Voot 20 ✉ 1200 – ✆ 0 2 770 05 55 Plan: **C2**
– www.alpiccolo.net – closed Saturday lunch and Sunday
Menu 18 € (lunch) – Carte 45/77 €
• Italian • Friendly •

A couple have harnessed their years of experience into creating this inviting restaurant. The care with which they rustle up authentic Italian dishes can be tasted in each morsel. Never over-the-top, they seek to enhance generous traditional flavours. Excellent wine list.

Le Coq en Pâte

Tomberg 259 ✉ 1200 – ✆ 0 2 762 19 71 Plan: **C2**
– www.lecoqenpate.be – closed Monday
Menu 18 € (lunch), 35/55 € 🍷 – Carte 36/48 €
• Italian • Neighbourhood •

The Bachetta family has been regaling diners since 1972. You will taste unfussy, scrumptious Italian food. The chef's talent and flair delight the palate in each creative dish, liberally sprinkled with Mediterranean flavours.

Foro Romano

rue Joseph II 19 ✉ 1000 – ✆ 0 2 280 29 76 Plan III: **J2**
– www.fororomano.be – closed Bank Holidays, Saturday and Sunday
Carte 35/51 €
• Italian • Neighbourhood •

This inviting restaurant specialises in cuisine with Italian accents. The international clientele enjoys the establishment's menu, of Puglian origins and the chef's generous, appetising cuisine. The owner presents an intriguing wine list.

Humus x Hortense

rue de Vergnies 2 ✉ 1050 – ✆ 0 474 65 37 06 Plan II: **F2**
– www.humusrestaurant.be – closed first 3 weeks September, Sunday and Monday
Menu 26 € (lunch), 46/54 € – *(booking essential) (tasting menu only)*
• Creative • Vintage •

The encounter between vegetables and an inspired and inventive chef could not fail to produce something special, which is light years from culinary tradition! Get ready to enjoy surprising, attractively presented dishes with contrasting flavours, washed down with equally intriguing cocktails – under the watchful eyes of the angels on the ceiling.

Origine

rue Général Leman 36 ✉ 1040 – ✆ 0 2 256 68 93 Plan: **C2**
– www.origine-restaurant.be – closed 1 week Easter, 15 July-15 August, 28 October-3 November, last week December-first week January, Saturday lunch, Sunday and Monday
Menu 15 € (lunch)/38 € – Carte approx. 35 €
• Modern French • Bistro • Friendly •

The whimsical décor of the Origine is depicted by colourful creatures and plants, setting the scene for a modern restaurant run by Xavier Lizen, who demonstrates great maturity despite his youth. The menu is renewed each month and illustrates the chef's international and original approach, in which each flavour lives up to our expectations.

Racines

chaussée d'Ixelles 353 ✉ 1050 – ✆ 0 2 642 95 90 – www.racinesbruxelles.com – closed 21 July-15 August, Saturday lunch and Sunday

Plan II: **F2**

Menu 36 € (lunch), 58/90 € – Carte 46/80 €

• Italian • Trattoria • Trendy •

Francesco and Ugo are proud of their Italian heritage. One of them pulls up a chair to walk you through the menu, rich in delicious specialties from their homeland, prepared creatively and masterfully. Organic biodynamic wines figure prominently on the wine list, which is definitely worth a close look.

GARE DU MIDI PLAN I

La Paix (David Martin)

rue Ropsy-Chaudron 49 (opposite abattoirs) ✉ 1070 – ✆ 0 2 523 09 58 – www.lapaix.eu – closed July, Christmas-New Year, Bank Holidays, Saturday, Sunday, Monday, Tuesday dinner and Wednesday dinner

Plan: **B2**

Menu 70/145 €

• Asian influences • Fashionable • Friendly •

A striking flock of origami birds on the ceiling brings life to the stylish La Paix. David Martin executes classic recipes with finesse, while also adding a personal touch and incorporating refined elements of Japanese cuisine. He loves to work with local vegetables and fish fresh from the tank. A fabulous culinary experience!

→ Tartelette croustillante de pastrami de veau de lait de Corrèze et bulot. Bœuf confit en cocotte au vinaigre de kriek. Millefeuille inversé à la vanille bleue de la Réunion.

La Brouette

boulevard Prince de Liège 61 ✉ 1070 – ✆ 0 2 522 51 69 – www.labrouette.be – closed 1 week Easter, August, 22 September, 4-7 January, Carnival holiday, Tuesday dinner, Saturday lunch, Sunday dinner and Monday

Plan: **A2**

Menu 28 € (lunch), 37/59 € – Carte 51/66 €

• Creative French • Friendly •

Herman Dedapper welcomes you with open arms to his neighbourhood restaurant, decorated in warm colours and adorned with his own photo work. He is an excellent sommelier and loves to share his passion for wine. The chef's generous, French-inspired dishes are sourced from high-quality produce.

René

place de la Résistance 14 ✉ 1070 – ✆ 0 2 523 28 76 – closed last week June, July, Monday and Tuesday

Plan: **A2**

Carte 27/58 €

• Belgian • Family •

This former chippy has been turned into a delightful vintage-style bistro by René, who takes us back in time to an era when cooking was simple and unfussy. Mussels, steak and nourishing stews are all served with generous portions of french fries – a treat for lovers of down-to-earth, wholesome food.

ATOMIUM QUARTER PLAN I

't Stoveke (Daniel Antuna)

Jetsestraat 52 ✉ 1853 Strombeek-Bever – ✆ 0476 50 07 29 – www.tstoveke.be – closed late July-early August, late December-early January, Saturday lunch, Sunday dinner, Tuesday and Wednesday

Plan: **B1**

Menu 36 € (lunch), 67/101 € – Carte 82/132 € – *(booking essential)*

• Modern cuisine • Cosy • Design •

The chef of 't Stoveke follows in the footsteps of some of the best-known chefs in the world, but has added his own personal touch. This has ensured that his cuisine remains resolutely up to date. The dishes reveal an explosion of flavours that are as much a delight to the eye as to the palate.

→ Gebakken eendenlever en gerookte paling met venkel, sjalot en biersausje. Zeebaars met zeekraal, grijze garnalen, tomatenfondue en champagnesaus. Aardbeien en rabarber met mascarpone, amandelcrunch en pistacheroomijs.

Wine in the City (Eddy Münster)

place Reine Astrid 34 ✉ 1090 – ✆ 0 24 20 09 20 Plan: **B2**
– www.wineinthecity.be – closed first week January, Sunday, Monday and Tuesday
Menu 45 € (lunch), 60/90 € – *(lunch only except Friday and Saturday) (booking essential)*

• Creative • Wine bar •

In this restaurant-cum-wine-bar, amid rows and rows of bottles, sample the wholesome fare of an enthusiastic and creative chef whose dishes frequently surprise. Excellent produce, faultless combinations and of course a magnificent wine list!

➜ Thon rouge au chou-rave en pickles, coriandre, noix de cajou et bouillon de dashi. Pigeon rôti aux textures de chou, salsifis, champignons persillés et purée de pomme de terre au beurre salé. Structures de fraise et rhubarbe, limonade à la verveine, shiso rouge et biscuit au spéculoos.

L'Auberge de l'Isard

Romeinsesteenweg 964 ✉ 1780 Wemmel Plan: **B1**
– ✆ 0 2 479 85 64 – www.isard.be – closed dinner on Bank Holidays, Sunday dinner, Monday and Tuesday
Menu 29 € (lunch), 37/52 € – Carte 46/65 €

• Classic French • Friendly •

To escape the bustle of Heysel and Brussels' ring road, head for the elegant villa of Roland Taildeman, who opened his restaurant in 1989. Guests are particularly taken with the extensive set menu. There is a wide and varied choice with one constant byword – taste.

La Brasserie de la Gare

chaussée de Gand 1430 ✉ 1082 Plan: **A2**
– ✆ 0 2 469 10 09 – www.brasseriedelagare.be
– closed Saturday lunch and Sunday
Menu 37 € – Carte 36/55 €

• Belgian • Brasserie • Neighbourhood •

For a typical Brussels experience, come and discover this old café, which has retained all of its retro charm. The chef's cooking honours tradition by having a pleasing simplicity and you enjoy succulent boar in season or a timeless steak tartare and chips... This is one of life's certainties!

Brasserie de l'Expo

avenue Houba de Strooper 188 ✉ 1020 Plan: **B1**
– ✆ 0 2 476 99 70 – www.brasseriedelexpo.be
– closed dinner 24 and 31 December
Menu 17 € (lunch)/37 € – Carte 41/57 €

• Seafood • Brasserie •

The memory of the 1958 Expo continues to linger in this delightful vintage brasserie opposite Heysel stadium. Right from the word go, the seafood bar leaves you in no doubt that fresh, quality ingredients take pride of place in the chef's cuisine. Brasserie fare at its best!

French Kiss

rue Léopold I 470 ✉ 1090 – ✆ 0 2 425 22 93 Plan: **B2**
– www.restaurantfrenchkiss.com – closed 24 July-14 August, 24 December-1 January and Monday
Menu 29 € (lunch)/37 € – Carte 38/65 €

• Meats and grills • Friendly •

A pleasant restaurant renowned for its excellent grilled dishes and impressive wine list. Dining area with a low ceiling and bright paintings adding colour to the brick walls.

Bruneau by Maxime Maziers

avenue Broustin 73 ✉ 1083 – ✆ 0 2 421 70 70 Plan: **B2**
– www.bruneau.be – closed first 2 weeks August, 25 December-2 January, Tuesday and Wednesday
Menu 55 € (lunch)/95 € – Carte 77/164 €
• Modern French • Elegant •

Jean-Pierre Bruneau's influence on the world of fine food needs no introduction. His signature dishes, such as carpaccio of langoustine and tournedos Rossini, are now part of Belgium's culinary heritage. His former second chef, talented Maxime Maziers, is continuing the adventure. Maziers adds a modern spin to a traditional menu.

La table d'Evan

Brusselsesteenweg 21 ✉ 1780 Wemmel – ✆ 0 2 460 52 39 Plan: **A1**
– www.evanrestaurants.be – closed 21 July-7 August, late December, Saturday lunch and Sunday
Menu 35 € (lunch), 55/110 € – Carte 72/100 €
• Mediterranean cuisine • Brasserie • Trendy •

Chef Evan's restaurant is modern, comfortable and free of unnecessary frills. On a constant quest for fine produce, he deploys his talent and experience to create delicious dishes. 'Quality before all else' is his motto – much to the delight of our taste buds!

Spectrum

Romeinsesteenweg 220 ✉ 1800 Vilvoorde – ✆ 0 2 267 00 45 Plan: **B1**
– www.restospectrum.be – closed Monday dinner, Saturday lunch and Sunday
Menu 39 € – Carte 38/65 €
• Market cuisine • Brasserie •

Could it be better food? And at a better price? On the contrary, the quality to price ratio at Spectrum is among the best in Brussels and the surrounding area. Classic cuisine, copious portions and modest prices – what more could you ask for?

AIRPORT & NATO — PLAN I

Maxime Colin

Pastoorkesweg 1 ✉ 1950 Kraainem – ✆ 0 2 720 63 46 Plan: **D2**
– www.maximecolin.be – closed 5-10 March, 28 July-12 August, 29 October-3 November, Sunday and Monday
Menu 40 € (lunch), 62/98 € – *(tasting menu only)*
• Creative French • Romantic • Friendly •

When you first enter chef Colin's establishment you will want to admire the setting. Located in the gardens of Jourdain Castle, the restaurant has a romantic interior and a handsome terrace beside a pond. The modern cuisine uses a wide variety of good quality produce.

Bovis

Heldenplein 16 ✉ 1930 Zaventem – ✆ 0 2 308 83 43 Plan: **D1**
– www.bovis-zaventem.be – closed Bank Holidays, Saturday and Sunday
Carte 47/75 €
• Meats and grills • Brasserie •

The strapline of this restaurant is 'simply meat'; it uses only the very best quality and ensures that each cut is aged until it reaches perfect maturity. All are served with handcut chips fried in beef fat, and can be accompanied by some interesting wines.

Brasserie Mariadal

Kouterweg 2 ✉ 1930 Zaventem – ✆ 0 2 720 59 30 Plan: **D1**
– www.brasseriemariadal.be
Menu 38 € – Carte 27/67 €
• Modern French • Brasserie •

Imagine a handsome castle surrounded by a moat, sporting an unusual interior decor. There is also a menu that can hold its own with the best brasseries with a few more personal creations. You will understand why the Mariadal leaves no one indifferent! Fine choice on the menu and good value for money.

ANTWERP
ANTWERPEN/ANVERS

RossHelen/iStock

ANTWERP IN...

→ **ONE DAY**
Grote Markt, Our Lady's Cathedral, MoMu, Het Zuid.

→ **TWO DAYS**
Rubens' House, Royal Museum of Fine Arts, a stroll to the Left Bank via the Sint-Anna tunnel.

→ **THREE DAYS**
Het Eilandje and MAS, a river trip, Kloosterstraat, Nationalestraat.

Antwerp calls itself the pocketsize metropolis, and with good reason. Although it's Europe's second largest port, it still retains a compact intimacy, defined by bustling squares and narrow streets. It's a place with many facets, not least its marked link to Rubens, the diamond trade and, in later years, the fashion collective The Antwerp Six. The city's centre teems with ornate gabled guild-houses, and in summer, open-air cafés line the area beneath the towering cathedral, giving the place a festive, almost bohemian air. It's a fantastic place to shop: besides clothing boutiques, there are antiques emporiums and diamond stores – to say nothing of

the chocolate shops with their appealing window displays. Bold regeneration projects have transformed the skyline and the waterfront's decrepit warehouses have started new lives as ritzy storerooms of 21C commerce. The nightlife here is the best in Belgium, while the beer is savoured the way others might treat a vintage wine.

The Old Town is defined by Grote Markt, Groenplaats and The Meir shopping street – these are a kind of dividing line between Antwerp's north and south. North of the centre is Het Eilandje, the hip former warehouse area; to the east is the Diamond District. Antique and bric-a-brac shops are in abundance in the 'designer heart' Het Zuid, south of the centre, which is also home to the best museums and art galleries.

EATING OUT

The menus of Flanders are heavily influenced by the lush meadows, the canals swarming with eels and the proximity of the North Sea – but the eating culture in Antwerp offers more than just seafood. With its centuries old connection to more exotic climes, there's no shortage of fragrant spices such as cinnamon in their dishes, especially in the rich stews so beloved by the locals. If you want to eat with the chic, hang around the Het Eilandje dockside or the rejuvenated ancient warehouses south of Grote Markt. For early risers, the grand cafés are a popular port of call, ideal for a slow coffee and a trawl through the papers. Overall the city boasts the same tempting Belgian specialities as Brussels (stewed eel in chervil sauce; mussels; dishes containing rabbit; beef stew and chicory), but also with a focus on more contemporary cuisine. Don't miss out on the local chocolate (shaped like a hand in keeping with the legend which gave Antwerp its name), and be sure to try their De Koninck beer, served in a glass designed like an open bowl.

✿✿ **'t Zilte** (Viki Geunes) XXXX

Hanzestedenplaats 5 Plan I: **B1**
– ✆ 0 3 283 40 40 – www.tzilte.be
– closed 1 week Easter, 2 weeks in July, Autumn break, late December, Saturday, Sunday and after 8.30pm
Menu 68 € (lunch), 135/185 € – Carte 160/193 €
• Creative • Design •

Savour the view of Antwerp at your feet while you sample sophisticated dishes, as 't Zilte is wonderfully located on the top floor of the Museum Aan de Stroom. Viki Geunes' joyful cooking is depicted by diverse textures and flavours, a whirlwind of international ingredients and desserts of which the chef is particularly proud.

→ Toro tonijn en noordzeekrab met kombu en koolrabi. Wagyu met aubergine, gepofte ui, artisjok en miso. Geitenyoghurt met zuring, ananas en sorbet van cedraat.

✿✿ **The Jane** (Nick Bril) XXX

Paradeplein 1 ✉ 2018 Plan III: **H1**
– ✆ 0 3 808 44 65 – www.thejaneantwerp.com
– closed late March-early April, late June-early July, late September-early October, 23 December-3 January, Sunday and Monday
Menu 145/165 € – *(booking essential) (tasting menu only)*
• Creative • Fashionable • Design •

This striking chapel, now a trend-setting temple, is unique in Belgium! Chef Nick Bril can be relied upon to introduce diners to mind-blowing flavours. His food is both sophisticated and simple, steeped in powerful flavours and yet amazingly harmonious. The Upper Room Bar serves cocktails.

→ Langoustines met eekhoorntjesbrood en courget. Paling met dashi en boerenkool. BBQ-appel met kaneel, chocolade, hazelnoot en koffie.

✿ **FRANQ** – Hotel FRANQ XXX

Kipdorp 10 – ✆ 0 3 555 31 80 – www.hotelfranq.com Plan: **D1**
– closed 14-22 April, 14-28 July, Saturday lunch and Sunday
Menu 35 € (lunch), 65/80 € – Carte 71/97 €
• Modern cuisine • Elegant •

You only need to take one step over the threshold of this mansion to get a grasp of FRANQ's ambitions. The premises, steeped in elegant, understated luxury, are ideal to sample creative, classical dishes. With flavoursome sauces and flawless culinary craftsmanship, the chef demonstrates his modern bent with subtle nuances.

→ Ravioli met langoustines, tomaat en mozzarella. Geglaceerde grietbot met jus van kokkels, crème van zoete pepers en boulangère-aardappel. Parfait van pistache zoals een Norvegiènne.

✿ **'t Fornuis** (Johan Segers) XXX

Reyndersstraat 24 – ✆ 0 3 233 62 70 Plan: **D2**
– closed 22 July-18 August, late December, Bank Holidays, Saturday and Sunday
Carte 75/120 €
• Classic cuisine • Romantic • Classic décor •

't Fornuis is a type of restaurant that has become rare nowadays: the interior of this pretty townhouse is rustic and authentic, and the service is as it was in days gone by. Behind the stove is a craftsman who has held a Michelin Star since 1986: Johan Segers. He returns to the roots of Belgian gastronomy to give his guests a deliciously nostalgic feel.

→ Wulken met champignons, kalfsballetjes en amandelen. In olijfolie gebakken inktvisjes met kruiden en groenten. Pannacotta met karamel.

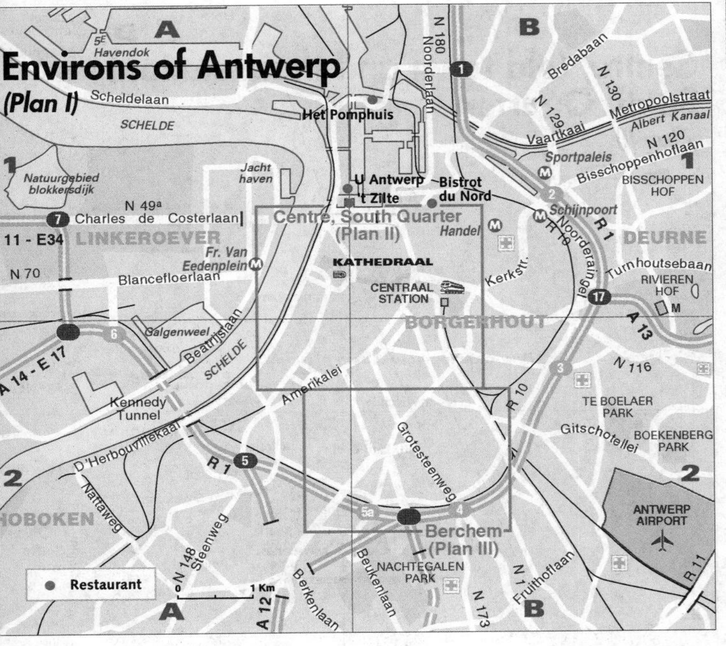

Environs of Antwerp (Plan I)

Het Gebaar (Roger van Damme)

XX

Leopoldstraat 24 – ✆ 03 232 37 10 Plan: **D2**
– www.hetgebaar.be – closed Bank Holidays, Saturday and Sunday
Carte 70/123 € – *(lunch only) (booking essential)*

• Creative • Cosy •

This restaurant is located in an elegant building on the edge of the botanical park. Luxury tea room cuisine, which the chef enriches with modern twists; mouthwatering desserts! Non-stop service until 6pm.

➜ Carpaccio van rund met peperknollenkaas, ganzenlever en pecorinocrème. Gegrilde tarbot met aardappelpuree, lauwwarme groenten en mosseltjesescabeche. Gekaramelliseerde appel met yuzu, basilicum, krokant bladerdeeg en chocolademousse.

Bistrot du Nord (Michael Rewers)

XX

Lange Dijkstraat 36 ✉ 2060 Plan I: **B1**
– ✆ 03 233 45 49 – www.bistrotdunord.be
– closed 24 December-3 January, Bank Holidays, Wednesday, Saturday and Sunday
Carte 51/102 €

• Traditional cuisine • Bourgeois • Intimate •

A lesson in tradition! The chef, an authentic craftsman, knows how to get the best out of fine produce. He admits to a weakness for tripe, but diners need have no fears - whatever your choice, your taste buds will be delighted.

➜ Zuurkool met buikspek en gerookte paling. Fazant Brabançonne. Bladerdeeg met crème chibouste en bosvruchten.

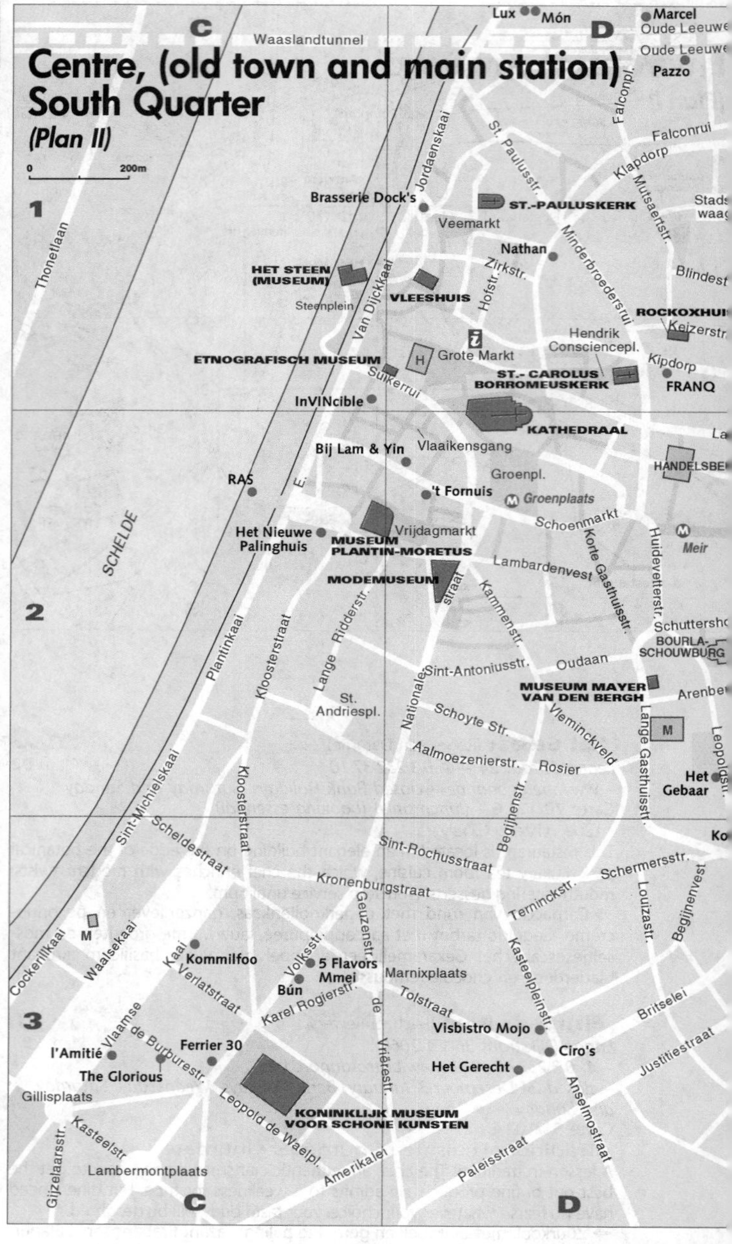
Centre, (old town and main station)
South Quarter
(Plan II)
0
200m
C
D
1
2
3
Waaslandtunnel
Lux
Món
Marcel
Oude Leeuwe
Pazzo
Falconpl.
Falconrui
Klapdorp
Jordaenskaai
St. Paulusstr.
Brasserie Dock's
ST.-PAULUSKERK
Veemarkt
Mutsaertstr.
Nathan
Minderbroedersrui
Zirkstr.
Blindest
HET STEEN (MUSEUM)
VLEESHUIS
Steenplein
Van Dijckkaai
Hofstr.
ROCKOXHUI
Keizerstr
Hendrik Consciencepl.
Grote Markt
ETNOGRAFISCH MUSEUM
Suikerrui
ST.- CAROLUS BORROMEUSKERK
Kipdorp
FRANQ
InVINcible
KATHEDRAAL
Vlaaikensgang
Bij Lam & Yin
Groenpl.
HANDELSBE
Thonetlaan
RAS
't Fornuis
Groenplaats
SCHELDE
Schoenmarkt
Het Nieuwe Palinghuis
MUSEUM PLANTIN-MORETUS
Vrijdagmarkt
Meir
Lambardenvest
Korte Gasthuisstr.
Huidevettersstr.
MODEMUSEUM
Kammenstr.
Lange Riddersstr.
Kloosterstraat
Plantinkaai
Schuttersh
BOURLA-SCHOUWBURG
Sint-Antoniusstr.
Oudaan
MUSEUM MAYER VAN DEN BERGH
Arenbe
St. Andriespl.
Nationalestraat
Schoyte Str.
Vleminckveld
Lange Gasthuisstr.
Aalmoezenierstr.
Rosier
Het Gebaar
Leopoldstr.
Sint-Michielskaai
Scheldestraat
Kloosterstraat
Begijnenstr.
Sint-Rochusstraat
Kronenburgstraat
Schermersstr.
Terninckstr.
Louizastr.
Begijnenvest
M
Cockerillkaai
Waalsekaai
Kommilfoo
Kaai
Verlatstraat
Volksstr.
5 Flavors Mmei
Bún
Geuzenstr.
Marnixplaats
Karel Rogierstr.
Tolstraat
Kasteelpleinstr.
Britselei
Visbistro Mojo
Ciro's
Vlaamse
de Burburestr.
Ferrier 30
l'Amitié
The Glorious
Het Gerecht
Vrièrestr.
de
Justitiestraat
Gillisplaats
KONINKLIJK MUSEUM VOOR SCHONE KUNSTEN
Leopold de Waelpl.
Anselmostraat
Kasteelstr.
Gijzelaarsstr.
Lambermontplaats
Amerikalei
Paleisstraat

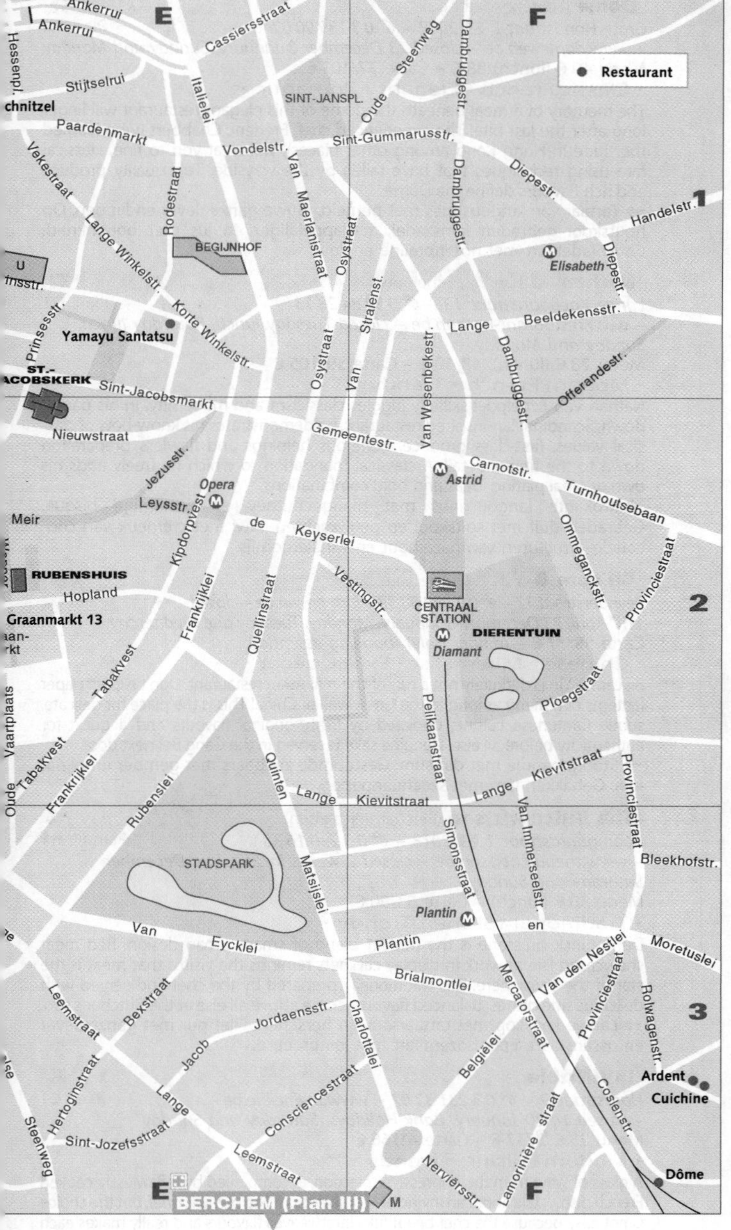

E
F
Restaurant
1
2
3
Ankerrui
Cassiersstraat
Steenweg
Oude
Dambruggestr.
Hessenpl.
Stijtselrui
SINT-JANSPL.
chnitzel
Italielei
Paardenmarkt
Vondelstr.
Sint-Gummarusstr.
Vekestraat
Van Maerlanistraat
Diepestr.
Rodestraat
Osystraat
Handelstr.
Lange Winkelstr.
BEGIJNHOF
Elisabeth
Korte Winkelstr.
Stralenst.
Beeldekensstr.
Prinsesstr.
Yamayu Santatsu
Lange
Van Wesenbekestr.
ST.-
JACOBSKERK
Sint-Jacobsmarkt
Offerandestr.
Nieuwstraat
Gemeentestr.
Carnotstr.
Astrid
Jezusstr.
Opera
Turnhoutsebaan
Leysstr.
Kipdorpvest
Meir
de Keyserlei
Ommeganckstr.
Vestingstr.
Provinciestraat
RUBENSHUIS
Hopland
Frankrijklei
Quellinstraat
CENTRAAL
STATION
Graanmarkt 13
DIERENTUIN
Diamant
Tabakvest
Ploegstraat
Vaartplaats
Oude
Pelikaanstraat
Kievitstraat
Quinten
Lange Kievitstraat
Rubenslei
Simonsstraat
Van Immerseelstr.
STADSPARK
Matsijslei
Bleekhofstr.
Plantin
Van Eycklei
Plantin en Moretuslei
Van den Nestlei
Brialmontlei
Mercatorstraat
Leemstraat
Bexstraat
Jordaensstr.
Charlottalei
Rolwagenstr.
Jacob
Belgiëlei
Ardent
Cuichine
Hertoginstraat
Lange
Conscienscestraat
Coslenstr.
Steenweg
Sint-Jozefsstraat
Leemstraat
Lamorinière straat
Nerviërsstr.
Dôme
BERCHEM (Plan III)
M

Dôme (Frédéric Chabbert)

Grote Hondstraat 2 ✉ 2018 – ☎ 0 3 239 90 03 – www.domeweb.be – closed 23 December-8 January, Sunday and Monday Plan: **F3**

Menu 40 € (lunch)/88 € – Carte 77/101 €

• Classic French • Elegant • Romantic •

The memory of a meal beneath the dome of this elegant restaurant will linger long after the last bite! The experienced chef, Frédéric Chabbert (who learned the trade in Hong Kong among other places), will treat you to fine, classical fare using techniques that have fallen by the wayside. Top quality produce and rich flavours define the Dôme.

➜ Tartaar van langoustines met pomelo, rauwe ganzenlever en limoen. Op houtskool gebraden lamszadel, aardappelaligot en jus met bonenkruid. Chocoladetaart met notenpraliné en zout.

Nathan (Nathan Van Echelpoel)

Lange Koepoortstraat 13 – ☎ 0 32 84 28 13 – www.restaurant-nathan.be – closed Tuesday lunch, Saturday lunch, Sunday and Monday Plan: **D1**

Menu 28 € (lunch), 48/68 € – Carte 59/105 €

• Modern French • Trendy •

Nathan Van Echelpoel skilfully juggles classicism and modernity. In his pared-down, Scandinavian-inspired restaurant, he demonstrates his know-how of classical values: first-class produce, generous helpings and flawless preparation down to the tiniest detail. A classical foundation to which he freely adds his own original plating ideas and bold combinations.

➜ Krokante langoustines met mangochutney en schuimige bisque. Gebraden duif met spitskool en peulvruchten. Kiwi met crémeux van chocolade, structuren van hazelnoot en vanilleroomijs.

Bij Lam & Yin (Lap Yee Lam)

Reynderstraat 17 – ☎ 0 3 232 88 38 – lam-en-yin.be – closed 1-17 April, 23 December-8 January, Monday, Tuesday and Wednesday Plan: **D2**

Carte 55/77 € – *(dinner only) (booking essential)*

• Chinese • Minimalist • Exotic décor •

Bij Lam & Yin is definitely not a run-of-the-mill Asian restaurant. Don't expect paper lanterns or a menu as long as the Great Wall of China! This is the place for delicate, subtle Cantonese cuisine, depicted by fresh, original flavours and a quest for authenticity before all else. Genuine saké is served in the Gang Bei next door.

➜ Stoommandje met dimsum. Gestoomde zeebaars met gember en pijpajuin. Gebakken lam met szechuanpeper.

The Butcher's son (Bert-Jan Michielsen)

Boomgaardstraat 1 ✉ 2018 – ☎ 0 3 230 16 38 – www.thebutchersson.be – closed 2 weeks in July, late December, Saturday and Sunday Plan III: **H1**

Menu 30 € (lunch) – Carte 53/90 €

• Traditional cuisine • Trendy •

De Koninck brasserie is the perfect blend of smart, urban design. Red meat showcased like artwork in display cabinets reminds the visitor that meat is the star of the show here; it is traditionally prepared by the chef and served with delicious side dishes. Balanced flavours come above all else at the Butcher's son.

➜ Lauwe kalfskop met tartaarsaus en hersenen. Filet pur met ganzenlever en ossenstaart. Frambozentaart met lemon curd.

InVINcible

Haarstraat 9 – ☎ 0 3 231 32 07 – www.invincible.be – closed 14-20 January, Bank Holidays, Saturday and Sunday Plan: **C1**

Menu 25 € 🍷/37 € – Carte 41/66 €

• Modern cuisine • Trendy •

A glass of wine from the impressive selection, accompanied by a flawlessly cooked French dish… talk about an invincible combination! The menu is brief, but the choice is not easy because the chef beautifully interweaves flavours and really makes each dish his own. Tip: a seat at the counter will complete this authentic experience.

Schnitzel

Paardenmarkt 53 – ✆ 03 256 63 86 Plan: **E1**
– www.schnitzelantwerpen.be – closed Saturday and Sunday
Carte 28/35 € – *(dinner only)*

• Classic cuisine • Neighbourhood • Traditional décor •

Simple but good is the motto of this establishment. The experienced chef deploys his talents to prepare delicious cooked meats and *beuling*, a sort of black pudding. He rustles up these ingredients into dishes designed to be shared. Refreshingly down to earth and wholesome!

Lux

Adriaan Brouwerstraat 13 – ✆ 03 233 30 30 Plan: **D1**
– www.luxantwerp.com – closed 23 July-6 August, 1 January, lunch on Bank Holidays, Saturday lunch, Sunday and Monday
Menu 35 € (lunch), 60/85 € – Carte 72/93 €

• Modern French • Chic •

This restaurant occupies the house of a former ship owner, and has a terrace that overlooks the port. There is a profusion of marble (columns, fireplaces), a wine and cocktail bar, à la carte options, plus an attractive lunch menu.

Ardent

Dageraadplaats 3 ✉ 2018 – ✆ 03 336 32 99 Plan: **F3**
– www.resto-ardent.be – closed Saturday lunch, Monday and Tuesday
Menu 29 € (lunch), 49/79 € – Carte 57/76 €

• Modern cuisine • Minimalist •

Passion is often said to be the distinctive character trait of great chefs. Wouter Van Steenwinkel is no exception to this rule and his tasteful restaurant will give you an insight into his many talents. You can expect well-thought out and balanced meals with perfectly blended flavours.

Graanmarkt 13

Graanmarkt 13 – ✆ 03 337 79 91 Plan: **E2**
– www.graanmarkt13.com – closed Sunday
Menu 35 € (lunch)/45 € – *(tasting menu only)*

• Organic • Minimalist • Trendy •

The days are long past when vegetables were little more than bland anonymous extras on the plate. Seppe Nobels proves that they are fully capable of taking the star role and he brilliantly and skilfully incorporates them into contemporary recipes rich in powerful flavours. Each dish is a new discovery!

Marcel

Van Schoonbekeplein 13 – ✆ 03 336 33 02 Plan: **D1**
– www.restaurantmarcel.be – closed late December and Sunday
Menu 25 € (lunch), 40/69 € – Carte 51/87 €

• Classic French • Brasserie • Vintage •

Welcome to Marcel's – a vintage bistro with a distinctly French feel. The culinary repertory mingles traditional recipes with touches of modernity, resulting in cuisine steeped in wholesome flavours. Terrace overlooking the MAS.

Món

Sint-Aldegondiskaai 30 – ✆ 03 345 67 89 Plan: **D1**
– www.monantwerp.com
Carte 34/63 €

• Meats and grills • Brasserie • Trendy •

The sculpture of a bull's head immediately gives you a foretaste of the menu, in which red meat takes pride of place. In fact, not just any meat but home raised Limousin beef prepared in a Josper charcoal fire. The cooking and accompaniments are a treat for your taste buds.

Het Nieuwe Palinghuis

Sint-Jansvliet 14 – ✆ 0 3 231 74 45 Plan: **C2**
– www.hetnieuwepalinghuis.be – closed June, Friday, Monday and Tuesday
Menu 44/172 € – Carte 63/171 €
• Seafood • Friendly •

Eel is king at this fish restaurant, only dethroned by Escaut lobster in season. The dining room and veranda are decorated with seascapes and old photographs of Antwerp. The perfect place to enjoy the pleasures of the North Sea.

Het Pomphuis

Siberiastraat ✉ 2030 – ✆ 0 3 770 86 25 Plan I: **B1**
– www.hetpomphuis.be – closed 24 December, 1 January and Saturday lunch
Menu 32 € (lunch)/54 € – Carte 62/82 €
• Modern cuisine • Vintage •

This immense former pumping station was magnificently transformed into a luxury brasserie with a terrace overlooking the port. The site's architectural interest is ideally paired to the establishment's up-to-the-minute, subtle menu.

RAS

Ernest Van Dijckkaai 37 – ✆ 0 32 34 12 75 Plan: **C2**
– www.ras.today – closed 24 December
Carte 44/74 €
• Modern cuisine • Elegant • Trendy •

The Zuiderterras has been treated to a recent makeover and most of the tables, set in bay windows, command fine views of the Schelde River. Charcoal sketches by Rinus Van de Velde add an arty touch to the interior. The plates are dressed according to modern tastes, while the recipes are predominantly classic.

U Antwerp

Nassaustraat 42 – ✆ 0 3 201 90 70 – www.u-eatsleep.be Plan I: **B1**
Menu 32 € (lunch), 55/65 € – Carte 48/85 €
• Modern cuisine • Trendy •

Arrange to meet in this delightful establishment in the Eilandje district and get ready to enjoy contemporary dishes from a modern, attractive menu concocted by Viki Geunes of 't Zilte (two stars). Finally, set your mind and body at rest and stay overnight in one of the comfortable rooms. Sheer bliss!

Cuichine

Draakstraat 13 ✉ 2018 – ✆ 0 485 02 05 37 Plan: **F3**
– www.cuichine.be – closed 8-15 April, first 2 weeks September, 24, 25 and 31 December, 1 and 2 January, Saturday lunch, Sunday and Monday
Menu 23 € (lunch)/40 € – Carte 44/62 €
• Chinese • Friendly •

Two childhood friends, both sons of restaurant owners, created Cuichine with the idea of serving dishes they used to eat at home. Their Cantonese recipes are well prepared from fresh produce and without fussy frills. Even better, the à la carte menu is well priced and the lunch menu unbeatable.

Ko'uzi

Leopoldplaats 12 – ✆ 0 3 232 24 88 – www.kouzi.be Plan: **D3**
– closed 2 weeks in August, Bank Holidays, Sunday, Monday and after 8pm
Carte 25/62 €
• Japanese • Minimalist • Design •

The interior design is as hip and minimalist as the food. Sushi and sashimi classics rub shoulders with other more inventive recipes. Enjoy delicious fare and the chance to buy different teas. The chef Kawada also organises sushi classes that are all the rage.

Pazzo

Oude Leeuwenrui 12 – ✆ 0 3 232 86 82 – www.pazzo.be Plan: **D1**
– closed late December-early January, Saturday and Sunday
Menu 24 € (lunch) – Carte 45/84 €
• Modern cuisine • Friendly •

This trendy brasserie with a lively atmosphere occupies a former warehouse near the docks. Enjoy Mediterranean- and Asian-inspired bistro cuisine and excellent wines.

Yamayu Santatsu

Ossenmarkt 19 – 0 3 234 09 49 – www.santatsu.be Plan: **E1**
– closed Sunday lunch and Monday
Menu 16 € (lunch), 23/45 € – Carte 29/55 €
• Japanese • Simple •
A lively and authentic Japanese restaurant that only uses the best hand picked ingredients, and prepares sushi in full view of diners. Assorted à la carte options with four different menus for two people.

SOUTH QUARTER AND BERCHEM

Kommilfoo (Olivier de Vinck de Winnezeele)

Vlaamse Kaai 17 – 0 3 237 30 00 Plan II: **C3**
– www.restaurantkommilfoo.be – closed first 3 weeks July, 25 December, Saturday lunch, Sunday and Monday
Menu 40 € (lunch), 70/85 € – Carte 80/114 €
• Creative • Cosy •
Smart yet casual, Kommilfoo will acquaint you with the creative and inventive talent of a dedicated chef. The dishes are both amusing and imaginative, with a clear desire to render contrasting tastes harmonious. Pyrenean goat, the house speciality, is on the menu all year long.
➜ Taco en carpaccio van langoustines met frisse rode quinoa, bisque en waterkers. Krokant gebakken kalfszwezerik met knolseldercrème, geglaceerde raapjes en kruidige kalfsjus. Crémeux met vanille, aardbeienroomijs, gemarineerde aardbeien en litchisap.

The Glorious

De Burburestraat 4a – 0 3 237 06 13 Plan II: **C3**
– www.theglorious.be – closed 16-24 April, 16-29 July, 24, 25 and 26 December, 1 and 2 January, Sunday and Monday
Menu 43 € (lunch)/65 € – Carte 78/108 €
• Modern French • Wine bar • Chic •
This former warehouse now houses a chic, well-designed restaurant. The sommelier is in charge of the renowned wine selection and the chef, Johan, tempts you with his cooking, which elevates classic dishes to a whole new level. Enjoy this glorious adventure surrounded by original baroque and art deco features.
➜ Millefeuille met langoustines, brunoise van gele en groene courgette en nantuasaus. Gebraden duif met gebakken eendenlever, primeurgroenten en jus met geplette jeneverbessen. Vanilleroomijs met warme chocoladesaus en krokante chocolade.

De Troubadour

Driekoningenstraat 72 ✉ 2600 Berchem Plan III: **H1**
– 0 3 239 39 16 – www.detroubadour.be – closed first 3 weeks August, Sunday and Monday
Menu 26 € (lunch), 37/47 €
• Modern cuisine • Trendy •
Out-going, sociable Johan Verbeeck welcomes diners with his inimitable style and fun-loving personality. Popular with gourmets since 1990, the establishment is depicted by a trendy vintage style. The menu and dishes seek to enhance and exalt the excellent seasonal ingredients and produce.

Bún

Volkstraat 43 – 0 3 235 85 89 – www.bunantwerp.be Plan II: **C3**
– closed 17-28 April, 17-21 July, 2-6 October, 9-13 January, Sunday and Monday
Carte 28/37 € – *(booking essential)*
• Vietnamese • Friendly •
Beyond the pleasantly exotic interior, it is the plate itself that will whisk you off to distant lands! Each successive appetising dish brings a promise of authenticity. The chef has achieved a fine balance between east and west in his street food cuisine, hence the well-deserved success.

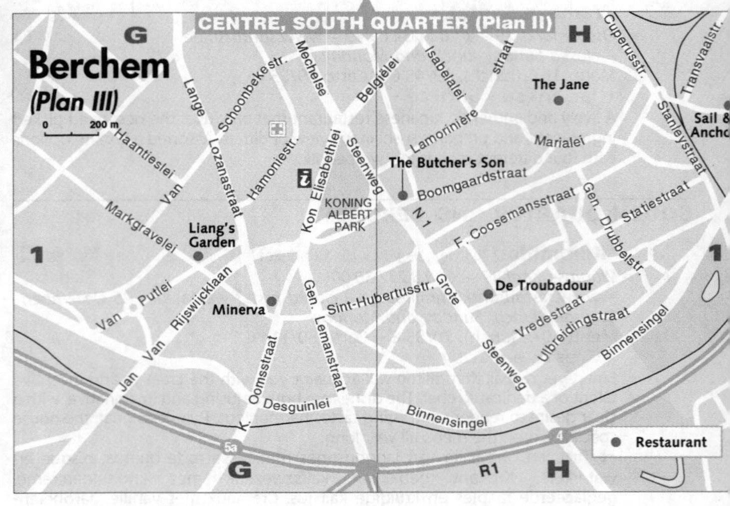

Ciro's

Amerikalei 6 ✉ 2018 – ✆ 0 3 238 11 47 – www.ciros.be Plan II: **D3**
– closed July, Saturday lunch and Monday
Menu 19 € (lunch) – Carte 37/69 €
• Belgian • Neighbourhood • Traditional décor •

The nostalgic interior, working class atmosphere and traditional Belgian fare will provide the opportunity to turn a meal at Ciro's into a taste of Antwerp's past. The vol-au-vent deluxe is the star of the show. Book ahead – you won't be disappointed!

5 Flavors Mmei

Volkstraat 37 – ✆ 0 3 281 30 37 – www.5flavors.be Plan II: **C3**
– closed Monday and Tuesday
Menu 16 € 🍷 (lunch), 30/80 € – Carte 23/50 €
• Chinese • Simple •

The most well-known and the most obvious can sometimes surprise – and this restaurant is a perfect example. The chef pays homage to Chinese tradition with fresh and sometimes surprising preparations, which put paid to many prejudices regarding the cuisine of his place of birth. The dim sum are to die for!

Minerva – Hotel Firean

Karel Oomsstraat 36 ✉ 2018 – ✆ 0 3 216 00 55 Plan III: **G1**
– www.restaurantminerva.be – closed 16 July-16 August, 24 December-10 January, Bank Holidays, Saturday and Sunday
Menu 38 € (lunch)/65 € – Carte 66/116 € – *(booking essential)*
• Classic cuisine • Elegant •

Minerva was also the name of the legendary Belgian luxury car, the repair workshops of which were located here. The site is now that of a well-oiled restaurant, serving good quality, traditional fare. You might be interested to know that all the meat is sliced in front of you!

Ferrier 30

Leopold de Waelplaats 30 – ✆ 0 3 216 50 62 – www.ferrier-30.be – closed Wednesday Plan II: **C3**

Menu 55/75 € – Carte 51/75 € – *(open until 11pm)*

• Italian • Design •

The best Italian restaurant in the area is doubtless Ferrier 30. The meat, fish and pasta dishes (lasagne al ragu, taglioni con prosciutto) are all steeped in authentic Italian flavours and are further enhanced by wines brought back by the owner in person.

Het Gerecht

Amerikalei 20 – ✆ 0 3 248 79 28 – www.hetgerecht.be – closed 8-22 April, 14 July-5 August, 22 December-7 January, Wednesday dinner, Saturday lunch, Sunday and Monday Plan II: **D3**

Menu 30 € (lunch), 56/68 € – Carte 52/80 € – *(set menu only at weekends)*

• Market cuisine • Cosy •

This restaurant is full of character. Peggy pampers her customers while Wim treats their taste buds to his talented creations. The photos adorning the walls are Wim's handiwork, as is the French inspired cuisine, which follows the seasons. The lunch menu is great.

Liang's Garden

Generaal Lemanstraat 54 – ✆ 0 3 237 22 22 – www.liangsgarden.eu – closed 8 July-4 August and Sunday Plan III: **G1**

Menu 27 € (lunch), 36/72 € – Carte 29/85 €

• Chinese • Traditional décor • Classic décor •

A stalwart of Chinese cuisine in the city! A spacious restaurant where the authentic menu covers specialities from Canton (dim sum), Peking (duck) and Szechuan (fondue).

l'Amitié

Vlaamse Kaai 43 – ✆ 0 3 257 50 05 – www.lamitie.net – closed 29 December-3 January, Saturday and Sunday Plan II: **C3**

Menu 30 € (lunch) – Carte 28/48 €

• Modern cuisine • Fashionable •

When you arrive in this fully renovated bistro, it won't be friendship, but something more akin to love that you will feel. Terroir-food takes pride of place and the first class ingredients are prepared according to modern techniques and served in small dishes. Scrumptious!

Sail & Anchor

Guldenvliesstraat 60 ✉ 2600 Berchem – ✆ 0 34 30 40 04 – www.sailandanchor.be – closed Sunday dinner, Monday and Tuesday Plan III: **H1**

Menu 70/135 € 🍷 – *(dinner only except Sunday) (tasting menu only)*

• Modern British • Vintage •

Michael Yates wavers between modern and traditional British cuisine. This English-born chef enjoys tweaking top-quality Belgian ingredients with his inimitable creativity. Amusing, refreshing, intriguing, but always a delight. Gracious Marijke is in her element to welcome you to this urban eatery.

Visbistro Mojo

Kasteelpleinstraat 56 – ✆ 0 3 237 49 00 – www.visbistro-mojo.be – closed Saturday lunch, Sunday and Monday Plan II: **D3**

Menu 21 € (lunch)/33 € – Carte 39/53 €

• Seafood • Bistro • Simple •

Fresh fish and shellfish are attractively displayed on the counter, bringing the promise of succulent fare. Chef Johan and his sister Nuria are determined to provide diners with excellent quality produce at reasonable prices. No frills, good wholesome food!

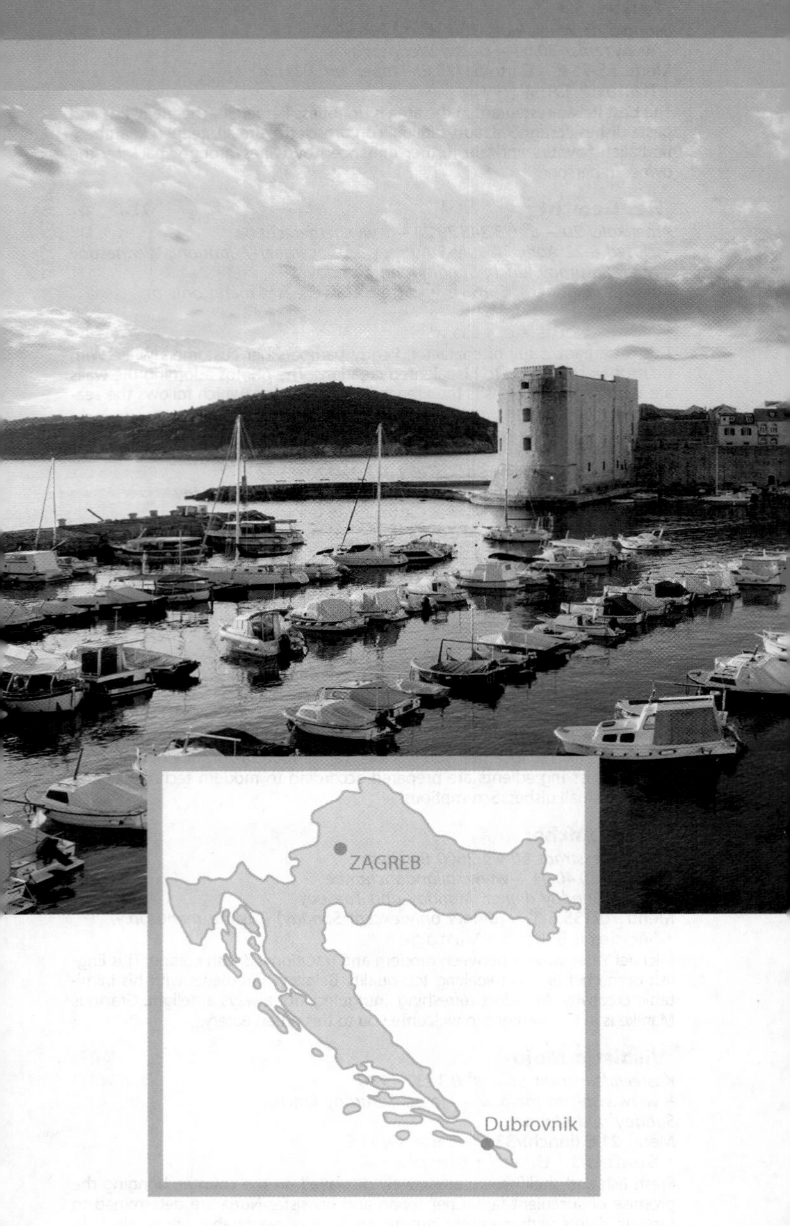

ZAGREB
Dubrovnik

CROATIA
CROATIA

phant/iStock

ZAGREB
ZAGREB

RudyBalasko/iStock

ZAGREB IN...

- **ONE DAY**
  Funicular, Upper Town (Gornji Grad).
- **TWO DAYS**
  Lower Town (Donji Grad), Upper Town (Gornji Grad).
- **THREE DAYS**
  Stone Gate, National Museum of Naïve Art, Church of St Mark, City Museum, Meštrović Gallery.

As both the capital and the largest city in the country, Zagreb is the cultural, scientific, religious, political and administrative centre of the Republic of Croatia, offering a melting-pot of Middle European and Mediterranean cultures.

It extends between Mt Medvednica (which protects it from the cold winter winds) to the north, and the River Sava, with its vast plain, to the south. Zagreb is home to almost a quarter of Croatia's population and over the centuries has been inhabited by people from all over Europe. This has given the city a rich and varied cultural life as well as an exciting and tumultuous history, which is reflected in the city's architecture (its streets, squares and palatial façades) and

unique atmosphere. A large yet manageable city, Zagreb has two distinct characters: the Baroque district, with its narrow alleyways, flights of steps and old buildings in the upper town offering a striking contrast to the large open areas and Art Nouveau-style palaces of the lower town.

With its lively streets for strolling around and its outdoor cafés for soaking up the sun, Zagreb is, above all, a carefree city – and one that will undoubtedly enchant visitors with its magical and timeless ambience.

EATING OUT

Year after year, the appeal of Croatia's capital as a tourist destination continues to grow. Its many restaurants and outdoor cafes, combined with its welcoming ambience, provide the backdrop for cuisine which is influenced more by the coast than inland, and by Istria, Dalmatia and neighbouring Italy rather than Austria, although the latter has also left a significant mark on the country thanks to its inclusion in the Austro-Hungarian Empire. The result is a cuisine with a strong Mediterranean influence, which includes vegetables, olive oil, fresh pasta, risottos and an equal balance of meat and fish on most menus, plus a focus on grilled dishes, while, in season, the best restaurants will include the renowned truffle in many of their dishes. A more distinctive culinary experience awaits in a small number of trendy restaurants which are gaining a reputation for their creative cuisine, although regional fare continues to hold its own in most places. Almost all restaurants are proud to offer a surprisingly good selection of local wines alongside options from outside the country.

Noel (Goran Kočiš)
Ul. Popa Dukljanina, 1 – ✆ (14) 844 297 – www.noel.hr – Closed Christmas, Easter and Sunday Plan: **D2**
Menu 430/690 HRK – Carte 428/608 HRK
• Modern cuisine • Fashionable • Design •
A fashionable restaurant with soft lighting and trendy, internationally inspired furnishings, where guests can enjoy exciting, colourful cuisine prepared by the owner-chef. The delicious modern and creative dishes served here are accompanied by a selection of Croatian, French and Italian wines carefully chosen by the sommelier/partner.
➜ Tataki trout, passion fruit, citrus and sunflower. Duck, red cabbage, fig and mangel. Schneenockerl.

Agava
Ul. Ivana Tkalčićeva 39 – ✆ (14) 829 826 – www.restaurant-agava.hr – Closed Christmas Plan: **B1**
Menu 450/600 HRK – Carte 200/500 HRK
• International • Bistro • Mediterranean •
Climb the many steps up to this homely restaurant, unusually set into the side of a hill, and you will be rewarded with views out over historic pedestrianised Tkalčićeva Street. The extensive, internationally influenced menu offers plenty of rustic Italian dishes as well as a selection of Croatian favourites.

Tač
Vrhovec 140 - Northwest : 2 km – ✆ (13) 776 757 – www.restac.hr – Closed Christmas, New Year, Easter and Monday
Carte 200/500 HRK
• Traditional cuisine • Family • Neighbourhood •
Despite its location in a residential district outside the city centre, this restaurant is a sound choice for its unfussy cuisine which pays little attention to passing trends. Instead, the couple in charge here focus on a Mediterranean-influenced menu offering fresh, simple dishes, many of which come from the female owner's native Istria. Announced at your table, daily specials can include ingredients such as fish, truffles, asparagus and artichokes, depending on the season and market availability.

Dubravkin Put
Dubravkin Put 2 – ✆ (14) 834 975 – www.dubravkin-put.com – Closed Christmas, New Year, Easter and Sunday Plan: **B1**
Carte 230/375 HRK
• Mediterranean cuisine • Romantic • Intimate •
This peaceful hideaway, surrounded by greenery, is located a short walk north of the city, and features a delightful terrace, perfect for an alfresco meal. Inside, it's spacious and contemporary, with a separate wine bar. International menus give a nod to Italy; home-grown wines dominate the wine list.

Zinfandel's
Esplanade H. Mihanoviceva 1 – ✆ (14) 566 644 – www.zinfandels.hr Plan: **B2**
Carte 305/515 HRK
• Modern cuisine • Intimate • Elegant •
Set in the finest hotel in Zagreb, built in 1925, this luxurious restaurant effortlessly combines the elegance of a bygone era with the ambience of a contemporary dining room. Ambitious menus offer Croatian classics alongside modern European dishes artistically presented and often with a playful element.

Apetit
Masarykova ul. 18 – ✆ (14) 811 077 – www.apetit.hr – Closed Christmas, Easter and Sundays in summer Plan: **B2**
Carte 180/360 HRK
• Mediterranean cuisine • Wine bar • Fashionable •
Wine bar meets contemporary restaurant at this fashionable destination, tucked away off a city street. The menu travels the globe, with regular sojourns to Italy and the Med and dishes are skilfully prepared, brightly coloured and full of flavour. Wine is taken seriously and the homemade pasta is a highlight.

Bistro Apetit by Marin Rendić

Jurjevska ul. 65A – ✆ (14) 677335 – www.bistroapetit.com – Closed Easter and Monday
Menu 371/560 HRK – Carte 320/410 HRK
• Mediterranean cuisine • Fashionable • Neighbourhood •
A delightful neighbourhood restaurant with a stylish modern look; floor to ceiling windows let in lots of light and open out onto a pretty, foliage-filled terrace. The seasonal, Italian-influenced menu is pleasingly concise, and the unfussy, vibrantly coloured dishes are fresh, flavoursome and fairly priced.

Le Bistro Esplanade

Esplanade H. Mihanoviceva 1 – ✆ (14) 566611 – www.lebistro.hr
Plan: **B2**
Menu 160 HRK – Carte 225/500 HRK
• French • Fashionable • Brasserie •
One of the capital's most popular places for meeting and eating is this smartly dressed yet informal all-day bistro, set in the city's top hotel. The classic French bistro menu offers soups and salads, steaks and schnitzel; try their signature dish, Esplanade Strukli, which has been served here since 1951.

ManO

Medvedgradska ul. 2 – ✆ (14) 669 342 – www.mano.hr – Closed Christmas, Easter, 1 January and Sunday
Plan: **B1**
Carte 230/570 HRK
• Meats • Fashionable • Design •
Exposed brick and high ceilings give a clue to this destination restaurant's previous life as a leather factory; nowadays it boasts an exclusive, clubby atmosphere and features soft, moody lighting and a bright open kitchen. Dishes range from the traditional to the more contemporary; go for one of the steaks.

Takenoko

Masarykova 22 – ✆ (16) 463 385 – www.takenoko.hr – Closed Christmas and Easter
Plan: **B2**
Carte 171/670 HRK – *(bookings advisable at dinner)*
• Japanese • Minimalist • Fashionable •
Japanese fusion is the name of the game at this trendy restaurant, simply decorated in black and cream. The wide-ranging menu offers a vast array of dishes, from sushi and sashimi to tempura and teriyaki, with wok dishes and western choices also included; portions are generous and cocktails add to the fun.

Time

Petrinjska 7 – ✆ (13) 333 660 – www.timerestaurant.hr – Closed Sunday
Plan: **C2**
Menu 60/100 HRK – Carte 240/550 HRK
• Fusion • Design • Fashionable •
This Japanese-style restaurant with soft lighting boasts a cocktail lounge and serves Japanese-fusion cuisine, including some top-quality fish options.

Boban

Gajeva 9 – ✆ (14) 811 549 – www.boban.hr – Closed Christmas, New Year and Easter
Plan: **B2**
Carte 115/305 HRK
• Traditional cuisine • Mediterranean • Fashionable •
An unpretentious city centre spot owned by Croatian footballer Zvonimir Boban. The ground floor café-bar serves sandwiches and snacks, but head instead to the red-brick, barrel-ceilinged basement restaurant to enjoy classic Italian dishes. Cooking is fresh and hearty; homemade pastas are the highlight.

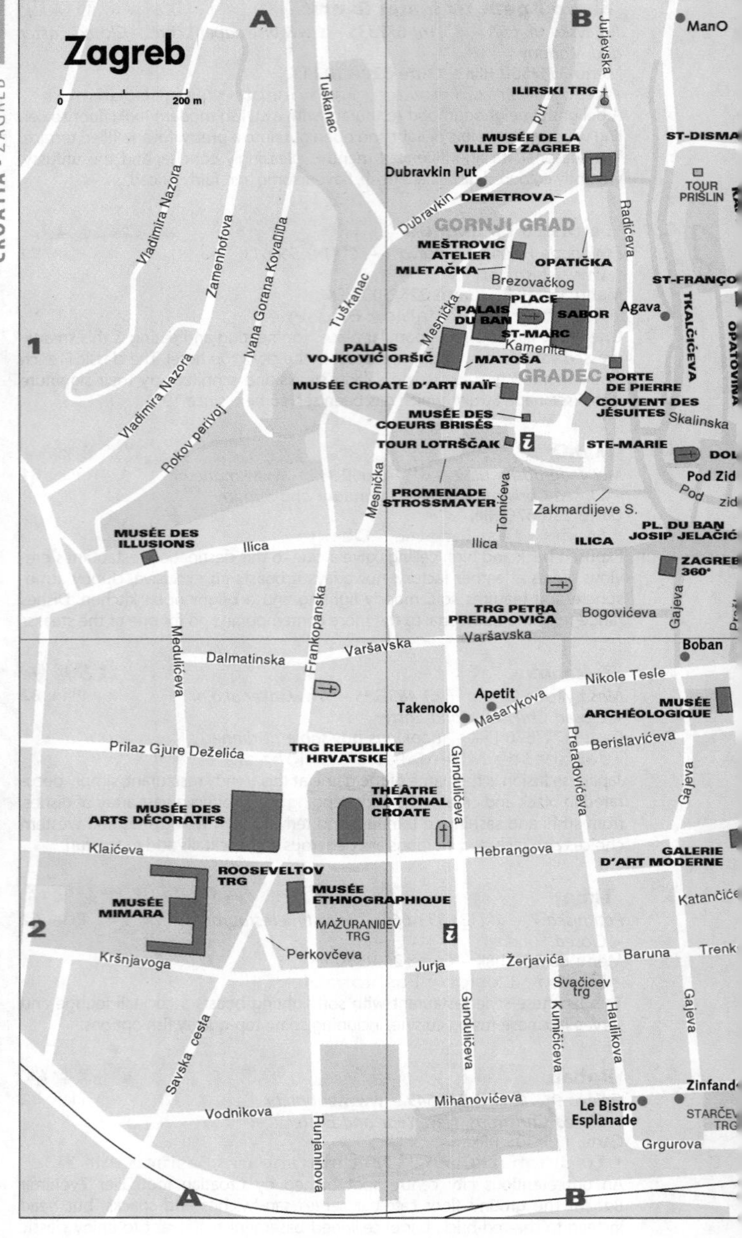
Zagreb
0
200 m
A
B
1
2
ManO
Jurjevska
ILIRSKI TRG
put
MUSÉE DE LA VILLE DE ZAGREB
ST-DISMA
TOUR PRISLIN
Dubravkin Put
DEMETROVA
Dubravkin
GORNJI GRAD
Radićeva
MEŠTROVIC ATELIER
OPATIČKA
MLETAČKA
Brezovačkog
ST-FRANÇO
PLACE
PALAIS DU BAN
SABOR
Agava
TKALČIĆEVA
OPATOVINA
ST-MARC
Kamenita
PALAIS VOJKOVIĆ ORŠIĆ
MATOŠA
GRADEC
PORTE DE PIERRE
MUSÉE CROATE D'ART NAÏF
COUVENT DES JÉSUITES
Skalinska
MUSÉE DES COEURS BRISÉS
TOUR LOTRŠČAK
STE-MARIE
DOL
Pod Zid
Pod zid
PROMENADE STROSSMAYER
Zakmardijeve S.
PL. DU BAN JOSIP JELAČIĆ
ILICA
ZAGREB 360°
Tomićeva
Mesnička
Tuškanac
Vladimira Nazora
Zamenhofova
Ivana Gorana Kovačića
Rokov perivoj
MUSÉE DES ILLUSIONS
Ilica
TRG PETRA PREFADOVIĆA
Bogovićeva
Gajeva
Varšavska
Boban
Dalmatinska
Frankopanska
Medulićeva
Nikole Tesle
Apetit
Takenoko
Masarykova
MUSÉE ARCHÉOLOGIQUE
Berislavićeva
Prilaz Gjure Deželića
TRG REPUBLIKE HRVATSKE
Gundulićeva
Preradovićeva
THÉÂTRE NATIONAL CROATE
MUSÉE DES ARTS DÉCORATIFS
Klaićeva
Hebrangova
GALERIE D'ART MODERNE
ROOSEVELTOV TRG
MUSÉE MIMARA
MUSÉE ETHNOGRAPHIQUE
MAŽURANIĆEV TRG
Katančiće
Perkovčeva
Kršnjavoga
Jurja
Žerjavića
Baruna
Trenk
Svačićev trg
Kumičićeva
Hatulikova
Savska cesta
Mihanovićeva
Zinfand
Le Bistro Esplanade
STARČEV TRG
Vodnikova
Runjaninova
Grgurova

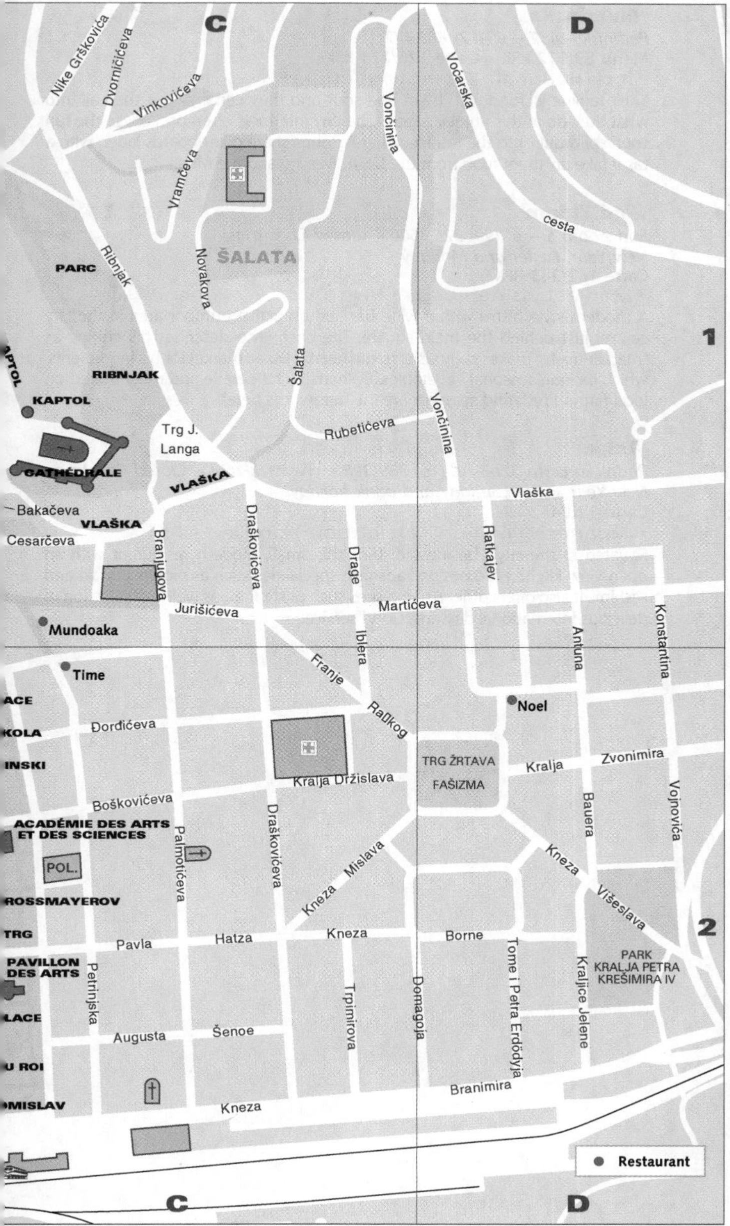
C
D
Nike Grškovića
Dvorničićeva
Vinkovićeva
Vramčeva
Vončinina
Voćarska
cesta
ŠALATA
PARC
Ribnjak
Novakova
Šalata
1
KAPTOL
RIBNJAK
KAPTOL
Rubetićeva
Vončinina
Trg J.
Langa
CATHÉDRALE
VLAŠKA
Vlaška
Bakačeva
VLAŠKA
Cesarčeva
Branjugova
Draškovićeva
Drage
Ratkajev
Jurišićeva
Martićeva
Mundoaka
Iblera
Antuna
Konstantina
Time
Franje
Račkog
Noel
ACE
KOLA
Đorđićeva
INSKI
TRG ŽRTAVA
FAŠIZMA
Kralja
Zvonimira
Kralja Držislava
Boškovićeva
ACADÉMIE DES ARTS
ET DES SCIENCES
Palmotićeva
Draškovićeva
Bauera
Vojnovića
POL.
Kneza
Mislava
Kneza
Višeslava
ROSSMAYEROV
TRG
2
Pavla
Hatza
Kneza
Borne
PAVILLON
DES ARTS
Petrinjska
Tome i Petra Erdődyja
Kraljice Jelene
PARK
KRALJA PETRA
KREŠIMIRA IV
Domagoja
Trpimirova
LACE
Augusta
Šenoe
U ROI
Branimira
MISLAV
Kneza
Restaurant
C
D

Mundoaka

Petrinjska ul. 2 – ✆ (17) 888 777 Plan: **C1**

Menu 89/112 HRK – Carte 126/223 HRK

• International • Friendly • Simple •

Their tagline is 'food with heart and soul' and they certainly put their all into what they do at this unique eatery. The tiny interior is often packed, so the fun soon spills out onto the terrace, where groups share giant boards laden with a tasty take on street food from the U.S.A., Mexico and the Med.

Pod Zidom

Pod zidom 5 – ✆ (99) 325 3600 – Closed Christmas, New Year, Easter and Monday Plan: **B1**

Carte 162/283 HRK

• Market cuisine • Cosy • Bistro •

A modern-style bistro with a wine bar and attractive outdoor area in the city centre, just behind the main square. The chef, who describes his cuisine as "market-fresh", makes daily visits to the nearby Dolac market for his ingredients, which include seasonal vegetables, Dalmatian charcuterie and meat reared on local farms. Fresh and seasonal are the buzzwords here!

Tekka

Radnička cesta 37b – ✆ (16) 389 398 – www.tekka.hr – Closed Christmas, New Year, Easter, Sunday and bank holidays

Carte 128/442 HRK

• Japanese • Design • Neighbourhood •

Situated in the city's business district, this small, modern restaurant with an open-view kitchen focuses on Japanese specialities such as nigiri, uramaki and sashimi. It also offers other Asian dishes such as stir fries, as well as a selection of delicious international desserts. Good service.

MarcinZielezny/iStock

DUBROVNIK
DUBROVNIK

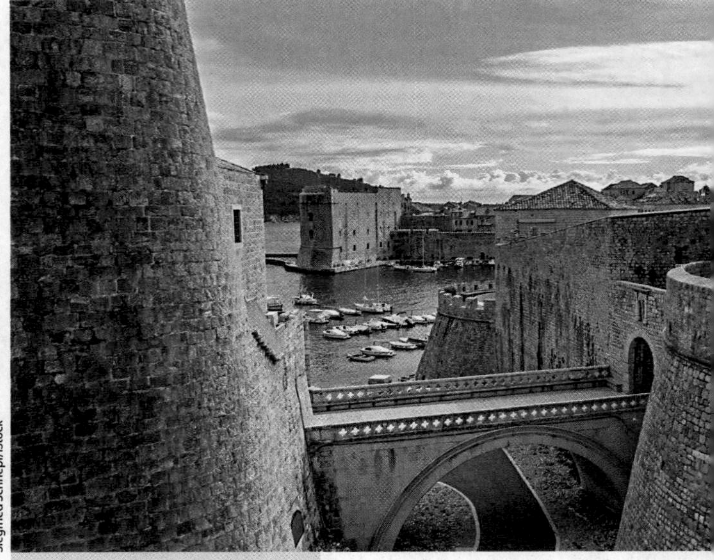

Siegfried Schnepf/iStock

DUBROVNIK IN...

→ **ONE DAY**
Walk along the city walls and visit the Old Port.

→ **TWO DAYS**
Luza Square, Rector's Palace, Dubrovnik Cathedral, Sponza Palace, Bell Tower, Church of St Blaise.

→ **THREE DAYS**
A boat trip to Lokrum Island, cable car to Mt Srd, Franciscan Monastery.

Perched on a rock and surrounded by high ramparts lapped by the sea, the former Ragusa in the historic region of Dalmatia is a real architectural gem. Nicknamed the 'pearl of the Adriatic' by the poet Lord Byron, the old town of Dubrovnik was declared a UNESCO World Heritage Site in 1979.

Although badly damaged during the Second World War and then again in the 1990s when it was heavily bombed by Serbian artillery during the civil war which followed the break-up of the former Yugoslavia, Dubrovnik has since regained its former glory,

attracting increasing numbers of tourists who are drawn here by its evocative atmosphere – the town now receives over one million visitors a year! Beautiful, romantic, distinctive – no adjective quite sums up the ambience of this extraordinary town. Its success is based on cultural and geographical factors which make it unique: the influence of Venetian, Gothic and Baroque architecture and the town's old walls combined with the crystal-clear Mediterranean and stunning features such as Lokrum Island and Srd mountain, which protects the town from the Scirocco and Bora winds.

EATING OUT

Although the narrow streets of the walled city are crowded with tourists from all around the world, Dubrovnik's cuisine remains firmly anchored in local traditions with a particular focus on simple, authentic fish and seafood dishes which are carefully cooked to preserve their fragrance and flavour. From vegetables and herbs to olive oil, the ingredients used are fresh and typical of the healthy Mediterranean diet. Visitors who love pasta will have no problem finding it here, where it is served with a wide variety of sauces, while other popular choices include risottos and an excellent selection of meat dishes. Alongside these international staples there is also evidence of a more elaborate and creative cuisine, which can be technically sophisticated and is often elegantly and beautifully presented. Finally, if you want to add a touch of romance to your dinner, it's worth knowing that some of the city's restaurants boast superb views of the Old Town or Port, while wine enthusiasts will be pleased to hear that they are also well catered for – the quality of Croatian wine will definitely surprise you!

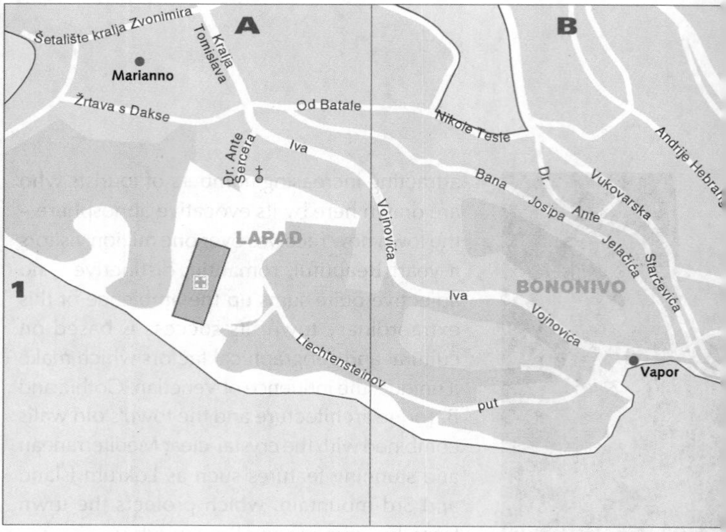

A
B
Šetalište kralja Zvonimira
Kralja Tomislava
Marianno
Žrtava s Dakse
Od Batale
Nikole Tesle
Andrije Hebranga
Dr. Ante Sercera
Iva
Bana
Dr.
Josipa
Ante
Vukovarska
Jelačića
Starčevića
Vojnovića
LAPAD
BONONIVO
1
Iva
Vojnovića
Liechtensteinov
put
Vapor

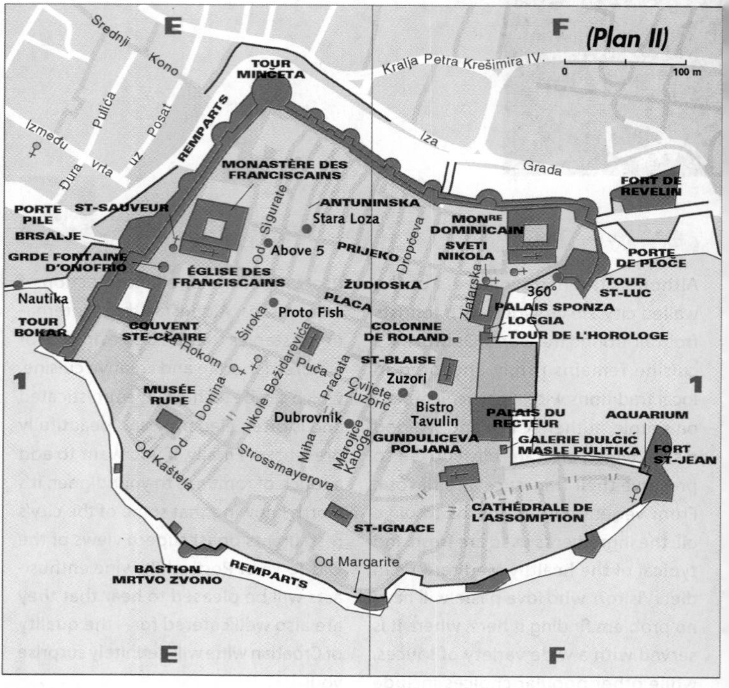

E
F
(Plan II)
0
100 m
Srednji
Kono
Kralja Petra Krešimira IV.
TOUR MINČETA
Pulića
Posat
Između
Đura
vrta
uz
REMPARTS
Iza
Grada
MONASTÈRE DES FRANCISCAINS
FORT DE REVELIN
PORTE PILE
ST-SAUVEUR
ANTUNINSKA
Stara Loza
Od Sigurate
Dropčeva
MON^RE DOMINICAIN
BRSALJE
Above 5
PRIJEKO
SVETI NIKOLA
PORTE DE PLOČE
GRDE FONTAINE D'ONOFRIO
ÉGLISE DES FRANCISCAINS
ŽUDIOSKA
Zlatarska
TOUR ST-LUC
360°
Nautika
PLACA
PALAIS SPONZA
Proto Fish
LOGGIA
TOUR BOKAR
COUVENT STE-CLAIRE
Široka
COLONNE DE ROLAND
TOUR DE L'HOROLOGE
Od Rokom
Nikole Božidarevića
Puča
ST-BLAISE
1
Pracata
Cvijete Zuzorić
Zuzori
1
MUSÉE RUPE
Domina
Bistro Tavulin
Dubrovnik
PALAIS DU RECTEUR
AQUARIUM
Od
Miha
Marojice Kaboge
GUNDULICEVA POLJANA
GALERIE DULČIĆ MASLE PULITIKA
FORT ST-JEAN
Od Kaštela
Strossmayerova
CATHÉDRALE DE L'ASSOMPTION
ST-IGNACE
Od Margarite
BASTION MRTVO ZVONO
REMPARTS
E
F

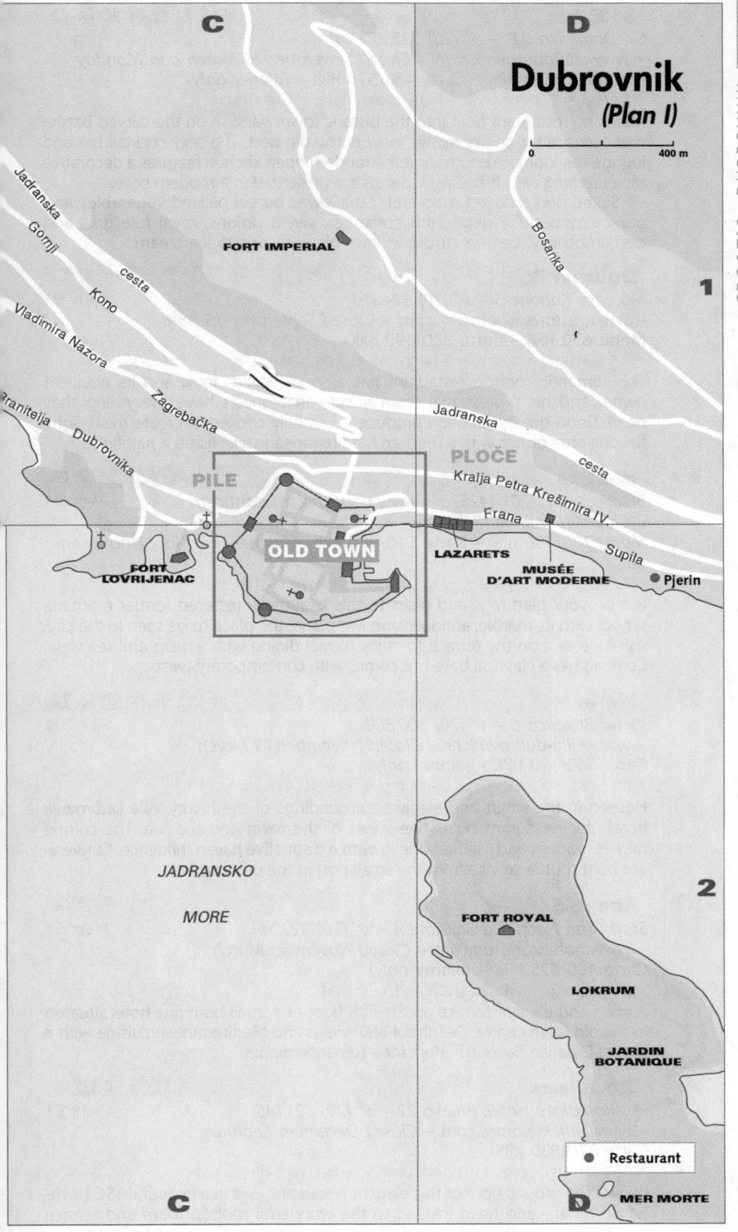

C
D
Dubrovnik
(Plan I)
0
400 m
Jadranska
Gornji
cesta
Kono
Vladimira Nazora
Zagrebačka
Branitelja
Dubrovnika
FORT IMPERIAL
Bosanka
1
Jadranska
cesta
PLOČE
PILE
Kralja Petra Krešimira IV
Frana
Supila
OLD TOWN
LAZARETS
MUSÉE
D'ART MODERNE
Pjerin
FORT
LOVRIJENAC
JADRANSKO
MORE
2
FORT ROYAL
LOKRUM
JARDIN
BOTANIQUE
Restaurant
MER MORTE
C
D

360°

Sv. Dominika B.B. – (20) 322 222 Plan: **F1**
– www.360dubrovnik.com – Closed November-26 March and Monday
Menu 820/820 HRK – Carte 480/570 HRK – *(dinner only)*
• Modern cuisine • Fashionable • Design •

A striking restaurant built into the historic town walls; sit on the curved battlement terrace for an impressive view of the old port. The sexy cocktail bar and lounge has intimate booths and the modern open kitchen features a decorative tank teeming with fish. Classic dishes are presented in a modern style.

→ Salted and smoked mackerel, cauliflower puree, pickled vegetables and garlic croquette. Pigeon with coriander, sweet onions, royal foie gras and bergamot jelly. Lemon curd and crumble with ricotta ice cream.

Dubrovnik

Marojice Kaboge 5 – (20) 324810 Plan: **E1**
– www.restorandubrovnik.com – Closed September-15 April
Menu 630 HRK – Carte 380/490 HRK
• Mediterranean • Elegant • Romantic •

This romantic rooftop restaurant has a smart, stylish look, and its ebullient owner and his professional team ensure that guests have everything they need. Good quality Croatian produce is carefully cooked to create fresh, light, flavoursome dishes with a modern Mediterranean style; fish is a highlight.

Nautika

Brsalje 3 – (20) 442526 – www.nautikarestaurant.com Plan: **E1**
– Closed November-February
Menu 780/780 HRK – Carte 510/900 HRK – *(dinner only) (booking essential)*
• Classic cuisine • Elegant • Fashionable •

Put on your glad rags and head to this beautifully restored former maritime school with its marble, antiques and live piano: the place to be seen in the city. Ask for a seat on the terrace to enjoy formal dining with a delightful sea view. Cooking has a classical base but comes with contemporary twists.

Pjerin

Vlaha Bukovca 6 – (20) 500 300 Plan: **D2**
– www.villa-dubrovnik.hr – Closed November-15 March
Carte 560/790 HRK – *(dinner only)*
• Mediterranean • Luxury • Mediterranean •

Housed in the smart and elegant surroundings of the luxury Villa Dubrovnik hotel, this restaurant boats fine views of the town and the sea. The cuisine here is modern and Mediterranean with a distinctive Italian influence. Convenient boat shuttle service from the small port in the old town.

Above 5

Stari Grad Hotel, Od Sigurate 4 – (20) 322244 Plan: **E1**
– www.hotelstarigrad.com – Closed November-March
Carte 450/625 HRK – *(dinner only)*
• Creative • Romantic • Elegant •

A quiet and elegant terrace on the fifth floor of a small boutique hotel situated in the old town centre. Delightful 360° views and Mediterranean cuisine with a hint of Croatian flavour. Perfect for a romantic dinner!

Stara Loza

Prijeko Palace Hotel, Prijeko 22 – (20) 321145 Plan: **E1**
– www.prijekopalace.com – Closed December-February
Carte 270/530 HRK
• Mediterranean cuisine • Elegant • Intimate •

Bypass the ground floor of this elegant restaurant - set in a beautiful 15C townhouse hotel - and head instead to the wonderful rooftop room and terrace which look over the old town and out to sea. Cooking mixes Croatian, Italian and Asian influences, with visually appealing dishes prepared by a skilled team.

Marianno

Mata Vodopića 2A – ✆ (20) 311333 Plan: **A1**
– www.restaurantmarianno.com – Closed Monday lunch in winter
Carte 260/400 HRK
• Classic cuisine • Cosy •

If you're looking for a change from the historic centre, why not head to Lapad bay where you'll find this restaurant situated just a few minutes from the beach and the delightful footpaths wending their way around the coast. Modern decor provides the backdrop for reinterpretations of classic fish and meat dishes, with an emphasis on fresh, local produce.

Proto Fish

Široka ul 1 – ✆ (20) 323235 Plan: **E1**
– www.esculaprestaurants.com – Closed December-February
Menu 680 HRK – Carte 289/890 HRK
• Fish and seafood • Mediterranean • Fashionable •

This long-standing, family-owned fish and seafood restaurant in the heart of the old town has a loyal local following and attracts many well-heeled tourists too. Those in the know head to the lovely hidden roof terrace to enjoy the carefully prepared seasonal Mediterranean dishes; go for the catch of the day.

Vapor

Bellevue Hotel, Pera Čingrije 7 – ✆ (20) 330000 Plan: **B1**
– www.adriaticluxuryhotels.com – Closed December-April
Menu 555 HRK – Carte 370/600 HRK – *(dinner only)*
• Modern cuisine • Fashionable • Design •

Floor to ceiling windows mean it's not only those on the terrace who can enjoy fantastic views of the Adriatic at this elegant restaurant, which is set in a luxury hotel built into the cliffside. Croatian produce is showcased in modern, eye-catching, boldly flavoured dishes with influences from the Med.

Bistro Tavulin

Cvijete Zuzorić 1 – ✆ (20) 323977 – www.tavulin.com Plan: **F1**
– Closed December-February
Carte 205/350 HRK
• Traditional cuisine • Neighbourhood • Bistro •

Aimed at tourists but offering more than your typical bistro is this old town restaurant with its rustic beamed dining room and neatly set pavement tables. The concise menu offers classic Croatian dishes with subtle modern touches and a Mediterranean edge; the set four course 'Dubrovnik Dinner' is a steal.

Zuzori

Cvijete Zuzoric 2 – ✆ (20) 324 076– www.zuzori.com Plan: **F1**
– Closed Christmas
Menu 350/400 HRK – Carte 384/539 HRK
• Mediterranean • Bistro • Friendly •

A bistro serving imaginative, out-of-the-ordinary cuisine with Mediterranean-style options as well as some interesting traditional local dishes. Attractive classic outdoor dining area in an alleyway in the town centre. Friendly service.

PRAGUE

CZECH REPUBLIC
ČESKÁ REPUBLIKA

MarekKijevsky/iStock

PRAGUE
PRAHA

satariel/iStock

PRAGUE IN…

→ **ONE DAY**
Old Town Square, the astronomical clock, Charles Bridge, Prague Castle, Petřín Hill.

→ **TWO DAYS**
Josefov, the National Theatre, Golden Lane.

→ **THREE DAYS**
Wenceslas Square, the National Museum, cross the bridge to look round Malá Strana.

Prague's history stretches back to the Dark Ages. In the ninth century a princely seat comprising a simple walled-in compound was built where the castle now stands; in the tenth century the first bridge over the Vltava arrived; and by the 13C the enchanting cobbled alleyways below the castle were complete. But Prague has come of age and Europe's most perfectly preserved capital now proffers consumer choice as well as medieval marvels. Its state-of-the-art shopping malls and pulsing nightlife bear testament to its popularity with tourists – the iron glove of communism long since having given way to western consumerism. These days there are practically two

versions of Prague: the lively, youthful, 'stag party capital', and the sedate, enchanting 'city of a hundred spires'.

The four main zones of Prague were originally independent towns in their own right. The river Vltava winds its way through their heart and is spanned by the iconic Charles Bridge. On the west side lie Hradcany – the castle quarter, built on a rock spur – and Malá Strana, Prague's most perfectly preserved district, located at the bottom of the castle hill. Over the river are Staré Město, the old town with its vibrant medieval square and outer boulevards, and Nové Město, the new town, which is the city's commercial heart and where you'll find Wenceslas Square and Prague's young partygoers.

EATING OUT

Since the late 1980s, Prague has undergone a bit of a foodie revolution. Global menus have become common currency and the heavy, traditional Czech cuisine is now often served – in the better establishments – with a creative flair and an international touch. Lunch is the main meal of the Czech day and many restaurants close well before midnight. Prague was and still is, to an extent, famous for its infinite variety of dumplings – these were the glutinous staple that saw locals through the long years of stark Communist rule. The favoured local dish is still pork, pickled cabbage and dumplings, and those on a budget can also mix the likes of schnitzel, beer and ginger cake for a ridiculously cheap outlay. Some restaurants include a tip in your final bill, so check closely to make sure you don't tip twice. Czechs consume more beer than anyone else in the world and there are some excellent microbrewery tipples to be had.

ON THE RIGHT BANK (Old Town, Staroměstské Námesti)

La Degustation Bohême Bourgeoise (Oldřich Sahajdák)

Haštalská 18 ✉ 110 00 – Ⓜ Náměsti Republiky – ✆ 222 311 234 – www.ladegustation.cz – Closed 1 week January, 24 December and Monday

Plan: **G1**

Menu 3450 CZK – *(dinner only) (booking essential) (tasting menu only)*

• Modern cuisine • Intimate • Fashionable •

It might be set in a historic building at the end of a narrow lane, but this restaurant is surprisingly stylish, with bespoke chandeliers hung above tables inlaid with slices of oak. Marie B Svobodová's 19C cookery school provides the inspiration for creative modern dishes which stimulate the taste buds.

➜ Kohlrabi with buttermilk and garlic. Pork neck, apple and mustard. Apricot with rum.

Field (Radek Kašpárek)

U Milosrdných 12 ✉ 110 00 – Ⓜ Staroměstská – ✆ 222 316 999 – www.fieldrestaurant.cz – Closed 24 December

Plan: **G1**

Menu 1300 CZK (weekday lunch)/3500 CZK – Carte 1160/1290 CZK – *(booking essential)*

• Modern cuisine • Design • Friendly •

Two friends run this stylishly understated restaurant, which has a warm, intimate feel. An eye-catching mural is projected overhead and the well-balanced Scandinavian cooking is equally stimulating. Alongside wine pairings are non-alcoholic drink matches, such as tomato, cucumber and chilli juice.

➜ Perch with leek, avocado and citrus. Lamb with carrot, Bryndza cheese and lovage. Rhubarb, yoghurt and caramel.

Divinis

Týnská 21 ✉ 110 00 – Ⓜ Náměsti Republiky – ✆ 222 325 440 – www.divinis.cz – Closed 2 weeks August, 24-26 December, Saturday lunch and Sunday

Plan: **G1**

Carte 885/1125 CZK – *(booking essential)*

• Italian • Friendly • Cosy •

You'll find this intimate, homely restaurant tucked away on a side street; it's run with great passion and has a friendly feel. Rustic, seasonal Italian dishes have original touches and are cooked with flair. The perfect accompaniment comes in the form of a large collection of wines from Italian growers.

Eska

Pernerova 49, Karlín (Northeast : 3 km. by Italská) ✉ 186 00 – Ⓜ Křižíkova – ✆ 731 140 884 – www.eska.ambi.cz – Closed 24 December

Carte 545/995 CZK

• Traditional cuisine • Design • Fashionable •

A café, bakery and restaurant in a converted fabric factory. The dining room has a stark, industrial feel with exposed bricks, pipework and girders, and the open kitchen adds to the buzz. Old family favourites are given modern makeovers; much use is made of traditional techniques like marinating and fermenting.

Sansho

Petrská 25 ✉ 110 00 – Ⓜ Florenc – ✆ 222 317 425 – www.sansho.cz – Closed Christmas, 31 December-1 January, Sunday, Monday and bank holidays

Plan: **H1**

Menu 1100 CZK (dinner) – Carte 510/890 CZK – *(booking essential at dinner)*

• Asian • Neighbourhood • Simple •

A fun neighbourhood eatery that uses organic and free range ingredients from the owner's butcher's shop. Dishes have an Asian base and could include the likes of soft shell crab sliders or dry sweet pork with coconut rice and papaya; at dinner, they serve a 6 course tasting menu. Some tables are for sharing.

Alcron – Alcron Hotel Prague

Štepánská 40 ✉ 110 00 – Ⓜ Muzeum – ✆ 222 820 000 Plan: **H2**
– www.alcron.cz – Closed Sunday and Monday
Menu 1400/2000 CZK – *(dinner only and lunch Friday-Saturday) (booking essential)*
• Modern cuisine • Intimate • Vintage •

An intimate, semi-circular restaurant dominated by an art deco mural of dancing couples by Tamara de Lempicka. Choose 'hot' or 'cold' dishes from an elaborate international menu. There's a good choice of wines and staff are attentive.

Salabka

K Bohnicím 2 (North : 8 km. via Trojská) ✉ 171 00 – ✆ 778 019 002
– www.salabka.cz – Closed 24 December-20 January, Sunday dinner and Monday
Menu 550/1450 CZK
• Modern cuisine • Fashionable • Design •

Set in a boutique winery on the outskirts of the city; vines have been grown on the hillside here since the 13C. Imaginative modern cooking focuses on local ingredients, with each plate containing many textures and flavours. The best tables are on the first floor overlooking the vines. Six spacious and stylish apartments.

Aromi

Náměstí Míru 6 ✉ 120 00 – Ⓜ Náměstí Míru Plan: **H3**
– ✆ 222 713 222 – www.aromi.lacollezione.cz
Menu 395 CZK (weekday lunch) – Carte 980/1310 CZK
• Italian • Brasserie • Neighbourhood •

A friendly team welcomes you to this bright modern restaurant. Simply prepared, classically based Italian dishes are given modern touches; the fresh fish display demonstrates the owners' commitment to sourcing good quality produce.

Bellevue

Smetanovo Nábreží 18 ✉ 110 00 – Ⓜ Staroměstská Plan: **G2**
– ✆ 222 221 443 – www.bellevuerestaurant.cz
– Closed 24 December
Menu 890/1680 CZK – Carte 1245/1815 CZK – *(booking essential at dinner)*
• Modern cuisine • Chic • Contemporary décor •

Sit on the pleasant terrace or in the contemporary, pastel-hued dining room of this elegant 19C townhouse and take in the view over Charles Bridge and the river. Ambitious, original modern dishes consist of many different elements.

Café Imperial – Hotel Imperial

Na Porící 15 ✉ 110 00 – Ⓜ Náměsti Republiky Plan: **H1**
– ✆ 246 011 440 – www.cafeimperial.cz
Carte 535/880 CZK – *(booking essential)*
• Traditional cuisine • Grand café • Vintage •

The Imperial hotel's restaurant is an impressive room, with a high ceiling and colourful mosaic-tiled walls and pillars. Menus list robust Czech dishes. It was the place to be seen in the 1920s and, as they say, Kafka's spirit lives on...

Casa De Carli

Vezenskská 5 ✉ 110 00 – Ⓜ Staromestská Plan: **G1**
– ✆ 224 816 688 – www.casadecarli.com – Closed Sunday
Carte 535/1175 CZK
• Italian • Friendly • Neighbourhood •

A contemporary family-run restaurant with bold artwork, and tables on the cobbled street. Flavoursome cooking has a subtle North Italian bias; the breads, pastas and ice creams are all homemade – go for one of the daily specials.

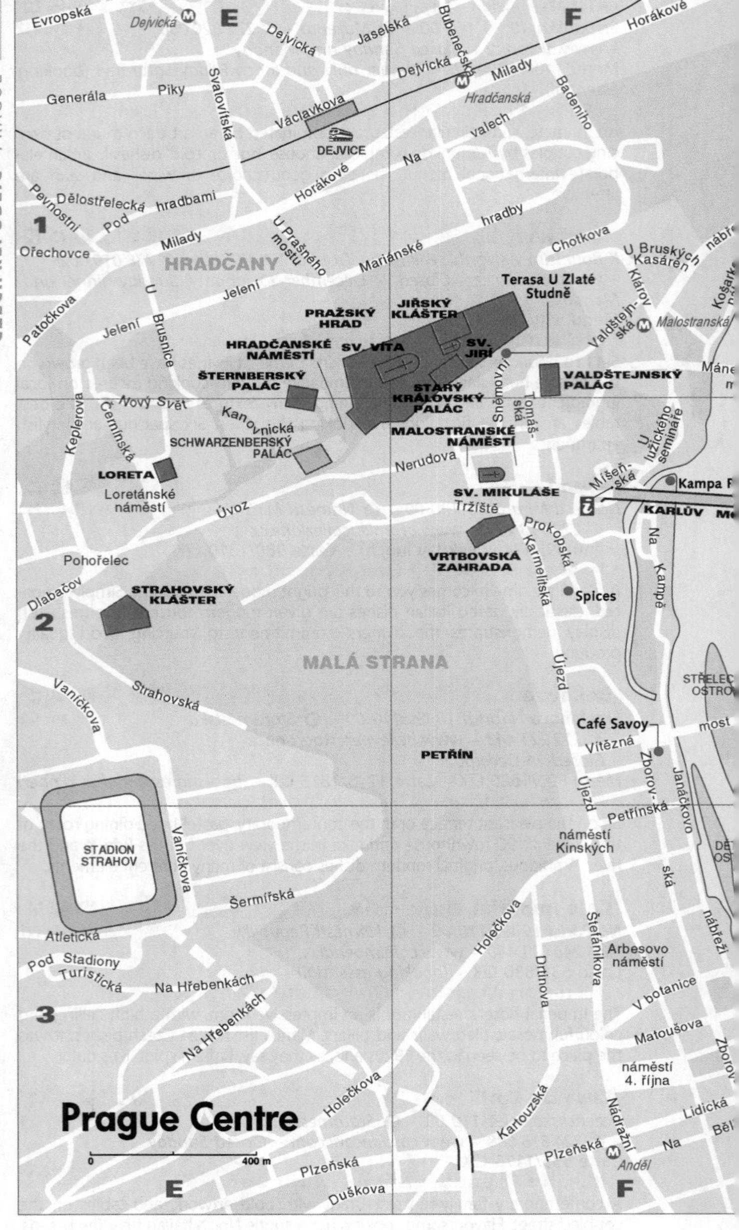

Prague Centre
0
400 m
E
F
1
2
3
Evropská
Dejvická
Dejvická
Jaselská
Bubenečská
Dejvická
Milady
Hradčanská
Horákové
Generála
Piky
Svatovítská
Václavkova
DEJVICE
Badeniho
Na
valech
Pevnostní
Dělostřelecká
Pod
hradbami
Horákové
U Prašného mostu
hradby
Ořechovce
Milady
HRADČANY
Mariánské
Chotkova
U Bruských Kasáren
Klárov
Terasa U Zlaté Studně
Patočkova
Jelení
Jelení
U Brusnice
PRAŽSKÝ HRAD
JIŘSKÝ KLÁŠTER
HRADČANSKÉ NÁMĚSTÍ
SV. VÍTA
SV. JIŘÍ
Valdštejnská
Malostranská
ŠTERNBERSKÝ PALÁC
STARÝ KRÁLOVSKÝ PALÁC
VALDŠTEJNSKÝ PALÁC
Sněmovní
Tomášská
Keplerova
Nový Svět
Černínská
Kanovnická
SCHWARZENBERSKÝ PALÁC
MALOSTRANSKÉ NÁMĚSTÍ
U lužického semináře
Nerudova
LORETA
Loretánské náměstí
SV. MIKULÁŠE
Míšeňská
Kampa
Tržiště
KARLŮV
Úvoz
Prokopská
Karmelitská
VRTBOVSKÁ ZAHRADA
Na Kampě
Pohořelec
Dlabačov
STRAHOVSKÝ KLÁŠTER
Spices
MALÁ STRANA
Újezd
Vaníčkova
Strahovská
Café Savoy
most
Vítězná
PETŘÍN
Zborovská
Janáčkovo
Újezd
Petřínská
STADION STRAHOV
Vaníčkova
náměstí Kinských
Šermířská
Holečkova
Štefánikova
nábřeží
Atletická
Pod Stadiony
Turistická
Na Hřebenkách
Drtinova
Arbesovo náměstí
V botanice
Na Hřebenkách
Matoušova
náměstí 4. října
Holečkova
Kartouzská
Nádražní
Lidická
Plzeňská
Na
Anděl
Plzeňská
Duškova

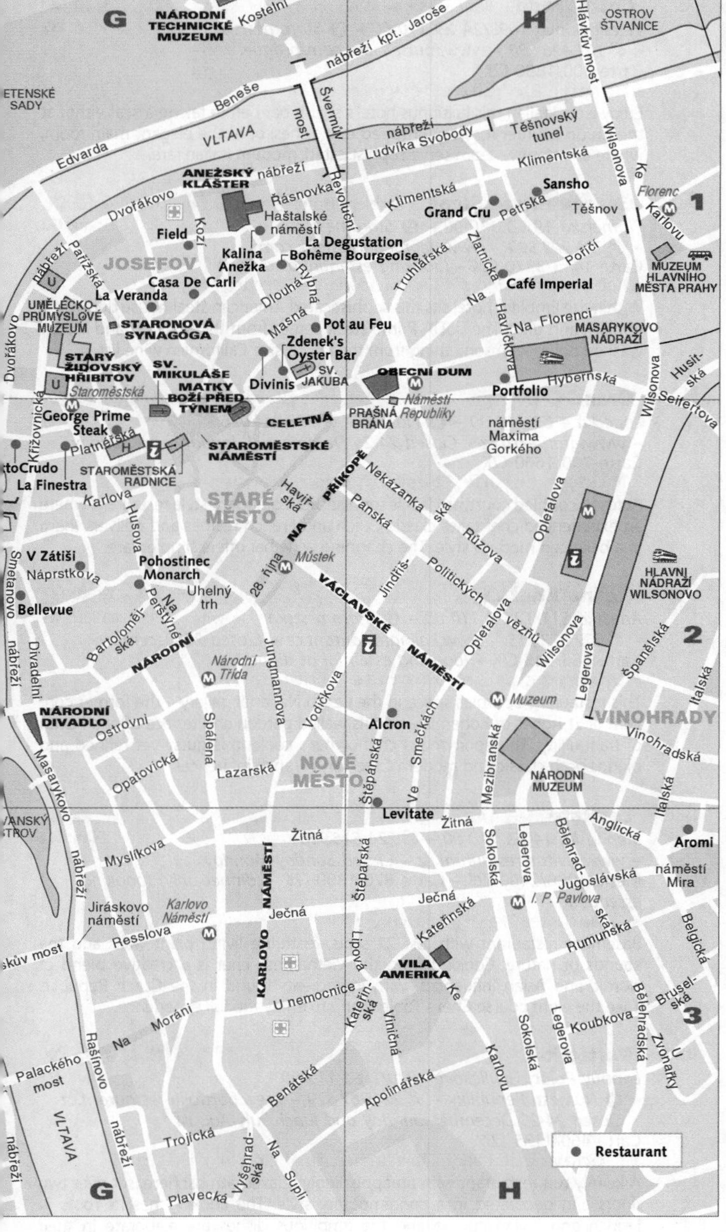
G
H
NÁRODNÍ TECHNICKÉ MUZEUM
Kostelní
nábřeží kpt. Jaroše
OSTROV ŠTVANICE
Hlávkův most
Beneše
Edvarda
VLTAVA
Švermův most
nábřeží Ludvíka Svobody
Těšnovský tunel
Wilsonova
Klimentská
ANEŽSKÝ KLÁŠTER
Řásnovka
Revoluční
Sansho
Grand Cru
Petrská
Těšnov
Florenc
Karlovu
Dvořákovo
Field
Kozí
Haštalské náměstí
La Degustation Bohême Bourgeoise
Kalina
Anežka
JOSEFOV
Pařížská
Truhlářská
Zlatnická
Poříčí
MUZEUM HLAVNÍHO MĚSTA PRAHY
Casa De Carli
La Veranda
Dlouhá
Rybná
Café Imperial
Na Poříčí
UMĚLECKO-PRŮMYSLOVÉ MUZEUM
STARONOVÁ SYNAGÓGA
Masná
Pot au Feu
Havlíčkova
Na Florenci
MASARYKOVO NÁDRAŽÍ
STARÝ ŽIDOVSKÝ HŘBITOV
SV. MIKULÁŠE
Zdenek's Oyster Bar
SV. JAKUBA
OBECNÍ DUM
Portfolio
Hybernská
Husitská
Staroměstská
MATKY BOŽÍ PŘED TÝNEM
Divinis
Náměstí Republiky
Seifertova
George Prime Steak
CELETNÁ
PRAŠNÁ BRÁNA
náměstí Maxima Gorkého
Platnéřská
Křižovnická
STAROMĚSTSKÉ NÁMĚSTÍ
toCrudo
La Finestra
STAROMĚSTSKÁ RADNICE
NA PŘÍKOPĚ
Nekázanka
Karlova
Husova
STARÉ MĚSTO
Havířská
Panská
Opletalova
Růžova
V Zátiši
Náprstkova
Smetanovo
Pohostinec Monarch
Můstek
Jindřišská
Politických vězňů
HLAVNÍ NÁDRAŽÍ WILSONOVO
Bellevue
Uhelný trh
Na Perštýně
28. října
VÁCLAVSKÉ NÁMĚSTÍ
Bartolomějská
NÁRODNÍ
Jungmannova
Opletalova
Wilsonova
Španělská
Legerova
nábřeží
Divadelní
Národní Třída
Vodičkova
Muzeum
Italská
NÁRODNÍ DIVADLO
Ostrovní
Spálená
Alcron
VINOHRADY
Vinohradská
Masarykovo
Opatovická
Lazarská
NOVÉ MĚSTO
Štěpánská
Ve Smečkách
Mezibranská
NÁRODNÍ MUZEUM
Levitate
Žitná
Anglická
Italská
Aromi
Myslíkova
KARLOVO NÁMĚSTÍ
Štěpařská
Sokolská
Legerova
Bělehradská
náměstí Míra
Jugoslávská
Jiráskovo náměstí
Karlovo Náměstí
Ječná
I. P. Pavlova
Resslova
Kateřinská
Rumunská
Belgická
Jiráskův most
Lipová
VILA AMERIKA
U nemocnice
Ke Karlovu
Na Moráni
Kateřinská
Viničná
Bruselská
Koubkova
Palackého most
Rašínovo nábřeží
Benátská
Apolinářská
Sokolská
Legerova
Bělehradská
U Zvonařky
VLTAVA
Trojická
Vyšehradská
Na Slupi
Plavecká
Restaurant
1
2
3

CottoCrudo – Four Seasons Hotel

Veleslavínova 1098/2A ✉ 110 00 – Ⓜ Staroměstská – ✆ 221 426 880 – www.fourseasons.com/prague
Plan: **G2**

Carte 800/1880 CZK

• Italian • Elegant • Design •

Enjoy a cocktail in this luxurious hotel's stylish bar before taking a seat either at the Crudo counter for Asian-inspired raw dishes, or in the elegant main room, where an attentive team serve sophisticated, modern Italian fare.

George Prime Steak – Emblem Hotel

Platnéřská 19 ✉ 110 00 – Ⓜ Staroměstská – ✆ 226 202 599 – www.georgeprimesteak.com
Plan: **G2**

Carte 1415/3370 CZK – *(booking essential at dinner)*

• Meats and grills • Fashionable • Design •

Within the Emblem hotel sits this sophisticated American steakhouse decorated in black and grey. The USDA Prime steak comes from the Midwest and is best washed down with something from the impressive Californian wine list.

Grand Cru

Lodecká 4 ✉ 110 00 – Ⓜ Florenc – ✆ 775 044 076 – www.grand-cru.cz – Closed 24-26 December, 1 January and Sunday
Plan: **H1**

Carte 700/1660 CZK

• Modern cuisine • Fashionable • Elegant •

Across a cobbled courtyard is this sophisticated orangery-style restaurant where an experienced chef takes classic Czech and French recipes and delivers them in a balanced modern style. The charming wine bar offers simpler fare.

Kalina Anežka

Anežská 811/12 ✉ 110 00 – Ⓜ Staromestská – ✆ 222 317 715 – www.kalinarestaurant.cz – Closed 25 December
Plan: **G1**

Carte 355/945 CZK – *(booking essential at dinner)*

• Modern cuisine • Intimate • Friendly •

This restaurant occupies space in the Czech National gallery – the former convent of St Agnes of Bohemia – and its walled garden and terrace offer a haven of tranquillity. The eponymous chef-owner's cooking is gutsy yet refined and blends both classic and modern Czech and French influences.

Levitate

Štěpánská 14 ✉ 110 00 – ✆ 724 516 996 – www.levitaterestaurant.cz – Closed Sunday-Monday
Plan: **H2**

Menu 1900/2400 CZK – Carte 870/1300 CZK – *(dinner only) (booking essential)*

• Creative • Design • Cosy •

Basement restaurant with just 22 seats, featuring living plant walls and the sounds of nature. Cooking from the Vietnamese chef is a creative blend of Nordic and Asian influences, with ingredients found in the Czech Republic. Take the eight course Chef's Table Menu to enjoy the full experience.

Portfolio

Lannův Palác, Havlíčkova 1030/1 ✉ 110 00 – Ⓜ Náměsti Republiky – ✆ 224 267 579 – www.portfolio-restaurant.cz – Closed 24-25 December, Sunday and lunch July-August
Plan: **H1**

Carte 460/1135 CZK

• Modern cuisine • Contemporary décor • Design •

A keenly run restaurant with an appealingly relaxed atmosphere, set over two floors and decorated in a contemporary style. The cooking has its roots in French and Italian cuisine and the ambitious dishes are elaborate in their construction.

Pot au Feu

XX AC

Rybná 13 ✉ 110 00 – Ⓜ Náměsti Republiky Plan: **G1**
– ✆ 739 654 884 – www.potaufeu.cz – Closed Christmas, Easter, Saturday lunch and Sunday-Monday
Menu 495/595 CZK – Carte 515/1335 CZK
• French • Intimate • Design •

The chef-owner's cooking is inspired by the French classics but also by his travels. The intimate interior comes with striking artwork and shelves packed with directly sourced French wines. Service is relaxed yet clued-up.

V Zátiši

XX AC

Liliová 1, Betlémské Nám. ✉ 110 00 – Ⓜ Můstek Plan: **G2**
– ✆ 222 221 155 – www.zatisi.cz – Closed 24 December
Menu 590/1390 CZK – Carte 985/1385 CZK – *(booking essential at dinner)*
• Modern cuisine • Cosy • Contemporary décor •

This modern city centre restaurant is a popular spot. Its name means 'timeless' and with its clever blend of modern Czech and Indian dishes, well-judged spicing and attractive presentation, it looks set to stand up to its name.

La Veranda

XX AC

Elišky Krásnohorské 2 ✉ 110 00 – Ⓜ Staroměstská Plan: **G1**
– ✆ 224 814 733 – www.laveranda.cz – Closed 24 December and Sunday
Carte 635/1195 CZK
• Mediterranean cuisine • Cosy • Friendly •

Sit surrounded by books in the colourfully decorated main room or head down to the intimate basement. Cooking takes its inspiration from the Med, with Italy playing a big part. Staff are friendly and welcoming.

Yamato

XX AC

U Kanálky 14 (East : 1 km. via Slezská and Vinohradská) ✉ 120 00 – Ⓜ Jiřiho z Poděbrad – ✆ 222 212 617 – www.yamato.cz – Closed Christmas, Saturday lunch and Sunday
Carte 520/5250 CZK – *(booking essential at dinner)*
• Japanese • Elegant • Friendly •

The chef is a local but he trained in Japan, so alongside an array of authentic dishes you'll find some original creations. A selection of Japanese beers and whiskies complement the cooking, and the place is run with real passion.

Benjamin

X

Norská 14 (East : 2 km. via Francouzská) ✉ 101 00 – Ⓜ Flora – ✆ 774 141 432 – www.benjamin14.cz – Closed Christmas, 1 January and Sunday-Tuesday
Menu 1200/1800 CZK – *(dinner only) (booking essential) (tasting menu only)*
• Modern cuisine • Cosy • Neighbourhood •

Ten seats around a horseshoe counter; come early for 5 courses or later for the full 8 course experience. Chefs interact with guests, presenting carefully executed, boldly flavoured dishes, which are inspired by the history and old recipes of Central Europe. Wine pairings are offered to match.

La Finestra

X AC

Platnérská 13 ✉ 110 00 – Ⓜ Staroměstská Plan: **G2**
– ✆ 222 325 325 – www.lafinestra.lacollezione.cz
Carte 1165/1385 CZK – *(booking essential at dinner)*
• Italian • Rustic • Cosy •

You'd never guess but from 1918-1945, this lovely restaurant with its red-brick vaulted ceiling was an Alfa Romeo showroom! Expect rustic Italian dishes and fine Italian wines, and be sure to stop off at their neighbouring shop.

Pohostinec Monarch

Na Perštýně 15 ✉ 110 00 – Ⓜ Můstek – ✆ 703 182 801 Plan: **G2**
– www.monarch.pohostinec.cz – Closed 24 December
Carte 500/1830 CZK
• Traditional cuisine • Pub • Friendly •

The baby sister of Grand Cru has a relaxed, pub-like atmosphere, a large bar and liberal use of black in its decoration. The kitchen, visible through a large hatch, focuses on traditional Czech cooking, with steaks a speciality.

Zdenek's Oyster Bar

Malá Štupartská 5 ✉ 110 00 – Ⓜ Náměsti Republiky Plan: **G1**
– ✆ 725 946 250 – www.oysterbar.cz
Carte 1345/2915 CZK
• Seafood • Bistro • Wine bar •

Deep in the heart of the city is this atmospheric, dimly lit restaurant with a pretty pavement terrace. Menus include tapas, caviar, elaborate seafood platters, dishes from the Josper grill and, of course, 8 different types of oyster.

ON THE LEFT BANK (Castle District, Lower Town)

Na Kopci

K Závěrce 2774/20 (Southwest : 6 km. by Radlická) ✉ 150 00 – Ⓜ Smíchovské Nádraží – ✆ 251 553 102 – www.nakopci.com – Closed Christmas
Carte 695/835 CZK – *(booking essential)*
• Traditional cuisine • Bistro • Simple •

Leave the city behind and escape to this buzzy bistro, whose name means 'on the hill'. The wallpaper is a montage of pictures of the owner's family, and the atmosphere is warm and welcoming. You can't book for lunch and by 12pm it's packed. Flavoursome Czech and French dishes are accompanied by local beers.

Terasa U Zlaté Studně – Golden Well Hotel

U Zlaté Studně 166/4 ✉ 118 00 – Ⓜ Malostranská Plan: **F1**
– ✆ 257 533 322 – www.terasauzlatestudne.cz
Menu 990/3100 CZK – Carte 1440/2510 CZK – *(booking essential)*
• Classic cuisine • Cosy • Elegant •

This long-standing restaurant opened in 1901 and, in fact, predates the hotel it sits atop. The intimate room has blue and gold walls and a picture window, while above is a heated terrace with a stunning panoramic view. The classic international menu displays influences ranging from the Med through to Asia.

Kampa Park

Na Kampe 8b, Malá Strana ✉ 118 00 – Ⓜ Malostranská Plan: **F2**
– ✆ 257 532 685 – www.kampagroup.com
Carte 1315/1915 CZK – *(booking essential at dinner)*
• Modern cuisine • Fashionable • Design •

Kampa Park is stunningly located by the water's edge, next to Charles Bridge. Choose from several dining areas: the best spots are the Winter Garden and the riverside terrace. The décor is contemporary, as is the interesting menu.

SaSaZu

Bubenské nábr. 306 (Northeast : 4 km by Italská) ✉ 170 04 – Ⓜ Vltavská – ✆ 284 097 455 – www.sasazu.com – Closed 24-25 December and lunch 1 January
Carte 615/1000 CZK – *(booking essential at dinner)*
• Asian • Exotic décor • Fashionable •

You'll find this chic restaurant and bar inside a cavernous warehouse in Prague Market. The extensive menu lists dishes under their cooking techniques, with all the sweet, sour, spicy and salty flavours of Southeast Asia present.

Spices – Mandarin Oriental Hotel

Nebovidská 459/1 ✉ 118 00 – Ⓜ Malostranská Plan: **F2**
– ✆ 233 088 777 – www.mandarinoriental.com/prague
Carte 795/1465 CZK – *(dinner only)*

• Asian • Intimate • Fashionable •

Softly backlit dark wood panels and decorative Chinoiserie items set the tone in this chic hotel restaurant. The pan-Asian menu is divided into three regions – Northeast, Southeast and Southwest – and there's a separate sushi list too.

Café Savoy

Vítězná 5 ✉ 150 00 – Ⓜ Anděl – ✆ 731 136 144 Plan: **F2**
– www.cafesavoy.ambi.cz – Closed 24 December
Carte 425/1190 CZK – *(booking essential)*

• Traditional cuisine • Elegant • Grand café •

This atmospheric grand café with its superb neo-renaissance ceiling has been open since 1893. Come for coffee and a cake from their patisserie, the daily lunch special and a beer, or generously sized Czech and French classics.

Aarhus
COPENHAGEN

DENMARK
DANMARK

Westersoe/iStock

COPENHAGEN
KØBENHAVN

AleksandarGeorgiev/iStock

COPENHAGEN IN...

➜ **ONE DAY**
Walk along Strøget, National Museum, Ny Carlsberg Glyptotek, Black Diamond, boat watching at Nyhavn.

➜ **TWO DAYS**
Tivoli Gardens, Vesterbro, Opera House, Christiania.

➜ **THREE DAYS**
Royal palaces at Frederiksstaden, train ride along the coast.

Some cities overwhelm you, and give the impression that there's too much of them to take in. Not Copenhagen. Most of its key sights are neatly compressed within its central Slotsholmen 'island', an area that enjoyed its first golden age in the early seventeenth century in the reign of Christian IV, when it became a harbour of great consequence. It has canals on three sides and opposite the harbour is the area of Christianshavn, home of the legendary freewheeling 'free-town' community of Christiania. Further up from the centre are Nyhavn, the much-photographed canalside with brightly coloured buildings where the sightseeing cruises leave from, and the elegant

Frederiksstaden, whose wide streets contain palaces and museums. West of the centre is where Copenhageners love to hang out: the Tivoli Gardens, a kind of magical fairyland. Slightly more down-to-earth are the western suburbs of Vesterbro and Nørrebro, which were run-down areas given a street credible spit and polish for the 21C, and are now two of the trendiest districts.

Once you've idled away some time in the Danish capital, you'll wonder why anyone might ever want to leave. With its waterfronts, quirky shops and cafés, the city presents a modern, user-friendly ambience – but it also boasts world class art collections, museums, and impressive parks, gardens and lakes, all of which bear the mark of an earlier time.

EATING OUT

Fresh regional ingredients have revolutionized the menus of Copenhagen's hip restaurants and its reputation for food just keeps getting bigger. The city's dining establishments manage to marry Danish dining traditions such as herring or frikkadeller meatballs with global influences to impressive effect. So impressive that in recent times the city has earned itself more Michelin stars, for its crisp and precise cooking, than any other in Scandinavia. Many good restaurants blend French methods and dishes with regional ingredients and innovative touches and there is a trend towards fixed price, no choice menus involving several courses, which means that dinner can be a pleasingly drawn-out affair, stretching over three or four hours. There's no need to tip, as it should be included in the cost of the meal. Danes, though, have a very good reputation as cheerful, helpful waiting staff, so you might feel like adding a bit extra. But be warned, many restaurants – and even hotels – charge between 2.5% and 5% for using a foreign credit card.

✿✿✿ **Geranium** (Rasmus Kofoed)

Per Henrik Lings Allé 4 (8th Fl), Parken National Stadium (3 km via Dag Hammaraskjölds Allé) ✉ 2100 Ø – ☎ 69 96 00 20 – www.geranium.dk – Closed 2 weeks Christmas, 2 weeks summer and Sunday-Tuesday
Menu 2500 DKK – *(booking essential) (surprise menu only)*
• Creative • Design • Elegant •

Unusually located on the 8th floor of the National Football Stadium, this luxurious restaurant feels as if it is inviting the outside in with its panoramic park views. Modern techniques and the finest organic and biodynamic ingredients are used to create pure, beautiful and balanced dishes.
➜ Fjord shrimp tartlet, söl and pickled elderflower. Chicken with morels, sprouts, smoked chicken fat and hops. Beeswax and pollen ice cream with rhubarb.

✿✿ **a|o|c** (Søren Selin)

Dronningens Tværgade 2 ✉ 1302 K Plan: **D2**
– Ⓜ Kongens Nytorv – ☎ 33 11 11 45 – www.aoc.dk – Closed Christmas, 3 weeks July, 1 week February, 1 week October, Sunday and Monday
Menu 1700/2000 DKK – *(dinner only) (booking essential) (tasting menu only)*
• Modern cuisine • Elegant • Romantic •

A spacious, simply decorated restaurant in the vaults of an eye-catching 17C building close to Nyhavn harbour; owned and run by an experienced sommelier and chef. Skilful, well-judged and, at times, playful cooking has a Danish heart and shows great originality, as well as a keen eye for detail, flavour and texture.
➜ Scallop with fermented asparagus, dill and mussel cream. Quail, flowers and roasted potato skin. Jerusalem artichoke, caramel and hazelnut ice cream.

✿✿ **Kadeau Copenhagen** (Nicolai Nørregaard)

Wildersgade 10B ✉ 1408 K – Ⓜ Christianshavn Plan: **D3**
– ☎ 33 25 22 23 – www.kadeau.dk – Closed 5 weeks July-August, 24-26 December, 1-2 January and Sunday-Tuesday
Menu 1950 DKK – *(dinner only and Saturday lunch) (booking essential) (tasting menu only)*
• Modern cuisine • Design • Fashionable •

You'll receive a warm welcome at this delightful restaurant, where the open kitchen adds a sense of occasion to the sophisticated room. The chefs have an innate understanding of how best to match fresh and aged produce, and use their experience in preserving and fermenting to add many elements to each dish.
➜ Hot and cold smoked salmon, elderflower and tomato water. Fire-baked celery root, honey and wood ants. Grilled, dried and fresh pumpkin with lavender.

✿✿ **noma** (René Redzepi)

Refshalevej 96 (3.5km by Torvegade and Prinsessegade D3) ✉ 1432 K – ☎ 32 96 32 97 – www.noma.dk – Closed 2 weeks mid-June, 2 weeks late September, first week March and Saturday dinner-Monday
Menu 2500 DKK – *(dinner only and Saturday lunch) (booking essential) (surprise menu only)*
• Creative • Rustic • Elegant •

An urban farm and restaurant with stunning lakeside views. Thought-provoking seasonal menus offer seafood in spring, vegetables in summer and game in autumn. Their considered and holistic approach creates beautifully executed, original dishes packed with flavour and delivered with confidence and pride.
➜ Fjord shrimps and summer preserves with chicken 'skin'. Celeriac shawarma. Flower pot cake with roses and flowers.

Kong Hans Kælder

XxX

Vingaardsstræde 6 ✉ 1070 K – Ⓜ Kongens Nytorv Plan: **C2**
– ✆ 33 11 68 68 – www.konghans.dk
– Closed 13-26 March, 17 April, 31 July-20 August, 23-27 December and Sunday-Tuesday
Menu 1700 DKK – Carte 965/2065 DKK – *(dinner only)*
(booking essential)

• Classic French • Elegant • Intimate •

A historic restaurant in a beautiful vaulted Gothic cellar in the heart of the city. Richly flavoured, classic French cooking uses luxury ingredients – signature dishes could include Danish Black lobster. There's a 5 course tasting menu and Gueridon trolleys add a theatrical element to proceedings.

➜ Scallops with smoked butter and caviar. Black lobster 'à la Kong Hans'. Chocolate soufflé and vanilla ice cream.

Era Ora

XxX

Overgaden Neden Vandet 33B ✉ 1414 K Plan: **D3**
– Ⓜ Christianshavn – ✆ 32 54 06 93
– www.era-ora.dk
– Closed 24-26 December, 1 January, Easter Monday and Sunday
Menu 480/1280 DKK – *(booking essential) (tasting menu only)*

• Italian • Elegant • Intimate •

Set on a quaint cobbled street by the canal; a grand, long-standing restaurant with an enclosed rear terrace and a formal air. Complex, innovative dishes feature lots of different ingredients (many imported from Italy) and are often explorative in their approach. The wine cellar boasts over 90,000 bottles.

➜ Langoustine, cherry gel and langoustine cream. Ravioli of almond, lemon cream and amaranth. 'Sweet Italian Traditions'.

Kiin Kiin

XX

Guldbergsgade 21 ✉ 2200 N Plan: **A1**
– ✆ 35 35 75 55 – www.kiin.dk
– Closed Christmas and Sunday
Menu 495/975 DKK – *(dinner only) (booking essential)*
(tasting menu only)

• Thai • Exotic décor • Intimate •

A charming restaurant, whose name means 'come and eat'. Start with refined versions of street food in the moody lounge, then head for the tasteful dining room decorated with golden Buddhas and fresh flowers. Menus offer modern, personal interpretations of Thai dishes, which have vibrant flavour combinations.

➜ Frozen red curry with lobster. Stir-fried beef with oyster sauce and krachai. Pandan ice cream with pistachio.

Alouette (Nick Curtin)

XX

Sturlasgade 14 (1st Floor) (through the arch)
(Southwest : 2.5 km by H.C. Andersens Boulevard and Langebro off Klaksvigsgade)
✉ 2300 S – Ⓜ Islands Brygge
– ✆ 3167 6606 – www.restaurantalouette.dk
– Closed Christmas and Sunday-Wednesday
Menu 695 DKK – *(dinner only) (booking essential) (surprise menu only)*

• Modern cuisine • Trendy • Design •

Graffiti-covered corridors and a freight lift lead to this light, modern restaurant in a former pencil factory. The confident chef understands that less is more; combining a handful of top notch ingredients in pared back, sublimely flavoured dishes. The open fire is used to great effect.

➜ Embered pumpkin, caviar and mulberry. Hegnsholt lamb, chanterelles and new cabbage. Plum wood smoked parfait and plums.

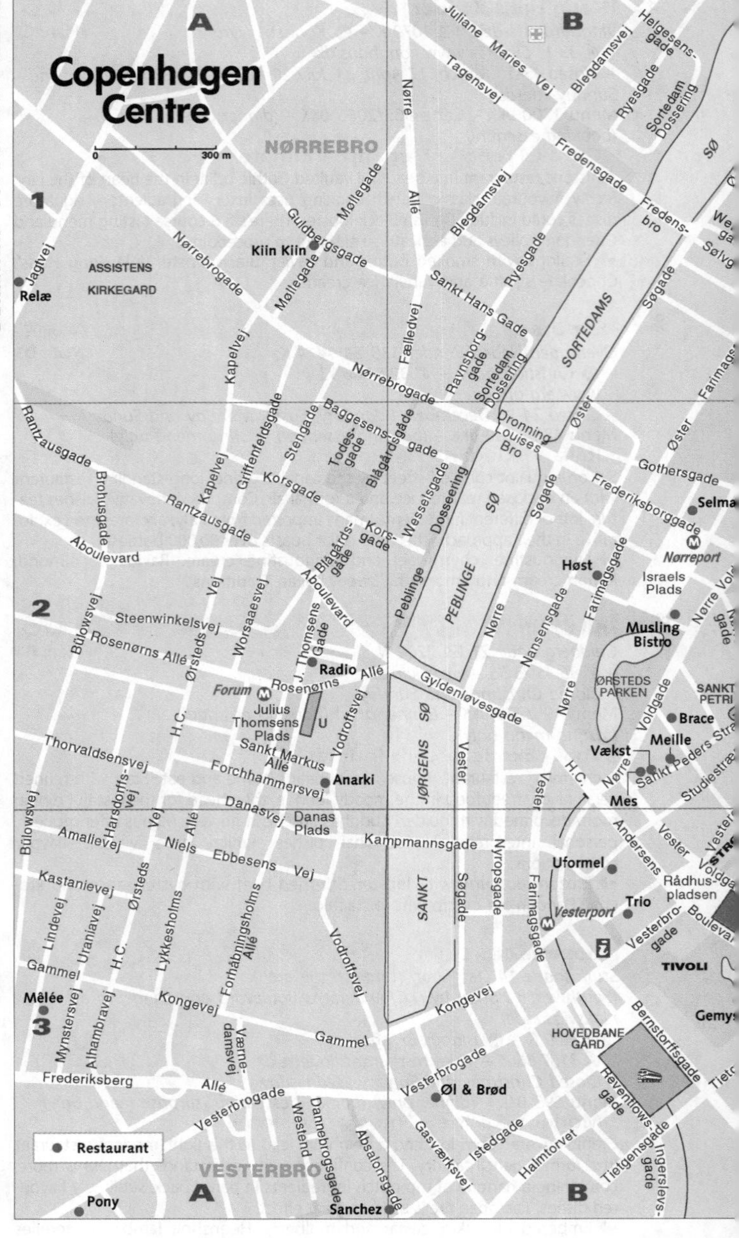
Copenhagen Centre
0
300 m
A
B
1
2
3
NØRREBRO
VESTERBRO
ASSISTENS
KIRKEGARD
Relæ
Jagtvej
Kiin Kiin
Guldbergsgade
Møllegade
Nørrebrogade
Kapelvej
Juliane Maries Vej
Tagensvej
Blegdamsvej
Helgesens-gade
Ryesgade
Sortedam Dossering
Fredensgade
Fredens-bro
Nørre Allé
Fælledvej
Sankt Hans Gade
Ravnsborg-gade
SORTEDAMS
SØ
Søgade
Farimagsgade
Øster
Dronning Louises Bro
Gothersgade
Frederiksborggade
Selma
Nørreport
Israels Plads
Høst
Musling Bistro
ØRSTEDS PARKEN
SANKT PETRI
Brace
Meille
Vækst
Mes
Sankt Peders Stræde
Studiestræde
Voldgade
Rantzausgade
Brohusgade
Baggesensgade
Todes-gade
Blågårdsgade
Stengade
Griffenfeldsgade
Korsgade
Wesselsgade
Dosseering
PEBLINGE
Peblinge
Nørre
Nansensgade
Aboulevard
Bülowsvej
Steenwinkelsvej
Rosenørns Allé
Ørsteds Vej
Worsaaesvej
J. Thomsens Gade
Radio
Forum
Julius Thomsens Plads
U
Vodroffsvej
Gyldenløvesgade
SANKT JØRGENS SØ
Vester Søgade
H.C.
Thorvaldsensvej
Sankt Markus Allé
Forchhammersvej
Anarki
Danasvej
Danas Plads
Harsdorffs-vej
Amalievej
Niels Ebbesens Vej
Kampmannsgade
Nyropsgade
Farimagsgade
H.C. Andersens Boulevard
Vester Voldgade
Uformel
Rådhus-pladsen
Trio
Vesterport
Vesterbro-gade
TIVOLI
Kastanievej
Lindevej
Uranlavej
Lykkesholms Allé
Forhåbningsholms Allé
Gammel Kongevej
Mêlée
Mynstersvej
Alhambravej
Værnedamsvej
Kongevej
HOVEDBANE GÅRD
Bernstorffsgade
Gemys
Frederiksberg Allé
Vesterbrogade
Øl & Brød
Reventlows-gade
Tietgensgade
Ingerslevs-gade
Westend
Dannebrogsgade
Absalonsgade
Gasværksvej
Istedgade
Halmtorvet
Restaurant
Pony
Sanchez

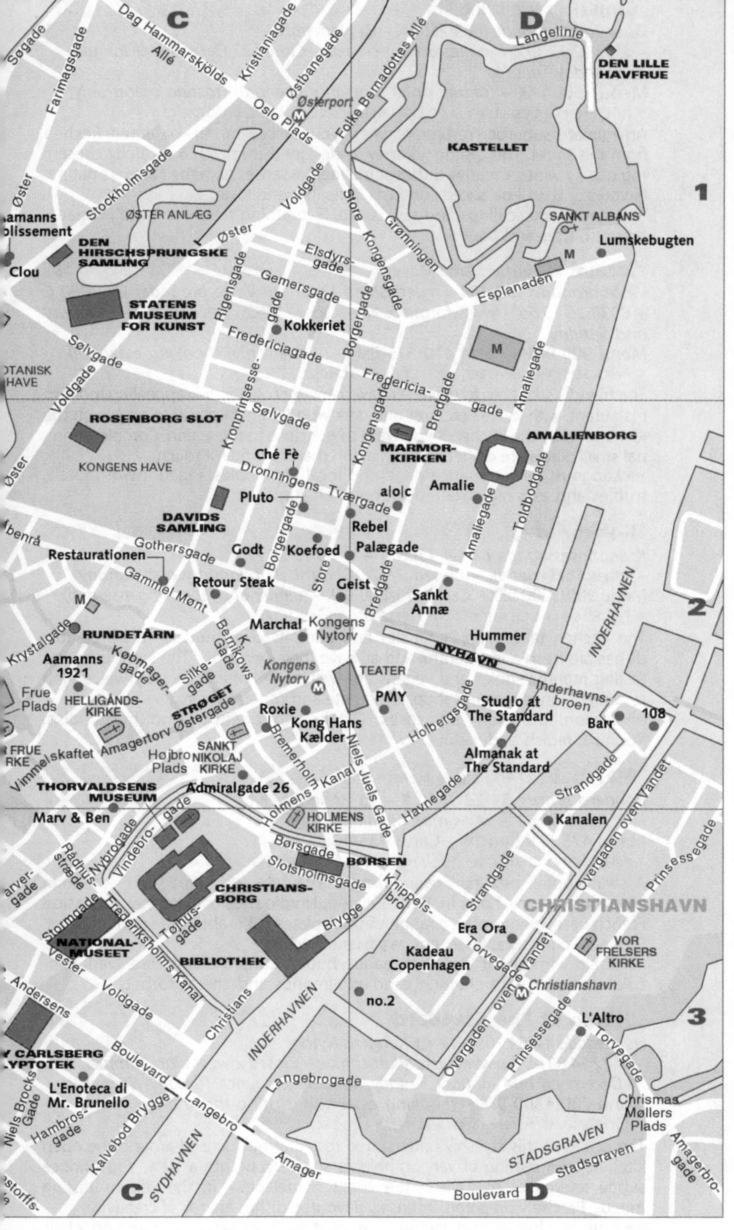

C
D
DEN LILLE HAVFRUE
KASTELLET
Østerport
Lumskebugten
DEN HIRSCHSPRUNGSKE SAMLING
Clou
STATENS MUSEUM FOR KUNST
Kokkeriet
ROSENBORG SLOT
KONGENS HAVE
AMALIENBORG
MARMOR-KIRKEN
Ché Fè
Pluto
a|o|c
Amalie
DAVIDS SAMLING
Rebel
Restaurationen
Godt
Koefoed
Palægade
Retour Steak
Geist
Sankt Annæ
RUNDETÅRN
Marchal
Hummer
NYHAVN
Aamanns 1921
TEATER
PMY
Studio at The Standard
Barr
108
Roxie
Kong Hans Kælder
Almanak at The Standard
THORVALDSENS MUSEUM
Admiralgade 26
Marv & Ben
Kanalen
HOLMENS KIRKE
BØRSEN
CHRISTIANS-BORG
CHRISTIANSHAVN
NATIONAL-MUSEET
BIBLIOTHEK
Era Ora
Kadeau Copenhagen
VOR FRELSERS KIRKE
Christianshavn
no.2
L'Altro
CARLSBERG GLYPTOTEK
L'Enoteca di Mr. Brunello
Chrismas Møllers Plads
STADSGRAVEN
SYDHAVNEN
INDERHAVNEN
1
2
3

Clou (Jonathan Berntsen)

Øster Farimagsgade 8 ✉ 2100 K – Ⓜ Nørreport Plan: C1
– ✆ 91 92 72 30 – www.restaurant-clou.dk – Closed 22 December-2 January and Sunday-Tuesday
Menu 1600 DKK – *(dinner only) (booking essential) (tasting menu only)*
• Modern cuisine • Intimate • Neighbourhood •

An intimate, suburban restaurant where you can see into the basement kitchen from the street. The tasting 'journey' is designed to match 6 carefully chosen, top quality wines. Creative dishes stimulate the senses with their intense natural flavours and well-balanced contrasts in texture and taste.

➜ Hand-dived scallops and raw cacao. 'Everything from the quail'. Banana, brown butter and liquorice.

formel B (Kristian Arpe-Møller)

Vesterbrogade 182-184, Frederiksberg (2 km on Vesterbrogade) ✉ 1800 C – ✆ 33 25 10 66 – www.formelb.dk – Closed 24-26 December, 1-5 January and Sunday
Menu 900 DKK – Carte 420/575 DKK – *(dinner only) (booking essential)*
• Modern cuisine • Fashionable • Design •

The friendly staff help to create a relaxed environment at this appealing modern restaurant, with its tree pictures and dark wood branches; ask for a table on the lower level by the kitchen if you want to get close to the action. Complex, original small plates are crafted with an assured and confident touch.

➜ Langoustine with sauce nage and local vegetables. Pigeon with morels, truffles and asparagus. Sea buckthorn 'en surprise'.

Kokkeriet

Kronprinsessegade 64 ✉ 1306 K – ✆ 33 15 27 77 Plan: C1
– www.kokkeriet.dk – Closed 24-26 December, 1 January and Sunday
Menu 900/1200 DKK – Carte 675/800 DKK – *(dinner only) (booking essential)*
• Modern cuisine • Intimate • Design •

The kitchen takes Danish classics and adds its own modern interpretation; dishes are fresh and colourful and all have their own story. The focus is on the tasting menu; veggies and vegans are well looked after. This very welcoming restaurant, once a corner shop, is intimate and contemporary.

➜ Scallop, pumpkin and roses. Oxtail with beetroot and horseradish. Yoghurt, radish and walnut.

Marchal – D'Angleterre Hotel

Kongens Nytorv 34 ✉ 1050 K – Ⓜ Kongens Nytorv Plan: C2
– ✆ 33 12 00 94 – www.marchal.dk
Menu 475 DKK (lunch) – Carte 435/1030 DKK
• Modern cuisine • Elegant • Romantic •

A stylish hotel restaurant overlooking the Square and named after the man who founded the hotel in 1755. Refined, Nordic-style cooking has a classical French base; menus offer a range of small plates – 3 is about the right amount. Dinner also includes an extensive caviar collection.

➜ Squid with caviar and champagne butter. Canard à la presse. Dark chocolate mousse with cherries, candied almonds and cherry sorbet.

Stud!o at The Standard

Havnegade 44 ✉ 1058 K – Ⓜ Kongens Nytorv Plan: D2
– ✆ 72 14 88 08 – www.thestandardcph.dk – Closed 2 weeks late summer, 22-26 December, 1-14 January, Sunday, Monday and lunch Tuesday-Wednesday.
Menu 700/1300 DKK – *(booking essential) (tasting menu only)*
• Creative • Fashionable • Design •

The action at this stylishly understated restaurant is focused around the open kitchen, with seating of varying heights so everyone has a view. You'll notice subtle references to Chile – the chef's homeland – in the various tasting menus. Precisely prepared, intensely flavoured dishes are full of creativity.

➜ Churro, cheese and truffle. Langoustine with passion fruit and chilli. Gooseberry served with coriander and olive oil.

108 (Kristian Baumann)

Strandgade 108 ✉ *1401 K* – Ⓜ *Christianshavn* Plan: **D2**
– ✆ *32 96 32 92* – *www.108.dk* – *Closed 22-27 December and 1 January*
Menu 1150 DKK – Carte 525/770 DKK – *(dinner only)*

• Modern cuisine • Neighbourhood • Design •

A former whale meat warehouse with floor to ceiling windows and water views; bare concrete and a semi-open kitchen give it a cool Nordic style. There's a Noma alumnus in the kitchen and plenty of pickled, cured and fermented ingredients on the 'no rules' menu, from which you pick as many dishes as you like.
➜ Brown beech mushrooms with smoked egg yolk sauce. Lobster claw and raspberries. Wild blackcurrant sorbet with hazelnut milk.

Relæ

Jægersborggade 41 ✉ *2200 N* – ✆ *36 96 66 09* Plan: **A1**
– *www.restaurant-relae.dk* – *Closed Christmas, 31 December, Sunday and Monday*
Menu 475/895 DKK – *(dinner only and lunch Friday-Saturday) (booking essential) (surprise menu only)*

• Modern cuisine • Minimalist • Fashionable •

This modern, understated restaurant never stands still. The open kitchen provides a real sense of occasion and you can feel the passion of the chefs as they explain the dishes they are serving. 5 and 10 course surprise menus showcase produce grown on their farm. Dishes are intensely flavoured and unrestrained.
➜ White asparagus and buttermilk. Havervadgård lamb, dill and beach herbs. Birch, malt and juniper.

L'Altro

Torvegade 62 ✉ *1400 K* – Ⓜ *Christianshavn* Plan: **D3**
– ✆ *32 54 54 06* – *www.laltro.dk* – *Closed 23-27 December, 1-9 January and Sunday*
Menu 395/530 DKK – *(dinner only) (booking essential) (tasting menu only)*

• Italian • Intimate • Traditional décor •

A long-standing restaurant with a downstairs wine bar and a warm, rustic style. It celebrates 'la cucina de la casa' – the homely Italian spirit of 'mama's kitchen'. Regularly changing set menus feature tasty family recipes from Umbria and Tuscany; dishes are appealing and rely on top quality imported ingredients.

Anarki

Vodroffsvej 47 ✉ *1900 C* – Ⓜ *Forum* – ✆ *22 13 11 34* Plan: **A2**
– *www.restaurant-anarki.dk* – *Closed July, Christmas, Easter and Monday*
Menu 395 DKK – Carte 275/435 DKK – *(dinner only)*

• Traditional cuisine • Neighbourhood • Bistro •

An unassuming and proudly run neighbourhood bistro, set just over the water in Frederiksberg. The interesting menu of gutsy, flavourful dishes draws inspiration from all over the world, so expect to see words like ceviche, paella and burrata as well as bakskuld – with plenty of offal and some great wines.

Enomania

Vesterbrogade 187 (2.5 km via Vesterbrogade) ✉ *1800 C* – ✆ *33 23 60 80*
– *www.enomania.dk* – *Closed 21 December-6 January, 8-17 February, 9-13 and 18-22 April, 6 July-5 August, 12-21 October, Saturday-Monday and bank holidays*
Menu 390 DKK – Carte 260/380 DKK – *(dinner only and lunch Thursday-Friday) (booking essential)*

• Italian • Wine bar • Simple •

A simple, bistro-style restaurant near Frederiksberg Park – its name means 'Wine Mania'. The wine cellar comes with a table for tasting and there's an excellent list of over 600 bins, mostly from Piedmont and Burgundy. These are complemented by straightforward, tasty Italian dishes from a daily 4 course menu.

Kødbyens Fiskebar

Den Hvide Kødby, Flæsketorvet 100 (1 km via Halmtorvet) ✉ 1711 V – ✆ 32 15 56 56 – www.fiskebaren.dk – Closed 24-26 December and 1 January
Menu 300 DKK (lunch) – Carte 300/565 DKK – *(dinner only and lunch Friday-Sunday)*

• Seafood • Simple • Fashionable •

This buzzy, industrial-style restaurant is set – somewhat incongruously – in a former butcher's shop in a commercial meat market. Menus feature freshly prepared 'hot' and 'cold' seafood dishes which are based around the latest catch, and oysters are a speciality. The terrace is a popular spot come summer.

Marv & Ben

Snaregade 4 ✉ 1205 K – Ⓜ Kongens Nytorv Plan: **C2/3**
– ✆ 33 91 01 91 – www.marvogben.dk – Closed Christmas
Menu 400/600 DKK – Carte 290/385 DKK – *(dinner only)*

• Modern cuisine • Bistro • Fashionable •

The young owners bring plenty of enthusiasm to this little restaurant, where dining is split over two dimly lit floors. Organic produce features in seasonal dishes which display purity and depth of flavour. Choose 'Four Favourites' (4 courses), 'Almost Everything' (6 courses) or from the à la carte.

Mêlée

Martensens Allé 16 ✉ 1828 C – Ⓜ Frederiksberg Plan: **A3**
– ✆ 35 13 11 34 – www.melee.dk – Closed Christmas, Easter and Sunday
Menu 395 DKK – Carte 335/445 DKK – *(dinner only) (booking essential)*

• French • Friendly • Bistro •

A bustling neighbourhood bistro with a friendly, laid-back atmosphere; run by an experienced team. Modern, country-style cooking is French-based but has Danish influences; menus may be concise but portions are generous and flavours are bold. An excellent range of wines from the Rhône Valley accompany.

Musling Bistro

Linnésgade 14 ✉ 1361 K – Ⓜ Nørreport – ✆ 34 10 56 56 Plan: **B2**
– www.muslingbistro.dk – Closed 24-26 December, 1 January, Sunday and Monday
Carte 315/495 DKK

• Seafood • Bistro • Fashionable •

A relaxed bar-cum-bistro next to the Nørrebro food market – find a space at the black ash counter, grab your cutlery from one of the pots, and choose from the list of modern craft beers and unusual wines. Fantastic fresh seafood is to the fore on the concise menu, and service is swift and efficient.

Pluto

Borgergade 16 ✉ 1300 K – Ⓜ Kongens Nytorv Plan: **C2**
– ✆ 33 16 00 16 – www.restaurantpluto.dk – Closed 24-25 December and 1 January
Menu 475 DKK – Carte 305/430 DKK – *(dinner only)*

• Mediterranean cuisine • Bistro • Rustic •

An appealing restaurant in a residential area, with concrete pillars and an intentionally 'unfinished' feel – sit at wooden tables, at the long metal bar or at communal marble-topped tables. The enticing menu is made up of small plates; cooking is rustic, unfussy and flavoursome.

PMY

Tordenskjoldsgade 11 ✉ 1055 K – Ⓜ Kongens Nytorv Plan: **D2**
– ✆ 50 81 00 02 – www.restaurant-pmy.com – Closed July, 23-27 December, 1-7 January, Sunday and Monday
Menu 275/395 DKK – *(dinner only) (booking essential)*

• South American • Friendly • Trendy •

Start with some snacks and a cocktail at this fun, laid-back restaurant, before moving on to fresh, zingy dishes bursting with Latin American flavours. Potato, Maize and Yuca feature highly on the small menu, which lists tasty, good value dishes from Peru, Mexico and Venezuela.

Rebel

Store Kongensgade 52 ✉ 1264 K – Ⓜ Kongens Nytorv Plan: **C/D2**
– ✆ 33 32 32 09 – www.restaurantrebel.dk – Closed 22 July-4 August, 2 weeks Christmas, Sunday and Monday
Carte 315/525 DKK – *(dinner only)*
• Modern cuisine • Bistro • Fashionable •

Located in a busy part of the city; a simply decorated, split-level restaurant with closely set tables and a buzzy vibe. Choose 3 or 4 dishes from the list of 12 starter-sized options; cooking is modern and refined, and relies largely on Danish produce. The atmospheric lower floor is often used for parties.

Mielcke & Hurtigkarl

Runddel 1 (2 km via Veseterbrogade and Frederiksberg Allé) ✉ 2000 C – ✆ 38 34 84 36 – www.mhcph.com – Closed 3 weeks Christmas, Sunday and Monday
Menu 800/950 DKK – *(dinner only) (booking essential)*
• Creative • Elegant • Exotic décor •

Set in a delightful spot in Frederiksberg Gardens, its walls painted with garden scenes, is this charming 1744 orangery with a fire-lit terrace. Dishes come from around the globe, with Asian influences to the fore – and an amazing array of herbs from the gardens.

Aamanns 1921

Niels Hemmingsens Gade 19-21 ✉ 1153 K Plan: **C2**
– Ⓜ Kongens Nytorv – ✆ 20 80 52 04 – www.aamanns.dk – Closed 24-25 and 31 December, 1 January and dinner Sunday-Monday
Menu 290/390 DKK – Carte 235/385 DKK
• Modern cuisine • Brasserie • Design •

An appealing restaurant with original stone arches. Lunch sees traditional smørrebrød, while dinner focuses on modern dishes. They grind and mill their own flours, marinate their herring for 6-12 months and gather the herbs for their snaps.

Amass

Refshalevej 153 (3 km via Torvgade and Prinsessgade) ✉ 1432 K – ✆ 43 58 43 30 – www.amassrestaurant.com – Closed January, 1 week summer, Christmas, Sunday, Monday and lunch September-April.
Menu 695/995 DKK – *(dinner only and Saturday lunch) (booking essential)*
• Danish • Minimalist • Friendly •

A large restaurant just outside the city. It has an urban, industrial feel courtesy of graffitied concrete walls and huge windows overlooking the old docks. Prices and the authenticity of ingredients are key; cooking is modern Danish.

Brace

Teglgårdstræde 8a ✉ 1452 K – Ⓜ Nørreport Plan: **B2**
– ✆ 28 88 20 01 – www.restaurantbrace.dk – Closed 1-21 January, 24-26 December, Easter and Sunday
Menu 515/775 DKK – Carte 325/495 DKK – *(dinner only and lunch Friday-Saturday) (booking essential)*
• Italian • Elegant • Fashionable •

The name of this smart restaurant, set in the heart of the city, refers to the building's external structure and to the solidarity of the tight-knit team. Dishes are a fusion of Danish and Italian, and come with colourful modern twists.

L' Enoteca di Mr. Brunello

Rysensteensgade 16 ✉ 1564 K Plan: **C3**
– Ⓜ København Hovedbane Gård – ✆ 33 11 47 20 – www.lenoteca.dk – Closed July-early August, Easter, Christmas, Sunday, Monday and bank holidays
Menu 495/695 DKK – Carte 560/595 DKK – *(dinner only)*
• Italian • Elegant • Neighbourhood •

Tucked away near the Tivoli Gardens and run by passionate, experienced owners. Refined, classic Italian cooking uses quality produce imported from Italy. The good value Italian wine list has over 150 different Brunello di Montalcinos.

Frederiks Have

XX

Smallegade 41, (entrance on Virginiavej) (1.5 km. via Gammel Kongevej) ✉ 2000 F – Ⓜ Fasanvej St. – ✆ 38 88 33 35 – www.frederikshave.dk – Closed Christmas, Easter and Sunday

Menu 295/400 DKK – Carte 355/565 DKK

• Danish • Neighbourhood • Family •

A sweet two-roomed neighbourhood restaurant hidden just off the main street in a residential area. Sit inside – surrounded by flowers and vivid local art – or outside, on the terrace. Good value menus offer a mix of traditional Danish and French dishes.

Geist

XX

Kongens Nytorv 8 ✉ 1050 K – Ⓜ Kongens Nytorv – ✆ 33133713 – www.restaurantgeist.dk – Closed 24-26 December and 1-2 January Plan: **C2**

Carte 370/560 DKK

• Modern cuisine • Design • Trendy •

A lively, fashionable restaurant with an open kitchen and floor to ceiling windows overlooking the square. Choose the large counter at the front, or more intimate dining at the rear. The cleverly crafted dishes display a light touch; 4 should suffice.

Godt

XX

Gothersgade 38 ✉ 1123 K – Ⓜ Kongens Nytorv – ✆ 33 15 21 22 – www.restaurant-godt.dk – Closed mid July-mid August, Christmas-New Year, Easter, Sunday, Monday and bank holidays Plan: **C2**

Menu 520/680 DKK – *(dinner only) (tasting menu only)*

• Classic cuisine • Friendly • Family •

2019 is the 25th anniversary of this family run restaurant which seats just 20 on two levels. The cooking is underpinned by a strong classical base and the dishes on the daily changing menu are satisfying and full of flavour. Old WWII shells act as candle holders.

Kiin Kiin VeVe

XX

Dampfærgevej 7 (North 2.5 km by Store Kongensgade and Folke Bernadottes Allé) ✉ 2100 Ø – ✆ 51 22 59 55 – www.veve.dk – Closed Christmas and Sunday-Tuesday

Menu 750 DKK – *(dinner only) (booking essential) (tasting menu only)*

• Vegetarian • Design • Contemporary décor •

A former bread factory houses this chic restaurant which serves sophisticated vegetarian cuisine. The 6 course tasting menu revolves around the seasons and offers some imaginative combinations. Wine and juice pairings accompany.

Koefoed

XX

Landgreven 3 ✉ 1301 K – Ⓜ Kongens Nytorv – ✆ 56 48 22 24 – www.restaurant-koefoed.dk – Closed 26-December-1 January, Sunday and Monday Plan: **C2**

Menu 295/495 DKK – Carte 425/500 DKK – *(booking essential at dinner)*

• Modern cuisine • Intimate • Romantic •

An intimate collection of rooms in an old coal cellar, where everything from the produce to the glassware celebrates Bornholm island. Modern cooking is accompanied by an impressive range of bordeaux wines. Lunch sees reinvented smørrebrød.

Lumskebugten

XX

Esplanaden 21 ✉ 1263 K – ✆ 33 15 60 29 – www.lumskebugten.dk – Closed 3 weeks July, Christmas, Easter and Sunday Plan: **D1**

Menu 375/485 DKK – Carte 300/630 DKK

• Traditional cuisine • Cosy • Classic décor •

A traditional quayside restaurant with period décor, charming staff and a warm ambience. Lunch means classic Danish dishes with plenty of herrings and smørrebrød; dinner offers a menu of traditional dishes with a Danish heart, like fried fish on the bone or Danish rib-eye steaks.

Palægade

Palægade 8 ✉ 1261 K – Ⓜ Kongens Nytorv – ✆ 70 82 82 88 Plan: **C/D2**
– www.palaegade.dk – Closed 24-26 December, 1-4 January and Sunday dinner
Menu 450 DKK – Carte 260/525 DKK

• Smørrebrød • Friendly • Simple •

More than 40 classic smørrebrød are available at lunch – with plenty of local beers and snaps to accompany them. Things become more formal in the evenings, when they serve highly seasonal dishes in a traditional Northern European style.

Restaurationen

Møntergade 19 ✉ 1116 K – Ⓜ Kongens Nytorv Plan: **C2**
– ✆ 33 14 94 95 – www.restaurationen.dk – Closed 29 June-26 August, 21 December-6 January, 14-22 April, Sunday and Monday
Menu 635 DKK – *(dinner only)*

• Classic cuisine • Chic • Romantic •

This friendly restaurant is over a quarter of a century old, and run by a well-known chef who also owns the next door wine bar. The dining room displays some impressive contemporary art and the modern Danish dishes are created with good quality local produce.

Trio

Axel Towers (9th Floor), Jernbanegade 11 ✉ 1608 V Plan: **B3**
– Ⓜ København Hovedbane Gård – ✆ 44 22 74 74 – www.restauranttrio.dk – Closed 3 weeks July, Christmas, Easter and Sunday
Menu 400/675 DKK – Carte 350/555 DKK

• Modern cuisine • Design • Fashionable •

The highest restaurant in the city is located on floors 9 and 10 of the striking Axel Towers building; enjoy a cocktail while taking in the view. Accomplished dishes take their influences from both classic French and modern Nordic cuisine.

Barr

Strandgade 93 ✉ 1401 – Ⓜ Christianshavn Plan: **D2**
– ✆ 32 96 32 93 – www.restaurantbarr.com – Closed 23-26 and 31 December, 1 January and 1 November.
Menu 600 DKK – Carte 385/545 DKK – *(dinner only and lunch Friday-Sunday) (booking essential)*

• Modern cuisine • Trendy • Rustic •

A laid-back quayside restaurant with wood-clad walls. Its name means 'Barley' and it has an amazing array of cask and bottled beers (some custom-brewed), along with beer pairings to match the food. Intensely flavoured, rustic dishes have classic Nordic roots but are taken to new heights; the sweet cake is a must.

Gemyse – Nimb Hotel

Tivoli Gardens, Bernstoffsgade 5 ✉ 1572 V Plan: **B3**
– Ⓜ København Hovedbane Gård – ✆ 88 70 00 80 – www.nimb.dk – Closed 25 February-3 April, 23 September-10 October, 4-15 November and 1-2 January
Menu 550 DKK – Carte 280/480 DKK

• Modern cuisine • Rustic • Romantic •

This delightful vegetable-orientated restaurant – part of the Nimb hotel – sits in the heart of Tivoli Gardens (when they are open, admission must be paid). It comes complete with a greenhouse and raised beds where they grow much of the produce. Dishes are well-prepared, attractively presented and very tasty.

Bib Gourmand?
Good quality, good value cooking!
'Bibs' are awarded for simple yet skilful cooking for under £28 or €40. The Michelin good tip for all the gourmets!

Kanalen

Wilders Plads 2 ✉ 1403 K – Ⓜ Christianshavn Plan: **D3**
– ✆ 32 95 13 30 – www.restaurant-kanalen.dk – Closed Christmas-New Year, Easter, 9-10 June, Sunday and bank holidays
Menu 250/655 DKK – Carte 395/780 DKK – *(booking essential)*
• Danish • Bistro • Cosy •

Find a spot on the delightful canalside terrace of this quaint, shack-like building – formerly the Harbour Police office – and watch the boats bobbing up and down as you eat. Alongside classic Danish flavours you'll find some light French and Asian touches; for dessert, the 'flødeboller' is a must.

Aamanns Etablissement

Øster Farimagsgade 12 ✉ 2100 Ø – Ⓜ Nørreport Plan: **C1**
– ✆ 20 80 52 02 – www.aamanns.dk – Closed 3 weeks July, 24-25 and 31 December, 1 January and dinner Sunday-Tuesday
Carte 145/365 DKK
• Danish • Bistro • Cosy •

The perfect setting for classic smørrebrød is this cosy, contemporary restaurant. Choose one of their fixed selections which feature their signature herrings and fried plaice – and order their homemade snaps, flavoured with handpicked herbs to accompany.

Admiralgade 26

Admiralgade 26 ✉ 1066 K – Ⓜ Kongens Nytorv Plan: **C2**
– ✆ 33 33 79 73 – www.admiralgade26.dk – Closed 23-26 and 31 December, 1-3 January, Sunday and bank holidays.
Menu 550 DKK (dinner) – Carte 275/395 DKK
• Modern cuisine • Intimate • Cosy •

This historic house dates from 1796 and sits in one of the oldest parts of the city. It's a relaxed place – a mix of wine bar, café and bistro – and, alongside an appealing modern menu, offers around 4,000 frequently changing wines.

Almanak at The Standard

Havnegade 44 ✉ 1058 K – Ⓜ Kongens Nytorv Plan: **D2**
– ✆ 72 14 88 08 – www.thestandardcph.dk – Closed 24 December, 1-2 January and Monday
Menu 575 DKK (dinner) – Carte 295/580 DKK
• Modern cuisine • Fashionable • Chic •

A chic restaurant on the ground floor of an impressive art deco customs building on the waterfront. At lunch, it's all about smørrebrød, while dinner sees a concise menu of updated Danish classics. An open kitchen adds to the theatre.

Ché Fè

Borgergade 17a ✉ 1300 K – Ⓜ Kongens Nytorv Plan: **C2**
– ✆ 33 11 17 21 – www.chefe.dk – Closed 23-26 December, 10 June, Easter Monday and Sunday
Menu 435 DKK – Carte 375/465 DKK – *(dinner only) (booking essential)*
• Italian • Simple • Neighbourhood •

An unassuming façade conceals an appealing trattoria with pastel hues and coffee sack curtains. Menus offer authentic Italian classics, including homemade pastas; virtually all ingredients are imported from small, organic producers.

Høst

Nørre Farimagsgade 41 ✉ 1364 K – Ⓜ Nørreport Plan: **B2**
– ✆ 89 93 84 09 – www.cofoco.dk/restauranter/hoest – Closed 24 December and 1 January
Menu 350/450 DKK – *(dinner only)*
• Modern cuisine • Friendly • Rustic •

A busy neighbourhood bistro with fun staff and a lively atmosphere; sit in the Garden Room. The great value monthly set menu comprises 3 courses but comes with lots of extras. Modern Nordic cooking is seasonal and boldly flavoured.

Hummer

Nyhavn 63a ✉ 1051 K – Ⓜ Kongens Nytorv Plan: **D2**
– ✆ 33 33 03 39 – www.restauranthummer.dk – Closed 23-27 December and Monday-Tuesday October-April
Menu 395 DKK – Carte 290/610 DKK

• Seafood • Friendly • Simple •

Lobster is the mainstay of the menu at this restaurant, situated among the brightly coloured buildings on the famous Nyhavn strip. Enjoy a meal on the sunny terrace or in the modish, nautically styled dining room.

Meille

Sankt Peders Stræde 24a ✉ 1453 K – Ⓜ Nørreport Plan: **B2**
– ✆ 53 65 14 53 – www.restaurant-meille.dk – Closed Christmas-New Year, Monday and lunch Tuesday-Wednesday
Menu 195/345 DKK – Carte lunch 200/250 DKK – *(booking essential at dinner)*

• Modern cuisine • Bistro • Fashionable •

Sister to Mes round the corner, 'Us' is a busy bistro with shelves full of cookbooks, wine bottles and jars of preserved, fermented and marinating produce. Lunch offers a classic smørrebrød selection; dinner sees a 3 or 5 course set menu of creative modern Nordic dishes with a rustic edge.

Mes

Jarmers Plads 1 ✉ 1551 V – Ⓜ Nørreport Plan: **B2**
– ✆ 25 36 51 81 – www.restaurant-mes.dk – Closed 24-26 December and Sunday
Menu 350 DKK – *(dinner only) (booking essential) (tasting menu only)*

• Danish • Intimate • Friendly •

A sweet little restaurant run by a tight-knit team. The frequently changing set menu lists classic dishes – some of which are pepped up with modern techniques. A 120 year old German cooling cabinet plays host to the wines.

no.2

Nicolai Eigtveds Gade 32 ✉ 1402 K Plan: **D3**
– Ⓜ Christianshaven – ✆ 33 11 11 68 – www.nummer2.dk – Closed 3 weeks July, Christmas, Easter, Saturday lunch and Sunday
Menu 325/475 DKK – Carte 300/425 DKK

• Modern cuisine • Design • Fashionable •

Set among smart offices and apartments on the edge of the dock is this elegant restaurant; a sister to a|o|c. Fresh, flavoursome dishes focus on quality Danish ingredients – highlights include the cured hams, cheeses and ice creams.

Øl & Brød

Viktoriagade 6 ✉ 1655 K Plan: **B3**
– Ⓜ København Hovedbane Gård – ✆ 33 31 44 22 – www.ologbrod.com – Closed Monday and dinner Tuesday-Wednesday
Menu 300/400 DKK – Carte 275/490 DKK – *(booking essential)*

• Modern cuisine • Neighbourhood • Cosy •

A cosy, hip neighbourhood restaurant where the emphasis is as much on aquavit and craft beers as it is on the refined and flavourful modern food. Lunch sees smørrebrød taken to a new level, while dinner offers a choice of 3 or 6 courses.

Pony

Vesterbrogade 135 ✉ 1620 V – ✆ 33 22 10 00 Plan: **A3**
– www.ponykbh.dk – Closed 6 weeks July-August, 1 week Christmas and Monday
Menu 425/485 DKK – *(dinner only) (booking essential)*

• Danish • Bistro • Neighbourhood •

A buzzy restaurant with chatty service; sit on high stools by the kitchen or in the retro dining room. Choose from the fixed price menu or try the more adventurous 4 course 'Pony Kick'. Refined, modern cooking has a nose-to-tail approach.

Radio

Julius Thomsens Gade 12 ✉ 1632 V – Ⓜ Forum Plan: **A2**
– ✆ 25102733 – www.restaurantradio.dk – Closed 3 weeks summer, 2 weeks Christmas-New Year, Sunday and Monday
Menu 350 DKK – *(dinner only and lunch Friday-Saturday) (booking essential) (tasting menu only)*
• Modern cuisine • Minimalist • Neighbourhood •
An informal restaurant with an unfussy urban style, wood-clad walls and cool anglepoise lighting. Oft-changing menus feature full-flavoured, good value dishes and use organic ingredients grown in the restaurant's nearby fields. Pick 3 or 5 dishes from the five understated choices.

Retour Steak

Ny Østergade 21 ✉ 1101 K – Ⓜ Kongens Nytorv Plan: **C2**
– ✆ 33 16 17 19 – www.retoursteak.dk – Closed 25 December and 1 January
Carte 240/625 DKK – *(dinner only) (booking essential)*
• Meats and grills • Bistro • Friendly •
A relaxed, informal restaurant with a stark white interior and contrasting black furnishings. A small menu offers simply prepared grills, good quality American rib-eye steaks and an affordable selection of wines.

Roxie – Herman K Hotel

Bremerholm 6 ✉ 1069 K – Ⓜ Kongens Nytorv Plan: **C2**
– ✆ 53 89 10 69 – www.roxie.dk – Closed 24-25 December, 1 January and lunch Monday-Thursday
Menu 400 DKK (lunch) – Carte 465/600 DKK – *(booking essential at dinner)*
• Modern cuisine • Design • Fashionable •
Little sister to Kadeau is this chic, industrial style restaurant set over three floors of a boutique hotel. The modern bistro dishes use lots of pickled, fermented and preserved produce and are full of interesting textures and flavours. Relaxed but professional service from a knowledgeable team.

Sanchez

Istedgade 60 ✉ 1650 K Plan: **A/B3**
– Ⓜ København Hovedbane Gård – ✆ 31 11 66 40
– www.lovesanchez.com – Closed Tuesday-Wednesday
Menu 375 DKK – Carte 200/300 DKK – *(dinner only and lunch Saturday-Sunday) (booking essential)*
• Mexican • Neighbourhood • Bistro •
Neighbourhood cantina offering Mexican small plates, powerful flavours and a lot of fun; grab a seat at the counter, order a Mezcal and watch the chefs at work. The best choice is the 'favourite servings', which is five dishes selected by the kitchen. Come for brunch at the weekend.

Uformel

Studiestraede 69 ✉ 1554 V – Ⓜ Vesterport – ✆ 70 99 91 11 Plan: **B3**
– www.uformel.dk – Closed 23-28 December and 1 January
Menu 800 DKK – Carte 360/600 DKK – *(dinner only) (booking essential)*
• Modern cuisine • Fashionable • Trendy •
The informal sister of Formel B, with gold table-tops, black cutlery, a smart open kitchen and a cocktail bar (a lively spot at the weekend!) Dishes are tasting plates and all are the same price; 4-6 is about the right amount.

Vækst

Sankt Peders Stræde 34 ✉ 1453 K – Ⓜ Nørreport Plan: **B2**
– ✆ 38 41 27 27 – www.cofoco.dk/en/restaurants/vaekst/ – Closed 24 December, 1 January and Sunday lunch
Menu 325 DKK – Carte 375/435 DKK
• Modern cuisine • Rustic • Trendy •
Dining outside 'inside' is the theme here, and you'll find plants, garden furniture and a full-sized greenhouse at the centre of the room. Interesting Danish cooking follows the seasons and is light, stimulating and full of flavour.

SMØRREBRØD *The following list of simpler restaurants and cafés/bars specialise in Danish open sandwiches and are generally open from 10.00am to 4.00pm.*

Selma

Rømersgade 20 ✉ 1362 K – ✆ 93 10 72 03 – www.selmacopenhagen.dk – Closed 3 weeks July, 24-25 December, New Year and dinner Sunday-Tuesday Plan: **B2**

Menu 325/345 DKK – Carte 300/450 DKK

• Smørrebrød • Simple • Friendly •

A sweet homely place, named after the owner-chef's daughter and run by a friendly young team. Lunchtime smørrebrød are modern in style whilst respecting tradition; dinner dispenses with the rye and sourdough bases to create dishes ideal for sharing. Excellent selection of craft beers.

Sankt Annæ

Sankt Annæ Plads 12 ✉ 1250 K – Ⓜ Kongens Nytorv – ✆ 33 12 54 97 – www.restaurantsanktannae.dk – Closed 15 July-4 August, Christmas-New Year, Sunday and bank holidays Plan: **D2**

Carte 220/440 DKK – *(lunch only) (booking essential)*

• Smørrebrød • Cosy • Classic décor •

An attractive terraced building with a traditional, rather quaint interior. There's a seasonal à la carte and a daily blackboard menu: prices can vary so check before ordering. The lobster and shrimp – fresh from local fjords – are a hit.

Amalie

Amaliegade 11 ✉ 1256 K – Ⓜ Kongens Nytorv – ✆ 33 12 88 10 – www.restaurantamalie.dk – Closed 3 weeks July, Christmas, Easter, Sunday and bank holidays Plan: **D2**

Menu 279 DKK – Carte 265/322 DKK – *(lunch only) (booking essential)*

• Smørrebrød • Intimate • Rustic •

A charming 18C townhouse by Amalienborg Palace, with two tiny, cosy rooms filled with old paintings and elegant porcelain. The Danish menu offers a large choice of smørrebrød, herring, salmon and salads. Service is warm and welcoming.

ENVIRONS OF COPENHAGEN

AT NORDHAVN North : 3 km by Østbanegade and Road 2

Paustian

Kalkbrænderiløbskaj 2 ✉ 2100 Ø – ✆ 39 18 55 01 – www.paustian.com – Closed July, 23 December-14 January and Sunday

Carte 300/570 DKK – *(lunch only)*

• Danish • Fashionable • Design •

A friendly, informal restaurant set in an impressive harbourside building designed by renowned architect Jørn Utzon. Traditional Danish cooking has French touches; watch the chefs at work in the open kitchen.

AT GENTOFTE North : 8 km by Ostbanegade and Road 2

Jordnær (Eric Kragh Vildgaard)

Gentofte Hotel, Gentoftegade 29 ✉ 2820 – ✆ 22 40 80 20 – www.restaurantjordnaer.dk – Closed 3 weeks July, 1 week February, 1 week October, 22 December-2 January and Sunday-Tuesday

Menu 850/1300 DKK – *(dinner only) (booking essential) (tasting menu only)*

• Danish • Romantic • Intimate •

The passionately run 'Down to Earth' is housed within an unassuming suburban hotel. The building dates from 1666 and the rustic modern room comes with grey painted timbers. Knowledgeably prepared dishes feature ingredients foraged by the largely self-taught chef and flavours are pure and harmonious.

→ Turbot with green asparagus and Noilly Prat. Pike-perch with ramps and fermented garlic. Camomile, honey and green rhubarb.

AT KLAMPENBORG North : 12 km by Folke Bernadottes Allé and Road 2

Den Røde Cottage

Strandvejen 550 (North: 12 km by Folke Bernadottes Allé and Road 2)
✉ 2930 – ✆ 31 90 46 14 – www.denroedecottage.dk – Closed Sunday dinner and Monday
Menu 575/825 DKK – *(dinner only and Sunday lunch) (booking essential) (tasting menu only)*
• Modern cuisine • Cosy • Rustic •

Run with real enthusiasm by a young team of friends, this cosy 'Red Cottage' sits in a charming spot in a wooded park close to the sea. Dishes reflect the changing seasons and the modern, well-balanced cooking respects the classics, whilst also having its own original style.

AT SØLLERØD North : 20 km by Tagensvej (take the train to Holte then taxi) - ✉ 2840 Holte

Søllerød Kro

Søllerødvej 35 ✉ 2840 – ✆ 45 80 25 05 – www.soelleroed-kro.dk – Closed 3 weeks July, 1 week February, Easter, Sunday dinner, Monday and Tuesday
Menu 395/1195 DKK – Carte 845/1310 DKK
• Modern cuisine • Inn • Elegant •

A characterful 17C thatched inn by a pond in a picturesque village, with a delightful courtyard terrace and three elegant, intimate rooms. In keeping with the surroundings, cooking has a classical heart but is presented in a modern style. Dishes have deceptive depth and the wine list is a tome of beauty.

→ Oscietra caviar 'en surprise'. Black lobster, vin jaune and creamed morels. Gourmandise desserts.

Jon Arnold Images/hemis.fr

AARHUS
AARHUS

Urilux/iStock

AARHUS IN...

→ **ONE DAY**
ARoS Art Museum, the Viking Museum, Aarhus Cathedral, stroll around the Latin Quarter.

→ **TWO DAYS**
Den Gamle By (open air 'living' museum), hire a bike and ride into the country.

→ **THREE DAYS**
Marselisborg Palace (summer residence of the Royal family), Moesgaard Museum.

Known as the world's smallest big city, Denmark's second city is a vibrant, versatile place, yet has the charm of a small town. It was originally founded by the Vikings in the 8th century and has been an important trading centre ever since. It's set on the Eastern edge of Jutland and is the country's main port; lush forests surround it, and there are beautiful beaches to the north and south. It's easy to enjoy the great outdoors, while also benefiting from the advantages of urban life.

There's plenty to see and do, and most of it is within walking distance: the city centre is awash with shops – from big chains to

quirky boutiques – as well as museums, bars and restaurants, and the student population contributes to its youthful feel. The most buzzing area is Aboulevarden; a pedestrianized street which runs alongside the river, lined with clubs and cafés. Cultural activities are also high on the agenda of the European Capital of Culture 2017: visit the 12th century Cathedral and the ARoS Art Museum with its colourful rooftop panorama; witness the 2000 year old Grauballe man on display at the Moesgaard prehistoric museum; or step back in time at Den Gamle By. This is not a place that stands still and bold redevelopment projects are reshaping the cityscape, with shiny new apartment and office blocks springing up around the harbour.

EATING OUT

Being a student city, Aarhus hums with café culture all year round; you'll find cosy coffee shops on almost every street, offering breakfasts, cakes, sandwiches and light lunches – some are also popular places to enjoy an evening drink, especially in the lively Aboulevarden area. Eating out is something the Danes excel at and restaurants range from friendly bistros to elegant fine dining establishments; most offer food with a Danish heart but influences come from around the globe. Local produce includes freshly caught fish landed at the harbour and vegetables from the island of Samso; restaurants tend to offer set menus of between 3 and 7 courses and these are a great way to sample a varied selection of dishes. They tend to open early – at around 6pm – while the bars and clubs stay open late, and often offer live music. Not to be overlooked are the city's classic Danish smørrebørd restaurants, where satisfying and wonderfully tasty open sandwiches are served, often along with a tempting selection of cakes and pastries. Tipping is not expected, but obviously greatly appreciated.

Frederikshøj (Wassim Hallal)

Oddervej 19-21 (South: 3.5 km by Spanien and Strandvejen) ✉ 8000 – ✆ 86 14 22 80 – www.frederikshoj.com – Closed 4 weeks midsummer, 1 week October, Christmas-New Year and Sunday-Tuesday
Menu 1145 DKK – *(dinner only) (booking essential) (tasting menu only)*
• Creative • Elegant • Luxury •

Set in the former staff lodge to the Royal Palace, this restaurant is smart, luxurious and contemporary with edgy artwork, iPad menus and floor to ceiling windows affording views over the gardens and out to sea. Dishes are elaborate, creative and visually impressive. Service is professional and knowledgeable.
➜ Potatoes from Samsø. Sweetbread. Rhubarb.

Domestic (Morten Rastad and Christoffer Norton)

Mejlgade 35B ✉ 8000 – ✆ 6143 7010 Plan: **B2**
– www.restaurantdomestic.dk – Closed 22 December-7 January, Easter, Sunday and Monday
Menu 550/950 DKK – *(dinner only) (booking essential) (tasting menu only)*
• Modern cuisine • Fashionable • Minimalist •

This restaurant sets itself the challenge of only using Danish ingredients – hence the name – so expect lots of techniques, creativity and imagination in their 4 or 8 course menus. It's housed in a period property that's been everything from a school to a dairy; the burnt oak dining tables are lovely.
➜ Squash, oyster and yoghurt. Pork with onion and unripe plums. Cherries with camomile and buttermilk.

Gastromé (William Jørgensen)

Rosensgade 28 ✉ 8000 – ✆ 28 78 16 17 Plan: **B2**
– www.gastrome.dk – Closed 25-26 December, Sunday and Monday
Menu 600/1100 DKK – *(dinner only) (tasting menu only)*
• Modern cuisine • Fashionable • Intimate •

This intimate Latin Quarter restaurant features a semi open plan kitchen and stark white walls punctuated with contemporary art. The menu is divided into a 'half throttle' of 4 courses and a 'full throttle' of 8, with wines to match. Complex cooking showcases modern techniques. Service is informative.
➜ Lobster with cauliflower and mousseline sauce. Quail, seasonal mushrooms, burnt potato and wild herbs. 'Rødgrød': berries, white chocolate and sour cream.

Substans (René Mammen)

Frederiksgade 74 ✉ 8000 – ✆ 86 23 04 01 Plan: **A2**
– www.restaurantsubstans.dk – Closed 24-25 December and Sunday-Tuesday
Menu 800/1200 DKK – *(dinner only) (tasting menu only)*
• Modern cuisine • Friendly • Simple •

Classically Scandic in style, with a fresh, uncluttered feel, Pondus' older, more adventurous sister is run by the same experienced husband and wife team. Creative, contemporary cooking uses top quality, mostly organic, ingredients. Dishes have original touches, distinct flavours and stimulating combinations.
➜ Scallop with tomatoes, camomile and pine. Pork with pumpkin, squash and coriander. Rhubarb, lilac, cream and hazel.

Hærværk

Frederiks Allé 105 ✉ 8000 – ✆ 50 51 26 51 Plan: **A2**
– www.restaurant-haervaerk.dk – Closed Sunday-Tuesday
Menu 455 DKK – *(dinner only) (tasting menu only)*
• Danish • Intimate • Rustic •

Run with plenty of passion and enthusiasm by a group of friends. The place has an ersatz industrial feel, thanks to the concrete floor, stark white décor and a glass-fronted fridge of hanging meats. The menu focuses on organic Danish produce in dishes that are earthy, natural and satisfying.

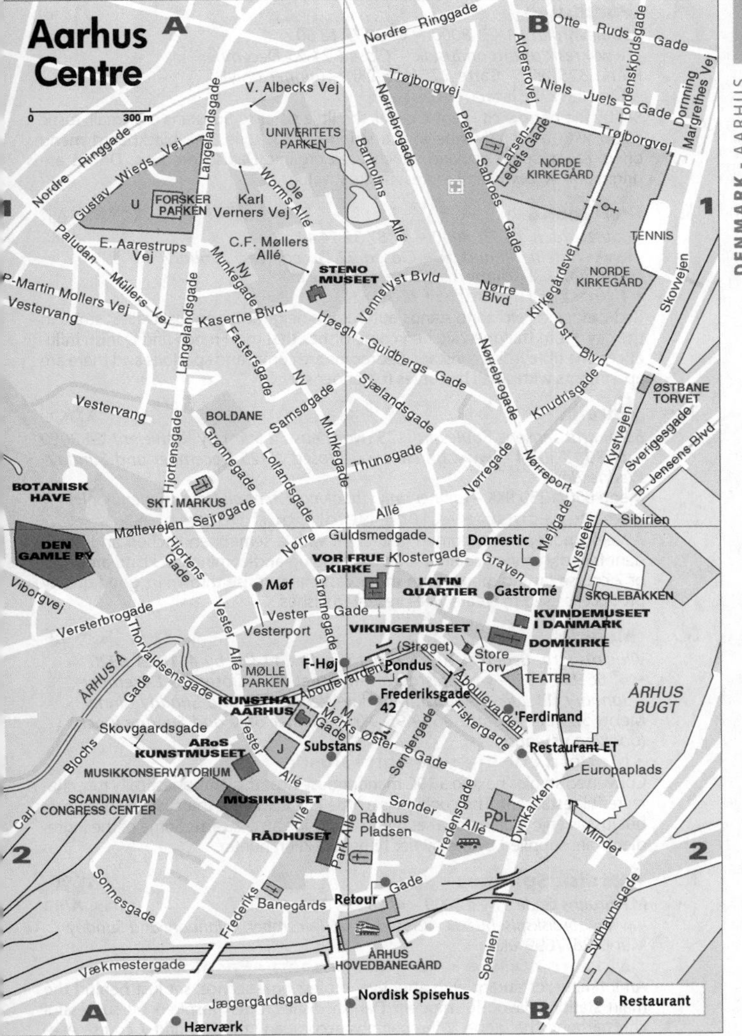

Aarhus Centre
0 300 m
Nordre Ringgade
Trøjborgvej
Nørrebrogade
Otte Ruds Gade
Aldersrovej
Niels Juels Gade
Tordenskjoldsgade
Dronning Margrethes Vej
V. Albecks Vej
UNIVERITETS PARKEN
Bartholins Allé
Peter Sabroes Gade
Larsen-Ledets Gade
NORDE KIRKEGÅRD
Gustav Wieds Vej
Langelandsgade
FORSKER PARKEN
Karl Verners Vej
Ole Worms Allé
TENNIS
Paludan Müllers Vej
E. Aarestrups Vej
C.F. Møllers Allé
STENO MUSEET
Vennelyst Bvld
Nørre Blvd
Kirkegårdsvej
Øst Blvd
Skovvejen
P-Martin Mollers Vej
Vestervang
Ny Munkegade
Kaserne Blvd.
Høegh - Guidbergs Gade
Fastersgade
ØSTBANE TORVET
Knudrisgade
Sjælandsgade
Samsøgade
BOLDANE
Grønnegade
Munkegade
Thunøgade
Kystvejen
Sverigesgade
B. Jensens Blvd
BOTANISK HAVE
Hjortensgade
SKT. MARKUS
Lollandsgade
Nørregade
Nørreport
Sibirien
Møllevejen
Sejrøgade
Allé
Mejlgade
DEN GAMLE BY
Hjortens Gade
Nørre
Guldsmedgade
Domestic
Klostergade
Graven
VOR FRUE KIRKE
Viborgvej
Møf
LATIN QUARTIER
Gastromé
SKOLEBAKKEN
Versterbrogade
Vester Allé
Vester Gade
Vesterport
KVINDEMUSEET I DANMARK
VIKINGEMUSEET
DOMKIRKE
Thorvaldsensgade
ÅRHUS Å
(Strøget)
Store Torv
F-Høj
Pondus
MØLLE PARKEN
Aboulevarden
TEATER
Frederiksgade 42
ÅRHUS BUGT
KUNSTHAL AARHUS
J. M. Mørks Gade
Fiskergade
'Ferdinand
Gade
Skovgaardsgade
Søndergade
Øster Gade
ARoS KUNSTMUSEET
Substans
Restaurant ET
Blochs
MUSIKKONSERVATORIUM
Europaplads
Vester Allé
SCANDINAVIAN CONGRESS CENTER
MUSIKHUSET
Sønder Allé
Fredensgade
POL.
Dynkarken
Carl
Rådhus Pladsen
RÅDHUSET
Park Allé
Mindet
Sonnesgade
Frederiks
Banegårds
Retour
Gade
Sydhavnsgade
ÅRHUS HOVEDBANEGÅRD
Vækmestergade
Spanien
Jægergårdsgade
Nordisk Spisehus
Restaurant
Hærværk
A
B
1
2

Pondus

Åboulevarden 51 ✉ 8000 – ✆ 28 77 18 50 Plan: **B2**
– www.restaurantpondus.dk – Closed 24-25 December
Menu 325 DKK – Carte 375/405 DKK – *(dinner only)*
• Danish • Bistro • Rustic •

Set by the narrow city centre canal, the little sister to Substans is a small, rustic bistro with a friendly vibe and a stripped-back style. The blackboard menu offers flavoursome cooking which uses organic Danish produce. Dishes are bright and colourful and represent great value.

Ferdinand

Åboulevarden 28 ✉ 8000 – ✆ 87 32 14 44 Plan: **B2**
– www.hotelferdinand.dk – Closed 22 December-5 January
Menu 445 DKK (dinner) – Carte 345/435 DKK
• French • Brasserie • Cosy •

Red-canopied Ferdinand stands out from its neighbours on the liveliest street in the city. From the open kitchen come dishes that mix French and Danish influences; the rib-eye is a constant. Bedrooms are comfy and spacious and there are apartments with small balconies for longer stays.

Ghrelin

Bernhardt Jensens Boulevard 125 (Northeast: 2.5 km by Kystvejen) ✉ 8000 – ✆ 30 13 30 04 – www.ghrelin.dk – Closed 24-25 December and Sunday-Wednesday
Menu 650/1250 DKK – *(dinner only) (booking essential) (tasting menu only)*
• Modern cuisine • Chic • Neighbourhood •

A sleek, modern two-roomed restaurant with a semi-open kitchen and confident friendly service, set in the heart of the up-and-coming dockland area. 3, 5 or 7 course tasting menus with the occasional surprise thrown in; good quality produce is used to create well-presented dishes.

Mejeriet

Vilhelmsborg, Bedervej 101, Mårslet (South : 11 km by 451) ✉ 8320 – ✆ 86 93 71 95 – www.restaurant-mejeriet.dk – Closed 23 December-3 January, 11 July-5 August, Monday-Wednesday and Sunday dinner
Menu 525 DKK – Carte 365/495 DKK – *(dinner only and Sunday lunch) (booking essential)*
• Modern cuisine • Design • Rustic •

Converted stables next to a 19C manor house host this enthusiastically run, characterful restaurant. The cooking is a little less elaborate than in previous years but just as enjoyable, with a set menu alongside an à la carte. Some of the ingredients are supplied by the owner himself, a keen hunter.

Nordisk Spisehus

M.P.Bruuns Gade 31 ✉ 8000 – ✆ 86 17 70 99 Plan: **A/B2**
– www.nordiskspisehus.dk – Closed 24-26 December, 1 January and Sunday
Menu 267/699 DKK
• Modern cuisine • Neighbourhood • Fashionable •

An intimate restaurant with attentive, professional service, set just behind the main station. Flavourful modern Danish dishes, often inspired by successful chefs around the globe. Wine pairings accompany the 3, 5 and 7 course evening tasting menus.

Restaurant ET

Åboulevarden 7 ✉ 8000 – ✆ 86 13 88 00 Plan: **B2**
– www.restaurant-et.dk – Closed 23 December-7 January and Sunday
Menu 369 DKK – Carte 246/497 DKK
• French • Design • Fashionable •

A bright, contemporary and smoothly run brasserie split between a number of floors, including the cellar which doubles as the private dining room. The familiar Gallic dishes are generous in size and robust in flavour and come accompanied by an extensive, exclusively French wine list.

Frederiksgade 42

Frederiksgade 42 ✉ 8000 – ✆ 606 89 606 Plan: **B2**
– www.frederiksgade42.dk – Closed 23 December-4 January, Sunday and Monday
Menu 368 DKK – Carte 324/344 DKK – *(dinner only)*
• Danish • Neighbourhood • Bistro •

The larger-than-life owner extends a warm welcome to customers at this delightful restaurant in the heart of the city. The seasonal menu is geared 80:20 in favour of vegetables against meat/fish; the well-priced plates are designed for sharing.

Møf

Vesterport 10 ✉ 8000 – ✆ 61 73 33 33 Plan: **A2**
– www.restaurantmoef.com – Closed 24-26 December, 1-2 January, Tuesday and Wednesday
Menu 349 DKK – Carte 397/517 DKK – *(dinner only) (booking essential)*
• Danish • Neighbourhood • Trendy •

Ask for a seat at the counter to watch the young chef-owners cook in the open kitchen. The three different menus presented at dinner allow for some flexibility; dishes are Danish at heart and made with local produce.

Retour

Banegårdspladsen 4 ✉ 8000 – ✆ 88 63 02 90 Plan: **B2**
– www.retouraarhus.dk – Closed 24-25 December and 1 January
Carte 240/595 DKK – *(dinner only)*
• Meats and grills • Fashionable • Bistro •

A busy restaurant close to station, now offering greater choice and not quite as steak-based as it was when it first opened. However, the Danish rib-eye with fluffy homemade chips is still a feature. The midweek set menu is a steal.

SMØRREBRØD *The following simpler café specializes in Danish open sandwiches*

F-Høj

Grønnegade 2 ✉ 8000 – www.fhoj.dk – Closed 4 weeks midsummer, 1 week October, Christmas-New Year, and Sunday-Tuesday Plan: **A2**
Carte 235/245 DKK – *(lunch only) (bookings not accepted)*
• Smørrebrød • Neighbourhood • Friendly •

A bright, busy café with a pavement terrace; fridges and cabinets display a tempting selection of desserts, cakes, biscuits and drinks. There are three hot and six cold dishes on the smørrebrød menu; two plus dessert should suffice.

HELSINKI

FINLAND
SUOMI

scanrail/iStock

Helsinki
Helsingfors

petriarttuirasikainen/iStock

HELSINKI IN…

→ **ONE DAY**
Harbour market place, Uspensky Cathedral, Lutheran Cathedral, Katajanokka, Mannerheimintie.

→ **TWO DAYS**
A ferry to Suomenlinna, Church in the Rock, the nightlife of Fredrikinkatu.

→ **THREE DAYS**
Central Park, the Sibelius monument, Esplanadi.

Cool, clean and chic, the 'Daughter of the Baltic' sits prettily on a peninsula, jutting out between the landmasses of its historical overlords, Sweden and Russia. Surrounded on three sides by water, Helsinki is a busy port, but that only tells a small part of the story: forests grow in abundance around here and trees reach down to the lapping shores. This is a striking city to look at: it was rebuilt in the 19C after a fire, and many of the buildings have a handsome neoclassical or art nouveau façade. Shoppers can browse the picturesque outdoor food and tourist markets stretching along the main harbour, where island-hopping ferries ply their trade.

In a country with over 200,000 lakes it would be pretty hard to escape a green sensibility, and the Finnish capital has made sure that concrete and stone have never taken priority over its distinctive features of trees, water and open space. There are bridges at every turn connecting the city's varied array of small islands, and a ten kilometre strip of parkland acts as a spine running vertically up from the centre. Renowned as a city of cool, it's somewhere that also revels in a hot nightlife and even hotter saunas – this is where they were invented. And if your blast of dry heat has left you wanting a refreshing dip, there's always a freezing lake close at hand.

EATING OUT

Local - and we mean local - ingredients are very much to the fore in the kitchens of Helsinki's restaurants. Produce is sourced from the country's abundant lakes, forests and seas, so your menu will assuredly be laden with the likes of smoked reindeer, reindeer's tongue, elk in aspic, lampreys, Arctic char, Baltic herring, snow grouse and cloudberries. Generally speaking, complicated, fussy preparations are overlooked for those that let the natural flavours shine through. In the autumn, markets are piled high with woodland mushrooms, often from Lapland, and chefs make the most of this bounty. Local alcoholic drinks include schnapps, vodka and liqueurs made from local berries: lakka (made from cloudberries) and mesimarja (brambleberries) are definitely worth discovering – you may not find them in any other European city. You'd find coffee anywhere in Europe, but not to the same extent as here: Finns are among the world's biggest coffee drinkers. In the gastronomic restaurants, lunch is a simpler affair, often with limited choice.

CENTRE

Palace

XXX

Eteläranta 10 (10th floor) ✉ 00130 – Ⓜ Rautatientori – ✆ (050) 502 0718 – www.palacerestaurant.fi – Closed Easter, July, 22 December-8 January and Saturday-Monday

Plan: **C2**

Menu 62/169 € – *(tasting menu only)*

• Modern cuisine • Elegant • Design •

On the 10th floor of a modernist building constructed in 1952 for the Olympic Games, with a sleek interior and harbourside views. Sophisticated, well balanced and beautifully presented dishes from a highly experienced Finnish chef, with luxurious ingredients in harmonious combinations of texture and flavour.

➜ Poached turbot, Jerusalem artichokes and white Alba truffle. Loin of venison with baked swede and juniper. Lemon & liquorice.

Ask (Filip Langhoff)

XX

Vironkatu 8 ✉ 00170 – Ⓜ Kaisaniemi – ✆ (040) 581 8100 – www.restaurantask.fi – Closed Easter, Christmas, Sunday-Tuesday and bank holidays

Plan: **C1**

Menu 65/119 € – *(dinner only and lunch Friday-Saturday) (tasting menu only)*

• Modern cuisine • Intimate • Cosy •

It may be hidden away but this welcoming restaurant is well-known. It's a charming place, run by a delightful, experienced couple, who offer modern Nordic cooking crafted almost entirely from organic ingredients. Dishes are light and original, produce is top quality and flavours are clearly defined.

➜ Smoked reindeer tartare with hazelnut. Pike-perch with Finnish caviar and nasturtium. Pancakes with spruce shoots and brown butter ice cream.

Demo (Tommi Tuominen)

XX

Uudenmaankatu 9-11 ✉ 00120 – Ⓜ Rautatientori – ✆ (09) 228 90 840 – www.restaurantdemo.fi – Closed 2 weeks July-August, 2 weeks Christmas, Easter, midsummer, Sunday and Monday

Plan: **C2**

Menu 65/105 € – *(dinner only) (booking essential) (tasting menu only)*

• Modern cuisine • Intimate • Romantic •

An unassuming-looking restaurant decorated in neutral tones and hung with huge cotton pendant lights. Classically based cooking combines French and Finnish influences to produce robust, satisfying dishes with a subtle modern edge. Choose 4-7 courses; the menu is presented verbally and changes almost daily.

➜ Duck liver mousse with truffle cream. Beef with sweetbread, fermented red onion and gem lettuce. White chocolate, lemon yoghurt and wood sorrel ice cream.

Olo (Jari Vesivalo)

XX

Pohjoisesplanadi 5 ✉ 00170 – Ⓜ Kaisaneimi – ✆ (010) 3206 250 – www.olo-ravintola.fi – Closed Christmas, Easter, midsummer, Sunday and Monday

Plan: **C2**

Menu 121 € – *(dinner only and lunch in December) (booking essential) (tasting menu only)*

• Modern cuisine • Design • Contemporary décor •

An attractive harbourside townhouse plays host to this cool, minimalist restaurant, whose four rooms have a delightfully understated feel. Local meats such as moose and elk feature in exciting, innovative dishes which are packed with flavour. Dinner arrives in up to 18 servings.

➜ Pike-perch with caviar and wasabi. Cod, butter sauce and white asparagus juice. Liquorice mousse, beetroot and blackcurrant leaf ice cream.

Grön (Toni Kostian)

Albertinkatu 36 ✉ 00180 – Ⓜ Kammpi Plan: **B2**
– ✆ (050) 3289181 – www.restaurantgron.com – Closed 22 December-6 January, Sunday and Monday
Menu 58 € – *(dinner only) (booking essential) (tasting menu only)*
• Finnish • Neighbourhood • Intimate •

A warmly run restaurant where the open kitchen is the focal point and the chefs bring the dishes to the table to explain them. Cooking has a satisfying earthiness and clever use is made of both fresh and fermented ingredients, with vegetables given equal billing with meat or fish. Natural wines are well-chosen.
➜ Lamb with milk, herbs and summer flowers. Potatoes with spring onion, fermented white asparagus and crayfish broth. Blueberries with woodruff parfait.

Ora (Sasu Laukkonen)

Huvilakatu 28A ✉ 00150 – ✆ (40) 0959 440 Plan: **C3**
– www.orarestaurant.fi – Closed 20 June-18 July, Christmas-New Year, Easter, 3rd week February, 1 week September-October and Sunday-Tuesday
Menu 89 € – *(dinner only) (booking essential) (tasting menu only)*
• Modern cuisine • Chic • Cosy •

This small, intimate restaurant is run by chef-owner Sasu Laukkonen. The cooking focuses on local ingredients and uses modern techniques to enhance classic Finnish flavours. Dishes are served and explained by the chefs themselves.
➜ White fish, kohlrabi with horseradish and hyssop. Pork neck with sunflower and cider sauce. Meadowsweet flower parfait, tomato, redcurrants and roses.

Boulevard Social

Bulevardi 6 ✉ 00120 – Ⓜ Rautatientori Plan: **C2**
– ✆ (010) 3229387 – www.boulevardsocial.fi – Closed Christmas, midsummer and Sunday
Menu 29/57 € – Carte 30/51 €
• Mediterranean cuisine • Fashionable •

Owned by the same people as next door Gaijin, this lively, informal restaurant offers an accessible range of authentic North African, Turkish and Eastern Mediterranean dishes; try the set or tasting menus to experience a cross-section of them all. If they're fully booked, ask for a seat at the counter.

Farang

Ainonkatu 3 (inside the Kunsthalle) ✉ 00100 Plan: **B2**
– Ⓜ Kamppi – ✆ (010) 322 9385 – www.farang.fi – Closed Christmas, midsummer, Easter, last 3 weeks July, Saturday lunch, Sunday and Monday
Menu 32/64 € – Carte 39/72 €
• South East Asian • Simple • Intimate •

This stylish, modern restaurant is housed in the Kunsthalle art centre. One room is decorated with large photos of Thai scenes and has communal tables; the other is more intimate and furnished in red, black and grey. Zesty, harmonious dishes take their influences from Vietnam, Thailand and Malaysia.

Gaijin

Bulevardi 6 ✉ 00120 – Ⓜ Rautatientori Plan: **C2**
– ✆ (010) 3229386 – www.gaijin.fi – Closed Christmas, midsummer and lunch Saturday-Monday
Menu 35/64 € – Carte 33/79 € – *(booking essential)*
• Asian • Fashionable •

Gaijin comes with dark, contemporary décor, a buzzing atmosphere, attentive service and an emphasis on sharing. Its experienced owners offer boldly flavoured, skilfully presented modern takes on Japanese, Korean and Northern Chinese recipes. The tasting menus are a great way to sample the different cuisines.

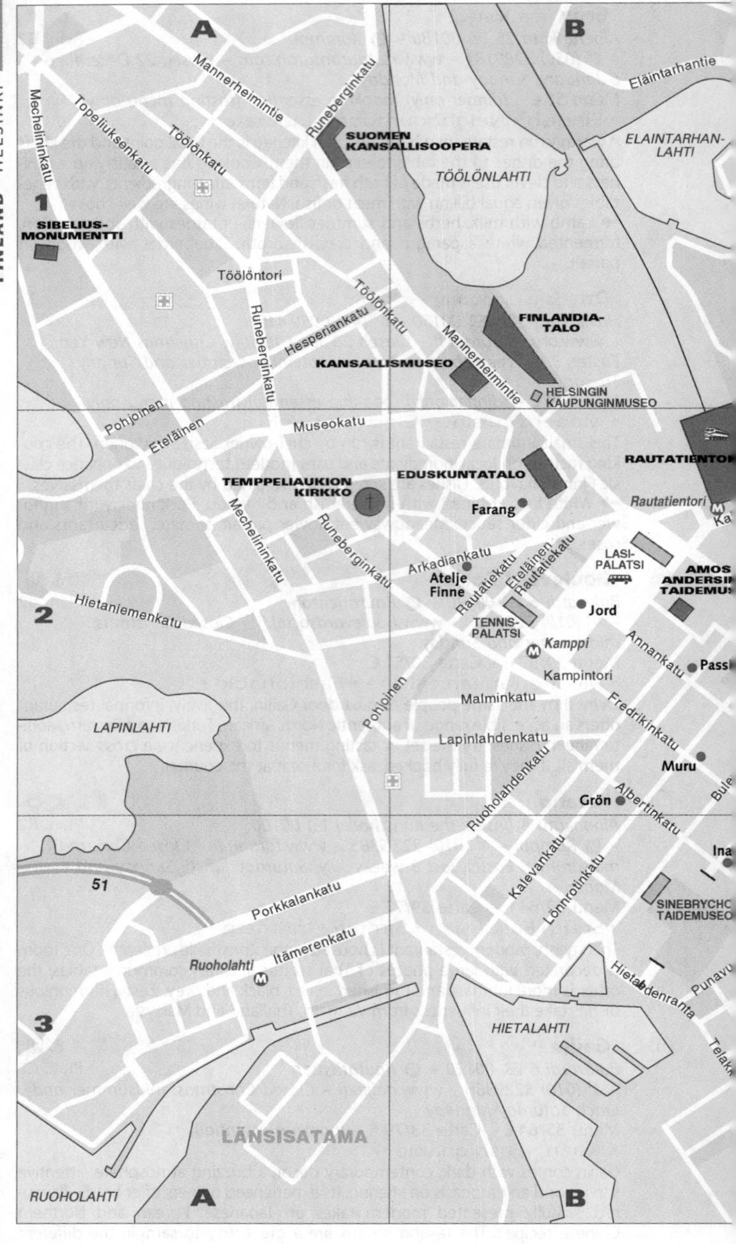

A
B
Mannerheimintie
Runeberginkatu
Eläintarhantie
ELAINTARHAN-
LAHTI
Mechelininkatu
Topeliuksenkatu
Töölönkatu
SUOMEN
KANSALLISOOPERA
TÖÖLÖNLAHTI
1
SIBELIUS-
MONUMENTTI
Töölöntori
Runeberginkatu
Töölönkatu
Hesperiankatu
Mannerheimintie
FINLANDIA-
TALO
KANSALLISMUSEO
HELSINGIN
KAUPUNGINMUSEO
Pohjoinen
Eteläinen
Museokatu
RAUTATIENTO
TEMPPELIAUKION
KIRKKO
EDUSKUNTATALO
Farang
Rautatientori
Mechelininkatu
Runeberginkatu
Arkadiankatu
Atelje
Finne
Rautatiekatu
Eteläinen
Rautatiekatu
LASI-
PALATSI
AMOS
ANDERSI
TAIDEMU
Hietaniemenkatu
2
TENNIS-
PALATSI
Jord
Kamppi
Annankatu
Kampintori
Passi
Malminkatu
Pohjoinen
Fredrikinkatu
LAPINLAHTI
Lapinlahdenkatu
Ruoholahdenkatu
Muru
Grön
Albertinkatu
Ina
51
Kalevankatu
Lönnrotinkatu
SINEBRYCHO
TAIDEMUSEO
Porkkalankatu
Itämerenkatu
Ruoholahti
Hietalahdenranta
Punavu
3
HIETALAHTI
Telakk
LÄNSISATAMA
RUOHOLAHTI
A
B

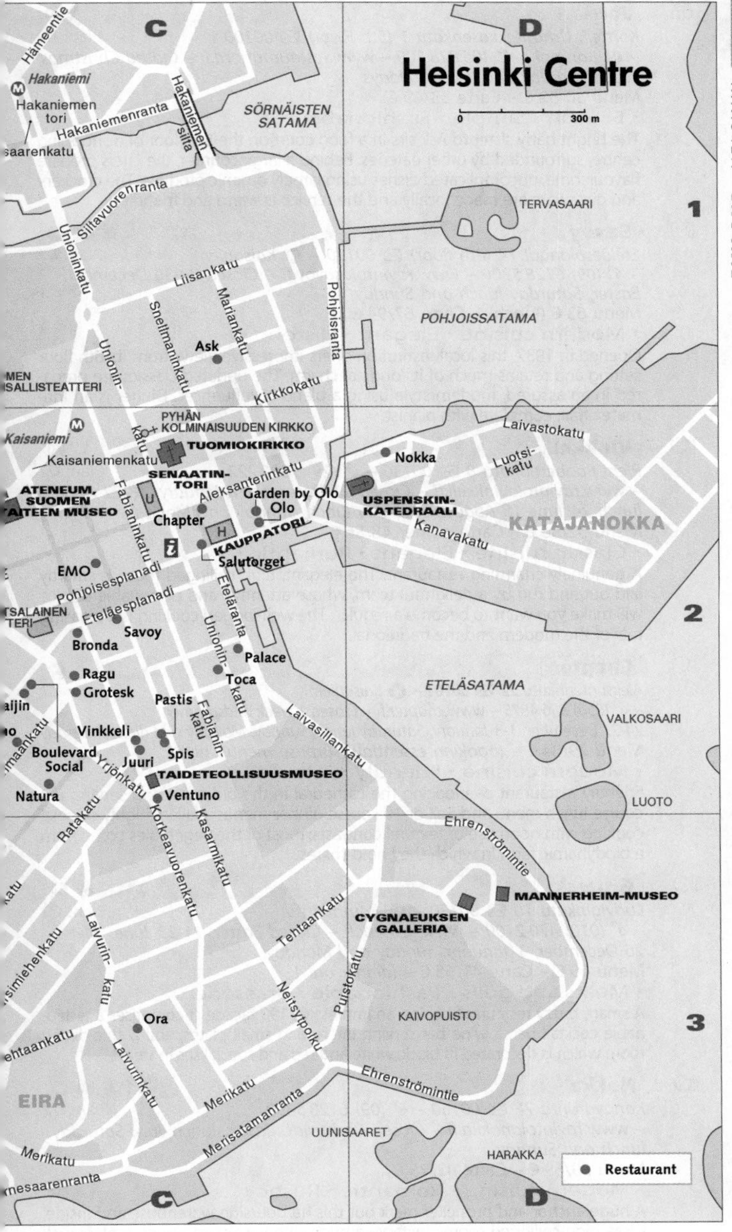
Helsinki Centre
0
300 m
C
D
Hämeentie
Hakaniemi
Hakaniemen tori
Hakaniemenranta
Hakaniemen silta
SÖRNÄISTEN SATAMA
Siltavuorenranta
Unioninkatu
Liisankatu
Snellmaninkatu
Mariankatu
Pohjoisranta
TERVASAARI
POHJOISSATAMA
Ask
Kirkkokatu
PYHÄN KOLMINAISUUDEN KIRKKO
TUOMIOKIRKKO
Kaisaniemi
Kaisaniemenkatu
SENAATINTORI
Aleksanterinkatu
ATENEUM, SUOMEN TAITEEN MUSEO
Fabianinkatu
Garden by Olo
Olo
Chapter
KAUPPATORI
Salutorget
Nokka
Laivastokatu
Luotsikatu
USPENSKIN-KATEDRAALI
Kanavakatu
KATAJANOKKA
EMO
Pohjoisesplanadi
Eteläesplanadi
Savoy
Bronda
Eteläranta
Palace
Toca
Ragu
Grotesk
Pastis
Vinkkeli
Boulevard Social
Juuri
Spis
Natura
Yrjönkatu
TAIDETEOLLISUUSMUSEO
Ventuno
ETELÄSATAMA
VALKOSAARI
LUOTO
Laivasillankatu
Ehrenströmintie
Ratakatu
Korkeavuorenkatu
Kasarmikatu
MANNERHEIM-MUSEO
CYGNAEUKSEN GALLERIA
Tehtaankatu
Laivurinkatu
Neitsytpolku
Puistokatu
KAIVOPUISTO
Ora
EIRA
Merikatu
Merisatamanranta
UUNISAARET
HARAKKA
Restaurant
1
2
3

Jord

Kortteli, Urho Kekkosenkatu 1 (5th Floor) ✉ 00100 – Ⓜ Kamppi – ✆ 405 828 100 – www.restaurantjord.fi – Closed Christmas, Easter, Sunday and bank holidays Plan: **B2**

Menu 30/52 € – Carte 33/49 €

• Finnish • Simple • Fashionable •

The bright baby sister to Ask sits in a food court on the 5th floor of a shopping centre, surrounded by other eateries. Behind a large counter, the chefs prepare flavoursome, uncomplicated dishes using largely organic produce. The crockery and glassware are made locally and the service is warm and friendly.

Savoy

Eteläesplanadi 14 (8th floor) ✉ 00130 – Ⓜ Kaisaniemi – ✆ (09) 6128 5300 – www.ravintolasavoy.fi – Closed 23-30 December, Easter, Saturday lunch and Sunday Plan: **C2**

Menu 63 € (lunch) – Carte 67/94 €

• Modern cuisine • Elegant • Historic •

Opened in 1937, this local institution offers impressive views from its 8th floor setting and retains much of its original charm. The updated classics are prepared in an assured, modern style using a blend of influences. Dinner is an intimate affair, complete with pianist.

Vinkkeli

Pieni Roobertinkatu 8 ✉ 00130 – ✆ (29) 1800 222 – www.ravintolavinkkeli.fi – Closed 21 December-7 January, 18-22 April, lunch 24 June-18 August, Saturday lunch, Sunday and Monday Plan: **C2**

Menu 32/56 € – Carte dinner 48/56 €

• Classic cuisine • Elegant • Romantic •

A genuinely charming restaurant. The elegant, high-ceilinged room is smartly laid out and run by a delightful team, whose attentive and personable service will make you want to become a regular. The well-judged cooking is a pleasing mix of the modern and the traditional.

Chapter

Aleksanterinkatu 22 ✉ 00101 – Ⓜ Kaisaniemi – ✆ (050) 356 4875 – www.chapter.fi – Closed 1 week midsummer, 24-27 December, 1-3 January, Saturday lunch, Sunday, Monday and dinner Tuesday Plan: **C2**

Menu 29/84 € – *(booking essential) (surprise menu only)*

• Modern cuisine • Friendly • Intimate •

Friendly restaurant overlooking the cathedral in the old town and serving a 3 course lunch menu and 5, 7 or 10 course dinner menus. Skilled, highly original cooking with good use of textural contrasts; most of the vegetables come from a biodynamic farm in which they hold shares.

Grotesk

Ludviginkatu 10 ✉ 00130 – Ⓜ Rautatientori – ✆ (010) 470 2100 – www.grotesk.fi – Closed Easter, 21-23 June, 24-26 December, 1 January, Sunday and Monday Plan: **C2**

Menu 49 € – Carte 41/65 € – *(dinner only)*

• Meats and grills • Fashionable • Brasserie •

A smart, buzzy restaurant behind an impressive 19C façade. It comprises a fashionable cocktail bar, a wine bar serving interesting small plates, and a chic dining room which is decorated in black, white and red and specialises in steaks.

Nokka

Kanavaranta 7F ✉ 00160 – ✆ (09) 6128 5600 – www.ravintolanokka.fi – Closed Christmas, Easter, lunch July, Saturday lunch and Sunday Plan: **D2**

Menu 59/69 € – Carte 42/75 €

• Modern cuisine • Romantic • Rustic •

A huge anchor and propeller mark out this harbourside warehouse and inside, three high-ceilinged rooms juxtapose brick with varnished wood. A glass wall allows you to watch farm ingredients being prepared in a modern Finnish style.

Ragu

Ludviginkatu 3-5 ✉ 00130 – Ⓜ Rautatientori Plan: **C2**
– ✆ (09) 596 659 – www.ragu.fi – Closed Christmas, Easter, midsummer and Sunday
Menu 45/57 € – Carte 48/56 € – *(dinner only)*
• Modern cuisine • Design • Chic •
Finland's famed seasonal ingredients are used in unfussy Italian recipes and the welcoming service and lively atmosphere also have something of an Italian feel. Choose the weekly 'Chef's Menu' to sample the latest produce. Vegetarian/vegan options available.

Salutorget

Pohjoisesplanadi 15 ✉ 00170 – Ⓜ Kaisaniemi Plan: **C2**
– ✆ (09) 6128 5950 – www.salutorget.fi – Closed Christmas, Easter, midsummer, Sunday and Bank holidays
Menu 36/44 € – Carte 35/57 €
• International • Brasserie • Elegant •
An old bank, located on the esplanade; now an elegant restaurant with impressive columns and attractive stained glass. The classic, brasserie-style menu has global influences. Enjoy afternoon tea in the plush cocktail bar.

Muru

Fredrikinkatu 41 ✉ 00120 – Ⓜ Kamppi Plan: **B2**
– ✆ (300) 472 335 – www.murudining.fi – Closed Christmas, New Year, Easter, 1 May, midsummer, Sunday, Monday and bank holidays
Menu 52 € – Carte 46/52 € – *(dinner only) (booking essential)*
• Modern cuisine • Neighbourhood • Trendy •
The charming team really enhance your experience at this cosy little bistro. It's a quirky place, with a wine bottle chandelier, a bar made from old wine boxes and a high level wine cellar. A blackboard lists snacks and around 7 main dishes but most diners choose the 4 course daily menu with a Gallic base.

Ateljé Finne

Arkadiankatu 14 ✉ 00100 – Ⓜ Kamppi Plan: **B2**
– ✆ (010) 281 8242 – www.ateljefinne.fi – Closed Christmas, Easter Monday, midsummer, Saturdays in July and Sunday
Carte 45/66 € – *(dinner only)*
• Modern cuisine • Bistro • Family •
This is the old studio of sculptor Gunnar Finne, who worked here for over 30 years. Local art decorates the small bistro-style dining rooms set over three levels. Regional dishes are given subtle modern and international twists.

Bronda

Eteläesplanadi 20 ✉ 00101 – Ⓜ Rautatientori Plan: **C2**
– ✆ (010) 322 9388 – www.ravintolabronda.fi – Closed Christmas, midsummer and Sunday
Menu 32/54 € – Carte 31/83 €
• Modern cuisine • Fashionable • Brasserie •
The floor to ceiling windows of this old furniture showroom flood it with light. Enjoy cocktails and snacks at the bar or comforting, boldly flavoured, Mediterranean sharing plates in the brasserie. Each dish arrives as it's ready.

EMO

Kluuvikatu 2 ✉ 00100 – Ⓜ Rautatientori Plan: **C2**
– ✆ (010) 505 0900 – www.emo-ravintola.fi – Closed Christmas, New Year, Easter Monday, midsummer, Saturday lunch and Sunday
Menu 39/54 € – Carte 45/74 €
• Modern cuisine • Fashionable • Intimate •
Expect modern cooking showcasing original combinations of flavours and textures, along with a broad range of European influences. It's a stylish, intimate restaurant run in a friendly and relaxed manner, and it benefits from a large pavement terrace on a pleasant pedestrianised street.

Garden by Olo

Pohjoiseplanadi 5 (Entrance on Helenankatu 2) ✉ 00170 Plan: **C2**
– ✆ (010) 320 6250 – www.olo-ravintola.fi – Closed July, 24-25 December, 2-15 January, Sunday and Monday
Menu 49/65 € – Carte 55/63 € – *(dinner only) (booking essential)*
• Modern cuisine • Simple •
The casual addendum to Olo occupies a glass-roofed inner courtyard and has a feeling of openness. The menu has a light, modern style and some occasional Asian notes; some dishes are designed for sharing. The cocktails are popular.

Inari

Albertinkatu 19a ✉ 00120 – ✆ (050) 514 8155 Plan: **B3**
– www.ravintolainari.fi – Closed Sunday-Tuesday
Menu 70 € – *(dinner only) (booking essential) (surprise menu only)*
• Creative • Rustic • Neighbourhood •
Hottest ticket in town is this relaxed restaurant, owned and run by Noma alumnus, Kim Mikkola. The set 7 course tasting menu offers Nordic cuisine with Asian influences to the fore and the ambitious, mostly plant-based dishes are well presented and full of flavour.

Juuri

Korkeavuorenkatu 27 ✉ 00130 – ✆ (09) 635 732 Plan: **C2**
– www.juuri.fi – Closed 23-27 December and midsummer
Carte 39/64 €
• Traditional cuisine • Bistro • Intimate •
A friendly bistro with colourful décor and a rustic feel. The focus here is on sharing: small, tapas-style plates showcase organic produce and classic Finnish recipes are given a modern makeover. They brew their own beer in the cellar.

Natura

Iso Roobertinkatu 11 ✉ 00120 – ✆ (040) 6891 111 Plan: **C2**
– www.restaurantnatura.com – Closed July, 23-26 December, 21-23 June, Monday and Tuesday
Menu 39/89 € – Carte 22/41 € – *(dinner only) (booking essential)*
• Finnish • Neighbourhood • Design •
Carefully chosen ingredients are bound together in appealing seasonal small plates at this intimate restaurant. Techniques mix the old and the new and dishes are full of colour. Go for the 'Classic' menu, accompanied by a pure wine.

Passio

Kalevankatu 13 ✉ 00100 – Ⓜ Kamppi Plan: **B2**
– ✆ (020) 7352 040 – www.passiodining.fi – Closed Christmas, midsummer, lunch Monday, Tuesday, Saturday and Sunday
Menu 30/52 €
• Modern cuisine • Friendly • Neighbourhood •
Exposed ducts, dimly lit lamps and leather-topped tables give Passio a faux industrial feel. Modern cooking showcases regional ingredients and flavours are well-defined. It's run by a local brewer, so be sure to try the artisan beers.

Pastis

Pieni Roobertinkatu 2 ✉ 00130 – ✆ (030) 04 72 336 Plan: **C2**
– www.pastis.fi – Closed Christmas-New Year, Easter, midsummer, 2 November, Sunday and lunch Monday and lunch in July
Menu 29 € (lunch) – Carte 40/54 € – *(booking essential)*
• Classic French • Bistro • Neighbourhood •
The clue is in the name: they serve classic French dishes, alongside several different brands of pastis. It's a popular place, so there's always a lively atmosphere. Come for Saturday brunch or have a private meal in Petit Pastis.

Spis

Kasarmikatu 26 ✉ 00130 – ✆ (045) 305 1211 Plan: **C2**
– www.spis.fi – Closed Sunday, Monday and bank holidays
Menu 57/77 € – *(dinner only) (booking essential) (tasting menu only)*
• Modern cuisine • Neighbourhood • Bistro •

An intimate restaurant seating just 18; the décor is 'faux derelict', with exposed brick and plaster walls. Creative, flavoursome cooking features Nordic flavours in attractive, imaginative combinations. Most dishes are vegetable-based.

Toca

Unioninkatu 18 ✉ 00130 – ✆ (044) 2379922 Plan: **C2**
– www.toca.fi – Closed July, 23 December-7 January, Sunday and Monday
Menu 45/65 € – *(dinner only) (booking essential) (tasting menu only)*
• Modern cuisine • Trendy •

A passionately run, popular little bistro with a modest, unfinished look. The 3 and 5 set course menus change daily depending on the seasonal produce available; cooking is an original mix of Italian simplicity and Finnish modernity.

Ventuno

Korkeavuorenkatu 21 ✉ 00130 – ✆ (010) 322 9395 Plan: **C2**
– www.ventuno.fi – Closed 24-26 December and midsummer
Carte 42/73 €
• Italian • Neighbourhood • Osteria •

Buzzy, modern day osteria open from early morning for coffee and pastries; sit in the area next to the glass-fronted wine cabinet. Authentic Italian dishes cover all the regions of Italy and are unfussy, full-flavoured and perfect for sharing. The all-Italian wine list is a labour of love.

PARIS
Lyons

FRANCE
FRANCE

Jerome_Correia/iStock

PARIS
PARIS

MaxOzerov/iStock

PARIS IN...

→ **ONE DAY**
Eiffel Tower, Notre-Dame Cathedral, a café on Boulevard St Germain, Musée d'Orsay, Montmartre.

→ **TWO DAYS**
The Louvre, Musée du Quai Branly.

→ **THREE DAYS**
Canal Saint-Martin, Centre Pompidou, Picasso Museum and the Marais.

The French capital is one of the truly great cities of the world, a metropolis that eternally satisfies the desires of its beguiled visitors. With its harmonious layout, typified by the grand geometric boulevards radiating from the Arc de Triomphe like the spokes of a wheel, Paris is designed to enrapture. Despite its ever-widening tentacles, most of the things worth seeing are contained within the city's ring road. Paris wouldn't be Paris sans its Left and Right Banks: the Right Bank comprises the north and west; the Left Bank takes in the city south of the Seine. A stroll along the Left Bank conjures

images of Doisneau's magical monochrome photographs, while the narrow, cobbled streets of Montmartre vividly call up the colourful cool of Toulouse-Lautrec.

The Ile de la Cité is the nucleus around which the city grew and the oldest quarters around this site are the 1st, 2nd, 3rd and 4th arrondissements on the Right Bank and 5th and 6th on the Left Bank. Landmarks are universally known: the Eiffel Tower and the Arc de Triomphe to the west, the Sacré-Coeur to the north, Montparnasse Tower to the south, and, of course, Notre-Dame Cathedral in the middle. But Paris is not resting on its laurels. New buildings and new cultural sensations are never far away: Les Grands Travaux are forever in the wings, waiting to inspire.

EATING OUT

Food plays such an important role in Gallic life that eating well is deemed a citizen's birth-right. Parisians are intensely knowledgeable about their food and wine - simply stroll around any part of the capital and you'll come across lavish looking shops offering perfectly presented treats. Restaurants, bistros and brasseries too can call on the best available bounty around: there are close to a hundred city-wide markets teeming with fresh produce. As Charles De Gaulle said: "How can you govern a country which has 246 varieties of cheese?" Whether you want to linger in a legendary café or dine in a grand salon, you'll find the choice is endless. The city's respect for its proud culinary heritage is palpable but it is not resting on its laurels. Just as other European cities with vibrant restaurant scenes started to play catch-up, so young chefs here took up the cudgels. By breaking away from formulaic regimes and adopting more contemporary styles of cooking, they have ensured that the reputation of the city remains undimmed.

RESTAURANTS FROM A TO Z

deepblue4you/iStock

✿✿✿ Alain Ducasse au Plaza Athénée – Hôtel Plaza Athénée

25 avenue Montaigne (8th) – Ⓜ Alma Marceau XXXXX
– ✆ 01 53 67 65 00 – www.alain-ducasse.com Plan: **G3**
– Closed 19 July-27 August, 20-30 December, Monday lunch, Tuesday lunch, Wednesday lunch, Saturday, Sunday
Menu 210 € (lunch)/395 € – Carte 250/395 €

• Creative • Luxury • Design •

Alain Ducasse has rethought his entire restaurant along the lines of 'naturality' – his culinary Holy Grail is to uncover the truth of each ingredient. Based on the trilogy fish-vegetables-cereals (here too, a respect for nature prevails), some of the dishes are really outstanding, and the setting is magnificent!

➜ Lentilles vertes du Puy et caviar, délicate gelée d'anguille fumée. Bar de l'Atlantique, courgette et pâtissons, wakame de pêche côtière. Chocolat de notre manufacture, céréales toastées, sorbet cacao-single malt.

✿✿✿ Alléno Paris au Pavillon Ledoyen (Yannick Alléno)

8 avenue Dutuit (8th) XXXXX
– Ⓜ Champs-Elysées Clemenceau Plan: **H3**
– ✆ 01 53 05 10 00 – www.yannick-alleno.com
– Closed Saturday lunch, Sunday
Menu 145 € (lunch)/380 € – Carte 188/380 €

• Modern Cuisine • Luxury •

This Parisian institution – in an elegant pavilion in the Champs-Élysées gardens – has been taken over by Yannick Alléno, who has set about writing a new chapter in its story. The chef creates a tour de force, immediately stamping his hallmark. He masterfully puts a new spin on haute cuisine, magnifying, for example, jus and sauces through clever extractions.

➜ Rouget cuit dans un coffre de tourteau au jus de coquillages. Tronçon de turbot étuvé, risotto de tout petits pois, lentilles et sarrasin au cerfeuil. Meringue au charbon de bois et cardamome, glace fleur d'oranger.

✿✿✿ Le Cinq – Hôtel Four Seasons George V XXXXX

31 avenue George V (8th) – Ⓜ George V Plan: **G3**
– ✆ 01 49 52 71 54 – www.restaurant-lecinq.com
Menu 145 € (lunch)/340 € – Carte 195/360 €

• Modern Cuisine • Luxury • Elegant •

After the fabulous years at Ledoyen, Christian Le Squer is now at the helm of this renowned establishment. The majesty of the Grand Trianon inspired decor remains intact, waiters in uniform still perform their dizzying ballet, and the expertise of the chef does the rest, keeping the finest tradition alive!

➜ Gratinée d'oignons contemporaine à la parisienne. Bar de ligne au caviar et lait ribot de mon enfance. Givré laitier au goût de levure.

✿✿✿ Épicure – Hôtel Le Bristol XXXXX

112 rue du Faubourg Saint-Honoré (8th) Plan: **H2**
– Ⓜ Miromesnil – ✆ 01 53 43 43 40 – www.lebristolparis.com
Menu 145 € (lunch)/340 € – Carte 173/287 €

• Modern Cuisine • Luxury • Classic Décor •

The bright dining room overlooking the garden boasts a restrained, distinguished elegance in which the glamour of the 18C shines forth. The virtuosity of Éric Fréchon's classic cuisine bears witness to his freedom of expression with regard to great tradition. He creates dishes that are fresh and endowed with the finest flavours!

➜ Macaronis farcis, truffe noire, artichaut et foie gras gratinés au vieux parmesan. Poularde de Bresse en vessie, suprêmes au vin jaune, écrevisses et girolles. Cacao du Guatemala, pépites de grué sablées à la fleur de sel, émulsion de lait fumé à la vanille.

❀❀❀ **Pierre Gagnaire**

6 rue Balzac (8th) – Ⓜ George V – ✆ 01 58 36 12 50 – www.pierregagnaire.com – Closed 3-26 August, 30 December-7 January, Saturday, Sunday

Plan: **G2**

Menu 90 € (lunch)/315 € – Carte 320/400 €

• Creative • Elegant • Chic •

The restaurant's chic and restrained contemporary decor is in complete contrast to the renowned inventiveness of this famous chef.

➜ Le jardin marin. Canard de Challans rôti et fumé sous une cloche au chocolat. Le grand dessert de Pierre Gagnaire.

❀❀ **L'Abeille** – Hôtel Shangri-La

10 avenue d'Iéna (16th) – Ⓜ Iéna – ✆ 01 53 67 19 90 – www.shangri-la.com – Closed 1-14 January, 28 July-26 August, Monday, Tuesday lunch, Wednesday lunch, Thursday lunch, Friday lunch, Saturday lunch, Sunday

Plan: **F3**

Menu 230 € – Carte 160/230 €

• Modern Cuisine • Luxury • Elegant •

The Shangri-La Hotel's 'French restaurant' has a name that gives a nod to the Napoleonic emblem of the bee. As you might expect, France's grand culinary tradition is honoured here under the auspices of a team that has inherited the best expertise. The menu promotes fine classicism and noble ingredients.

➜ Feuille à feuille de foie gras de canard et champignons, gelée de dashi. Pigeonneau de Racan rôti, betterave au foin, sauce d'un borchtch. Miel du maquis corse givré aux parfums de citron et d'eucalyptus.

❀❀ **Le Clarence**

31 avenue Franklin-D.-Roosevelt (8th) – Ⓜ Franklin D. Roosevelt – ✆ 01 82 82 10 10 – www.le-clarence.paris – Closed 4-27 August, 30 December-7 January, Monday, Tuesday lunch, Sunday

Plan: **H3**

Menu 90 € (lunch), 130/320 €

• Modern Cuisine • Luxury • Historic •

This superb 1884 mansion located close to the Champs-Elysées hosts the remarkable talent of Christophe Pelé (former chef of La Bigarrade, in Paris). He is an artist when it comes to marrying produce from land and sea. As for the sumptuous wine list, it is enough to make you dizzy before you have even had a glass!

➜ Seiche de casier, raviole de potimarron et jus à l'encre de seiche. Turbot, oseille et huile d'argan. Crémeux citron-safran.

❀❀ **Le Gabriel** – Hôtel La Réserve

42 avenue Gabriel (8th) – Ⓜ Champs-Elysées Clemenceau – ✆ 01 58 36 60 50 – www.lareserve-paris.com – Closed Saturday lunch

Plan: **H3**

Menu 95 € (lunch), 215/280 € – Carte 192/260 €

• Modern Cuisine • Elegant • Luxury •

The restaurant is nestled in the elegant setting of La Réserve and features Versailles wooden flooring and cuir de Cordoue with a gold patina. Chef Jérôme Banctel, no stranger to Paris' grandes maisons, cooks his own superb take on the classics, with a smattering of Asian touches and executed in the proper way. A success!

➜ Cœur d'artichaut de Macau en impression de fleur de cerisier et coriandre fraîche. Pigeon de Racan mariné au cacao et sarrasin croustillant. Grains de café et crème glacée au sirop de merisier.

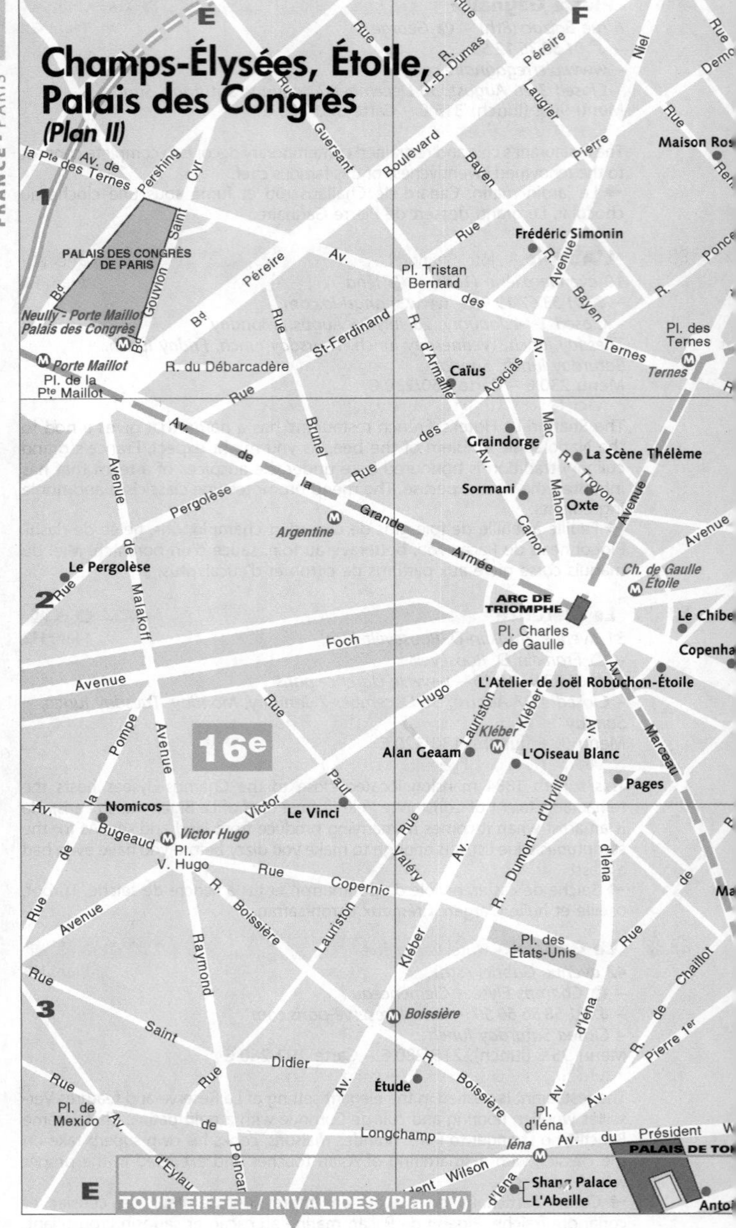
Champs-Élysées, Étoile, Palais des Congrès
(Plan II)
E
F
1
2
3
PALAIS DES CONGRÈS DE PARIS
Neuilly - Porte Maillot Palais des Congrès
Porte Maillot
Pl. de la Pte Maillot
Pl. Tristan Bernard
Frédéric Simonin
Maison Ros
Pl. des Ternes
Ternes
Caïus
Graindorge
La Scène Thélème
Sormani
Oxte
Argentine
Ch. de Gaulle Étoile
ARC DE TRIOMPHE
Pl. Charles de Gaulle
Le Chibe
Copenha
L'Atelier de Joël Robuchon-Étoile
Le Pergolèse
16e
Kléber
Alan Geaam
L'Oiseau Blanc
Pages
Nomicos
Le Vinci
Victor Hugo
Pl. V. Hugo
Pl. des États-Unis
Boissière
Étude
Pl. de Mexico
Pl. d'Iéna
Iéna
Shang Palace
L'Abeille
PALAIS DE TO
Antoi
TOUR EIFFEL / INVALIDES (Plan IV)
Av. de la Grande Armée
Avenue Foch
Avenue de Malakoff
Rue Pergolèse
Rue Brunel
Rue des Acacias
Av. Mac Mahon
Av. Carnot
Av. Marceau
Av. Kléber
Av. d'Iéna
Rue Copernic
R. Boissière
Rue Lauriston
Rue Paul Valéry
Av. Victor Hugo
Rue Hugo
Bd Pereire
Av. des Ternes
Rue Laugier
Rue Bayen
Avenue de Wagram
Rue de Chaillot
Rue Pierre 1er de Serbie
Av. du Président Wilson
Rue Saint Didier
Rue de Longchamp
Av. d'Eylau
Rue de la Pompe
Av. Bugeaud
Rue Raymond Poincaré
Rue Dumont d'Urville
Av. Niel
Rue Guersant
Bd Gouvion Saint Cyr
R. du Débarcadère
Rue St-Ferdinand
R. d'Armaillé
R. Troyon
R. J.-B. Dumas
Av. de la Pte des Ternes
Pershing
R. Poncelet
Rue Rennequin
Rue Demours
Rue Pierre Demours
Rue Saint Ferdinand

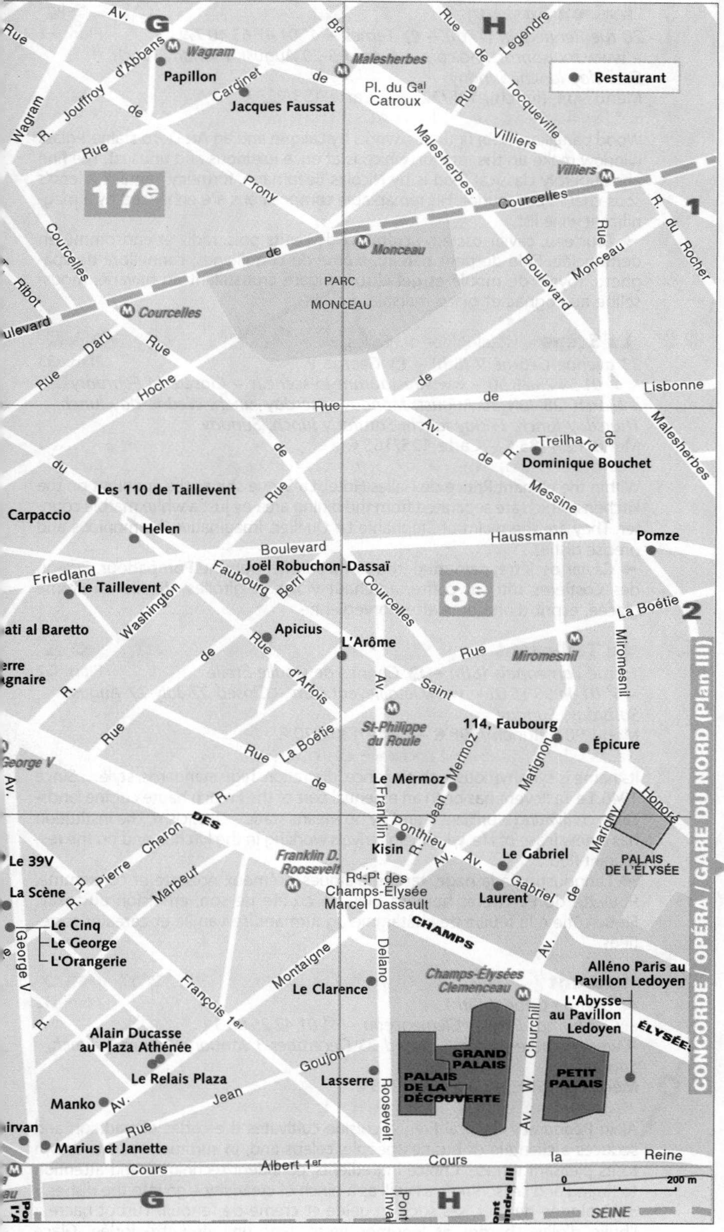
Restaurant
17e
8e
PARC MONCEAU
Papillon
Jacques Faussat
Les 110 de Taillevent
Carpaccio
Helen
Joël Robuchon-Dassaï
Le Taillevent
Apicius
L'Arôme
Dominique Bouchet
Pomze
114, Faubourg
Épicure
Le Mermoz
Kisin
Le Gabriel
Laurent
Le 39V
La Scène
Le Cinq
Le George
L'Orangerie
Le Clarence
Alain Ducasse au Plaza Athénée
Le Relais Plaza
Lasserre
Manko
Marius et Janette
Alléno Paris au Pavillon Ledoyen
L'Abysse au Pavillon Ledoyen
PALAIS DE L'ÉLYSÉE
GRAND PALAIS
PALAIS DE LA DÉCOUVERTE
PETIT PALAIS
Wagram
Malesherbes
Villiers
Monceau
Courcelles
Miromesnil
St-Philippe du Roule
Franklin D. Roosevelt
Champs-Élysées Clemenceau
Pl. du Gal Catroux
Rd-Pt des Champs-Élysée Marcel Dassault
CHAMPS ÉLYSÉES
SEINE
0 200 m
CONCORDE / OPÉRA / GARE DU NORD (Plan III)

Maison Rostang

20 rue Rennequin (17th) – Ⓜ Ternes – ✆ 01 47 63 40 77 Plan: **F1**
– www.maisonrostang.com – Closed 5-20 August, Monday lunch, Saturday lunch, Sunday

Menu 90 € (lunch), 185/225 € – Carte 153/223 €

• Classic Cuisine • Elegant • Luxury •

Wood panelling, Robj figurines, works by Lalique and an Art Deco stained-glass window make up the interior, which is at once luxurious and unusual. The fine and superbly classical food is by Nicolas Beaumann, formerly Yannick Alleno's sous-chef at Le Meurice. His remarkable compositions are enhanced by a magnificent wine list.

→ Tourteau, caviar osciètre, crémeux de petits pois, radis et consommé en demi-gelée. Sole de petit bateau, crème de coquillages, cannelloni de spaghetti, royale de moule et gel citron. Cigare croustillant au havane, mousseline au cognac et glace marsala.

La Scène – Hôtel Prince de Galles

33 avenue George V (8th) – Ⓜ George V Plan: **G3**
– ✆ 01 53 23 78 50 – www.restaurant-la-scene.fr – Closed 24 February-4 March, 28 July-30 August, Monday, Tuesday lunch, Wednesday lunch, Thursday lunch, Friday lunch, Saturday lunch, Sunday

Menu 125/185 € – Carte 125/165 €

• Modern Cuisine • Elegant • Luxury •

Within the elegant Prince de Galles Hotel, La Scène shines the spotlight on the kitchens, which are separated from the dining area by just a white marble counter. They are the realm of Stéphanie Le Quellec. Imaginative, harmonious and precise dishes.

→ Caviar osciètre, pain mi-perdu et mi-soufflé, pomme Pompadour. Pigeon des Costières rôti sur coffre, artichaut violet et girolles. Vanille en crème glacée, esprit d'une omelette norvégienne.

Le Taillevent

15 rue Lamennais (8th) – Ⓜ Charles de Gaulle-Etoile Plan: **G2**
– ✆ 01 44 95 15 01 – www.letaillevent.com – Closed 27 July-27 August, Saturday, Sunday

Menu 90 € (lunch)/198 € – Carte 130/220 €

• Classic Cuisine • Luxury • Elegant •

Its name is synonymous with elegance, discretion, high standards, style... Since 1946, Le Taillevent has been an essential part of the French haute cuisine landscape, cultivating a brilliant – and by no means static – classicism. The institution has a new lease of life, with fresh arrivals working in the kitchen and on the restaurant floor.

→ Langoustine à la nage, tartare d'algues, crémeux noisette et consommé. Poulette du Perche et homard bleu en croûte de son, émulsion au tokaji. Figue rôtie à la feuille de châtaignier, gourmandise vanille et céréales torréfiées.

Laurent

41 avenue Gabriel (8th) Plan: **H3**
– Ⓜ Champs-Elysées Clemenceau – ✆ 01 42 25 00 39
– www.le-laurent.com – Closed 23 December-3 January, Saturday lunch, Sunday

Menu 95/159 € – Carte 155/245 €

• Modern Cuisine • Elegant • Luxury •

Alain Pégouret's classical French cuisine cultivates the codes of tradition and seduces a clientele of businesspeople, celebs and, in summer, tourists drawn to its pleasant terrace. Choice ingredients, confident technique, and attention to timing and seasoning – as well as a pinch of creativity – go into the dishes.

→ Araignée de mer, ses sucs en gelée et crème de fenouil. Turbot nacré à l'huile d'olive, bardes et légumes verts dans une fleurette iodée. Glace vanille minute.

Apicius

20 rue d'Artois (8th) – Ⓜ St-Philippe du Roule – ✆ 01 43 80 19 66 – www.restaurant-apicius.com – Closed Sunday

Plan: **G2**

Menu 120 € (lunch), 180/250 € – Carte 160/230 €

• Modern Cuisine • Elegant • Luxury •

Apicius is located in a sumptuous 18C private mansion that calls to mind a small palace. Created by Jean-Pierre Vigato, a champion of fine dining, it is now linked to the destiny (and talent) of Mathieu Pacaud, who creates a symbiosis of tradition and creativity. Time passes, Apicius changes... but remains!

➜ Langoustines crues rafraîchies au caviar golden, tropézienne anisée en chaud-froid. Turbot rôti à l'huile de figuier, coques et couteaux à l'extraction d'oseille. Vacherin "enigma", copeaux meringués et sorbet noix de coco.

Lasserre

17 avenue Franklin-D.-Roosevelt (8th) – Ⓜ Franklin D. Roosevelt – ✆ 01 43 59 02 13 – www.restaurant-lasserre.com – Closed 1-31 August, Monday lunch, Tuesday lunch, Wednesday lunch, Thursday lunch, Friday lunch, Saturday lunch, Sunday

Plan: **H3**

Menu 190 € – Carte 130/175 €

• Classic Cuisine • Luxury • Chic •

One of the temples of Parisian gastronomy. The elegance of the interior (columns, draperies, tassels etc), the tableware, the quality of the service – it all comes together to magnify haute cuisine! Fashions come and go, Lasserre remains.

➜ Gratin de macaronis à l'artichaut et truffe noire. Turbot poché, sauce de laitue, asperges au caviar osciètre. Foisonné de chocolat du Pérou sous de fines feuilles à la fleur de sel.

L'Abysse au Pavillon Ledoyen – Hôtel Alléno Paris au Pavillon Ledoyen

8 avenue Dutuit (8th) – Ⓜ Champs-Elysées - Clemenceau – ✆ 01 53 05 10 00 – www.yannick-alleno.com – Closed Saturday, Sunday

Plan: **H3**

Menu 98 € (lunch), 170/280 €

• Japanese • Design • Minimalist •

A great Japanese sushi master, ingredients of stunning quality (ikejime fish from the Atlantic) and the creative touch of Yannick Alléno: L'Abysse takes us to the heady summits of Japanese gastronomy. Not to mention the tip-top service of a grand establishment and a sumptuous wine list, rich in sought-after sakes. N.B. the 12 seats at the counter are quickly snapped up.

➜ Orphie au sudachi, haricots noirs et betterave. Collection de sushis nigiris. Sélection d'amamis.

Le George – Hôtel Four Seasons George V

31 avenue George-V (8th) – Ⓜ George V – ✆ 01 49 52 72 09 – www.legeorge.com

Plan: **G3**

Menu 65 € (lunch)/110 € – Carte 65/120 €

• Italian • Elegant • Cosy •

In the kitchens of the George since September 2016, Simone Zanoni has made an impression with his light, Italian-inspired cooking, often served in tasting-size portions. Superb dining room or conservatory in the courtyard.

➜ Ravioli de pintade à la truffe et crème de parmesan. Bar de ligne poêlé et son jus iodé. Déclinaison de noisettes du Piémont et citron.

Il Carpaccio – Hôtel Le Royal Monceau

37 avenue Hoche (8th) – Ⓜ Charles de Gaulle-Etoile Plan: **G2**
– ✆ 01 42 99 88 12
– www.leroyalmonceau.com
– Closed 28 July-27 August, Monday, Sunday
Menu 120/145 € – Carte 97/133 €
• Italian • Elegant •

You reach the restaurant via a remarkable corridor decorated with thousands of shells. The restaurant decor, reminiscent of a winter garden, is also delightful. The menu is unapologetically simple and in the great tradition of Italian home cooking.

➜ Carpaccio de gambas rouges de Sicile, confiture de tomates et gingembre, caviar italien. Filet de saint-pierre, carpaccio de cèpe, poivron friggitello et mousserons. Baba au limoncello, crème citron, citron frais et semi-confit, sorbet au citron de Méditerranée.

Shang Palace – Hôtel Shangri-La

10 avenue d'Iéna (16th) – Ⓜ Iéna Plan: **F3**
– ✆ 01 53 67 19 92 – www.shangri-la.com
– Closed 15 August-11 September
Menu 48 € (lunch), 98/128 € – Carte 70/150 €
• Chinese • Exotic Décor •

The Shang Palace occupies one of the lower floors of the Shangri-La hotel. It gracefully recreates the decor of a luxury Chinese restaurant with its jade columns, sculpted screens and crystal chandeliers. The menu pays homage to the full flavours and authenticity of Cantonese gastronomy.

➜ Saumon Lo Hei. Poulet sauté et riz fermenté à l'osmanthe. Crème de mangue, pomélo et perles de sagou.

Antoine (Thibault Sombardier)

10 avenue de New York (16th) – Ⓜ Alma Marceau Plan: **F3**
– ✆ 01 40 70 19 28
– www.antoine-paris.fr
– Closed Monday, Sunday
Menu 49 € (lunch)/160 € – Carte 130/175 €
• Seafood • Elegant •

Under the aegis of chef Thibault Sombardier, this is one of Paris's top seafood restaurants (also serving other dishes). The menu changes daily to offer the best fresh fish and seafood, sourced directly from ports in Brittany, the Basque Country or Mediterranean; everything is made with savoir faire and inspiration. The contemporary decor is elegant. In short: don't miss this place.

➜ Pain soufflé de homard, estragon et champignons de Paris. Suprême de pintade fermière, crème d'échalote et raviole végétale. Écorce chocolat, caramel et cacahouètes.

L'Arôme (Thomas Boullault)

3 rue Saint-Philippe du Roule (8th) Plan: **G-H2**
– Ⓜ St-Philippe-du-Roule
– ✆ 01 42 25 55 98 – www.larome.fr
– Closed Saturday, Sunday
Menu 59 € (lunch), 109/159 €
• Modern Cuisine • Chic • Romantic •

Attractive restaurant run by Eric Martins (front of house) and Thomas Boullault (in the kitchen). Comfortable dining room with a warm atmosphere and an open kitchen. Modern cuisine.

➜ Pressé de tourteau breton, avocat, riz koshihikari et eau de tomate. Pavé de veau, ravioles de céleri à la ricotta, cédrat confit et jus aux girolles. Soufflé chaud à l'amande, marmelade et sorbet abricot.

Le Chiberta

3 rue Arsène-Houssaye (8th) – Ⓜ Charles de Gaulle-Etoile – ✆ 01 53 53 42 00 – www.lechiberta.com – Closed 5-25 August, Saturday lunch, Sunday Plan: **F2**

Menu 49 € (lunch)/110 € – Carte 90/120 €

• Creative • Minimalist •

Soft lighting and a simple, understated interior by J M Wilmotte (dark colours and unusual wine bottle walls) set the scene for inventive cuisine overseen by Guy Savoy. Market-fresh, weekly changed menu. It is a pleasure to watch the chefs at work behind the counter.

➜ Courgette, condiment mimosa et caviar et fleur de courgette croustillante. Ris de veau laqué, girolles persillées, chou pak-choï et carottes multicolores. Fraises, framboises, amandes, ganache à l'amaretto et sorbet fruits rouges.

Copenhague (Andreas Møller)

142 avenue des Champs-Elysées (8th) – Ⓜ George V – ✆ 01 44 13 86 26 – www.restaurant-copenhague-paris.fr – Closed 5 August-1 September, Saturday, Sunday Plan: **F2**

Menu 55 € (lunch), 75/115 € – Carte 69/84 €

• Danish • Contemporary Décor • Minimalist •

The Maison du Danemark on the Champs Élysées has long been a culinary ambassador of the food of the Great North. A tasteful, low-key interior ideally showcases its gourmet ambitions. Cod in a frothy sauce of grey shrimp, and smoked reindeer are two of the iconic Scandinavian dishes served here.

➜ Cuisine du marché.

Dominique Bouchet

11 rue Treilhard (8th) – Ⓜ Miromesnil – ✆ 01 45 61 09 46 – www.dominique-bouchet.com – Closed 5-18 August, Saturday, Sunday Plan: **H2**

Menu 58 € (lunch)/125 € – Carte 95/120 €

• Classic Cuisine • Elegant •

This is the sort of place you want to recommend to your friends: a contemporary interior that is at once chic and intimate, alert service, tasty and well put-together classic cuisine.

➜ Parmentier de homard, beurre blanc, ciboulette et caviar. Côte de veau de lait fumé au foin et blettes à la crème. Mont-Blanc en coque de meringue et confiture de cassis.

Étude (Keisuke Yamagishi)

14 rue du Bouquet-de-Longchamp (16th) – Ⓜ Boissière – ✆ 01 45 05 11 41 – www.restaurant-etude.fr – Closed 17 February-11 March, 4-26 August, Monday, Saturday lunch, Sunday Plan: **F3**

Menu 45 € (lunch), 80/130 €

• Modern Cuisine • Elegant •

Nourished by his meetings with small-scale producers, by the discovery of ingredients from afar – pepper from Taiwan with citrus notes, Iranian berries – the chef, Keisuke Yamagishi, cooks here like a tightrope walker, offering set menus named "Symphonie", "Ballade", "Prélude" in homage to Chopin. Each dish is a masterclass in harmony.

➜ Cuisine du marché.

Helen

3 rue Berryer (8th) – Ⓜ George V – ✆ 01 40 76 01 40 – www.helenrestaurant.com – Closed 3-27 August, 23 December-3 January, Monday, Saturday lunch, Sunday Plan: **G2**

Menu 48 € (lunch)/138 € – Carte 80/170 €

• Seafood • Elegant • Design •

Founded in 2012, Helen has already made its mark among the fish restaurants of Paris' chic neighbourhoods. If you love fish, you will be bowled over: from the quality of the ingredients (only wild fish sourced from fishermen who bring in the catch of the day on small boats) to the care taken over the recipes. Sober and elegant decor.

➜ Carpaccio de daurade royale au citron caviar. Bar de ligne aux olives taggiasche. Paris-brest.

Nomicos (Jean-Louis Nomicos)

Plan: E3

16 avenue Bugeaud (16th) – Ⓜ Victor Hugo – ✆ 01 56 28 16 16 – www.nomicos.fr – Closed Monday, Sunday
Menu 49 € (lunch), 75/145 € – Carte 120/180 €
• Modern Cuisine • Elegant •

After working at Lasserre – one of the temples of classical French cuisine – Jean-Louis Nomicos created this restaurant that bears his name. In a contemporary interior, refurbished by architect Marie Deroudilhe, he creates lovely cuisine with nods to the Mediterranean, in keeping both with his Marseille roots and exacting know-how.
➜ Macaroni aux truffes noires et foie gras de canard. Côte de veau de lait, girolles et petits pois. Archipel Nomicos, îles flottantes aux trois saveurs.

Penati al Baretto (Alberico Penati)

Plan: G2

9 rue Balzac (8th) – Ⓜ George V – ✆ 01 42 99 80 00 – www.penatialbaretto.eu – Closed Saturday lunch, Sunday
Menu 55 € (lunch) – Carte 75/115 €
• Italian • Classic Décor • Elegant •

Alberico Penati's Italian restaurant, opened mid-2014, has right away imposed itself as one of the best in the city! In accordance with the finest Italian tradition, generosity and refinement distinguish each recipe. The dishes are brimming with flavour as they explore all the regions of the peninsula. A succulent voyage.
➜ Purée de potiron de Mantoue aux fruits de mer, sauce salmoriglio. Thon rouge de Méditerranée aux tomates sautées, sauce au câpres. Cassata sicilienne.

Le Pergolèse (Stéphane Gaborieau)

Plan: E2

40 rue Pergolèse (16th) – Ⓜ Porte Maillot – ✆ 01 45 00 21 40 – www.lepergolese.com – Closed 3-25 August, Saturday, Sunday
Menu 56 € (lunch) – Carte 90/135 €
• Traditional Cuisine • Elegant •

Sun-drenched cuisine given a nice new spin by a Meilleur Ouvrier de France chef, and served in a pared-down and elegant decor.
➜ Moelleux de filets de sardines marinés aux herbes, fondue de poivrons en basquaise et sorbet tomate. Sole meunière farcie en duxelles, jus de cuisson en glaçage. Soufflé chaud aux saveurs de la saison.

L'Orangerie – Hôtel Four Seasons George V

Plan: G3

31 avenue George-V (8th) – Ⓜ George V – ✆ 01 49 52 72 24 – www.lorangerieparis.com
Menu 75 € (lunch), 95/125 € – Carte 100/150 €
• Modern Cuisine • Elegant •

This tiny restaurant (18 seats only) is between La Galerie restaurant and the handsome courtyard of the Four Seasons George V hotel. It features a concise, seasonal menu in which tradition is updated thanks to elegant, perfumed notes and a delicate blend of flavours.
➜ Langoustine et bouillon de riz au yuzu. Daurade sur le grill, tapioca de concombre et jus pimenté. Fleur de vacherin.

La Scène Thélème (Julien Roucheteau)

Plan: F2

18 rue Troyon (17th) – Ⓜ Charles de Gaulle - Étoile – ✆ 01 77 37 60 99 – www.lascenetheleme.fr – Closed 29 July-18 August, Monday, Saturday lunch, Sunday
Menu 49 € (lunch), 95/169 € – Carte 119/149 €
• Modern Cuisine • Contemporary Décor • Cosy •

An unusual restaurant, where theatre and gastronomy come together. On some evenings you can see a theatre performance before your meal. Chef Julien Roucheteau creates refined and visually strong dishes. Diners will also be delighted by the use of excellent gourmet ingredients, as well as the impeccable wait staff, from the restaurant manager to the sommelier. The scene is set for a memorable culinary intermission.
➜ Transparence de langoustines aux effluves de feuilles de shiso. Croustillant de ris de veau doré au beurre, fricassée de courgettes d'Albenga au curcuma frais et nèfle. Rhubarbe des champs cuite au sucre et sorbet à la rhubarbe fermentée.

Alan Geaam

19 rue Lauriston (16th) – Ⓜ Charles de Gaulle-Etoile Plan: **F2**
– ✆ 01 45 01 72 97 – www.alangeaam.fr – Closed Monday, Sunday
Menu 48 € (lunch), 80/100 €
• Creative • Elegant •

Everyone has heard of the American dream, but Alan Geaam prefers the French version! Moving to Paris at the age of 24, he has climbed the rungs of the ladder of gastronomy. His original recipes combine France's rich culinary heritage with touches from his native Lebanon and his commitment and passion can be sampled in each creation.

➜ Kebbeh d'anguille fumée. Pigeon laqué à la mélasse de Grenade. Cône de cèdre, praliné de graines de courge, miel et lait fermenté glacé.

114, Faubourg – Hôtel Le Bristol

114 rue du Faubourg-Saint-Honoré (8th) – Ⓜ Miromesnil Plan: **H2**
– ✆ 01 53 43 44 44 – www.lebristolparis.com – Closed Saturday lunch, Sunday lunch
Menu 119 € – Carte 84/115 €
• Modern Cuisine • Elegant •

This chic brasserie within the premises of Le Bristol has a lavish interior with gilded columns, floral motifs and a grand staircase. Savour dishes from the menu of fine brasserie classics cooked with care and lots of taste.

➜ Œuf king-crab, mayonnaise au gingembre et citron. Sole, pousses d'épinard, huile vierge aux câpres. Millefeuille à la vanille Bourbon, caramel au beurre demi-sel.

Frédéric Simonin

25 rue Bayen (17th) – Ⓜ Ternes – ✆ 01 45 74 74 74 Plan: **F1**
– www.fredericsimonin.com – Closed 4-26 August, Monday, Sunday
Menu 55 € (lunch), 105/155 € – Carte 120/140 €
• Modern Cuisine • Cosy • Elegant •

Black-and-white decor forms the backdrop to this chic restaurant close to Place des Ternes. Fine, delicate cuisine from a chef with quite a career behind him already.

➜ Chair de tourteau, gelée de tomate, onctuosité d'avocat et espuma à la coriandre. Veau normand cuit en cocotte, champignons et condiment d'ail noir. Soufflé chaud au caramel et glace au lait.

Pages (Ryuji Teshima)

4 rue Auguste-Vacquerie (16th) – Ⓜ Charles de Gaulle-Etoile Plan: **F2**
– ✆ 01 47 20 74 94 – www.restaurantpages.fr – Closed 5-26 August, Monday, Sunday
Menu 55 € (lunch), 105/175 €
• Creative • Minimalist • Elegant •

Ryuji Teshima, aka Teshi, knocked about in some top establishments, before deciding to deploy his own contemporary and personal vision of French food. His "surprise" menus create incredible associations of flavours that seem most unlikely on paper but that taste somehow undisputable when in the mouth. You can even put your head into the kitchen for a closer look!

➜ Carpaccio de bœuf ozaki. Poularde grillée et jaune d'œuf. Hojicha et chocolat.

L'Atelier de Joël Robuchon - Étoile

133 avenue des Champs-Elysées (8th) Plan: **F2**
– Ⓜ Charles de Gaulle-Étoile – ✆ 01 47 23 75 75 – www.joel-robuchon.com
Menu 49 € (lunch), 99/199 € – Carte 100/210 €
• Creative • Design • Minimalist •

Paris, London, Las Vegas, Tokyo, Taipei, Hong Kong, Singapore and back to Paris... A French and international destiny for these Ateliers with their finger on the pulse. The great chef, who passed away in 2018, devised a bold concept: a long counter with bar stools, red and black colour scheme... and precisely cooked dishes drawing on France, Spain and Asia.

➜ Langoustine en ravioli truffé à l'étuvée de chou vert. Côtelettes d'agneau de lait à la fleur de thym. Chocolat tendance, crémeux onctueux au chocolat araguani, sorbet cacao et biscuit Oréo.

Graindorge

XX

15 rue de l'Arc-de-Triomphe (17th) Plan: **F2**
– Ⓜ Charles de Gaulle-Étoile – ✆ 01 47 54 00 28 – www.le-graindorge.fr
– Closed 1-20 August, Monday lunch, Saturday lunch, Sunday
Menu 32 € (lunch), 37/55 € – Carte 50/70 €

• Flemish • Vintage • Friendly •

Potjevlesch (potted meat), bintje farcie (stuffed potatoes), waterzoï (a stew with Ostend grey prawns) and Boulogne kippers, Flemish-style hare during hunting season. Diners tuck into food prepared by a serious and industrious chef, whose know-how is no longer to be proven. Accompanied by good craft beers from outside Quiévrain (Angélus, Moinette Blonde). Pretty Art Deco interior.

Pomze

XX

109 boulevard Haussmann (8th) – Ⓜ St-Augustin Plan: **H2**
– ✆ 01 42 65 65 83 – www.pomze.com – Closed 23 December-2 January, Saturday lunch, Sunday
Menu 37 € – Carte 49/65 €

• Modern Cuisine • Minimalist •

The unusual concept behind Pomze is to take the humble apple as a starting point for a culinary voyage! From the food shop (where you will find cider and calvados) to the restaurant, this 'forbidden fruit' provides the central theme. Creative and intrepid dishes offer excellent value for money.

Kisin

X

9 rue de Ponthieu (8th) – Ⓜ Franklin D. Roosevelt Plan: **H3**
– ✆ 01 71 26 77 28 – www.udon-kisin.fr – Closed 1-15 August, Sunday
Menu 30/45 € – Carte 28/36 €

• Japanese • Simple •

When a bib gourmand chef from Tokyo arrives in Paris, the first thing he does is open a restaurant, tantalising and bewitching our senses. Diners will sample Japanese produce and genuine udon, made in front of the diner. Natural, additive-free ingredients, most of which are imported direct from the land of the rising sun. Healthy, wholesome and succulent.

Le Mermoz

X

16 rue Jean-Mermoz (8th) – Ⓜ Champs-Elysées Plan: **H2**
– ✆ 01 45 63 65 26 – Closed 29 July-19 August, Saturday, Sunday
Carte 32/41 €

• Market Cuisine • Bistro •

Manon Fleury, a former fencer who initially studied literature, trained under some of the best (Pascal Barbot, Alexandre Couillon). Her lunches are like bouquets of delicacies veal tartare, soft apricot and oregano –, seasonal and reasonably priced. For dinner, tapas-style plates are served up in a wine bar atmosphere.

Sormani

XXX

4 rue du Général-Lanrezac (17th) Plan: **F2**
– Ⓜ Charles de Gaulle-Étoile – ✆ 01 43 80 13 91
– www.restaurantsormani.fr – Closed 5-25 August, Saturday, Sunday
Carte 70/140 €

• Italian • Romantic • Elegant •

Fabric wallpaper, Murano glass chandeliers, mouldings and mirrors: all the elegance of Italy comes to the fore in this chic and hushed restaurant. The cooking of Pascal Fayet (grandson of a Florentine cabinet maker) pays a subtle homage to Italian cuisine. From the lobster ravioli and veal with ceps to the remarkable dessert, the "gigantesco".

Les 110 de Taillevent

195 rue du Faubourg-St-Honoré (8th) – Ⓜ Charles de Gaulle-Etoile – ✆ 01 40 74 20 20 – www.les-110-taillevent-paris.com – Closed 3-27 August
Plan: G2

Menu 44 € – Carte 50/150 €

• Traditional Cuisine • Cosy •

Under the aegis of the prestigious Taillevent name, this ultra-chic brasserie puts the onus on food and wine pairings. The concept is a success, with its remarkable choice of 110 wines by the glass, and nicely done traditional food (pâté en croûte, bavette steak with a peppercorn sauce etc). Elegant and inviting decor.

L'Oiseau Blanc – Hôtel The Peninsula

19 avenue Kleber (16th) – Ⓜ Kléber – ✆ 01 58 12 67 30 – www.peninsula.com/fr/
Plan: F2

Menu 69 € (lunch)/115 €

• Modern Cuisine • Design • Elegant •

This is the Peninsula's rooftop restaurant for 'contemporary French gastronomy'. Part of the luxury hotel that opened in 2014 near the Arc de Triomphe, the restaurant is presided over by a replica of the White Bird (in homage to the plane in which Nungesser and Coli attempted to cross the Atlantic in 1927) and offers stunning views.

Le Relais Plaza – Hôtel Plaza Athénée

25 avenue Montaigne (8th) – Ⓜ Alma Marceau – ✆ 01 53 67 64 00 – www.dorchestercollection.com/paris/hotel-plaza-athenee
Plan: G3

Menu 64 € – Carte 80/135 €

• Classic Cuisine • Elegant •

Within the Plaza Athénée is this chic and exclusive brasserie, popular with regulars from the fashion houses nearby. It is impossible to resist the charm of the lovely 1930s decor inspired by the liner SS Normandie. A unique atmosphere for food that has a pronounced sense of tradition. As Parisian as it gets.

Le 39V

39 avenue George-V (8th) – Ⓜ George V – ✆ 01 56 62 39 05 – www.le39v.com – Closed Saturday, Sunday
Plan: G3

Menu 40 € (lunch), 95/135 € – Carte 81/149 €

• Modern Cuisine • Design • Friendly •

The Temperature is rising at 39, avenue George V! On the 6th floor of this impressive Haussmann-style building overlooking the rooftops of Paris, diners can enjoy the chef's refined cuisine in a stylish setting. Dishes are based around a classic repertoire, top quality ingredients and fine flavours.

Jacques Faussat

54 rue Cardinet (17th) – Ⓜ Malesherbes – ✆ 01 47 63 40 37 – www.jacquesfaussat.com – Closed 28 July-28 August, 24 December-1 January, Saturday, Sunday
Plan: G1

Menu 42 € (lunch), 48/160 € – Carte 74/102 €

• Traditional Cuisine • Contemporary Décor • Friendly •

In a quiet neighbourhood, this comfortable, inviting restaurant, recently renovated in a contemporary style, offers a menu that evolves with the market and the inspiration of the chef, an endearing native of Gers, who combines traditional know-how and contemporary style. Whether just passing through or regulars, diners exit with a smile on their face. Good value for money.

Joël Robuchon-Dassaï

184 rue du Faubourg-Saint-Honoré (8th) – ✆ 01 76 74 74 70 – www.robuchon-dassai-laboutique.com – Closed Monday, Sunday
Plan: G2

Menu 49 € (lunch) – Carte 54/112 €

• Japanese • Chic • Contemporary Décor •

Pâtisserie, sandwich shop, tearoom, sake bar and restaurant... for an ode to Japan, a country of elegance and gastronomy, so dear to Joël Robuchon. The great chef joined forces with a famous sake house. Designer setting with 1970s touches, Japanese and French cuisine, attentive service down to every last detail. Inspiring.

Marius et Janette

Plan: **G3**

4 avenue George-V (8th) – Ⓜ Alma Marceau – ✆ 01 47 23 41 88 – www.mariusjanette.com

Menu 52 € (lunch) – Carte 91/180 €

• Seafood • Mediterranean • Friendly •

This seafood restaurant's name recalls Marseille's Estaque district. It has an elegant nautical decor and a pleasant street terrace in summertime.

Maxan

Plan: **F3**

3 rue Quentin Bauchart (8th) – Ⓜ George V – ✆ 01 40 70 04 78 – www.rest-maxan.com – Closed 4-20 August, Saturday lunch, Sunday

Menu 40 € – Carte 48/82 €

• Modern Cuisine • Elegant •

So this is the spot, a stone's throw from Avenue George V, where Maxan is to be found. The decor, in a palette of greys, is elegant and discreet, and it is not without pleasure that we reacquaint ourselves with the flavoursome market-based cuisine: button mushrooms, Scotch bonnet and poached egg...

Le Vinci

Plan: **E2-3**

23 rue Paul-Valéry (16th) – Ⓜ Victor Hugo – ✆ 01 45 01 68 18 – www.restaurantlevinci.fr – Closed 2-25 August, Saturday, Sunday

Menu 39 € – Carte 45/70 €

• Italian • Friendly •

The pleasing interior design and friendly service make Le Vinci a very popular choice a stone's throw from avenue Victor-Hugo. The impressive selection of pastas and risottos, as well as the à la carte meat and fish dishes vary according to the seasons.

Manko

Plan: **G3**

15 avenue Montaigne (8th) – Ⓜ Alma Marceau – ✆ 01 82 28 00 15 – www.manko-paris.com

Menu 65 € – Carte 40/80 €

• Peruvian • Elegant • Exotic Décor •

Star chef, Peruvian Gaston Acurio, and singer Garou are the driving force behind Manko. This restaurant, lounge and cabaret bar in the Théâtre des Champs-Elysées basement proposes Peruvian recipes peppered with Asian and African touches. The food is nicely done and ideal for sharing.

Shirvan

Plan: **G3**

5 place de l'Alma (8th) – Ⓜ Alma Marceau – ✆ 01 47 23 09 48 – www.shirvancafemetisse.fr

Menu 36 € (lunch) – Carte 40/100 €

• Modern Cuisine • Contemporary Décor • Vintage •

This restaurant near the Alma Bridge is the brainchild of Akrame Benallal. Starched white linen has made way for designer cutlery, earthenware goblets and a menu inspired by the Silk Road from Morocco to India, via Azerbaijan. A delicious melting pot of culinary flavours. Professional service, open almost all-day long.

Caïus

Plan: **F1**

6 rue d'Armaillé (17th) – Ⓜ Charles de Gaulle-Étoile – ✆ 01 42 27 19 20 – www.caius-restaurant.fr – Closed 1-23 August, Saturday, Sunday

Menu 45 €

• Creative • Friendly • Neighbourhood •

Each season, the particularly inventive chef of this chic and lively restaurant concocts playful and aromatic cuisine, enhanced with spices and "forgotten" ingredients. The wine list is short but top quality.

Oxte

5 rue Troyon (17th) – Ⓜ Ternes – ✆ 01 45 75 15 15 Plan: **F2**
– www.restaurant-oxte.com – Closed 5-25 August, Saturday lunch, Sunday
Menu 39/65 €

• Mexican • Trendy •

Opened in early 2018 in the Étoile neighbourhood, near the Arc de Triomphe, this trendy restaurant proposes delicious contemporary cuisine with Mexican influences. French ingredients are infused with condiments, herbs and spices by a talented and passionate Mexican chef. A success.

Papillon

8 rue Meissonier (17th) – Ⓜ Wagram Plan: **G1**
– ✆ 01 56 79 81 88 – www.papillonparis.fr – Closed 27 July-26 August, 22 December-2 January, Saturday, Sunday
Menu 36 € (lunch)/75 € – Carte 52/76 €

• Modern Cuisine • Bistro • Trendy •

Christophe Saintagne has accomplished his metamorphosis, opening his own place after running the kitchens at the Plaza Athénée then at Le Meurice. Blossoming in his elegant neo-bistro, he creates classic, noble cuisine with the emphasis firmly on taste and balance. A word of advice, be sure to book!

CONCORDE – OPÉRA – BOURSE – GARE DU NORD PLAN III

Le Meurice Alain Ducasse – Hôtel Le Meurice

228 rue de Rivoli (1th) – Ⓜ Tuileries – ✆ 01 44 58 10 55
– www.alainducasse-meurice.com/fr – Closed Plan: **J-K3**
23 February-11 March, 27 July-26 August, Saturday, Sunday
Menu 110 € (lunch), 380/580 € – Carte 260/345 €

• Modern Cuisine • Luxury • Romantic •

In the heart of the iconic luxury hotel, this is the epitome of a great French restaurant. Its lavish interior, inspired by the royal apartments of Versailles Palace, has been tastefully updated by Philippe Starck. Under the watchful eye of Alain Ducasse, executive chef Jocelyn Herland signs a menu that celebrates top quality produce. Stylish flair.

➜ Petit pâté chaud de pintade et foie gras, sauce Périgueux. Poulette fermière, girolles et céleri. Baba au rhum de votre choix, crème mi-montée.

La Table de l'Espadon – Hôtel Ritz

15 place Vendôme (1th) – Ⓜ Opéra – ✆ 01 43 16 33 74 Plan: **K3**
– www.ritzparis.com – Closed Monday lunch, Tuesday lunch, Wednesday lunch, Thursday lunch, Friday lunch, Saturday lunch, Sunday lunch
Menu 195/345 € – Carte 200/420 €

• Modern Cuisine • Elegant • Luxury •

The interior, submerged in golds and drapes, is stunning. In this magical setting, the precise cuisine of young Nicolas Sale shines. Choose the bait, then the line, and finally the bite: the announcement of the meals is packed with nods to fishing and swordfish. Taste, personality, intensity: a wind of modernity is blowing over the Ritz. Superb!

➜ La langoustine. Le bar de ligne. Le miel.

Le Grand Véfour (Guy Martin)

17 rue de Beaujolais (1th) – Ⓜ Palais Royal Plan: **L3**
– ✆ 01 42 96 56 27 – www.grand-vefour.com – Closed Saturday, Sunday
Menu 115 € (lunch)/315 € – Carte 210/290 €

• Creative • Classic Décor •

Bonaparte and Joséphine, Lamartine, Hugo, Sartre… For more than two centuries, the former Café de Chartres has been cultivating the legend. Nowadays it is Guy Martin who maintains the aura. Influenced by travel and painting – colours, shapes, textures – the chef 'sketches' his dishes like an artist… between invention and history.

➜ Ravioles de foie gras, crème foisonnée truffée. Parmentier de queue de bœuf aux truffes. Palet noisette et chocolat au lait, glace au caramel brun et sel de Guérande.

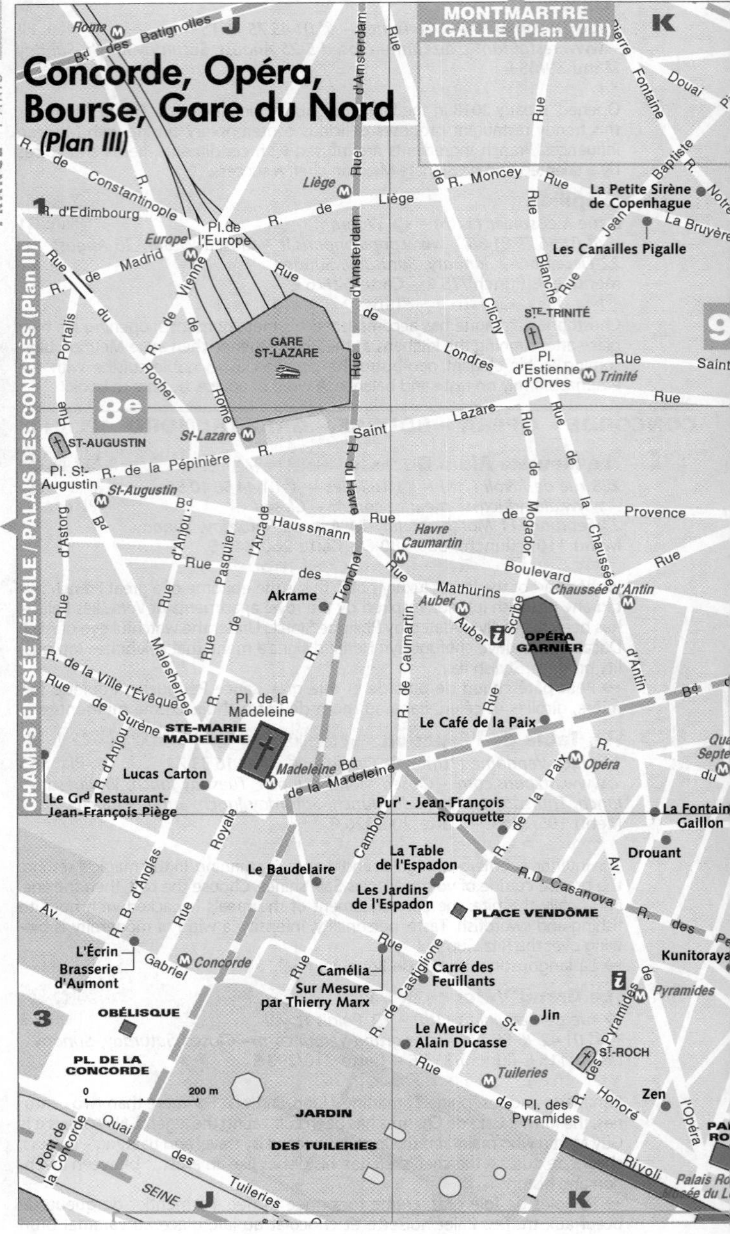
Concorde, Opéra, Bourse, Gare du Nord
(Plan III)
MONTMARTRE PIGALLE (Plan VIII)
CHAMPS ÉLYSÉE / ÉTOILE / PALAIS DES CONGRÈS (Plan II)
J
K
1
3
9
8e
Rome
Bd des Batignolles
R. de Constantinople
R. d'Edimbourg
Pl. de l'Europe
Europe
Rue de Madrid
R. de Liège
Liège
Rue d'Amsterdam
Rue de Londres
Rue de Rome
Rue de Vienne
R. du Rocher
Rue Portalis
GARE ST-LAZARE
St-Lazare
R. Saint Lazare
ST-AUGUSTIN
Pl. St-Augustin
St-Augustin
R. de la Pépinière
Bd Haussmann
Rue d'Astorg
Rue d'Anjou
Rue Pasquier
Rue de l'Arcade
R. du Havre
Havre Caumartin
Rue des Mathurins
Rue Tronchet
Akrame
Auber
Rue Auber
Rue Scribe
OPÉRA GARNIER
Chaussée d'Antin
Rue de la Chaussée d'Antin
Rue de Mogador
Rue de Provence
Boulevard
R. de Caumartin
Rue Malesherbes
R. de la Ville l'Évêque
Rue de Surène
R. d'Anjou
Pl. de la Madeleine
STE-MARIE MADELEINE
Madeleine
Bd de la Madeleine
Lucas Carton
Le Grd Restaurant-Jean-François Piège
Le Café de la Paix
R. de la Paix
Opéra
Pur' - Jean-François Rouquette
La Table de l'Espadon
Les Jardins de l'Espadon
Rue Cambon
Rue Royale
Le Baudelaire
R. B. d'Anglas
PLACE VENDÔME
R.D. Casanova
R. des Petits Champs
Av. de l'Opéra
La Fontaine Gaillon
Drouant
Kunitoraya
Pyramides
Av. Gabriel
L'Écrin
Brasserie d'Aumont
Concorde
Rue de Castiglione
Camélia
Sur Mesure par Thierry Marx
Carré des Feuillants
Rue St-Honoré
Jin
Le Meurice Alain Ducasse
R. des Pyramides
ST-ROCH
Tuileries
Pl. des Pyramides
Rue de Rivoli
Zen
OBÉLISQUE
PL. DE LA CONCORDE
0
200 m
JARDIN DES TUILERIES
Quai des Tuileries
SEINE
Pont de la Concorde
Palais Royal Musée du Louvre
Rue Moncey
Rue Blanche
Rue de Clichy
STE-TRINITÉ
Pl. d'Estienne d'Orves
Trinité
R. Jean Baptiste Pigalle
Rue Fontaine
Rue de Douai
Rue La Bruyère
La Petite Sirène de Copenhague
Les Canailles Pigalle

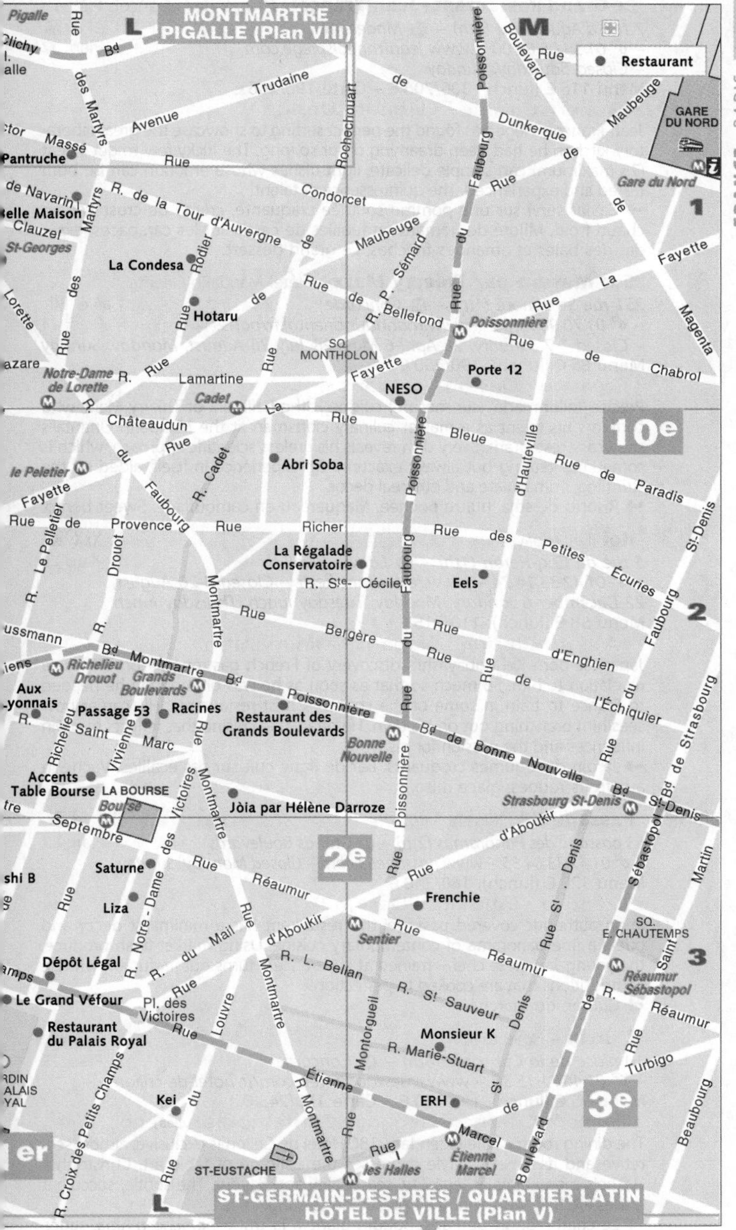
MONTMARTRE
PIGALLE (Plan VIII)
Restaurant
GARE DU NORD
Gare du Nord
Pantruche
Belle Maison
La Condesa
Hotaru
SQ. MONTHOLON
Porte 12
NESO
10e
Abri Soba
La Régalade Conservatoire
Eels
Aux Lyonnais
Passage 53
Racines
Restaurant des Grands Boulevards
Accents Table Bourse
LA BOURSE
Jòia par Hélène Darroze
2e
Saturne
Liza
Frenchie
SQ. E. CHAUTEMPS
Dépôt Légal
Le Grand Véfour
Restaurant du Palais Royal
Monsieur K
ERH
Kei
3e
ST-EUSTACHE
Pigalle
Notre-Dame de Lorette
Cadet
Poissonnière
le Peletier
Richelieu Drouot
Grands Boulevards
Bonne Nouvelle
Strasbourg St-Denis
Bourse
Sentier
Réaumur Sébastopol
Étienne Marcel
les Halles
Bd de Bonne Nouvelle
Bd Poissonnière
Bd Montmartre
Bd St-Denis
Bd de Strasbourg
Bd Sébastopol
Rue La Fayette
Rue de Dunkerque
Rue de Maubeuge
Rue de Chabrol
Rue de Paradis
Rue des Petites Écuries
Rue d'Enghien
Rue de l'Échiquier
Rue du Faubourg Poissonnière
Rue du Faubourg Montmartre
Rue Réaumur
Rue d'Aboukir
Rue Montmartre
Rue Étienne Marcel
Rue Turbigo
Rue Montorgueil
Rue du Louvre
Rue St-Denis
Boulevard de Magenta
ST-GERMAIN-DES-PRÉS / QUARTIER LATIN
HÔTEL DE VILLE (Plan V)

✿✿ **Le Grand Restaurant - Jean-François Piège** (Jean-François Piège)
7 rue d'Aguesseau (8th) – Ⓜ Madeleine – ✆ 01 53 05 00 00 – www.jeanfrancoispiege.com – Closed Saturday, Sunday
Plan: J2
Menu 116 € (lunch), 306/706 € – Carte 196/266 €
• Modern Cuisine • Elegant • Design •

Jean-François Piège has found the perfect setting to showcase the great laboratory kitchen he had been dreaming of for so long. The lucky few to get a seat (25 maximum) can sample delicate, light dishes whose emotion can be both tasted and experienced. The quintessence of talent!

➜ Caviar servi sur une pomme soufflée craquante, crème de crustacés en chaud-froid. Mijoté de homard en feuilles de cassis sur les carapaces, exsudat des baies et amandes fraîches. Le grand dessert.

✿✿ **Sur Mesure par Thierry Marx** – Hôtel Mandarin Oriental
251 rue St-Honoré (1th) – Ⓜ Concorde – ✆ 01 70 98 71 25 – www.mandarinoriental.fr/paris – Closed 1-7 January, 28 April-6 May, 28 July-26 August, Monday, Sunday
Plan: J3
Menu 85 € (lunch), 190/250 €
• Creative • Design • Elegant •

Precise 'tailor-made' (sur mesure) cuisine is the hallmark of Thierry Marx, who confirms his talent as a master culinary craftsman at the Mandarin Oriental's showcase restaurant. Every dish reveals his tireless scientific approach, which is sometimes teasing but always exacting. An experience in itself, aided by the stunning, immaculate and ethereal decor.

➜ Risotto de soja, huître pochée. Maquereau en camouflage. Sweet bento.

✿✿ **Kei** (Kei Kobayashi)
5 rue du Coq-Heron (1th) – Ⓜ Louvre Rivoli – ✆ 01 42 33 14 74 – www.restaurant-kei.fr – Closed 4-26 August, 22 December-6 January, Monday, Tuesday lunch, Thursday lunch
Plan: L3
Menu 58 € (lunch), 110/215 €
• Modern Cuisine • Elegant • Minimalist •

Japanese-born Kei Kobayashi's discovery of French gastronomy on TV was a revelation to him. So much so that as soon as he was old enough he headed to France to train in some of the country's best restaurants. His career now sees him branching out on his own. He offers fine cuisine that reflects his twin influences and the passion for his work.

➜ Jardin de légumes croquants. Bar de ligne cuit sur ses écailles. Vacherin aux fruits rouges, glace miso.

✿✿ **Passage 53** (Shinichi Sato)
53 passage des Panoramas (2th) – Ⓜ Grands Boulevards – ✆ 01 42 33 04 35 – www.passage53.com – Closed Monday, Sunday
Plan: L2
Menu 120 € (lunch), 180/240 €
• Creative • Intimate • Design •

In an authentic covered passage, this restaurant has a minimalist decor and offers a fine panorama of contemporary cuisine. Using market-fresh produce, the young Japanese chef – trained at L'Astrance – turns out irrefutably precise compositions that are cooked to perfection.

➜ Cuisine du marché.

✿ **L'Écrin** – Hôtel Crillon
10 place de la Concorde (8th) – Ⓜ Concorde – ✆ 01 44 71 15 30 – www.rosewoodhotels.com/fr/hotel-de-crillon
Plan: J3
Menu 95 € (lunch), 195/260 € – Carte 150/245 €
• Modern Cuisine • Elegant • Contemporary Décor •

The dining room of the legendary, 18C Hôtel de Crillon is exclusive, almost secretive and its timeless style expresses the epitome of table art. Christopher Hache's menu aims at legibility, seasonality and flavour. The subtle, succulent dishes are fully worthy of their prestigious setting.

➜ Le champignon de Paris. Boudin blanc à la truffe blanche d'Alba, sauce champagne. Fleur de lait, glace au miel et pollen.

Les Jardins de l'Espadon – Hôtel Ritz

15 place Vendome (1th) – Ⓜ Opéra – ✆ 01 43 16 33 74 Plan: **K3**
– www.ritzparis.com – Closed Monday dinner, Tuesday dinner, Wednesday dinner, Thursday dinner, Friday dinner, Saturday, Sunday
Menu 148 €

• Modern Cuisine • Romantic •

The Ritz's restaurant for gourmet lunchtimes. In this retractable conservatory that is lined with greenery and entered via a flower-decked, gilt-edged gallery, you can sample Nicolas Sale's appealing dishes: concise menu, inventive cuisine aligned with seasonal produce, flawless service... A success.

➔ Cannelloni de langoustine, chou pointu et sauce au vin de Meursault. Merlan de ligne et crème de charlotte à la grenobloise. Chocolat de Madagascar, textures de meringue et sauce chocolat frappé.

Lucas Carton (Julien Dumas)

9 place de la Madeleine (8th) – Ⓜ Madeleine – ✆ 01 42 65 22 90 Plan: **J2**
– www.lucascarton.com – Closed 27 July-21 August, Monday, Sunday
Menu 89/175 € – Carte 140/230 €

• Modern Cuisine • Historic • Chic •

The story of the Lucas Carton, the iconic name on Place de la Madeleine, continues. Youthful chef, Julien Dumas, has no equal for bringing out the best of fine produce. The vegetables from small producers and his marriage of acidic and bitter flavours are particularly noteworthy. Well-balanced dishes, rich in Mediterranean scents.

➔ Chou-fleur croustillant. Sarrasin et merlan croustillant. Chocolat et avocat.

Le Baudelaire – Hôtel Le Burgundy

6-8 rue Duphot (1th) – Ⓜ Madeleine – ✆ 01 71 19 49 11 Plan: **J3**
– www.leburgundy.com – Closed 22-30 December, Saturday lunch, Sunday
Menu 58 € (lunch), 110/150 € – Carte 110/134 €

• Modern Cuisine • Elegant •

Diners will appreciate the classic subdued atmosphere of this restaurant. Chef Guillaume Goupil (who worked under Stéphanie Le Quellec at the Prince de Galles) puts together light and modern dishes, taking evident delight in putting a spin on tradition. "Tea Time", with its lovely home-made pastries, proves popular in the afternoon.

➔ Langoustines rôties, ravioles d'herbes potagères et bisque à la cardamome verte. Ris de veau rôti, chapelure aux câpres, blettes glacées et girolles. Chocolat macaé, meringue cacao.

Carré des Feuillants (Alain Dutournier)

14 rue de Castiglione (1th) – Ⓜ Tuileries Plan: **K3**
– ✆ 01 42 86 82 82 – www.carredesfeuillants.fr – Closed Saturday, Sunday
Menu 68 € (lunch)/220 € – Carte 131/154 €

• Modern Cuisine • Elegant •

Elegant and minimalist contemporary restaurant on the site of the old Feuillants convent. Modern menu with strong Gascony influences. Superb wines and Armagnacs.

➔ Langoustines marinées, citron caviar, fleurette de légumes coraillée et noisettes grillées. Poularde "Belle Aurore", truffe fraîche, foie gras et ris de veau. Fraises de plein champ et rhubarbe, feuilleté gaufré et goyave.

Pur' - Jean-François Rouquette – Hôtel Park Hyatt Paris-Vendôme

5 rue de la Paix (2th) – Ⓜ Opéra – ✆ 01 58 71 10 60
– www.paris-restaurant-pur.fr – Closed 3-31 August, Monday lunch, Tuesday lunch, Wednesday lunch, Thursday lunch, Friday lunch, Saturday lunch, Sunday lunch Plan: **K3**
Menu 145/185 € – Carte 145/250 €

• Creative • Elegant •

Enjoy a sense of pure enjoyment as you dine in this restaurant. The highly elegant contemporary decor and creative dishes are carefully conjured by the chef using the finest ingredients. Attractive, delicious and refined.

➔ Ormeaux dorés au beurre d'algue, artichaut poivrade, vadouvan, tobiko. Turbot doucement étuvé, jus beurré de moules, huile de fleurs. Fine feuille de chocolat "crunchy", parfait glacé au riz, sauce cacao au vinaigre sakura.

Restaurant du Palais Royal

Galerie de Valois (1th) – Ⓜ Palais Royal Plan: **L3**
– ✆ 01 40 20 00 27 – www.restaurantdupalaisroyal.com – Closed 17 February-4 March, Monday, Sunday
Menu 55 € (lunch)/152 € – Carte 104/166 €

• Creative • Elegant •

Magnificently located beneath the arcades of the Palais Royal, this elegant restaurant is now the playground of young chef Philip Chronopoulos, formerly of the Atelier Etoile de Joël Robuchon. Philip concocts creative, striking meals, such as flash-fried scampi with girolle mushrooms and fresh almonds.

➜ Poulpe au piment fumé, pommes grenaille caramélisées. Cabillaud confit à l'huile d'argan, citron rôti et pousses d'épinard. Citron meringué, crémeux à la noix de coco.

Accents Table Bourse

24 rue Feydeau (2th) – Ⓜ Bourse – ✆ 01 40 39 92 88 Plan: **L2**
– www.accents-restaurant.com – Closed 1-31 July, Monday, Sunday
Menu 39 € (lunch), 62/73 € – Carte 43/62 €

• Modern Cuisine • Design • Contemporary Décor •

This pleasant place close to Bourse, run by a Japanese pastry chef, combines classic recipes and more cutting-edge creations. The flavours are pleasant, the preparations are precise, and the lièvre à la royale (hare – in season) is excellent. A delicious white chocolate cream flavoured with green tea is the icing on the cake of this impeccable experience. Very friendly, professional service.

➜ Cuisine du marché.

Akrame (Akrame Benallal)

7 rue Tronchet (8th) – Ⓜ Madeleine – ✆ 01 40 67 11 16 Plan: **J2**
– www.akrame.com – Closed 19-31 August, 24-30 December, Saturday, Sunday
Menu 65 € (lunch), 130/160 €

• Creative • Design •

Akrame Benallal now dons his chef's hat in this restaurant tucked away behind a heavy porte cochère (coach gateway). With a single, well put-together set menu, he unleashes great inventiveness to capitalise on excellent quality ingredients. The dishes are meticulously prepared. Needless to say, it's a hit!

➜ Cuisine du marché.

ERH

11 rue Tiquetonne (2th) – Ⓜ Étienne Marcel Plan: **M3**
– ✆ 01 45 08 49 37 – www.restaurant-erh.com – Closed 5-18 August, Monday, Sunday
Menu 35 € (lunch), 85/120 €

• Modern Cuisine • Elegant • Design •

The initials E, R and H stand for water, rice and man in French: a mysterious name for this unusual place on the same premises as a sake shop and a whisky bar. Japanese chef Keita Kitamura creates market-fresh French cuisine with a predilection for vegetables and fish. Character, flavours: an abundance of talent.

➜ Cuisine du marché.

Saturne (Sven Chartier)

17 rue Notre-Dame-des-Victoires (2th) – Ⓜ Bourse Plan: **L3**
– ✆ 01 42 60 31 90 – www.saturne-paris.fr – Closed 22 December-7 January, Saturday, Sunday
Menu 50 € (lunch)/90 €

• Creative • Trendy •

Saturn, god of agriculture, and, in French, an anagram of "natures". The credo of the chef, Sven Chartier, is to use great ingredients in emphatically creative cuisine, to sample in the form of a single set menu. The decor is Scandinavian (pale wood furniture, polished concrete). Yes, trendy and delicious can go hand in hand! Lunch set menu, with a choice of dishes.

➜ Foie gras grillé au barbecue et galette de courges. Poularde grillée, safran et feuille de figuier. Lait d'amande, fruits rouges et géranium.

Jin (Takuya Watanabe)

6 rue de la Sourdière (1th) – Ⓜ Tuileries – ✆ 01 42 61 60 71 Plan: **K3**
– Closed 5-23 August, 23 December-7 January, Monday, Sunday
Menu 95 € (lunch), 145/195 €
• Japanese • Elegant • Design •

A new showcase for Japanese cuisine, right in the heart of Paris! Jin is first and foremost about the know-how of Takuya Watanabe, the chef, who comes from Sapporo. Before your eyes, he creates delicious sushi and sashimi, using fish sourced from Brittany, Oléron and Spain. The whole menu is a treat.

➜ Cuisine du marché.

Sushi B

5 rue Rameau (2th) – Ⓜ Bourse – ✆ 01 40 26 52 87 Plan: **L3**
– www.sushi-b-fr.com – Closed 1-8 January, 1-9 May, 1-19 August, Monday, Tuesday
Menu 58 € (lunch), 130/160 €
• Japanese • Minimalist •

It is enjoyable to linger in this tiny restaurant (with just seven places) on the edge of the pleasant Square Louvois for its sleek, soothing interior, of course... but particularly to witness for oneself the chef's great talent. Like an excellent artisan, he uses only the freshest top-notch ingredients, which he handles with surgical precision.

➜ Cuisine du marché.

La Condesa (Indra Carrillo)

17 rue Rodier (9th) – Ⓜ Notre-Dame de Lorette Plan: **L1**
– ✆ 01 53 20 94 90 – www.lacondesa-paris.com – Closed 4 August-5 September, 23 December-3 January, Monday, Tuesday lunch, Wednesday lunch, Thursday lunch, Friday lunch, Saturday lunch, Sunday
Menu 38 € (lunch)/78 €
• Creative • Cosy • Chic •

Condesa is a district of Mexico City as well as the restaurant of Indra Carillo, who came from Mexico to study at the Paul Bocuse institute. He composes a high-flying culinary score with disconcerting ease, featuring a variety of cultures and influences. An excellent restaurant, further enhanced by the professional attentive personnel.

➜ Cuisine du marché.

Frenchie (Grégory Marchand)

5 rue du Nil (2th) – Ⓜ Sentier – ✆ 01 40 39 96 19 Plan: **M3**
– www.frenchie-restaurant.com – Closed 3-21 August, 22 December-2 January, Monday lunch, Tuesday lunch, Wednesday lunch, Saturday, Sunday
Menu 48 € (lunch)/78 €
• Modern Cuisine • Friendly • Trendy •

Young chef Grégory Marchand earned his stripes at several great restaurants in the UK and US, before setting up shop in the Sentier neighbourhood. His small restaurant is always packed, but he has his delicious contemporary cooking to "blame" for that!

➜ Asperges biscornues, jaune d'œuf fumé, crème de parmesan et orge soufflé. Poulette, polenta de maïs frais et tomate marinée à la marjolaine. Citron meyer, romarin et olives de Kalamata.

Racines (Simone Tondo)

8 passage des Panoramas (2th) – Ⓜ Grands Boulevards Plan: **L2**
– ✆ 01 40 13 06 41 – www.racinesparis.com – Closed 3-30 August, Saturday, Sunday
Carte 40/60 €
• Italian • Bistro •

After several years at the head of Roseval, in the 20th *arrondissement*, Simone Tondo, a young Sardinian chef, took over this bistro, which he had the judicious idea to turn into an old-fashioned osteria. The daily specials board offers a choice of Italian dishes made with the best ingredients of the moment and showcased with a skilful blend of simplicity and subtlety. Everything is fragrant and pleasant. The antithesis of over-complicated and convoluted cooking.

➜ Vitello tonnato. Tagliolini à la saucisse au fenouil. Tiramisu.

Restaurant des Grands Boulevards – Hôtel des Grands Boulevards

17 boulevard Poissonnière (2th) – Ⓜ Grands Boulevards – ✆ 01 85 73 33 32 – www.grandsboulevardshotel.com

Plan: **L2**

Menu 27 € (lunch) – Carte 35/60 €

• Italian • Contemporary Décor • Trendy •

Beneath the hotel's central glass roof, the decoration is modern and trendy, with a "summer on the Riviera" feel... and Italian flavours, under the direction of chef Giovanni Passerini. Just one example, his interpretation of a popular Tuscan dish – *gnudi* with herbs and parmesan – is a lesson in simplicity and delicacy. Efficient and friendly service.

Abri Soba

10 rue Saulnier (9th) – Ⓜ Cadet – ✆ 01 45 23 51 68 – Closed 12 August-1 September, Monday, Sunday lunch

Plan: **L2**

Menu 38 € – Carte 25/40 €

• Japanese • Bistro •

You may have heard of soba, Japanese pasta made with buckwheat, the reputation of which is currently snowballing around the planet. The chef of this restaurant has made soba his house speciality and serves it lunch and evening in an amazing variety of preparations: hot, cold, in stock or with finely sliced duck. Simply flavoursome – get out your chopsticks!

Les Canailles Pigalle

25 rue La Bruyère (9th) – Ⓜ St-Georges – ✆ 01 48 74 10 48 – www.restaurantlescanailles.fr – Closed 1-30 August, Saturday, Sunday

Plan: **K1**

Menu 36 € – Carte 54/63 €

• Modern Cuisine • Bistro • Friendly •

This pleasant restaurant was created in 2012 by two Bretons with impressive culinary backgrounds. They slip into the bistronomy (gastro bistro), serving bistro and seasonal dishes. Specialities: ox tongue carpaccio and sauce ravigote, and rum baba with vanilla whipped cream... Tuck in!

Dépôt Légal

6 rue des Petits-Champs (2th) – Ⓜ Bourse – ✆ 01 42 61 67 07 – www.depotlegalparis.com – Closed Sunday dinner

Plan: **L3**

Carte 30/45 €

• Modern Cuisine • Trendy • Contemporary Décor •

This atypical restaurant, run by Christophe Adam, a high-profile pastry chef with an impeccable CV (Le Gavroche in London, Hôtel de Crillon and Fauchon in Paris), proposes sweets and plates to share, from breakfast to dinner. At the entrance, a large glass counter presents the pastries, including numerous éclairs (taste the salted butter caramel one!). No lunch bookings taken, brunch on Sundays.

Le Pantruche

3 rue Victor-Massé (9th) – Ⓜ Pigalle – ✆ 01 48 78 55 60 – Closed 12-31 August, Saturday, Sunday

Plan: **L1**

Menu 36 € – Carte 39/50 €

• Modern Cuisine • Bistro •

'Pantruche' is slang for Paris... an apt name for this bistro with its chic retro decor, which happily cultivates a 1940s-1950s atmosphere. As for the food, the chef and his small team put together lovely seasonal dishes in keeping with current culinary trends.

Zen

8 rue de l'Échelle (1th) – Ⓜ Palais Royal – ✆ 01 42 61 93 99 – www.restaurantzenparis.fr

Plan: **K3**

Menu 35/55 € – Carte 25/58 €

• Japanese • Minimalist •

This enticing restaurant combines a refreshing contemporary interior design and authentic Japanese cooking. The menu is well-rounded and faithful to the classic sushi, grilled dishes and tempura, with house specialities of gyoza and chirashi. Ideal for a quick lunch or a relaxing 'zen' dinner.

Brasserie d'Aumont - Hôtel Crillon

10 place de la Concorde (8th) – Ⓜ Concorde Plan: **J3**
– ✆ 01 44 71 15 15 – www.rosewoodhotels.com/fr/hotel-de-crillon
Carte 65/120 €

• Modern Cuisine • Brasserie • Luxury •

The Brasserie d'Aumont sports a handsome Art deco interior, whose two connecting dining rooms are flanked by a shellfish counter with bar seats. Simply-laid tables and top-quality brasserie classics with a modern touch. Concise wine list and fine choice by the glass. Pleasant terrace. Smart and succulent.

Le Café de la Paix - Hôtel Intercontinental Le Grand

12 Boulevard des Capucines (9th) – Ⓜ Opéra
– ✆ 01 40 07 32 32 – www.paris.intercontinental.com Plan: **K2**
Menu 55 € – Carte 90/110 €

• Classic Cuisine • Elegant • Chic •

Frescoes, gilded wainscotting and furniture inspired by the Napoleon-III style: this luxurious, legendary restaurant, open from 7am to midnight, remains the haunt of well-heeled Parisians. It stands to reason: the pâté en croûte is wonderful, and it is a joy to delve into the layers of the vanilla mille-feuille. Fine brasserie cuisine.

Camélia - Hôtel Mandarin Oriental

251 rue St-Honoré (1th) – Ⓜ Concorde Plan: **J3**
– ✆ 01 70 98 74 00 – www.mandarinoriental.fr/paris
Menu 65 € (lunch)/98 € – Carte 67/113 €

• Modern Cuisine • Elegant • Design •

Keep it simple, concentrate on the flavour of the top-notch ingredients, draw inspiration from France's gastronomical classics and enhance them with Asian touches. This is the approach of Thierry Marx at Camélia; an elegant, soothing, zen place. An unequivocal success.

Drouant

16 place Gaillon (2th) – Ⓜ Quatre Septembre Plan: **K3**
– ✆ 01 42 65 15 16 – www.drouant.com
Menu 45 € (lunch) – Carte 45/83 €

• Traditional Cuisine • Elegant •

The Goncourt Prize has been awarded here since 1914. Under the Gardinier family, who recently took over the establishment, traditional dishes are getting a modern reboot. New menu, new chef: this legendary place is alive and well.

La Fontaine Gaillon

place Gaillon (2th) – Ⓜ Quatre Septembre Plan: **K2-3**
– ✆ 01 47 42 63 22 – Closed Saturday, Sunday
Menu 55 € (lunch) – Carte 80/120 €

• Seafood • Elegant •

Beautiful 17C townhouse supervised by Gérard Depardieu with a hushed setting and terrace around a fountain. Spotlight on seafood, accompanied by a pleasant selection of wines.

Our inspectors make regular and anonymous visits to restaurants to gauge the quality of products and services offered to an ordinary customer, and they settle their own bill. Our readers' comments are also a valuable source of information, which we can follow up with a visit of our own.

Porte 12

12 rue des Messagerie (10th) – Ⓜ Poissonnière Plan: **M1**
– ✆ 01 42 46 22 64 – www.porte12.com – Closed Monday, Tuesday lunch, Wednesday lunch, Thursday lunch, Friday lunch, Saturday lunch, Sunday
Menu 68/120 €

• Modern Cuisine • Design • Elegant •

Young French chef Vincent Crépel, who hails from the Basque Country, is developing a striking signature cuisine. Resolutely contemporary, it is inspired by his travels and his various professional experiences (notably in Asia). Verdict: his daring combinations work every time. A great place!

Aux Lyonnais

32 rue St-Marc (2th) – Ⓜ Richelieu Drouot Plan: **L2**
– ✆ 01 42 96 65 04 – www.auxlyonnais.com – Closed 28 July-27 August, 23 December-2 January, Monday, Saturday lunch, Sunday
Menu 34 € (lunch)/35 € – Carte 44/60 €

• Lyonnaise • Bistro • Vintage •

This bistro founded in 1890 has a delightfully retro decor, and serves delicious cuisine that explores the city's gastronomy: tablier de sapeur (crumbed tripe), pike quenelles with sauce Nantua, veal liver with persillade, and floating islands with pink pralines.

Belle Maison

4 rue de Navarin (9th) – Ⓜ Saint-Georges – ✆ 01 42 81 11 00 Plan: **L1**
– www.restaurant-bellemaison.com – Closed Monday, Sunday
Carte 41/58 €

• Seafood • Bistro • Trendy •

The three associates of Pantruche and Caillebotte are back behind the wheel in this Belle Maison, named after a beach on the Island of Yeu where they used to spend their holidays. The chef rustles up seafood-inspired dishes with disconcerting expertise: crab ravioles and gazpacho; line caught croaker, peas and girolles – a tantalising experience awaits!

Eels

27 rue d'Hauteville (10th) – Ⓜ Bonne Nouvelle Plan: **M2**
– ✆ 01 42 28 80 20 – www.restaurant-eels.com – Closed 3-28 August, 22 December-1 January, Monday, Sunday
Menu 29 € (lunch)/58 € – Carte 50/58 €

• Modern Cuisine • Trendy • Bistro •

At Eels, the dishes flirt with "bistronomie", and some of them focus on eel (the clue is in the name). The young chef, Adrien Ferrand, already has considerable experience under his belt (six years for William Ledeuil, first at Ze Kitchen Galerie, then KGB). And now he has a place of his own. A success!

Hotaru

18 rue Rodier (9th) – Ⓜ Notre-Dame de Lorette Plan: **L1**
– ✆ 01 48 78 33 74 – Closed Monday, Sunday
Menu 24 € (lunch) – Carte 26/53 €

• Japanese • Rustic • Simple •

A welcoming Japanese restaurant with a young chef who produces traditional, family cuisine with an emphasis on fish. Enjoy sushi, maki and sashimi, as well as a selection of cooked and fried dishes.

Jòia par Hélène Darroze

39 rue des Jeûneurs (2th) – Ⓜ Grands Boulevards Plan: **L2**
– ✆ 01 40 20 06 06 – www.joiahelenedarroze.com
Menu 29 € (lunch) – Carte 40/67 €

• Cuisine from South West France • Contemporary Décor •

Hélène Darroze's brand new venture is all about conviviality centred on dishes drawn from her memory of her native South-West France, with nods to the culinary traditions of the Basque Country, Landes and Béarn. Bold flavours, quality ingredients: a pleasant tribute to the family cuisine of the Darroze home, which her father concocted in Villeneuve de Marsan. The power of nostalgia!

ǁO **Kunitoraya** X ⇔ AC

5 rue Villedo (1th) – Ⓜ Pyramides – ☎ 01 47 03 07 74 Plan: **K3**
– www.kunitoraya.com – Closed 5-19 August, 23 December-2 January, Monday, Sunday dinner
Menu 32 € (lunch)/100 € – Carte 50/100 €
• Japanese • Vintage • Minimalist •

With its old zinc counter, mirrors and Métro-style tiling, Kunitoraya has the feel of a late-night Parisian restaurant from the early 1900s. Refined Japanese cuisine is based around "udon", a thick homemade noodle prepared with wholemeal flour imported from Japan.

ǁO **Liza** X AC

14 rue de la Banque (2th) – Ⓜ Bourse Plan: **L3**
– ☎ 01 55 35 00 66 – www.restaurant-liza.com – Closed Sunday dinner
Menu 38/48 € – Carte 40/50 €
• Lebanese • Trendy •

Originally from Beirut, Liza Asseily gives pride of place to her country's cuisine. In a contemporary interior dotted with Middle Eastern touches, opt for the shish taouk or mechoui kafta (lamb, hummus and tomato preserves). Dishes are meticulously prepared using fresh ingredients. A real treat!

ǁO **Monsieur K** X

10 rue Marie-Stuart (2th) – Ⓜ Sentier Plan: **M3**
– ☎ 01 42 36 01 09 – www.kapunkaparis.com – Closed Sunday
Menu 27 € (lunch)/39 € – Carte 30/50 €
• Thai • Friendly •

The chef is a true Asia enthusiast. He has travelled the length and breadth of Thailand to sample its many cuisines and to reproduce a replica of the best dishes. He is a perfectionist fighting for the good cause, and makes a mean Pad Thai.

ǁO **La Petite Sirène de Copenhague** X

47 rue Notre-Dame de Lorette (9th) – Ⓜ St-Georges Plan: **K1**
– ☎ 01 45 26 66 66 – Closed 23 February-11 March, 4-31 August, 21 December-5 January, Monday, Saturday lunch, Sunday
Menu 38 € (lunch)/44 € – Carte 50/82 €
• Danish • Bistro •

The Danish flag flying above the entrance provides a strong clue to the gourmet offerings inside. There is a daily menu chalked up on a slate board, as well as a more expensive à la carte, from which guests can feast on Danish specialities such as herrings.

ǁO **La Régalade Conservatoire** – Hôtel de Nell X ⇔ ♿ AC

7-9 rue du Conservatoire (9th) – Ⓜ Bonne Nouvelle Plan: **M2**
– ☎ 01 44 83 83 60 – www.charmandmore.com
Menu 39 €
• Modern Cuisine • Trendy • Friendly •

After his Régalades in the 1st arrondissements, Bruno Doucet has opened a third, this time close to Grands Boulevards inside the luxurious Hôtel de Nell. Here bistro-style goes chic, and the chef's cooking is as well-executed, generous and tasty as ever. Roll on the new venture!

TOUR EIFFEL – INVALIDES PLAN IV

✿✿✿ **Arpège** (Alain Passard) XXX ⇔ AC

84 rue de Varenne (7th) – Ⓜ Varenne Plan: **Q2**
– ☎ 01 47 05 09 06 – www.alain-passard.com – Closed Saturday, Sunday
Menu 175 € (lunch) – Carte 243/327 €
• Creative • Elegant •

Precious woods and a Lalique crystal decor provide the backdrop for the dazzling, vegetable-inspired cuisine of this culinary genius. He creates his astonishing dishes from organic produce grown in his three vegetable gardens!

→ Fines ravioles potagères multicolores, consommé éphémère. Aiguillettes de homard bleu au vin de Côtes-du-Jura. Millefeuille croustillant aux fruits de nos vergers.

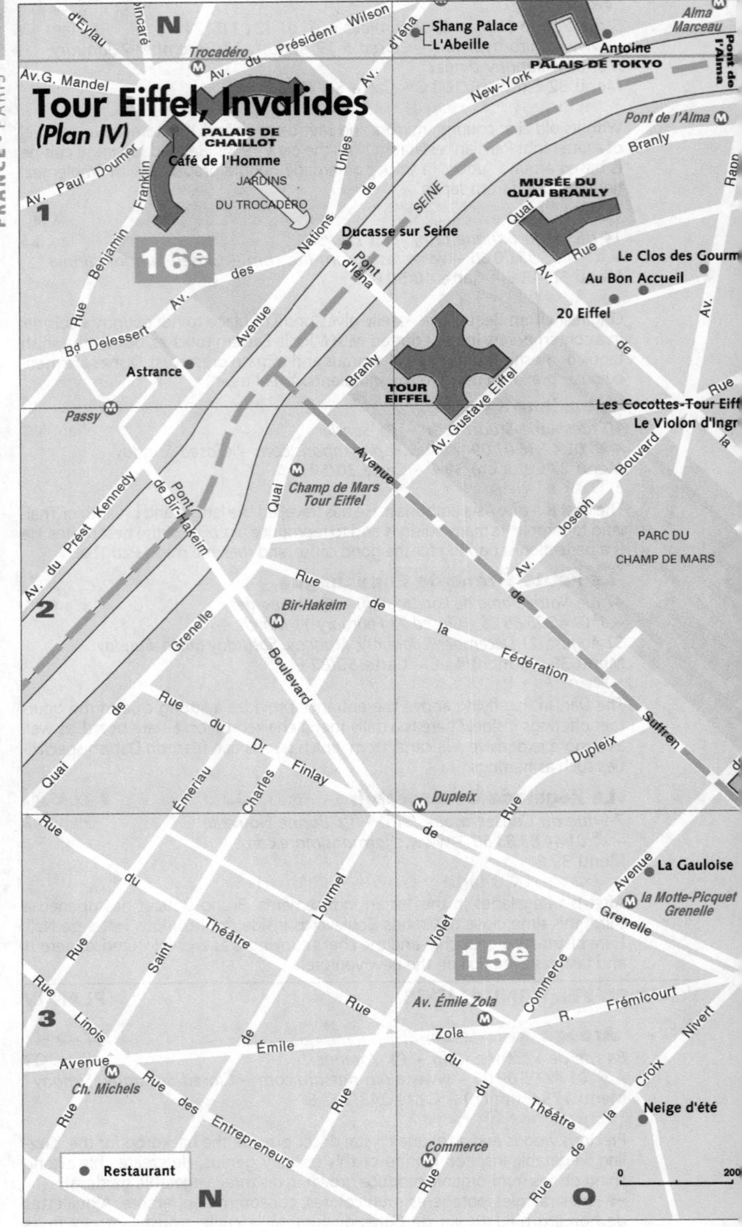
Tour Eiffel, Invalides
(Plan IV)
N
1
2
3
16e
15e
Shang Palace
L'Abeille
Antoine
PALAIS DE TOKYO
PALAIS DE CHAILLOT
Café de l'Homme
JARDINS DU TROCADÉRO
MUSÉE DU QUAI BRANLY
Ducasse sur Seine
Le Clos des Gourm
Au Bon Accueil
20 Eiffel
Astrance
TOUR EIFFEL
Les Cocottes-Tour Eiff
Le Violon d'Ingr
PARC DU CHAMP DE MARS
La Gauloise
Neige d'été
Trocadéro
Alma Marceau
Pont de l'Alma
Passy
Champ de Mars Tour Eiffel
Bir-Hakeim
Dupleix
la Motte-Picquet Grenelle
Av. Émile Zola
Commerce
Ch. Michels
SEINE
Restaurant
N
O
0
200

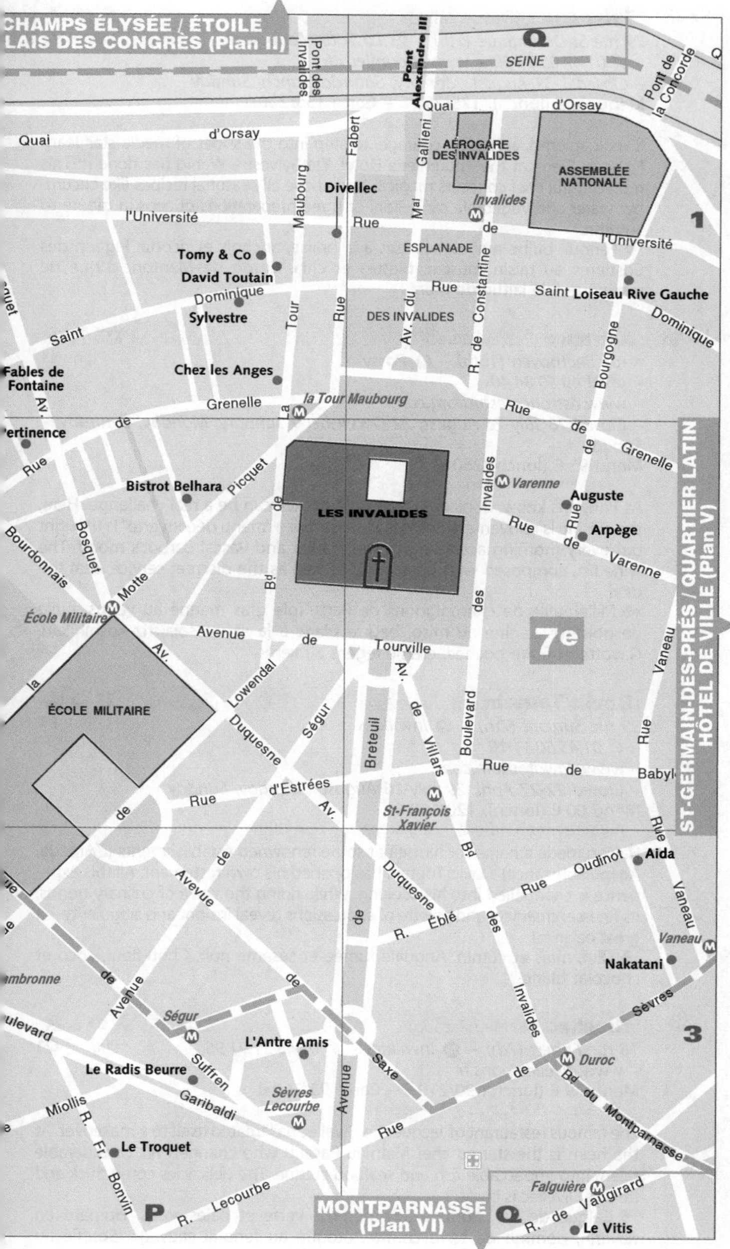
CHAMPS ÉLYSÉE / ÉTOILE
LAIS DES CONGRÈS (Plan II)
SEINE
Pont des Invalides
Pont Alexandre III
Pont de la Concorde
Quai d'Orsay
AÉROGARE DES INVALIDES
ASSEMBLÉE NATIONALE
Divellec
Invalides
Rue de l'Université
ESPLANADE DES INVALIDES
Tomy & Co
David Toutain
Sylvestre
Rue Saint Dominique
Loiseau Rive Gauche
Chez les Anges
Fables de Fontaine
la Tour Maubourg
Rue de Grenelle
Pertinence
Bistrot Belhara
LES INVALIDES
Varenne
Auguste
Arpège
Rue de Varenne
École Militaire
ÉCOLE MILITAIRE
Avenue de Tourville
7e
ST-GERMAIN-DES-PRÉS / QUARTIER LATIN HÔTEL DE VILLE (Plan V)
Rue de Babylone
St-François Xavier
Rue d'Estrées
Aida
Rue Oudinot
R. Éblé
Vaneau
Nakatani
Cambronne
Ségur
L'Antre Amis
Duroc
Le Radis Beurre
Sèvres Lecourbe
Le Troquet
Bd du Montparnasse
MONTPARNASSE (Plan VI)
Falguière
R. de Vaugirard
Le Vitis
R. Lecourbe

✿✿ **Sylvestre** (Sylvestre Wahid) XXX ✿ ⊖ AC

79 rue St-Dominique (7th) – Ⓜ La Tour Maubourg Plan: **P1**
– ✆ 01 47 05 79 00 – www.thoumieux.fr
– Closed 1-31 August, Monday, Saturday lunch, Sunday
Menu 98 € (lunch), 175/250 € – Carte 155/200 €
• Modern Cuisine • Elegant •

It took aplomb, and even courage, to step into the shoes of media star Jean-François Piège at the Thoumieux Hotel. Yet Sylvestre Wahid has done it! This multicultural chef concocts magical, and above all seasonal recipes like cucumber water and vegetable cannelloni or three preparations of ceps in tribute to autumn.

➜ Fenouil bulbe aux algues cuit à la braise, anchois et ricotta. Pigeon des Costières au raisin muscat, blettes et chia. Citron de Menton, coque de meringue à la laitue de mer.

✿✿ **Astrance** (Pascal Barbot) XXX ✿ AC

4 rue Beethoven (16th) – Ⓜ Passy Plan: **N1**
– ✆ 01 40 50 84 40
– www.astrancerestaurant.com
– Closed 26 July-26 August, 22 December-7 January, Monday, Saturday, Sunday
Menu 95 € (lunch)/250 €
• Creative • Minimalist • Elegant •

As Parisians know, booking a table at Astrance can be a real challenge! Here, the cuisine is reinvented every day: the surprise "menu découverte" is thought out every morning according to the market and Pascal Barbot's mood. The wine list, composed with great care, as well as the discreet service, seal the deal.

➜ Millefeuille de champignons de Paris, foie gras mariné au verjus, huile de noisette. Légine au miso, beurre blanc à la sauce soja, riz koshihikari. Gavotte et figue pochée, crème légère au xérès.

✿✿ **David Toutain** XX ⊖ AC

29 rue Surcouf (7th) – Ⓜ Invalides Plan: **P1**
– ✆ 01 45 50 11 10
– www.davidtoutain.com
– Closed 22-27 April, 29 July-16 August, Saturday, Sunday
Menu 60 € (lunch), 120/160 €
• Modern Cuisine • Design • Trendy •

Having made a name for himself at some renowned establishments (L'Arpège, Agapé Substance), David Toutain has opened his own restaurant. All this experience is channelled into his cooking. While riding the wave of culinary trends, its finesse, creativity and palette of expressions reveal insight and singularity – a great balance!

➜ Œuf, maïs et cumin. Anguille fumée et sésame noir. Chou-fleur, coco et chocolat blanc.

✿ **Divellec** (Mathieu Pacaud) XX ✿ ⊖ ♿ AC

18 rue Fabert (7th) – Ⓜ Invalides – ✆ 01 45 51 91 96 Plan: **P-Q1**
– www.divellec-paris.fr
Menu 49 € (lunch), 90/210 € – Carte 95/160 €
• Seafood • Chic • Elegant •

The famous restaurant of Jacques Le Divellec has treated itself to a makeover. At the helm is the starred chef Mathieu Pacaud who channels his considerable talent into impeccable fish and seafood cuisine. The delicacies come thick and fast. Le Divellec is back!

➜ Calque de bar, bonbons de pomme verte et baies roses. Homard en navarin, pomme de terre confite, étouffé au fenouil sauvage. Soufflé au chocolat grand cru.

Auguste (Gaël Orieux)

XX AC

54 rue de Bourgogne (7th) – Ⓜ Varenne Plan: **Q2**
– ✆ 01 45 51 61 09
– www.restaurantauguste.fr
– Closed Saturday, Sunday
Menu 39 € (lunch)/90 € – Carte 90/120 €
• Modern Cuisine • Elegant •

Intimate atmosphere, mirrors, white walls and pretty armchairs... Auguste is perfectly tailored to the cuisine of Gaël Orieux, a chef who is passionate about food and ingredients. His dishes? A quest for harmony and inventiveness, finely weaving together ingredients from land and sea. Affordable prices at lunch; they pull out all the stops at dinner.

➜ Huîtres creuses en gelée d'eau de mer, mousse raifort et poire comice. Ris de veau croustillant, cacahouètes caramélisées, girolles, abricot sec et vin jaune. Millefeuille parfumé à la fève tonka.

Loiseau rive Gauche

XX

5 rue de Bourgogne (7th) – Ⓜ Assemblée Nationale Plan: **Q1**
– ✆ 01 45 51 79 42
– www.bernard-loiseau.com
– Closed 4-27 August, Monday, Sunday
Menu 45 € (lunch), 82/105 €
• Creative • Elegant • Cosy •

A stone's throw from the Palais Bourbon, traditional cuisine that harks back (notably) to fine Burgundian roots. Vegetarians are also catered to here, thanks to the "Légumes en fête" set menu, devised by chef Maxime Laurenson. Wood panelling, Louis XV chairs and astonishing table design (no 20): the atmosphere feels resolutely luxurious.

➜ Cuisine du marché.

Nakatani (Shinsuke Nakatani)

XX AC

27 rue Pierre-Leroux (7th) – Ⓜ Vaneau Plan: **Q3**
– ✆ 01 47 34 94 14
– www.restaurant-nakatani.com
– Closed 1-12 August, Monday, Sunday
Menu 50 € (lunch), 105/145 €
• Modern Cuisine • Intimate • Romantic •

Japanese chef Shinsuke Nakatani (formerly at Hélène Darroze) is now standing on his own two feet. With a keen sense of seasoning, technique and the aesthetics of the dishes, he cooks fabulous French cuisine using seasonal ingredients. All this is served by discreet and efficient staff. Impeccable!

➜ Consommé de légumes. Bœuf Wagyu, girolles, pomme de terre de Noirmoutier, brocoletti, sarrasin et sauce au vin rouge. Biscuit vapeur aux courges, reine-claude et crème brûlée au thé.

Neige d'Été (Hideki Nishi)

XX

12 rue de l'Amiral-Roussin (15th) Plan: **O3**
– Ⓜ Avenue Émile Zola
– ✆ 01 42 73 66 66 – www.neigedete.fr
– Closed 4-26 August, Monday, Sunday
Menu 55 € (lunch)/130 €
• Modern Cuisine • Minimalist •

The name (meaning 'Summer Snow') is poetically Japanese, and that is no coincidence. This restaurant was opened in mid-2014 by a young Japanese chef, Hideki Nishi, who used to be at the George V. It also hints at the contrasts and minimalism that are the hallmarks of his work, which is always spot-on and full of counterpoints.

➜ Bretagne "vitrée", blinis au sarrasin. Poularde grillée au charbon de bois japonais. Crémeux chocolat au café.

Le Violon d'Ingres (Christian Constant)

135 rue St-Dominique (7th) – Ⓜ École Militaire – ✆ 01 45 55 15 05 – www.maisonconstant.com Plan: **O1**

Menu 49 € (lunch)/130 € – Carte 87/99 €

• Traditional Cuisine • Elegant •

Diners are fighting each other off for a spot at Christian Constant's restaurant! His recipes reveal the soul of an authentic cook, firmly in line with the finest tradition. Their execution shows off the know-how of a talented team. The interior decor was redone in 2013, which is an excuse to rediscover this place.

➜ Fine gelée d'araignée de mer, crémeux de tourteau à l'infusion d'herbes. Suprême de bar croustillant aux amandes, jus acidulé aux câpres et citron. Soufflé chaud au Grand Marnier.

Aida (Koji Aida)

1 rue Pierre-Leroux (7th) – Ⓜ Vaneau – ✆ 01 43 06 14 18 – www.aida-paris.net – Closed Monday, Tuesday lunch, Wednesday lunch, Thursday lunch, Friday lunch, Saturday lunch, Sunday lunch Plan: **Q3**

Menu 280 €

• Japanese • Elegant • Minimalist •

Be transported to the Land of the Rising Sun in this restaurant. It breathes authenticity and purity through its delicious Japanese cuisine full of finesse. The fish, presented alive and then prepared in front of you, couldn't be fresher. The art of simplicity and transparency at its best!

➜ Sashimi. Teppanyaki. Wagashi.

Pertinence (Kwen Liew et Ryunosuke Naito)

29 rue de l' Exposition (7th) – Ⓜ École Militaire – ✆ 01 45 55 20 96 – www.restaurantpertinence.com – Closed 28 July-12 September, Monday, Tuesday lunch, Sunday Plan: **P2**

Menu 45 € (lunch), 105/135 € – Carte 100/180 €

• Modern Cuisine • Design • Trendy •

This minimalist interior, depicted by light wood Knoll chairs, near the Champs Elysees is the fief of Japanese Ryu and Malaysian Kwen. Ryu carefully and expertly nurtures and coaxes market-fresh ingredients into succulent classical French dishes, brushing off the cobwebs of tradition on the way. We expect to hear much more from this quarter!

➜ Cuisine du marché.

Tomy & Co (Tomy Gousset)

22 rue Surcouf (7th) – Ⓜ Invalides – ✆ 01 45 51 46 93 – Closed Saturday, Sunday Plan: **P1**

Menu 48/80 €

• Modern Cuisine • Friendly • Bistro •

This establishment bears the hallmark of the unabashed talent of Tomy Gousset (ex-Meurice and Taillevent). Tomy plays a gourmet-bistro score whose modern notes reveal a deceptively simple melody. The establishment is determined to consume locally (organic veggies from Essonne). Booking would be a good idea!

➜ Tartelette de langue de bœuf, navets en pickles et sauce gribiche. Filet de canette Apicius, blettes et figues rôties, pommes dauphine. Tarte au chocolat à la fève tonka et glace praliné.

Au Bon Accueil

14 rue de Monttessuy (7th) – Ⓜ Alma Marceau – ✆ 01 47 05 46 11 – www.aubonaccueilparis.com – Closed 12-31 August, Saturday, Sunday Plan: **O1**

Menu 36/55 € – Carte 60/80 €

• Modern Cuisine • Bistro • Cosy •

In the shadow of the Eiffel Tower in a quiet street, this shy, but smart bistro serves appetising, market-fresh cuisine that mirror the seasons. Grilled squid, crushed potatoes and aioli; roast saddle and confit shoulder of lamb…

Chez les Anges

XX

54 boulevard de la Tour-Maubourg (7th) – Ⓜ La Tour Maubourg – ✆ 01 47 05 89 86 – www.chezlesanges.com – Closed 12-31 August, Saturday, Sunday Plan: **P1**

Menu 37/55 € – Carte 61/83 €

• Classic Cuisine • Elegant • Neighbourhood •

An elegant dining area for tasty, sincere cuisine that draws on both traditional and modern: langoustines, angel's hair and celeriac remoulade, or sole meunière and Bresse chicken. Accompanied by a fine wine and whisky list.

L'Antre Amis

X

9 rue Bouchut (15th) – Ⓜ Ségur – ✆ 01 45 67 15 65 – www.lantreamis.com – Closed 1-10 January, 1-31 August, Saturday, Sunday Plan: **P3**

Menu 35/45 € – Carte 48/60 €

• Modern Cuisine • Contemporary Décor •

The chef-patron at L'Antre Amis brings passion to his cooking. Using excellent produce sourced from Rungis Market (meat, fish, shellfish etc), he composes scrupulous dishes, precisely made and organised into a very short menu. To be accompanied by your choice from a fine wine list – around 150 varieties.

Le Clos des Gourmets

X

16 avenue Rapp (7th) – Ⓜ Alma Marceau – ✆ 01 45 51 75 61 – www.closdesgourmets.com – Closed 1-20 August, Monday, Sunday Plan: **O1**

Menu 30 € (lunch), 35/42 € – Carte 43/56 €

• Modern Cuisine • Trendy •

Sleek and welcoming modern bistro where the chef loves good food and cares enough to do it well. Asparagus crème brûlée, fennel slow cooked with mellow spices: the cuisine is honest and full of delicious flavours.

Les Cocottes - Tour Eiffel

X

135 rue St-Dominique (7th) – Ⓜ École Militaire – ✆ 01 45 50 10 28 – www.maisonconstant.com Plan: **O1**

Menu 28 € (lunch)/35 € – Carte 34/59 €

• Traditional Cuisine • Trendy •

The concept in this friendly eatery is based around bistro cuisine with a modern touch cooked in cast-iron casserole pots (cocottes), and includes popular dishes such as country paté, roast veal etc. No advance booking.

Le Radis Beurre

X

51 boulevard Garibaldi (15th) – Ⓜ Sèvres Lecourbe – ✆ 01 40 33 99 26 – www.restaurantleradisbeurre.com – Closed 1-21 August, 22 December-2 January, Saturday, Sunday Plan: **P3**

Menu 36 € – Carte 36/45 €

• Traditional Cuisine • Bistro •

It was in 2015 on Boulevard Garibaldi in Paris that chef Jérôme Bonnet found the perfect site for his restaurant. He prepares tasty, carefully created food that bears the hallmark of his southern upbringing. An example? Pig's trotters with duck foie gras and meat juices. You may even get to nibble on a few radishes with butter while you wait.

Le Troquet

X

21 rue François-Bonvin (15th) – Ⓜ Cambronne – ✆ 01 45 66 89 00 – www.restaurantletroquet.fr – Closed 5-26 August, Monday, Sunday Plan: **P3**

Menu 33 € (lunch), 35/41 €

• Traditional Cuisine • Bistro • Vintage •

A traditional bistro in all its splendour: authentic decor, moleskin banquettes, menu blackboards, mirrors, small tables that set a convivial mood etc. Diners come here as much for the atmosphere as the cooking. Delicious food, prepared with extremely fresh ingredients... and (often) the accent of South-West France.

20 Eiffel

20 rue de Monttessuy (7th) – Ⓜ Alma Marceau Plan: **O1**
– ✆ 01 47 05 14 20 – www.restaurant20eiffel.fr
– Closed 2-11 January, 5-16 May, 1-13 September, Monday, Sunday
Menu 33 € – Carte 49/55 €

• Traditional Cuisine • Classic Décor •

In a quiet street a stone's throw from the Eiffel Tower, this restaurant offers a understated interior full of light. On the menu, you can choose from a range of updated dishes, prepared by two chefs, all of which place the focus on flavour and taste. For example, a delicious fillet of wild Pollack with squash.

Café de l'Homme

6 place du Trocadéro-et-du-11-Novembre (16th) Plan: **N1**
– Ⓜ Trocadéro – ✆ 01 44 05 30 15 – www.cafedelhomme.com
Carte 52/86 €

• Modern Cuisine • Elegant • Trendy •

On the rooftop of the Palais de Chaillot, the huge 330m² terrace of the Café de l'Homme commands a matchless view of the nearby Eiffel Tower, guaranteed to leave you with unforgettable memories. Classical recipes (beef fillet and pepper sauce) rub shoulders with exotic creations (tataki of red tuna with yuzu and wasabi), each dish is a talented mix of creative culinary dedication.

La Gauloise

59 avenue de La Motte-Piquet (15th) Plan: **O3**
– Ⓜ La Motte Picquet Grenelle
– ✆ 01 47 34 11 64
Menu 31 € (lunch) – Carte 40/68 €

• Traditional Cuisine • Elegant • Vintage •

This Belle Epoque brasserie boasts the delightful air of Parisian life from yesteryear. It has a menu that features dishes such as poached eggs and vegetable pot-au-feu, pork crepinettes, turbot with a Béarnaise sauce, and onion soup. La Gauloise's attractive terrace is also much appreciated by diners.

Bistrot Belhara

23 rue Duvivier (7th) – Ⓜ École Militaire Plan: **P2**
– ✆ 01 45 51 41 77 – www.bistrotbelhara.com
– Closed 9-26 August, Monday, Sunday
Menu 34 € (lunch), 41/60 € – Carte 40/65 €

• Traditional Cuisine • Bistro •

Belhara is a site that is famous for its superb waves on the Basque coast - and this is the chef's nod to his origins. It is a tough call to summarise his impressive career path (Guérard, Loiseau, Ducasse etc). A convert to the bistro mode, Thierry Dufroux works wonders as he revisits the classics – the chef is definitely on the crest of the wave!

Les Fables de La Fontaine

131 rue St-Dominique (7th) – Ⓜ École Militaire Plan: **P1**
– ✆ 01 44 18 37 55 – www.lesfablesdelafontaine.net
Carte 50/75 €

• Modern Cuisine • Bistro • Friendly •

The former sous-chef of Les Fables has slipped effortlessly into the role of chef. He composes modern cuisine that is fragrant and bursting with colours, demonstrating an impressive maturity and undeniable talent. Relish your meal in a sleek, light and elegant bistro decor.

✿✿✿ Guy Savoy

11 quai de Conti (6th) – Ⓜ St-Michel Plan: **S1**
– ✆ 01 43 80 40 61
– www.guysavoy.com
– Closed 22 December-3 January, Monday, Saturday lunch, Sunday
Menu 250 € (lunch)/415 € – Carte 234/349 €
• Creative • Luxury • Romantic •

Guy Savoy, act II, in the Hôtel de la Monnaie, on the bank of the Seine. The setting is sumptuous – six rooms adorned with contemporary works lent by François Pinault –, and the host, true to himself: sincere and passionate, inventive without excess, unfailing generosity. Irresistible!

➜ Soupe d'artichaut à la truffe noire, brioche feuilletée aux champignons et aux truffes. Canette maturée aux épices douces et gratin de côtes de bettes. Mille feuilles ouvertes à la vanille de Tahiti.

✿✿ L'Atelier de Joël Robuchon - St-Germain

5 rue de Montalembert (7th) – Ⓜ Rue du Bac Plan: **R1**
– ✆ 01 42 22 56 56
– www.joel-robuchon.net
Menu 189 € – Carte 80/170 €
• Creative • Design • Minimalist •

A long counter flanked by bar stools, a small, intimate dining area, red and black colour scheme, a carefully designed half-light and stunning food (over 80 different dishes), prepared with a watchmaker's precision. A must in its genre, invented by the great chef, who died last year.

➜ Caviar sur un œuf de poule mollet et friand au saumon fumé. Côtelettes d'agneau de lait à la fleur de thym. Ganache onctueuse au chocolat araguani, glace au grué de cacao enrobé d'une saveur Oreo.

✿ Tour d'Argent

15 quai de la Tournelle (5th) – Ⓜ Maubert Mutualité Plan: **U2**
– ✆ 01 43 54 23 31
– www.tourdargent.com
– Closed Monday, Sunday
Menu 105 € (lunch), 350/380 € – Carte 200/350 €
• Modern Cuisine • Luxury • Elegant •

This institution dating back to 1582 is undergoing a velvet revolution! Chef Philippe Labbé serves modern, vivacious dishes, whose updated classicism continues to bear his inspired hallmark. The service is impeccable and the wine cellar boasts some 400,000 bottles. Tradition hand in hand with modernity.

➜ Quenelle "hommage au grand-père". Caneton Frédéric Delair. Crêpes "mademoiselle".

✿ Marsan - Hélène Darroze

4 rue d'Assas (6th) – Ⓜ Sèvres Babylone Plan: **R2**
– ✆ 01 42 22 00 11
– www.helenedarroze.com
Menu 65 € (lunch)/155 €
• Modern Cuisine • Contemporary Décor • Elegant •

Hélène Darroze has reopened her restaurant in 2019 after several months of refurbishment. Elegant, cosy décor, subtle, delicate cuisine in a single, seasonal menu that has not forgotten southwest France, so dear to her heart... The lucky few may even be able to eat at the table (6-8 seats) right in the kitchen to get even closer to the action!

➜ Cuisine du marché.

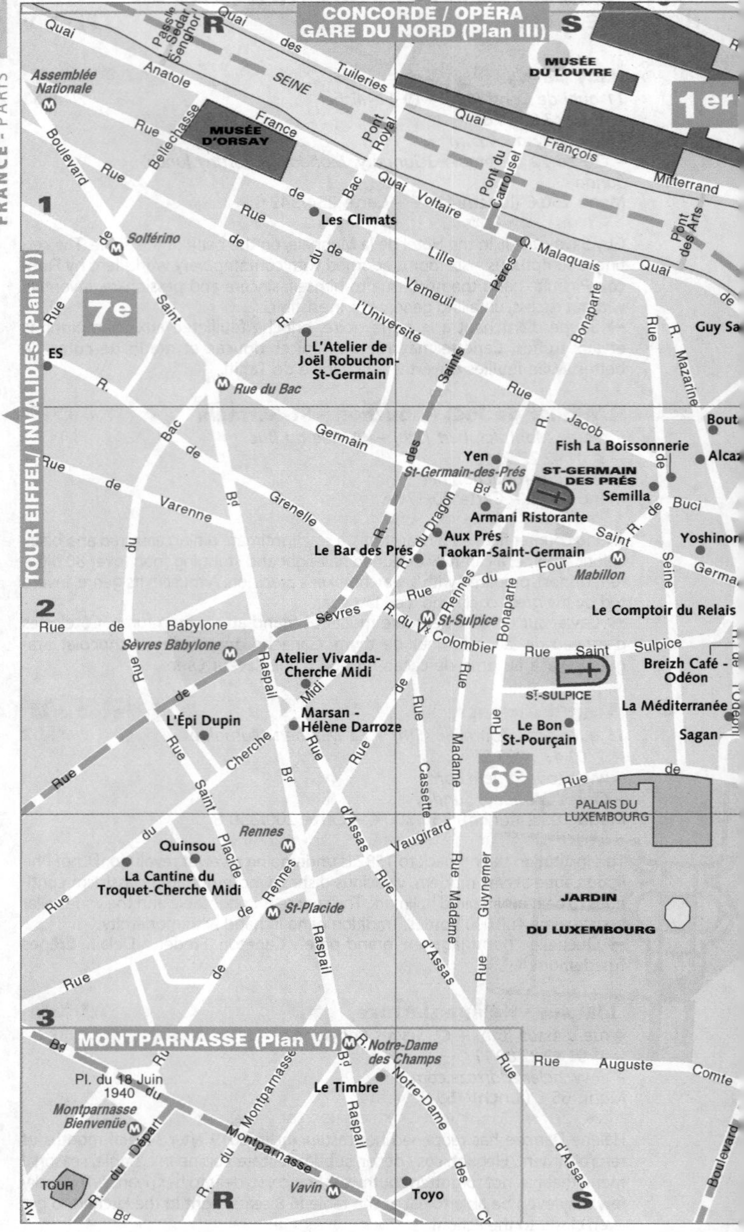
CONCORDE / OPÉRA
GARE DU NORD (Plan III)
TOUR EIFFEL/ INVALIDES (Plan IV)
MONTPARNASSE (Plan VI)
R
S
1
2
3
7e
6e
1er
MUSÉE DU LOUVRE
MUSÉE D'ORSAY
Assemblée Nationale
Solférino
Rue du Bac
St-Germain-des-Prés
Mabillon
St-Sulpice
Sèvres Babylone
Rennes
St-Placide
Notre-Dame des Champs
Montparnasse Bienvenüe
Vavin
ST-GERMAIN DES PRÉS
ST-SULPICE
PALAIS DU LUXEMBOURG
JARDIN DU LUXEMBOURG
Pl. du 18 Juin 1940
TOUR
SEINE
Quai Anatole France
Quai des Tuileries
Quai François Mitterrand
Quai Voltaire
Q. Malaquais
Quai de
Passerelle Sédar Senghor
Pont Royal
Pont du Carrousel
Pont des Arts
Boulevard Saint Germain
Rue de Bellechasse
Rue de Lille
Rue de Verneuil
Rue de l'Université
Rue du Bac
Rue des Saints Pères
Rue Bonaparte
Rue Mazarine
Rue Jacob
Rue de Seine
R. de Buci
Rue de Varenne
Rue de Grenelle
Rue de Babylone
Rue de Sèvres
Rue du Four
R. du Dragon
Rue de Rennes
R. du Vx Colombier
Rue Saint Sulpice
Rue du Cherche Midi
Bd Raspail
Rue Saint Placide
Rue d'Assas
Rue Cassette
Rue Madame
Rue Guynemer
Rue de Vaugirard
Rue Auguste Comte
Bd du Montparnasse
R. du Départ
R. Notre-Dame des Champs
Les Climats
L'Atelier de Joël Robuchon-St-Germain
Yen
Fish La Boissonnerie
Semilla
Armani Ristorante
Aux Prés
Taokan-Saint-Germain
Le Bar des Prés
Le Comptoir du Relais
Atelier Vivanda-Cherche Midi
Marsan - Hélène Darroze
L'Épi Dupin
Le Bon St-Pourçain
Breizh Café - Odéon
La Méditerranée
Sagan
Yoshinori
Guy Sa
Bout
Alcaz
Quinsou
La Cantine du Troquet-Cherche Midi
Le Timbre
Toyo

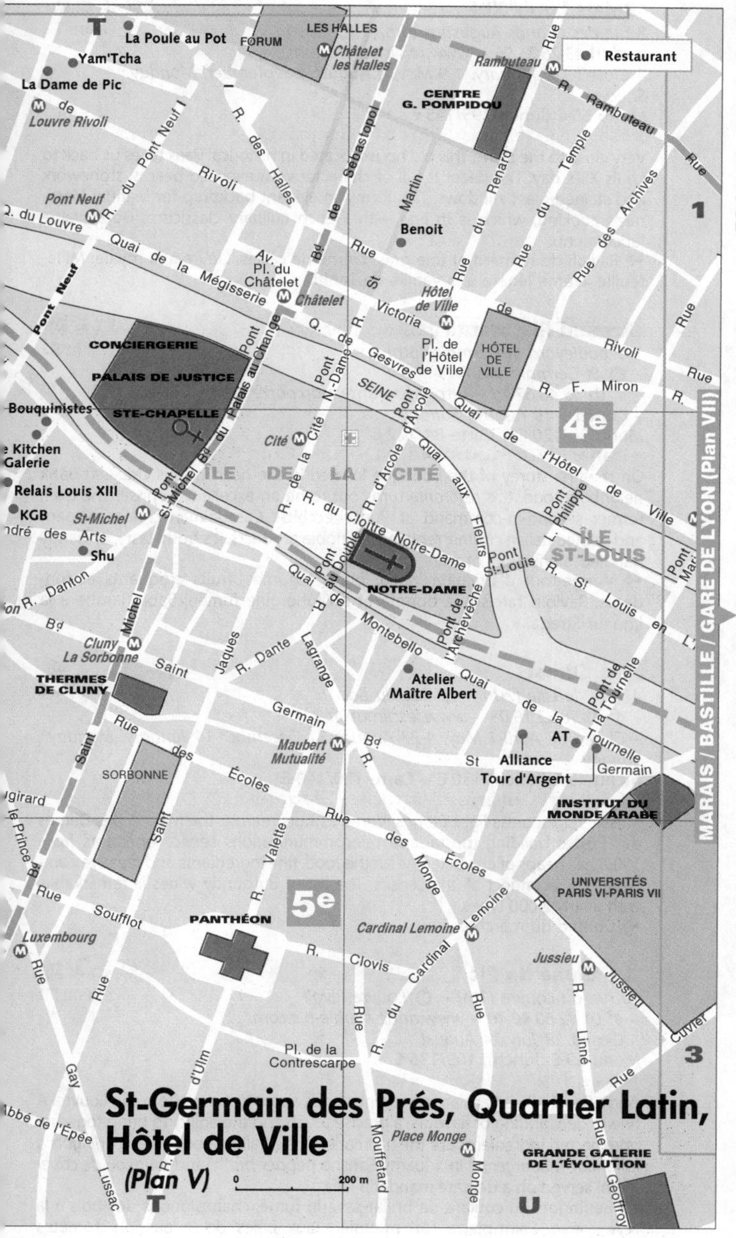

St-Germain des Prés, Quartier Latin, Hôtel de Ville (Plan V)

Relais Louis XIII (Manuel Martinez)

XXX

Plan: **T2**

8 rue des Grands-Augustins (6th) – Ⓜ Odéon – ✆ 01 43 26 75 96 – www.relaislouis13.com – Closed 1-8 January, 1-9 May, 4 August-4 September, Monday, Sunday

Menu 65 € (lunch), 95/145 €

• Classic Cuisine • Elegant • Bourgeois •

Very close to the Seine, this old house located in historical Paris takes us back to Louis XIII's day. The decor is full of character with exposed beams, stonework and stained-glass windows. This forms an elegant backdrop for Manuel Martinez's cooking, which is in line with French culinary classicism. Good value lunch menu.

➜ Ravioli de homard et foie gras, crème de cèpes. Lièvre à la royale. Millefeuille, crème légère à la vanille de Tahiti.

Armani Ristorante (Massimo Tringali)

XX

Plan: **S2**

149 boulevard St-Germain (6th) – Ⓜ St-Germain des Prés – ✆ 01 45 48 62 15 – http://ristorante.mori.paris/ – Closed 5-19 August, Sunday

Menu 90/120 € – Carte 84/122 €

• Italian • Contemporary Décor • Chic •

On the first storey of the boutique located in the heart of this chic Left Bank neighbourhood, this *ristorante* turns out to be an excellent surprise. The chef, former second-in-command at Porto-Vecchio's Casadelmar, creates elegant and refined Italian cuisine, replete with noble products. It's fresh, tasty, brilliantly handled: a fine work of art.

➜ Mange-tout d'artichaut violet, petits légumes, fruits croquants et fondants. Raviolis farcis à la burrata et à l'aubergine fumée. Baba flambé à la liqueur Strega.

Les Climats

XX

Plan: **R1**

41 rue de Lille (7th) – Ⓜ Rue du Bac – ✆ 01 58 62 10 08 – www.lesclimats.fr – Closed 28 April-1 May, 4-27 August, 31 December-14 January, Monday, Sunday

Menu 49 € (lunch)/130 € – Carte 120/140 €

• Modern Cuisine • Vintage • Elegant •

Mosaic floors, brass light fittings, Vert d'Estours marble: the Maison des Dames des Postes building (postal and telecommunications service operators from 1905) has heaps of character. As for the food, fine ingredients and creative combinations reconnect all the senses. The list of Burgundy wines is remarkable, with nearly 2 000 types.

➜ Cuisine du marché.

La Dame de Pic

XX

Plan: **T1**

20 rue du Louvre (1th) – Ⓜ Louvre Rivoli – ✆ 01 42 60 40 40 – www.anne-sophie-pic.com – Closed 28 July-24 August

Menu 59 € (lunch), 105/135 €

• Creative • Design • Elegant •

Anne-Sophie Pic's Parisian restaurant stands a stone's throw from the Louvre. A fine understanding of flavours, a precise touch and the ability to bring together unexpected ingredients are the hallmarks of the Valence-born chef: *berlingots à la fondue fribourgeoise* in a foamy Sansho pepper broth, and *tourteau de casier* (crab) served on a delicate mandarin jelly.

➜ Berlingots au coulant de brillat-savarin fumé, champignons des bois à la fève tonka. Saint-pierre rôti meunière aux baies de la passion, tomates anciennes et sauge. Chocolat aux arômes de citron et glace moelleuse.

Yam'Tcha (Adeline Grattard) XX

121 rue Saint-Honoré (1th) – Ⓜ Louvre Rivoli Plan: **T1**
– ✆ 01 40 26 08 07 – www.yamtcha.com – Closed 28 July-4 September, 23 December-9 January, Monday, Tuesday, Sunday
Menu 70 € (lunch)/150 €

• Creative • Elegant •

No pretension here; just superb flavour combinations: in rue St Honoré, Adeline Grattard works wonders. With a remarkable feel for her ingredients, she turns out simple and striking culinary pairings – with influences from France and Asia – designed in accordance with a selection of excellent teas. An energetic, spontaneous, moving accomplishment: this is great art.

➜ Spaghetti de patate douce, shiitakés et caviar. Ris de veau poché au fuyu et celtuce. Soupe de sésame noir et glace vanille.

Alliance (Toshitaka Omiya) XX AC

5 rue de Poissy (5th) – Ⓜ Maubert Mutualité Plan: **U2**
– ✆ 01 75 51 57 54 – www.restaurant-alliance.fr – Closed 29 July-19 August, Saturday, Sunday
Menu 55 € (lunch), 95/185 € – Carte 91/155 €

• Modern Cuisine • Contemporary Décor • Minimalist •

Alliance brings together two alumni of the restaurant Agapé Substance as partners in this new adventure. A starter of oyster, onion and lemon; foie gras, vegetable pot-au-feu and Corsican broth... The chef's dishes are flashes of simplicity, at once subtle and well executed. We will be going back for more.

➜ Foie gras de canard, légumes et consommé de canard. Poulette patte noire, corail de homard et chou pointu. Aloe vera, galanga et mélisse.

Benoit XX AC

20 rue St-Martin (4th) – Ⓜ Châtelet-Les Halles Plan: **U1**
– ✆ 01 42 72 25 76 – www.benoit-paris.com – Closed 28 July-26 August
Menu 39 € (lunch) – Carte 70/100 €

• Classic Cuisine • Bistro • Classic Décor •

Alain Ducasse supervises this chic and lively bistro, one of the oldest in Paris: Benoit celebrated its 100th anniversary in 2012! The classic food is prepared in time-honoured tradition, and respects the soul of this authentic and fine establishment.

➜ Langue de bœuf Lucullus, cœur de romaine à la crème moutardée. Sauté gourmand de ris de veau, crêtes et rognons de coq, foie gras et jus truffé. Profiteroles Benoit, sauce chocolat chaud.

ES (Takayuki Honjo) XX AC

91 rue de Grenelle (7th) – Ⓜ Solférino Plan: **R1**
– ✆ 01 45 51 25 74 – www.es-restaurant.fr – Closed 5-26 August, Monday, Tuesday lunch, Wednesday lunch, Thursday lunch, Sunday
Menu 55 € (lunch)/105 €

• Modern Cuisine • Minimalist •

A restaurant run by Takayuki Honjo, a young Japanese chef who is a fan of French cuisine. From the first mouthful, his talent jumps out at you. Foie gras and sea urchins, pigeon and cacao: all the pairings work, with never a wrong note; he masters the flavours and always has in mind the bigger picture. Clarity and harmony.

➜ Cuisine du marché.

Yoshinori (Yoshinori Morié) XX

18 rue Grégoire de Tours (6th) – Ⓜ Odéon Plan: **S2**
– ✆ 09 84 19 76 05 – www.yoshinori-paris.com – Closed Monday, Sunday
Menu 45 € (lunch), 70/95 €

• Modern Cuisine • Intimate • Contemporary Décor •

Yoshinori Morié's latest born is already sparkling in the culinary firmament. The Japanese chef regales us with his refined, vegetable-based, aesthetic cuisine, presented as a seasonal menu. For instance, tartare of milk-fed Corrèze veal with cauliflower, or monkfish with lotus blossom and mushrooms. So many unabashed odes to elegance and taste. Excellent set lunch menu. A real winner.

➜ Tartare de veau de lait, chou-fleur. Turbot breton, coulis de bourrache. Mousse coco, sorbet ananas et tagète.

La Poule au Pot

9 rue Vauvilliers (1th) – Ⓜ Châtelet-Les-Halles – ✆ 01 42 36 32 96 – www.lapouleaupot.com
Plan: **T1**
Menu 48 € – Carte 56/122 €
• Traditional Cuisine • Vintage •

The great classics of the French culinary repertoire are given a skilful overhaul here by Jean-François Piège and his faithful executive chef, Shinya Usami. Service on a silver platter, old-fashioned bistro decor, zinc counter: nothing is missing. It's Audiard's Paris down to a T, right down to the contents of your plate: duck galantine and full-bodied jelly, Colbert fried whiting and tartar sauce, platter of *tartes du jour*.

➜ Cuisses de grenouilles en persillade. Blanquette de veau à l'ancienne et bouquetière de légumes. Plateau de tartes comme dans mon enfance.

Quinsou (Antonin Bonnet)

33 rue de l'Abbé-Grégoire (6th) – Ⓜ St-Placide – ✆ 01 42 22 66 09 – www.quinsou.business.site – Closed 29 April-6 May, 5-19 August, 21 December-6 January, Monday, Tuesday lunch, Sunday
Plan: **R3**
Menu 35 € (lunch)/75 €
• Creative • Trendy • Trendy •

Opposite Ferrandi, the French School of Culinary Arts, Quinsou – "chaffinch" in Occitan – cooks up a storm, relished by the fine palates of the 6th arrondissement and beyond, with, for instance, monkfish, Hokkaido squash and curry sauce: Antonin Bonnet, former chef from Le Sergent Recruteur, brings the ingredients to life. A really great place.

➜ Cuisine du marché.

Ze Kitchen Galerie (William Ledeuil)

4 rue des Grands Augustins (6th) – Ⓜ St-Michel – ✆ 01 44 32 00 32 – www.zekitchengalerie.fr – Closed 29 July-19 August, Saturday, Sunday
Plan: **T2**
Menu 48 € (lunch), 85/98 €
• Creative • Contemporary Décor •

William Ledeuil has breathed his love of Southeast Asian flavours (Thailand, Vietnam and Japan) that inspire his creations into this establishment. Galanga, ka-chaï, curcuma, wasabi and ginger – herbs, roots, spices and condiments from all over the world at the service of French classics.

➜ Fleurs de courgette, curry rouge de crustacés, condiment kimchi. Bœuf Wagyu, condiment soubressade. Glace chocolat blanc, wasabi-fraise, pistache, turron.

La Méditerranée

2 place de l'Odéon (6th) – Ⓜ Odéon – ✆ 01 43 26 02 30 – www.la-mediterranee.com
Plan: **S2**
Menu 36 € – Carte 55/81 €
• Seafood • Mediterranean • Colourful •

The frescoes evoke the Mediterranean in this restaurant opposite the Théâtre de l'Odéon. The maritime inspired cuisine, in which particular attention is paid to the best ingredients, is influenced by the accents of the south. In summer dine beneath the azure blue awning.

Alcazar

62 rue Mazarine (6th) – Ⓜ Odéon – ✆ 01 53 10 19 99 – www.alcazar.fr – Closed 1-30 August
Plan: **S2**
Menu 40 € (lunch) – Carte 50/100 €
• Modern Cuisine • Brasserie • Trendy •

Alcazar's interior was designed by the architect and decorator Lola Gonzalez. Plants have the upper hand, endowing the space with the timeless elegance of a grand winter garden. The kitchen never fails to turn out an appetising menu of contemporary brasserie dishes, such as the excellent roasted free-range chicken and home-made chips, or the confit shoulder of lamb. Brunch on Sundays.

Atelier Maître Albert

1 rue Maître-Albert (5th) – Ⓜ Maubert Mutualité Plan: **U2**
– ✆ 01 56 81 30 01 – www.ateliermaitrealbert.com – Closed 4-19 August, 23 December-2 January, Saturday lunch, Sunday lunch
Menu 36 € (lunch), 39/78 € – Carte 40/70 €
• Traditional Cuisine • Friendly • Chic •

An attractive medieval fireplace and roasting spits take pride of place in this handsome interior designed by Jean-Michel Wilmotte. Guy Savoy is responsible for the mouthwatering menu.

Les Bouquinistes

53 quai des Grands-Augustins (6th) – Ⓜ St-Michel Plan: **T1**
– ✆ 01 43 25 45 94 – www.lesbouquinistes.com – Closed 4-19 August, 23 December-2 January
Menu 36 € (lunch), 44/78 € – Carte 50/66 €
• Modern Cuisine • Contemporary Décor •

Looking out over the bouquinistes – the booksellers lining the banks of the Seine – this restaurant set up by Guy Savoy has a trendy modern decor that calls to mind a New York loft. Discuss literature over chicory in remoulade dressing with œuf parfait and Mimolette cheese, confit suckling pig with slow-cooked lentils, or hazelnut floating islands.

Boutary

25 rue Mazarine (6th) – Ⓜ Odéon – ✆ 01 43 43 69 10 Plan: **S2**
– www.boutary-restaurant.com – Closed 22 July-13 August, Monday, Saturday lunch, Sunday
Menu 35 € (lunch)/86 € – Carte 60/75 €
• Modern Cuisine • Chic • Intimate •

In the middle of rue Mazarine, this old building hosts a Japanese-Korean chef with a fine track record. Armed with magnificent ingredients, he proposes fine and tasty recipes that pop with colours and brim with ideas. Taste has come home to roost here: a pleasant dining experience, not least as the bill won't break the bank.

AT

4 rue du Cardinal-Lemoine (5th) – Ⓜ Cardinal Lemoine Plan: **U2**
– ✆ 01 56 81 94 08 – www.atushitanaka.com – Closed Monday lunch, Sunday
Menu 55 € (lunch)/105 €
• Creative • Design • Minimalist •

A stone's throw from the banks of the Seine and the Tour d'Argent, the minimalist interior of this small restaurant embodies the quintessence of Japan. Chef Tanaka, formerly with Pierre Gagnaire, loves fresh ingredients and precise cooking and is forever surprising us with his creative recipes. Vaulted basement.

Atelier Vivanda - Cherche Midi

20 rue du Cherche-Midi (6th) – Ⓜ Sèvres Babylone Plan: **R2**
– ✆ 01 45 44 50 44 – www.ateliervivanda.com – Closed 4-18 August, 22 December-4 January, Monday, Sunday
Carte 40/53 €
• Steakhouse • Bistro • Friendly •

Welcome to the new bistrot à viande run by Akrame Benallal. Superb pieces of meat are of course on the menu: Black Angus beef (flank and marbled cuts), chicken supreme and Iberian pork chop, all lovingly prepared and accompanied by gratin dauphinois or homemade fries. Wildly good.

Aux Prés

27 rue du Dragon (6th) – Ⓜ St-Germain des Prés Plan: **S2**
– ✆ 01 45 48 29 68 – www.restaurantauxpres.com
Carte 60/90 €
• Modern Cuisine • Bistro • Vintage •

An openly vintage bistro (red banquette seating, smoked-glass mirrors, floral wallpaper) in St Germain and international cuisine by Cyril Lignac, whose creativity never strays entirely from its French country roots.

Le Bar des Prés

Plan: **S2**

25 rue du Dragon (6th) – Ⓜ St-Germain des Prés – ✆ 01 43 25 87 67 – www.lebardespres.com

Carte 55/75 €

• Modern Cuisine • Design • Contemporary Décor •

Cyril Lignac has placed a Japanese chef with a strong track record in the kitchens of Le Bar des Prés, next door to his restaurant Aux Prés. On the menu, extremely fresh sushi and sashimi, but also a few contemporary dishes: tartare of sea bream and petits pois with mint; galette craquante and crab with Madras curry. Cocktails courtesy of a mixologist.

Le Bon Saint-Pourçain

Plan: **S2**

10 bis rue Servandoni (6th) – Ⓜ Mabillon – ✆ 01 42 01 78 24 – Closed 5-25 August, Monday, Sunday

Carte 47/67 €

• Modern Cuisine • Bistro • Vintage •

Tucked away behind St Sulpice church in the heart of the high-brow Saint Germain des Prés district, this former 'bougnat' restaurant reopened in the spring of 2015. Bistro traditions with a modern twist depict the delicious food – doubtless due to the high quality fresh produce. Booking advisable!

Breizh Café - Odéon

Plan: **S2**

1 rue de l'Odéon (6th) – Ⓜ Odéon – ✆ 01 42 49 34 73 – https://breizhcafe.com/fr

Carte 26/52 €

• Breton • Contemporary Décor • Friendly •

The location, for a start, couldn't be better: a freestone building right on the Carrefour de l'Odéon is home to the youngest of Bertrand Larcher's crêperies. This Brittany-born chef spent time in Japan before settling down in France. Tuck into savoury galettes and sweet crêpes, made with organic flour and artisanal ingredients and accompanied by quality ciders and sakes.

La Cantine du Troquet - Cherche Midi

Plan: **R3**

79 rue du Cherche-Midi (6th) – Ⓜ St Placide – ✆ 01 43 27 70 06 – www.lacantinedutroquet.com – Closed Saturday, Sunday

Carte 38/50 €

• Traditional Cuisine • Bistro •

La Cantine du Troquet mark 4 on Paris's Left Bank shares the osmosis of its predecessors between decoration (brick walls and exposed stonework, tightly packed tables) and cuisine that is a fine celebration of tradition. Razor clams a la plancha, onglet de bœuf steak with a red wine sauce... This is generous, neat and tasty fare. Now, à table!

Le Comptoir du Relais – Hôtel Relais St-Germain

Plan: **S2**

5 carrefour de l'Odéon (6th) – Ⓜ Odéon – ✆ 01 44 27 07 50 – www.hotel-paris-relais-saint-germain.com

Menu 60 € – Carte 29/65 €

• Traditional Cuisine • Bistro • Friendly •

In this pocket-sized 1930s bistro, chef Yves Camdeborde delights customers with his copious traditional cuisine. Brasserie dishes are to the fore at lunchtime, with a more refined menu available in the evening.

L'Épi Dupin

Plan: **R2**

11 rue Dupin (6th) – Ⓜ Sèvres Babylone – ✆ 01 42 22 64 56 – www.epidupin.com – Closed 5-25 August, Monday, Saturday, Sunday

Menu 42/56 €

• Modern Cuisine • Friendly •

True to his beliefs, chef François Pasteau runs an eco-friendly establishment. He buys his fruit and vegetables locally, recycles organic waste, filters the drinking water on site, etc. This respect for the health of our planet and bodies can be tasted in his recipes, which provide an appetising tribute to French country traditions.

Fish La Boissonnerie

69 rue de Seine (6th) – Ⓜ Odéon – ✆ 01 43 54 34 69 – www.fishlaboissonnerie.com – Closed 23 December-3 January

Plan: **S2**

Menu 29 € (lunch) – Carte 40/60 €

• Modern Cuisine • Bistro • Friendly •

For almost 20 years this restaurant has been paying a fine tribute to the wine god Bacchus: 300 sorts of wine (Burgundy, Champagne, Côtes du Rhône appellations) accompany appealingly contemporary market-based cooking: broccoli soup with burrata and mint; pork chop with new potatoes and roasted onions.

KGB

25 rue des Grands-Augustins (6th) – Ⓜ St-Michel – ✆ 01 46 33 00 85 – www.zekitchengalerie.fr – Closed 27 July-20 August, 30 December-8 January, Monday, Sunday

Plan: **T2**

Menu 36 € (lunch), 55/66 €

• Modern Cuisine • Contemporary Décor • Colourful •

KGB stands for Kitchen Gallery Bis, 'bis' referring to the fact that this is the second KGB restaurant in Paris. A cross between an art gallery and a less than conventional restaurant, it has the same feel as its elder sibling. The original cuisine explores sweet and sour associations, flavoured with the spices of Asia.

Sagan

8 rue Casimir-Delavigne (6th) – Ⓜ Odéon – ✆ 06 69 37 82 19 – Closed 4-28 August, 23 December-7 January, Monday, Tuesday lunch, Wednesday lunch, Thursday lunch, Friday lunch, Saturday lunch, Sunday

Plan: **T2**

Carte 35/60 €

• Japanese • Minimalist • Intimate •

Near to Odéon, a tiny restaurant (15 covers) from the owner of Lengué in the 5th arrondissement. In an unadorned, hushed and intimate interior, diners sample inventive and often surprising Japanese food, such as Japanese-style ratatouille, tuna tataki, horsemeat sashimi and squab with Japanese pepper. Fine wine list.

Semilla

54 rue de Seine (6th) – Ⓜ Odéon – ✆ 01 43 29 11 62 – www.semillaparis.com – Closed 5-19 August, 23 December-3 January

Plan: **S2**

Menu 40 € (lunch) – Carte 50/75 €

• Modern Cuisine • Trendy • Friendly •

This bistro – a good "seed" (semilla in Spanish) – was founded in 2012 on the initiative of the owners of Fish La Boissonnerie, which is just opposite. Find a convivial atmosphere, trendy decor and, in the kitchens, a young and passionate team, who work exclusively with hand-picked suppliers. Delicious and well done!

Shu

8 rue Suger (6th) – Ⓜ St-Michel – ✆ 01 46 34 25 88 – www.restaurant-shu.com – Closed 28 April-6 May, 28 July-12 August, Monday lunch, Tuesday lunch, Wednesday lunch, Thursday lunch, Friday lunch, Saturday lunch, Sunday

Plan: **T2**

Carte 42/52 €

• Japanese • Minimalist • Friendly •

You have to stoop to get through the doorway that leads to this 17C cellar. In a minimalist decor, discover authentic and finely executed Japanese cuisine, in which the freshness of the ingredients works its magic in kushiage, sushi and sashimi.

Taokan - St-Germain

8 rue du Sabot (6th) – Ⓜ St-Germain des Prés – ✆ 01 42 84 18 36 – www.taokan.fr – Closed Sunday lunch

Plan: **S2**

Menu 24 € (lunch)/70 € – Carte 43/72 €

• Chinese • Trendy • Contemporary Décor •

Come inside this pretty restaurant, in the heart of St-Germain des Prés, to enjoy Chinese cuisine. Cantonese specialities feature; for example dim sum, steamed fish, duck breast with honey, and caramelised sliced chicken. Beautiful presentation and good ingredients: this is a real ambassador for Chinese food!

Yen

22 rue St-Benoît (6th) – Ⓜ St-Germain-des-Prés – ✆ 01 45 44 11 18 – www.yen-paris.fr – Closed Sunday Plan: **S2**
Menu 48 € (lunch)/70 € – Carte 40/90 €

• Japanese • Minimalist • Contemporary Décor •

The highly refined Japanese decor in this restaurant will appeal to fans of the minimalist look. The menu showcases the chef's speciality, soba – buckwheat noodles served hot or cold and prepared in front of you.

MONTPARNASSE – DENFERT PLAN VI

Cobéa (Philippe Bélissent)

11 rue Raymond-Losserand (14th) – Ⓜ Gaité – ✆ 01 43 20 21 39 – www.cobea.fr – Closed 28 July-19 August, Monday, Sunday Plan: **V2**
Menu 55 € (lunch), 90/120 €

• Modern Cuisine • Elegant •

Co, as in Jérôme Cobou, in the restaurant, Bé, as in Philippe Bélissent, in the kitchens, and A for Associates. Cobéa is the venture of two passionate young professionals, who have created a place in their image, that is, guided by the taste for good things! A feel for ingredients, harmony and strength of flavours and finesse. A delicious restaurant.

→ Écrevisses européennes, melon et jus des carapaces. Ris d'agneau meunière, figue et semoule. Fruits rouges en pavlova.

Montée (Takayuki Nameura)

9 rue Léopold-Robert (14th) – Ⓜ Notre-Dame-des-Champs – ✆ 01 43 25 57 63 – www.restaurant-montee.fr – Closed Monday, Sunday Plan: **W1**
Menu 40 € (lunch)/105 €

• Modern Cuisine • Elegant • Cosy •

A Japanese chef (from Kobe in this case) shares his love of French food in this establishment. His meticulously crafted dishes are rich in distinctive flavours, revealing his undisputed skill, know-how and personality. Finally, the stripped-back décor further enhances and amplifies the culinary experience.

→ Fois gras et banane fumée. Caille farcie aux raisins secs. Pomme, cidre et safran.

Bistrotters

9 rue Decrès (14th) – Ⓜ Plaisance – ✆ 01 45 45 58 59 – www.bistrotters.com – Closed 24 December-1 January Plan: **V2**
Menu 23 € (lunch), 33/37 €

• Modern Cuisine • Bistro • Simple •

A very lovely find in the southern reaches of the 14th arrondissement, close to Métro Plaisance. The values of bistronomie and Epicureanism are at the fore with hearty, elaborate fare made from fine ingredients (small producers from the Île-de-France area are preferred). Bistro interior and laid-back service.

Le Timbre

3 rue Ste-Beuve (6th) – Ⓜ Notre-Dame des Champs – ✆ 01 45 49 10 40 – www.restaurantletimbre.com – Closed 1-7 January, 27 July-27 August, Monday, Tuesday lunch, Sunday Plan: **W1**
Menu 32 € (lunch), 37/55 €

• Modern Cuisine • Bistro • Friendly •

A young chef with a varied career path (Australia, Belgium) is at the helm of this charming bistro – wooden tables, banquette seating, small open kitchen – where you can enjoy an informal dining experience. He proposes original and tasty market-sourced cuisine, accompanied by decent wines, most of which are organic or natural.

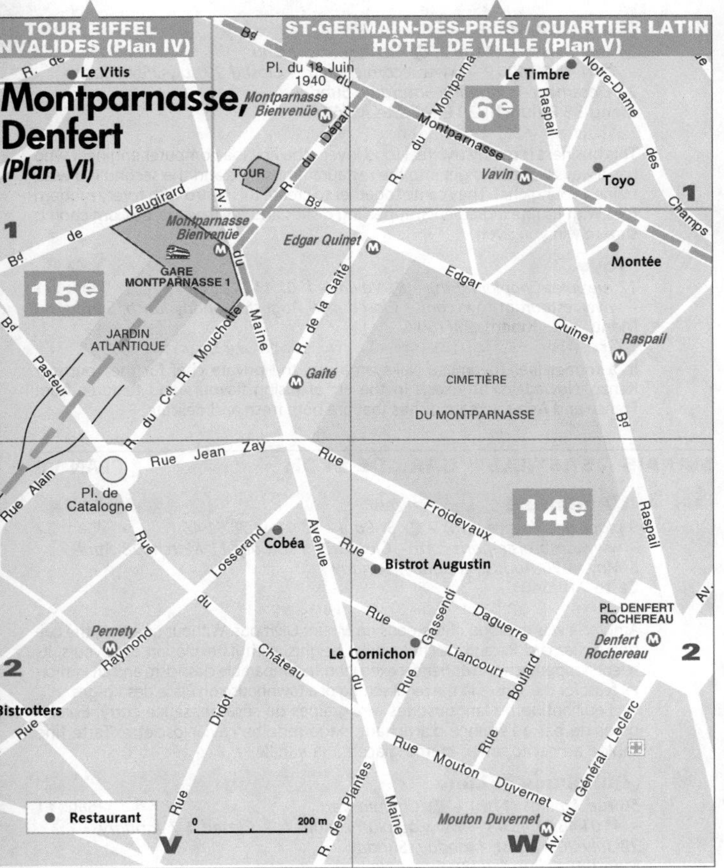

Le Vitis

Plan: **V1**

8 rue Falguière (15th) – Ⓜ Falguière – ✆ 01 42 73 07 02
– www.levitis.fr – Closed Monday, Sunday
Carte 35/39 €

• Traditional Cuisine • Bistro •

The Delacourcelle brothers, first encountered at Le Pré Verre (in the 5th arrondissement), are at the helm of this tiny bistro. Their recipes give diners well-made, bold and flavoursome dishes: pan-fried razor shells, tender suckling pig with mild spices... Excellent!

Bistrot Augustin

Plan: **W2**

79 rue Daguerre (14th) – Ⓜ Gaîté – ✆ 01 43 21 92 29
– www.augustin-bistrot.fr – Closed Sunday
Menu 39 €

• Traditional Cuisine • Bistro • Friendly •

This chic bistro with an intimate interior proposes market (and seasonal) cuisine with southern influences to whet the appetite. An example: the superb Périgord pork chop... Ingredients take pride of place here, and our taste buds aren't complaining!

Le Cornichon

34 rue Gassendi (14th) – Ⓜ Denfert Rochereau Plan: **W2**
– ✆ 01 43 20 40 19 – www.lecornichon.fr – Closed 29 July-25 August, 24 December-1 January, Saturday, Sunday
Menu 35 € (lunch)/39 € – Carte 45/65 €

• Modern Cuisine • Bistro • Friendly •

This business is run by two real food lovers: the first is a computer engineer who has always wanted to get into the restaurant business and the second is a well-trained young chef. They came together to create this bistro with a very modern feel. With its fine ingredients, appealing dishes and full flavours, Le Cornichon is sure to win you over!

Toyo

17 rue Jules-Chaplain (6th) – Ⓜ Vavin – ✆ 01 43 54 28 03 Plan: **W1**
– www.restaurant-toyo.com – Closed 4-19 August, Monday lunch, Sunday
Menu 39 € (lunch), 99/150 €

• Creative • Minimalist • Contemporary Décor •

In a former life, Toyomitsu Nakayama was the private chef for the couturier Kenzo. Nowadays, he excels in the art of fusing flavours and textures from France and Asia to create dishes that are both fresh and delicate.

MARAIS – BASTILLE – GARE DE LYON PLAN VII

L'Ambroisie (Bernard Pacaud)

9 place des Vosges (4th) – Ⓜ St-Paul – ✆ 01 42 78 51 45 Plan: **X2**
– www.ambroisie-paris.com – Closed 24 February-11 March, 28 April-6 May, 4-26 August, Monday, Sunday
Carte 210/340 €

• Classic Cuisine • Luxury • Elegant •

Ambrosia was the food of the gods on Mount Olympus. Without question, the cuisine of Bernard Pacaud reaches similar heights, with its explosion of flavours, its scientific approach and its perfect execution. Incomparable classicism and an immortal feast for the senses in the regal setting of a townhouse on Place des Vosges.

➜ Feuillantine de langoustines aux graines de sésame, sauce curry. Escalopines de bar à l'émincé d'artichaut, nage réduite, caviar osciètre. Tarte fine sablée au cacao amer, crème glacée à la vanille.

Qui plume la Lune

50 rue Amelot (11th) – Ⓜ Chemin Vert Plan: **Y1**
– ✆ 01 48 07 45 48 – www.quiplumelalune.fr – Closed 1-7 January, 28 July-20 August, Monday, Sunday
Menu 45 € (lunch)/130 €

• Modern Cuisine • Cosy • Intimate •

First, there is the place itself, which is cosy and romantic. Then, above all, the food, which is fresh, full of vitality, and made with hand-selected ingredients (organic, quality vegetables etc). A tasty culinary interlude.

➜ Huître grillée à la plancha, bouillon de bœuf maturé et caviar. Foie gras laqué au vin rouge et au jus de betterave. Mousse de lait à la vanille, tuile de lait au thé matcha et caramel à la verveine.

Restaurant H (Hubert Duchenne)

13 rue Jean-Beausire (4th) – Ⓜ Bastille – ✆ 01 43 48 80 96 Plan: **Y2**
– www.restauranth.com – Closed 1-7 May, 30 July-20 August, Monday, Sunday
Menu 35 € (lunch), 60/80 €

• Creative • Cosy • Intimate •

A good restaurant near Bastille may sound like a contradiction in terms, but at this eatery with barely 20 places, diners tuck into a single set menu (for example: mussels, cream of parsley and samphire greens). "H" stands for Hubert Duchenne, a young chef who learned the ropes from Akrame Benallal and Jean-François Piège. Inventive and skilful cooking.

➜ Cèpe en feuille de figuier et figue confite. Lieu jaune, amarente, écume d'un beurre noisette. Autour du café vert, citron, noisette.

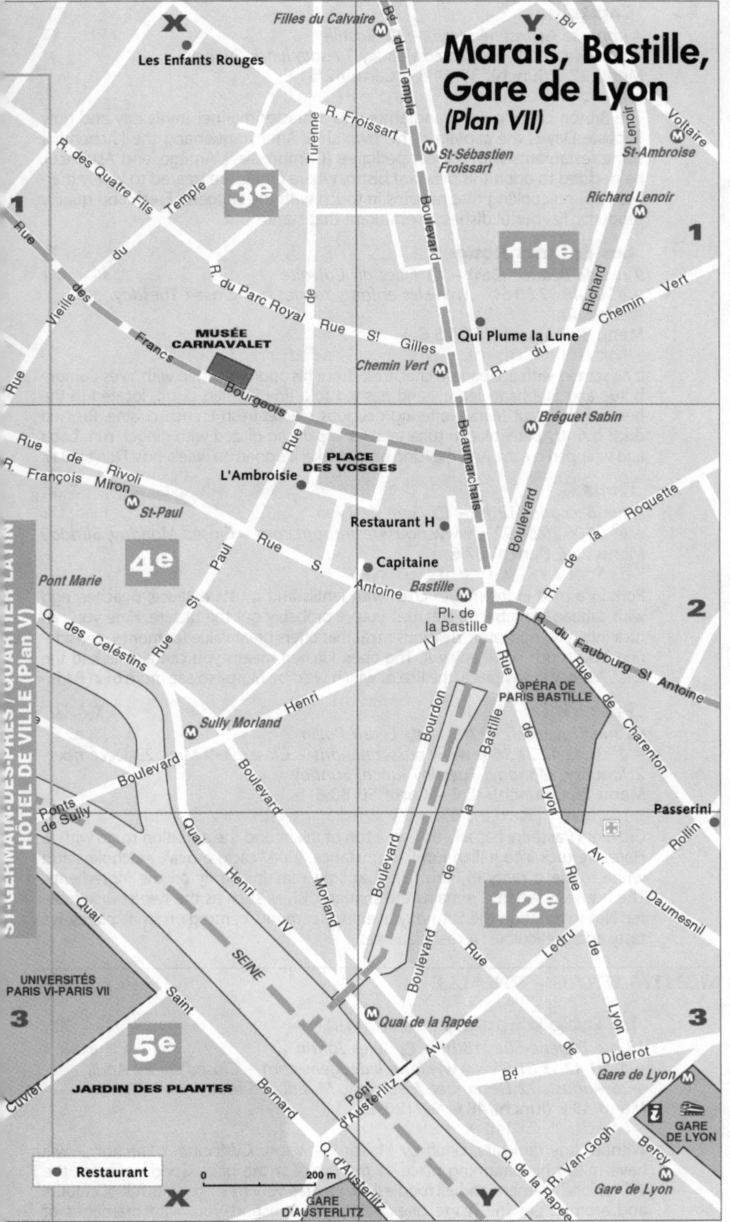
Marais, Bastille, Gare de Lyon
(Plan VII)
Les Enfants Rouges
Filles du Calvaire
St-Sébastien Froissart
St-Ambroise
Voltaire
Richard Lenoir
Chemin Vert
Bréguet Sabin
Qui Plume la Lune
MUSÉE CARNAVALET
PLACE DES VOSGES
L'Ambroisie
Restaurant H
Capitaine
St-Paul
Pont Marie
Bastille
Pl. de la Bastille
OPÉRA DE PARIS BASTILLE
Sully Morland
Passerini
Quai de la Rapée
Gare de Lyon
GARE DE LYON
GARE D'AUSTERLITZ
UNIVERSITÉS PARIS VI-PARIS VII
JARDIN DES PLANTES
3e
4e
5e
11e
12e
ST-GERMAIN-DES-PRÉS / QUARTIER LATIN HÔTEL DE VILLE (Plan V)
Restaurant
0
200 m

Capitaine

4 impasse Guéménée (4th) – Ⓜ Bastille Plan: **Y2**
– ✆ 01 44 61 11 76 – Closed Monday, Tuesday lunch, Sunday
Menu 27 € (lunch), 38/64 € – Carte 42/51 €
• Modern Cuisine • Bistro • Friendly •

The Breton chef's great-grandfather was a master mariner in his day and now Baptiste Day is the captain of his own ship. After frequenting the kitchens of some restaurants with a great pedigree (L'Ambroisie, L'Arpège, and Astrance), he decided to open this pleasant bistro, where diners are treated to lovely market-inspired cooking that remains in touch with the zeitgeist. Fresh and quality products, flavourful dishes: a restaurant that stands out.

Les Enfants Rouges

9 rue de Beauce (3th) – Ⓜ Filles du Calvaire Plan: **X1**
– ✆ 01 48 87 80 61 – www.les-enfants-rouges.fr – Closed Tuesday, Wednesday
Menu 38 € (lunch), 50/75 €
• Modern Cuisine • Bistro • Traditional •

It all started with a Japanese chef, fresh from his apprenticeship with Yves Camdeborde and Stéphane Jégo… and has led to a fine Parisian bistro, located in the heart of the Haut Marais, offering delicious market-fresh French cuisine. Pressed duck country pâté, bluefin tuna tataki *a la plancha* glazed with ginger, rum baba and whipped cream. And the icing on the cake: it's open on weekends! Don't delay.

Nous 4

3 rue Beccaria (12th) – Ⓜ Gare de Lyon Plan: **D2**
– ✆ 06 06 70 64 92 – www.nous4restaurant.com – Closed Monday, Sunday
Menu 25 € (lunch)/37 €
• Traditional Cuisine • Bistro •

Pork in a melt-in-the-mouth crust with lentils and mustard sauce; poached egg with cabbage and bacon cream… you've probably got the picture. Here you can tuck into a no-nonsense, delicious meal that offers great value for money, considering how much you'll enjoy it. The open kitchen means you can also talk to the chef. A really lovely place, the like of which we'd be happy to see more of in Paris.

Passerini

65 rue Traversière (12th) – Ⓜ Ledru Rollin Plan: **Y3**
– ✆ 01 43 42 27 56 – www.passerini.paris – Closed 1-9 May, 23 December-2 January, Monday, Tuesday lunch, Sunday
Menu 26 € (lunch)/48 € – Carte 50/80 €
• Italian • Contemporary Décor • Friendly •

Giovanni Passerini has a keen eye, a ton of talent and the ambition to go with it. Here, we tuck into Italian food, for instance, tripe "cacio e ova", artichokes and white truffle, a rarity in Paris. The spotlight remains firmly on the ingredients. The house "specialty" remains the sharing dishes, such as the two-course lobster. Not to mention the Saturday evening set menu, centred on small plates. It's tasty and meticulous. A real pleasure.

MONTMARTRE – PIGALLE — PLAN VIII

La Table d'Eugène (Geoffroy Maillard)

18 rue Eugène-Süe (18th) – Ⓜ Jules Joffrin Plan: **AA 1**
– ✆ 01 42 55 61 64 – www.latabledeugene.com – Closed 21-29 April, 4-26 August, 22 December-7 January, Monday, Sunday
Menu 45 € (lunch)/48 €, 99/130 €
• Modern Cuisine • Elegant •

Without any difficulty, Geoffroy Maillard – whose CV includes Frechon – will have raised his charming place to the ranks of the best. Good news for the 18th arrondissement and all foodies! He creates very fresh cuisine, full of colours and aromas. Let the "carte blanche" menu transport you, with marriages of dishes and wines. Strength and finesse.

→ Cuisine du marché.

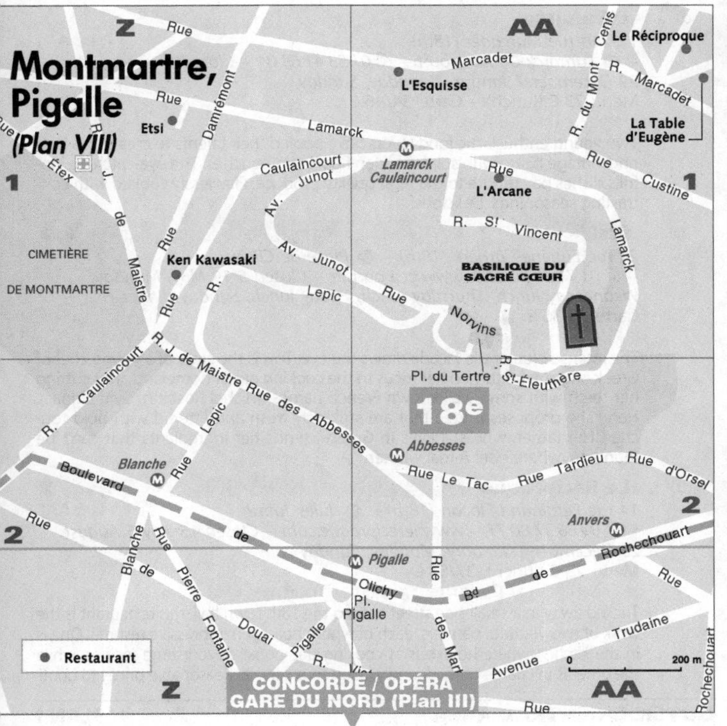

Ken Kawasaki

15 rue Caulaincourt (18th) – Ⓜ Blanche Plan: **Z1**
– ✆ 09 70 95 98 32 – www.restaurantkenkawasaki.fr – Closed 25 December-1 January, Wednesday lunch, Thursday lunch, Sunday
Menu 45 € (lunch)/70 €

• Creative • Minimalist •

This establishment invites you to celebrate a splendid marriage between Japanese and French cuisine. Japanese chef Ken Kawasaki has put together a fine team, who together prepare exquisitely graphic dishes, full of unusual flavours using market-fresh ingredients. Simply excellent.

➜ Cuisine du marché.

L'Arcane (Laurent Magnin)

39 rue Lamarck (18th) – Ⓜ Lamarck Caulaincourt Plan: **AA1**
– ✆ 01 46 06 86 00 – www.restaurantlarcane.com – Closed 30 July-26 August, Monday, Tuesday lunch, Sunday
Menu 49 € (lunch), 66/105 €

• Modern Cuisine • Cosy •

Let's try to get to the bottom of the secrets of this restaurant behind Sacré Cœur. The chef offers his take on tradition, and it has to be said that the pleasant surprises come thick and fast over the course of the meal: prawns three ways, skate wing à la grenobloise etc. An appealing place, the charms of which are liable to radiate well beyond Montmartre.

➜ Cuisine du marché.

L'Esquisse

151 bis rue Marcadet (18th) Plan: **AA1**
– Ⓜ Lamarck-Caulaincourt – ✆ 01 53 41 63 04 – Closed 4-19 August, 29 December-7 January, Monday, Sunday
Menu 23 € (lunch) – Carte 34/46 €

• Modern Cuisine • Bistro •

Two young enthusiastic food lovers have pooled their talents to create this inviting vintage bistro with solid wooden floors and benches. The eye-catching, no-frills dishes pay tribute to the high quality produce. Flawlessly cooked with contrasting seasonings. Delicious!

Etsi

23 rue Eugène-Carrière (18th) – Ⓜ Place de Clichy Plan: **Z1**
– ✆ 01 71 50 00 80 – www.etsi-paris.fr – Closed 5-19 May, Monday, Wednesday lunch, Thursday lunch, Friday lunch, Sunday dinner
Carte 25/35 €

• Greek • Tavern •

The intense blue of the façade draws the eye. This is the story of a young chef of Greek origin, who turned her focus to the cooking of her homeland after cutting her teeth with some well-known French names (Michel Rostang, Cyril Lignac). Here, she proposes mezze that are strikingly fresh and littered with bold touches. Her father, who still lives in Greece, sends her ingredients that can't be found anywhere else! A real winner.

Le Réciproque

14 rue Ferdinand-Flocon (18th) – Ⓜ Jules Joffrin Plan: **AA1**
– ✆ 09 86 37 80 77 – www.lereciproque.com – Closed 15 July-5 August, 23 December-1 January, Monday, Sunday
Menu 23 € (lunch), 37/54 €

• Traditional Cuisine • Contemporary Décor •

Tucked away in a small side street behind the 18th town hall, this restaurant is the work of two youthful partners, each of whom boasts an impressive résumé. One is in the kitchen where he excels at cooking traditional, flavoursome recipes, while the other is in charge of the friendly, courteous service. Reasonable prices to boot!

OUTSIDE CENTRAL AREA — PLAN I

Le Pré Catelan

route de Suresnes - Bois de Boulogne (16th) Plan: **A2**
– ✆ 01 44 14 41 14 – www.precatelanparis.com – Closed 24 February-11 March, 28 July-19 August, 27 October-4 November, Monday, Sunday
Menu 140 € (lunch), 220/280 € – Carte 260/310 €

• Creative • Luxury • Elegant •

Set within the Bois de Boulogne, the superb Napoleon-III pavilion installed here since 1905 is easily recognisable. In this dream location, Frédéric Anton works wonders: the precision and rigour passed on by his mentors (who include Robuchon) are his signature, along with his taste for original pairings. Topped off by a prestigious wine cellar and perfect service.

➜ Crabe, crème à l'aneth, avocat, caviar de France, pomélo et saveurs thaïes. Cabillaud aux algues, beurre au citron vert et brandade. Pomme soufflée croustillante, crème glacée au caramel, cidre et sucre pétillant.

La Grande Cascade

Bois de Boulogne (16th) – ✆ 01 45 27 33 51
– www.restaurantsparisiens.com – Closed 22 December-11 January
Menu 89/192 € – Carte 160/220 €

• Modern Cuisine • Classic Décor • Elegant •

A charming pavilion (1850) just a stone's throw from the large waterfall (Grande Cascade) in the Bois de Boulogne. To savour the refined cuisine here beneath the majestic rotunda or on the delightful terrace is a rare and elegant treat.

➜ Macaroni, truffe noire, foie gras et céleri gratinés au parmesan. Ris de veau croustillant aux herbes à tortue, carottes, gingembre-orange. Mille gaufres à la crème légère de vanille.

Le Quinzième - Cyril Lignac

14 rue Cauchy (15th) – Ⓜ Javel Plan: **A2-3**
– ✆ 01 45 54 43 43 – www.restaurantlequinzieme.com
– Closed Saturday, Sunday
Menu 69 € (lunch), 150/180 €

• Modern Cuisine • Elegant •

It would be wrong to only consider Cyril Lignac in terms of his notoriety: his precise and aesthetically pleasing dishes reveal associations of flavours as original as they are effective. For instance, lobster from Brittany or *pigeonneau royal* (squab), premium ingredients cooked to a T. A sure-fire winner.

➜ Langoustine dorée, tartare et fraises de Plougastel, vinaigre de fruits rouges. Homard breton confit au beurre de corail, gnocchis de pomme de terre. Chocolat Équateur, mousse légère alpaco et crémeux chocolat au lait.

Agapé

51 rue Jouffroy-D'Abbans (17th) – Ⓜ Wagram Plan: **B1**
– ✆ 01 42 27 20 18 – www.agape-paris.fr
– Closed Saturday, Sunday
Menu 52 € (lunch), 109/215 € – Carte 140/155 €

• Modern Cuisine • Elegant • Friendly •

Agapè… meant unconditional love of another in Ancient Greece. Here, you do indeed feel the love, as you taste this good quality food. The finesse of the flavours and the precision of the cooking makes it a sure-fire winner.

➜ Tartare de noix de veau, caviar et oignon grelot. Lotte de Saint-Gilles-Croix-de-Vie, pommes grenailles confites, tartare de bulots et beurre fumé. Pavlova aux fruits exotiques et crème glacée banane.

L'Archeste (Yoshiaki Ito)

79 rue de la Tour (16th) – Ⓜ Rue de la Pompe Plan: **A2**
– ✆ 01 40 71 69 68 – www.archeste.com
– Closed 1-31 August, Monday, Saturday lunch, Sunday
Menu 52 € (lunch), 110/180 €

• Creative • Minimalist • Contemporary Décor •

Yoshiaki Ito, former chef at Hiramatsu, astounds in this restaurant with a pared-down interior... in keeping with his work. The set menus (three or five courses at lunch, seven at dinner) are models of creativity and precision, espousing the seasons and always giving the best of excellent ingredients. Fine recipes from a repertoire of contemporary French cuisine, which have already garnered quite a following.

➜ Seiche et foie gras poché, salade romaine et sauce gribiche. Carré d'agneau de Lozére et légumes de saison. Vacherin revisité aux fruits de saison.

Comice (Noam Gedalof)

31 avenue de Versailles (16th) – Ⓜ Mirabeau Plan: **A2**
– ✆ 01 42 15 55 70
– www.comice.paris
– Closed 21 April-6 May, 11-26 August, 22 December-6 January, Monday, Tuesday lunch, Wednesday lunch, Sunday
Menu 46 € (lunch)/120 € – Carte 80/110 €

• Modern Cuisine • Elegant •

A Canadian couple had the excellent idea to open their first restaurant in Paris: the chef, Noam, draws inspiration from the foundations of French cuisine, which he gives a modern tweak. Etheliya manages the service and wine. From their complicity a vibrant array of flavours is born; for you to sample in an elegant, intimate interior. A success!

➜ Chou-fleur à la grenobloise. Veau corse, aubergines en persillade et jus de veau. Soufflé au chocolat et glace à la vanille.

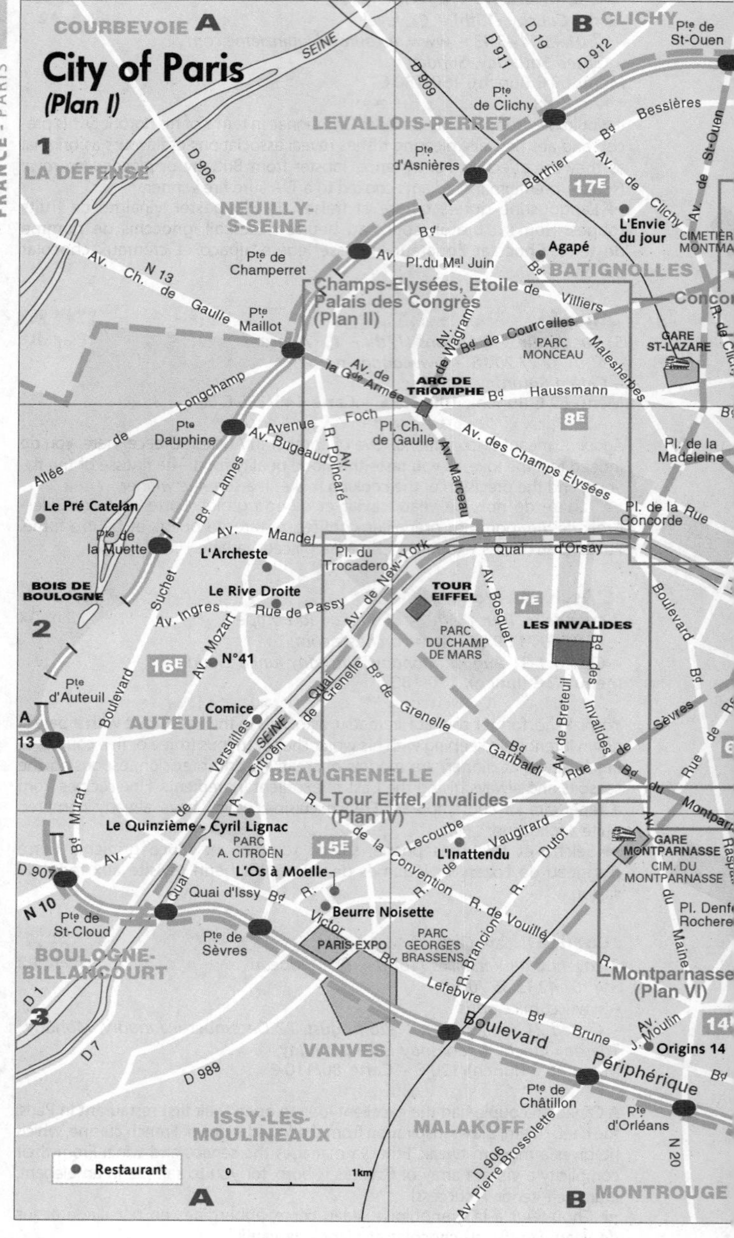
City of Paris
(Plan I)
COURBEVOIE
LA DÉFENSE
NEUILLY-S-SEINE
LEVALLOIS-PERRET
CLICHY
BATIGNOLLES
Champs-Elysées, Etoile
Palais des Congrès
(Plan II)
ARC DE TRIOMPHE
PARC MONCEAU
GARE ST-LAZARE
Pl. de la Madeleine
Pl. de la Concorde
TOUR EIFFEL
PARC DU CHAMP DE MARS
LES INVALIDES
Pl. du Trocadero
BOIS DE BOULOGNE
AUTEUIL
BEAUGRENELLE
Tour Eiffel, Invalides
(Plan IV)
PARC A. CITROËN
GARE MONTPARNASSE
CIM. DU MONTPARNASSE
Montparnasse
(Plan VI)
BOULOGNE-BILLANCOURT
PARIS EXPO
PARC GEORGES BRASSENS
VANVES
ISSY-LES-MOULINEAUX
MALAKOFF
MONTROUGE
Boulevard Périphérique
L'Envie du jour
Agapé
Le Pré Catelan
L'Archeste
Le Rive Droite
N°41
Comice
Le Quinzième - Cyril Lignac
L'Os à Moelle
Beurre Noisette
L'Inattendu
Origins 14
16E
17E
8E
7E
15E
Restaurant
0
1km

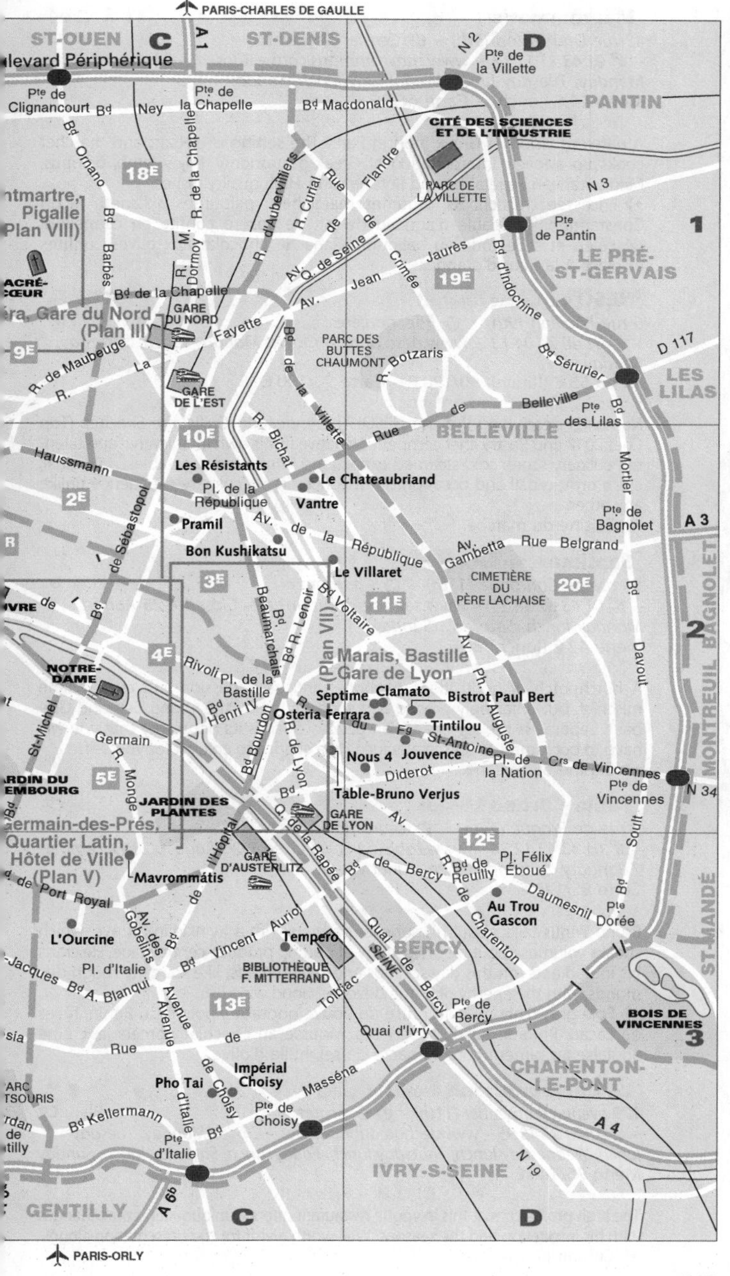
PARIS-CHARLES DE GAULLE
ST-OUEN
ST-DENIS
PANTIN
CITÉ DES SCIENCES ET DE L'INDUSTRIE
PARC DE LA VILLETTE
LE PRÉ-ST-GERVAIS
PARC DES BUTTES CHAUMONT
GARE DU NORD
GARE DE L'EST
LES LILAS
BELLEVILLE
Les Résistants
Le Chateaubriand
Vantre
Pramil
Bon Kushikatsu
Le Villaret
CIMETIÈRE DU PÈRE LACHAISE
NOTRE-DAME
Marais, Bastille Gare de Lyon (Plan VII)
Septime
Clamato
Bistrot Paul Bert
Osteria Ferrara
Tintilou
Nous 4
Jouvence
Table-Bruno Verjus
JARDIN DES PLANTES
GARE DE LYON
GARE D'AUSTERLITZ
Mavrommátis
Au Trou Gascon
L'Ourcine
Tempero
BIBLIOTHÈQUE F. MITTERRAND
BERCY
BOIS DE VINCENNES
CHARENTON-LE-PONT
Impérial Choisy
Pho Tai
IVRY-S-SEINE
GENTILLY
PARIS-ORLY

Mavrommatis

42 rue Daubenton (5th) – Ⓜ Censier Daubenton Plan: **C3**
– ✆ 01 43 31 17 17 – www.mavrommatis.com – Closed 3-28 August, Monday, Tuesday lunch, Wednesday lunch, Sunday
Menu 44 € (lunch) – Carte 66/96 €
• Greek • Elegant • Classic Décor •

A different vision of Greek food in Paris! The setting is elegant and the chef cooks up a lovely interpretation of Greek gastronomy. Enjoy lamb, octopus, Mediterranean vegetables and Retsina wine. High quality dishes.
➜ Fricassée d'artichauts, légumes maraîchers, palourdes à l'aneth façon Constantinople. Épaule d'agneau de lait de Lozère confite en cannelloni de céleri et selle rôtie au halloumi. Ganache chocolat aux olives confites et glace à la fleur d'oranger.

NESO (Guillaume Sanchez)

6 rue Papillon (9th) – Ⓜ Poissonnière Plan: **M1**
– ✆ 01 48 24 04 13 – www.neso.paris – Closed Monday lunch, Saturday, Sunday
Menu 55 € (lunch), 90/120 € – Carte 90/100 €
• Creative • Contemporary Décor •

Nomos is dead: long live the NESO! The endearing Guillaume Sanchez (Top Chef 2017 and Pastry chef competitions) reveals his own imaginative and talented culinary score: cold-steamed extractions, fermented vegetables... Original, often on the ball and occasionally disconcerting: a culinary experience unlike any other.
➜ Cuisine du marché.

Septime (Bertrand Grébaut)

80 rue de Charonne (11th) – Ⓜ Charonne Plan: **D2**
– ✆ 01 43 67 38 29 – www.septime-charonne.fr – Closed 4-26 August, Monday lunch, Saturday, Sunday
Menu 42 € (lunch)/80 €
• Modern Cuisine • Contemporary Décor • Friendly •

A hotchpotch of good ideas, freshness and ease, passion and even a little mischief, but unfailingly precise and spot on: led by the young Bertrand Grébaut, Septime is the joy of Parisian palates! Such is its popularity that you will have to book three weeks in advance for a chance to enjoy it for yourself.
➜ Cuisine du marché.

Table - Bruno Verjus

3 rue de Prague (12th) – Ⓜ Ledru Rollin Plan: **C2**
– ✆ 01 43 43 12 26 – www.table.paris – Closed 1-26 August, 23 December-7 January, Saturday lunch, Sunday
Carte 85/125 €
• Modern Cuisine • Design • Trendy •

Bruno Verjus talks about his supplier partners with a twinkle in his eye, which speaks volumes about his philosophy of putting produce centre stage. He crafts his ingredients (on this day scallops and sweetbreads) like so many rough diamonds, with the energy of a true devotee. Good wine list.
➜ Foie gras d'oie mi-cuit infusé de flouve odorante, poivre du Bénin, fèves de cacao. Pintade en deux services. Mousse au chocolat porcelana, crème anglaise au piment coréen, nacre de sel, huile d'olive.

Le Chateaubriand (Inaki Aizpitarte)

129 avenue Parmentier (11th) – Ⓜ Goncourt Plan: **C2**
– ✆ 01 43 57 45 95 – www.lechateaubriand.net – Closed Monday, Tuesday lunch, Wednesday lunch, Thursday lunch, Friday lunch, Saturday lunch, Sunday
Menu 75/140 €
• Modern Cuisine • Bistro • Friendly •

The high profile chef at this in vogue restaurant offers a unique menu that changes with his inspiration and the seasons. Well worth a visit for the presentation alone!
➜ Cuisine du marché.

Clamato

80 rue de Charonne (11th) – Ⓜ Charonne – ✆ 01 43 72 74 53 – www.clamato-charonne.fr – Closed Monday, Tuesday, Wednesday lunch, Thursday lunch, Friday lunch Plan: **D2**

Carte 35/60 €

• Seafood • Trendy •

The Septime's little sister is becoming something of a bistronomic hit, thanks to its fashionable interior and concise menu focused on seafood and vegetables. Each ingredient is selected carefully and meals are served in a genuinely friendly atmosphere. No bookings are taken – it's first come, first served!

L'Envie du Jour

106 rue Nollet (17th) – Ⓜ Brochant – ✆ 01 42 26 01 02 – www.lenviedujour.com – Closed 5 August-1 September, Monday, Sunday dinner Plan: **B1**

Menu 32/44 €

• Modern Cuisine • Friendly • Trendy •

Charlotte Gondor's dishes reveal precision, colour and flavour: eg. the hangar steak tataki or cod and salad of split peas, the presentation of which is so sharp it whets the appetite. A small selection of well-chosen wines accompanies your choice. A real treat.

Impérial Choisy

32 avenue de Choisy (13th) – Ⓜ Porte de Choisy – ✆ 01 45 86 42 40 Plan: **C3**

Carte 20/50 €

• Chinese • Simple •

A genuine Chinese restaurant frequented by many local Chinese people who use it as their lunchtime canteen. Hardly surprising given the delicious Cantonese specials on offer!

Jouvence

172 bis rue du Faubourg-St-Antoine (12th) – Ⓜ Faidherbe-Chaligny – ✆ 01 56 58 04 73 – www.jouvence.paris – Closed 1-31 August, Monday, Sunday Plan: **D2**

Menu 24 € (lunch) – Carte 37/49 €

• Modern Cuisine • Vintage • Trendy •

Situated on the corner of rue de Cîteaux, this former apothecary-style shop from the 1900s does not merely rest on its decorative laurels. They serve contemporary cuisine, replete with quality ingredients, such as prawn tempura, cucumber kimchi and celery juice. The young chef, formerly with Dutournier (Pinxo restaurant), certainly has talent.

N° 41

41 avenue Mozart (16th) – Ⓜ Ranelagh – ✆ 01 45 03 65 16 – www.n41.fr – Closed 11-22 August, 30 December-2 January Plan: **A2**

Carte 25/53 €

• Traditional Cuisine • Bistro •

This pleasant industrial-style bistro serves tasty, quality cuisine, such as eggs baked in ramekins and cream of foie gras. This restaurant has a modern feel and is run by a couple of restaurateurs who are passionate about what they do.

Origins 14

49 rue Jean-Moulin (14th) – Ⓜ Porte d'Orléans – ✆ 01 45 45 68 58 – www.origins14.com – Closed Monday lunch, Saturday, Sunday Plan: **B3**

Menu 24 € (lunch)/37 €

• Traditional Cuisine • Friendly •

After sharpening his wooden spoon under the masterful eye of Bruno Doucet, young Cornish-born chef Ollie Clarke has taken the plunge in the ex-Régalade, now Origins 14. Inspired by his love of French cuisine, he scrupulously sources and assembles fine ingredients accompanied with equally well-chosen wines.

L'Os à Moelle

3 rue Vasco-de-Gama (15th) – Ⓜ Lourmel – ✆ 01 45 57 27 27 – www.osamoelle-restaurant.com – Closed 22 December-2 January, Monday, Saturday lunch, Sunday

Plan: **A3**

Menu 29 € (lunch) – Carte 37/44 €

• Traditional Cuisine • Friendly • Bistro •

Thierry Faucher is still at the commands of L'Os à Moelle, where, in the early 2000s, he secured his position as one of the precursors of the bistronomie movement. Oysters and leeks in vinaigrette, calf's liver, swede mash with ginger, marrowbone, soup of the day... It's simple, delicious fare and truly enjoyable!

Pho Tai

13 rue Philibert-Lucot (13th) – Ⓜ Maison Blanche – ✆ 01 45 85 97 36

Plan: **C3**

Carte 25/35 €

• Vietnamese • Simple •

In a quiet street in the Asian quarter, this small Vietnamese restaurant stands out from the crowd. All credit to the chef, Mr Te, who arrived in France in 1968 and is a magnificent ambassador for Vietnamese cuisine. Dumplings, crispy chicken with fresh ginger, bo bun and phô soups: everything is full of flavour.

Les Résistants

16 rue du Château-d'Eau (10th) – Ⓜ République – ✆ 01 42 06 43 74 – www.lesresistants.fr – Closed 12-25 August, Monday, Sunday

Plan: **C2**

Menu 19 € (lunch) – Carte 33/40 €

• Modern Cuisine • Friendly • Trendy •

These résistants believe that taste and traceability should be the backbone of all food. Indeed, the credo of owner, Florent Piard, is none other than "good food that respects natural cycles!" and he amply proves his case in this cheerful establishment. The concise menu changes daily in keeping with market availability and the prices are never outlandish. Natural wines bien sûr!

Tempero

5 rue Clisson (13th) – Ⓜ Chevaleret – ✆ 09 54 17 48 88 – www.tempero.fr – Closed 4-26 August, 22 December-1 January, Monday dinner, Tuesday dinner, Wednesday dinner, Saturday, Sunday

Plan: **C3**

Menu 26 € (lunch), 28/48 € – Carte 32/50 €

• Creative • Bistro • Friendly •

A friendly little bistro, which is rather like its chef, Alessandra Montagne. Originally from Brazil, she worked at some fine Parisian establishments before opening her own place. Here she cooks with market-fresh ingredients, creating invigorating and reasonably priced dishes that draw on French, Brazilian and Asian cooking. A lovely fusion!

Le Villaret

13 rue Ternaux (11th) – Ⓜ Parmentier – ✆ 01 43 57 75 56 – Closed Saturday lunch, Sunday

Plan: **C2**

Menu 28 € (lunch), 35/60 € – Carte 50/70 €

• Traditional Cuisine • Friendly • Bistro •

The delicious aromas that greet you as soon as you walk in the door let you know you're in for a culinary treat! Chef-owner Olivier Gaslain is an enthusiastic cook, proposing traditional and generous cuisine made using seasonal ingredients (truffles and game, shown to best effect). Superb wine list (more than 800 varieties).

Ducasse sur Seine

XXX A/C

Port Debilly (16th) – Ⓜ Trocadéro – ✆ 01 58 00 22 08 – www.ducasse-seine.com

Plan: **N1**

Menu 100 € (lunch), 150/290 €

• Modern Cuisine • Design • Chic •

Well, no one can say that Alain Ducasse lacks for boldness or ideas, as the Ducasse sur Seine once again proves. An electric boat, moored on the quayside of Port Debilly in the swanky 16th arrondissement, offers a gastronomic cruise that is both ecological and silent. At the same time as you discover Parisian monuments, you will taste up-to-the-minute cuisine, masterfully crafted by a kitchen team worthy of the best restaurants. Well done, mon capitaine!

Au Trou Gascon

XX A/C

40 rue Taine (12th) – Ⓜ Daumesnil – ✆ 01 43 44 34 26 – www.autrougascon.fr – Closed Saturday, Sunday

Plan: **D3**

Menu 48 € (lunch)/88 € – Carte 66/87 €

• Cuisine from South West France • Elegant •

This institution, dedicated to the cuisine of Southwest France, transports diners to the area between the River Adour and the ocean. It has earned the loyalty of many long-standing regulars with its pâté en croûte with duck foie gras, lièvre à la royale (hare), and warm and crusty tourtière - not to mention the ever-popular cassoulet.

L'Inattendu

XX A/C

99 rue Blomet (15th) – Ⓜ Vaugirard – ✆ 01 55 76 93 12 – www.restaurant-inattendu.fr – Closed Monday, Sunday

Plan: **B3**

Menu 38 €

• Traditional Cuisine • Cosy •

This small, elegantly decorated restaurant is run by two experienced partners who have opened a fishmonger's next door – a real guarantee of fresh produce! Reliable, well-presented cuisine with the occasional unexpected surprise.

Bon Kushikatsu

X A/C

24 rue Jean-Pierre-Timbaud (11th) – Ⓜ Oberkampf – ✆ 01 43 38 82 27 – www.kushikatsubon.fr – Closed 14-28 August, Monday lunch, Tuesday lunch, Wednesday, Thursday lunch, Friday lunch, Saturday lunch, Sunday

Plan: **C2**

Menu 58 €

• Japanese • Intimate • Elegant •

This restaurant is an express trip to Osaka to discover the city's culinary speciality of kushikatsu (meat, vegetables or seafood skewers coated with breadcrumbs and deep-fried). Dish after dish reveals fine flavours, such as: beef sancho, peppered foie gras, and shiitake mushrooms. The courteous service transports you to Japan.

Beurre Noisette

X

68 rue Vasco-de-Gama (15th) – Ⓜ Lourmel – ✆ 01 48 56 82 49 – www.restaurantbeurrenoisette.com – Closed 4-19 August, Monday, Sunday

Plan: **A3**

Menu 32 € (lunch), 38/56 €

• Traditional Cuisine • Friendly •

A tasty bistro, with a following of regulars. Thierry Blanqui draws his inspiration from the market: blood pudding ravioli, chorizo; caramelised pork belly; rum baba, and good old, down-to-earth canaille dishes. Straddling the traditional and the new: most enjoyable. Always a good bet.

Bistrot Paul Bert

X

18 rue Paul-Bert (11th) – Ⓜ Faidherbe Chaligny – ✆ 01 43 72 24 01 – Closed Monday, Sunday

Plan: **D2**

Menu 19 € (lunch)/41 € – Carte 50/60 €

• Traditional Cuisine • Bistro • Vintage •

The façade of this pleasant bistro promises "cuisine familiale". Translate this as: feuilleté of calf sweetbreads with mushrooms, and roast venison with cranberries and celeriac purée. Generous, tasty dishes are prepared without frills. You will be asking for more but be sure to save some room for the rum baba!

Osteria Ferrara

7 rue du Dahomey (11th) – Ⓜ Faidherbe Chaligny Plan: **D2**
– ✆ 01 43 71 67 69 – Closed 27 July-18 August, 22 December-6 January, Saturday, Sunday
Carte 35/55 €

• Italian • Osteria • Bistro •

Gourmets come here, safe in the knowledge they have found sanctuary in this elegant interior. The Sicilian chef whips up mouth-watering Italian recipes based on excellent ingredients. Loin of veal à la Milanese with stir-fried spinach leaf. This Osteria has soul and a fine wine list to boot!

L'Ourcine

92 rue Broca (13th) – Ⓜ Les Gobelins Plan: **C3**
– ✆ 01 47 07 13 65 – www.restaurant-lourcine.fr – Closed 5-25 August, Monday, Sunday
Menu 38 €

• Traditional Cuisine • Bistro • Friendly •

Quality and modesty summarise nicely the spirit of L'Ourcine, a pleasant little bistro which offers inspired, seasonal cuisine. The menu du jour and the 'coups de cœur' set menu on the blackboard offer an array of great suggestions.

Pramil

9 rue Vertbois (3th) – Ⓜ Temple – ✆ 01 42 72 03 60 Plan: **C2**
– www.pramil.fr – Closed Monday, Sunday lunch
Menu 33/43 € – Carte 38/48 €

• Modern Cuisine • Bistro •

The elegant yet restrained decor helps focus the senses on the attractive and honest seasonal cuisine conjured up by Alain Pramil. He is a self-taught chef passionate about food who, in another life, was a physics teacher!

Le Rive Droite

80 rue de Passy (16th) – Ⓜ La Muette Plan: **A2**
– ✆ 01 44 14 38 70 – www.restaurant-lerivedroite.com – Closed Monday dinner, Tuesday dinner, Sunday
Menu 25 € (lunch)/42 € – Carte 40/50 €

• Modern Cuisine • Trendy • Cosy •

On the second floor of the Grande Épicerie, this is the third place (after Coretta and Neva) opened by Beatriz Gonzalez and Matthieu Marcant. In the kitchen, supported by her predominantly female staff (rare enough to be noteworthy), Beatriz masterfully cooks up a tasty menu in harmony with the seasons.

Tintilou

37 bis rue de Montreuil (11th) – Ⓜ Faidherbe-Chaligny Plan: **D2**
– ✆ 01 43 72 42 32 – www.letintilou.fr – Closed 1-21 August, Monday lunch, Saturday lunch, Sunday
Menu 25 € (lunch), 38/49 €

• Modern Cuisine • Friendly •

This 16C former relais de mousquetaires – frequented by Louis XIII's guards – is elegant and original. The flavoursome cuisine served here evokes travel. The menu is short and changes every month, presenting dishes with enigmatic marriages of flavour: salmon, pumpkin, fennel, botargo; wild duck and cocoa. Tasty simplicity!

Vantre

19 rue de la Fontaine-au-Roi (11th) – Ⓜ Goncourt Plan: **C2**
– ✆ 01 48 06 16 96 – www.vantre.fr – Closed Saturday, Sunday
Menu 21 € (lunch) – Carte 40/75 €

• Modern Cuisine • Bistro •

In the Middle Ages, a vantre was a "place of enjoyment" and indeed that's what it is today, for stomach and soul. Two partners, a chef – formerly sous-chef at Saturne – and a wine waiter (Le Bristol, Le Taillevent), offer food featuring select ingredients. More than 2 000 wine types, a friendly welcome… and well-deserved success.

instamatics/iStock

LYONS

LYON

matteo69/iStock

LYONS IN...

→ **ONE DAY**
Old town including funicular up Fourvière hill, Musée des Beaux-Arts.

→ **TWO DAYS**
Musée des Tissus, La Croix-Rousse, evening river trip, Opera House.

→ **THREE DAYS**
Traboule hunting (map in hand), antique shops in rue Auguste Comte.

Lyons is a city that needs a second look, because the first one may be to its disadvantage: from the outlying autoroute, drivers get a vision of the petrochemical industry. But strip away that industrial façade and look what lies within: the gastronomic epicentre of France; a wonderfully characterful old town of medieval and Renaissance buildings with a World Heritage Site stamp of approval; and the peaceful flow of two mighty rivers. Lyons largely came of age in the 16C thanks to its silk industry; many of the city's finest buildings were erected by Italian merchants who flocked here at the time. What they left behind was the largest Renaissance quarter in France, with glorious architecture and an imposing cathedral.

Nowadays it's an energised city whose modern industries give it a 21C feel but that hasn't pervaded the three-hour lunch ethos of the older quarters. The rivers Saône and Rhône provide the liquid heart of the city. Modern Lyons in the shape of the new Villeurbanne and La Part Dieu districts are to the east of the Rhône. The medieval sector, the old town, is west of the Saône. Between the two rivers is a peninsula, the Presqu'ile, which is indeed almost an island. This area is renowned for its red-roofed 16C and 17C houses. Just north of here on a hill is the old silk-weavers' district, La Croix-Rousse.

EATING OUT

Lyons is a great place for food. In the old town virtually every square metre is occupied by a restaurant but if you want a real encounter with the city, step inside a Lyonnais bouchon. These provide the true gastronomic heartbeat of the city - authentic little establishments where the cuisine revolves around the sort of thing the silk workers ate all those years ago: tripe, pigs' trotters, calf's head; fish lovers go for quenelles. For the most atmospheric example of the bouchon, try one in a tunnel-like recess inside a medieval building in the old town. Lyons also has plenty of restaurants serving dishes from every region in France and is a city that loves its wine: it's said that Lyons is kept afloat on three rivers: the Saône, the Rhône and the Beaujolais. Furthermore, the locals still enthusiastically embrace the true concept of lunch and so, unlike in many cities, you can enjoy a midday meal that continues for quite a few hours. With the reputation the city has for its restaurants, it's usually advisable to book ahead.

Les Loges – Hôtel Cour des Loges

XXX
Plan: E2

6 rue du Boeuf (5th) – Ⓜ Vieux Lyon
– ✆ 04 72 77 44 44 – www.courdesloges.com
– Closed Monday, Tuesday lunch, Wednesday lunch, Thursday lunch, Friday lunch, Saturday lunch, Sunday dinner
Menu 105/145 € – Carte 92/119 €
• Modern Cuisine • Romantic • Elegant •

Time seems to have stood still in this enchanting and romantic setting. Find a Florentine courtyard ringed by three floors of galleries and crowned by a contemporary glass ceiling. Savour the refined and inventive cuisine with flickering candlelight adding a final touch.

➜ Escalope de foie gras de canard et racines confites et arquebuse. Pigeonneau, pain croustillant de champignons et fruit épicé. Grands crus de cacao, chuao glacé et ceylan légèrement fumé.

Les Terrasses de Lyon – Hôtel Villa Florentine

XXX
Plan: E2

25 Montée St-Barthélémy (5th) – Ⓜ Fourvière
– ✆ 04 72 56 56 02 – www.villaflorentine.com
– Closed Monday, Sunday
Menu 49 € (lunch), 76/105 €
• Classic Cuisine • Elegant • Luxury •

In the heights of Fourvière; an elegant restaurant with a splendid view of the city. Classical cooking which places the emphasis on quality regional produce.

➜ Foie gras de canard poêlé aux crevettes grises, légumes croustillants. Suprême de pigeon d'Anjou fumé aux sarments de vigne, petits pois, fraises de Pusignan à la moutarde de pistache. Soufflé chaud au chocolat, sablé viennois à la fleur de sel, crème glacée à la fève tonka.

Têtedoie (Christian Têtedoie)

XXX
Plan: E2

4 rue Professeur-Pierre-Marion (5th) – Ⓜ Minimes
– ✆ 04 78 29 40 10 – www.tetedoie.com
Menu 48 € (lunch), 70/145 € – Carte 100/140 €
• Modern Cuisine • Design • Chic •

Perched on Fourvière hill, this restaurant, with its ultra-contemporary design, is a vantage point over the city. Christian Têtedoie applies his talent to exploring French tradition. His signature dish, casseroled lobster and calf's head cromesquis, is quite simply exquisite. Meanwhile, Le Phosphore, open all year round, creates modern cuisine and has another atmosphere entirely, while La Terrasse de l'Antiquaille serves dishes *a la plancha* in fine weather. Superb view of the city on all floors.

➜ Œuf parfait, brocoli, ail et champignons. Pigeon, girolles et verveine. Chocolat sakanti, citron et thym.

Au 14 Février (Tsuyoshi Arai)

XX
Plan: E2

36 rue du Bœuf (5th) – Ⓜ Vieux Lyon
– ✆ 04 78 92 91 39
– www.ly-au14fevrier.com
– Closed 5-19 August, 22 December-6 January, Monday, Tuesday lunch, Wednesday lunch, Thursday lunch, Friday lunch, Sunday
Menu 92 €
• Creative • Elegant • Cosy •

In rue du Bœuf, in the heart of Vieux Lyon, Japanese chef Tsuyoshi Arai sublimates outstanding produce (e.g. Maison Masse squab, Wagyu beef) by playing on textures and bitterness. Talent, precision, imagination, and extremely gracious service.

➜ Menu surprise.

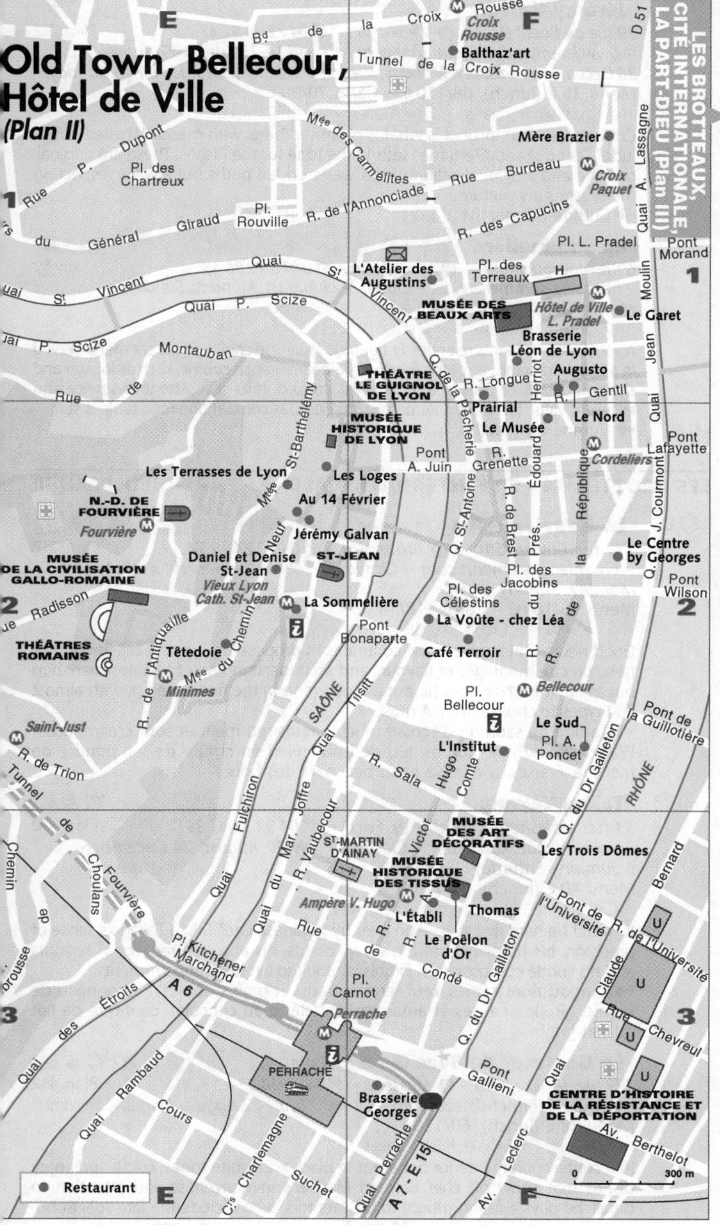
Old Town, Bellecour, Hôtel de Ville
(Plan II)
LES BROTTEAUX, CITÉ INTERNATIONALE, LA PART-DIEU (Plan III)
E
F
1
2
3
Bd de la Croix Rousse
Croix Rousse
Balthaz'art
Tunnel de la Croix Rousse
D 51
Mée des Carmélites
Mère Brazier
Rue Burdeau
Croix Paquet
Rue P. Dupont
Pl. des Chartreux
Pl. Rouville
R. de l'Annonciade
R. des Capucins
Quai A. Lassagne
Rue du Général Giraud
Pl. L. Pradel
Pont Morand
Quai St Vincent
L'Atelier des Augustins
Pl. des Terreaux
H
Quai P. Scize
MUSÉE DES BEAUX ARTS
Hôtel de Ville L. Pradel
Le Garet
Quai Jean Moulin
Brasserie Léon de Lyon
Rue de Montauban
THÉÂTRE LE GUIGNOL DE LYON
Augusto
R. Longue
R. Gentil
Q. de la Pêcherie
Prairial
Le Nord
MUSÉE HISTORIQUE DE LYON
Le Musée
Mée St-Barthélémy
Pont A. Juin
R. Grenette
Cordeliers
Pont Lafayette
Les Terrasses de Lyon
Les Loges
Au 14 Février
N.-D. DE FOURVIÈRE
Fourvière
Jérémy Galvan
Q. St-Antoine
R. de Brest
Prés. Édouard Herriot
R. de la République
Q. J. Courmont
Le Centre by Georges
MUSÉE DE LA CIVILISATION GALLO-ROMAINE
Daniel et Denise St-Jean
ST-JEAN
Pl. des Jacobins
Pont Wilson
Vieux Lyon Cath. St-Jean
Rue Radisson
La Sommelière
Pl. des Célestins
La Voûte - chez Léa
Mée Neuf
Pont Bonaparte
THÉÂTRES ROMAINS
Têtedoie
Mée du Chemin Neuf
Café Terroir
R. de l'Antiquaille
Minimes
SAÔNE
Quai Tilsitt
Pl. Bellecour
Bellecour
Saint-Just
Le Sud
Pont de la Guillotière
Pl. A. Poncet
L'Institut
R. de Trion
R. Sala
Hugo
Comte
Q. du Dr Gailleton
RHÔNE
Tunnel de Fourvière
Quai Fulchiron
Quai du Mar. Joffre
R. Vaubecour
MUSÉE DES ART DÉCORATIFS
Les Trois Dômes
ST-MARTIN D'AINAY
Victor
MUSÉE HISTORIQUE DES TISSUS
Chemin de Choulans
Ampère V. Hugo
Thomas
Pont de l'Université
R. de l'Université
L'Établi
Rue Bernard
Le Poêlon d'Or
Rue Claude
Pl Kitchener Marchand
Rue de Condé
U
Pl. Carnot
A 6
Quai des Étroits
Perrache
Rue Chevreul
PERRACHE
Quai Rambaud
Pont Gallieni
Brasserie Georges
Cours Suchet
Quai Perrache
CENTRE D'HISTOIRE DE LA RÉSISTANCE ET DE LA DÉPORTATION
Av. Berthelot
Crs Charlemagne
A 7 - E 15
Av. Leclerc
0
300 m
Restaurant

✿ **Jérémy Galvan** X A/C

29 rue du Boeuf (5th) – Ⓜ Vieux-Lyon – ✆ 04 72 40 91 47 Plan: **E2**
– www.jeremygalvanrestaurant.com – Closed 14-23 April, 4-27 August, 30 December-8 January, Monday, Wednesday lunch, Saturday lunch, Sunday
Menu 35 € (lunch), 68/110 € – Carte 70/90 €

• Creative • Cosy • Contemporary Décor •

Cuisine based on instinct is what is promised here, with menus labelled "Interlude", "Let go" and "Perfume" setting the tone for the dishes. These are original, creative and playful; deviating from well-trodden paths but always respecting the seasons and nature.

➜ Cuisine du marché.

✿ **La Sommelière** X A/C

6 rue Mourguet (5th) – Ⓜ Vieux Lyon – ✆ 04 78 79 86 45 Plan: **E2**
– https://la-sommeliere.net – Closed 5-25 August, Monday, Sunday
Menu 72 €

• Modern Cuisine • Intimate •

A sommelier owner, a relentlessly rigorous Japanese chef, a single set menu served in a tiny restaurant. As for the food: very elegant French cuisine, such as lobster and shellfish cream, or fillet of wild sea bass cooked in its skin. Attentive service and excellent value for money. Remember to book, as competition for a table is stiff.

➜ Cuisine du marché.

LES BROTTEAUX – CITÉ INTERNATIONALE – LA PART-DIEU PLAN III

✿✿ **Le Neuvième Art** (Christophe Roure) XXX ✿ ♿ A/C

173 rue Cuvier (6th) – Ⓜ Brotteaux – ✆ 04 72 74 12 74 Plan: **H2**
– www.leneuviemeart.com – Closed 17 February-4 March, 4-27 August, Monday, Sunday
Menu 95/160 € – Carte 118/145 €

• Creative • Design • Contemporary Décor •

Good news: Christophe Roure continues to propose the best! Subtle inventiveness, precise marriages of flavours and an understanding of textures mark him out as an artist. Nor does he put a foot wrong in the fine wine list, with almost 400 types to choose from. A must.

➜ Tartine de saumon d'Écosse mi-cuit, radis red-meat et sour cream. Bœuf Wagyu 'Blackmore' cuit au feu de bois, céleri en croûte de sel, poudre de menthe. Fraises, thé fraise et sorbet mara des bois.

✿✿ **Takao Takano** XX ♿ A/C

33 rue Malesherbes (6th) – Ⓜ Foch – ✆ 04 82 31 43 39 Plan: **G2**
– www.takaotakano.com – Closed 27 July-20 August, 24 December-5 January, Saturday, Sunday
Menu 40 € (lunch), 80/120 €

• Creative • Design • Elegant •

It would be hard not to be won over by Japanese chef Takao Takano's sense of precision, his humility before his ingredients, his absolute respect of flavours and his subtle compositions. Exquisite. Book to avoid disappointment.

➜ Langoustines saisies, œuf fermier battu et grains nobles. Pigeonneau de Pornic, girolles, cerises et amaretto. Tartelette au chocolat, confiture de lait à l'earl grey.

✿ **Le Gourmet de Sèze** (Bernard Mariller) XXX ⇔ ♿ A/C

129 rue de Sèze (6th) – Ⓜ Masséna – ✆ 04 78 24 23 42 Plan: **H2**
– www.le-gourmet-de-seze.com – Closed 27 July-22 August, Monday, Sunday
Menu 38 € (lunch), 60/120 €

• Classic Cuisine • Elegant • Cosy •

In a contemporary interior done out in black and white tones, come and enjoy dishes that show off chef Bernard Mariller's inventiveness and attention to detail: he pays a fitting tribute to his mentors, who include the late Joël Robuchon, Jacques Lameloise and Michel Troigros. Modern and tasty cuisine.

➜ Saint-Jacques d'Erquy. Pigeon de Bresse. Citron en trompe l'œil.

Les Brotteaux, Cité Internationale, La Part-Dieu (Plan III)

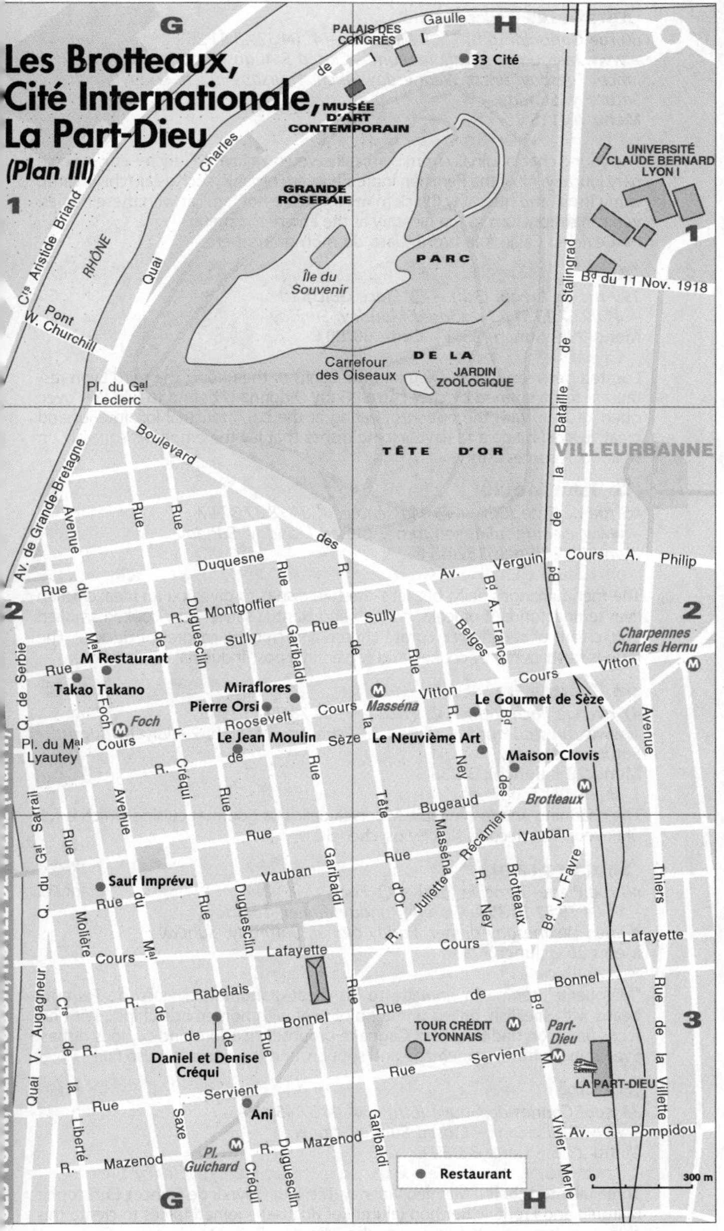

Miraflores (Carlos Camino)

60 rue Garibaldi (6th) – Ⓜ Massena – ✆ 04 37 43 61 26 – www.restaurant-miraflores.com – Closed 5 August-1 September, Monday lunch, Tuesday lunch, Wednesday lunch, Thursday lunch, Friday lunch, Saturday, Sunday Plan: **G2**

Menu 70/115 €

• Peruvian • Intimate • Elegant •

The young chef, originally from Peru, takes you on a joyful, French-Peruvian culinary journey. All of the Peruvian ingredients are organic, such as aji (chilli), camu camu (fruit) and huacatay (black mint). If you are not familiar with these names, you can simply turn to the glossary at the end of the menu.

➜ Ceviche. Caille à la brasa. Casa de mon grand père.

Ani

199 rue de Créqui (3th) – Ⓜ Place Guichard – ✆ 09 67 23 51 33 – Closed Monday, Sunday Plan: **G3**

Menu 23 € (lunch)/33 € – Carte 60/80 €

• Creative • Trendy • Trendy •

Located between La Part-Dieu and the banks of the Rhône, the third Lyon restaurant to be opened by chef-patron Gaby Didonna is bound to win you over: open kitchen, with the option of eating at the bar, industrial loft interior and creative, well-made and flavoursome dishes that lay the emphasis squarely on seafood. A success story.

Le Jean Moulin

45 rue de Sèze (6th) – Ⓜ Masséna – ✆ 04 78 37 37 97 – www.lejeanmoulin-lyon.com – Closed Monday, Sunday Plan: **G2**

Menu 25 € (lunch), 32/45 €

• Modern Cuisine • Contemporary Décor • Friendly •

The menu changes daily, but let's cite two dishes to give you an idea: chicken liver terrine, fondant of leeks, crayfish and Nantua sauce; slow-cooked smoked egg, cream of cauliflower, comté cheese and smoked magret of duck ... The food is fresh, perfectly cooked and served in a post-industrial, hip interior.

M Restaurant

47 avenue Foch (6th) – Ⓜ Foch – ✆ 04 78 89 55 19 – www.mrestaurant.fr – Closed 23 February-2 March, 29 July-18 August, Saturday, Sunday Plan: **G2**

Menu 28 € (lunch), 32/38 €

• Market Cuisine • Trendy • Friendly •

The charming and fashionable M serves delicious gourmet cuisine which is full of flavour. The decor is slightly psychedelic.

Sauf Imprévu

40 rue Pierre-Corneille (6th) – Ⓜ Foch – ✆ 04 78 52 16 35 – Closed Monday dinner, Tuesday dinner, Wednesday dinner, Friday dinner, Saturday, Sunday Plan: **G3**

Menu 26 € (lunch)/29 €

• Traditional Cuisine • Simple • Family •

"Marguerite" terrine in homage to his great-grandmother, coco de Paimpol beans with shellfish, grilled prime rib of beef with homemade chips... With his focus firmly on tradition, Félix Gagnaire proposes delicious and copious dishes. Everything is fresh, homemade and spot on, and the prices are also fair!

33 Cité

33 quai Charles-de-Gaulle (6th) – ✆ 04 37 45 45 45 – www.33cite.com – Closed Sunday dinner Plan: **H1**

Menu 28 € – Carte 33/50 €

• Traditional Cuisine • Brasserie • Contemporary Décor •

Three talented chefs – Mathieu Viannay (Meilleur Ouvrier de France), Christophe Marguin and Frédéric Berthod (alumni of Bocuse) – joined forces to create this chic, tasty brasserie. It opens onto the Tête-d'Or Park. On the menu find great brasserie specialities.

Pierre Orsi

XXXX

3 place Kléber (6th) – Ⓜ Masséna – ✆ 04 78 89 57 68 Plan: **G2**
– www.pierreorsi.com – Closed Monday, Sunday
Menu 60 € (lunch), 125/135 € – Carte 91/160 €
• Classic Cuisine • Bourgeois • Romantic •

First, you come face to face with the lovely ochre Florentine façade, then, on entering, you discover the elegance and luxurious comfort of an opulent bourgeois house. As for the food: the cuisine is fine and precise, of the moment, based on top-notch ingredients and accompanied by superb wines.

Maison Clovis

XX

19 boulevard des Brotteaux (6th) – Ⓜ Brotteaux Plan: **H2**
– ✆ 04 72 74 44 61 – www.maisonclovis.com – Closed 16-23 February, 7-11 May, 6-24 August, Monday, Sunday
Menu 32 € (lunch), 59/95 € – Carte 60/110 €
• Modern Cuisine • Contemporary Décor • Trendy •

Exotic wood furniture, metallic grey tones: the place is stylish and elegant, without being stuffy. A fine chef, Clovis Khoury creates seasonal creations that are truly original and at least as tasty.

L'Art et la Manière

X

102 Grande-Rue-de-la-Guillotière (7th) Plan I: **B2**
– Ⓜ Saxe-Gambetta – ✆ 04 37 27 05 83 – www.art-et-la-maniere.fr
– Closed 3-28 August, 29 December-6 January, Saturday, Sunday
Menu 21 € (lunch), 32/37 €
• Traditional Cuisine • Bistro • Friendly •

A bistro that champions conviviality, market-fresh cooking and lively, reasonably priced wines… and a good excuse to come and explore the Guillotière neighbourhood. The place has a loyal local following, so if you've not booked, instead try Les Bonnes Manières, their second eatery.

TOWN CENTRE — PLAN II

Mère Brazier (Mathieu Viannay)

XXX

12 rue Royale (1th) – Ⓜ Hôtel de Ville Plan: **F1**
– ✆ 04 78 23 17 20 – www.lamerebrazier.fr – Closed 18-24 February, 5-25 August, Saturday, Sunday
Menu 70 € (lunch), 105/170 € – Carte 153/250 €
• Modern Cuisine • Elegant • Chic •

The guardian of Lyon cuisine, Eugénie Brazier (1895-1977) is without doubt looking down on Mathieu Viannay – winner of the Meilleur Ouvrier de France award – with pride. An emblematic restaurant where high-powered classics and creativity continue to be served.

➜ Artichaut et foie gras. Volaille de Bresse demi-deuil. Paris-brest.

Les Trois Dômes – Hôtel Sofitel Lyon Bellecour

XXX

20 quai Gailleton (2th) – Ⓜ Bellecour – ✆ 04 72 41 20 97 Plan: **F3**
– www.les-3-domes.com – Closed 16-20 April, 1-31 August, Monday, Sunday
Menu 48 € (lunch), 82/125 € – Carte 90/145 €
• Modern Cuisine • Contemporary Décor • Minimalist •

On the top floor of the hotel; high-level cooking with the accent on delicious food and wine pairings. From a terrine of pot au feu with foie gras to leg of Limousin lamb, the classics are skillfully reworked. Magical views of the city from the elegant and contemporary dining room.

➜ Quenelles de brochet, sauce écrevisse et pousses d'épinard. Filet de bœuf de Salers, foie gras chaud, artichaut violet et sauce au vin rouge. Cigare au chocolat, crémeux Baileys et glace au safran.

Prairial (Gaëtan Gentil)

11 rue Chavanne (1th) – Ⓜ Cordeliers Plan: **F1**
– ✆ 04 78 27 86 93 – www.prairial-restaurant.com – Closed 30 April-13 May, 1-23 September, Monday, Thursday lunch, Sunday
Menu 34 € (lunch), 58/93 €

• Modern Cuisine • Minimalist • Contemporary Décor •

Gaëtan Gentil took over this restaurant in the city's Presqu'île district in the spring of 2015. In this pleasant setting, complete with a green wall, he creates his gastronomy "décomplexée": contemporary cuisine, resolutely creative, with vegetables at its core.

➜ Tomate, tagète, agastache et pamplemousse. Omble chevalier, girolles, sabayon de beurre noisette et reine-des-prés. Fine coque de meringue, myrtilles sauvages et sorbet à la feuille de cassissier.

Aromatic

15 rue du Chariot-d'Or (4th) – Ⓜ Croix-Rousse Plan I: **B1**
– ✆ 04 78 23 73 61 – www.aromaticrestaurant.fr – Closed Monday, Sunday
Menu 19 € (lunch), 33/43 €

• Modern Cuisine • Trendy •

Look out for this gem in the neighbourhood of La Croix Rousse! Partners Frédéric Taghavi and Pierre Julien Gay cook up tasty modern recipes based on ultra-fresh produce – including beautiful wild fish. Everything is mouth-watering, and the wild cod with its bouillabaisse jus is no exception... We're still licking our lips.

Augusto

6 rue Neuve (2th) – Ⓜ Cordelier – ✆ 04 72 19 44 29 Plan: **F1**
– www.augusto-restaurant-lyon.fr – Closed Monday, Sunday
Menu 19 € (lunch), 29/39 € – Carte 33/46 €

• Italian • Cosy •

Difficult not to rave about the work of Augusto, the very committed young Brazilian chef at the helm of this Italian restaurant. Fine ingredients, deployed with great precision, dishes brimming with flavour and colour – just as it should be. The place is delightful down to the last detail, not to mention the charming service.

Balthaz'art

7 rue des Pierres-Plantées (1th) – Ⓜ Croix-Rousse Plan: **F1**
– ✆ 04 72 07 08 88 – www.restaurantbalthazart.com – Closed 7-21 January, Monday, Tuesday lunch, Wednesday lunch, Sunday
Menu 18 € (lunch), 29/36 € – Carte 33/45 €

• Modern Cuisine • Bistro • Friendly •

You have to earn your meal at this restaurant located near the top of La Croix-Rousse! Housed in the former French Communist Party HQ, red dominates the interior, and Picasso and Modigliani prints hang on the walls. The imagination and beauty found in the decoration are also present in the dishes, which are paired with well-chosen wines.

Brasserie Léon de Lyon

1 rue Pleney (1th) – Ⓜ Hôtel de Ville – ✆ 04 72 10 11 12 Plan: **F1**
– www.leondelyon.com
Menu 30 € – Carte 43/55 €

• Traditional Cuisine • Elegant • Brasserie •

This Lyon institution, founded in 1904, has kept its affluent setting and its convivial atmosphere. Excellent ingredients combine to produce hearty gourmet dishes.

Brasserie Georges

30 cours de Verdun (2th) – Ⓜ Perrache Plan: **F3**
– ✆ 04 72 56 54 54 – www.brasseriegeorges.com
Menu 22/28 € – Carte 30/51 €

• Traditional Cuisine • Brasserie • Vintage •

'Good beer and good cheer since 1836' in the jealously guarded Art Deco setting of this brasserie that is a veritable institution. Lively atmosphere.

L'Établi

22 rue des Remparts-d'Ainay (2th) – Ⓜ Ampère Victor Hugo – ✆ 04 78 37 49 83 – www.letabli-restaurant.fr – Closed Saturday, Sunday Plan: **F3**

Menu 28 € (lunch), 49/64 €

• Modern Cuisine • Trendy •

This restaurant run by an alumnus of Christian Têtedoie is a real favourite. Unbeatable value for money, creative or unapologetically traditional dishes (onion soup and pot-au-feu), but always skilfully handled: from start to finish it's a wonderful treat. Not to spoil anything, the service is also attentive.

L'Institut – Hôtel Le Royal

20 place Bellecour (2th) – Ⓜ Bellecour – ✆ 04 78 37 23 02 – www.linstitut-restaurant.fr – Closed 5-26 August, 23 December-7 January, Monday, Sunday Plan: **F2**

Carte 51 €

• Modern Cuisine • Elegant • Contemporary Décor •

On Place Bellecour, the training restaurant of the Paul Bocuse Institute feels nothing like a school! In a contemporary decor designed by Pierre-Yves Rochon, with open kitchens giving onto the restaurant, the students deliver a high standard of service. The dishes are extremely well made and deserve a high mark.

L'Atelier des Augustins

11 rue des Augustins (1th) – Ⓜ Hôtel de Ville – ✆ 04 72 00 88 01 – www.latelierdesaugustins.com – Closed Monday, Saturday lunch, Sunday Plan: **F1**

Menu 35 € (lunch)/45 € – Carte 50/80 €

• Modern Cuisine • Contemporary Décor • Minimalist •

After stints in some fine establishments, the former chef of the embassies of France in London and Bamako, Nicolas Guilloton, left the world of diplomatic missions to open this refined Atelier. Here food remains an important matter. He creates lovely recipes that are full of colour and flavour, and are nicely modern!

Café Terroir

14 rue d'Amboise (2th) – Ⓜ Bellecour – ✆ 09 53 36 08 11 – www.cafeterroir.fr – Closed 5-13 May, 11 August-3 September, 23 December-8 January, Monday, Sunday lunch Plan: **F2**

Menu 21 € (lunch)/32 € – Carte 30/50 €

• Country cooking • Friendly • Bistro •

The philosophy of the two young owners of the Café Terroir, near the Célestins Theatre, is to source the best of the region's produce to create mouthwatering dishes. The house classics include shepherd's pie with farm reared Ain poultry, hot pistachio sausages, and Lyonnaise cream cheese dip.

Le Centre by Georges

14 rue Grolée (2th) – Ⓜ Cordeliers – ✆ 04 72 04 44 44 – www.lespritblanc.com Plan: **F2**

Menu 24 € (lunch), 26/32 € – Carte 40/75 €

• Steakhouse • Brasserie • Contemporary Décor •

Georges Blanc, the famous chef from the restaurant in Vonnas, is the mastermind behind this contemporary brasserie that opened in late 2012. It is dedicated to meat – and fine meats at that. Find Charolais, Wagyu beef, Aveyron lamb and Bresse chicken served with a large choice of accompaniments and sauces. Calling all carnivores!

Le Nord

18 rue Neuve (2th) – Ⓜ Hôtel de Ville – ✆ 04 72 10 69 69 – www.nordsudbrasseries.com Plan: **F1**

Menu 27/33 € – Carte 36/62 €

• Traditional Cuisine • Brasserie • Historic •

The smallest of the Bocuse brasseries, with a veranda giving onto the street and private lounges on the first floor. The kitchen team are well trained: the use of fresh ingredients is a dogma, and tradition goes hand in hand with generosity and flavour. Salade lyonnaise, saucisson chaud pistaché en brioche (brioche sausage roll), Burgundy snails etc: a reliable option.

Le Sud

11 place Antonin-Poncet (2th) – Ⓜ Bellecour – ✆ 04 72 77 80 00 – www.brasseries-bocuse.com
Plan: **F2**
Menu 27 € (lunch) – Carte 35/60 €
• Mediterranean Cuisine • Brasserie • Mediterranean •

There is an elegant Greek feel to the white and blue decor of this Bocuse brasserie situated a hop, skip and a jump from Place Bellecour. The name is no coincidence: here, it's the South – chicken pastilla with cinnamon and coriander; knuckle-joint of lamb in couscous; fresh cod with aioli – and even more so in summer, on the terrace!

Thomas

6 rue Laurencin (2th) – Ⓜ Bellecour – ✆ 04 72 56 04 76 – www.restaurant-thomas.com – Closed 26 July-11 August, 22 December-6 January, Saturday, Sunday
Plan: **F3**
Menu 22 € (lunch), 47/60 €
• Traditional Cuisine • Bistro • Friendly •

This cosy, modern bistro is under the auspices of a young chef who communicates his passion for delicious, refined cuisine (on a monthly changing menu). Game is a feature, as is one of the house classic desserts, pain perdu (French toast).

La Voûte - Chez Léa

11 place Antonin-Gourju (2th) – Ⓜ Bellecour – ✆ 04 78 42 01 33 – www.lavoutechezlea.com – Closed Sunday
Plan: **F2**
Menu 21 € (lunch), 29/40 € – Carte 32/49 €
• Lyonnaise • Traditional • Friendly •

One of the oldest restaurants in Lyon: in a welcoming atmosphere, tradition carries on with verve. A fine menu with tasty regional dishes and game in autumn.

BOUCHONS *Regional wine tasting and local cuisine in a typical Lyonnaise atmosphere*

Daniel et Denise Créqui

156 Rue de Créqui (3th) – Ⓜ Place Guichard – ✆ 04 78 60 66 53 – www.daniel-et-denise.fr – Closed Saturday, Sunday
Plan: **G3**
Menu 33/51 € – Carte 39/52 €
• Lyonnaise • Lyonnaise Bistro • Friendly •

Joseph Viola – *Meilleur Ouvrier de France* – reigns over this dyed-in-the-wool *bouchon*, with the patina of age. It serves traditional dishes perfectly made with superb ingredients, along with some seasonal suggestions. The cult dish is pâté en croûte with calf sweetbreads and foie gras.

Le Garet

7 rue du Garet (1th) – Ⓜ Hôtel de Ville – ✆ 04 78 28 16 94 – Closed 1-18 March, 26 July-27 August, Saturday, Sunday
Plan: **F1**
Menu 22 € (lunch)/29 € – Carte 25/43 €
• Lyonnaise • Lyonnaise Bistro • Friendly •

This veritable institution is well known among aficionados of Lyonnais cuisine. Calf's head, tripe, dumplings and andouillette sausages are served in a convivial atmosphere and in a typical setting.

Daniel et Denise Croix-Rousse

8 rue de Cuire (4th) – Ⓜ Croix-Rousse – ✆ 04 78 28 27 44 – www.daniel-et-denise.fr – Closed Monday, Sunday
Plan I: **B1**
Menu 33/51 € – Carte 38/55 €
• Lyonnaise • Lyonnaise Bistro • Bistro •

Daniel and Denise Croix-Rousse – the third in the series, after locations on rue de Créqui and in the St Jean quarter – is enjoying the same success as its older siblings. Fill up on hearty Lyon cuisine in a traditional *bouchon* (tavern) setting.

Daniel et Denise Saint-Jean

32 rue Tramassac (5th) – Ⓜ Vieux Lyon Plan: **E2**
– ✆ 04 78 42 24 62 – www.daniel-et-denise.fr – Closed Monday, Sunday
Menu 33 € – Carte 35/55 €

• Lyonnaise • Lyonnaise Bistro • Friendly •

A stone's throw from Cathédrale St-Jean, this Old Town *bouchon* is run by chef Joseph Viola (*Meilleur Ouvrier de France* in 2004), already known for Daniel and Denise in the 3rd *arrondissement*. On the menu, traditional Lyon cuisine to delight fans.

Le Musée

2 rue des Forces (2th) – Ⓜ Cordeliers – ✆ 04 78 37 71 54 Plan: **F2**
– Closed 1-31 August, 24 December-2 January, Monday, Saturday dinner, Sunday
Menu 26 € (lunch)/31 €

• Lyonnaise • Lyonnaise Bistro • Friendly •

A sincere and authentic bouchon with a decor of checked tablecloths, closely packed tables and a buzzing atmosphere. In the kitchen, the young chef creates the classics with real know-how, such as Lyonnaise pork, foie de veau persillé (calf's liver), trotters and brawn salad.

Le Poêlon d'or

29 rue des Remparts-d'Ainay (2th) – Ⓜ Ampère Plan: **F3**
– ✆ 04 78 37 65 60 – www.lepoelondor-restaurant.fr – Closed 3-25 August, Saturday, Sunday
Menu 18 € (lunch), 27/35 € – Carte 27/50 €

• Lyonnaise • Bistro • Friendly •

It's hard to say whether or not the chef does actually use a golden saucepan (poêlon d'or), but he must have a secret weapon – he revisits Lyon's terroir so well and creates food that is as tasty as it is perfectly put together - from the gâteau de foie de volaille (chicken liver) with tomato coulis, to the pike quenelle gratin with béchamel sauce. A must!

AROUND THE CENTRE — PLAN I

Auberge de l'Île Barbe

(Jean-Christophe Ansanay-Alex) Ile Barbe (9th) Plan: **B1**
– ✆ 04 78 83 99 49 – www.aubergedelile.com – Closed Monday, Tuesday lunch, Sunday dinner
Menu 60 € (lunch), 128/158 €

• Classic Cuisine • Elegant •

A country feel in the heart of the leafy île Barbe, an island in the Saône. The walls date from 1601 and there is a softly intimate atmosphere. The very refined cuisine has remarkable flavour associations and creative flights of fancy.

➜ Velouté de cèpe comme un cappuccino, vapeur de foie gras. Poitrine de poulette fermière, sauce suprême au citron confit, haricots beurre, pastèque et amandes. Soufflé chaud de pêche blanche.

Le Canut et les Gones

29 rue Belfort (4th) – Ⓜ Croix-Rousse Plan: **B1**
– ✆ 04 78 29 17 23 – www.lecanutetlesgones.com – Closed Monday, Sunday
Menu 22 € (lunch)/33 €

• Modern Cuisine • Bistro • Vintage •

A unique atmosphere, somewhere between bistro and secondhand shop – formica bar, wooden floorboards, vintage tapestry, collection of old clocks on the walls –, modern cuisine in tune with the seasons, a wine list boasting over 300 types... In a little-frequented area of La Croix-Rousse, this is definitely one to try out.

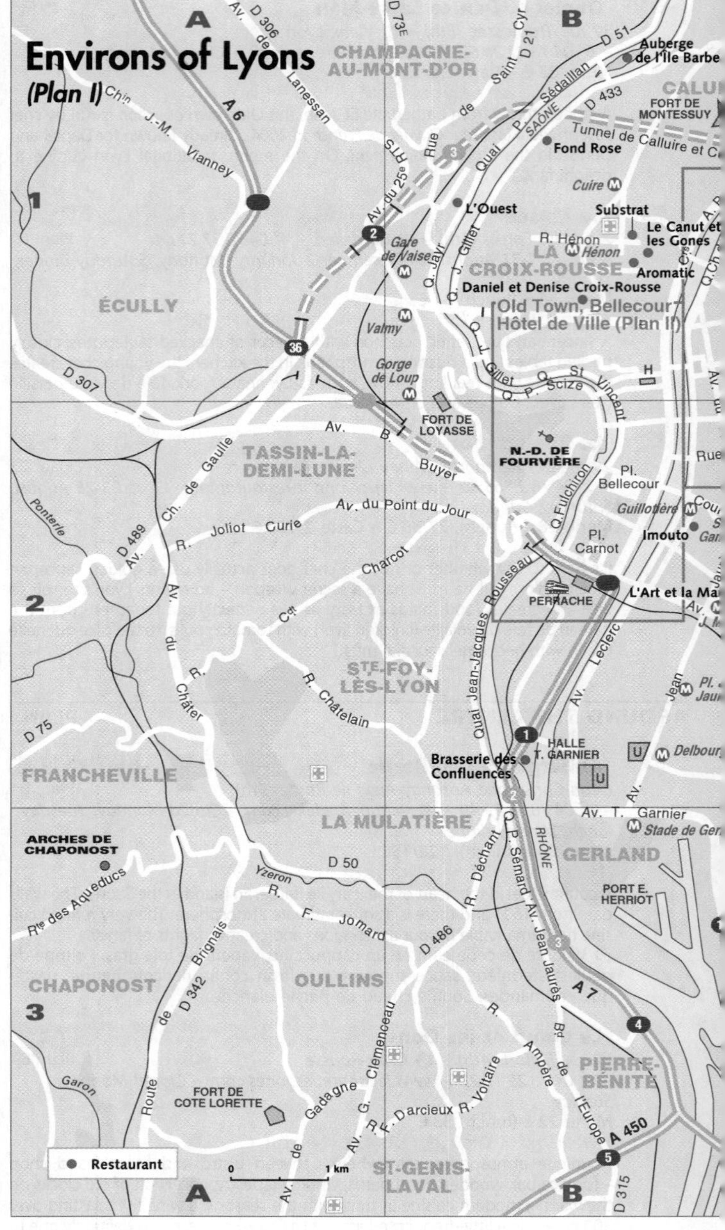
Environs of Lyons
(Plan I)
CHAMPAGNE-AU-MONT-D'OR
ÉCULLY
TASSIN-LA-DEMI-LUNE
STE-FOY-LÈS-LYON
FRANCHEVILLE
LA MULATIÈRE
CHAPONOST
OULLINS
ST-GENIS-LAVAL
PIERRE-BÉNITE
GERLAND
LA CROIX-ROUSSE
Auberge de l'Île Barbe
FORT DE MONTESSUY
Fond Rose
L'Ouest
Substrat
Le Canut et les Gones
Aromatic
Daniel et Denise Croix-Rousse
Old Town, Bellecour Hôtel de Ville (Plan II)
FORT DE LOYASSE
N.-D. DE FOURVIÈRE
Pl. Bellecour
Imouto
Pl. Carnot
PERRACHE
L'Art et la Ma
Brasserie des Confluences
HALLE T. GARNIER
ARCHES DE CHAPONOST
PORT E. HERRIOT
FORT DE COTE LORETTE
Tunnel de Calluire et Cu
Cuire
Hénon
Gare de Vaise
Valmy
Gorge de Loup
Guillotière
Delbour
Stade de Ger
Restaurant
0 1 km
A
B
1
2
3

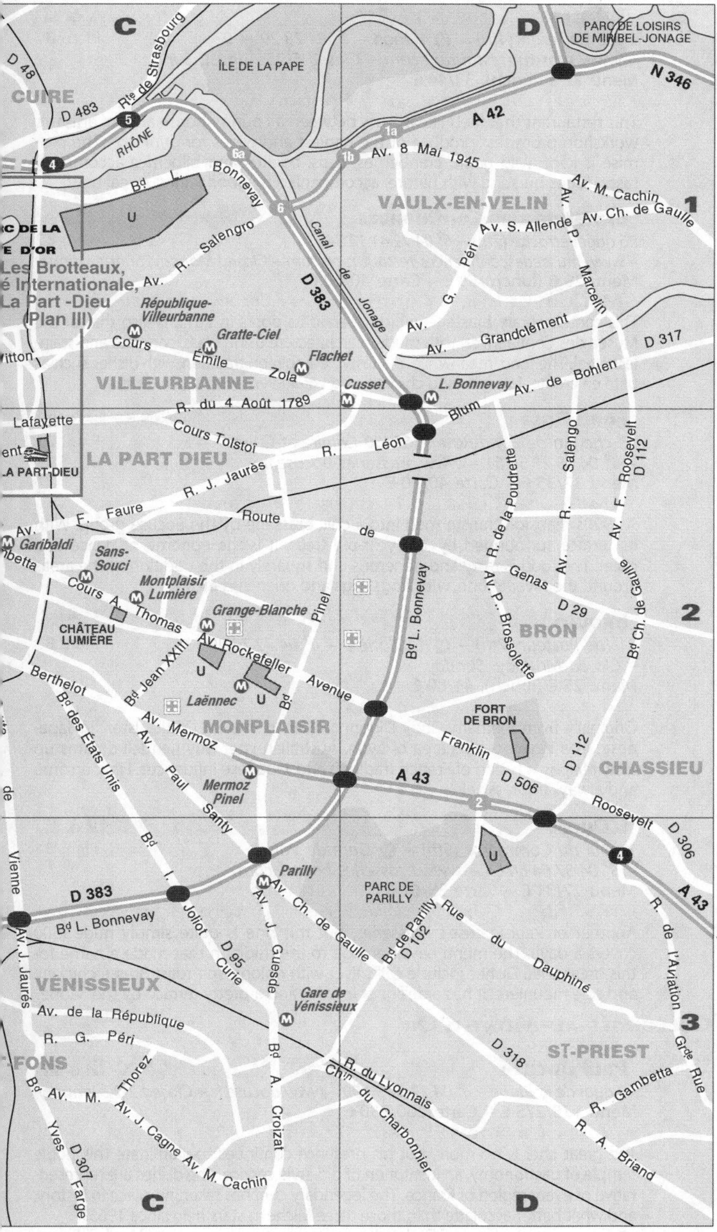

C
D
PARC DE LOISIRS DE MIRIBEL-JONAGE
ÎLE DE LA PAPE
N 346
A 42
CUIRE
D 48
D 483
Rte de Strasbourg
RHÔNE
Av. 8 Mai 1945
Av. M. Cachin
VAULX-EN-VELIN
1
Bd L. Bonnevay
Av. Ch. de Gaulle
Av. S. Allende
Av. P. Marcelin
Av. R. Salengro
Canal de Jonage
D 383
Av. G. Péri
Les Brotteaux, Cité Internationale, La Part-Dieu (Plan III)
République-Villeurbanne
Gratte-Ciel
Cours Émile Zola
Flachet
Cusset
L. Bonnevay
Av. Grandclément
D 317
Av. de Bohlen
VILLEURBANNE
R. du 4 Août 1789
Lafayette
Cours Tolstoï
R. Léon Blum
LA PART DIEU
LA PART-DIEU
R. J. Jaurès
Av. F. Faure
Route de Genas
R. de la Poudrette
Av. R. Salengo
Av. F. Roosevelt
D 112
Garibaldi
Sans-Souci
Montplaisir Lumière
Cours A. Thomas
Grange-Blanche
Pinel
Bd L. Bonnevay
Av. P. Brossolette
BRON
D 29
Bd Ch. de Gaulle
2
CHÂTEAU LUMIÈRE
Av. Rockefeller
Bd Jean XXIII
Laënnec
Bd Pinel
U
Avenue Franklin Roosevelt
Berthelot
Bd des États Unis
Av. Mermoz
Av. Paul Santy
MONPLAISIR
FORT DE BRON
D 112
CHASSIEU
Mermoz Pinel
A 43
D 506
2
4
D 306
Av. de Vienne
Bd I. Joliot Curie
D 383
Parilly
Av. J. Guesde
Av. Ch. de Gaulle
PARC DE PARILLY
Bd de Parilly
D 102
Rue du Dauphiné
R. de l'Aviation
Grde Rue
LYON-ST EXUPÉRY
Bd L. Bonnevay
Av. J. Jaurès
D 95
VÉNISSIEUX
Gare de Vénissieux
Av. de la République
R. G. Péri
Bd A. Croizat
D 318
ST-PRIEST
3
ST-FONS
R. du Lyonnais
Chin du Charbonnier
R. Gambetta
Bd Yves Farge
D 307
Av. M. Thorez
Av. J. Cagne
Av. M. Cachin
R. A. Briand

Substrat

7 rue Pailleron (4th) – Ⓜ Hénon – ✆ 04 78 29 14 93 – www.substrat-restaurant.com – Closed 5-25 August, Sunday

Plan: **B1**

Menu 22 € (lunch), 33/44 €

• Modern Cuisine • Bistro • Friendly •

This restaurant that feels like a cross between a country house and an artisan's workshop promises "produce of the harvest and wines for drinking". The promise is kept: wild garlic, cranberries, ceps, boletus and bilberries accompany tasty dishes bursting with nature, accompanied by good wines. A real treat!

Brasserie des Confluences

86 quai Perrache (2th) – ✆ 04 72 41 12 34 – www.museedesconfluences-restauration.com – Closed Monday, Sunday dinner

Plan: **B2**

Menu 29 € (lunch)/53 € – Carte 40/60 €

• Modern Cuisine • Contemporary Décor • Brasserie •

This contemporary brasserie, which opened its doors in 2015, is also that of the Musée des Confluences, with modern architecture using glass, concrete and stainless steel. The food, meanwhile, is a tasty new spin on tradition, with dishes such as pâté en croûte, foie gras and chicken, and vol-au-vent with sauce Nantua.

Fond Rose

23 chemin de Fond-Rose – 69300 Caluire-et-Cuire – ✆ 04 78 29 34 61 – www.brasseries-bocuse.fr

Plan: **B1**

Menu 32/35 € – Carte 40/70 €

• Traditional Cuisine • Brasserie • Elegant •

A 1920s mansion transformed into a chic brasserie by the Bocuse group. With its terrace surrounded by 100 year-old trees, it is the epitome of peace and quiet. The food is tasty and generous and squarely in the tradition of the areas around the River Saône, with frogs' legs and quenelles etc.

Imouto

21 rue Pasteur (7th) – Ⓜ Guillotière – ✆ 04 72 76 99 53 – Closed Monday, Sunday

Plan: **B2**

Menu 25 € (lunch), 41/80 €

• Fusion • Design • Simple •

Originally from Vietnam, Gaby Didonna opened Imouto ("little sister" in Japanese) in a working-class area of Lyon. Australian chef Guy Kendell dreams up tasty recipes, a fusion of French tradition and Japanese influences. Flavoursome and always impressive!

L'Ouest

1 quai du Commerce (9th) – Ⓜ Gare de Vaise – ✆ 04 37 64 64 64 – www.brasseries-bocuse.com

Plan: **B1**

Menu 27/31 € – Carte 35/67 €

• Traditional Cuisine • Brasserie • Contemporary Décor •

Another of Paul Bocuse's brasseries, but this one is quite simply huge (600 covers a day!). The menu pays homage to the tradition that made a name for this great chef. Dishes include calf's liver with onions, spit-roast Bresse chicken, and sole meunière. It has a designer interior and a pretty terrace by the Saone.

Collonges-au-Mont-d'Or

Paul Bocuse

40 quai de la Plage – ✆ 04 72 42 90 90 – www.bocuse.fr – Closed 2-22 January

Menu 175/275 € – Carte 200/250 €

• Classic Cuisine • Elegant • Luxury •

The great chef is no more, but his presence continues to illuminate this noble temple of gastronomy, an institution of old-style service. The dishes are representative of every region of France. The legendary chef has taken his place in history, and what better accolade than those three Michelin stars held since 1965!

➜ Soupe aux truffes V.G.E. Volaille de Bresse cuite en vessie "Mère Fillioux". Gâteau Président "Maurice Bernachon".

Charbonnières-les-Bains

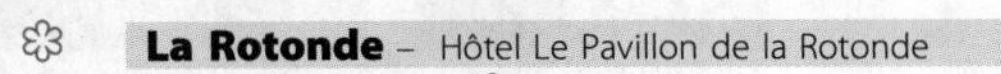

La Rotonde – Hôtel Le Pavillon de la Rotonde

avenue du Casino – ✆ 04 78 87 00 97
– www.restaurant-rotonde.com – Closed 30 July-23 August, Monday, Tuesday lunch, Saturday lunch, Sunday
Menu 39 € (lunch), 78/135 €

• Modern Cuisine • Elegant • Luxury •

In this pleasantly leafy area on the outskirts of town: a fine legacy of the Art Deco period which also houses the casino Le Lyon Vert. The menu is in a classic French vein and combines timeless dishes with new influences - not forgetting the great repertoire of Lyon cuisine.

➜ Pâté en croûte "Champion du Monde 2013". Lotte de petit bateau aux coquillages, émulsion marinière. Finger praliné au citron, noisettes et crème glacée au chocolat gianduja.

Hamburg
BERLIN
Munich

GERMANY
DEUTSCHLAND

bluejayphoto/iStock

BERLIN
BERLIN

TomasSereda/iStock

BERLIN IN...

→ **ONE DAY**
Unter den Linden, Museum Island, Nikolaiviertel, coffee at TV Tower.

→ **TWO DAYS**
Potsdamer Platz, Reichstag, Regierungsviertel including the Gemäldegalerie, concert at Philharmonie.

→ **THREE DAYS**
KaDeWe, Kurfürstendamm, Charlottenburg Palace.

Berlin's parliament faces an intriguing dilemma when it comes to where to call its heart, as, although they are homogeneous in many other ways, the east and the west of the city still lay claim to separate centres after 40 years of partition. Following the tempestuous 1990s, Berlin sought to resolve its new identity, and it now stands proud as one of the most dynamic and forward thinking cities in the world. Alongside its idea of tomorrow, it's never lost sight of its bohemian past, and many parts of the city retain the arty sense of adventure that characterised downtown Berlin during the 1920s: turn any corner and you might find a modernist art gallery, a tiny cinema or a cutting-edge club.

The eastern side of the River Spree, around Nikolaiviertel, is the historic heart of the city, dating back to the 13C. Meanwhile, way over to the west of the centre lie Kurfürstendamm and Charlottenburg; smart districts which came to the fore after World War II as the heart of West Berlin. Between the two lie imposing areas which swarm with visitors: Tiergarten is the green lung of the city, and just to its east is the great boulevard of Unter den Linden. Continuing eastward, the self-explanatory Museum Island sits snugly and securely in the tributaries of the Spree. The most southerly of Berlin's sprawling districts is Kreuzberg, renowned for its bohemian, alternative character.

EATING OUT

Many of Berlin's best restaurants are found within the grand hotels and you only have to go to Savignyplatz near Ku'damm to realise how smart dining has taken off. Dinner is the most popular meal and you can invariably eat late, as lots of places stay open until 2 or 3am. Berlin also has a reputation for simple, hearty dishes, inspired by the long, hard winter and, when temperatures drop, the city's comfort food has an irresistible allure – there's pork knuckle, Schnitzel, Bratwurst in mustard, chunky dumplings... and the real Berlin favourite, Currywurst. Bread and potatoes are ubiquitous but since reunification, many dishes have also incorporated a more global influence, so produce from the local forests, rivers and lakes may well be given an Asian or Mediterranean twist (Berlin now claims a wider range of restaurants than any other German city). Service is included in the price of your meal but it's customary to round up the bill. Be sure to try the local 'Berliner Weisse mit Schuss' – a light beer with a dash of raspberry or woodruff.

✿✿ **Lorenz Adlon Esszimmer**

Hotel Adlon Kempinski – Unter den Linden 77 (1st floor) Plan: **G1**
✉ 10117 – Ⓜ Brandenburger Tor – ✆ (030) 22 61 19 60 – www.lorenzadlon-esszimmer.de – Closed 2 weeks January, 3 weeks July and Sunday-Tuesday
Menu 175/205 € – *(dinner only) (booking essential)*
• Creative • Luxury • Elegant •

The Adlon inevitably conjures up an image of stylish fine dining, with its sumptuous interior, charming professional service including excellent wine recommendations and top-class creative cuisine. The food itself is conceived with great imagination and prepared with consummate skill using only the very best ingredients. The view of the Brandenburg Gate is the icing on the cake!

➜ Norwegischer Lachs, Rapssaat, Szechuan Pfeffer, Amarant, Tannenhonig, Dill. Taube, wilder Brokkoli, Zimtblüte, schwarzer Knoblauch. Himbeeren, karamellisierter Blätterteig, Crème von Jivara- und Opalisschokolade, Kakaoknusper, Milchhaut, Sauerkleeeis.

✿✿ **FACIL** – Hotel THE MANDALA

Potsdamer Str. 3 (5th floor) ✉ 10785 – Ⓜ Potsdamer Platz – ✆ (030) 5 90 05 12 34 – www.facil.de – Closed 2 weeks January, 13 July - 4 August and Saturday-Sunday Plan: **F2**
Menu 51 € (lunch)/198 € – Carte 119/151 € – *(booking advisable)*
• Creative • Chic • Elegant •

FACIL is an oasis of calm amid the hustle and bustle of the Potsdamer Platz. It is pleasantly light and airy, especially in the summer, with plenty of greenery outside even though it's on the fifth floor! The modern, creative food is beautifully presented.

➜ Steinbutt, Lauch und Verbene. Lammrücken, Tamarillo, Basilikum und grüne Oliven. Wilde Feige, Veilchen und Caramelia Schokolade.

✿✿ **Horváth** (Sebastian Frank)

Paul-Lincke-Ufer 44a ✉ 10999 – Ⓜ Schönleinstr. – ✆ (030) 61 28 99 92 – www.restaurant-horvath.de – Closed 4-10 February, 22 July - 4 August and Monday-Tuesday Plan I: **D2**
Menu 100/140 € – *(dinner only) (booking advisable)*
• Creative • Minimalist • Vintage •

Try Horváth if you fancy some really imaginative cuisine full of interesting combinations, full-bodied flavours and intensity. The food has its own particular style, which is elaborate yet harmonious. The service is friendly and accomplished, and in good weather you can sit outside in the garden overlooking the lively street.

➜ Melanzani, Minze und gefrorene Petersilie. Gegrilltes Störfilet, Paprikaaromen. Milchferkel, Rauchzwiebel, Wangerl und gedörrtes Wurzelwerk.

✿✿ **Rutz**

Chausseestr. 8 (1st floor) ✉ 10115 – Ⓜ Oranienburger Tor – ✆ (030) 24 62 87 60 – www.rutz-restaurant.de – Closed Sunday-Monday Plan I: **C2**
Menu 145/185 € – *(dinner only)*
• Modern cuisine • Design • Trendy •

Marco Müller's set Inspirations menu promises well-balanced, creative combinations of top-quality ingredients, skilfully showcasing particular flavours to give each dish its own special character. Diners enjoy their food in the modern interior accompanied by some expert wine suggestions drawn from a fine wine list.

➜ Muscheln und Bohnenkraut, Holundermilch, alter und neuer Kohlrabi. Rebholz und Kiefer, Ente, Rosenkohl. Junge Triebe, Ackersalatsud und Joghurt.

Rutz Weinbar – See below

✿✿ **Tim Raue** XX

Rudi-Dutschke-Str. 26 ✉ 10969 – Ⓜ Kochstr.
– ✆ (030) 25 93 79 30
– www.tim-raue.com
– Closed 23 December - 2 January and Sunday-Monday
Menu 138/198 € – Carte 125/161 € – *(Tuesday-Thursday: dinner only)*
Plan: **G2**

• Asian • Fashionable • Friendly •

Originality is what makes the cuisine of Tim Raue so unique! The chef uses top-quality produce and skilfully combines flavours, creating personal signature dishes which always feature Asian elements. The attentive and unpretentious service is a pleasure to experience, as is the minimalist and elegant decor of the interior.

➜ Weißer Spargel, Fish Maw und Sansho. Ikarimi Lachs, Tomate und Sternanis. Kalb, Erbse und Kamebishi.

✿ **GOLVET** XX

Potsdamer Str. 58 (8th floor) ✉ 10785
– Ⓜ Mendelsohn-Bartholdy-Park
– ✆ (030) 89064222 – www.golvet.de
– Closed 24 June - 9 July and Sunday-Monday
Menu 79/118 € – Carte 93/135 € – *(dinner only)*
Plan: **F2**

• International • Design •

GOLVET offers an impressive view over Potsdamer Platz, a stylish interior complete with open kitchen and artful, modern, pared-down cuisine made using the very best ingredients. Then of course, there's the top-quality service and excellent wine recommendations.

➜ Beuscherl vom Kalb mit Aubergine, Kalamaretti und jungem Knoblauch. Saibling aus dem Königssee mit geeistem Miso, Blumenkohl und Queller. Dessert vom Rhabarber mit Gurke, Dill und Litschi.

✿ **Pauly Saal** XX

Auguststr. 11 ✉ 10117 – Ⓜ Rosenthaler Pl.
– ✆ (030) 33 00 60 70 – www.paulysaal.com
– Closed Sunday-Monday
Menu 69/115 € – *(booking advisable)*
Plan I: **C2**

• Modern cuisine • Fashionable •

If you're looking for somewhere elegant yet relaxed to eat, this is it. The high-ceilinged hall in this former Jewish girls' school boasts a striking decorative rocket above the window into the kitchen and stylish Murano glass chandeliers. The food is modern with creative notes. At lunchtimes, the set menu is available from three courses.

➜ Makrele, Gurken, Miso, Salzkraut. Dorsch, Spargel, Kapuziner, Olivensamen. Rind, Karotten, Morcheln, Zucchini.

✿ **Richard** XX

Köpenicker Str. 174 (by Köpenicker Straße) ✉ 10997 – Ⓜ Schlesisches Tor
– ✆ (030) 49 20 72 42
– www.restaurant-richard.de
– Closed Sunday - Monday
Menu 68/100 € – *(dinner only)*

• Modern French • Fashionable • Trendy •

Yes, this really is it, but don't be put off by the somewhat lacklustre exterior. Inside the former Köpenicker Hof, built in 1900, the fine interior boasts an ornate ceiling, designer lighting and artwork (the owner Hans Richard is also a painter). It provides the perfect setting for the excellent, artful and reasonably priced set menu.

➜ Sellerie aus dem Salzteig mit Perigord Trüffel und Petersilie. Milchkalbsbries mit Morcheln und Vin Jaune. Taube vom Holzkohlegrill mit Aubergine und Dattel-Condiment.

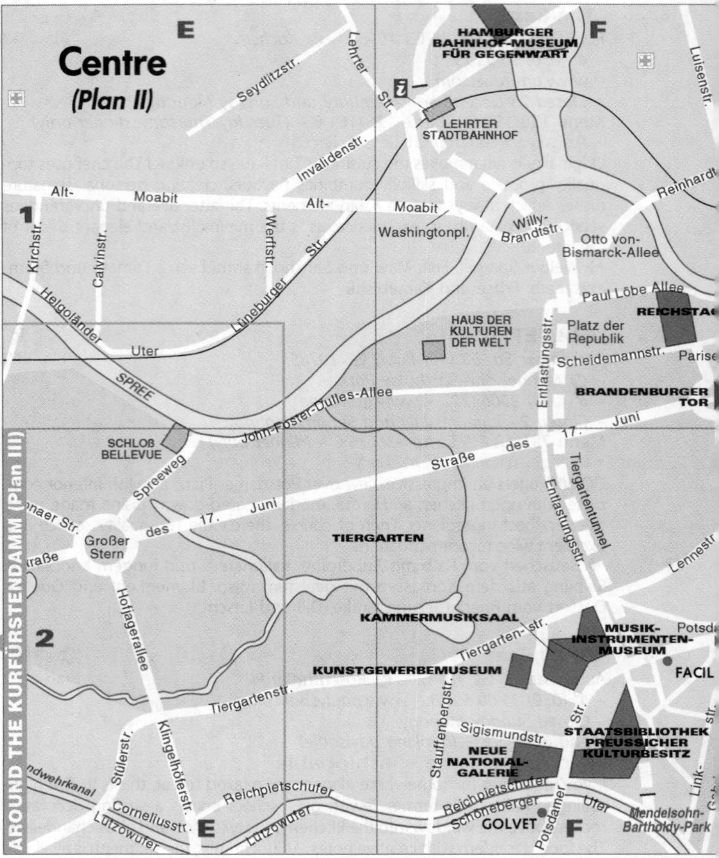

Centre
(Plan II)

AROUND THE KURFÜRSTENDAMM (Plan III)

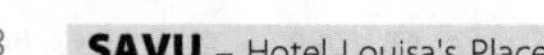

SAVU – Hotel Louisa's Place XX A/C

Kurfürstendamm 160 ✉ *10709 –* Ⓜ *Adenauerplatz* Plan I: **A3**
– ☏ *(030) 88475788 – www.savu.berlin – Closed Sunday*
Menu 65/95 € – *(dinner only)*
• Creative • Friendly •

SAVU – meaning "smoked" in Finnish – is relaxed and informal with an appealing Nordic touch. Behind a huge pane of glass, the kitchen staff prepare modern food with Scandinavian, Spanish and Italian influences. Note that there's no distinction between starter and main course here, you can mix and match all the dishes as you please. Friendly service from an accomplished front-of-house team.

➜ Heilbutt, Erbsencreme, Erbsen, Zitronen-Verbenejus. Poltinger Lammnuss und Zunge, Auberginenlasagne. Geräucherte Erdbeeren, Erdbeersorbet, Pistazienkuchen.

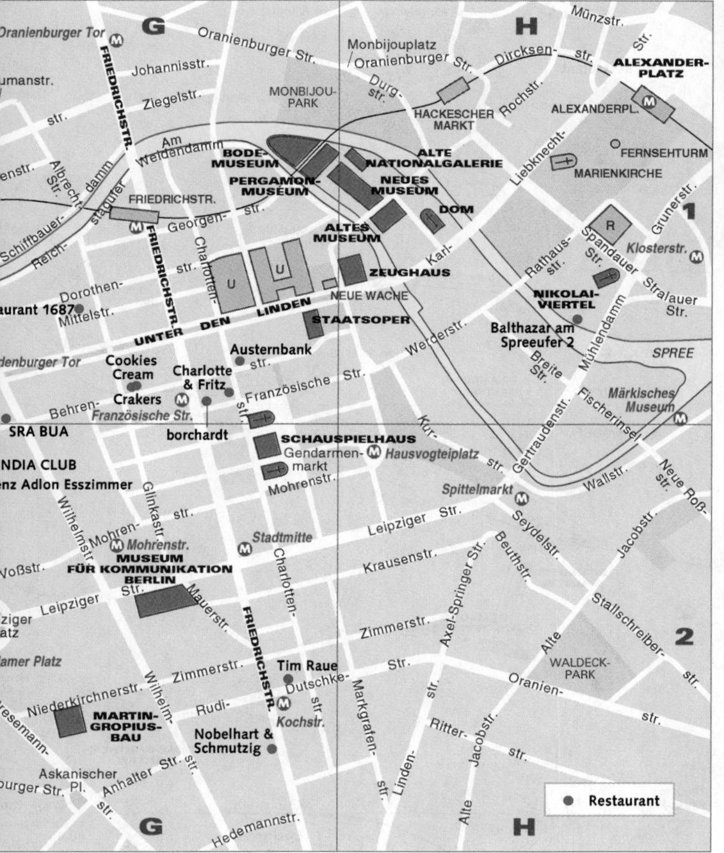

einsunternull XX

Hannoversche Str. 1 ✉ *10115* Plan I: **C2**
– Ⓜ *Oranienburger Tor*
– ✆ *(030) 27 57 78 10*
– *www.einsunternull.com*
– *Closed Sunday-Monday lunch, Wednesday*

Menu 59 € (lunch)/119 € (dinner)

• Creative • Design •

Everything is pared down to the essentials here, whether it's the minimalist-style interior or the creative cuisine. The food is simple and unfussy, the dishes have an original feel and great flavour. Interestingly, the restaurant preserves many of its seasonal ingredients.

➜ Pilzboden mit Roggen und Geflecht. In Asche gereifte Ente mit Mirabellen und Schmalz. Schwarzbrot mit Honig.

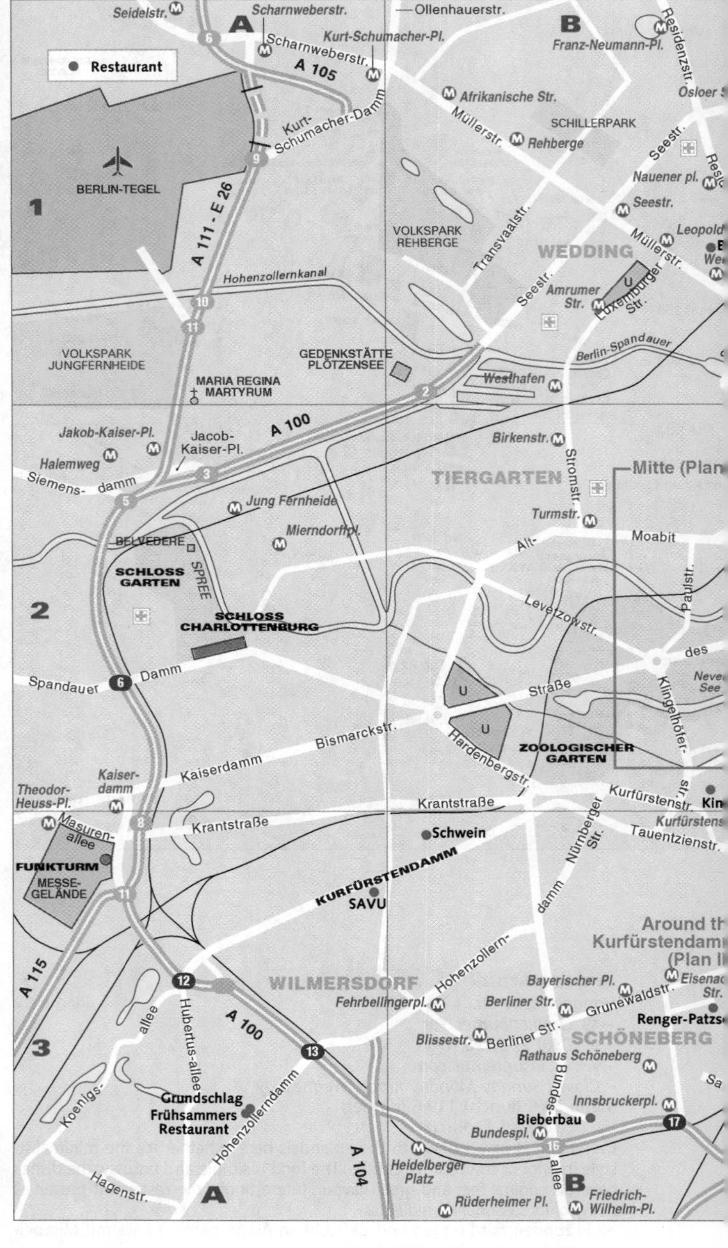

Restaurant
BERLIN-TEGEL
VOLKSPARK JUNGFERNHEIDE
MARIA REGINA MARTYRUM
GEDENKSTÄTTE PLÖTZENSEE
VOLKSPARK REHBERGE
SCHILLERPARK
WEDDING
TIERGARTEN
Mitte (Plan
SCHLOSS GARTEN
BELVEDERE
SPREE
SCHLOSS CHARLOTTENBURG
ZOOLOGISCHER GARTEN
FUNKTURM
MESSE-GELÄNDE
KURFÜRSTENDAMM
WILMERSDORF
SCHÖNEBERG
Around th Kurfürstendamm (Plan II
Schwein
SAVU
Grundschlag
Frühsammers Restaurant
Bieberbau
Renger-Patzsch
Seidelstr.
Scharnweberstr.
Kurt-Schumacher-Pl.
Ollenhauerstr.
Franz-Neumann-Pl.
Residenzstr.
Osloer S
Afrikanische Str.
Müllerstr.
Rehberge
Seestr.
Nauener pl.
Leopold
Amrumer Str.
Luxemburger Str.
Transvaalstr.
Berlin-Spandauer
Westhafen
Birkenstr.
Stromstr.
Turmstr.
Moabit
Alt-
Paulstr.
Levetzowstr.
des
Straße
Neuer See
Klingelhöfer-str.
Hardenbergstr.
Kurfürstenstr.
Tauentzienstr.
Krantstraße
Nürnberger Str.
Hohenzollern-damm
Bayerischer Pl.
Eisenacher Str.
Grunewaldstr.
Berliner Str.
Fehrbellingerpl.
Blissestr.
Rathaus Schöneberg
Innsbruckerpl.
Bundespl.
Bundes-allee
Heidelberger Platz
Rüderheimer Pl.
Friedrich-Wilhelm-Pl.
Hohenzollernkanal
A 105
Kurt-Schumacher-Damm
A 111 - E 26
A 100
Jakob-Kaiser-Pl.
Jacob-Kaiser-Pl.
Halemweg
Siemens-damm
Jung Fernheide
Mierndorffpl.
Spandauer Damm
Bismarckstr.
Kaiserdamm
Kaiser-damm
Theodor-Heuss-Pl.
Masuren-allee
A 115
Hubertus-allee
Koenigs-allee
Hohenzollerndamm
A 104
Hagenstr.

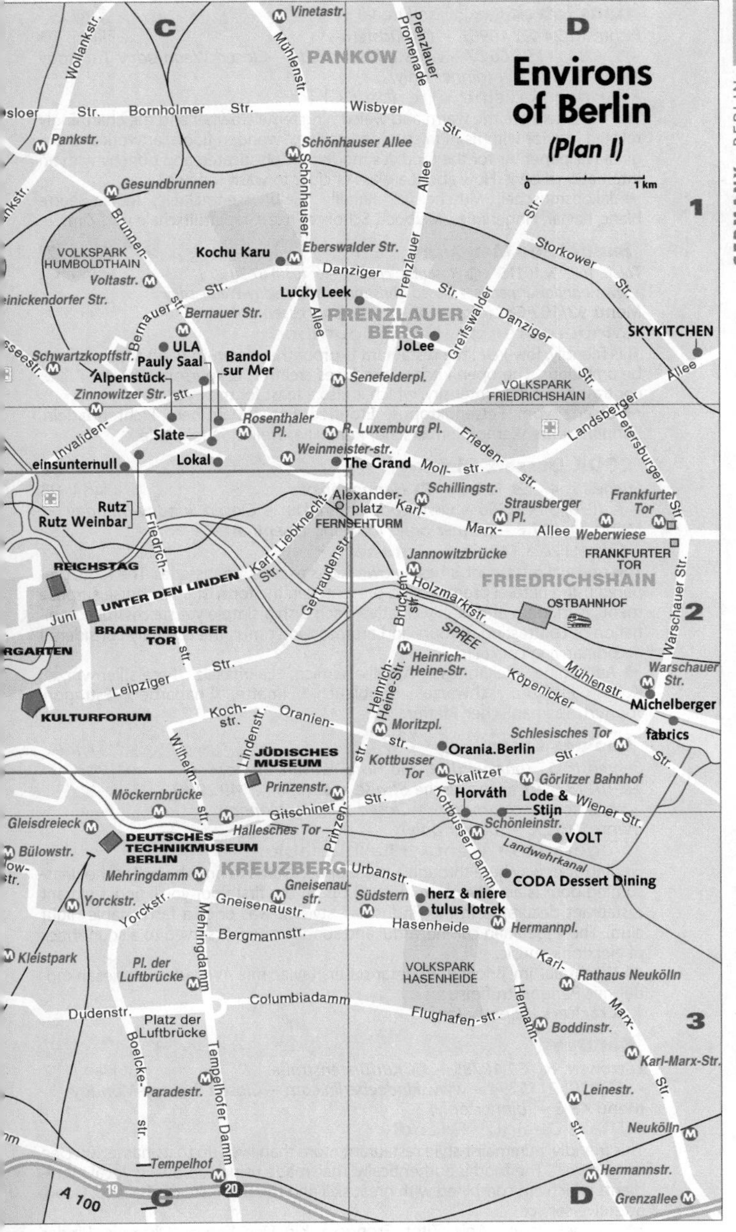
Environs of Berlin
(Plan I)
0
1 km
C
D
1
2
3
PANKOW
PRENZLAUER BERG
FRIEDRICHSHAIN
KREUZBERG
VOLKSPARK HUMBOLDTHAIN
VOLKSPARK FRIEDRICHSHAIN
VOLKSPARK HASENHEIDE
Kochu Karu
Lucky Leek
JoLee
SKYKITCHEN
ULA
Pauly Saal
Bandol sur Mer
Alpenstück
Slate
Lokal
einsunternull
The Grand
Rutz
Rutz Weinbar
REICHSTAG
UNTER DEN LINDEN
BRANDENBURGER TOR
KULTURFORUM
JÜDISCHES MUSEUM
DEUTSCHES TECHNIKMUSEUM BERLIN
FERNSEHTURM
OSTBAHNHOF
FRANKFURTER TOR
Michelberger
fabrics
Orania.Berlin
Horváth
Lode & Stijn
VOLT
CODA Dessert Dining
herz & niere
tulus lotrek
SPREE
Landwehrkanal
Vinetastr.
Pankstr.
Gesundbrunnen
Schönhauser Allee
Eberswalder Str.
Voltastr.
Bernauer Str.
Schwartzkopffstr.
Zinnowitzer Str.
Senefelderpl.
Rosenthaler Pl.
R. Luxemburg Pl.
Weinmeister-str.
Alexanderplatz
Schillingstr.
Strausberger Pl.
Frankfurter Tor
Weberwiese
Jannowitzbrücke
Heinrich-Heine-Str.
Warschauer Str.
Moritzpl.
Schlesisches Tor
Kottbusser Tor
Görlitzer Bahnhof
Prinzenstr.
Möckernbrücke
Gleisdreieck
Hallesches Tor
Bülowstr.
Mehringdamm
Gneisenaustr.
Südstern
Schönleinstr.
Hermannpl.
Yorckstr.
Kleistpark
Pl. der Luftbrücke
Platz der Luftbrücke
Rathaus Neukölln
Boddinstr.
Karl-Marx-Str.
Leinestr.
Neukölln
Paradestr.
Tempelhof
Hermannstr.
Grenzallee
Wollankstr.
Bornholmer Str.
Wisbyer Str.
Mühlenstr.
Prenzlauer Promenade
Prenzlauer Allee
Schönhauser Allee
Brunnenstr.
Danziger Str.
Storkower Str.
Greifswalder Str.
Bernauer Str.
Invalidenstr.
Friedenstr.
Landsberger Allee
Petersburger Str.
Mollstr.
Karl-Marx-Allee
Karl-Liebknecht-Str.
Gertraudenstr.
Holzmarktstr.
Brückenstr.
Friedrichstr.
Leipziger Str.
Kochstr.
Oranienstr.
Lindenstr.
Wilhelmstr.
Köpenicker Str.
Mühlenstr.
Skalitzer Str.
Wiener Str.
Gitschiner Str.
Kottbusser Damm
Urbanstr.
Gneisenaustr.
Yorckstr.
Bergmannstr.
Hasenheide
Mehringdamm
Karl-Marx-Str.
Hermannstr.
Columbiadamm
Dudenstr.
Flughafen-str.
Boelcke-str.
Tempelhofer Damm
A 100
19
20

tulus lotrek (Maximilian Strohe)

Fichtestr. 24 ✉ 10967 – Ⓜ Südstern Plan I: **D3**
– ✆ (030) 41 95 66 87 – www.tuluslotrek.de – Closed Wednesday-Thursday
Menu 99/129 € – *(dinner only)*

• Modern cuisine • Trendy • Chic •

The USPs here are the warm and welcoming female owner and the charmingly relaxed interior with its high stuccoed ceilings, wooden floors, artwork and original wallpaper. As for the food, it's modern, sophisticated and punchy with an international bent. How about a glass of cider to wash it down?

→ Jakobsmuschel, Muschelsud, Kamille. Gelbflossenmakrele, Molke-Beurre blanc, Kaviar, Fingerlimes. Maibock, Schokominze, Grapefruitschale und Zimt.

Bandol sur Mer (Andreas Saul)

Torstr. 167 ✉ 10115 – Ⓜ Rosenthaler Platz – ✆ (030) 67 30 20 51 Plan I: **C2**
– www.bandolsurmer.de – Closed Christmas and Tuesday-Wednesday
Menu 92/102 € – *(dinner only) (booking essential)*

• Modern French • Neighbourhood •

This friendly, low-key little restaurant is proof that down-to-earth food can also be ambitious. The open kitchen produces creative, flavoursome cuisine full of contrast and rich in intensity, which is also a feast for the eyes.

→ Essenz vom Felsenoktopus. Étouffée Ente, Mairüben, Fichtennadeln, Sonnenblumenkerne. Rumkirsche, Petersilie, weiße Schokolade.

CODA Dessert Dining

Friedelstr. 47 ✉ 12047 – Ⓜ Hermannplatz Plan I: **D3**
– ✆ (030) 91496396 – www.coda-berlin.com – Closed Sunday-Monday
Menu 51/117 € – *(dinner only) (booking essential)*

• Creative • Design • Intimate •

This unusual restaurant is best known for its excellent patisseries. The food, prepared using natural products and presented in the form of a six-course surprise menu, is modern and highly creative, each dish a simple yet successful combination of contrasting flavours and aromas. Don't miss the carefully considered accompanying cocktails.

→ Aubergine, Pekannuss, Apfelbalsamico, Lakritzsalz. Petersilienwurzel, Kokos, Pistazie, schwarzer Knoblauch, Limette. Rhabarber, Estragon, Joghurt, Tasmanischer Pfeffer.

Cookies Cream

Behrenstr. 55 (backyard off the Hotel Westin Grand) Plan: **G1**
✉ 10115 – Ⓜ Französische Straße – ✆ (030) 27 49 29 40
– www.cookiescream.com – Closed Sunday-Monday
Menu 59/72 € – *(dinner only)*

• Vegetarian • Trendy • Fashionable •

Finding your way here through a maze of backyards to ring the bell at the unassuming door is an adventure in itself! Up on the first floor you'll find a vibrant restaurant decorated in the "industrial" style (it was once a fashionable night club). The vegetarian cuisine, artful and sophisticated, is served to a soundtrack of electronic music.

→ Wachtelei im Brioche. Vegetarischer Kaviar mit Avocado. Parmesanknödel mit Perigordtrüffelsud.

Crackers – See below

Kin Dee

Lützowstr. 81 ✉ 10785 – Ⓜ Kurfürstenstraße Plan I: **B2**
– ✆ (030) 2155294 – www.kindeeberlin.com – Closed Sunday-Monday
Menu 48 € – *(dinner only)*

• Thai • Design • Friendly •

This friendly, minimalist-style restaurant more than lives up to its name, Kin Dee or "eat well". The food is authentically Thai, made using top-quality local ingredients which are combined with great skill and the real taste of Thailand. Good, attentive service.

→ Spargel, Kokos, Anis, Zimt, Erdnüsse. Kin Dee Kaprao Oktopus. Rinder Curry, Zucchini, Aubergine, Thai-Basilikum.

Nobelhart & Schmutzig

Friedrichstr. 218 ✉ 10969 – Ⓜ Kochstr. Plan: G2
– ✆ (030) 25 94 06 10 – www.nobelhartundschmutzig.com – Closed 2 weeks early January, August and Sunday-Monday
Menu 95/120 € – *(dinner only) (booking essential)*
• Creative • Trendy • Friendly •

This 'food bar' offers its own special mix of trendy, urban chic and relaxed but professional service. The cuisine also has its own particular style, consciously eschewing any hint of luxury or chichi. The powerful and creative food is made using predominantly regional Brandenburg produce.
➜ Hecht, Frühlingszwiebeln. Ei, Senf. Joghurt, Robinie.

Rutz Weinbar – Restaurant Rutz

Chausseestr. 8 (1st floor) ✉ 10115 Plan I: C2
– Ⓜ Oranienburger Tor – ✆ (030) 24 62 87 60 – www.rutz-restaurant.de – Closed Sunday-Monday
Carte 38/64 € – *(dinner only)*
• Country • Wine bar •

This genuinely German restaurant has a regionally inspired menu. It offers traditional specialities such as smoked Neuköllner Rauchknacker sausage and Mangalitza ham hock; in contrast to the more sophisticated Rutz.

Kochu Karu

Eberswalder Str. 35 ✉ 10437 – Ⓜ Eberswalder Str. Plan I: C1
– ✆ (030) 80 93 81 91 – www.kochukaru.de – Closed 23 July - 5 August and Sunday-Monday
Menu 37/54 € – Carte 28/49 € – *(dinner only) (booking advisable)*
• Korean • Minimalist • Neighbourhood •

This pretty little minimalist-style restaurant combines the best of Spain and Korea with passion to create ambitious, flavoursome tapas such as mackerel adobo with barley and apricots and chicory with buckwheat and wild orange. Main dishes include options such as beef ribs with red cabbage kimchi, ginko nuts and sherry jus.

Lokal

Linienstr. 160 ✉ 10115 – Ⓜ Rosenthaler Platz Plan I: C2
– ✆ (030) 28 44 95 00 – www.lokal-berlinmitte.de
Menu 30/45 € – Carte 34/54 € – *(dinner only) (booking advisable)*
• Country • Friendly •

Relaxed, friendly and pleasantly unpretentious, it is no surprise that Lokal is popular with Berliners and visitors alike. The food is fresh, flavoursome and seasonal and includes dishes such as ox cheek with swede, chicory and broccoli.

Lucky Leek

Kollwitzstr. 54 ✉ 10405 – Ⓜ Senefelderplatz Plan I: D1
– ✆ (030) 66 40 87 10 – www.lucky-leek.com – Closed Monday-Tuesday
Menu 36/59 € – Carte 37/42 € – *(dinner only)*
• Vegan • Neighbourhood • Trendy •

Lucky Leek is a genuinely modern restaurant with a friendly, personal note. Josita Hartanto cooks vegan cuisine including vegetable consommé with potato and cress ravioli, pear and chilli risotto with tandoori cabbage and nori tempeh rolls.

Charlotte & Fritz – Hotel The Regent

Charlottenstr. 49 ✉ 10117 – Ⓜ Französische Str. Plan: G1
– ✆ (030) 20336363 – www.charlotteundfritz.com – Closed Sunday-Monday
Menu 32 € (lunch) – Carte 50/131 €
• Country • Elegant • Friendly •

The restaurant in the luxury Hotel Regent is genuinely chic, classic and modern combining to create an elegant picture. The kitchens set great store by good local produce and menu options include breast and leg of corn-fed spring chicken.

SRA BUA – Hotel Adlon Kempinski

Behrenstr. 72 ✉ 10117 – Ⓜ Brandenburger Tor Plan: **G1**
– ✆ (030) 22 61 15 90 – www.srabua-berlin.de – Closed Sunday-Monday
Menu 39/74 € – Carte 50/90 € – *(dinner only)*
• Asian • Elegant • Exotic décor •

Authentic produce and a variety of South-East Asian influences combine at SRA BUA to produce ambitious fare which includes some interesting Izakaya-style bar food. The upmarket, minimalist-style interior is at once elegant and cosy and the service attentive.

Balthazar am Spreeufer 2

Spreeufer 2 ✉ 10178 – Ⓜ Märkisches Museum Plan: **H1**
– ✆ (030) 30882156 – www.balthazar-spreeufer.de – Closed November-Easter: Sunday
Menu 38/95 € – Carte 31/46 € – *(November-Easter: dinner only)*
• Classic cuisine • Friendly • Cosy •

This cosy, friendly restaurant offers classic cuisine. This ranges from Wiener Schnitzel with roast potatoes to redfish with pearl barley, and black salsify stew with chorizo. Its location on the River Spree makes the terrace particularly popular.

The Grand

Hirtenstr. 4 ✉ 10178 – Ⓜ Alexanderplatz Plan I: **C2**
– ✆ (030) 2789099555 – www.the-grand-berlin.com
Menu 30/60 € (dinner) – Carte 44/110 € – *(August: dinner only)*
• Grills • Trendy • Design •

The interior is chic with a shabby touch and the gallery tables overlooking the restaurant are particularly attractive. The main focus of the ambitious cuisine is steaks from the 800°C Southbend grill, which are on view in the glazed meat maturing cabinet. Reduced lunchtime menu with good value specials. Bar and club.

INDIA CLUB

Behrenstr. 72 ✉ 10117 – Ⓜ Brandenburger Tor Plan: **G2**
– ✆ (030) 20628610 – www.india-club-berlin.com
Carte 37/53 € – *(dinner only)*
• Indian • Elegant •

Authentic Indian food in Berlin! The self-styled 'rustic cuisine' from the north of India includes some delicious curries (try the lamb shank curry) as well as original tandoori dishes such as the 'maachi tikka'. The upmarket interior features dark wood and typically Indian colours and motifs.

Orania.Berlin – Hotel Orania.Berlin

Oranienplatz 17 ✉ 10999 – Ⓜ Moritzplatz Plan: **D2**
– ✆ (030) 6953968780 – www.orania.berlin
Carte 46/70 € – *(dinner only)*
• Modern cuisine • Elegant • Brasserie •

Stylish, warm and relaxed, the eye catcher at Orania.Berlin is the large open kitchen. The food is seasonal, creative and made using good regional produce with menu options including gilthead sea bream with bouillabaisse broth and supplì rice balls. The service is attentive and accomplished.

Restaurant 1687

Mittelstr. 30 ✉ 10117 – Ⓜ Friedrichstraße Plan: **G1**
– ✆ (030) 20630611 – www.1687.berlin – Closed Saturday lunch, Sunday
Carte 36/72 €
• Mediterranean cuisine • Design •

This tastefully stylish restaurant with its pretty terrace is set in a narrow side street off Unter den Linden. In the evenings it serves modern fare including calves' cheeks with liquorice, barley, black salsify and baby carrots and an exclusive seafood platter. Considerably simpler lunchtime menu.

Slate

Elisabethkirchstr. 2 ✉ 10115 – Ⓜ Rosenthaler Platz — Plan I: **C1**
– ✆ (030) 22327518 – www.slateberlin.com – Closed 1-14 January, 1-15 July amd Sunday-Monday
Menu 69/103 € – Carte 52/78 € – *(dinner only)*
• Modern cuisine • Design • Elegant •

Set in a nice residential area in Berlin's lively Mitte district, Slate is run with great commitment by a young team. The atmosphere is modern and elegant, the food flavoursome, creative and with a distinct seasonal feel.

fabrics – Hotel nhow

Stralauer Allee 3 ✉ 10245 – Ⓜ Warschauer Str. — Plan I: **D2**
– ✆ (030) 2902990 – www.nhow-berlin.com – Closed Sunday
Menu 35 € – Carte 21/52 €
• Modern cuisine • Design • Trendy •

Cool design throughout in white, pink and a trendy green, giving a light and airy feel. The top quality produce in the kitchen is used to create house specials including classics such as steak Chateaubriand. Small lunchtime menu.

Alpenstück

Gartenstr. 9 ✉ 10115 – Ⓜ Rosenthaler Platz — Plan I: **C1**
– ✆ (030) 21751646 – www.alpenstueck.de
Menu 30/48 € – Carte 31/47 € – *(dinner only) (booking advisable)*
• Country • Fashionable •

This relaxed and friendly restaurant uses regional produce in dishes such as pan-fried fillet of trout with beetroot, yellow turnip and fondant potatoes. At lunchtimes the restaurant's own bakery over the road sells fine pastries and small snacks. In the delicatessen you can buy Maultaschen (Swabian pasta squares) and fond (caramelised meat dripping for making gravy) to take home.

Austernbank

Behrensstr. 42 ✉ 10117 – Ⓜ Französische Str. — Plan: **G1**
– ✆ (030) 767752724 – www.austernbank-berlin.de – Closed Sunday-Monday
Carte 36/124 € – *(dinner only)*
• Seafood • Historic •

What were once the vaults of the former Disconto Bank provide an impressive setting with their high ceilings, striking pillars, lovely stone floors and tiled walls. The open kitchen serves a seafood menu, with the house speciality being oysters. There's also a pavement terrace and the Blaue Stunde smokers' bar on the first floor.

Crackers – Restaurant Cookies Cream

Friedrichstr. 158 ✉ 10115 – Ⓜ Französische Straße — Plan: **G1**
– ✆ (030) 6 80 73 04 88 – www.crackersberlin.com – Closed Sunday-Monday
Carte 41/69 € – *(dinner only)*
• International • Trendy • Chic •

You'll find this trendy eatery one floor below Cookies Cream. Ring the bell and the staff will lead you through the kitchen into a large and lively restaurant with a high ceiling and dim lights. The menu offers a range of ambitious meat and fish dishes.

Lode & Stijn

Lausitzer Str. 25 ✉ 10999 – Ⓜ Görlitzer Bahnhof — Plan I: **D3**
– ✆ (030) 65214507 – www.lode-stijn.de – Closed Sunday-Monday
Menu 65 € – *(dinner only) (booking essential)*
• Modern cuisine • Neighbourhood • Friendly •

As well as being a great place to eat Lode & Stijn offers a welcoming, relaxed and lively atmosphere, a nice retro feel and friendly service. The food –pleasantly uncomplicated and based on good seasonal produce – is Scandinavian.

Michelberger

Warschauer Str. 39 ✉ 10243 – Ⓜ Warschauer Str. Plan I: **D2**
– ✆ (030) 29778590 – www.michelbergerhotel.com – Closed Saturday lunch, Sunday, Monday dinner
Carte 21/33 €
• Modern cuisine • Bistro • Trendy •

Don't be put off by the Michelberger hotel's plain façade, as the team at the eponymous restaurant takes regional organic produce and transforms it into modern, tapas-style dishes which are great for sharing. The atmosphere is appropriately hip and trendy and there's a great interior courtyard. The simpler lunchtime menu includes a "lunch tray".

Schwein

Mommsenstr. 63 ✉ 10629 – Ⓜ George-Grosz-Platz Plan I: **B3**
– ✆ (030) 24356282 – www.schwein.online – Closed Sunday
Menu 59/75 € – Carte 53/61 € – *(dinner only)*
• Market cuisine • Bistro • Chic •

This trendy urban restaurant continues to offer ambitious seasonal cuisine which is pared down and punchy following its move westwards from Berlin's Mitte district to Charlottenburg, where the fresh new design and friendly atmosphere have met with great success. Wine is high on the agenda, alongside a range of cool long drinks.

VOLT

Paul-Lincke-Ufer 21 ✉ 10999 – Ⓜ Schönleinstr. Plan I: **D3**
– ✆ (030) 338402320 – www.restaurant-volt.de – Closed 1 week early January, 3 weeks July-August and Sunday-Monday
Menu 58/87 € – Carte 67/73 € – *(dinner only)*
• Modern cuisine • Design •

Matthias Gleiß's restaurant is very popular and you can see why. With its well-chosen industrial design features and good food – including vegetables sourced from local farmers – this former electricity substation built in 1928 fits perfectly into Kreuzberg's lively gastro scene.

herz & niere

Fichtestr. 31 ✉ 10967 – Ⓜ Südstern Plan I: **D3**
– ✆ (030) 69001522 – www.herzundniere.berlin – Closed Monday, May-September: Sunday-Monday
Menu 50/92 € – *(dinner only)*
• Country • Friendly • Cosy •

You'll find two set menus here: one focusing on offal dishes and the other vegetarian. Even if you order something in between, you won't be disappointed at this pleasant restaurant, its "nose to tail" principle ensuring that nothing goes to waste. The friendly front-of-house team also provide good wine suggestions.

AROUND THE KURFÜRSTENDAMM — PLAN III

5 - Cinco by Paco Pérez – Hotel Das Stue

Drakestr. 1 ✉ 10787 – Ⓜ Wittenbergplatz Plan: **L2**
– ✆ (030) 3 11 72 20 – www.5-cinco.com – Closed Sunday-Monday
Menu 130/165 € – Carte 94/159 € – *(dinner only) (booking advisable)*
• Creative • Design • Trendy •

You no longer have to make the journey to Miramar in Spain for Paco Pérez' Michelin-starred cuisine. You can now sample his upmarket creations in this modern restaurant – with 86 copper pans hanging from the centre of the ceiling – as you marvel at the intense activity in the kitchens. Choose the 'Experience Menu' or go à la carte.

➜ Weißer Spargel, Bottarga und Mandel. Taube, Mais, Mole und Huitlacoche. Rote Früchte mit geräuchertem Milcheis.

Hugos – Hotel InterContinental

Budapester Str. 2 (14th floor) ✉ 10787 – Ⓜ Zoologischer Garten Plan: **L2**
– ✆ (030) 26 02 12 63 – www.hugos-restaurant.de – Closed Sunday-Monday
Menu 110 € (Vegetarian)/155 € – *(dinner only) (booking advisable)*
• Modern cuisine • Chic • Elegant •

It is true that the view from the 14th floor is fantastic but this elegant, minimalist-style restaurant is known first and foremost for its classic, modern cuisine, which is both beautifully crafted and delicious.

➜ Périgord Trüffel und Knollensellerie, Apfelquitte, zweierlei Kohl, Kümmel. Kanadischer Hummer, Passionsfrucht, Gartenkresse, Vanille, Daikon Rettich. Australisches Roastbeef, Goldnavetten, Brunnenkresse, Birnenkraut.

Bieberbau (Stephan Garkisch)

Durlacher Str. 15 ✉ 10715 – Ⓜ Bundesplatz Plan I: **B3**
– ✆ (030) 8 53 23 90 – www.bieberbau-berlin.de – Closed 3 weeks July-August and Saturday-Sunday
Menu 48/70 € – *(dinner only) (booking advisable)*
• Modern cuisine • Cosy •

The atmosphere here is genuinely unique, not least thanks to Richard Bieber's remarkable stuccowork! The chef cooks modern seasonal fare, skilfully placing herbs and spices centre stage, while his partner oversees the charming front-of-house team. Excellent value for money!

➜ Falafel mit Brokkoli, Aprikose, Berberitze, Mandel und Waldmeister. Gebratener Zander mit Kohlrabi und Pfifferlingen. Karamellisiertes Holunderblüteneis mit Erdbeeren.

Colette Tim Raue

Passauer Str. 5 ✉ 10789 – Ⓜ Wittenbergplatz Plan: **L2**
– ✆ (030) 2 199 21 74 – www.brasseriecolette.de
Menu 24 € (lunch) – Carte 35/78 €
• Classic French • Brasserie •

A well-known name on the Berlin gastro scene, Colette Tim Raue has created a friendly, modern and uncomplicated brasserie, which could easily be in Paris. Try the paysanne pie, duck confit or lemon tart.

Nußbaumerin

Leibnizstr. 55 ✉ 10629 – Ⓜ Adenauerpl. – ✆ (030) 50 17 80 33 Plan: **J3**
– www.nussbaumerin.de – Closed Sunday and Bank Holidays
Carte 31/49 € – *(dinner only) (booking essential)*
• Austrian • Cosy • Neighbourhood •

Here in her cosy restaurant Johanna Nußbaumer recreates a little bit of Austria in the heart of Berlin. Specialities include breaded fried chicken, Wiener Schnitzel, sirloin steak, and a range of Austrian stews and sweet dishes. The excellent wines also hail from her home country.

Renger-Patzsch

Wartburgstr. 54 ✉ 10823 – Ⓜ Eisenacher Str. Plan I: **B3**
– ✆ (030) 7 84 20 59 – www.renger-patzsch.com – Closed Sunday
Menu 36/50 € – Carte 31/41 € – *(dinner only)*
• Traditional cuisine • Inn • Cosy •

Traditional, tasty and well-executed dishes such as Alsatian sauerkraut with shoulder of pork or flammekueche. The restaurant owes its name to one of the pioneers of landscape photography - a number of his black and white photos adorn the walls. A great place to eat and a very popular one. Wonderful terrace.

GRACE – Hotel Zoo Berlin

Kurfürstendamm 25 ✉ 10719 – Ⓜ Uhlandstr. Plan: **K2**
– ✆ (030) 88437750 – www.grace-berlin.com – Closed August and Sunday-Monday
Menu 69/99 € – Carte 40/106 € – *(dinner only) (booking advisable)*
• International • Chic • Design •

Combining stylish, modern design and vintage flair, Grace is a really smart place to eat. The food is modern and international and includes such delights as creamy rock shrimps with cucumber, coriander, peanuts and chilli.

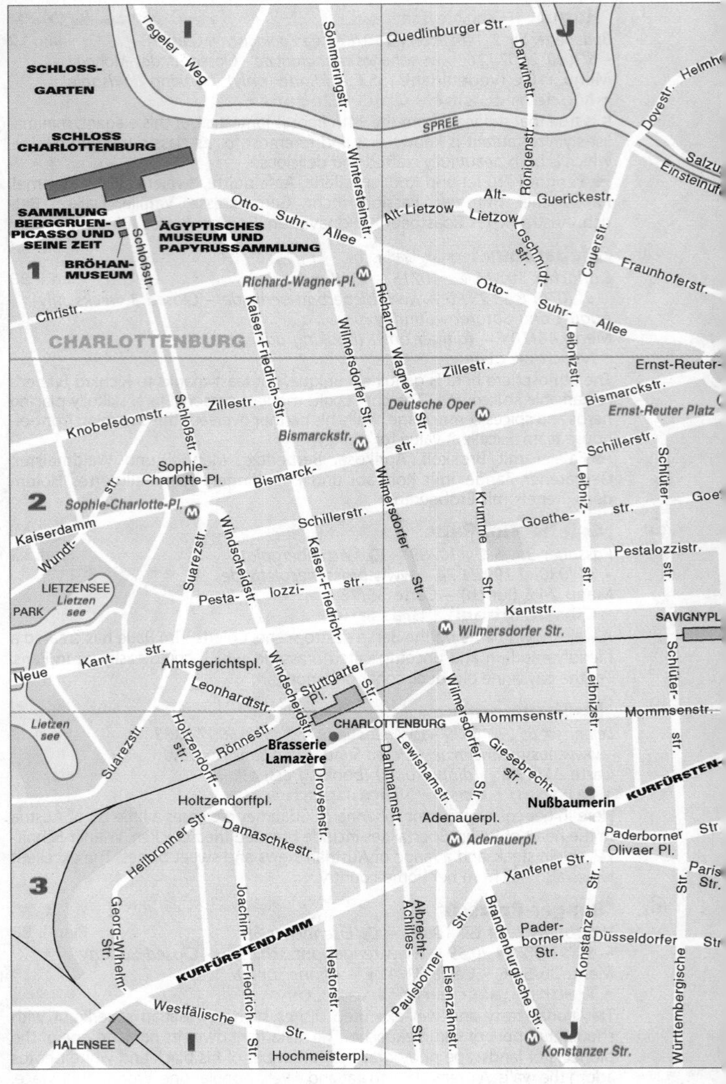
SCHLOSS-
GARTEN
SCHLOSS
CHARLOTTENBURG
SAMMLUNG
BERGGRUEN-
PICASSO UND
SEINE ZEIT
BRÖHAN-
MUSEUM
ÄGYPTISCHES
MUSEUM UND
PAPYRUSSAMMLUNG
Tegeler Weg
Sömmeringstr.
Quedlinburger Str.
Darwinstr.
SPREE
Röntgenstr.
Dovestr.
Helmholtz
Salzu
Einsteinufe
Otto-Suhr-Allee
Alt-Lietzow
Guerickestr.
Loschmidt-str.
Cauerstr.
Fraunhoferstr.
Wintersteinstr.
Schloßstr.
Richard-Wagner-Pl.
Christr.
CHARLOTTENBURG
Kaiser-Friedrich-Str.
Wilmersdorfer Str.
Richard-Wagner-Str.
Leibnizstr.
Ernst-Reuter-
Zillestr.
Bismarckstr.
Ernst-Reuter Platz
Deutsche Oper
Knobelsdomstr.
Bismarckstr.
Schillerstr.
Schlüter-str.
Sophie-Charlotte-Pl.
Krumme Str.
Goethe-str.
Kaiserdamm
Wundt-str.
Suarezstr.
Windscheidstr.
LIETZENSEE PARK
Lietzen see
Pestalozzistr.
Kantstr.
SAVIGNYPL
Wilmersdorfer Str.
Neue Kant-str.
Amtsgerichtspl.
Leonhardtstr.
Stuttgarter Pl.
CHARLOTTENBURG
Mommsenstr.
Holtzendorff-str.
Rönnestr.
Brasserie Lamazère
Lewishamstr.
Giesebrechtstr.
Dahlmannstr.
Droysenstr.
Holtzendorffpl.
Nußbaumerin
KURFÜRSTEN-
Adenauerpl.
Heilbronner Str.
Damaschkestr.
Paderborner Str
Olivaer Pl.
Xantener Str.
Paris Str.
Georg-Wilhelm-Str.
Joachim-Friedrich-Str.
Albrecht-Achilles-Str.
Brandenburgische Str.
Paderborner Str.
Konstanzer Str.
Düsseldorfer Str
KURFÜRSTENDAMM
Nestorstr.
Paulsborner Str.
Eisenzahnstr.
Württembergische Str.
Westfälische Str.
HALENSEE
Hochmeisterpl.
Konstanzer Str.
I
J
1
2
3

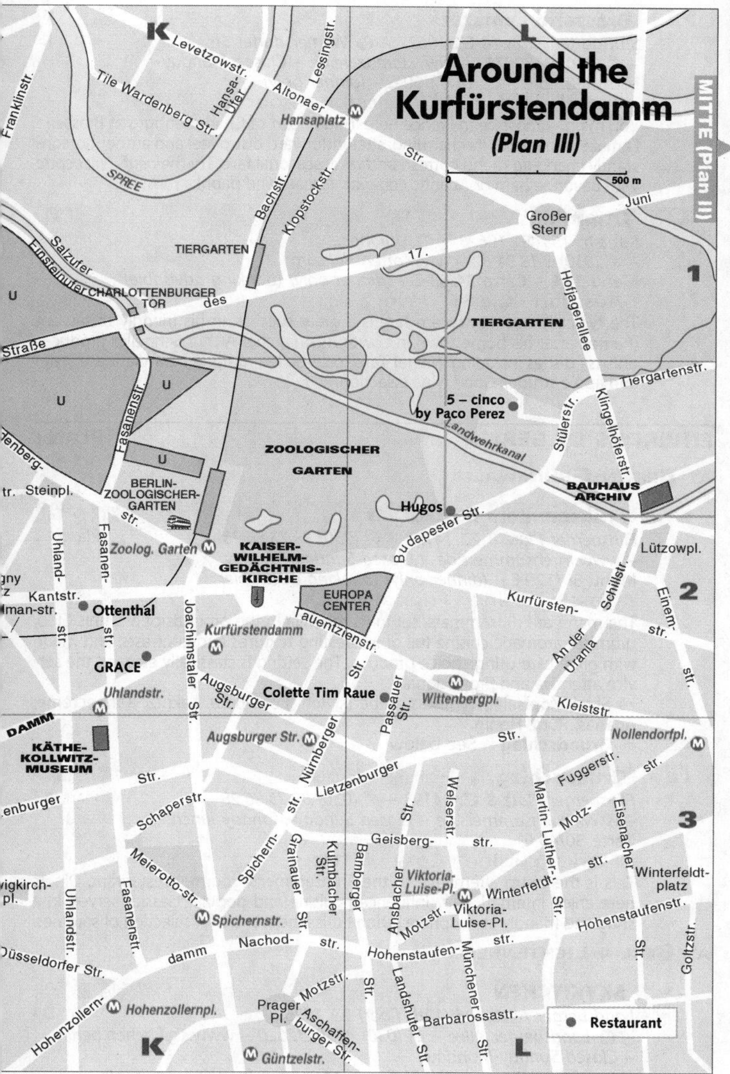
Around the Kurfürstendamm
(Plan III)
0
500 m
K
L
1
2
3
Levetzowstr.
Tile Wardenberg Str.
Hansa-Ufer
Altonaer Str.
Lessingstr.
Hansaplatz
Franklinstr.
SPREE
Bachstr.
Klopstockstr.
Großer Stern
Juni
17.
TIERGARTEN
Salzufer
Einsteinufer
CHARLOTTENBURGER TOR
des
Straße
TIERGARTEN
Hofjägerallee
Tiergartenstr.
5 – cinco by Paco Perez
Landwehrkanal
Stülerstr.
Klingelhöferstr.
Fasanenstr.
ZOOLOGISCHER GARTEN
BAUHAUS ARCHIV
BERLIN-ZOOLOGISCHER-GARTEN
Steinpl.
Hugos
Budapester Str.
Lützowpl.
Zoolog. Garten
KAISER-WILHELM-GEDÄCHTNIS-KIRCHE
Uhland-str.
Fasanen-str.
Kantstr.
Ottenthal
EUROPA CENTER
Kurfürsten-str.
Schillstr.
Einem-str.
Joachimstaler Str.
Tauentzienstr.
Kurfürstendamm
GRACE
Augsburger Str.
Nürnberger Str.
Colette Tim Raue
Passauer Str.
Wittenbergpl.
An der Urania
Kleiststr.
Uhlandstr.
DAMM
KÄTHE-KOLLWITZ-MUSEUM
Augsburger Str.
Nollendorfpl.
Lietzenburger Str.
Fuggerstr.
Schaperstr.
Weiserstr.
Martin-Luther-Str.
Motz-str.
Eisenacher Str.
Geisberg-str.
Meierotto-str.
Spichern-str.
Grainauer Str.
Kulmbacher Str.
Bamberger Str.
Ansbacher Str.
Viktoria-Luise-Pl.
Winterfeldt-str.
Winterfeldtplatz
Uhlandstr.
Fasanenstr.
Spichernstr.
Motzstr.
Viktoria-Luise-Pl.
Hohenstaufenstr.
Nachod-str.
damm
Düsseldorfer Str.
Hohenstaufen-str.
Münchener Str.
Goltzstr.
Motzstr.
Prager Pl.
Aschaffenburger Str.
Landshuter Str.
Hohenzollern-damm
Hohenzollernpl.
Barbarossastr.
Güntzelstr.
Restaurant

Brasserie Lamazère

Stuttgarter Platz 18 ✉ 10627 – Ⓜ Wilmersdorfer Str. – ✆ (030) 31800712 – www.lamazere.de – Closed Monday Plan: **I3**
Menu 38/45 € – Carte 42/60 € – *(dinner only)*
• French • Brasserie • Neighbourhood •
You might almost be in France here in the heart of Charlottenburg at Brasserie Lamazère thanks to its charming, straightforward bistro feel and authentic, constantly changing menu of fresh and tasty seasonal fare. Try the *oeufs en cocotte* with Bayonne ham or Atlantic cod with tomato and paprika mussels.

Ottenthal

Kantstr. 153 ✉ 10623 – Ⓜ Uhlandstr. – ✆ (030) 3 13 31 62 – www.ottenthal.com Plan: **K2**
Menu 34 € – Carte 34/63 € – *(dinner only) (booking advisable)*
• Austrian • Classic décor •
The typically Austrian tavern fare is a great success. In his friendly restaurant (named after his home town in Lower Austria) chef Arthur Schneller produces unfussy dishes including Wiener Tafelspitz (boiled rump of beef Viennese style) and apple strudel. Good wine selection.

ENVIRONS OF BERLIN — PLAN I

AT BERLIN-GRUNEWALD

Frühsammers Restaurant

Flinsberger Platz 8 ✉ 14193 – ✆ (030) 89 73 86 28 – www.fruehsammers.de – Closed Sunday-Tuesday Plan: **A3**
Menu 89/129 € – *(dinner only) (booking advisable)*
• Classic cuisine • Friendly •
The menu at Frühsammers, set in its red villa in the grounds of a tennis Club, promises aromatic cuisine full of interesting textures and contrasts, and made with great care using choice produce. The setting is classically elegant, the service attentive and professional.
➜ Skrei, Kopfsalat, Hibiskus, Kapern. Reh, Rote Bete, Lakritz. Kaffeecrème, Ananas, Rum, Honig.
Grundschlag – See below

Grundschlag – Frühsammers Restaurant

Flinsberger Platz 8 ✉ 14193 – ✆ (030) 89 73 86 28 – www.fruehsammers.de – Closed Sunday-Monday lunch Plan: **A3**
Carte 30/49 €
• Market cuisine • Cosy • Bistro •
This is the bistro alternative to the Frühsammer's gourmet restaurant. Diners here enjoy internationally influenced cuisine and popular classics served in a snug and friendly atmosphere – don't miss the wonderful selection of sardines!

AT BERLIN-LICHTENBERG

SKYKITCHEN

Landsberger Allee 106 (12th floor) ✉ 10369 – Ⓜ Landsberger Allee – ✆ (030) 4530532620 – www.skykitchen.berlin – Closed Sunday-Monday Plan: **D1**
Menu 54 € (Vegetarian)/141 € – *(dinner only) (booking advisable)*
• Modern cuisine • Fashionable •
It is worth making your way out to Lichtenberg to sample the 'voyage culinaire' on offer on the 12th floor of Andel's Hotel. The 3 to 11 course set menu showcases a creative, modern cuisine full of contrasts, with local and international influences. The setting is relaxed yet stylishly chic, and the view is wonderful. The SKYBAR is two floors further up.
➜ Bio Ei, luftgetrockneter Schinken, Meerrettich, Crème fraîche. Perlhuhn, Aubergine, Kichererbse, Hühnerhaut. Thai Mango, Gartenkräuter, Mandel, Amarettini.

AT BERLIN-WEDDING

Ernst (Dylan Watson-Brawn) XX AC

Gerichtstr. 54 ✉ 13347 – Ⓜ Wedding Plan: **B1**
– www.ernstberlin.de – Closed 2 weeks January, 2 weeks August and Monday-Tuesday
Menu 165 € – *(dinner only) (booking essential)*
• Creative • Design • Fashionable •

Somewhat unprepossessing from the outside, inside Ernst tells quite a different story. Diners ring the bell on the great stainless-steel door to enter this sober industrial-style restaurant where 12 counter seats face the open kitchen. "Less is more" is the order of the day here and the pared-down dishes on the 25-course set menu are made using the very best ingredients. An impressive three-hour epicurean experience.

➜ Mushroom Dashi. Fresh Cheese. Blood Orange.

HAMBURG
HAMBURG

ponomarevvb/iStock

HAMBURG IN...

- **ONE DAY**
  Boat trip from Landungsbrücken, Speicherstadt, Kunsthalle, Fishmarket (Sunday morning). Elbphilharmonie.
- **TWO DAYS**
  Steamboat on the Alster, Hamburg History Museum, St Pauli by night.
- **THREE DAYS**
  Arts and Crafts Museum, canal trip, concert at Musikhalle.

With a maritime role stretching back centuries, Germany's second largest city has a lively and liberal ambience. Hamburg is often described as 'The Gateway to the World', and there's certainly a visceral feel here, particularly around the big, buzzy and bustling port area. Locals enjoy a long-held reputation for their tolerance and outward looking stance, cosmopolitan to the core. Space to breathe is seen as very important in Hamburg: the city authorities have paid much attention to green spaces, and the city can proudly claim an enviable amount of parks, lakes and tree-lined canals.

There's no cathedral here (at least not a standing one, as war-destroyed St Nikolai remains a ruin), so the Town Hall acts as the central landmark. Just north of here are the Binnenalster (inner) and Aussenalster (outer) lakes. The old walls of the city, dating back over eight hundred years, are delineated by a distinct semicircle of boulevards that curve attractively in a wide arc south of the lakes. Further south from here is the port and harbour area, defined by Landungsbrücken to the west and Speicherstadt to the east. The district to the west of the centre is St Pauli, famed for its clubs and bars, particularly along the notorious Reeperbahn, which pierces the district from east to west. The contrastingly smart Altona suburb and delightful Blankenese village are west of St Pauli.

EATING OUT

Being a city immersed in water, it's no surprise to find Hamburg is a good place for fish. Though its fishing industry isn't the powerhouse of old, the city still boasts a giant trawler's worth of seafood places to eat. Eel dishes are mainstays of the traditional restaurant's menu, as is the herring stew with vegetables called Labskaus. Also unsurprisingly, considering it's the country's gateway to the world, this is somewhere that offers a vast range of international dishes. Wherever you eat, the portions are likely to be generous. There's no problem with finding somewhere early: cafés are often open at seven, with the belief that it's never too early for coffee and cake. Bakeries also believe in an early start, and the calorie content here, too, can be pretty high. Bistros and restaurants, usually open by midday, are proud of their local ingredients, so keep your eyes open for Hamburgisch on the menu. Service charges are always included in the bill, so tipping is not compulsory, although most people will round it up and possibly add five to ten per cent.

✿✿✿ The Table Kevin Fehling XxX

Shanghaiallee 15 ✉ 20457 – Ⓜ HafenCity Universität Plan I: **C2**
– ✆ (040) 22 86 74 22 – www.the-table-hamburg.de
– Closed 23 December-7 January, 7-15 April, 21 July-12 August and Sunday-Monday
Menu 210 € – *(dinner only) (booking essential)*
• Creative • Design •

This relaxed restaurant really is one of a kind! Diners sit at a long, curved table as the chefs – a study of concentration – combine fine international ingredients to perfection before their eyes with the precision, subtlety and stunning presentation for which Kevin Fehling is famed. Excellent wine recommendations.

→ Hummer mit Kressenpüree, Lardo, Yuzu und Champagnerschaum. Challans Entenbrust mit Kürbis, Shiso, Erdnuss, Passionsfrucht-Hollandaise und Curryjus. Haselnuss- Crémeux mit Gänselebereis, Rhabarber, Lavendel und Himbeere.

✿✿ Haerlin XxXxX

Fairmont Hotel Vier Jahreszeiten – Neuer Jungfernstieg 9 Plan: **F2**
✉ 20354 – Ⓜ Jungfernstieg – ✆ (040) 34 94 33 10 – www.fairmont-hvj.de
– Closed 1-6 January, 4-10 March, 8 July-4 August, 7-13 October and Sunday-Monday
Menu 145/210 € – *(dinner only) (booking advisable)*
• Creative French • Luxury • Elegant •

The food at Haerlin is powerful and intensely flavoured. The dishes brought to your table are creative and technically perfect, and use nothing but the very best ingredients. The culinary quality is matched by the exquisite interior where everything is of the finest quality. The view over the Inner Alster Lake adds the finishing touch.

→ Pochierte Gillardeau Auster mit grünen Erbsen und geröstetem Zwiebelsaft. Wolfsbarsch in Bouillabaissejus mit heller Miso und Zucchini. Mango und Olivenöl mit Basilikum und Koriander.

✿ Lakeside – Hotel The Fontenay XxX

Fontenay 10 ✉ 20354 – Ⓜ Stephansplatz Plan I: **C2**
– ✆ (040) 60566050 – www.thefontenay.de
– Closed Sunday-Monday
Menu 165 € – Carte 101/160 € – *(dinner only) (booking essential)*
• Creative • Design • Elegant •

Set on the seventh floor, this light and airy restaurant with its smart, bold interior in elegant white offers a sensational view over Hamburg. More than a match for the upmarket setting, the seasonal cuisine based on top-quality ingredients is full of creativity and fine contrasts. Excellent wine suggestions.

→ Förde Garnele, Lardo, Kaviar, Auster. Taube, Kalbsbries, Rote Bete. Schokolade, Shiso, Vanille, Apfel.

✿ bianc XxX

Am Sandtorkai 50 ✉ 20457 – Ⓜ Baumwall Plan I: **C3**
– ✆ (040) 18119797 – www.bianc.de
– Closed 14-28 January, 12-26 August and Sunday-Monday
Menu 80/160 € – *(dinner only) (booking advisable)*
• Creative • Design • Friendly •

Mediterranean cuisine in a modern and creative style – this is the approach adopted by Matteo Ferrantino whose personal signature dishes reveal both his talent and his vast experience. Located among the office buildings in the harbourside HafenCity district, the restaurant's piazza ambience designed by Julia Erdmann provides an elegant setting in which to enjoy superb cuisine.

→ Hummer, Karotten, Orange. Huhn, Jakobsmuschel, Mais, Kapern. Joghurt, Himbeere, Rhabarber.

100/200 (Thomas Imbusch)

Brandshofer Deich 68 ✉ 20539 – Ⓜ Brooksfleet – ✆ (040) 30925191 – www.100200.kitchen– Closed Sunday-Monday Plan I : **D3**

Menu 95/119 € – *(dinner only)*

• Creative • Chic • Fashionable •

100/200 promises industrial chic in an urban loft-style decor with an eye-catching open kitchen that is visible from all sides and boasts a smart Molteni oven. It's here at between 100° and 200°C – hence the name – that the chefs produce a creative surprise menu based on the "nose to tail" principle, which they then serve up themselves at stylish tree-trunk tables. Ticket-type booking system.

➜ Odefey´s Huhn mit Sauce Rouennaise. Lunge "Bordelaiser Art". Brioche mit Renekloden.

SE7EN OCEANS

Ballindamm 40 (2nd floor) (Europa-Passage) ✉ 20095 – Ⓜ Jungfernstieg – ✆ (040) 32 50 79 44 – www.se7en-oceans.de – Closed 4-11 February, 5-25 August and Sunday-Monday Plan: **G2**

Menu 43 € (lunch)/129 € – Carte 56/85 €

• Classic French • Chic • Design •

Ideal for escaping the crowds, this modern eatery has a great view of the Inner Alster Lake and the Jungfernstieg promenade. It offers peace and quiet in the midst of the Europa Passage shopping centre and serves classic international cuisine. The glass front opens up in the summer.

➜ Bretonische Makrele, Gurke, Dill. Steinköhler, Sellerie, Brunnenkresse. Westfälisches Juvenilferkel, Mairüben, Zwiebeln.

Tschebull

Mönckebergstr. 7 ✉ 20095 – Ⓜ Mönchebergstr. – ✆ (040) 32 96 47 96 – www.tschebull.de – Closed Sunday and Bank Holidays Plan: **H2**

Menu 32 € (lunch) – Carte 34/68 € – *(booking advisable)*

• Austrian • Cosy •

In the centre of this exclusive shopping arcade sits a little piece of Austria, courtesy of Carinthian chef Alexander Tschebull. As you would expect, the Austrian classics, such as Tafelspitz (Viennese-style boiled beef) and Fiaker (beef) goulash are excellent, as are the more modern dishes. These include skrei cod with potato and caper champ, radish and pearl onions.

Brook

Bei den Mühren 91 ✉ 20457 – Ⓜ Meßberg – ✆ (040) 37 50 31 28 – www.restaurant-brook.de – Closed Sunday-Monday Plan: **G3**

Menu 19 € (lunch)/45 € – Carte 37/54 €

• International • Fashionable •

The most popular dishes at this relaxed modern restaurant include classics such as braised calves' cheeks, but fish fresh from the famous fish market just round the corner are also firm favourites, as is the very reasonable set lunchtime menu. It is worth coming here in the evenings too, when you can enjoy views of the illuminated warehouse district.

Cox

Lange Reihe 68 ✉ 20099 – Ⓜ Hauptbf. Nord – ✆ (040) 24 94 22 – www.restaurant-cox.de – Closed Saturday lunch, Sunday lunch Plan: **H1**

Menu 20 € (lunch) – Carte 36/52 €

• International • Bistro • Cosy •

More casual and urban than chic and elegant, Cox is a bistro in the best sense of the word. A colourful mix of diners enjoys a varied selection of dishes including braised lamb shanks, grass-fed beef rissoles and cod. Good value lunchtime menu.

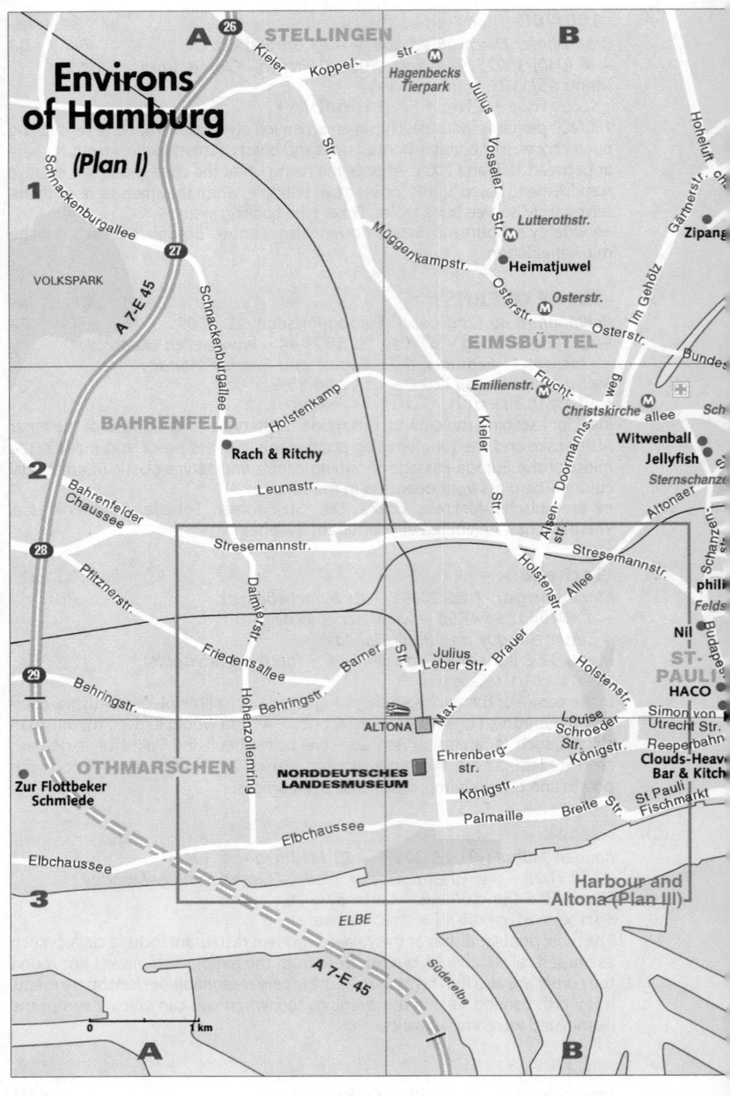
Environs of Hamburg
(Plan I)
A
B
1
2
3
STELLINGEN
Hagenbecks Tierpark
Kieler
Koppel-
str.
Julius Vosseler Str.
Hoheluft ch
Gärtnerstr.
Zipang
Str.
Lutterothstr.
Müggenkampstr.
Heimatjuwel
Osterstr.
Im Gehölz
VOLKSPARK
Schnackenburgallee
A 7-E 45
EIMSBÜTTEL
Bundes
Emilienstr.
Frucht-
Doormanns-weg
Christskirche
allee
Witwenball
Jellyfish
Sternschanze
BAHRENFELD
Holstenkamp
Rach & Ritchy
Leunastr.
Kieler Str.
Alsen-str.
Altonaer
Bahrenfelder Chaussee
Stresemannstr.
Holstenstr.
Allee
Schanzen-
Pfitznerstr.
Daimlerstr.
phili
Felds
Nil
Budapest
Friedensallee
Barner Str.
Julius Leber Str.
Brauer
ST-PAULI
HACO
Behringstr.
Hohenzollernring
Max
Simon von Utrecht Str.
ALTONA
Louise Schroeder Str.
Reeperbahn
Königstr.
Clouds-Heav
Bar & Kitch
OTHMARSCHEN
Zur Flottbeker Schmiede
NORDDEUTSCHES LANDESMUSEUM
Ehrenberg-str.
Königstr.
Palmaille
Breite Str.
St Pauli Fischmarkt
Elbchaussee
Harbour and Altona (Plan III)
ELBE
Süderelbe
0
1 km
26
27
28
29

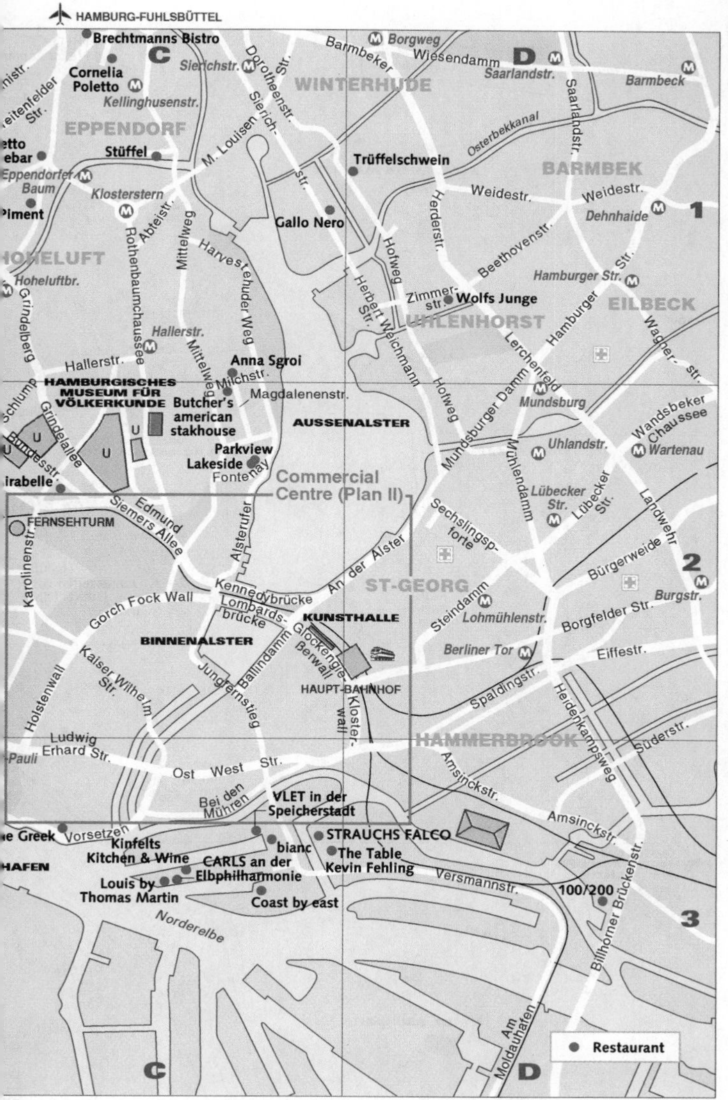
HAMBURG-FUHLSBÜTTEL
Brechtmanns Bistro
Cornelia Poletto
Kellinghusenstr.
EPPENDORF
Stüffel
Eppendorfer Baum
Klosterstern
Piment
HOHELUFT
Hoheluftbr.
Hallerstr.
Hallerstr.
HAMBURGISCHES MUSEUM FÜR VÖLKERKUNDE
Butcher's american stakhouse
Parkview Lakeside
Fontenay
Anna Sgroi
Milchstr.
Magdalenenstr.
Sierichstr.
WINTERHUDE
Borgweg
Barmbeker
Wiesendamm
Saarlandstr.
Barmbeck
BARMBEK
Osterbekkanal
Trüffelschwein
Gallo Nero
Weidestr.
Dehnhaide
Beethovenstr.
Hamburger Str.
Zimmerstr.
Wolfs Junge
UHLENHORST
EILBECK
Mundsburg
Uhlandstr.
Wartenau
Lübecker Str.
AUSSENALSTER
Commercial Centre (Plan II)
FERNSEHTURM
Edmund Siemers Allee
Gorch Fock Wall
Kennedybrücke
Lombardsbrücke
An der Alster
ST-GEORG
KUNSTHALLE
BINNENALSTER
Jungfernstieg
Ballindamm
Glockengießerwall
HAUPT-BAHNHOF
Klosterwall
Steindamm
Lohmühlenstr.
Berliner Tor
Bürgerweide
Borgfelder Str.
Burgstr.
Eiffestr.
Spaldingstr.
Heidenkampsweg
HAMMERBROOK
Süderstr.
Amsinckstr.
Ludwig Erhard Str.
Ost West Str.
Bei den Mühren
VLET in der Speicherstadt
Vorsetzen
Kinfelts Kitchen & Wine
bianc
STRAUCHS FALCO
The Table Kevin Fehling
CARLS an der Elbphilharmonie
Louis by Thomas Martin
Coast by east
Versmannstr.
100/200
Billhorner Brückenstr.
Norderelbe
Am Moldauhafen
Restaurant
C
D
1
2
3

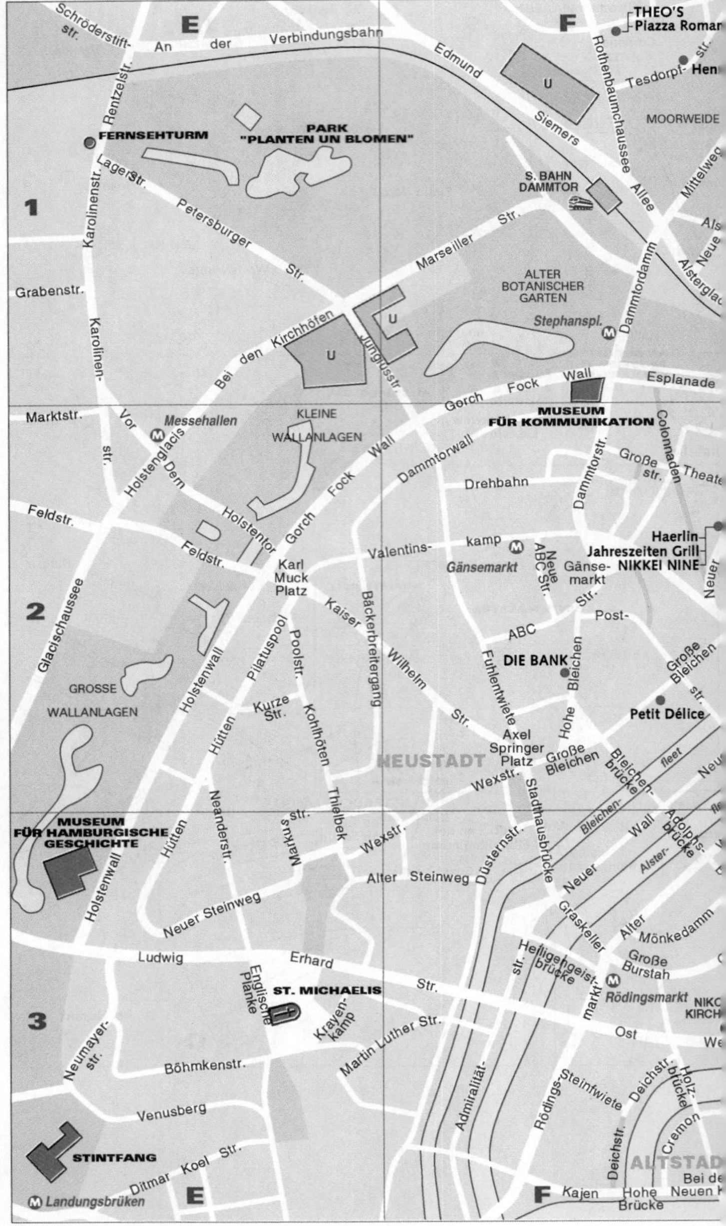
E
F
1
2
3
THEO'S Piazza Roman
FERNSEHTURM
PARK "PLANTEN UN BLOMEN"
S. BAHN DAMMTOR
MOORWEIDE
ALTER BOTANISCHER GARTEN
Stephanspl.
Esplanade
MUSEUM FÜR KOMMUNIKATION
KLEINE WALLANLAGEN
Messehallen
Karl Muck Platz
Gänsemarkt
Haerlin
Jahreszeiten Grill
NIKKEI NINE
DIE BANK
Petit Délice
Axel Springer Platz
NEUSTADT
GROSSE WALLANLAGEN
MUSEUM FÜR HAMBURGISCHE GESCHICHTE
ST. MICHAELIS
Rödingsmarkt
STINTFANG
Landungsbrüken
Schröderstift-str.
An der Verbindungsbahn
Edmund Siemers Allee
Rothenbaumchaussee
Tesdorpf-str.
Rentzelstr.
Lagerstr.
Petersburger Str.
Marseiller Str.
Karolinenstr.
Grabenstr.
Bei den Kirchhöfen
Jungiusstr.
Dammtordamm
Gorch Fock Wall
Marktstr.
Vor Dem Holstentor
Holstenglacis
Dammtorwall
Drehbahn
Dammtorstr.
Große Theaterstr.
Colonnaden
Feldstr.
Valentinskamp
Neue ABC Str.
Gänsemarkt
Glacischaussee
Kaiser Wilhelm Str.
Bäckerbreitergang
Pilatuspool
Poolstr.
Post-str.
ABC Str.
Fuhlentwiete
Hohe Bleichen
Große Bleichen
Holstenwall
Kurze Str.
Kohlhöfen
Hütten
Thielbek
Wexstr.
Stadthausbrücke
Bleichenbrücke
Neanderstr.
Markusstr.
Bleichenfleet
Neuer Wall
Adolphsbrücke
Alsterfleet
Düsternstr.
Alter Steinweg
Neuer Steinweg
Graskeller
Alter Mönkedamm
Große Burstah
Heiligengeistbrücke
Ludwig Erhard Str.
Englische Planke
Krayenkamp
Martin Luther Str.
Ost West
Neumayerstr.
Böhmkenstr.
Admiralitätstr.
Rödingsmarkt
Steinfwiete
Deichstr.
Holzbrücke
Cremon
Venusberg
Ditmar Koel Str.
Kajen
Hohe Brücke
ALTSTAD
Bei de Neuen

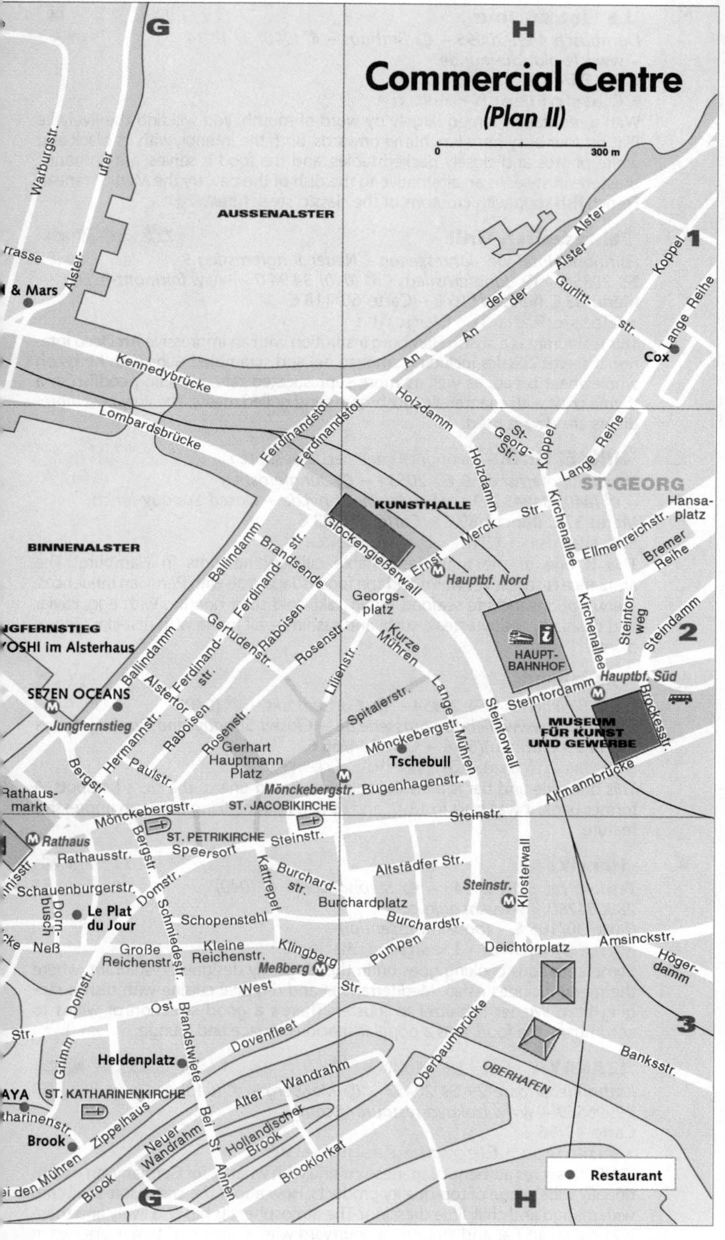
Commercial Centre
(Plan II)
0
300 m
G
H
1
2
3
AUSSENALSTER
BINNENALSTER
KUNSTHALLE
ST-GEORG
HAUPT-BAHNHOF
MUSEUM FÜR KUNST UND GEWERBE
ST. JACOBIKIRCHE
ST. PETRIKIRCHE
ST. KATHARINENKIRCHE
OBERHAFEN
Hauptbf. Nord
Hauptbf. Süd
Jungfernstieg
Mönckebergstr.
Rathaus
Steinstr.
Meßberg
Cox
Tschebull
Le Plat du Jour
Heldenplatz
Brook
& Mars
SEVEN OCEANS
YOSHI im Alsterhaus
Kennedybrücke
Lombardsbrücke
Ferdinandstor
Holzdamm
An der Alster
Gurlitt-str.
Koppel
Lange Reihe
St-Georg-Str.
Kirchenallee
Ellmenreichstr.
Hansa-platz
Bremer Reihe
Steintor-weg
Steindamm
Ernst Merck Str.
Glockengießerwall
Georgsplatz
Ballindamm
Brandsende
Ferdinand-str.
Gertudenstr.
Raboisen
Rosenstr.
Lilienstr.
Kurze Mühren
Lange Mühren
Spitalerstr.
Steintorwall
Steintordamm
Brockesstr.
Mönckebergstr.
Bugenhagenstr.
Altmannbrücke
Steinstr.
Gerhart Hauptmann Platz
Alstertor
Hermannstr.
Paulstr.
Bergstr.
Rathaus-markt
Rathausstr.
Speersort
Kattrepel
Burchard-str.
Altstädter Str.
Burchardplatz
Burchardstr.
Klosterwall
Schauenburgerstr.
Domstr.
Schmiedestr.
Dorn-busch
Schopenstehl
Neß
Große Reichenstr.
Kleine Reichenstr.
Klingberg
Pumpen
Deichtorplatz
Amsinckstr.
Höger-damm
West Str.
Ost
Brandstwiete
Dovenfleet
Oberbaumbrücke
Banksstr.
Grimm
Wandrahm
Alter Wandrahm
Holländischer Brook
Neuer Wandrahm
Zippelhaus
Bei St Annen
Brooklorkat
Bei den Mühren
Warburgstr.
Alster-ufer
Restaurant

Le Plat du Jour

Dornbusch 4 ✉ 20095 – Ⓜ Rathaus – ✆ (040) 32 14 14 – www.le-plat-du-jour.de Plan: **G3**
Carte 34/45 €
• Classic French • Bistro •
With a reputation forged largely by word of mouth, you will find the lively Le Plat du Jour busy from lunchtime onwards. Both the interior, with its black and white photos and closely packed tables, and the food it serves, are authentic brasserie in style. As an alternative to the dish of the day, try the Mediterranean French fish soup with croutons or the classic 'steak frites'.

Jahreszeiten Grill

Fairmont Hotel Vier Jahreszeiten – Neuer Jungfernstieg 9 ✉ 20354 – Ⓜ Jungfernstieg – ✆ (040) 34 94 0 – www.fairmont-hvj.de Plan: **F2**
Menu 33 € (lunch)/116 € – Carte 60/118 €
• Classic French • Elegant •
This restaurant is a stylish Hamburg institution with an impressive Art Deco interior. It serves classics including smoked eel and scrambled eggs with herbs on wholewheat bread, as well as more sophisticated fare, including codfish in a thyme crust with chanterelle mushrooms and grilled meats. The very best ingredients are always used.

NIKKEI NINE – Fairmont Hotel Vier Jahreszeiten

Neuer Jungfernstieg 9 ✉ 20534 – Ⓜ Jungfernstieg – ✆ (040) 34943399 – www.fairmont-hvj.de – closed Sunday lunch Plan: **F2**
Menu 32 € (lunch)/89 € – Carte 47/183 €
• Japanese • Chic • Exotic décor •
This is one of the most fashionable culinary hotspots in Hamburg! The ambience is stylish yet warm and the food is Japanese with Peruvian influences. Menu options include seafood toban yaki, cold soba noodles with egg, caviar and dashi soy, wagyu steak, sushi and sashimi – all made with first-class ingredients.

DIE BANK

Hohe Bleichen 17 ✉ 20354 – Ⓜ Gänsemarkt – ✆ (040) 2380030 – www.diebank-brasserie.de – Closed Sunday and Bank Holidays Plan: **F2**
Menu 29 € (lunch)/59 € – Carte 44/66 €
• International • Brasserie • Trendy •
This brasserie and bar is a fashionable venue and one of the city's hotspots. A former bank, it was built in 1897, and its first floor banking hall is an impressive feature.

Henriks

Tesdorpfstr. 8 ✉ 20148 – Ⓜ Stephanspl. – ✆ (040) 288084280 – www.henriks.cc Plan: **F1**
Carte 30/105 € – *(booking essential)*
• International • Design • Elegant •
Some ambitious cooking goes on in this elegantly designed restaurant, where the menu includes Asian, Mediterranean and regional cuisine with dishes ranging from Wiener Schnitzel to lobster. There's a good selection of wines to accompany the food, plus a popular spacious terrace and lounge.

IZAKAYA – Hotel Sir Nikolai

Katharinenstrasse 29 ✉ 20457 – Ⓜ Meßberg – ✆ (040) 29996669 – www.izakaya-restaurant.com Plan: **G3**
Carte 45/96 €
• Japanese • Elegant • Fashionable •
IZAKAYA serves authentic Japanese cuisine with what is, for Germany, an exceptionally wide range of top-quality products. How about the crispy soft-shell crab with mango and chilli lime dressing? The atmosphere is hip and lively and there is also a smart bar and an interior courtyard with a glass roof that is opened in fine weather.

Parkview – Hotel The Fontenay XX

Fontenay 10 ✉ 20354 – Ⓜ Stephansplatz – ☎ (040) 60566050 – www.thefontenay.de Plan I: C2

Menu 34 € (weekday lunch) – Carte 37/99 €

• International • Friendly •

If you're looking for something casual but stylish Parkview may be the answer. The relaxed atmosphere is complemented – thanks to the floor-to-ceiling windows – by a lovely view of the Alster and the park, friendly service and good international cuisine. Try the pan-fried fillet of sea bass with its skin on with sautéed Mediterranean vegetables, pesto and gnocchi. Great terrace.

Piazza Romana – Hotel Grand Elysée XX

Rothenbaumchaussee 10 ✉ 20148 – Ⓜ Stephanspl. – ☎ (040) 41 41 27 34 – www.grand-elysee.com Plan: F1

Carte 27/59 €

• Italian • Classic décor •

If you fancy carpaccio di vitello, a plate of linguine or tiramisu, then the Italian cuisine on offer at this restaurant is for you.

STRAUCHS FALCO XX

Koreastr. 2 ✉ 20457 – Ⓜ Hafen City Universität – ☎ (040) 2 26 16 15 11 – www.falco-hamburg.de Plan I: C3

Carte 28/93 €

• International • Fashionable •

Strauchs Falco serves a wide range of good Mediterranean dishes, steaks and classic fare. The restaurant itself is modern in style with an open kitchen and a large terrace in summer. The tapas bar on the first floor doubles up as a café during the day.

THEO'S – Hotel Grand Elysée XX

Rothenbaumchaussee 10 ✉ 20148 – Ⓜ Stephanspl. – ☎ (040) 41 41 28 55 – www.grand-elysee.com – Closed Sunday Plan: F1

Carte 44/81 € – *(dinner only)*

• Steakhouse • Brasserie •

At THEO'S you can enjoy exclusive cuts of meat from the Southbend Broiler just like a New York steakhouse. Whatever you do, don't miss the Uckermärker steaks – the cattle are raised to the restaurant's specification!

VLET in der Speicherstadt XX

Sandtorkai 23/24 (entrance by Kibbelstegbrücke 1, 1st floor, Block N) ✉ 20457 – Ⓜ Baumwall – ☎ (040) 334753750 – www.vlet.de – Closed Sunday Plan I: C3

Menu 69/89 € – Carte 53/78 € – *(dinner only)*

• Modern cuisine • Trendy •

The deliberate warehouse feel, typical of Hamburg's Speicherstadt area, makes an ideal venue for fashionable cuisine. It is best to park in the Contipark and cross the Kibbelstegbrücke bridge to reach the restaurant.

YOSHI im Alsterhaus XX

Jungfernstieg 16 (Alsterhaus, 4th floor, direct Elevator, entrance Poststr. 8) ✉ 20354 – Ⓜ Jungfernstieg – ☎ (040) 36099999 – www.yoshi-hamburg.de – Closed Sunday and Bank Holidays Plan: G2

Menu 26 € (weekday lunch)/95 € – Carte 22/113 €

• Japanese • Fashionable •

Christened 'Gourmet Boulevard', the fourth floor of Hamburg's upmarket Alsterhaus shopping plaza is the meeting place for enthusiasts of Japanese food and culture. The teriyaki and sushi dishes prepared by the Japanese chefs achieve a perfect marriage of the traditional and the modern. Popular roof terrace.

Basil & Mars

Alsterufer 1 ✉ 20354 – Ⓜ Stephansplatz – ✆ (040) 41 35 35 35 – www.basilundmars.com – Closed Saturday lunch, Sunday Plan: **G1**
Menu 47 € (dinner) – Carte 38/65 €
• Modern cuisine • Trendy •

This restaurant close to the Kennedy Bridge is chic and fashionable but also pleasantly relaxed. The food prepared in the kitchens is a modern mix of regional, Mediterranean and Southeast Asian influences, such as 12-hour short ribs, grilled octopus and sashimi salad. A simpler lunchtime menu is served Monday to Friday.

CARLS an der Elbphilharmonie

Am Kaiserkai 69 ✉ 20457 – Ⓜ Baumwall – ✆ (040) 300322400 – www.carls-brasserie.de Plan I: **C3**
Menu 39/42 € – Carte 38/75 €
• Country • Brasserie •

This elegant brasserie is at the New Elbe Philharmonic Hall. It serves up French cuisine with a North German slant alongside great views of the port. Savoury tarts and nibbles in the bistro; spices and other gourmet treats in the delicatessen.

Coast by east

Großer Grasbrook 14 ✉ 20457 – Ⓜ Überseequartier – ✆ (040) 30993230 – www.coast-hamburg.de Plan I: **C3**
Carte 44/74 €
• Fusion • Friendly • Fashionable •

With a great location close to the water on the Marco Polo Terrace at the edge of the Hafencity, Coast serves an interesting mix of European and Southeast Asian food and creative sushi delicacies. Downstairs in the basement you will find the Enoteca, which serves Italian cuisine. From 6pm you can park in the Unilever garage next door.

The Greek

Vorsetzen 53 ✉ 20459 – Ⓜ Baumwall – ✆ (040) 31807370 – www.thegreek.hamburg Plan I: **C3**
Menu 20 € (weekday lunch) – Carte 33/55 €
• Greek • Fashionable •

There's no standard Gyros-style fare here; the three floors of this modern restaurant in the port serve upmarket, modern Greek cuisine. Dishes include shoulder of lamb with aubergine caviar, pitta bread and cardamom yoghurt and moraitiko hilopitaki (traditional Greek pasta with lobster). There's a shorter lunchtime menu.

Heldenplatz

Brandstwiete 46 ✉ 20457 – Ⓜ Meßberg – ✆ (040) 30372250 – www.heldenplatz-restaurant.de – Closed end December-early January and Monday-Tuesday Plan: **G3**
Menu 55/69 € – Carte 48/65 € – *(dinner only)*
• Modern French • Fashionable •

Great news for night owls: at Heldenplatz you will find the whole menu available until 2am! Options including Iberico pork with aubergines, red onions and tamarillos, followed by chocolate tart with peanuts, caramel and lemon. The surroundings are relaxed and modern, and all the wines on offer are sold by the glass.

Kinfelts Kitchen & Wine

Am Kaiserkai 56 ✉ 20457 – Ⓜ Baumwall – ✆ (040) 300 68 369 – www.kinfelts.de– Closed Monday Plan I : **C3**
Menu 49/69 € – Carte 43/50 €
• Market cuisine • Chic • Brasserie •

His reputation made at the starred Trüffelschwein, Kirill Kinfelt now runs a second restaurant close to the Elbphilharmonie concert hall. It serves seasonal, regional cuisine that is ambitious yet hearty in a chic, modern setting. The fine selection of wines betrays the presence of a highly skilled sommelier. Good-value lunchtime menu.

LOUIS - by Thomas Martin

Am Kaiserkai 69 ✉ 20457 – Ⓜ Baumwall – ✆ (040) 300322413 – www.louisrestaurant.de Plan I: C3

Carte 42/48 € – *(dinner only)*

• Market cuisine • Elegant • Cosy •

Situated opposite the Elbphilharmonie concert hall and the shipping piers, this stylish and elegant restaurant boasts lovely views. The imaginative international dishes created under the guidance of award-winning chef Thomas Martin are designed for sharing.

La Mirabelle

Bundesstr. 15 ✉ 20146 – Ⓜ Hallerstr. – ✆ (040) 4107585 – www.la-mirabelle-hamburg.de – Closed 1-14 January, Sunday-Monday and Bank Holidays Plan I: C2

Menu 35/63 € – Carte 54/67 € – *(dinner only)*

• Classic French • Cosy • Family •

As the name suggests, the cuisine is French, flavoursome and without frills. Try the delicious sounding Atlantic cod with mustard sauce. Cheese lovers beware: the restaurant boasts some 50 different French cheeses!

Petit Délice

Große Bleichen 21 (at Galleria Passage) ✉ 20354 – Ⓜ Jungfernstieg – ✆ (040) 343470 – www.petit-delice-hamburg.de – Closed Sunday and Bank Holidays Plan: F2

Menu 25 € (lunch) – Carte 37/73 €

• Classic French • Neighbourhood •

Petit Délice serves classic cuisine with a regional influence in a warm and lively atmosphere. The menu includes roast pumpernickel with scrambled eggs and smoked eel and monkfish served with sweetheart cabbage and cucumber relish. Lovely terrace overlooking the Fleet. Traiteur next door serves simpler fare.

NORTH OF THE CENTRE — PLAN I

Piment (Wahabi Nouri)

Lehmweg 29 ✉ 20251 – Ⓜ Eppendorfer Baum – ✆ (040) 42 93 77 88 – www.restaurant-piment.de – closed Wednesday and Sunday Plan: C1

Menu 78/108 € – *(dinner only) (booking advisable)*

• Creative • Neighbourhood •

Wahabi Nouri has an instinctive feel for a product, enabling him to create original dishes in which the high quality of the ingredients is the main focus, while his North African origins also shine through. Friendly, professional service, plus helpful advice on wine selection.

→ Geflämmte Gelbflossen Makrele, Tatar, Zitronengranité, kandierter Apfel. Gemüse Couscous mit Arganöl und Orangenblütenschaum. Étouffée Taube mit B'stilla und Ras el Hanout Jus.

Trüffelschwein (Kirill Kinfelt)

Mühlenkamp 54 ✉ 22303 – Ⓜ Sierichstr. – ✆ (040) 69 65 64 50 – www.trueffelschwein-restaurant.de – Closed 1-3 January, 18-24 March, 15-28 July and Sunday-Monday Plan: D1

Menu 89/139 € – *(dinner only) (booking advisable)*

• Modern cuisine • Friendly •

The cuisine is modern, elaborate and sophisticated right down to the last detail. The attractive interior, which is warm and minimalist in style, makes a great setting for this fine food.

→ Raviolo, Rote Bete, Trüffel. Geschmorte Iberico Backe, Trüffel, Karotte, Mandel. Lammhaxe, Aubergine, Spargel, Gewürze.

Jellyfish

Weidenallee 12 ✉ 20357 – Ⓜ Christkirche – ✆ (040) 4 10 54 14 – www.jellyfish-restaurant.de – Closed 23 December-6 January and Tuesday

Plan: **B2**

Menu 98/134 € – *(dinner only)*

• Seafood • Fashionable •

A relaxed restaurant with a pleasantly minimalist interior and a charmingly trendy feel, Jellyfish provides the ideal setting for fine, creative cuisine, which is full of contrasts and made using top-quality sea food. As for wine, you can always rely on the suggestions from the experienced staff.

→ Makrele, Lauchvinaigrette, Jalapeno. Pulpo, Spargel, Salsa verde, Holzkohle. Kabeljau, Aal, Birne, Bohne, Speck.

Stüffel

Isekai 1 ✉ 20249 – Ⓜ Keilinghusenstr. – ✆ (040) 60902050 – www.restaurantstueffel.de – Closed Monday

Plan: **C1**

Menu 37/56 € – Carte 35/58 €

• Market cuisine • Chic • Bistro •

The riverside location here is every bit as appealing as the seasonal cuisine with Mediterranean and regional influences in which top-quality produce combines to create dishes such as fillet of spined loach with tomato, bread and basil salad. You can eat in the stylish modern bistro or outside on the waterfront. The wine list is well chosen and if you're lucky the owner himself will advise you on your choice.

Brechtmanns Bistro

Erikastr. 43 ✉ 20251 – Ⓜ Kellerhusenstr. – ✆ (040) 41305888 – www.brechtmann-bistro.de

Plan: **C1**

Menu 32 € – Carte 31/56 €

• Asian influences • Minimalist •

Brechtmanns is an extremely popular, friendly minimalist-style bistro serving South East Asian-inspired market-fresh cuisine including crispy tuna fish tartare with cucumber, wasabi and sweet and sour pineapple, and boiled topside of beef in broth with root vegetables and apple.

Zipang

Eppendorfer Weg 171 ✉ 20253 – Ⓜ Eppendorfer Baum – ✆ (040) 43 28 00 32 – www.zipang.de – Closed Sunday-Monday

Plan: **B1**

Menu 32 € (lunch)/65 € (dinner) – Carte 32/63 € – *(Bank Holidays: dinner only)*

• Japanese • Minimalist •

The minimalist interior at Zipang has clean lines, muted colours and a smart silver sheen. This makes a perfect match for chef Toshiharu Minami's mix of traditional and modern Japanese cooking styles. The restaurant is popular with Japanese diners – always a good sign.

Gallo Nero

Sierichstr. 46 ✉ 22301 – Ⓜ Sierichstr. – ✆ (040) 27092229 – www.gallo-nero.net

Plan: **C1**

Menu 49/89 € – Carte 39/68 €

• Italian • Mediterranean décor •

A restaurant, wine shop and "alimentari con cucina" with three lovely terraces, this Winterhuder institution promises authentic Italian cuisine made using top-quality produce including dishes such as burrata con datterino e culatello di Zibello and calamaretti alla griglia… all washed down with a selection of good Italian reds and some lovely Rieslings.

Butcher's american steakhouse

Milchstr. 19 ✉ 20148 – Ⓜ Stephansplatz – ✆ (040) 446082 – www.butchers-steakhouse.de – Closed Saturday lunch, Sunday lunch and Bank Holidays lunch

Plan: **C2**

Carte 60/173 €

• Steakhouse • Family • Cosy •

At Butcher's american steakhouse you can enjoy fine Nebraska beef that the chef presents to the table personally. A cosy restaurant is dominated by dark wood and warm colours.

Cornelia Poletto X

Eppendorfer Landstr. 80 ✉ 20249 – Ⓜ Kellenhusenstr. – ✆ (040) 4802159 – www.cornelia-poletto.de – Closed Sunday-Monday and Bank Holidays Plan: **C1**

Menu 59/98 € – Carte 45/86 €

• Italian • Friendly • Cosy •

Cornelia Poletto (who Germans will know from the television if not from her previous restaurant) serves Italian specialities in the restaurant and sells them (spices, wine, pasta, cheese) in the shop. Booked out almost daily.

Heimatjuwel X

Stellinger Weg 47 ✉ 20255 – Ⓜ Lutterothstr. – ✆ (040) 42106989 – www.heimatjuwel.de – Closed 1 week March, 2 weeks August, Sunday-Tuesday lunch, Wednesday lunch, Saturday lunch Plan: **B1**

Menu 44/87 € – Carte 49/55 €

• Creative • Minimalist • Rustic •

Marcel Görke, no stranger to the Hamburg culinary scene, runs this rustic, minimalist-style little restaurant with its friendly, informal atmosphere. It serves creative, fully-flavoured regional cuisine that represents great value for money. There is a very short and simple lunchtime menu. Small pavement terrace.

Poletto Winebar X

Eppendorfer Weg 287 ✉ 20251 – Ⓜ Eppendorfer Baum – ✆ (040) 38 64 47 00 – www.poletto-winebar.de Plan: **C1**

Menu 32 € – Carte 35/62 €

• Italian • Cosy •

This lively wine bar is definitely one of the places to be in Eppendorf. The food is flavoursome, and Italian in style, and includes classics such as vitello tonnato and tiramisu, alongside excellent cold meats straight from the Berkel meat slicer. The adjacent wine shop has a great selection.

Witwenball X

Weidenallee 20 ✉ 20357 – Ⓜ Christskirche – ✆ (040) 53630085 – www.witwenball.com – Closed Monday Plan: **B2**

Menu 35 € (Vegetarian) – Carte 38/58 € – *(dinner only)*

• Modern cuisine • Cosy •

Where once people danced, you will now find fresh, flavoursome fare – try the zander with cauliflower, purple curry and raisins. Good, predominantly German wines are served in a relaxed and friendly atmosphere. Lovely big marble bar.

Wolfs Junge X

Zimmerstr. 30 ✉ 22085 – Ⓜ Mundsburg – ✆ (040) 20965157 – www.wolfs-junge.de– Closed Sunday-Monday, Saturday lunch Plan: **D1**

Menu 24 € (lunch)/79 € (dinner)

• Market cuisine • Friendly • Minimalist •

The accent here is on sustainable, regional cuisine, the very epitome of "nose to tail" eating. The ingredients are sourced from selected producers with some of the vegetables and herbs grown by the restaurant itself. Serves simple midday fare such as home-made bratwurst and an ambitious, creative set menu including Angeln Saddleback, kimchi and fermented onion in the evenings.

HARBOUR – ALTONA — PLAN III

Landhaus Scherrer (Heinz O. Wehmann) XXX

Elbchaussee 130 ✉ 22763 – Ⓜ Königstr. – ✆ (040) 8 83 07 00 30 – www.landhausscherrer.de – Closed Sunday Plan: **I1**

Menu 72/128 € – Carte 63/101 €

• Classic French • Elegant •

Heinz O. Wehmann has been at the helm at Landhaus Scherrer since 1980. He is still serving classic cuisine in this elegant restaurant where Otto Bachmann's large erotic painting remains the decorative focus. Adding a modern note, the 600 plus wines on the wine list are presented to you on an iPad.

→ Gebratene Pilgermuschel mit Stängelrübe und Krustentierschaum. Steinbutt an der Gräte gebraten mit Fenchel, Tomate und Olive. Maibockrücken mit Pfifferlingen und Lauchpüree.

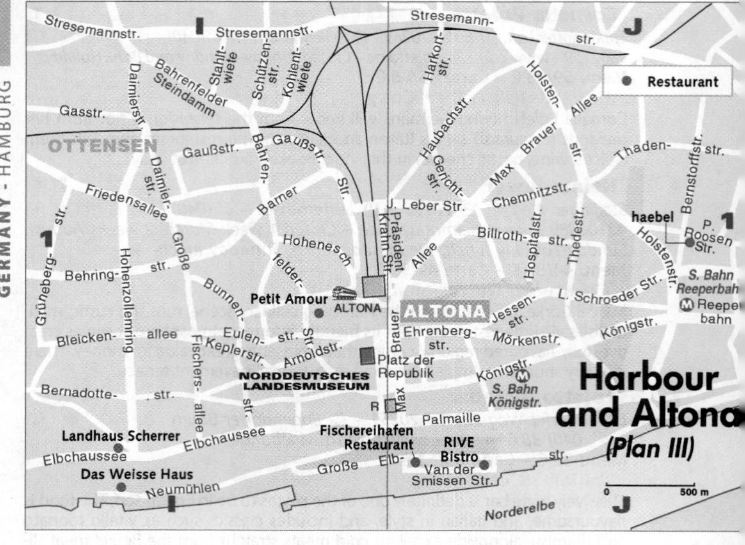

Petit Amour (Boris Kasprik)

XX

Spritzenplatz 11 ✉ 22765 – Ⓜ Altona – ✆ (040) 30 74 65 56 – www.petitamour-hh.com – Closed end January-early February 2 weeks, 4 weeks June-July and Sunday-Monday

Plan: **I1**

Menu 115/185 € – *(dinner only) (booking advisable)*

• Creative French • Chic • Cosy •

This is a very popular restaurant for a number of reasons… The upmarket design (modern and minimalist yet warm and friendly), the professional service and wine suggestions, and the unfussy, ambitious cuisine with international influences.

➜ Terrine von der Foie Gras und grünem Tee mit Rhabarber und Brioche. Steinbutt unter Kartoffelschuppen mit Vin Jaunejus, grünem Spargel und Morcheln. Geeiste Gariguette Erdbeeren, grüne Mandeln und konfierte Orange.

Nil

X

Neuer Pferdemarkt 5 ✉ 20359 – Ⓜ Feldstr. – ✆ (040) 4 39 78 23 – www.restaurant-nil.de – Closed Tuesday except in December

Plan I: **B2**

Menu 30/42 € – Carte 32/50 € – *(dinner only)*

• International • Neighbourhood • Friendly •

Located in Hamburg's fashionable Schanze district, Nil is cosy, though perhaps a little cramped, and serves a range of well-cooked dishes including young goat bratwurst with lentils, parsnips and apple mustard and pan-fried skrei with baked carrots and coriander. There is an attractive garden to the rear and cookery courses next door.

RIVE Bistro

X

Van-der-Smissen Str. 1 ✉ 22767 – Ⓜ Königstr. – ✆ (040) 3 80 59 19 – www.rive.de – Closed Monday

Plan: **J1**

Menu 30 € (weekday lunch) – Carte 35/87 € – *(booking advisable)*

• Seafood • Brasserie •

Sitting right on the port, this bistro is run by the same team as Tschebull. It serves good quality, flavoursome seafood and grilled meats alongside classic dishes such as Hamburger Pannfisch and Wiener Schnitzel. In summer the wonderful terrace is a must! Hot food served throughout the day.

philipps

Turnerstr. 9 ✉ 20357 – Ⓜ Feldstr. – ✆ (040) 63 73 51 08 – www.philipps-restaurant.de – Closed Sunday-Monday Plan I: **B2**

Menu 38/60 € – Carte 32/60 €

• International • Trendy • Friendly •

Hidden away in a side street, phillips is a great place to eat. Walk down the few stairs to this friendly little restaurant with low ceilings, a relaxed atmosphere and international menu. It promises flavoursome and skilfully prepared dishes such as ox cheeks with leek champ.

Fischereihafen Restaurant

Große Elbstr. 143 ✉ 22767 – Ⓜ Königstr. – ✆ (040) 381816 – www.fischereihafenrestaurant.de Plan: **J1**

Menu 25 € (lunch)/65 € – Carte 38/98 €

• Seafood • Classic décor •

This fish restaurant overlooking the port is a veritable Hamburg institution. The service is excellent, as is the great value lunchtime menu.

East – Hotel East

Simon-von-Utrecht-Str. 31 ✉ 20359 – Ⓜ St. Pauli – ✆ (040) 309933 – www.east-hamburg.de Plan I: **B2**

Carte 38/105 € – *(dinner only)*

• Fusion • Design • Fashionable •

The atmosphere in this former factory building draws on many styles and influences. Far Eastern charm combines skilfully with Western industrial heritage. A restaurant not to be missed.

Clouds - Heaven's Bar & Kitchen

Reeperbahn 1 (at 23. floor der Tanzenden Türme) ✉ 20359 – Ⓜ St. Pauli – ✆ (040) 30993280 – www.clouds-hamburg.de – Closed Saturday lunch, Sunday lunch Plan I: **B3**

Carte 50/130 € – *(booking essential) (bar lunch)*

• Modern French • Design • Fashionable •

Set high above the River Elbe and St Michael's church, Clouds offers a truly amazing view and good modern cuisine including a selection of meat cuts and a classic steak tartare prepared at your table. The interior is stylishly urban and from May onwards the Heaven's Nest roof terrace serves drinks and snacks.

HACO

Clemens-Schultz Str. 18 ✉ 20359 – Ⓜ St. Pauli – ✆ (040) 74203939 – www.restaurant-haco.com – Closed 23 December-6 January and Sunday-Monday Plan I: **B2**

Carte 49/96 € – *(dinner only)*

• Modern cuisine • Cosy • Friendly •

There is a trendy and relaxed feel to this attractive corner restaurant (the name "HACO" is derived from "HAmburg" and "COrner"). The modern Scandinavian style of the furnishings is also reflected in the produce-oriented cuisine which is also a real delight for vegetarians and vegans.

Das Weisse Haus

Neumühlen 50 ✉ 22763 – Ⓜ Königstr. – ✆ (040) 3909016 – www.das-weisse-haus.de – Closed Monday Plan: **I1**

Menu 39/60 € – Carte 37/47 €

• International • Friendly •

In the little white building on the Elbpromenade your host Patrick Voelz proposes a range of international dishes alongside a now established seasonal surprise menu. The atmosphere is casual and friendly and you can sit outside too.

haebel

Paul-Roosen-Str. 31 ✉ *22767* – Ⓜ *S. Bahhn Reeperbahn* Plan: **J1**
– ✆ *(0151) 72423046* – *www.haebel.hamburg*– *Closed Sunday-Monday*
Menu 74/85 € – *(Tuesday to Friday dinner only)*
• Creative French • Contemporary décor • Bistro •

This tiny, bistro-style restaurant with its open kitchen serves a Nordic/French-inspired surprise menu that showcases excellent ingredients, which are subsequently fashioned into a range of creative and pleasingly pared-down dishes.

ELBE-WESTERN DISTRICTS

Süllberg - Seven Seas

(Karlheinz Hauser) Süllbergsterrasse 12 (by Elbchaussee) ✉ *22587*
– ✆ *(040) 8 66 25 20* – *www.karlheinzhauser.de* – *Closed January-12 February and Monday-Tuesday*
Menu 130 € (Vegetarian)/190 € – *(dinner only)*
• Modern French • Luxury •

The Süllberg is a Blankenese institution and along with the Seven Seas has become one of Hamburg's top gourmet addresses. It offers a genuinely upmarket dining experience, from the classy interior to Karlheinz Hauser's fragrant, classic cuisine, as well as the accomplished and attentive service and expert wine recommendations. The rooms are as attractive and stylish as the restaurant.

→ Thunfisch "roh mariniert", Ananas, grüne Olive, Ponzu. Loup de Mer "Eau de Moule", Muscheln, Rhabarber, Hijiki Algen. Frühjahrs Trüffel "Los Ancones Schokolade", Ingwer, Kaffee, Mandarine.

Deck 7 – See below

Jacobs Restaurant

Hotel Louis C. Jacob – Elbchaussee 401 (by Elbchaussee) ✉ *22609*
– ✆ *(040) 82 25 54 06* – *www.hotel-jacob.de* – *Closed Monday-Tuesday*
Menu 102/148 € – Carte 66/115 € – *(Wednesday to friday dinner only) (booking advisable)*
• Classic French • Chic •

Thomas Martin's food – classic, simple, free of fancy flourishes, and placing great emphasis on top-quality ingredients – is available from an à la carte menu. The dining experience is rounded off by the accomplished service, the stylish decor and the magnificent lime tree shaded terrace overlooking the Elbe.

→ Samtsuppe vom Hummer, Riesling-Beerenauslese, Estragon-Royale. Bretonischer Steinbutt mit Beurre Blanc. Karamellisierte Altländer Apfeltarte, Crème Chantilly.

HYGGE Brasserie & Bar

Hotel Landhaus Flottbek – Baron-Voght-Str. 179 (by Stresemannstraße)
✉ *22607* – ✆ *(040) 82 27 41 60* – *www.hygge-hamburg.de* – *Closed Saturday lunch, Sunday lunch*
Menu 36/60 € – Carte 35/60 € – *(dinner only)*
• Country • Brasserie • Elegant •

In Danish, 'hygge' describes a feeling of warmth, cosiness and well-being - just the atmosphere conjured up in this chic, stylish and relaxed timber-framed restaurant with an open hearth at its centre. The food is seasonal and regional, and includes dishes such as cod fillet with braised cucumbers, horseradish and mash. The bar-lounge is a trendy spot.

Zur Flottbeker Schmiede

Baron-Voght-Str. 79 ✉ *20038* – ✆ *(040) 20918236* Plan I: **A3**
– *www.zurflottbekerschmiede.de* – *Closed 1-7 January and Monday*
Carte 22/47 € – *(dinner only)*
• Portuguese • Bistro • Family •

Hamburg offers a taste of Portugal in this old listed forge building, where a traditional German ambience (with authentic decor and an old open fireplace) combines with a more informal southern European feel. The menu focuses on Portuguese-Mediterranean cuisine, with a selection of delicious tapas.

Weinwirtschaft Kleines Jacob

Hotel Louis C. Jacob – Elbchaussee 404 (by Elbchaussee) ✉ 22609 – ✆ (040) 82 25 55 10 – www.kleines-jacob.de
Menu 36 € – Carte 36/67 € – *(dinner only and Sunday lunch) (booking advisable)*

• Classic cuisine • Wine bar • Cosy •

No wonder so many people describe Kleines Jakob as their favourite restaurant with its wine bar charm, candlelit tables and attentive service. The dishes coming out of the open kitchens include chicken fricassee vol-au-vents and rice. All the wines come from vineyards in German-speaking countries.

Deck 7 – Restaurant Süllberg - Seven Seas

Süllbergsterrasse 12 (by Elbchaussee) ✉ 22587 – ✆ (040) 86 62 52 77 – www.karlheinzhauser.de
Menu 32 € – Carte 35/73 €

• Country • Cosy • Elegant •

In defiance of many a passing trend, this restaurant with its smart, brown leather upholstered chairs and parquet flooring has opted for the versatility of a classic yet modern interior. In summer, eat outside with stunning views of the Elbe.

Rach & Ritchy

Holstenkamp 71 ✉ 22525 – ✆ (040) 89726170 Plan I: **A2**
– www.rach-ritchy.de – Closed Saturday lunch, Sunday-Monday and Bank Holidays lunch
Carte 34/70 € – *(booking advisable)*

• Meats and grills • Friendly • Fashionable •

TV chef Christian Rach is now a household name. It is the second member of the duo, Richard 'Ritchy' Mayer, who does the cooking in his fashionable, modern grill restaurant. Specialities include succulent steaks from the glass-fronted maturing cabinet.

MUNICH
MÜNCHEN

gameover2012/iStock

MUNICH IN...

→ **ONE DAY**
The old town, Frauenkirche, English Garden, Wagner (if possible!) at the National Theatre.

→ **TWO DAYS**
Schwabing, Pinakothek, Hofbräuhaus.

→ **THREE DAYS**
Olympic Park, Schloss Nymphenburg, Deutsches Museum, an evening in a traditional Bavarian inn.

Situated in a stunning position not far north of the Alps, Munich is a cultural titan. Famously described as the 'village with a million inhabitants', its mix of German organisation and Italian lifestyle makes for a magical mix, with an enviable amount of Italian restaurants to seek out and enjoy. This cultural capital of Southern Germany boasts over forty theatres and dozens of museums; temples of culture that blend charmingly with the Bavarian love of folklore and lederhosen. Perhaps in no other world location – certainly not in Western Europe – is there such an enjoyable abundance of folk festivals and groups dedicated to playing

the local music. And there's an abundance of places to see them, too: Munich is awash with Bierhallen, Bierkeller, and Biergarten.

The heart of Munich is the Old Town, with its epicentre the Marienplatz in the south, and Residenz to the north: there are many fine historic buildings around here. Running to the east is the River Isar, flanked by fine urban thoroughfares and green areas for walks. Head north for the area dissected by the Ludwigstrasse and Leopoldstrasse – Schwabing – which is full of students as it's the University district. To the east is the English Garden, a denizen of peace. West of here, the Museums district, dominated by the Pinakothek, is characterised by bookshops, antique stores and galleries.

EATING OUT

Munich is a city in which you can eat well - especially if you're a meat-eater – and in large quantities. The local specialities are meat and potatoes, with large dollops of cabbage on the side; you won't have trouble finding roast pork and dumplings or meatloaf and don't forget the local white veal sausage, weisswurst. The meat is invariably succulent, and cabbage is often adorned with the likes of juniper berries. Potatoes, meanwhile, have a tendency to evolve into soft and buttery dumplings. And sausage? Take your pick from over 1,500 recognised species. Other specialities include Schweinshaxe (knuckle of pork) and Leberkäs (meat and offal pâté). Eating out in Munich, or anywhere in Bavaria, is an experience in itself, with the distinctive background din of laughter, singing and the clinking of mugs of Bavarian Weissbier. It's famous for the Brauereigaststätten or brewery inn; be prepared for much noise, and don't be afraid to fall into conversation with fellow diners and drinkers. The many Italian restaurants in the city provide an excellent alternative.

✿✿✿ **Atelier** – Hotel Bayerischer Hof

Promenadeplatz 2 ✉ 80333 – Ⓜ Marienplatz Plan: **G2**
– ✆ (089) 2 12 00 – www.bayerischerhof.de – Closed 5 weeks July-September, 24 December - 8 January and Sunday-Monday
Menu 165/220 € – *(dinner only)*

• Creative French • Elegant • Design •

With its artistic interior designed by Axel Vervoordt, this restaurant more than lives up to its name. You will find the cuisine of young and talented chef Jan Hartwig equally modern and individual in style. His tasty culinary creations are masterpieces of balance and intensity.

➜ Bayerische Forelle, Kimizu mit Gartenkräutern, Kartoffelstampf und Schinken-Zwiebelsud. Rehrücken, Wirsingsalat, Petersilienwurzel, Herzkirschen und Pfeffer. Karamellisierter Blätterteig, Johannisbeerstrauch, Piemonteser Haselnüsse, Vanilleessig.

✿✿ **Alois - Dallmayr Fine Dining**

Dienerstr. 14 (1st floor) ✉ 80331 – Ⓜ Marienplatz Plan: **G2**
– ✆ (089) 2135100 – www.dallmayr.com– Closed 14-30 April, 9-18 June, 4 August-3 September and Sunday-Wednesday lunch, Bank Holidays
Menu 70/155 € (dinner) – Carte 60/105 €

• Modern French • Elegant •

Whether you try the delicatessen or the gourmet restaurant, there's one thing you can be sure of at this distinguished and long-established eatery: top quality produce. After a change of name and with a smart, new interior, it now serves distinctive, modern cuisine that is well-balanced and pleasingly pared down. The service and wine recommendations are equally good.

➜ Rinderfilet, Tofu, Edamame. Schwarzfederhuhn, Senfsaat, Vin Jaune. Pflaume, Vanille, Lorbeer.

✿ **Schuhbecks Fine Dining**

Pfisterstr. 9 ✉ 80331 – Ⓜ Marienplatz Plan: **H2**
– ✆ (089) 2166900 – www.schuhbeck.de – Closed 2 weeks early January, 3 weeks August and Sunday-Monday
Menu 78/116 €

• Modern cuisine • Friendly • Elegant •

Another of Alfons Schuhbeck's restaurants in the Platzl, Fine Dining promises an interior that is elegant without being overly formal and a friendly and professional front-of-house team. Culinary offerings include two seasonal set menus that are modern, harmonious, tasty and based on the finest ingredients.

➜ Gillardeau Auster mit Zitrone. Bretonischer Steinbutt, Spargel, Mole, Quinoa, Jalapeno. Passionsfrucht, Mango, Joghurt, Koriander.

✿ **Les Deux**

Maffeistr. 3a (1st Floor) ✉ 80333 – Ⓜ Marienplatz Plan: **G2**
– ✆ (089) 7 10 40 73 73 – www.lesdeux-muc.de – Closed Sunday and Bank Holidays
Menu 48 € (weekday lunch)/120 € – Carte 73/154 € – *(booking advisable)*

• Modern French • Friendly • Fashionable •

"Les Deux" are host Fabrice Kieffer and chef de cuisine Edip Sigl and their chic designer restaurant enjoys a prime city location. The cuisine is modern yet classic, the service pleasant and friendly, the wine list attractive.

➜ Entenleberparfait, Ingwer, Miso, Popcorn, Alge. Tranche vom Bretonischen Steinbutt, Ratatouille, Basilikum, Safran. Französische Entenbrust, Sellerie, Blaukraut, Markklößchen, Buchenpilze, Purple Curry.

Brasserie – See below

Schwarzreiter – Hotel Vier Jahrszeiten Kempinski

Maximilianstr. 17 ✉ 80539 – Ⓜ Lehel – ✆ (089) 21 250 Plan: **H2**
– www.schwarzreiter.com – Closed August and Sunday-Monday
Menu 92/119 € – *(dinner only)*

• Modern cuisine • Elegant •

Chic and upmarket without being overly formal, Schwarzreiter is this classic Munich hotel's fine dining restaurant. The 'Young Bavarian Cuisine' served here is sophisticated food of the very highest calibre, and the friendly and professional front-of-house team will be only too pleased to provide wine recommendations.

→ Steinpilze, bayerischer Reis, Kerbelknolle. Eifeler Ur-Lamm, Bohne, Birne, Speck. Slyrs Whiskey, dunkle Schokolade, Tabak, Pflaume.

Tian

Frauenstr. 4 ✉ 80469 – Ⓜ Isartor – ✆ (089) 885656712 Plan: **G3**
– www.taste-tian.com – Closed Sunday-Monday and Bank Holidays
Menu 37 € (lunch)/112 € – Carte 65/71 €

• Vegetarian • Fashionable •

Even though this restaurant focuses exclusively on vegetarian and vegan cuisine, the resulting dishes are still full of flavour. Guests can look forward to dishes demonstrating creativity, finesse and intensity from either the shorter lunch menu or the evening menu and it is possible to select dishes from either menu at lunchtime. Add to all this a trendy design, an attractive bar, a stylish inner courtyard terrace and a prime location on the Viktualienmarkt.

→ Lauchherzen, Kartoffel, Trüffel. Zucchiniblüte, Pfifferlinge, Petersilie. Weinbergpfirsich, Basilikum, Mascarpone.

Showroom

Lilienstr. 6 ✉ 81669 – Ⓜ Isartor – ✆ (089) 44 42 90 82 Plan I: **C3**
– www.showroom-restaurant.de – Closed 6-27 August, Saturday-Sunday and Bank Holidays
Menu 115/135 € – *(dinner only) (booking essential)*

• Creative • Friendly • Trendy •

Showroom offers a winning formula that combines a relaxed atmosphere and creative cuisine with the emphasis on good, fresh produce. Presented in the form of a surprise menu, each dish is a perfectly judged blend of flavours served up by the excellent front-of-house team.

→ Hamachi, Rharbarer, Radieschen, Johannisbeeren. Wagyu, Steinpilze, Brioche, Tinte, Curry, Brokkoli. Guave, Avocado, Basilikum, Pininenkerne, Rum.

Colette Tim Raue

Klenzestr. 72 ✉ 80469 – Ⓜ Frauenhoferstraße Plan I: **B3**
– ✆ (089) 23 00 25 55 – www.brasseriecolette.de
Menu 49 € – Carte 37/72 € – *(dinner only)*

• French • Brasserie •

Tim Raue really has his finger on the pulse with his new culinary concept at Colette. It is as relaxed as a French brasserie, friendly with pleasantly informal service, and offers good food at great prices. The first class ingredients speak for themselves in dishes such as *boeuf bourguignon* with speck, mushrooms and shallots.

Schuhbecks in den Südtiroler Stuben

Platzl 6 ✉ 80331 – Ⓜ Isartor – ✆ (089) 2166900 Plan: **H2**
– www.schuhbeck.de – Closed 1 week early January and Sunday
Carte 35/70 €

• Country • Rustic • Elegant •

You will find a new culinary concept here as Bavarian delicacies meet Italian specialities in this decidedly elegant restaurant. The motto is 'share and enjoy' and rather than the classic menu sequence, diners are free to order starters or mains as they wish. Also available at the Platzl: ice cream, chocolate, spices and wine.

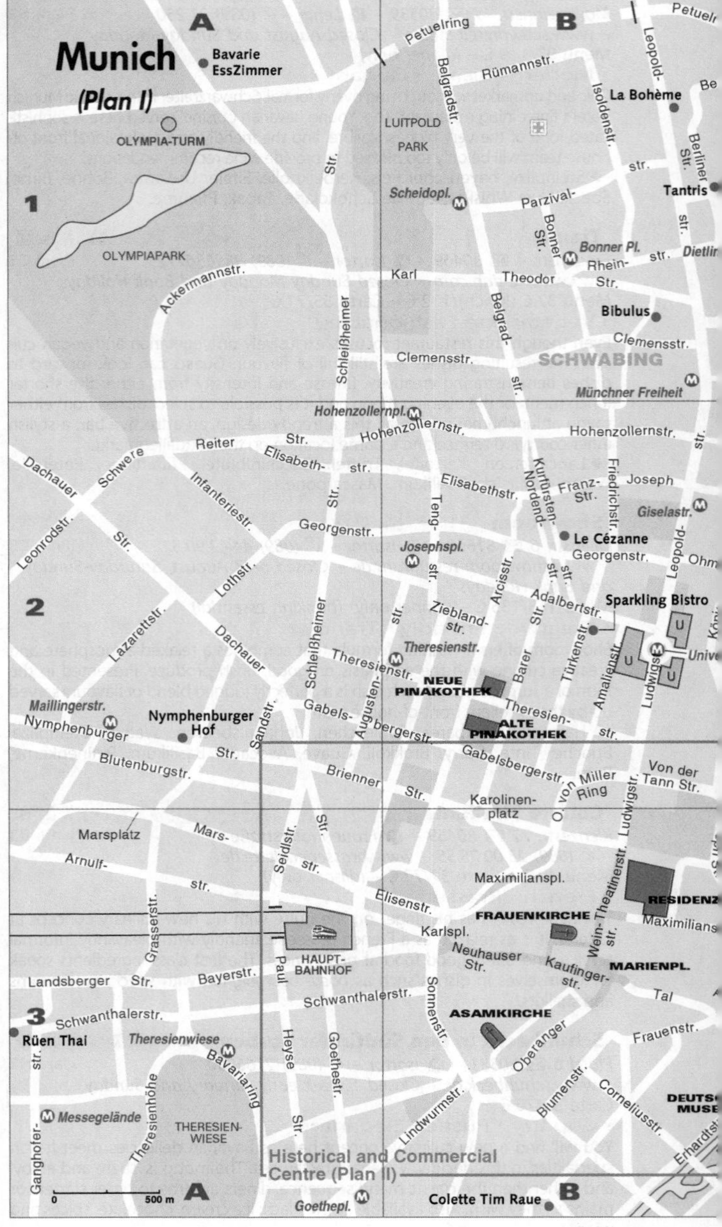

Munich
(Plan I)
A
B
1
2
3
Bavarie EssZimmer
OLYMPIA-TURM
OLYMPIAPARK
Petuelring
Rümannstr.
Belgradstr.
LUITPOLD PARK
Scheidopl.
La Bohème
Tantris
Parzival-str.
Bonner Str.
Bonner Pl.
Rhein-str.
Dietlin
Ackermannstr.
Karl Theodor Str.
Belgrad-str.
Bibulus
Clemensstr.
SCHWABING
Münchner Freiheit
Schleißheimer Str.
Hohenzollernpl.
Hohenzollernstr.
Dachauer Str.
Schwere Reiter Str.
Elisabeth-str.
Elisabethstr.
Infanteriestr.
Kurfürsten-Nordend-
Franz-Joseph Str.
Friedrichstr.
Giselastr.
Leonrodstr.
Georgenstr.
Josephspl.
Le Cézanne
Leopold-str.
Lothstr.
Teng-str.
Arcisstr.
Adalbertstr.
Sparkling Bistro
Ziebland-str.
Lazarettstr.
Theresienstr.
Barer Str.
Türkenstr.
Amalienstr.
Ludwigstr.
Univ
NEUE PINAKOTHEK
ALTE PINAKOTHEK
Augusten-str.
Maillingerstr.
Nymphenburger Str.
Nymphenburger Hof
Sandstr.
Gabelsbergerstr.
Blutenburgstr.
Brienner Str.
Von der Tann Str.
O. von Miller Ring
Karolinen-platz
Marsplatz
Mars-str.
Arnulf-str.
Seidlstr.
Maximilianspl.
Elisenstr.
RESIDENZ
FRAUENKIRCHE
Maximilians
Grasserstr.
Karlspl.
HAUPT-BAHNHOF
Neuhauser Str.
Wein-Theatinerstr.
MARIENPL.
Landsberger Str.
Bayerstr.
Paul Heyse Str.
Kaufinger-str.
Schwanthalerstr.
Sonnenstr.
Tal
Rüen Thai
Theresienwiese
Bavariaring
ASAMKIRCHE
Oberanger
Frauenstr.
Goethestr.
Blumenstr.
Corneliusstr.
Messegelände
Theresienhöhe
THERESIEN-WIESE
Lindwurmstr.
Ganghofer-str.
Historical and Commercial Centre (Plan II)
0 500 m
Goethepl.
Colette Tim Raue
Erhardtstr.

FRANZ-JOSEF-STRAUSS

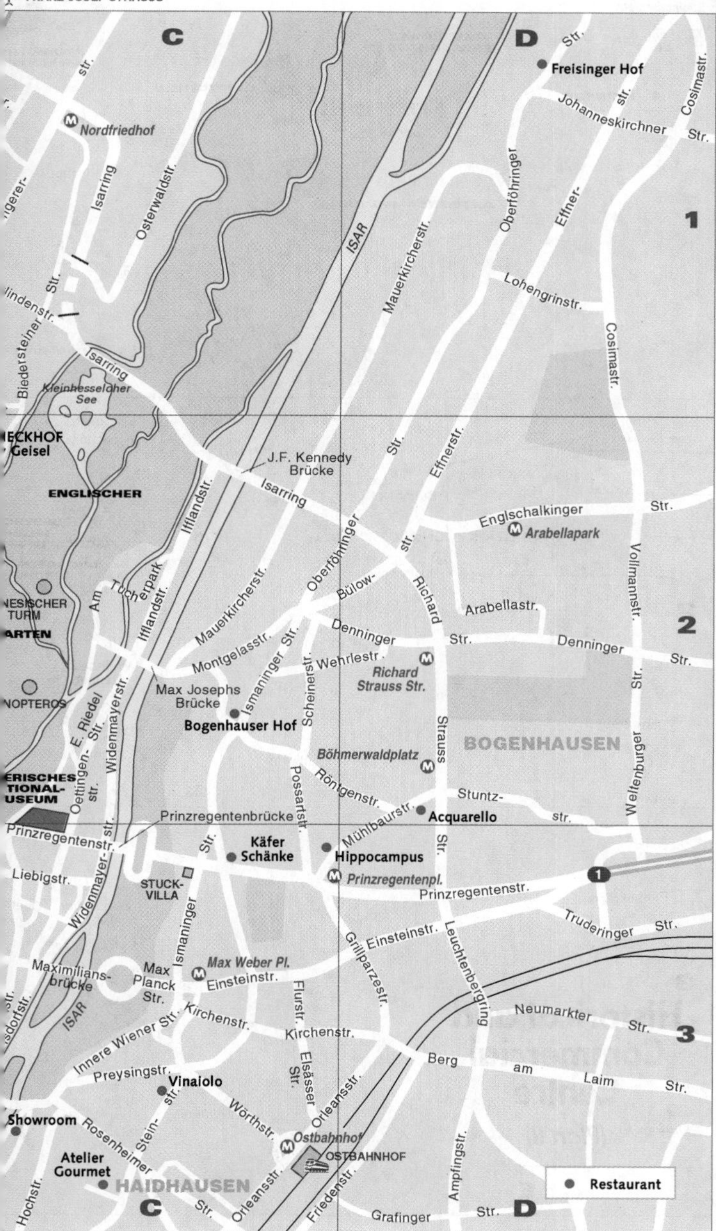

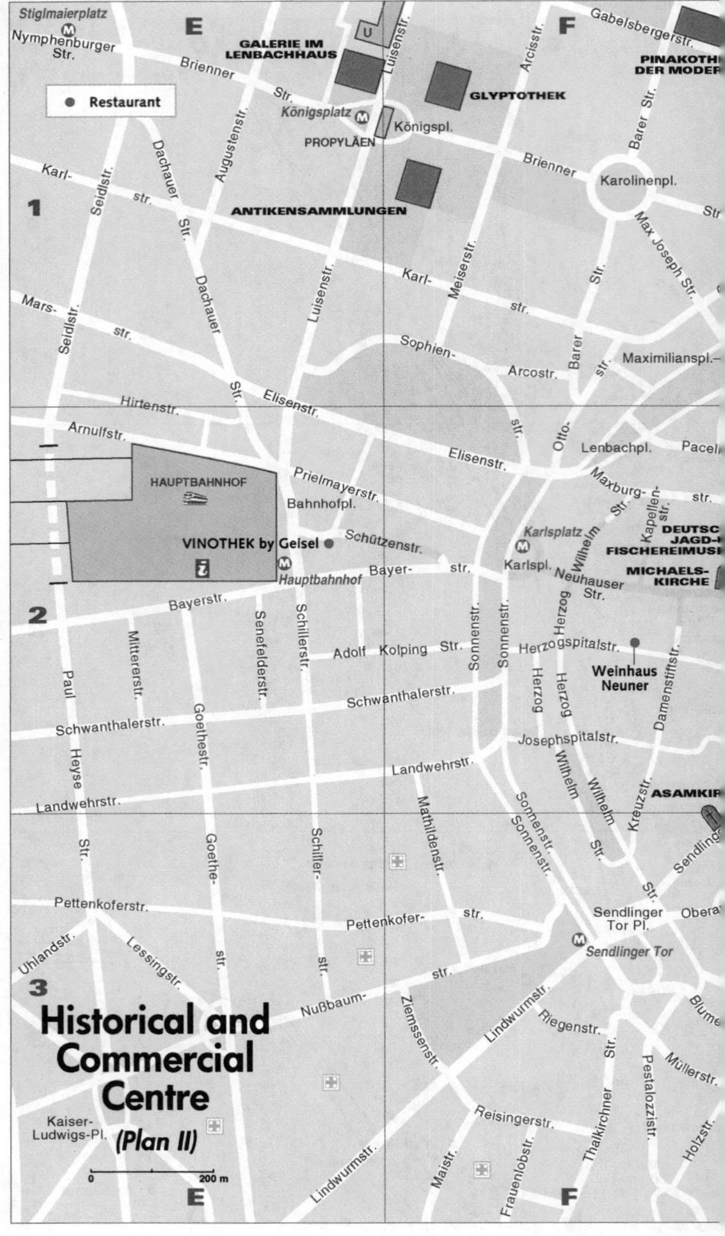

Historical and Commercial Centre
(Plan II)
Restaurant
GALERIE IM LENBACHHAUS
GLYPTOTHEK
PINAKOTHEK DER MODERNE
PROPYLÄEN
ANTIKENSAMMLUNGEN
HAUPTBAHNHOF
VINOTHEK by Geisel
Weinhaus Neuner
DEUTSCHES JAGD- und FISCHEREIMUSEUM
MICHAELS-KIRCHE
ASAMKIRCHE
Stiglmaierplatz
Königsplatz
Königspl.
Karolinenpl.
Maximiliansplatz
Lenbachpl.
Karlsplatz
Karlspl.
Hauptbahnhof
Bahnhofpl.
Sendlinger Tor Pl.
Sendlinger Tor
Kaiser-Ludwigs-Pl.
Nymphenburger Str.
Brienner Str.
Karlstr.
Marsstr.
Seidlstr.
Dachauer Str.
Augustenstr.
Luisenstr.
Arcisstr.
Gabelsbergerstr.
Barer Str.
Max Joseph Str.
Meiserstr.
Sophienstr.
Arcostr.
Hirtenstr.
Arnulfstr.
Elisenstr.
Prielmayerstr.
Ottostr.
Maxburgstr.
Kapellenstr.
Schützenstr.
Bayerstr.
Neuhauser Str.
Herzog Wilhelm Str.
Adolf Kolping Str.
Herzogspitalstr.
Damenstiftstr.
Mittererstr.
Senefelderstr.
Schillerstr.
Sonnenstr.
Paul Heyse Str.
Schwanthalerstr.
Goethestr.
Josephspitalstr.
Landwehrstr.
Mathildenstr.
Kreuzstr.
Sendlinger Str.
Oberanger
Pettenkoferstr.
Uhlandstr.
Lessingstr.
Nußbaumstr.
Ziemssenstr.
Lindwurmstr.
Riegenstr.
Thalkirchner Str.
Pestalozzistr.
Müllerstr.
Blumenstr.
Reisingerstr.
Maistr.
Frauenlobstr.
Holzstr.
Paceliistr.
E
F
1
2
3
0
200 m

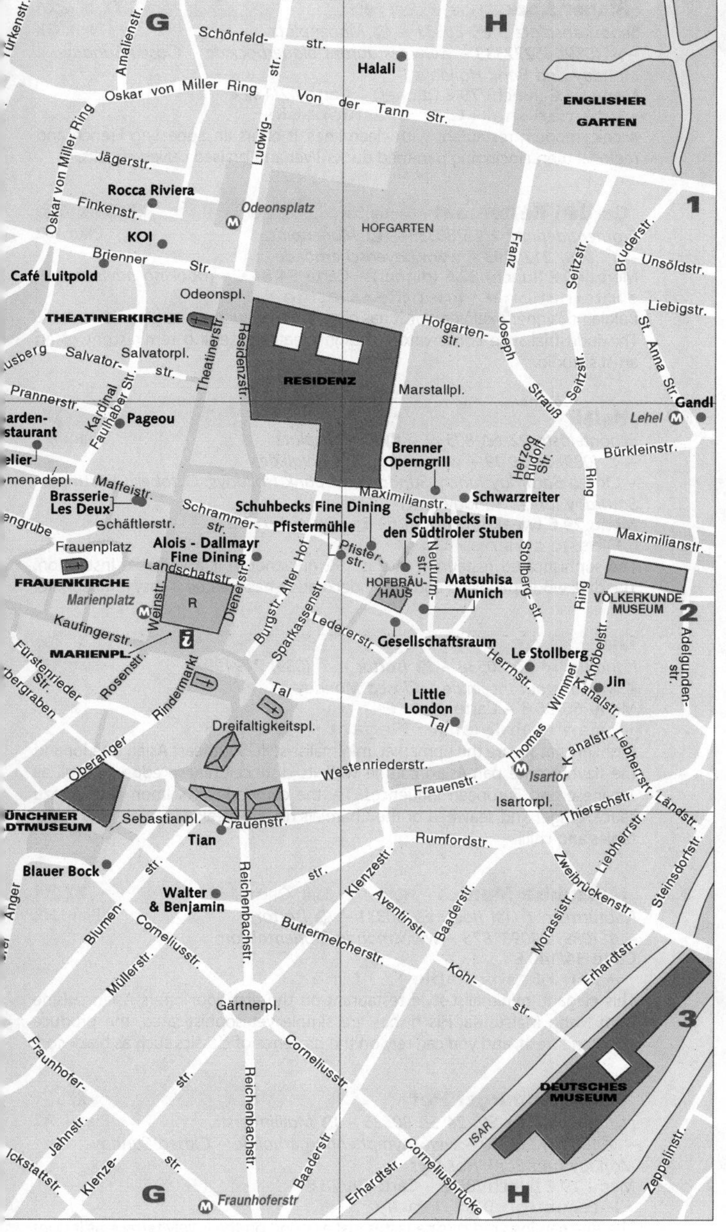

G
H
Schönfeld-str.
Halali
Amalienstr.
Oskar von Miller Ring
Von der Tann Str.
ENGLISHER GARTEN
Ludwig-str.
Jägerstr.
Rocca Riviera
Finkenstr.
Odeonsplatz
HOFGARTEN
1
KOI
Brienner Str.
Café Luitpold
Odeonspl.
Franz Joseph Strauß Ring
Seitzstr.
Bruderstr.
Unsöldstr.
Liebigstr.
THEATINERKIRCHE
Theatinerstr.
Residenzstr.
RESIDENZ
Hofgarten-str.
St. Anna Str.
Salvatorpl.
Salvator-str.
Marstallpl.
Prannerstr.
Kardinal Faulhaber Str.
Gandl
Lehel
Pageou
Bürkleinstr.
Brenner Operngrill
Herzog Rudolf Str.
Maffeistr.
Brasserie Les Deux
Maximilianstr.
Schwarzreiter
Schrammer-str.
Schuhbecks Fine Dining
Schuhbecks in den Südtiroler Stuben
Schäftlerstr.
Pfistermühle
Frauenplatz
Alois - Dallmayr Fine Dining
Pfister-str.
Neuturm-str.
Stollberg-str.
FRAUENKIRCHE
Landschaftstr.
Alter Hof
HOFBRÄU-HAUS
Matsuhisa Munich
Marienplatz
Weinstr.
R
Dienerstr.
Burgstr.
VÖLKERKUNDE MUSEUM
2
Kaufingerstr.
Sparkassenstr.
Ledererstr.
Gesellschaftsraum
Adelgunden-str.
MARIENPL.
Rosenstr.
Herrnstr.
Le Stollberg
Fürstenrieder Str.
Rindermarkt
Knöbelstr.
Jin
Thomas Wimmer Ring
Kanalstr.
Tal
Little London
Dreifaltigkeitspl.
Liebherrstr.
Oberanger
Westenriederstr.
Isartor
Frauenstr.
Isartorpl.
Thierschstr.
Lándstr.
Sebastianpl.
Tian
Rumfordstr.
Blauer Bock
Anger
Walter & Benjamin
Reichenbachstr.
Klenzestr.
Aventinstr.
Baaderstr.
Zweibrückenstr.
Morassistr.
Steinsdorfstr.
Blumen-str.
Corneliusstr.
Buttermelcherstr.
Kohl-str.
Müllerstr.
Erhardtstr.
Gärtnerpl.
3
Fraunhofer-str.
DEUTSCHES MUSEUM
ISAR
Jahnstr.
Erhardtstr.
Corneliusbrücke
Zeppelinstr.
Klenze-str.
Fraunhoferstr

Blauer Bock – Hotel Blauer Bock XX

Sebastiansplatz 9 ✉ 80331 – Ⓜ Marienplatz Plan: **G3**
– ✆ (089) 45222333 – www.restaurant-blauerbock.de – Closed Sunday-Monday and Bank Holidays
Menu 34 € (lunch)/79 € (dinner) – Carte 42/162 €
• International • Chic • Fashionable •
A chic, modern restaurant with clean lines. It offers an appealing French and regional menu including pan-fried ducks' liver and braised calves' cheeks.

Garden-Restaurant – Hotel Bayerischer Hof XX

Promenadeplatz 2 ✉ 80333 – Ⓜ Marienplatz Plan: **G2**
– ✆ (089) 2120993 – www.bayerischerhof.de
Menu 40 € (lunch)/82 € (dinner) – Carte 54/84 € – *(booking advisable)*
• International • Friendly • Design •
Belgian designer Axel Vervoordt has given this restaurant a very particular look. The industrial-style conservatory design creates a setting reminiscent of an artist's studio.

Halali XX

Schönfeldstr. 22 ✉ 80539 – Ⓜ Odeonsplatz Plan: **H1**
– ✆ (089) 28 59 09 – www.restaurant-halali.de
– Closed Saturday lunch, Sunday and Bank Holidays; October-Christmas: Saturday lunch, Sunday lunch
Menu 29 € (weekday lunch)/69 € – Carte 41/77 €
• Classic cuisine • Cosy •
The sophisticated restaurant in this 19C guesthouse is a veritable institution. The dark wood panelling and lovely decoration has created a cosy atmosphere.

Jin XX

Kanalstr. 14 ✉ 80538 – Ⓜ Isartor – ✆ (089) 21949970 Plan: **H2**
– www.restaurant-jin.de – Closed Monday
Menu 66/96 € – Carte 31/61 €
• Asian • Minimalist • Elegant •
Highlights at Jin are the upmarket, minimalist-style Southeast Asian interior and the flavoursome pan-Asian cuisine with its distinct Chinese edge, as well as Japanese and European influences. Try the carpaccio of salmon with ponzu sauce, ginger and seaweed or the Charolais rib-eye steak with wok-fried vegetables and chilli.

Matsuhisa Munich – Hotel Mandarin Oriental XX

Neuturmstr. 1 (1st floor) ✉ 80331 – Ⓜ Isartor Plan: **H2**
– ✆ (089) 290981875 – www.mandarinoriental.com
Carte 34/140 €
• Asian • Fashionable •
This elegant, minimalist-style restaurant on the first floor offers Asian cuisine from Nobu Matsuhisa. His dishes are simple yet sophisticated, the produce good and fresh, and you can rely on the presence of classics such as black cod.

Nymphenburger Hof XX

Nymphenburger Str. 24 ✉ 80335 – Ⓜ Maillingerstr. Plan I: **A2**
– ✆ (089) 1233830 – www.nymphenburgerhof.de – Closed Sunday-Monday and Bank Holidays
Menu 29 € (lunch)/85 € – Carte 38/78 €
• International • Friendly •
The Austrian inspired cuisine tastes just as good on the lovely terrace as it does in the friendly restaurant. Live piano music is also played on some evenings.

Pageou

XX

Kardinal-Faulhaber-Str. 10 (1st floor) ✉ 80333 – Ⓜ Marienplatz – ✆ (089) 24231310 – www.pageou.de – Closed Sunday-Monday and Bank Holidays

Plan: **G2**

Menu 35 € (lunch)/129 € – Carte 59/96 €

• Mediterranean cuisine • Cosy •

Behind the magnificent historical façade, Ali Güngörmüs (previously chef at Le Canard Nouveau in Hamburg) serves Mediterranean cuisine with north African influences in the relaxed atmosphere of the tasteful interior. Quiet, attractive terrace in the courtyard. Business lunch menu.

Pfistermühle – Hotel Platzl

XX

Pfisterstr. 4 ✉ 80331 – Ⓜ Marienplatz – ✆ (089) 23703865 – www.pfistermuehle.de – Closed Sunday

Plan: **G2**

Menu 52/74 € (dinner) – Carte 46/73 €

• Country • Rustic • Cosy •

A separate entrance leads into the former ducal mill (1573) where you can sample regional fare in a stylish Bavarian setting (including a lovely vaulted ceiling). Try dishes such as braised calves' cheeks with parsnip puree, creamy savoy cabbage and dried fruit sauce.

Rocca Riviera

XX A/C

Wittelsbacherplatz 2 ✉ 80331 – Ⓜ Odeonsplatz – ✆ (089) 28724421 – www.roccariviera.com – Closed Saturday lunch, Sunday

Plan: **G1**

Menu 28/86 € – Carte 33/82 €

• Mediterranean cuisine • Fashionable • Chic •

Rocca Riviera is a relaxed and stylish restaurant with a pleasant atmosphere not far from the Odeonsplatz. It serves Mediterranean-French fusion cuisine on a sharing plate basis, as well as meat and fish from the charcoal grill.

Le Stollberg

XX

Stollbergstr. 2 ✉ 80539 – Ⓜ Isartor – ✆ (089) 24243450 – www.lestollberg.de – Closed 2 weeks June, Sunday and Bank Holidays

Plan: **H2**

Menu 57/73 € – Carte 45/61 €

• Classic cuisine • Friendly • Elegant •

After spells at several good restaurants, the charming Anette Huber has started her own venture with this modern restaurant. The classic, French and seasonal cuisine includes offerings such as calves' kidneys in red wine sauce with mashed potato. Good value lunch. Open throughout the day on Saturdays.

Weinhaus Neuner

X A/C

Herzogspitalstr. 8 ✉ 80331 – Ⓜ Karlsplatz – ✆ (089) 2603954 – www.weinhaus-neuner.de

Plan: **F2**

Menu 25 € (weekday lunch)/65 € – Carte 45/69 €

• Traditional cuisine • Traditional décor •

With its cross-vaulted ceiling, herringbone parquet and wood panelling, this old restaurant has lost nothing of its traditional charm. The food is just what you would expect from an upmarket Munich restaurant – try the flaky pastry crust chicken fricassee pie.

Brasserie – Restaurant Les Deux

X

Maffeistr. 3a ✉ 80333 – Ⓜ Marienplatz – ✆ (089) 7 10 40 73 73 – www.lesdeux-muc.de – Closed Sunday and Bank Holidays

Plan: **G2**

Carte 37/92 € – *(booking advisable)*

• International • Bistro • Brasserie •

If you like a lively, modern bistro, you'll enjoy the seasonal, international dishes - including gnocchi with asparagus and black tiger prawns - on offer on the ground floor of Les Deux. Or perhaps you'd prefer one of the 'old' or 'new' classics: mini burger or beef tartare with imperial caviar for example?

Brenner Operngrill

Maximilianstr. 15 ✉ 80331 – Ⓜ Lehel Plan: **H2**
– ✆ (089) 4 52 28 80 – www.brennergrill.de
Carte 26/57 €
• Grills • Trendy •
A place to see and be seen... The bar, café and restaurant housed in this impressive hall with its high-vaulted ceiling (once the stables of this great residence) are a hot item on the Munich culinary scene. Homemade pasta, as well as meat and fish served hot from the open grill in the centre of the room.

Cafe Luitpold

Brienner Str. 11 ✉ 80333 – Ⓜ Odeonsplatz Plan: **G1**
– ✆ (089) 2428750 – www.cafe-luitpold.de – Closed Sunday dinner and Monday dinner except Bank Holidays
Menu 36/69 € – Carte 24/50 €
• Traditional cuisine • Friendly • Traditional décor •
Guests can sit in the lively coffee house atmosphere of Cafe Luitpold and enjoy its good, fresh cuisine. There is also a museum on the first floor from which you can see right into the bakery – make sure you try the tarts, pralines and other delicacies!

Gandl

St.-Anna-Platz 1 ✉ 80538 – Ⓜ Lehel Plan: **H1**
– ✆ (089) 29162525 – www.gandl.de – Closed Sunday and Monday dinner
Menu 22 € (weekday lunch)/60 € – Carte 36/66 €
• Classic cuisine • Cosy • Bistro •
Gandl is located in a former colonial goods store, which has retained some of its old shelving and still sells one or two items. The food ranges from classic French to international. If you are here in summer don't miss the terrace overlooking the square.

Gesellschaftsraum

Bräuhausstr. 8 ✉ 80331 – Ⓜ Isartor Plan: **H2**
– ✆ (089) 55077793 – www.der-gesellschaftsraum.de – Closed Sunday
Menu 65/95 € (dinner) – Carte 62/68 €
• Creative • Trendy • Fashionable •
If you like things casual, urban and trendy, you will find the atmosphere in this restaurant in the centre of the old town to your taste. The food is creative, modern and ambitious, and the service is pleasantly relaxed.

KOI

Wittelsbacherplatz 1 ✉ 80333 – Ⓜ Odeonsplatz Plan: **G1**
– ✆ (089) 89081926 – www.koi-restaurant.de – Closed Saturday lunch, Sunday and Bank Holidays
Carte 39/124 €
• Japanese • Friendly • Bistro •
You can look forward to an interesting mix of visual and culinary styles on the two floors at Koi. The kitchens produce a combination of Japanese and European cuisine, including sushi and Robata-grilled meats, all based on fresh produce.

Little London

Tal 31 ✉ 80331 – Ⓜ Marienplatz – ✆ (089) 222239470 Plan: **H2**
– www.little-london.de – Closed August: Sunday-Monday
Carte 45/209 € – *(dinner only)*
• Grills • Friendly •
This lively steakhouse at the Isartor is fronted by a large, classic bar with a great selection of gins and whiskeys and makes a great place to enjoy some top-quality meat. The Nebraska steaks, but also the roast topside of veal and shoulder of lamb, are in particular demand.

Sparkling Bistro

Amalienstr. 89 (Amalien Passage) ✉ 80799 – Ⓜ Universität Plan I: **B2**
– ✆ (089) 46138267 – www.bistro-muenchen.de – Closed 27 December-7 January, Saturday lunch, Sunday-Monday lunch and Bank Holidays
Menu 30 € (lunch)/100 €

• Modern cuisine • Bistro • Friendly •

This pretty, friendly bistro is a little out of the way, but well worth searching for. It's run with dedication and a personal touch as evidenced by the ambitious cuisine prepared using top-quality, market-fresh produce. In the evenings diners choose from the Exkursion menu, at midday a reduced lunchtime offering.

VINOTHEK by Geisel – Hotel EXCELSIOR by Geisel

Schützenstr. 11 ✉ 80335 – Ⓜ Hauptbahnhof Plan: **E2**
– ✆ (089) 551377140 – www.excelsior-hotel.de – Closed Sunday lunch
Menu 45 € (dinner) – Carte 41/69 €

• Country • Rustic •

Diners here eat in a friendly rustic atmosphere under a lovely vaulted ceiling. The excellent wine list is accompanied by a menu of Mediterranean-inspired food. This includes selected fish in bouillabaisse broth with artichokes, celery and rouille crostini, as well as pasta dishes and classics such as roast beef with sautéed potatoes.

Walter & Benjamin

Rumfordstr. 1 ✉ 80469 – Ⓜ Frauenhoferstr. Plan: **G3**
– ✆ (089) 26024174 – www.walterundbenjamin.de – Closed 1-7 January, Sunday-Monday and Bank Holidays
Menu 54/80 € – Carte 41/65 € – *(Tuesday to Friday dinner only)*

• Modern cuisine • Fashionable •

You'll find this relaxed and friendly restaurant-cum-wine bar not far from the Viktualienmarkt. The food is modern and ambitious, the skrei with carrots and parsley particularly appetising. There is also a great selection of wines with the accent on old world and organic names. Snacks and home-baked cakes are available throughout the day on Saturdays.

ENVIRONS — PLAN I

Tantris

Johann-Fichte-Str. 7 ✉ 80805 – Ⓜ Dietlindenstr. Plan: **B1**
– ✆ (089) 3 61 95 90 – www.tantris.de – Closed 22 December-16 January, 14 April-1 May, 1-11 September, Bank Holidays, January-September: Sunday-Tuesday, October-December: Sunday-Monday and Bank Holidays
Menu 100 € (weekday lunch)/225 € – Carte 101/173 € – *(booking advisable)*

• Classic French • Vintage •

Tantris is quite simply THE place to eat with its near legendary 1970s-style and Hans Haas' sublime, product-based classic cuisine. The cult setting and fine dining are accompanied by a well-practised, friendly and professional front-of-house team, as well as good wine recommendations.

➜ Lauchpüree mit Kaviar und Nussbutter. Lauwarme Seeforelle mit Fenchel-Safranpüree und Limonen-Buttermilchfond. Medaillons vom Rehrücken mit Balsamicokirschen und Briochenockerl.

EssZimmer

Am Olympiapark 1 (3th floor, elevator) (at BMW Welt) ✉ 80809 Plan: **A1**
– Ⓜ Olympiazentrum – ✆ (089) 3 58 99 18 14 – www.esszimmer-muenchen.de – Closed 2 weeks January, August, Sunday-Monday and Bank Holidays
Menu 135/195 € – *(dinner only) (booking advisable)*

• Modern French • Chic • Cosy •

There is a double pleasure on offer at EssZimmer: a view of the impressive shipping hall at BMW Welt with its smart exhibition pieces, as well as the chance to enjoy Bobby Bräuer's delicate cuisine. Dine in the elegant, modern setting with a choice of two set menus. Free parking.

➜ Felsenrotbarbe, Bärlauch, Safran, Yuzu. Salzwiesenlamm, Bries, Zunge, Pak Choi. Holunder, Himbeere, Basilikum, Tonic.

Bavarie – See below

WERNECKHOF by Geisel

Werneckstr. 11 ✉ 80802 – Ⓜ Münchner Freiheit Plan: **C2**
– ✆ (089) 38 87 95 68 – www.geisels-werneckhof.de – Closed 24-30 December, end July-mid August and Sunday-Monday
Menu 150/180 € – *(Tuesday to Friday dinner only) (booking essential)*

• Creative • Cosy • Traditional décor •

The cuisine prepared by Tohru Nakamura is anything but 'off the peg'. The finesse and fluency with which he combines top-quality produce, classic principles and Japanese influences to create elegant, creative dishes is genuinely impressive and clearly bears his inimitable signature.

→ Tuna, Avocado, Dahlienknolle und geräucherte Ponzu. Burgaud Ente "Hanami" mit Kirschblüten und Mandeln. Mango, Yuzu, Thaibasilikum und schwarzer Sesam.

Acquarello (Mario Gamba)

Mühlbaurstr. 36 ✉ 81677 – Ⓜ Böhmerwaldplatz Plan: **D2**
– ✆ (089) 4 70 48 48 – www.acquarello.com – Closed 1-3 January, Monday, Saturday lunch, Sunday lunch, Bank Holidays lunch
Menu 49 € (weekday lunch)/119 € – Carte 82/108 €

• Mediterranean cuisine • Friendly • Mediterranean décor •

The Latin flair of this friendly, elegant restaurant is the perfect match for the Italian/Mediterranean and French cuisine which Mario Gamba and his team have been preparing here since 1994. The food is light, sophisticated, made with the very best ingredients and accompanied by Italian wines. The service is attentive and professional.

→ Gambas, Rotweinbutter, Birne, Sesam, Sauerrahm, Chili. Ravioli, Walnuss, Ricotta, Parmesansabayon. Brasato, Ragout, Brotmantel, Selleriepüree, kleines Gemüse.

Gabelspiel (Florian Berger)

Zehentbauernstr. 20 (South: 4 km by Steinstr.) ✉ 81539 – Ⓜ Silberhornstr. – ✆ (089) 12253940 – www.restaurant-gabelspiel.de – Closed 1-9 January and Sunday-Monday
Menu 58/89 € – *(dinner only)*

• Modern cuisine • Family •

Gabelspiel offers a genuinely pleasant and entirely unpretentious, informal atmosphere. The food is fresh, ambitious and modern and comes in the form of a selection menu. Try the prawn, ponzu and radish fusion or the pigeon, falafel and spring onion étouffée with poppadoms.

→ Seeforelle vom Birnbaum, Karotte, Kardamom, Sanddorn. Verkohlte Sardine, Quinoa, Paprika, Sonnenblumenkerne. Zweierlei vom Kalb, Artischocke, Kräuterjus.

Freisinger Hof – Hotel Freisinger Hof

Oberföhringer Str. 189 ✉ 81925 – ✆ (089) 95 23 02 Plan: **D1**
– www.freisinger-hof.de – Closed 28 December-9January
Carte 34/58 €

• Country • Inn •

This is just what you imagine a traditional Bavarian restaurant to be like. Dating back to 1875, it stands just outside the city gates and serves typical Bavarian and Austrian cuisine. Dishes include Krosser saddle of suckling pig, and Vienna-style beef boiled in broth.

La Bohème

Leopoldstr. 180 ✉ 80804 – Ⓜ Dietlindenstr. Plan: **B1**
– ✆ (089) 23762323 – www.boheme-schwabing.de
Menu 35/69 € – Carte 37/98 € – *(dinner only and Sunday lunch)*

• Market cuisine • Fashionable • Trendy •

La Bohème offers a trendy urban setting in which to enjoy its modern cuisine. Simpler lunchtime offerings give way to an ambitious evening menu – try the sea bass with bouillabaisse vegetables and pearl barley Risotto. The restaurant serves brunch on Sundays, and also organises occasional magic shows and music evenings.

Le Cézanne

Konradstr. 1 ✉ 80801 – Ⓜ Giselastr. – ✆ (089) 39 18 05 – www.le-cezanne.de – Closed 3 weeks August and Monday, Bank Holidays Plan: **B2**

Menu 45/50 € – Carte 27/56 € – *(dinner only) (booking advisable)*

• French • Family • Friendly •

In this friendly corner restaurant the chef cooks dishes from his French homeland. You can choose from the blackboard or the small menu of classic dishes. In summer, enjoy your meal outdoors or by the open, glass façade.

Bogenhauser Hof

Ismaninger Str. 85 ✉ 81675 – Ⓜ Böhmerwaldplatz – ✆ (089) 98 55 86 – www.bogenhauser-hof.de – Closed 24 December-7 January, Sunday and Bank Holidays Plan: **C2**

Menu 88 € – Carte 47/80 €

• Classic cuisine • Traditional décor • Cosy •

This elegant yet comfortable restaurant, housed in a building dating back to 1825, serves classic cuisine prepared using the finest ingredients, which explains why it has so many regulars. It also has a leafy garden complete with mature chestnut trees.

Bibulus

Siegfriedstr. 11 ✉ 80803 – Ⓜ Münchner Freiheit – ✆ (089) 396447 – www.bibulus-ristorante.de – Closed Saturday lunch and Sunday Plan: **B1**

Menu 26 € (lunch)/79 € – Carte 38/65 €

• Italian • Elegant •

It says something when a restaurant is popular with the locals, and the people of Schwabing clearly appreciate the uncomplicated and flavoursome Italian food. It is especially nice outside in the little square under the plane trees. Charming service.

Hippocampus

Mühlbaurstr. 5 ✉ 81677 – Ⓜ Prinzregentenplatz – ✆ (089) 475855 – www.hippocampus-restaurant.de – Closed Monday, Saturday lunch Plan: **C3**

Menu 30 € (weekday lunch)/70 € – Carte 49/64 €

• Italian • Elegant •

Hippocampus offers friendly service, an informal atmosphere and ambitious Italian cuisine. Beautiful fixtures and fittings help create the elegant yet warm and welcoming interior.

Käfer-Schänke

Prinzregentenstr. 73 (1st floor) ✉ 81675 – Ⓜ Prinzregentenplatz – ✆ (089) 4168247 – www.feinkost-kaefer.de/schaenke – Closed Sunday and Bank Holidays Plan: **C3**

Menu 40 € (lunch)/109 € – Carte 53/113 € – *(booking advisable)*

• International • Cosy •

The name "Käfer" has become synonymous with Munich's restaurant scene. The presence of a delicatessen under the same roof as this cosy restaurant guarantees the top-class ingredients, used to make its popular classics. There are also a number of stylish function rooms for special occasions.

Acetaia

Nymphenburger Str. 215 (by Nymphenburger Str.) ✉ 80639 – ✆ (089) 13929077 – www.restaurant-acetaia.de – Closed Saturday lunch

Menu 70 € (dinner)/105 € – Carte 50/70 €

• Italian • Cosy •

Serving Italian cuisine in a comfortable Art Nouveau setting, Acetaia takes its name from the aged balsamic vinegar you will find on sale here. Walkers will enjoy a stroll along the Nymphenburger Canal to the palace with its lovely grounds.

Vinaiolo

Steinstr. 42 ✉ 81667 – Ⓜ Ostbahnhof Plan: **C3**
– ✆ (089) 48950356 – www.vinaiolo.de – Closed Saturday lunch
Menu 59 € (dinner) – Carte 51/61 €

• Italian • Cosy • Friendly •

Experience a touch of dolce vita in the old town of Haidhausen. The service exudes Mediterranean charm, the cuisine is typically Italian and the cosy and authentic atmosphere is accentuated by furnishings from an old grocer's shop in Trieste.

Atelier Gourmet

Rablstr. 37 ✉ 81669 – Ⓜ Ostbahnhof Plan: **C3**
– ✆ (089) 487220 – www.ateliergourmet.de – Closed 15-23 April, 10-18 June, 26 August-9 September and Sunday
Menu 42/86 € – *(dinner only)*

• Classic French • Bistro •

Small, intimate, lively and popular, Atelier Gourmet is quite simply a great little restaurant. The food is fresh, delicious and good value for money thanks to chef Bousquet. It is served in a casual, friendly atmosphere with efficient service and good wine recommendations from the female owner. Try the capon and duck crépinette.

Bavarie – Restaurant EssZimmer

Am Olympiapark 1 (2nd floor, elevator) (at BMW Welt) Plan: **A1**
✉ 80809 – ✆ (089) 3 58 99 18 18 – www.feinkost-kaefer.de
– Closed 3 weeks August, Sunday dinner and Bank Holidays dinner
Menu 34/65 € – Carte 38/50 €

• International • Bistro • Fashionable •

Grounded in the principles of regionality and sustainability, the Bavarie concept on offer here creates a combination of Bavarian and French cuisine based on local produce. Dishes include goose liver crème brûlée and Gutshof Polting lamb. The terrace offers views of the Olympia Park and Tower.

Rüen Thai

Kazmairstr. 58 ✉ 80339 – Ⓜ Messegelände Plan: **A3**
– ✆ (089) 503239 – www.rueen-thai.de – Closed 1 week April, 3 weeks June-July
Menu 52/78 € – Carte 30/56 € – *(Friday to Sunday and Bank Holidays dinner only)*

• Thai • Family • Bourgeois •

True to his roots, Anuchit Chetha has dedicated himself to the cuisine of southern Thailand, preparing a range of dishes including gung pla and nüe san kua, as well as a finger food menu. In addition to specialising in interesting spice combinations, he is also passionate about wine – the restaurant boasts a cellar containing a number of real rarities.

mcbrugg/iStock

ATHENS

GREECE
ELLÁDA

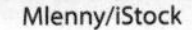
Mlenny/iStock

ATHENS
ATHÍNA

tanukiphoto/iStock

ATHENS IN...

→ **ONE DAY**
Acropolis (Parthenon), Agora and Temple of Hephaestus, Plaka.

→ **TWO DAYS**
Kolonaki, National Archaeological Museum, Filopappou Hill.

→ **THREE DAYS**
Monastiraki flea-market (Sunday), Benaki Museum, Technopolis, National Gardens, Lykavittos Hill.

Inventing democracy, the theatre and the Olympic Games... and planting the seeds of philosophy and Western Civilisation – Athens was central to all of these, a city that became a byword for glory and learning, a place whose golden reputation could inspire such awe that centuries later just the mention of its name was enough to turn people misty-eyed. It's a magical place, built upon eight hills and plains, with a history stretching back at least 3,000 years. Its short but highly productive golden age resulted in the architectural glory of The Acropolis, while the likes of Plato, Aristotle and Socrates were in the business of changing the mindset of society.

The Acropolis still dominates Athens and can be seen peeking through alleyways and turnings all over the city. Beneath it lies a teeming metropolis, part urban melting pot, part über-buzzy neighbourhood. Plaka, below the Acropolis, is the old quarter, and the most visited, a mixture of great charm and cheap gift shops. North and west, Monastiraki and Psiri have become trendy zones; to the east, Syntagma and Kolonaki are notably modern and smart, home to the Greek parliament and the famous. The most northerly districts of central Athens are Omonia and Exarcheia, distinguished by their rugged appearance and steeped in history; much of the life in these parts is centred round the polytechnic and the central marketplace.

EATING OUT

In recent times, a smart wave of restaurants has hit the city and, with many chefs training abroad before returning home, this is a good time to eat out in the shadow of The Acropolis. If you want the full experience, dine with the locals rather than the tourists and make your reservation for late evening, as Greeks rarely go out for dinner before 10pm. The trend towards a more eclectic restaurant scene now means that you can find everything from classical French and Italian cuisine to Asian and Moroccan dishes, and even sushi. Modern tavernas offer good attention to detail, but this doesn't mean they're replacing the wonderfully traditional favourites. These older tavernas, along with mezedopoleia, are the backbone of Greek dining, and most visitors wouldn't think their trip was complete without eating in one; often the waiter will just tell you what's cooking that day - and you're usually very welcome to go into the kitchen and make your selection. Greece is a country where it is customary to tip good service; ten per cent is the normal rate.

✿✿ Spondi

XXX

5 Pyronos, off Varnava Sq, Pangrati ✉ 116 36 Plan: **D3**
– ✆ (210) 7564 021 – www.spondi.gr – Closed Easter
Menu 79/140 € – Carte 95/140 € – *(dinner only)*

• French • Romantic • Elegant •

A discreet, intimate restaurant with two delightful courtyards and two charming dining rooms – one built from reclaimed bricks in the style of a vaulted cellar. Top quality seasonal ingredients are used in imaginative, deftly executed, stunningly presented modern French dishes. Greek, French and Italian wines feature on an impressive list.

→ Pineapple tomato with lemon verbena, feta and black olive. Milk-fed lamb with pea and lemon. Greek yoghurt with candied mango, banana sorbet and cardamom.

✿ Hytra

XX

Onassis Cultural Centre (6th Floor), 107-109 Syngrou Ave C3 (Southwest: 2.5 km) ✉ 11745 – ✆ (210) 331 6767 – www.hytra.gr – Closed 11 March and 26-29 April
Menu 59 € – Carte 69/86 € – *(dinner only)*

• Modern cuisine • Design • Fashionable •

Take the express lift up to the 6th floor of the striking Onassis Cultural Centre; here you'll find a sultry restaurant looking out over Syngrou. Classic Greek recipes are executed in a refined modern manner – for something a little different try the cocktail pairings. They also offer a bistro menu at the bar.

→ Amberjack with horseradish, sour cream and pine oil. Pork with sea buckthorn and marigold. Almond parfait, cherries and wild berry marmalade.

Athiri

X

15 Plateon ✉ 104 35 – Ⓜ Keramikós Plan: **A2**
– ✆ (210) 3462 983 – www.athirirestaurant.gr – Closed 2 weeks August, 1 week Easter, 1-5 January, Sunday dinner in winter and Monday
Menu 39 € – Carte 30/39 €

• Greek • Neighbourhood • Friendly •

In winter, sit inside, surrounded by blue, white and grey hues; in summer, head out to the courtyard and well-spaced tables surrounded by lush green plants. Local, seasonal ingredients are simply prepared in order to reveal their natural flavours. Dishes are generous, good value and have creative touches.

Nolan

X

31-33 Voulis St ✉ 105 57 – Ⓜ Syntagma Plan: **C3**
– ✆ (210) 3243545 – www.nolanrestaurant.gr
– Closed 12-18 August, Easter, Christmas and Sunday
Carte 25/40 €

• Fusion • Fashionable • Minimalist •

This small, contemporary bistro stands out from the other restaurants in this busy neighbourhood. The young chef has Greek, German and Asian roots and his cooking fuses influences from all three countries along with many other international flavours. Dishes provide plenty of appeal and are great for sharing.

Oikeîo

X

15 Ploutarhou St ✉ 106 75 – Ⓜ Evangelismos Plan: **D2**
– ✆ (210) 7259 216 – Closed 25-26 December and 3 days Easter
Carte 16/28 €

• Greek • Rustic • Traditional décor •

A sweet little restaurant in a chic neighbourhood, with tables on two different levels, as well as outside. The décor is traditional and the place has a warm, cosy feel. Menus offer great value family-style dishes made with fresh ingredients and feature the likes of sardines, moussaka and octopus in vinegar.

7 Food Sins

Square Filomousou Etaireias 1 ✉ 10558 – Ⓜ Syntagma – ☎ (210) 7011108 – www.7foodsins.com
Plan: **C3**

Carte 32/42 € – *(dinner only)*

• Greek • Neighbourhood • Intimate •

A vibrant, personally run restaurant in the centre of busy Plaka; its name refers to their philosophy, which is built around 7 sins of eating, including using your hands, feeding friends and being gluttonous. Appealing modern menus offer well priced, tasty Greek and Mediterranean dishes.

GB Roof Garden – Grande Bretagne Hotel

1 Vas Georgiou A, Constitution Sq ✉ 105 64 – Ⓜ Syntagma – ☎ (210) 3330 766 – www.gbroofgarden.gr
Plan: **C2**

Carte 47/138 € – *(booking essential)*

• Mediterranean cuisine • Fashionable • Elegant •

Set on the 8th floor of the Grande Bretagne hotel, this elegant rooftop restaurant offers spectacular views across Syntagma Square towards The Acropolis. Sunny, modern Mediterranean cooking uses fresh ingredients and is accompanied by an extensive wine list. Service is smooth and efficient.

Electra Roof Garden – Electra Palace Hotel

18-20 Nikodimou St ✉ 105 57 – Ⓜ Syntagma – ☎ (210) 3370 000 – www.electrahotels.gr
Plan: **C3**

Menu 35 € – Carte 30/54 € – *(dinner only)*

• Mediterranean cuisine • Romantic • Elegant •

Set on the top floor of the Electra Palace hotel, this superbly located restaurant offers unrivalled views of The Acropolis and downtown Athens. Well-made dishes are a mix of traditional Greek and more international flavours.

Première – Athenaeum InterContinental Hotel

89-93 Syngrou Ave (9th floor) (Southwest: 2.5 km) ✉ 117 45 – ☎ (210) 9206 981 – www.intercontinental.com/athens – Closed Sunday and Monday

Menu 75/95 € – Carte 60/80 € – *(dinner only)*

• Mediterranean cuisine • Friendly • Minimalist •

Start with a drink in the cocktail bar then head through to the elegant restaurant or out onto the terrace to take in views of The Acropolis. Top quality produce features in carefully crafted modern dishes; go for the tasting menu, where dishes are matched with unusual Greek wines.

CTC

27 Diocharous ✉ 11528 – Ⓜ Evangelismos – ☎ (210) 722 8812 – www.ctc-restaurant.com – Closed 15 July-1 September, Sunday and Monday
Plan: **D2**

Menu 38/90 € – *(dinner only) (booking essential) (surprise menu only)*

• Modern cuisine • Intimate • Fashionable •

Its name is short for "the art of feeding" and the sleek, intimate room seats just 28, with a private table on the mezzanine. Surprise menus take you on a gastronomic journey; the chef has worked in both Greece and France, so dishes are a modern blend of Greek and Gallic elements.

Cookoovaya

2A Chatzigianni Mexi St ✉ 115 28 – Ⓜ Evangelismos – ☎ (210) 723 5005 – www.cookoovaya.gr – Closed 25 April-1 May, 11-21 August and 1 January
Plan: **D2**

Carte 43/70 €

• Greek • Friendly • Fashionable •

Five of the city's leading chefs have come together to open this bustling restaurant, where rustic, homely cooking is the order of the day and generous dishes are designed for sharing. The homemade pies from the wood-oven are a hit.

A
B
1
2
3
Liosion
Paloniou
Michail
Acharnon
Pl. Egiptou
Tritis Septemvriou
Boumpoulinas
Spyridonos Trikoupi
Ioulianou
Metsovou
Maroneias
Leoforos Konstantinoupoleos
T. Diligianni
Voda
28 Oktovriou
V. Irakleiou
Larissis
Sidirodromon
Ipeirou
ETHNIKÓ ARHEOLOGIKÓ MOUSSÍO
Neof. Metaxa
Tositsa
Marni
Stournari
Ioanninon
POLITEHNÍOU
Psaron
Akominatou
(Patission)
Chiou
Pl. Vathis
Pl. Kaningos
PELOPONISSOS
Emmanouil Benaki
Favierou
Lenorman
Solonos
Akadimias
Satovriandou
Karolou
Metaxourghio
Omonia
Pl. Karaïskaki
OMONOIA
Ag. Konstantinou
Menandrou
El. venizelou
Athinas
L. Konstantinoupoleos
Deligiorgi
Achilleos
Alexandrou
Stadiou
Sokratous
Pl. Kodzia
METAXOURGÍO
Kolokynthous
Panepistimio
Thermopylon
Myllerou
Sofokleous
Tsaldari
KENDRIKÍ AGORÁ
Pl. Klafthmonos
Keramikou
Evripidou
Pl. Eleftherias
Praxitelous
Megalou
Plataion
Panagi
Aristofanous
Aiolou
Kriezi
Sarri
Athiri
Kolokotroni
(Peiraios)
Athinaidos
Iera Odos
KAPNIKARÉA
Keramikós
KERAMIKÓS
PL. MONASTIRÁKI
Ermou
Mitropoleos
Voutadon
MIKRÍ MITRÓPOLI
Thissio
Adrianou
Monastiraki
Eptachalkou
Thessalonikis
Peiraios
THISSÍO
ROMAÏKÍ AGORÁ
MONASTIRÁKI
PLÁKA
ARHÉA AGORÁ
Aktaiou
Nileos
Apostolou Pavlou
Akamantos
Theorias
ÁRIOS PÁGOS
Kymaion
ASTEROSKOPÍO
AKRÓPOLI
LÓFOS NIMFÓN
Pavlou
ODIOU IRÓDOU ATIKOÚ
THÉATRO DIONÍSSOU
Aeropagitou
Thessalonikis
Trion Ierarchon
Dimofontos
Apolloniou
PNÍKA
Dionysiou
Karyatidon
Rovertou Gkalli
Parthenonos
Garivaldi
LÓFOS FILOPÁPOU

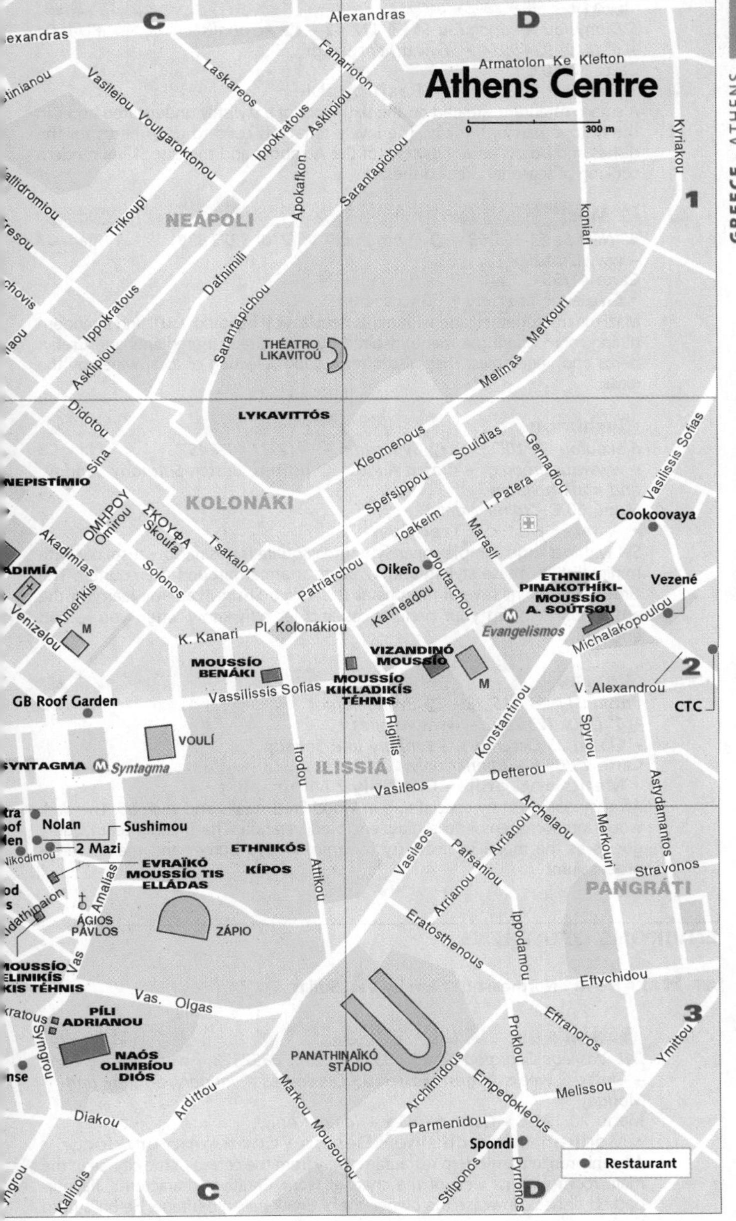
Athens Centre
0
300 m
C
D
1
2
3
NEÁPOLI
KOLONÁKI
ILISSIÁ
PANGRÁTI
LYKAVITTÓS
THÉATRO LIKAVITOÚ
Alexandras
Armatolon Ke Klefton
Fanarioton
Laskareos
Vasileiou Voulgaroktonou
Ippokratous
Asklipiou
Apokafkon
Sarantapichou
Trikoupi
Dafnimili
Kyriakou
Koniari
Melinas
Merkouri
Didotou
Sina
Kleomenous
Souidias
Gennadiou
Vasilissis Sofias
Spefsippou
I. Patera
Ioakeim
Marasli
Tsakalof
Akadimias
Omirou
Skoufa
Solonos
Amerikis
Venizelou
Patriarchou
Ploutarchou
Karneadou
Michalakopoulou
K. Kanari
Pl. Kolonákiou
Cookoovaya
Oikeîo
Vezené
ETHNIKÍ PINAKOTHÍKI-MOUSSÍO A. SOÚTSOU
Evangelismos
VIZANDINÓ MOUSSÍO
M
MOUSSÍO BENÁKI
MOUSSÍO KIKLADIKÍS TÉHNIS
Vassilissis Sofias
GB Roof Garden
V. Alexandrou
CTC
VOULÍ
Syntagma
Irodou
Rigillis
Konstantinou
Spyrou
Defterou
Vasileos
Astydamantos
Nolan
Sushimou
2 Mazi
ETHNIKÓS KÍPOS
EVRAÏKÓ MOUSSÍO TIS ELLÁDAS
Attikou
Archelaou
Arrianou
Pafsaniou
Merkouri
Stravonos
Amalias
ÁGIOS PÁVLOS
ZÁPIO
Eratosthenous
Ippodamou
Vas. Olgas
Eftychidou
PÍLI ADRIANOU
NAÓS OLIMBÍOU DIÓS
Syngrou
PANATHINAÏKÓ STÁDIO
Proklou
Effranoros
Ymittou
Archimidous
Empedokleous
Melissou
Arditou
Markou Mousourou
Diakou
Parmenidou
Spondi
Pyrronos
Stilponos
Kallirois
Restaurant

Sense – AthensWas Hotel XX
5 Dionysiou Areopagitou St ✉ 117 42 – Ⓜ Acropolis – ✆ (210) 924 9954 – www.athenswas.gr Plan: **C3**
Carte 30/50 €
• Greek • Brasserie • Fashionable •
A smart restaurant situated on the sixth floor of a stylishly understated hotel, in the historic part of the city. The lovely terrace is used to grow herbs for the dishes and boasts amazing views of the Acropolis and the city. Skilful modern cooking of seasonal Greek dishes.

2 Mazi XX
48 Nikis St ✉ 105 58 – Ⓜ Syntagma – ✆ (210) 3222 839 – www.2mazi.gr Plan: **C3**
Carte 41/55 €
• Greek • Trendy • Historic •
Mazi means 'together' and within this neoclassical building you'll find a modern dining room offering a menu inspired by fresh Greek ingredients and Cretan herbs and vegetables. They also offer a good selection of local wines by the glass.

Sushimou X
6 Skoufou ✉ 105 57 – Ⓜ Syntagma – ✆ (211) 4078457 – www.sushimou.gr – Closed August, Christmas, Easter, Saturday-Sunday and bank holidays Plan: **C3**
Menu 60 € – *(dinner only)*
• Asian • Bistro • Trendy •
Set within a large complex near Syntagma Square is this narrow sushi bar with minimalist Japanese styling and 12 seats arranged around the counter. The Greek chef spent several months at the Tokyo Sushi Academy learning the art; simply tell him your preferences and let him know when you've had enough.

Vezené X
Vrasida 11 ✉ 115 28 – Ⓜ Evangelismos – ✆ (210) 723 2002 – www.vezene.gr – Closed 25 December, 1 January and Sunday Plan: **D2**
Carte 25/64 € – *(dinner only)*
• Meats and grills • Friendly • Minimalist •
An easy-going eatery specialising in wood-fired steaks and seafood. The dark wood interior opens into a glass-enclosed veranda. The friendly team guide guests as the menu evolves. Try the mini Wagyu burger and the sliced-to-order salumi.

ENVIRONS OF ATHENS

AT HALANDRI Northeast : 11 km by Vas. Sofias

Botrini's (Ettore Botrini) XXX
24b Vasileos Georgiou ✉ 152 33 – ✆ (210) 6857323 – www.botrinis.com – Closed 3 weeks August, Easter, 25 December, 1 January, Sunday and Monday
Menu 70/120 € – Carte 65/85 € – *(dinner only)*
• Mediterranean cuisine • Design • Contemporary décor •
A keenly run, ultra-modern restaurant away from the centre of the city; sit in the main room with its view of the chefs at work. Creative, characterful, flavour-packed dishes showcase the owner-chef's Greek-Italian heritage. He hails from Corfu and ingredients from the island are well used.
➜ Swordfish carpaccio. "The cuttlefish became tsigareli". Bounty Colada.

AT MAROUSSI Northeast : 12.5 km by Vas. Sofias

Aneton

Stratigou Lekka 19 ✉ 151 22 – Ⓜ Maroussi – ✆ (210) 8066 700 – www.aneton.gr – Closed August, 25 December and Easter
Carte 25/65 € – *(dinner only and Sunday lunch) (booking essential)*
• Greek • Friendly • Intimate •

It's worth travelling into the smart city suburbs to seek out this appealing neighbourhood restaurant. Menus follow the seasons; in summer they have a Mediterranean base and some Middle Eastern spicing, while in winter, hearty stews and casseroles feature. The hands-on owner really brings the place to life.

AT PIRAEUS Southwest: 8 km by Singrou

Varoulko Seaside (Lefteris Lazarou)

Akti Koumoundourou, 54-56 Mikrolimano Marina (Southeast: 1.5 km by coastal road) ✉ 185 33 – Ⓜ Piraeus – ✆ (210) 522 8400 – www.varoulko.gr – Closed Easter, Christmas and 31 December
Menu 60 € – Carte 42/59 € – *(booking essential)*
• Seafood • Classic décor • Friendly •

Varoulko sits in a great spot in Mikrolimano Marina – the chef's old neighbourhood. Watch the yachts glide by from the maritime-themed dining room which opens onto the water. Greek and Mediterranean dishes feature organic vegetables, Cretan olive oil and the freshest seafood; squid and octopus feature highly.
→ Grilled squid with fish roe, roasted lettuce and ouzo jellies. Grouper with Jerusalem artichoke mousse, mustard pickle and cocoa. Chocolate crémeux with Breton biscuit and raspberry sorbet.

BUDAPEST

HUNGARY
MAGYARORSZÁG

focusstock/iStock

Budapest
BUDAPEST

jon chica parada/iStock

BUDAPEST IN...

- **ONE DAY**
  Royal Palace, the Parliament Building, a trip on the Danube.
- **TWO DAYS**
  Gellert Baths, a stroll down Váci utca, a concert at the State Opera House.
- **THREE DAYS**
  Museum of Applied Arts, Margaret Island, coffee and cake at Gerbeaud.

No one knows quite where the Hungarian language came from: it's not quite Slavic, not quite Turkic, and its closest relatives appear to be in Finland and Siberia. In much the same way, Hungary's capital is a bit of an enigma. A lot of what you see is not as old as it appears. Classical and Gothic buildings are mostly neoclassical and neo-Gothic, and the fabled baroque of the city is of a more recent vintage than in other European capitals. That's because Budapest's frequent invaders and conquerors, from all compass points of the map, left little but rubble behind them when they left; the grand look of today took shape for the most part no earlier than the mid-19C.

It's still a beautiful place to look at, with hilly Buda keeping watch – via eight great bridges – over sprawling Pest on the other side of the lilting, bending Danube. These were formerly two separate towns, united in 1873 to form a capital city. It enjoyed its heyday around that time, a magnificent city that was the hub of the Austro-Hungarian Empire. Defeats in two world wars and fifty years behind the Iron Curtain put paid to the glory, but battered Budapest is used to rising from the ashes and now it's Europe's most earthily beautiful capital, particularly when winter mists rise from the river to shroud it in a thick white cloak. In summer the days can swelter, and the spas are definitely worth a visit.

EATING OUT

The city is most famous for its coffee houses so, before you start investigating restaurants, find time to tuck into a cream cake with a double espresso in, say, the Ruszwurm on Castle Hill, the city's oldest, and possibly cosiest, café. In tourist areas, it's not difficult to locate goulash on your menu, and you never have to travel far to find beans, dumplings and cabbage in profusion. Having said that, Budapest's culinary scene has moved on apace since the fall of communism, and Hungarian chefs have become much more inventive with their use of local, seasonal produce. Pest is where you'll find most choice but even in Buda there are plenty of worthy restaurants. Lots of locals like to eat sausage on the run and if you fancy the idea, buy a pocket knife. Sunday brunch is popular in Budapest, especially at the best hotels. Your restaurant bill might well include a service charge; don't feel obliged to pay it, as tipping is entirely at your own discretion – though you may find the persistence of the little folk groups that pop up in many restaurants hard to resist.

✿✿ Onyx XxX

Vörösmarty tér 7-8 ✉ 1051 – Ⓜ Vörösmarty tér – ✆ (030) 508 0622 – www.onyxrestaurant.hu – Closed 2 weeks January, 3 weeks August, Tuesday and Wednesday lunch, Sunday and Monday Plan: **E2**

Menu 18900/36900 HUF – *(booking essential) (tasting menu only)*

• Modern cuisine • Elegant • Intimate •

In the city's heart is this glitzy restaurant where you sit on gilt chairs, under sparkling chandeliers, surrounded by onyx adornments. Passionate, highly skilled cooking keeps classic Hungarian flavours to the fore but also has interesting modern twists. Dishes are precisely prepared and intensely flavoured.

➜ Water buffalo tartare, pine and mushroom. Saddle of lamb with fondant potato and summer truffle. 'Túró Rudi' with forest fruits.

✿ Costes XxX

Ráday utca 4 ✉ 1092 – Ⓜ Kálvin tér – ✆ (1) 219 0696 – www.costes.hu – Closed Christmas, Monday and Tuesday Plan: **F3**

Carte 21000/26600 HUF – *(dinner only) (booking essential)*

• Modern cuisine • Design • Elegant •

A sophisticated restaurant with immaculately dressed tables, run by a confident, experienced service team. The talented chef uses modern techniques and a deft touch to produce accomplished, innovative dishes with clear flavours. Most diners choose the 4-7 course set menus and their interesting wine pairings.

➜ Smoked sturgeon, caviar, potato and leek. Venison with celeriac 'carbonara' and pine cone. Honeycomb with sunflower ice cream and lemon cream.

✿ Babel XX

Piarista Köz 2 ✉ 1052 – Ⓜ Ferenciek ter – ✆ (70) 6000 800 – www.babel-budapest.hu – Closed 13-29 January, 11-27 August, Sunday and Monday Plan: **E2**

Menu 25000 HUF – *(dinner only) (booking essential) (tasting menu only)*

• Modern cuisine • Elegant • Design •

A stylish, intimate restaurant run with a real passion by the owner and his young team. Innovative, flavourful cooking: dishes on the Babel Classic menu are informed by the chef's Transylvanian heritage and each has a story to tell, while dishes on the Tasting Menu are more ambitious, with some playful elements.

➜ Octopus with paprika and balsamic. Poultry broth with celeriac. "Bicaz Gorge".

✿ Borkonyha Winekitchen (Ákos Sárközi) XX

Sas utca 3 ✉ 1051 – Ⓜ Bajcsy-Zsilinszky út – ✆ (1) 266 0835 – www.borkonyha.hu – Closed Sunday and bank holidays Plan: **E2**

Carte 9050/15850 HUF – *(booking essential)*

• Modern cuisine • Fashionable • Friendly •

A bustling wine-orientated restaurant close to the Basilica. The fortnightly menu features well-executed dishes with an elaborate modern style and subtle Hungarian influences. Top ingredients are sourced from the surrounding countries. 48 of the 200 wines are offered by the glass; many are from local producers.

➜ Duck liver with baked apple and celeriac. Saddle of venison with textures of beetroot. Autumn apple.

✿ Costes Downtown – Prestige Hotel XX

Vigyázó Ferenc utca 5 ✉ 1051 – Ⓜ Vörösmarty tér – ✆ (1) 920 1015 – www.costesdowntown.hu Plan: **E1**

Menu 7900 HUF (weekday lunch)/24000 HUF – Carte 8500/21600 HUF

• Modern cuisine • Fashionable • Contemporary décor •

Costes' more relaxed younger sister is set on the ground floor of the Prestige Hotel; ask for one of the booths or a table with a view of the kitchen. Quality produce comes from local suppliers and the creative modern dishes are full of colour, with distinct textures and flavours.

➜ Quail, swiss chard and lentils. Mangalica saddle and cheek with capers. Cottage cheese noodles with apricot and lavender.

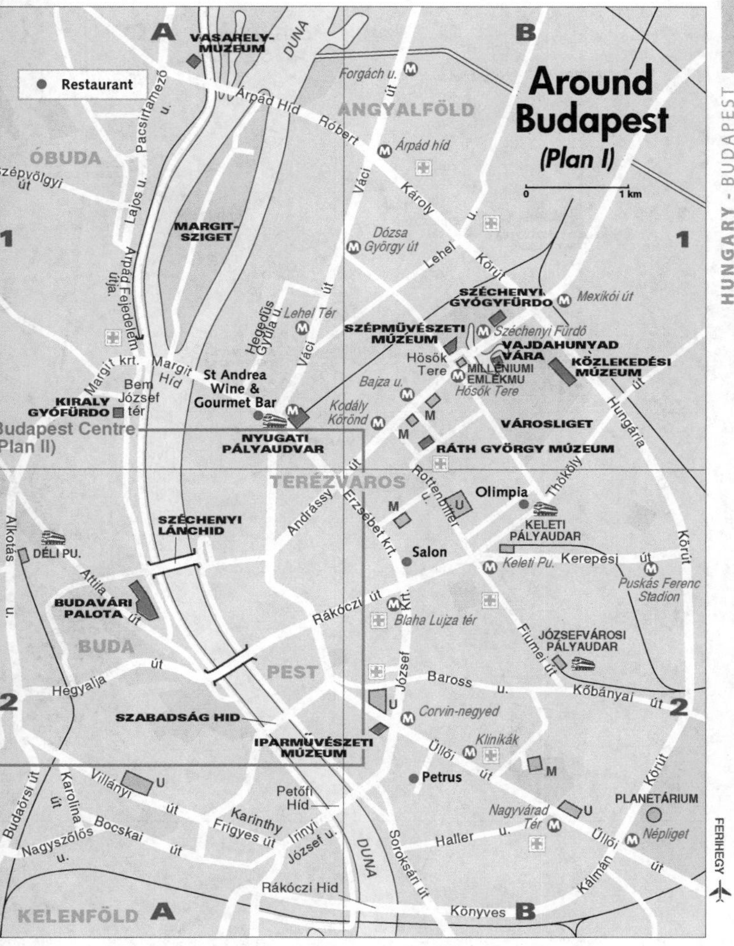

Stand (Tamás Széll and Szabina Szulló) XX [A/C]

Székely Mihály utca 2 ✉ 1061 – Ⓜ Opera – ✆ (30) 785 9139 – www.standrestaurant.hu – Closed 2 weeks late January, 2 weeks early August, Sunday and Monday Plan: **F2**

Menu 7500/19500 HUF

• Modern cuisine • Design • Fashionable •

Smart formal restaurant with contemporary monochrome styling and a kitchen on view behind glass. The cooking is modern, but the unfussy dishes have their heart in the Hungarian classics; the confident kitchen taking a just a handful of top quality ingredients and allowing them to shine.

➜ Pumpkin spaghetti with seaberry and pumpkin seeds. Suckling pig, black pudding and stuffed cabbage. Plums with kefir and fig leaf ice cream.

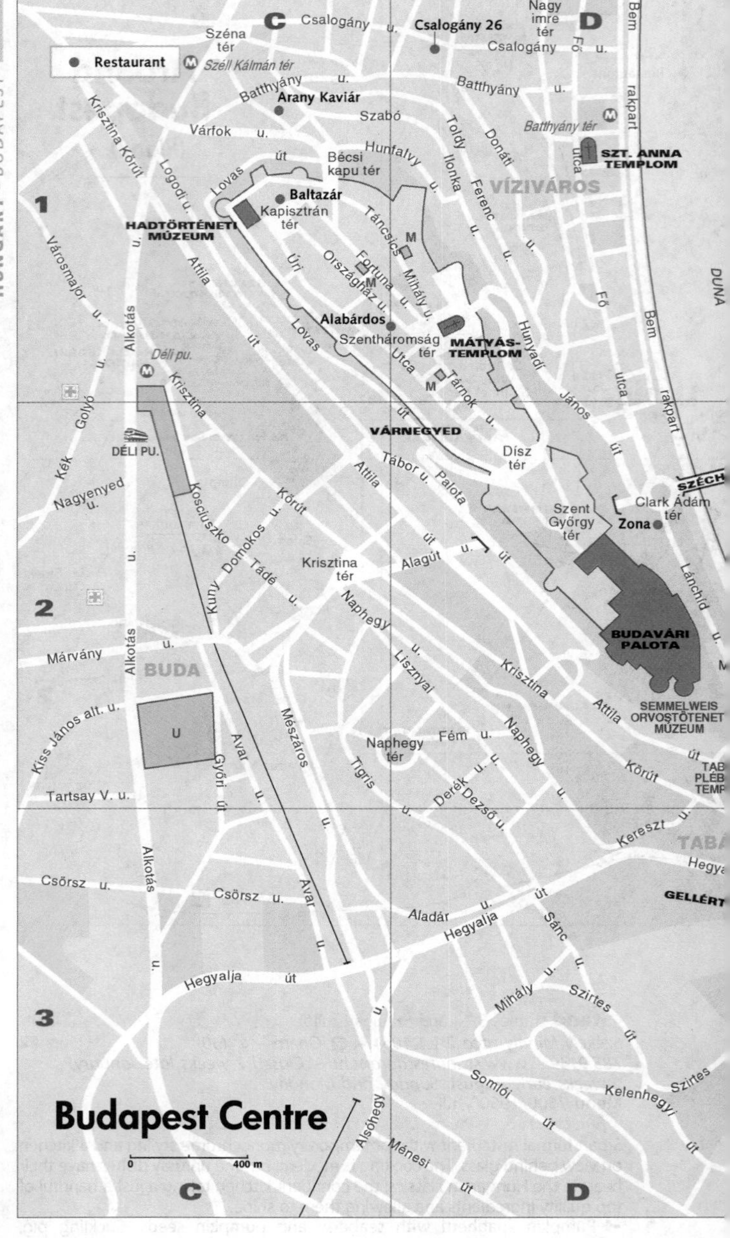

Restaurant
Széll Kálmán tér
Csalogány 26
Arany Kaviár
Baltazár
Alabárdos
Zona
HADTÖRTÉNETI MÚZEUM
MÁTYÁS-TEMPLOM
SZT. ANNA TEMPLOM
BUDAVÁRI PALOTA
SEMMELWEIS ORVOSTÖTENET MÚZEUM
VÍZIVÁROS
VÁRNEGYED
BUDA
DÉLI PU.
Déli pu.
Batthyány tér
Bécsi kapu tér
Kapisztrán tér
Szentháromság tér
Dísz tér
Szent György tér
Clark Ádám tér
Krisztina tér
Naphegy tér
Széna tér
Nagy imre tér
DUNA
Budapest Centre
0 400 m

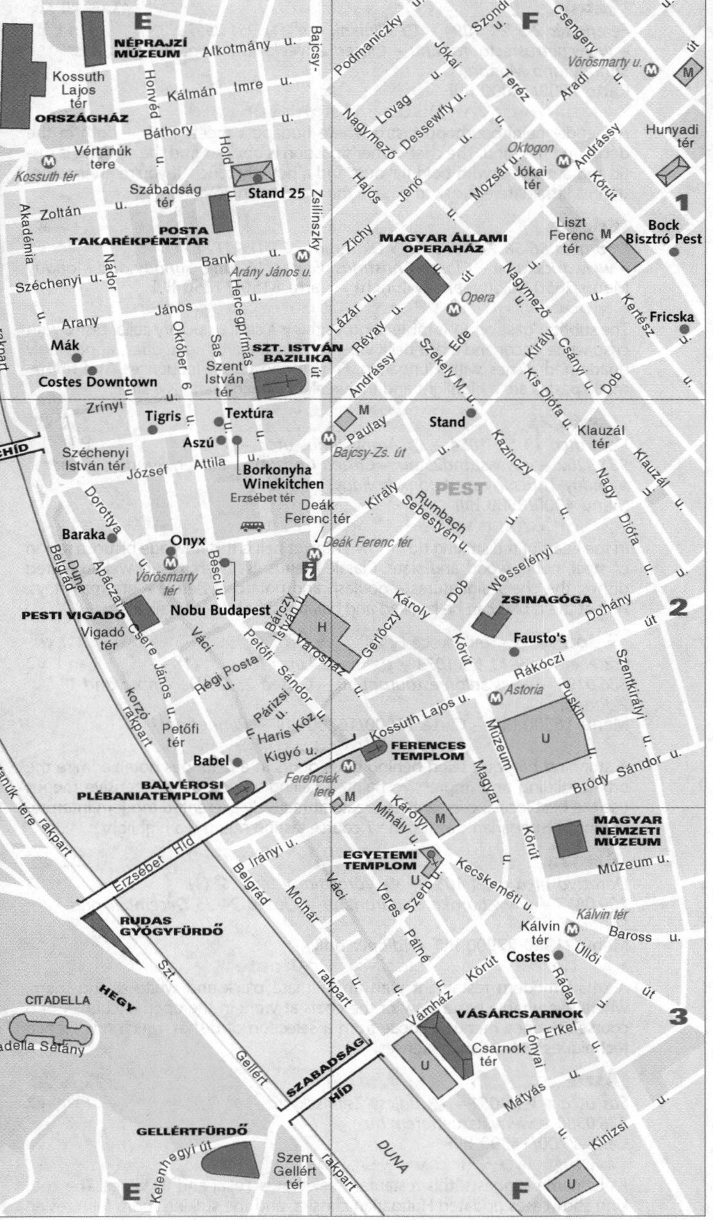
E
F
1
2
3
NÉPRAJZI MÚZEUM
Kossuth Lajos tér
ORSZÁGHÁZ
Vértanúk tere
Kossuth tér
Alkotmány u.
Kálmán Imre u.
Honvéd u.
Báthory u.
Hold u.
Stand 25
Szábadság tér
Zoltán u.
Akadémia u.
POSTA TAKARÉKPÉNZTAR
Bank u.
Arány János u.
Széchenyi u.
Nádor u.
Arany János u.
Hercegprímás u.
Október 6 u.
Sas u.
Szent István tér
SZT. ISTVÁN BAZILIKA
Mák
Costes Downtown
Zrínyi u.
Tigris
Textúra
Aszú
Attila u.
Borkonyha Winekitchen
Széchenyi István tér
József Attila u.
Erzsébet tér
Deák Ferenc tér
Deák Ferenc tér
Dorottya u.
Baraka
Onyx
Vörösmarty tér
Bécsi u.
Nobu Budapest
Duna Belgrád
Apáczai Csere János u.
PESTI VIGADÓ
Vigadó tér
Váci u.
Régi Posta u.
Petőfi Sándor u.
Párizsi u.
Haris Köz u.
Bárczy István u.
Városház u.
H
Gerlóczy u.
korzó rakpart
Petőfi tér
Babel
Kigyó u.
Kossuth Lajos u.
FERENCES TEMPLOM
Ferenciek tere
BALVÉROSI PLÉBANIATEMPLOM
Erzsébet Híd
Irányi u.
Belgrád rakpart
Molnár u.
Váci u.
Veres Pálné u.
Szerb u.
EGYETEMI TEMPLOM
Károlyi Mihály u.
M
U
RUDAS GYÓGYFÜRDŐ
Szt. Gellért rakpart
HEGY
CITADELLA
Citadella Sétány
SZABADSÁG HÍD
GELLÉRTFÜRDŐ
Kelenhegyi út
Szent Gellért tér
rakpart
DUNA
Bajcsy-Zsilinszky út
Podmaniczky u.
Jókai u.
Szondi u.
Csengery u.
Vörösmarty u.
Teréz
Aradi u.
Hunyadi tér
Lovag u.
Nagymező u.
Dessewffy u.
Oktogon
Andrássy
Körút
Jókai tér
Mozsár u.
Hajós u.
Jenő u.
Zichy
Liszt Ferenc tér
Bock Bisztró Pest
MAGYAR ÁLLAMI OPERAHÁZ
Opera
Lázár u.
Révay u.
Andrássy út
Székely M. u.
Ede
Király u.
Csányi u.
Kertész u.
Fricska
Kis Diófa u.
Dob u.
Paulay
Bajcsy-Zs. út
Stand
Kazinczy
Klauzál tér
Klauzál u.
PEST
Király
Rumbach Sebestyén u.
Nagy Diófa u.
Wesselényi
Dob
Károly Körút
ZSINAGÓGA
Dohány
Fausto's
Rákóczi út
Astoria
Puskin
Szentkirályi u.
Múzeum Körút
Brody Sándor u.
Magyar
MAGYAR NEMZETI MÚZEUM
Múzeum u.
Kecskeméti u.
Kálvin tér
Kálvin tér
Baross u.
Üllői út
Costes
Ráday u.
Körút
Vámház
VÁSÁRCSARNOK
Erkel u.
Csarnok tér
Lónyai u.
Mátyás u.
Kinizsi u.

Petrus

Ferenc tér 2-3 ✉ 1094 – Ⓜ Klinikák – ✆ (1) 951 2597 – www.petrusrestaurant.hu – Closed 2 weeks late August, Christmas, Sunday and Monday Plan I: **B2**

Carte 7500/13000 HUF

• Classic French • Bistro • Neighbourhood •

A friendly neighbourhood bistro where Budapest meets Paris – both in the décor and the food. The chef-owner's passion is obvious and the cooking is rustic and authentic, with bold flavours and a homely touch. If you're after something a little different, ask to dine in the old Citroën 2CV!

Fricska

Dob utca 56-58 ✉ 1073 – Ⓜ Oktogon – ✆ (1) 951 8821 – www.fricska.eu – Closed Christmas, Easter, 16 June, Sunday and Monday Plan: **F1**

Menu 2650 HUF (weekday lunch) – Carte 8150/11850 HUF

• Modern cuisine • Bistro • Contemporary décor •

The subtitle 'gastropub' is misleading, as this is a contemporary cellar bistro with crisp white décor and a laid-back vibe. The blackboard menu offers appealingly unadorned dishes with Hungarian, French and Italian influences. The homemade pastas are a highlight and the weekday lunch menu is a steal.

Stand 25

Hold utca 13 ✉ 1054 – Ⓜ Arany János utca – ✆ (30) 961 3262 – www.stand25.hu – Closed Christmas, Easter, Sunday, dinner Monday-Thursday and bank holidays Plan: **E1**

Menu 4900/8500 HUF

• Traditional cuisine • Simple • Bistro •

In the heart of the striking downtown market hall is this new age bistro: a fusion of steel, neon, wood and slate. Classic menus list fresh, rustic, well-executed dishes; the chefs' signatures – goulash and potato casserole – are mainstays. Half of the tables can be booked and half are set aside for walk-ins.

Salon – New York Palace Hotel

Erzsébet krt. 9-11 ✉ 1073 – Ⓜ Blaha Lujza tér – ✆ (1) 886 6191 – www.salonrestaurant.hu – Closed 25-26 December and 1-2 January Plan I: **B2**

Menu 16500 HUF – Carte 11000/16200 HUF – *(dinner only)*

• Hungarian • Classic décor • Luxury •

A stunning baroque salon behind glass doors in a luxurious hotel; admire the ornate gilding and impressive painted ceiling as you dine. Extensive menus use the best local ingredients to create attractively presented modern interpretations of Hungarian classics; the 7 course tasting menu is a highlight.

Baraka

Dorottya utca 6 ✉ 1051 – Ⓜ Vörösmarty tér – ✆ (1) 200 0817 – www.barakarestaurant.hu – Closed 24-25 December and Sunday Plan: **E2**

Menu 21900/27900 HUF – *(dinner only)*

• Modern cuisine • Elegant • Intimate •

A smart modern restaurant with an intimate black and white dining room, where every table has a view of the chefs at work in the open kitchen. 4 or 6 course set price menus; choose from a selection of dishes which mix French techniques with Asian influences.

Aszú

Sas utca 4 ✉ 1051 – Ⓜ Bajcsy-Zsilinszky út – ✆ (1) 328 0360 – www.aszuetterem.hu Plan: **E2**

Carte 7700/14300 HUF

• Hungarian • Elegant • Design •

As its name suggests, this restaurant celebrates Tokaj and its wines. The cooking showcases updated Hungarian classics, and the striking room features an ornate mirrored wall, a golden-hued vaulted ceiling and handcrafted wooden carvings.

Fausto's

Dohány utca 5 ✉ 1072 – Ⓜ Astoria – ✆ (30) 589 1813 – www.fausto.hu – Closed Christmas, Sunday and bank holidays
Plan: **F2**
Carte 13200/20500 HUF – *(booking essential)*
• Italian • Cosy • Intimate •

Expect a friendly welcome at this personally run eatery. Dine on sophisticated modern Italian dishes at linen-laid tables in the restaurant or on simpler, more classically based fare in the laid-back, wood-furnished osteria; the daily home-made pasta is a hit. Good quality Hungarian and Italian wines feature.

Nobu Budapest – Kempinski H. Corvinus

Erzsébet tér 7-8 ✉ 1051 – Ⓜ Deák Ferenc tér – ✆ (1) 429 4242 – www.noburestaurants.com – Closed 24 December
Plan: **E2**
Carte 10400/15900 HUF
• Japanese • Minimalist • Fashionable •

A minimalist restaurant in a stylish hotel, with well-spaced wooden tables, Japanese lanterns, fretwork screens and an open kitchen. Numerous menus offer a huge array of Japanese-inspired dishes; some come with matching wine flights.

St. Andrea Wine & Gourmet Bar

Bajcsy-Zsilinszky utca 78 ✉ 1055 – Ⓜ Nyugati pályaudvar – ✆ (1) 269 0130 – www.standreaborbar.hu – Closed Christmas, Easter, Saturday lunch, Sunday and bank holidays
Plan I: **A1**
Menu 4800/16000 HUF – Carte 7100/16500 HUF
• Modern cuisine • Elegant • Wine bar •

A stylish bar-cum-restaurant with wine-themed décor; owned by a small boutique winery. Well-presented, creative dishes are designed to match their wines – some of which aren't sold anywhere else in the world!

Textúra

Sas utca 6 ✉ 1051 – Ⓜ Bajcsy-Zsilinszky út – ✆ (1) 617 9495 – www.texturaetterem.hu – Closed 1 week January, 24-26 December, Sunday and bank holidays
Plan: **E2**
Carte 13000/15000 HUF
• Hungarian • Design • Fashionable •

A stylish, design-led brasserie with a relaxed atmosphere, a living wall of moss and a central wooden 'tree'; set almost opposite its sister restaurant, Borkonyha Winekitchen. Seasonal, Hungarian influenced dishes are ambitious and creative.

Tigris

Mérleg utca 10 ✉ 1051 – Ⓜ Bajcsy-Zsilinszky út – ✆ (1) 317 3715 – www.tigrisrestaurant.hu – Closed 1 week August, 24 December and Sunday
Plan: **E2**
Carte 12500/19500 HUF – *(booking essential at dinner)*
• Hungarian • Traditional décor • Neighbourhood •

A traditional bistro in a historic building designed by a Hungarian architect; it exudes a luxurious feel. Classic dishes have an appealing, earthy quality and feature foie gras specialities. The wine list champions up-and-coming producers.

Bock Bisztró Pest

Erzsébet krt. 43-49 ✉ 1073 – Ⓜ Oktogon – ✆ (1) 321 0340 – www.bockbisztro.hu – Closed Monday and bank holidays
Plan: **F1**
Carte 5500/13000 HUF – *(booking essential)*
• Hungarian • Bistro • Rustic •

A busy, buzzy bistro; its shelves packed with wine. Choose something from the à la carte or try one of the blackboard specials – the friendly, knowledgeable staff will guide you. Cooking is gutsy and traditional with a modern twist.

Mák

Vigyázó Ferenc utca 4 ✉ 1051 – Ⓜ Vörösmarty tér — Plan: **E1**
– ✆ (30) 723 9383 – www.mak.hu – Closed 1 week August, Christmas, Sunday and Monday
Menu 4800 HUF (weekday lunch)/18000 HUF – Carte 9000/14800 HUF
• Modern cuisine • Bistro • Rustic •

A rustic restaurant with whitewashed brick walls, semi-vaulted ceilings and a relaxed feel: its name means 'poppy seed'. The talented young chef prepares creative dishes which play with different texture and flavour combinations.

Olimpia

Alpár utca 5 ✉ 1076 – Ⓜ Keleti pályaudvar — Plan I: **B2**
– ✆ (1) 321 0680 – www.olimpiavendeglo.com – Closed August, Christmas, Saturday, Sunday and Monday
Menu 3050/8500 HUF
• Modern cuisine • Neighbourhood • Friendly •

The local area might be uninspiring but as you step over the threshold of this bright basement restaurant, all is forgotten. Fresh, light cooking is unfussy at lunch and more complex in the evening; dinner is a surprise menu served at 7pm.

BUDA — PLAN II

Alabárdos

Orszaghaz Utca 2 ✉ 1014 – Ⓜ Széll Kármán tér — Plan: **D1**
– ✆ (1) 356 0851 – www.alabardos.hu – Closed 25-26 December and Sunday
Menu 14900/18900 HUF – Carte 10700/17900 HUF – *(dinner only and Saturday lunch) (booking essential)*
• Hungarian • Elegant • Intimate •

Set in a series of 15C buildings opposite the castle and named after its guards, this professionally run restaurant has stood here for over 50 years. It's formal yet atmospheric, with subtle modern touches and a delightful terrace. Cooking is rich and flavourful and features classic dishes with a modern edge.

Arany Kaviár

Ostrom utca 19 ✉ 1015 – Ⓜ Széll Kálmán tér — Plan: **C1**
– ✆ (1) 201 6737 – www.aranykaviar.hu – Closed 24-26 December, 20 August, Monday and bank holidays
Menu 6500 HUF (weekday lunch)/19500 HUF – Carte 10500/29500 HUF
• Russian • Intimate • Elegant •

Choose between an opulent, richly appointed room and a larger, more modern extension which opens onto the garden. French and Russian influences guide the creative, ambitious cooking; Hungarian and Siberian caviar is a speciality.

Csalogány 26

Csalogány utca 26 ✉ 1015 – Ⓜ Batthyány tér — Plan: **D1**
– ✆ (1) 201 7892 – www.csalogany26.hu
– Closed 2 weeks summer, 2 weeks winter, Sunday, Monday and bank holidays
Menu 3100/16000 HUF – Carte 7000/12100 HUF
• Modern cuisine • Bistro • Friendly •

A homely neighbourhood restaurant with a simple bistro style. The passionate father and son team prepare tasty dishes in a modern manner. Choose from the à la carte, the daily blackboard or, at dinner, an 8 course tasting menu.

Baltazár

Országház utca 31 ✉ 1014 – Ⓜ Széll Kálmán tér – ✆ (1) 300 7050 – www.baltazarbudapest.com
Plan: **C1**

Carte 6500/17240 HUF

• Meats and grills • Design • Bistro •

A hidden gem, tucked back to the north of the Old Town, away from the crowds. Sit on the pretty terrace or head into the striking bistro, where stage spotlights illuminate boldly painted concrete walls. Cooking focuses on Hungarian classics and meats from the Josper grill. Its bedrooms are also ultra-modern.

Vendéglõ a KisBíróhoz

Szarvas Gábor utca 8/d (Northwest: 3.5 km by Attila utca, Kristina Körut and Szilágyi Erzsébet off Kutvölgyi utca) ✉ 1125 – ✆ (1) 376 6044 – www.vendegloakisbirohoz.hu – Closed bank holidays

Menu 3900 HUF – Carte 5500/13000 HUF

• Hungarian • Bistro • Neighbourhood •

A contemporary glass and wood building with a large terrace, in a peaceful suburban location. Wine takes centre stage: staff will recommend a match for your dish from the extensive list. Cooking is hearty and classical with a modern edge.

Zona

Lánchíd utca 7-9 ✉ 1013 – ✆ (30) 422 5981 – www.zonabudapest.com – Closed 24 December and 1 January
Plan: **D2**

Menu 3590 HUF (weekday lunch) – Carte 6120/15800 HUF

• Modern cuisine • Design • Trendy •

A contemporary restaurant with floor to ceiling windows overlooking the river and a huge shelving unit packed with wines. Gold glass balls illuminate sleek wooden tables. Modern dishes follow the seasons and arrive smartly presented.

REYKJAVÍK

ICELAND
ICELAND

Boyloso/iStock

Reykjavik
REYKJAVIK

dennisvdw/iStock

REYKJAVIK IN...

→ **ONE DAY**
Hallgrímskirkja Church, Harpa Concert Hall, Laugavegur: the main shopping street.

→ **TWO DAYS**
Saga Museum, the Old Harbour (Grandi).

→ **THREE DAYS**
A trip out to the Blue Lagoon or a glacier tour.

Europe's youngest landmass is a country of extremes; a dramatic wilderness where volcanic springs sit beside vast glaciers and long summer days are offset by dark winters. Its largest city, Reykjavik, lays claim to being the world's most northern capital and its settlement by a Norseman over 1100 years ago is recounted in the Icelandic Sagas. Two thirds of Icelanders live in Reykjavik, in low, colourful buildings designed to fend off the North Atlantic winds and brighten spirits through the long, dark nights. Other buildings echo nature itself: the geometric shapes of the Hallgrímskirkja Church – whose soaring tower keeps watch

over the city – mirror the lava flows, while the Harpa Concert Hall is cleverly designed to reflect both the city and nature – its cascading LEDs alluding to the incredible spectacle of the Aurora Borealis. The historic city centre, known as 101, lies between the harbour and an inland lake, and is a bustling, bohemian place filled with independent boutiques and fashionable bars. Head out further east and you can discover the secrets of the Blue Lagoon's healing thermal waters and the Golden Circle, which comprises three of Iceland's greatest natural wonders: the Þingvellir National Park (where you can walk between two tectonic plates); the Haukadalur Geothermal Field with its geysers and mud pools; and the spectacular Gullfoss Waterfall – the largest in Europe.

EATING OUT

Eating out is an important part of Icelandic life but it can be expensive, so choose wisely and avoid the tourist traps. There's a pleasing informality to most restaurants so it's easy to enjoy good cooking in relaxed surroundings, but the city is small, so reservations are recommended. Lunch is a low-key affair, with dinner being the main event, and cooking tends to be quite contemporary – the local chefs are proud of their heritage and have a great way of updating traditional recipes. Clarity of flavour leads the way and there's a pleasing reliance on the island's natural produce: seafood (particularly cod) and lamb take centre stage, and popular techniques include smoking and preserving. Rye bread is a typical accompaniment and you'll find the cultured dairy product skyr – once eaten by Vikings and farmers – in everything from starters to desserts. Icelanders love their cosy coffee shops (be sure to accompany your drink with a traditional *kleina* doughnut), and the Sandholt Bakery, run by the 4th generation, is worth a visit.

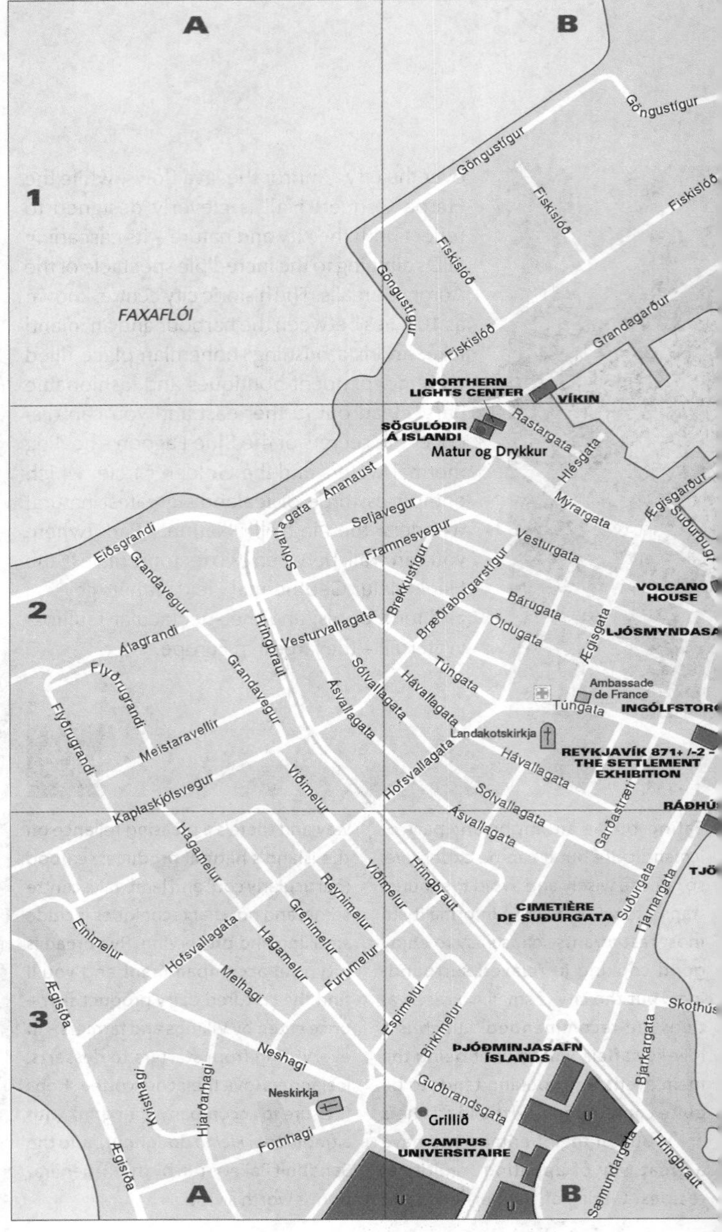
A
B
1
2
3
FAXAFLÓI
Göngustígur
Fiskislóð
Grandagarður
NORTHERN LIGHTS CENTER
VÍKIN
SÖGULÓÐIR Á ISLANDI
Matur og Drykkur
Rastargata
Hlésgata
Ánanaust
Mýrargata
Ægisgarður
Suðurbugt
Eiðsgrandi
Sólvallagata
Seljavegur
Framnesvegur
Vesturgata
Grandavegur
Brekkustígur
Bræðraborgarstígur
Bárugata
VOLCANO HOUSE
Álagrandi
Hringbraut
Vesturvallagata
Öldugata
Ægisgata
LJÓSMYNDASA
Flyðrugrandi
Túngata
Ambassade de France
INGÓLFSTOR
Ásvallagata
Hávallagata
Landakotskirkja
Meistaravellir
REYKJAVÍK 871+ /-2 - THE SETTLEMENT EXHIBITION
Hofsvallagata
Víðimelur
Kaplaskjólsvegur
Garðastræti
RÁÐHÚ
Hagamelur
Reynimelur
Suðurgata
Tjarnargata
TJÖ
CIMETIÈRE DE SUÐURGATA
Grenimelur
Einimelur
Furumelur
Melhagi
Ægisíða
Espimelur
Skothús
Birkimelur
Neshagi
ÞJÓÐMINJASAFN ÍSLANDS
Bjarkargata
Kvisthagi
Hjarðarhagi
Neskirkja
Guðbrandsgata
Grillið
Fornhagi
CAMPUS UNIVERSITAIRE
U
Sæmundargata

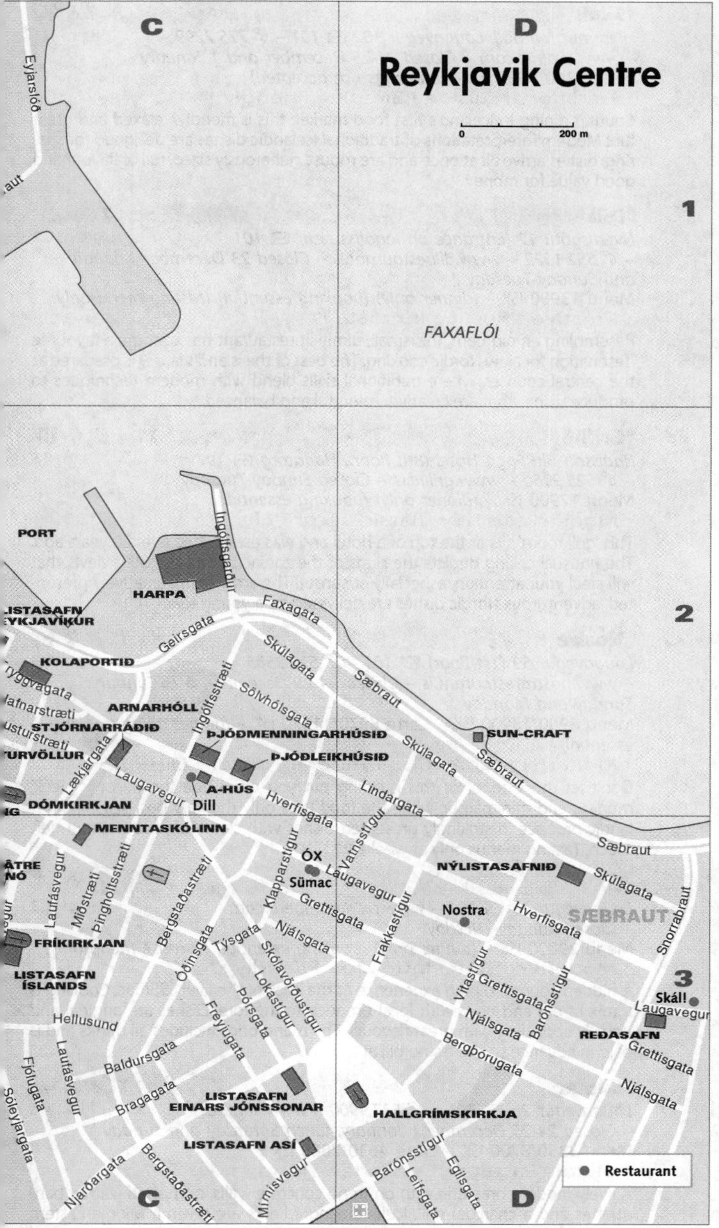
Reykjavik Centre
0
200 m
C
D
1
2
3
FAXAFLÓI
Eyjarslóð
PORT
HARPA
LISTASAFN
REYKJAVÍKUR
KOLAPORTIÐ
ARNARHÓLL
STJÓRNARRÁÐIÐ
ÞJÓÐMENNINGARHÚSIÐ
ÞJÓÐLEIKHÚSIÐ
A-HÚS
Dill
DÓMKIRKJAN
MENNTASKÓLINN
ÓX
Sümac
SUN-CRAFT
NÝLISTASAFNIÐ
Nostra
SÆBRAUT
Skál!
REÐASAFN
FRÍKIRKJAN
LISTASAFN
ÍSLANDS
LISTASAFN
EINARS JÓNSSONAR
HALLGRÍMSKIRKJA
LISTASAFN ASÍ
Ingólfsgarður
Faxagata
Geirsgata
Skúlagata
Sæbraut
Tryggvagata
Hafnarstræti
Austurstræti
Ingólfsstræti
Sölvhólsgata
Lækjargata
Laugavegur
Hverfisgata
Lindargata
Vatnsstígur
Klapparstígur
Grettisgata
Njálsgata
Frakkastígur
Vitastígur
Barónsstígur
Snorrabraut
Bergþórugata
Laufásvegur
Miðstræti
Þingholtsstræti
Bergstaðastræti
Óðinsgata
Týsgata
Skólavörðustígur
Lokastígur
Þórsgata
Freyjugata
Hellusund
Baldursgata
Bragagata
Fjólugata
Sóleyjargata
Njarðargata
Mímisvegur
Leifsgata
Egilsgata
Restaurant

Skál!

Hlemmur Mathöll, Laugavegur 107 ✉ 101 – ✆ 775 2299 – www.skalrvk.com – Closed 24-25 December and 1 January
Plan: **D3**
Carte 3300/5550 ISK – *(bookings not accepted)*
• Traditional cuisine • Simple • Friendly •
Counter dining in Iceland's first food market; this is friendly, relaxed and great fun! Modern interpretations of traditional Icelandic dishes are designed for sharing; dishes arrive all at once and are robust, generously sized, full of flavour and good value for money.

Dill

Hverfisgötu 12 (Entrance on Ingólfsstræti) ✉ 101 – ✆ 552 1522 – www.dillrestaurant.is – Closed 23 December-1 January and Sunday-Tuesday
Plan: **C2**
Menu 13900 ISK – *(dinner only) (booking essential) (tasting menu only)*
• Creative • Rustic • Intimate •
Resembling an old barn, this small, dimly-lit restaurant has become a favourite destination for New Nordic cooking. The best of the island's larder is prepared at the central counter, where traditional skills blend with modern techniques to produce dishes that are creative, colourful and balanced.

Grillið

Radisson Blu Saga Hotel (8th floor), Hagatorg ✉ 107 – ✆ 525 9960 – www.grillid.is – Closed Sunday-Tuesday
Plan: **B3**
Menu 12900 ISK – *(dinner only) (booking essential)*
• Modern cuisine • Classic décor • Elegant •
This 'grill room' sits at the top of a hotel and was established over 50 years ago. The unusual ceiling depicts the signs of the zodiac but it's the 360° views that will steal your attention, especially at sunset. The array of imaginatively presented, adventurous Nordic dishes are delivered by a young team.

Nostra

Laugavegur 59 (1st floor) ✉ 101 – ✆ 519 3535 – www.nostrarestaurant.is – Closed 24-25 December, 6-16 January, Sunday and Monday
Plan: **D3**
Menu 8900/13900 ISK – Carte 8970/11970 ISK – *(dinner only) (booking essential)*
• Modern cuisine • Contemporary décor • Design •
Don't let the exterior of this building put you off; inside the décor is sleek, modern and minimalistic while the food uses only the very best seasonal Icelandic produce in strikingly presented dishes with clarity of flavour and a deft touch. Tasting menus only at weekends.

ÓX

Laugavegur 28 ✉ 101 – www.ox.dinesuperb.com – Closed Sunday-Tuesday
Plan: **C3**
Menu 29000 ISK – *(dinner only) (booking essential) (surprise menu only)*
• Modern cuisine • Intimate • Friendly •
A hidden counter dining experience at the back of the lively Sümac. Cooking is a mix of old and new, with local produce to the fore. Dishes are original and visually appealing with great flavours. The menu price includes all drinks and is paid in advance so there's no bill at the end.

Sümac

Laugavegur 28 ✉ 101 – ✆ 537 9900 – www.sumac.is – Closed 24-25 December,1 January, lunch Saturday and Sunday
Plan: **C3**
Menu 3850/8700 ISK – Carte 4630/7880 ISK
• Middle Eastern • Brasserie • Trendy •
A lively modern brasserie with on-trend concrete walls, burnished leather banquettes and a charcoal grill. Icelandic ingredients are given a Middle Eastern twist, with influences from North Africa to the Lebanon. Cooking is rustic and full of flavour; go for the sharing meze menus.

VOX

Hilton Reykjavik Nordica Hotel, Suðurlandsbraut 2 (East: 2.75 km by 41)
✉ 108 – ✆ 444 5050 – www.vox.is

Menu 4000 ISK – Carte 7350/12030 ISK

• Modern cuisine • Contemporary décor • Elegant •

A stylish restaurant and bar set off the lobby of the Hilton hotel. At lunch there's a popular hot and cold buffet; at dinner, choices include an à la carte and 'Season' and 'Seafood' tasting menus. Cooking is modern and creative.

Matur og Drykkur

Grandagarður 2 ✉ 101 – ✆ 571 8877 Plan: **B2**
– www.maturogdrykkur.is – Closed 24 December, 1 January and Sunday lunch

Menu 3690 ISK (lunch) – Carte 4070/10070 ISK

• Traditional cuisine • Simple • Trendy •

This simple little eatery is named after an Icelandic cookbook and shares its premises with the Saga Museum. Old recipes are given modern twists, resulting in delicious dishes with a creative edge. The à la carte is supplemented by great value 'Icelandic Snacks', along with various tasting menus at dinner.

DUBLIN

Republic of IRELAND
ÉIRE

Warchi/iStock

DUBLIN
BAILE ÁTHA CLIATH

gianliguori/iStock

DUBLIN IN...

➜ **ONE DAY**
Trinity College, Grafton Street, St Stephen's Green, Merrion Square, Temple Bar.

➜ **TWO DAYS**
Christ Church Cathedral, Dublin Castle, Chester Beatty Library, the quayside.

➜ **THREE DAYS**
O'Connell Street, Parnell Square, Dublin Writers' Museum, DART train to the coast.

For somewhere touted as the finest Georgian city in the British Isles, Dublin enjoys a very young image. When the 'Celtic Tiger' roared to prominence in the 1990s, Ireland's old capital took on a youthful expression, and for the first time revelled in the epithets 'chic' and 'trendy'. Nowadays it's not just the bastion of Guinness drinkers and those here for the 'craic', but a twenty-first century city with smart restaurants, grand new hotels, modern architecture and impressive galleries. Its handsome squares and façades took shape 250 years ago, designed by the finest architects of the time. Since then, it's gone through uprising, civil war and independence

from Britain, and now holds a strong fascination for foreign visitors.

The city can be pretty well divided into three. Southeast of the river is the classiest, defined by the glorious Trinity College, St Stephen's Green, and Grafton Street's smart shops. Just west of here is the second area, dominated by Dublin Castle and Christ Church Cathedral – ancient buildings abound, but it doesn't quite match the sleek aura of the city's Georgian quarter. Across the Liffey, the northern section was the last part to be developed and, although it lacks the glamour of its southern neighbours, it does boast the city's grandest avenue, O'Connell Street, and its most celebrated theatres.

EATING OUT

It's still possible to indulge in Irish stew but nowadays you can also dine on everything from tacos and Thai to Malaysian and Middle Eastern cuisine, particularly in the Temple Bar area. The city makes the most of its bay proximity, so seafood features highly, with smoked salmon and oysters the favourites; the latter washed down with a pint of Guinness. Meat is particularly tasty in Ireland, due to the healthy livestock and a wet climate, and Irish beef is world famous for its fulsome flavour. However, there's never been a better time to be a vegetarian in Dublin, as every type of veg from spinach to seaweed now features, and chefs insist on the best seasonal produce, cooked for just the right amount of time to savour all the taste and goodness. Dinner here is usually served until about 10pm, though many global and city centre restaurants stay open later. If you make your main meal at lunchtime, you'll pay considerably less than in the evening: the menus are often similar, but the bill in the middle of the day will probably be about half the price.

✿✿ **Patrick Guilbaud** (Guillaume Lebrun)

21 Upper Merrion St ✉ D2 – ✆ (01) 6764192 Plan: **F3**
– www.restaurantpatrickguilbaud.ie – Closed 17 March, 25-31 December, Sunday, Monday and bank holidays
Menu 60/120 € – *(booking essential)*

• Modern French • Elegant • Luxury •

A truly sumptuous restaurant in an elegant Georgian house; the eponymous owner has run it for over 35 years. Accomplished, original cooking uses luxurious ingredients and mixes classical French cooking with modern techniques. Dishes are well-crafted and visually stunning with a superb balance of textures and flavours.

→ Blue lobster ravioli with coconut scented lobster cream, toasted almonds and curry dressing. Caramelised veal sweetbread, with parsnip, Mimolette and coffee. Lime soufflé with lime leaf ice cream.

✿ **Chapter One** (Ross Lewis)

The Dublin Writers Museum, 18-19 Parnell Sq ✉ D1 – ✆ (01) 8732266 – www.chapteronerestaurant.com – Closed 2 weeks August, 2 weeks Christmas, Sunday, Monday and bank holidays Plan: **E1**
Menu 44/80 € – *(dinner only and Friday lunch) (booking essential)*

• Modern cuisine • Intimate • Design •

Good old-fashioned Irish hospitality meets with modern Irish cooking in this stylish basement restaurant beneath the Writers Museum. The series of interconnecting rooms have an understated elegance and striking bespoke art hangs on the walls. Boldly flavoured dishes showcase produce from local artisan producers.

→ Haddock with smoked eel, tartare of mackerel and yuzu. Salt marsh duck with tart of Braeburn apple, smoked bacon and pickled walnut. Flavours and textures of Irish milk and honey.

✿ **L'Ecrivain** (Derry Clarke)

109a Lower Baggot St ✉ D2 – ✆ (01) 6611919 – www.lecrivain.com – Closed Sunday and bank holidays Plan: **F3**
Menu 35 € (lunch) – Carte 67/88 € – *(dinner only and Friday lunch) (booking essential)*

• Modern cuisine • Fashionable • Design •

A well-regarded restaurant with an attractive terrace, a glitzy bar and a private dining room which screens live kitchen action. The refined, balanced menu has a classical foundation whilst also displaying touches of modernity; the ingredients used are superlative. Service is structured yet has personality.

→ Scallops with cauliflower, white asparagus and Lardo di Colonnata. Irish beef fillet with celeriac, morels and a wild garlic jus. Pistachio nougat and cream with honey ice cream.

✿ **Greenhouse** (Mickael Viljanen)

Dawson St ✉ D2 – ✆ (01) 676 7015 – www.thegreenhouserestaurant.ie – Closed 2 weeks July, 2 weeks Christmas, Sunday and Monday Plan: **E3**
Menu 42/90 €

• Modern cuisine • Elegant • Fashionable •

Stylish restaurant with turquoise banquettes and smooth service. Menus include a good value set lunch, midweek set and tasting menus and a 5 course 'Surprise' on Friday and Saturday evenings. Accomplished, classically based cooking has stimulating flavour combinations and creative modern overtones.

→ Foie gras royale with apple, walnut and smoked eel. Anjou pigeon with artichoke and truffle sauce. Passion fruit soufflé with ginger sauce.

Pichet

XX AC

14-15 Trinity St ✉ D2 – ✆ (01) 6771060 Plan: **E2**
– www.pichet.ie – Closed 25 December and 1 January
Menu 28 € (lunch and early dinner)/49 € – Carte 32/46 € – *(booking essential)*
• Classic French • Fashionable • Brasserie •
You can't miss the bright red signs and blue and white striped canopies of this buzzy brasserie – and its checkerboard flooring makes it equally striking inside. Have snacks at the bar or classic French dishes in the main room. A good selection of wines are available by the glass or pichet.

Delahunt

X

39 Camden Street Lower ✉ D2 – ✆ (01) 598 4880 Plan: **D3**
– www.delahunt.ie – Closed 15 August-1 September, Sunday and Monday
Menu 34/39 € – *(dinner only and lunch Thursday-Saturday) (booking essential)*
• Modern cuisine • Bistro • Fashionable •
An old Victorian grocer's shop mentioned in James Joyce's 'Ulysses'; the clerk's snug is now a glass-enclosed private dining room. Precisely executed, flavoursome dishes are modern takes on time-honoured recipes. Lunch offers two choices per course and dinner, four; they also serve snacks in the upstairs bar.

Bastible

X

111 South Circular Rd ✉ D8 – ✆ (01) 473 7409 Plan II: **G1**
– www.bastible.com – Closed Sunday dinner, Monday and Tuesday
Menu 26/48 € – *(dinner only and lunch Friday-Sunday) (booking essential)*
• Modern cuisine • Simple • Neighbourhood •
The name refers to the cast iron pot which once sat on the hearth of every family home; they still use it here to make the bread. Modern cooking showcases one main ingredient with minimal accompaniments; menus offer 3 choices per course.

Clanbrassil House

X

6 Clanbrassil St Upper ✉ D8 – ✆ (01) 453 9786 Plan II: **G1**
– www.clanbrassilhouse.com – Closed Sunday and Monday
Menu 25 € (early dinner) – Carte 30/47 € – *(dinner only and Saturday lunch) (booking essential)*
• Modern cuisine • Rustic • Simple •
Bastible's younger sister is a small place seating just 25. The concise menu focuses on the charcoal grill, with everything from homemade sausages to prime cuts. The hash brown chips are a favourite; the early evening menu is a steal; and if you're in a group you can share dishes 'family-style'.

Etto

X

18 Merrion Row ✉ D2 – ✆ (01) 6788872 – www.etto.ie Plan: **E3**
– Closed last 2 weeks August, 25 December-7 January, 15-23 April, Sunday-Tuesday and lunch Wednesday
Menu 25 € (weekday lunch)/28 € – Carte 29/45 € – *(booking essential)*
• Mediterranean cuisine • Rustic • Neighbourhood •
The name of this rustic restaurant means 'little' and it is totally apt! Blackboards announce the daily wines and the Worker's Lunch special. Flavoursome dishes rely on good ingredients and have Italian influences; the chef understands natural flavours and follows the 'less is more' approach.

Pig's Ear

X

4 Nassau St ✉ D2 – ✆ (01) 6703865 – www.thepigsear.ie Plan: **E2**
– Closed first week January, Sunday and bank holidays
Menu 24 € (lunch and early dinner) – Carte 31/49 € – *(booking essential)*
• Modern cuisine • Bistro • Friendly •
Look out for the bright pink door of this three storey Georgian townhouse overlooking Trinity College Gardens. The first and second floors have a homely retro feel while the third floor is a private dining room with its own kitchen and library. Irish produce features in refined yet comforting dishes.

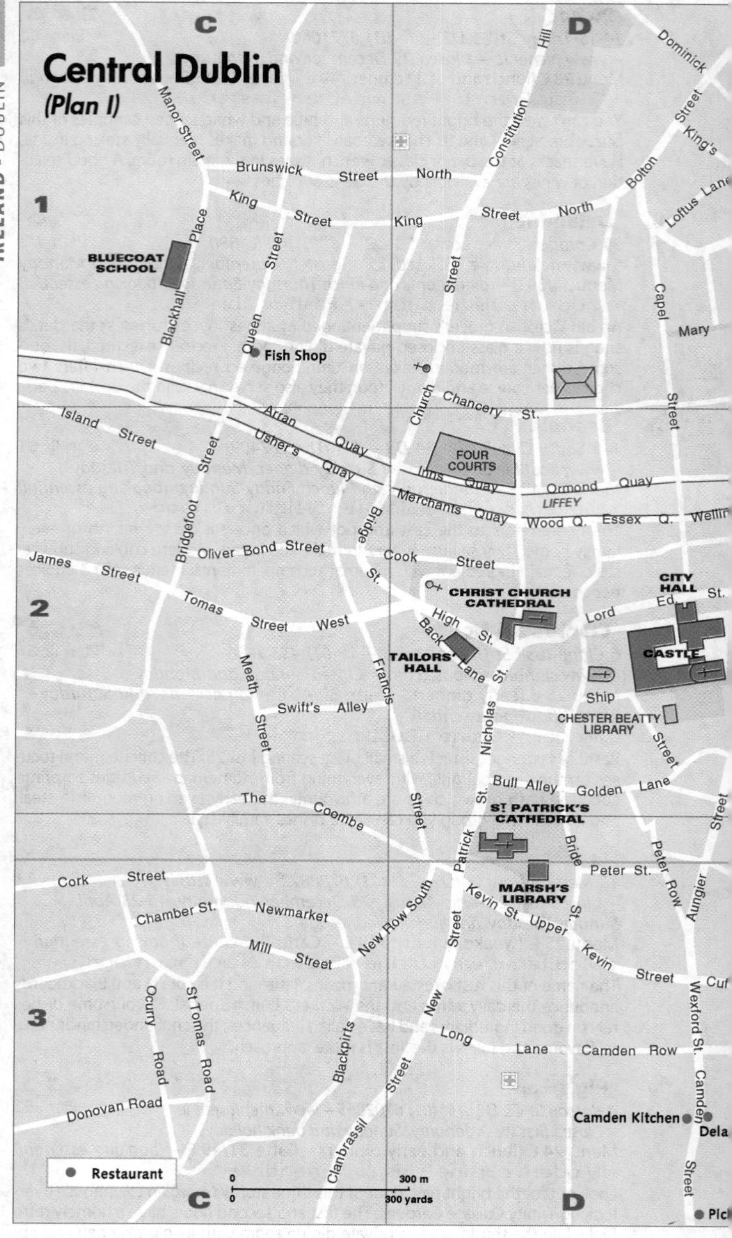

Central Dublin
(Plan I)
C
D
1
2
3
BLUECOAT SCHOOL
Fish Shop
FOUR COURTS
LIFFEY
CHRIST CHURCH CATHEDRAL
TAILORS' HALL
CITY HALL
CASTLE
CHESTER BEATTY LIBRARY
ST PATRICK'S CATHEDRAL
MARSH'S LIBRARY
Camden Kitchen
Restaurant
300 m
300 yards

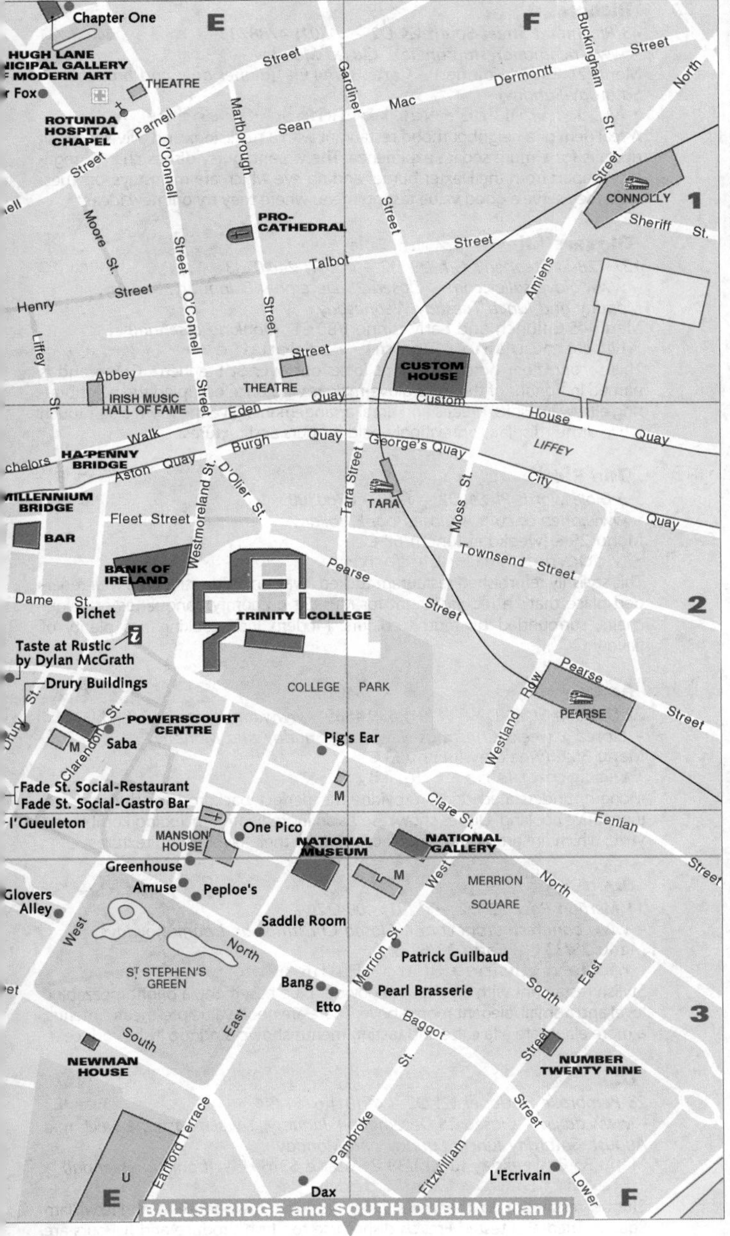
Chapter One
E
F
HUGH LANE MUNICIPAL GALLERY OF MODERN ART
THEATRE
ROTUNDA HOSPITAL CHAPEL
PRO-CATHEDRAL
CONNOLLY
CUSTOM HOUSE
THEATRE
IRISH MUSIC HALL OF FAME
HA'PENNY BRIDGE
MILLENNIUM BRIDGE
LIFFEY
TARA
BAR
BANK OF IRELAND
TRINITY COLLEGE
COLLEGE PARK
PEARSE
Pichet
Taste at Rustic by Dylan McGrath
Drury Buildings
POWERSCOURT CENTRE
Saba
Pig's Ear
Fade St. Social-Restaurant
Fade St. Social-Gastro Bar
l'Gueuleton
MANSION HOUSE
One Pico
NATIONAL MUSEUM
NATIONAL GALLERY
Greenhouse
Amuse
Peploe's
Glovers Alley
MERRION SQUARE
Saddle Room
Patrick Guilbaud
ST STEPHEN'S GREEN
Bang
Etto
Pearl Brasserie
NEWMAN HOUSE
NUMBER TWENTY NINE
L'Ecrivain
Dax
1
2
3
BALLSBRIDGE and SOUTH DUBLIN (Plan II)

Richmond

43 Richmond Street South ✉ D2 – ✆ (01) 4788783 Plan II: **G1**
– www.richmondrestaurant.ie – Closed Monday
Menu 24 € (early dinner) – Carte 33/44 € – *(dinner only and brunch Saturday-Sunday)*
• Modern cuisine • Neighbourhood • Friendly •
A real gem of a neighbourhood restaurant with a rustic look and a lively feel; sit upstairs for a more sedate experience. The vibrant, gutsy dishes change regularly – apart from the Dexter burger and rib-eye which are mainstays; on Tuesdays they serve a good value tasting menu where they try out new ideas.

Glovers Alley – Fitzwilliam Hotel

127-128 St Stephen's Grn ✉ D2 – ✆ (01) 244 0733 Plan: **E3**
– www.gloversalley.com – Closed 25 December-8 January, Sunday, Monday and lunch Tuesday-Wednesday
Menu 45 € (lunch and early dinner)/80 € – *(booking essential)*
• Modern cuisine • Design • Fashionable •
This second floor hotel restaurant looks out over St Stephen's Green and is named in honour of the city's glove-makers who once occupied the neighbouring alleyway. Pinks, greens and floral arrangements give the room a soft touch while dishes display contrastingly bold flavours and textures.

One Pico

5-6 Molesworth Pl ✉ D2 – ✆ (01) 6760300 Plan: **E3**
– www.onepico.com – Closed bank holidays
Menu 29 € (weekday lunch)/68 €
• Modern cuisine • Elegant •
This stylishly refurbished restaurant tucked away on a side street is a well-regarded place that's a regular haunt for MPs. Sit on comfy banquettes or velour chairs, surrounded by muted colours. Modern Irish cooking has plenty of flavour.

Amuse

22 Dawson St ✉ D2 – ✆ (01) 639 4889 – www.amuse.ie Plan: **E3**
– Closed 2 weeks Christmas-New Year, Sunday and Monday
Menu 35 € (weekday lunch)/55 €
• Modern cuisine • Friendly •
Modern, understated décor provides the perfect backdrop for the intricate, innovative cooking. Dishes showcase Asian ingredients – including kombu and yuzu; which are artfully arranged according to their flavours and textures.

Bang

11 Merrion Row ✉ D2 – ✆ (01) 4004229 Plan: **E3**
– www.bangrestaurant.com – Closed Christmas and bank holidays
Menu 25/33 € – Carte 38/61 €
• Modern cuisine • Bistro • Fashionable •
Stylish restaurant with an intimate powder blue basement, a bright mezzanine level and a small, elegant room above. There are good value pre-theatre menus, a more elaborate à la carte and tasting menus showcasing top Irish produce.

Dax

23 Pembroke St Upper ✉ D2 – ✆ (01) 6761494 Plan: **E3**
– www.dax.ie – Closed 25 December-4 January, 1 week Easter, 1 week mid August, Saturday lunch, Sunday and Monday
Menu 35 € (weekday lunch)/39 € – Carte 53/69 € – *(booking essential)*
• French • Bistro • Classic décor •
Clubby restaurant in the cellar of a Georgian townhouse near Fitzwilliam Square. Tried-and-tested French dishes use top Irish produce and flavours are clearly defined. The Surprise Menu best showcases the kitchen's talent.

Fade St. Social - Restaurant

4-6 Fade St ✉ D2 – ☎ (01) 604 0066 Plan: **E2**
– www.fadestreetsocial.com – Closed 25-26 December
Menu 35 € (lunch and early dinner) – Carte 36/73 € – *(dinner only and lunch Thursday-Friday)*

• Modern cuisine • Brasserie • Fashionable •

Have cocktails on the terrace then head for the big, modern brasserie. Dishes use Irish ingredients but have a Mediterranean feel; they specialise in sharing and wood-fired dishes, and use large cuts of meat such as chateaubriand.

Mr Fox

38 Parnell Sq. West ✉ D1 – ☎ (01) 8747778 Plan: **E1**
– www.mrfox.ie – Closed Sunday, Monday and bank holidays
Menu 22 € (lunch and early dinner) – Carte 34/48 €

• Modern cuisine • Intimate • Neighbourhood •

In the basement of a striking Georgian house you'll find this light-hearted restaurant with a lovely tiled floor and a small terrace. The charming team present tasty international dishes, some of which have a playful touch.

Pearl Brasserie

20 Merrion St Upper ✉ D2 – ☎ (01) 6613572 Plan: **F3**
– www.pearl-brasserie.com – Closed 25 December and Sunday
Menu 35/39 € – Carte 47/70 €

• Classic French • Brasserie •

Formal basement restaurant with a small bar-lounge and two surprisingly airy dining rooms; sit in a stylish booth in one of the old coal bunkers. Intriguing modern dishes have a classical base and Mediterranean and Asian influences.

Peploe's

16 St Stephen's Grn. ✉ D2 – ☎ (01) 6763144 Plan: **E3**
– www.peploes.com – Closed 25-26 December, Good Friday and lunch bank holidays
Menu 38 € (lunch) – Carte 46/70 € – *(booking essential)*

• Mediterranean cuisine • Cosy • Brasserie •

Atmospheric cellar restaurant – formerly a bank vault – named after the artist. The comfy room has a warm, clubby feel and a large mural depicts the owner. The well-drilled team present Mediterranean dishes and an Old World wine list.

Saddle Room - Shelbourne Hotel

27 St Stephen's Grn. ✉ D2 – ☎ (01) 6634500 Plan: **E3**
– www.shelbournedining.ie
Menu 28 € (weekday lunch)/47 €

• Meats and grills • Elegant • Fashionable •

Renowned restaurant with a history as long as that of the hotel in which it stands. The warm, inviting room features intimate gold booths and a crustacea counter. The menu offers classic dishes and grills.

Suesey Street

26 Fitzwilliam Pl ✉ D2 – ☎ (01) 669 4600 Plan II: **H1**
– www.sueseystreet.ie – Closed 25-30 December, Sunday and Monday
Menu 30 € (weekday dinner) – Carte 38/59 €

• Modern cuisine • Intimate • Cosy •

An intimate restaurant with sumptuous, eye-catching décor, set in the basement of a Georgian townhouse; sit on the superb courtyard terrace. Refined, modern cooking brings out the best in home-grown Irish ingredients.

Camden Kitchen

3a Camden Mkt, Grantham St ✉ D8 – ☎ (01) 4760125 Plan: **D3**
– www.camdenkitchen.ie – Closed 24-26 December, Sunday and Monday
Menu 24/29 € – Carte 31/50 €

• Classic cuisine • Bistro • Neighbourhood •

A simple, modern, neighbourhood bistro set over two floors; watch the owner cooking in the open kitchen. Tasty dishes use good quality Irish ingredients prepared in classic combinations. Service is relaxed and friendly.

Drury Buildings

Plan: E2

52-55 Drury St ✉ D2 – ✆ (01) 960 2095 – www.drurybuildings.com – Closed 25-26 December

Menu 24/42 € – Carte 31/59 €

• Italian • Trendy • Brasserie •

A hip, laid-back 'New York loft': its impressive terrace has a retractable roof and reclaimed furniture features in the stylish cocktail bar, which offers cicchetti and sharing boards. The airy restaurant serves rustic Italian dishes.

Fade St. Social - Gastro Bar

Plan: E2

4-6 Fade St ✉ D2 – ✆ (01) 604 0066 – www.fadestreetsocial.com – Closed 25-26 December and 1 January

Menu 40 € (early dinner) – Carte 25/57 € – *(dinner only and lunch Saturday-Sunday) (booking essential)*

• International • Fashionable • Tapas bar •

Buzzy restaurant with an almost frenzied feel. It's all about a diverse range of original, interesting small plates, from a bacon and cabbage burger to a lobster hotdog. Eat at the kitchen counter or on leather-cushioned 'saddle' benches.

Fish Shop

Plan: C1

6 Queen St ✉ D7 – ✆ (01) 430 8594 – www.fish-shop.ie – Closed Sunday-Tuesday

Menu 29/45 € – *(dinner only and lunch Friday-Saturday) (tasting menu only)*

• Seafood • Rustic • Friendly •

A very informal little restaurant where they serve a daily changing seafood menu which is written up on the tiled wall. Great tasting, supremely fresh, unfussy dishes could be prepared raw or roasted in the wood-fired oven.

l'Gueuleton

Plan: E2

1 Fade St ✉ D2 – ✆ (01) 6753708 – www.lgueuleton.com – Closed 25-26 December

Menu 29 € (early dinner) – Carte 26/52 €

• Classic French • Bistro • Rustic •

Friendly staff run this long-standing restaurant, which has a shabby-chic bistro feel and a large pavement terrace. The established kitchen team have a good understanding of French country classics; cooking is good value, flavoursome and relies on local seasonal produce. The cocktail bar is open 'til late.

Locks

Plan II: G1

1 Windsor Terr ✉ D8 – ✆ (01) 416 3655 – www.locksrestaurant.ie – Closed Sunday dinner and Monday

Menu 25 € (early dinner) – Carte 35/55 € – *(dinner only and lunch Friday-Sunday) (booking essential)*

• Modern cuisine • Bistro • Neighbourhood •

Locals love this restaurant overlooking the canal – downstairs it's buzzy, while upstairs is more intimate, and the personable team add to the feel. Natural flavours are to the fore and dishes are given subtle modern touches; for the best value menus come early in the week or before 7pm.

Pickle

Plan: D3

43 Lower Camden St ✉ D2 – ✆ (01) 555 7755 – www.picklerestaurant.com – Closed 25-27 December

Menu 22 € (early dinner) – Carte 32/57 € – *(dinner only and lunch Wednesday-Friday)*

• Indian • Fashionable • Neighbourhood •

It might not look much from the outside but inside the place really comes alive. Spices are lined up on the kitchen counter and dishes are fresh and vibrant; the lamb curry with bone marrow is divine. Try a Tiffin Box for lunch.

Saba

26-28 Clarendon St ✉ D2 – ✆ (01) 679 2000 – www.sabadublin.com – Closed 25-26 December Plan: **E2**
Menu 15 € (weekday lunch)/35 € – Carte 32/48 €
• Thai • Fashionable • Simple •

Trendy, buzzy restaurant and cocktail bar. Simple, stylish rooms have refectory tables, banquettes and amusing photos. Fresh, visual, authentic cooking is from an all-Thai team, with a few Vietnamese dishes and some fusion cooking too.

Taste at Rustic by Dylan McGrath

17 South Great George's St (2nd Floor) ✉ D2 – ✆ (01) 526 7701 – www.tasteatrustic.com – Closed 25-26 December, 1 January and Sunday-Tuesday Plan: **E2**
Carte 34/74 € – *(dinner only)*
• Asian • Rustic •

Dylan McGrath's love of Japanese cuisine inspires dishes which explore the five tastes; sweet, salt, bitter, umami and sour. Ingredients are top-notch and flavours, bold and masculine. Personable staff are happy to recommend dishes.

BALLSBRIDGE — PLAN II

Chop House

2 Shelbourne Rd ✉ D4 – ✆ (01) 6602390 – www.thechophouse.ie – Closed Saturday lunch Plan: **J1**
Carte 28/57 €
• Meats and grills • Pub • Neighbourhood •

An imposing pub not far from the stadium. For warmer days there's a small terrace; in colder weather head up the steps, through the bar and into the bright conservatory. The relaxed lunchtime menu is followed by more ambitious dishes in the evening when the kitchen really comes into its own.

Old Spot

14 Bath Ave ✉ D4 – ✆ (01) 660 5599 – www.theoldspot.ie – Closed 25-26 December and Good Friday Plan: **J1**
Menu 27 € – Carte 27/51 €
• Traditional cuisine • Pub • Friendly •

The appealing bar has a stencilled maple-wood floor and a great selection of snacks and bottled craft beers, while the relaxed, characterful restaurant filled with vintage posters serves pub classics with a modern edge.

ENVIRONS OF DUBLIN

AT CLONTARF Northeast : 5.5 km by R105

Pigeon House

11b Vernon Ave (East : 1.5 km by Clontarf Rd on Vernon Ave (R808)) ✉ D3 – ✆ (01) 8057567 – www.pigeonhouse.ie – Closed 25-26 December
Menu 29 € (dinner) – Carte 30/46 €
• Modern cuisine • Neighbourhood • Bistro •

Slickly run neighbourhood bistro that's open for breakfast, lunch and dinner. It's just off the coast road in an up-and-coming area and has a lovely front terrace and a lively feel. Cooking is modern and assured. The bar counter is laden with freshly baked goodies and dishes are full of flavour.

Fishbone

324 Clontarf Rd (East : 1.5 km on Clontarf Rd) ✉ D3 – ✆ (01) 536 9066 – www.fishbone.ie – Closed 25-26 December
Menu 18/22 € – Carte 30/48 €
• Seafood • Neighbourhood •

A friendly little restaurant opposite the Bull Bridge, with a cocktail bar at its centre and a glass-enclosed kitchen to the rear. Prime seafood from the plancha and charcoal grill is accompanied by tasty house sauces.

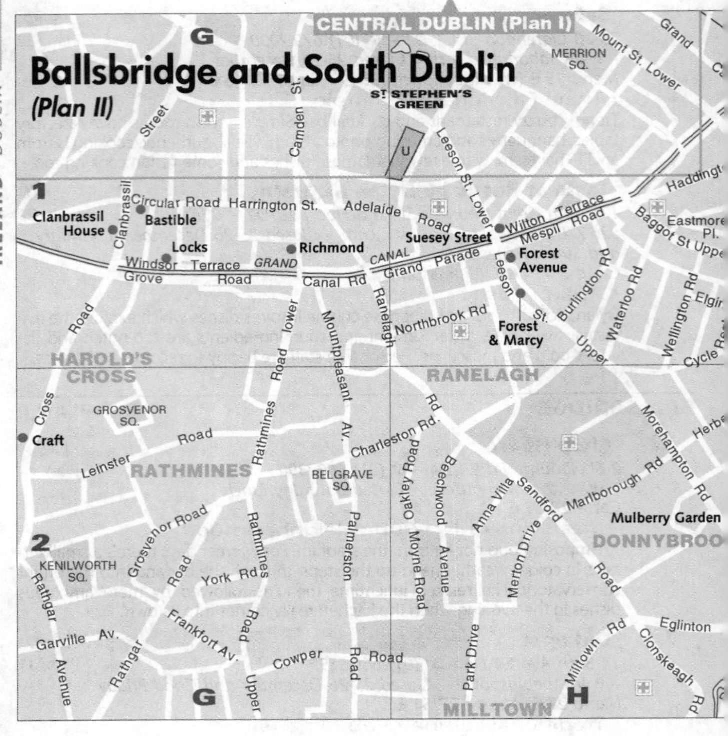

AT DONNYBROOK

Mulberry Garden

Mulberry Ln (off Donnybrook Rd) ✉ *D4 – ✆ (01) 269 3300* Plan: **H2**
– www.mulberrygarden.ie – Closed first week January and Sunday-Wednesday
Menu 49 € – *(dinner only) (booking essential)*
• Modern cuisine • Cosy • Intimate •
Delightful restaurant hidden away in the city suburbs; its interesting L-shaped dining room set around a small courtyard terrace. Choice of two dishes per course on the weekly menu; original modern cooking relies on tasty local produce.

AT DUNDRUM South : 7.5 km by R 117

Ananda

Sandyford Rd, Dundrum Town Centre ✉ *D14 – ✆ (01) 296 0099*
– www.anandarestaurant.ie – Closed 25-26 December
Menu 21 € (lunch) – Carte 35/56 € – *(dinner only and lunch Friday-Sunday)*
• Indian • Exotic décor • Fashionable •
Its name means 'bliss' and it's a welcome escape from the bustle of the shopping centre. The stylish interior encompasses a smart cocktail bar, attractive fretwork and vibrant art. Accomplished Indian cooking is modern and original.

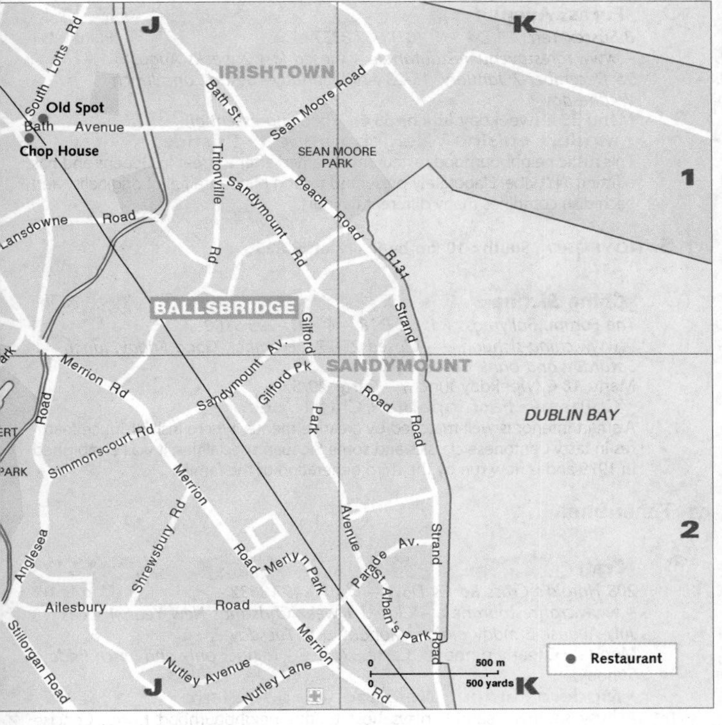

AT FOXROCK Southeast : 13 km by N 11

Bistro One XX

3 Brighton Rd ✉ *D18 – ✆ (01) 289 7711 – www.bistro-one.ie – Closed 25 December-3 January, 3 April, Sunday dinner, Monday and lunch Tuesday-Thursday*

Menu 29 € (lunch) – Carte dinner 29/52 € – *(booking essential)*

• Traditional cuisine • Neighbourhood •

Long-standing neighbourhood bistro above a parade of shops; run by a father-daughter team and a real hit with the locals. Good value daily menus list a range of Irish and Italian dishes. They produce their own Tuscan olive oil.

AT RANELAGH

Forest & Marcy X

126 Leeson St Upper ✉ *D4 – ✆ (01) 660 2480* Plan II: **H1**

– www.forestandmarcy.ie – Closed 25 December-7 January, 20-28 April, last two weeks August and Monday-Tuesday

Menu 49 € – Carte 33/42 € – *(dinner only) (booking essential)*

• Modern cuisine • Fashionable • Wine bar •

There's a lively buzz to this lovely little wine kitchen with high-level seating. Precisely prepared, original dishes burst with flavour; many are prepared at the counter and the chefs themselves often present and explain what's on the plate. They offer a tasting menu only Friday-Sunday.

Forest Avenue

8 Sussex Terr. ✉ D4 – ✆ (01) 667 8337 Plan II: **H1**
– www.forestavenuerestaurant.ie – Closed last 2 weeks August, 25 December-7 January, 15-23 April, Sunday-Tuesday and lunch Wednesday
Menu 35 € (weekday lunch)/68 € – *(booking essential)*
• Modern cuisine • Neighbourhood • Rustic •
This rustic neighbourhood restaurant is named after a street in Queens and has a fitting 'NY' vibe. Elaborately presented tasting plates are full of originality and each dish combines many different flavours.

AT SANDYFORD South : 10 km by R 117 off R 825

China Sichuan

The Forum, Ballymoss Rd. ✉ D18 – ✆ (01) 293 5100
– www.china-sichuan.ie – Closed 25-27 December, Good Friday, lunch Saturday and bank holidays
Menu 16 € (weekday lunch) – Carte 29/57 €
• Chinese • Fashionable • Classic décor •
A smart interior is well-matched by creative menus, where Irish produce features in tasty Cantonese classics and some Sichuan specialities. It was established in 1979 and is now run by the third generation of the family.

AT TERENURE

Craft

208 Harold's Cross Rd ✉ D6W – ✆ (01) 497 8632 Plan II: **G2**
– www.craftrestaurant.ie – Closed 1 week Christmas-New Year, 1 week July-August, Sunday dinner, Monday and Tuesday
Menu 29 € (early dinner) – Carte 37/50 € – *(dinner only and lunch Friday-Sunday)*
• Modern cuisine • Neighbourhood • Bistro •
A busy southern suburb plays host to this neighbourhood bistro. Concise menus evolve with seasonal availability and the lunch and early evening menus really are a steal. Dishes are modern and creative with vibrant colours and fresh, natural flavours. Sweet service from a local team completes the experience.

Sime/Photononstop

Milan
ROME

ITALY
ITALIA

MasterLu/iStock

Rome
ROMA

ROMAOSLO/iStock

ROME IN...

→ **ONE DAY**
Capitol, Forum, Colosseum, Pantheon, Trevi Fountain, Spanish Steps.

→ **TWO DAYS**
Via Condotti, Piazza Navona and surrounding churches, Capitoline museums.

→ **THREE DAYS**
A day on the west bank of the Tiber at Trastevere, Vatican City.

Rome wasn't built in a day, and, when visiting, it's pretty hard to do it justice in less than three. The Italian capital is richly layered in Imperial, Renaissance, baroque and modern architecture, and its broad piazzas, hooting traffic and cobbled thoroughfares all lend their part to the heady fare: a theatrical stage cradled within seven famous hills. Being Eternal, Rome never ceases to feel like a lively, living city, while at the same time a scintillating monument to Renaissance power and an epic centre of antiquity. Nowhere else offers such a wealth of classical remains; set alongside palaces and churches, and bathed in the

soft, golden light for which it is famous. When Augustus became the first Emperor of Rome, he could hardly have imagined the impact his city's language, laws and calendar would have upon the world.

The River Tiber snakes its way north to south through the heart of Rome. On its west bank lies the characterful and 'independent' neighbourhood of Trastevere, while north of here is Vatican City. Over the river the Piazza di Spagna area to the north has Rome's smartest shopping streets, while the southern boundary is marked by the Aventine and Celian hills, the latter overlooking the Colosseum. Esquiline's teeming quarter is just to the east of the city's heart; that honour goes to The Capitol, which gave its name to the concept of a 'capital' city.

EATING OUT

Despite being Italy's capital, Rome largely favours a local, traditional cuisine, typically found in an unpretentious trattoria or osteria. Although not far from the sea, the city doesn't go in much for fish, and food is often connected to the rural, pastoral life with products coming from the surrounding Lazio hills, which also produce good wines. Pasta, of course, is not to be missed, and lamb is favoured among meats for the main course. So too, the 'quinto quarto': a long-established way of indicating those parts of the beef (tail, tripe, liver, spleen, lungs, heart, kidney) left over after the best bits had gone to the richest families. For international cuisine combined with a more refined setting, head for the elegant hotels: very few other areas of Italy have such an increasing number of good quality restaurants within a hotel setting. Locals like to dine later in Rome than say, Milan, with 1pm, or 8pm the very earliest you'd dream of appearing for lunch or dinner. In the tourist hotspots, owners are, of course, only too pleased to open that bit earlier.

✿✿ **Il Pagliaccio** (Anthony Genovese) XXX
via dei Banchi Vecchi 129/a ✉ 00186 Plan: **E2**
– ☏ 06 68809595
– www.ristoranteilpagliaccio.com
– Closed 3 weeks in August, 25 January-8 February, Sunday, Tuesday lunch and Monday
Menu 75 € (lunch)/170 € – Carte 95/145 €
• Creative • Elegant • Luxury •

The appearance of the menu – no more than a simple list of the ingredients used – hides the fact that this restaurant serves some of the most original and sophisticated dishes in Rome. The chef here has real passion for the aesthetics and ingredients of the Far East, as well as a new awareness of the vegetarian requirements of his guests, which means that many of the dishes are also available as a vegetable-based version.

→ Tortello di maiale, caciocavallo e pomodoro. Agnello, aglio nero e avocado bruciato. Cioccolato mediterraneo.

✿ **Imàgo** – Hotel Hassler XXXX
piazza Trinità dei Monti 6 ✉ 00187 – Ⓜ Spagna Plan: **F1**
– ☏ 06 69934726 – www.imagorestaurant.com
– Closed 2 weeks in January
Menu 130/170 € – Carte 100/164 € – *(dinner only)*
• Modern cuisine • Luxury • Friendly •

This restaurant continues to be a perennial favourite, thanks to its large windows and unforgettable views of Rome. Modern cuisine made with high quality ingredients.

→ Risotto cacio, pepi e sesami. Pollo ai peperoni alla romana. Dolce mozzarella di bufala.

✿ **Pipero** XXX
corso Vittorio Emanuele 246 ✉ 00186 Plan: **E2-3**
– ☏ 0668139022 – www.piperoroma.com
– Closed Sunday
Menu 110/140 € – Carte 85/165 € – *(dinner only)*
• Creative • Elegant • Romantic •

This establishment long-favoured by food enthusiasts in the capital has moved to new premises. Alessandro Pipero now presides over an elegant, stylish contemporary restaurant opposite the Chiesa Nuova, with a mezzanine area for guests wanting a bit more privacy. In the kitchen, Luciano Monosilio uses just a few ingredients to create seemingly simple dishes which are nonetheless full of character.

→ Genovese di polpo in raviolo. Piccione sale e scalogno. Croccante di cioccolato e menta.

✿ **Acquolina** (Angelo Troiani) – Hotel The First Roma XXX
via del Vantaggio 14 – Ⓜ Spagna Plan: **B2**
– ☏ 06 3200655 – www.acquolinaristorante.it
– Closed 13-21 August and Sunday
Menu 95/135 € – Carte 67/159 € – *(dinner only)*
• Seafood • Minimalist • Intimate •

In a refined setting adorned with original art works, paintings and sculptures, the chef at this restaurant creates fish-based dishes inspired by the culinary traditions of the Mediterranean, accompanied by a selection of excellent wines. The natural light which pours through the large picture windows facing the tables adds a sophisticated ambience.

→ Linguine, vongole, zenzero e prezzemolo. Polpo, mele, rucola e finta maionese. Passion cheesecake.

✿ **Il Convivio-Troiani** (Angelo Troiani) XXX

vicolo dei Soldati 31 ✉ 00186 Plan: **E2**
– ✆ 06 6869432
– www.ilconviviotroiani.com
– Closed 1 week in August, 24-26 December and Sunday
Menu 110/125 € – Carte 84/142 € – *(dinner only)*
• Modern cuisine • Elegant • Chic •

Situated in the maze of alleyways not far from Piazza Navona, Il Convivio welcomes its guests in three elegant, themed dining rooms – the cloister room, carriage room and art room. The menu offers skilful reinterpretations of classic dishes from Lazio and Italy with the occasional imaginative twist.

➜ Amatriciana de Il Convivio. Piccione, ciliegie, scorzonera e tartufo nero. "Sottobosco".

✿ **Enoteca al Parlamento Achilli** XX

via dei Prefetti 15 ✉ 00186 – Ⓜ Spagna Plan: **F2**
– ✆ 06 86761422
– www.enotecalparlamento.com
– Closed 14-31 August, Sunday and bank holidays
Menu 100/160 € – Carte 88/107 €
• Creative • Elegant •

Although little suggests from the outside that this city centre building houses a restaurant, the elegant wine bar leads to two successive dining rooms furnished in wood. The cuisine is highly individual, based on striking contrasts and bold presentation, making it perfect for those looking for a change from traditional fare. Some tables are reserved for bistro dining, where the food is simpler and more regional in style.

➜ Passata di zucchine trombette e gamberi in leggera frittura. Baccalà in vago pensar di carbonara. Gamberi suzette.

✿ **Glass Hostaria** (Cristina Bowerman) XX

vicolo del Cinque 58 ✉ 00153 Plan: **E3**
– ✆ 06 58335903 – www.glasshostaria.it
– Closed 2-24 July, 8-31January and Monday
Menu 90/120 € – Carte 61/102 € – *(dinner only)*
• Creative • Design • Fashionable •

Situated in the heart of Trastevere, this restaurant boasts an ultra-modern design with an interesting play of light. The excellent cuisine also features highly modern touches.

➜ Linguine, zenzero, lime, prezzemolo e percebes (crostaceo). Colombaccio, platano, burro di arachidi, polvere di lampone ed erbe fritte. Cioccolato, sesamo e datterino.

✿ **Per Me Giulio Terrinoni** XX

vicolo del Malpasso 9 ✉ 00186 Roma Plan: **E3**
– ✆ 06 6877365 – www.giulioterrinoni.it
– Closed 10 days in August
Menu 80/140 € – Carte 86/146 € – *(number of covers limited, pre-book)*
• Creative • Contemporary décor • Intimate •

This restaurant in Vicolo del Malpasso in the historic centre of Rome, famous for its "tappi" (tapas-style snacks), fully expresses the strong personality of its chef, as well as his striking originality. This is a place of experimentation, technical expertise and imagination, where creativity and top-quality ingredients are constant throughout. However, the food varies slightly between lunch (more informal) and dinner, when tasting menus (including the outstanding "Terra e Mare") take centre stage.

➜ Carpaccio di scampi, foie gras marinato e gel di cipolla rossa. Variazione di rana pescatrice, coppa, trippa, coda e diplomatico. Cake alla vaniglia, mousse al limone e gelato al basilico.

Environs of Rome
(Plan I)

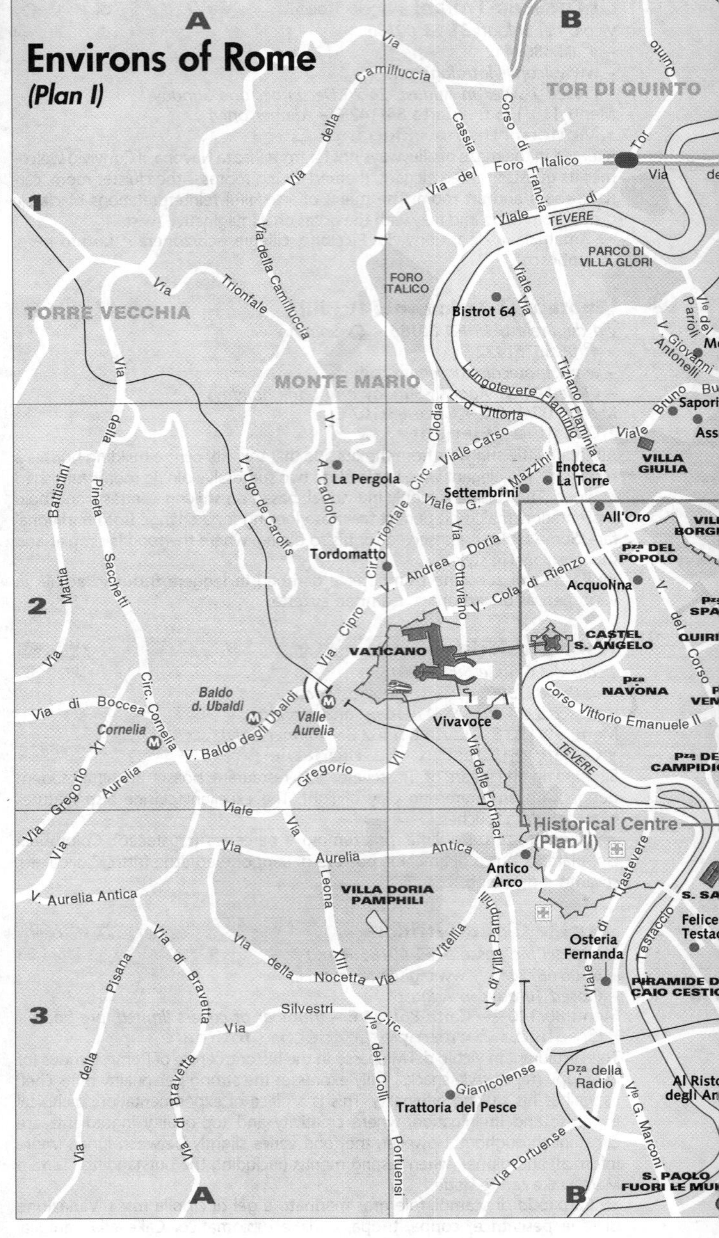

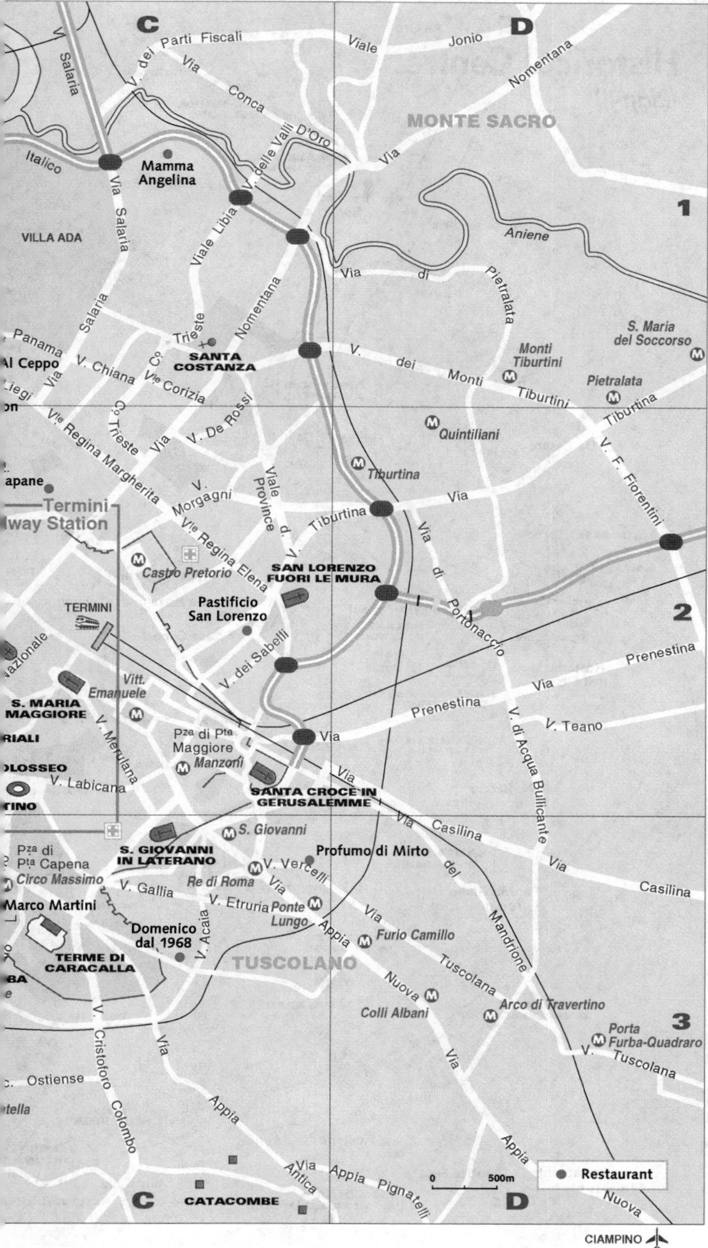
C
D
V. dei Parti Fiscali
Viale Jonio
Via Conca D'Oro
Nomentana
MONTE SACRO
V. Salaria
Italico
Mamma Angelina
Via Salaria
V. delle Valli
Viale Libia
Via
1
Aniene
VILLA ADA
Via di Pietralata
Nomentana
Salaria
Trieste
Panama
SANTA COSTANZA
V. dei Monti Tiburtini
S. Maria del Soccorso
Monti Tiburtini
Pietralata
V. Chiana
Via
V.le Corizia
Co. Trieste
Tiburtina
Quintiliani
V.le Regina Margherita
Via
V. De Rossi
V. F. Fiorentini
Tiburtina
V. Morgagni
Viale Province
Via Tiburtina
Via di Portonaccio
V.le Regina Elena
d. V.
Castro Pretorio
SAN LORENZO FUORI LE MURA
TERMINI
Pastificio San Lorenzo
2
V. dei Sabelli
Prenestina
Via Prenestina
Vitt. Emanuele
S. MARIA MAGGIORE
V. Merulana
V. di Acqua Bullicante
V. Teano
Pza di Pta Maggiore
Via
Manzoni
Via
V. Labicana
SANTA CROCE IN GERUSALEMME
Via Casilina
S. Giovanni
Pza di Pta Capena
S. GIOVANNI IN LATERANO
Profumo di Mirto
V. Vercelli
del Mandrione
Via Casilina
Circo Massimo
Re di Roma
Via
V. Gallia
Marco Martini
V. Etruria
Ponte Lungo
Via
Domenico dal 1968
V. Acaia
Appia
Furio Camillo
Tuscolana
TERME DI CARACALLA
TUSCOLANO
Nuova
Colli Albani
Arco di Travertino
3
Porta Furba-Quadraro
V. Tuscolana
V. Cristoforo Colombo
Via
Via
Ostiense
Appia
Appia
Via Antica
Via Appia Pignatelli
0
500m
Restaurant
Nuova
C
CATACOMBE
D
CIAMPINO

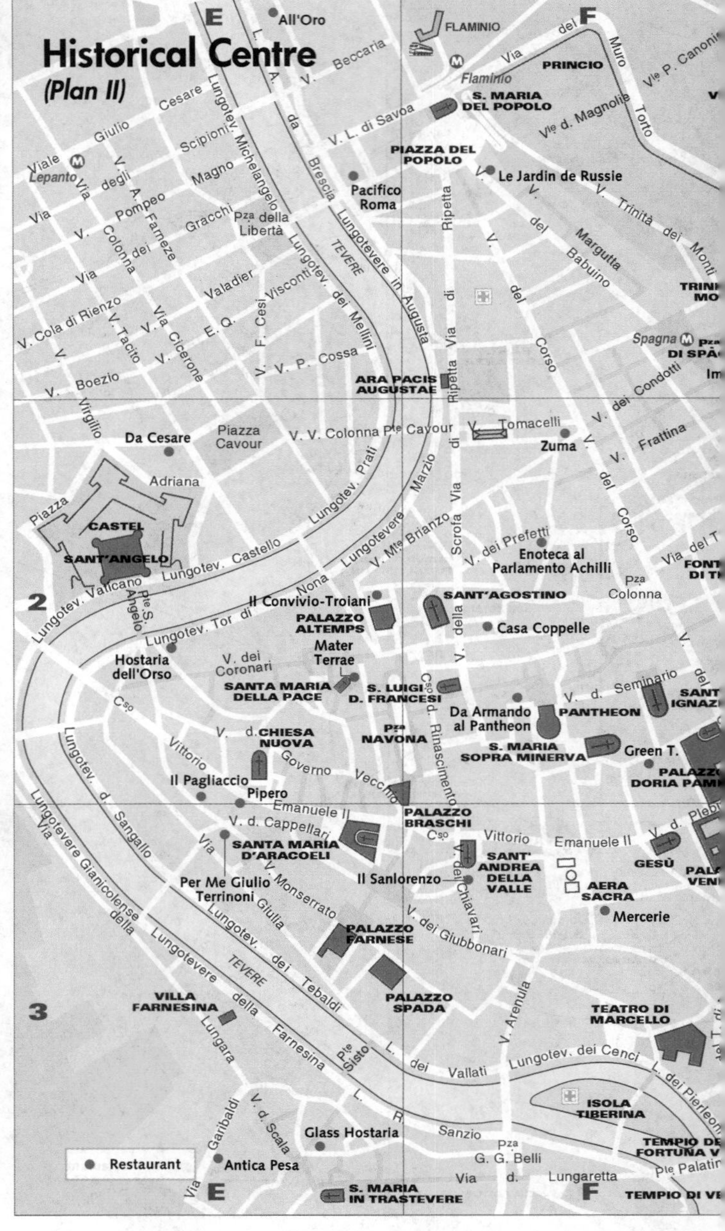
Historical Centre
(Plan II)
E
F
2
3
All'Oro
FLAMINIO
Flaminio
S. MARIA DEL POPOLO
PRINCIO
PIAZZA DEL POPOLO
Le Jardin de Russie
Pacifico Roma
Pza della Libertà
TEVERE
TRINI MO
Spagna
Pza DI SPA
ARA PACIS AUGUSTAE
Da Cesare
Piazza Cavour
Zuma
CASTEL SANT'ANGELO
Enoteca al Parlamento Achilli
Pza Colonna
Il Convivio-Troiani
PALAZZO ALTEMPS
SANT'AGOSTINO
Casa Coppelle
Hostaria dell'Orso
Mater Terrae
SANTA MARIA DELLA PACE
S. LUIGI D. FRANCESI
Da Armando al Pantheon
PANTHEON
SANT IGNAZ
CHIESA NUOVA
Pza NAVONA
S. MARIA SOPRA MINERVA
Green T.
PALAZZ DORIA PAMP
Il Pagliaccio
Pipero
PALAZZO BRASCHI
SANTA MARIA D'ARACOELI
Per Me Giulio Terrinoni
Il Sanlorenzo
SANT' ANDREA DELLA VALLE
AERA SACRA
GESÙ
PAL VEN
Mercerie
PALAZZO FARNESE
PALAZZO SPADA
VILLA FARNESINA
TEATRO DI MARCELLO
ISOLA TIBERINA
TEMPIO DI FORTUNA V
Glass Hostaria
Antica Pesa
Pza G. G. Belli
S. MARIA IN TRASTEVERE
TEMPIO DI VE
Restaurant

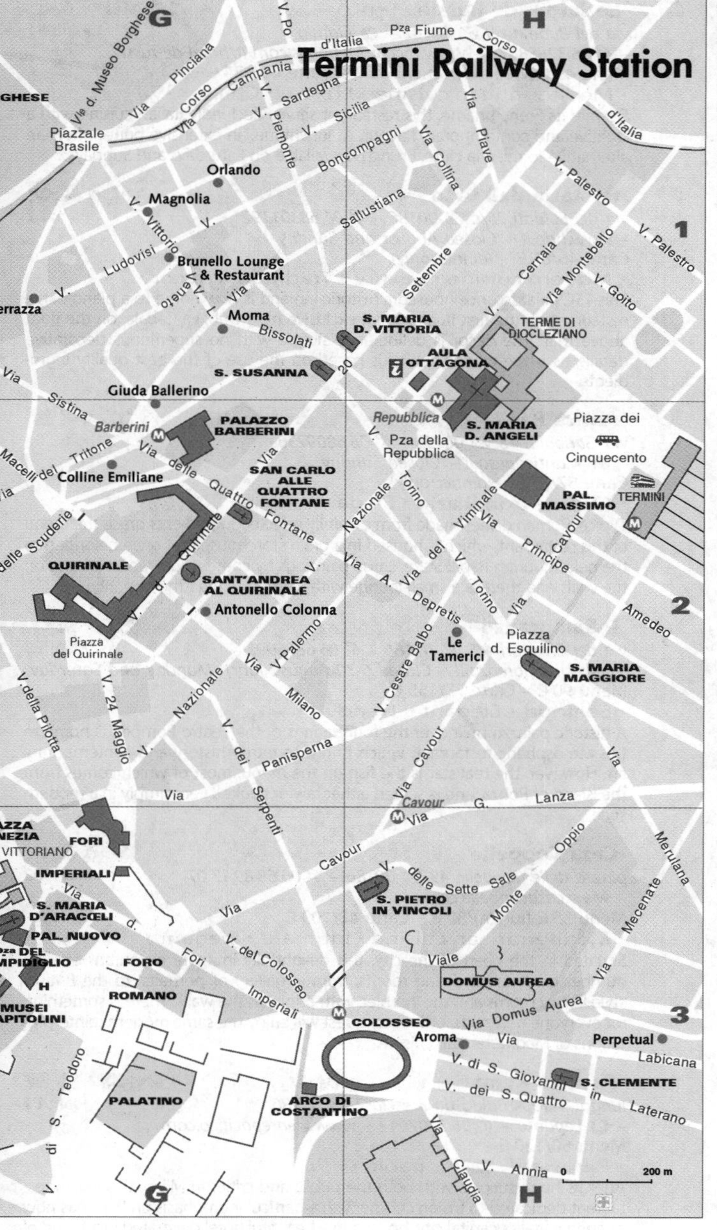
Termini Railway Station
Orlando
Magnolia
Brunello Lounge & Restaurant
Moma
S. MARIA D. VITTORIA
TERME DI DIOCLEZIANO
AULA OTTAGONA
S. SUSANNA
Giuda Ballerino
PALAZZO BARBERINI
Barberini
Repubblica
S. MARIA D. ANGELI
Piazza dei Cinquecento
Pza della Repubblica
Colline Emiliane
SAN CARLO ALLE QUATTRO FONTANE
PAL. MASSIMO
TERMINI
QUIRINALE
SANT'ANDREA AL QUIRINALE
Antonello Colonna
Piazza del Quirinale
Le Tamerici
Piazza d. Esquilino
S. MARIA MAGGIORE
Cavour
FORI IMPERIALI
VITTORIANO
S. MARIA D'ARACŒLI
PAL. NUOVO
FORO ROMANO
MUSEI CAPITOLINI
S. PIETRO IN VINCOLI
DOMUS AUREA
COLOSSEO
Aroma
Perpetual
S. CLEMENTE
PALATINO
ARCO DI COSTANTINO
0
200 m
G
H
1
2
3

Le Jardin de Russie – Hotel De Russie

via del Babuino 9 ✉ 00187 – Ⓜ Flaminio – ✆ 06 32888870 – www.roccofortehotels.com/it/hotel-de-russie
Plan: **F1**
Menu 45 € (weekday lunch)/65 € – Carte 66/124 €
• Mediterranean cuisine • Luxury • Chic •
Despite its French name, this restaurant serves decidedly Italian cuisine with a creative and contemporary flavour. At lunchtime, an extensive buffet offers an alternative to the à la carte. Brunch is available on Saturdays and Sundays.

Hostaria dell'Orso

via dei Soldati 25/c ✉ 00186 – ✆ 06 68301192 – www.hdo.it – Closed August and Sunday
Plan: **E2**
Carte 46/85 € – *(dinner only)*
• Modern cuisine • Luxury • Traditional décor •
This 15C palazzo once housed a historic inn and is now home to a piano bar, a restaurant on the first floor and an exclusive nightclub, La Cabala, on the floor above that. The decor is deliberately simple with no superfluous decorative details, as is the cuisine, which is based on the use of the best quality ingredients.

Antica Pesa

via Garibaldi 18 ✉ 00153 – ✆ 06 5809236 – www.anticapesa.it – Closed Sunday
Plan: **E3**
Carte 57/77 € – *(dinner only)*
• Cuisine from Lazio • Elegant • Cosy •
Typical Roman dishes made from carefully selected ingredients grace the menu of this restaurant, which is housed in a grain storehouse that once belonged to the neighbouring Papal State. Large paintings by contemporary artists hang on the walls and there is a small lounge with a fireplace near the entrance.

Il Sanlorenzo

via dei Chiavari 4/5 ✉ 00186 – ✆ 06 6865097 – www.ilsanlorenzo.it – Closed 6-30 August, lunch Monday and Saturday
Plan: **F3**
Menu 90 € – Carte 73/155 €
• Seafood • Elegant • Trendy •
A historic palazzo built over the foundations of the Teatro Pompeo is home to this atmospheric restaurant, which brings together history and contemporary art. However, the real star is the fish on the menu, most of which comes from the island of Ponza, and is served either raw or cooked very simply in a modern style.

Casa Coppelle

piazza delle Coppelle 49 ✉ 00186 – ✆ 06 68 89 17 07 – www.casacoppelle.com
Plan: **F2**
Menu 55 € (lunch)/80 € – Carte 48/109 €
• Mediterranean cuisine • Intimate • Elegant •
Situated in the heart of the city, this delightfully intimate restaurant offers a number of different dining rooms, from a 'gallery of portraits' to the British-style library rooms and the 'herbier' with prints on the walls. There is something for everyone here, although every guest will enjoy the same modern reinterpretations of Mediterranean cuisine.

Pacifico Roma – Hotel Palazzo Dama

lungotevere Arnaldo da Brescia 2 ✉ 00186 – Ⓜ Lepanto – ✆ 06 3207042 – www.wearepacifico.com
Plan: **E1**
Menu 60/120 € – Carte 38/104 €
• Peruvian • Fashionable •
After its huge success with both the public and critics in Milan, this Italian restaurant dedicated to fusion cuisine with a particular emphasis on Peru has now opened in Italy's capital city, housed in a beautiful hotel decorated in a blend of Art Nouveau and fashionable designer style.

Mater Terrae – Hotel Raphaël

XX A/C — Plan: **E2**

largo Febo 2 ✉ 00186 – ✆ 06 68283762 – www.raphaelhotel.com – closed Monday
Menu 90/110 € – Carte 60/94 €
• Vegetarian • Luxury • Intimate •

This evocatively named restaurant focuses on vegetarian and organic cuisine, which is served on its stunning terraces overlooking the rooftops and domes of the historic centre of Rome.

Mercerie

XX A/C — Plan: **F3**

Via di San Nicola de' Cesarini 4/5 ✉ 00186 – ✆ 3479714949 – www.mercerie.eu
Menu 30/80 € – Carte 28/51 € – *(dinner only)*
• Street Food • Trendy • Minimalist •

High-quality street food has arrived in the capital in the form of this modern, fashionable restaurant which bears the signature of famous chef Igles Corelli. The flavours here are typically Italian, with a few Roman and Lazian favourites on the menu. Dishes are also available to take away.

Le Tamerici

XX A/C — Plan: **H2**

Vicolo Scavolino, 79 ✉ 00186 – Ⓜ Barberini – ✆ 06 69200700 – www.letamerici.com
Menu 60/90 € – Carte 44/120 €
• Mediterranean cuisine • Elegant • Cosy •

Just a few metres from the Trevi Fountain, this unusual top-quality restaurant stands out among the many ordinary tourist-style options available in this district. Excellent modern Mediterranean cuisine served in a quiet and elegant setting.

Zuma

XX ♿ A/C — Plan: **F2**

via della Fontanella di Borghese 48 ✉ 00186 – Ⓜ Spagna – ✆ 06 99266622 – www.zumarestaurant.com – Closed 14-21 August
Menu 145 € – Carte 61/86 €
• Fusion • Fashionable • Trendy •

An international chain dedicated to contemporary Japanese food, Zuma has chosen the fourth and fifth floors (with a terrace) of Palazzo Fendi for its first Italian restaurant. The striking and decidedly fashionable cuisine consists of a delicious sushi corner, the robata grill and a selection of modern and creative dishes. A huge success ever since it opened.

Da Armando al Pantheon

X A/C — Plan: **F2**

salita dè Crescenzi 31 – Ⓜ Spagna – ✆ 06 68803034 – www.armandoalpantheon.it – Closed August, Saturday dinner and Sunday
Carte 36/65 € – *(number of covers limited, pre-book)*
• Roman • Family • Friendly •

Just a few meters from the Pantheon, this small family-run restaurant has been delighting locals and visitors for years with its traditional cuisine. Booking ahead is essential if you want to be sure of a table.

Felice a Testaccio

X A/C — Plan: **B3**

via Mastrogiorgio 29 ✉ 00153 – ✆ 06 5746800 – www.feliceatestaccio.com – Closed 1 week in August
Carte 36/49 €
• Traditional cuisine • Friendly • Traditional décor •

The simple, family, trattoria-style atmosphere of Felice a Testaccio is so popular that it is now almost essential to book ahead for a table. Make sure you try the legendary roast lamb with potatoes, as well as the *cacio e pepe* tonnarelli pasta and the tiramisù. Without a doubt, one of the standard-bearers of Latium cuisine.

Green T.

Via del Piè di Marmo 28 ✉ 00186 – ✆ 06 679 8628 Plan: **F2**
– www.green-tea.it – Closed 1 week in August and Sunday
Menu 10 € (lunch)/18 € – Carte 26/77 €
• Chinese • Minimalist • Friendly •
Owner Yan introduces tea lovers to the "Tao of Tea" (an introduction and tasting of this ancient beverage) in this original restaurant situated on four floors of a building not far from the Pantheon. The menu features the type of fine Chinese cuisine which has graced official banquets in China ever since the time of Chairman Mao.

ST-PETER'S BASILICA (Vatican City and Monte Mario) PLAN I-II

La Pergola – Hotel Rome Cavalieri

via Cadlolo 101 ✉ 00136 – ✆ 06 35092152 Plan: **A2**
– www.romecavalieri.com – Closed 3 weeks in August, January, Sunday and Monday
Menu 225 € – Carte 135/239 € – *(dinner only) (booking essential)*
• Modern cuisine • Luxury • Romantic •
This superb restaurant is suspended above the Eternal City in the magnificent setting of a panoramic roof garden. Mediterranean cuisine (chef Heinz Beck's constant passion), a systematic search for the best quality ingredients, and an added dose of creativity all come together in La Pergola. The restaurant's success speaks for itself.
➜ Fiore di zucca in pastella su fondo di crostacei e zafferano con caviale. Fagottelli "La Pergola". Sfera ghiacciata ai lamponi su crema al tè con lamponi cristallizzati

Enoteca la Torre – Hotel Villa Laetitia

lungotevere delle Armi 22/23 ✉ 00195 – Ⓜ Lepanto Plan: **B2**
– ✆ 0645668304 – www.enotecalatorreroma.com – Closed 10 days in August, Monday lunch and Sunday
Menu 60 € (weekday lunch)/130 € – Carte 90/135 €
• Modern cuisine • Liberty • Romantic •
This restaurant has a distinctly refined and elegant look. The antique furniture, flowers, columns and stucco all contribute to an Art Nouveau feel that would not be out of place in Paris. The cuisine continues to celebrate creativity with excellent results.
➜ Risotto al limone, tartufi di mare, asparagi e yogurt di bufala. Agnello alla Villeroy. Soffice di cheesecake, frutti di bosco fermentati e melissa.

Tordomatto (Adriano Baldassarre)

via Pietro Giannone 24 ✉ 00195 – ✆ 06 69352895 Plan: **A-B2**
– www.tordomattoroma.com – Closed lunch Monday and Tuesday
Menu 65/120 € – Carte 70/120 €
• Modern cuisine • Fashionable • Minimalist •
Herbs in pots on the window sills add an attractive touch to this restaurant situated just a stone's throw from the Vatican Museums. According to the chef "the cuisine is traditional and yet at the same time creative, with a real focus on local traditions as we believe that dishes should always reflect their locality". His bold and intelligent dishes more than live up to this claim.
➜ Quaglia, ostrica, patate, prezzemolo e alghe. Spaghettone ai funghi e dragoncello. Tiramisù di zabaione e zafferano, gelato di liquirizia e cacao.

Antico Arco

piazzale Aurelio 7 ✉ 00152 – ✆ 06 5815274 Plan: **B3**
– www.anticoarco.it
Carte 57/90 €
• Creative • Chic • Cosy •
The chef at this modern, bright and fashionable restaurant selects the best Italian ingredients to create innovative dishes based on traditional specialities.

Da Cesare

Plan: **E2**

via Crescenzio 13 ✉ 00193 – Ⓜ Lepanto – ✆ 06 6861227 – www.ristorantecesare.com – Closed 13 August-6 September, Sunday dinner
Carte 36/91 €
• Classic cuisine • Trattoria • Traditional décor •
As the Florentine lily on the glass at the entrance implies, the specialities of this place are Tuscan in origin, as well as seafood-based. Friendly atmosphere, ample wine list.

Settembrini

Plan: **B2**

via Settembrini 27 ✉ 00195 – Ⓜ Lepanto – ✆ 06 3232617 – www.viasettembrini.com – Closed Sunday dinner
Menu 28 € (lunch) – Carte 40/52 € – *(bookings advisable at dinner)*
• Modern cuisine • Bistro • Minimalist •
In just over 10 years, this fashionable bistro has become one of the leading restaurants in Rome. Recent changes have moved the dining room to the living area, which was previously occupied by the café. The cuisine served is simple, fresh and contemporary in feel. If you like unusual settings, ask for the table surrounded by bottles in the wine cellar.

Trattoria del Pesce

Plan: **B3**

via Folco Portinari 27 ✉ 00186 – ✆ 349 3352560 – www.trattoriadelpesce.it – Closed 14-20 August and lunch Monday
Carte 33/78 €
• Seafood • Bistro • Family •
A good selection of fresh and raw fish dishes served in a welcoming, vaguely bistro-style restaurant with young and competent staff. Parking can be difficult, but your patience is definitely rewarded!

PARIOLI — PLAN I-II

Assaje – Hotel Aldrovandi Villa Borghese

Plan: **B2**

via Ulisse Aldrovandi 15 – Ⓜ Policlinico – ✆ 06 3223993 – www.aldrovandi.com
Menu 80/140 € – Carte 80/110 € – *(dinner only)*
• Modern cuisine • Mediterranean décor • Luxury •
Assaje means 'abundance' in the Neapolitan dialect and the focus of this restaurant is on Mediterranean cuisine. The menu offers imaginative, modern dishes alongside more traditional, classic fare with a range of fish and meat options available.
→ Ostriche con crema di cetriolo, caviale e lattuga di mare. Battuta di fassona con senape rustica, ravanelli e tartufo nero. Paccheri di ananas con cremoso all'anice stellato, gelato di fior di latte e amarene.

Metamorfosi (Roy Caceres)

Plan: **B1**

via Giovanni Antonelli 30/32 ✉ 00197 – ✆ 06 8076839 – www.metamorfosiroma.it – Closed Saturday lunch and Sunday
Menu 110/140 € – Carte 86/130 € – *(dinner only)*
• Creative • Elegant • Cosy •
Enjoy excellent fusion cuisine with an eclectic and international feel. These are prepared by a young Colombian chef and his colleagues who hail from all four corners of the globe. Whether the dishes come from Lazio or South America, they are all colourful, exciting and full of flavour.
→ Riso "opercolato" funghi e nocciole. Anguilla di Comacchio, farro franto e carpione gelato. Mela, pinoli e gelsomino.

All'Oro (Riccardo Di Giacinto)

Plan: **B2**

Hotel The H'All Tailor Suite – via Giuseppe Pisanelli 25
✉ 00196 – ✆ 06 97996907 – www.ristorantealloro.it
Menu 88/150 € – Carte 87/133 € – *(dinner only)*
• Creative • Design • Intimate •

One of the dining rooms is decorated in a modern, pleasantly sophisticated New York style, while the other is vaguely English in feel. The menu continues to focus on creative cuisine with the occasional regional influence.

➜ Cappelletti in "brodo asciutto" con parmigiano, zafferano e limone. Vitello alla piemontese: grissini, giardiniera, salsa tonnata, terra di prezzemolo e caviale. Tiramisù All'Oro.

Bistrot 64

Plan: **B1**

via Guglielmo Calderini 64 ✉ 00196 – ✆ 06 3235531 – www.bistrot64.it – Closed 15 days in August, 1 week in January and Tuesday
Menu 50/90 € – Carte 60/80 € – *(dinner only)*
• Mediterranean cuisine • Bistro • Fashionable •

This restaurant boasts the attractive, informal decor of a bistro combined with surprisingly creative and imaginative cuisine. Courteous and attentive service.

➜ Spaghetto di patate con burro e alici. Manzo marinato al koji e asparagi. Bianco: yogurt, panna, fragola e cocco.

Sapori del Lord Byron – Hotel Lord Byron

Plan: **B2**

via G. De Notaris 5 ✉ 00197 – ✆ 06 3220404 – www.lordbyronhotel.com – Closed Sunday
Carte 42/74 € – *(dinner only)*
• Italian • Luxury • Classic décor •

Mirror-covered walls, dark octagonal tables and fine marble decor all add to the delightful Art Deco style of this restaurant. The food consists of delicious specialities from all over Italy, magnificently reinterpreted by the creative chef.

Al Ceppo

Plan: **C1**

via Panama 2 ✉ 00198 – ✆ 06 8551379 – www.ristorantealceppo.it – Closed 10-25 August, Saturday lunch June-September, Monday lunch rest of the year
Menu 25 € (weekday lunch) – Carte 42/78 €
• Mediterranean cuisine • Elegant • Traditional décor •

Elegant bistro-style wood panelling welcomes guests to this rustic yet elegant restaurant which serves Mediterranean cuisine reinterpreted with a contemporary twist. Specialities include grilled fish and meat dishes prepared in front of guests in the dining room.

Marzapane

Plan: **C2**

via Velletri 39 ✉ 00198 – ✆ 06 6478 1692 – www.marzapaneroma.com – Closed 10-25 August, 2-10 January, Tuesday lunch and Monday
Menu 30 € (weekday lunch)/95 € – Carte 48/90 €
• Creative • Classic décor • Cosy •

There is skill and expertise to the fore in the kitchen but also a young and informal atmosphere. The cuisine is modern with a twist.

Mamma Angelina

Plan: **C1**

viale Arrigo Boito 65 ✉ 00199 – ✆ 06 8608928 – Closed August and Wednesday
Menu 25/35 € – Carte 27/41 €
• Seafood • Trattoria • Neighbourhood •

After the antipasto buffet, the cuisine in this restaurant follows two distinct styles – fish and seafood, or Roman specialities. The paccheri pasta with seafood and fresh tomatoes sits in both camps!

La Terrazza – Hotel Eden XXXX

via Ludovisi 49 ✉ 00187 – Ⓜ Barberini – ✆ 06 47812752 Plan: **G1**
– www.dorchestercollection.com – Closed 7-21 August, 17-31 January and Tuesday
Menu 130/280 € – Carte 126/182 € – *(dinner only)*
• Modern cuisine • Luxury • Elegant •

Sitting in the modern, elegant dining room of La Terrazza, your attention is drawn to the spectacular roof-garden restaurant overlooking the city's rooftops. Also competing for your attention is the creative and original cuisine which has a hint of local flavour, although the main influence here is the chef's imagination.

➜ Spaghetti cacio e pepe del Madagascar, profumati ai boccioli di rosa. Stracotto di intercostata di manzo con asparagi e cipolla bianca. Variazione di limone amalfitano.

Aroma – Hotel Palazzo Manfredi XXX

via Labicana 125 ✉ 00184 – Ⓜ Colosseo Plan: **H3**
– ✆ 06 97615109 – www.aromarestaurant.it
Menu 110/180 € – Carte 104/188 € – *(bookings advisable at dinner)*
• Creative • Luxury • Romantic •

The brand-new open-view kitchen is the first thing guests see when they arrive at this delightful roof-garden restaurant which offers views of Ancient Rome from the Colosseum to the dome of St Peter's. The name pays tribute to both the city and the aromas provided by the creative and imaginative Mediterranean cuisine served here. There's also now a bistro-style eatery offering more informal dining.

➜ Rigatoni di kamut con crema di cicerchia e rafano, datterini e zucchine romanesche. Guazzetto di scorfano e gallinella con sfere di patate e lattuga di mare croccante. "Primavera": albicocca, miele e lavanda.

Marco Martini Restaurant XX

viale Aventino 121 ✉ 00186 – ✆ 06 45597350 Plan: **C3**
– www.marcomartinichef.com – Closed 14-21 August, 7-14 January, Saturday lunch and Sunday
Menu 200 € – Carte 67/97 € – *(booking advisable)*
• Creative • Trendy • Bistro •

Chef Martini and his team create modern and imaginative cuisine in this restaurant which boasts a winter garden-style dining room with a contemporary feel as well as a terrace-cum-lounge for aperitifs and snacks, dominated by a life-size marble Superman. The gourmet menu is also available at lunchtime if you book ahead.

➜ Tortello di mortadella, pizza bianca e pistacchi. Rombo, patate e carbonara. Cioccolato affumicato, scorzanera e Vermouth.

Moma X

via San Basilio 42/43 ✉ 00186 – Ⓜ Barberini Plan: **G1**
– ✆ 0642011798 – www.ristorantemoma.it – Closed Sunday
Menu 50/75 € – Carte 51/94 € – *(bar lunch)*
• Creative • Contemporary décor •

A plain, simple and contemporary-style restaurant on the first floor of a palazzo to the rear of Via Veneto, where all the attention is focused on the quality of the food. Unexpectedly elegant and creative, and occasionally based on original combinations, the dishes here showcase the personality of the talented young chef.

➜ Crudo di ricciola, mela verde e rafano. Triglia e 'nduja, salsa ai ricci di mare e ramolacci. Ricotta, visciole e pepe.

Domenico dal 1968 X

via Satrico 21 ✉ 00183 – ✆ 06 70494602 Plan: **C3**
– www.domenicodal1968.it – Closed 3 weeks in August, Sunday dinner and Monday
Carte 35/51 €
• Roman • Simple • Family •

It's well worth heading off the usual tourist trail to experience this authentic Roman trattoria, where you can try specialities such as fish broth with broccoli and local tripe. The restaurant also serves a selection of fish-based dishes which vary according to market availability.

Profumo di Mirto

viale Amelia 8/a ✉ 00181 – ☎ 06 786206 Plan: **C3**
– www.profumodimirto.it – Closed August and Monday
Menu 25 € (weekday lunch)/55 € – Carte 28/81 €
• Seafood • Family • Friendly •

The cuisine at this restaurant pays tribute to its owners' native Sardinia, in addition to other typical Mediterranean fare. There's a focus on fish and seafood reinterpreted in delicious, home-style dishes, including specialities such as ravioli with sea bass, prawns cooked in Vernaccia di Oristano and *seadas* fritters.

Al Ristoro degli Angeli

via Luigi Orlando 2 ✉ 00154 – ☎ 06 51436020 Plan: **B3**
– www.ristorodegliangeli.it – Closed Sunday
Carte 26/60 € – *(dinner only)*
• Roman • Vintage • Simple •

Situated in the Garbatella district, this restaurant with a bistro feel is embellished with vintage tables, chairs and lighting. The menu focuses on dishes from Lazio, such as mezze maniche pasta alla gricia (with bacon and cheese) flavoured with lemon, and sour-cherry tart. Delicious fish and vegetable options are also available.

Magnolia – Grand Hotel Via Veneto

via Sicilia 24 ✉ 00187 – Ⓜ Barberini – ☎ 06 487881 Plan: **G1**
– www.magnoliarestaurant.it – Closed August
Menu 135 € – Carte 87/170 € – *(dinner only)*
• Creative • Luxury • Elegant •

The superb cloister-style courtyard at this restaurant is the perfect setting for alfresco dining in fine weather. The dishes here resemble works of art in their composition, clever use of colour and beautiful presentation and strike a truly innovative note. Contemporary culinary technique is to the fore here.

Antonello Colonna

scalinata di via Milano 9/a ✉ 00184 – Ⓜ Termini Plan: **G2**
– ☎ 06 47822641 – www.antonellocolonna.it – Closed August, Sunday and Monday
Menu 95/30 € – Carte 80/124 € – *(dinner only)*
• Creative • Contemporary décor • Elegant •

This open-plan, glass-walled restaurant within the imposing Palazzo delle Esposizioni serves as a backdrop for creative cuisine inspired by traditional dishes. There's also a smoking area for cigar lovers, as well as a bistro below (also open at lunchtime) serving quicker meals.

Giuda Ballerino! – Hotel Sina Bernini Bristol

piazza Barberini 23 ✉ 00187 – Ⓜ Barberini Plan: **G2**
– ☎ 06 42010469 – www.giudaballerino.com – Closed 2 weeks in January and Sunday
Menu 35/90 € – Carte 84/142 €
• Modern cuisine • Elegant • Contemporary décor •

The kitchen opens into the dining room in this restaurant on the 8th floor of the historic Hotel Bernini, where large windows provide magnificent views of Rome. This is the elegant setting for Giuda Ballerino's modern restaurant, which is decorated with icons from some of the chef's favourite comics strips, such as Dylan Dog. Creative cuisine and an excellent wine list.

Brunello Lounge & Restaurant – Regina Hotel Baglioni

via Vittorio Veneto 72 ✉ 00187 – Ⓜ Barberini Plan: **G1**
– ☎ 06 421111 – www.baglionihotels.com
Menu 75/85 € – Carte 64/125 €
• Modern cuisine • Intimate • Elegant •

This warm, elegant restaurant has a faintly Oriental feel. It provides the perfect setting to enjoy superb Mediterranean cuisine, as well as international dishes that will appeal to foreign visitors to the capital.

Orlando

XX A/C
Plan: G1

via Sicilia 41 ✉ 00186 – ✆ 06 42016102 – www.orlandoristorante.it
Menu 20 € (weekday lunch)/70 € – Carte 45/101 €
• Sicilian • Regional décor •
An elegant, contemporary-style restaurant just a stone's throw from Via Veneto. It serves traditional Sicilian cuisine with a modern twist.

Osteria Fernanda

XX A/C
Plan: B3

via Crescenzo Del Monte 18/24 ✉ 00186 – ✆ 06 5894333 – www.osteriafernanda.com – Closed 13-20 August, 1 week in February, Saturday lunch and Sunday
Menu 55/69 € – Carte 42/72 €
• Creative • Minimalist • Neighbourhood •
In the district famous for its Porta Portese market, this restaurant run by two talented business partners is definitely worth a visit. One of the partners manages the front of house, while the other shows real passion in his creative cuisine made from locally sourced ingredients, as well as produce from further afield.

Perpetual

XX ♿ A/C
Plan: H3

piazza Iside 5 ✉ 00186 Roma – Ⓜ Manzoni – ✆ 0669367085 – www.perpetualrome.it
Menu 66/85 € – Carte 69/91 € – *(dinner only)*
• Modern cuisine • Minimalist • Trendy •
Situated to the rear of a tranquil piazza next to the ruins of the Temple of Isis, this modern restaurant serves gourmet cuisine. Designed by a renowned Spanish architect, the dining room offers views of the pastry kitchen at work. At lunchtime, guests can take advantage of the bistro-style service, also available outdoors in summer.

Colline Emiliane

X A/C
Plan: G2

via degli Avignonesi 22 ✉ 00187 – Ⓜ Barberini – ✆ 06 4817538 – Closed August, Sunday dinner and Monday
Carte 41/51 €
• Emilian • Trattoria •
Just a stone's throw from Piazza Barberini, this simple, friendly, family-run restaurant has just a few tables arranged close together. It serves typical dishes from the Emilia region, including fresh pasta stretched by hand in the traditional way.

Pastificio San Lorenzo

X A/C
Plan: C2

via Tiburtina 196 ✉ 00186 – ✆ 06 33974628 – www.pastificiosanlorenzo.com – Closed in July, August and Sunday
Menu 32/38 € – Carte 35/62 € – *(bookings advisable at dinner) (bar lunch)*
• Modern cuisine • Fashionable • Friendly •
The name of this modern restaurant with an international feel hints at its origins. An old industrial building once home to a pasta factory, the site subsequently became a centre for artists – right in the middle of the San Lorenzo university district – and it has retained a lively ambience despite its location away from the city's main tourist sites. The food doesn't disappoint with its intriguing blend of regional flavours and modern influences. Simpler, more restricted menu at lunchtime.

MILAN
MILANO

da-kuk/iStock

MILAN IN...

→ **ONE DAY**
Duomo, Leonardo da Vinci's 'The Last Supper' (remember to book first), Brera, Navigli.

→ **TWO DAYS**
Pinacoteca Brera, Castello Sforzesco, Parco Sempione, Museo del Novecento, a night at La Scala.

→ **THREE DAYS**
Giardini Pubblici and its museums, trendy Savona district.

If it's the romantic charm of places like Venice, Florence or Rome you're looking for, then best avoid Milan. If you're hankering for a permanent panorama of Renaissance chapels, palazzi, shimmering canals and bastions of fine art, then you're in the wrong place. What Milan does is relentless fashion, churned out with oodles of attitude and style. Italy's second largest city is constantly reinventing itself, and when Milan does a makeover, it invariably does it with flair and panache. That's not to say that Italy's capital of fast money and fast fashion doesn't have an eye for its past. The centrepiece of the whole city is the

magnificent gleaming white Duomo, which took five hundred years to complete, while up la via a little way, La Scala is quite simply the world's most famous opera house. But this is a city known primarily for its sleek and modern towers, many housing the very latest threads from the very latest fashion gurus.

Just north of Milan's centre lies Brera, with its much prized old-world charm, and Quadrilatero d'Oro, with no little new-world glitz; the popular Giardini Pubblici are a little further north east from here. South of the centre is the Navigli quarter, home to rejuvenated Middle Age canals, while to the west are the green lungs of the Parco Sempione. For those into art or fashion, the trendy Savona district is also a must.

EATING OUT

For a taste of Italy's regional cuisines, Milan is a great place to be. The city is often the goal of those leaving their home regions in the south or centre of the country; many open trattoria or restaurants, with the result that Milan offers a wide range of provincial menus. Excellent fish restaurants, inspired by recipes from the south, are a big draw despite the fact that the city is a long way from the sea. Going beyond the local borders, the emphasis on really good food continues and the quality of internationally diverse places to eat is better in Milan than just about anywhere else in Italy, including Rome. You'd expect avant-garde eating destinations to be the thing in this city of fashion and style, and you'd be right: there are some top-notch cutting-edge restaurants, thanks to Milan's famous tendency to reshape and experiment as it goes. For those who want to try out the local gastronomic traditions, risotto allo zafferano is not to be missed, nor is the cotoletta alla Milanese (veal cutlet) or the casoeula (a winter special made with pork and cabbage).

✿✿ Seta by Antonio Guida – Hotel Mandarin Oriental Milano

via Monte di Pietà 18 ✉ 20121 – Ⓜ Montenapoleone – ✆ 02 87318897 – www.mandarinoriental.com – Closed 5-26 August, 1-8 January, Saturday lunch and Sunday

Plan: **G1**

Menu 70 € (weekday lunch)/190 € – Carte 93/168 €

• Creative • Design • Luxury •

A complete dining experience offering sophisticated elegance, glamour and beautifully presented cuisine which is classic and modern, light and yet luxurious. Antonio Guida creates a menu which includes meat and fish dishes, combining the flavours of northern Italy with the scents of the south, with outstanding results.

➜ Risotto all'anice stellato con scorzonera e polvere di cavolo nero. Anguilla laccata al vino rosso con fegato grasso e salsa al rosmarino. Fragola con croccante al gianduia, caprino, salsa al litchi e gelato alla mandorla.

✿✿ Vun Andrea Aprea – Hotel Park Hyatt Milano

via Silvio Pellico 3 ✉ 20121 – Ⓜ Duomo – ✆ 02 88211234 – www.ristorante-vun.it – Closed August, 2 weeks in December, Sunday and Monday

Plan: **G2**

Menu 115/165 € – *(dinner only)*

• Modern cuisine • Elegant • Fashionable •

In this elegant and cosmopolitan restaurant decorated in neutral colours and adorned with drapery, Neapolitan chef Andrea Aprea serves the best of traditional Italian cuisine and a few dishes with the immediately recognisable character of his native city.

➜ Caprese... dolce salato. Baccalà, pizzaiola disidratata, olive verdi. Gianduja e lamponi.

✿ Cracco

galleria Vitttorio Emauele II ✉ 20123 Milano – Ⓜ Duomo – ✆ 02 876774 – www.ristorantecracco.it

Plan: **G2**

Menu 190 € – Carte 134/179 €

• Italian • Elegant • Luxury •

Arranged over several floors, this restaurant, one of the most versatile in the city, is connected directly to the Galleria thanks to skilful reconstruction work. Cracco is not just a restaurant – there's also a bar, a bistro serving snacks, a pastry shop and a wine boutique which is well worth a visit, plus the venue is often used to host special events. The menu features creative dishes alongside more traditional fare.

➜ Spaghettone al sugo di pomodoro giallo abbrustolito, astice e basilico. Triglie di scoglio, zuppa di piselli, menta e pomodoro. Petto d'anatra arrosto, agretti, ciliegie e lumache al prezzemolo.

✿ Il Ristorante Trussardi alla Scala

piazza della Scala 5 (palazzo Trussardi) ✉ 20121 – Ⓜ Duomo – ✆ 02 80688201 – www.trussardiallascala.com – Closed 2 weeks in August, 2 weeks December-January, Saturday lunch and Sunday

Plan: **G1**

Menu 140/160 € – Carte 75/160 €

• Modern cuisine • Luxury •

Combinations which are surprising but never overly bold or excessive, a careful choice of ingredients, and the use of seasonal produce are the hallmarks of this restaurant which specialises in gourmet reintrepretations of traditional Italian cuisine. The setting in a palazzo facing the Piazza della Scala is an added bonus.

➜ Riso agli agrumi, scampi e ginepro. Costoletta di vitello alla milanese. Soufflé alla lavanda.

Felix Lo Basso - Hotel Townhouse Duomo

piazza Duomo 21 (5° piano) 20122 – Duomo Plan: **G2**
– 02 49528914 – www.felixlobassorestaurant.it – Closed 13-27 August, 1-8 January, Saturday lunch and Sunday
Menu 112/190 € – Carte 108/168 €

• Creative • Contemporary décor • Elegant •

Puglian chef Felice Lo Basso's premises offer breathtaking views of the Duomo. He continues to prove his talent with his recognised trademark of light, creative and colourful cuisine, which is often playful and always focuses on the use of top-quality Italian ingredients.

➜ Rivisitazione di riso, cozze e patate. La parmigiana di mia mamma in un risotto. Polpo arrosto in salsa barbecue, spuma di patate, misticanza di erbe e fiori.

Savini

galleria Vittorio Emanuele II 20121 – Duomo Plan: **G2**
– 02 72003433 – www.savinimilano.it – Closed 3 weeks in August, 1-7 January, Saturday lunch and Sunday
Menu 95/160 € – Carte 86/128 €

• Creative • Luxury • Chic •

The entrance to this restaurant is through the Caffè Savini, which offers a selection of Italy's most famous dishes. A lift takes diners to the first floor, where the gourmet restaurant has been delighting guests with its mix of Milanese favourites and more creative fare since 1867.

Armani - Armani Hotel Milano

via Manzoni 31 20121 – Montenapoleone Plan: **G1**
– 02 8883 8702 – www.armanihotelmilano.com – Closed 5-27 August, 1-8 January, Sunday and Monday
Menu 110/240 € – Carte 84/203 € – *(dinner only) (booking advisable)*

• Modern cuisine • Luxury • Design •

Elegant and carefully prepared contemporary cuisine served on the seventh floor of a palazzo which is totally dedicated to the world of Armani. Superb views of Milan combine with a decor of black marble and backlit onyx to create an exclusive and fashionable ambience.

Don Carlos - Grand Hotel et de Milan

via Manzoni 29 20121 – Montenapoleone Plan: **G1**
– 02 72314640 – www.ristorantedoncarlos.it – Closed August
Carte 78/119 € – *(dinner only) (number of covers limited, pre-book)*

• Modern cuisine • Romantic • Vintage •

The tribute paid to Verdi by the Grand Hotel is accompanied in the small Don Carlos dining rooms by a homage to Italian and Milanese cuisine. Amid a setting of sketches, pictures and paintings dedicated to the world of opera, this restaurant is a favourite with music-lovers who come here after attending a performance in La Scala opera house nearby. Also perfect for a romantic dinner.

Il Ristorante Niko Romito - Hotel Bulgari

via privata Fratelli Gabba 7/b 20121
– Montenapoleone – 02 8058051 Plan: **G1**
– www.bulgarihotels.com
Menu 65 € – Carte 69/140 € – *(bar lunch)*

• Modern cuisine • Fashionable • Minimalist •

Overlooking an unexpected yet beautiful garden, this attractive restaurant boasts the same exclusive style as the rest of the hotel. The cuisine showcases top quality Italian produce in dishes that are modern and contemporary in flavour.

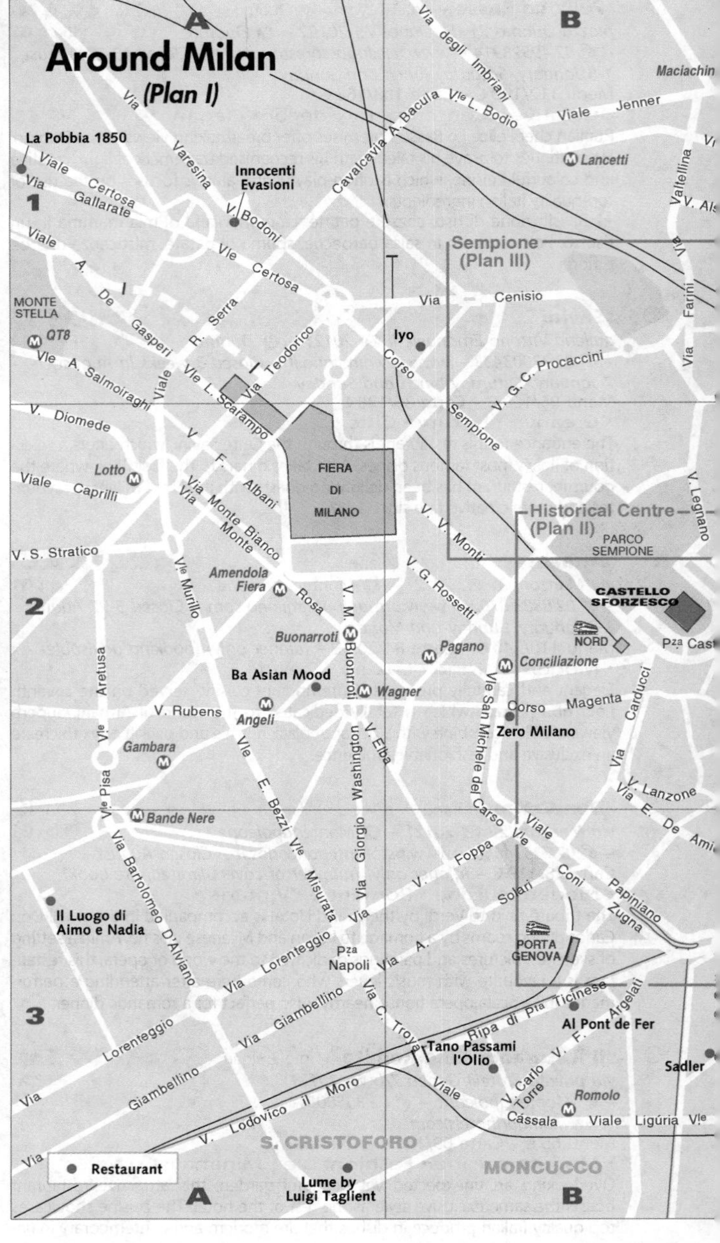
Around Milan
(Plan I)
A
B
1
2
3
La Pobbia 1850
Innocenti
Evasioni
Iyo
Ba Asian Mood
Zero Milano
Il Luogo di
Aimo e Nadia
Tano Passami
l'Olio
Al Pont de Fer
Sadler
Lume by
Luigi Taglient
Sempione
(Plan III)
Historical Centre
(Plan II)
PARCO
SEMPIONE
CASTELLO
SFORZESCO
FIERA
DI
MILANO
MONTE
STELLA
QT8
Lotto
Amendola
Fiera
Buonarroti
Pagano
Conciliazione
Wagner
Angeli
Gambara
Bande Nere
Lancetti
Maciachin
Romolo
NORD
PORTA
GENOVA
Pza Cas
Pza
Napoli
S. CRISTOFORO
MONCUCCO
Via degli Imbriani
Vle L. Bodio
Viale Jenner
Cavalcavia A. Bacula
Via Valtellina
V. Als
Via Farini
Via Varesina
V. Bodoni
Viale Certosa
Via Gallarate
Vle Certosa
Viale A. De Gasperi
Viale R. Serra
Via Teodorico
Via Cenisio
Corso Sempione
V. G. C. Procaccini
Vle A. Salmoiraghi
Vle L. Scarampo
V. Diomede
V. F. Albani
Viale Caprilli
Via Monte Bianco
Via Monte Rosa
V. V. Monti
V. Legnano
V. S. Stratico
Vle Murillo
V. G. Rossetti
V. M. Buonrroti
Vle San Michele del Carso
Corso Magenta
Via Carducci
Vle Aretusa
V. Rubens
Vle Pisa
Vle E. Bezzi
Via Giorgio Washington
V. Elba
V. Lanzone
Via E. De Ami
Viale Coni Zugna
Viale Papiniano
Via Foppa
Via Solari
Vle Misurata
Via Bartolomeo D'Alviano
Via Lorenteggio
Via A.
Via Giambellino
Via C. Troya
Ripa di Pta Ticinese
V. F. Argelati
V. Carlo Torre
Viale Cassala
Viale Ligúria
V. Lodovico il Moro
Restaurant

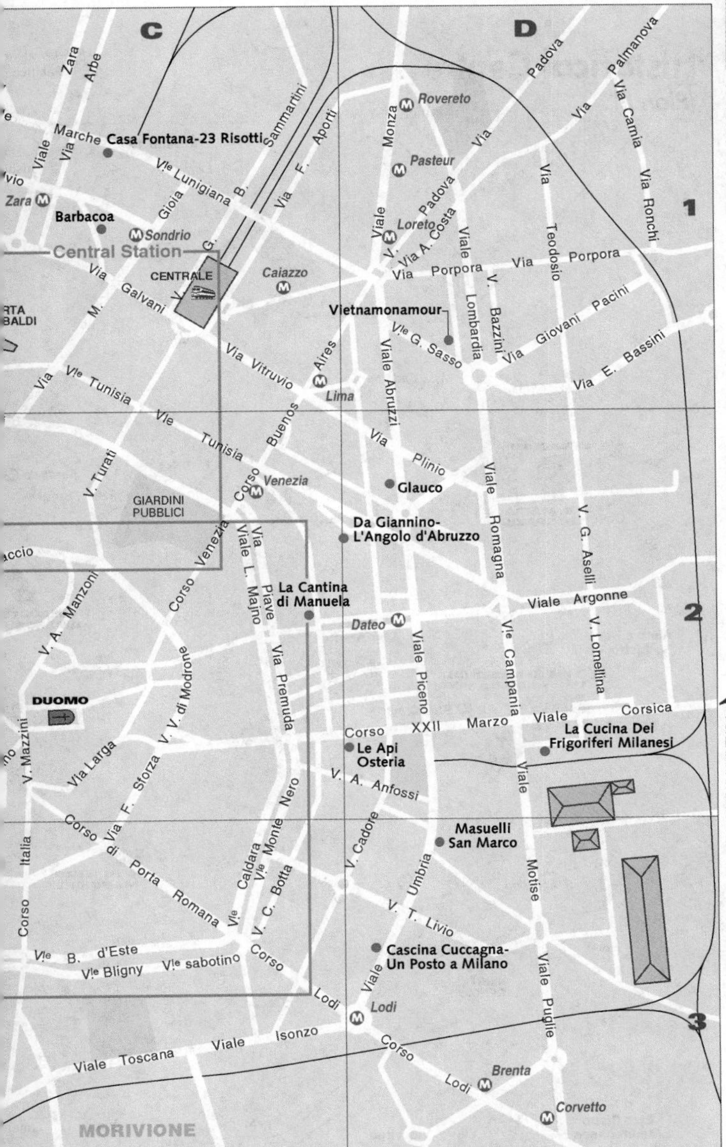

C D

1

Casa Fontana-23 Risotti
Barbacoa
Central Station
CENTRALE
Vietnamonamour
GIARDINI PUBBLICI
Glauco
Da Giannino-L'Angolo d'Abruzzo
La Cantina di Manuela
DUOMO
Le Api Osteria
La Cucina Dei Frigoriferi Milanesi
Masuelli San Marco
Cascina Cuccagna-Un Posto a Milano
MORIVIONE

2

3

FORLANINI DI LINATE EST

0 1 Km

C D

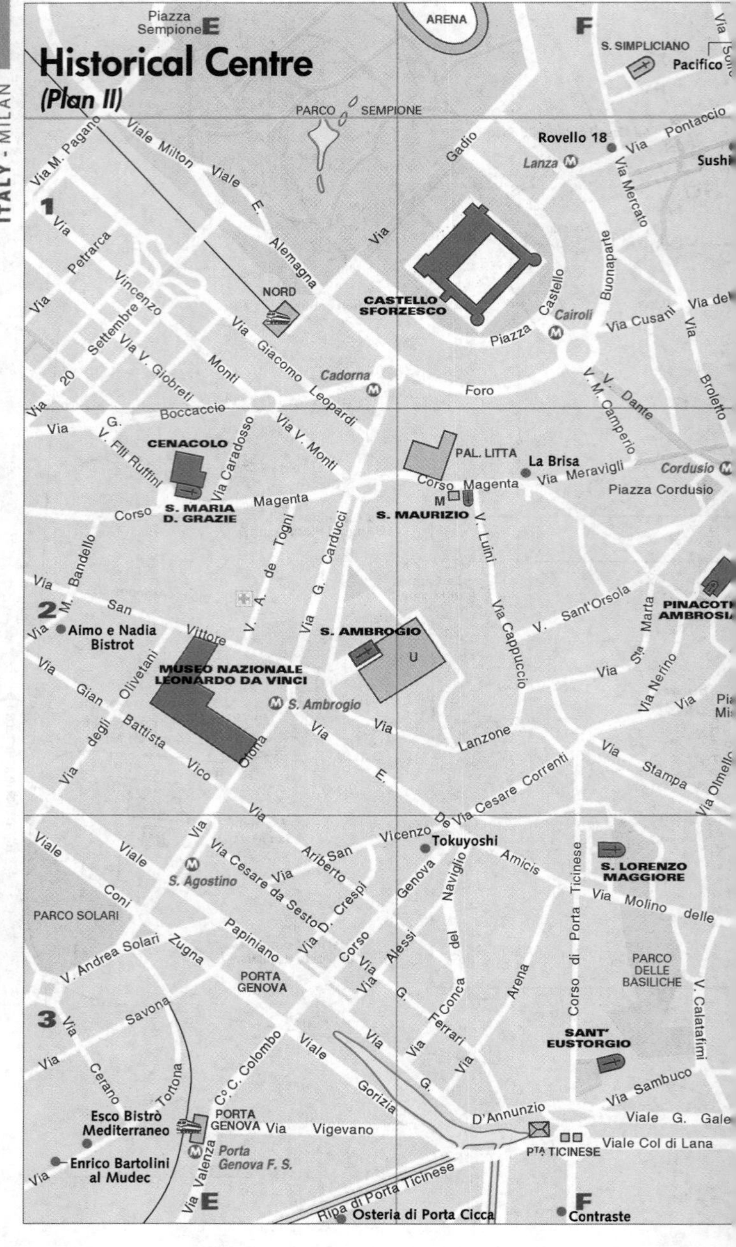
Historical Centre
(Plan II)
Piazza Sempione
E
F
ARENA
S. SIMPLICIANO
Pacifico
PARCO SEMPIONE
Via M. Pagano
Viale Milton
Viale E. Alemagna
Rovello 18
Via Pontaccio
Lanza
Sushi
Gadio
Via Mercato
1
Via Petrarca
Vincenzo
Via Buonaparte
NORD
CASTELLO SFORZESCO
Piazza Castello
Cairoli
Via Cusani
Via del
Via 20 Settembre
Via V. Giobreti
Via Giacomo Leopardi
Monti
Cadorna
Foro
V. V. Dante
V. M. Camperio
Via Broletto
Via G. Boccaccio
V. Flli Ruffini
CENACOLO
Via Caradosso
Via V. Monti
PAL. LITTA
La Brisa
Via Meravigli
Cordusio
Piazza Cordusio
Corso Magenta
S. MARIA D. GRAZIE
M
S. MAURIZIO
V. Luini
Via Bandello
Via A. de Togni
Via G. Carducci
Via M.
San Vittore
2
Aimo e Nadia Bistrot
S. AMBROGIO
U
Via Cappuccio
V. Sant'Orsola
Via Sta Marta
PINACOTI AMBROSIA
MUSEO NAZIONALE LEONARDO DA VINCI
Via Olivetani
Via Gian Battista Vico
S. Ambrogio
Via Lanzone
Via Nerino
Via Stampa
Via degli
Olona
Via E. De Amicis
Via Cesare Correnti
Via Olmetto
Via San Vicenzo
Tokuyoshi
Viale Coni
Via Cesare da Sesto
S. Agostino
Via Ariberto
Via D. Crespi
Corso Genova
Naviglio
Corso di Porta Ticinese
S. LORENZO MAGGIORE
Via Molino delle
PARCO SOLARI
Papiniano
Via Alessi
Via del
PARCO DELLE BASILICHE
V. Andrea Solari
Zugna
PORTA GENOVA
Via G. Ferrari
Conca
Arena
V. Calatafimi
3
Via Savona
SANT' EUSTORGIO
Via Cerano
Tortona
C.so C. Colombo
Viale Gorizia
Via Sambuco
Esco Bistrò Mediterraneo
PORTA GENOVA
Via Vigevano
D'Annunzio
Viale G. Gale
PTA TICINESE
Viale Col di Lana
Porta Genova F. S.
Enrico Bartolini al Mudec
Via Valenza
Ripa di Porta Ticinese
Osteria di Porta Cicca
Contraste

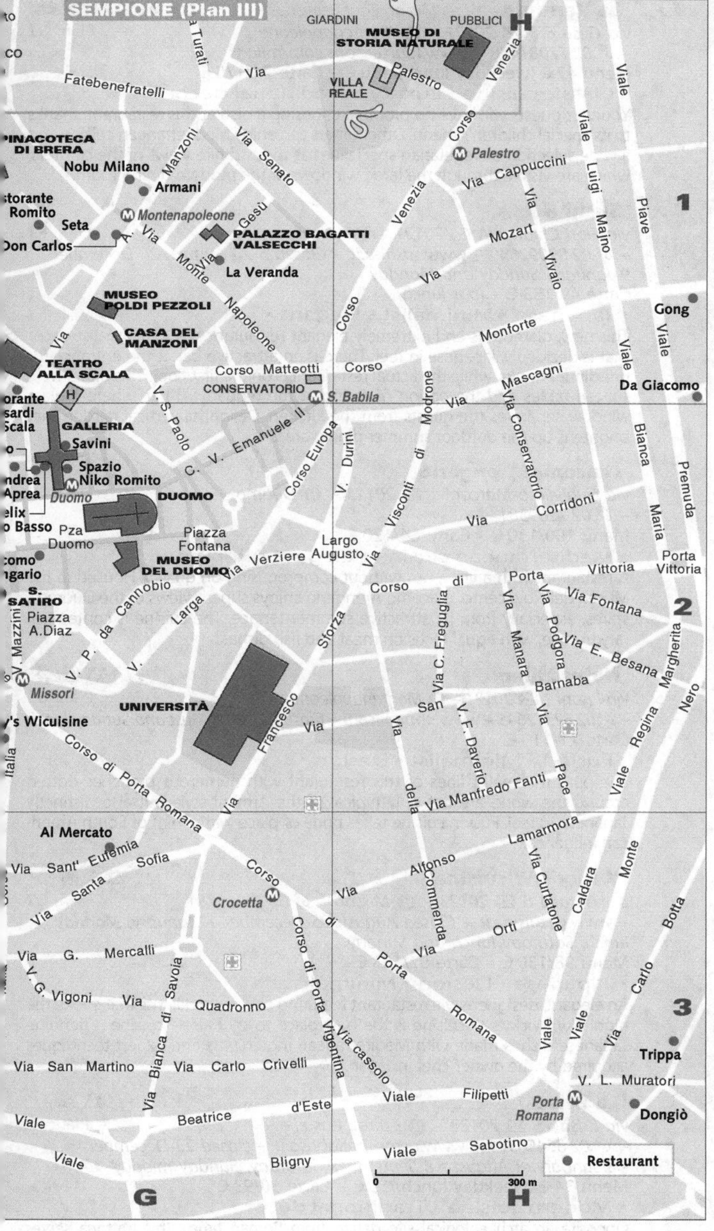
SEMPIONE (Plan III)
GIARDINI PUBBLICI
MUSEO DI STORIA NATURALE
VILLA REALE
PINACOTECA DI BRERA
Nobu Milano
Armani
Seta
Don Carlos
Montenapoleone
PALAZZO BAGATTI VALSECCHI
La Veranda
MUSEO POLDI PEZZOLI
CASA DEL MANZONI
TEATRO ALLA SCALA
CONSERVATORIO
S. Babila
Palestro
GALLERIA
Savini
Spazio Niko Romito
Duomo
DUOMO
Piazza Fontana
MUSEO DEL DUOMO
Largo Augusto
S. SATIRO
Piazza A.Diaz
Missori
UNIVERSITÀ
Al Mercato
Crocetta
Porta Romana
Gong
Da Giacomo
Porta Vittoria
Trippa
Dongiò
Restaurant
1
2
3
G
H
300 m

La Veranda – Hotel Milano Four Seasons

via Gesù 6/8 ✉ 20121 – Ⓜ Montenapoleone Plan: **G1**
– ☎ 02 77081478 – www.fourseasons.com/milan
Menu 42 € (weekday lunch)/130 € – Carte 74/175 €
• Classic cuisine • Luxury • Traditional décor •

Younger guests will have no problem choosing a dish at this restaurant, thanks to its special children's menu. Other diners can enjoy Mediterranean cuisine and a wide selection of vegetarian specialities as they admire views of the cloisters, which are visible through the large windows of the modern dining room.

Sushi B

via Fiori Chiari 1/A ✉ 20121 – Ⓜ Lanza Plan: **F1**
– ☎ 02 89092640 – www.sushi-b.it – Closed 5-20 August, 24 December-9 January, Sunday and Monday
Carte 49/133 € – *(bar lunch)*
• Japanese • Minimalist • Elegant •

This new, glamorous and extremely elegant restaurant has a minimalist decor that is decidedly Japanese in feel. There is an attractive bar at the entrance for pre-dinner drinks, while the actual restaurant is on the first floor. This offers well-spaced tables and the option of eating at the teppanyaki bar, where a glass window separates the guests from the kitchen. Delightful vertical garden that brightens up the outdoor summer dining area.

Giacomo Arengario

via Guglielmo Marconi 1 ✉ 20123 – Ⓜ Duomo Plan: **G2**
– ☎ 02 72093814
Menu 100/130 € – Carte 64/120 €
• Mediterranean cuisine • Elegant • Romantic •

A restaurant with a view, but without compromising on quality. Housed in the Museo del Novecento, Giacomo Arengario enjoys superb views of the Duomo's spires, especially from its attractive summer terrace. The cuisine is contemporary in style, with equal focus on meat and fish dishes.

Nobu Milano

via Pisoni 1 ✉ 20121 – Ⓜ Montenapoleone Plan: **G1**
– ☎ 02 62312645 – www.armani.com – Closed 13-20 August and Sunday lunch
Carte 71/110 €
• Fusion • Minimalist • Design •

The pure minimalist lines of this restaurant with numerous branches dotted around the world are not only typical of the Armani style but also distinctly Japanese in feel. Fusion cuisine takes pride of place with a hint of South American influence.

Wicky's Wicuisine

corso Italia 6 ✉ 20123 – Ⓜ Missori – ☎ 02 89093781 Plan: **G2**
– www.wicuisine.it – Closed August, 25 December-1° January, Monday lunch, Saturday lunch and Sunday
Menu 98/130 € – Carte 57/153 €
• Japanese • Design • Minimalist •

An elegant, designer-style restaurant featuring colours and lights that evoke the night sky, Wicky's Wicuisine is the best place to try Kaiseki cuisine – genuine Japanese dishes made with Mediterranean ingredients and expert techniques acquired by the owner-chef in Japan.

La Brisa

via Brisa 15 ✉ 20123 – Ⓜ Cairoli Castello. Plan: **F2**
– ☎ 02 86450521 – www.ristorantelabrisa.it – closed 23 December - 3 January, 8 August - 8 September, Saturday, Sunday midday
Menu 34 € (weekday lunch)/55 € – Carte 50/93 €
• Modern cuisine • Traditional décor •

Opposite an archaeological site dating from Roman times, this trattoria serves modern, regional cuisine. Summer dining on the veranda overlooking the garden.

Da Giacomo

XX A/C
Plan: H1

via P. Sottocorno 6 ✉ 20129 – ✆ 02 76023313 – www.giacomoristorante.com
Carte 52/107 €

• Seafood • Friendly • Neighbourhood •

This old Milanese trattoria dates from the early 20C. Seafood enthusiasts will be delighted by the numerous fish specialities on offer. The menu also includes a few meat dishes, as well as Alba truffles, Caesars' mushrooms and cep mushrooms in season.

Masuelli San Marco

X A/C
Plan: D3

viale Umbria 80 ✉ 20135 – Ⓜ Lodi TIBB – ✆ 02 55184138 – www.masuellitrattoria.it – Closed 25 August-9 September, 26-30 December, 1-7 January, Monday lunch and Sunday
Menu 22 € (weekday lunch) – Carte 39/71 €

• Lombardian • Vintage • Inn •

A rustic atmosphere with a luxurious feel in a typical trattoria, with the same management since 1921; cuisine strongly linked to traditional Lombardy and Piedmont recipes.

Al Mercato

X ♿ A/C
Plan: G3

via Sant'Eufemia 16 ✉ 20121 – Ⓜ Missori – ✆ 02 87237167 – www.al-mercato.it – Closed August
Carte 54/88 € – *(dinner only) (number of covers limited, pre-book)*

• Modern cuisine • Simple • Contemporary décor •

The tiny dining room serves as a backdrop for gourmet cuisine in the evening and a more restricted menu at lunchtime. In another part of the restaurant, the lively Burger Bar (no reservations; the queue can be long) offers various tasty snacks, including the inevitable hamburger.

Rovello 18

X 🍇 A/C
Plan: F1

via Tivoli 2 ang. Corso Garibaldi ✉ 20123 – Ⓜ Lanza – ✆ 02 72093709 – www.rovello18.it – Closed 3 weeks in August, Sunday lunch and Saturday
Carte 42/130 €

• Italian • Vintage • Traditional décor •

A simple setting for cuisine which focuses on carefully chosen ingredients presented with the minimum of fuss. Although the menu features a few specialities from Milan, most of the dishes served here are classically Italian in style.

Spazio Niko Romito

X A/C
Plan: G2

galleria Vittorio Emanuele II (3° piano del Mercato del Duomo) ✉ 20123 – Ⓜ Duomo – ✆ 02 878400 – www.nikoromitoformazione.it – Closed 14-31 August
Carte 39/65 €

• Creative • Design •

This restaurant on the top floor of the Mercato del Duomo acts as a training ground for youngsters from the cookery school run by Romito (3-star Michelin restaurant in Abruzzo); although you would never guess from the food that these chefs are beginners. Three rooms offer views of the kitchen, Galleria and cathedral respectively and the food made from top quality produce is full of flavour.

Enjoy good food without spending a fortune!
Look out for the Bib Gourmand symbol
to find restaurants offering good food at great prices!

Alice-Eataly Smeraldo (Viviana Varese)

piazza XXV Aprile 10 ✉ 20123 – Ⓜ Porta Garibaldi FS – ✆ 02 49497340 – www.aliceristorante.it – Closed Sunday

Plan: L2

Menu 55 € (weekday lunch)/150 € – Carte 87/144 €

• Creative • Design • Fashionable •

In 2014, the famous Teatro Smeraldo in Milan became the setting for a large Eataly complex, in which the Alice restaurant is certainly one of the highlights. The attractive designer-style decor makes the perfect backdrop for the imaginative cuisine that includes a number of fish dishes.

➜ Lasagnetta multicolore con baccalà, spuma di baccalà alle erbe aromatiche, catalogna saltata e bergamotto. Capitone con salsa di fondo bruno al profumo d'oriente, zuppa di cipollotto di Tropea e crema di cavolo rosso fermentato. Meringa con spuma di zabaglione, vellutata di mandorla, mandorle croccanti di Noto, sorbetto al caffè, cioccolato amaro Oriado e pepe timut.

Berton

via Mike Bongiorno 13 ✉ 20123 – Ⓜ Gioia – ✆ 02 67075801 – www.ristoranteberton.com – Closed 2 weeks in August, Christmas Holidays, Saturday and Monday lunch, Sunday

Plan: L1

Menu 120 €, 110/135 € – Carte 85/188 €

• Creative • Design • Minimalist •

Light, modern and minimalist in style, the restaurant decor echoes the cuisine served here, which uses just a few ingredients to create original and beautifully presented dishes.

➜ Risotto con gambero crudo e corallo di crostacei. Carrè d'agnello arrosto, friggitelli con ricotta, cipolla e salsa verde. Uovo di yogurt e mango.

Joia (Pietro Leemann)

via Panfilo Castaldi 18 ✉ 20124 – Ⓜ Repubblica – ✆ 02 29522124 – www.joia.it – Closed 14-20 August, 24 December-7 January, Sunday

Plan: M2

Menu 90/130 € – Carte 83/120 €

• Vegetarian • Minimalist • Chic •

The pupil of a great master, the chef here became a vegetarian after a gradual philosophical and spiritual transformation in Asia. After many years, his focus is now on natural food, which is avant-garde, experimental, skilfully prepared and beautifully presented. Full of flavour, the menu here is 80% vegan and gluten free.

➜ Perseveranza (ravioli napoletani, uno farcito di sugo napoletano, uno di ricotta e aglio degli orsi, con emulsione di pecorino sardo, taccole e macchie di vino ridotto). Anima Mundi (tortino di patate, lenticchie e ortiche, con erbe del nostro orto e fragole, caprino di mandorle). Macondo (cioccolato e nocciole biodinamiche, salse di mango e more di gelso, spuma di armelline e gelato di fragole allo zenzero).

La Cucina Dei Frigoriferi Milanesi

via Piranesi 10 ✉ 20121 – ✆ 02 3966 6784 – www.lacucinadeifrigoriferimilanesi.it – Closed Saturday lunch and Sunday

Plan: D2

Menu 14 € (weekday lunch)/33 € – Carte 35/49 €

• Modern cuisine • Contemporary décor •

An interesting location in the artistic-cultural setting of the Frigoriferi Milanesi industrial complex for this restaurant with a modern feel both in its decor and its cuisine. The restaurant offers an "unstructured" menu, which instead of dividing the courses into the traditional antipasti, starters and main courses, consists of different dishes which can be selected however guests prefer.

Dongiò

X AC

via Corio 3 ✉ 20135 – Ⓜ Porta Romana – ✆ 02 5511372 Plan: **H3**
– Closed 3 weeks in August, Saturday lunch and Sunday
Carte 26/40 €
• Calabrian • Family • Rustic •

A taste of Calabria in Milan. This family-run restaurant is simply furnished and always busy – a typical traditional trattoria of the type that is more and more difficult to find. The house speciality is *spaghettoni alla tamarro* (with a sausage and tomato sauce), while the menu also features fresh pasta, 'nduja sausage and the ever-present peperoncino.

Serendib

X AC

via Pontida 2 ✉ 20121 – Ⓜ Moscova – ✆ 02 6592139 Plan: **K2**
– www.serendib.it
Menu 15 € – Carte 24/40 €
• Indian • Simple • Oriental décor •

Serendib, the old name for Sri Lanka, means "to make happy" – an ambitious promise, but one which this restaurant manages to keep! True to its origins, the tempting menu focuses on Indian and Sri Lankan cuisine, including dishes such as biriyani rice and chicken curry.

Trippa

X AC

Via Giorgio Vasari, 3 ✉ 20135 – Ⓜ Porta Romana Plan: **H3**
– ✆ 327 668 7908 – www.trippamilano.it – Closed 2 weeks in August and Sunday
Carte 32/54 € – *(dinner only)*
• Italian • Trattoria • Vintage •

Simple, informal and with a slightly retro feel, this restaurant serves a range of dishes from all over Italy, including the tripe which gives the restaurant its name. Unfussy and uncomplicated, the cuisine prepared by the skilful young chef using top-quality ingredients makes this one of the best trattorias in Italy. House specialities include Milanese risotto with grilled marrow, *vitello tonnato* and, of course, the ever-present tripe!

Da Giannino-L'Angolo d'Abruzzo

X AC

via Pilo 20 ✉ 20129 – Ⓜ Porta Venezia Plan: **D2**
– ✆ 02 29406526
Carte 29/39 €
• Cuisine from Abruzzo • Traditional décor • Friendly •

A warm welcome combined with a simple but lively atmosphere and typical dishes from the Abruzzo region make this a popular place to eat. Generous portions and excellent roast dishes.

Acanto – Hotel Principe di Savoia

XXXX AC

piazza della Repubblica 17 ✉ 20124 – Ⓜ Repubblica Plan: **M2**
– ✆ 02 62302026 – www.dorchestercollection.com – Closed 8-23 August
Menu 35 € (weekday lunch)/120 € – Carte 82/126 € – *(bar lunch)*
• Modern cuisine • Luxury • Chic •

Large elegant spaces full of light characterise this modern restaurant which pampers its guests with excellent, attentive service and classic contemporary-style cuisine. There's an original "La Tavolozza dello Chef" formula at lunchtime, which offers a choice of dishes combining a starter with a main course and a side dish.

Terrazza Gallia – Excelsior Hotel Gallia

XXXX AC

piazza Duca d'Aosta 9 – Ⓜ Centrale FS Plan: **M1**
– ✆ 02 67853514 – www.excelsiorhotelgallia.com
Menu 75/95 € – Carte 61/137 €
• Creative • Luxury • Contemporary décor •

Situated on the seventh floor with panoramic views of the city, this restaurant is an excellent choice for a light lunch, a cocktail or an informal dinner. Two young brothers from Naples are at the helm here, creating traditional Italian and Lombardian dishes with a creative and contemporary touch.

Daniel

XXX

via Castelfidardo 7, angolo via San Marco ✉ 20121 Plan: **L2**
– Ⓜ Moscova – ✆ 02 63793837 – www.danielcanzian.com – Closed 3 weeks in August, Saturday lunch and Sunday
Menu 18 € (weekday lunch)/80 € – Carte 54/97 €

• Italian • Contemporary décor • Elegant •

One of the first things to strike you in this restaurant is the open-view kitchen, where the young friendly chef happily interacts with diners. His menu focuses on traditional Italian classics, as well as a few more inventive offerings, all of which are prepared using the very best ingredients. Simpler fare available at lunchtime.

Barbacoa

XX

via delle Abbadesse 30 ✉ 20123 – Ⓜ Zara Plan: **C1**
– ✆ 02 6883883 – www.barbacoa.it
Menu 50 € – *(dinner only)*

• Grills • Intimate • Cosy •

Meat-lovers will be in their element here. For a fixed price, guests help themselves to as much as they want from the buffet (mainly salads and vegetables), while waiters move from table to table serving a selection of around fifteen meat options, all barbecued in churrasceria style over a traditional Brazilian rodizio. A unique flavour of South America in Milan.

Glauco

XX

via Achille Maiocchi 29 ✉ 20123 – Ⓜ Lima Plan: **D2**
– ✆ 0220241973 – www.ristoranteglaucomilano.com
Menu 75/120 € – Carte 72/142 €

• Seafood • Intimate •

Intimate, welcoming and modern, this restaurant serves fish and seafood prepared by a young chef with plenty of experience behind him. Most of the fish comes from Sicily.

Gong

XX

corso Concordia 8 ✉ 20123 – ✆ 02 76023873 Plan: **H1**
– www.gongmilano.it – Closed 14-19 August and Monday lunch
Menu 70/90 € – Carte 38/129 €

• Chinese • Minimalist • Elegant •

Italy meets the Far East in this elegant restaurant with a menu that includes Chinese specialities, internationally influenced dishes and plenty of other tempting delicacies. The imposing onyx gongs which lend their name to the restaurant are a striking feature in the dining room.

Pacifico

XX

via Moscova 29 ✉ 20123 Milano – Ⓜ Moscova Plan: **F1**
– ✆ 02 8724 4737 – www.wearepacifico.com – Closed 7-21 August
Menu 50 € – Carte 34/86 €

• Peruvian • Bistro • Elegant •

Cosmopolitan Milan has warmly embraced this lively restaurant, which acts as an ambassador for Peruvian cuisine with the occasional Asian influence. There is an excellent choice of ceviche – raw fish or seafood dishes marinated in lemon and flavoured with spices such as chilli pepper and coriander – which are a typical speciality of Latin American countries along the Pacific coast.

Trattoria Trombetta

XX

largo Bellintani 1 ✉ 20123 – Ⓜ Porta Venezia Plan: **M2**
– ✆ 02 35941975 – www.trattoriatrombetta.eu – Closed Monday
Menu 60 € – Carte 41/69 €

• Modern cuisine • Neighbourhood • Friendly •

A typical modern Milanese trattoria with a relaxed atmosphere. The dishes focus on Lombardy and, in a broader sense, Italy, with particular attention paid to the use of seasonal produce. Brunch is served on Sundays alongside a more concise menu.

Il Liberty

XX A/C

viale Monte Grappa 6 ✉ 20124 – ✆ 02 29011439 Plan: **L2**
– www.il-liberty.it – Closed 12-19 August, 1°-7 January, Saturday lunch and Sunday
Menu 20 € (lunch)/80 € – Carte 48/87 € – *(number of covers limited, pre-book)*

• Creative • Cosy • Cosy •

Occupying an Art Nouveau-style palazzo, this small restaurant with two rooms and a loft area has a friendly, welcoming atmosphere. The menu includes a selection of fish and meat dishes, with a choice of simpler and more reasonably priced options at lunchtime.

Vietnamonamour

X A/C

via A. Pestalozza 7 ✉ 20131 – Ⓜ Piola Plan: **D1**
– ✆ 02 70634614 – www.vietnamonamour.com – Closed Monday lunch and Sunday
Menu 13 € (weekday lunch)/25 € – Carte 31/58 €

• Vietnamese • Romantic •

This restaurant would certainly have been appreciated by the French writer Marguerite Duras, who would have rediscovered the ambience of her native Vietnam here. If you're not familiar with Vietnamese dishes, don't be put off by the menu – everything will be clearly explained when you order and you're sure to fall under the spell of this fascinating country.

Le Api Osteria

X A/C

Via Carlo Foldi 1 ✉ 20123 – ✆ 0284575100 Plan: **D2**
– www.leapiosteria.com
Menu 16 € (weekday lunch)/53 € – Carte 40/64 € – *(pre-book)*

• Modern cuisine • Simple •

After a number of years working in Italy and elsewhere in Europe, chef Hide Matsumoto has at last opened his own restaurant, where his gently creative Mediterranean cuisine takes centre stage in the simply decorated dining room.

Casa Fontana-23 Risotti

X A/C

piazza Carbonari 5 ✉ 20125 – Ⓜ Sondrio Plan: **C1**
– ✆ 02 6704710 – www.23risotti.it – Closed 2 weeks in August, 1-12 January, Monday and Saturday lunch in summer
Carte 43/72 €

• Lombardian • Traditional décor • Cosy •

Despite the obligatory 25min wait for your food, this restaurant is well worth a visit for its excellent risottos. Attractive pictures of rice fields on the walls.

Pisacco

X A/C

via Solferino 48 ✉ 20121 – Ⓜ Moscova Plan: **L2**
– ✆ 02 91765472 – www.pisacco.it – Closed 12-19 August and Monday
Menu 14 € (lunch)/50 € – Carte 36/63 €

• Modern cuisine • Trendy • Colourful •

A modern and informal restaurant with attentive service and reasonable prices. Excellent selection of creative dishes, as well as some reinterpretations of classic favourites, such as polenta and baccalà (salted cod) and Caesar salad.

Un Posto a Milano-Cascina Cuccagna

X A/C

via Cuccagna 2 ✉ 20121 Milano – ✆ 02 5457785 Plan: **D3**
– www.unpostoamilano.it – Closed Monday
Menu 15 € (weekday lunch)/20 € – Carte 29/60 €

• Classic cuisine • Country house • Traditional décor •

Occupying an old restored farmhouse in urban Milan, the Cascina Cuccagna is both a restaurant and a cultural centre. It is surrounded by greenery, providing a delightful oasis in the city. At lunchtime, choose from a copious and reasonably priced buffet. The evening menu is more elaborate but still offers good value for money.

La Cantina di Manuela

via Carlo Poerio 3 ✉ 20129 – ✆ 02 76318892 Plan: **C2**
– www.lacantinadimanuela.it
Carte 32/58 €
• Modern cuisine • Bistro • Colourful •
The dining room in this young, dynamic restaurant is surrounded by bottles of wine. Elaborate dishes feature on the menu, with antipasti available in the evening. At lunchtime these are replaced by various salads aimed at a business clientele in a hurry. Milanese-style cutlets are the house speciality.

FIERAMILANOCITY - SEMPIONE - NAVIGLI

(viale Fulvio Testi, Niguarda, viale Fermi, viale Certosa, corso Sempione, piazza Carlo Magno, via Monte Rosa, San Siro, via Novara, via Washington, Ripa di porta Ticinese, Corso S. Gottardo) **PLAN I**

Enrico Bartolini al Mudec

via Tortona 56 ✉ 20123 – Ⓜ Porta Genova Plan: **E3**
– ✆ 02 84293701 – www.enricobartolini.net – Closed 2 weeks in August, Monday lunch and Sunday
Menu 145/180 € – Carte 110/195 €
• Creative • Contemporary décor • Trendy •
This elegant, contemporary-style restaurant on the third floor of the Museo delle Culture offers an original location and attentive, solicitous service. The apparent simplicity of the menu sets the tone for a concert of dishes which feature extraordinary soloists backed by choirs of ingredients and variations on the same theme, all arranged across several courses which are striking for their imaginative quality. The conductor of this culinary orchestra is young Bartolini, poised and composed on the outside yet full of passion and energy within.
➜ Alici in incontro tra saor e carpione con caviale, ostriche e cren. Piccione arrosto e "bentornati" grissini bolliti. Soufflè ai limoni dolci, gelato allo yogurt, lamponi e liquirizia.

Il Luogo di Aimo e Nadia (Alessandro Negrini e Fabio Pisani)

via Montecuccoli 6 ✉ 20147 – Ⓜ Primaticcio
– ✆ 02 416886 – www.aimoenadia.com Plan: **A3**
– Closed August, 1-8 January, Saturday lunch and Sunday
Menu 45 € (weekday lunch)/195 € – Carte 90/186 €
• Creative • Design •
Although Aimo and Nadia are no longer at the helm of this restaurant, their style of cuisine is echoed by two excellent chefs. They have maintained the restaurant's tradition of creating Italian regional dishes with a modern twist. The focus has always been on top-quality ingredients (even before it was fashionable), making this restaurant in Via Montecuccoli one of the cradles of this culinary ethos. This is now kept alive through exciting, memorable cuisine created by two fine chefs.
➜ Stoccafisso ragno mantencato all'olio extravergine di oliva. Il piccione: petto, con pralinato di porcini essiccati e nocciole, e coscia. Amari: cioccolato venezuelano, arance amare di Sicilia, caffé arabica.

Contraste (Matias Perdomo)

via Meda 2 ✉ 20123 – ✆ 02 49536597 Plan: **F3**
– www.contrastemilano.it – Closed 2 weeks in August, 1°-10 January, Tuesday from 12 September to 15 Juin, Sunday rest of the year
Menu 100/140 € – *(dinner only)*
• Modern cuisine • Elegant • Historic •
Glittering red silicon chandeliers hover above diners at this restaurant, which is decorated here and there with Art Nouveau touches. The cuisine is traditional yet reinterpreted in presentation and appearance, offering contrasting flavours that leave guests impressed and delighted.
➜ Cozze cacio e pepe con granita di salicornia. Rognoncini di coniglio, anguilla affumicata e sorbetto d'aceto. Tarte tatin alle mele con gelato di pasta frolla.

Lume by Luigi Taglienti

via Watt 37 ✉ 20123 – ✆ 02 80888624 Plan: **A3**
– www.lumemilano.com – Closed 14-26 August, 10 days in January, Sunday dinner and Monday
Menu 40 € (weekday lunch), 120/170 € – Carte 93/250 €
• Modern cuisine • Design • Minimalist •

Offering a delightful experience for all the senses, this restaurant has recently been extended with an outdoor area, Orto di Lume, a garden blooming with plants whose fruits are used in the imaginative dishes created by chef Luigi Taglienti. The cuisine focuses on the culinary heritage of Italian flavours, combined with the liberal use of various sauces.

➜ Musetto di vitello cotto a lungo nello spumante con insalata di mostarda dolce. Lasagna tradizionale alla bolognese. Omelette a sorpresa, fior di latte, amarena e pan di spezie al cassis.

Sadler

via Ascanio Sforza 77 ✉ 20141 – Ⓜ Romolo Plan: **B3**
– ✆ 02 58104451 – www.sadler.it – Closed 2 weeks in August, 1 week in January and Sunday
Menu 85 € (weekdays)/185 € – Carte 78/158 € – *(dinner only)*
• Creative • Elegant •

One of the first chefs to focus on the aesthetics of a dish, with a focus on modern, geometric and colourful presentation, Sadler prepares beautiful creations which can be compared with contemporary art, of which he is an avid fan. Dishes are listed with the year in which they were invented: starting with the famous padellata di crostacei (sautéed shellfish) of 1996. The menu features a selection of mainly fish and seafood dishes which tell the story of the gastronomic history of Milan and other areas of Italy.

➜ Risotto al nero di seppia e oro con spaghetti di calamari e contrasto di mango. Padellata di crostacei, con carciofi di riviera alla carbonella e spuma al dragoncello. Varietà di cioccolato in differenti forme e sapori.

Innocenti Evasioni (Tommaso Arrigoni)

via privata della Bindellina ✉ 20155 – Ⓜ Portello Plan: **A1**
– ✆ 02 33001882 – www.innocentievasioni.com – Closed 6-31 August, 1-10 January and Sunday
Menu 50/80 € – Carte 55/90 € – *(dinner only)*
• Creative • Elegant •

Although his colleague in the kitchen has moved on, the owner-chef at this restaurant continues to prepare creative cuisine, including reinterpretations of Milanese dishes. Meat and fish specialities feature on the menu, to be enjoyed in the unexpectedly delightful garden with just a few sought-after tables.

➜ Spaghetti di Gragnano al pesto di nocciole e foglie di sedano, capperi e zeste di limone. Polpo rosolato, patata affumicata, cima di rapa, pomodoro e pane croccante alla cipolla. Sorbetto di albicocche e alloro, burro bianco al rum, pralinato e lamponi croccanti.

Iyo

via Piero della Francesca 74 ✉ 20154 Plan: **B1**
– Ⓜ Gerusalemme – ✆ 02 45476898 – www.iyo.it – Closed 2 weeks in August, Christmas Holidays, Monday and Tuesday lunch
Menu 95 € – Carte 41/140 €
• Japanese • Design • Contemporary décor •

The presence of international chefs from Italy and Japan in this restaurant ensures that Iyo's distinctive culinary style is kept alive. The cuisine served here is always original, creative and inspired by Japan, and looks towards the future. The wine list is also excellent, with its selection of around 800 wines and a good choice of sake, with different varieties to accompany different dishes.

➜ Kakisu - ostrica e gelée d'ostrica, kombu, granita di daikon all'aceto di riso e yuzu. Asado - manzo, crema di mais abbrustolito, funghi cardoncelli affumicati e salvia in tempura. La sfera - meringa al lime, mousse al cioccolato bianco, sorbetto al kabosu e composta di sedano, mela verde e menta.

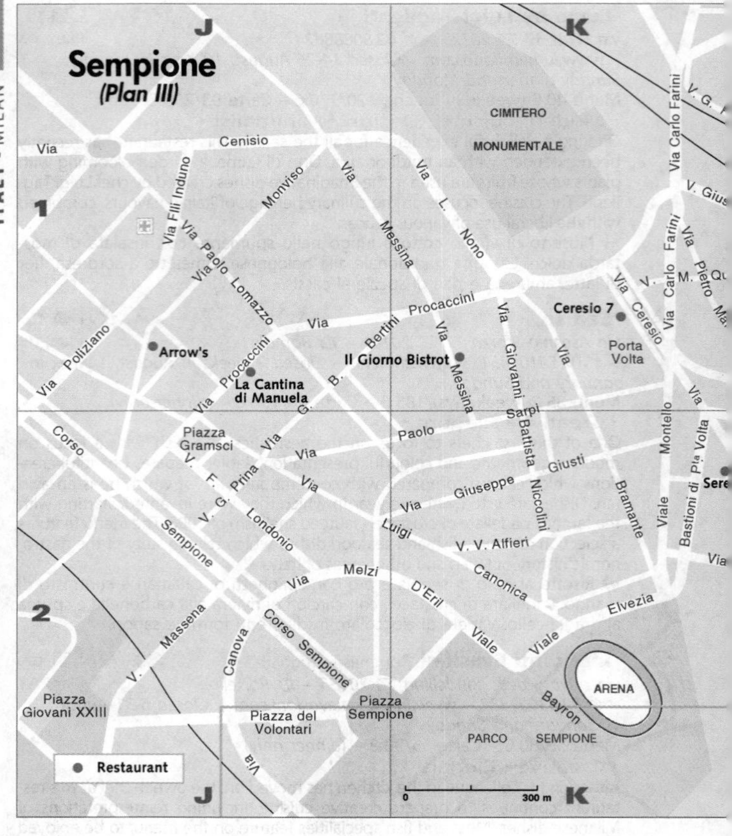

✿ Tano Passami l'Olio (Gaetano Simonato) XX A/C

via Villoresi 16 ✉ *20143 –* ✆ *02 8394139* Plan: **B3**
– www.tanopassamilolio.it – Closed August, 24 December-6 January and Sunday
Menu 65/135 € – Carte 100/145 € – *(dinner only)*
• Creative • Elegant • Classic décor •

A far cry from the busy, noisy atmosphere of the Navigli district, this restaurant offers hushed dining rooms with a classic, elegant feel. The cuisine is decidedly original and striking for its unusual combinations and refined presentation. Excellent olive oils are also available to add additional flavour to your meal. Smoking room available.

➜ Spaghetti alla chitarra ripieni di bottarga di uovo di gallina in crema di burrata e grana. Carrè d'agnello col suo fondo di cottura e miele con carciofo alla menta. Bavarese di anice stellato con sfera d'isomalto con mousse di carota e mou.

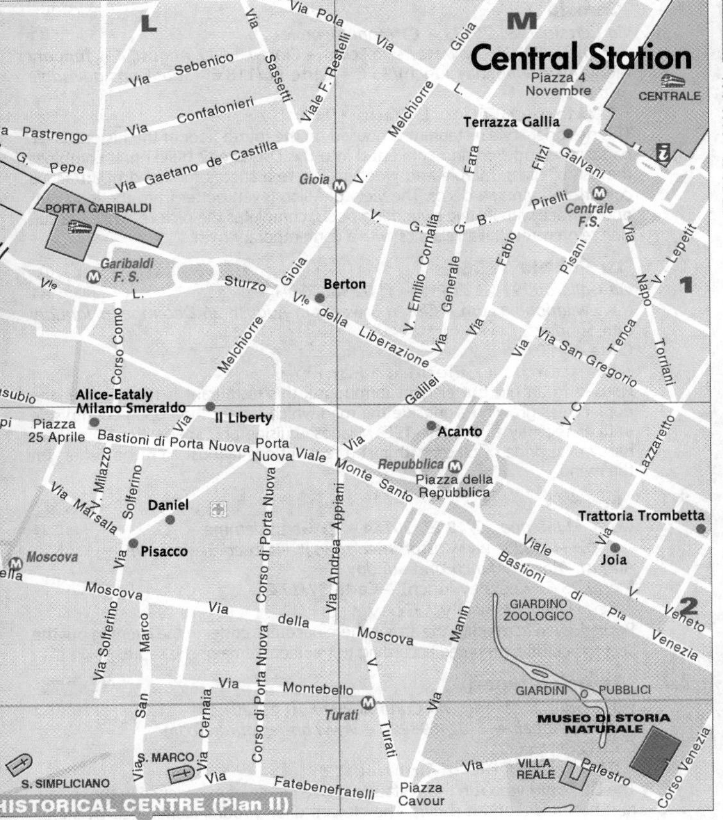

Tokuyoshi

XX ♿ A/C

Plan: **F3**

via San Calocero 3 ✉ 20123
– Ⓜ Sant'Ambrogio
– ✆ 0284254626
www.ristorantetokuyoshi.com
– Closed 3 weeks in August, 2 weeks in January and Monday
Menu 110/140 € – Carte 75/160 € – *(dinner only)*

• Creative • Minimalist • Trendy •

Mention creative cuisine in Milan and Yoji Tokuyoshi immediately comes to mind. With typical Japanese humility and precision, this chef has been serving imaginative cuisine in his eponymous restaurant for the past couple of years. His original dishes full of decisive flavours take diners on a culinary voyage around his native Japan and adopted home of Italy, the country that has nurtured his professional development.

➜ Pane, burro e alici. "Piccione con sasso". Babà allo Chateau d'Yquem.

Ceresio 7

XXX

via Ceresio 7 ✉ 20123 – Ⓜ Monumentale Plan: **K1**
– ✆ 0231039221 – www.ceresio7.com – Closed 14-17 August, 1-4 January
Menu 40 € (weekday lunch)/95 € – Carte 66/118 € – *(bookings advisable at dinner)*

• Modern cuisine • Design • Trendy •

This designer-style restaurant is housed on the fourth floor of the historic ENEL palazzo, remodelled and converted into the Dsquared2 building. It combines the use of brass, marble and wood to create a successful blend of attractive colours and vintage decor. The view of Milan (even better from the long outdoor terrace with its two swimming pools) completes the picture, while the cuisine reinterprets Italian classics with a contemporary twist.

La Pobbia 1850

XXX

via Gallarate 92 ✉ 20151 – ✆ 02 38006641 Plan: **A1**
– www.lapobbia.com – Closed 3 weeks in August, 26 December-6 January and Sunday
Carte 44/70 €

• Lombardian • Elegant • Family •

Housed in an old but elegant farmhouse, this restaurant is named after the poplar trees growing alongside the road which ran through open countryside until as recently as the late 19C. Milanese cuisine and specialities from Lombardy take pride of place, with just a few options (almost all meat dishes) on the menu.

Arrow's

XX

via A. Mantegna 17/19 ✉ 20154 – Ⓜ Gerusalemme Plan: **J1**
– ✆ 02 341533 – www.ristorantearrows.it – Closed 3 weeks in August, Monday lunch and Sunday
Menu 25 € (weekday lunch) – Carte 37/77 €

• Seafood • Family • Cosy •

Packed, even at midday, the atmosphere becomes cosier in the evening but the seafood cuisine, prepared according to tradition, remains the same.

Ba Asian Mood

XX

via R. Sanzio 22, ang. via Carlo Ravizza 10 ✉ 20123 Plan: **A2**
– Ⓜ De Angeli – ✆ 024693206 – www.ba-restaurant.com
Carte 28/116 €

• Chinese • Chic • Minimalist •

The Liu family who run this restaurant have plenty of experience in the restaurant business – and it shows. The elegant dining room, illuminated by subtle lighting, has an international, almost fashionable appeal, while the typically Chinese cuisine is carefully prepared using top-quality ingredients with the occasional Italian influence.

La Cantina di Manuela

XX

via Procaccini 41 ✉ 20154 – Ⓜ Gerusalemme Plan: **J1**
– ✆ 02 3452034 – www.lacantinadimanuela.it
Carte 32/58 €

• Modern cuisine • Neighbourhood • Friendly •

As its name suggests ("cantina" is the Italian for cellar), this restaurant offers a good selection of wines, many of which are available by the glass and to take away. Modern cuisine with a focus on Italian recipes and meat specialities.

Aimo e Nadia BistRo

X

via Matteo Bandello 14 ✉ 20121 – Ⓜ Conciliazione Plan: **E2**
– ✆ 0248026205 – www.bistroaimoenadia.com
Menu 30 € (lunch) – Carte 47/68 €

• Italian • Chic • Trendy •

This bistro with a small yet charming and original dining room is a simpler and more informal version of the famous 2-star restaurant. The focus is the same, with an emphasis on Italian ingredients used in dishes which bring out their full flavour and integrity.

Osteria di Porta Cicca

ripa di Porta Ticinese 51 ✉ 20143 – Ⓜ Porta Genova Plan: **E3**
– ✆ 02 8372763 – www.osteriadiportacicca.com – Closed 14-21 August and Monday
Menu 40/70 € – Carte 37/85 €
• Modern cuisine • Romantic • Cosy •
A welcoming, intimate ambience with a hint of Provence in an attractive canal side setting. The only sign of a traditional osteria is in the name – the cuisine is modern and innovative in style.

Esco Bistrò Mediterraneo

via Tortona 26 ✉ 20123 – Ⓜ Porta Genova Plan: **E3**
– ✆ 028358144 – www.escobistromediterraneo.it – Closed 13-26 August, Saturday lunch and Sunday
Menu 16 € (weekday lunch)/55 € – Carte 42/58 €
• Mediterranean cuisine • Trendy • Friendly •
A modern restaurant which is informal and welcoming, and where your first (but not only) impression is that of finding yourself in an architect's studio, as a guest of the owner. Attractive, contemporary-style cuisine with a hint of Piedmontese flavour.

Al Pont de Ferr

Ripa di Porta Ticinese 55 ✉ 20143 Plan: **B3**
– Ⓜ Porta Genova FS – ✆ 02 89406277 – www.pontdeferr.it – Closed 24 December-6 January
Menu 20 € (weekday lunch)/130 € – Carte 34/90 €
• Creative • Osteria • Trendy •
Excellent cuisine with a playful touch and an emphasis on Italy's fine culinary traditions, which have been given a new, contemporary twist by chef Ivan. The wine cellar continues to be enhanced by a constant search for new wines and innovative producers, with a good selection also available by the glass. The lunchtime business menu offers smaller portions of the same delicious cuisine.

Zero Milano

corso Magenta 87 ✉ 20123 – Ⓜ Conciliazione Plan: **B2**
– ✆ 02 45474733 – www.zeromagenta.com
Menu 48/64 € – Carte 21/79 € – *(dinner only)*
• Japanese • Minimalist • Chic •
There's absolutely zero compromise on attention and quality in this restaurant, where the cuisine is made from top-quality ingredients. Although traditional Japanese specialities feature on the menu, more often the dishes are the result of a blend of Japanese and Western styles. In a dark dining room with subtle lighting the amber-coloured tables are offset by onyx walls, while the traditional sushi bar offers guests a great view of the skilful chef at work. The success of this Italian-run restaurant with a Japanese chef has led to the recent opening of an offshoot in Tokyo!

LUXEMBOURG

LUXEMBOURG
LËTZEBUERG

SerrNovik/iStock

LUXEMBOURG
LËTZEBUERG

Xantana/iStock

LUXEMBOURG CITY IN...

→ **ONE DAY**
Place d'Armes, Ducal Grand Palace, National Museum of History and Art, Chemin de la Corniche.

→ **TWO DAYS**
Luxembourg City History Museum, Bock Casemates, the Grund.

→ **THREE DAYS**
Kirchberg Plateau, Museum of Modern Art, concert at Luxembourg Philharmonic Hall.

Luxembourg may be small but it's perfectly formed. Standing high above two rivers on a sandstone bluff, its commanding position over sheer gorges may be a boon to modern visitors, but down the centuries that very setting has rendered it the subject of conquest on many occasions. Its eye-catching geography makes it a city of distinctive districts, linked by spectacular bridges spanning lush green valleys.

The absolute heart of the city is the old town, its most prominent landmarks the cathedral spires and the city squares with their elegant pastel façades – an ideal backdrop to the 'café culture' and a

worthy recipient of UNESCO World Heritage Status. Winding its way deep below to the south west is the river Pétrusse, which has its confluence with the river Alzette in the south east. Follow the Chemin de la Corniche, past the old city walls and along the Alzette's narrow valley to discover the ruins of The Bock, the city's first castle, and the Casemates, a labyrinth of rocky 17C and 18C underground defences. Directly to the south of the old town is the railway station quarter, while down at river level to the east is the altogether more attractive Grund district, whose northerly neighbours are Clausen and Pfaffenthal. Up in the north east, connected by the grand sounding Pont Grand-Duchesse Charlotte, is Kirchberg Plateau, a modern hub of activity for the EU.

EATING OUT

The taste buds of Luxembourg have been very much influenced by French classical cuisine, particularly around and about the Old Town, an area that becomes a smart open-air terrace in summer. Look out for the local speciality Judd mat Gaardebounen, smoked neck of pork with broad beans. The centre of town is an eclectic place to eat as it runs the gauntlet from fast-style pizzeria to expense account restaurants favoured by businessmen. A good bet for atmosphere is the Grund, which offers a wide variety of restaurants and price ranges, and is certainly the area that boasts the most popular cafés and pubs. A few trendy places have sprouted over recent times near the Casemates, and these too are proving to be pretty hot with the younger crowd. A service charge is included in your bill but if you want to tip, ten per cent is reasonable. The Grand Duchy produces its own white and sparkling wines on the borders of the Moselle. Over the last decade it has produced some interesting varieties but you'll rarely find these abroad, as they're eagerly snapped up by the locals.

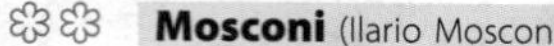

Mosconi (Ilario Mosconi)

13 rue Münster ✉ 2160 – ✆ 54 69 94 – www.mosconi.lu Plan: **A1**
– closed 1 week Easter, last 3 weeks August, 24 December-early January, Bank Holidays, Saturday lunch, Sunday and Monday
Menu 50 € (lunch) – Carte 100/140 €
• Italian • Elegant • Luxury •

Ilario and Simonetta Mosconi are an enthusiastic couple that proudly pay homage to the gastronomic traditions of Italy. Their Italian cuisine is as full of flair as it is steeped in flavours. The secret of their success no doubt lies in the infinite care and attention they devote to choosing their suppliers.
→ Tartare de sardines marinées et citron confit. Veau à la milanaise, asperges vertes et jus de veau à la crème de truffe blanche. Caramalle à la sicilienne, sauce à l'orange et pistaches.

Clairefontaine (Arnaud Magnier)

9 place de Clairefontaine ✉ 1341 – ✆ 46 22 11 Plan: **B1**
– www.restaurantclairefontaine.lu – closed 1 week Easter, last 2 weeks August-first week September, Christmas-New Year, first week January, Bank Holidays, Saturday and Sunday
Menu 59 € (lunch)/104 € – Carte 82/126 €
• Creative French • Elegant •

This attractive restaurant with a terrace stands on an elegant square. It has traditional decor with old wooden panelling and contemporary furnishings. Creative, modern cuisine and astute wine pairings.
→ Carpaccio et tartare de Saint-Jacques au céleri et à la truffe. Poularde de Bresse contisée à la truffe et cuite en vessie, farce au foie gras et purée aux truffes. Soufflé au Grand Marnier et madeleines à l'orange.

La Cristallerie – Hôtel Le Place d'Armes

18 place d'Armes (1er étage) ✉ 1136 – ✆ 274 73 74 21 Plan: **A1**
– www.la-cristallerie.com – closed 14-22 April, 28 July-19 August, 25 December-2 January, 17-25 February, Saturday lunch, Sunday and Monday
Menu 58/228 € – Carte 123/198 €
• Modern French • Classic décor • Elegant •

In terms of decor, this crystal glassworks is the epitome of stylish, classical elegance. The chef amply demonstrates how subtle touches of creativity can enhance fine ingredients. His well-balanced creations feature the occasional Asian influence.
→ Cuisses de grenouilles poêlées aux épices satay. Coeur de ris de veau aux asperges sauvages. Douceur de café, à la pomme, gingembre et pêche blanche.

La Bergamote

2 place de Nancy ✉ 2212 – ✆ 26 44 03 79 – www.labergamote.lu
– closed late December, Bank Holidays, Saturday lunch, Sunday and Monday
Menu 30 € (lunch)/37 € – Carte 49/69 €
• Modern cuisine • Trendy • Friendly •

Have you ever actually tasted bergamot? The subtle, fresh taste of this small citrus fruit is a recurring ingredient in the sun-drenched cuisine of this restaurant. Vitello tonnato, roast sea bream and shrimp polenta, without forgetting a few modern, French touches...

Kamakura

4 rue Münster ✉ 2160 – ✆ 47 06 04 – www.kamakura.lu Plan: **B1**
– closed 2 weeks Easter, last 2 weeks August-early September, late December-early January, Bank Holidays, Saturday lunch and Sunday
Menu 15 € (lunch), 37/65 € – Carte 47/79 €
• Japanese • Minimalist •

Authenticity is the hallmark of this minimalist restaurant founded in 1988, which makes no concessions to Western tastes! Seasonal specialties like fresh tuna and Kobe beef (wagyu) reveal delicious aromas, rich in sophisticated and varied flavours.

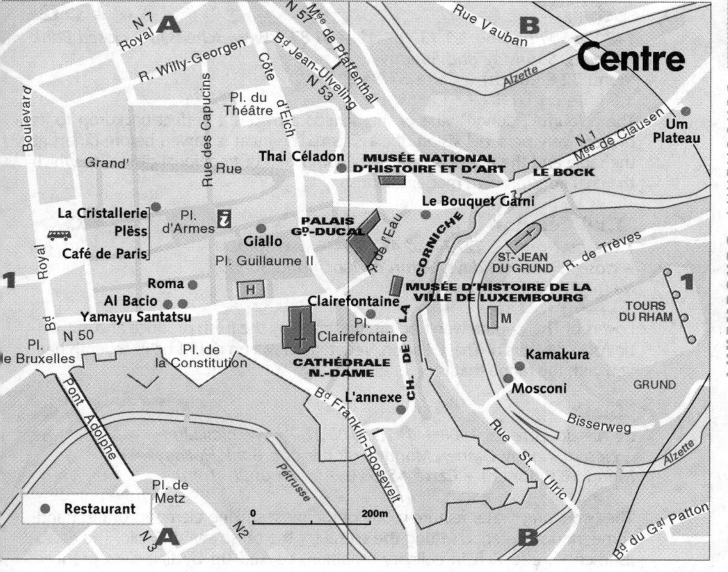

Le Bouquet Garni

XX (dinner)

32 rue de l'Eau ✉ 1449 – ✆ 26 20 06 20 Plan: **B1**

– www.lebouquetgarni.lu – closed Bank Holidays, Sunday and Monday

Menu 32 € (lunch)/55 €

• Classic French • Romantic • Rustic •

This 18C abode is steeped in charm and bare stones and low ceilings set the inviting scene. The Bouquet Garni seeks to enhance and develop the strength of classical dishes. The chef focuses on the essential without unnecessary frills, offering diners an attractive repertory.

Plëss – Hôtel Le Place d'Armes

XX A/C

18 place d'Armes ✉ 1136 – ✆ 274 73 74 11 Plan: **A1**

– www.hotel-leplacedarmes.com

Menu 44 € (lunch)/56 € – Carte 59/81 €

• Classic cuisine • Brasserie •

Plëss means 'square' in Luxembourgish – an obvious reference to the Place d'Armes, which is where this lovely contemporary brasserie is located, right in the heart of town. Carvery and plancha meat features prominently. A mouth-watering "plëss-ure"!

Roma

XX

5 rue Louvigny ✉ 1946 – ✆ 22 36 92 – www.roma.lu Plan: **A1**

– closed Sunday dinner and Monday

Carte 41/61 €

• Italian • Friendly •

The first Italian restaurant to be opened in Luxembourg, in 1950, the Roma continues to brilliantly uphold authentic, traditional cuisine, including homemade pasta. Theme festivals and a varied menu transform each meal into a feast.

Schéiss

142 Val Sainte-Croix ✉ 1370 – ✆ 24 61 82 – www.scheiss.lu – closed Bank Holidays, Saturday and Sunday
Menu 32 € (lunch) – Carte 57/84 €
• Classic cuisine • Design •

The colourful "lounge" vibe of the Schéiss provides a perfect backdrop to its owners' very personal vision of classicism. The meat is carved before diners at the table and the menu is essentially composed of traditional dishes, to which the chef adds his own modern flourish.

Thai Céladon

1 rue du Nord ✉ 2229 – ✆ 47 49 34 – www.thai.lu – closed Bank Holidays, Saturday lunch and Sunday Plan: **A1**
Menu 47/57 € – Carte 42/51 €
• Thai • Intimate •

Lovers of Thai cuisine won't be disappointed by the fresh produce and authentic Asian flavours of Thai Céladon. Vegetarians will no doubt be in seventh heaven with the range that is on offer.

Giallo

24 rue du Curé ✉ 1368 – ✆ 26 20 00 27 – www.giallo.lu – closed Sunday Dinner, Monday dinner and Bank Holidays Plan: **A1**
Menu 18 € (lunch) – Carte 45/63 € – *(open until 11pm)*
• Italian • Design •

The two-storey water feature is one of the most striking elements of this handsome modern interior, setting the scene for the oh so stylish Giallo. The establishment is also rich in culinary ambition, backed up by first-class produce, which is perhaps unsurprising when the aim is to serve authentic Italian cuisine.

Al Bacio

24 rue Notre-Dame ✉ 2240 – ✆ 27 99 48 81 – closed 2 weeks Easter, last 3 weeks August, late December-early January, Bank Holidays, Monday dinner, Tuesday dinner and Sunday Plan: **A1**
Menu 15 € (lunch), 39/42 €
• Italian • Trendy • Simple •

Hey presto! The characteristic bustle of Italian towns forms the backdrop to this popular restaurant. The regulars return for authentic, super fresh food. The menu changes according to seasonal availability. The themed menu (evenings only) is definitely to be recommended.

Yamayu Santatsu

26 rue Notre-Dame ✉ 2240 – ✆ 46 12 49 – closed last week July-first 2 weeks August, late December-early January, Bank Holidays, Sunday and Monday Plan: **A1**
Menu 16 € (lunch) – Carte 28/61 €
• Japanese • Minimalist •

Don't be misled by the low-key interior, you are in the right place to taste the best sushi in the city of Luxemburg. The chef prepares it at the last minute at the sushi bar and is a stickler for super fresh fish. An assured choice since 1989.

L'annexe

7 rue du Saint Esprit ✉ 1475 – ✆ 26 26 25 07 – www.lannexe.lu – closed 24 December-1 January, Saturday lunch and Sunday Plan: **B1**
Menu 13 € (lunch), 33/42 € – Carte 36/59 €
• Market cuisine • Friendly • Contemporary décor •

Set in a lively, friendly district, this annexe specialises in good wholesome victuals that any self-respecting brasserie would be proud of. The chef's traditional brasserie dishes, which are occasionally more sophisticated, are as mouth-watering as they are generous. Lovely terrace.

Les Jardins d'Anaïs

2 place Sainte Cunégonde ✉ 1367 Clausen – ✆ 28 99 80 00 – www.jardinsdanais.lu – closed Saturday and Sunday
Menu 41 € (lunch), 80/135 € – Carte approx. 100 €
• Modern French • Elegant •

Undeniably classy. Attentive staff. Understated elegant interior and a delightful conservatory. The experienced chef pursues his sophisticated culinary adventure crafting traditional recipes, in which nothing is left to chance. Quality is the name of the game here, extending of course to the lavishly, luxurious guest rooms.

➜ L'œuf parfait iodé au caviar, toast Melba d'herbes, petit pois et crème de haddock fumé. Ris de veau au croustillant de fruit à coques, poireau et asperges vertes au vin jaune. Baba au rhum et diplomate aux fruits confits.

La Cantine du Châtelet

2 boulevard de la Pétrusse ✉ 2320 – ✆ 40 21 01 – www.chatelet.lu – closed 22 December-1 January, Monday dinner, Saturday lunch and Sunday
Menu 29 € (lunch), 37/55 € – Carte 43/67 €
• Market cuisine • Elegant • Contemporary décor •

A lounge-inspired dining room and trendy vibe on the left-hand side and a more classical ambience on the right: choose your setting depending on your mood. Creative fare with varied, international influences. Steak tartare and risotto are house favourites, but the chef's choice set menu really showcases his immense talent.

Bick Stuff

95 rue de Clausen ✉ 1342 Clausen – ✆ 26 09 47 31 – www.bickstuff.lu – closed week after Pentecost, 2 weeks in August, late December, Thursday dinner, Saturday lunch, Sunday dinner and Monday
Menu 19 € (lunch), 36/46 € – Carte 52/80 €
• Home cooking • Classic décor •

A family-run establishment where you will instantly feel at home. Bick is a local word which literally means 'beak' in English but loosely translates as 'food'. Owners Virginie and Denis Laissy have the same goal: to serve good food in a relaxed atmosphere. Chef Denis rustles up reassuringly classical recipes, adding his own distinctive touch. We recommend the set menu.

Brasserie des Jardins

27b boulevard Marcel Cahen ✉ 1311 Belair – ✆ 26 25 93 48 – www.brasseriedesjardins.lu – closed 24 and 31 December
Menu 18 € (lunch)/37 € – Carte 43/62 €
• Traditional cuisine • Brasserie • Contemporary décor •

If only we lived next-door to this modern brasserie... Run by a highly professional team, it boasts a fine terrace. However, the star is the traditional fare, prepared with skill and attention to detail. The chef's touches of modernity are always perfectly balanced. High-quality ingredients in good hands!

Oro e Argento – Hôtel Sofitel Europe

6 rue du Fort Niedergrünewald (European Centre) ✉ 2015 Kirchberg – ✆ 43 77 68 70 – www.sofitel.com – closed Saturday lunch and Sunday
Menu 41 € (lunch), 52/80 € – Carte 58/82 €
• Italian • Intimate •

An attractive Italian restaurant in a luxury hotel. Contemporary cuisine is served to a backdrop of plush decor with a Venetian touch. Intimate atmosphere and stylish service.

Airfield

6 rue de Trèves ✉ 2632 Findel – ✆ 288 39 51 – www.airfield.lu – closed 25 August-12 September, 23 December-7 January, Sunday and Monday
Carte 43/78 €

· Modern cuisine · Friendly ·

A former hunting lodge of the Grand Duke's family, located near the airport, is now a practical hotel with two different dining experiences: bustling brasserie or plush restaurant. Creative recipes that delight patrons. Flawlessly crafted and perfectly tuned to modern tastes.

Um Plateau

6 Plateau Altmünster ✉ 1123 Clausen – ✆ 26 47 84 26 Plan: **B1**
– www.umplateau.lu – closed Saturday lunch and Sunday
Menu 28 € (lunch) – Carte 39/66 €

· Modern cuisine · Chic ·

Diners appreciate the smart lounge ambience and cosy interior of this restaurant. After a glass of wine in the lively bar, treat yourself to a meal in which fine produce takes pride of place. Authentic flavours and painstaking preparations are the hallmarks of this establishment.

F. Troiani/agefotostock

AMSTERDAM
Rotterdam

NETHERLANDS
NEDERLAND

AleksandarGeorgiev/iStock

AMSTERDAM
AMSTERDAM

AndreyKrav/iStock

AMSTERDAM IN…

- **ONE DAY**
  A trip on a canal boat, Rijksmuseum, Anne Frank Museum, Van Gogh Museum.
- **TWO DAYS**
  Begijnhof, shopping in the '9 Straatjes', Vondelpark, evening in a brown café.
- **THREE DAYS**
  The Jordaan, Plantage and Entrepotdok, red light district.

Once visited, never forgotten; that's Amsterdam's great claim to fame. Its endearing horseshoe shape – defined by 17C canals cut to drain land for a growing population – allied to finely detailed gabled houses, has produced a compact city centre of aesthetically splendid symmetry and matchless consistency. Exploring the city on foot or by bike is the real joy here and visitors rarely need to jump on a tram or bus.

'The world's biggest small city' displays a host of distinctive characteristics, ranging from the world-famous red light district to the cosy and convivial brown cafés, from the wonderful art galleries

and museums to the quirky shops, and the medieval churches to the tree-lined waterways with their pretty bridges. There's the feel of a northern Venice, but without the hallowed and revered atmosphere. It exists on a human scale, small enough to walk from one end to the other. Those who might moan that it's just too small should stroll along to the former derelict docklands on the east side and contemplate the shiny new apartments giving the waterfront a sleek, 21C feel. Most people who come here, though, are just happy to cosy up to old Amsterdam's sleepy, relaxed vibe. No European city does snug bars better: this is the place to go for cats kipping on beat-up chairs and candles flickering on wax-encrusted tables…

EATING OUT

Amsterdam is a vibrant and multicultural city and, as such, has a wide proliferation of restaurants offering a varied choice of cuisines, where you can eat well without paying too much. Head for an eetcafe and you'll get a satisfying three course meal at a reasonable price. The Dutch consider the evening to be the time to eat your main meal, so some restaurants shut at lunchtime. Aside from the eetcafe, you can top up your middle-of-day fuel levels with simple, home-cooked meals and local beers at a bruin (brown) café, or for something lighter, a café specialising in coffee and cake. If you wish to try local specialities, number one on the hit list could be rijsttafel or 'rice table', as the Dutch have imported much from their former colonies of Indonesia. Fresh raw herring from local waters is another nutritious local favourite, as are apple pies and pancakes of the sweet persuasion; often enjoyed with a hot chocolate. Restaurants are never too big but are certainly atmospheric and busy, so it's worth making reservations.

✿✿ **Spectrum** – Hotel Waldorf Astoria
Herengracht 542 ✉ 1017 CG Plan: **G1**
– ✆ (0 20) 718 46 43 – www.restaurantspectrum.com
– closed 27 April, 28 July-19 August, 1-21 January, Sunday and Monday
Menu 98/168 € – Carte 81/135 € – *(dinner only)*
• Creative • Luxury • Elegant •

Extraordinarily beautiful and classy! This refined, classic restaurant offers a true fine dining experience. The food is elegant, with a unique interplay of textures and tastes that is spot on, creating a wonderful harmony where every bite surprises. Definitely worth a visit!

➜ Carabinerogarnaal met runderrib en sherryroomsausje, gember, watermeloen en gebrande paprika. Kabeljauwrug met fenergiek, morieljes, wortel en konijnniertjes. Avocadosorbet met appel, komkommer en yoghurt.

✿✿ **&Moshik** (Moshik Roth)
Oosterdokskade 5 ✉ 1011 AD Plan: **H1**
– ✆ (0 20) 260 20 94 – www.moshikrestaurant.com
– closed Monday and Tuesday
Menu 145/190 € – Carte 117/245 € – *(dinner only except Friday and Sunday)*
• Creative • Design •

Moshik Roth invites you on an adventure. This fashionable establishment will take you from one pleasant surprise to the next. The chef knows how to combine inventiveness with refinement for a fantastic flavour experience, extracting the best from top-quality ingredients with absolute precision.

➜ Kabeljauw met angelicavinaigrette, kruidnagel en aardpeer. Eend uit Challans met gnocchi in roomsausje en gefermenteerde noten. Moderne pavlova van duindoornbes, kokos en mandarijn.

✿ **Bord'Eau** – Hotel de l'Europe
Nieuwe Doelenstraat 2 ✉ 1012 CP Plan: **G2**
– ✆ (0 20) 531 16 19 – www.bordeau.nl
– closed Saturday lunch, Sunday and Monday
Menu 48 € (lunch), 110/138 € – Carte 98/114 €
• Creative • Elegant • Chic •

Bord'Eau is a delightful luxurious restaurant with a classy feel which is evident throughout, from the stylish decor to the beautifully dressed plates. The chef uses ingredients from all corners of the world to create strongly contrasting flavours in delicate combinations. Make sure you try the cheese – the selection is great!

➜ Coquilles met Thaise garnalenconsommé, yuzu en groene papaja. Gebakken tarbot met olijfjes, knolselderij en gezouten citroen. Rode Roos : lychee met rode biet, geitenkaas en olijfolie.

✿ **Bougainville** – Hotel TwentySeven
Dam 27 ✉ 1012 JS – ✆ 020 218 21 80 Plan: **G2**
– www.restaurantbougainville.com
– closed Sunday and Monday
Menu 75/100 € – Carte 100/125 € – *(dinner only) (booking advisable)*
• Modern cuisine • Elegant •

Warm materials and luxurious designs give Restaurant Bougainville an intimate atmosphere, and its splendour is emphasized by the stunning view of the Dam. Let your taste buds travel from west to east enjoying dishes prepared by the highly technical chef, who has a creative, refined and intuitive style of cooking. The sommelier's selection is just as impressive as the cuisine.

➜ Carpaccio van coquilles met tamarillo, krab, avocado en groene kerrie. Hoevekip met za'atar kruiden, worteltexturen en Albuferasaus. Inspiratie op de Cariño cocktail.

The Duchess

XXX

Spuistraat 172 ✉ *1012 VT – ✆ (0 20) 811 33 22 – www.the-duchess.com*

Plan: **F1**

Carte 60/85 € – *(open until 11pm)*

• Mediterranean cuisine • Chic • Elegant •

The grandeur of this former ticket office is impressive. This is a magnificent venue, where the use of dark marble and the Belle Époque atmosphere lend The Duchess real flair. The beautiful Molteni kitchen turns out generous, classic dishes. Where else would you find such a delicious, traditional beef Wellington?

➜ Kreeft en koningskrab met avocado en tomaat. Runderhaas Wellington. Tartelette Tropézienne met oranjebloesembrioche, vanilleschuimpje en geroosterde amandelen.

Vinkeles – Hotel The Dylan

XXX

Keizersgracht 384 ✉ *1016 GB – ✆ (020) 530 20 10 – www.vinkeles.com – closed 29 April-5 May, 5-20 August, 1-8 January, Sunday and Monday*

Plan: **F2**

Menu 95/140 € – Carte 79/298 € – *(dinner only)*

• Creative • Friendly • Elegant •

The original features of this 18C bakery make Vinkeles a special place to eat, especially in combination with the stylish interior. The food deserves the highest praise, as the creative chef succeeds in bringing excitement and nuance to the plate, while never losing sight of natural flavours.

➜ Langoustines met tijgermelk, koolrabi, rozenwater en geitenkaas. Anjouduifje "au sang" met ingelegde bramen, gyoza van de bout en een sausje met eendenlever. Creatie van cheesecake, havermout, koriander en mandarijnsorbet.

The White Room by Jacob Jan Boerma – NH Grand Hotel Krasnapolsky

XXX

Dam 9 ✉ *1012 JS – ✆ (020) 554 94 54 – www.restaurantthewhiteroom.com – closed 27 April-8 May, 28 July-20 August, 1-16 January, Tuesday lunch, Wednesday lunch, Sunday and Monday*

Plan: **G1**

Menu 40 € (lunch)/69 € – Carte approx. 96 € – *(booking essential at dinner) (set menu only at weekends)*

• Modern cuisine • Classic décor • Elegant •

You can imagine yourself as an Austrian prince or princess in this white and gold dining room, which dates from 1885 and magnificently combines classical elegance with modern furnishings. Citrus flavours and exotic spices are combined in a creative interplay. The chef is a strong technician and understands what refinement really means.

➜ Amsterdams tuintje : groentenpalet met kruiden en specerijen. Tarbot met bloemkool, lardo di Colonnata en beurre noisette. Perzik met room, ras-el-hanout en citroen.

Bridges Dining – Hotel Sofitel The Grand

XXX

O.Z. Voorburgwal 197 ✉ *1012 EX – ✆ (0 20) 555 35 60 – www.bridges-amsterdam.nl – closed Monday lunch*

Plan: **G2**

Menu 42 € (lunch)/64 € – Carte 54/95 €

• Seafood • Elegant •

The dishes on offer in this beautiful fish restaurant combine refinement, surprise, originality and quality, and are worthy of the utmost praise. Overall, good quality, reasonably priced cuisine.

➜ Cilinder van tonijn en sesam met wasabi, roomkaas en sojavinaigrette. Krokant gebakken rode mul en langoustine met lardo, waldorfslaatje en verjus. Hazelnootgebakje met appel, kersmeringue en roomijs.

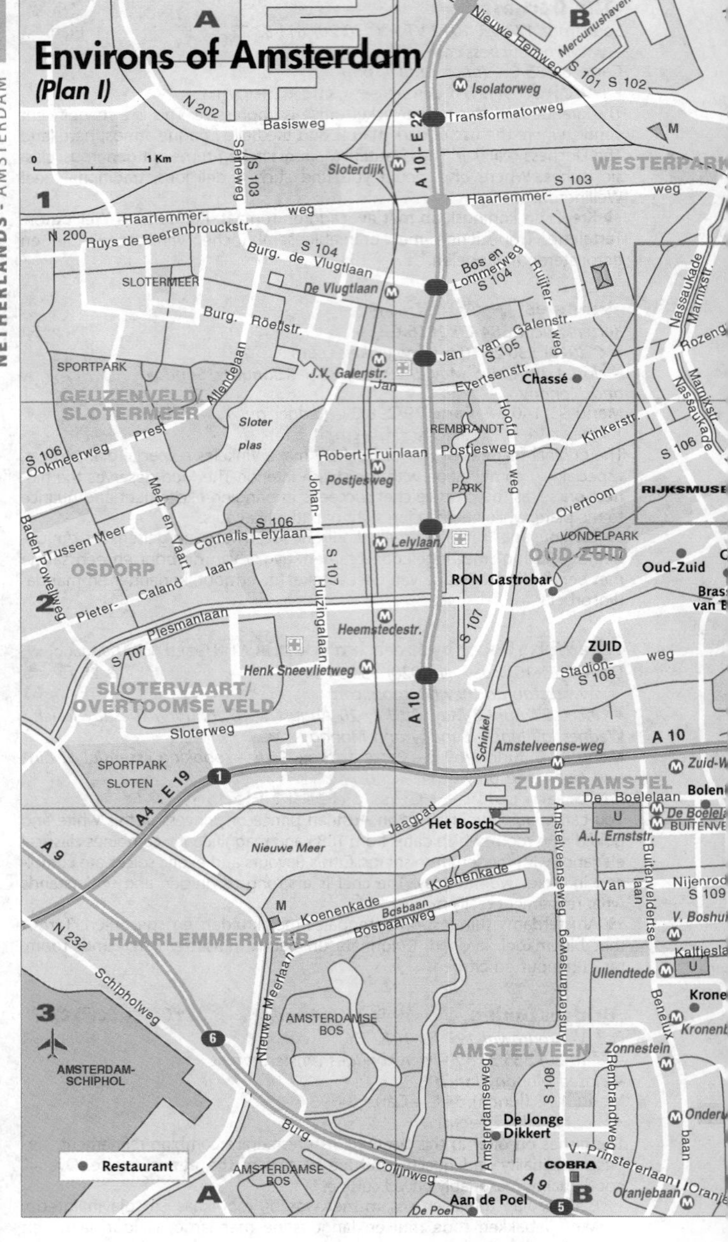
Environs of Amsterdam
(Plan I)
A
B
1
2
3
Restaurant
Chassé
RON Gastrobar
Oud-Zuid
Het Bosch
De Jonge Dikkert
Aan de Poel
COBRA
SLOTERMEER
GEUZENVELD/ SLOTERMEER
OSDORP
SLOTERVAART/ OVERTOOMSE VELD
HAARLEMMERMEER
AMSTERDAMSE BOS
AMSTELVEEN
ZUIDERAMSTEL
OUD-ZUID
WESTERPARK
VONDELPARK
REMBRANDT PARK
SPORTPARK
SPORTPARK SLOTEN
AMSTERDAM-SCHIPHOL
Nieuwe Meer
Sloter plas
Isolatorweg
Sloterdijk
De Vlugtlaan
J.V. Galenstr.
Postjesweg
Lelylaan
Heemstedestr.
Henk Sneevlietweg
Zuid
Transformatorweg
Basisweg
Haarlemmerweg
Nieuwe Hemweg
Mercuriushaven
Ruys de Beerenbrouckstr.
Burg. de Vlugtlaan
Bos en Lommerweg
Burg. Röellstr.
Jan van Galenstr.
Jan Evertsenstr.
Kinkerstr.
Robert-Fruinlaan
Overtoom
Cornelis Lelylaan
Pieter-Calandlaan
Plesmanlaan
Sloterweg
Amstelveense-weg
Amstelveenseweg
Amsterdamseweg
Buitenveldertse laan
Rembrandtweg
V. Prinstererlaan
Burg. Colijnweg
Koenenkade
Bosbaanweg
Nieuwe Meerlaan
Schipholweg
Jaagpad
Stadionweg
Huizingalaan
Johan-Huizingalaan
Ookmeerweg
Tussen Meer
Baden Powellweg
Meer en Vaart
Allendelaan
Seineweg
Hoofdweg
Ruijterweg
Nassaukade
Marnixstr.
A 10 - E 22
A 10
A4 - E 19
A 9
N 200
N 202
N 232
S 101
S 102
S 103
S 104
S 105
S 106
S 107
S 108
S 109
De Boelelaan
A.J. Ernststr.
Ullendtede
Zonnestein
Oranjebaan
De Poel
RIJKSMUSE
Bolen
Kronen
Kaltjesla
Nijenrod
V. Boshu
Brass van B
Zuid-W
BUITENVE

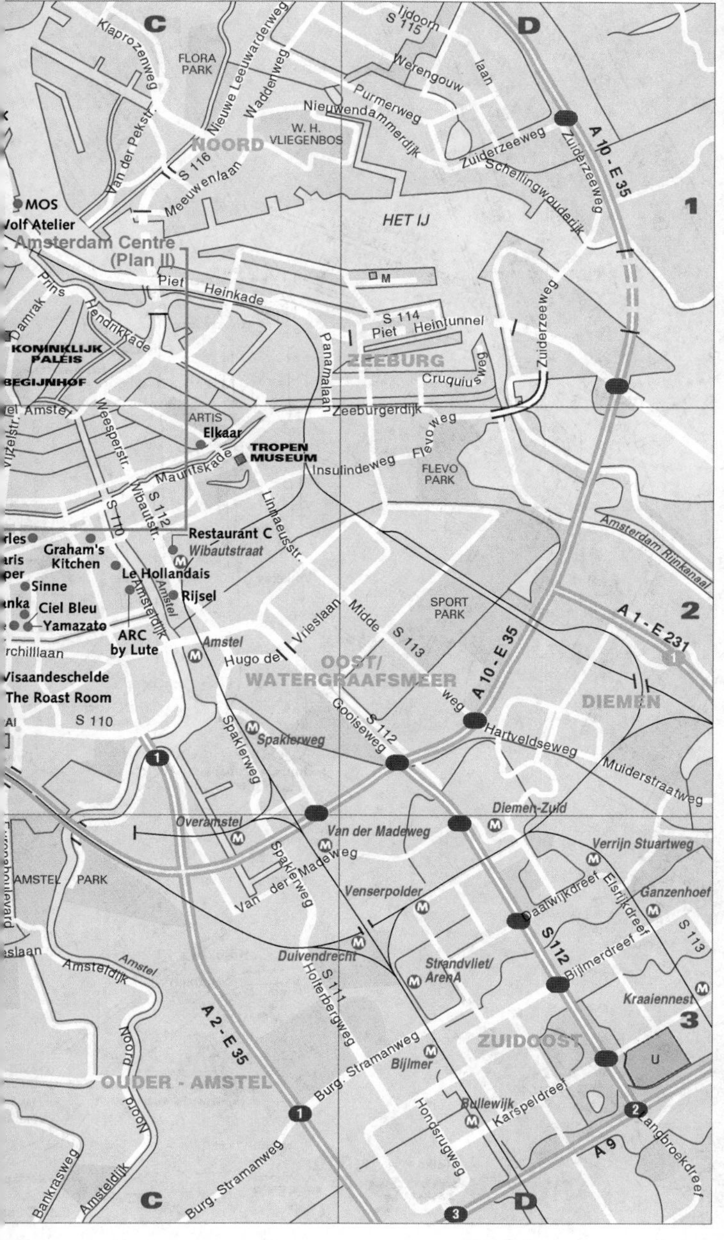

C
D
Klaprozenweg
FLORA PARK
Nieuwe Leeuwarderweg
Waddenweg
IJdoorn
S 115
Werengouw
laan
Purmerweg
Nieuwendammerdijk
W. H. VLIEGENBOS
NOORD
Van der Pekstr.
S 116
Meeuwenlaan
Zuiderzeeweg
Schellingwouderdijk
A 10 - E 35
1
HET IJ
MOS
Wolf Atelier
Amsterdam Centre (Plan II)
Piet Heinkade
Prins Hendrikkade
Damrak
KONINKLIJK PALEIS
BEGIJNHOF
M
S 114
Piet Heintunnel
Panamalaan
ZEEBURG
Cruquiusweg
Zeeburgerdijk
Amstel
ARTIS
Elkaar
Weesperstr.
TROPEN MUSEUM
Mauritskade
Insulindeweg
Flevoweg
FLEVO PARK
S 112
Wibautstr.
S 110
Linnaeusstr.
Restaurant C
Wibautstraat
Graham's Kitchen
Le Hollandais
Sinne
Ciel Bleu
Yamazato
Rijsel
Amsteldijk
Amstel
ARC by Lute
Amsterdam Rijnkanaal
SPORT PARK
Vrieslaan
Middenweg
S 113
A 10 - E 35
2
A 1 - E 231
Hugo de
OOST/ WATERGRAAFSMEER
Visaandeschelde
The Roast Room
S 110
DIEMEN
Spaklerweg
Gooiseweg
S 112
Hartveldseweg
Muiderstraatweg
Overamstel
Van der Madeweg
Diemen-Zuid
Verrijn Stuartweg
AMSTEL PARK
Van der Madeweg
Spaklerweg
Venserpolder
Daalwijkdreef
Elsrijkdreef
Ganzenhoef
S 113
Amstel
Amsteldijk
Duivendrecht
S 111
Holterbergweg
Strandvliet/ ArenA
S 112
Bijlmerdreef
Kraaiennest
3
A 2 - E 35
Noord
ZUIDOOST
U
Burg. Stramanweg
Bijlmer
OUDER - AMSTEL
Noord
Bullewijk
Karspeldreef
Hondsrugweg
Langbroekdreef
A 9
Bankrasweg
Amsteldijk
Burg. Stramanweg
C
D

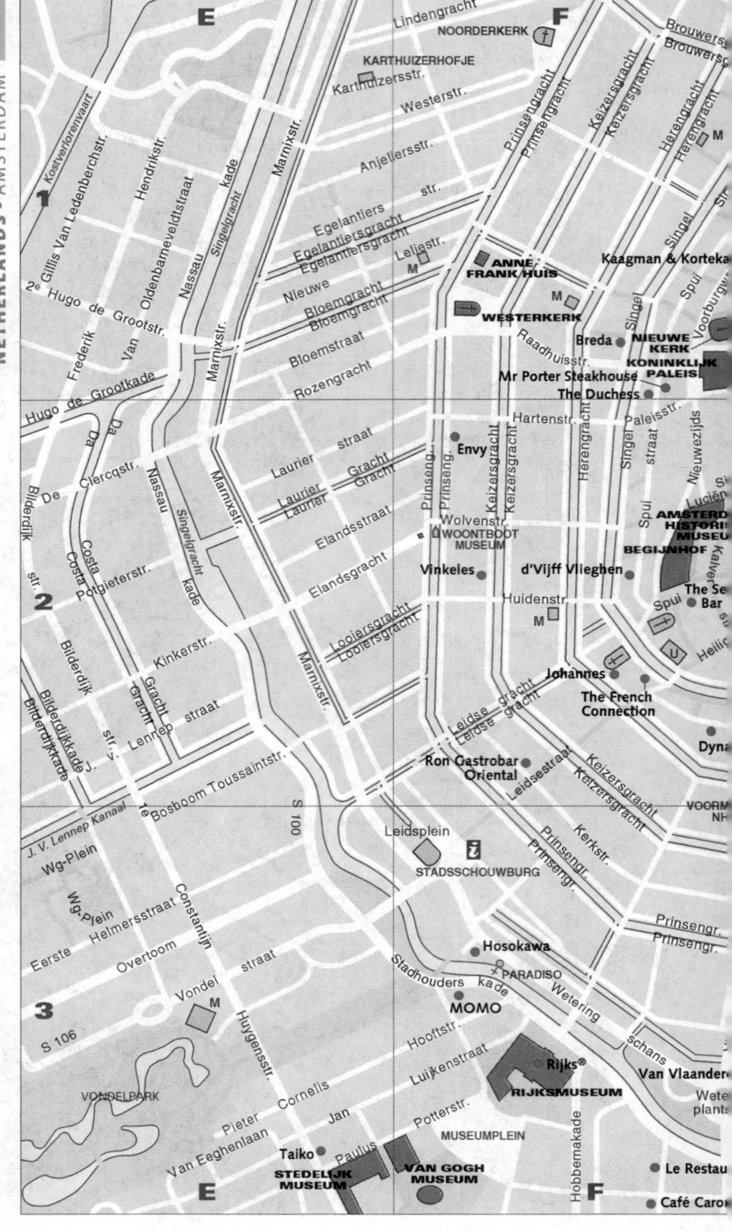
E
F
1
2
3
Lindengracht
NOORDERKERK
KARTHUIZERHOFJE
Karthuizersstr.
Westerstr.
Anjeliersstr.
Egelantiers str.
Egelantiersgracht
Leliestr.
Nieuwe Leliestr.
Bloemgracht
Bloemstraat
Rozengracht
ANNE FRANK HUIS
WESTERKERK
Raadhuisstr.
Prinsengracht
Keizersgracht
Herengracht
Singel
Brouwersgracht
Kaagman & Kortekaas
Spui
Voorburgwal
Breda
NIEUWE KERK
KONINKLIJK PALEIS
Mr Porter Steakhouse
The Duchess
Hartenstr.
Paleisstr.
Nieuwezijds
Envy
Prinseng.
Wolvenstr.
WOONTBOOT MUSEUM
AMSTERDAM HISTORISCH MUSEUM
BEGIJNHOF
Kalverstr.
Vinkeles
d'Vijff Vlieghen
Huidenstr.
The Seven Bar
Johannes
The French Connection
Leidsegracht
Ron Gastrobar Oriental
Leidsestraat
Kerkstr.
Prinsengr.
Kostverlorenvaart
Gillis Van Ledenberchstr.
Hendrikstr.
Van Oldenbarneveldtstraat
Nassaukade
Singelgracht
Marnixstr.
Marnixkade
2e Hugo de Grootstr.
Frederik
Van
Hugo de Grootkade
Da Costa
De Clercqstr.
Laurierstraat
Lauriergracht
Elandsstraat
Elandsgracht
Looiersgracht
Bilderdijkstr.
Potgieterstr.
Kinkerstr.
J. v. Lennepstraat
Bilderdijkkade
Bosboom Toussaintstr.
1e Constantijn Huygensstr.
J. V. Lennep Kanaal
Wg-Plein
Eerste Helmersstraat
Overtoom
Vondelstraat
S 100
S 106
Leidsplein
STADSSCHOUWBURG
Hosokawa
PARADISO
Stadhouderskade
Weteringschans
MOMO
Hooftstr.
Luijkenstraat
Rijks
RIJKSMUSEUM
Van Vlaanderen
VONDELPARK
Pieter Cornelis
Jan Luijkenstraat
Paulus Potterstr.
Van Eeghenlaan
MUSEUMPLEIN
Taiko
STEDELIJK MUSEUM
VAN GOGH MUSEUM
Hobbemakade
Le Restaurant
Café Caron
M

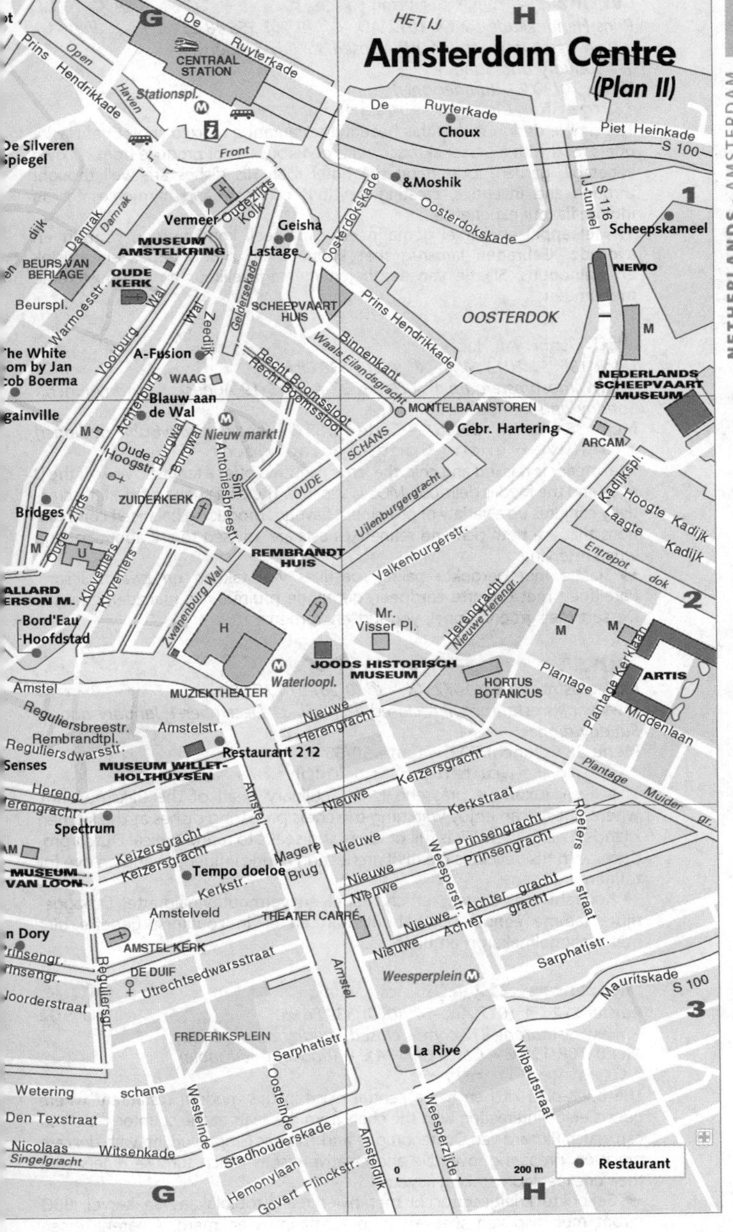
Amsterdam Centre
(Plan II)
HET IJ
Centraal Station
De Ruyterkade
Prins Hendrikkade
Stationspl.
Damrak
Beurs van Berlage
Oude Kerk
Museum Amstelkring
Scheepvaart Huis
Oosterdok
NEMO
Nederlands Scheepvaart Museum
Montelbaanstoren
Nieuw markt
Waag
Zuiderkerk
Rembrandt Huis
Joods Historisch Museum
Muziektheater
Waterloopl.
Hortus Botanicus
Artis
Museum Willet-Holthuysen
Museum van Loon
Theater Carré
Amstel Kerk
De Duif
Frederiksplein
Weesperplein
Choux
&Moshik
Scheepskameel
Vermeer
Geisha
Lastage
De Silveren Spiegel
A-Fusion
Blauw aan de Wal
Gebr. Hartering
Bridges
Bord'Eau Hoofdstad
Restaurant 212
Senses
Spectrum
Tempo doeloe
La Rive
Restaurant
0
200 m
G
H
1
2
3

✿ **Vermeer** – Hotel NH Barbizon Palace

Prins Hendrikkade 59 ✉ 1012 AD – ✆ (0 20) 556 48 85 – www.restaurantvermeer.nl – closed 15 July-5 August, 1-7 January and Sunday Plan: **G1**

Menu 70/90 € – *(dinner only)*

• Organic • Design • Elegant •

The simple design makes this beautiful restaurant a relaxed spot. Chef Naylor offers food with a personal touch, with generous use of produce from his own vegetable garden, located on the hotel roof. His dishes are well thought through and inventive, creating delicious contrasts and harmonies for an intense flavour experience.

➜ Met appel en zurkel gemarineerde makreel, komkommer, yoghurt en avocado. Gebraden lamsrug met knoflook en munt, gebakken artisjok en walnootjus. Slaatje van aardbeien met agavelikeur en chiboustcrème met limoen.

✿ **MOS** (Egon van Hoof)

IJdok 185 ✉ 1013 MM – ✆ (0 20) 638 08 66 – www.mosamsterdam.nl – closed 27 April, 5-19 August, Saturday lunch, Sunday and Monday Plan I: **C1**

Menu 38 € (lunch), 55/95 € – Carte 71/83 € – *(bookings advisable at dinner)*

• Creative French • Contemporary décor • Trendy •

The interior is relaxed and chic, the large windows offer a fantastic view of the IJ river, and the food is delicious. MOS is sublime. The chef shows how a little creativity conjures up a variety of prominent flavours, producing balanced combinations that are both rich and refined. Guests are advised to ask about parking when reserving.

➜ Slaatje met gerookte paling, pastilles van takuan en zwarte sesam. Parelhoen met gepofte aardpeer, gebrande pruimen en macadamiasausje. Dessert met groene appel, yoghurt en verbena.

✿ **RIJKS®**

Museumstraat 2 ✉ 1077 XX – ✆ (0 20) 674 75 55 – www.rijksrestaurant.nl – closed 27 April, 31 December-1 January and Sunday dinner Plan: **F3**

Menu 38 € (lunch)/70 € – Carte 50/65 €

• Creative • Contemporary décor • Brasserie •

This lively luxurious brasserie is the culinary pearl of the Rijksmuseum, where guests can enjoy watching the chefs preparing dishes at the kitchen islands. Chef Bijdendijk is full of ideas and seeks to refine typical Dutch produce, with his delicious creativity reflecting exotic influences and an eye for refinement.

➜ Koolrabi met oester, rettich, appel en vermouthvinaigrette. Drooggerijpte tamme eend : borst, bout, hart en ei. In zoutkorst gepofte biet met amandelmakaron en hibiscus.

✿ **Restaurant 212** (R. van Oostenbrugg & T. Groot)

Amstel 212 ✉ 1017 AH – ✆ (020) 334 86 85 – www.restaurant-212.com – closed Sunday and Monday Plan: **G2**

Menu 108/138 € – Carte 64/174 € – *(booking advisable)*

• Creative • Trendy •

The open-plan kitchen has a central place in this modern restaurant where guests enjoy interacting with the chefs from the seats at the counter. Here you can watch Richard van Oostenbrugge and Thomas Groot working with delicate precision, preparing inventive and creative dishes which surprise diners with their unexpectedly striking flavours.

➜ Gekookte krieltjesgnocchi met rivierkreeft, robiolakaas en kervel. BBQ tarbot met rasp van spek en ui, ossenstaartjus en merg. Amarenakersen met smoky Bourbon, citrus, zwarte olijf en krokante walnoot.

Lastage (Rogier van Dam)

Geldersekade 29 ✉ 1011 EJ – ✆ (0 20) 737 08 11 Plan: **G1**
– www.restaurantlastage.nl – closed 27 and 28 April, 29 July-16 August, 31 December-8 January and Monday
Menu 47/89 € – *(dinner only)*

• Creative • Friendly • Bistro •

Lastage is an appealing little restaurant which will immediately make you feel welcome. Chef Van Dam delights the taste buds with dishes that are full of personality. Nothing on the plate is unnecessary – every ingredient adds interest and is there to enhance the dish. For the quality, the prices are more than reasonable. This is a little establishment with big flavours!

➜ Geelvinmakreel met avocado, groene kerrie en gambapoffertje. Met eendenlever en salie gevulde kwartel, snijbiet en pepersausje. Citroenmeringue met bros van honingkaramel, pecannoten en geitenyoghurtsorbet.

Hoofdstad – Hotel de l'Europe

Nieuwe Doelenstraat 2 ✉ 1012 CP – ✆ (0 20) 531 16 19 Plan: **G2**
– www.hoofdstadbrasserie.nl
Menu 37 € – Carte 60/102 € – *(open until 11pm)*

• Classic cuisine • Bistro • Friendly •

On the terrace of this luxurious canal-side brasserie, with its views of bridges and passing boats, Amsterdam really comes into its own. The delicious dishes, which are uncomplicated yet always full of flavour, can also be enjoyed indoors. Sole meunière and charcoal-grilled entrecote are just two of the kitchen's culinary delights.

Van Vlaanderen

Weteringschans 175 ✉ 1017 XD – ✆ (0 20) 622 82 92 Plan: **F3**
– www.restaurant-vanvlaanderen.nl – closed 23 July-6 August, 1-14 January, Sunday and Monday
Menu 30 € (lunch), 37/53 € – *(dinner only except Friday)*

• Modern cuisine • Classic décor •

Van Vlaanderen has long been recognised as the place to go for the good things in life. The restaurant's success lies in its pleasant location right in the centre of Amsterdam with its own jetty on the patio, and attentive service of a young, spirited team whose enthusiasm is evident in the modern, original versions of the classic dishes served here. A heart-warming experience.

A-Fusion

Zeedijk 130 ✉ 1012 BC – ✆ (020) 330 40 68 Plan: **G1**
– www.a-fusion.nl
Menu 34 € – Carte 23/43 € – *(open until 11pm)*

• Asian • Brasserie • Bistro •

A fusion of Chinese and Japanese cuisine in the heart of Amsterdam's Chinatown. This restaurant boasts a grill, a sushi bar and a wok kitchen. Be sure to try the prawn dim sum, the beef with black pepper sauce and the oysters with ginger. Alternatively, give the cooks carte blanche to come up with some surprising choices.

Scheepskameel

Kattenburgerstraat 7 ✉ 1018 JA – ✆ (020) 337 96 80 Plan: **H1**
– www.scheepskameel.nl – closed 24 December-1 January, Sunday and Monday
Menu 35/75 € – Carte 31/125 € – *(dinner only)*

• Traditional cuisine • Brasserie • Trendy •

Scheepskameel is a lively, relaxed establishment, providing honest, straightforward food. Everything here starts with top-quality ingredients, prepared without fuss and beautifully seasoned. The wine list is comprised entirely of German wines and accompanies the food perfectly.

Tempo doeloe

X AC

Utrechtsestraat 75 ✉ 1017 VJ Plan: **G3**
– ✆ (0 20) 625 67 18 – www.tempodoeloerestaurant.nl
– closed 27 April, 25, 26 and 31 December-1 January, Monday lunch, Tuesday lunch and Sunday
Menu 24/38 € – Carte 35/63 €

• Indonesian • Traditional décor • Exotic décor •

Regular diners at Tempo doeloe or 'Times Gone By' find it difficult to hide their enthusiasm when they visit this restaurant. They know that an Indonesian feast like no other in Amsterdam awaits them. The food here is authentically Indonesian, with no concessions to Western tastes. Selamat makan!

La Rive - Hotel Amstel

XXXX AC P

Prof. Tulpplein 1 ✉ 1018 GX Plan: **H3**
– ✆ (0 20) 520 32 64 – www.restaurantlarive.com
– closed 6-24 January
Menu 90/125 € – Carte 130/145 € – *(dinner only)*

• Modern French • Chic • Elegant •

On entering this refined establishment, guests will immediately sense its rich history, although it is the Amstel that really steals the show here, thanks to the wonderful location on the riverbank. This is a classic restaurant, where the chef also works with the latest trends, taking inspiration from Asia and playing with the acidity balance of his food.

De Silveren Spiegel

XXX

Kattengat 4 ✉ 1012 SZ Plan: **G1**
– ✆ (020) 624 65 89 – www.desilverenspiegel.com
– closed 27 April, 5-13 January and Sunday
Menu 53/93 € – Carte approx. 73 € – *(dinner only) (booking essential)*

• Creative French • Historic • Friendly •

The authentic interior of these two buildings with stepped gables, dating back to 1614, has stood the test of time, retaining features such as a warm open hearth with matching tiles. In stark contrast with the decor, the food is modern down to the last detail. The young chef works mainly with Dutch ingredients and has a well-deserved reputation.

John Dory

XX

Prinsengracht 999 ✉ 1017 KM Plan: **G3**
– ✆ (020) 622 90 44 – www.johndory.nl
– closed 31 December-1 January, Sunday and Monday
Menu 40/90 € – *(dinner only except Friday and last Sunday of the month) (tasting menu only)*

• Seafood • Friendly • Intimate •

The charm and character of this 1680s warehouse is fantastic. The seats around the open kitchen are in demand for those wishing to discover what 'vistronomie' is. The quality of the fish, which comes directly from the North Sea, shines through here, and comes with all kinds of creative garnishes. The refinement of the 4-10 course menu will surprise you!

MOMO - Hotel Park

XX AC

Hobbemastraat 1 ✉ 1071 XZ – ✆ (0 20) 671 74 74 Plan: **F3**
– www.momo-amsterdam.com
Menu 25 € (lunch), 50/100 € – Carte 57/120 € – *(open until 11pm) (bar lunch)*

• Asian influences • Trendy • Brasserie •

MOMO is still one of the city's hotspots, offering fusion cuisine in a fashionable setting. Bento (Japanese lunchboxes) are served at lunchtime, followed by a menu designed for sharing in the evening.

Taiko – Hotel Conservatorium XX ♿ A/C

Van Baerlestraat 27 ✉ 1071 AN – ✆ (0 20) 570 00 00 – www.taikorestaurant.nl – closed Sunday Plan: **E3**

Menu 95/115 € – Carte 78/160 € – *(dinner only)*

• Asian influences • Elegant • Intimate •

This cosmopolitan restaurant has an intimate and stylish ambience, with an open kitchen where you can watch the sushi master at work. Prepare for a feast! Asian ingredients and recipes are used to create an intense harmony of flavours, with an extensive menu comprising both traditional and modern dishes, which are as pure as they are delicate.

Blauw aan de Wal XX

O.Z. Achterburgwal 99 ✉ 1012 DD – ✆ (020) 330 22 57 – www.blauwaandewal.com – closed Sunday Plan: **G2**

Menu 45/67 € – *(dinner only until 11pm) (booking advisable) (tasting menu only)*

• Market cuisine • Rustic • Friendly •

A popular restaurant at the end of a cul-de-sac in the lively red light district. Discreet décor, simple and tasty modern cuisine, good wine selection and a shady terrace.

Dynasty XX A/C

Reguliersdwarsstraat 30 ✉ 1017 BM – ✆ (020) 626 84 00 – www.restaurantdynasty.nl – closed 27 December-31 January and Tuesday Plan: **F2**

Menu 45/50 € – Carte 35/80 € – *(dinner only)*

• Chinese • Elegant • Exotic décor •

A pleasant, long-standing restaurant featuring cuisine from around Asia. The trendy, exotic décor is warm and colourful. There's a lovely terrace at the back and service is attentive.

Hosokawa XX A/C

Max Euweplein 22 ✉ 1017 MB – ✆ (0 20) 638 80 86 – www.hosokawa.nl – closed 27 April, 31 December and 1 January Plan: **F3**

Menu 50/95 € – Carte 31/110 € – *(dinner only)*

• Teppanyaki • Fashionable • Design •

Experienced chef Hiromichi Hosokawa has mastered Japanese cuisine down to the fine details. In 1992 he opened this smart restaurant, where he continues to prepare traditional teppanyaki, robatayaki and sushi dishes. Characteristic Japanese precision, finesse and full flavours are part and parcel of the experience.

Ron Gastrobar Oriental XX A/C

Kerkstraat 23 ✉ 1017 GA – ✆ (0 20) 223 53 52 – www.rongastrobaroriental.nl – closed 27 April, 31 December and 1 January Plan: **F2**

Menu 24 € (lunch), 39/63 € – Carte 30/60 € – *(dinner only until 11pm) (booking advisable)*

• Chinese • Oriental décor • Trendy •

Subtle lighting, Asian decor and natural materials set the mood at this stylish restaurant, while a renowned bartender shakes cocktails at the extensive bar. Full of flavour, the delicious dishes offer a contemporary take on traditional Chinese cuisine.

Senses – Hotel The Albus XX

Vijzelstraat 45 ✉ 1017 HE – ✆ (0 20) 530 62 66 – www.sensesrestaurant.nl – closed 27 April, 25 and 26 December Plan: **G2**

Menu 40 € 🍷 (lunch), 43/79 €

• Modern cuisine • Intimate • Bistro •

Lars Bertelsen is a chef bursting with creativity, as guests will notice in the presentation, diverse textures and sometimes surprising flavour combinations in his food. He is also highly talented, as proven by the entire experience at Senses. The restyling of the cosy, colourful room emphasises his ambition.

d'Vijff Vlieghen

Spuistraat 294 (via Vlieghendesteeg 1) ✉ 1012 VX Plan: **F2**
– ✆ (0 20) 530 40 60 – www.vijffvlieghen.nl – closed 27 April, 5-18 August and 24 December-4 January
Menu 39/80 € 🍷 – Carte 40/55 € – *(dinner only)*
• Traditional cuisine • Historic • Rustic •
The classic dishes on offer at these charming 17C premises are all prepared with typical Dutch products. Various attractive, country-style dining rooms where original Rembrandt sketches decorate the walls.

Envy

Prinsengracht 381 ✉ 1016 HL – ✆ (0 20) 344 64 07 Plan: **F2**
– www.envy.nl
Menu 28 € (lunch), 47/67 € – Carte 32/55 € – *(dinner only except Friday, Saturday and Sunday)*
• Mediterranean cuisine • Fashionable • Brasserie •
Looking for a place to eat in trendy surroundings? Then head for this stylish trattoria, where the menu offers a beautiful range of creative recipes in tapas-style portions and the combination of subtle and pronounced flavours adds overall depth to the dishes. Note that the number of tables available for advance booking is very limited.

Wolf Atelier

Westerdoksplein 20 ✉ 1013 AZ – ✆ (0 20) 344 64 28 Plan I: **C1**
– www.wolfatelier.nl – closed 25 December, 1 January and Sunday
Menu 23 € (lunch), 43/75 € – Carte approx. 50 €
• Modern French • Contemporary décor • Design •
Michael Wolf plays with flavours and modern combinations, offering diners the opportunity to test them out (as well as a choice of regular dishes), then refines them to retain their best features. The name Atelier is therefore particularly appropriate in this trendy, industrial-style restaurant, which is located on an old railway bridge with a beautiful view of the IJ.

BAK

Van Diemenstraat 408 ✉ 1013 CR – ✆ (0 20) 737 25 53 Plan I: **C1**
– www.bakrestaurant.nl – closed 27 April, 29 July-13 August, Monday and Tuesday
Menu 33/70 € – *(dinner only except Saturday and Sunday) (tasting menu only)*
• Vegetarian • Vintage • Friendly •
Take the stairs to the third floor of this unobtrusive warehouse (you'll need to ring the bell in the evening) to discover the industrial-style BAK restaurant with its lovely view over the IJ river. The focus here is on original, vegetarian dishes made from sustainably produced ingredients which are full of surprising and delicious flavours.

Bistrot Neuf

Haarlemmerstraat 9 ✉ 1013 EH – ✆ (0 20) 400 32 10 Plan: **G1**
– www.bistrotneuf.nl
Menu 22 € (lunch), 35/53 € – Carte 37/81 €
• Classic cuisine • Lyonnaise bistro • Friendly •
With its clean, modern design, this relaxed bistro is ideally located in a lively area of Amsterdam. Traditional French dishes exhibit original Amsterdam flair and are impeccably cooked to bring out the true flavours of the ingredients. Efficient service.

Breda

Singel 210 ✉ 1016 AB – ✆ (0 20) 622 52 33 Plan: **F1**
– www.breda-amsterdam.com – closed 27 April, 26 December and 1 January
Menu 30 € (lunch), 60/80 € – *(bookings advisable at dinner) (surprise menu only)*
• Modern cuisine • Brasserie •
Welcome to Breda: dazzling, a touch retro, and luxurious too, but above all a place for delicious food. Choose from surprise menus featuring a range of inventive dishes created by the chef. International, varied and tasty.

Choux

De Ruyterkade 128 ✉ 1011 AC – ✆ (020) 210 30 90 – www.choux.nl – closed 22 and 27 April, 10 June, 4-12 August, 31 December-7 January, Monday dinner, Saturday lunch and Sunday

Plan: **H1**

Menu 30 € (lunch), 38/69 € – Carte approx. 39 €

• Modern French • Fashionable • Trendy •

Giving prominence to vegetables may not always be the obvious choice, but at this trendy restaurant it works beautifully. The continually surprising ingredients, creative preparations and intense flavours ensure complete fulfilment, taking diners on a wonderful voyage of discovery.

The French Connection

Singel 460 ✉ 1017 AW – ✆ (0 20) 737 30 51 – www.tfcrestaurant.nl – closed Sunday and Monday

Plan: **F2**

Menu 42/68 € – Carte approx. 50 € – *(dinner only)*

• Creative French • Friendly • Intimate •

France is clearly the theme here, from the rustic interior to the Gallic menu. The experienced chef serves up tasty dishes which deliver a creative take on classic French recipes, while also demonstrating refined precision and offering great value for money.

Gebr. Hartering

Peperstraat 10hs ✉ 1011 TL – ✆ (020) 421 06 99 – www.gebr-hartering.nl – closed 24, 25, 26 and 31 December-1 January

Plan: **H2**

Menu 55/80 € – Carte 50/79 € – *(dinner only)*

• French • Bistro • Rustic •

Niek and Paul Hartering share a love of ingredients. This cheerful venue proposes a short menu, which changes regularly, as the fusion cuisine depends on the ingredients at their best on the day. Flavours don't lie.

Geisha

Prins Hendrikkade 106a ✉ 1011 AJ – ✆ (0 20) 626 24 10 www.restaurantgeisha.nl – closed 27 April, 25 and 31 December, 1 January and Sunday

Plan: **G1**

Menu 33/55 € – Carte 24/68 € – *(dinner only)*

• Asian • Exotic décor • Fashionable •

This trendy Geisha spoils guests with the delicacies of Southeast Asia. The traditional precision and freshness are certainly part of the deal, and are supplemented with more innovative dishes. You can also enjoy hors-d'oeuvres-style options at the bar, accompanied by a choice of delicious cocktails.

Kaagman & Kortekaas

Sint Nicolaasstraat 43 ✉ 1012 NJ – ✆ (0 20) 233 65 44 – www.kaagmanenkortekaas.nl – closed Sunday and Monday

Plan: **F1**

Menu 50 € – *(dinner only) (booking essential)*

• Market cuisine • Friendly • Trendy •

Giel Kaagman and Bram Kortekaas focus on quality in their informal bistro. The chef likes to work with game and poultry, making his own charcuterie and terrines. These are cleverly worked into dishes that present an up-to-date take on traditional flavours.

The Seafood Bar

Spui 15 ✉ 1012 WX – ✆ (0 20) 233 74 52 – www.theseafoodbar.com – closed 24 and 31 December dinner

Plan: **F2**

Menu 16 € (lunch), 38/49 € – Carte 29/69 €

• Brasserie • Contemporary décor •

You will not be surprised to find that this trendy establishment is a mecca for lovers of seafood. The delicacies glisten on the display counters and look mouthwatering on the plate, prepared with the minimum of fuss. The extensive array of fresh ingredients guarantees a superb meal.

✿✿ **Ciel Bleu** – Hotel Okura, 23rd floor

Ferdinand Bolstraat 333 ✉ 1072 LH Plan: **C2**
– ✆ (0 20) 678 74 50 – www.okura.nl
– closed 4-25 August, 30 December-6 January and Sunday
Menu 185/195 € – *(dinner only)*
• Creative • Elegant •

At Ciel Bleu visitors can expect a spectacle: the view of the city is fantastic and the modern elegance of the decor is a feast for the eyes. The technically accomplished chef reveals his true character, producing an astonishing variety of international cuisine, surprising in its creativity and unexpected combinations of flavours.

➜ Koningskrab met kaviaar, roomijs van beurre blanc en gezouten citroen. Dorsetlam met polenta, groene asperges en foyotsaus. Banaan met gianduja, pinda en bruine rum.

✿ **Yamazato** – Hotel Okura

Ferdinand Bolstraat 333 ✉ 1072 LH Plan: **C2**
– ✆ (0 20) 678 74 50 – www.okura.nl
– closed 8-19 July and Monday
Menu 45 € (lunch), 95/125 € – Carte 38/172 €
• Japanese • Minimalist • Chic •

The intimate, spartan interior and view of the Japanese garden produce a Zen feel. Ladies in kimonos bring authentic kaiseki dishes to the table, showcasing the subtlety and technical accomplishment of Japanese cuisine. This place honours tradition, as visitors will also discover when ordering a simple bento box lunch.

➜ Omakase en nigiri sushi. Tempura van kreeft. Shabu shabu, dunne plakjes entrecote en groenten in een bouillon.

✿ **RON Gastrobar** (Ron Blaauw)

Sophialaan 55 ✉ 1075 BP Plan: **B2**
– ✆ (0 20) 496 19 43 – www.rongastrobar.nl
– closed 27 April and 31 December-1 January
Menu 24 € (lunch), 39/68 € – Carte approx. 60 €
• Creative French • Fashionable • Trendy •

Ron Blaauw returns to basics here, creating cuisine that is pure and prepared with quality ingredients. This urban gastro-bar combines a hip, lively ambience with top class cuisine without the frills. It also means little formality but original, delicious food and sensational flavours. Phenomenal value for money, which is also reflected in the wine list.

➜ Gebakken ganzenlever met gemarineerde bietjes, krenten in madeira en parmezaanschuim. Barbecue spare ribs met huisgemaakte sambal. Surprise ei.

✿ **Bolenius** (Luc Kusters)

George Gershwinlaan 30 ✉ 1082 MT Plan: **B2**
– ✆ (0 20) 404 44 11 – www.bolenius-restaurant.nl
– closed 3-19 August, 26 December-2 January, Bank Holidays, Saturday lunch and Sunday
Menu 49 € (lunch), 79/99 € – Carte 72/123 €
• Creative • Design • Elegant •

Luc Kusters is an ambassador of Dutch cuisine with his creativity turning home-grown produce (the vegetable garden is right next to the restaurant) into wonderful dishes. Vegetables play an important role in his exciting culinary experience, really exploring the power of natural flavours. The sleek and minimalistic style of Bolenius has indeed a class of its own.

➜ Spaghetti van asperge met kokkels. Lam en paling met kuit en aubergine. Peer en pastinaak met drop, granen en chocolade.

Le Restaurant (Jan de Wit)

Frans Halsstraat 26H ✉ 1072 BR – ✆ (020) 379 22 07 Plan II: **F3**
– www.lerestaurant.nl – closed 23 April-1 May, 16 July-3 August, 24 December-4 January, Sunday and Monday
Menu 65/85 € – *(dinner only) (number of covers limited, pre-book) (tasting menu only)*

• Market cuisine • Bistro •

Jan de Wit's Le Restaurant is a cosy establishment with a bistro feel. His formula for success remains the same: a simple but spectacular menu. The best of market produce is prepared without too much fuss and plated up in its authentic form to convince diners with its powerful flavours. The price-pleasure ratio is spot on.

→ Ceviche van makreel en coquilles, asperges en dashi. Tamme eend van de Japanse grill met amandel, romanesco en emulsie van gepofte knoflook. Hollandse aardbeien met rabarber, chartreusesabayon en kaffirlimoen.

Sinne (Alexander Ioannou)

Ceintuurbaan 342 ✉ 1072 GP – ✆ (0 20) 682 72 90 Plan: **C2**
– www.restaurantsinne.nl – closed Monday and Tuesday
Menu 39/87 € – *(dinner only except Sunday) (booking essential)*

• Modern cuisine • Trendy •

The open-plan kitchen at the back of this warm and friendly restaurant is reminiscent of a theatre scene. Chef Ioannou adds the finishing touch to dishes where French, Mediterranean and Oriental influences meet. The result is remarkable – dishes full of wonderful and complex flavours at affordable prices.

→ Ceviche van makreel met limoendressing, rettich en gepofte mais. Eendenborst op de barbecue met rode kerrie, linzen, boleten en eigen jus. Bananencremeux met gezouten pinda, chocoladeganache en kalamansi.

Brasserie van Baerle

Van Baerlestraat 158 ✉ 1071 BG – ✆ (0 20) 679 15 32 Plan: **B2**
– www.brasserievanbaerle.nl – closed 27 April, 31 December-1 January, Monday lunch and Saturday lunch
Menu 37 € – Carte 48/56 €

• Classic cuisine • Vintage •

This retro brasserie attracts regular customers, mainly from the local area because of its appealing menu, tasty steak tartare and well-matched wines. Courtyard terrace.

Le Hollandais

Amsteldijk 41 ✉ 1074 HV – ✆ (0 20) 679 12 48 Plan: **C2**
– www.lehollandais.nl – closed 27 April, 1-25 August, 22 December-6 January, Sunday and Monday
Menu 37/65 € 🍷 – Carte 51/61 € – *(dinner only)*

• Classic cuisine • Vintage • Bistro •

Feeling a little nostalgic? Then this is the place for you, as Le Hollandais really turns the clock back. The dining hall is reminiscent of the 1970s and the chef still serves up generous dishes with rich flavours, just like the old days. You will experience classic French cuisine the way it is meant to taste.

Serre – Hotel Okura

Ferdinand Bolstraat 333 ✉ 1072 LH – ✆ (0 20) 678 74 50 – www.okura.nl – closed 18 February-1 March Plan: **C2**
Menu 37/40 € – Carte 42/58 €

• Modern cuisine • Brasserie •

Like Okura's other restaurants, quality is the focus of this chic brasserie, with its magnificent canal-side terrace. Excellent ingredients go into the international cuisine served here. The chef selects techniques from diverse cuisines, unifying them in straightforwardly delicious dishes.

Arles

Govert Flinckstraat 251 ✉ 1073 BX – ✆ (0 20) 679 82 40 Plan: **C2**
– www.arles-amsterdam.nl – closed late December-early January
Menu 37 € – *(dinner only)*

• Modern French • Bistro • Intimate •

This attractive bistro brings a touch of Provence to Amsterdam, with framed photos of the chef's native city Arles adorning the walls. The chef, a fan of jazz music, creates neo-bistro-style dishes which offer a fresh reinterpretation of familiar French flavours. The fixed-price menu, which changes every month, is a real winner!

Café Caron

Frans Halsstraat 28 ✉ 1072 BS – ✆ (0 20) 675 86 68 Plan II: **F3**
– www.cafecaron.nl – closed 27 April and 31 January
Menu 37 € – Carte 37/49 € – *(dinner only)*

• Classic French • Bistro • Friendly •

This cosy bistro is run by Alain Caron (a well-known TV personality and chef) and his family. The ambience here is typically French, as is the menu which features traditional, generous bistro-style dishes which are a work of art in their own right. Trying out the set menu here is a real joy.

Elkaar

Alexanderplein 6 ✉ 1018 CG – ✆ (0 20) 330 75 59 Plan: **C2**
– www.etenbijelkaar.nl – closed 27 April, 24 December-7 January, Sunday and Monday
Menu 37/55 € – Carte 45/55 €

• Modern French • Family •

If you are looking for a relaxed meal out together, this friendly establishment with a pleasant summer terrace is a great option. The set menu is a good choice, offering a selection from the à la carte menu. The chef combines quality ingredients in a contemporary manner, creating beautiful flavours without overcomplicating things.

Oud-Zuid

Johannes Verhulststraat 64 ✉ 1071 NH – ✆ (0 20) 676 60 58 – www.restaurantoudzuid.nl – closed 27 April, 25, 26 and 31 December-1 January Plan: **B2**
Menu 28 € (lunch)/37 € – Carte 47/64 €

• Traditional cuisine • Brasserie •

This characterful restaurant with a brasserie-style dining room presents traditional dishes with a modern touch. For music lovers, Oud-Zuid is less than a 10 min walk from the Concertgebouw.

Rijsel

Marcusstraat 52b ✉ 1091 TK – ✆ (0 20) 463 21 42 Plan: **C2**
– www.rijsel.com – closed 1-14 August and Sunday
Menu 36/75 € – Carte 40/105 € – *(dinner only) (booking essential)*

• Traditional cuisine • Simple •

Rijsel's simple interior resembles a classroom, and the restaurant happens to share its entrance with a school. In the open kitchen you can see the master at work preparing his delicious French cuisine. He has an excellent knowledge of ingredients and his traditional dishes also include a nod to Flemish food.

Het Bosch

Jollenpad 10 ✉ 1081 KC – ✆ (0 20) 644 58 00 Plan: **B3**
– www.hetbosch.com – closed 23 December-6 January and Sunday
Menu 40 € (lunch), 45/65 € – Carte 38/50 €

• Modern French • Fashionable • Trendy •

From this contemporary restaurant diners enjoy a breathtaking view of the Nieuwe Meer marina. In this dream location the chef entertains diners with lavish, up-to-date dishes prepared with real know-how.

Le Garage

Ruysdaelstraat 54 ✉ 1071 XE – ✆ (0 20) 679 71 76 – www.restaurantlegarage.nl – closed Saturday and Sunday
Plan: **B2**
Menu 37 € – Carte 46/60 € – *(dinner only)*
• French • Fashionable •
Red velour, mirrors and small lamps all combine to create a luxurious brasserie interior which gives Le Garage a genuine showbiz look! The impressive and extensive menu offers a wide choice of enticing traditional French dishes which are full of flavour – with occasional touches of creativity which make the food just a little bit more special.

The Roast Room

Europaplein 2 ✉ 1078 GZ – ✆ (020) 723 96 14 – www.theroastroom.nl – closed 26 and 27 April, Saturday lunch and Sunday lunch
Plan: **C2**
Menu 35 € (lunch)/45 € – Carte 50/85 € – *(open until 11.30pm)*
• Meats and grills • Trendy • Fashionable •
An impressive steakhouse. Glass, steel, wood and meat are the dominant features of the Roast Bar (brasserie on the ground floor) and the Rotisserie (restaurant upstairs). See the meat hanging ready to cook, smell it on the grill and taste the results when it has been cooked to perfection. Excellent side dishes complete the picture.

Sazanka – Hotel Okura

Ferdinand Bolstraat 333 ✉ 1072 LH – ✆ (0 20) 678 74 50 – www.okura.nl – closed 22 July-2 August
Plan: **C2**
Menu 90/125 € – Carte 63/111 € – *(dinner only)*
• Teppanyaki • Friendly •
After being greeted by ladies dressed in kimonos, you sit down around the teppenyaki grill and the show begins. Seven to ten people can be accommodated here to watch the teppan-chef juggle with all kinds of produce. It is an entertaining spectacle that results in delicious Japanese dishes.

ARC. by Lute

Hotel Pestana Amsterdam Riverside – Amsteldijk 67 ✉ 1074 HZ – ✆ (020) 220 69 02 – www.arc.amsterdam
Plan: **C2**
Menu 38 € (lunch), 48/99 € – Carte 56/76 €
• Modern cuisine • Fashionable • Elegant •
Boasting a terrace shaded by a large tree, this stylish restaurant has a contemporary, cosmopolitan and trendy feel. Peter Lute's creations do full justice to the fine location, demonstrating modern techniques and international influences in dishes bursting with flavour. A fashionable venue offering truly delicious cuisine!

Graham's Kitchen

Hemonystraat 38 ✉ 1074 BS – ✆ (0 20) 364 25 60 – www.grahamskitchen.amsterdam – closed 27 December-2 January, Sunday and Monday
Plan: **C2**
Menu 39/63 € – *(dinner only)*
• Modern British • Friendly • Intimate •
Graham Mee's cuisine not only reflects his English origins, but also demonstrates his creative flair and his ability to prepare strong dishes, thanks to his experience in top-class establishments. The restaurant's cosy interior is equally attractive, with an eye-catching mural forming part of the decor.

Maris Piper

Frans Halsstraat 76 ✉ 1072 BV – ✆ (0 20) 737 24 79 – www.maris-piper.com – closed 27 April, 26 December and 1 January
Plan: **C2**
Carte 39/83 €
• Modern cuisine • Contemporary décor •
There is a chic, London-style atmosphere in this large luxurious brasserie. The menu is equally good with dishes which are not unnecessarily complex yet full of strong flavours and prepared by a chef who delights his guests with his internationally influenced dishes. The Chef's Table (only in the evening) is a real experience.

Restaurant C XX

Wibautstraat 125 ✉ 1091 GL – ✆ (0 20) 210 30 11 Plan: **C2**
– www.c.amsterdam – closed 27 April and 1 January
Menu 25 € (lunch), 35/75 € – Carte 41/48 € – *(open until 11pm)*
• Creative French • Trendy • Chic •

The contemporary, chic Restaurant Celsius is a dazzling spot, especially the kitchen bar. The reference to degrees emphasises the precision the chefs strive for, because that is what makes the difference between good food and delicious cuisine. Creativity in the combination of strong flavours and textures makes C a top choice.

Visaandeschelde XX (dinner)

Scheldeplein 4 ✉ 1078 GR – ✆ (020) 675 15 83 Plan: **C2**
– www.visaandeschelde.nl – closed 27 April, 31 December-1 January, Saturday lunch and Sunday lunch
Menu 40 € (lunch), 45/65 € – Carte 57/98 € – *(open until 11pm)*
• Seafood • Traditional décor •

The Scheldeplein is the place to come for tasty fish. The attractive nautical décor and the lively atmosphere contribute to the success it has achieved since 1999. Guests love to come and enjoy fresh delicacies plucked straight from the sea. A creative approach to classic combinations gives the flavours plenty of punch!

ZUID X

Stadionweg 320 ✉ 1076 PK – ✆ 020 210 3321
– www.restaurantzuid.amsterdam – closed 1 January and Mondays from June to August
Menu 28 € (lunch), 35/53 € – Carte 35/46 €
• Modern French • Trendy • Fashionable •

Zuid-Amsterdam is booming, as is demonstrated by establishments such as ZUID. This pleasant restaurant is open throughout the day; whether you choose a sandwich or a three-course dinner, you can rest assured it will be delicious. The cuisine is modern, varied and international in flavour. No fuss and plenty of fun!

AT SCHIPHOL AIRPORT

Aan de Poel (Stefan van Sprang) XXXX

Handweg 1 ✉ 1185 TS Amstelveen – ✆ (0 20) 345 17 63 – www.aandepoel.nl – closed 27 April-1 May, 28 July-12 August, 27 December-10 January, Saturday lunch, Sunday and Monday Plan I: **B3**
Menu 55 € (lunch)/119 € – Carte 96/147 €
• Elegant •

A successful marriage of technical skill and brilliant produce ensures that every dish is a feast for the senses. Here, contemporary cuisine can be savoured in one of its most beautiful and tasteful forms. What's more, this restaurant benefits from a superb lakeside setting, a chic and sophisticated designer interior and a skilled sommelier.

→ Tonijn en ganzenlever met pistache en baconvinaigrette. Gegrilde sukade met een ganzenleverterrine en morieljessaus. Geblazen suikerbal met structuren van bramen en lavendel.

De Jonge Dikkert XX

Amsterdamseweg 104a ✉ 1182 HG Amstelveen Plan I: **B3**
– ✆ (0 20) 643 33 33 – www.jongedikkert.nl – closed 3 weeks in August, 24 and 31 December-5 January, Saturday lunch and Sunday lunch
Menu 35 € (lunch), 36/68 € – Carte 47/57 €
• Country • Romantic • Inn •

De Jonge Dikkert has given this 17C windmill a new lease of life with its modern decor, intimate atmosphere and attractive dining room with wooden beams. Here the chef uses predominantly Dutch produce (up to 80%!) in his creative, contemporary-style dishes, resulting in a surprisingly refined cuisine.

Kronenburg

XX

Prof. E.M. Meijerslaan 6 ✉ 1183 AV Amstelveen Plan I: **B3**
– ✆ (0 20) 345 54 89 – www.restaurant-kronenburg.nl – closed 27 April, 11-27 August, Saturday lunch and Sunday
Menu 29/42 € – Carte 28/50 €

• Modern cuisine • Trendy • Fashionable •

This is a welcome oasis in the Kronenburg business quarter, where you can dine surrounded by lush greenery beside a lake, enjoying the beautiful setting through the glass façade of the terrace. The light, airy interior is equally stunning. The young chef here creates modest-sized dishes with sophisticated, diverse and delicious modern flavours.

Den Burgh

XX

Rijnlanderweg 878 ✉ 2132 ML Hoofddorp – ✆ 0 23 888 56 66 – www.denburgh.nl – closed Saturday lunch and Sunday
Menu 30 € (lunch)/49 € – Carte 43/67 €

• Market cuisine • Contemporary décor • Chic •

Stylishly modernised and elegantly furnished, Den Burgh has the typical charm of a farmhouse dating from 1859. The main bar, lined with golden pennies, is a real eye-catcher. The restaurant also boasts an excellent location next to a business park and close to the airport. The menu focuses on local produce, featuring traditionally flavoured dishes with a modern look.

Rotterdam

ROTTERDAM

DutchScenery/iStock

ROTTERDAM IN...

→ **ONE DAY**
Blaak area including Kijk-Kubus and Boompjestorens, Oude Haven, Museum Boijmans Van Beuningen.

→ **TWO DAYS**
More Museumpark, Delfshaven, take in the view from Euromast, cruise along the Nieuwe Maas.

→ **THREE DAYS**
Kop Van Zuid, a show at the Luxor Theatre.

Rotterdam trades on its earthy appeal, on a rough and ready grittiness that ties in with its status as the largest seaport in the world; it handles 350 million tonnes of goods a year, with over half of all the freight that is heading into Europe passing through it. Flattened during the Second World War, Rotterdam was rebuilt on a grand scale, jettisoning the idea of streets full of terraced houses in favour of a modern cityscape of concrete and glass, and there are few places in the world that have such an eclectic range of buildings to keep you entertained (or bewildered): try the Euromast Space Tower, the Groothandelsgebouw

(which translates as 'wholesale building'), the 'Cube Houses' or the fabulous sounding Boompjestorens for size. The city is located on the Nieuwe Maas but is centred around a maze of other rivers – most importantly the Rhine and the Maas – and is only a few dozen kilometres inland from the North Sea. It spills over both banks, and is linked by tunnels, bridges and the metro; the most stunning connection across the water is the modern Erasmusbridge, whose graceful, angular lines of silver tubing have earned it the nickname 'The Swan', and whose sleek design has come to embody the Rotterdam of the new millennium. It's mirrored on the southern banks by the development of the previously rundown Kop Van Zuid area into a sleek, modern zone.

EATING OUT

Rotterdam is a hot place for dining, in the literal and metaphorical sense. There are lots of places to tuck into the flavours of Holland's colonial past, in particular the spicy delicacies of Indonesia and Surinam. The long east/west stretch of Oude and Nieuwe Binnenweg is not only handy for many of the sights, it's also chock-full of good cafés, café-bars and restaurants, and the canal district of Oudehaven has introduced to the city a good selection of places to eat while taking in the relaxed vibe. Along the waterfront, various warehouses have been transformed into mega-restaurants, particularly around the Noordereiland isle in the middle of the river, while in Kop Van Zuid, the Wilhelminapier Quay offers quality restaurants and tasty views too. Many establishments are closed at lunchtime, except business restaurants and those that set a high gastronomic standard and like to show it off in the middle of the day as well as in the evening. The bill includes a service charge, so tipping is optional: round up the total if you're pleased with the service.

CENTRE

✿✿ **Parkheuvel** (Erik van Loo) XxxX

Heuvellaan 21 ✉ 3016 GL – ✆ (0 10) 436 05 30 Plan: **A3**
– www.parkheuvel.nl – closed 22 and 27 April, 10 May, 10 June, 31 July-20 August, 27 December-8 January, 25-28 February, Saturday lunch, Monday and Tuesday
Menu 43 € (lunch), 105/145 € – Carte 112/186 €
• Creative • Elegant •

The elegant Parkheuvel, beautifully situated beside the river Maas, is a big name in Dutch gastronomy. It received its first Michelin Star in 1990 – and Erik van Loo upholds this tradition with cuisine that's well-crafted, meticulously prepared and has a natural generosity. His signature dishes are must-tries!

➜ Noordzeekrab en kaviaar met zoetzure komkommer, chlorofyl en boekweitblini's. Zuiglam met tomaat, gefermenteerde knoflook, tuinboontjes en tortellini. Parkheuvels Snickers met pinda, karamel en nougatine.

✿✿ **Fred** (Fred Mustert) XxxX (dinner)

Honingerdijk 263 ✉ 3063 AM – ✆ (0 10) 212 01 10
– www.restaurantfred.nl – closed 4-18 August, 25 December-1 January, Saturday lunch and Sunday
Menu 48 € (lunch), 97/140 € – Carte 86/108 €
• Creative French • Chic • Elegant •

Fred Mustert takes his guests on a culinary adventure in this stylish restaurant, which boasts decorative highlights such as a leather and 24-carat gold work of art and an impressive lighting installation. Less really is more according to chef Mustert, who creates well-balanced culinary masterpieces which are exciting, modern and with no unnecessary frills.

➜ Gebakken langoustines met meloen, bleekselderij en vinaigrette van milde kerrie. Zeetong met artisjok, asperges en beurre blanc met citroen. Parfait van nougat, compote van banaan, vanilleschuim en café glacé.

✿✿ **FG - François Geurds** XxX

Katshoek 37B ✉ 3032 AE Plan: **A1**
– ✆ (0 10) 425 05 20 – www.fgrestaurant.nl
– closed Sunday and Monday
Menu 45 € (lunch), 125/205 € – Carte 108/220 €
• Creative • Fashionable • Chic •

François Geurds has a clear vision and he brings it to life in this restaurant, which is urban, trendy and original. The chef adopts a style that is very detailed, sometimes even playful, but always keeps his focus on the flavours of his high quality ingredients and sauces. FG could easily stand for Fantastically Good!

➜ Oester met kombu, rabarber en ganzenlever. Piepkuiken met langoustine en kaviaar. Dessertcreatie met drop, banaan, venkel en dragon.

✿ **Amarone** (Jan van Dobben) XxX

Meent 72a ✉ 3011 JN Plan: **B1**
– ✆ (0 10) 414 84 87 – www.restaurantamarone.nl
– closed 5-26 August, 31 December-7 January, Bank Holidays, Saturday lunch and Sunday
Menu 38 € (lunch), 65/85 € – Carte 71/140 €
• Modern French • Chic •

A cosy open fire and a warm and fashionable interior… elegance is a quality this restaurant and the wine after which it is named share. Amarone has a prominent place on the impressive wine list, which beautifully complements the creative dishes from Jan van Dobben. Combinations are well-thought-through and, although the flavours can sometimes provide contrasts, they are always in harmony.

➜ Rode mul met knolselderij, zwarte knoflook en nori. Zeetong met sambai, beukenzwammen, paksoi en uiencrème. Champagnemousse met rabarber, yoghurt en rozensorbetijs.

Fitzgerald

XXX

Gelderseplein 49 ✉ 3011 WZ – ✆ (0 10) 268 70 10 Plan: **B2**
– www.restaurantfitzgerald.nl – closed 27 April, 28 July-12 August, 27 December-7 January, Monday lunch, Saturday lunch and Sunday
Menu 32 € (lunch), 49/89 € – Carte 66/101 €

• Modern French • Elegant •

Italian marble combined with design and vintage features, big windows and a beautiful enclosed garden all lend Fitzgerald a special allure. The modern, sometimes surprising twists the chef gives his dishes take them to a higher level and create a fantastic exchange of flavours. The sommelier complements this with excellent wines.

➜ Langoustines met avocado, kimchi, garnalen en zeebanaan. Gebraden duif met aubergine, tamarinde en kastanje. Ananas met appelkappers en karamelroomijs.

Joelia (Mario Ridder) – Hotel Hilton

XXX

Coolsingel 5 ✉ 3012 AA – ✆ (010) 710 80 34 – www.joelia.eu Plan: **A1**
Menu 45 € (lunch), 105/165 € – Carte 97/158 €

• Creative French • Design • Trendy •

Joelia proves that refinement does not need to be complex. Her eclectic decor beautifully combines vintage and design to unique effect. Her cuisine is creative without being fussy, and serves one aim: to achieve a harmony of subtle perfumes and intense flavours.

➜ Gouden gebak van brioche met ganzenlever en truffel. Hazenrug met rode biet en knolselderij. Soufflé met vanille, roomijs en bessencompote.

The Millèn (Wim Severein)

XXX

Weena 686 ✉ 3012 CN – ✆ (010) 430 23 33 Plan: **A1**
– www.restaurantthemillen.nl – closed 24 December-2 January, Saturday lunch, Sunday and Monday
Menu 30 € (lunch), 60/95 € – Carte 58/75 € – *(booking essential)*

• Modern cuisine • Design • Elegant •

The Millennium Tower is a landmark in Rotterdam and, thanks to the arrival of this elegant design restaurant, it is now also a destination for foodies. Wim Severein shows his knowledge and inventiveness here by bringing together top quality ingredients and allowing them to interact with one other with a certain playfulness. His colourful compositions really are delicious!

➜ Geroosterde langoustines met pastinaak, zoute vinger, zuurdesem en schaaldierengelei. Boerenduif met een parmentier van de pootjes, hazelnoot, gnocchi en koffie. Chocoladeganache met eucalyptus en bramensorbetijs.

FG Food Labs (François Geurds)

X

Katshoek 41 ✉ 3032 AE – ✆ (0 10) 425 05 20 Plan: **A1**
– www.fgfoodlabs.nl
Menu 43 € (lunch), 80/125 € – Carte 55/73 €

• Creative • Fashionable • Design •

This 'taste laboratory' housed in a trendy version of a train tunnel is definitely part of the Rotterdam scene. The emphasis is on new flavours and textures and on pushing culinary boundaries. This results in inventive cuisine that is bold and full of character.

➜ Nitro vijzel 'lab style'. Porkbelly 48 uur gegaard. Blanc-manger van amandelen.

In den Rustwat

XXX

Honingerdijk 96 ✉ 3062 NX – ✆ (0 10) 413 41 10 Plan: **C2**
– www.idrw.nl – closed 23 July-12 August, 31 December-8 January, Saturday lunch, Sunday and Monday
Menu 35 € (lunch), 37/62 € – Carte 52/79 €

• Modern cuisine • Intimate •

In den Rustwat adds an exotic touch to metropolitan Rotterdam with its thatched roof, history dating back to the 16C and an idyllic setting close to an arboretum. The food here is anything but traditional, offering contemporary-style dishes with an abundance of ingredients and cooking methods.

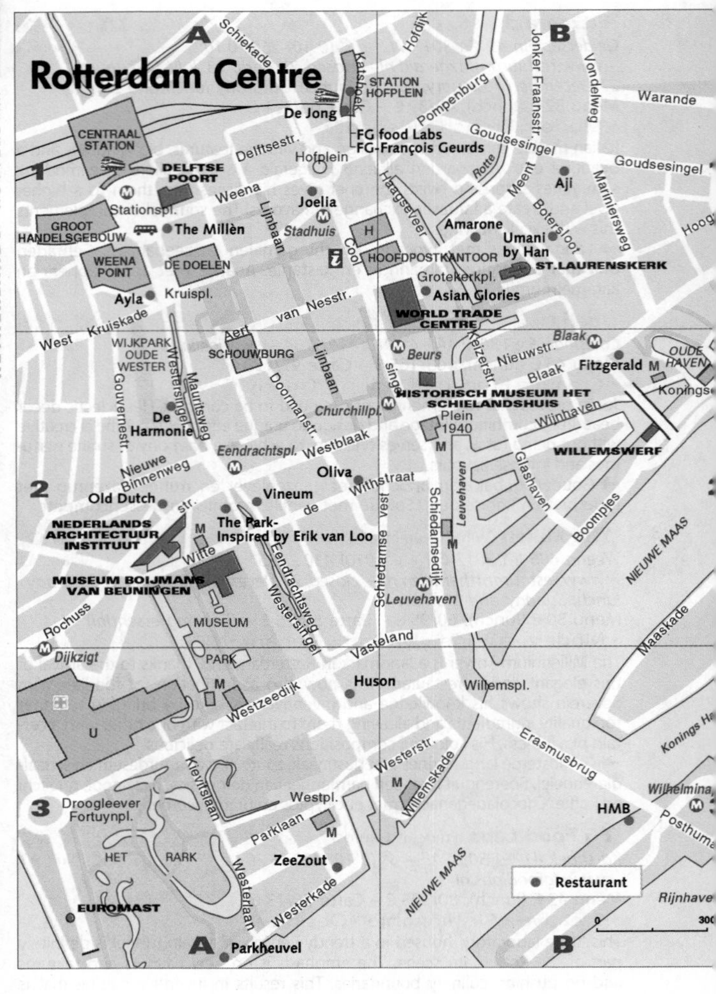

Asian Glories

XX AC

Leeuwenstraat 15a ✉ 3011 AL Plan: **B1**
– ✆ (0 10) 411 71 07 – www.asianglories.nl
– closed Wednesday
Menu 32/52 € – Carte 33/52 €
• Chinese • Family •

Asian Glories offers authentic, high quality Chinese cuisine, which focuses on the culinary traditions of Canton and Szechuan. Specialities on the menu include Peking duck and the delicious dim sum, a type of Oriental dumpling that is served either boiled or fried.

Gym & Gin

Kralingseweg 224 ✉ 3062 CG – ✆ (010) 210 45 10 – www.gymandgin.nl – closed first week August, 28 December-7 January and Sunday
Menu 29 € (lunch), 36/45 € – Carte 37/54 €
• International • Vintage • Trendy •
The name Gym & Gin stands for the balance we have to find between hedonism and health, although hedonism comes first here. The colourful decor, a balance between vintage and modern, makes for a wonderful backdrop for exploring the well-composed dishes. The originality of chef Huson's flavour bombs is exciting and refreshing.

Huson

Scheepstimmermanslaan 14 ✉ 3011 BS – ✆ (010) 413 03 71 – www.huson.nl – closed Saturday lunch and Sunday dinner after 7.30pm
Plan: **A3**
Menu 33 € 🍷 (lunch), 36/80 € – Carte 44/61 €
• Modern cuisine • Friendly • Vintage •
Huson is a trendy establishment where a lively industriousness always prevails. Here guests' mouths will water at the marvellous pairing of creativity with international ingredients in small dishes which are as subtle as they are exuberant. The chef is a dab hand at beautifully balancing fullness of flavour with freshness, as his signature dishes show.

The Park - Inspired by Erik van Loo

Parkhotel – Westersingel 70 ✉ 3015 LB – ✆ (0 10) 440 81 65 – www.thepark.nl – closed Saturday lunch and Sunday lunch
Plan: **A2**
Menu 29 € (lunch), 37/80 € – Carte 28/52 €
• Modern cuisine • Trendy •
The food at this blue-tinted luxury brasserie doesn't lie: they understand the meaning of taste here. The dishes are creatively inspired and beautifully composed. Every dish is perfectly seasoned and fits into the complete picture. So it makes sense when you hear that The Park is inspired by Erik van Loo, the chef of Michelin two star establishment Parkheuvel.

Ayla

Kruisplein 153 ✉ 3014 DD – ✆ (010) 254 00 05 – www.ayla.nl
Plan: **A1**
Carte 24/46 € – *(open until 11.30pm)*
• Mediterranean cuisine • Tapas bar • Mediterranean décor •
The air is sultry and Mediterranean scents quietly fill the room. Welcome to Ayla, where guests can enjoy the international atmosphere all day long. This is a relaxed spot where experienced chefs put all their skill into enhancing southern European flavours. Dishes are not unnecessarily complicated and are simply delicious.

Kwiezien

Delistraat 20 ✉ 3072 ZK – ✆ (0 10) 215 14 40 – www.kwiezien.nl – closed 25 and 26 December, 1 January, Sunday, Monday and Tuesday
Menu 35/50 € – *(dinner only)*
• Market cuisine • Family •
Sit back and enjoy the tempting range of dishes which this cosy restaurant has put together. Karin and Remco work exclusively with fresh ingredients and are constantly in search of inspiring combinations. The rich palette of flavours they create is sometimes daring but they always pull it off.

Umami by Han

Binnenrotte 140 ✉ 3011 HC – ✆ (0 10) 433 31 39 – www.umami-restaurant.com – closed 31 December
Plan: **B1**
Menu 27 € – Carte approx. 19 € – *(dinner only) (booking advisable)*
• Asian • Fashionable •
The trendy, modern interior with bright colours immediately catches the eye, but the trump card of this restaurant is its rock solid concept... a range of Asian dishes with a French twist from which you can choose your heart's desire. A wonderful journey of discovery at amazing prices!

Old Dutch

Rochussenstraat 20 ✉ 3015 EK – ✆ (0 10) 436 03 44 Plan: **A2**
– www.olddutch.net – closed Bank Holidays, Saturday and Sunday
Menu 40 € (lunch), 45/63 € – Carte 54/98 €

• Classic French • Classic décor •

With its serving staff decked out in suits and bow ties, this traditional restaurant with an incredibly spacious terrace has the atmosphere of a gentlemen's club. Familiar produce is given a fresh twist. Meat is even sliced at your table.

Allure

Cargadoorskade 107 ✉ 3071 AW – ✆ (0 10) 486 65 29
– www.restaurant-allure.nl – closed Saturday lunch and Monday
Menu 30 € (lunch), 38/63 € – Carte approx. 55 €

• Market cuisine • Design •

Allure fully lives up to its name. The experience starts with a warmly designed interior hung with modern art, which fits beautifully with the fantastic view of the marina. Then comes the champagne trolley, followed by top quality ingredients worked into modern French dishes with an international twist. Finally, there's the well-stocked cheese trolley.

HMB

Holland Amerika Kade 104 ✉ 3072 MC – ✆ (0 10) 760 06 20 – www.hmb-restaurant.nl – closed 22-30 April, 29 July-13 August, 27 December-8 January, Saturday lunch, Sunday and Monday Plan: **B3**
Menu 38 € (lunch), 65/90 € – Carte 52/93 € – *(booking advisable)*

• International • Fashionable •

HMB stands for hummingbird, and in keeping with its name, the interior of this restaurant is elegantly playful. The large windows also provide a stunning view of the Rotterdam skyline. The delicious, beautifully presented dishes are prepared with care and attention using ingredients from different international culinary traditions.

De Harmonie 23

Westersingel 95 ✉ 3015 LC – ✆ (0 10) 436 36 10 Plan: **A2**
– restaurant23.deharmonierotterdam.nl – closed 27 December-9 January, Bank Holidays, Saturday lunch, Sunday and Monday
Menu 53/100 € – Carte 56/80 €

• Creative • Elegant • Trendy •

The magnificently restored interior of De Harmonie 23 adds power to the ambition of chef Somer. His creativity is beautifully expressed here, making the name of his restaurant a reality, with authenticity and honesty combining to exciting effect. The extensive tasting menu allows diners to truly discover his cuisine.

Vineum

Eendrachtsweg 23 ✉ 3012 LB – ✆ (010) 720 09 66 Plan: **A2**
– www.vineum.nl – closed 27 April, 25 and 26 December, 31 December-1 January, Saturday lunch and Sunday
Menu 35/55 € – Carte 46/72 €

• Modern French • Friendly • Wine bar •

The wine list is the heart and soul of this restaurant with a pleasant city garden at the back. The variety and quality of the wines is truly remarkable, supported by cuisine that showcases excellent ingredients. The experienced chef brings freshness to the plate, using produce at its best.

Zeezout

Westerkade 11b ✉ 3016 CL – ✆ (0 10) 436 50 49 Plan: **A3**
– www.restaurantzeezout.nl – closed Sunday lunch and Monday
Menu 35 € (lunch), 50/69 € – Carte 57/65 €

• Seafood • Design •

Fish, fish and more fish. In the shipping quarter of one of the most important port cities in the world diners can enjoy the best the water has to offer. Their pure flavours seduce time and again, with dishes such as the salt-crusted sea bream topping the list. The stylishly decorated dining room also offers a view of the River Maas.

Aji

Pannekoekstraat 40A ✉ 3011 LK – ✆ (0 10) 767 01 69 Plan: **B1**
– www.restaurantaji.nl – closed 22 July-7 August, Sunday and Monday
Menu 25 € (lunch) – Carte 39/51 € – *(open until 11pm)*
• South American • Vintage •

Aji (a type of chilli pepper) is one of the ingredients that Pelle Swinkels discovered on his travels through Asia and South America – travels which have had a strong influence on his menu. He mixes these influences with basic French techniques to create delicious and intriguing dishes with an adventurous feel which is echoed in the restaurant's bold, vintage lounge-style decor.

C.E.O baas van het vlees

Sumatraweg 1 ✉ 3072 ZP – ✆ (0 10) 290 94 54
– www.ceobaasvanhetvlees.nl – closed Sunday and Monday
Carte 41/83 € – *(dinner only until 11pm)*
• Meats and grills • Contemporary décor • Bistro •

A lively bistro where prime quality American meat takes pride of place on the menu. All you have to decide is how you would like your meat cooked and whether you would like French fries and homemade mayonnaise as part of your meal.

De Jong

Raampoortstraat 38 ✉ 3032 AH – ✆ (010) 465 79 55 Plan: **A1**
– www.restaurantdejong.nl – closed Monday and Tuesday
Menu 47/62 € – *(dinner only)*
• Organic • Neighbourhood •

Chef Jim de Jong loves vegetables and herbs. He grows them himself and is inventive in preparing them, always placing their natural flavours front and centre. In this old train tunnel, decorated in vintage style, he shows diners how surprising and delicious organic cuisine can be. Eating at De Jong is an adventure every time.

Oliva

Witte de Withstraat 15a ✉ 3012 BK – ✆ (0 10) 412 14 13 Plan: **A2**
– www.restaurantoliva.nl – closed 25 December-1 January
Menu 37/49 € – Carte 27/52 € – *(dinner only)*
• Italian • Bistro •

Enjoy down-to-earth Italian cuisine in this delightful trattoria. The menu changes daily and the dishes are made from ingredients imported straight from Italy. Authentic and delicious.

OSLO

NORWAY
NORGE

konstantin32/iStock

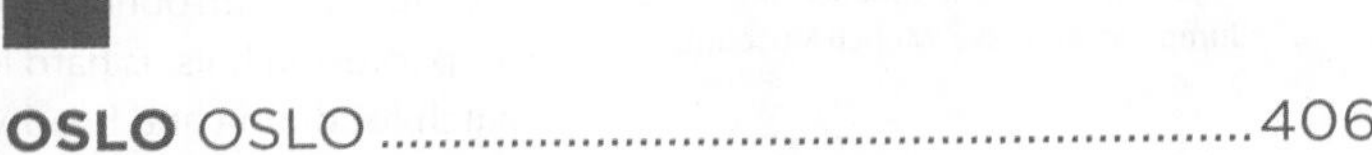

OSLO
OSLO

LeoPatrizi/iStock

OSLO IN...

→ **ONE DAY**
Aker Brygge, Karl Johans Gate, Oslo Opera House.

→ **TWO DAYS**
Akershus, Astrup Fearnley Museum, ferry trip to Bygdøy.

→ **THREE DAYS**
Vigeland Park, Holmenkollen Ski Jump, Grunerlokka, Munch Museum.

Oslo has a lot going for it – and one slight downside: it's one of the world's most expensive cities. It also ranks high when it comes to its standard of living, however, and its position at the head of Oslofjord, surrounded by steep forested hills, is hard to match for drama and beauty. It's a charmingly compact place to stroll round, particularly in the summer, when the daylight hours practically abolish the night and, although it may lack the urban cool of some other Scandinavian cities, it boasts its fair share of trendy clubs and a raft of Michelin Stars. There's a real raft, too: Thor Hyerdahl's famous Kon-Tiki – one of the star turns in a city that loves its museums.

Oslo's uncluttered feel is enhanced by parks and wide streets and, in the winter, there are times when you feel you have the whole place to yourself. Drift into the city by boat and land at the smart harbour of Aker Brygge; to the west lies the charming Bygdøy peninsula, home to museums permeated with the smell of the sea. Northwest is Frogner, with its famous sculpture park, the place where locals hang out on long summer days. The centre of town, the commercial hub, is Karl Johans Gate, bounded at one end by the Royal Palace and at the other by the Cathedral, while further east lie two trendy multi-cultural areas, Grunerlokka and Grønland, the former also home to the Edvard Munch Museum.

EATING OUT

Oslo has a very vibrant dining scene, albeit one that is somewhat expensive, particularly if you drink wine. The cooking can be quite classical and refined but there are plenty of restaurants offering more innovative menus too. What is in no doubt is the quality of the produce used, whether that's the ever-popular game or the superlative shellfish, which comes from very cold water, giving it a clean, fresh flavour. Classic Norwegian dishes often include fruit, such as lingonberries with venison. Lunch is not a major affair; most prefer just a snack or sandwich at midday while making dinner the main event of the day. You'll find most diners are seated by 7pm and are offered a 6, 7 or 8 course menu which they can reduce at their will, with a paired wine menu alongside. It doesn't have to be expensive, though. Look out for konditoris (bakeries) where you can pick up sandwiches and pastries, and kafeterias which serve substantial meals at reasonable prices. Service is a strength; staff are generally very polite, speak English and are fully versed in the menu.

CENTRE

PLAN I

✿✿✿ **Maaemo** (Esben Holmboe Bang) XxX AC

Schweigaardsgate 15B ✉ 0191 – Ⓜ Grønland – ☎ 22 17 99 69 – www.maaemo.no – Closed Christmas, Easter and Sunday-Tuesday Plan: **D2**

Menu 2800 NOK – *(dinner only and lunch Friday-Saturday) (booking essential) (tasting menu only)*

• Modern cuisine • Design • Fashionable •

Maaemo means 'Mother Earth' and this striking restaurant is all about connecting with nature. Service is perfectly choreographed and dishes are brought down from the mezzanine feature kitchen and finished at the table by the chefs themselves. Innovative, intricate cooking awakens the senses with sublime flavour combinations – some dishes take several days to construct.

➜ Oysters and aged caviar with mussel and dill sauce. Reindeer with preserved plums. Norwegian strawberries with rhubarb root and wood sorrel.

✿ **Statholdergaarden** (Bent Stiansen) XxX

Rådhusgata 11 (entrance on Kirkegata) ✉ 0151 – Ⓜ Stortinget – ☎ 22 41 88 00 – www.statholdergaarden.no – Closed 14 July-6 August, 23 December-3 January, 14-23 April, Sunday and bank holidays Plan: **C3**

Menu 1195 NOK – Carte 1020/1180 NOK – *(dinner only) (booking essential)*

• Classic cuisine • Intimate • Elegant •

A charming 17C house in the city's heart. Three elegant rooms feature an array of antiques and curios, and have wonderfully ornate stucco ceilings hung with chandeliers. Expertly rendered classical cooking uses seasonal Norwegian ingredients in familiar combinations. Service is well-versed and willing.

➜ Langoustine, radish, broccoli and black garlic. Lamb with salsify, kale and rosemary sauce. Raspberry with mascarpone and elderflower.

Statholderens Mat og Vin Kjeller – See below

✿ **Galt** (Bjørn Svensson) XX AC

Frognerveien 12B ✉ 0263 – ☎ (47) 48514886 – www.galt.no – Closed 22 December-3 January, 20-23 April, Sunday and Monday Plan: **A2**

Menu 865 NOK – Carte 515/715 NOK – *(dinner only)*

• Modern cuisine • Rustic • Chic •

The friends who previously ran Fauna and Oscarsgate have created this warm, intimate restaurant with an appealingly rustic feel. The set menu of 6 courses is nicely balanced, flavour combinations have been well thought through, and the contrast in textures is a particular strength.

➜ Langoustine, watercress and rye. Duck with leek, barley and tarragon sauce. Milk ice cream, blueberries, chocolate and verbena.

✿ **Kontrast** (Mikael Svensson) XX AC

Maridalsveien 15 ✉ 0178 – ☎ 21 60 01 01 – www.restaurant-kontrast.no – Closed 2 weeks Christmas-New Year, 2 weeks Easter, Sunday and Monday Plan: **D1**

Menu 1150/1600 NOK – Carte 595/960 NOK – *(dinner only)*

• Scandinavian • Design • Fashionable •

A modern restaurant with a stark, semi-industrial feel created by a concrete floor, exposed pipework and an open kitchen. Seasonal, organic Norwegian produce is used to create refined, original, full-flavoured dishes whose apparent simplicity often masks their complex nature. The service is well-paced.

➜ Langoustine served '3 ways' with rosehip. Mangalitsa pork with Swiss chard and pickled fennel. Hen's egg preserved in elderflower syrup.

Smalhans X

Ullevålsveien 43 ✉ 0171 – ☎ 22 69 60 00 – www.smalhans.no – Closed 7-28 July, 22 December-2 January, 17-23 April and lunch Monday and Tuesday Plan: **C1**

Menu 450/650 NOK (dinner) – Carte lunch 440/490 NOK – *(booking essential at dinner)*

• Traditional cuisine • Neighbourhood • Simple •

A sweet neighbourhood café with friendly staff and an urban feel. Coffee and homemade cakes are served in the morning, with a short selection of dishes including soup and a burger on offer between 12pm and 4pm. A daily hot dish is available from 4-6pm, while set menus and sharing plates are served at dinner.

À L'aise

XXX

Essendrops gate 6 ✉ 0368 – Ⓜ Majorstuen Plan: **A1**
– ✆ 210 55 700 – www.alaise.no – Closed 3 weeks July-August, Christmas, Easter, Sunday and Monday
Carte 960/1245 NOK – *(dinner only)*

• Modern cuisine • Intimate • Elegant •

This elegant, sophisticated restaurant is run by an engaging, knowledgeable team. The experienced chef is something of a Francophile: expect refined Gallic dishes packed with flavour and crafted from French and Norwegian produce.

Feinschmecker

XXX

Balchens gate 5 ✉ 0265 – ✆ 22 12 93 80 Plan: **A2**
– www.feinschmecker.no – Closed 3 weeks summer, Christmas, Easter and Sunday
Menu 895 NOK – Carte 665/1000 NOK – *(dinner only)*

• Traditional cuisine • Classic décor • Neighbourhood •

This long-standing restaurant – run by a charming team – has a cosy, welcoming atmosphere and a loyal local following. The well-presented dishes are classically based, with French influences. Wine pairings are available.

Festningen

XX

Myntgata 9 ✉ 0151 – ✆ 22 83 31 00 Plan: **C3**
– www.festningenrestaurant.no – Closed 22 December-4 January, 10 days Easter and Sunday
Menu 315/595 NOK – Carte 615/875 NOK

• Modern cuisine • Brasserie • Fashionable •

A smart, contemporary brasserie with a terrace and lovely views over the water to Aker Brygge; it was once a prison and its name means 'fortress'. The experienced kitchen create unfussy, attractively presented modern Nordic dishes using fresh local produce. The impressive wine list is strong on burgundy.

BA 53

XX

Bygdoy Allé 53 ✉ 0265 – ✆ 21 42 05 90 Plan: **A2**
– www.ba53.no – Closed July, Christmas, Easter and Sunday
Carte 400/640 NOK – *(dinner only and Saturday lunch)*

• Modern cuisine • Fashionable • Neighbourhood •

A moody cocktail bar combines with a relaxed, softly lit brasserie to create this stylish neighbourhood hotspot. Menus offer a mix of Nordic classics and more modern dishes; four per person is ample.

Bokbacka

XX

Skovveien 15 ✉ 0257 – ✆ 41 26 01 44 Plan: **A2**
– www.bokbacka.no – Closed 14 July-11 August, 21 December-3 January, 14-22 April, Sunday-Monday and bank holidays
Menu 795 NOK – *(dinner only) (tasting menu only)*

• Modern cuisine • Fashionable • Neighbourhood •

A unique 'food bar' with clean, light styling and fun, idiosyncratic features; most seats are arranged around the open kitchen, with only 4 other tables. Many of the theatrically presented dishes on the set omakase-style menu have a story.

Brasserie Paleo – Hotel Rosenkrantz

XX

Rosenkrantz gate 1 ✉ 0159 – Ⓜ National Theatrer Plan: **C2**
– ✆ 23 31 55 80 – www.brasseriepaleo.no – Closed early July-early August, Christmas, Easter and Sunday
Carte 545/595 NOK

• Scandinavian • Design • Brasserie •

With a name which reflects its philosophy, and a contemporary urban style, this is not your typical hotel restaurant. Watch the chefs prepare attractive modern Scandinavian dishes in the open kitchen. Service is professional and friendly.

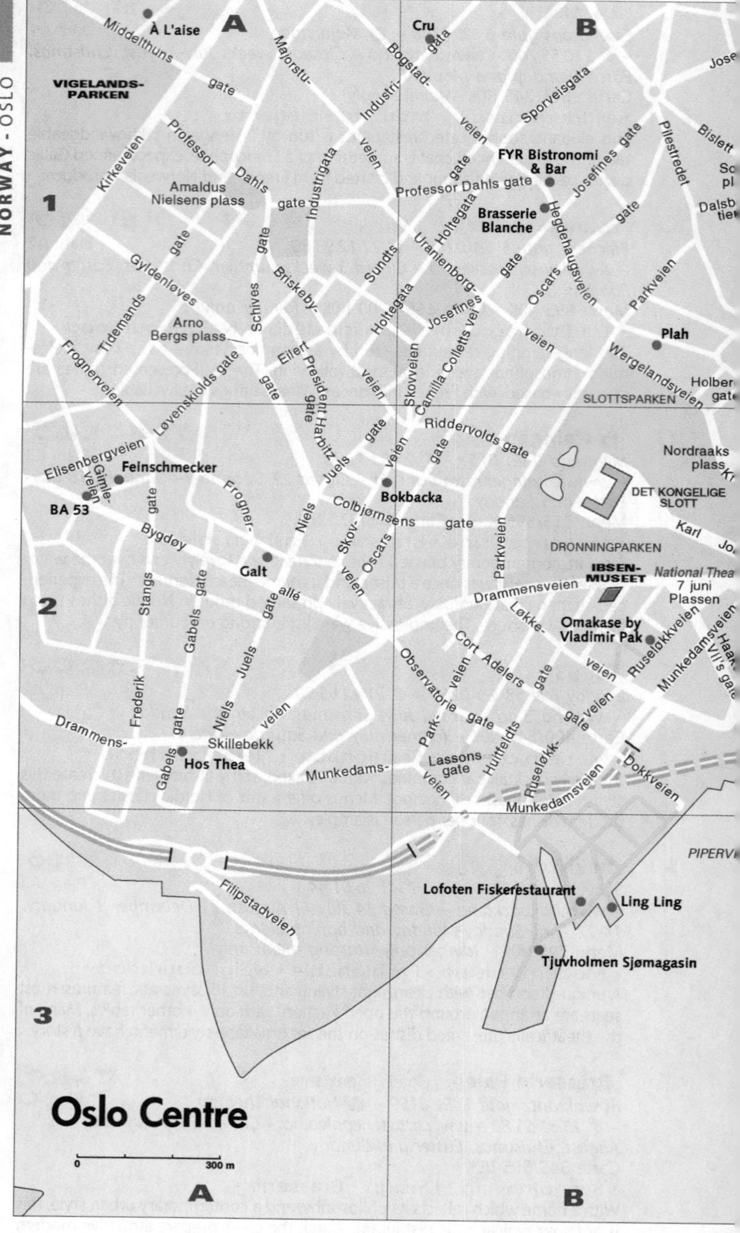
Oslo Centre
A
B
1
2
3
À L'aise
Cru
VIGELANDS-PARKEN
FYR Bistronomi & Bar
Brasserie Blanche
Amaldus Nielsens plass
Arno Bergs plass
Plah
SLOTTSPARKEN
Feinschmecker
BA 53
Bokbacka
Galt
Nordraaks plass
DET KONGELIGE SLOTT
DRONNINGPARKEN
IBSEN-MUSEET
National Thea
7 juni Plassen
Omakase by Vladimir Pak
Hos Thea
PIPERV
Lofoten Fiskerestaurant
Ling Ling
Tjuvholmen Sjømagasin
0
300 m

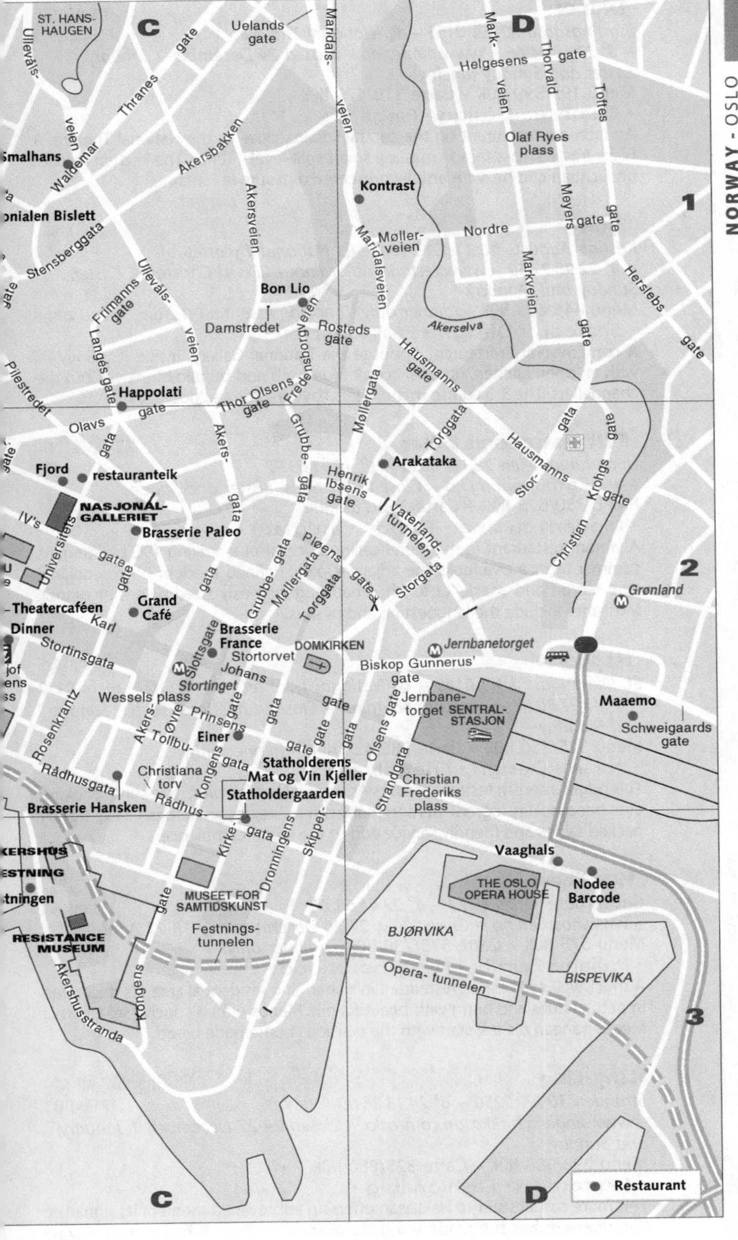

C
D
1
2
3
Smalhans
Kontrast
Bon Lio
Happolati
Fjord
restauranteik
NASJONAL-GALLERIET
Brasserie Paleo
Arakataka
Theatercaféen
Grand Café
Dinner
Brasserie France
DOMKIRKEN
Jernbanetorget
SENTRAL-STASJON
Maaemo
Einer
Statholderens Mat og Vin Kjeller
Statholdergaarden
Brasserie Hansken
Vaaghals
Nodee Barcode
THE OSLO OPERA HOUSE
MUSEET FOR SAMTIDSKUNST
RESISTANCE MUSEUM
BJØRVIKA
BISPEVIKA
Grønland
Stortinget
Stortorvet
Akerselva
Restaurant

Dinner

Stortingsgata 22 ✉ 0161 – Ⓜ National Theatret Plan: **C2**
– ✆ 23 10 04 66 – www.dinner.no – Closed 24 December-2 January , Easter and Sunday lunch
Menu 195/399 NOK – Carte 310/475 NOK
• Chinese • Design • Elegant •
An intimate restaurant on the central square, close to the National Theatre. A black frosted glass façade masks a smart split-level interior. The kitchen focuses on Sichuan cuisine, with artfully presented dim sum at lunch.

Fjord

Kristian Augusts gt. 11 ✉ 0164 – Ⓜ National Theatret Plan: **C2**
– ✆ 22 98 21 50 – www.restaurantfjord.no – Closed Christmas, Easter, Sunday and Monday
Menu 445/695 NOK – *(dinner only) (booking essential) (tasting menu only)*
• Seafood • Design • Fashionable •
A contemporary restaurant opposite the National Gallery. Inside it's dimly lit, with an open kitchen, unusual cobalt blue walls and buffalo horns set into the chandeliers. The 3-6 course menu offers flavoursome seafood dishes.

FYR Bistronomi & Bar

Underhaugsveien 28 ✉ 0354 – ✆ 45 91 63 92 Plan: **B1**
– www.fyrbistronomi.no – Closed Christmas, Easter and Sunday
Menu 350/695 NOK – Carte 360/785 NOK
• Modern cuisine • Trendy • Intimate •
A vibrant restaurant in the barrel-ceilinged cellar of a striking 19C building; its summer terrace overlooks the adjacent park. Refined modern bistro cooking: smørrebrød and snacks at lunch; creative, generously sized dishes at dinner. Must-tries include the langoustine and oysters.

Happolati

St. Olavs Plass 2 ✉ 0165 – Ⓜ National Theatret Plan: **C1/2**
– ✆ 47 97 80 87 – www.happolati.no – Closed Christmas, Easter, Sunday and Monday
Menu 525/750 NOK – Carte 385/425 NOK – *(dinner only)*
• Asian • Design • Friendly •
This bright, modish restaurant fuses Asian and Nordic styles; its assured cooking uses good quality ingredients and many dishes are designed for sharing. Tightly packed tables and friendly service add to the vibrant ambience.

Hos Thea

Gabels gate 11 ✉ 0272 – ✆ 22 44 68 74 Plan: **A2**
– www.hosthea.no – Closed July, 24-26 December and 18-22 April
Menu 575 NOK – Carte 575/730 NOK – *(dinner only)*
• Italian • Family • Neighbourhood •
A small, well-established restaurant in a charming residential area. It's decorated in natural hues and hung with beautiful oils. Menus offer a concise selection of Mediterranean dishes; start with the delicious homemade bread.

Ling Ling

Stranden 30 ✉ 0250 – ✆ 24 13 38 00 Plan: **B3**
– www.lingling.hakkasan.com/oslo – Closed 24-27 December, 1 January and Sunday
Menu 298/988 NOK – Carte 325/880 NOK
• Cantonese • Fashionable •
This more casual sister to Hakkasan offers an abbreviated menu of its signature Cantonese dishes but made using Norwegian produce. It has a great marina location, a cool lounge-bar and a terrific rooftop bar and terrace come summer.

Nodee Barcode

XX Plan: D3

Dronning Eufemais gate 28 ✉ 0191 – Ⓜ Jernbanetorget – ✆ 22 93 34 50 – www.nodee.no – Closed 24 December-1 January, 18-22 April, Sunday and bank holidays

Menu 335/658 NOK – Carte 310/970 NOK

• Asian • Fashionable • Trendy •

A moody, elegant restaurant serving an all-encompassing Asian menu featuring dim sum, sushi and dishes cooked on the Robata grill – crispy Peking duck is their speciality. There's a bar and terrace on the 13th floor and on the 14th floor is Nodee Sky, with its appealing set menu and city views.

Plah

XX Plan: B1

Hegdehaugsveien 22 ✉ 0167 – ✆ 22 56 43 00 – www.plah.no – Closed 2 weeks July, Christmas, Easter and Sunday-Monday

Menu 595/845 NOK – Carte 735/845 NOK – *(dinner only)*

• Thai • Neighbourhood • Friendly •

Norwegian ingredients blend with Thai flavours at this well-run restaurant. Choose between the à la carte and 2 tasting menus: 'Journey Through Thailand' or 'Journey Through The Jungle' (vegetarian). Dishes are eye-catching, imaginative and full of flavour. Their neighbouring bar serves Thai street food.

Theatercaféen – Continental Hotel

XX Plan: C2

Stortingsgaten 24-26 ✉ 0117 – Ⓜ National Theatret – ✆ 22 82 40 50 – www.theatercafeen.no – Closed 4 weeks July-August and Easter

Menu 655 NOK (dinner) – Carte 550/950 NOK

• Traditional cuisine • Luxury • Romantic •

A truly grand café, with tiled flooring, art deco lights, pillars and a vaulted ceiling; it's been a meeting point for the good and the great of the Norwegian cultural scene since 1900. Lunch offers lighter dishes, sandwiches, pastries and cakes; dinner is the time for more classic dishes.

Tjuvholmen Sjømagasin

XX Plan: B3

Tjuvholmen Allé 14 ✉ 0252 – ✆ 23 89 77 77 – www.sjomagasinet.no – Closed Christmas, Easter, Sunday and bank holidays

Menu 355/685 NOK – Carte 600/775 NOK

• Seafood • Fashionable • Brasserie •

A vast restaurant with three dining rooms, a crab and lobster tank, a superb terrace and a wet fish shop. Its name means 'sea store' and menus are fittingly seafood based. Shellfish is from the nearby dock – the langoustines are fantastic.

restauranteik

XX Plan: C2

Clarion Collection H. Savoy, Universitetsgata 11 ✉ 0164 – Ⓜ National Theatret – ✆ 22 36 07 10 – www.restauranteik.no – Closed July, Easter, Christmas, Sunday and Monday

Menu 395 NOK – *(dinner only) (tasting menu only)*

• Modern cuisine • Friendly • Minimalist •

Colourful abstract screens adorn the walls of this hotel restaurant close to the National Gallery. There's an inventive European element to the cooking, which is also informed by the chef's travels. The wine list offers a good range of older vintages, especially from Burgundy and Bordeaux.

Brasserie Blanche

X Plan: B1

Josefinesgate 23 ✉ 0351 – ✆ 23 20 13 10 – www.blanche.no – Closed 9-31 July, 23-26 December and Monday

Menu 395 NOK – Carte 352/595 NOK – *(dinner only)*

• French • Cosy • Brasserie •

A cosy French restaurant housed in an 18C building which was originally a stable and later spent time as a garage and an interior furnishings store. It has a small front terrace, a bar decorated with wine boxes and a wall made of corks. The chef is a Francophile and creates flavoursome classic French dishes.

Omakase by Vladimir Pak

Ruseløkkveien 3, 1st floor ✉ 0251 – ✆ 4568 5022 Plan: **B2**
– www.omakaseoslo.no – Closed Christmas, Easter, Sunday and bank holidays
Menu 1350 NOK – *(dinner only)*
• Sushi • Design •
This restaurant comprises a three-sided counter with seats for 15. The fish and shellfish come largely from Norwegian waters and the rice is American. The no-choice menu offers around 18 servings of Edomae-style sushi, although there can be surprises, like reindeer; some wine pairings are equally original.

Arakataka

Mariboes gate 7 ✉ 0183 – Ⓜ Stortinget – ✆ 23 32 83 00 Plan: **D2**
– www.arakataka.no – Closed July, Christmas-New Year and Easter
Menu 650 NOK – Carte 455/525 NOK – *(dinner only)*
• Norwegian • Fashionable • Friendly •
A smart glass-fronted restaurant with a central food bar, an open kitchen and a buzzy atmosphere. Choose from a concise menu of seasonal Norwegian small plates – they recommend 3 savoury dishes plus a dessert per person.

Bon Lio

Fredensborgveien 42 ✉ 0177 – ✆ 46 77 72 12 Plan: **C1**
– www.bonlio.no – Closed 2 weeks July, Christmas, Easter, Sunday and Monday
Menu 865 NOK – *(dinner only) (booking essential) (surprise menu only)*
• Modern cuisine • Simple • Cosy •
A lively, fun gastro-bar in a characterful 200 year old cottage. The Norwegian owner grew up in Mallorca and showcases local and imported ingredients in a surprise 12-17 course tapas-style menu. Spanish beers and wines accompany.

Brasserie France

Øvre Slottsgate 16 ✉ 0157 – Ⓜ Stortinget Plan: **C2**
– ✆ 23 10 01 65 – www.brasseriefrance.no – Closed 23 December-2 January, Easter, Sunday and lunch Monday
Menu 370/495 NOK – Carte 480/730 NOK
• French • Brasserie • Traditional décor •
This lively Gallic brasserie in a pedestrianised shopping street has several private dining rooms. Brasserie classics range from bouillabaisse to steak frites; for dessert, choose from the 'eat-as-much-as-you-like' pastry trolley.

Brasserie Hansken

Akersgate 2 ✉ 0158 – Ⓜ Stortinget – ✆ 22 42 60 88 Plan: **C2**
– www.brasseriehansken.no – Closed Christmas-New Year, Monday in July and Sunday
Carte 595/775 NOK
• Modern cuisine • Family • Brasserie •
A delightfully traditional brasserie, centrally located by City Hall, with various charming dining areas and a fantastic terrace. Classical cooking follows the seasons and mixes French and Scandic influences; seafood is a speciality.

Cru

Ingelbrecht, Knudssøns gate 1 ✉ 0365 – Ⓜ Majorstuen Plan: **B1**
– ✆ 23 98 98 98 – www.cru.no – Closed 1 July-2 August, 22 December-2 January, Easter and Sunday
Menu 595 NOK – Carte 500/530 NOK – *(dinner only and Saturday lunch)*
• Norwegian • Wine bar • Trendy •
Upstairs, in the rustic restaurant, they serve a set 4 course menu with inventive British touches and 4 optional extra courses. Downstairs, in the wine bar, you can enjoy everything from nibbles to a full meal from the à la carte.

Einer

Prinsens gate 18 ✉ 0152 – Ⓜ Stortinget Plan: **C2**
– ✆ 22 41 55 55 – www.restauranteiner.no – Closed 2 weeks July, Christmas, Easter, Sunday and Monday
Menu 650/850 NOK – *(dinner only) (booking essential) (tasting menu only)*
• Modern cuisine • Friendly • Design •
Personally run restaurant serving 4 and 6 course tasting menus with an emphasis on Norwegian seafood. Understated, full-flavoured modern dishes use original combinations alongside traditional techniques such as fermenting, pickling and smoking. The wine matches are well worth choosing.

Grand Café – Grand H.Oslo by Scandic

Karl Johans Gate 31 ✉ 0159 – Ⓜ Stortinget Plan: **C2**
– ✆ 98 18 20 00 – www.grandcafeoslo.no
– Closed Easter and Christmas
Carte 425/585 NOK
• Modern cuisine • Classic décor • Vintage •
This iconic restaurant dates from 1874; look out for the colourful mural depicting past regulars including Edvard Munch and Henrik Ibsen. The concise menu lists flavour-filled Nordic and international dishes. The cellar wine bar opens Tues-Sat and offers snacks, charcuterie and over 1,500 bottles of wine.

Kolonialen Bislett

Sofiesgate 16 ✉ 0170 – ✆ 901 15 098 Plan: **C1**
– www.kolonialenbislett.no
– Closed July, Sunday and bank holidays
Carte 540/620 NOK – *(dinner only and Saturday lunch) (booking essential)*
• Modern cuisine • Brasserie • Neighbourhood •
Close to the stadium you'll find this cosy, modern bistro – previously a grocer's shop for nearly 80 years. The concise, keenly priced menu includes oysters, cured meats and wholesome Norwegian classics that have been brought up-to-date.

Lofoten Fiskerestaurant

Stranden 75 ✉ 0250 – ✆ 22 83 08 08 Plan: **B3**
– www.lofotenfiskerestaurant.no – Closed Christmas
Menu 395/565 NOK – Carte 455/645 NOK
• Seafood • Brasserie • Simple •
A traditional fjord-side restaurant hung with bright modern artwork and offering lovely views from its large windows and sizeable terrace. Watch as fresh, simply cooked fish and shellfish are prepared in the semi-open kitchen.

Statholderens Mat og Vin Kjeller – Statholdergaarden

Rådhusgate 11 (entrance from Kirkegata) ✉ 0151 Plan: **C3**
– Ⓜ Stortinget – ✆ 22 41 88 00 – www.statholdergaarden.no – Closed July, 22 December-3 January, Sunday and bank holidays
Menu 750 NOK – Carte 750/980 NOK – *(dinner only) (booking essential)*
• Norwegian • Rustic • Simple •
The informal sister of Statholdergaarden – set over three rooms in the old vaults beneath it. One wall of the large entranceway is filled with wine bottles. Choose from a huge array of small plates or go for the 10 course tasting menu.

Vaaghals

Dronning Eufemias gate 8 ✉ 0151 – Ⓜ Jernbanetorget Plan: **D3**
– ✆ 92 07 09 99 – www.vaaghals.com – Closed last 3 weeks July, 22 December-3 January, Easter and Sunday
Menu 715 NOK (dinner) – Carte 475/815 NOK
• Scandinavian • Brasserie • Fashionable •
A bright, contemporary restaurant with an open kitchen and a terrace; located on the ground floor of one of the modern 'barcode' buildings. Scandinavian menus feature dry-aged meat; many of the dinner dishes are designed for sharing.

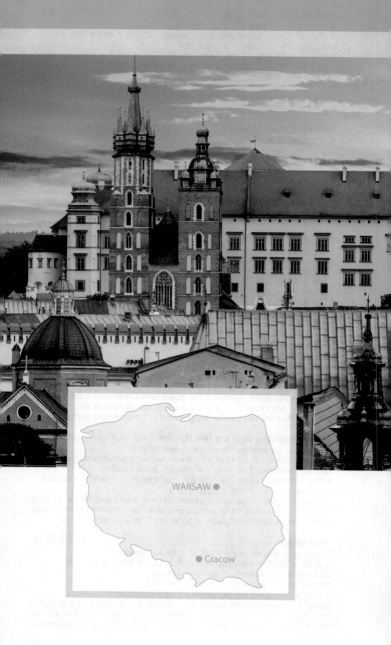
WARSAW
Cracow

POLAND
POLSKA

Velishchuk/iStock

WARSAW
WARSZAWA

fotorince/iStock

WARSAW IN…

- **ONE DAY**
  Royal Castle, Warsaw History Museum, National Museum, Lazienki Park.
- **TWO DAYS**
  Monument to the Ghetto Heroes, Saxon Gardens, concert at Grand Theatre or Philharmonic Hall.
- **THREE DAYS**
  The Royal Route, Marshal Street, Solidarity Avenue, Wilanow.

When UNESCO added Warsaw to its World Heritage list, it was a fitting seal of approval for its inspired rebuild, after eighty per cent of the city was destroyed during World War II. Using plans of the old city, architects painstakingly rebuilt the shattered capital throughout the 1950s, until it became an admirable mirror image of its former self. Now grey communist era apartment blocks sit beside pretty, pastel-coloured aristocratic buildings, their architecture ranging from Gothic to baroque, rococo to secession.

Nestling against the River Vistula, the Old Town was established at the end of the 13C, around what is now the Royal Castle, and a

century later the New Town, to the north, began to take shape. To the south of the Old Town runs 'The Royal Route', so named because, from the late middle ages, wealthy citizens built summer residences with lush gardens along these rural thoroughfares. Continue southwards and you're in Lazienki Park with its palaces and pavilions, while to the west lie the more commercial areas of Marshal Street and Solidarity Avenue, once the commercial heart of the city. The northwest of Warsaw was traditionally the Jewish district, until it was destroyed during the war; today it has been redeveloped with housing estates and the sobering Monument to the Ghetto Heroes.

EATING OUT

The centuries-old traditional cuisine of Warsaw was influenced by neighbouring Russia, Ukraine and Germany, while Jewish dishes were also added to the mix. Over the years there has been a growing sophistication to the cooking and a lighter, more contemporary style has become evident, with time-honoured classics - such as the ubiquitous pierogi (dumplings with various fillings) and the ever-popular breaded pork dish 'bigos' - having been updated with flair. These are accompanied, of course, by chilled Polish vodka, which covers a bewildering range of styles. Warsaw also has a more global side, with everything from stalls selling falafel to restaurants serving Vietnamese, and a large Italian business community has ensured there are a good number of Italian restaurants too. Stylised settings are popular, such as a burghers' houses or vaulted cellars; wherever you eat, check that VAT has been included within the prices (it's not always) and add a ten per cent tip. If it's value for money you're after, head for a Milk Bar, a low priced cafeteria selling traditional dairy-based food.

atelier Amaro (Wojciech Modest Amaro)

XXX Plan: **D2**

Plac Trzech Krzyży 10/14 ✉ 00 507 – ✆ 792 222 211 – www.atelieramaro.pl – Closed first two weeks August, Christmas-New Year, Easter, Sunday, Monday and lunch Tuesday and Saturday
Menu 150/420 PLN – *(booking essential) (tasting menu only)*

• Modern cuisine • Design • Elegant •

Owner-chef Wojciech Modest Amaro is a huge advocate of seasonal Polish ingredients; menus are based on 'Nature's Calendar' and showcase foraged herbs and flowers. Ambitious, innovative dishes are full of colour and use many modern techniques; the Polish spirit matches are a must.

→ Sturgeon with dill and gin. Duck, beet and hay. Elderflower with acorn and milk.

Senses (Andrea Camastra)

XXX Plan: **C1**

ul. Bielanska 12 ✉ 00-085 – Ⓜ Ratusz – ✆ (22) 331 9697 – www.sensesrestaurant.pl – Closed Easter, middle 2 weeks August, Christmas and Sunday
Menu 320/550 PLN – *(dinner only) (booking essential) (tasting menu only)*

• Modern cuisine • Elegant • Romantic •

As with the buildings between which it is housed, this formal restaurant connects tradition with modernity. Of the 3 set menus, most opt for the 7 course dinner to best experience cooking that is innovative, creative and at times theatrical, but also underpinned by classic Polish flavours.

→ Mushrooms with leeks, pork and flatbread. Beef goulash, chana masala and aubergine. Tiramisu.

Brasserie Warszawska

XX Plan I: **B2**

ul. Górnośląska 24 ✉ 00 484 – ✆ (22) 628 94 23 – www.brasseriewarszawska.pl – Closed Christmas, Easter and Sunday
Carte 40/175 PLN

• Modern cuisine • Brasserie • Vintage •

A smart brasserie with a zinc-topped bar, a black and white tiled floor, and caricatures of its regulars on the walls. Modern European dishes are executed with care and passion. Meats come from their own butcher's shop and mature steaks are a feature, with a choice of cuts from Poland, Ireland and Australia.

Alewino

X Plan: **D2**

ul. Mokotowska 48 ✉ 00 543 – ✆ (22) 628 38 30 – www.alewino.pl – Closed Christmas, Easter, Sunday and lunch Monday
Carte 104/139 PLN – *(booking essential at dinner)*

• Polish •

Alewino started life as a wine shop before developing into a rustic, modern wine-bar-cum-restaurant. Choose a spot in one of 4 cosy rooms or in the garden. Menus might be concise but the portions are generous, with classic Polish recipes reworked in a modern manner. Over 250 wines accompany.

Butchery and Wine

X Plan: **D2**

ul. Zurawia 22 ✉ 00 515 – Ⓜ Centrum – ✆ (22) 502 3118 – www.butcheryandwine.pl – Closed Christmas, Easter and 1 November
Carte 65/250 PLN – *(booking essential)*

• Meats and grills • Friendly • Trendy •

A keenly run modern bistro in a long, narrow room. The name says it all: staff wear butcher's aprons, there's a diagram of cuts above the kitchen pass and the emphasis is on offal and meat – particularly beef – which is served on wooden boards. Wines from around the world provide the perfect match.

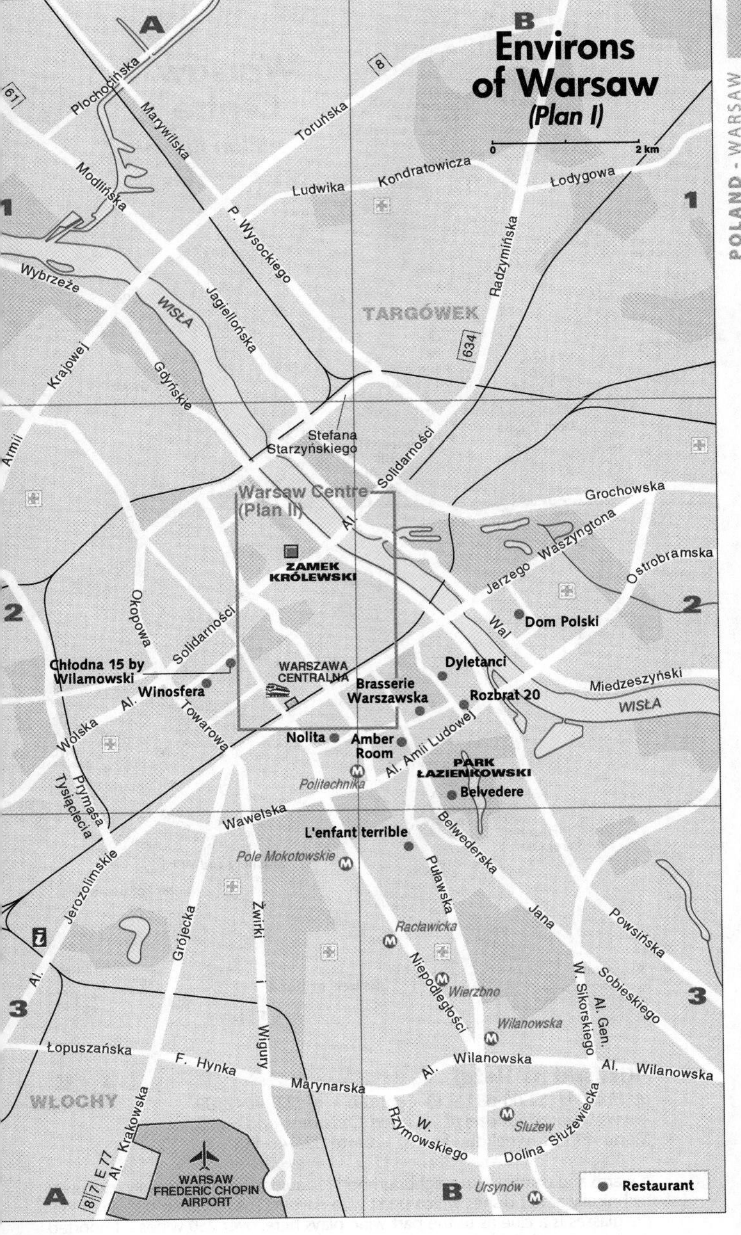

Environs of Warsaw
(Plan I)
0
2 km
A
B
1
2
3
Płochocińska
Marywilska
Toruńska
Modlińska
Ludwika
Kondratowicza
Łodygowa
P. Wysockiego
Radzymińska
Wybrzeże
WISŁA
Jagiellońska
TARGÓWEK
Krajowej
Gdyńskie
Armii
Stefana Starzyńskiego
Solidarności
Warsaw Centre (Plan II)
Al.
Grochowska
ZAMEK KRÓLEWSKI
Jerzego Waszyngtona
Ostrobramska
Okopowa
Solidarności
Wał
Dom Polski
Chłodna 15 by Wilamowski
Winosfera
WARSZAWA CENTRALNA
Dyletanci
Brasserie Warszawska
Rozbrat 20
Miedzeszyński
WISŁA
Wolska
Al.
Towarowa
Nolita
Amber Room
Al. Armii Ludowej
PARK ŁAZIENKOWSKI
Prymasa Tysiąclecia
Politechnika
Belvedere
Wawelska
L'enfant terrible
Belwederska
Pole Mokotowskie
Jerozolimskie
Puławska
Żwirki
Grójecka
Racławicka
Jana
Powsińska
Al.
Niepodległości
Wierzbno
W. Sikorskiego
Sobieskiego
Wilanowska
Al. Gen.
Łopuszańska
F. Hynka
Wigury
Wilanowska
Al.
Wilanowska
Al.
Marynarska
WŁOCHY
Al. Krakowska
W. Rzymowskiego
Służew
Służewiecka
Dolina
E 77
WARSAW FREDERIC CHOPIN AIRPORT
Ursynów
Restaurant
61
8
634
7

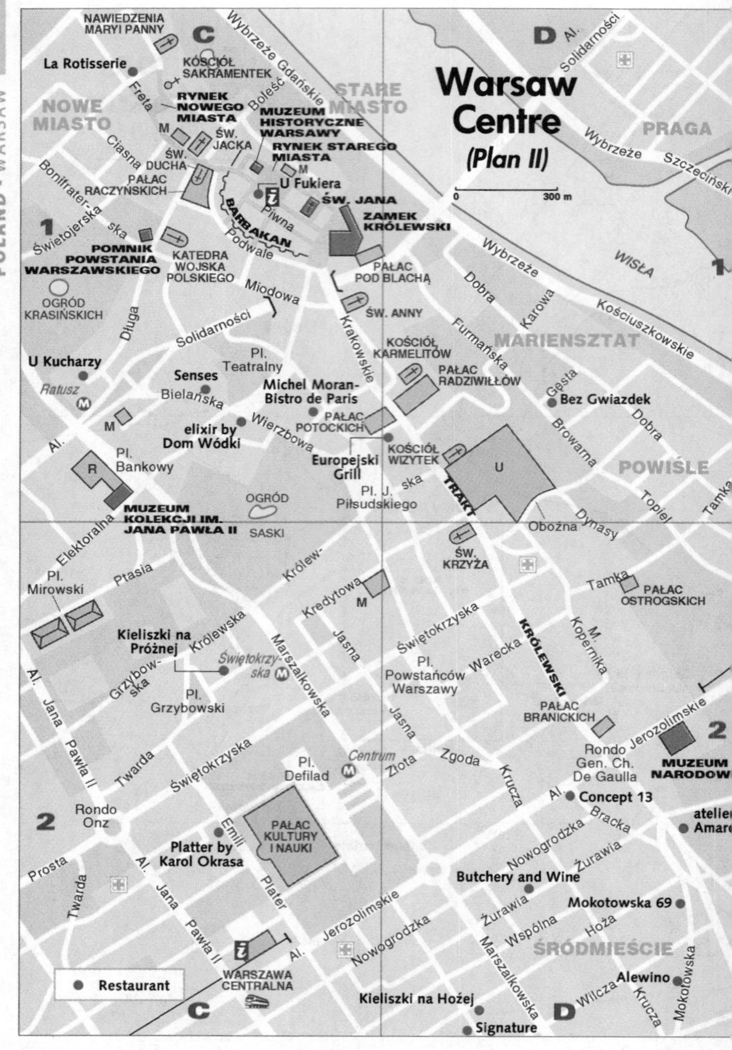

Kieliszki na Hożej

Plan: **D2**

ul. Hoża 41 ✉ *00 681 – Ⓜ Centrum – ☎ (22) 4042109 – www.kieliszkinahozej.pl – Closed Christmas and Sunday*

Menu 49 PLN (weekday lunch) – Carte 82/146 PLN

• Modern cuisine • Wine bar • Friendly •

A warm and characterful neighbourhood restaurant serving carefully executed, technically adroit dishes which burst with flavour. The towering display of Riedel glasses is a clue as to the part wine plays here: over 230 wines – imported directly – are available by the glass.

Kieliszki na Próżnej

ul. Próżna 12 ✉ 00 107 – Ⓜ Świętokrzyska – ✆ (501) 764 674 – www.kieliszkinaproznej.pl – Closed Christmas and Sunday

Plan: C2

Carte 78/160 PLN

• Modern cuisine • Design • Wine bar •

A huge rack of glasses welcomes you into a parquet-floored room with a striking black & white wildlife mural and zinc ducting. Small growers feature on the 220-strong wine list and all wines are available by the glass. A concise menu offers light, modern interpretations of Polish classics; lunch is a steal.

Amber Room

al Ujazdowskie 13 ✉ 00 567 – ✆ (600) 800 999 – www.amber-room.pl – Closed Christmas, Easter and bank holidays

Plan I: B2

Menu 64 PLN (weekday lunch) – Carte 130/250 PLN

• Modern cuisine • Chic • Intimate •

A grand dining room in an attractive villa; home to the exclusive 'Round Table of Warsaw'. Modern cooking uses top ingredients and has original touches. Service is attentive and well-paced, and there's a great selection of Krug champagne.

Belvedere

Lazienki Park, ul Agrykoli 1 (Entry from ul Parkowa St) ✉ 00 460 – ✆ (22) 55 86 701 – www.belvedere.com.pl – Closed 22-30 December

Plan I: B2

Menu 81 PLN (weekday lunch) – Carte 106/193 PLN – *(booking essential)*

• Modern cuisine • Chic • Romantic •

An impressive Victorian orangery in Lazienki Park; large arched windows keep it light, despite it being packed with shrubs and trees. Dishes are classic in both style and presentation. Smartly uniformed staff provide formal service.

Michel Moran - Bistro de Paris

Pl. Pilsudskiego 9 ✉ 00 078 – Ⓜ Ratusz – ✆ (22) 826 01 07 – www.restaurantbistrodeparis.com – Closed Christmas, Easter, Sunday and bank holidays

Plan: C1

Menu 89 PLN (weekday lunch) – Carte 170/246 PLN

• French • Elegant • Chic •

A smart, marble-floored restaurant at the rear of the Opera House, with striking columns and colourful glass panels. The large menu offers reworked Polish and French dishes, with produce imported from France; the 'Classics' are a hit.

Platter by Karol Okrasa – InterContinental Hotel

ul. Emilii Plater 49 ✉ 00 125 – Ⓜ Centrum – ✆ (22) 328 8730 – www.platter.pl – Closed August, Saturday lunch and Sunday

Plan: C2

Menu 210/330 PLN – Carte 155/230 PLN

• Modern cuisine • Chic • Intimate •

A first floor hotel restaurant with smart red and black décor. Menus change with the seasons and offer modern Polish dishes and European classics. Cooking is refined, sophisticated and flavoursome, and relies on native ingredients.

Chłodna 15 by Wilamowski

ul. Chlodna 15 ✉ 00 891 – Ⓜ Rondo ONZ – ✆ (730) 737 644 – www.chlodna15.pl – Closed 23 July-13 August, 23-30 December, 20 January-3 February, Sunday and Monday

Plan: A2

Menu 59 PLN (weekday lunch) – Carte 115/615 PLN

• French • Intimate • Romantic •

The Polish chef spent time working in some of the best restaurants in France and the UK before returning home to open this smart French eatery. The menu changes daily according to the ingredients available, including fish sourced from French markets and vegetables freshly picked by the chef.

Concept 13

XX

Vitkac (5th Floor), ul. Bracka 9 ✉ 00 501 – Ⓜ Centrum – ✆ (22) 3107373 – www.likusrestauracje.pl – Closed Sunday dinner and bank holidays Plan: **D2**

Menu 59 PLN (weekday lunch) – Carte 105/190 PLN

• Modern cuisine • Design • Fashionable •

A vast restaurant on top of a chic department store, with black furnishings, a glass-walled kitchen and a smart terrace. Dishes are modern, appealing and well-presented. They also have a wine bar and an impressive deli on the floor below.

Dom Polski

XX

ul. Francuska 11 ✉ 03 906 – ✆ (22) 616 24 32 – www.restauracjadompolski.pl – Closed 24 December Plan I: **B2**

Carte 75/165 PLN

• Polish • Classic décor • Elegant •

A Mediterranean-style villa with attractive gardens and a lovely terrace, set in a smart residential area. Various small rooms are set over two floors. Extensive menus offer refined yet hearty dishes; duck and goose are the specialities.

Europejski Grill – Raffles Europejski Warsaw

XX

Krakowskie Przedmieście 13 ✉ 00 071 – ✆ (22) 255 95 90 – www.raffles.com/warsaw Plan: **D1**

Menu 65 PLN (weekday lunch) – Carte 100/220 PLN

• Modern cuisine • Design • Intimate •

A sophisticated restaurant set in the lovingly restored Europejski Hotel, which overlooks the historic Pilsudski square. Menus feature meat and fish cooked over a charcoal grill alongside modern versions of Polish classics. Try the vodka distilled to celebrate the hotel's reopening.

Mokotowska 69

XX

ul. Mokotowska 69 ✉ 02 530 – ✆ (22) 628 73 84 – www.mokotowska69.pl – Closed 25 December and Easter Plan: **D2**

Carte 94/190 PLN

• International • Traditional décor • Romantic •

This unusual circular building has a cosy, romantic atmosphere and the welcoming team make you feel well-looked-after. Menus focus on seafood and prime quality American Black Angus, Scottish Aberdeen Angus and Japanese Kobe steaks.

Nolita

XX

ul. Wilcza 46 ✉ 00 679 – ✆ (22) 29 20 424 – www.nolita.pl – Closed 2 weeks August, Christmas-New Year, Easter, Saturday lunch, Sunday and bank holidays Plan I: **A2**

Menu 99 PLN (weekday lunch) – Carte 177/255 PLN – *(booking essential)*

• Modern cuisine • Design • Intimate •

Whitewashed stone and black window blinds are matched inside by a smart monochrome theme, where an open kitchen takes centre stage. Bold, modern dishes feature many flavours and take their influences from across the globe.

La Rotisserie – Mamaison Le Régina Hotel

XX

ul. Koscielna 12 ✉ 00 218 – ✆ (22) 531 60 00 – www.mamaison.com/leregina – Closed 24 December Plan: **C1**

Menu 228 PLN – Carte 172/219 PLN – *(booking essential)*

• Modern cuisine • Chic • Intimate •

A small but stylish hotel restaurant with an arched ceiling and an intimate feel. Refined modern dishes have Polish origins and arrive attractively presented. When the weather's right, the courtyard is the place to be.

Rozbrat 20

XX

ul. Rozbrat 20 ✉ 00 447 – ✆ (22) 416 6266 – www.rozbrat20.com.pl – Closed Christmas and Sunday

Plan I: **B2**

Menu 72/249 PLN – Carte 95/195 PLN

• Modern cuisine • Friendly • Bistro •

What was once a corner bakery and wine shop has become a smart, cosy neighbourhood restaurant; sit in the front room to watch the chefs at work. Modern cooking with pronounced flavours and an emphasis on seasonal Polish ingredients – give the lesser known Polish wines a try.

Signature – H15 Hotel

XX

ul. Poznańska 15 ✉ 00 680 – Ⓜ Politechnika – ✆ (22) 553 87 55 – www.signaturerestaurant.pl – Closed Christmas-New Year, Easter, 1-3 May and lunch Saturday-Sunday

Plan: **D2**

Menu 48/120 PLN – Carte 80/163 PLN

• Modern cuisine • Intimate • Bistro •

Black and white photos of old Hollywood Stars hang against white, pink and green walls in this striking hotel restaurant. Cooking is a modern take on traditional Polish recipes and the playful puddings are particularly memorable.

U Fukiera

XX

Rynek Starego Miasta 27 ✉ 00 272 – ✆ (22) 831 10 13 – www.ufukiera.pl – Closed 24-25 and 31 December

Plan: **C1**

Carte 91/207 PLN

• Polish • Traditional décor • Elegant •

An immaculately kept house in the heart of the Old Town, overlooking a historic cobbled square. The fiercely traditional interior comprises several intimate, homely rooms, including a 17C vaulted cellar. Cooking is hearty and classical.

U Kucharzy

XX

Państwowego Muzeum Archeologicznego, ul. Długa 52 ✉ 00 238 – Ⓜ Ratusz – ✆ (22) 826 79 36 – www.gessler.pl – Closed Christmas and Easter

Plan: **C1**

Menu 25/210 PLN – Carte 65/185 PLN

• Traditional cuisine • Historic • Traditional décor •

'The Cook' is located in a 16C former arsenal and two of the original cannons sit in its large inner courtyard. The day's ingredients are on display in the open kitchen and the chef comes to the table to carve your meat himself.

Bez Gwiazdek

X

Wiślana 8 ✉ 00 317 – ✆ (22) 628 04 45 – Closed 2 weeks August, Christmas, Easter, Sunday dinner and Monday

Plan: **D1**

Menu 100/180 PLN – *(dinner only and Sunday lunch)*

• Modern cuisine • Neighbourhood • Cosy •

A cosy neighbourhood restaurant minutes from the castle. Monthly changing menus focus on one of the 16 Polish regions; showcasing ingredients and traditional recipes which have been brought up to date. The team's pride and enthusiasm is clear; wine recommendations add to the experience.

Dyletanci

X

ul. Rozbrat 44A ✉ 00 415 – ✆ (692) 887 234 – www.dyletanci.pl – Closed Christmas, Easter and Sunday

Plan I: **B2**

Menu 135 PLN (dinner) – Carte 107/158 PLN

• Modern cuisine • Friendly • Wine bar •

The brainchild of an experienced chef and a wine importer, Dyletanci has a welcoming modern bistro style and walls laden with wines sourced from across the globe. Seasonal ingredients are prepared in a contemporary manner.

Winosfera

ul. Chlodna 31 ✉ 00 867 – Ⓜ Rondo ONZ Plan I: **A2**
– ✆ (22) 526 25 00 – www.winosfera.pl – Closed Christmas, Easter, Sunday and bank holidays
Menu 49 PLN (weekday lunch) – Carte 95/190 PLN
• Modern cuisine • Design • Trendy •

Winosfera sits within an old factory – it retains its industrial feel and, in a nod to the famed cinema which once stood here, comes with a screening room for private events. Modern European menus cover Italy, France and Poland.

elixir by Dom Wódki

ul. Wierzbowa 9-11 ✉ 00 094 – Ⓜ Ratusz Plan: **C1**
– ✆ (22) 828 22 11 – www.restauracjaelixir.pl – Closed Christmas, New Year and Easter
Menu 39 PLN (lunch) – Carte 100/150 PLN
• Polish • Wine bar • Fashionable •

A smart, very fashionable bar and restaurant is the setting for this marriage of modern Polish cuisine and top quality vodkas. The likes of local herring, dumplings and beef tartare are paired with over 500 vodkas from around the world.

L'enfant terrible

ul. Sandomierska 13 (entrance on Rejtana St.) Plan I: **B3**
✉ 02 567 – Ⓜ Pol Mokotowskie – ✆ (22) 119 57 05 – www.eterrible.pl – Closed Christmas, New Year, Easter, lunch Saturday and Monday and Sunday dinner
Carte 136/157 PLN
• Modern cuisine • Neighbourhood • Romantic •

This delightfully rustic restaurant is owned by a self-taught chef, who picks up the day's produce on his 40km drive into work. The atmosphere is welcoming and dishes are modern and well-presented; the sourdough bread is fantastic.

bphotographer/iStock

CRACOW

KRAKÓW

martin-dm/iStock

CRACOW IN…

→ **ONE DAY**
St Mary's Church, Cloth Hall, Wawel, main building of National Museum.

→ **TWO DAYS**
Kazimierz, Oskar Schindler's Factory, 'Footsteps of Pope Jean Paul II' tour.

→ **THREE DAYS**
Auschwitz-Birkenau, Wieliczka salt mine.

Cracow was deservedly included in the very first UNESCO World Heritage List. Unlike much of Poland, this beautiful old city – the country's capital from the 11C to the 17C – was spared Second World War destruction because the German Governor had his HQ here. So Cracow is still able to boast a hugely imposing market square – the biggest medieval square in Europe – and a hill that's crowned not just with a castle, but a cathedral too. Not far away there's even a glorious chapel made of salt, one hundred metres under the ground.

Cracow is a city famous for its links with Judaism and its Royal Route, but also for its cultural inheritance. During the Renaissance,

it became a centre of new ideas that drew the most outstanding writers, thinkers and musicians of the day. It has thousands of architectural monuments and millions of artefacts displayed in its museums and churches; but it's a modern city too, with an eye on the 21C. The heart and soul of Cracow is its old quarter, which received its charter in 1257. It's dominated by the Market Square and almost completely encircled by the Planty gardens. A short way to the south, briefly interrupted by the curving streets of the Okol neighbourhood, is Wawel Hill, and further south from here is the characterful Jewish quarter of Kazimierz. The smart residential areas of Piasek and Nowy Swiat are to the west.

EATING OUT

Even during the communist era, Cracow had a reputation as a good place to eat. In the 1990s, hundreds of new restaurants opened their doors, often in pretty locations with medieval or Renaissance interiors or in intimate cellars. Many Poles go misty-eyed at the thought of Bigos on a cold winter's day; it's a game, sausage and cabbage stew that comes with sauerkraut, onion, potatoes, herbs and spices, and is reputed to get better with reheating on successive days. Pierogi is another favourite: crescent-shaped dumplings which come in either savoury or sweet style. Barszcz is a lemon and garlic flavoured beetroot soup that's invariably good value, while in Kazimierz, specialities include Jewish dumplings - filled with onion, cheese and potatoes - and Berdytchov soup, which imaginatively mixes honey and cinnamon with beef. There are plenty of restaurants specialising in French, Greek, Vietnamese, Middle Eastern, Indian, Italian and Mexican food too. Most restaurants don't close until around midnight and there's no pressure to rush your drinks and leave.

Copernicus - Copernicus Hotel XxX
ul. Kanonicza 16 ✉ 31 002 – ☎ (12) 424 34 21 – www.copernicus.hotel.com.pl Plan: **E3**
Menu 220/430 PLN (dinner) – Carte lunch 147/187 PLN – *(booking essential)*
• Modern cuisine • Intimate • Elegant •
Set off the atrium of a charming hotel; an intimate split-level restaurant of less than 10 tables, boasting an ornate hand-painted Renaissance ceiling. 5, 7 and 12 course menus offer well-crafted Polish and European dishes.

Trzy Rybki - Stary Hotel XxX
ul. Szczepanska 5 ✉ 31 011 – ☎ (12) 384 08 06 – www.stary.hotel.com.pl/en/restaurants/trzy-rybki-restaurant/ Plan: **E1**
Menu 170/290 PLN – Carte 180/200 PLN
• Modern cuisine • Elegant • Design •
Thick stone walls give this stylish restaurant in the Stary hotel's basement plenty of character. A glass-fronted case stretching along one wall displays an impressive collection of wines. Well-prepared dishes have subtle Italian leanings.

Albertina XX
ul. Dominikańska 3 ✉ 31 043 – ☎ (12) 333 4110 – www.albertinarestaurant.pl – Closed 24-25 December, Easter Sunday and 1 November Plan: **F2**
Carte 130/220 PLN
• Modern cuisine • Design • Chic •
A sophisticated modern restaurant with a basement wine bar. Menus show the chef's passion for hunting and fishing – venison is a speciality and they offer lobster and oyster menus. Eye-catching dishes capture the ingredients' true flavours.

Amarylis - Queen Hotel XX
ul. Józefa Dietla 60 ✉ 31 039 – ☎ (12) 433 33 06 – www.queenhotel.pl Plan: **F3**
Carte 120/143 PLN
• Modern cuisine • Design • Intimate •
Head down to the hotel's basement and sit in either a traditional brick room or a more modern space furnished in black and white. Cooking mixes Polish and global influences and dishes are well-presented and full of flavour.

Corse XX
ul Poselska 24 ✉ 31 002 – ☎ (12) 421 62 73 – www.corserestaurant.pl – Closed 24-25 December and Easter Plan: **F2**
Carte 62/200 PLN
• Mediterranean cuisine • Traditional décor • Bistro •
A nautically-themed restaurant featuring model ships, paintings of clippers and old ships' lamps. Good-sized menus offer Mediterranean-influenced dishes which use Polish produce; they specialise in seafood but offer more besides.

Cyrano de Bergerac XX
ul Slawkowska 26 ✉ 31 014 – ☎ (12) 411 72 88 – www.cyranodebergerac.pl – Closed Christmas, Easter and 1 November Plan: **E1**
Carte 105/280 PLN – *(booking essential at dinner)*
• Polish • Intimate • Rustic •
An atmospheric restaurant in the barrel-ceilinged cellars of a 17C townhouse. Tapestries, antiques and old implements fill the room, and there's a lovely enclosed rear terrace. Polish ingredients are showcased in refined French dishes.

Jarema

XX 🏠 A/C ⚡ Plan: **F1**

Pl. Matejki 5 ✉ 31 157 – ✆ (12) 429 36 69
– www.jarema.pl – Closed 25 December
Carte 64/140 PLN

• Traditional cuisine • Traditional décor • Vintage •

A charming restaurant with a homely feel. Hunting trophies fill the walls and there's live violin and piano music every night. Family recipes are handed down through the generations and focus on dishes from the east of the country.

Kogel Mogel

XX 🏠 A/C ⚡ Plan: **F2**

ul. Sienna 12 ✉ 31 041 – ✆ (12) 426 49 68
– www.kogel-mogel.pl – Closed 24-25 December and Easter
Carte 76/142 PLN

• Polish • Brasserie • Fashionable •

A smart, lively brasserie; the wine room with its original painted ceiling is a popular spot, as is the enclosed terrace. Extensive menus offer refined, modern versions of classic Polish and Cracovian dishes. Live music is a feature.

Leonardo

XX A/C ⇔ Plan: **F1**

ul. Szpitalna 20-22 ✉ 31 024 – ✆ (12) 429 6850
– www.leonardo.com.pl – Closed Christmas, Easter and 1 November
Carte 95/255 PLN – *(booking essential at dinner)*

• Classic cuisine • Intimate • Classic décor •

Set in the basement of a small shopping mall, Leonardo pays homage to da Vinci, with reproduction etchings and an ornithopter on display. Menus take inspiration from France and Italy; cooking is hearty yet refined and uses prime ingredients.

Pod Baranem

XX A/C ⚡ Plan: **F3**

ul. Sw. Gertrudy 21 ✉ 31 049 – ✆ (12) 429 40 22
– www.podbaranem.com – Closed 25 December and Easter
Carte 66/158 PLN – *(booking essential at dinner)*

• Polish • Neighbourhood • Family •

A traditional family-run restaurant set over 5 rooms, with rug-covered stone floors, homely furnishings and contemporary artwork by Edward Dwurnik. The large menu offers classic Polish cuisine; sharing dishes must be ordered in advance.

Szara

XX 🏠 ⚡ Plan: **E/F2**

Rynek Glówny 6 ✉ 31 042 – ✆ (12) 421 66 69
– www.szara.pl – Closed 24 December
Carte 91/174 PLN

• International • Brasserie • Classic décor •

A well-regarded family-run restaurant on the Grand Square, featuring a lovely terrace, a hand-painted Gothic ceiling and a pleasant brasserie atmosphere. Menus mix Polish, French and Swedish classics; cooking is authentic and hearty.

Pod Nosem

X 🏠 ⇔ Plan: **E3**

ul. Kanonicza 22 ✉ 31 002 – ✆ (12) 376 00 14
– www.podnosem.com – Closed 24 December
Menu 59 PLN (weekday lunch) – Carte 100/185 PLN

• Polish • Cosy • Romantic •

The bright ground floor of this characterful medieval-style restaurant is hung with tapestries and the white wooden banquettes have tapestry seat cushions to match; while downstairs, amongst the brick and stone, it's more dimly lit. Classic Polish recipes are given appealing modern updates. Above the restaurant are 3 richly furnished suites with prices to match.

Bianca

X 🏠 Plan: **F2**

Plac Mariacki 2 ✉ 31 042 – ✆ (12) 422 18 71
– www.biancaristorante.pl – Closed 24-25 December and Easter
Carte 82/133 PLN

• Italian • Bistro • Intimate •

Sit on the small terrace opposite St Mary's Basilica and watch the world go by. Classical menus cover all regions of Italy and the pastas and ragus are freshly made; be sure to try the delicious saltimbocca with its sharp, lemony tang.

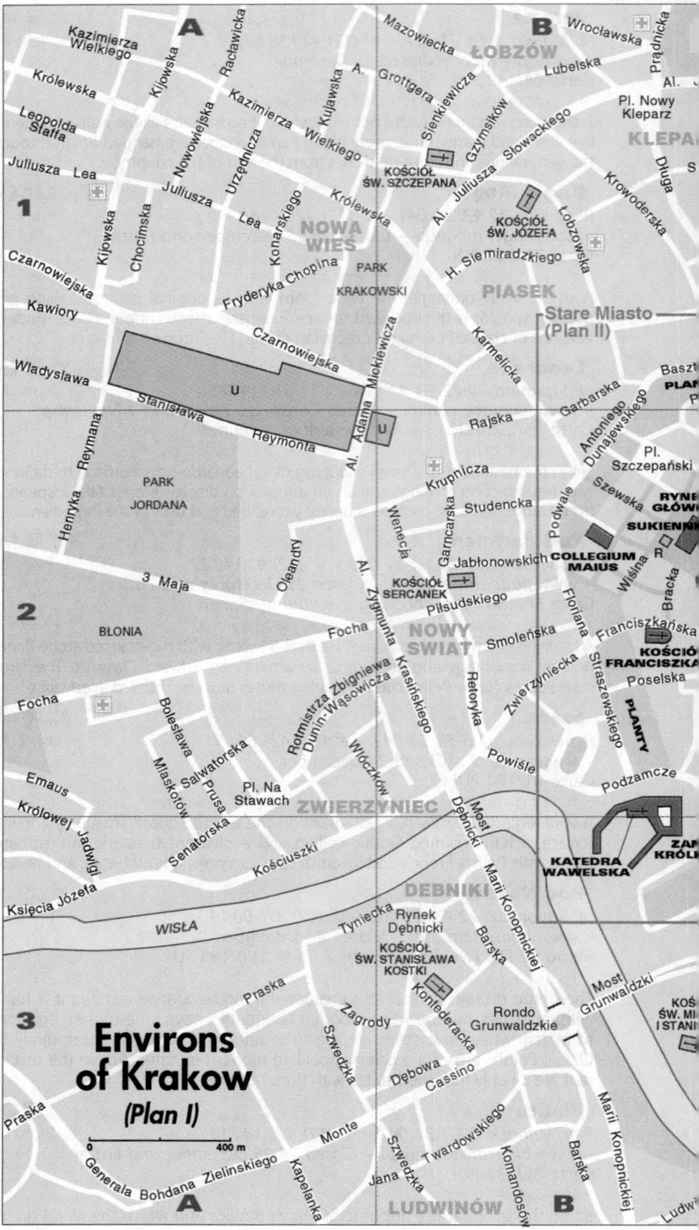

Environs of Krakow

(Plan I)

0 400 m

A B 1 2 3

Kazimierza Wielkiego
Królewska
Leopolda Staffa
Juliusza Lea
Kijowska
Chocimska
Nowowiejska
Racławicka
Urzędnicza
Konarskiego
Kujawska
A. Grottgera
Mazowiecka
ŁOBZÓW
Wrocławska
Prądnicka
Lubelska
Al.
Pl. Nowy Kleparz
KLEPA
Długa
Sienkiewicza
Gzymsików
Słowackiego
Al. Juliusza
KOŚCIÓŁ ŚW. SZCZEPANA
KOŚCIÓŁ ŚW. JÓZEFA
Krowoderska
Łobzowska
NOWA WIEŚ
PARK KRAKOWSKI
Fryderyka Chopina
H. Siemiradzkiego
PIASEK
Czarnowiejska
Kawiory
Wladyslawa
Stanisława
Reymonta
U
Al. Adama Mickiewicza
Stare Miasto (Plan II)
Karmelicka
Baszt
PLAN
Garbarska
Antoniego Dunajewskiego
Rajska
Pl. Szczepański
Krupnicza
Henryka Reymana
PARK JORDANA
Studencka
Szewska
RYNEK GŁÓWNY
SUKIENNICE
Wenecja
Garncarska
Podwale
COLLEGIUM MAIUS
Jabłonowskich
Wiślna
Bracka
R
Oleandry
Al. Zygmunta
KOŚCIÓŁ SERCANEK
3 Maja
Piłsudskiego
BŁONIA
Focha
NOWY SWIAT
Smoleńska
Floriana Straszewskiego
Franciszkańska
KOŚCIÓŁ FRANCISZKANÓW
Poselska
Zwierzyniecka
Krasińskiego
Retoryka
PLANTY
Rotmistrza Zbigniewa Dunin-Wąsowicza
Bolesława Prusa
Salwatorska
Mlaskotów
Włóczków
Powiśle
Podzamcze
Emaus
Pl. Na Stawach
ZWIERZYNIEC
Królowej Jadwigi
Senatorska
Most Dębnicki
KATEDRA WAWELSKA
ZAMEK KRÓLEWSKI
Kościuszki
Księcia Józefa
DEBNIKI
WISŁA
Tyniecka
Rynek Dębnicki
Marii Konopnickiej
Barska
KOŚCIÓŁ ŚW. STANISŁAWA KOSTKI
Praska
Konfederacka
Most Grunwaldzki
Rondo Grunwaldzkie
KOŚCIÓŁ ŚW. MICHAŁA I STANISŁAWA
Zagrody
Szwedzka
Dębowa
Cassino
Monte
Twardowskiego
Generała Bohdana Zielińskiego
Kapelanka
Jana
Komandosów
LUDWINÓW
Ludwinowska

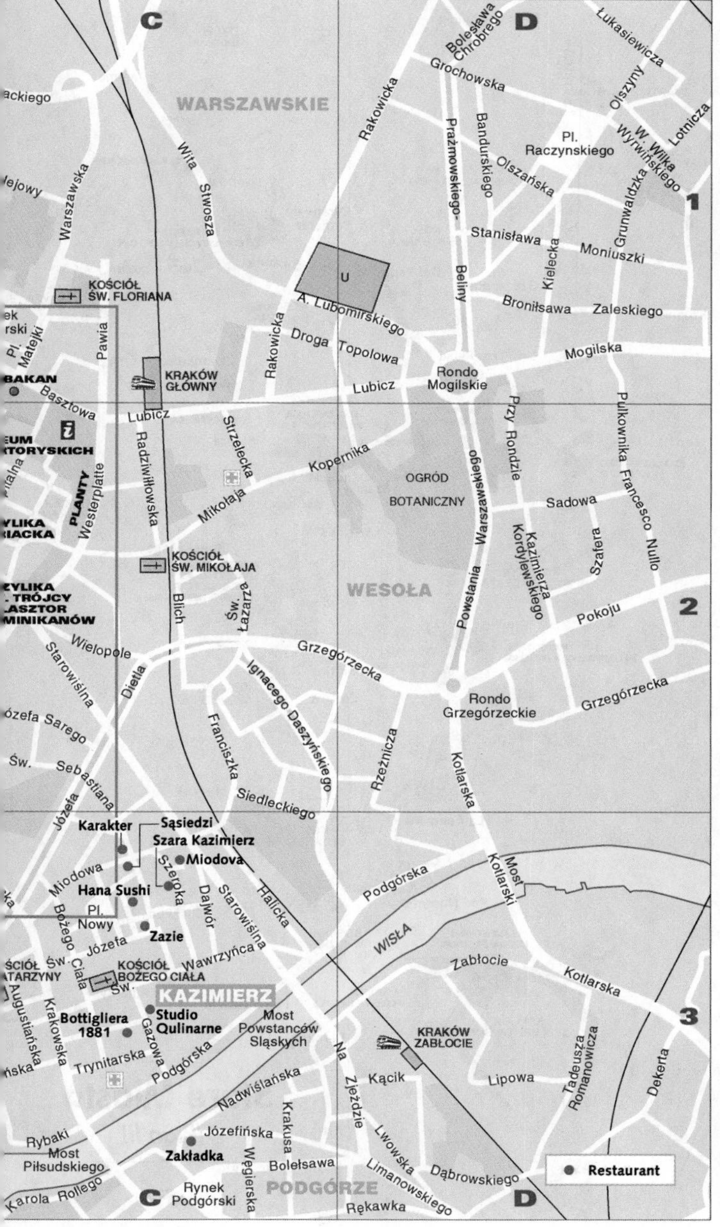
C
D
WARSZAWSKIE
Bolesława Chrobrego
Łukasiewicza
Grochowska
Olszyny
Lotnicza
Rakowicka
Prażmowskiego
Bandurskiego
Pl. Raczynskiego
W. Wilka Wyrwińskiego
Olszańska
Wita Stwosza
Warszawska
Grunwaldzka
1
Stanisława
Moniuszki
Kielecka
U
Beliny
KOŚCIÓŁ ŚW. FLORIANA
A. Lubomirskiego
Bronisława
Zaleskiego
Pl. Matejki
Pawia
Rakowicka
Droga
Topolowa
Mogilska
KRAKÓW GŁÓWNY
Rondo Mogilskie
Lubicz
Basztowa
Lubicz
Przy Rondzie
Pułkownika Francesco Nullo
Strzelecka
Radziwiłłowska
Kopernika
OGRÓD BOTANICZNY
PLANTY
Westerplatte
Mikołaja
Warszawskiego
Sadowa
Kazimierza Kordylewskiego
Szafera
KOŚCIÓŁ ŚW. MIKOŁAJA
Św. Łazarza
Blich
WESOŁA
Powstania
2
Pokoju
Wielopole
Grzegórzecka
Starowiślna
Dietla
Ignacego Daszyńskiego
Rondo Grzegórzeckie
Grzegórzecka
Franciszka
Sarego
Rzeźnicza
Kotlarska
Sebastiana
Siedleckiego
Józefa
Karakter
Sąsiedzi
Szara Kazimierz
Miodowa
Most Kotlarski
Miodowa
Szeroka
Podgórska
Hana Sushi
Dajwór
Starowiślna
Halicka
Pl. Nowy
Bożego
Zazie
WISŁA
Józefa
Wawrzyńca
Zabłocie
Ciała
Św.
KOŚCIÓŁ BOŻEGO CIAŁA
Kotlarska
KAZIMIERZ
Augustiańska
Krakowska
Bottigliera 1881
Studio Qulinarne
Most Powstanców Sląskych
KRAKÓW ZABŁOCIE
3
Gazowa
Trynitarska
Podgórska
Na Zjeździe
Kącik
Lipowa
Tadeusza Romanowicza
Dekerta
Nadwiślańska
Krakusa
Rybaki
Józefińska
Lwowska
Most Piłsudskiego
Zakładka
Węgierska
Bolesława
Limanowskiego
Dąbrowskiego
Restaurant
Karola Rollego
Rynek Podgórski
PODGÓRZE
Rękawka

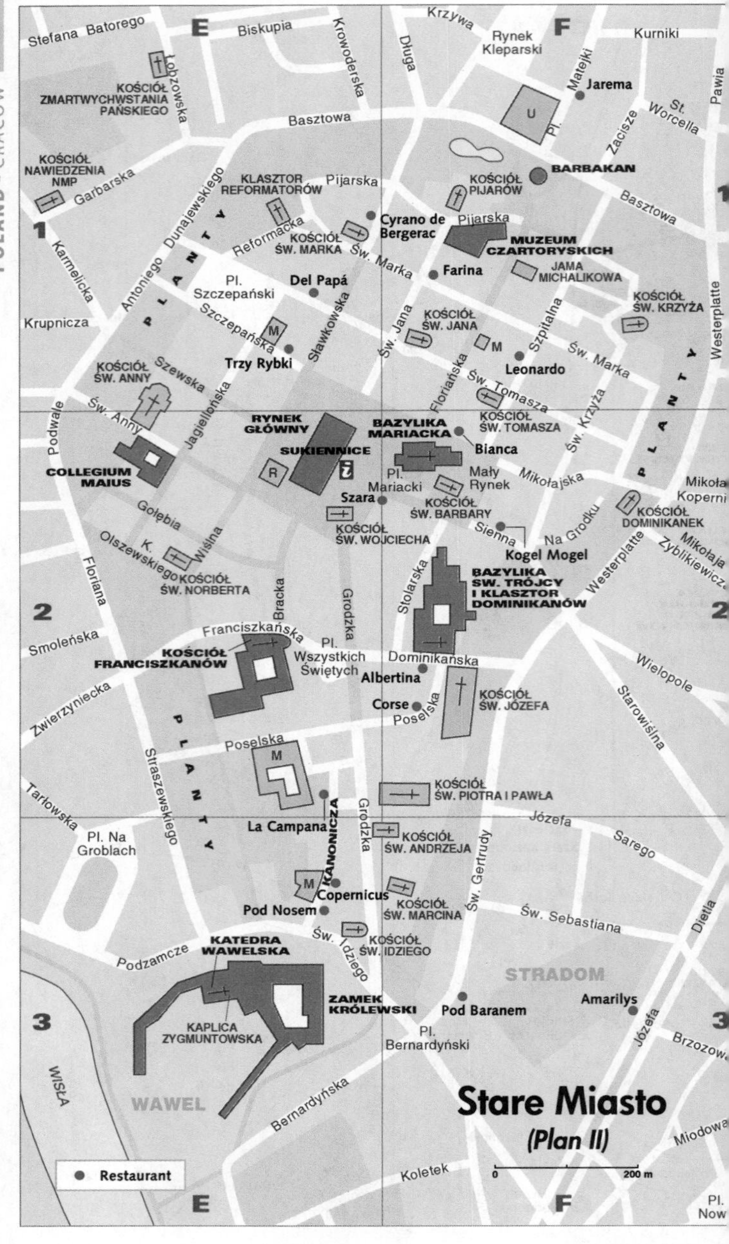
Stare Miasto
(Plan II)
Restaurant
0
200 m
E
F
1
2
3
STRADOM
WAWEL
WISŁA
PLANTY
KOŚCIÓŁ ZMARTWYCHWSTANIA PAŃSKIEGO
KOŚCIÓŁ NAWIEDZENIA NMP
KLASZTOR REFORMATORÓW
KOŚCIÓŁ ŚW. MARKA
KOŚCIÓŁ PIJARÓW
BARBAKAN
MUZEUM CZARTORYSKICH
JAMA MICHALIKOWA
KOŚCIÓŁ ŚW. KRZYŻA
KOŚCIÓŁ ŚW. JANA
KOŚCIÓŁ ŚW. ANNY
RYNEK GŁÓWNY
SUKIENNICE
BAZYLIKA MARIACKA
KOŚCIÓŁ ŚW. TOMASZA
COLLEGIUM MAIUS
KOŚCIÓŁ ŚW. BARBARY
KOŚCIÓŁ ŚW. WOJCIECHA
KOŚCIÓŁ DOMINIKANEK
KOŚCIÓŁ ŚW. NORBERTA
BAZYLIKA ŚW. TRÓJCY I KLASZTOR DOMINIKANÓW
KOŚCIÓŁ FRANCISZKANÓW
KOŚCIÓŁ ŚW. JÓZEFA
KOŚCIÓŁ ŚW. PIOTRA I PAWŁA
KOŚCIÓŁ ŚW. ANDRZEJA
KOŚCIÓŁ ŚW. MARCINA
KOŚCIÓŁ ŚW. IDZIEGO
KATEDRA WAWELSKA
ZAMEK KRÓLEWSKI
KAPLICA ZYGMUNTOWSKA
Jarema
Cyrano de Bergerac
Farina
Del Papá
Trzy Rybki
Leonardo
Bianca
Szara
Kogel Mogel
Albertina
Corse
La Campana
Copernicus
Pod Nosem
Pod Baranem
Amarilys
Stefana Batorego
Biskupia
Krowoderska
Krzywa
Długa
Rynek Kleparski
Kurniki
Matejki
Pl.
Pawia
Św. Worcella
Łobzowska
Basztowa
Zacisze
Garbarska
Pijarska
Dunajewskiego
Reformacka
Św. Marka
Karmelicka
Antoniego
Pl. Szczepański
Szczepańska
Sławkowska
Św. Jana
Szpitalna
Westerplatte
Krupnicza
Szewska
Floriańska
Św. Tomasza
Podwale
Św. Anny
Jagiellońska
Św. Krzyża
Pl. Mariacki
Mały Rynek
Mikołajska
Mikołaja Kopernika
Gołębia
Wiślna
Sienna
Na Grodku
K. Olszewskiego
Zyblikiewicza
Floriana
Bracka
Grodzka
Stolarska
Smoleńska
Franciszkańska
Pl. Wszystkich Świętych
Dominikańska
Wielopole
Zwierzyniecka
Poselska
Starowiślna
Straszewskiego
Tarłowska
Kanonicza
Józefa
Sarego
Pl. Na Groblach
Św. Gertrudy
Św. Sebastiana
Dietla
Podzamcze
Św. Idziego
Pl. Bernardyński
Józefa
Brzozowa
Bernardyńska
Miodowa
Koletek
Pl. Nowy

La Campana

ul. Kanonicza 7 ✉ 31 000 – ✆ (12) 430 22 32 — Plan: E2
– www.lacampana.pl – Closed 24-25 December and Easter
Carte 76/152 PLN

• Italian • Cosy • Rustic •

Discreetly set under an archway, with a charming country interior featuring pine dressers and an olive branch frieze; it also boasts a beautiful walled garden. The wide-ranging Italian menu features imported produce – the hams are a hit.

Del Papá

ul. Św. Tomasza 6 ✉ 31 014 – ✆ (507) 097 522 — Plan: E1
– www.delpapa.pl – Closed Christmas and Easter
Carte 60/115 PLN

• Italian • Bistro • Friendly •

A simple Italian trattoria: dine in the bistro-style room, the characterful Italian 'street' or on the partially covered rear terrace. Wide-ranging menus echo the seasons and pasta is a highlight – pick your variety, sauce and portion size.

Farina

ul. Sw. Marka 16 ✉ 31 018 – ✆ (12) 422 16 80 — Plan: F1
– www.farina.com.pl – Closed 24 December
Carte 95/325 PLN

• Seafood • Cosy • Friendly •

A pretty little restaurant set over three rooms; all of them cosy and candlelit but each with its own character. Seafood is the speciality, with fish arriving from France several times a week and then cooked whole over salt and herbs.

at KAZIMIERZ — PLAN I

Zazie

ul. Józefa 34 ✉ 31 056 – ✆ (500) 410 829 — Plan: C3
– www.zaziebistro.pl – Closed 24-25 December and Easter
Menu 31 PLN (weekday lunch) – Carte 58/89 PLN – *(booking essential at dinner)*

• French • Bistro • Cosy •

You'll find this bistro in a corner spot on a pleasant square. Inside it has a lively vibe; ask for a table in the attractive cellar, with its pleasing mix of French memorabilia and brick and stone walls. Great value Gallic dishes range from quiches and gratins to roast duck and beef Bourguignon.

Studio Qulinarne

ul. Gazowa 4 ✉ 31 060 – ✆ (12) 430 69 14 — Plan: C3
– www.studioqulinarne.pl – Closed Christmas, Easter and Sunday
Menu 210/280 PLN – *(dinner only)*

• Modern cuisine • Intimate • Elegant •

A passionately run, restyled bus garage with folding glass doors, a cocktail bar and an intimate enclosed terrace. The airy interior features exposed timbers, unusual lighting and black linen. Tasting menus have a playful, innovative edge. The wine list offers a rich, diverse selection.

Szara Kazimierz

ul. Szeroka 39 ✉ 31 053 – ✆ (12) 429 12 19 — Plan: C3
– www.szarakazimierz.pl – Closed 24-25 December
Carte 82/147 PLN

• Polish • Brasserie • Neighbourhood •

A friendly brasserie in a pleasant spot on the square. Sit out the front, on the enclosed rear terrace, or inside, surrounded by photos of Gaultier models. Menus reflect the owners' heritage by mixing Polish and Swedish classics.

Bottiglieria 1881

ul. Bochenska 5 ✉ 31 061 – ✆ (660) 66 17 56 Plan: **C3**
– www.1881.com.pl – Closed Christmas-New Year, Easter, Sunday and Monday
Carte 125/145 PLN

• Creative • Wine bar • Design •

This century old cellar is found in the Jewish district. Old wine boxes decorate the room, hand-crafted wood and stone feature and the large cave offers over 100 different wines. The menu is a concise collection of modern dishes.

Hana Sushi

ul.Kupa 12 ✉ 31 057 – ✆ (608) 576 255 Plan: **C3**
– www.hanasushikrakow.pl – Closed Monday
Carte 55/230 PLN

• Japanese • Simple • Neighbourhood •

This simple Japanese-style restaurant has made a real impact in the city. The chef-owner is a Sushi Master who trained in Tokyo and the sushi is prepared with finesse. They also serve some Korean dishes like ramen and bibimbap.

Karakter

Brzozowa 17 ✉ 31 050 – ✆ (795) 818 123 – Plan: **C3**
Closed 24-25 December, Easter and Monday lunch
Menu 35 PLN (weekday lunch) – Carte 63/97 PLN – *(booking essential at dinner)*

• Modern cuisine • Rustic • Simple •

Karakter is a lively spot, with loud music, cocktails and a minimalist feel. The charming young team serve an extensive menu with a focus on offal; horse meat tartare is one of their signatures. Refined cooking blends many different flavours.

Miodova

ul. Szeroka 3 ✉ 31 053 – ✆ (12) 432 5083 Plan: **C3**
– www.miodova.pl – Closed 24-25 December and 1 November
Carte 100/160 PLN

• Polish • Friendly • Fashionable •

In a cobbled square in the busy Jewish district you'll find 'Honey', an ultra-modern restaurant set over 3 floors. It's a comfortable place, with sofa-style banquettes and colourful cushions. Regional specialities are given modern twists.

Sąsiedzi – Boutique L'Otel

ul. Miodowa 25 ✉ 31 055 – ✆ (12) 654 83 53 Plan: **C3**
– www.oberza.pl – Closed 23-26 December, Easter and 1 November
Carte 85/160 PLN

• Polish • Intimate • Neighbourhood •

With its relaxed, welcoming atmosphere and delightful team, its name, 'Neighbourhood', sums it up well. Dine on the small terrace or in one of several charming cellar rooms. Honest, good value cooking uses old Polish recipes.

at PODGÓRZE — PLAN I

Zakładka

ul. Józefińska 2 ✉ 30 529 – ✆ (12) 442 74 42 Plan: **C3**
– www.zakladkabistro.pl – Closed 24-25 December
Carte 60/105 PLN

• French • Bistro • Neighbourhood •

Zakladka is set over a footbridge in an old tenement building, and run by a well-known local chef. With chequered floors and red banquettes, the characterful front rooms have a classic bistro feel; the French dishes are equally traditional.

Tomeyk/iStock

LISBON

PORTUGAL
PORTUGAL

SeanPavonePhoto/iStock

Lisbon
Lisboa

LeoPatrizi/iStock

LISBON IN…

- **ONE DAY**
  Alfama, Castelo São Jorge, Bairro Alto.
- **TWO DAYS**
  Baixa, Calouste Gulbenkian Museum, Parque das Nações.
- **THREE DAYS**
  Museu Nacional de Arte Antiga, Belém.

Sitting on the north bank of the River Tagus, beneath huge open skies and surrounded by seven hills, Lisbon boasts an atmosphere that few cities can match. An enchanting walk around the streets has an old-time ambience all of its own, matched only by a jaunt on the trams and funiculars that run up and down the steep hills. At first sight Lisbon is all flaky palaces, meandering alleyways and castellated horizon quarried from medieval stone; but there's a 21C element, too. Slinky new developments line the riverside, linking the old and new in a glorious jumble which spills down the slopes to the water's edge. The views of the water from various vantage points all over Lisbon and the vistas of the 'Straw Sea' – so

named because of the golden reflections of the sun – reach out to visitors, along with the sounds of fado, the city's alluring folk music, which conjures up a melancholic yearning.

The compact heart of the city is the Baixa, a flat, 18C grid of streets flanked by the hills. To the west is the elegant commercial district of Chiado and the funky hilltop Bairro Alto, while immediately to the east is Alfama, a tightly packed former Moorish quarter with kasbah-like qualities. North of here is the working-class neighbourhood of Graça and way out west lies the spacious riverside suburb of Belém, while up the river to the east can be found the ultra-modern Parque das Nações.

EATING OUT

Lisboetas love their local agricultural produce and the cuisine of the region can be characterised by its honesty and simplicity. The city has an age-old maritime tradition and there are a number of fishing ports nearby, so ocean-fresh fish and seafood features in a range of dishes. One thing the locals love in particular is bacalhau (cod), and it's said that in Lisbon, there's a different way to prepare it for every day of the year: it may come oven-baked, slow-cooked or cooked in milk, and it can be served wrapped in cabbage, with tocino belly pork or in a myriad of other ways. While eating in either a humble tasca, a casa de pasto or a restaurante, other specialities to keep an eye out for are clams cooked with garlic and coriander, traditional beef, chicken and sausage stew with vegetables and rice, bean casserole with tocino belly pork, and lamprey eel with rice. Enjoy them with a vinho verde, the wine of the region. A service charge will be included on your bill but it's customary to leave a tip of about ten per cent.

✿✿ **Belcanto** (José Avillez) XxX

Largo de São Carlos 10 ✉ 1200-410 – Ⓜ Baixa-Chiado Plan: **A2**
– ✆ 213 42 06 07 – www.belcanto.pt – Closed Sunday and Monday
Menu 165/185 € – Carte 106/112 €
• Creative • Contemporary décor •

This restaurant is located in the city's Bairro Alto, a district popular with tourists. Once through the front door you will enjoy one of the best gourmet experiences in Portugal, thanks to the cuisine of outstanding chef José Avillez. In the attractive dining room, renovated in a classically elegant style, the superb menus are of the utmost creativity and a demonstration of the very highest level of culinary skill.

→ Carabineiro do Algarve em dois serviços. Salmonete braseado, com molho de fígados e xerém de amêijoas à Bulhão Pato. Chocolate.

✿✿ **Alma** (Henrique Sá Pessoa) XX

Anchieta 15 ✉ 1200-023 – Ⓜ Baixa-Chiado Plan: **A2**
– ✆ 213 47 06 50 – www.almalisboa.pt – Closed Monday
Menu 110/120 € – Carte 55/75 €
• Creative • Contemporary décor •

Located in the heart of the Chiado district in an 18C building that was once a warehouse for the famous Bertrand bookshop, the oldest in the world. The interior is one of striking contrasts and provides the backdrop for seasonal à la carte options and interesting set menus that encompass traditional, international and Mediterranean dishes.

→ Escalope de foie-gras, maçã, granola e café. Calçada de bacalhau, puré de cebolada e gema de ovo. Bomba de chocolate e caramelo salgado, sorvete de avelã.

Tágide XxX

Largo da Academia Nacional de Belas Artes 18-20 Plan: **A2**
✉ 1200-005 – Ⓜ Baixa-Chiado – ✆ 213 40 40 10
– www.restaurantetagide.com – Closed 7 days January and Sunday
Menu 60/80 € – Carte 40/65 €
• Modern cuisine • Classic décor •

Climb a few steps to Tágide's elegant dining room embellished with chandeliers and attractive azulejo tilework. It offers updated traditional cuisine and has a tapas bar at the entrance.

Pesca XX

Rua da Escola Politécnica 27 ✉ 1250-099 – Ⓜ Rato – ✆ 213 46 06 33
– www.restaurantepesca.pt – Closed Monday
Menu 50/80 € – Carte 48/95 €
• Creative • Fashionable •

Pesca occupies a stone house in the upper part of Lisbon. The focus here is on traditional and Mediterranean cuisine using locally sourced products, which are carefully prepared and superbly presented.

Solar dos Presuntos XX

Rua das Portas de Santo Antão 150 ✉ 1150-269 Plan: **A1**
– Ⓜ Avenida – ✆ 213 42 42 53 – www.solardospresuntos.com – Closed 7 days Christmas, 21 days August, Sunday and bank holidays
Carte 33/57 €
• Traditional cuisine • Trendy •

A culinary icon in the city, which has been satisfying discerning palates for over 40 years. The extensive, traditional à la carte menu focuses on high-quality ingredients, particularly rice and seafood.

O Faz Figura

Rua do Paraíso 15-B ✉ 1100-396
– ✆ 218 86 89 81 – www.fazfigura.com
– Closed Monday dinner
Menu 25/50 € – Carte 30/45 €
• Modern cuisine • Trendy •

Next to the National Pantheon (Santa Engrácia church), near Alfama. A well-organised operation with classic facilities, in an elegant setting, and traditional cuisine with a creative touch.

Casa de Linhares

Plan: **B2**

Beco dos Armazéns do Linho 2 ✉ 1100-037
– Ⓜ Terreiro do Paço
– ✆ 910 18 81 18 – www.casadelinhares.com
Menu 50/65 € – Carte 37/61 € – *(dinner only) (booking essential)*
• Portuguese • Regional décor •

This restaurant occupies a Renaissance mansion that has been converted into one of the most popular *Fado* music venues in Lisbon. Impressive menu of traditional Portuguese cuisine.

Mini Bar Teatro

Rúa António Maria Cardoso 58 ✉ 1200-027 Plan: **A2**
– Ⓜ Baixa-Chiado – ✆ +351 211 30 53 93 – www.minibar.pt
Menu 45/55 € – Carte 13/44 € – *(dinner only)*
• Creative • Bistro •
An informal, enticing and relaxed eatery in the Bairro Alto theatre district. Diners are in for a pleasant surprise as the dishes on the menu have been created by José Avillez – Michelin-starred chef at the Belcanto restaurant.

Páteo - Bairro do Avillez

Rua Nova da Trindade 18 ✉ 1200-466 Lisboa Plan: **A2**
– Ⓜ Baixa-Chiado – ✆ 215 83 02 90 – www.bairrodoavillez.pt
Carte 41/65 € – *(booking essential)*
• Seafood • Mediterranean décor •
This restaurant occupies the central patio of an attractive gastronomic complex. The focus is on the high quality of the produce used and delicious seafood takes centre stage.

Taberna - Bairro do Avillez

Rua Nova da Trindade 18 ✉ 1200-466 Plan: **A2**
– Ⓜ Baixa-Chiado – ✆ 215 83 02 90 – www.bairrodoavillez.pt
Carte 20/30 €
• Traditional cuisine • Tavern •
The tavern-charcuterie format here is part of the successful Bairro do Avillez gastronomic complex. Traditional cuisine presented in the form of petiscos and main dishes.

Tapisco

Rua Dom Pedro V 81 ✉ 1250-026 Plan: **A1**
– ✆ 213 42 06 81 – www.tapisco.pt
Carte 25/38 € – *(bookings not accepted)*
• Traditional cuisine • Fashionable •
A contemporary eatery which perfectly lives up to its name – a combination of the words "tapas" and "petiscos". Guests here can enjoy plenty of dishes that are made for sharing.

O Asiático

Rua da Rosa 317 ✉ 1250-083 – ✆ 211 31 93 69 Plan: **A1**
– www.oasiatico.com
Carte 31/40 € – *(dinner only except Friday, Saturday and Sunday)*
• Asian • Fashionable •
India, Thailand, China and Japan are all represented by this chef, who has spent time living in Asia. He creates attractive fusion cuisine based around Portuguese ingredients and the dishes are perfect for sharing.

A Cevicheria

Dom Pedro V 129 ✉ 1200-093 – ✆ 218 03 88 15 Plan: **A1**
Carte 20/35 € – *(bookings not accepted)*
• Peruvian • Fashionable •
Peruvian cooking with a Portuguese edge. The setting is tight on space but highly original, and includes a huge octopus hanging from the ceiling! There's always a queue to get in here.

100 Maneiras

Rua do Teixeira 35 ✉ 1200-459 – ✆ 910 30 75 75 Plan: **A1**
– www.100maneiras.com
Menu 60 € – *(dinner only) (tasting menu only)*
• Creative • Traditional décor •
A small restaurant in a narrow street in the Bairro Alto district. The young chef offers a creative tasting menu, which is fresh, light and imaginatively presented.

Eleven (Joachim Koerper)

Rua Marquês de Fronteira ✉ 1070-051 – Ⓜ São Sebastião – ☎ 213 86 22 11 – www.restauranteleven.com – Closed Sunday
Menu 94/175 € – Carte 70/135 €
• Creative • Elegant •
Housed in a designer-style building above the Amália Rodrigues gardens, this light, airy and modern restaurant boasts splendid views of the Eduardo VII park and the city. Creative gourmet cuisine features on the menu.
➜ Foie gras de pato, soja, rum e laranja. Lavagante sobre espinafres e shiso, caviar e champagne. Soufflé de maracujá com gelado de banana.

Varanda

Hotel Four Seasons H. Ritz Lisbon – Rua Rodrigo da Fonseca 88 ✉ 1099-039 – Ⓜ Marquês de Pombal – ☎ 213 81 14 00 – www.fourseasons.com
Menu 84/114 € – Carte 80/120 € – *(dinner only)*
• Modern cuisine • Elegant •
The terrace overlooking the Eduardo VII park is as impressive as the cuisine here, which includes an extensive buffet at lunchtime and more gastronomic dining in the evening.

Bistrô 4 – Hotel Porto Bay Liberdade

Rua Rosa Araújo 8 ✉ 1250-195 – Ⓜ Avenida – ☎ 210 01 57 00 – www.portobay.com
Menu 22 € – Carte 26/58 €
• French • Bistro •
A restaurant with plenty of personality, featuring a spacious dining room with a classic-contemporary feel, where the bistro-style menu combines French, Portuguese and seasonal dishes.

Go Juu

Rua Marqués Sá da Bandeira 46 ✉ 1050-149 – Ⓜ S. Sebastião – ☎ 218 28 07 04 – www.gojuu.pt – Closed 20 August-3 September, Sunday dinner and Monday
Menu 20/25 € – Carte 30/89 €
• Japanese • Design •
Enjoy authentic Japanese cooking in this unique, almost minimalist space featuring a profusion of wood and a sushi bar in the dining room. There's also an exclusive area for Go Juu's club members.

Adega Tia Matilde

Rua da Beneficência 77 ✉ 1600-017 – Ⓜ Praça de Espanha – ☎ 217 97 21 72 – www.adegatiamatilde.pt – Closed Saturday dinner and Sunday
Menu 22 € – Carte 35/50 €
• Traditional cuisine • Family •
A classic Lisbon address occupying a modest family house that opened its doors in 1926. The focus here is on traditional cuisine that stands out for its authenticity and flavour.

O Talho

Carlos Testa 18 ✉ 1050-046 – Ⓜ S. Sebastião – ☎ 213 15 41 05 – www.otalho.pt
Carte 31/48 €
• Meats and grills • Fashionable •
A highly original restaurant given that access to it is via a modern butcher's shop. Not surprisingly, the menu here is centred around meat and its by-products.

PARQUE DAS NAÇÕES

D'Avis

Av. D. João II-1 (Parque das Nações) ✉ 1990-083 – ☎ 218 68 13 54 – Closed Sunday and bank holidays
Carte 20/30 €
• Cuisine from Alentejo • Rustic •
This oasis of rusticity imbued with the spirit of the Alentejo region is in the very modern setting of the Expo '98 site. The counter at the entrance sells regional products, while the two cosy dining rooms are decorated with a variety of traditional and antique objects. Highly authentic Alentejo cuisine.

A Casa do Bacalhau

Rua do Grilo 54 ✉ 1900-706 – ☎ 218 62 00 00 – www.acasadobacalhau.com – Closed Sunday July-August and Sunday dinner the rest of the year
Menu 25/50 € – Carte 29/44 €
• Portuguese • Contemporary décor •
This highly interesting restaurant combines a contemporary look with a vaulted dining room whose origins date back to the 18C. As the name suggests, you will discover the myriad ways of cooking cod here!

WEST

Loco (Alexandre Silva)

Rua dos Navegantes 53 ✉ 1250-731 – Ⓜ Rato – ☎ 213 95 18 61 – www.loco.pt – Closed 4-17 June, 12-25 November, Sunday and Monday
Menu 96/126 € – *(dinner only) (booking essential) (tasting menu only)*
• Modern cuisine • Fashionable •
Located next to the Basílica da Estrela, Loco has just the one dining room with a surprising design and views of the kitchen. Alexandre Silva, famous for winning the first *Top Chef de Portugal* competition, showcases his cuisine via two enticing and creative tasting menus, which make full use of locally sourced ingredients.
→ Lula marinada com ovas de polvo e oleo de pimento, caldo crú de caranguejo. Lingua de vaca com molho de moscatel roxo e pickle de batata. Ervilhas, alho negro e malaguetas verdes.

Solar dos Nunes

Rua dos Lusíadas 68-72 ✉ 1300-372 – ☎ 213 64 73 59 – www.solardosnunes.pt – Closed Sunday
Carte 30/40 €
• Traditional cuisine • Rustic •
This welcoming restaurant stands out for the magnificent mosaic-style floor in the main dining room and its walls covered with appreciative newspaper and magazine reviews. Impressive fish display, as well as a live seafood tank. Traditional Portuguese menu and an excellent wine list.

BELÉM

Feitoria – Hotel Altis Belém

Doca do Bom Sucesso ✉ 1400-038 – ☎ 210 40 02 08 – www.restaurantefeitoria.com – Closed 2-16 January, Sunday and Monday
Menu 85/135 € – Carte 72/87 € – *(dinner only)*
• Modern cuisine • Contemporary décor •
A restaurant of a very high standard, featuring a bar for a pre-dinner drink and a dining room arranged in a contemporary style. The chef offers creative, modern cuisine steeped in tradition, with a focus on high quality products and top-notch presentation.
→ Bivalves com arroz carolino e salicornia queimada. Peixe fresco da lota de Peniche, caldo das barrigas, espargos e caviar. Ananás dos Açores, pimenta selvagem e especiarias.

Thomas Demarczyk/iStock

Barcelona
MADRID

SPAIN
ESPAÑA

RudyBalasko/iStock

Madrid
MADRID

benedek/iStock

MADRID IN...

→ **ONE DAY**
Puerta del Sol, Plaza Mayor, Palacio Real, Museo del Prado.

→ **TWO DAYS**
Museo Thyssen-Bornemisza, Retiro, Gran Vía, tapas at a traditional taberna.

→ **THREE DAYS**
Chueca, Malasaña, Centro de Arte Reina Sofía.

The renaissance of Madrid has seen it develop as a big player on the world cultural stage, attracting more international music, theatre and dance than it would have dreamed of a few decades ago. The nightlife in Spain's proud capital is second to none and the superb art museums which make up the city's 'golden triangle' have all undergone thrilling reinvention in recent years. This is a city that might think it has some catching up to do: it was only made the capital in 1561 on the whim of ruler, Felipe II. But its position was crucial: slap bang in the middle of the Iberian Peninsula. Ruled by Habsburgs and Bourbons, it soon made a mark in Europe, and the contemporary big wigs of Madrid are now having the same effect – this time with a 21C twist.

The central heart of Madrid is compact, defined by the teeming Habsburg hubs of Puerta del Sol and Plaza Mayor, and the mighty Palacio Real – the biggest official royal residence in the world, with a bewildering three thousand rooms. East of here are the grand squares, fountains and fine museums of the Bourbon District, with its easterly boundary, the Retiro park. West of the historical centre are the capacious green acres of Casa de Campo, while the affluent, regimented grid streets of Salamanca are to the east. Modern Madrid is just to the north, embodied in the grand north-south boulevard Paseo de la Castellana.

EATING OUT

Madrileños know how to pace themselves. Breakfast is around 8am, lunch 2pm or 3pm, the afternoon begins at 5pm and dinner won't be until 10pm or 11pm. Madrid is the European capital which has best managed to absorb the regional cuisine of the country, largely due to massive internal migration to the city, and it claims to have the highest number of bars and restaurants per capita than anywhere else in the world. If you want to tuck into local specialities, you'll find them everywhere around the city. Callos a la Madrileña is Madrid-style tripe, dating back to 1559, while sopas de ajo (garlic soup) is a favourite on cold winter days. Another popular soup (also a main course) is cocido Madrileño, hearty and aromatic and comprised of chickpeas, meat, tocino belly pork, potatoes and vegetables, slowly cooked in a rich broth. To experience the real Madrid dining ambience, get to a traditional taberna in the heart of the old neighbourhood: these are distinguished by a large clock, a carved wooden bar with a zinc counter, wine flasks, marble-topped tables and ceramic tiles.

✿✿ La Terraza del Casino (Paco Roncero)

XXXX
Alcalá 15-3° ✉ 28014 – Ⓜ Sevilla Plan: **C2**
– ✆ 915 32 12 75
– www.casinodemadrid.es
– Closed August, Sunday, Monday and bank holidays
Menu 79/185 € – Carte 95/121 €
• Creative • Elegant •

This unique restaurant is accessed via an impressive 19C staircase leading to a cutting-edge space on the top floor. Chef Paco Roncero welcomes guests on a gastronomic journey which offers guests a more visual and interactive experience in the dining room.

➜ Kokotxas de merluza al pil-pil de curry. Lenguado a la mantequilla negra. Crema tostada, mandarina y pasión.

✿✿ DSTAgE (Diego Guerrero)

XX
Regueros 8 ✉ 28004 – Ⓜ Alonso Martínez Plan: **C1**
– ✆ 917 02 15 86
– www.dstageconcept.com
– Closed Holy Week, 1-16 August, Saturday and Sunday
Menu 95/150 € – *(booking essential) (tasting menu only)*
• Creative • Trendy •

This restaurant has an urban and industrial look and a relaxed feel that reflects the personality of the chef. The name is an acronym of his core philosophy: 'Days to Smell Taste Amaze Grow & Enjoy'. Discover cuisine that brings disparate cultures, ingredients and flavours together from Spain, Mexico and Japan.

➜ Tomate garum. Morcilla de Beasain, puerro joven y ceniza. Cebolla, vinagre, fresas silvestres y nasturtium.

✿ El Club Allard

XXXX
Ferraz 2 ✉ 28008 – Ⓜ Plaza España Plan: **A1**
– ✆ 915 59 09 39 – www.elcluballard.com
– Closed 11-20 August, Sunday dinner and Monday
Menu 115/145 € – Carte 82/120 €
• Creative • Classic décor •

This unique restaurant occupies a listed Modernist building dating back to 1908, although you won't find any trace of this on the outside. In the elegant interior, with its mix of classic and contemporary decor, the creative cuisine showcases the personal and oriental influence of the chef. If you're looking for an even more exclusive experience, make sure you book "La Pecera".

➜ Guisadito con cigala y verduras encurtidas. Rubio con caldo de las espinas y pan de picada realizado al momento. Pedacito de cielo, torrija de remolacha, helado de vainilla y leche quemada.

✿ Cebo – Hotel Urban

XXX
Carrera de San Jerónimo 34 ✉ 28014 – Ⓜ Sevilla Plan: **C2**
– ✆ 917 87 77 70 – www.cebomadrid.com – Closed August, Sunday, Monday and bank holidays
Menu 80/110 € – *(tasting menu only)*
• Creative • Design •

A meticulously appointed modern space with a hint of designer decor, and a splendid bar where dishes are completed in front of guests. The creative cuisine is a statement of intent for a culinary experience that is built around a unique fusion of regional cooking from around Spain.

➜ Nieve de gazpacho, camarones y remojón de olivas gordas. Bacalao a la riojana y mollejas de cordero. Aromas de naranja, mandarina, horchata, Mediterráneo y flor de azahar.

Corral de la Morería Gastronómico

XX AC

Morería 17 ✉ 28005 – Ⓜ La Latina – ✆ 913 65 84 46 Plan: **A3**
– www.corraldelamoreria.com – Closed July-15 August, Sunday and Monday
Menu 49/65 € – *(dinner only) (tasting menu only)*
• Modern cuisine • Contemporary décor •
A unique restaurant thanks to the two completely different dining spaces within it: Tablao, from where you can watch the show; and the separate gastronomic restaurant with just four tables, where the modern cooking is built around seasonality. An impressive array of tapas, set menus and à la carte choices.
➜ Cocochas de merluza en tinta negra. Pichón, asado y reposado, tomate anisado y hojas de espinacas. Ruibarbo, regaliz, aire de champagne y helado de piel de limón.

La Candela Restò (Samy Ali Rando)

XX AC

Amnistía 10 ✉ 28013 – Ⓜ Ópera – ✆ 911 73 98 88 Plan: **A2**
– www.lacandelaresto.com – Closed Holy Week, Sunday dinner, Monday and Tuesday lunch
Menu 69/100 € – *(tasting menu only)*
• Creative • Vintage •
An impressive, original and bold restaurant that is a faithful representation of the places in which the chef has lived. The highly unusual dining room with its retro-vintage ambience is the setting for innovative cuisine that is a perfect combination of different culinary cultures from around the world.
➜ Solo Salmón. Harumaki. Basta.

Yugo (Julián Mármol)

X AC

San Blas 4 ✉ 28014 – Ⓜ Atocha – ✆ 914 44 90 34 Plan: **C3**
– www.yugothebunker.com – Closed 12-18 August, Sunday and Monday lunch
Menu 65/150 € – Carte 80/115 €
• Japanese • Exotic décor •
A Japanese restaurant that transports guests to the atmosphere of the country's traditional pubs (izakayas) with its decor of wood, masks and flags. The cuisine here, a fusion of Japanese and Mediterranean cooking, has been adapted to European tastes. The room in the basement, available for the exclusive use of club members, is known as "The Bunker".
➜ Sashimi Moriawase. Nigiri de vieira salvaje con mantequilla de wasabi. Bombón de chocolate y té verde.

Atlantik Corner

X AC

Ventura de la Vega 11 ✉ 28014 – Ⓜ Sevilla Plan: **C2**
– ✆ 910 71 72 45 – www.atlantikcorner.com – Closed Monday
Menu 15/45 € – Carte 31/45 €
• Market cuisine • Fashionable •
An interesting option with a relaxed bistro-style atmosphere in which the cuisine has a global and Atlantic focus. The basis of its à la carte is Galician and Portuguese, though with a nod to Brazilian, Mexican and Moroccan cooking.

Triciclo

X AC

Santa María 28 ✉ 28014 – Ⓜ Antón Martin Plan: **C3**
– ✆ 910 24 47 98 – www.eltriciclo.es – Closed 7 days February, 7 days July-August and Sunday
Menu 52/75 € – Carte 34/58 €
• Creative • Bistro •
A restaurant that is on everyone's lips! Triciclo's simplicity is compensated for by a high degree of culinary expertise. This is showcased in well-prepared and attractively presented dishes that encompass personal and traditional, as well as Oriental and fusion influences.

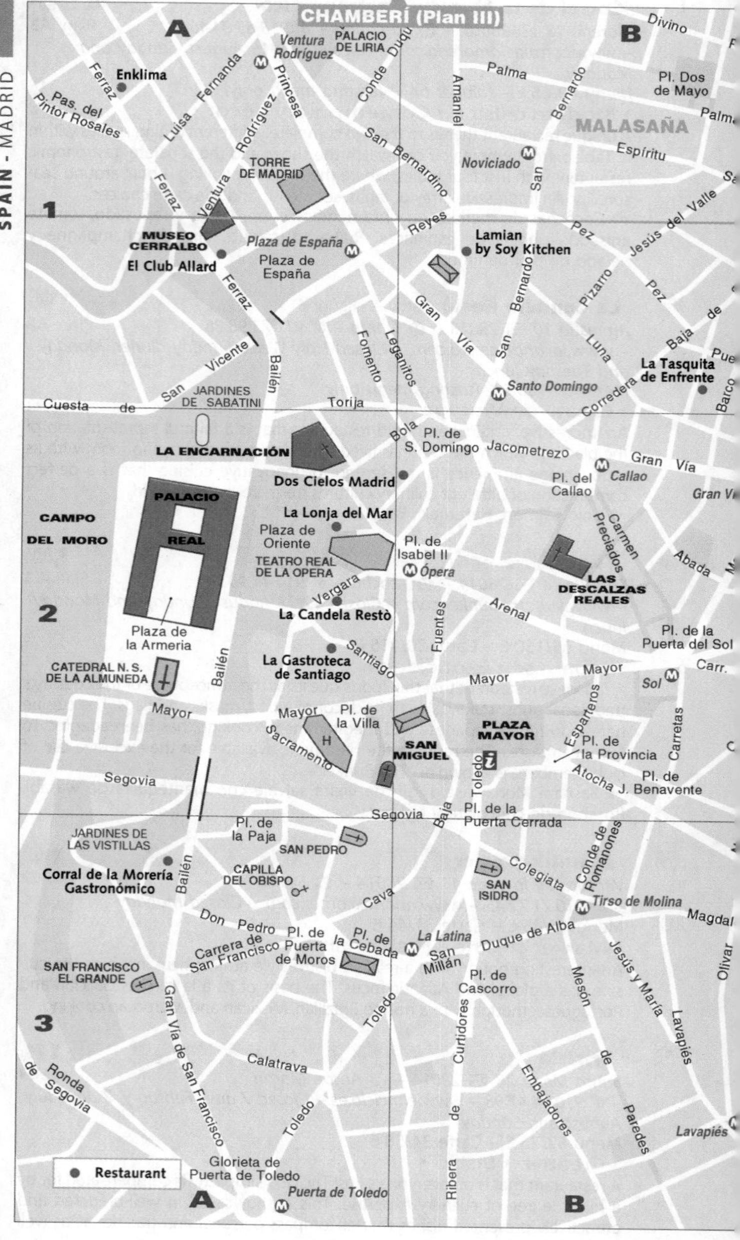

CHAMBERÍ (Plan III)
A
B
1
2
3
Enklima
Pas. del Pintor Rosales
Ferraz
Luisa Fernanda
Ventura Rodríguez
PALACIO DE LIRIA
Princesa
Conde Duque
Amaniel
Palma
San Bernardo
Divino
Pl. Dos de Mayo
MALASAÑA
Espíritu
Noviciado
San Bernardino
TORRE DE MADRID
Rodríguez
Ventura
MUSEO CERRALBO
El Club Allard
Plaza de España
Plaza de España
Reyes
Lamian by Soy Kitchen
Pez
Jesús del Valle
Pizarro
Gran Vía
San Bernardo
Luna
Baja de
La Tasquita de Enfrente
Santo Domingo
Corredera
Barco
Ferraz
San Vicente
Bailén
Fomento
Leganitos
JARDINES DE SABATINI
Cuesta de
Torija
Bola
Pl. de S. Domingo
Jacometrezo
LA ENCARNACIÓN
Gran Vía
Callao
Pl. del Callao
Dos Cielos Madrid
PALACIO REAL
CAMPO DEL MORO
La Lonja del Mar
Plaza de Oriente
TEATRO REAL DE LA OPERA
Pl. de Isabel II
Ópera
Carmen
Preciados
Abada
LAS DESCALZAS REALES
Vergara
La Candela Restò
Arenal
Fuentes
Plaza de la Armeria
Santiago
La Gastroteca de Santiago
Pl. de la Puerta del Sol
CATEDRAL N. S. DE LA ALMUNEDA
Bailén
Mayor
Mayor
Sol
Carr.
Mayor
Mayor
Pl. de la Villa
Sacramento
SAN MIGUEL
PLAZA MAYOR
Esparteros
Pl. de la Provincia
Carretas
Toledo
Atocha
Pl. de J. Benavente
Segovia
Segovia
Baja
Pl. de la Puerta Cerrada
JARDINES DE LAS VISTILLAS
Pl. de la Paja
SAN PEDRO
Corral de la Morería Gastronómico
Bailén
CAPILLA DEL OBISPO
SAN ISIDRO
Colegiata
Conde de Romanones
Tirso de Molina
Magdal
Cava
Don Pedro
Carrera de San Francisco
Pl. de Puerta de Moros
Pl. de la Cebada
La Latina
San Millán
Duque de Alba
Pl. de Cascorro
Jesús y María
Mesón de Paredes
Olivar
SAN FRANCISCO EL GRANDE
Gran Vía de San Francisco
Toledo
Cuitidores
Embajadores
Lavapiés
Calatrava
Ronda de Segovia
Toledo
Ribera de
Lavapiés
Restaurant
Glorieta de Puerta de Toledo
Puerta de Toledo

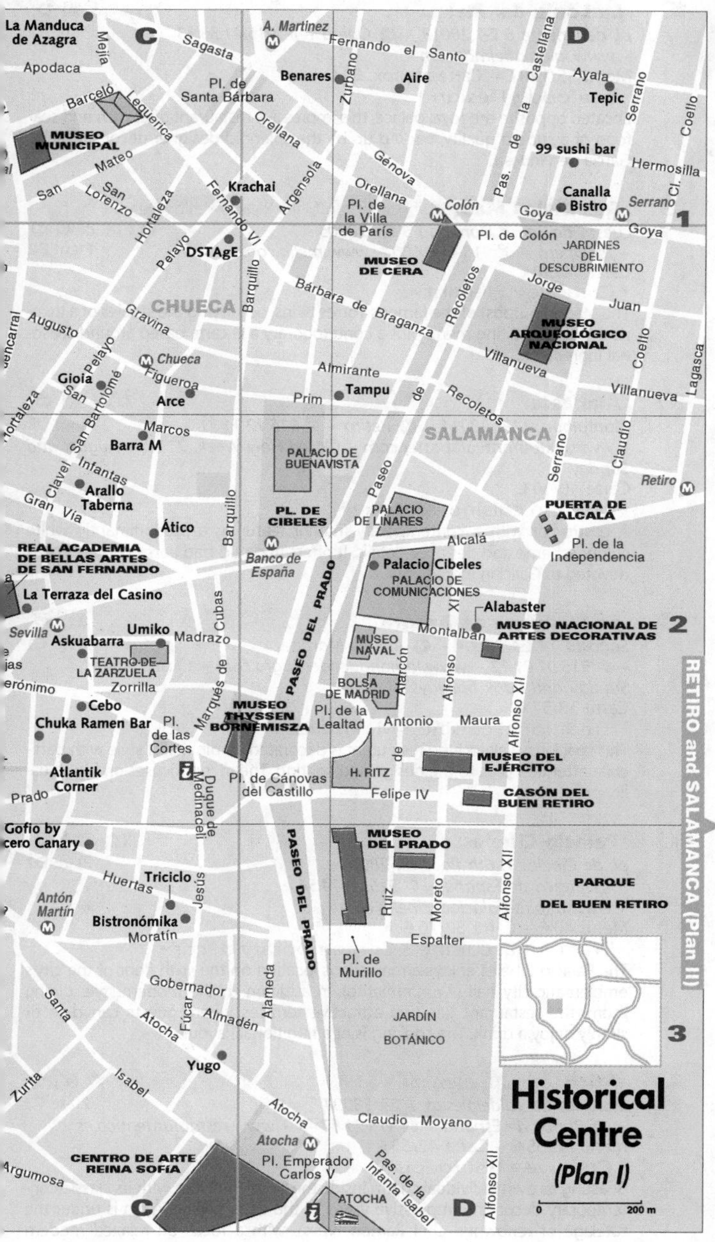
Historical Centre
(Plan I)
RETIRO and SALAMANCA (Plan II)
0
200 m
C
D
1
2
3
La Manduca de Azagra
Benares
Aire
Tepic
99 sushi bar
Canalla Bistro
Krachai
DSTAgE
MUSEO MUNICIPAL
MUSEO DE CERA
MUSEO ARQUEOLÓGICO NACIONAL
CHUECA
SALAMANCA
Gioia
Arce
Tampu
Barra M
Arallo Taberna
Ático
PALACIO DE BUENAVISTA
PL. DE CIBELES
PALACIO DE LINARES
PUERTA DE ALCALÁ
REAL ACADEMIA DE BELLAS ARTES DE SAN FERNANDO
La Terraza del Casino
Palacio Cibeles
PALACIO DE COMUNICACIONES
Alabaster
MUSEO NACIONAL DE ARTES DECORATIVAS
Umiko
Askuabarra
TEATRO DE LA ZARZUELA
MUSEO NAVAL
BOLSA DE MADRID
Cebo
Chuka Ramen Bar
MUSEO THYSSEN BORNEMISZA
Atlantik Corner
H. RITZ
MUSEO DEL EJÉRCITO
CASÓN DEL BUEN RETIRO
Gofio by Cícero Canary
MUSEO DEL PRADO
PARQUE DEL BUEN RETIRO
Triciclo
Bistronómika
JARDÍN BOTÁNICO
Yugo
CENTRO DE ARTE REINA SOFÍA
ATOCHA
PASEO DEL PRADO
A. Martínez
Colón
Serrano
Chueca
Banco de España
Retiro
Sevilla
Antón Martín
Atocha
Sagasta
Fernando el Santo
Pl. de Santa Bárbara
Apodaca
Mejía
Barceló
Lequerica
Orellana
Génova
Zurbano
Pas. de la Castellana
Ayala
Serrano
Coello
Hermosilla
Cl. Serrano
Goya
Pl. de Colón
JARDINES DEL DESCUBRIMIENTO
Jorge Juan
Villanueva
Lagasca
Mateo
San Lorenzo
Hortaleza
Fernando VI
Argensola
Pl. de la Villa de París
Pelayo
Barquillo
Bárbara de Braganza
Recoletos
Augusto Figueroa
Gravina
Almirante
Prim
Paseo de Recoletos
Claudio Coello
San Bartolomé
Marcos
Infantas
Clavel
Gran Vía
Alcalá
Pl. de la Independencia
Cubas
Madrazo
Marqués de Cubas
Montalbán
Alfonso XI
Alfonso XII
Alarcón
Zorrilla
Jerónimo
Pl. de las Cortes
Pl. de la Lealtad
Antonio Maura
Ruiz de Alarcón
Prado
Duque de Medinaceli
Pl. de Cánovas del Castillo
Felipe IV
Huertas
Jesús
Moratín
Ruiz
Moreto
Espalter
Pl. de Murillo
Gobernador
Fúcar
Almadén
Alameda
Santa Isabel
Zurita
Claudio Moyano
Pl. Emperador Carlos V
Pas. de la Infanta Isabel
Argumosa

La Lonja del Mar

pl. de Oriente 6 ✉ 28013 – Ⓜ Ópera – ✆ 915 41 33 33 – www.lalonjadelmar.com
Plan: **A2**
Menu 55/120 € – Carte approx. 59 €
• Seafood • Design •
Located opposite the royal palace, this impressive restaurant offers fish and seafood of a superb quality, backed up by the splendid designer decor of Nacho García de Vinuesa.

Dos Cielos Madrid – Hotel Gran Meliá Palacio de los Duques

cuesta de Santo Domingo 5 ✉ 28005 – Ⓜ Ópera – ✆ 915 41 67 00 – www.melia.com
Plan: **B2**
Carte 70/90 €
• Creative • Elegant •
The Madrid outpost of the famous Torres twins, occupying the stables of a luxurious palace. Tasting menu plus a contemporary à la carte based around seasonal ingredients.

Alabaster

Montalbán 9 ✉ 28014 – Ⓜ Retiro – ✆ 915 12 11 31 – www.restaurantealabaster.com – Closed Holy Week, 21 days August and Sunday
Plan: **D2**
Carte 40/60 €
• Modern cuisine • Trendy •
A gastro-bar with a contemporary interior featuring a predominantly white colour scheme and designer details. It offers updated traditional cuisine that is devoted to Galician ingredients.

La Manduca de Azagra

Sagasta 14 ✉ 28004 – Ⓜ Alonso Martínez – ✆ 915 91 01 12 – www.lamanducadeazagra.com – Closed August, Sunday and bank holidays
Plan: **C1**
Carte 38/57 €
• Traditional cuisine • Minimalist •
This spacious, well-located restaurant is decorated in minimalist style with particular attention paid to the design and lighting. The menu focuses on high quality produce.

Palacio Cibeles

pl. de Cibeles 1, 6th floor ✉ 28014 – Ⓜ Banco de España – ✆ 915 23 14 54 – www.adolfo-palaciodecibeles.com
Plan: **D2**
Menu 40 € – Carte 52/70 €
• Traditional cuisine • Contemporary décor •
The Palacio Cibeles enjoys a marvellous location on the sixth floor of the city's emblematic city hall (Ayuntamiento). In addition to the modern-style dining room, the restaurant has two attractive terraces where guests can dine or simply enjoy a drink. The cooking is of a traditional flavour.

Ático – Hotel The Principal Madrid

Marqués de Valdeiglesias 1 ✉ 28004 – Ⓜ Banco de España – ✆ 915 21 87 43 – www.restauranteatico.es
Plan: **C2**
Menu 40/65 € – Carte 42/55 €
• Creative • Bourgeois •
Boasting its own individual charm inside the Hotel Principal, with its classic-contemporary decor and impressive views of the city's skyline. Ático is under the tutelage of renowned chef Ramón Freixa, with a focus on relaxed modern cuisine.

Arce

Augusto Figueroa 32 ✉ 28004 – Ⓜ Chueca – ✆ 915 22 04 40 – www.restaurantearce.com – Closed Holy Week, 15 days August, Monday and Tuesday Plan: **C1**

Menu 65/80 € – Carte 47/65 €

• Classic cuisine • Classic décor •

A family-run business that prides itself on doing things well, hence the classic cuisine with a focus on quality ingredients and lots of flavour. Extensive à la carte, set menus and the option of half-*raciones*.

Askuabarra

Arlabán 7 ✉ 28014 – Ⓜ Sevilla – ✆ 915 93 75 07 – www.askuabarra.com – Closed Sunday dinner in October-May, Sunday in June-September and Monday Plan: **C2**

Carte 35/57 €

• Market cuisine • Rustic •

Run by two brothers who have grown up in this profession, hence the value they attach to the use of top-quality products. A modern take on seasonal cuisine, including the house speciality – steak tartare.

Bistronómika

Santa María 39 ✉ 28014 – Ⓜ Antón Martín – ✆ 911 38 62 98 – www.bistronomika.com – Closed 2 weeks August, Sunday dinner and Monday Plan: **C3**

Carte 35/50 €

• Traditional cuisine • Simple •

A modestly sized restaurant with a profusion of wood whose raison d'être is the sea. Fresh grilled fish is at the heart of everything, although meat also features on the menu.

Chuka Ramen Bar

Echegaray 9 ✉ 28014 – Ⓜ Sevilla – ✆ 640 65 13 46 – www.chukaramenbar.com – Closed August, Sunday, Monday and Tuesday lunch Plan: **C2**

Carte 26/37 €

• Japanese • Oriental décor •

The menu at this bar features a fusion of Chinese and Japanese cooking, and includes legendary dishes such as noodle-based ramen, alongside other popular street food style recipes.

Enklima

Ferraz 36 ✉ 28008 – Ⓜ Ventura Rodríguez – ✆ 911 16 69 91 – www.enklima.com – Closed 20 days August, Sunday and Monday Plan: **A1**

Menu 52/70 € – *(tasting menu only)*

• Fusion • Simple •

A compact and intimate eatery run by an enterprising couple. The menu here features highly personal fusion cuisine with lots of exotic combinations that will please contemporary tastes.

Gioia

San Bartolomé 23 ✉ 28004 – Ⓜ Chueca – ✆ 915 21 55 47 – www.gioiamadrid.es – Closed 21 days August, Sunday dinner and Monday Plan: **C1**

Menu 29 € – Carte 28/42 €

• Italian • Romantic •

An attractive restaurant on two levels run by a couple from Piedmont. Classic Italian cooking complemented by more contemporary dishes. Try the "uovo morbido" with poached eggs and truffles and the unusual "riso e oro" risotto.

Gofio by Cícero Canary

Lope de Vega 9 ✉ 28014 – Ⓜ Antón Martin Plan: **C3**
– ✆ 915 99 44 04 – www.gofiomadrid.com – Closed 24 December-7 January, 15 days August, Monday and Tuesday except bank holidays and the day before bank holidays
Menu 35/80 € – *(tasting menu only)*

• Regional cuisine • Bistro •

A homage to the cuisine of the Canary Islands in this modest bistro that recreates the culinary flavours of the islands in a modern yet informal way, with a focus on high levels of technical skill and reasonable prices. The main difference between the menus here is the number of courses that feature on them.

Krachai

Fernando VI-11 ✉ 28004 – Ⓜ Alonso Martínez Plan: **C1**
– ✆ 918 33 65 56 – www.krachai.es – Closed 20 days August and Sunday dinner
Menu 14/35 € – Carte 25/55 €

• Thai • Oriental décor •

The Krachai is split between two dining rooms, each with attractive lighting and a contemporary feel. The Thai cuisine on offer is listed on the menu according to the way it is prepared.

Lamian by Soy Kitchen

pl. Mostenses 4 ✉ 28015 – Ⓜ Plaza de España Plan: **B1**
– ✆ 910392231 – www.lamianconcept.com – Closed Monday
Carte 25/40 €

• Fusion • Bistro •

Named after a type of Chinese noodle, this restaurant is the perfect place to try ramen. Its menu features an interesting fusion of Spanish and Oriental cuisine.

Tampu

Prim 13 ✉ 28004 – Ⓜ Chueca – ✆ 915 64 19 13 Plan: **D1**
– Closed Sunday dinner and Monday
Carte 30/45 €

• Peruvian • Design •

A mix of slate, wood and wicker, plus a Quechua name that is in reference to old lodgings built along the Inca Trail. Classic Peruvian cuisine, including ceviches, raw fish tiraditos, and potato-based causas.

Umiko

Los Madrazo 18 ✉ 28014 – Ⓜ Sevilla – ✆ 914 93 87 06 Plan: **C2**
– www.umiko.es – Closed 15 days August, Sunday and Monday lunch
Carte 40/58 €

• Japanese • Minimalist •

A fun and different Asian restaurant whose aim is to combine traditional Japanese cuisine with the more traditional cooking of Madrid. The finishing touches to most of the dishes are added at the bar.

La Gastroteca de Santiago

pl. Santiago 1 ✉ 28013 – Ⓜ Ópera – ✆ 915 48 07 07 Plan: **A2**
– www.lagastrotecadesantiago.es – Closed 15-31 August, Sunday dinner and Monday
Carte 40/65 €

• Modern cuisine • Cosy •

A small, cosy restaurant with two large windows and modern decor. Friendly staff, contemporary cuisine and a kitchen that is partially visible to diners.

La Tasquita de Enfrente

Ballesta 6 ✉ 28004 – Ⓜ Gran Vía – ✆ 915 32 54 49 Plan: **B1**
– www.latasquitadeenfrente.com – Closed August and Sunday
Menu 79/110 € – Carte 51/73 € – *(booking essential)*

• International • Family •

An informal eatery with the benefit of a very loyal clientele. Its French-inspired cuisine with a contemporary touch is based around products of the highest quality.

Arallo Taberna

Plan: C2

Reina 31 ✉ 28004 – Ⓜ Chueca – ☏ 690 67 37 96 – www.arallotaberna.com – Closed Holy Week and August

Tapa 3 € **Ración** approx. 12 €

• Fusion • Fashionable •

An urban gastro-bar that breaks with tradition by opting for a fusion of Spanish and Oriental cuisine that demonstrates a subtle combination of textures and flavours. Don't miss the dumplings!

Barra M

Plan: C2

Libertad 8 ✉ 28004 – Ⓜ Chueca – ☏ 916 68 46 78 – www.barraeme.pacificogrupo.com – Closed 23-26 December, Sunday, Monday dinner and Tuesday dinner

Tapa 6 € **Ración** approx. 18 €

• Fusion • Design •

This unusual eatery, dominated by one striking table-counter, champions street food through an enticing fusion of Asian and Peruvian cooking. Perfect for foodies!

RETIRO – SALAMANCA PLAN II

Ramón Freixa Madrid

Plan: E1

Hotel Único Madrid – Claudio Coello 67 ✉ 28001 – Ⓜ Serrano – ☏ 917 81 82 62 – www.ramonfreixamadrid.com – Closed Christmas, Holy Week, August, Sunday, Monday and bank holidays

Menu 80/165 € – Carte 110/125 €

• Creative • Design •

A magical contradiction between traditional and cutting-edge cuisine is the culinary philosophy of Ramón Freixa, a Catalan chef who showcases flavours and classic combinations alongside plenty of creativity. His elegant dining room is connected to a glass-fronted terrace and an open-air space perfect for a pre- or post-dinner drink.

➜ El estudio del tomate 2019. Tortilla líquida de bacalao con guisantes lágrima y velo de menta. Miel, flores y pimientas.

Kabuki Wellington (Ricardo Sanz)

Plan: E2

Hotel Wellington – Velázquez 6 ✉ 28001 – Ⓜ Retiro – ☏ 915 77 78 77 – www.restaurantekabuki.com – Closed Holy Week, 21 days August, Saturday lunch, Sunday and bank holidays

Menu 93 € – Carte 70/130 €

• Japanese • Design •

An emblematic restaurant reflecting the gastronomic connection between Japan and the Mediterranean. Elegant dining room on two levels plus an enticing sushi bar offering a fusion of Japanese culinary culture, the very best local products, and a mastery of cutting, slicing and exquisite textures.

➜ Sashimi de salmonete en su carcasa. Bol de arroz tostado a la mantequilla con huevo roto y anguila asada. Chocoreto en texturas.

Álbora

Plan: E2

Jorge Juan 33 ✉ 28001 – Ⓜ Velázquez – ☏ 917 81 61 97 – www.restaurantealbora.com – Closed August and Sunday

Menu 69/89 € – Carte 55/75 €

• Modern cuisine • Design •

An attractive modern setting with two distinct sections: the gastro-bar on the ground floor and the gastronomic restaurant upstairs. Enjoy high level cuisine that makes full use of seasonal ingredients, with some dishes available in smaller half portions.

➜ Créme brûlée de bogavante con guarnición crema y caviar. Cabezada Joselito y jugo de cebolla roja. Torrija caramelizada con su helado de canela.

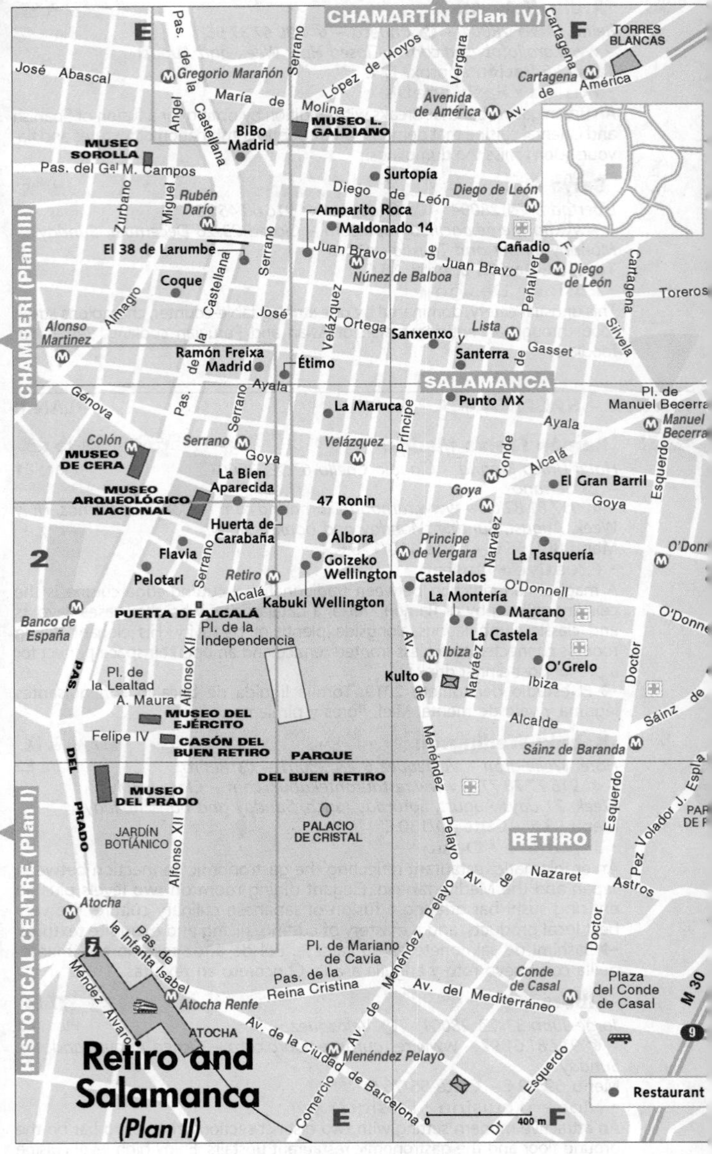
CHAMARTÍN (Plan IV)
CHAMBERÍ (Plan III)
HISTORICAL CENTRE (Plan I)
SALAMANCA
RETIRO
MUSEO SOROLLA
MUSEO L. GALDIANO
MUSEO DE CERA
MUSEO ARQUEOLÓGICO NACIONAL
PUERTA DE ALCALÁ
MUSEO DEL EJÉRCITO
CASÓN DEL BUEN RETIRO
PARQUE DEL BUEN RETIRO
MUSEO DEL PRADO
JARDÍN BOTÁNICO
PALACIO DE CRISTAL
TORRES BLANCAS
ATOCHA
BiBo Madrid
Surtopía
Amparito Roca
Maldonado 14
El 38 de Larumbe
Cañadio
Coque
Sanxenxo
Santerra
Ramón Freixa Madrid
Étimo
Punto MX
La Maruca
El Gran Barril
La Bien Aparecida
47 Ronin
Huerta de Carabaña
Álbora
La Tasquería
Flavia
Goizeko Wellington
Pelotari
Castelados
Kabuki Wellington
La Montería
Marcano
La Castela
O'Grelo
Kulto
Restaurant
Retiro and Salamanca (Plan II)

Punto MX (Roberto Ruiz)

General Pardiñas 40 ✉ 28001 – Ⓜ Goya Plan: **F2**
– ✆ 914 02 22 26 – www.puntomx.es – Closed 23 December-7 January, Holy Week, 15 days August, Sunday and Monday
Menu 75/120 € – *(booking essential) (tasting menu only)*

• Mexican • Minimalist •

An impressive Mexican restaurant that steers clear of stereotypes with its modern look, "mezcal bar" at the entrance, and cuisine in which chef Roberto Ruiz offers his personal vision of Mexican cooking that combines its basic flavours with Spanish ingredients, many of which come from his own vegetable garden.

➜ Aguachile tatemado y rape curado. Tuétano a la brasa. Chocolate y maíz.

La Tasquería (Javier Estévez)

Duque de Sesto 48 ✉ 28009 – Ⓜ Goya Plan: **F2**
– ✆ 914 51 10 00 – www.latasqueria.com – Closed 10 days January, 21 days August and Sunday dinner
Carte 33/45 €

• Modern cuisine • Bistro •

A new-generation, reasonably priced *tasca* that works miracles through the transformation of modest offal products (veal, pork, lamb) into modern, delicate and elegant dishes. The decor here is urban with rustic and industrial detail and includes an open-view kitchen.

➜ Morro, brava y pulpo. Manitas, alcachofa y cigalas. Chocolate, vainilla y frambuesa.

Castelados

Antonio Acuña 18 ✉ 28009 – Ⓜ Principe de Vergara Plan: **F2**
– ✆ 910 51 56 25 – www.castelados.com – Closed 20 days August and Sunday dinner
Carte 30/45 €

• Traditional cuisine • Traditional décor •

A restaurant with a relaxed, lively atmosphere which follows the same philosophy as its nearby older sibling, La Castela. Traditional cooking based around excellent raw ingredients and interesting daily suggestions that include impressive fresh fish dishes.

La Castela

Doctor Castelo 22 ✉ 28009 – Ⓜ Ibiza – ✆ 915 74 00 15 Plan: **F2**
– www.lacastela.com – closed August and Sunday dinner
Carte 25/40 €

• Traditional cuisine • Traditional décor •

La Castela continues the tradition of Madrid's historic taverns. Choose from the lively tapas bar or the simply furnished dining room where you can enjoy cooking with a traditional flavour, including an impressive choice of daily specials.

La Maruca

Velázquez 54 ✉ 28001 – Ⓜ Velázquez – ✆ 917 81 49 69 Plan: **E2**
– www.restaurantelamaruca.com
Carte 25/42 €

• Traditional cuisine • Friendly •

A bright, casual and contemporary restaurant offering high standard, traditional cuisine. There is a predominance of typical and very reasonably priced Cantabrian dishes.

La Montería

Lope de Rueda 35 ✉ 28009 – Ⓜ Ibiza – ✆ 915 74 18 12 Plan: **F2**
– www.lamonteria.es – Closed Sunday dinner
Menu 42/46 € – Carte 33/42 €

• Traditional cuisine • Simple •

This family-run business has a bar and intimate dining room, which are both contemporary in feel. The chef creates updated traditional cuisine including game dishes. Don't leave without trying the monterías (stuffed mussels)!

Tepic

Ayala 14 ✉ 28001 – Ⓜ Goya – ✆ 915 22 08 50 Plan I: **D1**
– www.tepic.es – Closed Sunday dinner
Menu 31 € – Carte 30/45 €

• Mexican • Rustic •

A uniquely styled Mexican restaurant where the rustic yet contemporary space is characterised by a profusion of wood and a predominance of white. High quality Mexican cuisine features alongside an interesting menu of beers, tequila and mezcal.

Goizeko Wellington – Hotel Wellington

Villanueva 34 ✉ 28001 – Ⓜ Retiro – ✆ 915 77 01 38 Plan: **E2**
– www.goizekogaztelupe.com – Closed Holy Week, 1-21 August, Saturday lunch, Sunday and bank holidays
Menu 85/120 € – Carte 52/74 €

• Spanish • Classic décor •

The contemporary-classic dining room and the two private rooms have been exquisitely designed. The cuisine on offer is a fusion of traditional, international and creative cooking, and is enriched with a few Japanese dishes.

Sanxenxo

José Ortega y Gasset 40 ✉ 28006 Plan: **F1**
– Ⓜ Núñez de Balboa – ✆ 915 77 82 72 – www.sanxenxo.es – Closed Holy Week, 1-15 August and Sunday dinner
Menu 50 € – Carte 45/66 €

• Seafood • Classic décor •

A classic address in a superb setting dominated by the finest materials, including wood and granite. Fish and seafood of the very highest quality.

Étimo

Ayala 27 ✉ 28005 – Ⓜ Goya – ✆ 913 27 36 07 Plan: **E1**
– www.etimo.es – Closed 5-26 August, Sunday and Monday
Menu 65/80 € – *(tasting menu only)*

• Creative • Fashionable •

Étimo's interior design comes as a pleasant surprise, combining the past and present and providing the backdrop for consistent, highly technical and delicately prepared contemporary cuisine. A chef's table is also available.

BiBo Madrid

paseo de la Castellana 52 ✉ 28046 Plan: **E1**
– Ⓜ Gregorio Marañón – ✆ 918 05 25 56 – www.grupodanigarcia.com
Carte 35/55 €

• Modern cuisine • Bistro •

The magic of southern Spain is transported to this restaurant. The striking, light design inspired by the entrance gateway to the Málaga Fair provides the backdrop for the more informal cuisine of award-winning chef Dani García.

Huerta de Carabaña

Lagasca 32 ✉ 28001 – Ⓜ Serrano – ✆ 910 83 00 07 Plan: **E2**
– www.huertadecarabana.es – Closed August and Sunday dinner
Carte 55/70 €

• Traditional cuisine • Contemporary décor •

A traditional culinary dominion where the very best fresh vegetables from Carabaña, 50km outside of Madrid, reign supreme. Choose between the bistro-style dining room and a second room offering more gastronomic fare.

Santerra

General Pardiñas 56 ✉ 28001 – Ⓜ Núñez de Balboa Plan: **F1**
– ✆ 914 01 35 80 – www.santerra.es – Closed Holy Week, 15 days August, Sunday, Monday dinner and bank holidays
Carte 46/58 €

• Traditional cuisine • Contemporary décor •

A restaurant with lots of personality that showcases daily the traditional cooking of La Mancha through delicious game dishes and stews. Make sure you order the croquettes!

Surtopía

XX A/C
Plan: E1

Núñez de Balboa 106 ✉ 28006 – Ⓜ Núñez de Balboa – ✆ 915 63 03 64 – www.surtopia.es – Closed 1-7 January, Holy Week, 13 August-4 September, Sunday and Monday
Menu 35/45 € – Carte 38/56 €

• Andalusian • Contemporary décor •

A restaurant with a modern ambience that translates to the cuisine, featuring the aromas and flavours of Andalucia and showcasing contemporary techniques and interesting innovative touches.

Amparito Roca

XX ♿ A/C
Plan: E1

Juan Bravo 12 ✉ 28006 – Ⓜ Núñez de Balboa – ✆ 913 48 33 04 – www.restauranteamparitoroca.com – Closed Sunday and Monday dinner
Carte 42/55 €

• Traditional cuisine • Cosy •

A restaurant that takes its name from a famous pasodoble, where the focus is on honest cuisine that flies the flag for the very best ingredients. A classic-contemporary dining room with some surprising decorative details.

La Bien Aparecida

XX A/C
Plan: E2

Jorge Juan 8 ✉ 28001 – ✆ 911 59 39 39 – www.restaurantelabienaparecida.com
Menu 75 € – Carte 47/68 €

• Traditional cuisine • Fashionable •

Named after the patron saint of Cantabria, this restaurant is laid out on two floors with different atmospheres. Updated traditional cuisine featuring fine textures and strong flavours.

Cañadío

XX A/C
Plan: F1

Conde de Peñalver 86 ✉ 28005 – Ⓜ Diego de León – ✆ 912 81 91 92 – www.restaurantecanadio.com – Closed 15 days August
Carte 35/60 €

• Traditional cuisine • Friendly •

The name will ring a bell with those familiar with Santander, given the location of this, the original Cañadio restaurant, on one of the city's most famous squares. Café-bar for tapas, two contemporary dining rooms, and well-prepared traditional cuisine.

47 Ronin

XX ♿ A/C
Plan: E2

Jorge Juan 38 ✉ 28001 – Ⓜ Velázquez – ✆ 913 48 50 34 – www.47-ronin.es – Closed 1-3 January, 5-29 August, Sunday dinner and Monday
Menu 45/125 € – Carte 40/58 €

• Japanese • Oriental décor •

Creative Japanese cuisine featuring modern techniques, fine textures and an enticing adaptation of Japanese recipes to Spanish ingredients, to produce dishes that are impressive on the eye.

El Gran Barril

XX ♿ A/C
Plan: F2

Goya 107 ✉ 28009 – Ⓜ Goya – ✆ 914 31 22 10 – www.elgranbarril.com
Carte 52/70 €

• Seafood • Traditional décor •

Hidden behind the glass façade of this building is a comfortable restaurant with a public bar and several modern dining rooms, the larger of which on the lower floor boasts a live shellfish pool. Top-quality fish, seafood and savoury rice dishes.

O grelo

XX AC

Menorca 39 ✉ 28009 – Ⓜ Ibiza – ✆ 914 09 72 04 Plan: **F2**
– www.restauranteogrelo.com – Closed Sunday dinner
Carte 35/70 €
• Galician • Classic décor •

Experience the excellence of traditional Galician cuisine at this restaurant serving a huge variety of seafood. Having undergone gradual renovation, O grelo has a more modern look, which includes a reasonably popular gastro-bar, a main dining room and three private sections.

Maldonado 14

XX AC

Maldonado 14 ✉ 28006 – Ⓜ Núñez de Balboa Plan: **E1**
– ✆ 914 35 50 45 – www.maldonado14.com – Closed Holy Week, 5-27 August, Sunday and bank holidays dinner
Menu 35/55 € – Carte 38/60 €
• Traditional cuisine • Classic décor •

A single dining room on two levels, both featuring classic decor, quality furnishings and wood floors. The à la carte menu has a traditional feel and includes delicious homely desserts, such as the outstanding apple tart.

99 sushi bar

XX AC

Hermosilla 4 ✉ 28001 – Ⓜ Serrano – ✆ 914 31 27 15 Plan I: **D1**
– www.99sushibar.com – Closed 30 July-26 August, Sunday and bank holidays
Menu 90 € – Carte 44/65 €
• Japanese • Minimalist •

A good restaurant in which to discover the flavours and textures of Japanese cuisine. There is a small bar where sushi is prepared in front of diners, an attractive glass-fronted wine cellar, and a modern dining room featuring typical Japanese decor and furnishings.

El 38 de Larumbe

XX AC

paseo de la Castellana 38 ✉ 28006 – Ⓜ Rubén Darío Plan: **E1**
– ✆ 915 75 11 12 – www.larumbe.com – Closed 15 days August, Sunday dinner and bank holidays dinner
Carte 42/59 €
• Modern cuisine • Classic décor •

This restaurant has two highly distinct dining areas – one has a gastro-bar feel, and the other has a more refined setting for à la carte dining. Updated traditional cuisine with the option of ordering half-raciones.

Canalla Bistro

X AC

Goya 5 (Platea Madrid) ✉ 28001 – Ⓜ Serrano Plan I: **D1**
– ✆ 915 77 00 25 – www.plateamadrid.com
Carte 35/45 €
• Modern cuisine • Contemporary décor •

At this bistro, discover the informal cuisine of Valencian chef Ricard Camarena who is keen to leave his stamp on the city via his highly urban cooking. His dishes are perfect for sharing.

Flavia

X AC

Gil de Santivañes 2 ✉ 28001 – Ⓜ Colón Plan: **E2**
– ✆ 914 93 90 51 – www.flaviamadrid.com
Menu 17 € – Carte 25/45 €
• Italian • Mediterranean décor •

A modern, urban trattoria laid out over several floors. Tasty, traditional cuisine is prepared using original ingredients imported from Italy.

Kulto

Plan: F2

Ibiza 4 ✉ 28009 – Ⓜ Ibiza – ✆ 911 73 30 53 – www.kulto.es – Closed Monday and Tuesday
Carte 45/62 €

• Modern cuisine • Friendly •

This restaurant is pleasant, modern and bright and just a stone's throw from the Retiro park. Contemporary cuisine that showcases seasonal ingredients and a fusion of international flavours and influences.

Marcano

Plan: F2

Doctor Castelo 31 ✉ 28009 – Ⓜ Ibiza – ✆ 914 09 36 42 – www.restaurantemarcano.com – Closed Holy Week, Sunday in August and Sunday dinner the rest of the year
Carte 50/75 €

• International • Simple •

The cooking here focuses on well-defined flavours. This is demonstrated by the range of traditional and international dishes, the latter with a European and Asian twist.

Pelotari

Plan: E2

Recoletos 3 ✉ 28001 – Ⓜ Colón – ✆ 915 78 24 97 – www.pelotari-asador.com – Closed Sunday
Carte 40/60 €

• Basque • Rustic •

This typical Basque eatery specialising in roasted meats is run by its owners, with one in the kitchen and the other front of house. There are four regional style dining rooms, two of which can be used as private rooms.

CHAMBERÍ PLAN III

Coque (Mario Sandoval)

Plan II : E1

Marqués de Riscal 11 ✉ 28010 – Ⓜ Rubén Darío – ✆ 916 04 02 02 – www.restaurantecoque.com – Closed 24-31 December, 29 July-27 August, Sunday and Monday
Menu 145/195 € – *(tasting menu only)*

• Creative • Design •

The Sandoval brothers have landed in the Spanish capital ready to create a stir! Their cuisine goes much further that what you see on the plate, dissecting the culinary experience into several distinct areas (cocktail bar, wine cellar, kitchen, dining room etc), each of which is designed to surprise and elicit different emotions. Superb wine cellar!

→ Guisante lágrima en texturas con ají amarillo, menta fresca y raíz de perifollo. Escabeche de foie y suprema de pato azulón en barrica de oloroso. Fresini de frutos rojos con esponja de naranja sanguina y yogur ácido.

Santceloni – Hotel Hesperia Madrid

Plan: H2

paseo de la Castellana 57 ✉ 28046 – Ⓜ Gregorio Marañón – ✆ 912 10 88 40 – www.restaurantesantceloni.com – Closed Holy Week, August, Saturday lunch, Sunday and bank holidays
Menu 185 € – Carte 120/158 €

• Creative • Elegant •

Elegance, comfort and good service are the perfect cocktail for a culinary experience that you won't forget in a hurry. In the completely glass-fronted kitchen chef Óscar Velasco creates traditional and international dishes that showcase plenty of creativity. Extensive wine cellar.

→ Cigalas a la plancha en hojas de lechuga. Lasaña de pato, pistachos, cardamomo y suero de Idiazabal. Rábano daikon, maíz, regaliz y fruta de la pasión.

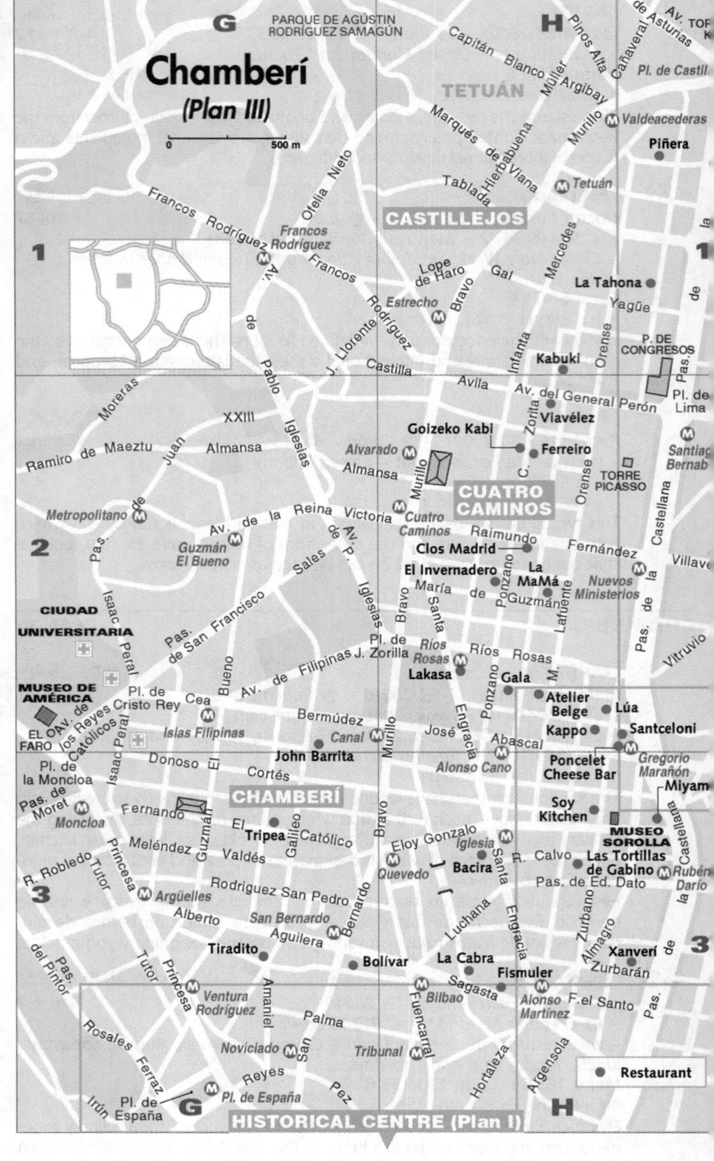
Chamberí
(Plan III)
0
500 m
G
H
1
2
3
PARQUE DE AGÚSTIN RODRÍGUEZ SAMAGÚN
TETUÁN
CASTILLEJOS
CUATRO CAMINOS
CHAMBERÍ
CIUDAD UNIVERSITARIA
MUSEO DE AMÉRICA
EL FARO
TORRE PICASSO
P. DE CONGRESOS
MUSEO SOROLLA
HISTORICAL CENTRE (Plan I)
Restaurant
La Tahona
Piñera
Kabuki
Viavélez
Goizeko Kabi
Ferreiro
Clos Madrid
El Invernadero
La MaMá
Lakasa
Gala
Atelier Belge
Lúa
Kappo
Santceloni
Poncelet Cheese Bar
Miyama
Soy Kitchen
Las Tortillas de Gabino
John Barrita
Tripea
Bacira
Xanverí
Tiradito
Bolívar
La Cabra
Fismuler
Valdeacederas
Tetuán
Estrecho
Francos Rodríguez
Alvarado
Cuatro Caminos
Metropolitano
Guzmán El Bueno
Nuevos Ministerios
Santiago Bernabéu
Ríos Rosas
Islas Filipinas
Canal
Gregorio Marañón
Alonso Cano
Moncloa
Quevedo
Iglesia
Rubén Darío
Argüelles
San Bernardo
Bilbao
Alonso Martínez
Ventura Rodríguez
Noviciado
Tribunal
Pl. de España
Capitán Blanco Argibay
Pinos Alta
Cañaveral
Av. de Asturias
Pl. de Castilla
Müller
Marqués de Viana
Hierbabuena
Murillo
Tablada
Ofelia Nieto
Francos Rodríguez
Av. de Pablo Iglesias
Lope de Haro
Gal
Mercedes
Bravo Murillo
Yagüe
J. Llorente
Castilla
Avila
Infanta
Orense
Av. del General Perón
Pl. de Lima
Pas. de la Castellana
Moreras
XXIII
Ramiro de Maeztu
Juan
Almansa
Zorita
C.
Av. de la Reina Victoria
Raimundo Fernández Villaverde
Pas. de Juan XXIII
Sales
Av. de P. Iglesias
María de Guzmán
Ponzano
Lafuente
Santa Engracia
Isaac Peral
Pas. de San Francisco
Bueno
Pl. de J. Zorilla
Ríos Rosas
Av. de Filipinas
Vitruvio
Pl. de Cristo Rey
Cea Bermúdez
Av. de los Reyes Católicos
José Abascal
Pl. de la Moncloa
Pas. de Moret
Donoso Cortés
Fernando El Católico
Guzmán El Bueno
Galileo
Meléndez Valdés
Eloy Gonzalo
R. Calvo
Pas. de Ed. Dato
R. Robledo
Tutor
Princesa
Rodriguez San Pedro
Alberto Aguilera
San Bernardo
Luchana
Zurbano
Almagro
Zurbarán
Pas. del Pintor
Amaniel
Palma
Fuencarral
Sagasta
F. el Santo
Rosales
Ferraz
Irún
San
Reyes
Pez
Hortaleza
Argensola

Clos Madrid

Plan: **H2**

Raimundo Fernández Villaverde 28 ✉ 28003 – Ⓜ Cuatro Caminos – ✆ 910 64 88 05 – www.restauranteclosmadrid.es – Closed 15-21 April, 5-18 August, Saturday lunch and Sunday
Menu 50/70 € – Carte 50/60 €
• Modern cuisine • Contemporary décor •
The Madrid outpost of Marcos Granda, the owner of the award-winning Skina in Marbella. In the contemporary-style dining room, the creative cuisine is bang up-to-date and based around the most select ingredients. The name Clos is a French word for a high-quality wine estate surrounded by a wall.
➜ Arroz de pichón. Merluza y su pil-pil. Uvas, fresas silvestres y chantilly.

El Invernadero (Rodrigo de la Calle)

Plan: **H2**

Ponzano 85 ✉ 28003 – Ⓜ Rios Rosas – ✆ 628 93 93 67 – www.elinvernaderorestaurante.com – Closed Sunday, Monday and bank holidays
Menu 95/135 € – *(booking essential) (tasting menu only)*
• Modern cuisine • Cosy •
Chef Rodrigo de la Calle is back in the Spanish capital! In the natural-cum-contemporary dining room, discover the "green revolution" that has broken down borders and where vegetables are the key to his unique menu. Flavour, fantasy and a delicate touch are to the fore here, with the option of always being able to order a fish or meat dish.
➜ Alcachofa-trigo verde. Lechuga-trufa. Pera-goji.

Lúa (Manuel Domínguez)

Plan: **H2**

Eduardo Dato 5 ✉ 28003 – Ⓜ Rubén Darío – ✆ 913 95 28 53 – www.restaurantelua.com – Closed Sunday
Menu 68/90 € – *(tasting menu only)*
• Modern cuisine • Cosy •
Lúa has two completely different ambiences. One a gastrobar at the entrance serving an à la carte of half and full *raciones*, the other a more gastronomic setting on the lower level. Here, guests can enjoy contemporary cuisine with a strong Galician influence focused around an impressive tasting menu.
➜ Sopa de ají amarillo con pez mantequilla y quisquilla. Raya en caldeirada y ajada. Cremoso de queso San Simón con sopa de violetas.

Bacira

Plan: **H3**

Castillo 16 ✉ 28010 – Ⓜ Iglesia – ✆ 918 66 40 30 – www.bacira.es – Closed 24 December-2 January, Sunday dinner and Monday
Menu 43/68 € – Carte 23/45 € – *(booking essential)*
• Fusion • Vintage •
Bacira has an attractive vintage style and is run by three young owner-chefs. Fresh, fusion-style cooking sees a mix of Mediterranean, Oriental and Japanese dishes which are designed for sharing and served in an informal atmosphere.

Gala

Plan: **H2**

Espronceda 14 ✉ 28003 – Ⓜ Alonso Cano – ✆ 914 42 22 44 – www.restaurantegala.com – Closed 15 days August, Sunday and Monday dinner
Menu 35/50 € – Carte 29/45 €
• Modern cuisine • Intimate •
A small but long-established restaurant with a single contemporary dining room. The market-inspired cooking has been brought bang up-to-date. It is supported by different set menus and interesting day-long gastronomic events with a variety of themes. Make sure you try the sirloin steak tartare.

Tripea

Vallehermoso 36 (Mercado de Vallehermoso, Puesto 44) Plan: **G3**
✉ 28005 – Ⓜ Quevedo – ✆ 918 28 69 47 – www.tripea.es – Closed 19 August-3 September, Sunday and Monday
Menu 35 € – Carte 30/40 €
• Fusion • Friendly •

This unique restaurant occupying three stalls in the Mercado de Vallehermoso has a frontage completely dominated by the kitchen plus a large shared table in the aisle. Interesting fusion of Asian and Peruvian cuisine, including specialities such as spicy chicken curry.

La MaMá

María Panes 6 ✉ 28003 – Ⓜ Nuevos Ministerios Plan: **H2**
– ✆ 910 61 97 64 – www.lamamarestaurante.com – Closed 24 December-1 January, Holy Week, 12-25 August, Sunday dinner, Monday, Tuesday dinner and Wednesday dinner
Menu 19/40 € – Carte 27/42 €
• Traditional cuisine • Friendly •

Simplicity in its decor and a culinary philosophy that focuses on emotion combine with traditional home cooking that respects timeless flavours yet adds an innovative touch. Almost everything on the menu can be order as a half-ración.

Las Tortillas de Gabino

Rafael Calvo 20 ✉ 28010 – Ⓜ Rubén Darío Plan: **H3**
– ✆ 913 19 75 05 – www.lastortillasdegabino.com – Closed Holy Week, 15 days August, Sunday and bank holidays
Carte 30/48 €
• Traditional cuisine • Cosy •

A restaurant with two modern dining rooms decorated with wood panelling, as well as a separate private dining section. Its seasonally inspired, seasonal menu is complemented by a superb selection of tortillas that changes throughout the year; the trufada, velazqueña and pulpo are particular favourites here.

Benares

Zurbano 5 ✉ 28010 – Ⓜ Alonso Martínez Plan I: **D1**
– ✆ 913 19 87 16 – www.benaresmadrid.com – Closed 6-22 August and Sunday dinner
Menu 39/100 € – Carte 45/65 €
• Indian • Classic décor •

Benares follows in the footsteps of its London namesake with its restaurant and cocktail bar. Updated Indian cuisine, an excellent wine cellar, and a charming terrace on an inner patio.

La Cabra

Francisco de Rojas 2 ✉ 28010 – Ⓜ Bilbao Plan: **H3**
– ✆ 914 45 77 50 – www.restaurantelacabra.com – Closed 1-4 January, Holy Week, August and Sunday
Carte 45/60 €
• Creative • Contemporary décor •

A gastronomic restaurant which, under the baton of chef Javier Aranda, is branching out in a new culinary direction featuring plenty of creativity. A delightful wine cellar completes the picture.

Atelier Belge

Bretón de los Herreros 39 ✉ 28003 – Ⓜ Alonso Cano Plan: **H2**
– ✆ 915 45 84 48 – www.restaurantegourmand.es – Closed Sunday dinner and Monday
Menu 14/59 € – Carte 44/67 €
• Belgian • Cosy •

Authentic Belgian cuisine showcasing interesting creative touches. Its mussel specialities and the skate with capers and black butter are particularly worth trying. Superb beer menu.

Lakasa

XX

pl. del Descubridor Diego de Ordás 1 ✉ 28003 Plan: **H2**
– Ⓜ Rios Rosas – ✆ 915 33 87 15 – www.lakasa.es – Closed Holy Week, Sunday, Monday and bank holidays

Carte 36/73 €

• Traditional cuisine • Fashionable •

A restaurant enjoying lots of popularity thanks to its gastrobar and main dining room serving market-fresh cooking and daily recommendations. Every dish can also be served as a half-*ración*.

Soy Kitchen

XX

Zurbano 59 ✉ 28010 – Ⓜ Gregorio Marañón Plan: **H3**
– ✆ 913 19 25 51 – www.soykitchen.es – Closed 15 days August and Sunday dinner

Menu 50/65 € – *(tasting menu only)*

• Fusion • Trendy •

The chef here, who hails from Beijing, creates unique dishes that combine Asian (Chinese, Korean, Japanese…) and Spanish and Peruvian influences. Dishes are full of colour and flavour.

Xanverí

XX

Zurbarán 18 ✉ 28010 – Ⓜ Rubén Darío Plan: **H3**
– ✆ 910 57 77 33 – www.xanveri.com – Closed Holy Week, 21 days August and Sunday dinner

Carte 40/50 €

• Modern cuisine • Contemporary décor •

It's back to his roots for chef César Anca with this restaurant offering an extensive and well-thought-out menu including lots of snack-style options, delicious Alicante-style rice dishes and even an R&D section!

Aire

X

Orfila 7 ✉ 28010 – Ⓜ Alonso Martínez Plan I: **D1**
– ✆ 911 70 42 28 – www.grupolos4elementos.com – Closed 15 days August and Sunday dinner

Carte 36/57 €

• Classic cuisine • Contemporary décor •

This charming, bistro-style restaurant is the first stage of a unique project. Everything revolves around poultry here (chicken, pigeon, pheasant, goose, partridge, etc).

Fismuler

X

Sagasta 29 ✉ 28005 – Ⓜ Alonso Martínez Plan: **H3**
– ✆ 918 27 75 81 – www.fismuler.com – Closed 31 December-6 January, Holy Week, 15 days August and Sunday

Menu 43 € – Carte 35/53 €

• Traditional cuisine • Fashionable •

Gastronomy meets interior design in this restaurant with an austere retro-industrial feel. Despite this, the service and ambience are relaxed, with a menu that features pleasantly updated traditional cuisine.

Kappo

X

Bretón de los Herreros 54 ✉ 28003 Plan: **H2**
– Ⓜ Gregorio Marañón – ✆ 910 42 00 66 – www.kappo.es – Closed Holy Week, 21 days August, Sunday and Monday

Menu 65 € – *(tasting menu only)*

• Japanese • Fashionable •

An intimate, contemporary address with an enticing sushi bar as its main focus. Diners order from a single yet extensive menu of modern Japanese cuisine.

Miyama

paseo de la Castellana 45 ✉ 28046 Plan: **H3**
– Ⓜ Gregorio Marañón – ✆ 913 91 00 26 – www.restaurantemiyama.com – Closed 7-31 August, Sunday and bank holidays
Carte 45/70 €
• Japanese • Contemporary décor •
This restaurant is hugely popular in the city. An extensive sushi bar and simply laid tables share space in the single dining area. The high quality, traditional Japanese cuisine is a hit, including with Japanese visitors.

Tiradito

Conde Duque 13 ✉ 28015 – Ⓜ San Bernardo Plan: **G3**
– ✆ 915 41 78 76 – www.tiradito.es – Closed 15 days August, Sunday dinner and Monday
Carte 40/58 €
• Peruvian • Trendy •
A young and easy-going restaurant serving 100% traditional Peruvian cuisine. Dishes on the menu include ceviches, tiraditos, picoteos and tapas criollas.

Bolívar

Manuela Malasaña 28 ✉ 28004 – Ⓜ San Bernardo Plan: **G3**
– ✆ 914 45 12 74 – www.restaurantebolivar.com – Closed 5-31 August and Sunday
Menu 20/38 € – Carte 30/45 €
• Traditional cuisine • Family •
A small restaurant in the bohemian Malasaña district in which the single dining room is divided into two sections with a modern feel. Traditional cuisine inspired by the seasons.

John Barrita

Vallehermoso 72 ✉ 28015 – Ⓜ Canal – ✆ 918 58 84 51 Plan: **G2**
– www.johnbarrita.com – Closed Holy Week and 21 days August
Tapa 4 € **Ración** approx. 10 €
• Traditional cuisine • Vintage •
A casual eatery with an industrial look that will definitely take you back in time. Here, the menu focuses on highly elaborate, top-quality sandwiches with an emphasis on fun presentation.

Poncelet Cheese Bar

José Abascal 61 ✉ 28003 – Ⓜ Gregorio Marañon Plan: **H2**
– ✆ 913 99 25 50 – www.ponceletcheesebar.es – Closed Sunday dinner and Monday
Tapa 6 € **Ración** approx. 14 €
• Cheese, fondue and raclette • Design •
An innovative designer space where cheese is king, with a menu featuring 150 options if you include the cheese plates, fondues and raclettes. However, dishes without cheese are still available!

CASTILLEJOS – CUATRO CAMINOS PLAN III

Kabuki

av. Presidente Carmona 2 ✉ 28020 Plan: **H1**
– Ⓜ Santiago Bernabeu – ✆ 914 17 64 15 – www.grupokabuki.com – Closed Holy Week, 6-28 August, Saturday lunch, Sunday and bank holidays
Carte 65/95 €
• Japanese • Minimalist •
A Japanese restaurant with a simple minimalist look that deliberately shifts the focus to the cooking created here. You're best advised to go with the daily recommendations which you can enjoy in the same way as a traditional Omakase (chef's choice) menu. Booking ahead is recommended as it is always full.
→ Maguro picante, sushi de fusión mediterránea. Costilla de wagyu en teriyaki. Mochi de moscatel con helado de queso fresco.

Ferreiro
XX

Comandante Zorita 32 ✉ 28020 – Ⓜ Alvarado – ✆ 915 53 93 42 – www.restauranteferreiro.com

Plan: **H2**

Menu 38/40 € – Carte 40/60 €

• Traditional cuisine • Classic décor •

Classic-contemporary dining rooms act as a backdrop for traditional cuisine with strong Asturian roots in this restaurant. Extensive menu that is supplemented by a good choice of specials.

Goizeko Kabi
XX

Comandante Zorita 37 ✉ 28020 – Ⓜ Alvarado – ✆ 915 33 01 85 – www.goizeko-gaztelupe.com – Closed Sunday dinner

Plan: **H2**

Menu 55/70 € – Carte 46/72 €

• Basque • Contemporary décor •

A classic restaurant which has been given a new contemporary feel. Traditional Basque cuisine, with the option of choosing half-raciones from the menu.

Piñera
XX

Rosario Pino 12 ✉ 28020 – Ⓜ Valdeacederas – ✆ 914 25 14 25 – www.restaurantepinera.com – Closed 21 days August and Sunday

Plan: **H1**

Menu 45/75 € – Carte 51/63 €

• Traditional cuisine • Contemporary décor •

Owner-chef Carlos Posadas has given this restaurant a new feel, with two very different dining rooms. Traditional cuisine with a modern twist.

Viavélez
XX

av. General Perón 10 ✉ 28020 – Ⓜ Santiago Bernabeu – ✆ 915 79 95 39 – www.restauranteviavelez.com – Closed August, Sunday and Monday lunch in summer, Sunday dinner and Monday the rest of the year

Plan: **H2**

Menu 32/65 € – Carte 35/55 €

• Creative • Trendy •

Viavélez boasts a stylish tapas bar plus a modern dining room in the basement where you can enjoy creative dishes that remain faithful to Asturian cuisine. The taberna does not close for holidays.

La Tahona
XX

Capitán Haya 21 (beside) ✉ 28020 – Ⓜ Cuzco – ✆ 915 55 04 41 – www.asadordearanda.com – Closed 6-31 August and Sunday dinner

Plan: **H1**

Menu 36/55 € – Carte 38/50 €

• Meats and grills • Classic décor •

Part of the El Asador de Aranda chain. La Tahona's dining rooms have a medieval Castillian ambience with a wood fire at the entrance taking pride of place. The suckling lamb (lechazo) is the star dish here!

CHAMARTÍN — PLAN IV

DiverXO (Dabiz Muñoz)
XXX

Hotel NH Collection Eurobuilding – Padre Damián 23 ✉ 28036 – Ⓜ Cuzco – ✆ 915 70 07 66 – www.diverxo.com – Closed Holy Week, 21 days August, Sunday and Monday

Plan: **I2**

Menu 195/250 € – *(booking essential) (tasting menu only)*

• Creative • Design •

This restaurant is an exciting and groundbreaking culinary wonderland, and a journey into the highly personal world of this chef. To a backdrop of stunning modern design, enjoy world cuisine that will challenge your palate, intensifying sensations and reaching its apogee in presentation worthy of the finest canvas.

→ Ensalada de papaya verde con berberechos al vapor, "ventresca" de cochinillo crujiente y aliño de hibiscus agridulce. Royal de pato a las cinco especias chinas y "gochuyang", y pato asado al carbón. Ganache de coco, ajo negro, chicle de grosella, albahaca y regaliz.

✿ **A'Barra** XXXX

Del Pinar 15 ✉ 28014 – Ⓜ Gregorio Marañón Plan: **I3**
– ✆ 910 21 00 61 – www.restauranteabarra.com – Closed Holy Week, August and Sunday
Menu 65/105 € – Carte 55/87 €
• Traditional cuisine • Design •

Both the decor, featuring a profusion of high-quality wood, and the spacious layout come as a pleasant surprise. Choose between the calm setting of the dining room and a large circular bar, which is more geared towards show cooking. Elaborate, modern cuisine with an emphasis on choice ingredients.

➜ Endivia, caviar, naranja y crema agria. Cabezada Joselito, manzana y sidra. Maratonca.

✿ **Gaytán** (Javier Aranda) XX

Príncipe de Vergara 205 (beside) ✉ 28002 Plan: **I3**
– Ⓜ Concha Espina
– ✆ 913 48 50 30 – www.chefjavieraranda.com
– Closed 5 days Christmas, Holy Week, August, Sunday and Monday
Menu 40/140 € – *(tasting menu only)*
• Modern cuisine • Minimalist •

This gastronomic restaurant has been designed to cause a stir. The minimalist interior decor is unexpected, dominated by the presence of original columns and a large open kitchen, which is the epicentre of activity here. Its different tasting menus demonstrate an interesting creativity.

➜ Quisquillas con aguachile de anémona. Despiece de cordero lechal. Milhojas.

Zalacaín XXXX

Álvarez de Baena 4 ✉ 28006 – Ⓜ Gregorio Marañón Plan: **I3**
– ✆ 915 61 48 40 – www.restaurantezalacain.com – Closed Holy Week, August, Satuday lunch, Sunday and bank holidays
Menu 90 € – Carte 62/98 €
• Classic cuisine • Elegant •

A legendary address with a new renovated look. Here, the classic-contemporary setting provides the backdrop for cuisine that combines past and present, including an impressive tasting menu and half-ración options.

Aderezo XX

Añastro 48 ✉ 28033 Plan: **J1**
– ✆ 917 67 01 58 – www.aderezorestaurante.es
– Closed August and Sunday
Menu 24/59 € – Carte 40/60 €
• Traditional cuisine • Classic décor •

This pleasant restaurant has a classic yet contemporary ambience, a bar for a pre-lunch or pre-dinner drink, and a superb fish display cabinet. Impressive cooking based around high quality ingredients and traditional recipes.

Rocacho XX

Padre Damián 38 ✉ 28036 – Ⓜ Cuzco – ✆ 914 21 97 70 Plan: **I2**
– www.rocacho.com
Carte 45/65 €
• Traditional cuisine • Contemporary décor •

A restaurant with a modern look where top-quality products take centre stage, including superb fish and meat cooked on the charcoal grill, plus a choice of savoury rice dishes.

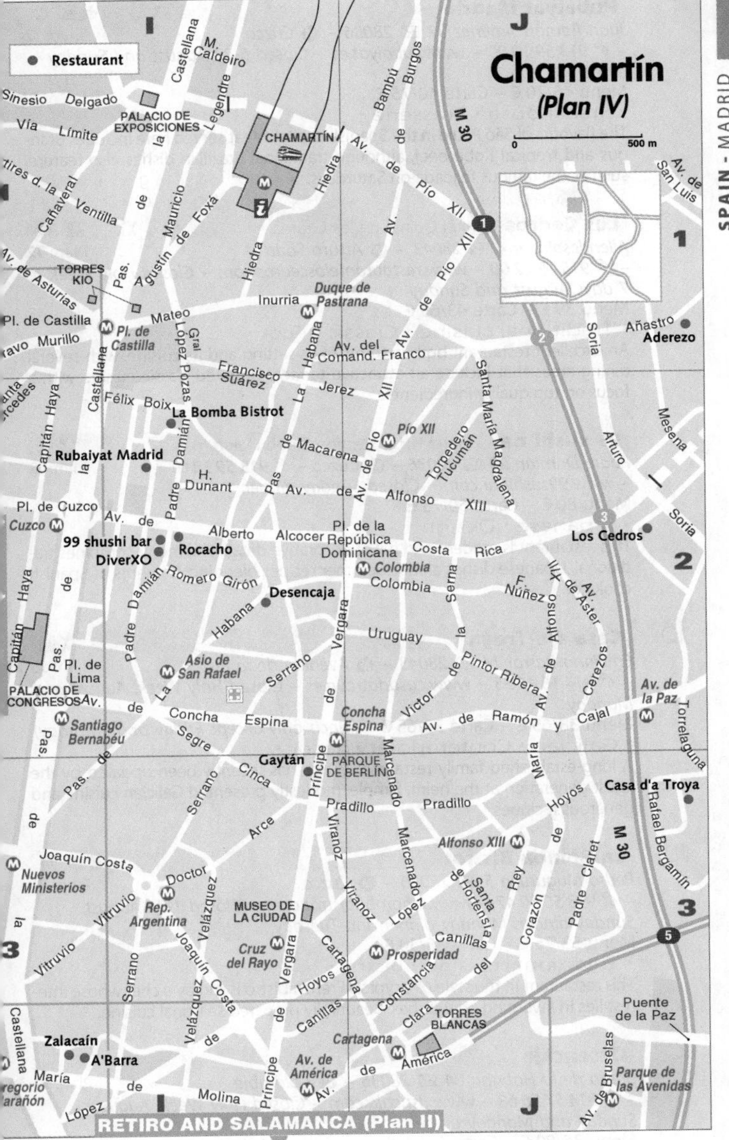
Chamartín
(Plan IV)
0
500 m
Restaurant
I
J
1
2
3
Aderezo
La Bomba Bistrot
Rubaiyat Madrid
99 shushi bar
DiverXO
Rocacho
Desencaja
Los Cedros
Gaytán
Casa d'a Troya
Zalacaín
A'Barra
PALACIO DE EXPOSICIONES
CHAMARTÍN
TORRES KIO
Pl. de Castilla
Duque de Pastrana
Pío XII
Pl. de Cuzco
Cuzco
Pl. de la República Dominicana
Colombia
Asio de San Rafael
Pl. de Lima
PALACIO DE CONGRESOS
Santiago Bernabéu
Concha Espina
PARQUE DE BERLÍN
Alfonso XIII
Av. de la Paz
Nuevos Ministerios
Rep. Argentina
MUSEO DE LA CIUDAD
Cruz del Rayo
Prosperidad
TORRES BLANCAS
Cartagena
Av. de América
Puente de la Paz
Parque de las Avenidas
Sinesio Delgado
Vía Límite
M. Caldeiro
Castellana
Legendre
Mauricio
Agustín de Foxá
Av. de Asturias
Mateo Inurria
Hiedra
Bambú
Burgos
Av. de Pío XII
M 30
Av. de San Luis
Gral López Pozas
Francisco Suárez
Av. del Comand. Franco
Jerez
La Habana
Añastro
Soria
Félix Boix
Capitán Haya
Padre Damián
Macarena
H. Dunant
Av. de Alfonso XIII
Torpedero Tucumán
Santa María Magdalena
Arturo
Mesena
Av. de Alberto Alcocer
Costa Rica
Romero Girón
Habana
Uruguay
Serna
F. Núñez
Av. de Alfonso XIII
Av. de Aster
Serrano
Vergara
Pintor Ribera
Cerezos
Víctor de la Serna
Av. de Ramón y Cajal
Torrelaguna
Av. de Concha Espina
Segre
Cinca
Príncipe de Vergara
Marcenado
Pradillo
María de Hoyos
Rafael Bergamín
Arce
Viranoz
Joaquín Costa
Doctor
Vitruvio
Velázquez
López de Hoyos
Santa Hortensia
Rey
Corazón de María
Padre Claret
Canillas
Cartagena
Constancia
Clara del Rey
América
Bruselas
Av. de Bruselas
María de Molina
Gregorio Marañón
López de Hoyos
Paseo de la Castellana
RETIRO AND SALAMANCA (Plan II)

Rubaiyat Madrid

Juan Ramón Jiménez 37 ✉ 28036 – Ⓜ Cuzco Plan: **I2**
– ✆ 913 59 10 00 – www.rubaiyat.es – Closed 6-23 August and Sunday dinner
Menu 46/70 € – Carte 40/75 €
• Steakhouse • Brasserie •
The flavours of São Paulo in the Spanish capital. Meat served here includes Brangus and tropical Kobe beef, although traditional Brazilian dishes also feature, such as the famous feijoada on Saturdays.

Los Cedros - Hotel Quinta de los Cedros

Allendesalazar 4 ✉ 28043 – Ⓜ Arturo Soria Plan: **J2**
– ✆ 915 15 22 00 – www.restauranteloscedros.com – Closed Holy Week, 7 days August and Sunday
Menu 39 € – Carte 43/65 €
• Traditional cuisine • Classic décor •
An excellent restaurant both in terms of its setting and its cuisine, with several dining areas that include an attractive terrace. Updated classic cuisine with a focus on top quality ingredients.

99 sushi bar - Hotel NH Collection Eurobuilding

Padre Damián 23 ✉ 28036 – Ⓜ Cuzco – ✆ 913 59 38 01 Plan: **I2**
– www.99sushibar.com – Closed Sunday dinner
Menu 80 € – Carte 60/75 €
• Japanese • Design •
This restaurant is modern and full of decorative detail. The menu combines traditional Japanese dishes alongside other recipes blending elements of Spanish cooking.

Casa d'a Troya

Emiliano Barral 14 ✉ 28043 – Ⓜ Avenida de la Paz Plan: **J3**
– ✆ 914 16 44 55 – www.casadatroya.es – Closed Holy Week, August and Monday
Menu 38/65 € – Carte 35/65 € – *(lunch only except Friday and Saturday)*
• Galician • Contemporary décor •
A long-established family restaurant which has recently been updated by the latest generation at the helm. Simple, modestly presented Galician cuisine and generous raciones.

La Bomba Bistrot

Pedro Muguruza 5 ✉ 28036 – Ⓜ Cuzco Plan: **I2**
– ✆ 913 50 30 47 – www.labombabistrot.com – Closed 1-24 August, Sunday dinner, Monday dinner and Tuesday
Menu 53/75 € – Carte 38/50 €
• Traditional cuisine • Bistro •
This restaurant in the style of a typical French bistro is run by a chef whose interest lies in inventing new dishes. Beautifully prepared seasonal cuisine.

Desencaja

paseo de la Habana 84 ✉ 28036 – Ⓜ Colombia Plan: **I2**
– ✆ 914 57 56 68 – www.dsncaja.com – Closed Holy Week, August, Sunday and Monday dinner
Menu 36/80 € – Carte 40/65 €
• Traditional cuisine • Contemporary décor •
A restaurant which is constantly changing while also managing to retain its identity, and always looking to meet the culinary needs of its guests. The menu changes according to market availability, including a few interesting game dishes.

AT NORTH

Filandón

Fuencarral-El Pardo Rd (km 1,9 - M 612) ✉ 28049 – ✆ 917 34 38 26 – www.filandon.es – Closed 2 weeks January, 30 July-20 August, Holy Week, Sunday dinner and Monday
Carte 40/65 €

• Traditional cuisine • Contemporary décor •

This rustic yet modern restaurant is situated in the middle of the countryside. It specialises in rotisserie-style cuisine with a focus on high quality ingredients and grilled fish dishes. The lenguado evaristo (grilled sole) is particularly mouthwatering.

El Oso

av. de Burgos 214 (service area La Moraleja, at Burgos) ✉ 28050 – ✆ 917 66 60 60 – www.restauranteeloso.com – Closed Sunday dinner
Menu 45/65 € – Carte 40/65 €

• Asturian • Regional décor •

A small house on two floors featuring several dining rooms with a contemporary look. All of which are spacious, bright and adorned with a typically Asturian decor. Cooking from the same region, based around fresh produce.

BARCELONA
BARCELONA

MasterLu/iStock

BARCELONA IN...

→ **ONE DAY**
Catedral de Santa Eulalia, Las Ramblas, La Pedrera, Museu Picasso, Sagrada Familia.

→ **TWO DAYS**
Montjuïc, Parc Güell, Nou Camp Stadium, Barceloneta Waterfront, Tibidabo.

→ **THREE DAYS**
Barri Gotic and Palau de la Musica Catalana, Via Laietana, Sitges.

It can't be overestimated how important Catalonia is to the locals of Barcelona: pride in their region of Spain runs deep in the blood. Barcelona loves to mix the traditional with the avant-garde, and this exuberant opening of arms has seen it grow into a pulsating city for visitors. Its rash of theatres, museums and concert halls is unmatched by most other European cities, and many artists and architects, including Picasso, Miró, Dalí, Gaudí and Subirachs, have chosen to live here.

The 19C was a golden period in the city's artistic development, with the growth of the great Catalan Modernism movement, but it

was knocked back on its heels after the Spanish Civil War and the rise to power of the dictator Franco, who destroyed hopes for an independent Catalonia. After his death, democracy came to Spain and since then, Barcelona has relished its position as the capital of a restored autonomous region. Go up on the Montjuïc to get a great overview of the city below. Barcelona's atmospheric old town is near the harbour and reaches into the teeming streets of the Gothic Quarter, while the newer area is north of this; its elegant avenues in grid formation making up Eixample. The coastal quarter of Barça has been transformed with the development of trendy Barceloneta. For many, though, the epicentre of this bubbling city is Las Ramblas, scything through the centre of town.

EATING OUT

Barcelona has long had a good gastronomic tradition, and geographically it's been more influenced by France and Italy than other Spanish regions. But these days the sensual enjoyment of food has become something of a mainstream religion here. The city has hundreds of tapas bars; a type of cuisine which is very refreshing knocked back with a draught beer. The city's location brings together produce from the land and the sea, with a firm emphasis on seasonality and quality produce. This explains why there are myriad markets in the city, all in great locations. Specialities to look out for include Pantumaca: slices of toasted bread with tomato and olive oil; Escalibada, which is made with roasted vegetables; Esqueixada, a typically Catalan salad, and Crema Catalana, a light custard. One little known facet of Barcelona life is its exquisite chocolate and sweet shops. Two stand out: Fargas, in the Barri Gothic, is the city's most famous chocolate shop, while Cacao Sampaka is the most elegant chocolate store you could ever wish to find.

Caelis (Romain Fornell) – Hotel Ohla Barcelona

Via Laietana 49 ✉ 08003 – Ⓜ Urquinaona – ✆ 935 10 12 05 Plan: **F1**
– www.caelis.com – Closed Sunday, Monday and Tuesday lunch
Menu 92/135 € – Carte approx. 106 €
• Creative • Elegant •

Elegant, contemporary and with an open kitchen surrounded by a bar where guests can also enjoy the cuisine on offer here. The award-winning French chef showcases his creative talents via several menus, from which you can also choose single, individually priced dishes.

➜ El huevo de Xavier en su nido y con sabayón trufado. Macarrones "mar y montaña" con alcachofas y bogavante. Limón cristal.

Koy Shunka (Hideki Matsuhisa)

Copons 7 ✉ 08002 – Ⓜ Urquinaona – ✆ 934 12 79 39 Plan: **F1**
– www.koyshunka.com – Closed Christmas, Holy Week, August, Sunday dinner and Monday
Menu 89/132 € – Carte 55/95 €
• Japanese • Contemporary décor •

In this restaurant, the name of which translates as "intense seasonal aromas", our senses are opened to the flavours, emotions and unique world of Japanese cuisine. The head chef, a master of his art who relies on a team of young chefs, combines the classic flavours and textures of Japan with Mediterranean ingredients.

➜ "Espardenyes" a la plancha y berenjena asiática. Anguila del Delta del Ebro. Chocolate, fresón y pera.

La Barra de Carles Abellán

passeig Joan de Borbó 19 ✉ 08003 – Ⓜ Barceloneta Plan: **H2**
– ✆ 937 60 51 29 – www.carlesabellan.com – Closed 21 days January, 14 days August, Tuesday in Winter, Sunday dinner in Summer and Monday
Tapa 7 € **Ración** approx. 18 € – Menu 70 €
• Market cuisine • Mediterranean décor •

A bright and relaxed tapas bar in which the cuisine and decor created by interior designer Lázaro Rosa-Violán come as a pleasant surprise. Extensive menu dedicated to the sea and its myriad flavours, in many instances with dishes cooked on the Japanese robata grill that takes centre stage in the dining room.

➜ Calamar relleno a la brasa con yema picante. Raya de playa a la madrileña. Fresas del Maresme con nata.

Dos Palillos

Elisabets 9 ✉ 08001 – Ⓜ Catalunya – ✆ 933 04 05 13 Plan: **E2**
– www.dospalillos.com – Closed 24 December-8 January, 6-27 August, Sunday, Monday, Tuesday lunch and Wednesday lunch
Tapa 9 € – Menu 90/100 € – Carte 40/51 €
• Asian • Contemporary décor •

A highly original dining option both for its unique "show cooking" concept and its culinary philosophy. This is centred on the fusion of oriental cuisine and typically Spanish products. There are two counters for dining, one at the entrance (no reservations taken and only for à la carte dining), and another further inside, which has a more gastronomic focus with its tasting menus.

➜ Sopa wonton de bogavante yin yang. Angulas vivas y angulas escaldadas. Helado de soja ahumada con caqui maduro caramelizado.

Senyor Parellada

L'Argenteria 37 ✉ 08003 – Ⓜ Jaume I Plan: **G2**
– ✆ 933 10 50 94 – www.senyorparellada.com
Menu 18 € – Carte 25/48 €
• Regional cuisine • Cosy •

This family-run restaurant stands out for its almost timeless elegance and classic-cum-colonial style, which pays a small homage to its past as an inn, with a nod to the constant coming-and-going of travellers who once stayed here. Traditional Catalan cuisine, including classic dishes and an enticing "travellers' menu".

Marea Alta

av. Drassanes 6-8, Building Colón, 24th floor ✉ 08001 – Ⓜ Drassanes – ✆ 936 31 35 90 – www.restaurantemareaalta.com – Closed Monday

Plan: **F3**

Menu 75/100 € – Carte 50/70 €

• Seafood • Mediterranean décor •

A restaurant offering marvellous views from its 24th floor location. Here, the focus is on the flavours of the sea, including grilled dishes that showcase the high-quality products used here.

Torre d'Alta Mar

passeig Joan de Borbó 88 ✉ 08039 – Ⓜ Barceloneta – ✆ 932 21 00 07 – www.torredealtamar.com – Closed 24-26 December, 12-20 August, Sunday lunch and Monday lunch

Plan: **H3**

Menu 39/98 € – Carte 65/95 €

• Modern cuisine • Contemporary décor •

A restaurant whose outstanding feature is its location on top of a 75m-high metal tower. Highly contemporary glass-fronted circular dining room with superb views of the sea, port and city. Traditional à la carte menu featuring contemporary touches.

Bravo 24 – Hotel W Barcelona

pl. de la Rosa dels Vents 1 (Moll De Llevant) ✉ 08039 – ✆ 932 95 26 36 – www.carlesabellan.com

Plan I: **C3**

Menu 90/130 € – Carte 60/80 €

• Traditional cuisine • Fashionable •

Located on the mezzanine of the W hotel in Barcelona, Bravo 24 has a resolutely contemporary feel, in which wood takes pride of place, plus an attractive summer terrace. Traditionally inspired cuisine enhanced by contemporary touches, as well as an impressive array of raciones!

El Cercle

dels Arcs 5-1º ✉ 08002 – Ⓜ Plaça Catalunya – ✆ 936 24 48 10 – www.elcerclerestaurant.com

Plan: **F2**

Menu 28/65 € – Carte 31/47 €

• Classic cuisine • Classic décor •

This restaurant, housed in the Reial Cercle Artístic, offers different types of cuisine ranging from Japanese specialities to modern Catalan fare in several different settings (terrace, library and Japanese bar).

Fonda España – Hotel España

Sant Pau 9 ✉ 08001 – Ⓜ Liceu – ✆ 935 50 00 10 – www.hotelespanya.com – Closed Sunday dinner

Plan: **F2**

Menu 28/79 € – Carte 35/60 € – *(dinner only August)*

• Traditional cuisine • Cosy •

An icon of Modernism serving updated traditional cuisine bearing the hallmark of chef Martín Berasategui. Enticing dining options including its "Journey through Modernism" menu.

Informal by Marc Gascons – Hotel The Serras

Plata 4 ✉ 08002 – Ⓜ Drassanes – ✆ 931 69 18 69 – www.restauranteinformal.com

Plan: **G2**

Menu 29/49 € – Carte 38/78 €

• Mediterranean cuisine • Bistro •

A hotel restaurant with its own separate entrance bearing the hallmark of Els Tinars. The à la carte menu is designed for sharing and includes Catalan and seasonal Mediterranean dishes.

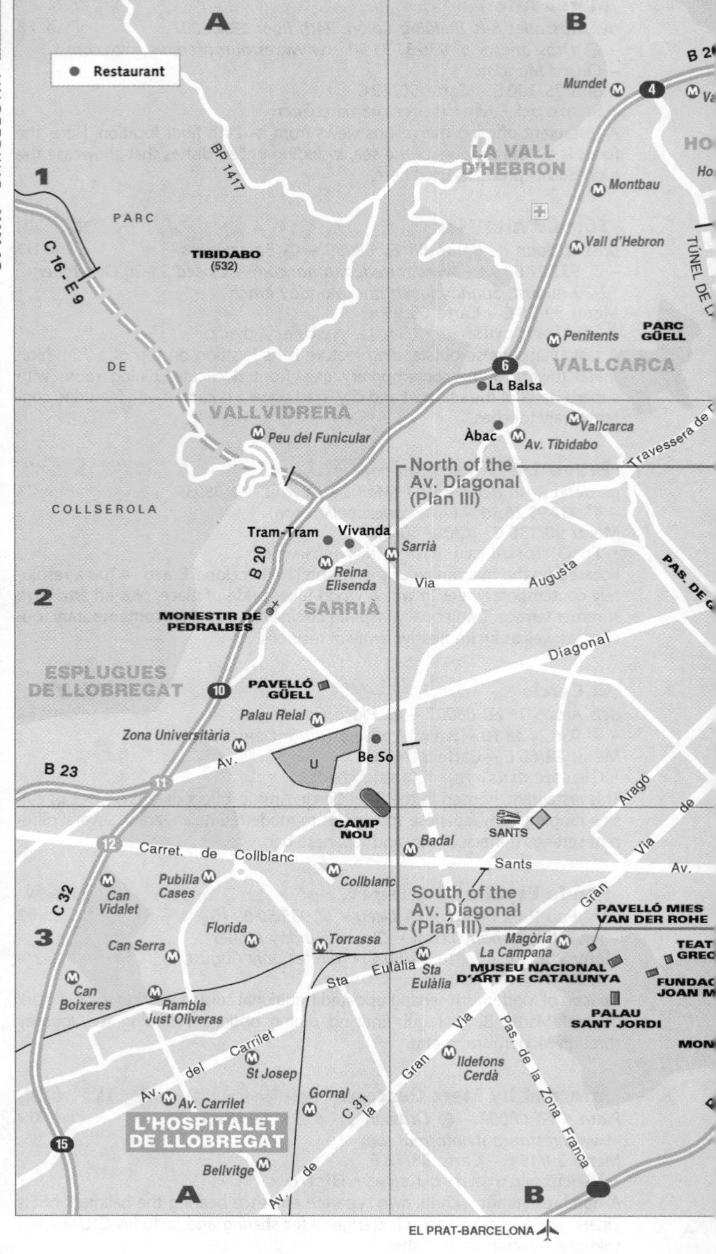

A
B
Restaurant
Mundet
Montbau
Vall d'Hebron
Penitents
LA VALL D'HEBRON
PARC GÜELL
VALLCARCA
TÚNEL DE L
BP 1417
PARC
TIBIDABO (532)
DE
C 16 - E 9
COLLSEROLA
La Balsa
Àbac
Vallcarca
Av. Tibidabo
Travessera de
VALLVIDRERA
Peu del Funicular
North of the Av. Diagonal (Plan III)
Tram-Tram
Vivanda
Sarrià
Reina Elisenda
B 20
Via Augusta
PAS. DE G
MONESTIR DE PEDRALBES
SARRIÀ
Diagonal
ESPLUGUES DE LLOBREGAT
PAVELLÓ GÜELL
Palau Reial
Zona Universitària
Av.
Be So
B 23
U
CAMP NOU
Badal
SANTS
Aragó
Gran Via de
Carret. de Collblanc
Sants
Av.
Pubilla Cases
Collblanc
Can Vidalet
C 32
South of the Av. Diagonal (Plan III)
PAVELLÓ MIES VAN DER ROHE
Florida
Torrassa
Magòria La Campana
Can Serra
Sta Eulàlia
MUSEU NACIONAL D'ART DE CATALUNYA
TEAT GREC
FUNDAC JOAN M
Can Boixeres
Rambla Just Oliveras
PALAU SANT JORDI
Carrilet
St Josep
Gran Via
Ildefons Cerdà
Pas. de la Zona Franca
Av. del
Av. Carrilet
Gornal
C 31
la
L'HOSPITALET DE LLOBREGAT
Bellvitge
Av. de
EL PRAT-BARCELONA

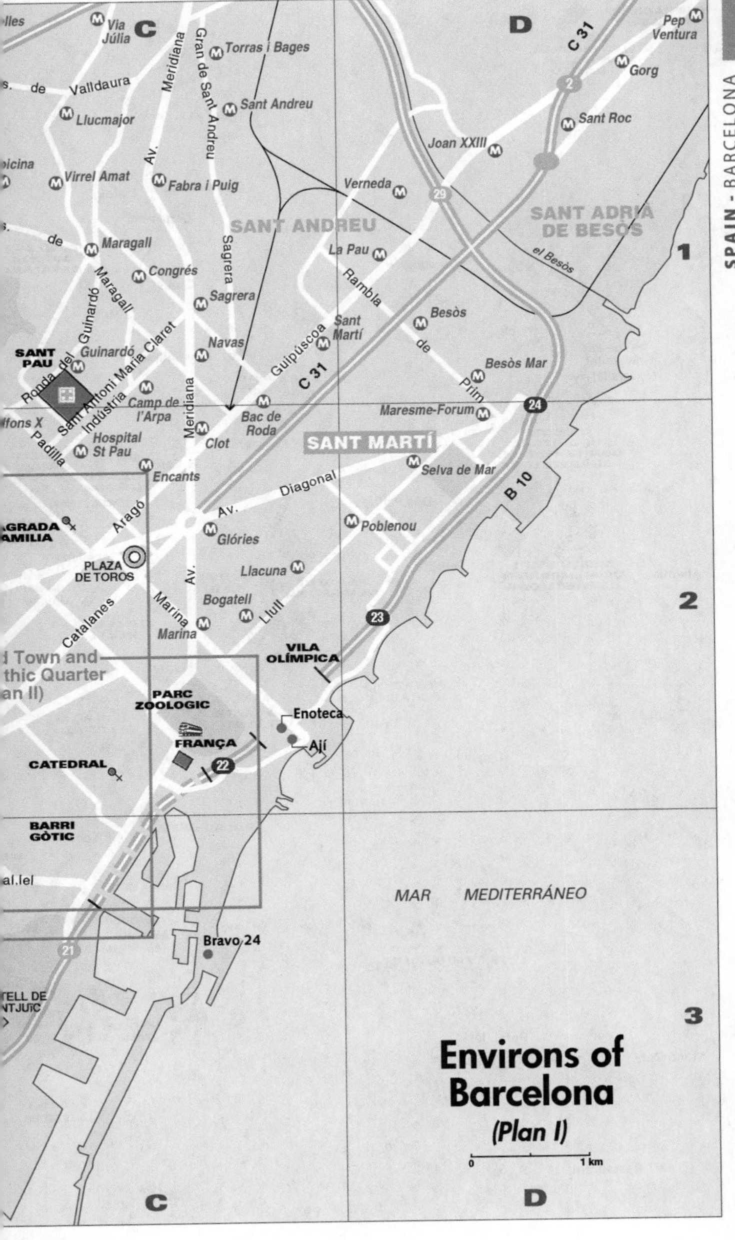
C
D
Via Júlia
Torras i Bages
Pep Ventura
Gorg
Valldaura
Meridiana
Gran de Sant Andreu
Sant Andreu
Sant Roc
Llucmajor
Joan XXIII
Virrel Amat
Fabra i Puig
Verneda
SANT ANDREU
SANT ADRIÀ DE BESÒS
el Besòs
Maragall
La Pau
Congrés
Sagrera
Rambla de Prim
Besòs
Navas
Sant Martí
Guinardó
Guipúscoa
C 31
SANT PAU
Ronda del Guinardó
Sant Antoni Maria Claret
Besòs Mar
Camp de l'Arpa
Indústria
Bac de Roda
Maresme-Forum
Hospital St Pau
Clot
Padilla
SANT MARTÍ
Encants
Selva de Mar
Av. Diagonal
B 10
Aragó
Glòries
Poblenou
PLAZA DE TOROS
Llacuna
Catalanes
Av. Marina
Bogatell
Llull
Marina
VILA OLÍMPICA
PARC ZOOLOGIC
Enoteca
FRANÇA
Ají
CATEDRAL
BARRI GÒTIC
MAR MEDITERRÁNEO
Bravo 24
1
2
3
Environs of Barcelona (Plan I)
0
1 km

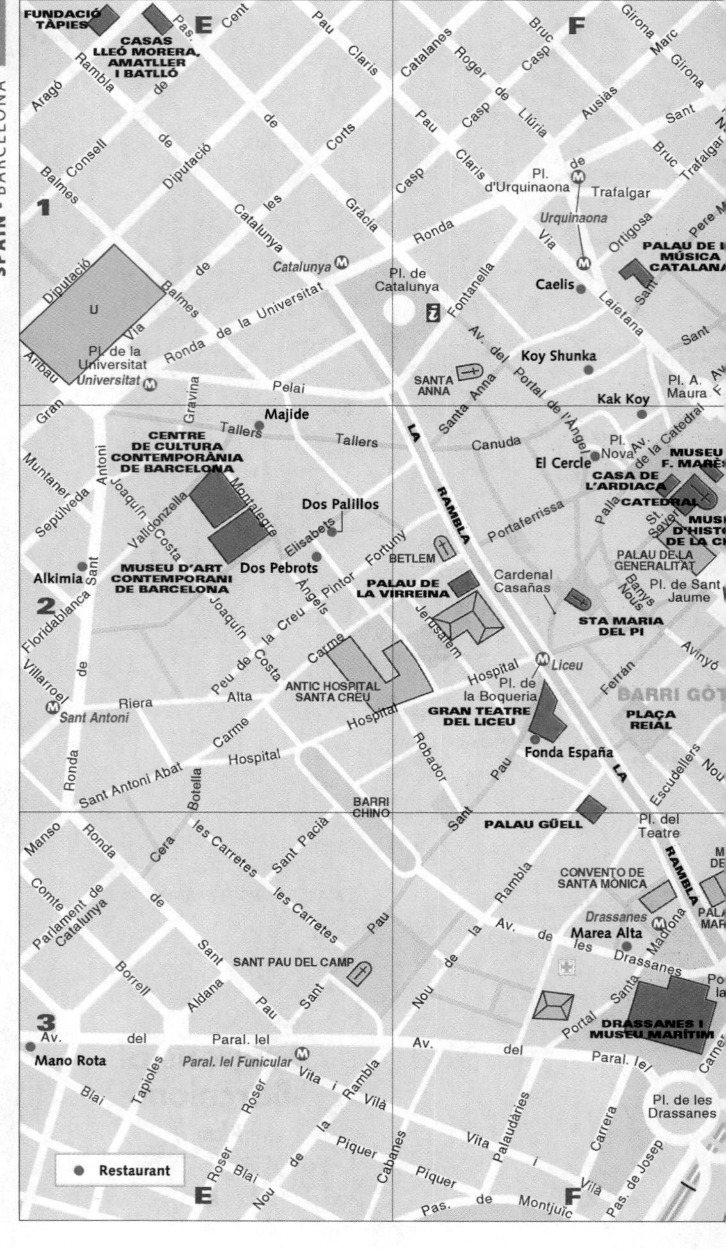

E
F
1
2
3
FUNDACIÓ TÀPIES
CASAS LLEÓ MORERA, AMATLLER I BATLLÓ
U
Pl. de la Universitat
Universitat
Catalunya
Pl. de Catalunya
Pl. d'Urquinaona
Urquinaona
PALAU DE LA MÚSICA CATALANA
Caelis
Koy Shunka
SANTA ANNA
Pl. A. Maura
Kak Koy
Majide
CENTRE DE CULTURA CONTEMPORÀNIA DE BARCELONA
Dos Palillos
MUSEU D'ART CONTEMPORANI DE BARCELONA
Dos Pebrots
Alkimia
BETLEM
PALAU DE LA VIRREINA
El Cercle
Pl. Nova
CASA DE L'ARDIACA
CATEDRAL
MUSEU F. MARÈS
PALAU DE LA GENERALITAT
Pl. de Sant Jaume
Cardenal Casañas
STA MARIA DEL PI
LA RAMBLA
Liceu
Pl. de la Boqueria
ANTIC HOSPITAL SANTA CREU
GRAN TEATRE DEL LICEU
Fonda España
BARRI GÒT
PLAÇA REIAL
Sant Antoni
BARRI CHINO
PALAU GÜELL
Pl. del Teatre
CONVENTO DE SANTA MÒNICA
Drassanes
Marea Alta
SANT PAU DEL CAMP
DRASSANES I MUSEU MARÍTIM
Mano Rota
Paral. lel Funicular
Av. del Paral. lel
Pl. de les Drassanes
Restaurant

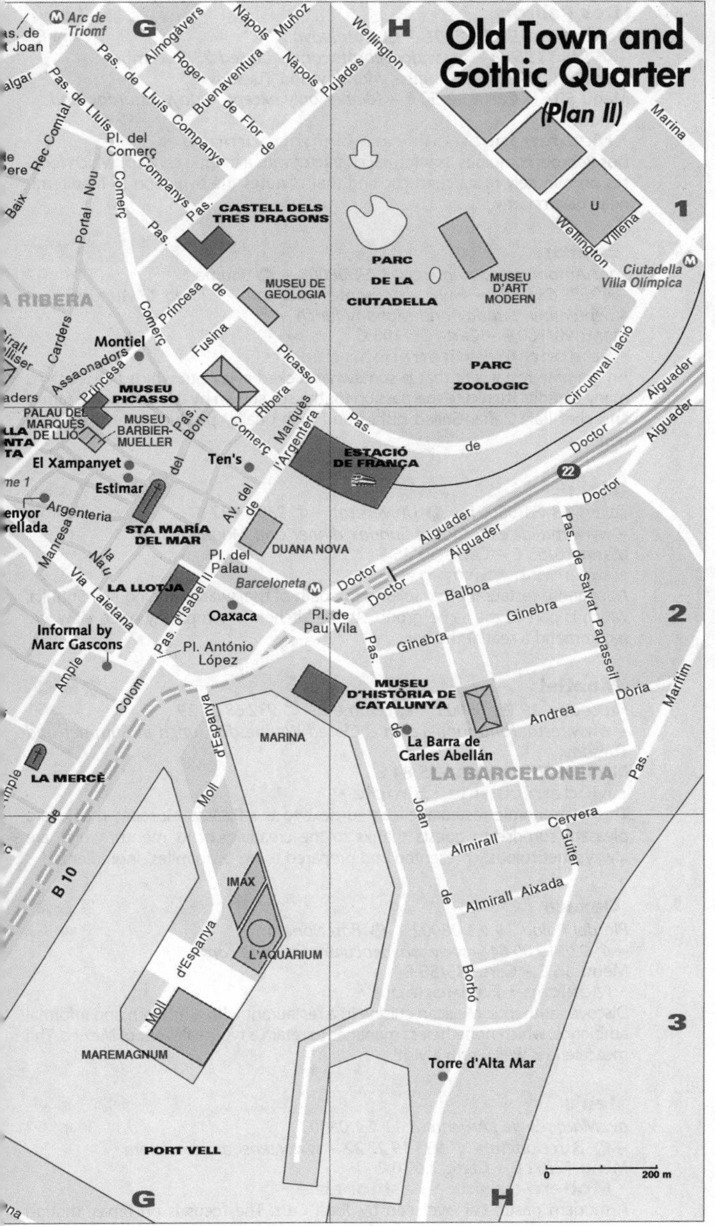
Old Town and Gothic Quarter
(Plan II)
CASTELL DELS TRES DRAGONS
MUSEU DE GEOLOGIA
PARC DE LA CIUTADELLA
MUSEU D'ART MODERN
PARC ZOOLOGIC
Ciutadella Villa Olímpica
MUSEU PICASSO
MUSEU BARBIER-MUELLER
PALAU DEL MARQUÈS DE LLIÓ
Montiel
El Xampanyet
Estimar
Ten's
ESTACIÓ DE FRANÇA
STA MARÍA DEL MAR
DUANA NOVA
LA LLOTJA
Oaxaca
Barceloneta
Pl. del Palau
Pl. de Pau Vila
Pl. António López
Informal by Marc Gascons
MUSEU D'HISTÒRIA DE CATALUNYA
La Barra de Carles Abellán
LA BARCELONETA
MARINA
LA MERCÈ
IMAX
L'AQUÀRIUM
MAREMAGNUM
Torre d'Alta Mar
PORT VELL
Pl. del Comerç
Arc de Triomf
0
200 m
B 10
22

Dos Pebrots

Doctor Dou 19 ✉ 08001 – Ⓜ Catalunya – ✆ 938 53 95 98 – www.dospebrots.com – Closed 23 December-7 January, 29 July-21 August, Monday and Tuesday

Plan: **E2**

Menu 50 € – Carte 30/50 € – *(dinner only except Friday, Saturday and Sunday)*

• Mediterranean cuisine • Neighbourhood •

Dos Pebrots combines its informal character with a unique concept which focuses on minutely researched cooking that narrates the evolution of Mediterranean gastronomy.

Estimar

Sant Antoni dels Sombrerers 3 ✉ 08003 – Ⓜ Jaume I – ✆ 932 68 91 97 – www.restaurantestimar.com – Closed 13 August-4 September, Sunday and Monday lunch

Plan: **G2**

Menu 90/160 € – Carte 56/106 €

• Seafood • Mediterranean décor •

An intimate restaurant that is somewhat tucked away but which has received many plaudits thanks to the passion for the sea shown by the Gotanegra family and chef Rafa Zafra. Grilled dishes and high-quality products are to the fore here.

Majide

Tallers 48 ✉ 08001 – Ⓜ Universitat – ✆ 930 16 37 81 – www.majide.es – Closed Sunday dinner and Monday lunch

Plan: **E2**

Menu 16/65 € – Carte 30/45 €

• Japanese • Simple •

A Japanese restaurant that follows the path of the award-winning Koy Shunka, which is part of the same group. As the kitchen is completely open view, we recommend a seat at the bar.

Montiel

Flassaders 19 ✉ 08003 – Ⓜ Jaume I – ✆ 932 68 37 29 – www.restaurantmontiel.com – Closed Wednesday lunch in Summer and Tuesday

Plan: **G1**

Menu 36/75 € – Carte 35/84 €

• Modern cuisine • Simple •

This gastronomic restaurant located next to the Picasso Museum provides a pleasant surprise to guests thanks to the creativity of its menus, which are always meticulously presented and prepared using "zero miles" ingredients.

Oaxaca

Pla del Palau 19 ✉ 08002 – Ⓜ Barceloneta – ✆ 933 19 00 64 – www.oaxacacuinamexicana.com

Plan: **G2**

Menu 56 € – Carte 35/55 €

• Mexican • Fashionable •

Discover authentic Mexican cuisine in a restaurant with a modern and informal ambience, which nonetheless manages to retain a typical flavour of Mexico. The mezcalería is well worth a visit!

Ten's

av. Marqués de l'Argentera 11 ✉ 08003 – Ⓜ Barceloneta – ✆ 933 19 22 22 – www.tensbarcelona.com

Plan: **G2**

Menu 48/62 € – Carte 22/36 €

• Modern cuisine • Fashionable •

A modern gastro-bar overseen by Jordi Cruz. The focus is on tapas, though raciones and superb oysters also feature prominently. Menus take centre stage here at weekends.

Kak Koy

Ripoll 16 ✉ 08002 – Ⓜ Urquinaona – ✆ 933 02 84 14 – www.kakkoy.com – Closed Christmas, Holy Week, August, Sunday and Tuesday lunch

Plan: **F2**

Tapa 8 € **Ración** approx. 15 €

• Japanese • Cosy •

Japanese cuisine with a Mediterranean influence that has adopted the tapas and *raciones* concept. The traditional Japanese robata grill takes centre stage here.

El Xampanyet

Montcada 22 ✉ 08003 – Ⓜ Jaume I – ✆ 933 19 70 03 – Closed 15 days January, Holy Week, August, Sunday dinner and Monday

Plan: **G2**

Tapa 5 € **Ración** approx. 15 €

• Traditional cuisine • Traditional décor •

This old tavern with a long-standing family tradition boasts a typical atmosphere with its azulejo tiles, wineskin bottles and barrels. Varied selection of tapas with an emphasis on cured meats and high-quality canned products.

SOUTH of AV. DIAGONAL — PLAN III

Lasarte – Hotel Monument H.

Mallorca 259 ✉ 08008 – Ⓜ Passeig de Gràcia – ✆ 934 45 32 42 – www.restaurantlasarte.com – Closed 1-9 January, Holy Week, 21 days August, Sunday, Monday and bank holidays

Plan: **K2**

Menu 215/245 € – Carte 109/162 €

• Creative • Design •

This impeccable contemporary-style restaurant is constantly changing and has the personal stamp of Martín Berasategui and his team. The original and imaginative cuisine bears the innovative hallmark of the chef, whose creativity is evident in the à la carte options and tasting menus alike.

➜ Ravioli de wagyu y anguila glaseada, crema yodada, raifort y caviar. Pez rey con salsa de crustáceos, cangrejo real, tomate en crudo y azafrán. Bombón de nuez de Pecán, rocas de leche, café y whisky ahumado.

Moments – Hotel Mandarin Oriental Barcelona

passeig de Gràcia 38-40 ✉ 08007 – Ⓜ Passeig de Gràcia – ✆ 931 51 87 81 – www.mandarinoriental.com – Closed 14-29 January, 26 August-12 September, Sunday and Monday

Plan: **K2**

Menu 77/176 € – Carte 122/223 €

• Creative • Elegant •

Accessed via the hotel lobby, Moments stands out for its design, which includes a private chef's table. Here, Raül Balam, the son of famous chef Carme Ruscadella, conjures up intelligent, creative cuisine which respects flavours, showcases textures and is able to reinterpret tradition through contemporary eyes.

➜ Arroz caldoso de colas de gambas, homenaje a los pescadores de Sant Pol de Mar. Foie-gras con contrastes dulces, ácidos y picantes. Nuestra versión de la tarta ópera.

Cocina Hermanos Torres (Sergio y Javier Torres)

Taquígraf Serra 20 ✉ 08029 – Ⓜ Entença – ✆ 934 10 00 20 – www.cocinahermanostorres.com – Closed August, Sunday and Monday

Plan: **I2**

Menu 120/135 € – Carte 82/105 €

• Creative • Design •

The most personal offering to date from the Torres twins who have transformed an industrial warehouse into a unique gastronomic space in which the open kitchen surrounded by tables takes centre stage. The creative dishes on offer are inspired by tradition, rekindling memories of childhood, travels and the flavours of different regions around Spain.

➜ Tartar de rubia gallega. Paletilla de cordero lechal, pólvora de Duc y almendras. Flor de almendra de leche.

North and South of Av. Diagonal

(Plan III)

● Restaurant

0 — 300 m

Silvestre
99 Sushi Bar
Hisop
Tunateca Balfegó
Via Veneto
Paco Meralgo
Gaig
Cocina Hermanos Torres
Nectari
Da Paolo
Enigma
Hoja Santa
Niño Viejo
Espai Kru
Rias de Galicia

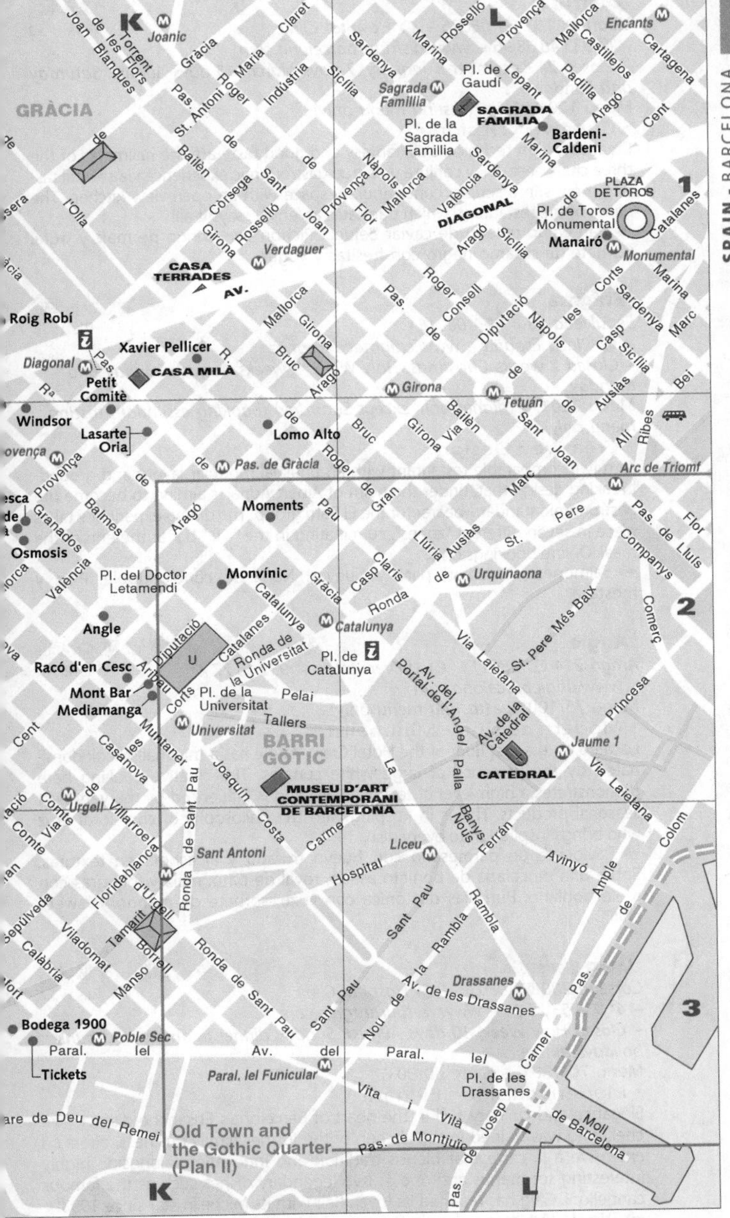
GRÀCIA
Joanic
Sagrada Família
SAGRADA FAMILIA
Bardeni-Caldeni
PLAZA DE TOROS
Pl. de Toros Monumental
Manairó
Monumental
DIAGONAL
Verdaguer
CASA TERRADES
Roig Robí
Xavier Pellicer
CASA MILÀ
Diagonal
Petit Comitè
Windsor
Lasarte Oria
Lomo Alto
Girona
Tetuán
Pas. de Gràcia
Arc de Triomf
Moments
Osmosis
Monvínic
Pl. del Doctor Letamendi
Urquinaona
Angle
Catalunya
Pl. de Catalunya
Racó d'en Cesc
Mont Bar
Mediamanga
Pl. de la Universitat
Universitat
BARRI GÒTIC
MUSEU D'ART CONTEMPORANI DE BARCELONA
CATEDRAL
Jaume 1
Urgell
Sant Antoni
Liceu
Drassanes
Bodega 1900
Poble Sec
Tickets
Paral. lel Funicular
Pl. de les Drassanes
Old Town and the Gothic Quarter (Plan II)

✿✿

Disfrutar

XX ♿ A/C

Villarroel 163 ✉ 08036 – Ⓜ Hospital Clinic Plan: **J2**
– ✆ 933 48 68 96 – www.disfrutarbarcelona.com
– Closed 24 December-8 January, 7 days March, 15 days August, Saturday and Sunday
Menu 120/185 € – *(tasting menu only)*

• Creative • Design •

Creativity, high technical skill, fantasy and good taste are the hallmarks of the three chefs here. They conjure up a true gastronomic experience via several tasting menus in a simple, contemporary space with an open-view kitchen. The name of the restaurant, which translates as 'enjoy', says it all!

➜ Pan chino relleno de caviar Beluga. Pichón con abrigo de maíz y trufa. Cornete de sésamo negro con fresitas y yogur.

✿

Enigma

XXX ♿ A/C

Sepúlveda 38-40 ✉ 08015 Plan: **J3**
– Ⓜ Plaza España – www.enigmaconcept.es
– Closed 2 weeks Christmas, Holy Week, 3 weeks August, Sunday and Monday
Menu 220 € – *(dinner only except Saturday) (booking essential) (tasting menu only)*

• Creative • Design •

A truly incomparable restaurant with an unusual modular layout and groundbreaking design that, under the helm of Albert Adrià, is aiming to become the gastronomic standard-bearer for the El Barri group. The dining experience takes place in seven different "zones", culminating in the "41º" bar at the end of the meal. Online bookings only.

➜ Salmonete, escamas, paté y huevas. Nuez de conejo doble. Piña y mostaza.

✿

Angle

XXX ♿ A/C

Aragó 214 ✉ 08011 – Ⓜ Universitat – ✆ 932 16 77 77 Plan: **K2**
– www.anglebarcelona.com
Menu 75/100 € – *(tasting menu only)*

• Modern cuisine • Minimalist •

Located on the first floor of the Hotel Cram, Angle has a minimalist look dominated by the presence of large white curtains. The creative cooking here demonstrates a high level of technical skill and is influenced by the very best seasonal products. This is in keeping with the philosophy of chef Jordi Cruz who brings inspiration to every dish.

➜ Raviolone de parmesano con huevo trufado y alcachofa en texturas. Sobre una pincelada de boniato asado, royal de pato, maíz y foie gras con mole poblano. Burbujas de tónica con yuzu, sorbete de mango y "sweet chili".

✿

Gaig (Carles Gaig)

XXX ♿ A/C

Còrsega 200 ✉ 08036 – Ⓜ Hospital Clinic Plan: **J2**
– ✆ 934 53 20 20 – www.restaurantgaig.com
– Closed Holy Week, 10 days August, Sunday dinner, Monday and bank holidays dinner
Menu 70/130 € – Carte 60/90 €

• Modern cuisine • Elegant •

Elegance and culinary skill in the heart of Barcelona's Ensanche district. The chef, who was trained in the kitchen of the former family business, offers an extensive à la carte that blends tradition and innovation, alongside highly interesting set menus and one or two legendary dishes such as the famous cannelloni. Gaig has retained its love affair with its Michelin star since 1993!

➜ Trío de tártars, gamba de Palamós, lubina y atún bluefin. Codorniz salvaje y foie a la moda de Alcántara. Limón y yogur.

Alkimia (Jordi Vilà)

Plan II: E2

Ronda San Antoni 41, 1º ✉ 08011 – Ⓜ Universitat – ✆ 932 07 61 15 – www.alkimia.cat – Closed 22 January-4 February, 13-26 August, Saturday and Sunday
Menu 98/158 € – Carte 65/95 €

• Modern cuisine • Design •

Alkimia boasts a striking design, with an avant-garde nod to the maritime world and a brand-new "unplugged" concept that complements its main gastronomic dining room. The contemporary cuisine (based around locally sourced ingredients) is sublime, with perfect textures and defined flavours that blend harmoniously together.

➜ Tartar de pescado, gamba, cigala y caviar. Bogavante en dos servicios, con suquet seco de galanga y arroz caldoso a banda. "Menjar blanc" con fruta fresca y gelée de cava.

Hoja Santa (Paco Méndez)

Plan: J3

av. Mistral 54 ✉ 08015 – Ⓜ Espanya – ✆ 933 48 21 94 – www.hojasanta.es – Closed 24 December-15 January, Holy Week, 14 days August, Sunday and Monday
Menu 130/160 € – *(dinner only except Saturday) (tasting menu only)*

• Mexican • Friendly •

Guests can enjoy fine Mexican cuisine at this restaurant named after an indigenous bush. The ambience here is relaxed and contemporary, featuring decor made up of ethnic and colonial details. The enticing combinations of flavours and, above all, the spicy dishes adapted to European tastes, ensure a thoroughly enjoyable dining experience.

➜ Flor de calabacín con ocosingo. Mole de ajo negro con aguacate. Garibaldi de naranja.

Oria – Hotel Monument H.

Plan: K2

passeig de Gràcia 75 ✉ 08008 – Ⓜ Passeig de Gràcia – ✆ 935 48 20 33 – www.monument-hotel.com
Menu 40 € – Carte 63/81 €

• Modern cuisine • Trendy •

The spacious, modern and elegant Oria restaurant opens onto the lobby of the hotel. Here, the cuisine is overseen by chef Martín Berasategui, which translates into dishes that are exquisitely prepared and full of interesting flavours. The à la carte is complemented by a 40-euro "Menú Ejecutivo" and a "Menú a medida", which can be tailored to your specific budget from the same amount upwards.

➜ Steak tartare con jugo de olivas verdes y bombones líquidos de Kalamata. Dorada asada con perlas de hinojo y caracolas de mar. Souflé de almendra con helado de miel.

Pakta

Plan: J3

Lleida 5 ✉ 08004 – Ⓜ Espanya – ✆ 936 24 01 77 – www.pakta.es – Closed Christmas, Holy Week, 3 weeks August, Sunday and Monday
Menu 120/150 € – Carte 45/70 € – *(dinner only except Saturday) (booking essential)*

• Peruvian • Design •

A colourful, contemporary and informal restaurant that evokes Peruvian culture. This is evident both in its name (that means 'together' or 'union' in the Quechua language) and its decor with walls and ceilings adorned with striking fabrics. However, the cuisine is very much Japanese, showcasing lots of technical prowess and meticulous presentation. Bookings need to be made online.

➜ Ceviche de corvina salvaje con leche de tigre de almendras. Nigiri de espardeña. Kakigori de coco.

Xerta – Hotel Ohla Eixample

Còrsega 289 ✉ 08008 – Ⓜ Diagonal – ✆ 937 37 90 80 Plan: **K1-2**
– www.xertarestaurant.com – Closed Sunday and Monday
Menu 38/105 € – Carte 58/81 €

• Creative • Design •

This elegant, contemporary restaurant oozes personality thanks to its striking skylights, vertical garden and large open-view kitchen. Choose from a concise à la carte with a contemporary Mediterranean focus and several set menus. Everything is centred around the very best products from the Ebro Delta and fantastic fish sourced from the daily fish market.

➜ Arroz de ortigas y espardeñas. Pichón con setas. Agua y jabón.

Tickets

av. del Paral.lel 164 ✉ 08015 – Ⓜ Espanya Plan: **K3**
– www.ticketsbar.es – Closed 24 December-16 January, Holy Week, 2 weeks August, Sunday and Monday
Tapa 12 € – *(dinner only except Saturday) (booking essential)*

• Creative • Colourful •

A unique and highly enjoyable restaurant with lots of colour and several cutting-edge bar counters. The innovative cuisine on offer, prepared in front of diners, plays homage to the legendary dishes that were once created at El Bulli. Don't miss the desserts here, which showcase an overwhelming abundance of imagination.

➜ Olivas esféricas. Pulpo crujiente con kimchi. Tarta de queso Coulommiers.

Petit Comitè

passatge de la Concepció 13 ✉ 08008 – Ⓜ Diagonal Plan: **K2**
– ✆ 936 33 76 27 – www.petitcomite.cat – Closed 14 days August
Menu 65 € – Carte 45/80 €

• Regional cuisine • Design •

This contemporary restaurant is decorated with lots of plates. The focus is on local cuisine prepared using Spanish ingredients, including enticing themed daily specials.

Racó d'en Cesc

Diputació 201 ✉ 08011 – Ⓜ Universitat Plan: **K2**
– ✆ 934 51 60 02 – www.elracodencesc.com – Closed Holy Week, August, Sunday and bank holidays
Menu 40 € – Carte 40/53 €

• Modern cuisine • Classic décor •

A restaurant with a small terrace, a bistro-style section and a classic dining room, with a different creative Catalan menu in each. A wide choice of craft beers is also available.

Rías de Galicia

Lleida 7 ✉ 08004 – Ⓜ Espanya – ✆ 934 24 81 52 Plan: **J3**
– www.riasdegalicia.com
Menu 80/120 € – Carte 70/100 €

• Seafood • Classic décor •

Goose barnacles, lamprey, oysters and tuna are among the many culinary treasures from the Atlantic and Mediterranean on offer here. The wine cellar is home to some impressive labels and vintages.

Windsor

Còrsega 286 ✉ 08008 – Ⓜ Diagonal – ✆ 932 37 75 88 Plan: **K2**
– www.restaurantwindsor.com – Closed 6-9 December, 1-7 January, Holy Week, 5-25 August and Sunday
Menu 32/99 € – Carte 55/75 €

• Modern cuisine • Classic décor •

This restaurant, with its updated classic decor, is enhanced by an exquisite terrace and several dining rooms that allow for different configurations. Contemporary Catalan cuisine.

Be So - Hotel Sofía

XX AC — Plan I: A2

pl. de Pius XII-4 ✉ 08028 – Ⓜ Maria Cristina – ✆ 935 08 10 20 – www.sofiabarcelona.com – Closed Sunday and Monday

Menu 80/120 € – Carte 68/99 €

• Traditional cuisine • Contemporary décor •

A restaurant with lots of personality that stands out thanks to its elegant decor, dominated by golden tones, and its updated traditional cuisine. Meticulous presentation.

Manairó

XX ♿ AC — Plan: L1

Diputació 424 ✉ 08013 – Ⓜ Monumental – ✆ 932 31 00 57 – www.jordiherrera.es – Closed 1-7 January, Sunday and bank holidays

Menu 45/90 € – Carte 60/75 €

• Creative • Contemporary décor •

A unique restaurant, both in terms of its modern decor and intimate lighting. Contemporary, meticulously presented cuisine with its roots in Catalan cooking.

Monvínic

XX ♿ AC — Plan: K2

Diputació 249 ✉ 08007 – Ⓜ Catalunya – ✆ 932 72 61 87 – www.monvinic.com – Closed August, Saturday lunch, Sunday and Monday lunch

Menu 27/80 €

• Modern cuisine • Wine bar •

This restaurant impresses through its contemporary design and philosophy, with everything revolving around the world of wine. A modern take on traditional cuisine, as well as a splendid wine cellar.

Nectari

XX AC — Plan: J3

València 28 ✉ 08015 – Ⓜ Tarragona – ✆ 932 26 87 18 – www.nectari.es – Closed 15 days September and Sunday

Menu 39/83 € – Carte 54/76 €

• Modern cuisine • Classic décor •

Nectari has just two small contemporary-style dining rooms and one private area where the Mediterranean-inspired menu features a variety of creative and innovative touches.

Tunateca Balfegó

XX ♿ AC — Plan: J2

Av. Diagonal 439 ✉ 08036 – ✆ 937 97 64 60 – www.tunatecabalfego.com – Closed 14-21 April, 5-19 August and Sunday

Menu 52/72 € – Carte 31/51 €

• Modern cuisine • Contemporary décor •

If you're interested in different cuts of tuna and ways of preparing it, you won't want to miss this restaurant decorated in varying tones of blue and featuring attractive decorative details alluding to this magnificent fish.

Xavier Pellicer

XX ♿ AC — Plan: K1

Provença 310 ✉ 08037 – Ⓜ Diagonal – ✆ 935 25 90 02 – www.xavierpellicer.com – Closed Sunday

Menu 28 € – Carte 40/50 €

• Market cuisine • Contemporary décor •

The most personal offering to date from this chef, who continues to champion healthy and organic cuisine. Dining options here include one space which is more informal and another, "El Menjador", with a more gastronomic focus.

El Bar

X AC — Plan: J3

Calabria 118 ✉ 08015 – Ⓜ Rocafort – ✆ 934 26 03 82 – www.elbarbarcelona.com – Closed Sunday dinner and Monday

Menu 22 € – Carte 33/53 €

• Catalan • Tapas bar •

A restaurant that lives up to its name more in terms of its size and simple decor rather than its menu which is both extensive and consistent in quality. Choose from a wide variety of tapas plus a choice of more elaborate dishes.

Espai Kru

Plan: J3

Lleida 7 ✉ 08004 – Ⓜ Espanya – ✆ 934 23 45 70 – www.espaikru.com – Closed Sunday dinner and Monday
Menu 100 € – Carte 40/65 €
• International • Fashionable •
Located on the first floor, Espai Kru has an impressive appearance, enhanced by an open-view kitchen, a private dining room and a cocktail bar. The extensive international fusion menu features both raw and cooked ingredients.

Gresca

Plan: K2

Provença 230 ✉ 08036 – Ⓜ Diagonal – ✆ 934 51 61 93 – www.gresca.net – Closed 7 days Christmas, Holy Week, 15 days August, Saturday and Sunday
Menu 21/70 € – Carte 35/65 €
• Modern cuisine • Minimalist •
A good option for those keen to try contemporary dishes that showcase seasonal ingredients. Its top-quality cooking has extended to the bar next door (Gresca Bar), which is more focused on the world of wine.

Lomo Alto

Plan: K2

Aragó 283-285 ✉ 08007 – Ⓜ Passeig de Gràcia – ✆ 935 19 30 00 – www.lomoalto.barcelona
Menu 95 € – Carte 50/70 €
• Meats and grills • Friendly •
A mecca for meat-lovers laid out on two floors (Lomo Bajo and Lomo Alto) with impressive vaulted windows. The mature beef is sourced from old Iberian breeds and cooked on the grill.

Mano Rota

Plan II : E3

Creus dels Molers 4 ✉ 08004 – Ⓜ Poble Sec – ✆ 931 64 80 41 – www.manorota.com – Closed 31 December-7 January, Sunday and Monday lunch
Menu 18/60 € – Carte 35/50 €
• Modern cuisine • Neighbourhood •
Mano Rota boasts an industrial feel and champions a specific concept: a restaurant with a bar. Its interesting menu includes traditional and contemporary recipes, as well as international dishes from Peru and Japan.

Osmosis

Plan: K2

Aribau 100 ✉ 08036 – Ⓜ Diagonal – ✆ 934 54 52 01 – www.restauranteosmosis.com – Closed 24-29 December and Sunday
Menu 42/72 € – *(tasting menu only)*
• Modern cuisine • Contemporary décor •
A restaurant with a pleasant, modern ambience arranged over two floors. The contemporary tasting menu, available in both long and short formats, is created using seasonal, market-fresh ingredients.

Da Paolo

Plan: I3

av. de Madrid 63 ✉ 08028 – Ⓜ Badal – ✆ 934 90 48 91 – www.dapaolo.es – Closed 3 weeks August and Sunday
Menu 12/20 € – Carte 25/35 €
• Italian • Classic décor •
Italian restaurant located near the Nou Camp stadium. Both simple and well-presented, it has a large pleasant dining room and an elaborate menu.

Sergi de Meià

Plan: K2

Aribau 106 ✉ 08036 – Ⓜ Diagonal – ✆ 931 25 57 10 – www.restaurantsergidemeia.cat – Closed Sunday and Monday
Menu 24/68 € – Carte 45/70 €
• Regional cuisine • Simple •
The owner-chef unashamedly promotes 100% Catalan cuisine. He rediscovers the flavours of yesteryear and always focuses on organic and locally sourced products.

Bodega 1900

Plan: **K3**

Tamarit 91 ✉ 08015 – Ⓜ Poble Sec – ☏ 933 25 26 59 – www.bodega1900.com – Closed 24 December-14 January, Holy Week, 2 weeks August, Sunday and Monday

Tapa 4 € **Ración** approx. 13 €

• Traditional cuisine • Neighbourhood •

This restaurant has all the charm of an old-fashioned grocery store. The small menu features grilled dishes, Iberian specialities and homemade preserves, all of excellent quality.

Mediamanga

Plan: **K2**

Aribau 13 ✉ 08011 – Ⓜ Universitat – ☏ 938 32 56 94 – www.mediamanga.es

Tapa 7 € **Ración** approx. 22 €

• Modern cuisine • Vintage •

A gastro-bar with an eclectic ambience featuring Modernist and Art Deco elements. The contemporary cuisine here is high on detail and is perfect for sharing.

Mont Bar

Plan: **K2**

Diputació 220 ✉ 08011 – Ⓜ Universitat – ☏ 933 23 95 90 – www.montbar.com – Closed 14-29 January and 19-29 August

Tapa 4.50 € **Ración** approx. 17 €

• Traditional cuisine • Bistro •

This charming and unusual gastro-bar serves traditional cuisine prepared using top quality ingredients. Friendly and professional service.

Niño Viejo

Plan: **J3**

av. Mistral 54 ✉ 08015 – Ⓜ Poble Sec – ☏ 933 48 21 94 – www.ninoviejo.es – Closed 24 December-15 January, Holy Week, 14 days August, Sunday and Monday

Tapa 5 € **Ración** approx. 15 € – *(dinner only except Thursday, Friday and Saturday)*

• Mexican • Exotic décor •

Unusual, lively, colourful and informal – this taco bar with an ethnic feel serves delicious homemade tacos, antojitos and spicy salsas. High quality Mexican cuisine.

Paco Meralgo

Plan: **J2**

Muntaner 171 ✉ 08036 – Ⓜ Hospital Clínic – ☏ 934 30 90 27 – www.restaurantpacomeralgo.com

Tapa 6 € **Ración** approx. 12 €

• Traditional cuisine • Mediterranean décor •

The Paco Meralgo has two bars and two separate entrances, although its most impressive feature is its display cabinets filled with fresh, varied, top quality seafood. A private room is also available.

SANT MARTÍ — PLAN I

Enoteca – Hotel Arts

Plan: **C2**

Marina 19 ✉ 08005 – Ⓜ Ciutadella-Vila Olímpica – ☏ 934 83 81 08 – www.enotecapacoperez.com – Closed 1-16 December, 3-18 March, Sunday and Monday

Menu 175 € – Carte 105/147 € – *(dinner only except Saturday)*

• Modern cuisine • Mediterranean décor •

A bright, fresh look with a penchant for varying tones of white that encapsulates the essence of the Mediterranean. This restaurant, which is under the baton of chef Paco Pérez, enhances the flavours of the Catalan coast with delicate international touches and the occasional nod to Asian fusion cooking.

➜ Espardenyes desnudas en fricandó con guiso de tendones. Pichón, huitlacoche, mole de mil días y dumplings. Torrija de cacao, trufa melanosporum, toffee, miel y limón.

Ají

Marina 19 ✉ 08005 – Ⓜ Ciutadella-Vila Olímpica Plan: **C2**
– ✆ 935 11 97 67 – www.restaurantaji.com – Closed 1-15 January, Sunday and Monday
Menu 21/45 € – Carte 31/50 €
• Peruvian • Bistro •

The name, which translates as "chilli pepper" in Peruvian Spanish and "taste" in Japanese, gives us a good insight into the culinary intentions of this restaurant. Japanese cuisine with a focus on well-defined textures and flavours.

NORTH of AV. DIAGONAL PLAN III

✿✿✿ **ABaC** – Hotel ABaC

av. del Tibidabo 1 ✉ 08022 – Ⓜ Av. Tibidabo Plan I: **B2**
– ✆ 933 19 66 00 – www.abacrestaurant.com
Menu 180/210 € – *(tasting menu only)*
• Creative • Design •

Discover the unique culinary vision of the bold, media-friendly chef Jordi Cruz who has raised technical skill, creativity and gastronomic perfection to even higher levels. His dishes tell stories that are complex yet at the same time intelligent and understandable, and which evolve in line with seasonal products.

→ Salmón gallego y yema curada, huevas de trucha, mantequilla de soja y texturas de nori. Magret de pato, jugo de cilantro y lavanda con romesco y jugo de zanahorias escabechadas. Coco helado, sorbete de coco tostado, vainilla y barquillo con perfume de limón.

✿ **Via Veneto**

Ganduxer 10 ✉ 08021 – Ⓜ Hospital Clínic Plan: **I2**
– ✆ 932 00 72 44 – www.viavenetorestaurant.com – Closed August, Saturday lunch and Sunday
Menu 80/165 € – Carte 70/100 €
• Classic cuisine • Classic décor •

A famous property in attractive Belle Époque-style with a dining room laid out on several levels and a number of private dining areas. Impressively updated classic menu with game in season and interesting tasting menus. Guests can visit the superb wine cellar here, featuring an outstanding collection of Spanish and French wines.

→ Tartar de cigala con ajoblanco sobre pan negro molido. Pescado de lonja sobre emulsión de mejillones de roca y rocas de azafrán. Biscuit glacé de piñones de "Cap Roig" con helado de miel de trufa negra.

✿ **Hofmann**

La Granada del Penedès 14-16 ✉ 08006 Plan: **J1**
– Ⓜ Diagonal – ✆ 932 18 71 65
– www.hofmann-bcn.com
– Closed Christmas, Holy Week, August, Saturday lunch, Sunday and bank holidays
Menu 38/95 € – Carte 59/76 €
• Modern cuisine • Classic décor •

The word gastronomy reflects the great passion of May Hofmann, the founder-chef who set the guidelines to be followed in one of the country's most influential restaurant schools. Her daughter Silvia and the current students continue her work, producing cuisine that is full of creativity.

→ Canelón de ternera con foie, crema trufada y teja de parmesano crujiente. Arroz meloso de pato ahumado, colmenillas y foie asado. Crujientes de vainilla.

Hisop (Oriol Ivern)

XX A/C

passatge de Marimon 9 ✉ 08021 – Ⓜ Hospital Clínic – ✆ 932 41 32 33 – www.hisop.com – Closed 1-7 January, Holy Week, Saturday lunch, Sunday and bank holidays

Plan: **J2**

Menu 65 € – Carte 56/64 €

• Creative • Minimalist •

Because of its size, this restaurant named after an aromatic medicinal plant offers guests an intimate and modern dining experience. In its minimalist dining room, enjoy fresh and creative dishes based around traditional recipes, always prepared using local and seasonal products. Interesting wine pairing options.
➔ Foie "after eight". Salmonete con mayonesa de moluscos. Chocolate con burrata y miel de caña.

Vivanda

Major de Sarrià 134 ✉ 08017 – Ⓜ Reina Elisenda – ✆ 932 03 19 18 – www.vivanda.cat – Closed Sunday dinner and Monday

Plan I: **A2**

Carte 25/35 €

• Traditional cuisine • Cosy •

A unique restaurant offering a traditional menu centred around small dishes (slightly larger than half raciones) advertised as *platos del mes* (dishes of the month). Attractive tree-shaded terrace and a modern interior combining standard tables for restaurant dining and bar tables for tapas.

Tram-Tram

XXX A/C

Major de Sarrià 121 ✉ 08017 – Ⓜ Reina Elisenda – ✆ 932 04 85 18 – www.tram-tram.com – Closed Holy Week, 15 days August, Sunday and Tuesday dinner from 15 June-15 September, Sunday dinner and Monday rest of the year

Plan I: **A2**

Menu 33/90 € – Carte 40/65 €

• Modern cuisine • Family •

A classically furnished restaurant, the name of which pays homage to this old form of transport. Updated traditional cuisine with the occasional international influence, and the option of ordering one of the set menus.

La Balsa

XX A/C

Infanta Isabel 4 ✉ 08022 – ✆ 932 11 50 48 – www.labalsarestaurant.com – Closed August, Sunday dinner and Monday

Plan I: **B1**

Menu 20/60 € – Carte 35/62 €

• Mediterranean cuisine • Cosy •

A classic address whose renovation has transformed it into a small architectural jewel nestled amid a haven of peace and quiet. Good Mediterranean cooking with a focus on quality products, which you can also enjoy on La Balsa's charming outdoor terraces.

99 sushi bar

XX A/C

Tenor Viñas 4 ✉ 08002 – Ⓜ Muntaner – ✆ 936 39 62 17 – www.99sushibar.com – Closed August and Sunday dinner

Plan: **J2**

Menu 90 € – Carte 55/75 €

• Japanese • Design •

High-quality Japanese cuisine in keeping with other restaurants in the chain. Eat at the bar if there's space so you can enjoy the preparation of the attractive cuisine here at close quarters.

Roig Robí

XX A/C

Sèneca 20 ✉ 08006 – Ⓜ Diagonal – ✆ 932 18 92 22 – www.roigrobi.com – Closed 1-7 January, 6-26 August, Saturday lunch and Sunday

Plan: **K1**

Menu 40/66 € – Carte 40/65 €

• Regional cuisine • Classic décor •

A pleasant restaurant in a classic setting that includes a winter garden-style dining room laid out around a patio-garden. Catalan cuisine with a choice of different menus.

Silvestre

Santaló 101 ✉ 08021 – Ⓜ Muntaner – ✆ 932 41 40 31 Plan: **J1**
– www.restaurante-silvestre.com – Closed Holy Week, 21 days August, Saturday dinner July-August, Saturday lunch, Sunday and bank holidays
Menu 26/50 € – Carte 27/43 €

• Traditional cuisine • Cosy •

Cosy and welcoming with various private dining areas that add an intimate feel. Traditional and international cuisine, including appealing fixed menus and the option of half-raciones.

Bardeni-Caldeni

Valencia 454 ✉ 08013 – Ⓜ Sagrada Familia Plan: **L1**
– ✆ 932 32 58 11 – www.bardeni.es – Closed Holy Week, 14 days August, Sunday and Monday
Tapa 9 € **Ración** approx. 15 €

• Meats and grills • Design •

A restaurant in which meat is very much centre stage. The ambience is that of an old butcher's shop, with a bar to the rear where guests can also eat.

AT SANTA COLOMA de GRAMENET

Lluerna (Víctor Quintillà)

av. Pallaresa 104 ✉ 08921 Santa Coloma de Gramenet – Ⓜ Santa Coloma – ✆ 933 91 08 20 – www.lluernarestaurant.com – Closed 14-22 April, 4-26 August, Sunday, Monday and bank holidays dinner
Menu 43/80 € – Carte 48/63 €

• Modern cuisine • Design •

A restaurant with a modern decor in which the kitchen, "hidden" behind three glass doors, is as much the centre of attraction as the dining room. The cuisine on offer, an updated take on traditional cooking, is focused where possible around locally sourced products but without completely turning its back on ingredients and influences from elsewhere. Interesting selection of tasting menus.

→ Arroz de gambas de playa. Pescado de playa sobre pil pil de almejas. Coulant de avellanas, albaricoque y fruta de la pasión.

Ca n'Armengol

Prat de La Riba 1 ✉ 08921 Santa Coloma de Gramenet – Ⓜ Santa Coloma – ✆ 933 91 68 55 – www.canarmengol.net – Closed Holy Week, 2 weeks August, Sunday dinner, Monday and Tuesday dinner
Menu 12/35 € – Carte 30/45 €

• Traditional cuisine • Classic décor •

A family-run restaurant with a classic ambience. There are two entrances: one directly through to the old bar, where customers can dine from the set menu, and the other to the dining rooms and private section reserved for à la carte dining. Traditionally based cuisine with the option of half-raciones (portions).

Verat

av. Pallaresa 104 ✉ 08921 Santa Coloma de Gramenet – Ⓜ Santa Coloma – ✆ 936 81 40 80 – www.barverat.com – Closed 14-22 April, 3-20 August, Sunday and Monday
Menu 18/30 € – Carte 20/30 €

• Fusion • Neighbourhood •

The "low cost" version of its older sibling, the Lluerna restaurant next door. In its atmosphere of informality and great simplicity, the cooking is based around small dishes and fusion-style raciones, both on its à la carte and its reasonably priced set menus.

Tomas Sereda/iStock

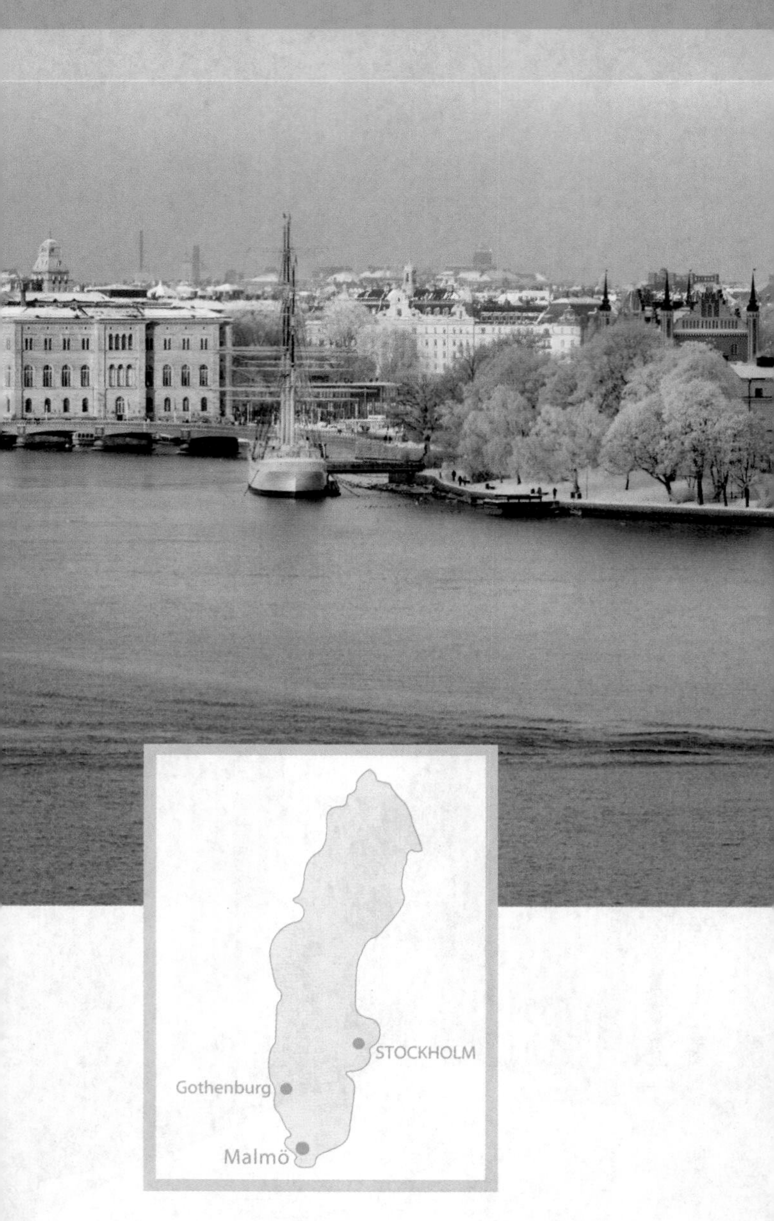
STOCKHOLM
Gothenburg
Malmö

SWEDEN
SVERIGE

mikdam/iStock

STOCKHOLM
STOCKHOLM

adisa/iStock

STOCKHOLM IN...

→ **ONE DAY**
Gamla Stan, City Hall, Vasa or Skansen museums, an evening in Södermalm.

→ **TWO DAYS**
Coffee in Kungsholmen, museums in Skeppsholmen, a stroll around Djurgården.

→ **THREE DAYS**
Shopping in Norrmalm, boat trip round the archipelago.

Stockholm is the place to go for clean air, big skies and handsome architecture. And water. One of the great beauties of the city is the amount of water that runs through and around it; it's built on 14 islands, and looks out on 24,000 of them. An astounding two-thirds of the area within the city limits is made up of water, parks and woodland, and there are dozens of little bridges to cross to get from one part of town to another. It's little wonder Swedes appear so calm and relaxed.

It's in Stockholm that the salty waters of the Baltic meet head-on the fresh waters of Lake Mälaren, reflecting the broad boulevards

and elegant buildings that shimmer along their edge. Domes, spires and turrets dot a skyline that in the summertime never truly darkens. The heart of the city is the Old Town, Gamla Stan, full of alleyways and lanes little changed from their medieval origins. Just to the north is the modern centre, Norrmalm: a buzzing quarter of shopping malls, restaurants and bars. East of Gamla Stan you reach the small island of Skeppsholmen, which boasts fine views of the waterfront; directly north from here is Östermalm, an area full of grand residences, while southeast you'll find the lovely park island of Djurgården. South and west of Gamla Stan are the two areas where Stockholmers particularly like to hang out, the trendy (and hilly) Södermalm, and Kungsholmen.

EATING OUT

Everyone thinks that eating out in Stockholm is invariably expensive, but with a little forward planning it doesn't have to be. In the middle of the day, most restaurants and cafés offer very good value set menus. Keep in mind that, unlike in Southern Europe, the Swedes like to eat quite early, so lunch can often begin at around 11am and dinner may start from 6pm. Picking wild food is a birthright of Swedes, and there's no law to stop you going into forest or field to pick blueberries, cloudberries, cranberries, strawberries, mushrooms and the like. This love of outdoor, natural fare means that Stockholmers have a special bond with menus which relate to the seasons: keep your eyes open for restaurants that feature husmanskost (traditional Swedish dishes), along with huge buffet-style smörgåsbords. These days, however, you might find that your classic meatball, dumpling, herring or gravlax dish comes with a modern twist.

✿✿✿ **Frantzén** (Björn Frantzén) XXX

Klara Norra Kyrkogata 26 ✉ 111 22 – Ⓜ T-Centralen – ✆ (08) 20 85 80 – www.restaurantfrantzen.com – Closed 16 June-18 July, 23 December-10 January and Sunday-Tuesday Plan: **B2**

Menu 3200 SEK – *(booking essential) (tasting menu only)*

• Modern cuisine • Design • Fashionable •

A unique restaurant set over 3 floors of a 19C property; ring the doorbell, enjoy an aperitif in the living room and have the day's luxurious ingredients explained. A beautiful wood counter borders the sleek kitchen and the chefs present, finish and explain the flavour-packed dishes personally. Cooking is modern and creative but also uses classic techniques.

➜ Langoustine with Koshihikari rice, onions and ginger butter emulsion. Guinea fowl with blond miso, vin jaune, walnuts and smoked morels. Tea, milk and honey.

✿✿ **Gastrologik** (Jacob Holmström and Anton Bjuhr) XX

Artillerigatan 14 ✉ 114 51 – Ⓜ Östermalmstorg – ✆ (08) 662 3060 – www.gastrologik.se – Closed Christmas-New Year, midsummer, Sunday and Monday Plan: **C2**

Menu 1595 SEK – *(dinner only) (booking essential) (surprise menu only)*

• Creative • Minimalist • Design •

Everything starts with the ingredients for the two chef-owners; they met as apprentices – one is from the north, the other the south – so both bring something different. The day's produce decides the Surprise menu – 20 or so beautiful dishes that are creative in their contrasts of flavour and texture.

➜ Shrimps with horseradish, dill and shrimp pancake. Quail with peas, hay broth and quail fat. Yoghurt curd, frozen gooseberries and lilac infusion.

✿ **Operakällaren** XXXXX

Operahuset, Karl XII's Torg ✉ 111 86 – Ⓜ Kungsträdgården – ✆ (08) 676 58 01 – www.operakallaren.se – Closed 1 December-15 January, July, midsummer, Sunday and Monday Plan: **C2**

Menu 1050/1550 SEK – *(dinner only)*

• Classic cuisine • Luxury • Historic •

Sweden's most opulent restaurant sits within the historic Opera House, and the stunning, high-ceilinged room boasts original gilt panelling decorated with frescoes and carvings. Carefully constructed dishes are underpinned by classic techniques. The wine list boasts extensive vintages of the world's great wines.

➜ Tartare of beef with beetroot and quail's egg. Saddle of roe deer with cabbage, game jus and cranberries. Prunes flambé in rum.

✿ **Ekstedt** (Niklas Ekstedt) X

Humlegårdsgatan 17 ✉ 11446 – Ⓜ Östermalmstorg – ✆ (08) 611 1210 – www.ekstedt.nu – Closed Christmas, New Year, midsummer, Sunday and Monday Plan: **C1**

Menu 890/1250 SEK – *(dinner only) (booking essential) (tasting menu only)*

• Meats and grills • Design • Friendly •

An unassuming façade hides a very relaxed, friendly, yet professionally run brasserie, where ingredients are cooked in a wood-burning oven, over a fire-pit or smoked through a chimney using birch wood. Dishes are inventive but well-balanced – they are given their finishing touches at the stone bar.

➜ Dried deer, leek, bleak roe and charcoal cream. Wild duck roasted over birch with forest mushrooms, capers and lovage. Wood oven-baked almond cake, blueberries and apple.

Mathias Dahlgren-Matbaren – Grand Hotel

Plan: **C2**

Södra Blasieholmshamnen 6 ✉ 103 27
– Ⓜ Kungsträdgården
– ✆ (08) 679 35 84 – www.mdghs.com
– Closed 12 July-5 August, 22 December-6 January, Saturday lunch, bank holiday lunch and Sunday
Carte 465/1275 SEK

• Modern cuisine • Fashionable • Design •

This popular hotel restaurant is both fun and charmingly run. The open kitchen specialises in flavoursome, well-balanced dishes from an appealing menu divided into the headings 'From our country', 'From other countries' and 'From the plant world'. They keep some seats at the counter for those who haven't booked.

→ Langoustine from Bohuslän. Roe deer and wild mushrooms. Baked white chocolate, toffee, sour cream and nuts.

Agrikultur (Filip Fastén)

Roslagsgatan 43 (Northwest : 2.5 km. by Birger Jarlsgatan) ✉ 113 54
– ✆ (08) 15 02 02 – www.agrikultur.se
– Closed 1 June-16 August, Christmas, Easter and Sunday-Monday
Menu 945 SEK – *(dinner only) (booking essential) (tasting menu only)*

• Modern cuisine • Cosy • Neighbourhood •

A lovely little restaurant with a certain homespun charm. The passionate young team deliver a multi-course menu which follows a local, seasonal and sustainable ethos. Creative cooking sees modernised Swedish classics prepared using some more traditional methods, and the Aga and wood-burning oven play a key part.

→ Jerusalem artichoke, green pepper and sesame seeds. Cabbage, whey, mushroom and red deer. Cherries, long pepper and lemon thyme.

Sushi Sho (Carl Ishizaki)

Plan: **A1**

Upplandsgatan 45 ✉ 113 28 – Ⓜ Odenplan
– ✆ (08) 30 30 30 – www.sushisho.se
– Closed July, Christmas, New Year, midsummer, Sunday and Monday
Menu 685 SEK – *(dinner only and Saturday lunch) (booking essential) (surprise menu only)*

• Japanese • Neighbourhood • Friendly •

With its white tiled walls and compact counter seating, the room couldn't be simpler; the food, by contrast, is sublime. Meals are served omakase-style, with the chef deciding what's best each day and dishes arriving as they're ready. Top quality seafood from local waters features alongside some great egg recipes.

→ Mackerel saba-bosushi with white kombu and sesame. Soy-cured egg yolk with char, okra and roasted rice.

Volt (Peter Andersson and Fredrik Johnsson)

Plan: **C1**

Kommendörsgatan 16 ✉ 114 48 – Ⓜ Stadion
– ✆ (08) 662 34 00 – www.restaurangvolt.se
– Closed 15 July-11 August, Christmas, New Year and Sunday-Monday
Menu 750/950 SEK – *(dinner only and Saturday lunch) (booking essential)*

• Creative • Intimate • Neighbourhood •

An intimate, welcoming restaurant run by a young but experienced team. Cooking is natural in style, with the largely organic produce yielding clear, bold flavours – natural wines also feature. Ingredients are arranged in layers, so that each forkful contains a little of everything; choose 4 or 6 courses.

→ Lettuce, chicken and beach rose. Lamb, onion and sourdough. Plum with fennel and cream.

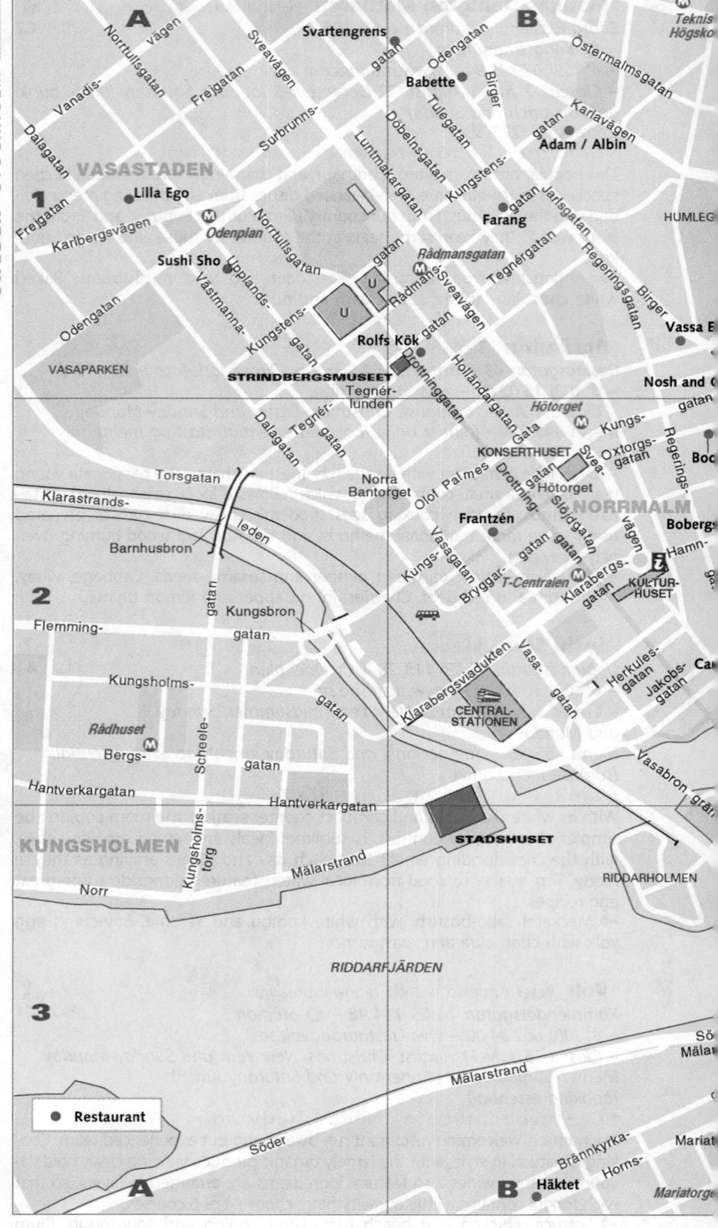

A
B
1
2
3
VASASTADEN
NORRMALM
KUNGSHOLMEN
RIDDARHOLMEN
RIDDARFJÄRDEN
VASAPARKEN
HUMLEG
Svartengrens
Babette
Adam / Albin
Lilla Ego
Farang
Sushi Sho
Rolfs Kök
Vassa E
Nosh and C
Boc
Bobergs
Frantzén
Ca
Häktet
STRINDBERGSMUSEET
KONSERTHUSET
KULTURHUSET
CENTRALSTATIONEN
STADSHUSET
Odenplan
Rådmansgatan
Hötorget
T-Centralen
Rådhuset
Tekniska Högsko
Mariatorget
Tegnérlunden
Norra Bantorget
Barnhusbron
Kungsbron
Vasabron
Restaurant

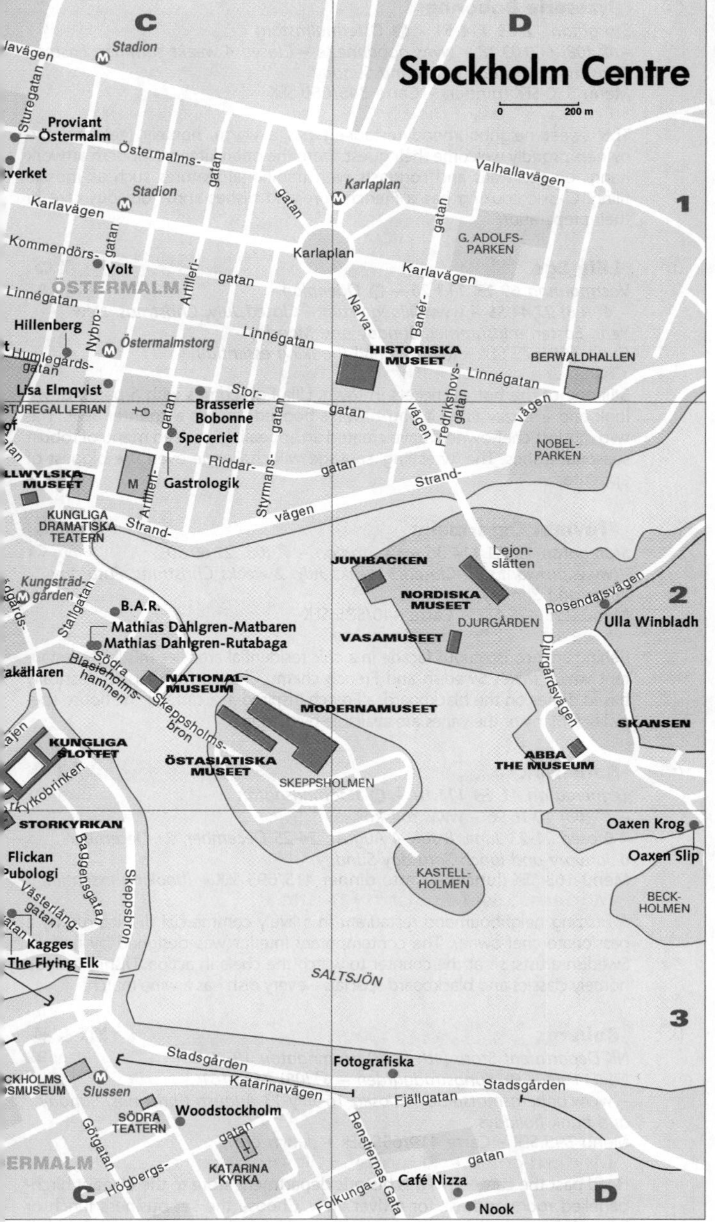
Stockholm Centre
0
200 m
C
D
1
2
3
Stadion
Proviant Östermalm
Östermalms-gatan
Valhallavägen
Karlaplan
Karlavägen
Kommendörs-gatan
Volt
ÖSTERMALM
Linnégatan
Artilleri-gatan
G. ADOLFS-PARKEN
Narva-vägen
Banér-gatan
Hillenberg
Nybro-gatan
Östermalmstorg
Humlegårds-gatan
HISTORISKA MUSEET
BERWALDHALLEN
Lisa Elmqvist
Stor-gatan
Fredrikshovs-gatan
STUREGALLERIAN
Brasserie Bobonne
Speceriet
Gastrologik
Riddar-gatan
Styrmans-gatan
NOBEL-PARKEN
Strand-vägen
M
KUNGLIGA DRAMATISKA TEATERN
Lejon-slätten
JUNIBACKEN
NORDISKA MUSEET
Rosendalsvägen
Kungsträdgården
B.A.R.
Stallgatan
Mathias Dahlgren-Matbaren
Mathias Dahlgren-Rutabaga
DJURGÅRDEN
Ulla Winbladh
VASAMUSEET
Djurgårdsvägen
Södra Blasieholms-hamnen
NATIONAL-MUSEUM
Skeppsholms-bron
MODERNAMUSEET
SKANSEN
KUNGLIGA SLOTTET
ÖSTASIATISKA MUSEET
ABBA THE MUSEUM
Kyrkobrinken
SKEPPSHOLMEN
STORKYRKAN
Oaxen Krog
Oaxen Slip
Flickan
Baggensgatan
Skeppsbron
KASTELL-HOLMEN
BECK-HOLMEN
Västerlång-gatan
Kagges
The Flying Elk
SALTSJÖN
Stadsgården
Fotografiska
Katarinavägen
Fjällgatan
Slussen
SÖDRA TEATERN
Woodstockholm
Renstiernas Gata
Götgatan
KATARINA KYRKA
Högbergs-gatan
Café Nizza
Folkunga-gatan
Nook

Brasserie Bobonne

Storgatan 12 ✉ 114 51 – Ⓜ Östermalmstorg Plan: **C1**
– ✆ (08) 660 03 18 – www.bobonne.se – Closed 4 weeks summer, Easter, Christmas, Saturday lunch and Sunday
Menu 550 SEK (dinner) – Carte 345/650 SEK
• French • Cosy • Bistro •

This sweet neighbourhood restaurant has a warm, homely feel, and the owners proudly welcome their guests from the open kitchen. Modern artwork hangs on the walls and contrasts with traditional features such as mosaic tiling. Classic cooking has a French core and dishes show obvious care in their preparation.

Lilla Ego

Västmannag 69 ✉ 113 26 – Ⓜ Odenplan Plan: **A1**
– ✆ (08) 27 44 55 – www.lillaego.com – Closed July, Christmas, New Year, Easter, midsummer, Sunday and Monday
Carte 465/675 SEK – *(dinner only) (booking essential)*
• Modern cuisine • Bistro • Friendly •

Still one of the hottest tickets in town, Lilla Ego comes with a pared-down look and a buzzy vibe; if you haven't booked, try for a counter seat. The two modest chef-owners have created an appealingly priced menu of robust seasonal dishes. The 'wrestling' sausage will challenge even the biggest of appetites.

Proviant Östermalm

Sturegatan 19 ✉ 114 36 – Ⓜ Stadion – ✆ (08) 22 60 50 Plan: **C1**
– www.proviant.se – Closed 3 weeks July, 2 weeks Christmas, Saturday lunch and Sunday
Menu 295/425 SEK – Carte 440/585 SEK
• Swedish • Bistro • Intimate •

Behind an inconspicuous façade in a chic residential area lies this lively restaurant which mixes Swedish and French charm. Choose from rustic, classically based dishes on the blackboard, a French-inspired à la carte or the house specialities. Many of the wines are available by the glass.

Rolfs Kök

Tegnérgatan 41 ✉ 111 61 – Ⓜ Rådmansgatan Plan: **B1**
– ✆ (08) 10 16 96 – www.rolfskok.se
– Closed 21-23 June, 8 July-4 August, 24-25 December, 31 December-6 January and lunch Saturday-Sunday
Menu 165 SEK (lunch) – Carte dinner 415/695 SEK – *(booking essential)*
• Modern cuisine • Bistro • Rustic •

A buzzing neighbourhood restaurant in a lively commercial district, run by a passionate chef-owner. The contemporary interior was designed by famous Swedish artists; sit at the counter to watch the chefs in action. Dishes include homely classics and blackboard specials – every dish has a wine match.

Bobergs

NK Department Store (4th floor), Hamngatan 18-20 Plan: **B2**
✉ 111 47 – Ⓜ Kungsträdgården – ✆ (08) 762 8161
– www.bobergsmatsal.se – Closed 16 July-13 August, Christmas, Sunday and bank holidays
Menu 395 SEK – Carte 419/655 SEK – *(lunch only)*
• Modern cuisine • Elegant • Classic décor •

Head past the canteen in this historic department store to the elegant birch-panelled room and ask for a river view. Choose the set business lunch or from the seasonal à la carte; classic cooking mixes French and Swedish influences.

Hillenberg

XX

Humlegårdsgatan 14 ✉ 114 34 – Ⓜ Östermalmstorg Plan: **C1**
– ✆ (08) 519 421 53 – www.hillenberg.se – Closed 24 December, 1 January, Sunday and lunch mid July-mid August
Carte 425/840 SEK – *(booking essential at lunch)*
• Modern cuisine • Design • Brasserie •

Perfectly pitched for busy Humlegårdsgatan is this stylish take on a classic brasserie. It has a smart, elegant feel and a hugely impressive wine cellar. Appealing Swedish classics are immensely satisfying yet exhibit a subtle modern touch and sense of finesse.

AG

XX

Kronobergsgatan 37 (2nd Floor), Kungsholmen (via Flemminggatan A2) ✉ 112 33 – Ⓜ Fridshemsplan – ✆ (08) 410 681 00 – www.restaurangag.se – Closed 6 July-5 August, 24-25 December, 30 December-6 January and Sunday
Carte 345/935 SEK – *(dinner only)*
• Meats and grills • Rustic • Fashionable •

An industrial, New York style eatery on the 2nd floor of an old silver factory. Swedish, American and Scottish beef is displayed in huge cabinets and you choose your accompaniments. Expect a great wine list and smooth service.

Farang

XX

Tulegatan 7 ✉ 113 53 – Ⓜ Rådmansgatan Plan: **B1**
– ✆ (08) 673 74 00 – www.farang.se – Closed July and Sunday-Monday
Menu 285/575 SEK (lunch) – Carte dinner 410/640 SEK
• South East Asian • Minimalist • Fashionable •

The unusual front door harks back to its Stockholm Electric Company days, and behind it lies a stylish restaurant and bar – the former sits in the old machine hall. Zingy, aromatic dishes focus on Southeast Asia and are full of colour.

Hantverket

XX

Sturegatan 15 ✉ 114 36 – Ⓜ Stadion Plan: **C1**
– ✆ (08) 121 321 60 – www.restauranghantverket.se – Closed July, Christmas, New Year, Easter, Saturday lunch and Sunday
Menu 295 SEK (weekday lunch) – Carte 295/460 SEK
• Modern cuisine • Rustic • Fashionable •

Exposed ducting contrasts with chunky tables and leafy plants at this buzzy restaurant. It has a cool lounge-bar, counter seats and a mix of raised and regular tables. Cooking has an artisanal Swedish heart and service is bright and breezy.

Nosh and Chow

XX

Norrlandsgatan 24 ✉ 111 43 – Ⓜ Hötorget Plan: **B2**
– ✆ (08) 503 389 60 – www.noshandchow.se – Closed Easter, 24 December, 1 January, midsummer, Saturday lunch and Sunday
Menu 315 SEK (lunch) – Carte 300/725 SEK
• International • Brasserie • Fashionable •

This former bank has been transformed into a glitzy cocktail bar and brasserie which displays a smart mix of New York and New England styling. Filling dishes blend French, American and Swedish influences with other global flavours.

Vassa Eggen – Elite H. Stockholm Plaza

XX

Birger Jarlsgatan 29 ✉ 103 95 – Ⓜ Östermalmstorg Plan: **B1**
– ✆ (08) 21 61 69 – www.vassaeggen.com – Closed midsummer, Christmas, Saturday lunch and Sunday
Menu 550 SEK (lunch) – Carte 445/740 SEK
• Meats and grills • Fashionable • Rustic •

A pleasant bar leads through to a dimly lit hotel dining room where bold artwork hangs on the walls. Hearty Swedish cooking relies on age-old recipes, with a particular focus on meat; whole beasts are butchered and hung on-site.

Adam / Albin

Rådmansgatan 16 ✉ 114 25 – Ⓜ Tekniska Högskolan Plan: **B1**
– ✆ (08) 411 5535 – www.adamalbin.se – Closed Christmas, Sunday, bank holidays and restricted opening in summer
Menu 895/1595 SEK – *(dinner only) (booking essential)*
• Modern cuisine • Intimate • Neighbourhood •

Owners Adam and Albin have stamped their mark on this charming restaurant, which comes with Italian marble clad walls and a mix of individual and communal tables. Snacks are followed by a 5 or 10 course menu, where refined, eye-catching dishes blend the ethos of a Scandic kitchen with Asian flavours.

B.A.R.

Blasieholmsgatan 4a ✉ 111 48 – Ⓜ Kungsträdgården Plan: **C2**
– ✆ (08) 611 53 35 – www.restaurangbar.se – Closed Christmas-New Year, Saturday lunch and Sunday
Carte 345/595 SEK
• Seafood • Brasserie • Fashionable •

This bright, buzzy restaurant is just a cast away from the waterfront and has a semi-industrial fish-market style. Choose your seafood from the fridge or the tank, along with a cooking style, a sauce and one of their interesting sides.

Babette

Roslagsgatan 6 ✉ 113 55 – Ⓜ Tekniska Högskolan Plan: **B1**
– ✆ (08) 5090 2224 – www.babette.se – Closed 23-25 and 31 December, 1 January and 17-24 June
Carte 185/545 SEK – *(dinner only)*
• Modern cuisine • Neighbourhood • Bistro •

You'll feel at home in this modern neighbourhood bistro. Cooking is rustic and unfussy and the daily selection of small plates and pizzas makes dining flexible. They limit their bookings so that they can accommodate walk-ins.

Boqueria

Jakobsbergsgatan 17 ✉ 111 44 – Ⓜ Hötorget Plan: **B2**
– ✆ (08) 307400 – www.boqueria.se – Closed 24-25 December, 1 January and midsummer
Carte 300/450 SEK
• Spanish • Tapas bar • Fashionable •

A vibrant, bustling tapas restaurant with high-level seating, located in a smart mall. Appealing menus offer tapas and a range of authentic dishes for two or more to share. Sangria and pintxos can be enjoyed in their nearby bar.

Carousel

Gustav Adolfs Torg 20 ✉ 111 53 – Ⓜ Kungsträdgården Plan: **B2**
– ✆ (08) 10 27 57 – www.restaurantcarousel.se – Closed Christmas, New Year, midsummer and Sunday
Carte 295/765 SEK
• Swedish • Classic décor • Historic •

Enjoy a drink under the impressive original ceiling in the bar before taking a seat near the carousel or out on the terrace. The experienced chefs carefully prepare flavoursome dishes which follow the seasons and have classic Swedish roots.

Lisa Elmqvist

Humlesgårdsgatan 1 ✉ 114 39 – Ⓜ Östermalmstorg Plan: **C1**
– ✆ (08) 553 40410 – www.lisaelmqvist.se – Closed 24 December, midsummer, Sunday and bank holidays
Carte 503/960 SEK – *(booking essential at lunch)*
• Seafood • Family • Bistro •

While the original 19C market hall is being restored, this established family-run restaurant is operating from the temporary marketplace next door. Top quality seafood from the day's catch features in unfussy, satisfying combinations.

Mathias Dahlgren-Rutabaga – Grand Hotel

Plan: C2

Södra Blasieholmshamnen 6 ✉ 103 27 – Ⓜ Kungsträdgården – ✆ (08) 679 35 84 – www.mdghs.se – Closed 22 December-6 January, 12 July-5 August, Sunday and Monday
Menu 495/795 SEK – *(dinner only) (booking essential) (tasting menu only)*
• Vegetarian • Simple • Fashionable •

A light, bright restaurant offering something one doesn't usually find in grand hotels – vegetarian cuisine. The two set menus come with flavours from across the globe; choose the chef's table for a more personal experience.

Speceriet

Plan: C2

Artillerigatan 14 ✉ 114 51 – Ⓜ Östermalmstorg – ✆ (08) 662 30 60 – www.speceriet.se – Closed Christmas, New Year, midsummer, Saturday lunch, Sunday and lunch mid July-mid September
Carte 370/595 SEK
• Classic cuisine • Simple •

The more casual addendum to the Gastrologik restaurant will get you in the mood for sharing. Sit at communal tables and enjoy the 'dish of the day' at lunchtime or a wider selection of mix and match dishes at dinner.

Sturehof

Plan: C2

Stureplan 2 ✉ 114 46 – Ⓜ Östermalmstorg – ✆ (08) 440 57 30 – www.sturehof.com
Menu 650 SEK – Carte 265/875 SEK
• Seafood • Brasserie • Fashionable •

This bustling city institution dates back over a century and is a wonderful mix of the traditional and the modern. It boasts a buzzing terrace, several marble-topped bars and a superb food court. Classic menus focus on seafood.

Svartengrens

Plan: B1

Tulegatan 24 ✉ 113 53 – Ⓜ Tekniska Högskolan – ✆ (08) 612 65 50 – www.svartengrens.se – Closed Christmas, 31 December and midsummer
Menu 725 SEK – Carte 295/905 SEK – *(dinner only)*
• Meats and grills • Friendly • Neighbourhood •

The eponymous chef-owner has created a modern bistro specialising in sustainable meat and veg from producers in the archipelago. Along with smoking and pickling, the dry-aging is done in-house, and the cuts change daily.

AT GAMLA STAN (OLD STOCKHOLM)

Kagges

Plan: C3

Lilla Nygatan 21 ✉ 111 28 – Ⓜ Gamla Stan – www.kagges.com – Closed first three weeks January, Christmas, midsummer and Monday-Tuesday
Menu 495 SEK – Carte 300/600 SEK – *(dinner only) (booking essential)*
• Swedish • Fashionable • Cosy •

This cosy restaurant with a lively buzz is run by two enthusiastic friends. Ask for a seat at the counter to watch the team prepare constantly evolving seasonal small plates with plenty of colour and a Swedish heart. 4 plates per person is about right – or go for the 4 course Chef's Choice of the Day menu.

Djuret

Plan: C3

Lilla Nygatan 5 ✉ 111 28 – Ⓜ Gamla Stan – ✆ (08) 506 400 84 – www.djuret.se – Closed July, Christmas, New Year, Sunday and Monday
Menu 620 SEK – *(dinner only) (booking essential) (tasting menu only)*
• Meats and grills • Rustic • Neighbourhood •

Various rooms make up this atmospheric restaurant, including one part-built into the city walls and looking into the impressive wine cellar. Monthly set menus are formed around 3 key ingredients, and the masculine cooking has big, bold flavours.

SWEDEN - STOCKHOLM

Pubologi

XX

Stora Nygatan 20 ✉ 111 27 – Ⓜ Gamla Stan Plan: **C3**
– ☎ (08) 506 400 86 – www.pubologi.se – Closed July, Christmas, New Year and Sunday-Tuesday
Menu 325 SEK – *(dinner only) (tasting menu only)*
• Swedish • Cosy • Neighbourhood •

Book a window table at this charming modern bistro for views out over the cobbled street. The 5 course set menu offers refined, rustic dishes; flavours are strong and punchy and seasonality is key. The wine list is impressive.

Flickan

X

Yxsmedsgränd 12 ✉ 111 28 – Ⓜ Gamla Stan Plan: **C3**
– ☎ (08) 506 40080 – www.restaurangflickan.se – Closed July, Christmas, New Year and Sunday-Tuesday
Menu 995 SEK – *(dinner only) (booking essential) (tasting menu only)*
• Modern cuisine • Fashionable • Intimate •

Pass through the busy bar to this small 16-seater restaurant, where you'll be greeted by a welcoming team. The 13 course set menu keeps Swedish produce to the fore, and modern dishes have the occasional Asian or South American twist.

The Flying Elk

X

Mälartorget 15 ✉ 111 27 – Ⓜ Gamla Stan Plan: **C3**
– ☎ (08) 20 85 83 – www.theflyingelk.se – Closed 24 December, 1 January and midsummer
Carte 400/610 SEK – *(dinner only)*
• Modern cuisine • Inn • Friendly •

A good night out is guaranteed at this lively corner spot, which is modelled on a British pub and has several different bars. Choose from bar snacks, pub dishes with a twist or a popular tasting menu of refined modern classics.

AT DJURGÅRDEN

Oaxen Krog (Magnus Ek)

XX

Beckholmsvägen 26 (off Djurgårdsvägen) ✉ 11521 Plan: **D3**
– ☎ (08) 551 531 05 – www.oaxen.com – Closed Christmas, New Year, Easter, midsummer, Sunday and Monday
Menu 2100 SEK – *(dinner only) (booking essential)*
• Creative • Design • Friendly •

A rebuilt boat shed in a delightful waterside location. Diners are led through a door in Oaxen Slip into an oak-furnished room with a slightly nautical feel. Creative, beautifully constructed Nordic dishes are allied to nature and the seasons – they're delicate and balanced but also offer depth of flavour.

➜ Langoustine, fermented pear, gooseberry, horseradish and juniper. Lamb with hogweed and peas. Unripe strawberries with pineapple weed granité and yoghurt.

Ulla Winbladh

XX

Rosendalsvägen 8 ✉ 115 21 – ☎ (08) 534 897 01 Plan: **D2**
– www.ullawinbladh.se – Closed 24-25 December
Carte 315/660 SEK – *(booking essential)*
• Swedish • Classic décor • Cosy •

Ulla Winbladh was originally built as a steam bakery for the 1897 Stockholm World Fair and is set in charming parkland beside the Skansen open-air museum. Sit on the terrace or in the older, more characterful part of the building. Hearty Swedish dishes include sweet and sour herring and fish roe.

Oaxen Slip

Beckholmsvägen 26 (off Djurgårdsvägen) ✉ 115 21 Plan: **D3**
– ✆ (08) 551 53105 – www.oaxen.com – Closed Christmas and New Year
Menu 395 SEK (weekday lunch) – Carte 400/750 SEK

• Traditional cuisine • Bistro •

A bright, bustling bistro next to the old slipway; try for a spot on the delightful terrace. Light floods the room and boats hang from the girders in a nod to the local shipbuilding industry. The food is wholesome and heartening and features plenty of seafood – whole fish dishes are a speciality.

AT SÖDERMALM

Bar Agrikultur

Skånegatan 79 (by Folkungagatan and Nytorgsgatan) ✉ 116 35 – Ⓜ Medborgarplatsen – www.baragrikultur.se – Closed Christmas, Easter and midsummer
Carte 275/435 SEK – *(dinner only)*

• Swedish • Cosy • Neighbourhood •

The trendy Södermalm district is home to this intimate wine bar, whose menu lists fresh tasty small plates which showcase the region's produce. The three stainless steel tanks contain home-distilled gin – flavours are changed regularly using various herbs, oils or fruits. Bookings only taken for early tables.

Nook

Åsögatan 176 ✉ 116 32 – Ⓜ Medborgarplatsen – ✆ (08) 702 1222 – www.nookrestaurang.se – Closed July, Christmas, Sunday and Monday Plan: **D3**
Menu 400 SEK – *(dinner only)*

• Modern cuisine • Intimate • Friendly •

This modern restaurant offers great value. Drop into the bar for Asian-influenced snacks or head to the intimately lit dining room for one of two set menus. Creative cooking blends Swedish ingredients with Korean influences; order 3 days ahead for the suckling pig feast.

Fotografiska

Stadsgårdshamnen 22 ✉ 116 45 – Ⓜ Slussen – ✆ (08) 50 900 500 – www.fotografiska.se – Closed July, 24 December, midsummer, Sunday and Monday Plan: **D3**
Menu 540 SEK – Carte 400/440 SEK – *(dinner only)*

• Country • Rustic • Design •

Take in lovely water views from the photography museum. From the room to the food, there's a green ethos, courtesy of reclaimed wood and ethical produce. Fresh, flavoursome dishes are largely vegetarian; go for 1 cold, 2 warm and 1 sweet.

ICHI

Timmermansgatan 38b (South : 0.25 km from Mariatorget subway station) ✉ 118 55 – Ⓜ Mariatorget – ✆ (08) 88 91 30 – www.ichisthlm.se – Closed Christmas-New Year, Easter, 4 weeks in summer and Sunday-Tuesday
Menu 670 SEK – *(dinner only) (tasting menu only)*

• Creative • Intimate • Trendy •

The chef-owner of this intimate little restaurant takes the best Swedish ingredients and showcases them in creative modern dishes which are underpinned by Japanese techniques. Sit at the counter or in front of the open kitchen to make the most of the experience. A good range of sakes accompanies.

Café Nizza

Åsögatan 171 ✉ 116 32 – Ⓜ Medborgarplatsen Plan: **D3**
– ✆ (08) 640 99 50 – www.cafenizza.se – Closed Christmas and midsummer
Menu 595 SEK – Carte 475/605 SEK – *(dinner only and Sunday lunch) (booking essential)*

• Swedish • Bistro • Neighbourhood •

Drop in for a drink and some bar snacks or a 4 course set menu of unfussy, flavoursome dishes with a mix of Swedish and French influences. The small room has chequerboard flooring, a granite-topped bar and a bustling Parisian feel.

Häktet

Hornsgatan 82 ✉ 118 21 – Ⓜ Zinkensdamn Plan: **B3**
– ✆ (08) 84 59 10 – www.haktet.se – Closed 24 and 31 December, 1 January, midsummer Saturday lunch and Sunday
Carte 395/600 SEK

• Modern cuisine • Bistro • Simple •

From 1781-1872 this was a debtors' prison. It has a characterful courtyard terrace and three bars – one in the style of a speakeasy, with a secret door. The simple bistro at the back serves classic Swedish dishes with a modern edge.

Woodstockholm

Mosebacke Torg 9 ✉ 116 46 – Ⓜ Slussen Plan: **C3**
– ✆ (08) 36 93 99 – www.woodstockholm.com – Closed Christmas, Sunday and Monday
Menu 565 SEK – Carte 395/610 SEK – *(dinner only)*

• Modern cuisine • Bistro • Neighbourhood •

A chef-turned-furniture-maker owns this neighbourhood restaurant overlooking the park. Cooking follows a theme which changes every 2 months and dishes are simple yet full of flavour. In summer, the private room opens as a wine bar.

ENVIRONS OF STOCKHOLM

AT ÄLVSJÖ Southwest : 11 km by Hornsgaten and E20/E4

Aloë (Niclas Jönsson and Daniel Höglander)

Svartlösavägen 52 ✉ 125 33 – ✆ (08) 556 361 68 – www.aloerestaurant.se – Closed 22 December-March and Sunday-Tuesday
Menu 1600 SEK – *(dinner only) (booking essential) (surprise menu only)*

• Creative • Rustic • Intimate •

Unusually hidden in an old suburban supermarket, this warm, welcoming restaurant is run by two talented chefs. Snacks at the kitchen counter are followed by a locally-influenced surprise menu with a seafood bias. Creative dishes stimulate the senses with their intense flavours and original combinations.
➜ Squid, shimeji and dashi. Autumn lamb with figs and ras el hanout. White peach, goat's milk and black sesame.

AT LILLA ESSINGEN West : 5.5 km by Norr Mälarstrand

Lux Dag för Dag

Primusgatan 116 ✉ 112 67 – ✆ (08) 619 01 90 – www.luxdagfordag.se – Closed 4 weeks July-August, 2 weeks Christmas-New Year, Sunday and Monday
Menu 650 SEK (dinner) – Carte 300/725 SEK

• Modern cuisine • Brasserie • Neighbourhood •

A bright, modern, brasserie-style restaurant in an old waterside Electrolux factory dating back to 1916. Generously proportioned dishes might look modern but they have a traditional base; sourcing Swedish ingredients is paramount.

AT BOCKHOLMEN ISLAND Northwest : 7 km by Sveavägen and E18

Bockholmen

Bockholmsvägen ✉ 170 78 – Ⓜ Bergshamra – ✆ (08) 624 22 00 – www.bockholmen.com – Closed 22 December-10 January, midsummer, lunch October-April and Monday
Carte 425/625 SEK – *(booking essential)*
• Swedish • Traditional décor • Country house •
With charming terraces leading down to the water, and an outside bar, this 19C summer house is the perfect place to relax on a summer's day. It's set on a tiny island, so opening times vary. Wide-ranging menus include weekend brunch.

AT EDSVICKEN Northwest : 8 km by Sveavägen and E 18 towards Norrtälje

Ulriksdals Wärdshus

Ulriksdals Slottspark (Northwest: 8 km by Sveavägen and E 18 towards Norrtälje then take first junction for Ulriksdals Slott) ✉ 170 79 – Ⓜ Bergshamra – ✆ (08) 85 08 15 – www.ulriksdalswardshus.se – Closed Monday
Carte 255/540 SEK – *(booking essential)*
• Traditional cuisine • Inn • Romantic •
A charming 19C wood-built inn located on the edge of a woodland; start with drinks on the terrace overlooking the lake. Every table in the New England style room has an outlook over the attractive gardens and there's a characterful wine cellar. Classic Swedish dishes are supplemented by a smörgåsbord at lunch.

GOTHENBURG
GÖTEBORG

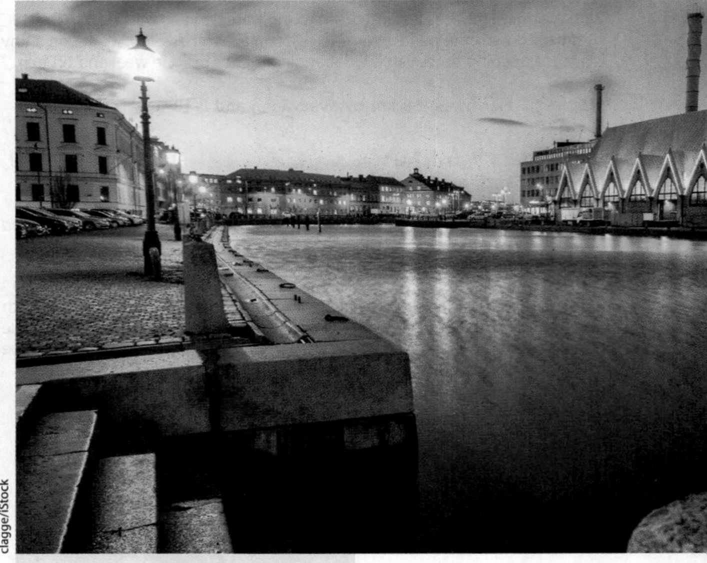

clagge/iStock

GOTHENBURG IN...

- **ONE DAY**
  The Old Town, Stadsmuseum, The Museum of World Culture.
- **TWO DAYS**
  Liseberg amusement park, The Maritiman, Art Museum, a stroll around Linné.
- **THREE DAYS**
  A trip on a Paddan boat, a visit to the Opera House.

Gothenburg is considered to be one of Sweden's friendliest towns, a throwback to its days as a leading trading centre. This is a compact, pretty city whose roots go back four hundred years. It has trams, broad avenues and canals and its centre is boisterous but never feels tourist heavy or overcrowded. Gothenburgers take life at a more leisurely pace than their Stockholm cousins over on the east coast. The mighty shipyards that once dominated the shoreline are now quiet; go to the centre, though, and you find the good-time ambience of Avenyn, a vivacious thoroughfare full of places in which to shop, eat and drink. But for those still itching for a feel of

the heavy industry that once defined the place, there's a Volvo museum sparkling with chrome and shiny steel.

The Old Town is the historic heart of the city: its tight grid of streets has grand façades and a fascinating waterfront. Just west is the Vasastan quarter, full of fine National Romantic buildings. Further west again is Haga, an old working-class district which has been gentrified, its cobbled streets sprawling with trendy cafes and boutiques. Adjacent to Haga is the district of Linné, a vibrant area with its elegantly tall 19th century Dutch-inspired buildings. As this is a maritime town, down along the quayside is as good a place to get your bearings as any.

EATING OUT

Gothenburg's oldest food market is called Feskekörka or 'Fish Church'. It does indeed look like a place of worship but its pews are stalls of oysters, prawns and salmon, and where you might expect to find an organ loft, you'll find a restaurant instead. Food – and in particular the piscine variety – is a big reason for visiting Gothenburg. Its restaurants have earned a plethora of Michelin stars, which are dotted all over the compact city. If you're after something a little simpler, head for one of the typical Swedish Konditoris (cafés) – two of the best are Brogyllen and Ahlströms. If you're visiting between December and April, try the traditional cardamom-spiced buns known as 'semla'. The 19C covered food markets, Stora Saluhallen at Kungstorget and Saluhallen Briggen at Nordhemsgatan in Linnestaden, are worth a visit. Also in Kungstorget is the city's most traditional beer hall, Ölhallen 7:an; there are only 6 others in town. Gothenburgers also like the traditional food pairing 'SOS', where herring and cheese are washed down with schnapps.

Upper House – Upper House Hotel

Gothia Towers (25th Floor), Mässans gata 24 ✉ 402 26 – ✆ (031) 708 82 00 – www.upperhouse.se – Closed 10 July-7 August, 24 December, 1 January, Sunday and Monday

Plan: **D3**

Menu 1400 SEK – *(dinner only) (booking essential) (surprise menu only)*

• Creative • Elegant • Chic •

A small but very comfortable restaurant with just 6 tables and superb views from its perch on the 25th floor. The single Surprise Menu is made up of numerous elaborate, creative and visually appealing dishes that offer complex layers of flavour. The chefs deliver and explain the dishes themselves.

→ Old potatoes and truffle. Plaice, ramson and sturgeon caviar. Selles-sur-Cher cheese and French toast.

Thörnströms Kök (Håkan Thörnström)

Teknologgatan 3 ✉ 411 32 – ✆ (031) 16 20 66 – www.thornstromskok.com – Closed 6 July-14 August, 22 December-3 January, Easter and Sunday

Plan: **C3**

Menu 675 SEK – Carte 755/905 SEK – *(dinner only) (booking essential)*

• Classic cuisine • Neighbourhood • Romantic •

An elegant, long-standing restaurant with a stunning wine cave; set in a quiet residential area and run by a welcoming, knowledgeable team. There's a good choice of menus, including 4 different tasting options. Precise, confident, classically based cooking uses top quality produce to create pronounced flavours.

→ Rabbit with roasted cheese, black truffle and Puy lentils. Turbot with grilled butter sauce and horseradish. Rhubarb and fennel with flaxseed, vanilla and caramel.

28+

Götabergsgatan 28 ✉ 411 34 – ✆ (031) 20 21 61 – www.28plus.se – Closed 1 July-21 August, Christmas, Sunday and Monday

Plan: **C3**

Menu 895 SEK – Carte 655/705 SEK – *(dinner only)*

• Modern cuisine • Romantic • Intimate •

This passionately run basement restaurant has been a Gothenburg institution for over 30 years. Modern cooking showcases prime seasonal ingredients, skilfully blending French and Swedish influences to create intricate, flavourful dishes. There's an exceptional cheese selection and an outstanding wine list.

→ Calves' sweetbreads and Jerusalem artichokes. Mirin-glazed haddock with white asparagus. Gateau Marcel with cottage cheese.

SK Mat & Människor (Stefan Karlsson)

Johannebergsgatan 24 ✉ 412 55 – ✆ (031) 812 580 – www.skmat.se – Closed 4 weeks summer, 2 weeks Christmas, Sunday and bank holidays

Plan: **C3**

Menu 650 SEK – Carte 560/605 SEK – *(dinner only) (booking essential)*

• Modern cuisine • Design • Neighbourhood •

The main focal point of this buzzy restaurant is the 360° open kitchen; not only can you watch the chefs at work but they also deliver your food. The effort put into sourcing and the reverence with which ingredients are treated is commendable and dishes are exciting and packed with flavour.

→ Cured cod with smoked mayonnaise and dried cod roe. Duck with glazed cherries and tarragon. Blueberries, grain-infused cream and crispy buckwheat.

Koka

Viktoriagatan 12 ✉ 411 25 – ✆ (031) 701 79 79 Plan: **B3**
– www.restaurangkoka.se – Closed 8 July-16 August, Christmas, Midsummer and Sunday-Tuesday
Menu 545/945 SEK – Carte 625/715 SEK – *(dinner only)*

• Modern cuisine • Design • Neighbourhood •

An understatedly elegant room with wooden planks on the floors and walls – and wooden furniture to match. Choose 3, 5 or 7 courses from the set daily menu; dishes are light and refreshingly playful in their approach and fish features highly. Well-chosen wines and smooth service complete the picture.

➜ Crab with yellow beetroot and quince. Duck breast, goats' curd and pickled spruce shoots. Cherries with bitter almond, potato and butterscotch.

Bhoga (Gustav Knutsson)

Norra Hamngatan 10 ✉ 411 14 – ✆ (031) 13 80 18 Plan: **B2**
– www.bhoga.se – Closed 4-21 August, 22 December-3 January, Sunday and Monday
Menu 600/900 SEK – *(dinner only) (tasting menu only)*

• Creative • Design • Fashionable •

A chic, contemporary restaurant with an elegant feel; passionately run by two well-travelled friends and their charmingly attentive team. Top quality seasonal ingredients are used in imaginative ways, creating provocative yet harmonious texture and flavour combinations. Wine pairings are original.

➜ Marinated scallops with kelp, apple and gooseberries. Lamb, ramson, leek and brown butter. Cherries with salted meringue, cream and woodruff.

Familjen

Arkivgatan 7 ✉ 411 34 – ✆ (031) 20 79 79 Plan: **C3**
– www.restaurangfamiljen.se – Closed 24-25 December, midsummer and Sunday
Menu 395/495 SEK – Carte 395/545 SEK – *(dinner only) (booking essential)*

• Scandinavian • Design • Neighbourhood •

A lively, friendly eatery divided into three parts: a bar with bench seating and an open kitchen; a bright red room with a characterful cellar and a glass wine cave; and a superb wrap-around terrace. Cooking is good value and portions are generous. There's an appealing wine, beer and cocktail list too.

Project

Södra vägen 45 ✉ 412 54 – ✆ (031) 18 18 58 Plan: **C3**
– www.projectgbg.com – Closed Christmas and Sunday-Tuesday
Menu 400 SEK – Carte 445/565 SEK – *(dinner only) (booking essential)*

• Modern cuisine • Neighbourhood • Fashionable •

A young couple and their charming service team run this cosy little bistro just outside the city centre. The modern, creative, full-flavoured dishes are Swedish at heart with some global influences; the delicious bread takes 5 days to make and the homemade butter takes 2 days.

Somm

Lorensbergsgatan 8 ✉ 411 36 – ✆ (031) 28 28 40 Plan: **C3**
– www.somm.se – Closed July, Christmas, midsummer and Sunday
Menu 395 SEK – Carte 550/645 SEK – *(dinner only)*

• Modern cuisine • Rustic • Cosy •

A simply but warmly decorated neighbourhood bistro with contemporary artwork and a cosy, friendly feel. Quality seasonal ingredients are used to create tasty modern dishes, which feature on an à la carte and various tasting menus. The wine list offers great choice and the service is charming and professional.

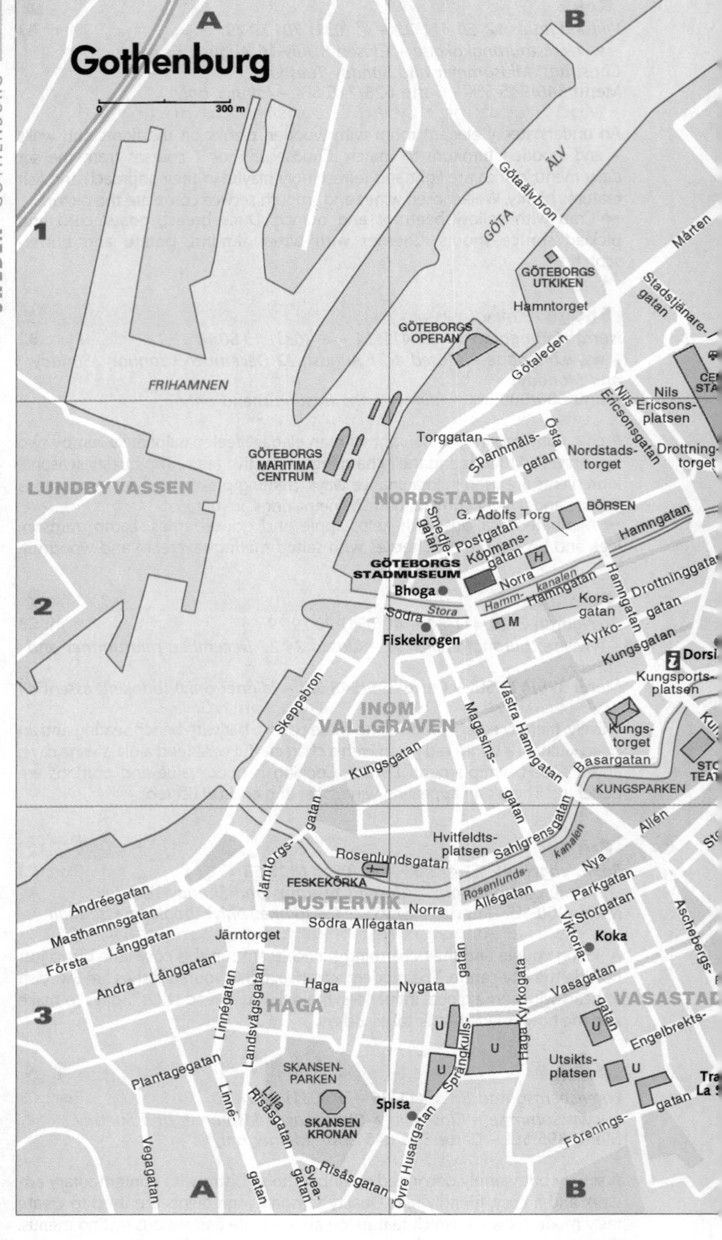

Gothenburg
0
300 m
A
B
1
2
3
GÖTA ÄLV
Götaälvbron
Mårten
Stadstjänare-gatan
GÖTEBORGS UTKIKEN
Hamntorget
GÖTEBORGS OPERAN
Götaleden
FRIHAMNEN
Nils Ericsonsgatan
Nils Ericsons-platsen
Drottning-torget
Torggatan
Spannmåls-gatan
Östa
Nordstads-torget
GÖTEBORGS MARITIMA CENTRUM
LUNDBYVASSEN
NORDSTADEN
BÖRSEN
G. Adolfs Torg
Smedje-gatan
Postgatan
Köpmans-gatan
Hamngatan
GÖTEBORGS STADMUSEUM
Bhoga
Norra Hamngatan
Stora Hamn-kanalen
Södra
Fiskekrogen
M
Kors-gatan
Kyrko-gatan
Drottninggatan
Hamngatan
Kungsgatan
Kungsports-platsen
Skeppsbron
INOM VALLGRAVEN
Magasins-gatan
Västra Hamngatan
Kungs-torget
Basargatan
KUNGSPARKEN
Kungsgatan
Allén
Järntorgs-gatan
Hvitfeldts-platsen
Sahlgrensgatan
Rosenlundsgatan
Rosenlunds-kanalen
FESKEKÖRKA
PUSTERVIK
Norra Allégatan
Nya Parkgatan
Storgatan
Södra Allégatan
Andréegatan
Masthamnsgatan
Järntorget
Första Långgatan
Andra Långgatan
Koka
Viktoria-gatan
Aschebergs-
Haga
Nygata
Vasagatan
HAGA
Linnégatan
Landsvägsgatan
U
Sprängkulls-gatan
Haga Kyrkogata
Engelbrekts-gatan
Utsikts-platsen
Plantagegatan
SKANSEN-PARKEN
Spisa
Lilla Risåsgatan
SKANSEN KRONAN
Risåsgatan
Övre Husargatan
Förenings-gatan
Vegagatan
Svea-gatan

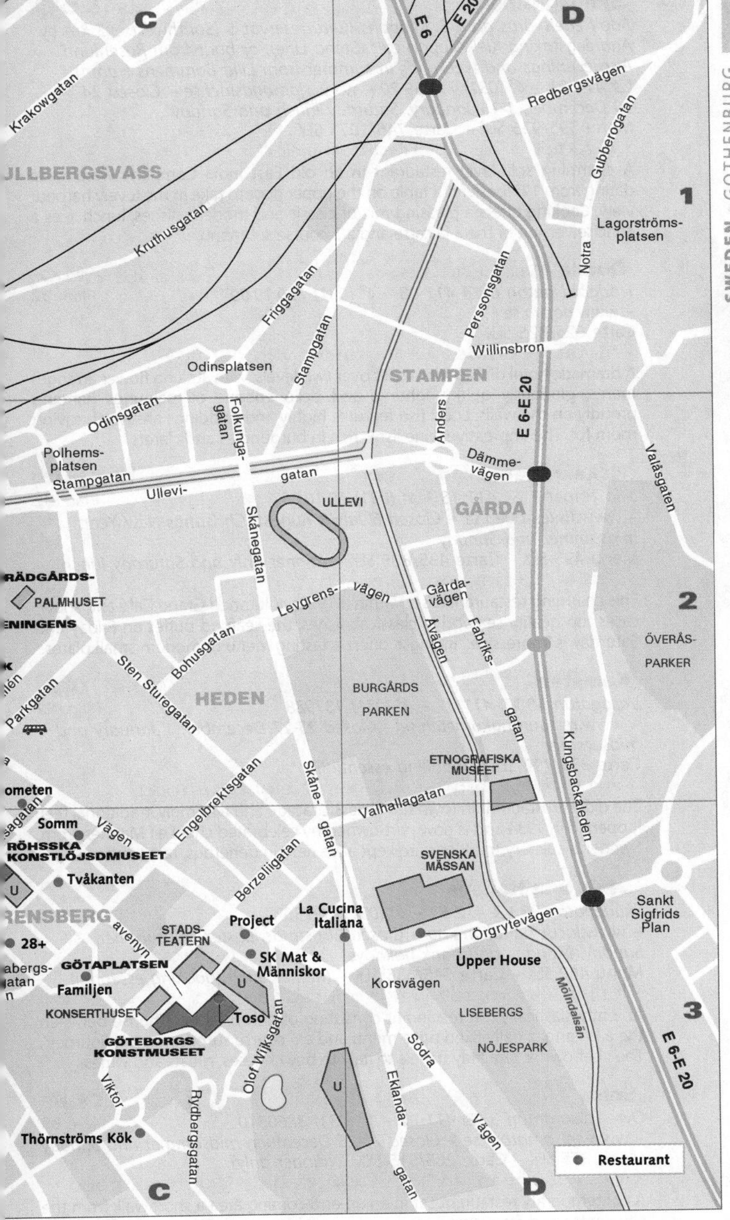
C
D
E 6
E 20
Krakowgatan
Redbergsvägen
Gubberogatan
ULLBERGSVASS
Kruthusgatan
1
Lagorströms-
platsen
Notra
Perssonsgatan
Friggagatan
Stampgatan
Willinsbron
Odinsplatsen
STAMPEN
E 6-E 20
Odinsgatan
Folkunga-
gatan
Anders
Polhems-
platsen
Stampgatan
Dämme-
vägen
Ullevi-
gatan
ULLEVI
GÅRDA
Valåsgatan
Skånegatan
RÄDGÅRDS-
PALMHUSET
Levgrens-
vägen
Gårda-
vägen
2
ENINGENS
Bohusgatan
Åvägen
Fabriks-
gatan
ÖVERÅS-
PARKER
Sten Sturegatan
Parkgatan
HEDEN
BURGÅRDS
PARKEN
ETNOGRAFISKA
MUSEET
Kungsbackaleden
Engelbrektsgatan
Skåne-
gatan
ometen
Valhallagatan
Somm
Vägen
RÖHSSKA
KONSTLÖJSDMUSEET
Berzeliigatan
SVENSKA
MÄSSAN
Tvåkanten
U
La Cucina
Italiana
RENSBERG
Project
Sankt
Sigfrids
Plan
avenyn
STADS-
TEATERN
Örgrytevägen
28+
SK Mat &
Människor
Upper House
GÖTAPLATSEN
Familjen
Korsvägen
KONSERTHUSET
Toso
LISEBERGS
NÖJESPARK
Mölndalsån
3
E 6-E 20
GÖTEBORGS
KONSTMUSEET
Olof Wijksgatan
Södra
Viktor
Eklanda-
gatan
Vägen
Rydbergsgatan
Thörnströms Kök
Restaurant

Sjömagasinet

Adolf Edelsvärds gata 5, Klippans Kulturreservat 5 (Southwest: 3.5 km by Andréeg taking Kiel-Klippan exit (Stena Line), or boat from Rosenlund. Also evenings and weekends in summer from Lilla Bommens Hamn)
414 51 – (031) 775 59 20 – www.sjomagasinet.se – Closed 24-30 December, 1-15 January, Saturday lunch and Sunday
Menu 595/925 SEK – Carte 745/1075 SEK
• Swedish • Rustic • Traditional décor •

A charming split-level restaurant in an old East India Company warehouse dating from 1775; ask for a table on the upper floor to take in the lovely harbour view. Cooking offers a pleasing mix of classic and modern dishes; lunch sees a concise version of the à la carte and a 3 course set menu.

Dorsia – Dorsia Hotel

Trädgårdsgatan 6 411 08 – (031) 790 10 00 – www.dorsia.se Plan: **B2**
Carte 625/825 SEK
• Modern cuisine • Exotic décor • Romantic •

A dramatic hotel dining room split over two levels, with striking flower arrangements, gloriously quirky lighting, and belle époque oil paintings hanging proudly on the walls. Local fish features highly and puddings are worth saving room for. The impressive wine list is rich in burgundies and clarets.

Fiskekrogen

Lilla Torget 1 411 18 – (031) 10 10 05 – www.fiskekrogen.se – Closed 6 July-8 August, Christmas-New Year, midsummer and Sunday Plan: **B2**
Menu 495 SEK – Carte 435/805 SEK – *(dinner only and Saturday lunch)*
• Seafood • Elegant • Classic décor •

This charming restaurant is set within a 1920s columned Grand Café and showcases top quality seafood in classical dishes; the seafood buffet on Friday and Saturday is impressive. 'Bifångst' offers a tasting menu of modern small plates.

Kometen

Vasagatan 58 411 37 – (031) 137988 – www.restaurangkometen.se – Closed 23-27 December, 1 January and midsummer Plan: **C2**
Carte 335/790 SEK – *(booking essential)*
• Swedish • Traditional décor • Neighbourhood •

The oldest restaurant in town has a classic façade and a homely, traditional feel; it opened in 1934 and is now part-owned by celebrated chef Leif Mannerström. Sweden's culinary traditions are kept alive here in generous, tasty dishes.

La Cucina Italiana

Skånegatan 33 412 52 – (031) 166 307 – www.lacucinaitaliana.nu – Closed Christmas, Easter, midsummer, Sunday, Monday and bank holidays Plan: **C/D3**
Menu 460 SEK – Carte 545/635 SEK – *(dinner only) (booking essential)*
• Italian • Intimate • Neighbourhood •

An enthusiastically run restaurant consisting of only 5 tables. Choose between the à la carte, a daily fixed price menu and a 6 course surprise tasting 'journey'. The chef-owner regularly travels to Italy to buy cheeses, meats and wines.

Spisa

Övre Husargatan 3 411 22 – (031) 3860610 – www.spisamatbar.se – Closed 24-25 December, midsummer and Sunday Plan: **B3**
Menu 375 SEK – Carte 285/515 SEK – *(dinner only)*
• Mediterranean cuisine • Fashionable • Neighbourhood •

A contemporary restaurant set in an up-and-coming area a short walk from the city centre and frequented by a lively, sociable crowd. The menu offers tasty sharing plates with French, Spanish and Italian origins. Try a cocktail too.

Toso

Götaplatsen ✉ 412 56 – ✆ (031) 787 98 00 – www.toso.nu – Closed Christmas
Plan: **C3**
Carte 300/460 SEK – *(dinner only)*
• Asian • Bistro • Exotic décor •
There's something for everyone at this modern Asian restaurant, where terracotta warriors stand guard and loud music pumps through the air. Dishes mix Chinese and Japanese influences; start with some of the tempting small plates.

Trattoria La Strega

Aschebergsgatan 23B ✉ 411 27 – ✆ (031) 18 15 01 – www.trattorialastrega.se – Closed 1 July-8 August, 23 December-6 January and Monday
Plan: **B3**
Menu 480 SEK – Carte 280/430 SEK – *(dinner only) (booking essential)*
• Italian • Friendly • Bistro •
A lively little trattoria in a quiet residential area; run by a charming owner. Sit at a candlelit table to enjoy authentic, boldly flavoured Italian cooking and well-chosen wines. Signature dishes include pasta with King crab ragout.

Tvåkanten

Kungsportsavenyn 27 ✉ 411 36 – ✆ (031) 18 21 15 – www.tvakanten.se – Closed Christmas, Easter, midsummer and bank holidays
Plan: **C3**
Menu 515 SEK (lunch) – Carte 475/750 SEK
• Traditional cuisine • Brasserie • Neighbourhood •
With its welcoming hum and friendly team, it's no wonder this long-standing family-run restaurant is always busy. The dimly-lit, brick-walled dining room is the place to eat. Homely lunches are followed by more ambitious dinners.

vRÅ

Clarion Hotel Post, Drottningtorget 10 ✉ 411 03 – ✆ (031) 61 90 60 – www.restaurangvra.se – Closed mid-July-mid-August, Christmas, Sunday and Monday
Plan: **C2**
Menu 495/1050 SEK – Carte 335/545 SEK – *(dinner only)*
• Japanese • Fashionable • Simple •
A cosy, modern hotel restaurant with an open kitchen; run by an attentive, knowledgeable team. Their tagline is 'Swedish ingredients, Japanese flavours' and the produce is top quality. Menus include a set price four courses, and a 'chef's choice' 7 courses.

MALMÖ
MALMÖ

Allard1/iStock

MALMÖ IN…

→ **ONE DAY**
Lilla Torg and the Form/Design Centre, Western Harbour.

→ **TWO DAYS**
Modern Museum, Contemporary Art Exhibition at the Konsthall.

→ **THREE DAYS**
Skt Petri Church, an evening at the Malmö Opera.

Malmö was founded in the 13C under Danish rule and it wasn't until 1658 that it entered Swedish possession and subsequently established itself as one of the world's biggest shipyards. The building of the 8km long Oresund Bridge in 2000 reconnected the city with Denmark and a year later, the Turning Torso apartment block was built in the old shipyard district, opening up the city to the waterfront. Once an industrial hub, this 'city of knowledge' has impressively green credentials: buses run on natural gas and there are 400km of bike lanes. There's plenty of green space too; you can picnic in Kungsparken or Slottsparken, sit by the lakes in Pildammsparken or pet the farm animals in 'Folkets'.

At the heart of this vibrant city lie three squares: Gustav Adolfs Torg, Stortorget and Lilla Torg, connected by a pedestrianised shopping street. You'll find some of Malmö's oldest buildings in Lilla Torg, along with bustling open-air brasseries; to the west is Scandinavia's oldest surviving Renaissance castle and its beautiful gardens – and beyond that, the 2km Ribersborg Beach with its open-air baths. North is Gamla Väster with its charming houses and galleries, while south is Davidshall, filled with designer boutiques and chic eateries. Further south is Möllevångstorget, home to a throng of reasonably priced Asian and Middle Eastern shops.

EATING OUT

The gloriously fertile region of Skane puts a wealth of top quality produce on Malmö's doorstep. Dishes rich in dairy and meat – perhaps a little meatier than expected given its waterside proximity – are staple fare and wild herbs and foraged ingredients are the order of the day; wild garlic, asparagus, potatoes and rhubarb are all celebrated here. The locals eat early, so don't be surprised if you're one of just a handful of diners at 1pm or 8pm. The popular social phenomenon 'fika' is a tradition observed by most, preferably several times a day, and involves the drinking of coffee accompanied by something sweet; usually cake or cinnamon buns. Hot meals are popular midday – look out for the great value dagens lunch, which often offers the dish of the day plus salad, bread and water for under 100kr – or for lunch on the run, grab a tunnbrödsrull (sausage and mashed potato in a wrap) from a Korv kiosk. Local delicacies include äggakaka (thick pancakes and bacon), wallenbergare (minced veal patties with mashed potato and peas), marinated herring, eel and goose.

✿✿ Vollmers (Mats Vollmer)

XX AC

Tegelgårdsgatan 5 ✉ 21133 – ✆ (040) 57 97 50 – www.vollmers.nu – Closed Christmas, Sunday and Monday Plan: **E2**

Menu 1600 SEK – *(dinner only) (booking essential) (tasting menu only)*

• Creative • Elegant • Intimate •

An intimate restaurant with charming, professional service, set in a pretty 19C townhouse. The talented Mats Vollmer showcases some of the area's finest seasonal ingredients in a set 8 course menu of intricate and elaborate modern dishes, which are innovative, perfectly balanced and full of flavour.

→ Duck, spring onion and havgus cheese. Salsify with buttermilk and cress. Raspberry, cream and violet.

✿ SAV (Sven Jensen and Alexander Fohlin)

XX P

Vindåkravägen 3, Tygelsjö (South 10.5 km by Trelleborgsvägen E22/E6) ✉ 21875 – ✆ (072) 022 85 20 – www.savrestaurang.nu – Closed 24 December-8 January, 17-20 April, 21 June-6 August, Sunday-Tuesday

Menu 625/895 SEK – *(dinner only) (booking essential) (surprise menu only)*

• Creative • Cosy • Rustic •

Flickering candles and crackling fires provide a warm welcome at this charming 19C farmhouse. The two young chefs pick many of the ingredients and explain their surprise menu personally. Dishes belie their apparent simplicity – inspired combinations of tastes, textures and temperatures all play their part.

→ Celery, pine spruce, unripe currants and hazelnut. Beef with yeast, dill and blackcurrant. Wild blueberry with hay and pine syrup.

✿ Bloom in the Park

XX AC

Pildammsvägen 17 (Southwest : 2 km.by Stora Nygatan and Fersens väg) ✉ 214 66 – ✆ (040) 793 63 – www.bloominthepark.se – Closed 24 December, 1 January, Easter, Sunday and bank holidays

Menu 495/695 SEK – *(dinner only) (surprise menu only)*

• Creative • Design • Chic •

A delightful lakeside lodge with a waterside terrace for drinks; run by an ebullient owner. There is no written menu or wine list; instead, the kitchen prepares a balanced set meal of modern dishes with international influences, which are accompanied by thoughtfully paired wines.

→ Cod, wasabi, peas and grapefruit. Variations of lamb with cabbage, truffle and walnuts. Chocolate, Sichuan pepper, passion fruit and white chocolate.

Bastard

X AC

Mäster Johansgatan 11 ✉ 211 21 – ✆ (040) 12 13 18 – www.bastardrestaurant.se – Closed 25 December, Easter, midsummer, Sunday and Monday Plan: **E1**

Menu 395 SEK – Carte 305/510 SEK – *(dinner only)*

• Modern cuisine • Simple • Trendy •

Popular with the locals, this is a bustling venue with an edgy, urban vibe. Style-wise, schoolroom meets old-fashioned butcher's, with vintage wood furniture, tiled walls, moody lighting and an open kitchen. Small plates offer nose-to-tail eating with bold, earthy flavours; start with a 'Bastard Plank' to share.

Namu

X AC

Landbygatan 5 ✉ 21134 – ✆ (040) 12 14 90 – www.namu.nu – Closed Christmas, 31 December-1 January, Sunday and Monday Plan: **E1/2**

Menu 395/595 SEK (dinner) – Carte 375/570 SEK

• Korean • Friendly • Simple •

Colourful, zingy food from a past Swedish MasterChef winner blends authentic Korean flavours with a modern Scandinavian touch. Dishes are satisfying – particularly the fortifying ramen – and desserts are more than an afterthought. Cookbooks line the shelves and friendly service adds to the lively atmosphere.

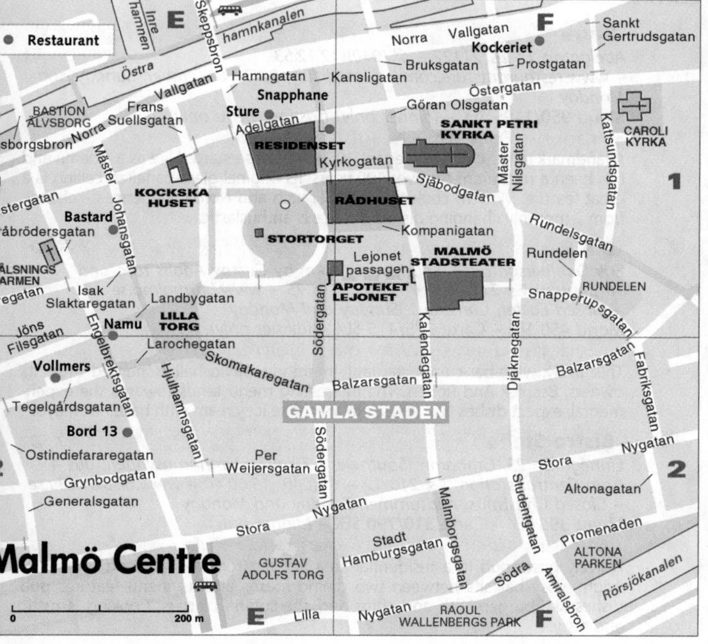

Atmosfär

XX

Fersens väg 4 (Southwest : 1 km. by Regementsgatan) ✉ 211 42 – ✆ (040) 12 50 77 – www.atmosfar.com – Closed Christmas, midsummer, Saturday lunch and Sunday

Menu 330 SEK (dinner) – Carte 350/500 SEK

• Swedish • Neighbourhood •

A formal yet relaxed eatery on the main road; dine at the bar, in the restaurant or on the pavement terrace. The menu consists of small plates, of which three or four should suffice. Fresh Skåne cooking is delivered with a light touch.

Kockeriet

XX

Norra Vallgatan 28 ✉ 211 25 – ✆ (040) 796 06 – www.kockeriet.se – Closed 24-25 and 31 December, 1 January, Easter, midsummer and Sunday

Plan: **F1**

Menu 645/795 SEK – *(dinner only) (tasting menu only)*

• Modern cuisine • Rustic • Intimate •

Well-known TV chef Tariq Taylor uses this characterful timbered 17C grain warehouse to deliver his own brand of modern cuisine, founded on ingredients from his kitchen garden and his worldly travels. Menus take on a tasting format. The beef from the on-view ageing cabinets is particularly good.

Snapphane – Mayfair Hotel Tunneln

XX

Adelgatan 4 ✉ 211 22 – ✆ (040) 15 01 00 – www.snapphane.nu – Closed 22-26 December, 1 January, Easter and Sunday

Plan: **E1**

Menu 595 SEK – Carte 415/615 SEK – *(dinner only) (booking essential)*

• Modern cuisine • Trendy • Intimate •

An elegant, intimate bistro with an open-plan kitchen at its centre. Innovative modern cooking uses top quality ingredients and dishes are well-presented, well-balanced and full of flavour. Service is friendly and professional.

Sture XX

Adelgatan 13 ✉ 21122 – ✆ (040) 12 12 53 Plan: **E1**
– www.restaurantsture.com – Closed July, 22-30 December, Sunday and Monday
Menu 950/1195 SEK – *(dinner only) (tasting menu only)*
• French • Friendly • Neighbourhood •

A landmark in the city, this elegant 19C townhouse started life as a cinema and has been a restaurant for over 100 years. Its original glass-panelled ceiling is a great feature. Modern cooking blends French and Nordic influences – choose from 7 monthly changing dishes. Service is enthusiastic.

B.A.R. X

Erik Dahlbersgatan 3 (Southwest : 1 km by Gustav Adolfs torg and Torggatan) ✉ 211 48 – ✆ (040) 17 01 75 – www.barmalmo.se – Closed Easter, Christmas, Sunday and Monday
Menu 450 SEK – Carte 275/415 SEK – *(dinner only)*
• Modern cuisine • Wine bar • Neighbourhood •

This lively wine-bar-cum-restaurant in trendy Davidshall is named after its owners, Besnick And Robert. The interesting menu tends towards the experimental; expect dishes like Jerusalem artichoke ice cream with hazelnut mayo.

Bistro Stella X

Linnégatan 25, Limhamn (Southwest: 7 km by Limhamnsvägen: bus 4 from Central station) ✉ 216 12 – ✆ (040) 15 60 40 – www.bistrostella.se – Closed Christmas, midsummer, Sunday and Monday
Menu 395 SEK – Carte 310/790 SEK – *(dinner only)*
• Modern cuisine • Neighbourhood • Pub •

A lively gastropub in a residential area not far from the Øresund Bridge. Its bright, cosy bar sits between two dining rooms and its menu features pub dishes like burgers, fish and chips and charcuterie platters. Cooking is rustic and tasty.

Bord 13 X

Engelbrektsg 13 ✉ 211 33 – ✆ (042) 58788 Plan: **E2**
– www.bord13.se – Closed Christmas, Easter, midsummer, Sunday and Monday
Menu 350/650 SEK – *(dinner only) (tasting menu only)*
• Creative • Wine bar • Friendly •

Sister to B.A.R. restaurant, is the bright, spacious and stylish 'Table 13', which offers a set 3 or 6 course menu and a diverse selection of biodynamic wines. Original Nordic cooking has some interesting texture and flavour combinations.

Mrs Brown X

Storgatan 26 (Southwest : 1 km. by Amiralsgatan) ✉ 211 42 – ✆ (040) 97 22 50 – www.mrsbrown.se – Closed Easter, 24 December and Sunday
Carte 380/460 SEK – *(dinner only and Saturday lunch)*
• Traditional cuisine • Wine bar • Trendy •

This retro brasserie's bar opens at 3pm for drinks and nibbles, while the kitchen opens at 6pm. Make sure you try one of the cocktails. Well-presented unfussy cooking has a modern edge and showcases the region's ingredients.

Mutantur X

Erik Dahlbergsgatan 12-14 (Southwest : 1 km. by Gustav Adolfs torg and Torggatan) ✉ 211 42 – ✆ (076) 101 72 05 – www.restaurantmutantur.se – Closed 3 weeks midsummer, 23-26 and 30-31 December, 1-2 January, Saturday and Sunday
Carte 350/550 SEK – *(dinner only) (bookings not accepted)*
• Modern cuisine • Fashionable • Neighbourhood •

Semi-industrial styling means concrete floors, brick-faced walls and exposed ducting; there's also an open kitchen and counter dining. The extensive menu offers snacks and small plates with a Nordic style and some Asian influences; they recommend between 3 and 5 per person.

Zurich
BERN
Geneva

SWITZERLAND

SUISSE, SCHWEIZ, SVIZZERA

AleksandarGeorgiev/iStock

BERN
BERNE

LeeYiuTung/iStock

BERN IN...

→ **ONE DAY**
River walk, Old Town (cathedral, clock tower, arcades), Museum of Fine Arts, cellar fringe theatre.

→ **TWO DAYS**
Zentrum Paul Klee, Einstein's house, Stadttheater.

→ **THREE DAYS**
Bern Museum of History, Swiss Alpine Museum, Rose Garden.

To look at Bern, you'd never believe it to be a capital city. Small and beautifully proportioned, it sits sedately on a spur at a point where the River Aare curves gracefully back on itself. The little city is the best preserved medieval centre north of the Alps – a fact recognised by UNESCO when it awarded Bern World Heritage status – and the layout of the streets has barely changed since the Duke of Zahringen chose the superbly defended site to found the city over 800 years ago. Most of the buildings date from between the 14 and 16C – when Bern was at the height of its power – and the cluster of

cobbled lanes, surrounded by ornate sandstone arcaded buildings and numerous fountains and wells, give it the feel of a delightfully overgrown village. (Albert Einstein felt so secure here that while ostensibly employed as a clerk in the Bern patent office he managed to find the time to work out his Theory of Relativity.)

The Old Town stretches eastwards over a narrow peninsula, and is surrounded by the arcing River Aare. The eastern limit of the Old Town is the Nydeggbrücke bridge, while the western end is marked out by the Käfigturm tower, once a city gate and prison. On the southern side of the Aare lies the small Kirchenfeld quarter, which houses some impressive museums, while the capital's famous brown bears are back over the river via the Nydeggbrücke.

EATING OUT

ern is a great place to sit and enjoy meal. Pride of place must go to the ood range of alfresco venues in the quares of the old town – popular spots o enjoy coffee and cake. Hiding away n the arcades are many delightful din- ng choices; some of the best for loca- ion alone are in vaulted cellars that reathe historic ambience. If you want o feel what a real Swiss restaurant is ke, head for a traditional rustic eatery omplete with cow-bells and sample he local dishes like the Berner Platte – heaving plate of hot and cold meats, served with beans and sauerkraut – or treberwurst, a sausage poached with fermented grape skins. There's no shortage of international restaurants either, and along with Germany, France and Italy also have their country's cuisine well represented here – it's not difficult to go from rösti to risotto. And, of course, there's always cheese – this is the birthplace of raclette - and tempting chocolates waiting in the wings. A fifteen percent service charge is always added but it's customary to round the bill up.

Meridiano – Hotel Allegro

Plan: **B1**

Kornhausstr. 3 ✉ 3000 – ✆ 031 339 52 45 – www.allegro-hotel.ch – Closed Saturday lunch and Sunday-Monday

Menu 88 CHF (lunch)/165 CHF – Carte 101/125 CHF

• Modern cuisine • Trendy •

This elegant restaurant with its wonderful view and stunning terrace is absolutely *the* place to eat in Bern. The food is modern and sophisticated, fully-flavoured and intense, and made with top-quality Swiss ingredients.

➜ Carabinero, Erbse, Lardo vom Wollschwein. Stör, lauwarme Vichyssoise, Brunnenkresse. Joghurt, Kaffirlimette, San Mauro Olivenöl.

Kirchenfeld

Plan: **C2**

Thunstr. 5 ✉ 3005 – ✆ 031 351 02 78 – www.kirchenfeld.ch – Closed Sunday-Monday

Menu 75 CHF (dinner) – Carte 44/91 CHF

• Traditional cuisine • Brasserie •

Eating in this loud and lively restaurant is great fun! Try the flavoursome zander fish served on Mediterranean couscous and one of the sweets, which include lemon tart and chocolate cake, displayed on the dessert trolley. At lunchtimes the restaurant is full of business people who swear by the daily set menu.

milles sens - les goûts du monde

Plan: **A2**

Spitalgasse 38 (Schweizerhofpassage, 1st floor) ✉ 3011 – ✆ 031 329 29 29 – www.millesens.ch – Closed mid July-early August and Saturday-Sunday; September-June: Saturday lunch, Sunday

Menu 69/120 CHF – Carte 65/106 CHF

• International • Fashionable •

If you are looking for a lively, modern restaurant, this minimalist-style establishment is for you. The mouthwatering menu promises Aargau chicken tagine, Gurten highland beef duo, and exotic Thai green vegetable curry. At midday there is also an interesting business lunch menu.

VUE – Hotel Bellevue Palace

Plan: **B2**

Kochergasse 3 ✉ 3011 – ✆ 031 320 45 45 – www.bellevue-palace.ch/vue

Menu 62/68 CHF (weekday lunch) – Carte 66/142 CHF

• Modern cuisine • Classic décor •

Ambitious, contemporary seasonal cuisine with traditional roots is served in this tastefully decorated setting. The terrace affords magnificent views over the Aare.

Casa Novo

Plan: **D1**

Läuferplatz 6 ✉ 3011 – ✆ 031 992 44 44 – www.casa-novo.ch – Closed 23 September-8 October, 23 December-7 January and Saturday lunch, Sunday-Monday

Menu 38 CHF (lunch)/109 CHF – Carte 68/109 CHF

• Mediterranean cuisine • Friendly •

The great location on the River Aare means that the terrace is a real highlight here. The seasonal Mediterranean food on offer includes meagre with crustacean emulsion, beluga lentils and ratatouille as well Swiss classics such as hand-chopped steak tartare. There is also a wine shop and you'll find the Klösterli car park just over the river.

Jack's Brasserie – Hotel Schweizerhof

Plan: **A1**

Bahnhofplatz 11 ✉ 3001 – ✆ 031 326 80 80 – www.schweizerhof-bern.ch

Menu 65 CHF (weekday lunch)/95 CHF – Carte 70/110 CHF

• Classic cuisine • Brasserie •

The restaurant at the Schweizerhof provides an elegant setting, with its decor, pretty alcoves, parquet flooring and stylish lighting. The menu features typical brasserie-style fare, alongside a number of popular classics including the Wiener schnitzel.

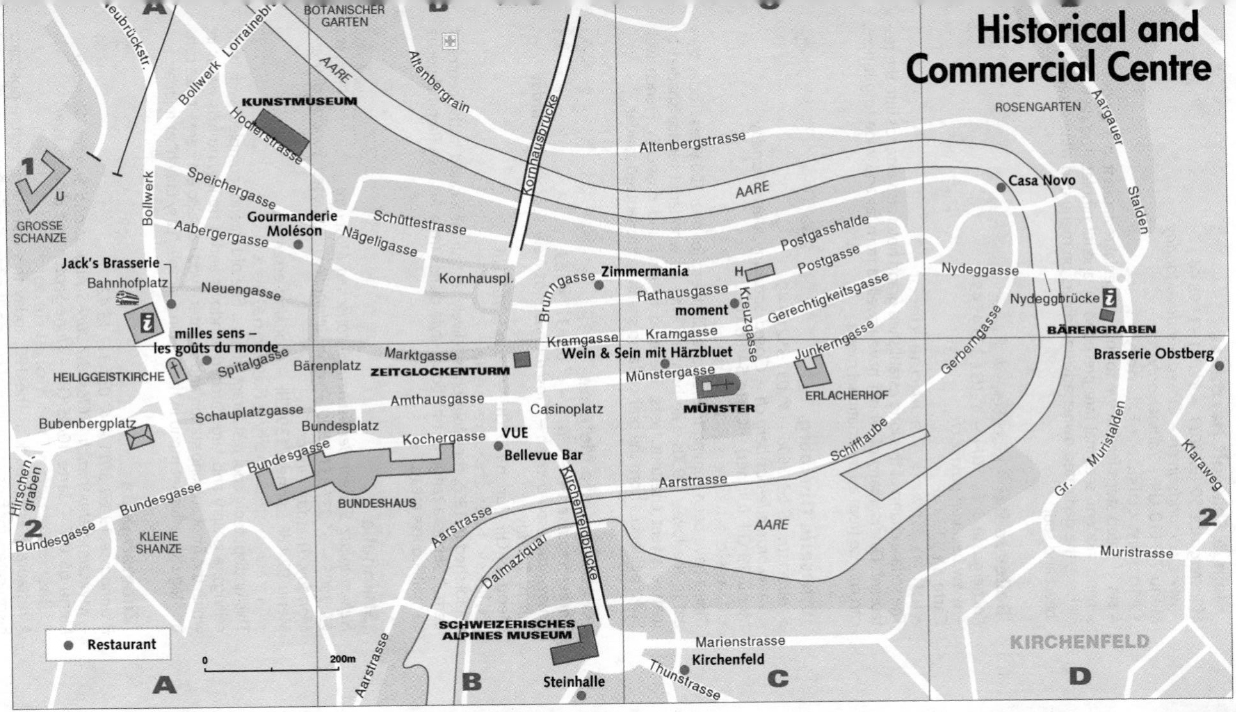

Historical and Commercial Centre

Wein & Sein mit Härzbluet

XX

Münstergasse 50 ✉ 3011 – ✆ 031 311 98 44 Plan: **C2**
– www.weinundsein.ch – Closed Sunday-Monday
Menu 78/118 CHF – *(dinner only)*

• Modern cuisine • Friendly •

A set of steep steps lead down to this congenial restaurant in a vaulted cellar serving modern, seasonal fare preceded by aperitif nibbles. The name says it all here, the dedicated owner advising diners on menu and wine choices with "heart and soul".

Bellevue Bar – Hotel Bellevue Palace

X

Kochergasse 3 ✉ 3011 – ✆ 031 320 45 45 Plan: **B2**
– www.bellevue-palace.ch
Carte 54/113 CHF

• International • Traditional décor •

The sedate charm of this long established grand hotel also extends into the restaurant. Diners, many of whom have travelled from far and wide to get here, can choose from an international menu.

Brasserie Obstberg

X

Bantigerstr. 18 ✉ 3006 – ✆ 031 352 04 40 Plan: **D2**
– www.brasserie-obstberg.ch – Closed Saturday lunch, Sunday
Menu 79 CHF (dinner) – Carte 54/86 CHF

• Classic cuisine • Brasserie •

Diners have been coming to Brasserie Obstberg for over 100 years. Today they eat in the lovely, 1930s-style brasserie with its wonderful terrace shaded by mature sweet chestnut trees. The food is fresh and classically French with Swiss influences from the braised lamb shank to the sautéed zander.

Gourmanderie Moléson

X

Aarbergergasse 24 ✉ 3011 – ✆ 031 311 44 63 Plan: **A1**
– www.moleson-bern.ch – Closed Christmas-New Year and Saturday lunch, Sunday
Menu 59 CHF (lunch)/77 CHF – Carte 55/87 CHF

• Classic French • Brasserie •

Established in 1865, the Moléson is a lively restaurant located in the centre of Bern. It serves a range of traditional-style dishes from Alsatian flammekueche to multi-course meals.

Steinhalle

X

Helvetiaplatz 5 (near Bernischen Historischen Museum) Plan: **B2**
✉ 3005 – ✆ 031 351 51 00 – www.steinhalle.ch – Closed Sunday dinner-Monday, Tuesday dinner
Menu 92 CHF (dinner)/139 CHF – *(booking essential)*

• Creative • Friendly • Fashionable •

This undisputedly cool restaurant offers a fine old interior complete with high ceilings, a gallery and large arched windows and a trendy, no-frills decor in which the front cooking station and counter – you can also eat here – takes centre stage. Creative set menu in the evening, simple "Easy Lunch" at midday.

Zimmermania

X

Brunngasse 19 ✉ 3011 – ✆ 031 311 15 42 Plan: **B1**
– www.zimmermania.ch – Closed 7 July-5 August and Sunday-Monday
Menu 65 CHF – Carte 40/95 CHF – *(June-September: dinner only)*

• Classic French • Traditional décor •

A restaurant as far back as the 19C, today this charming, picture-postcard bistro caters for fans of traditional cuisine. It offers classics such as calf's head vinaigrette, entrecôte Café de Paris and slow cooked stews.

moment

Gerechtigkeitsgasse 56 ✉ 3011 – ✆ 031 332 10 20 – www.moment-bern.ch – Closed Sunday-Monday

Plan: **C1**

Menu 42 CHF (lunch)/110 CHF (dinner)

• Creative • Fashionable •

Set in the historic heart of Bern, this trendy, modern restaurant spread over two floors serves creative cuisine that is sophisticated yet uncomplicated with regional and seasonal accents. Enticing menu options served up by the relaxed front-of-house team include veal with potatoes and dried green beans. Reduced lunchtime menu.

ENVIRONS OF BERN

Essort

Jubiläumstr. 97 (South: 2 km by Kirchenfeldbrücke) ✉ 3005 – ✆ 031 368 11 11 – www.essort.ch – Closed 1 week early January, 2 weeks early October, Saturday lunch and Sunday-Monday

Menu 68 CHF (lunch)/119 CHF (dinner)

• International • Friendly •

In the former US embassy the Lüthi family runs a modern restaurant. It produces international fare in its open kitchen, which is inspired by the owners' countless trips abroad. In summer, dine alfresco at one of the lovely tables laid outside under the mature trees.

Süder

Weissensteinstr. 61 (South: 3 km by Kirchenfeldbrücke) ✉ 3007 – ✆ 031 371 57 67 – www.restaurant-sueder.ch – Closed 1-10 January, 2 weeks July and Saturday lunch, Sunday-Monday

Menu 69 CHF (dinner)/89 CHF – Carte 51/90 CHF

• Swiss • Bourgeois •

This down-to-earth corner restaurant with its lovely wood panelling has many regulars. They are attracted by the good, honest, fresh Swiss cooking, such as the veal ragout. In the summer it is no surprise that the tables in the garden are particularly popular.

Waldheim

Waldheimstr. 40 (North-West: 3 km by Bundesgasse) ✉ 3012 – ✆ 031 305 24 24 – www.waldheim-bern.ch – Closed Saturday lunch, Sunday-Monday

Menu 56 CHF – Carte 44/91 CHF

• Traditional cuisine • Neighbourhood •

This pretty restaurant is panelled in light wood and located in a quiet residential area. It boasts a healthy number of regulars thanks to the fresh Swiss cuisine (try the marinated leg of lamb, spit-roasted to a perfect pink) and the friendly service.

GENEVA
GENEVE

Onfokus/iStock

GENEVA IN...

→ **ONE DAY**
St Peter's Cathedral, Maison Tavel, Jet d'Eau, Reformation Wall.

→ **TWO DAYS**
MAMCO (or the Art & History Museum), a lakeside stroll, a trip to Carouge.

→ **THREE DAYS**
A day in Paquis, including time relaxing at the Bains des Paquis.

In just about every detail except efficiency, Geneva exudes a distinctly Latin feel. It boasts a proud cosmopolitanism, courtesy of a whole swathe of international organisations (dealing with just about every human concern), and of the fact that roughly one in three residents is non-Swiss. Its renowned savoir-vivre challenges that of swishy Zurich, and along with its manicured city parks, it boasts the world's tallest fountain and the world's longest bench. It enjoys cultural ties with Paris and is often called 'the twenty-first arrondissement' – it's also almost entirely surrounded by France.

The River Rhône snakes through the centre, dividing the city into the southern left bank - the old town – and the northern right bank – the 'international quarter' (home to the largest UN office outside New York). The east is strung around the sparkling shores of Europe's largest alpine lake, while the Jura Mountains dominate the right bank, and the Alps form a backdrop to the left bank. Geneva is renowned for its orderliness: the Reformation was born here under the austere preachings of Calvin, and the city has provided sanctuary for religious dissidents, revolutionaries and elopers for at least five centuries. Nowadays, new arrivals tend to be of a more conservative persuasion, as they go their elegant way balancing international affairs alongside la belle vie.

EATING OUT

With the number of international organisations that have set up camp here, this is a place that takes a lot of feeding, so you'll find over 1,000 dining establishments in and around the city. If you're looking for elegance, head to a restaurant overlooking the lake; if your tastes are for home-cooked Sardinian fare, make tracks for the charming Italianate suburb of Carouge; and if you fancy something with an international accent, trendy Paquis has it all at a fair price and on a truly global scale, from Mexican to Moroccan and Jordanian to Japanese. The old town, packed with delightful brasseries and alpine-style chalets, is the place for Swiss staples: you can't go wrong here if you're after a fondue, rustic longeole (pork sausage with cumin and fennel) or a hearty papet vaudois (cream and leek casserole); for a bit of extra atmosphere, head downstairs to a candlelit, vaulted cellar. Although restaurants include a fifteen per cent service charge, it's customary to either round up the bill or give the waiter a five to ten per cent tip.

Le Chat Botté – Hôtel Beau Rivage

Quai du Mont-Blanc 13 ✉ 1201 – ✆ 022 716 69 20 Plan: **F3**
– www.beau-rivage.ch – Closed 25 March-8 April, 30 July-13 August and Saturday-Sunday
Menu 75 CHF (weekday lunch)/220 CHF – Carte 115/185 CHF

• Modern French • Elegant • Luxury •

This appealingly named restaurant ('Puss in Boots') serves contemporary-style cuisine with traditional roots, using culinary techniques that create harmonious flavours. The food is complemented by the expert work of the sommelier, who skilfully guides guests through the impressive wine list.

➜ Grenouillles de Vallorbe, pousses d'épinard, mousse de lait d'ail. Scampi d'Afrique du Sud, pomme croustillante, truffe d'éte. Framboises de pays, Arlette croustillante, mélisse et poivre de Tasmanie.

Il Lago – Four Seasons Hôtel des Bergues

Quai des Bergues 33 ✉ 1201 – ✆ 022 908 71 10 Plan: **F3**
– www.fourseasons.com/geneva
Menu 78 CHF (lunch)/130 CHF – Carte 115/189 CHF – *(booking essential)*

• Italian • Classic décor • Elegant •

Offering a taste of Italy on Lake Geneva, this restaurant combines decorative features such as pilasters and paintings with elegant Italian cuisine which is light, subtle and fragant. A delightful dining experience!

➜ Tortelli de fromage, parfumés au citron et à la menthe. Bar de ligne rôti, artichauts violets et émulsion au citron. Ananas rôti aux saveurs exotiques et crumble.

Bayview – Hôtel Président Wilson

Quai Wilson 47 ✉ 1211 – ✆ 022 906 65 52 Plan: **F2**
– www.hotelpresidentwilson.com – Closed 1-13 January, 16-24 April, 29July-25 August and Sunday-Monday
Menu 68 CHF (lunch)/170 CHF (dinner) – Carte 116/200 CHF

• Modern French • Design • Elegant •

With its chic, carefully designed decor and large bay windows facing the lake, this restaurant provides the ideal setting to enjoy the elegant cuisine. French classics are reinterpreted with creativity and subtlety, and the carefully produced dishes are chic and contemporary.

➜ Rafraîchi de King Crab à la livèche et craquant de pain sarde. Ris de veau de nos alpages, laqué, blé soufflé et cecina, jus acidulé. Tarte soufflée au chocolat Guanaja 70%.

Le Bologne

Rue Necker 9 ✉ 1201 – ✆ 022 732 86 80 Plan: **E3**
– www.lebologne.com – Closed 2 weeks end July-early August, 2 weeks end December and Saturday-Sunday
Menu 38 CHF – Carte 60/87 CHF

• Modern cuisine • Bistro • Vintage •

Located alongside the city's Fine Arts School, this vintage bistro boasts a decor of cement tiles, globe lights and bare bulbs, in addition to a bar, and bistro-style banquettes and chairs. The cuisine here focuses on carefully prepared and high-quality seasonal products to create dishes such as celeriac risotto and foie gras, and grilled red tuna with roasted beetroot.

Côté Square

Rue du Mont-Blanc 10 ✉ 1201 – ✆ 022 716 57 58 Plan: **F3**
– www.bristol.ch – Closed 1-6 January, 19-28 April and Saturday-Sunday
Menu 57 CHF (weekday lunch)/115 CHF – Carte 80/101 CHF

• French • Cosy •

This restaurant has a classic elegance. Wood panelling and paintings add an aristocratic air, enhanced by the occasional notes emanating from the attractive black piano near the bar. Enjoy delicious dishes showcasing a variety of textures and flavours, at tables covered with immaculate white cloths.

Le Jardin – Hôtel Le Richemond
Rue Adhémar-Fabri 8 ✉ 1201 – ✆ 022 715 71 00 Plan: **F3**
– www.lerichemond.com – Closed Saturday lunch and Sunday, except season
Menu 60 CHF (weekday lunch)/130 CHF – Carte 93/132 CHF
• Modern French • Elegant • Cosy •
This restaurant is situated in the Le Richemond hotel, facing the lake. It serves French cuisine with contemporary flavours and a focus on produce from the region. The terrace is a must in fine weather.

Rasoi by Vineet – Hôtel Mandarin Oriental
Quai turrettini 1 ✉ 1201 – ✆ 022 909 00 00 Plan: **E3**
– www.mandarinoriental.fr/geneva – Closed Sunday-Monday
Menu 85/115 CHF – Carte 42/70 CHF
• Indian • Elegant • Contemporary décor •
All the fragrances and colours of Indian cuisine are interpreted here with incredible refinement. Enjoy the cuisine of the sub-continent at its best in this chic and elegant restaurant where you can imagine yourself as a 21C maharaja!

Windows – Hôtel D'Angleterre
Quai du Mont-Blanc 17 ✉ 1201 – ✆ 022 906 55 14 Plan: **F3**
– www.hoteldangleterre.ch
Menu 58 CHF (weekday lunch)/180 CHF – Carte 82/143 CHF
• Creative French • Elegant • Friendly •
Housed in the Hôtel D'Angleterre, this restaurant offers superb views of Lake Geneva, the Jet d'Eau and the mountains in the distance. The menu features delicacies such as scallop carpaccio with lime, avocado tartare and fleur de sel, and half a baked lobster with little gem lettuce and potatoes.

L'Arabesque – Hôtel Président Wilson
Quai Wilson 47 ✉ 1211 – ✆ 022 906 67 63 Plan: **F2**
– www.hotelpresidentwilson.com
Menu 49 CHF (weekday lunch)/95 CHF – Carte 68/86 CHF
• Lebanese • Elegant • Exotic décor •
The attractive decor features gold mosaics, white leather and black lacquerware, evoking the magic of the Orient; in particular the Lebanon, from where the authentic aromas of dishes such as bastorma (dried beef with spices) and houmous (chickpea purée) transport diners to the land of the cedar tree!

Café Calla – Hôtel Mandarin Oriental
Quai Turrettini 1 ✉ 1201 – ✆ 022 909 00 00 Plan: **E3**
– www.mandarinoriental.fr/geneva
Menu 55 CHF (weekday lunch) – Carte 60/131 CHF
• Mediterranean cuisine • Contemporary décor •
Situated on the lakeside, the Mandarin Oriental's chic brasserie specialises in Mediterranean flavours, offering dishes from all over the region, such as aubergine caviar, chicken and lemon tagine, and Italian-style veal picatta.

Il Vero – Grand Hôtel Kempinski
Quai du Mont-Blanc 19 ✉ 1201 – ✆ 022 908 92 24 Plan: **F3**
– www.kempinski-geneva.com
Menu 81 CHF – Carte 77/193 CHF
• Italian • Fashionable • Design •
Situated on the second floor of the hotel, Il Vero takes us on a voyage to Italy, with pasta and meat dishes prepared in the best Italian tradition taking pride of place on the menu. It's no surprise, therefore, to see that some of the specialities here are Italian favourites such as vitello tonnato, bucatini Verdi and the ever-popular tiramisu. All to be enjoyed in a cosy setting with theatrical Italian feel.

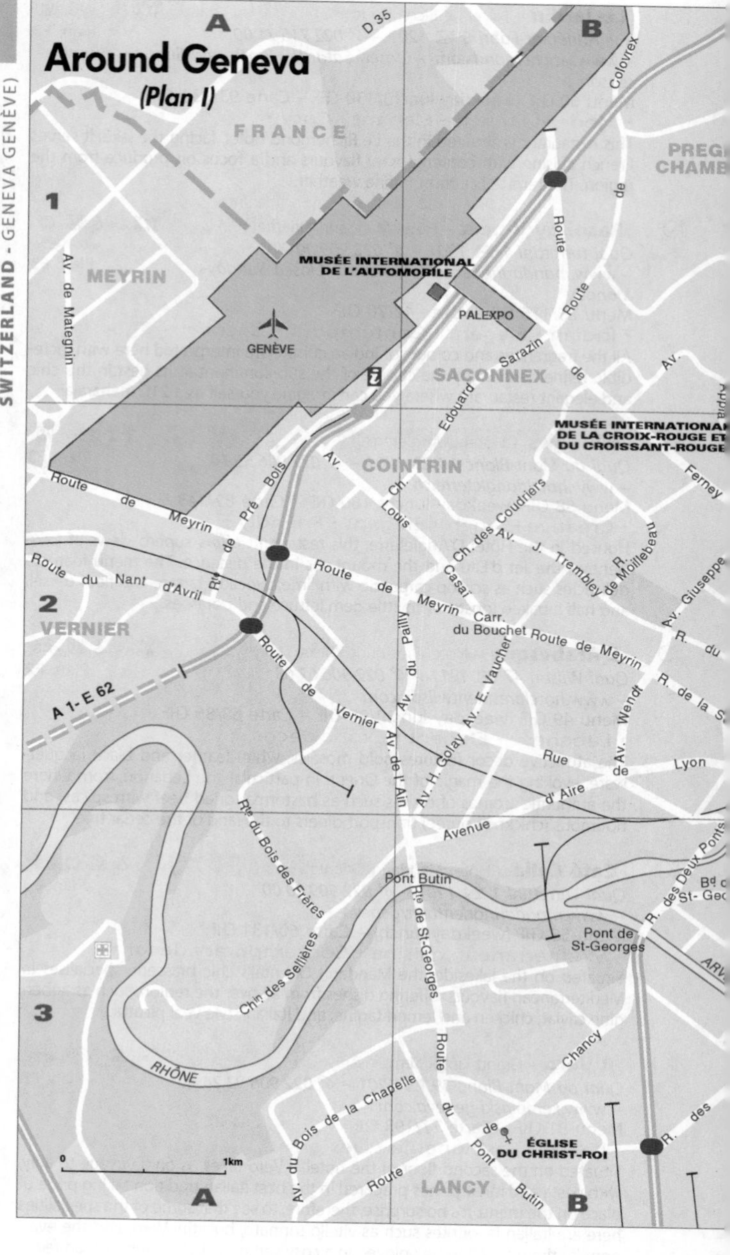
Around Geneva
(Plan I)
A
B
1
2
3
FRANCE
D 35
Colovrex
PREGNY-CHAMBÉSY
MEYRIN
Av. de Mategnin
MUSÉE INTERNATIONAL DE L'AUTOMOBILE
PALEXPO
GENÈVE
SACONNEX
COINTRIN
Route de Colovrex
Route Edouard Sarazin
Av. de la Paix
MUSÉE INTERNATIONAL DE LA CROIX-ROUGE ET DU CROISSANT-ROUGE
Route de Ferney
Route de Meyrin
Rte de Pré Bois
Av. Louis Casaï
Ch. des Coudriers
Av. J. Trembley
R. de Moillebeau
Av. Giuseppe Motta
Route du Nant d'Avril
VERNIER
Route de Vernier
Carr. du Bouchet
Route de Meyrin
Av. E. Vaucher
Av. du Pailly
Av. Wendt
R. du
R. de la S
A 1- E 62
Av. de l'Ain
Av. H. Golay
Rue de Lyon
Avenue d'Aire
Rte du Bois des Frères
Pont Butin
Rte de St-Georges
R. des Deux Ponts
Bd de St-Georges
Pont de St-Georges
ARVE
Chin des Sellières
RHÔNE
Route de Chancy
Route du Pont Butin
Av. du Bois de la Chapelle
ÉGLISE DU CHRIST-ROI
R. des
LANCY
0
1km

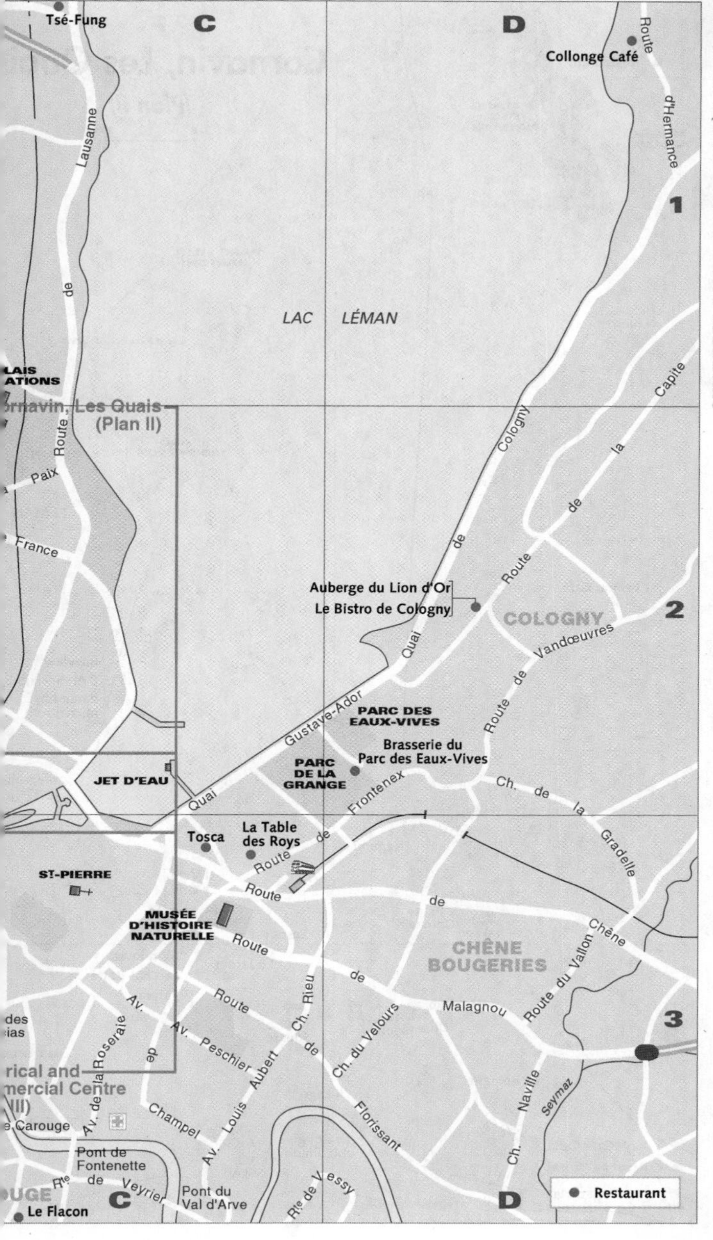

Tsé-Fung
C
D
Collonge Café
Route d'Hermance
Route de Lausanne
LAC LÉMAN
1
2
3
Cornavin, Les Quais (Plan II)
Paix
France
Quai de Cologny
Route de la Capite
Auberge du Lion d'Or
Le Bistro de Cologny
COLOGNY
Route de Vandœuvres
Quai Gustave-Ador
PARC DES EAUX-VIVES
Brasserie du Parc des Eaux-Vives
PARC DE LA GRANGE
JET D'EAU
Route de Frontenex
Ch. de la Gradelle
Tosca
La Table des Roys
ST-PIERRE
Route de Chêne
MUSÉE D'HISTOIRE NATURELLE
CHÊNE BOUGERIES
Route de Malagnou
Route du Vallon
Ch. Rieu
Route de Florissant
Ch. du Velours
Av. de la Roseraie
Av. Peschier
Route de Champel
Av. Louis Aubert
Ch. Naville
Seymaz
Pont de Fontenette
Rte de Veyrier
Pont du Val d'Arve
Rte de Vessy
Le Flacon
Restaurant

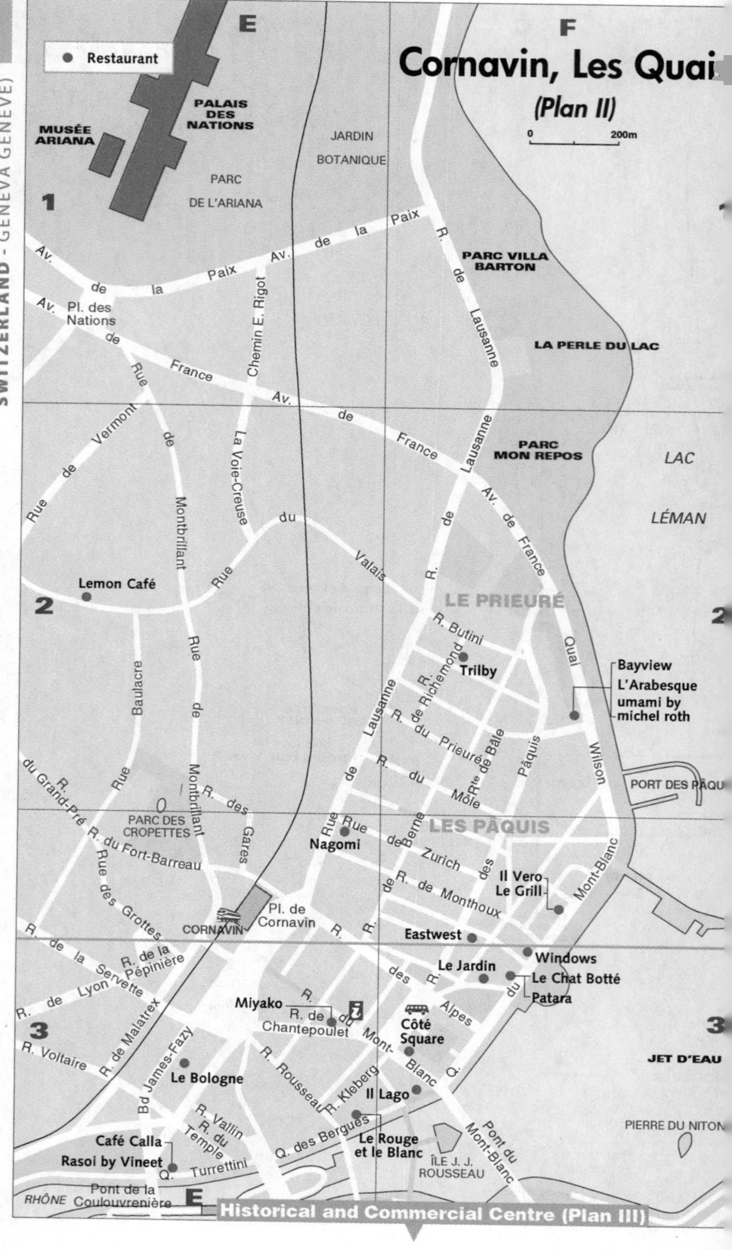
Cornavin, Les Quai
(Plan II)
Restaurant
0 200m
E
F
1
2
3
MUSÉE ARIANA
PALAIS DES NATIONS
PARC DE L'ARIANA
JARDIN BOTANIQUE
PARC VILLA BARTON
LA PERLE DU LAC
PARC MON REPOS
LAC LÉMAN
LE PRIEURÉ
LES PÂQUIS
PORT DES PÂQU
JET D'EAU
PIERRE DU NITON
ÎLE J. J. ROUSSEAU
RHÔNE
PARC DES CROPETTES
CORNAVIN
Pl. de Cornavin
Pl. des Nations
Av. de la Paix
Av. de France
R. de Lausanne
Chemin E. Rigot
La Voie-Creuse
Rue de Vermont
Rue de Montbrillant
Rue du Valais
Rue Baulacre
R. du Grand-Pré
R. du Fort-Barreau
Rue des Grottes
R. des Gares
R. Butini
R. de Richemond
R. du Prieuré
Rte de Bâle
Pâquis
R. du Môle
Rue de Berne
Rue de Zurich
R. de Monthoux
R. des Alpes
R. du Mont-Blanc
R. de Chantepoulet
Quai Wilson
Q. du Mont-Blanc
Pont du Mont-Blanc
R. de la Servette
R. de la Pépinière
R. de Lyon
R. de Malatrex
R. Voltaire
Bd James-Fazy
R. Rousseau
R. Kleberg
R. Vallin
R. du Temple
Q. des Bergues
Q. Turrettini
Pont de la Coulouvrenière
Lemon Café
Trilby
Bayview
L'Arabesque
umami by michel roth
Nagomi
Il Vero
Le Grill
Eastwest
Windows
Le Jardin
Le Chat Botté
Patara
Miyako
Côté Square
Le Bologne
Il Lago
Le Rouge et le Blanc
Café Calla
Rasoi by Vineet
Historical and Commercial Centre (Plan III)

Patara – Hôtel Beau-Rivage

Quai du Mont-Blanc 13 ✉ 1201 – ✆ 022 731 55 66 Plan: **F3**
– www.patara-geneva.ch – Closed 25 March-8 April, 30 July-13 August, 2 weeks Christmas-New Year
Menu 42 CHF (lunch)/125 CHF – Carte 62/108 CHF
• Thai • Exotic décor • Romantic •

Thai specialities served in one of the most beautiful luxury hotels in Geneva. Stylised gold motifs on the walls evoke the exotic ambience of Thailand, while the delicious specialities on the menu add to the sense of discovery.

Trilby – Hôtel N'vY

Rue de Richemont 18 ✉ 1202 – ✆ 022 544 66 66 Plan: **F2**
– www.hotelnvygeneva.com
Menu 69/80 CHF – Carte 53/87 CHF
• International • Fashionable • Elegant •

You might want to doff your own trilby as you enter this elegant and welcoming restaurant. The speciality is the outstanding beef, whether it is Scottish (Black Angus), Japanese (Wagyu Kobe) or Swiss (Simmental), accompanied by a choice of original sauces.

Eastwest – Hôtel Eastwest

Rue des Pâquis 6 ✉ 1201 – ✆ 022 708 17 07 Plan: **F3**
– www.eastwesthotel.ch
Menu 32/79 CHF – Carte 67/90 CHF – *(Brunch: Saturday and Sunday lunch)*
• Modern cuisine • Design • Cosy •

Eastwest avoids the rather formal menus of the nearby hotels to offer a more relaxed style of cuisine where a hint of Asia is evident in the dishes. Well-prepared fare, as well as a range of snack options, makes this restaurant a good choice.

Le Grill – Grand Hôtel Kempinski

Quai du Mont-Blanc 19 ✉ 1201 – ✆ 022 908 92 20 Plan: **F3**
– www.kempinski.com/geneva
Menu 45 CHF (weekday lunch)/95 CHF – Carte 71/117 CHF
• Meats and grills • Fashionable • Friendly •

A chic and original restaurant. It offers views of Lake Geneva, as well as of the kitchens, rotisserie and cold rooms where the splendid cuts of meat are stored (300g Parisian entrecôte, beef fillet, rack of lamb, etc). The meat is cooked to perfection and the set menu works well.

Lemon Café

Rue du Vidollet 4 ✉ 1202 – ✆ 022 733 60 24 Plan: **E2**
– www.lemon-cafe.ch – Closed 22 July-9 August, 23 December-4 January and Saturday-Sunday
Menu 50 CHF – Carte 49/84 CHF
• Modern cuisine • Bistro • Neighbourhood •

At this restaurant the chef delights guests with his travel-inspired dishes. Just some of the options are cod ceviche with a Peruvian flavour, pork spare ribs cooked for 12 hours and served with Maxim's potatoes, and lemon cheesecake.

Miyako

Rue Chantepoulet 11 ✉ 1201 – ✆ 022 738 01 20 Plan: **E3**
– www.miyako.ch – Closed Sunday
Menu 34 CHF (lunch)/108 CHF – Carte 64/157 CHF
• Japanese • Simple •

This aptly named restaurant (Miyako is the Japanese for heart) plunges you into the heart of Japan. It has tatami flooring, teppanyaki cuisine, fresh fish and attentive service. Arigato!

Nagomi
Plan: E3

Rue de Zurich 47 ✉ 1200 – ✆ 022 732 38 28 – www.restaurant-nagomi.ch – Closed 22 July-4 August, 25 December-8 January and Saturday lunch, Sunday
Menu 130 CHF – Carte 60/84 CHF

• Japanese • Simple •

This extraordinary restaurant run by a Japanese family is located in the Le Paquis district of the city. It is divided into two distinct dining spaces, one for sushi prepared by the father, the other for tempura dishes cooked by the son! In both places, the atmosphere is authentic, the service unfussy, and the ingredients of the highest quality. A feast for the all senses with the focus on simplicity. No credit cards.

Le Rouge et le Blanc
Plan: E3

Quai des Bergues 27 ✉ 1201 – ✆ 022 731 15 50 – www.lerougeblanc.ch – Closed Sunday
Carte 59/80 CHF – *(dinner only)*

• Traditional cuisine • Wine bar • Friendly •

A good wine selection, rib of beef as the house speciality (for two or three people), plates of tapas that vary according to market availability, and a relaxed and convivial atmosphere. This restaurant makes a good choice for an enjoyable meal out. Open evenings only.

umami by michel roth – Hôtel Président Wilson
Plan: F2

Quai Wilson 47 ✉ 1211 – ✆ 022 906 64 52 – www.hotelpresidentwilson.com – Closed October-May and Sunday dinner
Menu 59 CHF (lunch) – Carte 76/136 CHF

• Japanese • Exotic décor • Fashionable •

Dine at this restaurant and you will soon realise that there is far more to Japanese cuisine than sushi and sashimi. Creativity is very much to the fore, with the occasional French influence thrown in for good measure. The maki rolls sautéed with foie gras, green apple and ginger are a delicious combination.

LEFT BANK — PLAN III

Tosca
Plan: C3

Rue de la Mairie 8 ✉ 1207 – ✆ 022 707 14 44 – www.tosca-geneva.ch – Closed 23 December-7 January, 1 week Easter and Saturday-Sunday
Menu 110/140 CHF – Carte 74/108 CHF

• Tuscan • Chic •

This popular new addition to Geneva's dining scene does not disappoint! The beautifully presented Italian cuisine (with an obvious emphasis on Tuscany) is made from top-quality ingredients and is full of flavour. A fine selection of Tuscan wines and friendly, professional service complete the picture.

→ La tomate mozzarella revisitée par notre chef. Ravioli del Plin à la pintade, réduction de Parmesan et sauce salmis. Filet Mignon de veau à la cendre de romarin, déclinaison de pommes de terre et girolles.

La Bottega (Francesco Gasbarro)
Plan: G2

Rue de La Corraterie 21 – ✆ 022 736 10 00 – www.labottegatrattoria.com – Closed 1 week during Easter, 2 weeks early August, 23 December-9 January and Saturday lunch, Sunday
Menu 58 CHF (weekday lunch)/180 CHF – Carte 102/132 CHF

• Friendly • Neighbourhood •

There isn't a menu at La Bottega, just a whole heap of inspiration! The chef here presents a re-worked version of Italian cuisine with the help of top-quality Swiss ingredients. The modern, delicious dishes come full of surprises to delight guests.

→ Cappelletti di Piccione Burro e timo. Risotto estratto di barbabietola e gorgonzola. Cavolfiore cioccolato bianco e capperi.

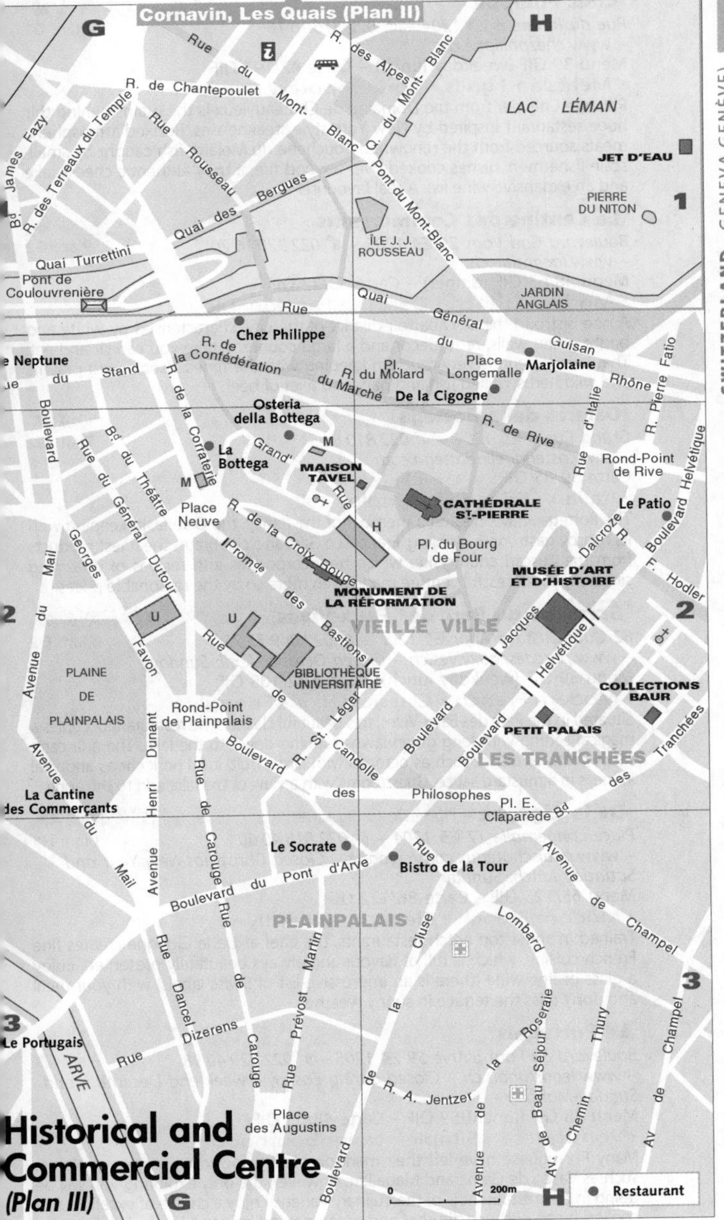
Cornavin, Les Quais (Plan II)
LAC LÉMAN
JET D'EAU
PIERRE DU NITON
ÎLE J. J. ROUSSEAU
JARDIN ANGLAIS
Chez Philippe
Neptune
Marjolaine
De la Cigogne
Osteria della Bottega
La Bottega
MAISON TAVEL
CATHÉDRALE ST-PIERRE
Le Patio
Place Neuve
Pl. du Bourg de Four
MUSÉE D'ART ET D'HISTOIRE
MONUMENT DE LA RÉFORMATION
VIEILLE VILLE
BIBLIOTHÈQUE UNIVERSITAIRE
COLLECTIONS BAUR
PETIT PALAIS
LES TRANCHÉES
PLAINE DE PLAINPALAIS
Rond-Point de Plainpalais
Rond-Point de Rive
Place Longemalle
Pl. du Molard
Pont de Coulouvrenière
La Cantine des Commerçants
Pl. E. Claparède
Le Socrate
Bistro de la Tour
PLAINPALAIS
Le Portugais
ARVE
Place des Augustins
0 200m
Restaurant

Historical and Commercial Centre
(Plan III)

Chez Philippe

XX Plan: G1

Rue du Rhône 8 ✉ 1204 – ✆ 022 316 16 16 – www.chezphilippe.ch

Menu 39 CHF (weekday lunch) – Carte 42/197 CHF

• Meats and grills • Contemporary décor •

Philippe Chevrier from the Domaine de Châteauvieux is the brains behind this huge restaurant inspired by New York-style steakhouses. Relaxed atmosphere, meats sourced from the renowned Boucherie du Molard, fish caught by small-scale fishermen, dishes cooked over a wood fire, a truly authentic cheesecake and an expansive wine list. A real favourite!

La Cantine des Commerçants

X Plan: G2

Boulevard Carl Vogt 29 ✉ 1205 – ✆ 022 328 16 70 – www.lacantine.ch

Menu 48/65 CHF (dinner) – Carte 53/72 CHF

• Modern French • Design • Fashionable •

A neo-bistro in the old abattoir district of the city, characterised by white and bright green walls, retro decor and a large counter where you can sit and eat. The varied menu is very much in keeping with the times: risotto with prawns and wild herbs, grilled fish and pan-fried fillet of beef.

Osteria della Bottega

X Plan: G2

Grand Rue 3 ✉ 1204 – ✆ 022 810 84 51 – www.osteriadellabottega.com

Carte 59/85 CHF

• Italian • Friendly • Simple •

The Bottegas have created a member of the family, the Osteria. In keeping with its nearby gastronomic sibling, Francesco Gasbarro celebrates the finest products from the Tuscan countryside which he incorporates into recipes of disarming simplicity. A successful venture made even more so by the reasonable prices.

Brasserie du Parc des Eaux-Vives

XX Plan: D2

82 Quai Gustave Ador ✉ 1207 – ✆ 022 849 75 75 – www.parcdeseauxvives.ch – Closed October-April: Sunday

Menu 39 CHF (weekday lunch) – Carte 72/105 CHF

• Modern French • Classic décor • Friendly •

Situated in the Parc des Eaux-Vives, this beautiful classic-style restaurant occupies a magical setting with long green lawns running down to the lake. The à la carte menu features dishes such as octopus with citrus fruit, local pork chops and veal kidneys in a mustard sauce. Guestrooms with a view of the lake add to the appeal.

De la Cigogne – Hôtel De la Cigogne

XX Plan: H1

Place Longemalle 17 ✉ 1204 – ✆ 022 818 40 60 – www.relaischateaux.com/cigogne – Closed Christmas-New Year and Saturday lunch, Sunday

Menu 65/125 CHF – Carte 86/122 CHF

• Modern French • Elegant • Friendly •

Trained in some top-notch restaurants, the chef at De la Cigogne creates fine French cuisine, which is full of flavour and always beautifully presented. Enjoy a glass of fine wine (there is an impressive list of Swiss labels) with your meal and don't miss the terrace in sunny weather.

Le Portugais

XX Plan: G3

Boulevard du Pont d'Arve 59 ✉ 1205 – ✆ 022 329 40 98 – www.leportugais.ch – Closed during Easter, 1 week end December and Sunday-Monday

Menu 38 CHF (lunch)/59 CHF – Carte 48/85 CHF

• Portuguese • Simple • Neighbourhood •

Many Portuguese have left their mark on history, including famous explorers such as Vasco de Gama and Magellan. However, the only exploring you will be doing in this restaurant is of the culinary variety. Enjoy a choice of excellent fish cooked by an enthusiastic chef and accompanied by good local wine. Friendly, rustic ambience. Obrigado!

Bistro de la Tour

Plan: **H3**

Boulevard de la Tour 2 ✉ 1205 – ✆ 022 321 97 66 – www.bistrodelatour.ch – Closed 15 July-19 August, 22 December-8 January and Saturday-Sunday

Menu 29 CHF (weekday lunch) – Carte 64/99 CHF

• World cuisine • Neighbourhood • Intimate •

Seasonal produce is the hallmark of the Bistro de la Tour, situated on the boulevard of the same name. The menu focuses on fresh ingredients, which change regularly, with flavoursome dishes that include the occasional surprise. Friendly and welcoming owner.

Le Neptune

Plan: **G1**

Rue de la Coulouvrenière 38 ✉ 1204 – ✆ 022 320 15 05 – www.leneptune.ch – Closed 2 weeks early January, 2 weeks end July-early August and Tuesday-Friday, Saturday lunch

Menu 45 CHF (weekday lunch)/107 CHF – Carte 81/106 CHF

• Modern cuisine • Minimalist • Trendy •

Located close to the lake shore and the Bâtiment des Forces Motrices (a former power station that has been converted into a concert hall), this restaurant with its Scandinavian decor has a clear focus on healthy, nature-based dishes that showcase locally sourced organic products, including delicious homemade sourdough bread. In fine weather, enjoy alfresco dining on the small terrace.

Marjolaine

Plan: **H1**

Rue du Rhône 49 ✉ 1204 – ✆ 022 320 49 49 – www.marjolaine.ch – Closed 15 July-18 August and Sunday

Menu 52/90 CHF – Carte 46/103 CHF

• Italian • Brasserie •

Situated opposite the lake and the Jardin Anglais, this lively brasserie with a timeless decor is the latest creation of Philippe Chevrier. Mediterranean cuisine takes pride of place here, with dishes such as braised beef and rosemary ravioli and baked turbot with potatoes and olives featuring on the menu.

Le Patio

Plan: **H2**

Boulevard Helvétique 19 ✉ 1207 – ✆ 022 736 66 75 – www.lepatio-restaurant.ch – Closed 19-28 April, 29 July-18 August, 24 December-6 January, May-August: Saturday-Sunday

Menu 45 CHF (lunch)/120 CHF (dinner) – Carte 47/120 CHF

• Creative French • Friendly • Bistro •

Philippe Chevrier (chef at the Domaine de Châteauvieux in Satigny) has chosen an original concept here: cuisine that is almost exclusively based on lobster and beef. The menu includes dishes such as lobster tartare and oxtail parmentier, which are fresh, delicious and full of flavour. A highly enjoyable dining experience!

Le Socrate

Plan: **H3**

Rue Micheli-du-Crest 6 ✉ 1205 – ✆ 022 320 16 77 – www.lesocrate.ch – Closed Saturday lunch, Sunday

Carte 62/68 CHF

• Traditional cuisine • Vintage • Friendly •

A bistro with a delightfully retro dining room adorned with old posters. Sample simple, honest and delicious dishes at tables set close together. A place where good food and conversation are to the fore, in an atmosphere that a certain Greek philosopher would have appreciated!

La Table des Roys

Rue du Nant 7 ✉ 1200 – ✆ 022 736 64 13 – www.latabledesroys.com – Closed 2 weeks early January, 2 weeks early August and Sunday-Monday

Plan: C3

Menu 37 CHF (weekday lunch)/80 CHF

• Traditional cuisine • Bistro •

This former café-bar has given way to a respected local bistro. The owner-chef creates tasty, traditional dishes based around local products (lamb from the Valais, beef from Choulex, vegetables), some of which are cooked on the spit. Cookery classes are available here on Monday evenings.

ENVIRONS AND COINTRIN AIRPORT

PLAN I

Domaine de Châteauvieux

(Philippe Chevrier) Chemin de Châteauvieux 16 (West: 10 km) – ✆ 022 753 15 11 – www.chateauvieux.ch – Closed 2 weeks Christmas-New Year, 1 week during Easter, 2 weeks July-August and Sunday-Monday

Menu 96 CHF (weekday lunch)/290 CHF – Carte 186/229 CHF

• Creative • Rustic • Inn •

Off the beaten track, standing above the Geneva countryside and its vineyards, this large traditional house teeming with cachet and individual charm cultivates a true sense of excellence! A culinary technician as much as he is an artist, Philippe Chevrier follows a unique path to unearth truly natural flavours that reconnect with the basics. Delightful rooms for those wishing to stay the night.

➜ Médaillons de homard bleu de Bretagne aux artichauts et girolles, noisettes grillées, émulsion des carapaces parfumée à l'estragon. Pigeon des "Deux Sèvres" poché en vessie aux aromates, ragoût de maïs aux cébettes, jus aux herbes. Pavlova rhubarbe, brunoise et sorbet fraise parfumé à l'hibiscus.

Auberge du Lion d'Or (Thomas Byrne et Gilles Dupont)

Place Pierre-Gautier 5 – ✆ 022 736 44 32 – www.dupont-byrne.ch – Closed 24 December-13 January and Saturday-Sunday

Plan: D2

Menu 68 CHF (weekday lunch)/210 CHF – Carte 121/163 CHF

• Modern cuisine • Elegant • Chic •

Two heads are often better than one and the two chefs at this restaurant certainly combine their talents to good effect. They offer an excellent choice of produce, original combinations and cuisine that is full of flavour - not to mention a romantic view of the lake. A great dining option!

➜ "Tarshimi" de thon rouge Albacore, salade d'algues marines, tobeko. Ravioles de crabe royal du Kamtchatka et langoustine "Asia", émulsion de crustacés à la citronnelle et gingembre. Bar d'Atlantique cuit en croûte de sel marin, sauce Niçoise.

Le Bistro de Cologny – See below

Tsé Fung – Hôtel La Réserve

Route de Lausanne 301 – ✆ 022 959 59 59 – www.tsefung.ch

Plan: C1

Menu 78 CHF (lunch)/188 CHF (dinner) – Carte 73/284 CHF

• Chinese • Exotic décor • Chic •

Cantonese - and Chinese cooking in general - can count on Frank Xu to act as its gastronomic ambassador here. His culinary creations are authentic and delicious in equal measure and meticulously prepared with the very best ingredients, including his quite outstanding dim sum, Peking duck and Szechuan eggplant. Exquisite and exotic red and black decor.

➜ Rouleaux de riz rouge aux crevettes. Canard laqué pekinoise en deux services. Filet de turbot sauté aux champignons, sauce aux haricots noirs.

La Chaumière by Serge Labrosse-La Table du 7

Chemin de la Fondelle 16 – ✆ 022 784 30 66 – www.lachaumiere.ch – Closed Christmas and Sunday-Monday

Plan: **C3**

Menu 115/155 CHF – *(dinner only) (booking essential)*

• Modern French • Cosy •

Serge Labrosse's restaurant is all the enticement you'll need to head out of the city. In its bright interior, savour fine cuisine prepared using the very best ingredients which is served as part of surprise menus featuring 5, 6 or 7 courses. A brasserie menu is available for guests in a hurry.

➜ Croque-monsieur de pied de cochon, burrata et truffe. Suprême de volaille fermière sauce au vin jaune. Agneau de Vessy, aubergine fumée et petits pois.

Le Cigalon (Jean-Marc Bessire)

Route d'Ambilly 39 (South-East: 5 km by Route de Chêne) – ✆ 022 349 97 33 – www.le-cigalon.ch – Closed 21 July-12 August, during Easter, 22 December-6 January and Sunday-Monday

Menu 54 CHF (weekday lunch)/155 CHF – Carte 86/118 CHF

• Seafood • Elegant • Romantic •

Judging by the fresh fish on the menu, you would be forgiven for thinking that the Breton coast lies just outside the doors of this restaurant. Le Cigalon has specialised in seafood for over 20 years, with delicacies such as fish soup, scallops and monkfish from Roscoff all featuring on the menu. Table d'hôte meals for five guests are also available.

➜ Pressé de rouget grondin aux parfums de bouillabaisse, rouille sétoise. Baby langouste rôtie entière dans sa carapace, émulsion crustacés. Légine Australe laquée et grillée, riz noir Vénéré, parfum curry.

Le Flacon

Rue Vautier 45 – ✆ 022 342 15 20 – www.leflacon.ch – Closed 1 week July-August, 2 weeks Christmas and Saturday lunch, Sunday-Monday

Plan: **C3**

Menu 69 CHF (lunch)/115 CHF – Carte 72/104 CHF

• Modern cuisine • Contemporary décor •

An enchanting restaurant where the young chef, only just in his 30s, creates delicious cuisine from his open-view kitchen. He demonstrates a fine command of flavour and ingredient combinations, as well as a real eye for detail in his beautifully presented dishes.

➜ Bar mariné, nectarine, navet et amande. Turbot, courgette, asperge blanche, noisette et mousseline de pomme rate. Agneau du Bourbonnais, oignon doux, carotte et panisse.

Le Bistrot Le Lion d'Or

Rue Ancienne 53 – ✆ 022 342 18 13 – www.lebistrot.ch – Closed Christmas-New Year and Sunday-Monday

Plan: **C3**

Menu 58/85 CHF – Carte 48/82 CHF

• Classic French • Bistro •

The team from Bistrot Laz Nillo has taken over the restaurant in this hotel dating from 1750. In a light, relaxed atmosphere, they create delicious French dishes full of flavour, such as the chicken salad with lime, rice vinegar and bird's eye chilli pepper. Pleasant terrace in a tranquil setting.

Collonge Café

Chemin du Château-de-Bellerive 3 – ✆ 022 777 12 45 Plan: **D1**
– www.collonge-cafe.ch – Closed Christmas-New Year and Sunday dinner-Monday; October-May: Monday
Menu 38 CHF (weekday lunch)/90 CHF – Carte 71/99 CHF

• Modern cuisine • Contemporary décor •

This reasonably priced auberge is the fiefdom of Angelo and Viviana Citiulo. In this resolutely modern setting of glass, wood and concrete, the cuisine continues to have a foot in Italian cuisine but also has a more global feel thanks to dishes such as soft-shelled crab with a cauliflower and yuzu couscous, and confit of suckling pig with raspberries, spring onions and peppers.

Le Bistro de Cologny – Restaurant Auberge du Lion d'Or

Place Pierre-Gautier 5 – ✆ 022 736 57 80 Plan: **D2**
– www.dupont-byrne.ch – Closed 24 December-13 January
Carte 71/88 CHF

• Traditional cuisine • Bistro • Inn •

Echoing the success of the gourmet Lion d'Or restaurant, this bistro annexe is much more than just an add on, offering delicious dishes such as sole from Brittany and veal fillet with cep mushrooms. The stunning views from the terrace allow diners to make the most of the 'bistronomic' set menu at weekends.

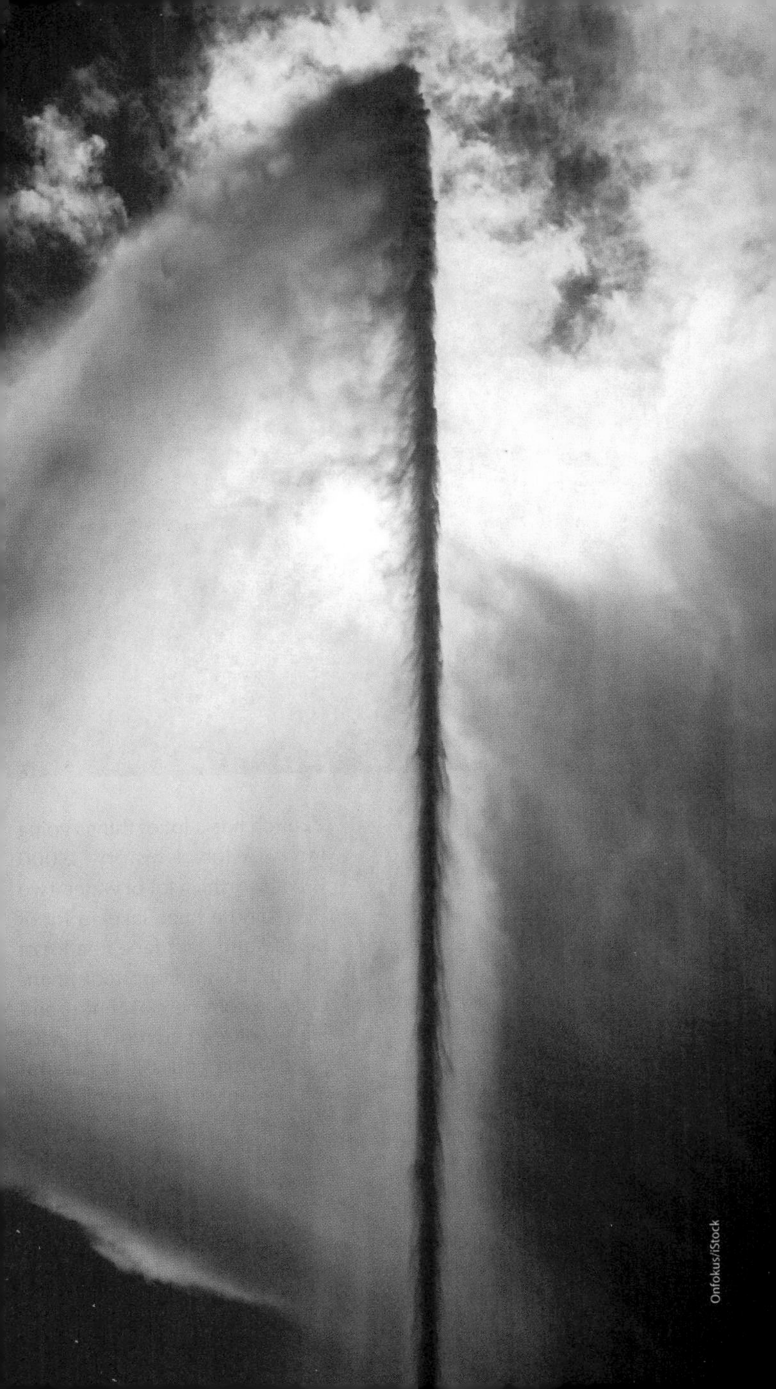

Onfokus/iStock

ZURICH
ZÜRICH

Juergen Sack/iStock

ZURICH IN...

→ **ONE DAY**
Old Town, Bahnhofstrasse, Zurich West, Grossmünster.

→ **TWO DAYS**
Watch chessplayers on Lindenhof, see Chagall's windows at Fraumünster, Kunsthaus, Cabaret Voltaire, Café Odeon.

→ **THREE DAYS**
Utoquai, Zürichhorn Park, night at the Opera House.

Zurich has a lot of things going for it. A lot of history (2,000 years' worth), a lot of water (two rivers and a huge lake), a lot of beauty and, let's face it, a lot of wealth. It's an important financial and commercial centre, and has a well-earned reputation for good living and a rich cultural life. The place strikes a nice balance – it's large enough to boast some world-class facilities but small enough to hold onto its charm and old-world ambience. The window-shopping here sets it apart from many other European cities – from tiny boutiques and specialist emporiums to a shopping boulevard that's famed across the globe. Although it's not Switzerland's political capital, it's the spiritual one because of its

pulsing arts scene: for those who might think the Swiss a bit staid, think again – this is where the nihilistic, anti-art Dada movement began. The attractive Lake Zurich flows northwards into the city, which forms a pleasingly symmetrical arc around it. From the lake, the river Limmat bisects Zurich: on its west bank lies the Old Town, the medieval hub, where the stylishly vibrant Bahnhofstrasse shopping street follows the line of the old city walls. Across the Limmat on the east side is the magnificent twin-towered Grossmünster, while just beyond is the charmingly historic district of Niederdorf and way down south, is the city's largest green space, the Zürichhorn Park.

EATING OUT

Zurich stands out in Switzerland (along with Geneva) for its top-class restaurants serving international cuisine. Zurich, though, takes the prize when it comes to trendy, cutting-edge places to dine, whether restaurant or bar, whether along the lakeside or in the converted loft of an old factory. In the middle of the day, most locals go for the cheaper daily lunchtime menus, saving themselves for the glories of the evening. The city is host to many traditional, longstanding Italian restaurants, but if you want to try something 'totally Zurcher', you can't do any better than tackle geschnetzeltes with rösti: sliced veal fried in butter, simmered with onions and mushrooms, with a dash of white wine and cream, served with hashed brown potatoes. A good place for simple restaurants and bars is Niederdorf, while Zurich West is coming on strong with its twenty-first century zeitgeist diners. It's customary to round up a small bill or leave up to ten percent on a larger one.

Florhof – Hotel Florhof

XX

Florhofgasse 4 ✉ 8001 – ✆ 044 250 26 26 Plan: **D2**
– www.hotelflorhof.ch – Closed 23 December-9 January and Saturday lunch, Sunday-Monday
Menu 51 CHF (lunch)/170 CHF – Carte 55/104 CHF
• Mediterranean cuisine • Cosy •

Fancy some flambéed tuna fish sashimi or pan-fried fillet of zander with peas, carrots and a ginger, coriander and macadamia nut gremolata? Try for a table on the lovely terrace – a little corner of peace and quiet in the heart of Zurich.

Stapferstube da Rizzo

XX

Culmannstr. 45 ✉ 8006 – ✆ 044 350 11 00 Plan: **D1**
– www.stapferstube.com – Closed Sunday
Menu 46 CHF (lunch) – Carte 49/110 CHF
• Italian • Rustic •

Southern Italian Giovanni Rizzo has been calling the shots here at Stapferstube, a well-known Zurich eatery, for some time. As a result, the cooking has a strong Italian feel, as evidenced by the delicious pan-fried squid with garlic, herbs and chilli. The food is served in a friendly, rustic setting and outdoors in summer. Conveniently, the restaurant has its own car park.

Bauernschänke

X

Rindermarkt 24 ✉ 8001 – ✆ 044 262 41 30 Plan: **D2**
– www.bauernschaenke.ch – Closed 22 July-5 August and Saturday lunch, Sunday
Carte 43/91 CHF – *(booking essential at dinner)*
• Country • Inn • Cosy •

Set in a small alleyway and over 100 years old, Bauernschänke offers a cosy, rustic interior, fresh regional cuisine and excellent value for money – try the marinated zander with Nostrano cucumber and dill. Unusually here the menu makes no difference between starters, entremets and main courses. Smaller lunchtime menu.

Drei Stuben

X

Beckenhofstr. 5 ✉ 8006 – ✆ 044 350 33 00 Plan: **C1**
– www.dreistuben-zuerich.ch – Closed Saturday lunch, Sunday
Menu 59/106 CHF – Carte 61/108 CHF
• Traditional cuisine • Rustic •

The floors, ceilings and walls here are all done out in rustic wood, lending a comfortable, cosy atmosphere to this restaurant – just what you would expect from a local hostelry with a 300-year-old tradition of serving food. There is also a lovely garden with mature trees. You are offered ambitious, traditional yet contemporary international food.

Bianchi

XX

Limmatquai 82 ✉ 8001 – ✆ 044 262 98 44 Plan: **D2**
– www.ristorante-bianchi.ch
Carte 49/109 CHF – *(booking advisable)*
• Seafood • Fashionable •

This bright, modern restaurant is located in a quiet spot on the banks of the River Limmat. It serves Mediterranean cuisine and diners are invited to take their pick from the fish and shellfish on offer at the generous buffet.

Conti

XX

Dufourstr. 1 ✉ 8008 – ✆ 044 251 06 66 Plan: **D3**
– www.bindella.ch – Closed 4 weeks mid July-mid August
Menu 56/62 CHF – Carte 78/100 CHF
• Italian • Mediterranean décor •

This restaurant is set immediately next to the opera. You'll find an interior of classical dignity with a lovely high stucco ceiling, an exhibition of paintings, and Italian cuisine.

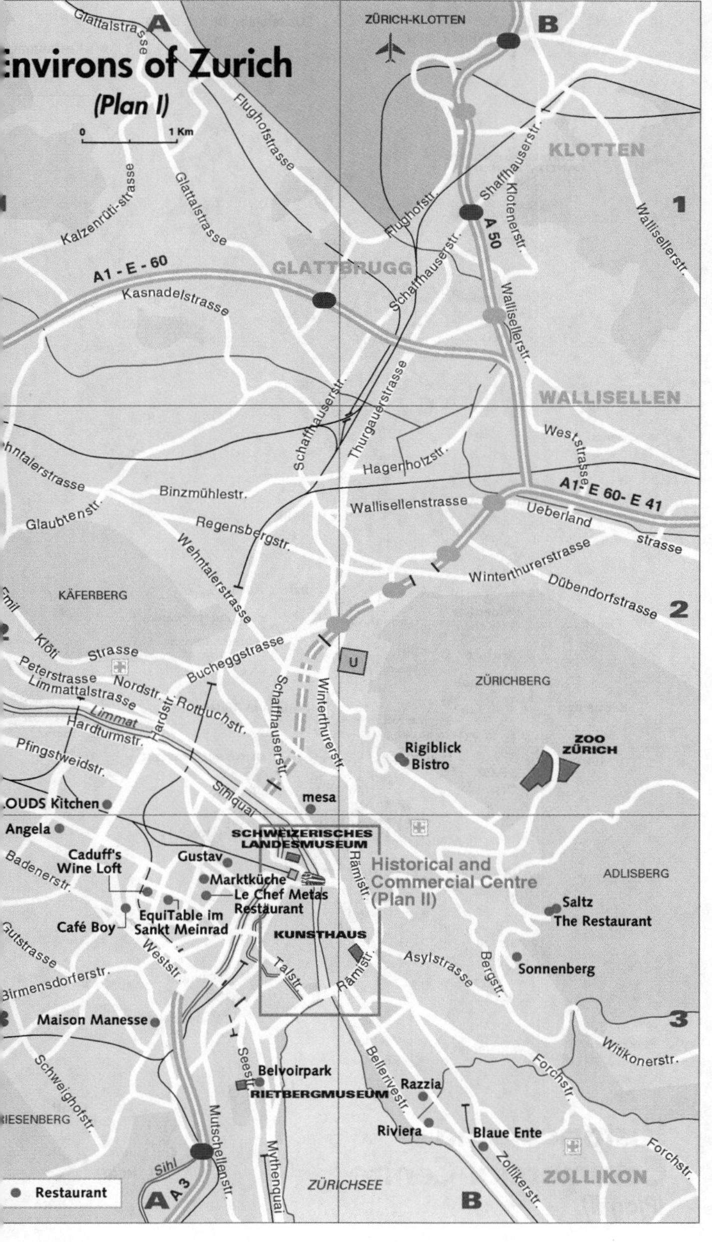
Environs of Zurich
(Plan I)
0
1 Km
A
B
1
2
3
ZÜRICH-KLOTTEN
KLOTTEN
GLATTBRUGG
WALLISELLEN
KÄFERBERG
ZÜRICHBERG
ADLISBERG
ZOLLIKON
ZÜRICHSEE
Glattalstrasse
Flughofstrasse
Kalzenrüti-strasse
A1 - E - 60
Kasnadelstrasse
Flughofstr.
Schaffhauserstr.
Shaffhauserstr.
Klotenerstr.
A 50
Wallisellerstr.
Thurgauerstrasse
Hagenholzstr.
Weststrasse
A1- E 60- E 41
Wallisellenstrasse
Ueberland strasse
Winterthurerstrasse
Dübendorfstrasse
Binzmühlestr.
Glaubtenstr.
Regensbergstr.
Wehntalerstrasse
Emil Klöti Strasse
Peterstrasse
Limmattalstrasse
Nordstr.
Rotbuchstr.
Bucheggstrasse
Hardstr.
Limmat
Hardturmstr.
Pfingstweidstr.
Sihlquai
Winterthurerstr.
U
Rigiblick Bistro
ZOO ZÜRICH
mesa
CLOUDS Kitchen
Angela
Caduff's Wine Loft
Gustav
Marktküche
Le Chef Metas Restaurant
EquiTable im Sankt Meinrad
Café Boy
SCHWEIZERISCHES LANDESMUSEUM
Historical and Commercial Centre (Plan II)
Rämistr.
KUNSTHAUS
Talstr.
Asylstrasse
Bergstr.
Saltz The Restaurant
Sonnenberg
Badenerstr.
Gutstrasse
Weststr.
Birmensdorferstr.
Maison Manesse
Schweighofstr.
RIESENBERG
Seestr.
Belvoirpark
RIETBERGMUSEUM
Bellerivestr.
Razzia
Riviera
Blaue Ente
Witikonerstr.
Forchstr.
Zollikerstr.
Mutschellenstr.
Mythenquai
Sihl
A 3
Restaurant

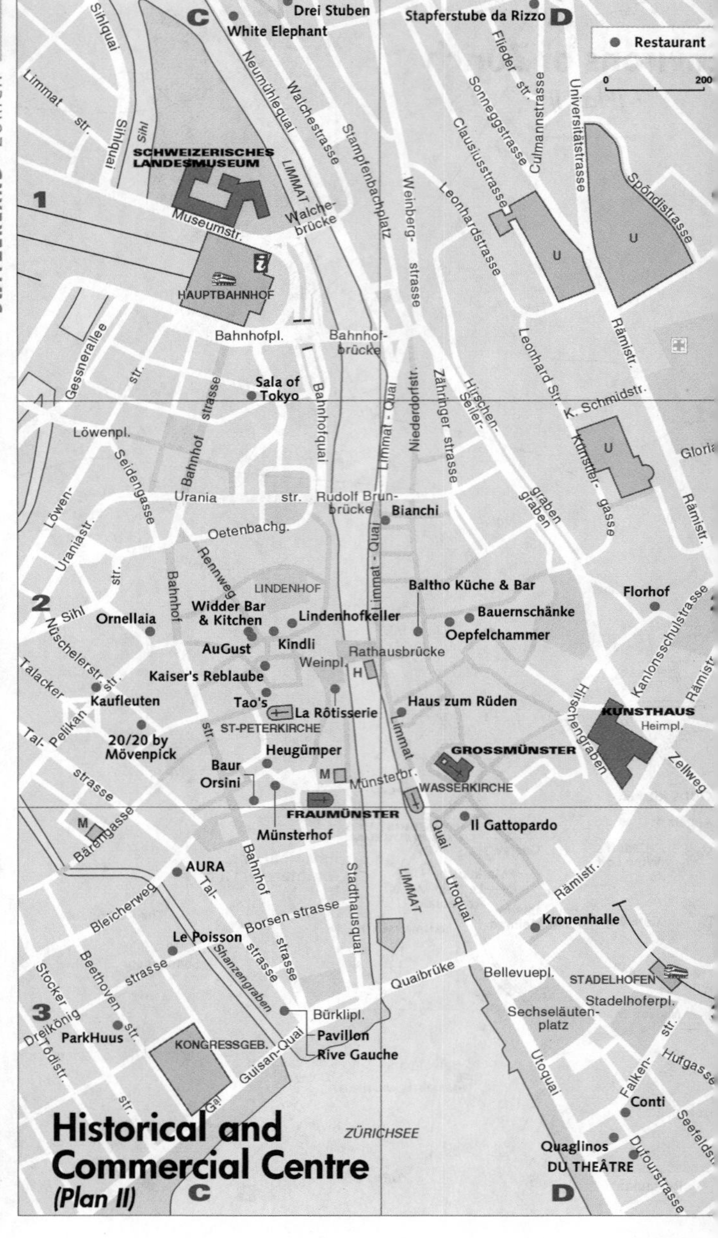

Historical and Commercial Centre
(Plan II)

Haus zum Rüden

Limmatquai 42 (1st Floor) ✉ 8001 – ✆ 044 261 95 66 Plan: **D2**
– www.hauszumrueden.ch – Closed 24 December-6 January and Saturday lunch, Sunday-Monday
Menu 36 CHF (weekday lunch)/165 CHF – Carte 73/116 CHF
• Modern cuisine • Elegant •

This guild house on the Münsterbrücke bridge dates back to 1348, as does the unique 11m-wide wooden barrel-vaulted ceiling in the Gothic Room. It serves Mediterranean crossover cuisine with Southeast Asian and North African influences. The modern Rüden Bar (complete with terrace) also serves a small selection of food.

Kronenhalle

Rämistr. 4 ✉ 8001 – ✆ 044 262 99 00 Plan: **D3**
– www.kronenhalle.com
Carte 66/142 CHF – *(booking advisable)*
• Traditional cuisine • Classic décor •

This building, constructed in 1862, is a Zurich institution, and is located on Bellevue Square. Be sure to take a look at the art collection put together over a period of decades. The atmosphere is traditional, as is the cooking.

Quaglinos – Hotel Europe

Dufourstr. 4 ✉ 8008 – ✆ 043 456 86 86 Plan: **D3**
– www.europehotel.ch
Carte 39/108 CHF
• Classic French • Bistro •

A lively and authentic Quaglinos brasserie based on the tried and tested bistro formula. It offers typical French savoir vivre and, of course, classic French cuisine including duck foie gras and 'Café de Paris' entrecote.

Il Gattopardo – Hotel Rössli

Rössligasse 7 (1st floor) ✉ 8001 – ✆ 079 605 01 08 Plan: **D3**
– www.ilgattopardo.ch – Closed Sunday
Menu 65/125 CHF – Carte 68/88 CHF – *(dinner only)*
• Italian • Family •

Located on the first floor of the Hotel Rössli, this charming family-run restaurant is decorated with lovely blue and white terracotta tiles. Try the 'spaghetti mafiosi' or the branzino al sale grosso (sea bass cooked in salt). Specialities include truffles in winter and asparagus in the spring.

Oepfelchammer

Rindermarkt 12 (1st floor) ✉ 8001 – ✆ 044 251 23 36 Plan: **D2**
– www.oepfelchammer.ch – Closed 15 July-13 August, 23 December-7 January, Sunday-Monday and Bank Holidays
Menu 69 CHF – Carte 63/84 CHF
• Traditional cuisine • Rustic • Wine bar •

The oldest remaining wine tavern in Zurich dating back to the 14C, Oepfelchammer once played host to 19C Swiss poet Gottfried Keller. In keeping with the quaint rustic charm, it serves traditional Swiss fare. Don't be afraid to try your hand at the famed "beam challenge"!

White Elephant

Neumühlequai 42 ✉ 8006 – ✆ 044 360 73 22 Plan: **C1**
– www.whiteelephant.ch – Closed Saturday lunch, Sunday lunch
Menu 39 CHF (weekday lunch) – Carte 60/98 CHF
• Thai • Exotic décor •

This restaurant in the Marriott Hotel is a must for fans of authentic Thai cuisine. Made with market fresh produce, the food is authentic and authentically spicy! Whatever you do, don't miss the curries.

DU THÉÂTRE

Dufourstr. 20 ✉ 8008 – ✆ 044 251 48 44 Plan: **D3**
– www.du-theatre.ch – Closed 1 week Christmas-New Year and Saturday lunch, Sunday
Carte 51/98 CHF

• Traditional cuisine • Fashionable • Bistro •

Established in 1890, this fashionable restaurant full of historic charm is located close to the Zurich Opera. It offers traditional and Southeast Asian cuisine ranging from beef tartare to chicken teriyaki with poached egg and mushrooms, as well as 'Sashimi Du Théâtre'. There's a smaller lunchtime menu.

LEFT BANK OF THE RIVER LIMMAT — PLAN II

Pavillon – Hotel Baur au Lac

Talstr. 1 ✉ 8001 – ✆ 044 220 50 22 Plan: **C3**
– www.aupavillon.ch – Closed 15-26 February, 8-22 October and Saturday lunch, Sunday, Bank Holidays
Menu 98 CHF (lunch)/205 CHF – Carte 119/224 CHF

• Classic French • Elegant • Friendly •

Star architect Pierre-Yves Rochon designed this elegant restaurant and the almost 360° glazed rotunda with its country views is wonderful. The exquisite classic cuisine is prepared by Laurent Eperon and includes dishes such as roast sea bass with Périgord truffles.

➜ Jakobsmuschel, Topinambur, schwarzer Trüffel, Kaviar. Kalbshaxe, Pelmeni à la Bordelaise, Gremolata. Honig, Milch, Brioche.

Ornellaia

St. Annagasse 2 ✉ 8001 – ✆ 044 212 00 22 Plan: **C2**
– www.ristorante-ornellaia.ch – Closed Sunday
Menu 65 CHF (lunch)/140 CHF – Carte 118/146 CHF

• Italian • Mediterranean décor •

This gem of a restaurant with its upmarket modern Tuscan interior and professional front-of-house team occupies a building that once housed a bank. Staff in the show kitchen prepare authentic Italian cuisine that is full of imagination and made using the very best produce. Many of the wines on the impressive wine list come from the eponymous winery.

➜ Tagliatelle mit Zucchini, Miesmuscheln und Safran. Rote Crevetten mit süss-saurem Gemüse. Kalbsentrecôte mit Zitronenkruste und Eierschwämmchen.

20/20 by Mövenpick

Nüschelerstr. 1 ✉ 8001 – ✆ 044 211 45 70 Plan: **C2**
– www.moevenpick-wein.com/20-20 – Closed mid July-mid August, Saturday lunch, Sunday-Monday and Bank Holidays
Menu 105/125 CHF – Carte 82/103 CHF – *(dinner only) (booking advisable)*

• Modern cuisine • Elegant •

You'll find a casual wine bar on the ground floor here and a gourmet restaurant with elegant, traditional Swiss pine panelling and modern touches on the first. The food is classically based with a certain refinement and accompanied by some excellent wines, almost all available by the glass. Slightly simpler lunchtime menu.

➜ Blauer Hummer, Mais, Safran, Estragon, Dill. Steinbutt, Eierschwämmli, Sellerie, Peterli. Kokosnuss und Maracuja, Meringue, Melisse.

AuGust – Hotel Widder

Rennweg 7 ✉ 8001 – ✆ 044 224 28 28 Plan: **E2**
– www.au-gust.ch – Closed mid July-mid August and Sunday-Monday
Carte 47/122 CHF

• Meats and grills • Brasserie •

Diners here enjoy fresh, flavoursome cuisine in a charming, classic brasserie setting. Dishes include some excellent terrines and sausages – try the meatloaf or a dish of venison goulash. Parties of six and over should book.

Kaufleuten

Plan: C2

Pelikanplatz ✉ 8001 – ✆ 044 225 33 33 – www.kaufleuten.ch – Closed Sunday
Carte 44/84 CHF

• Market cuisine • Brasserie •

This lively brasserie located in the fashionable venue of the same name is much in demand, not least thanks to its good food. Try the duck ravioli with leek salad or the veal cutlet – sliced for you at your table – before moving on to the bar or club.

Baur – Hotel Savoy Baur en Ville

Plan: C2

Poststr. 12 (at Paradeplatz) ✉ 8001 – ✆ 044 215 25 25 – www.savoy-zuerich.ch – Closed Saturday-Sunday
Menu 72 CHF – Carte 84/146 CHF

• Classic French • Elegant • Classic décor •

This restaurant has a stylish, elegant feel that is perfect for its classic French cuisine. Details such as the unusual rock crystal chandeliers together with the luxury fittings and smart table settings set the scene.

Rive Gauche – Hotel Baur au Lac

Plan: C3

Talstr. 1 ✉ 8001 – ✆ 044 220 50 60 – www.agauche.ch – Closed 14 July-11 August
Menu 49 CHF – Carte 66/170 CHF

• Classic cuisine • Cosy •

A 'brasserie de luxe', Rive Gauche offers chic, stylish design, attentive and accomplished service and modern cuisine with an attractive bar to boot. Menu offerings range from octopus carpaccio and vegan ravioli to steak and the Wagyu beefburger.

Heugümper

Plan: C2

Waaggasse 4 ✉ 8001 – ✆ 044 211 16 60 – www.restaurantheuguemper.ch – Closed 16 July-10 August, 23 December-6 January, January-September: Saturday-Sunday, October-December: Saturday lunch, Sunday
Menu 120 CHF (dinner) – Carte 71/98 CHF

• Modern cuisine • Elegant • Romantic •

This venerable townhouse in the heart of Zurich serves international food with a Southeast Asian Twist, in its smart modern interior. At lunchtime they offer a smaller menu.

Kaiser's Reblaube

Plan: C2

Glockengasse 7 ✉ 8001 – ✆ 044 221 21 20 – www.kaisers-reblaube.ch – Closed end July-mid August, January-October: Saturday lunch, Sunday-Monday; November-December: Saturday lunch, Sunday
Menu 58 CHF (weekday lunch)/135 CHF – Carte 66/97 CHF

• Classic cuisine • Rustic • Cosy •

Enjoy modern cooking with a traditional influence in this house that was built in 1260 along a small, narrow alley. Comfortable little restaurant on the first-floor and a wine bar on the ground floor.

Kindli – Hotel Kindli

Plan: C2

Pfalzgasse 1 ✉ 8001 – ✆ 043 888 76 76 – www.kindli.ch – Closed Sunday and Bank Holidays
Carte 67/116 CHF

• Classic French • Inn •

The restaurant's charming character comes in part from its wonderful old wood panelling and the bistro-style, communal arrangement of its beautifully laid tables.

La Rôtisserie – Hotel Storchen XX

Weinplatz 2 (access via Storchengasse 16) ✉ 8001 – ✆ 044 227 27 27 – www.storchen.ch

Plan: C2

Menu 110 CHF (dinner) – Carte 74/94 CHF

• Classic French • Classic décor • Intimate •

The classically traditional Rôtisserie boasts a lovely high-ceilinged dining room with large arched windows and an elegant atmosphere and serves French cuisine with Swiss influences. Try the veal ravioli with sage foam, the zander Café de Paris or the woodland game. The lovely terrace looks over the River Limmat.

Lindenhofkeller XX

Pfalzgasse 4 ✉ 8001 – ✆ 044 211 70 71 – www.lindenhofkeller.ch – Closed 3 weeks end July-August, 1 week Christmas, Saturday-Sunday and Bank Holidays

Plan: C2

Menu 49 CHF (weekday lunch)/125 CHF – Carte 49/125 CHF

• Classic cuisine • Elegant • Romantic •

With its homely, romantic touch, this elegant cellar restaurant and wine lounge fits harmoniously into the contemplative Old Town scene. Classic cooking exhibits a modern touch.

Orsini – Hotel Savoy Baur en Ville XX

Poststr. 12 (at Paradeplatz) ✉ 8001 – ✆ 044 215 25 25 – www.savoy-zuerich.ch

Plan: C2

Menu 76 CHF – Carte 62/144 CHF

• Italian • Elegant • Classic décor •

This elegant restaurant has been serving classic Italian cuisine for over 30 years. The sumptuous poppy design on the carpet, repeated in the filigree motif in the oil paintings on the walls, adds a special touch.

ParkHuus – Hotel Park Hyatt XX

Beethoven Str. 21 ✉ 8002 – ✆ 043 883 10 75 – www.zurich.park.hyatt.ch – Closed Saturday lunch, Sunday

Plan: C3

Menu 59 CHF (lunch)/175 CHF – Carte 53/141 CHF

• Modern cuisine • Fashionable •

The restaurant here is every bit as contemporary and international as the hotel, and the modern dishes that emerge from the show kitchen are made using good Swiss produce. There is also an impressive glazed wine cellar accessible via a spiral staircase.

Le Poisson – Hotel Glärnischhof XX

Claridenstr. 30 ✉ 8022 – ✆ 044 286 22 22 – www.lepoisson.ch – Closed Saturday lunch, Sunday and Bank Holidays

Plan: C3

Menu 59/120 CHF – Carte 53/130 CHF

• Seafood • Classic décor •

It is all about seafood here, with menu options ranging from bouillabaisse to sea bass and lobster claws. Diners can look forward to house classics but should also take a look at some of the kitchen team's new dishes. The interior is tastefully decorated.

Tao's XX

Augustinergasse 3 ✉ 8001 – ✆ 044 448 11 22 – www.taos-zurich.ch – Closed Sunday

Plan: C2

Carte 62/143 CHF

• Fusion • Exotic décor • Elegant •

A touch of the exotic in the middle of Zurich! Elegant upstairs, a little more informal on the ground floor. Smokers can use Tao's Lounge Bar that offers a Euro-Asian menu. Grilled meats.

Widder Bar & Kitchen – Hotel Widder

Plan: **C2**

Rennweg 7 ✉ 8001
– ✆ 044 224 24 12 – www.widderhotel.com
– Closed mid July-mid August and Sunday
Menu 55 CHF (lunch) – Carte 48/100 CHF
• International • Cosy •

The venerable Widder restaurant is now ultramodern and trendy, sporting the motto "Follow the flavour". Patrons eat in smart dining rooms, at the bar or right opposite the open kitchen. You'll find international dishes available to share including dim sum with North Sea prawns, coriander and tomato soy sauce.

AURA

Plan: **C3**

Bleicherweg 5 ✉ 8001 – ✆ 044 448 11 44
– www.aura-zurich.ch – Closed Saturday lunch, Sunday
Carte 44/129 CHF
• Meats and grills • Trendy • Design •

A stylishly urban restaurant, a top-flight events venue, a lounge or a club? AURA is a little bit of each, but above all the place to be for lovers of modern crossover cuisine with a weakness for grilled food – just watch the chefs at work! Located on Paradeplatz in the old stock exchange building.

Münsterhof

Plan: **C2**

Münsterhof 6 ✉ 8001 – ✆ 044 262 33 00
– www.mhof.ch – Closed end December-early January and Sunday-Monday
Menu 41 CHF (weekday lunch) – Carte 55/98 CHF
• Classic cuisine • Rustic • Friendly •

Set in a historic 11C building, Münsterhof offers a rustic dining room on the ground floor and something a little more elegant upstairs. The menus are the same and include homemade tortellini with veal and Lake Zurich bouillabaisse, not to mention an excellent steak tartare.

Sala of Tokyo

Plan: **C1**

Schützengasse 5 ✉ 8001
– ✆ 044 271 52 90 – www.sala-of-tokyo.ch
– Closed Saturday lunch and Sunday-Monday
Menu 75 CHF (lunch)/200 CHF (dinner) – Carte 46/320 CHF
• Japanese • Fashionable •

Following a move to Zurich's vibrant business and shopping district, Sala of Tokyo continues to offer authentic Japanese cuisine made using the very best ingredients. Try the shabu shabu, sushi and sashimi and tempura or the fish and Kobe beef from the robata grill. The designer interior is sober, modern and upmarket.

ENVIRONS OF ZURICH — PLAN I

The Restaurant

Plan: **B3**

Hotel The Dolder Grand – Kurhausstr. 65 ✉ 8032
– ✆ 044 456 60 00 – www.thedoldergrand.com – Closed 17 February-4 March and Saturday lunch, Sunday-Monday
Menu 98 CHF (weekday lunch)/278 CHF – Carte 163/242 CHF
• Creative • Luxury • Elegant •

For years now this stylish restaurant above the rooftops of Zurich has been the home of elaborate, creative cuisine full of contrasts made using only the finest ingredients. If you fancy trying a little of everything, go for the tasting menu. Charming service, excellent wine selection.

➜ Bretonischer Hummer mit Erdbeeren, Rande, Estragon und Senf. Weisser Spargel mit Ei, Kresse und Kaviar. Kalb mit Emmentaler, Pfifferlingen, Lattich und Meerrettich.

❀❀ Ecco Zürich – Hotel Atlantis by Giardino

Döltschiweg 234 (by Birmensdorferstrasse) ✉ 8055 – ✆ 044 456 55 55 – www.ecco-restaurant.ch – Closed 7 January-6 February and Sunday-Monday

Menu 160/260 CHF – *(dinner only)*

• Creative • Design • Elegant •

This creative concept is already well known from the Ecco restaurants in Ascona and St. Moritz, but here Stefan Heilemann brings his own personal touch. He cooks innovative food with fine, intelligent contrasts and great depth. The interior is genuinely elegant, while the service is friendly and professional.

➜ Gamba Carabiniera, Tomate, Koriander, Thai Salsa. Steinbutt aus der Bretagne, Blumenkohl, Erdnuss, rotes Curry. Japanisches Wagyu Entrecôte Kagoshima, gegrilltes Carpaccio, Zwiebel, Sauerrahm.

❀ Rigiblick

Germaniastr. 99 ✉ 8044 Plan: **B2**

– ✆ 043 255 15 70 – www.restaurantrigiblick.ch

– Closed 11-24 February, 15 July-18 August and Sunday-Tuesday

Menu 120/250 CHF – *(dinner only) (booking essential)*

• Modern cuisine • Elegant • Intimate •

Set in a smart residential district overlooking Zurich, the amazing view alone is a great draw, though it is more than matched by the attractive modern interior and sophisticated cuisine. The food, which includes vegetarian options, is made using local organic products. Those who wish to stay longer will appreciate the pretty apartments.

➜ Konfierter Saibling, Flaacher Spargel, Rinderherz, Nussbutter. Eierschwämmli, Kohlrabi, Fichtensprossen. Geschmorte Kalbsbacke, pochiertes Mark, Süsskartoffel von Stuckis Hof, eingelegte Zitrone.

🍽 **Bistro** – See below

❀ Gustav

Gustav-Gull-Platz 5 ✉ 8004 Plan: **A3**

– ✆ 044 250 65 00 – www.gustav-zuerich.ch

– Closed 1-6 January, Saturday lunch, Sunday and Bank Holidays, June-September: Sunday-Monday

Menu 56 CHF (weekday lunch)/145 CHF – Carte 82/114 CHF

• Italian • Design • Fashionable •

Set in an apartment block right next to the main railway station, this elegant restaurant also boasts a café, a bar and a lovely interior courtyard. The Italian food on offer includes turbot and calamari *alla romana* and boned shoulder of veal with polenta.

➜ Raviolone mit Ricotta, Eigelb, Carciofini, Salbeibutter. Rindsfilet mit Rucola-Parmiganokruste, marinierte Tomaten. Aprikose, weisse Schokolade, Tonkabohnenchantilly, Pistaziencrumble.

❀ mesa

Weinbergstr. 75 ✉ 8006 Plan: **A2**

– ✆ 043 321 75 75 – www.mesa-restaurant.ch

– Closed 24 December-10 January, 15 July-14 August and Saturday lunch, Sunday-Monday

Menu 78 CHF (lunch)/135 CHF

• Modern cuisine • Minimalist • Elegant •

Tasteful and pleasantly unpretentious, mesa boasts a friendly atmosphere, great service and excellent, produce-based food that is tasty and full of contrast. Wine lovers will be pleased to hear that even the rare wines on offer here are available by the glass.

➜ Salat aus 33 Blüten und Kräutern mit Aceto Balsamico. Freilandei mit Tessiner Polenta, jungem Spinat und Trüffel-Vinaigrette. Flat Iron mit Kartoffelcrème und Zucchetti.

EquiTable im Sankt Meinrad

Plan: **A3**

Stauffacherstr. 163 ✉ *8004 – ✆ 043 534 82 77 – www.equi-table.ch – Closed Sunday-Monday*
Menu 120/180 CHF – *(dinner only)*

• Modern cuisine • Fashionable •

Just as Sankt Meinrad's parent company deals only in fair trade and organic products, so its kitchen team under Fabian Fuchs uses nothing but the best ingredients in its modern cuisine. The whole experience is rounded off by the friendly service and informal atmosphere.

➜ Milchkuh, Meerrettich, Apfel, Radisli. Zander, Zwiebel, Alpenstörkaviar. Basilikum, Ziegenfrischkäse, Walderdbeeren.

Maison Manesse

Plan: **A3**

Hopfenstr. 2 ✉ *8045 – ✆ 044 462 01 01 – www.maisonmanesse.ch – Closed 3 weeks July-August, Christmas-New Year and Sunday-Monday*
Menu 130 CHF (Vegetarian)/142 CHF – Carte 75/95 CHF

• Creative • Rustic • Family •

If you like relaxed dining, you will enjoy this friendly, informal restaurant and its excellent, creative cuisine prepared using top-quality produce. A must for wine lovers, the 1 200 bottles on its wine list include a number of rarities and old vintages. Much reduced lunchtime menu.

➜ Rindstatar. Stundenei mit Erbsenpüree, geräucherten Pilze und Bärlauch. Zürich Zander mit grilliertem Mönchsbart, Rhabarber und Dillöl.

Belvoirpark

Plan: **A3**

Seestr. 125 ✉ *8002 – ✆ 044 286 88 44 – www.belvoirpark.ch – Closed 2 weeks Christmas, during Easter and Sunday-Monday*
Menu 86 CHF (dinner)/119 CHF – Carte 58/118 CHF

• Classic cuisine • Classic décor • Historic •

Belvoirpark is located in a smart, period villa in the park of the same name and doubles as a teaching facility for Zurich's School of Hotel Management. The interior is elegant, the cuisine predominantly classic. Dishes such as the steak tartare and crêpes Suzette are prepared in the traditional manner at your table.

Da Angela

Plan: **A3**

Hohlstr. 449 ✉ *8048 – ✆ 044 492 29 31 – www.daangela.ch – Closed 23 December-7 January, end July-early August and Saturday lunch, Sunday, Bank Holidays*
Carte 57/125 CHF

• Italian • Traditional décor •

It's no wonder that this long-established restaurant with its traditional charm is so popular. It serves really good classic Italian cuisine including home-made pasta – try the cappelletti Angela – and the ever popular ossobuco.

Café Boy

Plan: **A3**

Kochstr. 2 ✉ *8004 – ✆ 044 240 40 24 – www.cafeboy.ch – Closed 2 weeks end December and Saturday-Sunday*
Menu 61 CHF (dinner)/82 CHF – Carte 58/88 CHF

• Traditional cuisine • Bistro •

Once home to left-wing political activists, Café Boy is now a simple, lively bistro serving fresh, traditional cuisine. There is a passion for wine as you can see from the extensive selection. Simpler lunchtime menu.

Hide & Seek – Hotel Atlantis by Giardino

Döltschiweg 234 (by Birmensdorferstrasse) ✉ *8055 – ✆ 044 456 55 55 – www.atlantisbygiardino.ch*
Carte 51/123 CHF

• International • Chic • Fashionable •

This restaurant with a fusion theme offers a mix of modern European, Middle Eastern and Southeast Asian cuisine and design. The menu includes Thai fishcakes and zander with black quinoa, vanilla carrots and orange *beurre blanc.*

Marktküche

Plan: **A3**

Feldstr. 98 ✉ 8004 – ✆ 044 211 22 11 – www.marktkueche.ch – Closed 24 December-7 January, 22 July-11 August and Sunday-Monday

Menu 99/129 CHF – Carte 64/83 CHF – *(dinner only)*

• Vegetarian • Trendy •

The name says it all here, where market-fresh vegetables are the order of the day on a menu which is both meat- and fish-free. Modern, vegetarian and full of flavour, menu options include artichoke, parsnip, Höngg truffle, foam and spinach – all sampled in a lively atmosphere.

Sonnenberg

Plan: **B3**

Hitzigweg 15 ✉ 8032 – ✆ 044 266 97 97 – www.dersonnenberg.ch – Closed 1-6 January

Menu 39 CHF (weekdays) – Carte 44/138 CHF – *(booking advisable)*

• Classic French • Chic •

Sonnenberg's elevated location above Zurich provides a wonderful view over the city and lake. The cuisine includes various Sonnenberg specials including traditional Swiss veal chops and boiled beef, as well as Piedmont gnocchi with King crab and the classic ossobuco. The terrace is truly idyllic.

Blaue Ente

Plan: **B3**

Seefeldstr. 223 ✉ 8008 – ✆ 044 388 68 40 – www.blaue-ente.ch – Closed Saturday lunch, Sunday and Bank Holidays

Carte 52/83 CHF – *(booking advisable)*

• Country • Trendy • Friendly •

Historic industrial architecture outside and a trendy and lively atmosphere (and some fine old machinery) inside. The service is attentive and straightforward while the flavoursome food is made using local produce. The flour even comes from the restaurant's own mill next door. There is a more ambitious evening menu.

CLOUDS Kitchen

Plan: **A3**

Maagplatz 5 (at Prime Tower, 35th floor) ✉ 8005 – ✆ 044 404 30 00 – www.clouds.ch

Menu 89/114 CHF – Carte 65/114 CHF – *(booking essential)*

• International • Chic • Elegant •

One of Zurich's culinary hotspots, CLOUDS boasts stunning views of the city. But it's not just the spectacle outside that deserves attention. The interesting mix of Mediterranean, Southeast Asian and classic cuisine includes lobster cocktail, slow-cooked pork belly and Japanese sea bass with pak choi. Meanwhile, the Bistro serves simpler fare.

Caduff's Wine Loft

Plan: **A3**

Kanzleistr. 126 ✉ 8004 – ✆ 044 240 22 55 – www.wineloft.ch – Closed 24 December-4 January, Saturday lunch and Sunday

Menu 30/120 CHF – Carte 47/108 CHF

• Classic French • Trendy • Neighbourhood •

This former engineering works serves tasty seasonal cuisine, including pheasant terrine with black chanterelle mushrooms and pistachios, followed perhaps by a raw-milk cheese. The walk-in wine cellar boasts over 2 000 different bottles!

Le Chef Metas Restaurant

Plan: **A3**

Kanonengasse 29 ✉ 8004 – ✆ 044 240 41 00 – www.restaurant-lechef.ch – Closed July-August, 1 week December and Sunday-Monday

Menu 79 CHF – Carte 47/115 CHF

• International • Cosy •

Known not only for her cookery books and television programmes, the charismatic Meta Hiltebrand's attractive and lively restaurant also enjoys great popularity – not least because of the food which includes dishes such as Le Chef Vitello and a Seafood Duet (lobster and yellow-fin tuna). There is even a very popular surprise menu.

Razzia
XX
Plan: **B3**
Seefeldstr. 82 ✉ 8008 – ✆ 044 296 70 70
– www.razzia-zuerich.ch – Closed Saturday lunch, Sunday
Carte 63/108 CHF – *(booking advisable)*
• International • Trendy • Brasserie •
One of the city's culinary hot spots, set in a former cinema. The small tables in this stylish high-ceilinged restaurant with its attractive stuccowork are highly coveted. Menu offerings range from Thai beef salad to misoyaki black cod and Wiener schnitzel.

Saltz – Hotel The Dolder Grand
XX
Plan: **B3**
Kurhausstr. 65 ✉ 8032 – ✆ 044 456 60 00
– www.thedoldergrand.com
Menu 54 CHF – Carte 89/167 CHF
• International • Fashionable • Friendly •
The original, modern design takes Switzerland as its theme while the international food concentrates on the essentials. The menu includes burrata with datterini tomatoes, hamachi sashimi, sea bass baked in a salt crust or, if you prefer, a dish of *Zürcher Geschnetzeltes* – veal strips in a cream and white wine sauce.

Bistro – Restaurant Rigiblick
X
Plan: **B2**
Germaniastr. 99 ✉ 8044 – ✆ 043 255 15 70
– www.restaurantrigiblick.ch – Closed 11-24 February, 15 July-18 August
Menu 35/65 CHF – Carte 57/102 CHF
• Modern cuisine • Bistro • Fashionable •
The friendly alternative to Rigiblick offers a relaxed bistro ambience and regional fare using seasonal produce. This includes wild boar stew with red cabbage, spätzli and caramelised chestnuts. The great terrace has a view over the city.

Riviera
X
Plan: **B3**
Dufourstr. 161 ✉ 8008 – ✆ 044 422 04 26
– www.enoteca-riviera.ch – Closed 1-10 January, 24 July-14 August and Saturday lunch, Sunday-Monday
Menu 75/125 CHF (dinner) – Carte 59/97 CHF
• Italian • Rustic •
Riviera boasts a charming rustic interior complete with green wood panelling. The food is authentic Italian and includes home-made pasta and ossobuco. Smaller lunchtime menu. There is also a wine shop.

Edinburgh
LONDON

UNITED KINGDOM
UNITED KINGDOM

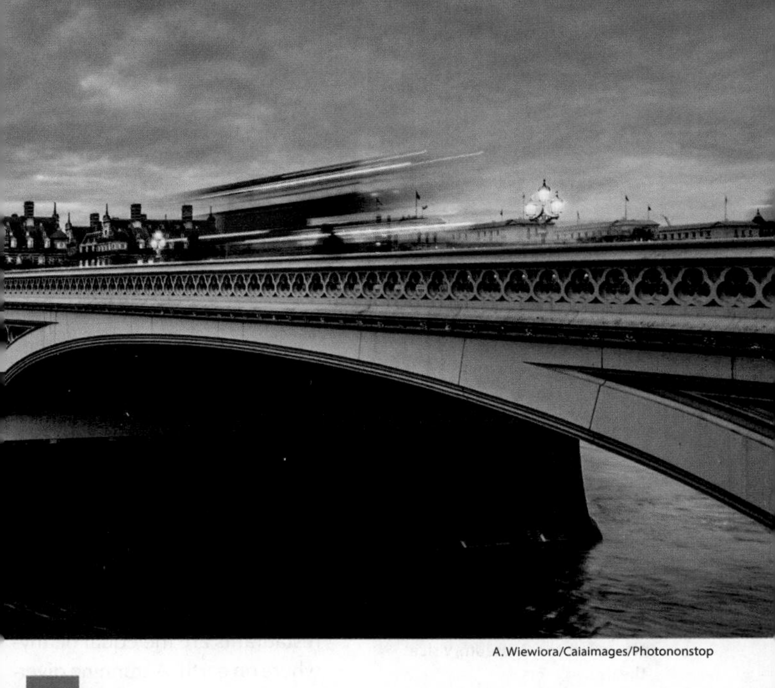

A. Wiewiora/Caiaimages/Photononstop

LONDON
LONDON

coldsnowstorm/iStock

LONDON IN…

➔ **ONE DAY**
British Museum, Tower of London, St Paul's Cathedral, Tate Modern.

➔ **TWO / THREE DAYS**
National Gallery, London Eye, Natural History Museum, visit a theatre.

➔ **THREE DAYS**
Science Museum, Victoria and Albert Museum, National Portrait Gallery.

The term 'world city' could have been invented for London. Time zones radiate from Greenwich, global finances zap round the Square Mile and its international restaurants are the equal of anywhere on earth. A stunning diversity of population is testament to the city's famed tolerance; different lifestyles and languages are as much a part of the London scene as cockneys and black cabs. London grew over time in a pretty haphazard way, swallowing up surrounding villages, but retaining an enviable acreage of green 'lungs': a comforting 30 per cent of London's area is made up of open space.

The drama of the city is reflected in its history. From Roman settlement to banking centre to capital of a 19C empire, the city's pulse has never missed a beat; it's no surprise that a dazzling array of theatres, restaurants, museums, markets and art galleries populate its streets. London's piecemeal character has endowed it with distinctly different areas, often breathing down each other's necks. North of Piccadilly lie the playgrounds of Soho and Mayfair, while south is the gentleman's clubland of St James's. On the other side of town are Clerkenwell and Southwark, artisan areas that have been scrubbed down and freshened up. The cool sophistication of Kensington and Knightsbridge is to the west, while a more touristy aesthetic is found in the heaving piazza zone of Covent Garden.

EATING OUT

London is one of the food capitals of the world, where you can eat everything from Turkish to Thai and Polish to Peruvian. Those wishing to sample classic British dishes also have more choice these days as more and more chefs are rediscovering home-grown ingredients, regional classics and traditional recipes. Eating in the capital can be pricey, so check out good value pre- and post-theatre menus, or try lunch at one of the many eateries that drop their prices, but not their standards, in the middle of the day. "Would I were in an alehouse in London! I would give all my fame for a pot of ale and safety", says Shakespeare's Henry V. Samuel Johnson agreed, waxing lyrical upon the happiness produced by a good tavern or inn. Pubs are often open these days from 11am to 11pm (and beyond), so this particular love now knows no bounds, and any tourist is welcome to come along and enjoy the romance. It's not just the cooking that has improved in pubs but wine too; woe betide any establishment in this city that can't distinguish its Gamay from its Grenache.

RESTAURANTS - ALPHABETICAL LIST

Alena Kravchenko/iStock

MAYFAIR

🏵🏵🏵 Alain Ducasse at The Dorchester – Dorchester Hotel

Park Ln ✉ W1K 1QA – Ⓜ Hyde Park Corner Plan: **G4**
– ✆ (020) 76298866 – www.alainducasse-dorchester.com
– Closed 3 weeks August, first week January, 26-30 December, Easter, Saturday lunch, Sunday and Monday
Menu £ 70/105 – *(booking essential)*
• French • Elegant • Luxury •

Alain Ducasse's elegant London outpost understands that it's all about making the diner feel at ease so expect service that is as charming as it is professional. The kitchen uses the best British or French produce to create stunning and visually striking dishes, including some that showcase the flavours of Southern France. The best tables are in the main room.

➜ Dorset crab, celeriac and caviar. Halibut with oyster and seaweed. 'Baba like in Monte Carlo'.

🏵🏵🏵 The Araki (Mitsuhiro Araki)

12 New Burlington St ✉ W1S 3BF – Ⓜ Oxford Circus Plan: **H3**
– ✆ (020) 7287 2481 – www.the-araki.com – Closed last 2 weeks August, Christmas-first week January and Monday
Menu £ 300 – *(dinner only) (booking essential) (tasting menu only)*
• Japanese • Intimate • Minimalist •

There are two sittings at Mitsuhiro Araki's 9-seater sushi counter, at 18.00 and 20.30, and payment is taken in advance. Only an omakase menu is served. His exquisite nigiri comes in manageable sizes and you can expect tuna and mackerel from Spanish waters, salmon from Scotland and caviar from Cornwall. The rice, grown by his father-in-law back in Japan, is extraordinary.

➜ Tuna tartare. Nigiri sushi. Wagashi.

🏵🏵 Hélène Darroze at The Connaught – Connaught Hotel

Carlos Pl. ✉ W1K 2AL – Ⓜ Bond Street
– ✆ (020) 71078880 – www.the-connaught.co.uk Plan: **G3**
Menu £ 55/105 – *(booking essential)*
• Modern cuisine • Luxury • Elegant •

From a Solitaire board of 13 marbles, each bearing the name of an ingredient, you choose 5, 7 or 9 (courses); this highlights the quality of produce used. The cooking is lighter these days yet still with the occasional unexpected flavour. The warm service ensures the wood-panelled room never feels too formal.

➜ Foie gras with black truffle, apple, celery and brioche. Venison with Sarawak pepper, butternut, grapes and Stichelton. Chocolate, cardamom and vanilla.

🏵🏵 Sketch (The Lecture Room & Library)

9 Conduit St (1st floor) ✉ W1S 2XG – Ⓜ Oxford Circus Plan: **H3**
– ✆ (020) 76594500 – www.sketch.london
– Closed 25 December, 1 January, 2 weeks late August-early September, Sunday, Monday and lunch Tuesday-Thursday.
Carte £ 102/131 – *(booking essential)*
• Modern French • Luxury • Elegant •

Mourad Mazouz and Pierre Gagnaire's 18C funhouse is awash with colour, energy and vim and the luxurious 'Lecture Room & Library' provides the ideal setting for the sophisticated French cooking. Relax and enjoy artfully presented, elaborate dishes that provide many varieties of flavours and textures.

➜ Live langoustines. Organic rack of pork with sage, mango vinegar and seasonal fruit. Pierre Gagnaire's 'Grand Dessert'.

✿✿ **Le Gavroche** (Michel Roux Jnr) XXXX ✿ A/C ⇔

Plan: **G3**

43 Upper Brook St ✉ W1K 7QR – Ⓜ Marble Arch
– ✆ (020) 74080881
– www.le-gavroche.co.uk
– Closed 2 weeks Christmas, Saturday lunch, Sunday, Monday and bank holidays
Menu £ 70/175 – Carte £ 68/197 – *(booking essential)*

• French • Intimate • Luxury •

In an age of tedious calorie counting there is something exhilarating about Michel Roux and head chef Rachel Humphrey's unapologetically extravagant French dishes. The ingredients are of the highest order, and the cheese board is one of London's best. A charming service team guide you through your meal and the hum of satisfaction that pervades the room says it all.

→ Artichoke with foie gras, truffles and chicken mousse. Butter poached lobster with white wine, asparagus and claw tart. Apricot and Cointreau soufflé.

✿✿ **Greenhouse** XXX ✿ A/C ⇔

Plan: **G4**

27a Hay's Mews ✉ W1J 5NY – Ⓜ Hyde Park Corner
– ✆ (020) 74993331
– www.greenhouserestaurant.co.uk
– Closed Saturday lunch, Sunday and bank holidays
Menu £ 45/100

• Creative • Fashionable • Elegant •

A charming setting reached via a mews and a small garden. This pastoral theme continues inside with a pale green colour scheme. The classical cuisine uses the finest ingredients from around Europe; the depth of the wine list is astounding. This discreet, sleek restaurant comes with well-judged service.

→ Native lobster with chicken, kohlrabi and cardamom leaf. Welsh lamb with aubergine, gomasio, harissa and soya. 'Ajuba Head' - chocolate with walnut and nutmeg.

✿✿ **Umu** XXX ✿ A/C

Plan: **H3**

14-16 Bruton Pl. ✉ W1J 6LX – Ⓜ Bond Street
– ✆ (020) 74998881
– www.umurestaurant.com
– Closed Christmas, New Year and Sunday
Menu £ 45/155 – Carte £ 46/151

• Japanese • Fashionable • Design •

Stylish, discreet interior using natural materials, with central sushi bar. Extensive choice of Japanese dishes; choose one of the seasonal kaiseki menus for the full experience. Over 160 different labels of sake.

→ Cornish cuttlefish with bottarga and tosazu sauce. Charcoal-grilled Wagyu tataki with vegetables and a sesame and ponzu sauce. Japanese seasonal tiramisu with matcha tea and ginjo sake.

✿ **Alyn Williams at The Westbury** XXXX ✿ ♿ A/C ⇔

Plan: **H3**

Westbury Hotel – 37 Conduit St ✉ W1S 2YF
– Ⓜ Bond Street – ✆ (020) 7183 6426 – www.alynwilliams.com
– Closed first 2 weeks January, last 2 weeks August, Sunday and Monday
Menu £ 30/90

• Modern cuisine • Design • Elegant •

Confident, cheery service ensures the atmosphere never strays into terminal seriousness; rosewood panelling and a striking wine display add warmth. The cooking is creative and even playful, but however elaborately constructed the dish, the combinations of flavours and textures always work.

→ Orkney scallop with yuzu caramel, white asparagus, morels and seaweed. Roasted halibut with fennel compote, cashews and coconut. Gariguette strawberry tartlet, lemon, vanilla curd and basil.

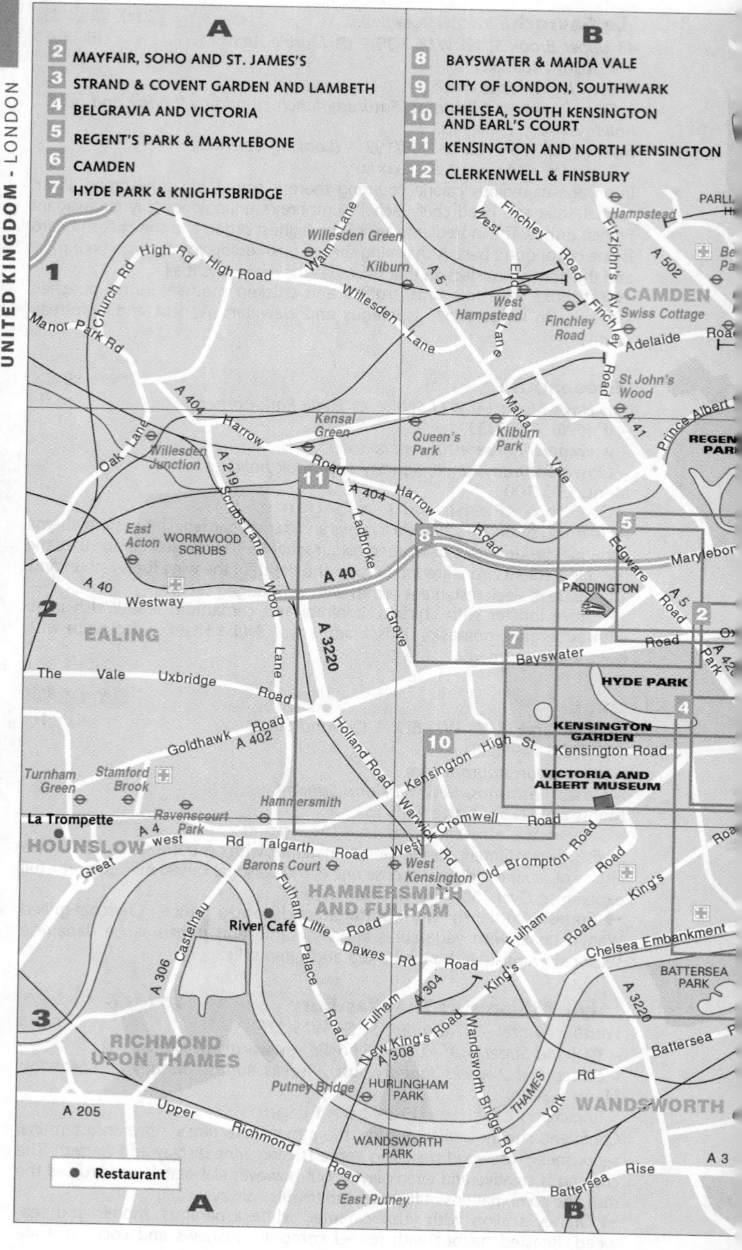
A
B
2 MAYFAIR, SOHO AND ST. JAMES'S
3 STRAND & COVENT GARDEN AND LAMBETH
4 BELGRAVIA AND VICTORIA
5 REGENT'S PARK & MARYLEBONE
6 CAMDEN
7 HYDE PARK & KNIGHTSBRIDGE
8 BAYSWATER & MAIDA VALE
9 CITY OF LONDON, SOUTHWARK
10 CHELSEA, SOUTH KENSINGTON AND EARL'S COURT
11 KENSINGTON AND NORTH KENSINGTON
12 CLERKENWELL & FINSBURY
1
2
3
Willesden Green
Walm Lane
Kilburn
A 5
High Rd
High Road
Church Rd
Willesden Lane
Manor Park Rd
West End Lane
West Hampstead
Finchley Road
Finchley Road
Fitzjohn's Av.
Hampstead
A 502
CAMDEN
Swiss Cottage
Adelaide Road
Finchley Road
St John's Wood
A 41
Prince Albert
REGENT'S PARK
PARLI
A 404
Harrow Road
Oak Lane
Willesden Junction
A 219
Kensal Green
Queen's Park
Kilburn Park
Maida Vale
Scrubs Lane
A 404
Harrow Road
Ladbroke Grove
East Acton
WORMWOOD SCRUBS
A 40
A 40
Westway
Wood Lane
A 3220
Marylebone
PADDINGTON
Edgware Road
A 5
EALING
The Vale
Uxbridge Road
Bayswater Road
HYDE PARK
KENSINGTON GARDEN
Kensington Road
Goldhawk Road
A 402
Holland Road
Kensington High St.
VICTORIA AND ALBERT MUSEUM
Turnham Green
Stamford Brook
Ravenscourt Park
Hammersmith
La Trompette
HOUNSLOW
A 4
Great west Rd
Talgarth Road
Cromwell Road
Warwick Rd
West Kensington
Barons Court
Old Brompton Road
HAMMERSMITH AND FULHAM
Fulham Road
King's Road
River Café
Lillie Road
Dawes Rd
A 306
Castelnau
Fulham Palace Road
Fulham Road
King's Road
A 304
Chelsea Embankment
BATTERSEA PARK
A 3220
RICHMOND UPON THAMES
New King's Road
A 308
Wandsworth Bridge Rd
THAMES
Battersea
York Rd
WANDSWORTH
Putney Bridge
HURLINGHAM PARK
A 205
Upper Richmond Road
WANDSWORTH PARK
East Putney
Battersea Rise
A 3
Restaurant

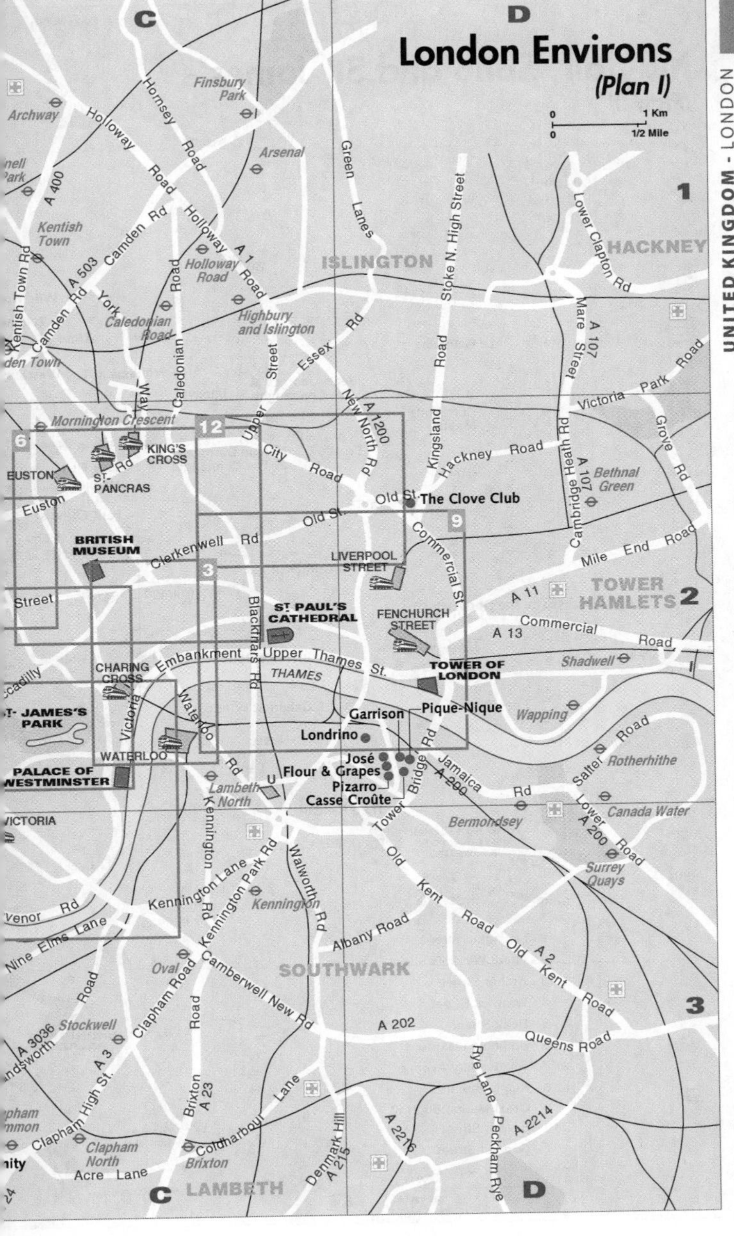
London Environs
(Plan I)
0 1 Km
0 1/2 Mile
C
D
1
2
3
Finsbury Park
Archway
Holloway Road
Hornsey Road
Arsenal
Green Lanes
Stoke N. High Street
Lower Clapton Rd
HACKNEY
A 400
Kentish Town
Kentish Town Rd
Camden Rd
A 503
York Way
Caledonian Road
Holloway Road
A 1
ISLINGTON
Highbury and Islington
Essex Rd
Upper Street
Mare Street
A 107
Victoria Park Road
Camden Town
Mornington Crescent
KING'S CROSS
ST. PANCRAS
EUSTON
Euston Rd
City Road
New North Rd
A 1200
Kingsland Road
Hackney Road
Cambridge Heath Rd
Grove Rd
Bethnal Green
Old St.
The Clove Club
Commercial St.
Mile End Road
BRITISH MUSEUM
Clerkenwell Rd
LIVERPOOL STREET
TOWER HAMLETS
A 11
Street
ST. PAUL'S CATHEDRAL
FENCHURCH STREET
Commercial Road
A 13
Blackfriars Rd
Embankment
Upper Thames St.
THAMES
TOWER OF LONDON
Shadwell
Piccadilly
CHARING CROSS
ST. JAMES'S PARK
Victoria
Waterloo Rd
Garrison
Pique-Nique
Wapping
Londrino
José
Flour & Grapes
Pizarro
Casse Croûte
Tower Bridge Rd
Jamaica Rd
A 200
Salter Road
Rotherhithe
WATERLOO
PALACE OF WESTMINSTER
Lambeth North
VICTORIA
Kennington Rd
Bermondsey
Lower Road
A 200
Canada Water
Surrey Quays
Kennington Lane
Kennington Park Rd
Walworth Rd
Kennington
Old Kent Road
Grosvenor Rd
Nine Elms Lane
Albany Road
Oval
Clapham Road
Camberwell New Rd
SOUTHWARK
A 2
Road
Stockwell
A 3036
Wandsworth
A 3
A 202
Queens Road
Clapham High St.
Brixton Road
A 23
Coldharbour Lane
Rye Lane
Peckham Rye
A 2216
A 2214
Clapham Common
Clapham North
Brixton
Acre Lane
Denmark Hill
A 215
LAMBETH
6
12
3
9

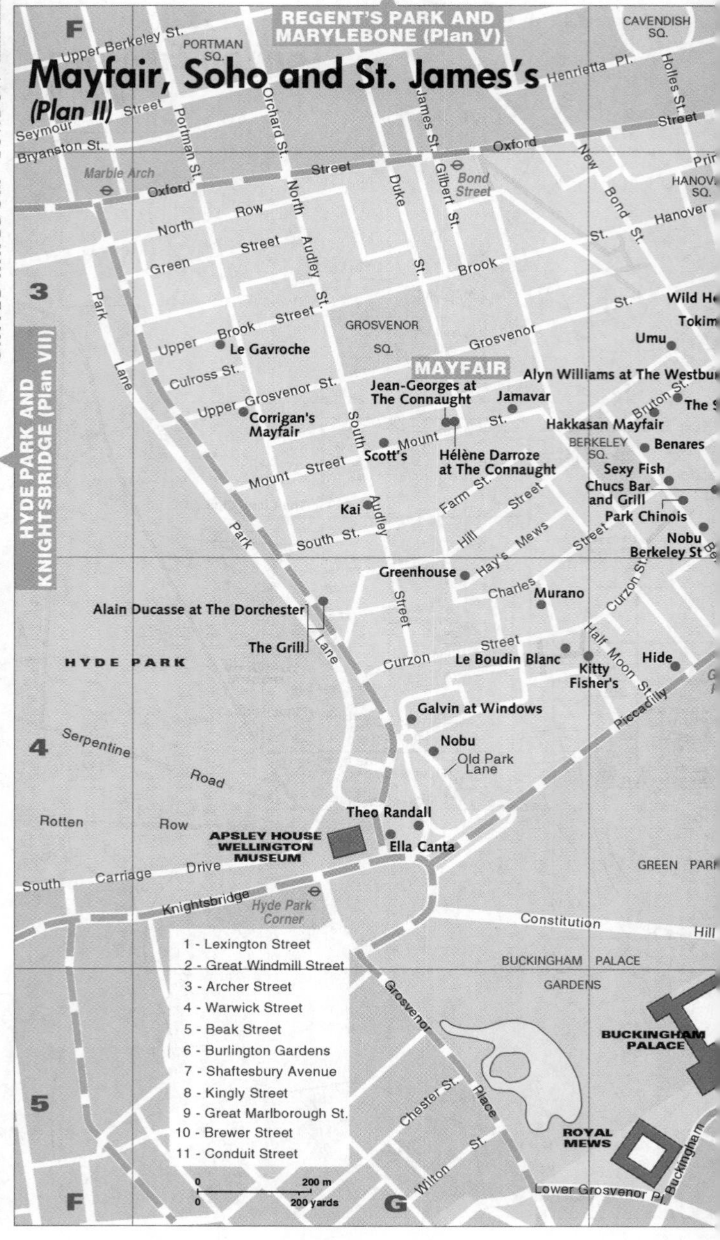

Mayfair, Soho and St. James's
(Plan II)
REGENT'S PARK AND MARYLEBONE (Plan V)
HYDE PARK AND KNIGHTSBRIDGE (Plan VII)
MAYFAIR
Le Gavroche
Corrigan's Mayfair
Scott's
Jean-Georges at The Connaught
Hélène Darroze at The Connaught
Jamavar
Kai
Umu
Alyn Williams at The Westbu
Hakkasan Mayfair
Benares
Sexy Fish
Chucs Bar and Grill
Park Chinois
Nobu Berkeley St
Greenhouse
Murano
Alain Ducasse at The Dorchester
The Grill
Le Boudin Blanc
Kitty Fisher's
Hide
Galvin at Windows
Nobu
Theo Randall
Ella Canta
APSLEY HOUSE WELLINGTON MUSEUM
HYDE PARK
GREEN PARK
BUCKINGHAM PALACE GARDENS
BUCKINGHAM PALACE
ROYAL MEWS
GROSVENOR SQ.
BERKELEY SQ.
PORTMAN SQ.
CAVENDISH SQ.
Marble Arch
Bond Street
Hyde Park Corner
1 - Lexington Street
2 - Great Windmill Street
3 - Archer Street
4 - Warwick Street
5 - Beak Street
6 - Burlington Gardens
7 - Shaftesbury Avenue
8 - Kingly Street
9 - Great Marlborough St.
10 - Brewer Street
11 - Conduit Street
0 200 m
0 200 yards

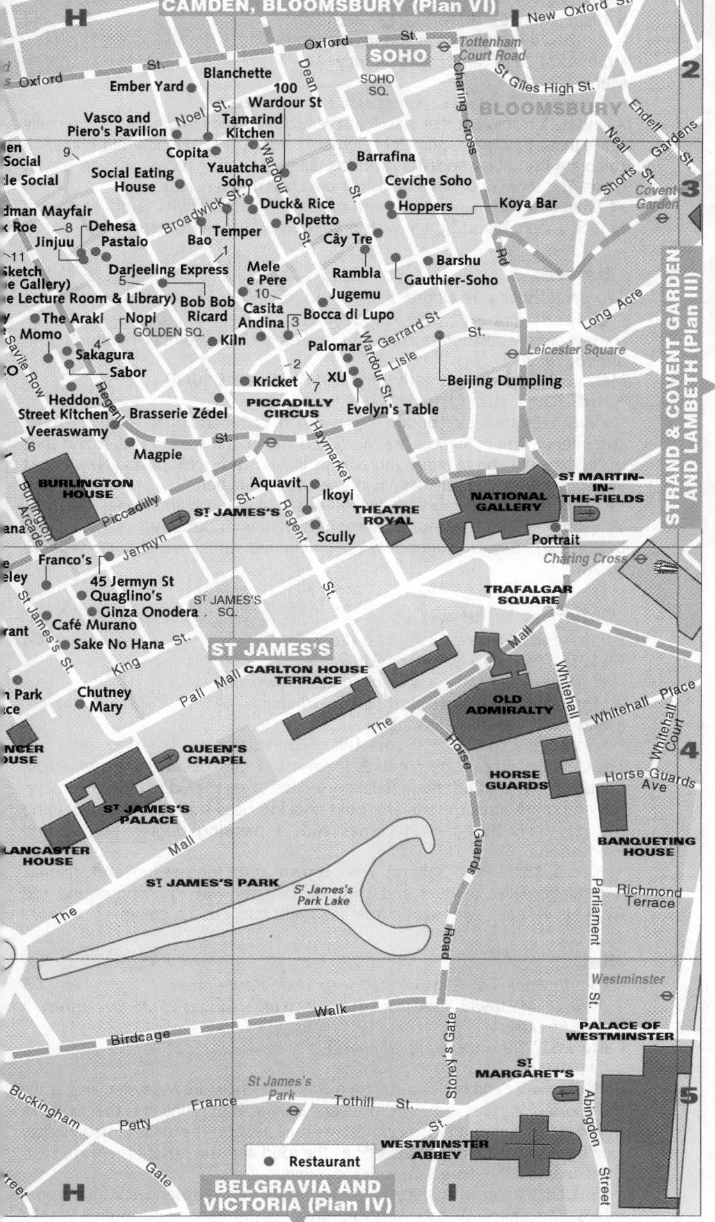
CAMDEN, BLOOMSBURY (Plan VI)
H
I
New Oxford St.
Oxford St.
SOHO
Tottenham Court Road
SOHO SQ.
St Giles High St.
Charing Cross Rd
BLOOMSBURY
Endell St.
Neal St.
Shorts Gardens
Covent Garden
2
3
4
5
Ember Yard
Blanchette
100 Wardour St
Noel St.
Dean St.
Vasco and Piero's Pavilion
Tamarind Kitchen
Copita
Wardour St.
Barrafina
Social Eating House
Yauatcha Soho
Ceviche Soho
Broadwick St.
Duck& Rice
Hoppers
Koya Bar
Polpetto
Dehesa
Pastaio
Jinjuu
Temper
Bao
Cây Tre
Barshu
Darjeeling Express
Mele e Pere
Rambla
Gauthier-Soho
Bob Bob Ricard
Jugemu
Casita Andina
Bocca di Lupo
The Araki
Nopi
GOLDEN SQ.
Momo
Kiln
Palomar
Gerrard St
Lisle St.
Long Acre
Leicester Square
Savile Row
Sakagura
Sabor
Kricket
XU
Beijing Dumpling
Heddon Street Kitchen
Regent St.
Brasserie Zédel
PICCADILLY CIRCUS
Evelyn's Table
Veeraswamy
Haymarket
STRAND & COVENT GARDEN AND LAMBETH (Plan III)
Magpie
BURLINGTON HOUSE
Burlington Arcade
Aquavit
Ikoyi
ST MARTIN-IN-THE-FIELDS
NATIONAL GALLERY
Piccadilly
ST JAMES'S
THEATRE ROYAL
Scully
Portrait
Jermyn St.
Franco's
Charing Cross
45 Jermyn St
Quaglino's
ST JAMES'S SQ.
TRAFALGAR SQUARE
Ginza Onodera
Café Murano
St James's St.
Sake No Hana
King St.
ST JAMES'S
CARLTON HOUSE TERRACE
The Mall
Pall Mall
Chutney Mary
OLD ADMIRALTY
Whitehall
Whitehall Place
Whitehall Court
QUEEN'S CHAPEL
Horse Guards Road
HORSE GUARDS
Horse Guards Ave
ST JAMES'S PALACE
LANCASTER HOUSE
BANQUETING HOUSE
ST JAMES'S PARK
St James's Park Lake
Richmond Terrace
Parliament St.
Westminster
Birdcage Walk
PALACE OF WESTMINSTER
Storey's Gate
ST MARGARET'S
St James's Park
Tothill St.
France
Petty
Buckingham Gate
Abingdon Street
WESTMINSTER ABBEY
Restaurant
BELGRAVIA AND VICTORIA (Plan IV)

The Square

XXXX Plan: H3

6-10 Bruton St. ✉ W1J 6PU – Ⓜ Green Park – ✆ (020) 74957100 – www.squarerestaurant.com – Closed 24-26 December and Sunday

Menu £ 37/85

• Creative French • Elegant • Intimate •

A landmark restaurant that wasn't just refurbished and re-launched – you really sense that a new era begun. Chef Clément Leroy, a proud Frenchman, is keen to celebrate the UK's wonderful produce, albeit with imaginative or even playful twists. The room now has a sleeker, more contemporary look.

➜ Orkney scallop with coffee and marsala. Aged Herdwick lamb 'earth and sea'. St John's Wood honey with grapefruit and sweet potato.

Benares

XXX Plan: H3

12a Berkeley Square House, Berkeley Sq. ✉ W1J 6BS – Ⓜ Green Park – ✆ (020) 76298886 – www.benaresrestaurant.com – Closed lunch 25 December,1 January and Sunday lunch

Menu £ 29 (lunch and early dinner)/98 – Carte £ 50/79

• Indian • Chic • Intimate •

No Indian restaurant in London enjoys a more commanding location or expansive interior. The influences are many and varied; the spicing is deft and they make excellent use of British ingredients like Scottish scallops and New Forest venison. The Chef's Table has a window into the kitchen.

➜ Crispy soft shell crab with puy lentil salad, kasundi and honey dressing. Venison, kale and chestnut mushroom biryani with butternut purée. Peanut butter parfait, with almond cake, cumin marshmallow and jaggery ice cream.

Galvin at Windows

XXX Plan: G4

London Hilton Hotel, 22 Park Ln (28th floor) ✉ W1K 1BE – Ⓜ Hyde Park Corner – ✆ (020) 72084021 – www.galvinatwindows.com – Closed Saturday lunch and Sunday dinner

Menu £ 37 (weekday lunch)/82

• Modern cuisine • Friendly • Romantic •

The cleverly laid out room makes the most of the spectacular views across London from the 28th floor. Relaxed service takes the edge off the somewhat corporate atmosphere. The bold cooking uses superb ingredients and the classically based food comes with a pleasing degree of flair and innovation.

➜ Cured Loch Fyne salmon with brown crab mousseline and celeriac remoulade. Fillet of beef and short-rib beignet with ox tongue and red wine jus. Pavlova with exotic fruit salsa and coconut ice cream.

Kai

XXX Plan: G3

65 South Audley St ✉ W1K 2QU – Ⓜ Hyde Park Corner – ✆ (020) 74938988 – www.kaimayfair.co.uk – Closed 25-26 December and 1 January

Carte £ 51/199 – *(booking essential)*

• Chinese • Intimate • Chic •

Both the owner and his long-standing chef Alex Chow are Malaysian and, while the cooking features dishes from several provinces in China, it is the southern region of Nanyang which is closest to their hearts. The unashamedly glitzy look of the restaurant is as eclectic as the food and the service team are switched on and fully conversant with the menu.

➜ Seared scallop with spicy XO sauce, lotus root crisp and stir-fried vegetables. Kagoshima Wagyu with foie gras, sesame ginger paste and Wagyu infused rice. Coconut parfait with chocolate and mango sorbet.

Murano (Angela Hartnett)

20 Queen St ✉ W1J 5PP – Ⓜ Green Park Plan: **G4**
– ✆ (020) 74951127 – www.muranolondon.com – Closed Christmas and Sunday
Menu £ 28/70

• Italian • Fashionable • Elegant •

Angela Hartnett's Italian-influenced cooking exhibits an appealing lightness of touch, with assured combinations of flavours, borne out of confidence in the ingredients. This is a stylish, elegant room run by a well-organised, professional and friendly team who put their customers at ease.

➜ Scallops, whipped cod's roe, dill, cucumber and horseradish. Lamb saddle, crispy shoulder, morels and wild garlic. Blood orange polenta cake and cream cheese sorbet.

Hide

85 Piccadilly ✉ W1J 7NB – Ⓜ Green Park Plan: **H4**
– ✆ (020) 3146 8666 – www.hide.co.uk – Closed 25 December
Menu £ 42/95 – Carte £ 42/72

• Modern British • Design • Fashionable •

A collaboration between Hedonism Wines and chef Ollie Dabbous; the striking decor is inspired by the park opposite. 'Above' offers only tasting menus while 'Ground' is an all-day operation. Both share the same commitment to producing immaculately drafted dishes that emphasise the natural flavours of ingredients.

➜ Celeriac, avocado and angelica seed. Slow-roast goose with birch sap and kale. Jasmine and wild pea flower religieuse.

Gymkhana

42 Albemarle St ✉ W1S 4JH – Ⓜ Green Park Plan: **H3**
– ✆ (020) 3011 5900 – www.gymkhanalondon.com – Closed 1-3 January, 25-27 December and Sunday
Menu £ 25 (weekday lunch) – Carte £ 25/67 – *(booking essential)*

• Indian • Fashionable • Elegant •

If you enjoy Trishna then you'll love Karam Sethi's Gymkhana – that's if you can get a table. Inspired by Colonial India's gymkhana clubs, the interior is full of wonderful detail and plenty of wry touches; ask to sit downstairs. The North Indian dishes have a wonderful richness and depth of flavour.

➜ Dosa, Chettinad duck and coconut. Wild muntjac biryani with pomegranate and mint raita. Saffron and pistachio kulfi falooda.

Hakkasan Mayfair

17 Bruton St ✉ W1J 6QB – Ⓜ Green Park Plan: **H3**
– ✆ (020) 79071888 – www.hakkasan.com – Closed 24-25 December
Menu £ 42 (lunch and early dinner)/120 – Carte £ 38/115 – *(booking essential)*

• Chinese • Minimalist • Trendy •

If coming for lunchtime dim sum then sit on the ground floor; for dinner ask for a table in the moodily lit and altogether sexier basement. The Cantonese cuisine uses top quality produce and can be delicate one minute; robust the next. There are also specialities specific to this branch.

➜ Soft shell crab with red chilli. Pan-fried Wagyu beef in spicy Sichuan sauce. Apple and sesame croustillant.

Pollen Street Social (Jason Atherton)

8-10 Pollen St ✉ W1S 1NQ – Ⓜ Oxford Circus Plan: **H3**
– ✆ (020) 7290 7600 – www.pollenstreetsocial.com – Closed Sunday and bank holidays
Menu £ 37 (lunch) – Carte £ 64/78 – *(booking essential)*

• Creative • Fashionable • Elegant •

The restaurant where it all started for Jason Atherton when he went solo. Top quality British produce lies at the heart of the menu and the innovative dishes are prepared with great care and no little skill. The room has plenty of buzz, helped along by the 'dessert bar' and views of the kitchen pass.

➜ Slow-cooked Copper Maran egg with turnip purée, parmesan, sage and kombu crumb. Lake District lamb loin & fillet with peas, broad beans and seaweed. Pistachio soufflé with 70% chocolate and vanilla ice cream.

Veeraswamy

Victory House, 99 Regent St (Entrance on Swallow St.) Plan: **H3**
W1B 4RS – Piccadilly Circus – (020) 77341401 – www.veeraswamy.com
Menu £ 26/45 – Carte £ 40/76

• Indian • Design • Historic •

It may have opened in 1926 but this celebrated Indian restaurant keeps producing wonderfully authentic and satisfying dishes from all parts of the country; dishes inspired by royal recipes are worth exploring. The room is awash with colour and is run with charm and obvious pride; ask for a window table.

→ Venison mutta kebab with tamarind glaze. Goan roast duck vindaloo. Rasmalai with tandoori fruit.

Sabor (Nieves Barragán Mohacho)

35-37 Heddon St W1B 4BR – Oxford Circus – (020) 3319 8130 – www.saborrestaurants.co.uk – Closed 24-26 December, 1-2 January, Sunday dinner and Monday Plan: **H3**
Carte £ 24/40

• Spanish • Tapas bar • Mediterranean décor •

A truly joyful and authentic tapas bar. Start with the pan con tomate at the ground floor counter. Bookings are only taken for El Asador upstairs, where succulent suckling pig and melt-in-the-mouth octopus are the must-haves. You'll be licking your lips for hours.

→ Pulpo a feira. Segovian suckling pig. Cuajada de turrón with oloroso cream.

Park Chinois

17 Berkeley St W1J 8EA – Green Park – (020) 3327 8888 – www.parkchinois.com – Closed 25 December Plan: **H3**
Menu £ 26 (lunch) – Carte £ 53/124 – *(booking essential)*

• Chinese • Exotic décor •

Old fashioned glamour, strikingly rich surroundings and live music combine to great effect at this sumptuously decorated restaurant. The menu traverses the length of China, with dim sum at lunchtimes and afternoon tea at weekends.

Scott's

20 Mount St W1K 2HE – Bond Street – (020) 74957309 – www.scotts-restaurant.com – Closed 25-26 December Plan: **G3**
Carte £ 39/66

• Seafood • Fashionable • Chic •

Scott's is proof that a restaurant can have a long, proud history and still be fashionable, glamorous and relevant. It has a terrific clubby atmosphere and if you're in a two then the counter is a great spot. The choice of prime quality fish and shellfish is impressive.

Corrigan's Mayfair

28 Upper Grosvenor St. W1K 7EH – Marble Arch – (020) 7499 9943 – www.corrigansmayfair.com – Closed 25-26 December, 1 January, Saturday lunch, Sunday and bank holidays Plan: **G3**
Menu £ 28 (lunch and early dinner) – Carte £ 42/76

• Modern British • Elegant •

Richard Corrigan's flagship celebrates British and Irish cooking, with game a speciality. The room is comfortable, clubby and quite glamorous and feels as though it has been around for years.

Ella Canta

InterContinental London Park Lane Hotel, 1 Hamilton Pl, Park Ln W1J 7QY – Hyde Park Corner – (020) 7318 8715 – www.ellacanta.com – Closed Sunday dinner and Monday lunch Plan: **G4**
Menu £ 25 (weekday lunch) – Carte £ 34/63

• Mexican • Design • Exotic décor •

Martha Ortiz is one of Mexico's most celebrated chefs and she now has a London outpost here at the InterContinental. The cooking draws on themes of history, philosophy and fantasy to create dishes that are colourful, creative and original. Great drinks list and charming staff.

Momo

XX AC

Plan: **H3**

25 Heddon St. ✉ W1B 4BH – Ⓜ Oxford Circus
– ✆ (020) 7434 4040 – www.momoresto.com – Closed 25 December
Menu £ 20 (weekday lunch) – Carte £ 32/49

• Moroccan • Exotic décor • Intimate •

An authentic Moroccan atmosphere comes courtesy of the antiques, kilim rugs, Berber artwork, bright fabrics and lanterns – you'll feel you're eating near the souk. Go for the classic dishes: zaalouk, briouats, pigeon pastilla, and tagines with mountains of fluffy couscous.

Sketch (The Gallery)

XX AC

Plan: **H3**

9 Conduit St ✉ W1S 2XG – Ⓜ Oxford Circus
– ✆ (020) 76594500 – www.sketch.london – Closed 25 December and 1 January
Carte £ 43/86 – *(dinner only) (booking essential)*

• Modern cuisine • Trendy • Intimate •

The striking 'Gallery' has a smart look from India Mahdavi and artwork from David Shrigley. At dinner the room transmogrifies from art gallery to fashionable restaurant, with a menu that mixes the classic, the modern and the esoteric.

Black Roe

XX AC

Plan: **H3**

4 Mill St ✉ W1S 2AX – Ⓜ Oxford Circus
– ✆ (020) 3794 8448 – www.blackroe.com – Closed Sunday
Carte £ 26/66

• World cuisine • Trendy • Neighbourhood •

Poke, made famous in Hawaii, is the star here. You can choose traditional ahi over the sushi rice or something more original like scallop and octopus. Other options include dishes with assorted Pacific Rim influences, along with others cooked on the Kiawe wood grill.

Bombay Bustle

XX AC

Plan: **H3**

29 Maddox St ✉ W1S 2PA – Ⓜ Oxford Circus
– ✆ (020) 7290 4470 – www.bombaybustle.com – Closed 25-25 December and 1-2 January
Menu £ 16 (lunch) – Carte £ 29/42

• Indian • Fashionable • Exotic décor •

Tiffin tin carriers on Mumbai's railways inspired Jamavar's second London restaurant. A charming train theme runs through it; the ground floor is the livelier; downstairs is more 'first class'. Before a curry, biryani or dish from the tandoor order some tasting plates, made from family recipes.

Chucs Bar and Grill

XX AC

Plan: **H3**

30b Dover St. ✉ W1S 4NB – Ⓜ Green Park
– ✆ (020) 3763 2013 – www.chucsrestaurant.com – Closed 25-26 and dinner 24 and 31 December, 1 January and bank holidays
Carte £ 36/69 – *(booking essential)*

• Italian • Elegant • Cosy •

Like the shop to which it's attached, Chucs caters for those who summer on the Riviera and are not afraid of showing it. It's decked out like a yacht and the concise but not inexpensive menu offers classic Mediterranean dishes.

Goodman Mayfair

XX AC

Plan: **H3**

26 Maddox St ✉ W1S 1QH – Ⓜ Oxford Circus
– ✆ (020) 7499 3776 – www.goodmanrestaurants.com – Closed Sunday and bank holidays
Carte £ 31/107 – *(booking essential)*

• Meats and grills • Brasserie • Classic décor •

A worthy attempt at recreating a New York steakhouse; all leather and wood and macho swagger. Beef is dry or wet-aged in-house and comes with a choice of four sauces; rib-eye is the speciality.

Heddon Street Kitchen

3-9 Heddon St ✉ *W1B 4BE* – Ⓜ *Oxford Circus* Plan: **H3**
– ✆ *(020) 7592 1212* – *www.gordonramsayrestaurants.com*
Menu £ 23 (lunch and early dinner) – Carte £ 26/63
• Modern cuisine • Brasserie • Trendy •

Gordon Ramsay's follow up to Bread Street is spread over two floors and is about all-day dining: breakfast covers all tastes, there's weekend brunch, and an à la carte offering an appealing range of European dishes executed with palpable care.

Indian Accent

16 Albemarle St ✉ *W1S 4HW* – Ⓜ *Green Park* Plan: **H3**
– ✆ *(020) 7629 9802* – *www.indianaccent.com* – *Closed Christmas, New Year, Sunday and bank holidays*
Menu £ 30/55
• Indian • Elegant • Fashionable •

The third branch, after New Delhi and NYC, is set over two levels, with a bright, fresh look. The kitchen takes classic dishes from all regions of India and blends them with European and Asian notes and techniques. The resulting dishes are colourful, sophisticated and full of flavour.

Jamavar

8 Mount St ✉ *W1K 3NF* – Ⓜ *Bond Street* Plan: **G3**
– ✆ *(020) 7499 1800* – *www.jamavarrestaurants.com*
– *Closed 25-26 December, 1 January and Sunday*
Menu £ 24 (lunch and early dinner) – Carte £ 32/54 – *(booking essential at dinner)*
• Indian • Exotic décor • Elegant •

Leela Palaces & Resorts are behind this smartly dressed Indian restaurant. The menus, including vegetarian, look to all parts of India, with a bias towards the north. The 'small plates' section includes Malabar prawns, and kid goat shami kebab; from the tandoor the stone bass tikka is a must; and the biryanis are also good.

Jean-Georges at The Connaught – Connaught Hotel

Carlos Pl. ✉ *W1K 2AL* – Ⓜ *Bond Street* – ✆ *(020) 7107 8861*
– *www.the-connaught.co.uk* Plan: **G3**
Carte £ 57/88
• Modern cuisine • Intimate • Elegant •

Low-slung bespoke marble-topped tables and comfy sofas make this room at the front of The Connaught hotel somewhere between a salon and a restaurant. It has something for all tastes, from Asian-inspired dishes to fish and chips. The truffle-infused pizza is a best seller.

Nobu

Metropolitan by COMO Hotel, 19 Old Park Ln Plan: **G4**
✉ *W1Y 1LB* – Ⓜ *Hyde Park Corner* – ✆ *(020) 74474747*
– *www.noburestaurants.com* – *Closed 25 December*
Carte £ 24/73 – *(booking essential)*
• Japanese • Fashionable • Minimalist •

Nobu restaurants are now all over the world but this was Europe's first and opened in 1997. It retains a certain exclusivity and is buzzy and fun. The menu is an innovative blend of Japanese cuisine with South American influences.

Nobu Berkeley St

15 Berkeley St. ✉ *W1J 8DY* – Ⓜ *Green Park* Plan: **H3**
– ✆ *(020) 72909222* – *www.noburestaurants.com* – *Closed 25 December*
Carte £ 30/92 – *(booking essential)*
• Japanese • Fashionable • Trendy •

This branch of the glamorous chain is more of a party animal than its elder sibling at The Metropolitan. Start with cocktails then head upstairs for Japanese food with South American influences; try dishes from the wood-fired oven.

Sakagura

XX

Plan: H3

8 Heddon St ✉ W1B 4BS – Ⓜ Oxford Circus – ✆ (020) 3405 7230 – www.sakaguralondon.com – Closed 25 December

Carte £ 21/53

• Japanese • Exotic décor • Contemporary décor •

A contemporary styled Japanese restaurant part owned by the Japan Centre and Gekkeikan, a sake manufacturer. Along with an impressive drinks list is an extensive menu covering a variety of styles; highlights include the skewers cooked on the robata charcoal grill.

Sexy Fish

XX

Plan: H3

Berkeley Sq. ✉ W1J 6BR – Ⓜ Green Park – ✆ (020) 3764 2000 – www.sexyfish.com – Closed 25-26 December

Carte £ 44/58

• Seafood • Design • Elegant •

Everyone will have an opinion about the name but what's indisputable is that this is a very good looking restaurant, with works by Frank Gehry and Damien Hirst, and a stunning ceiling by Michael Roberts. The fish comes with various Asian influences but don't ignore the meat dishes like the beef rib skewers.

StreetXO

XX

Plan: H3

15 Old Burlington St ✉ W1S 2JL – Ⓜ Oxford Circus – ✆ (020) 3096 7555 – www.streetxo.com – Closed 23-26 December, 1 January and Monday lunch

Menu £ 25 (weekday lunch) – Carte £ 45/68

• Creative • Trendy • Design •

The menu at Madrid chef David Muñoz's London outpost is inspired by European, Asian and even South American cuisines. Dishes are characterised by explosions of colour and a riot of different flavours, techniques and textures. The quasi-industrial feel of the basement room adds to the moody, noisy atmosphere.

Theo Randall

XX

Plan: G4

InterContinental London Park Lane Hotel, 1 Hamilton Pl, Park Ln ✉ W1J 7QY – Ⓜ Hyde Park Corner – ✆ (020) 73188747 – www.theorandall.com – Closed 25 December

Menu £ 29 (weekday lunch) – Carte £ 35/63

• Italian • Classic décor • Chic •

There's an attractive honesty about Theo Randall's Italian food, which is made using the very best of ingredients. The somewhat corporate nature of the hotel in which it is located can sometimes seem a little at odds with the rustic style of food but the room is bright, relaxed and well run.

Tokimeitē

XX

Plan: H3

23 Conduit St ✉ W1S 2XS – Ⓜ Oxford Circus – ✆ (020) 3826 4411 – www.tokimeite.com – Closed Sunday and bank holidays

Menu £ 25 (lunch) – Carte £ 40/106

• Japanese • Chic • Intimate •

Yoshihiro Murata, one of Japan's most celebrated chefs, teamed up with the Zen-Noh group to open this good looking, intimate restaurant on two floors. Their aim is to promote Wagyu beef in Europe, so it's understandably the star of the show.

Wild Honey

XX

Plan: H3

12 St George St. ✉ W1S 2FB – Ⓜ Oxford Circus – ✆ (020) 7758 9160 – www.wildhoneyrestaurant.co.uk – Closed 25-26 December, 1 January, Sunday and bank holidays except Good Friday

Menu £ 35 (lunch and early dinner) – Carte £ 33/59

• Modern cuisine • Design • Intimate •

The elegant wood panelling and ornate plasterwork may say 'classic Mayfair institution' but the personable service team keep the atmosphere enjoyably easy-going. The kitchen uses quality British ingredients and a French base but is not afraid of the occasional international flavour.

Le Boudin Blanc

5 Trebeck St ✉ W1J 7LT – Ⓜ Green Park Plan: **G4**
– ✆ (020) 74993292 – www.boudinblanc.co.uk – Closed 24-26 December and 1 January
Menu £ 19 (lunch) – Carte £ 28/57
• French • Rustic • Neighbourhood •
Appealing, lively French bistro in Shepherd Market, spread over two floors. Satisfying French classics and country cooking are the draws, along with authentic Gallic service. Good value lunch menu.

Little Social

5 Pollen St ✉ W1S 1NE – Ⓜ Oxford Circus Plan: **H3**
– ✆ (020) 7870 3730 – www.littlesocial.co.uk – Closed Sunday and bank holidays
Menu £ 25 – Carte £ 38/65 – *(booking essential)*
• French • Bistro • Fashionable •
Jason Atherton's lively French bistro, opposite his Pollen Street Social restaurant, has a clubby feel and an appealing, deliberately worn look. Service is breezy and capable and the food is mostly classic with the odd modern twist.

Kitty Fisher's

10 Shepherd Mkt ✉ W1J 7QF – Ⓜ Green Park Plan: **H4**
– ✆ (020) 3302 1661 – www.kittyfishers.com – Closed Christmas, New Year, Easter, Sunday and bank holidays
Carte £ 36/70 – *(booking essential)*
• Modern cuisine • Bistro • Cosy •
Warm, intimate and unpretentious restaurant – the star of the show is the wood grill which gives the dishes added depth. Named after an 18C courtesan, presumably in honour of the profession for which Shepherd Market was once known.

Magpie

10 Heddon St ✉ W1B 4BX – Ⓜ Oxford Circus Plan: **H3**
– ✆ (020) 3903 9096 – www.magpie-london.com – Closed Sunday dinner and bank holidays
Menu £ 25 (lunch) – Carte £ 25/38
• Modern cuisine • Fashionable • Bistro •
From the same team as Hackney's Pidgin. Sharing plates using an eclectic array of ingredients make for some original flavour pairings. This former gallery has an open feel and benefits from a large glass roof at the back; ask for one of the side booths.

Soho

Yauatcha Soho

15 Broadwick St ✉ W1F 0DL Plan: **I3**
– Ⓜ Tottenham Court Road – ✆ (020) 74948888 – www.yauatcha.com – Closed 25 December
Carte £ 25/65
• Chinese • Design • Trendy •
2019 is its 15th birthday but it still manages to feel fresh and contemporary, with its bright ground floor and moody basement, featuring low banquettes, an aquarium bar and a star-lit ceiling. Dishes are colourful with strong flavours and excellent texture contrasts; dim sum is the highlight – try the venison puff.
➜ Scallop shu mai. Stir-fried rib-eye of beef. Chocolate pebble.

Barrafina

26-27 Dean St ✉ W1D 3LL – Ⓜ Tottenham Court Road Plan: **I3**
– ✆ (020) 7440 1456 – www.barrafina.co.uk – Closed bank holidays
Carte £ 20/40 – *(bookings not accepted)*
• Spanish • Tapas bar • Fashionable •
In 2016 the original Barrafina moved to this brighter, roomier site fashioned out of what was previously a part of Quo Vadis restaurant. Dishes burst with flavour – do order some dishes from the blackboard specials – the staff are fun and the L-shaped counter fills up quickly, so be prepared to wait.
➜ Ham croquetas. Chorizo, potato and watercress. Santiago tart.

Social Eating House

58 Poland St ✉ *W1F 7NR – Ⓜ Oxford Circus* Plan: **H3**
– ✆ (020) 79933251 – www.socialeatinghouse.com – Closed Christmas, Sunday and bank holidays
Menu £ 27/36 – Carte £ 49/60

• Modern cuisine • Fashionable • Brasserie •

The coolest joint in Jason Atherton's stable comes with distressed walls, moody lighting and a laid-back vibe – it also has a terrific speakeasy-style bar upstairs. The 'Sampler' menu is a good way of experiencing the full breadth of the kitchen's skill at producing dishes with punchy, well-judged flavours.

→ Truffled Royal Legbar egg, Iberico de Bellota with Jerusalem artichoke. Slow-cooked rump of salt marsh lamb with olive oil mash, pickled turnips and sauce niçoise. Peanut butter parfait with cherry sorbet, almond and griottine cherry.

Brasserie Zédel

20 Sherwood St ✉ *W1F 7ED – Ⓜ Piccadilly Circus* Plan: **H3**
– ✆ (020) 7734 4888 – www.brasseriezedel.com – Closed 25 December
Menu £ 11/20 – Carte £ 18/43

• French • Brasserie •

A grand French brasserie, which is all about inclusivity and accessibility, in a bustling subterranean space restored to its original art deco glory. Expect a roll-call of classic French dishes and some very competitive prices.

Bao

53 Lexington St ✉ *W1F 9AS – Ⓜ Tottenham Court Road* Plan: **H3**
– ✆ (020) 30111632 – www.baolondon.com – Closed 24-26 December, 1 January and Sunday dinner
Carte £ 17/27 – *(bookings not accepted)*

• Asian • Simple • Cosy •

There are some things in life worth queueing for – and that includes the delicious eponymous buns here at this simple, great value Taiwanese operation. The classic bao and the confit pork bao are standouts, along with 'small eats' like trotter nuggets. There's also another Bao in Windmill St.

Copita

27 D'Arblay St ✉ *W1F 8EP – Ⓜ Oxford Circus* Plan: **H3**
– ✆ (020) 7287 7797 – www.copita.co.uk – Closed Sunday and bank holidays
Carte £ 20/41 – *(bookings not accepted)*

• Spanish • Tapas bar • Rustic •

Perch on one of the high stools or stay standing and get stuck into the daily menu of small, colourful and tasty dishes. Staff add to the atmosphere and everything on the Spanish wine list comes by the glass or copita.

Hoppers

49 Frith St ✉ *W1D 4SG – Ⓜ Tottenham Court Road* Plan: **I3**
– ✆ (020) 3011 1021 – www.hopperslondon.com – Closed 25-27 December and 1-3 January.
Menu £ 20 (lunch) – Carte £ 15/30 – *(bookings not accepted)*

• South Indian • Simple • Rustic •

Street food inspired by the flavours of Tamil Nadu and Sri Lanka features at this fun little spot from the Sethi family (Trishna, Gymkhana). Hoppers are bowl-shaped pancakes made from fermented rice and coconut – ideal with a creamy kari. The 'short eats' are great too, as are the prices, so expect a queue.

Kiln

58 Brewer St ✉ *W1F 9TL – Ⓜ Piccadilly Circus* Plan: **H3**
– www.kilnsoho.com
Carte £ 10/22 – *(bookings not accepted)*

• Thai • Simple • Cosy •

Sit at the far counter to watch chefs prepare fiery Thai food in clay pots, woks and grills. The well-priced menu includes influences from Laos, Myanmar and Yunnan – all prepared using largely British produce. The counter is for walk-ins only but parties of four can book a table downstairs.

Kricket

12 Denman St ✉ W1D 7HH – Ⓜ Piccadilly Circus – ✆ (020) 7734 5612 – www.kricket.co.uk – Closed 25-26 December, 1 January and Sunday

Plan: **I3**

Carte £ 20/27 – *(bookings not accepted)*

• Indian • Simple •

From Brixton pop-up to a permanent spot in Soho; not many Indian restaurants have a counter, an open kitchen, sharing plates and cocktails. The four well-priced dishes under each heading of 'Meat, 'Fish' and 'Veg' are made with home-grown ingredients. Bookings are only taken for groups of 4 or more at the communal tables downstairs.

Palomar

34 Rupert St ✉ W1D 6DN – Ⓜ Piccadilly Circus – ✆ (020) 7439 8777 – www.thepalomar.co.uk – Closed dinner 24-26 December

Plan: **I3**

Carte £ 17/40

• World cuisine • Trendy • Cosy •

A hip slice of modern-day Jerusalem in the heart of theatreland, with a zinc kitchen counter running back to an intimate wood-panelled dining room. Like the atmosphere, the contemporary Middle Eastern cooking is fresh and vibrant.

Polpetto

11 Berwick St ✉ W1F 0PL – Ⓜ Tottenham Court Road – ✆ (020) 7439 8627 – www.polpo.co.uk

Plan: **I3**

Carte £ 14/24

• Italian • Simple • Rustic •

Order a negroni at the bar then start ordering some of those Italian-inspired small plates. Look for the daily specials on the blackboard but don't forget old favourites like the pork and beef meatballs. It's fun, busy and great for a quick bite.

Gauthier - Soho

21 Romilly St ✉ W1D 5AF – Ⓜ Leicester Square – ✆ (020) 74943111 – www.gauthiersoho.co.uk – Closed Sunday, Monday and bank holidays except Good Friday

Plan: **I3**

Menu £ 30/75

• French • Intimate • Neighbourhood •

Detached from the rowdier elements of Soho is this charming Georgian townhouse, with dining spread over three floors. Alex Gauthier offers assorted menus of his classically based cooking, with vegetarians particularly well looked after.

Bob Bob Ricard

1 Upper James St ✉ W1F 9DF – Ⓜ Oxford Circus – ✆ (020) 31451000 – www.bobbobricard.com

Plan: **H3**

Carte £ 38/86

• Traditional British • Vintage • Elegant •

Small but perfectly formed, BBR actually sees itself as a glamorous grand salon; ask for a booth. The menu is all-encompassing – from pies and burgers to oysters and caviar. Prices are altered depending on how busy they are, with up to a 25% reduction at off-peak times.

Tamarind Kitchen

167-169 Wardour St ✉ W1F 8WR – Ⓜ Tottenham Court Road – ✆ (020) 72874243 – www.tamarindkitchen.co.uk – Closed 25-26 December, 1 January

Plan: **I3**

Menu £ 18 (lunch) – Carte £ 22/35

• Indian • Exotic décor •

A more relaxed sister to Tamarind in Mayfair, this Indian restaurant comes with endearingly earnest service and a lively buzz. There's a nominal Northern emphasis to the fairly priced menu, with Awadhi kababs a speciality, but there are also plenty of curries and fish dishes.

Temper

Plan: **H3**

25 Broadwick St ✉ *W1F 0DF* – Ⓜ *Oxford Circus*
– ✆ *(020) 3879 3834 – www.temperrestaurant.com*
– Closed 25-26 December, 1 January and Monday lunch
Carte £ 20/40

• Barbecue • Contemporary décor •

A fun, basement restaurant all about barbecue and meats. The beasts are cooked whole, some are also smoked in-house and there's a distinct South African flavour to the salsas that accompany them. Kick off with some tacos – they make around 1,200 of them every day.

Vasco and Piero's Pavilion

Plan: **H2**

15 Poland St ✉ *W1F 8QE* – Ⓜ *Oxford Circus*
– ✆ *(020) 7437 8774 – www.vascosfood.com – Closed Saturday lunch, Sunday and bank holidays*
Carte £ 28/48 – *(booking essential at lunch)*

• Italian • Friendly • Neighbourhood •

Regulars and tourists have been flocking to this institution for over 40 years; its longevity is down to a twice daily changing menu of Umbrian-influenced dishes rather than the matter-of-fact service or simple decoration.

100 Wardour St

Plan: **I3**

100 Wardour St ✉ *W1F 0TN*
– Ⓜ *Tottenham Court Road* – ✆ *(020) 7314 4000*
– www.100wardourst.com – Closed 25-26 December and Sunday-Monday
Menu £ 42 – Carte £ 31/58

• Modern cuisine • Contemporary décor •

For a night out with a group of friends, this D&D place is worth considering. At night, head downstairs for cocktails, live music (well, this was once The Marquee Club) and a modern, Med-influenced menu with the odd Asian touch. During the day, the ground floor offers an all-day menu.

Nopi

Plan: **H3**

21-22 Warwick St ✉ *W1B 5NE* – Ⓜ *Piccadilly Circus*
– ✆ *(020) 74949584 – www.ottolenghi.co.uk – Closed 25-26 December, 1 January and Sunday dinner*
Carte £ 31/49

• Mediterranean cuisine • Design • Fashionable •

The bright, clean look of Yotam Ottolenghi's charmingly run all-day restaurant matches the fresh, invigorating food. The sharing plates take in the Mediterranean, the Middle East and Asia and the veggie dishes stand out.

Barshu

Plan: **I3**

28 Frith St. ✉ *W1D 5LF* – Ⓜ *Leicester Square*
– ✆ *(020) 72878822 – www.barshurestaurant.co.uk*
– Closed 24-25 December
Carte £ 19/53

• Chinese • Exotic décor •

The fiery and authentic flavours of China's Sichuan province are the draw here; help is at hand as the menu has pictures. It's well run and decorated with carved wood and lanterns; downstairs is better for groups.

Beijing Dumpling

Plan: **I3**

23 Lisle St ✉ *WC2H 7BA* – Ⓜ *Leicester Square*
– ✆ *(020) 7287 6888 – Closed 24-25 December*
Menu £ 17/25 – Carte £ 14/38 – *(bookings not accepted)*

• Chinese • Neighbourhood • Simple •

This relaxed little place serves freshly prepared dumplings of both Beijing and Shanghai styles. Although the range is not as comprehensive as the name suggests, they do stand out, especially varieties of the famed Xiao Long Bao.

Blanchette

9 D'Arblay St ✉ W1F 8DR – Ⓜ Oxford Circus Plan: **H2**
– ✆ (020) 7439 8100 – www.blanchettelondon.co.uk
Menu £ 20 (lunch and early dinner) – Carte £ 18/49 – *(booking essential)*
• French • Simple • Fashionable •
Run by three frères, Blanchette takes French bistro food and gives it the 'small plates' treatment. It's named after their mother – the ox cheek Bourguignon is her recipe. Tiles and exposed brick add to the rustic look.

Bocca di Lupo

12 Archer St ✉ WID 7BB – Ⓜ Piccadilly Circus Plan: **I3**
– ✆ (020) 77342223 – www.boccadilupo.com – Closed 25 December and 1 January
Carte £ 26/63 – *(booking essential)*
• Italian • Tapas bar • Intimate •
Atmosphere, food and service are all best when sitting at the marble counter, watching the chefs at work. Specialities from across Italy come in large or small sizes and are full of flavour and vitality. Try also their gelato shop opposite.

Casita Andina

31 Great Windmill St ✉ W1D 7LP – Ⓜ Piccadilly Circus Plan: **I3**
– ✆ (020) 33279464 – www.andinalondon.com/casita
Carte £ 18/37
• Peruvian • Rustic •
Respect is paid to the home-style cooking of the Andes at this warmly run and welcoming Peruvian picantería. Dishes are gluten-free and as colourful as the surroundings of this 200 year old house.

Cây Tre

42-43 Dean St ✉ W1D 4PZ – Ⓜ Tottenham Court Road Plan: **I3**
– ✆ (020) 7317 9118 – www.thevietnamesekitchen.co.uk – Closed 25 December
Menu £ 25 – Carte £ 14/27
• Vietnamese • Minimalist •
Bustling Vietnamese restaurant offering specialities from all parts of the country. Dishes are generously sized and appealingly priced; their various versions of pho are always popular. Come in a group to compete with the noise.

Ceviche Soho

17 Frith St ✉ W1D 4RG – Ⓜ Tottenham Court Road Plan: **I3**
– ✆ (020) 7292 2040 – www.cevicherestaurants.com
– Closed 24-26 December and 1 January
Carte £ 17/29 – *(booking essential)*
• Peruvian • Friendly • Fashionable •
This is where it all started for this small group that helped London discover Peruvian food. It's as loud and cramped as it is fun and friendly. Start with a pisco-based cocktail then order classics like tiradito alongside dishes from the grill such as ox heart anticuchos.

Darjeeling Express

Top Floor, Kingly Ct. Carnaby St ✉ W1B 5PW Plan: **H3**
– Ⓜ Oxford Circus – ✆ (020) 7287 2828 – www.darjeeling-express.com
– Closed 25-26 and 31 December, 1 January and Sunday
Carte £ 22/29 – *(booking essential)*
• Indian • Brasserie • Family •
With Royal Mughlai ancestry and a great love of food gained from cooking traditional family recipes, the owner couldn't be better qualified. Her open kitchen is run by a team of housewives; the influences are mostly Bengali but there are also dishes from Kolkata to Hyderabad. Lively and great fun.

Dehesa

Plan: **H3**

25 Ganton St ✉ W1F 9BP – Ⓜ Oxford Circus – ✆ (020) 7494 4170 – www.dehesa.co.uk – Closed 25 December

Menu £ 15 (weekday lunch) – Carte £ 20/35

• Mediterranean cuisine • Tapas bar • Fashionable •

Repeats the success of its sister restaurant, Salt Yard, by offering flavoursome and appealingly priced Spanish and Italian tapas. Busy, friendly atmosphere in appealing corner location. Good drinks list too.

Duck & Rice

Plan: **I3**

90 Berwick St ✉ WIF 0QB – Ⓜ Tottenham Court Road – ✆ (020) 3327 7888 – www.theduckandrice.com – Closed 25 December

Carte £ 21/49

• Chinese • Intimate • Trendy •

Something a little different – a converted pub with a Chinese kitchen – originally set up by Alan Yau. Beer and snacks are the thing on the ground floor; upstairs, with its booths and fireplaces, is for Chinese favourites and comforting classics.

Ember Yard

Plan: **H2**

60 Berwick St ✉ W1F 8DX – Ⓜ Oxford Circus – ✆ (020) 7439 8057 – www.emberyard.co.uk – Closed 25-26 December and 1 January

Carte £ 29/48

• Mediterranean cuisine • Tapas bar • Fashionable •

Those familiar with the Salt Yard Group will recognise the Spanish and Italian themed menus – but their 4th fun outlet comes with a focus on cooking over charcoal or wood. There's even a seductive smokiness to some of the cocktails.

Evelyn's Table

Plan: **I3**

The Blue Posts, 28 Rupert St ✉ W1D 6DJ – Ⓜ Piccadilly Circus – www.theblueposts.co.uk – Closed 25-26 December and Sunday

Carte £ 25/43 – *(dinner only)*

• Modern cuisine • Simple • Friendly •

A former beer cellar of a restored 18C inn – much is made of the whole cramped, underground, speakeasy thing. Watching the chefs behind the counter is all part of the appeal; their modern European dishes are designed for sharing, with fish from Cornwall a highlight.

Jinjuu

Plan: **H3**

15 Kingly St ✉ W1B 5PS – Ⓜ Oxford Circus – ✆ (020) 8181 8887 – www.jinjuu.com – Closed 1 January and 25 December

Menu £ 14 (weekday lunch) – Carte £ 27/57

• Asian • Design • Fashionable •

American-born celebrity chef Judy Joo's restaurant is a celebration of her Korean heritage. The vibrant dishes, whether Bibimbap bowls or Ssam platters, burst with flavour and are as enjoyable as the fun surroundings. There's another branch in Mayfair.

Jugemu

Plan: **I3**

3 Winnett St ✉ W1D 6JY – Ⓜ Piccadilly Circus – ✆ (020) 7734 0518 – Closed Christmas, New Year and Sunday

Carte £ 10/50 – *(dinner only)*

• Japanese • Simple • Cosy •

Like all the best izakaya, this one is tucked away down a side street and easy to miss. It has three small tables and a 9-seater counter from where you can watch the chef-owner at work. Popular with a homesick Japanese clientele, it keeps things traditional; the sashimi is excellent.

Koya Bar

50 Frith St ✉ W1D 4SQ – Ⓜ Tottenham Court Road Plan: **I3**
– ✆ (020) 74949075 – www.koya.co.uk – Closed 25 December and 1 January
Carte £ 14/32 – *(bookings not accepted)*
• Japanese • Simple • Friendly •

A simple, sweet place serving authentic Udon noodles and small plates; they open early for breakfast. Counter seating means everyone has a view of the chefs; bookings aren't taken and there is often a queue, but the short wait is worth it.

Mele e Pere

46 Brewer St ✉ W1F 9TF – Ⓜ Piccadilly Circus Plan: **I3**
– ✆ (020) 7096 2096 – www.meleepere.co.uk – Closed 25-26 December and 1 January
Menu £ 20 (lunch and early dinner) – Carte £ 22/39
• Italian • Friendly • Neighbourhood •

There's a small dining room on the ground floor but all the fun happens downstairs, where you'll find a large vermouth bar with vintage posters and plenty of seating in the buzzy vaulted room. The rustic Italian dishes hit the spot and the pre-theatre menu is great value.

Pastaio

19 Ganton St ✉ W1F 9BN – Ⓜ Oxford Circus Plan: **H3**
– ✆ (020) 3019 8680 – www.pastaio.london – Closed 25 December and 1 January
Carte £ 24/28 – *(bookings not accepted)*
• Italian • Osteria • Simple •

Get ready to queue and even share a table – but at these prices who cares? This buzzy spot, a stone's throw from Carnaby Street, is all about pasta. It's made in-house daily by the all Italian team, with short and long semolina pasta extruded through bronze dies. The tiramisu is great too.

Rambla

64 Dean St ✉ W1D 4QQ – Ⓜ Tottenham Court Road Plan: **I3**
– ✆ (020) 7734 8428 – www.ramblalondon.com – Closed Christmas
Carte £ 22/39
• Spanish • Tapas bar • Simple •

The owner's childhood in Barcelona is celebrated here with an interesting range of Catalan-inspired dishes, which are punchy in flavour and designed to be shared. It's a simple, unpretentious place dominated by an open kitchen; the best seats are at the counter.

XU

30 Rupert St ✉ W1D 6DL – Ⓜ Piccadilly Circus Plan: **I3**
– ✆ (020) 3319 8147 – www.xulondon.com – Closed 25-26 December
Menu £ 18 (lunch) – Carte £ 22/38 – *(booking essential)*
• Asian • Chic • Vintage •

They've squeezed a lot into the two floors to create the feel of 1930s Taipei, including an emerald lacquered tea kiosk and mahjong tables. Don't miss the numbing beef tendon and classics like Shou Pa chicken. Tofu is made in-house and Chi Shiang rice is flown in from Taiwan.

St James's

Ritz Restaurant – Ritz Hotel

150 Piccadilly ✉ W1J 9BR – Ⓜ Green Park Plan: **H4**
– ✆ (020) 73002370 – www.theritzlondon.com
Menu £ 57/67 – Carte £ 73/123
• Modern British • Luxury • Historic •

Executive Chef John Williams MBE and his team take classic dishes, including some Escoffier recipes, and add their own subtle touches of modernity. Needless to say, the ingredients are luxurious. Thanks to the lavishness of its Louis XVI decoration, there is nowhere grander than The Ritz. The faultless service adds to the experience.

➜ Artichoke royale with truffle, pear and Ragstone cheese. Native lobster with broad beans, almond and lemon verbena. Apple mousseline with marigold and buttermilk sorbet.

Seven Park Place – St James's Hotel and Club

7-8 Park Pl ✉ SW1A 1LS – Ⓜ Green Park Plan: **H4**
– ✆ (020) 73161615 – www.stjameshotelandclub.com – Closed Sunday and Monday
Menu £ 28/95 – *(booking essential)*

• Modern cuisine • Cosy • Fashionable •

2019 sees William Drabble celebrate 10 years as head chef and it's a rare night if he's not at the stove. He starts with premier ingredients, most of which he sources himself; he then uses classic flavour combinations and tried-and-tested techniques. The gilded 9-table restaurant is intimate and discreet.

➜ Lobster tail with cauliflower and truffle butter sauce. Fillet of turbot with chestnut purée and wild mushrooms. Dark chocolate ganache with caramelised banana.

Aquavit

St James's Market, 1 Carlton St ✉ SW1Y 4QQ Plan: **I3**
– Ⓜ Piccadilly Circus – ✆ (020) 7024 9848 – www.aquavitrestaurants.com – Closed 23-27 December
Menu £ 24 (lunch) – Carte £ 34/58

• Scandinavian • Brasserie • Elegant •

Unlike the original in NYC, this Aquavit comes in the form of a warmly lit, relaxed brasserie. The Scandinavian cooking may also be less intricate but it's still immeasurably appealing. Kick things off by heading straight to the smörgåsbord section and some wonderful herring or shrimp.

➜ Crab with rye brioche and fennel. Turbot with horseradish, beetroot and Sandefjord sauce. Douglas fir panna cotta with queen's sorbet and sorrel.

Ikoyi (Jeremy Chan)

1 St. James's Market ✉ SW1Y 4AH – Ⓜ Piccadilly Circus Plan: **I3**
– ✆ (020) 3583 4660 – www.ikoyilondon.com – Closed 25 -26 December, 1 January and Sunday
Menu £ 25 (lunch and early dinner) – Carte £ 46/54 – *(booking essential)*

• Creative • Simple • Design •

The somewhat colourless development that is St James's Market is the unlikely setting for one of the most innovative and original restaurants to open in the capital in recent times. The two owners, friends since childhood, have put together a kitchen that uses home-grown ingredients enlivened with flavours from West Africa.

➜ Mushroom suya, malted barley and pine. Duck, uda, candied bacon and bitter leaf. Black benne & blackcurrant.

Chutney Mary

73 St James's St ✉ SW1A 1PH – Ⓜ Green Park Plan: **H4**
– ✆ (020) 7629 6688 – www.chutneymary.com – Closed 25 December
Menu £ 29 (lunch) – Carte £ 39/70

• Indian • Elegant • Design •

One of London's pioneering Indian restaurants, set in the heart of St James's. Elegant surroundings feature bold art and Indian artefacts. Spicing is understated, classics are done well, and some regional dishes have been subtly updated.

The Wolseley

160 Piccadilly ✉ W1J 9EB – Ⓜ Green Park Plan: **H4**
– ✆ (020) 74996996 – www.thewolseley.com
Carte £ 25/76 – *(booking essential)*

• Modern cuisine • Fashionable •

This feels like a grand and glamorous European coffee house, with its pillars and high vaulted ceiling. Appealing menus offer everything from caviar to a hotdog. It's open from early until late and boasts a large celebrity following.

Franco's

61 Jermyn St ✉ SW1Y 6LX – Ⓜ Green Park Plan: **H4**
– ✆ (020) 74992211 – www.francoslondon.com – Closed Sunday and bank holidays
Menu £ 32 – Carte £ 36/64 – *(booking essential)*
• Italian • Traditional décor • Romantic •

Have an aperitivo in the clubby bar before sitting down to eat at one of London's oldest yet rejuvenated Italian restaurants. The kitchen focuses on the classics and they live up to expectations; the regulars, of whom there are many, all have their favourites.

45 Jermyn St

45 Jermyn St. ✉ SW1 6DN – Ⓜ Piccadilly Circus Plan: **H4**
– ✆ (020) 72054545 – www.45jermynst.com
Menu £ 26 (early dinner) – Carte £ 30/67
• Traditional British • Brasserie • Elegant •

Style and comfort go hand in hand at this bright, contemporary brasserie. The menu is a mix of European and British classics; the beef Wellington and lobster spaghetti are finished off at your table. Sodas, coupes and floats pay tribute to its past as Fortnum's Fountain restaurant.

Cafe Murano

33 St. James's St ✉ SW1A 1HD – Ⓜ Green Park Plan: **H4**
– ✆ (020) 3371 5559 – www.cafemurano.co.uk – Closed Sunday dinner
Menu £ 23 (lunch and early dinner) – Carte £ 30/42 – *(booking essential)*
• Italian • Fashionable •

Angela Hartnett and her chef have created an appealing and flexible menu of delicious North Italian delicacies – the lunch menu is very good value. It's certainly no ordinary café and its popularity means pre-booking is essential.

Ginza Onodera

15 Bury St ✉ SW1Y 6AL – Ⓜ Green Park Plan: **H4**
– ✆ (020) 7839 1101 – www.onodera-group.com – Closed 25 December and 1 January
Menu £ 23 (lunch) – Carte £ 29/70
• Japanese • Elegant • Design •

Re-fitted and re-launched in 2017 on the site of what was Matsuri for over 20 years. A staircase leads down to the smart restaurant and the three counters: sushi, teppanyaki and the robata grill. The emphasis is on traditional Japanese cuisine and top-end ingredients.

Portrait

National Portrait Gallery (3rd floor), St Martin's Pl. Plan: **I3**
✉ WC2H 0HE – Ⓜ Charing Cross – ✆ (020) 73122490
– www.npg.org.uk/portraitrestaurant – Closed 24-26 December
Menu £ 20/33 – Carte £ 37/87 – *(lunch only and dinner Thursday-Saturday) (booking essential)*
• Modern cuisine • Contemporary décor •

Set on the top floor of the National Portrait Gallery with views of local landmarks. Carefully prepared modern European food; dishes are sometimes created in celebration of current exhibitions. Good value pre-theatre and weekend set menus.

Quaglino's

16 Bury St ✉ SW1Y 6AJ – Ⓜ Green Park Plan: **H4**
– ✆ (020) 79306767 – www.quaglinos-restaurant.co.uk – Closed Easter Monday and Sunday dinner
Menu £ 33 – Carte £ 36/52
• Modern cuisine • Design • Romantic •

This colourful, glamorous restaurant manages to be cavernous and cosy at the same time, with live music and a late night bar adding a certain sultriness to proceedings. The kitchen specialises in contemporary brasserie-style food.

Sake No Hana

XX AC

Plan: H4

23 St James's ✉ SW1A 1HA – Ⓜ Green Park – ✆ (020) 7925 8988 – www.sakenohana.com – Closed 25-26 December, Sunday and bank holiday Mondays

Menu £ 34 (lunch and early dinner)/45 – Carte £ 39/123

• Japanese • Minimalist • Fashionable •

A modern Japanese restaurant within a Grade II listed '60s edifice – and proof that you can occasionally find good food at the end of an escalator. As with the great cocktails, the menu is best enjoyed when shared with a group.

Scully

X ♿ AC

Plan: I3

4 St James's Market ✉ SW1Y 4AH – Ⓜ Piccadilly Circus – ✆ (020) 3911 6840 – www.scullyrestaurant.com – Closed dinner Sunday and bank holidays

Carte £ 21/46 – *(booking essential)*

• World cuisine • Friendly •

The eponymous chef-owner's travels and family heritage inform his style of food. The small plates feature an array of international influences and the bold, diverse flavours give them an appealing vitality. The kitchen makes good use of the shelves of pickles and spices.

STRAND – COVENT GARDEN – LAMBETH PLAN III

Strand and Covent Garden

L'Atelier de Joël Robuchon

X ♿ AC

Plan: I3

13-15 West St. ✉ WC2H 9NE – Ⓜ Leicester Square – ✆ (020) 70108600 – www.joelrobuchon.co.uk – Closed 25 December

Menu £ 45 (lunch and early dinner) – Carte £ 65/117

• French • Elegant • Contemporary décor •

Ground floor L'Atelier, with counter dining and chefs on view; La Cuisine upstairs offers table dining in an intimate setting just a few nights a week. Assured, accomplished cooking with an emphasis on the Mediterranean; dishes are creative and well-balanced, with a pleasing simplicity to their presentation.

→ Langoustine and truffle ravioli with Savoy cabbage. Oxtail braised with chestnuts, bone marrow and black truffle. Exotic fruit soufflé with coconut ice cream.

Cinnamon Bazaar

X AC

Plan: J3

28 Maiden Ln ✉ WC2E 7JS – Ⓜ Leicester Square – ✆ (020) 7395 1400 – www.cinnamon-bazaar.com

Menu £ 17/24 – Carte £ 20/38

• Indian • Exotic décor • Friendly •

Vivek Singh's latest venture provides relaxed, all-day contemporary Indian dining in the heart of Covent Garden, with a bright, colourful interior evoking a marketplace. Menus are influenced by the trade routes of the subcontinent, with twists that encompass Afghanistan, the Punjab and the Middle East.

Delaunay

XXX AC

Plan: J3

55 Aldwych ✉ WC2B 4BB – Ⓜ Temple – ✆ (020) 74998558 – www.thedelaunay.com – Closed 25 December

Carte £ 31/70 – *(booking essential)*

• Modern cuisine • Elegant • Fashionable •

The Delaunay was inspired by the grand cafés of Europe but, despite sharing the same buzz and celebrity clientele as its sibling The Wolseley, is not just a mere replica. The all-day menu is more mittel-European, with great schnitzels and wieners.

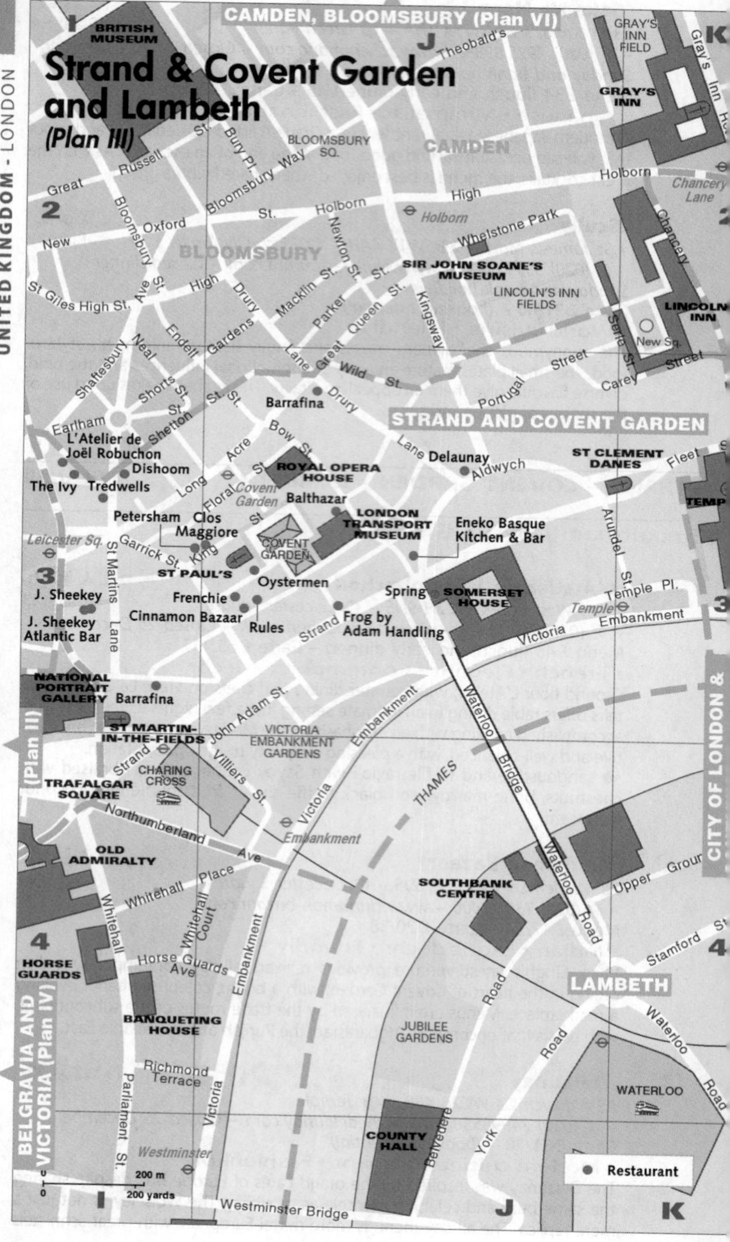
Strand & Covent Garden and Lambeth
(Plan III)
CAMDEN, BLOOMSBURY (Plan VI)
STRAND AND COVENT GARDEN
CITY OF LONDON &
(Plan II)
BELGRAVIA AND VICTORIA (Plan IV)
LAMBETH
CAMDEN
BLOOMSBURY
BRITISH MUSEUM
GRAY'S INN FIELD
GRAY'S INN
BLOOMSBURY SQ.
SIR JOHN SOANE'S MUSEUM
LINCOLN'S INN FIELDS
LINCOLN'S INN
New Sq.
Chancery Lane
Holborn
Leicester Sq.
Temple
Embankment
Westminster
ROYAL OPERA HOUSE
Covent Garden
COVENT GARDEN
LONDON TRANSPORT MUSEUM
ST PAUL'S
ST CLEMENT DANES
TEMP
SOMERSET HOUSE
NATIONAL PORTRAIT GALLERY
ST MARTIN-IN-THE-FIELDS
CHARING CROSS
TRAFALGAR SQUARE
VICTORIA EMBANKMENT GARDENS
THAMES
OLD ADMIRALTY
SOUTHBANK CENTRE
HORSE GUARDS
BANQUETING HOUSE
JUBILEE GARDENS
COUNTY HALL
WATERLOO
Barrafina
L'Atelier de Joël Robuchon
Dishoom
The Ivy
Tredwells
Petersham
Clos Maggiore
Balthazar
Delaunay
Eneko Basque Kitchen & Bar
Oystermen
Spring
J. Sheekey
Frenchie
Cinnamon Bazaar
Rules
Frog by Adam Handling
J. Sheekey Atlantic Bar
Barrafina
Theobald's
Gray's Inn Rd
Great Russell St.
Bury Pl.
Bloomsbury Way
Bloomsbury St.
New Oxford St.
Holborn
High Holborn
Whelstone Park
Newton St.
St Giles High St.
High
Drury
Macklin St.
Parker St.
Kingsway
Great Queen St.
Endell St.
Shaftesbury Ave
Neal St.
Shorts Gardens
Earlham St.
Shelton St.
Drury Lane
Wild St.
Portugal Street
Carey Street
Serle St.
Bow St.
Long Acre
Floral St
King St
Garrick St.
Aldwych
Fleet
Arundel St.
Temple Pl.
St Martins Lane
Strand
Victoria Embankment
Waterloo Bridge
John Adam St.
Villiers St.
Northumberland Ave
Whitehall Place
Whitehall Court
Whitehall
Horse Guards Ave
Richmond Terrace
Parliament St.
Westminster Bridge
Belvedere Road
York Road
Waterloo Road
Upper Ground
Stamford St
200 m
200 yards
Restaurant
1
2
3
4
I
J
K

The Ivy

XXX Plan: I3

9 West St ✉ *WC2H 9NE – Ⓜ Leicester Square – ✆ (020) 7836 4751 – www.the-ivy.co.uk – Closed 25 December*
Menu £ 24 (weekday lunch) – Carte £ 32/74

• Traditional British • Fashionable • Classic décor •

This landmark restaurant has had a facelift and while the glamorous clientele remain, it now has an oval bar as its focal point. The menu offers international dishes alongside the old favourites and personable staff anticipate your every need.

J.Sheekey

XX Plan: I3

28-32 St Martin's Ct ✉ *WC2N 4AL – Ⓜ Leicester Square – ✆ (020) 7240 2565 – www.j-sheekey.co.uk – Closed 25-26 December*
Carte £ 40/72 – *(booking essential)*

• Seafood • Fashionable •

Festooned with photographs of actors and linked to the theatrical world since opening in 1890. Wood panels and alcove tables add famed intimacy. Accomplished seafood cooking.

Rules

XX Plan: J3

35 Maiden Ln ✉ *WC2E 7LB – Ⓜ Leicester Square – ✆ (020) 78365314 – www.rules.co.uk – Closed 25-26 December*
Carte £ 39/70 – *(booking essential)*

• Traditional British • Traditional décor • Elegant •

London's oldest restaurant boasts a fine collection of antique cartoons, drawings and paintings. Tradition continues in the menu, specialising in game from its own estate.

Spring

XX Plan: J3

New Wing, Somerset House, Strand (Entrance on Lancaster Pl) ✉ *WC2R 1LA – Ⓜ Temple – ✆ (020) 3011 0115 – www.springrestaurant.co.uk – Closed Sunday*
Menu £ 32 (lunch) – Carte £ 41/63

• Italian • Fashionable • Elegant •

Spring occupies the 'new wing' of Somerset House that for many years was inhabited by the Inland Revenue. It's a bright, feminine space under the aegis of chef Skye Gyngell. Her cooking is Italian-influenced and ingredient-led.

Balthazar

XX Plan: J3

4-6 Russell St. ✉ *WC2B 5HZ – Ⓜ Covent Garden – ✆ (020) 3301 1155 – www.balthazarlondon.com – Closed 25 December*
Menu £ 23 (lunch and early dinner) – Carte £ 31/73 – *(booking essential)*

• French • Brasserie • Classic décor •

Those who know the original Balthazar in Manhattan's SoHo district will find the London version of this classic brasserie uncannily familiar in looks, vibe and food. The Franglais menu keeps it simple and the cocktails are great.

Clos Maggiore

XX Plan: J3

33 King St ✉ *WC2E 8JD – Ⓜ Leicester Square – ✆ (020) 7379 9696 – www.closmaggiore.com – Closed 24-25 December*
Menu £ 30 (weekday lunch)/37 – Carte £ 44/64

• French • Classic décor • Romantic •

One of London's most romantic restaurants – but be sure to ask for the enchanting conservatory with its retractable roof. The sophisticated French cooking is joined by a wine list of great depth. Good value and very popular pre/post theatre menus.

Eneko Basque Kitchen & Bar

XX Plan: J3

One Aldwych Hotel – 1 Aldwych ✉ *WC2B 4BZ – Ⓜ Temple – ✆ (020) 7300 0300 – www.eneko.london*
Menu £ 22 (lunch and early dinner) – Carte £ 26/89

• Basque • Design • Elegant •

Set in the One Aldwych Hotel, this stylish, ultra-modern restaurant features curved semi-private booths and a bar which seems to float above like a spaceship. Menus offer a refined reinterpretation of classic Basque dishes.

Frog by Adam Handling

XX

34-35 Southampton St ✉ WC2E 7HG Plan: **J3**
– Ⓜ Charing Cross – ✆ (020) 7199 8370 – www.frogbyadamhandling.com – Closed Sunday
Menu £ 35 (lunch and early dinner) – Carte £ 48/61

• Modern cuisine • Fashionable • Design •

The chef put his name in the title to signify that this is the flagship of his bourgeoning group. His dishes, which change regularly, are attractive creations and quite detailed in their composition. The well-run room is not without some understated elegance.

Petersham

XX

2 Floral Court ✉ WC2E 9FB – Ⓜ Covent Garden Plan: **I3**
– ✆ (020) 7305 7676 – www.petershamnurseries.com
Carte £ 42/73

• Mediterranean cuisine • Elegant • Chic •

Along with a deli, shop and florist is this elegant restaurant with contemporary art, Murano glass and an abundance of fresh flowers. The Italian-based menu uses produce from their Richmond nursery and Devon farm. The lovely terrace is shared with La Goccia, their more informal spot for sharing plates.

Tredwells

XX

4a Upper St Martin's Ln ✉ WC2H 9EF Plan: **I3**
– Ⓜ Leicester Square – ✆ (020) 3764 0840 – www.tredwells.com – Closed 24-26 December and 1 January
Menu £ 30 (lunch and early dinner) – Carte £ 29/57

• Modern British • Brasserie • Fashionable •

Chef-owner Chantelle Nicholson's contemporary cooking makes good use of British ingredients and also displays the occasional Asian twist. It's set over three floors, with a subtle art deco feel. A good choice for a Sunday roast.

J.Sheekey Atlantic Bar

X

33-34 St Martin's Ct. ✉ WC2 4AL – Ⓜ Leicester Square Plan: **I3**
– ✆ (020) 72402565 – www.jsheekeyatlanticbar.co.uk – Closed 25-26 December
Carte £ 22/49

• Seafood • Intimate •

An addendum to J. Sheekey restaurant. Sit at the bar to watch the chefs prepare the same quality seafood as next door but at slightly lower prices; fish pie and fruits de mer are the popular choices. Open all day.

Barrafina

X

10 Adelaide St ✉ WC2N 4HZ – Ⓜ Charing Cross Plan: **I3**
– ✆ (020) 7440 1456 – www.barrafina.co.uk – Closed Christmas, New Year and bank holidays
Carte £ 27/52 – *(bookings not accepted)*

• Spanish • Tapas bar • Trendy •

The second Barrafina is not just brighter than the Soho original – it's bigger too, so you can wait inside with a drink for counter seats to become available. Try more unusual tapas like ortiguillas, frit Mallorquin or the succulent meats.

Barrafina

X

43 Drury Ln ✉ WC2B 5AJ – Ⓜ Covent Garden Plan: **J3**
– ✆ (020) 7440 1456 – www.barrafina.co.uk – Closed 25-26 December, 27 May and 26 August
Carte £ 27/52 – *(bookings not accepted)*

• Spanish • Tapas bar • Simple •

The third of the Barrafinas is tucked away at the far end of Covent Garden; arrive early or prepare to queue. Fresh, vibrantly flavoured fish and shellfish dishes are a real highlight; tortillas y huevos also feature.

Dishoom

Plan: I3

12 Upper St Martin's Ln ✉ WC2H 9FB – Ⓜ Leicester Square – ✆ (020) 7420 9320 – www.dishoom.com – Closed dinner 24 December, 25-26 December and 1-2 January

Carte £ 14/28 – *(bookings not accepted)*

• Indian • Trendy •

Expect long queues at this group's original branch. It's based on a Bombay café, of the sort opened by Iranian immigrants in the early 20C. Try vada pau (Bombay's version of the chip butty), a curry or grilled meats; and finish with kulfi on a stick. It's lively, a touch chaotic but great fun.

Frenchie

Plan: J3

16 Henrietta St ✉ WC2E 8QH – Ⓜ Covent Garden – ✆ (020) 78364422 – www.frenchiecoventgarden.com – Closed 25-26 December and 1 January

Menu £ 27 (lunch) – Carte £ 45/60

• Modern cuisine • Bistro • Design •

A well-run modern-day bistro – younger sister to the Paris original, which shares the name given to chef-owner Greg Marchand when he was head chef at Fifteen. The adventurous, ambitious cooking is informed by his extensive travels.

Oystermen

Plan: J3

32 Henrietta St ✉ WC2E 8NA – Ⓜ Covent Garden – ✆ (020) 7240 4417 – www.oystermen.co.uk – Closed 25 December-1 January

Carte £ 28/48

• Seafood • Rustic • Simple •

Covent Garden isn't an area usually associated with independent restaurants but this bustling and modestly decorated little spot is thriving. From its tiny open kitchen come oysters, crabs and expertly cooked fish.

BELGRAVIA – VICTORIA — PLAN IV

BELGRAVIA

Marcus – Berkeley Hotel

Plan: G4

Wilton Pl ✉ SW1X 7RL – Ⓜ Knightsbridge – ✆ (020) 72351200 – www.marcusrestaurant.com – Closed Sunday

Menu £ 55/120

• Modern cuisine • Elegant • Intimate •

Marcus Wareing's eponymous restaurant inside the glamorous Berkeley Hotel is elegant and stylish, but also has a relaxed, easy-going feel. There's a steadfast Britishness to the menu which uses superlative produce like Isle of Gigha halibut, Cornish turbot and Galloway beef. The kitchen eschews complication and lets the main ingredient speak for itself.

→ Pheasant egg with short-rib ragu, wild garlic and asparagus. Middle White suckling pig with bacon broth and agnolotti. Salted milk chocolate aero with sorrel and clementine.

Céleste – The Lanesborough Hotel

Plan: G4

Hyde Park Corner ✉ SW1X 7TA – Ⓜ Hyde Park Corner – ✆ (020) 7259 5599 – www.lanesborough.com

Menu £ 39 (lunch) – Carte £ 72/100

• Creative French • Elegant • Luxury •

With its crystal chandeliers, immaculately dressed tables, Wedgwood blue friezes and fluted columns, this is a room in which you feel truly cosseted. The menu is overseen by Éric Fréchon, head chef of Le Bristol in Paris, so expect some of his specialities. However, the kitchen is unafraid of adding its own decidedly modern touches.

→ Fluffy organic Scotch egg. Lamb saddle with nori crust, kohlrabi purée and gnocchi. Coffee ice cream with caramelised pecan nuts and milk chocolate Chantilly.

Pétrus

1 Kinnerton St ✉ SW1X 8EA – Ⓜ Knightsbridge Plan: **F5**
– ✆ (020) 75921609 – www.gordonramsayrestaurants.com/petrus
– Closed 21-27 December and 1 January
Menu £ 45/105
• French • Elegant • Fashionable •

Gordon Ramsay's Belgravia restaurant is a sophisticated and elegant affair. The service is discreet and professional, and the cooking is rooted in classical techniques but isn't afraid of using influences from further afield. The superb wine list has Château Pétrus going back to 1928.

→ Steak tartare with crispy tendons, wasabi leaf and egg yolk. Fillet of Cornish brill with rouille, confit peppers and shellfish bisque. 'Black Forest' kirsch mousse with Amarena and Morello cherry sorbet.

Amaya

Halkin Arcade, 19 Motcomb St ✉ SW1X 8JT Plan: **F5**
– Ⓜ Knightsbridge – ✆ (020) 78231166 – www.amaya.biz
Menu £ 26/85 – Carte £ 33/82
• Indian • Design • Minimalist •

London has many open kitchens but at this Indian restaurant the shooting flames and enticing aromas from the tawa, tandoor and sigri grills will instantly alert your tastebuds that something interesting is about to happen. The service is as bright and lively as the surroundings.

→ Turmeric and tarragon chicken tikka. Tandoori wild prawns. Lime tart with limoncello jelly and blackberry compote.

Zafferano

15 Lowndes St ✉ SW1X 9EY – Ⓜ Knightsbridge Plan: **F5**
– ✆ (020) 72355800 – www.zafferanorestaurant.com – Closed 25 December
Menu £ 27 (weekday lunch) – Carte £ 36/85 – *(booking essential)*
• Italian • Fashionable • Neighbourhood •

The immaculately coiffured regulars continue to support this ever-expanding, long-standing and capably run Italian restaurant. They come for the reassuringly familiar, if rather steeply priced dishes from all parts of Italy.

Victoria

Dining Room at The Goring – Goring Hotel

15 Beeston Pl ✉ SW1W 0JW – Ⓜ Victoria Plan: **H5**
– ✆ (020) 73969000 – www.thegoring.com – Closed Saturday lunch
Menu £ 52/64
• Traditional British • Elegant • Classic décor •

A paean to all things British and the very model of discretion and decorum – the perfect spot for those who 'like things done properly' but without the stuffiness. The menu is an appealing mix of British classics and lighter, more modern dishes, all prepared with great skill and understanding.

→ Orkney scallop and kedgeree with shiso and lime. Salt-marsh lamb with haggis bun, shallot purée and seaweed tapenade. Brown sugar cake with poached pear, pine caramel and ginger ice cream.

Quilon – St James' Court Hotel

41 Buckingham Gate ✉ SW1E 6AF – Ⓜ St James's Park Plan: **H5**
– ✆ (020) 78211899 – www.quilon.co.uk – Closed 25 December
Menu £ 31/60 – Carte £ 42/57
• Indian • Design • Elegant •

A meal here will remind you how fresh, vibrant, colourful and healthy Indian food can be. Chef Sriram Aylur and his team focus on India's southwest coast, so the emphasis is on seafood and a lighter style of cooking. The room is stylish and comfortable and the service team, bright and enthusiastic.

→ Lobster broth with coriander and coconut cream. Venison chilli fry with onions and curry leaves. Baked yoghurt with palm jaggery, orange, mango and lychee.

A. Wong (Andrew Wong)

Plan: **H6**

70 Wilton Rd ✉ SW1V 1DE – Ⓜ Victoria – ✆ (020) 7828 8931 – www.awong.co.uk – Closed 23 December-4 January, Monday lunch and Sunday

Carte £ 24/54 – *(booking essential)*

• Chinese • Neighbourhood •

A modern Chinese restaurant with a buzzy ground floor and a sexy basement. The talented eponymous chef reinvents classic Cantonese dishes using creative, modern techniques; retaining the essence of a dish, whilst adding an impressive lightness and intensity of flavour. Service is keen, as are the prices.

➜ Crab claw and cured scallop with wasabi mayonnaise. Roasted char sui with sausage and foie gras. Poached meringue, orange sorbet, pomelo and passion fruit tofu.

The Cinnamon Club

Plan: **I5**

30-32 Great Smith St ✉ SW1P 3BU – Ⓜ St James's Park – ✆ (020) 7222 2555 – www.cinnamonclub.com – Closed bank holidays except 25 December

Menu £ 28 (weekday lunch) – Carte £ 37/84

• Indian • Historic • Elegant •

Locals and tourists, business people and politicians – this smart Indian restaurant housed in the listed former Westminster Library attracts them all. The fairly elaborate dishes arrive fully garnished and the spicing is quite subtle.

Roux at Parliament Square

Plan: **I5**

Royal Institution of Chartered Surveyors, Parliament Sq. ✉ SW1P 3AD – Ⓜ Westminster – ✆ (020) 73343737 – www.rouxatparliamentsquare.co.uk – Closed 2 weeks August, Christmas, New Year, Saturday, Sunday and bank holidays

Menu £ 42/79

• Modern cuisine • Elegant •

Light floods through the Georgian windows of this comfortable restaurant within the offices of the Royal Institute of Chartered Surveyors. Carefully crafted, elaborate and sophisticated cuisine, with some interesting flavour combinations.

Rex Whistler

Plan: **I6**

Tate Britain, Millbank ✉ SW1P 4RG – Ⓜ Pimlico – ✆ (020) 78878825 – www.tate.org.uk/visit/tate-britain/rex-whistler-restaurant – Closed 24-26 December

Menu £ 36 – *(lunch only)*

• Modern cuisine • Classic décor • Traditional décor •

A hidden gem, tucked away on the lower ground floor of Tate Britain; its most striking element is Whistler's restored mural, 'The Expedition in Pursuit of Rare Meats', which envelops the room. The menu is stoutly British and the remarkably well-priced wine list has an unrivalled 'half bottle' selection.

Aster

Plan: **H5**

150 Victoria St ✉ SW1E 5LB – Ⓜ Victoria – ✆ (020) 3875 5555 – www.aster-restaurant.com – Closed Sunday

Carte £ 36/55

• Modern cuisine • Contemporary décor • Fashionable •

Aster has a deli, a café, a bar and a terrace, as well the restaurant; a stylish, airy space on the first floor. The Finnish chef brings a Nordic slant to the modern French cuisine, with dishes that are light, refined and full of flavour.

Enoteca Turi

Plan: **G6**

87 Pimlico Rd ✉ SW1W 8PU – Ⓜ Sloane Square – ✆ (020) 7730 3663 – www.enotecaturi.com – Closed 25-26 December, 1 January, Sunday and bank holiday lunch

Menu £ 25 (lunch) – Carte £ 39/59

• Italian • Neighbourhood •

In 2016 Putney's loss was Pimlico's gain when, after 25 years, Giuseppe and Pamela Turi had to find a new home for their Italian restaurant. They brought their warm hospitality and superb wine list with them, and the chef has introduced a broader range of influences from across the country.

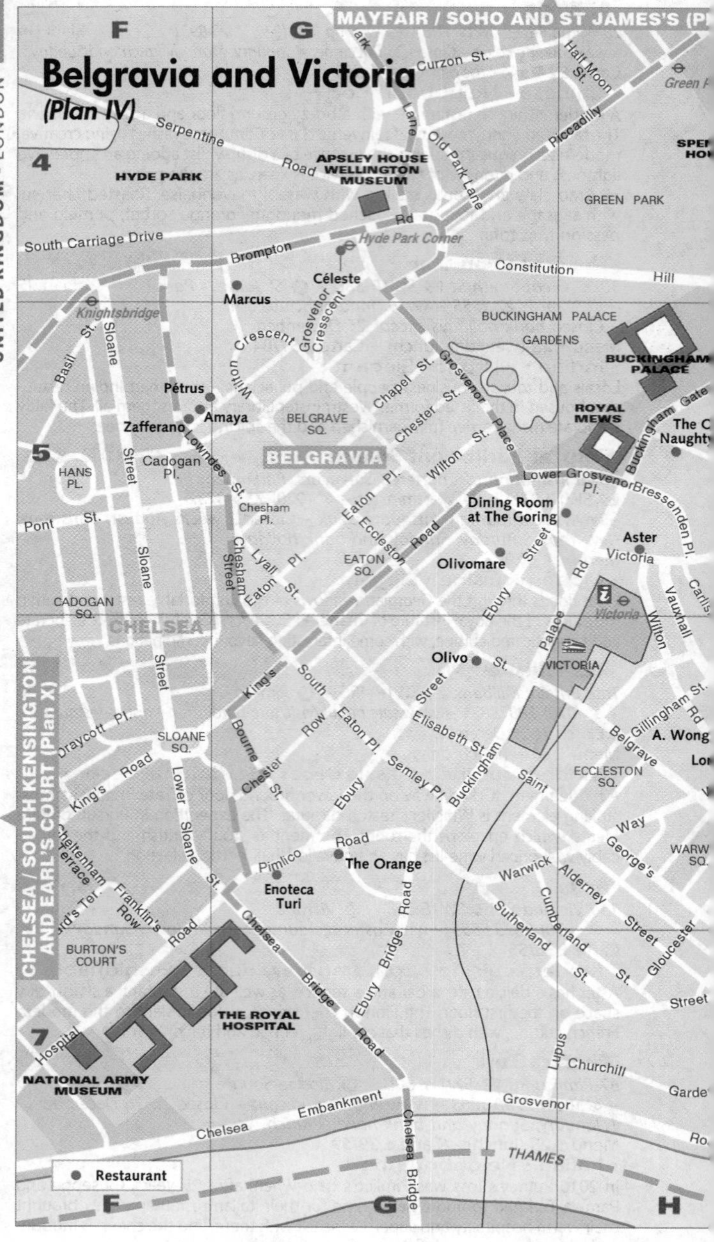
Belgravia and Victoria
(Plan IV)
MAYFAIR / SOHO AND ST JAMES'S
F
G
H
4
5
7
HYDE PARK
Serpentine Road
South Carriage Drive
APSLEY HOUSE WELLINGTON MUSEUM
Curzon St.
Half Moon St.
Piccadilly
Old Park Lane
Lane
GREEN PARK
Brompton Rd
Hyde Park Corner
Constitution Hill
Céleste
Marcus
Knightsbridge
Grosvenor Crescent
Wilton Crescent
BUCKINGHAM PALACE GARDENS
BUCKINGHAM PALACE
ROYAL MEWS
Buckingham Gate
Basil St.
Sloane St.
Pétrus
Amaya
Zafferano
BELGRAVE SQ.
Chapel St.
Chester St.
Grosvenor Place
Wilton St.
BELGRAVIA
HANS PL.
Sloane Street
Cadogan Pl.
Lowndes St.
Chesham Pl.
Eaton Pl.
Lower Grosvenor Pl.
Bressenden Pl.
Dining Room at The Goring
Aster
Victoria
Pont St.
Chesham Street
Lyall St.
Eccleston
EATON SQ.
Road
Olivomare
Street
Rd
Sloane
Eaton Pl.
CADOGAN SQ.
CHELSEA
Ebury
Victoria
Vauxhall
Wilton
Palace
VICTORIA
Olivo
St.
Street
King's
South
Row
Eaton Pl.
Elisabeth St.
Gillingham St.
Rd
A. Wong
Belgrave
Draycott Pl.
SLOANE SQ.
Road
King's
Lower Sloane St.
Bourne St.
Chester St.
Ebury
Semley Pl.
Buckingham
Saint
ECCLESTON SQ.
Way
George's
Road
Pimlico
The Orange
Enoteca Turi
Warwick
Alderney
WARW SQ.
Cheltenham Terrace
Franklin's Row
Road
Chelsea Bridge Road
Ebury Bridge Road
Sutherland St.
Cumberland St.
Street
Gloucester
BURTON'S COURT
THE ROYAL HOSPITAL
Hospital
NATIONAL ARMY MUSEUM
Lupus St.
Churchill
Street
Chelsea Embankment
Grosvenor
Chelsea Bridge
THAMES
CHELSEA / SOUTH KENSINGTON AND EARL'S COURT (Plan X)
Restaurant

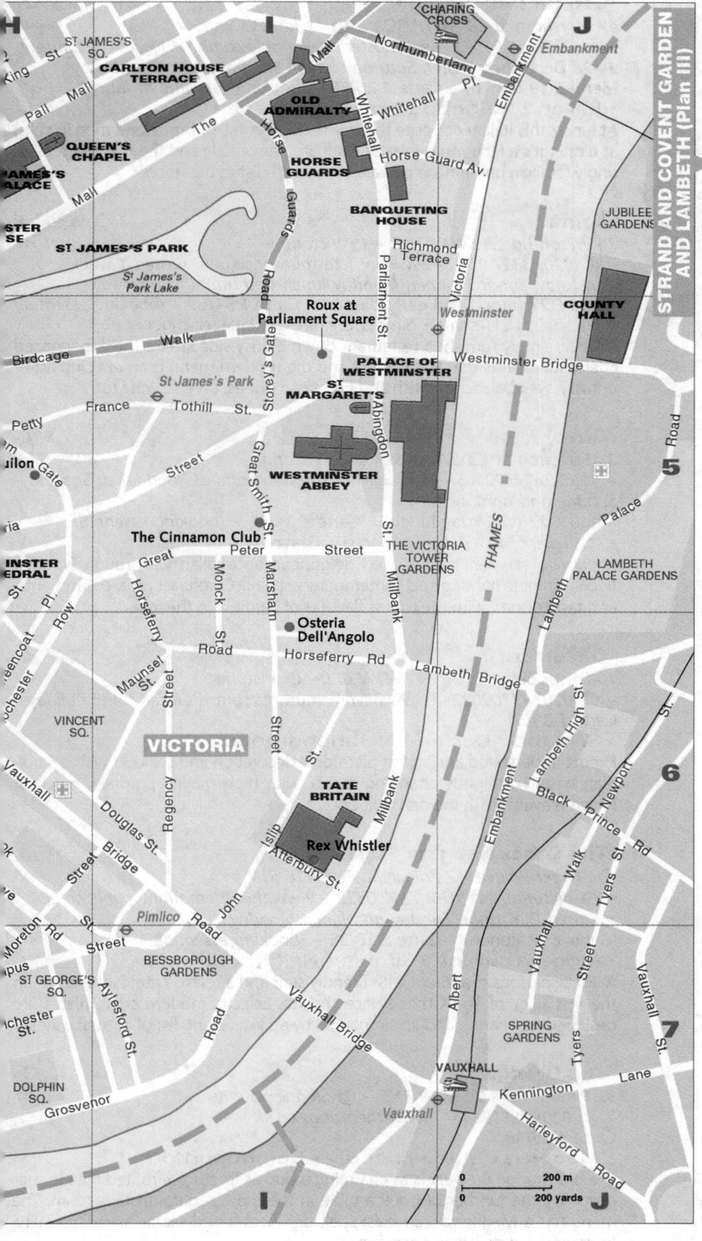
CHARING CROSS
Northumberland Pl.
Embankment
CARLTON HOUSE TERRACE
ST JAMES'S SQ.
OLD ADMIRALTY
Whitehall
Horse Guards Road
HORSE GUARDS
Horse Guard Av.
QUEEN'S CHAPEL
BANQUETING HOUSE
ST JAMES'S PARK
St James's Park Lake
Richmond Terrace
Parliament St.
Victoria Embankment
JUBILEE GARDENS
COUNTY HALL
Westminster
Roux at Parliament Square
Birdcage Walk
PALACE OF WESTMINSTER
Westminster Bridge
St James's Park
ST MARGARET'S
Tothill St.
Storey's Gate
Abingdon St.
WESTMINSTER ABBEY
Great Smith St.
Petty France
The Cinnamon Club
Great Peter Street
THE VICTORIA TOWER GARDENS
THAMES
LAMBETH PALACE GARDENS
Lambeth Palace Road
Horseferry Road
Monck St.
Marsham Street
Millbank
Osteria Dell'Angolo
Lambeth Bridge
Lambeth High St.
Maunsel St.
VINCENT SQ.
VICTORIA
Regency Street
TATE BRITAIN
Rex Whistler
Atterbury St.
Vauxhall Bridge Road
Douglas St.
Black Prince Rd
Newport St.
Tyers St.
Vauxhall Walk
Vauxhall Street
Pimlico
John Islip St.
BESSBOROUGH GARDENS
ST GEORGE'S SQ.
Aylesford St.
Grosvenor Road
DOLPHIN SQ.
Vauxhall Bridge
Albert Embankment
SPRING GARDENS
VAUXHALL
Kennington Lane
Harleyford Road
Vauxhall St.
0 200 m
0 200 yards
STRAND AND COVENT GARDEN AND LAMBETH (Plan III)
UNITED KINGDOM - LONDON

Osteria Dell' Angolo

47 Marsham St ✉ SW1P 3DR – Ⓜ St James's Park Plan: I6
– ✆ (020) 32681077 – www.osteriadellangolo.co.uk – Closed 1-4 January, 24-28 December, Easter, Saturday lunch, Sunday and bank holidays
Menu £ 19 (lunch) – Carte £ 26/50 – *(booking essential at lunch)*
• Italian • Neighbourhood • Brasserie •

At lunch, this Italian opposite the Home Office is full of bustle and men in suits; at dinner it's a little more relaxed. Staff are personable and the menu is reassuringly familiar; homemade pasta and seafood dishes are good.

Lorne

76 Wilton Rd ✉ SW1V 1DE – Ⓜ Victoria Plan: H6
– ✆ (020) 3327 0210 – www.lornerestaurant.co.uk – Closed 1 week Christmas, Sunday dinner, Monday lunch and bank holidays
Menu £ 27 (lunch and early dinner) – Carte £ 34/52 – *(booking essential)*
• Modern cuisine • Simple • Neighbourhood •

A small, simply furnished restaurant down a busy side street. The experienced chef understands that less is more and the modern menu is an enticing list of unfussy, well-balanced British and European dishes. Diverse wine list.

Olivo

21 Eccleston St ✉ SW1W 9LX – Ⓜ Victoria Plan: G6
– ✆ (020) 77302505 – www.olivorestaurants.com – Closed lunch Saturday-Sunday and bank holidays
Menu £ 27 (weekday lunch) – Carte £ 34/51 – *(booking essential)*
• Italian • Neighbourhood • Bistro •

A popular, pleasant and relaxed neighbourhood Italian with rough wooden floors, intimate lighting and contemporary styling. Carefully prepared, authentic and tasty dishes, with the robust flavours of Sardinia to the fore.

Olivomare

10 Lower Belgrave St ✉ SW1W 0LJ – Ⓜ Victoria Plan: G5
– ✆ (020) 77309022 – www.olivorestaurants.com – Closed bank holidays
Carte £ 39/51
• Seafood • Design • Neighbourhood •

Expect understated and stylish piscatorial decoration and seafood with a Sardinian base. Fortnightly changing menu, with high quality produce, much of which is available in the deli next door.

The Other Naughty Piglet

The Other Palace, 12 Palace St ✉ SW1E 5JA Plan: H5
– Ⓜ Victoria – ✆ (020) 7592 0322 – www.theothernaughtypiglet.co.uk – Closed Christmas, Sunday and lunch Monday
Menu £ 22 (lunch) – Carte £ 18/35 – *(booking essential)*
• Modern cuisine • Simple • Neighbourhood •

A light, spacious restaurant with friendly staff and a relaxed atmosphere, set on the first floor of The Other Palace theatre. Eclectic modern small plates are designed for sharing and accompanied by an interesting list of natural wines.

The Orange

37 Pimlico Rd ✉ SW1W 8NE – Ⓜ Sloane Square. Plan: G6
– ✆ (020) 78819844 – www.theorange.co.uk
Carte £ 25/48
• Modern cuisine • Friendly • Neighbourhood •

The old Orange Brewery is as charming a pub as its stucco-fronted façade suggests. Try the fun bar or book a table in the more sedate upstairs room. The menu has a Mediterranean bias; spelt or wheat-based pizzas are a speciality. Bedrooms are stylish and comfortable.

Locanda Locatelli (Giorgio Locatelli)

Plan: G2

8 Seymour St. ✉ W1H 7JZ – Ⓜ Marble Arch – ✆ (020) 79359088 – www.locandalocatelli.com – Closed 24-26 December and 1 January
Carte £ 49/74

• Italian • Fashionable • Elegant •

Giorgio Locatelli's Italian restaurant may be well into its second decade but it still looks as dapper as ever. The service is smooth and the room was designed with conviviality in mind. The hugely appealing menu covers all regions; unfussy presentation and superb ingredients allow natural flavours to shine.

→ Burrata with blood orange, black olive and fennel bread crisps. Tagliatelle with kid goat ragu, chilli and pecorino. Liquorice semifreddo with lime jelly, caviar and Branca Menta sauce.

Roganic

Plan: G2

5-7 Blandford St ✉ W1U 3DB – Ⓜ Bond Street – ✆ (020) 3370 6260 – www.roganic.uk – Closed 22 December-7 January, 25 August-2 September, Sunday and Monday.
Menu £ 35/95 – *(booking essential) (tasting menu only)*

• Creative British • Minimalist • Friendly •

Simon Rogan's London outpost is certainly not a copy of his L'Enclume restaurant in the Lake District but is intended to deliver elements of it. Much of the produce, however, comes from their farm in Cartmel. The cuisine style – which uses plenty of techniques including pickling and curing – will leave you feeling closer to nature.

→ Cured mackerel with radishes and sorrel sauce. Cornish lamb with broad beans and courgettes. Caramelised apple tart with Douglas fir ice cream.

Texture (Agnar Sverrisson)

Plan: G2

34 Portman St ✉ W1H 7BY – Ⓜ Marble Arch – ✆ (020) 72240028 – www.texture-restaurant.co.uk – Closed 2 weeks August, 1 week Easter, Christmas-New Year, Sunday, Monday and lunch Tuesday-Wednesday
Menu £ 29/95 – Carte £ 70/95

• Creative • Design • Fashionable •

Technically skilled but light and invigorating cooking from an Icelandic chef-owner, who uses ingredients from his homeland. Bright restaurant with high ceiling and popular adjoining champagne bar. Pleasant service from keen staff, ready with a smile.

→ Salmon gravlax with Oscietra caviar, mustard and sorrel. Lightly salted cod with avocado, Jersey Royals, romanesco and wild garlic. Icelandic skyr with vanilla, Gariguette strawberries and rye bread crumbs.

Portland

Plan: H2

113 Great Portland St ✉ W1W 6QQ – Ⓜ Great Portland Street – ✆ (020) 7436 3261 – www.portlandrestaurant.co.uk – Closed 23 December-3 January and Sunday
Menu £ 30/75 – Carte dinner £ 43/61 – *(booking essential)*

• Modern cuisine • Intimate • Simple •

The look is just the right side of austere, service is knowledgeable and wine is given equal billing to the food. One glance at the menu and you know you'll eat well: it changes daily and the combinations just sound right. The kitchen trusts the quality of the ingredients and lets natural flavours shine.

→ Asparagus, frozen egg yolk, nettles and ricotta gnudi. Gloucester Old Spot loin with braised treviso and lardo with quince. Bergamot custard, Douglas fir ice cream and burnt meringue.

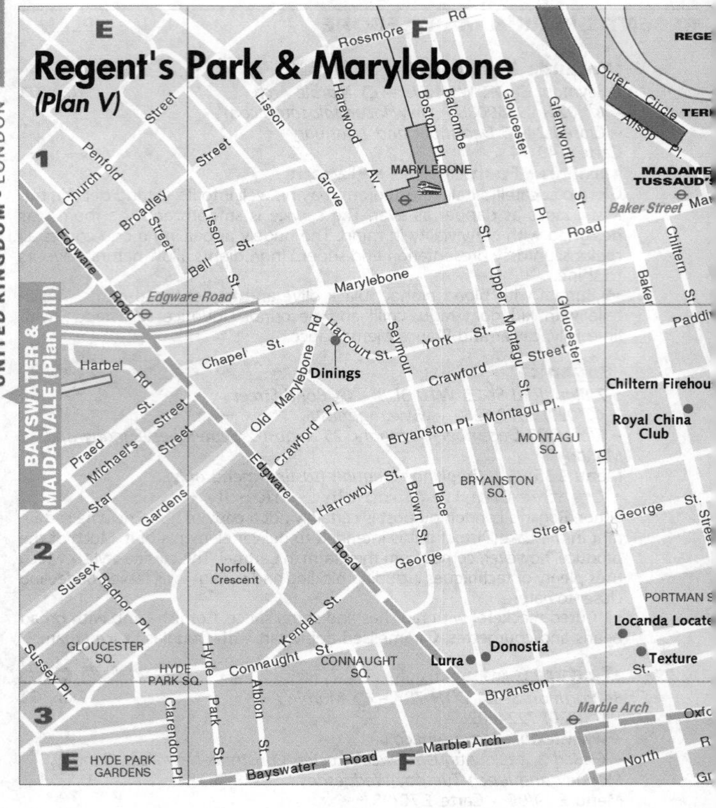

Trishna (Karam Sethi)

Plan: **G2**

15-17 Blandford St. ✉ W1U 3DG – Ⓜ Baker Street – ✆ (020) 79355624 – www.trishnalondon.com – Closed 25-27 December and 1-3 January

Menu £ 28/65 – Carte £ 32/59

• Indian • Neighbourhood • Friendly •

A double-fronted, modern Indian restaurant dressed in an elegant, understated style. The coast of southwest India provides the influences and the food is vibrant, satisfying and executed with care – the tasting menus provide a good all-round experience, and much thought has gone into the matching wines.

➜ Aloo tokri chaat. Dorset brown crab with butter, pepper, chilli and garlic. Baked yoghurt with apricot chutney.

Picture Fitzrovia

Plan: **H2**

110 Great Portland St. ✉ W1W 6PQ – Ⓜ Oxford Circus – ✆ (020) 7637 7892 – www.picturerestaurant.co.uk – Closed Sunday and bank holidays

Menu £ 23 (lunch) – Carte £ 23/33

• Modern British • Simple • Friendly •

An ex Arbutus and Wild Honey triumvirate created this cool, great value restaurant. The look may be a little stark but the delightful staff add warmth. The small plates are vibrant and colourful, and the flavours are assured.

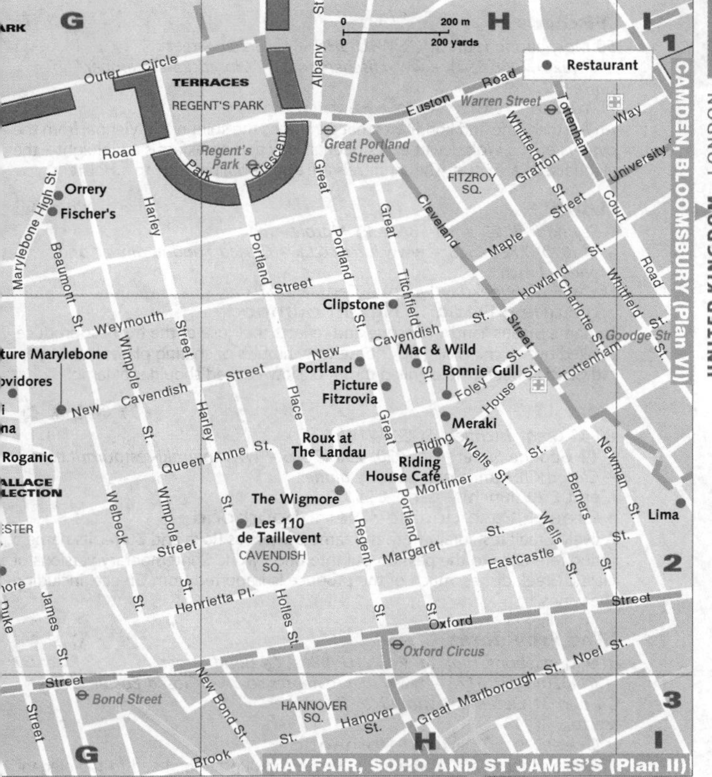

ꟾO **Orrery** XXX

55 Marylebone High St ✉ W1U 5RB Plan: **G1**
– Ⓜ Regent's Park – ✆ (020) 7616 8000
– www.orrery-restaurant.co.uk
Menu £ 25/59 – *(booking essential)*

• Modern cuisine • Neighbourhood • Design •

The most recent redecoration left this comfortable restaurant, located in what were converted stables from the 19C, looking lighter and more contemporary; the bar and terrace are also smarter. Expect quite elaborate, modern European cooking, strong on presentation and with the occasional twist.

ꟾO **Chiltern Firehouse** – Chiltern Firehouse Hotel XX

1 Chiltern St ✉ WIU 7PA – Ⓜ Baker Street Plan: **G2**
– ✆ (020) 7073 7676
– www.chilternfirehouse.com
Carte £ 37/63

• World cuisine • Fashionable • Design •

How appropriate – one of the hottest tickets in town is a converted fire station. The room positively bursts with energy but what makes this celebrity hangout unusual is that the food is rather good. Nuno Mendes' menu is full of vibrant North and South American dishes that are big on flavour.

Fischer's

XX A/C

50 Marylebone High St ✉ W1U 5HN – Ⓜ Baker Street Plan: **G1**
– ✆ (020) 7466 5501 – www.fischers.co.uk – Closed 25 December
Carte £ 23/59

• Austrian • Brasserie • Fashionable •

An Austrian café and konditorei that summons the spirit of old Vienna; from the owners of The Wolseley et al. It's open all day and breakfast is a highlight – the viennoiserie are great. The schnitzels are also good; upgrade to a Holstein.

Lurra

XX A/C

9 Seymour Pl ✉ W1H 5BA – Ⓜ Marble Arch Plan: **F2**
– ✆ (020) 7724 4545 – www.lurra.co.uk – Closed Sunday dinner and Monday lunch
Menu £ 25 (weekday lunch) – Carte £ 27/70

• Basque • Design • Neighbourhood •

Its name means 'land' in Basque and reflects their use of the freshest produce, cooked over a charcoal grill. Choose tasty nibbles or sharing plates like 14 year old Galician beef, whole grilled turbot or slow-cooked shoulder of lamb.

Meraki

XX ♿ A/C

80-82 Great Titchfield St ✉ W1W 7QT Plan: **H2**
– Ⓜ Goodge Street – ✆ (020) 7305 7686 – www.meraki-restaurant.com – Closed Christmas and Sunday dinner
Menu £ 20 (lunch) – Carte £ 25/60

• Greek • Fashionable • Neighbourhood •

A lively Greek restaurant from the same owners as Roka and Zuma; its name a fitting reference to the passion put into one's work. Contemporary versions of classic Greek dishes; much of the produce is imported from Greece, including the wines.

The Providores

XX A/C

109 Marylebone High St. ✉ W1U 4RX – Ⓜ Bond Street Plan: **G2**
– ✆ (020) 7935 6175 – www.theprovidores.co.uk – Closed Easter, dinner 24 and 31 December and 25-26 December
Carte £ 36/48

• Creative • Trendy • Romantic •

Tables and tapas are shared in the buzzing ground floor; head to the elegant, slightly more sedate upstairs room for innovative fusion cooking, with ingredients from around the world. New Zealand wine list; charming staff.

Roux at The Landau - Langham Hotel

XX A/C

1c Portland Pl., Regent St. ✉ W1B 1JA Plan: **H2**
– Ⓜ Oxford Circus – ✆ (020) 79650165 – www.rouxatthelandau.com – Closed Monday
Menu £ 25 (weekday lunch) – Carte £ 33/71

• French • Elegant • Design •

There's been a change to a more informal style for this restaurant run under the aegis of the Roux organisation – it's now more akin to a modern bistro in looks and atmosphere and is all the better for it. The cooking is classical French and informed by the seasons; shellfish is a highlight.

Royal China Club

XX A/C

40-42 Baker St ✉ W1U 7AJ – Ⓜ Baker Street Plan: **G2**
– ✆ (020) 7486 3898 – www.royalchinagroup.co.uk – Closed 25-27 December
Carte £ 35/80

• Chinese • Oriental décor •

Service is fast-paced and to the point, which is understandable considering how busy this restaurant always is. The large menu offers something for everyone and the lunchtime dim sum is very good; at dinner try their more unusual Cantonese dishes.

Les 110 de Taillevent

Plan: **H2**

16 Cavendish Sq ✉ W1G 9DD – Ⓜ Oxford Circus – ✆ (020) 3141 6016 – www.les-110-taillevent-london.com
Menu £ 28 (lunch) – Carte £ 38/76

• French • Elegant • Design •

Ornate high ceilings and deep green banquettes create an elegant look for this French brasserie deluxe, which is more food orientated than the Paris original. It also offers 110 wines by the glass: 4 different pairings for each dish, in 4 different price brackets.

Bonnie Gull

Plan: **H2**

21a Foley St ✉ W1W 6DS – Ⓜ Goodge Street – ✆ (020) 7436 0921 – www.bonniegull.com – Closed 25 December-3 January
Carte £ 31/45 – *(booking essential)*

• Seafood • Simple • Traditional décor •

Sweet Bonnie Gull calls itself a 'seafood shack' – a reference perhaps to its modest beginnings as a pop-up. Start with something from the raw bar then go for classics like Cullen skink, Devon cock crab or fish and chips. There's another branch in Soho.

The Michelin plate?
Restaurant or pub, traditional or modern, regional or international cooking: this symbol highlights restaurants where you will have a good meal!

Clipstone

Plan: **H2**

5 Clipstone St ✉ W1W 6BB – Ⓜ Great Portland Street – ✆ (020) 76370871 – www.clipstonerestaurant.co.uk – Closed Christmas, New Year and Sunday
Menu £ 24 (lunch) – Carte £ 34/40

• Modern cuisine • Fashionable • Neighbourhood •

Another wonderful neighbourhood spot from the owners of Portland, just around the corner. The sharing menu is a lesson in flavour and originality; choose one charcuterie dish, one from the seasonal vegetable-based section, one main and a dessert. Cocktails and 'on-tap' wine add to the fun.

Dinings

Plan: **F2**

22 Harcourt St. ✉ W1H 4HH – Ⓜ Edgware Road – ✆ (020) 77230666 – www.dinings.co.uk – Closed Christmas
Carte £ 25/67 – *(booking essential)*

• Japanese • Cosy • Simple •

It's hard not to be charmed by this sweet little Japanese place, with its ground floor counter and basement tables. Its strengths lie with the more creative, contemporary dishes; sharing is recommended but prices can be steep.

Donostia

Plan: **F2**

10 Seymour Pl ✉ W1H 7ND – Ⓜ Marble Arch – ✆ (020) 3620 1845 – www.donostia.co.uk – Closed Christmas, New Year and lunch Sunday-Monday
Menu £ 20 (weekday lunch) – Carte £ 20/43

• Basque • Tapas bar • Fashionable •

The two young owners were inspired to open this pintxos and tapas bar by the food of San Sebastián. Sit at the counter for Basque classics like cod with pil-pil sauce, chorizo from the native Kintoa pig and slow-cooked pig's cheeks.

Jikoni

19-21 Blandford St ✉ W1U 3DH – Ⓜ Baker Street Plan: **G2**
– ✆ (020) 7034 1988 – www.jikonilondon.com – Closed Monday and lunch Tuesday
Menu £ 20 (weekday lunch) – Carte £ 24/48
• Indian • Elegant • Neighbourhood •

Indian tablecloths and colourful cushions create a homely feel at this idiosyncratic restaurant. Born in Kenya of Indian parents and brought up in London, chef Ravinder Bhogal takes culinary inspiration from these sources and more.

Lima

31 Rathbone Pl ✉ W1T 1JH – Ⓜ Goodge Street Plan: **I2**
– ✆ (020) 3002 2640 – www.limalondongroup.com – Closed 24-26 December, 1 January and bank holidays
Menu £ 19 (weekday lunch) – Carte £ 30/59
• Peruvian • Neighbourhood • Intimate •

Lima is one of those restaurants that just makes you feel good about life – and that's even without the pisco sours. The Peruvian food at this informal, fun place is the ideal antidote to times of austerity: it's full of punchy, invigorating flavours and fantastically vivid colours.

Mac & Wild

65 Great Titchfield St ✉ W1W 7PS – Ⓜ Oxford Circus Plan: **H2**
– ✆ (020) 7637 0510 – www.macandwild.com – Closed Sunday dinner
Carte £ 21/62
• Scottish • Friendly • Neighbourhood •

The owner of this 'Highland restaurant' is the son of an Ardgay butcher – it is all about their wild venison and top quality game and seafood from Scotland. Don't miss the 'wee plates' like the deliriously addictive haggis pops. There's also a choice of over 100 whiskies.

Opso

10 Paddington St ✉ W1U 5QL – Ⓜ Baker Street Plan: **G1**
– ✆ (020) 7487 5088 – www.opso.co.uk – Closed 23 December-3 January
Carte £ 14/55
• Greek • Neighbourhood •

A modern Greek restaurant which has proved a good fit for the neighbourhood – and not just because it's around the corner from the Hellenic Centre. It serves small sharing plates that mix the modern with the traditional.

Picture Marylebone

19 New Cavendish St ✉ W1G 9TZ – Ⓜ Bond Street Plan: **G2**
– ✆ (020) 7935 0058 – www.picturerestaurant.co.uk – Closed Sunday, Monday and bank holidays
Menu £ 23 (lunch) – Carte £ 27/33
• Modern British • Design • Friendly •

This follow-up to Picture Fitzrovia hit the ground running. The cleverly created à la carte of flavoursome small plates lists 3 vegetable, 3 fish and 3 meat choices, followed by 3 desserts – choose one from each section.

Riding House Café

43-51 Great Titchfield St ✉ W1W 7PQ Plan: **H2**
– Ⓜ Oxford Circus – ✆ (020) 79270840 – www.ridinghousecafe.co.uk – Closed 25-26 December
Carte £ 25/49
• Modern cuisine • Rustic • Fashionable •

It's less a café, more a large, quirkily designed, all-day New York style brasserie and cocktail bar. The small plates have more zing than the main courses. The 'unbookable' side of the restaurant is the more fun part.

Zoilo

Plan: G2

9 Duke St. ✉ W1U 3EG – Ⓜ Bond Street – ✆ (020) 7486 9699 – www.zoilo.co.uk – Closed Sunday

Menu £ 19 (lunch) – Carte £ 29/53

• Argentinian • Friendly • Wine bar •

It's all about sharing so plonk yourself at the counter and discover Argentina's regional specialities. Typical dishes include braised pig head croquettes or grilled scallops with pork belly, and there's an appealing all-Argentinian wine list.

The Wigmore – Langham Hotel

Plan: H2

15 Langham Place, Upper Regent St ✉ W1B 1JA – Ⓜ Oxford Circus – ✆ (020) 7965 0198 – www.the-wigmore.co.uk

Carte £ 26/40

• Traditional British • Pub • Fashionable •

The impressively high ceiling can only mean one thing – this was once a bank. Booths, high tables, a sizeable bar and bold emerald green tones lend a clubby feel to this addendum to The Langham. Classic, hearty British dishes are given an update.

CAMDEN — PLAN VI

Bloomsbury

Kitchen Table at Bubbledogs (James Knappett)

XX

Plan: H2

70 Charlotte St ✉ W1T 4QG – Ⓜ Goodge Street – ✆ (020) 76377770 – www.kitchentablelondon.co.uk – Closed first 2 weeks January, 2 weeks September, 23-27 December and Sunday-Tuesday

Menu £ 125 – *(dinner only) (booking essential) (tasting menu only)*

• Modern cuisine • Fashionable • Friendly •

Behind a curtain you'll find a counter where chef-owner James Knappett and his team prepare a no-choice menu of around 12 dishes. The produce is some of the best you can find and the small dishes come with a clever creative edge. The chefs interact with their customers over the counter and are helped out by James' wife Sandia, who is charm personified.

➜ Orkney scallops with warm charcoal cream and Exmouth caviar. Duck with black garlic, blood orange purée, turnip and shiso. Milk ice cream with rhubarb and charred black pepper meringue.

Pied à Terre

XXX

Plan: I2

34 Charlotte St ✉ W1T 2NH – Ⓜ Goodge Street – ✆ (020) 76361178 – www.pied-a-terre.co.uk – Closed 23 December-9 January, Saturday lunch, Sunday and bank holidays

Menu £ 38/80 – *(booking essential)*

• Creative • Elegant • Intimate •

One of the reasons for the impressive longevity of David Moore's restaurant has been its subtle reinventions: nothing ever too grandiose – just a little freshening up with some new art or clever lighting to keep the place looking relevant and vibrant. The cooking is still based on classical French techniques but dishes now display a more muscular edge.

➜ Smoked quail spelt risotto with coral mushrooms and watercress. Poached turbot with langoustine and spinach. Pink and red pavlova with raspberries, kaffir lime and a lavender custard.

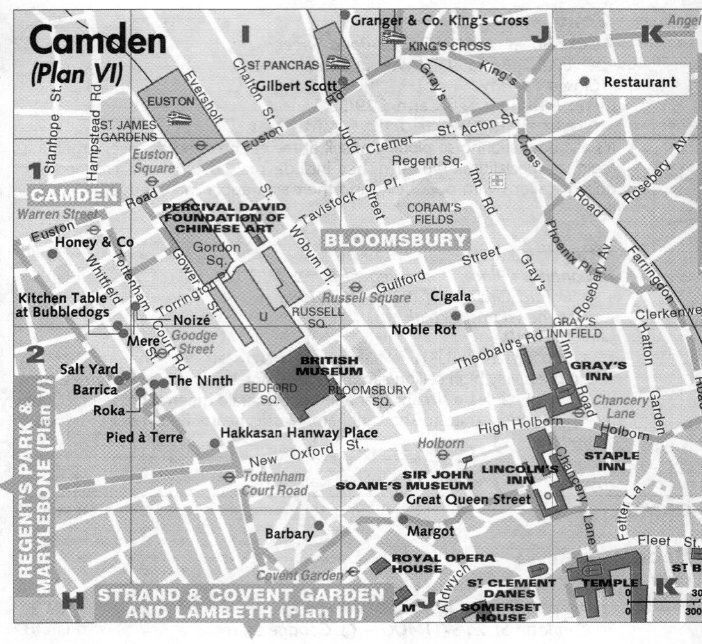

Hakkasan Hanway Place

XX A/C

8 Hanway Pl. ✉ *W1T 1HD* – Ⓜ *Tottenham Court Road* Plan: I2
– ✆ (020) 79277000 – www.hakkasan.com
– Closed 24-25 December
Carte £ 35/135
• Chinese • Trendy • Fashionable •

There are now Hakkasans all over the world but this was the original. It has the sensual looks, air of exclusivity and glamorous atmosphere synonymous with the 'brand'. The exquisite Cantonese dishes are prepared with care and consistency by the large kitchen team; lunch dim sum is a highlight.

➜ Dim sum platter. Grilled Chilean sea bass in honey. Chocolate and olive oil ganache.

The Ninth (Jun Tanaka)

X A/C

22 Charlotte St ✉ *W1T 2NB* – Ⓜ *Goodge Street* Plan: I2
– ✆ (020) 3019 0880 – www.theninthlondon.com
– Closed Christmas-New Year, Sunday and bank holidays
Menu £ 27 (lunch) – Carte £ 39/66
• Mediterranean cuisine • Brasserie • Fashionable •

Jun Tanaka's first restaurant – the ninth in which he has worked – is this neighbourhood spot with a lively downstairs and more intimate first floor. Cooking uses classical French techniques with a spotlight on the Med; dishes look appealing but the focus is firmly on flavour. Vegetables are a highlight.

➜ Salted beef cheek, oxtail consommé and sauce ravigote. Chargrilled sea bream, lemon confit and miso. Pain perdu with vanilla ice cream.

Barbary

Plan: I3

16 Neal's Yard ✉ WC2H 9DP – Ⓜ Covent Garden – www.thebarbary.co.uk – Closed dinner 24-26 December

Carte £ 16/36 – *(bookings not accepted)*

• World cuisine • Tapas bar • Rustic •

A sultry, atmospheric restaurant from the team behind Palomar: a tiny place with 24 non-bookable seats squeezed around a horseshoe-shaped, zinc-topped counter. The menu of small sharing plates lists dishes from the former Barbary Coast. Service is keen, as are the prices.

Barrica

Plan: H2

62 Goodge St ✉ W1T 4NE – Ⓜ Goodge Street – ☎ (020) 7436 9448 – www.barrica.co.uk – Closed 25-31 December, 1 January, Easter, Sunday and bank holidays

Carte £ 22/38 – *(booking essential)*

• Spanish • Tapas bar • Friendly •

All the staff at this lively little tapas bar are Spanish, so perhaps it's national pride that makes them run it with a passion lacking in many of their competitors. When it comes to the food, authenticity is high on the agenda. Dishes pack a punch and are fairly priced.

Salt Yard

Plan: H2

54 Goodge St. ✉ W1T 4NA – Ⓜ Goodge Street – ☎ (020) 76370657 – www.saltyard.co.uk – Closed 31 December-1 January and dinner 24-25 December

Carte £ 20/28

• Mediterranean cuisine • Tapas bar • Intimate •

A ground floor bar and buzzy basement restaurant specialising in good value plates of tasty Italian and Spanish dishes, ideal for sharing. Ingredients are top-notch; charcuterie is a speciality. Super wine list and sincere, enthusiastic staff.

Mere

Plan: H1/2

74 Charlotte St ✉ W1T 4QH – Ⓜ Goodge Street – ☎ (020) 7268 6565 – www.mere-restaurant.com – Closed Sunday and bank holidays

Menu £ 35 (weekday lunch) – Carte £ 46/64

• Modern cuisine • Fashionable • Elegant •

Monica Galetti's first collaboration with her husband, David, is an understatedly elegant basement restaurant flooded with natural light. Global, ingredient-led cooking features French influences with a nod to the South Pacific.

Noizé

Plan: I1

39 Whitfield St ✉ W1T 2SF – Ⓜ Goodge Street – ☎ (020) 7323 1310 – www.noize-restaurant.co.uk – Closed 2 weeks August, 23 December-3 January, Easter, Saturday lunch, Sunday and Monday

Carte £ 34/56

• Modern French • Neighbourhood • Bistro •

A softly spoken Frenchman, an alumnus of Pied à Terre, took over the former Dabbous site and created a delightfully relaxed, modern bistro. The unfussy French food is served at fair prices; sauces are a great strength. The wine list, with plenty of depth and fair mark-ups, is another highlight.

Roka

Plan: I2

37 Charlotte St ✉ W1T 1RR – Ⓜ Goodge Street – ☎ (020) 7636 5228 – www.rokarestaurant.com – Closed 25 December

Carte £ 42/75

• Japanese • Fashionable • Design •

The original Roka, where people come for the lively atmosphere as much as the cooking. The kitchen takes the flavours of Japanese food and adds its own contemporary touches; try specialities from the on-view Robata grill.

Cigala

54 Lamb's Conduit St. ✉ WC1N 3LW – Ⓜ Russell Square – ✆ (020) 74051717 – www.cigala.co.uk – Closed 24-26 December and 1 January Plan: **J1**

Menu £ 24 (weekday lunch) – Carte £ 34/46 – *(booking essential)*

• Spanish • Neighbourhood • Friendly •

Longstanding Spanish restaurant, with a lively and convivial atmosphere, friendly and helpful service and an appealing and extensive menu of classics. The dried hams are a must and it's well worth waiting the 30 minutes for a paella.

Honey & Co

25a Warren St ✉ W1T 5LZ – Ⓜ Warren Street – ✆ (020) 73886175 – www.honeyandco.co.uk – Closed 24-26, 31 December, 1-3 January and Sunday Plan: **H1**

Menu £ 35 – *(booking essential)*

• World cuisine • Simple • Neighbourhood •

The husband and wife team at this sweet little café were both Ottolenghi head chefs so expect cooking full of freshness and colour. Influences stretch beyond Israel to the wider Middle East. Open from 8am; packed at night.

Noble Rot

51 Lamb's Conduit St ✉ WC1N 3NB – Ⓜ Russell Square – ✆ (020) 7242 8963 – www.noblerot.co.uk – Closed 25-26 December and Sunday Plan: **J1**

Menu £ 16 (weekday lunch) – Carte £ 33/49

• Traditional British • Rustic • Wine bar •

A wine bar and restaurant from the people behind the wine magazine of the same name. Unfussy cooking comes with bold, gutsy flavours; expect fish from the Kent coast as well as classics like terrines, rillettes and home-cured meats.

Holborn

Margot

45 Great Queen St ✉ WC2 5AA – Ⓜ Holborn – ✆ (020) 34094777 – www.margotrestaurant.com – Closed 25 December Plan: **J3**

Menu £ 25 (lunch and early dinner) – Carte £ 30/61

• Italian • Elegant • Fashionable •

Bucking the trend of casual eateries is this glamorous, elegant Italian, where a doorman greets you, staff sport tuxedos and the surroundings are sleek and stylish. The seasonal, regional Italian cooking has bags of flavour and a rustic edge.

Great Queen Street

32 Great Queen St ✉ WC2B 5AA – Ⓜ Holborn – ✆ (020) 72420622 – www.greatqueenstreetrestaurant.co.uk – Closed Christmas-New Year, Sunday dinner and bank holidays Plan: **J2**

Menu £ 18 (weekday lunch) – Carte £ 22/42 – *(booking essential)*

• Modern British • Rustic • Neighbourhood •

The menu is a model of British understatement and is dictated by the seasons; the cooking, confident and satisfying and served in generous portions. Lively atmosphere and enthusiastic service. Highlights include the shared dishes like the suet-crusted steak and ale pie for two.

KING'S CROSS ST PANCRAS — PLAN VI

Gilbert Scott - St Pancras Renaissance Hotel

Euston Rd ✉ NW1 2AR – Ⓜ King's Cross St Pancras – ✆ (020) 7278 3888 – www.thegilbertscott.co.uk Plan: **J0**

Menu £ 30 (lunch and early dinner) – Carte £ 28/61

• Traditional British • Brasserie • Elegant •

Named after the architect of this Gothic masterpiece and run under the aegis of Marcus Wareing, this restaurant has the splendour of a Grand Salon but the buzz of a brasserie. The appealing menu showcases the best of British produce, whilst incorporating influences from further afield.

Dinner by Heston Blumenthal – Mandarin Oriental Hyde Park Hotel

66 Knightsbridge, ✉ SW1X 7LA – Ⓜ Knightsbridge – ✆ (020) 7201 3833 – www.dinnerbyheston.com – Closed 17-31 October

Plan: **F4**

Menu £ 45 (weekday lunch) – Carte £ 58/121

• Traditional British • Design • Fashionable •

Heston Blumenthal's menu celebrates British culinary triumphs through the ages, with the date of origin given to each dish along with information about its provenance. An impressively well-manned kitchen works with obvious intelligence, calm efficiency and attention to detail to produce dishes that look deceptively simple but taste sublime.

➜ Mandarin, chicken liver parfait and grilled bread (c.1500). Hereford rib-eye with mushroom ketchup and triple cooked chips (c.1830). Tipsy cake with spit-roast pineapple (c.1810).

Bar Boulud – Mandarin Oriental Hyde Park Hotel

66 Knightsbridge ✉ SW1X 7LA – Ⓜ Knightsbridge – ✆ (020) 72013899 – www.mandarinoriental.com

Plan: **F4**

Menu £ 19 (weekday lunch) – Carte £ 26/57

• French • Brasserie • Fashionable •

Daniel Boulud's London outpost is fashionable, fun and frantic. His hometown is Lyon but he built his considerable reputation in New York, so charcuterie, sausages and burgers are the highlights.

Zuma

5 Raphael St ✉ SW7 1DL – Ⓜ Knightsbridge – ✆ (020) 75841010 – www.zumarestaurant.com – Closed 25 December

Plan: **F5**

Carte £ 31/150 – *(booking essential)*

• Japanese • Fashionable •

Now a global brand but this was the original. The glamorous clientele come for the striking surroundings, bustling atmosphere and easy-to-share food. Go for the more modern dishes and those cooked on the robata grill.

BAYSWATER – MAIDA VALE

PLAN VIII

Hereford Road

3 Hereford Rd ✉ W2 4AB – Ⓜ Bayswater – ✆ (020) 77271144 – www.herefordroad.org – Closed 24 December-3 January and August bank holiday

Plan: **C2**

Menu £ 16 (weekday lunch) – Carte £ 25/32 – *(booking essential)*

• Traditional British • Neighbourhood • Bistro •

Converted butcher's shop specialising in tasty British dishes without frills, using first-rate, seasonal ingredients; offal a highlight. Booths for six people are the prized seats. Friendly and relaxed feel.

Kateh

5 Warwick Pl ✉ W9 2PX – Ⓜ Warwick Avenue – ✆ (020) 7289 3393 – www.katehrestaurant.co.uk – Closed 25-26 December

Plan: **D1**

Carte £ 21/38 – *(dinner only and lunch Saturday-Sunday) (booking essential)*

• Mediterranean cuisine • Neighbourhood • Intimate •

Booking is imperative if you want to join the locals who have already discovered what a little jewel they have in the form of this buzzy, busy Persian restaurant. Authentic stews, expert chargrilling and lovely pastries and teas.

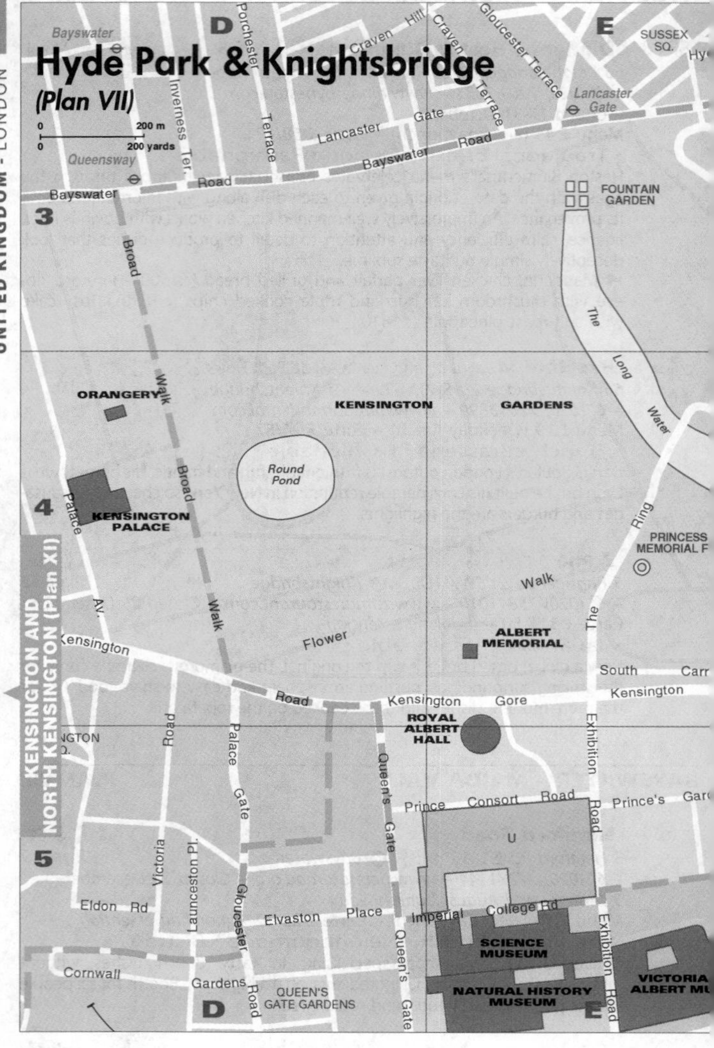

KENSINGTON AND NORTH KENSINGTON (Plan XI)

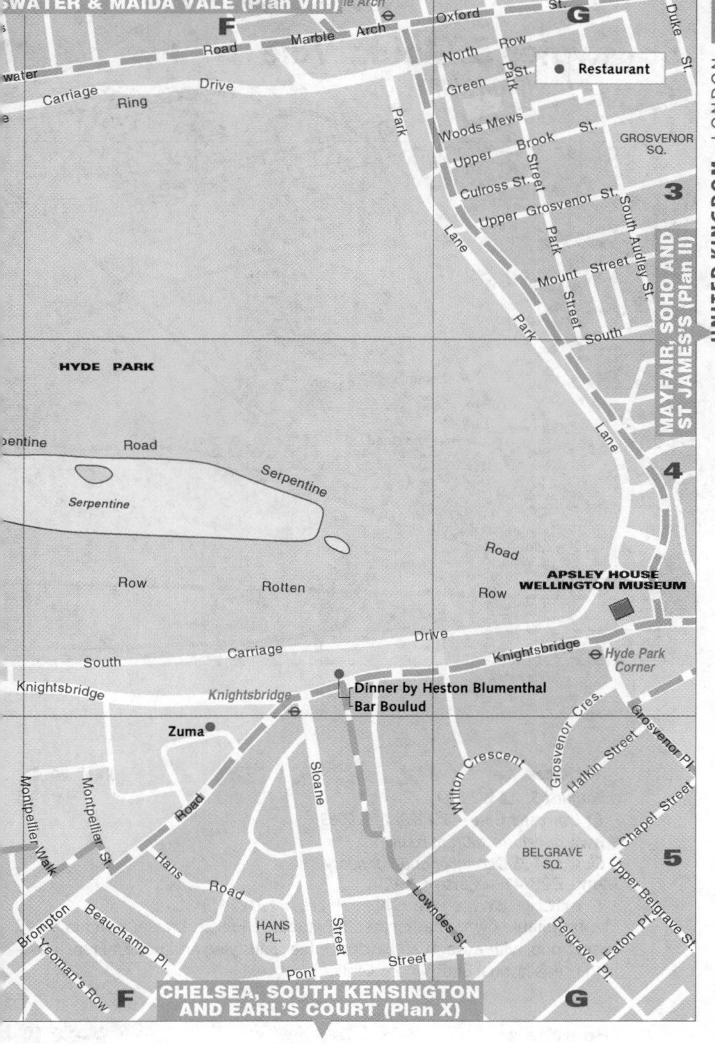

SWATER & MAIDA VALE (Plan VIII)
Restaurant
HYDE PARK
Serpentine
GROSVENOR SQ.
APSLEY HOUSE WELLINGTON MUSEUM
Hyde Park Corner
Knightsbridge
Dinner by Heston Blumenthal
Bar Boulud
Zuma
BELGRAVE SQ.
HANS PL.
MAYFAIR, SOHO AND ST JAMES'S (Plan II)
CHELSEA, SOUTH KENSINGTON AND EARL'S COURT (Plan X)

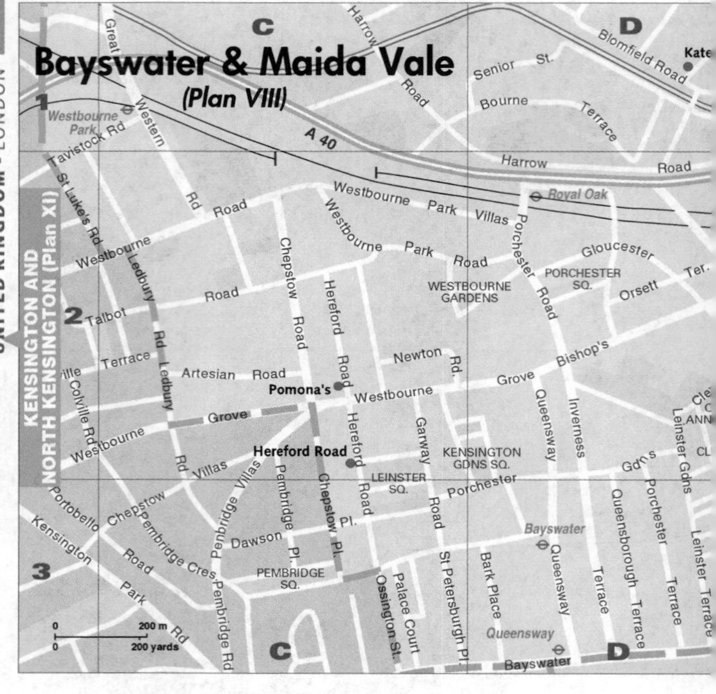

Angelus

XX ♿ AC

4 Bathurst St ✉ W2 2SD
Plan: **E3**
– Ⓜ Lancaster Gate – ✆ (020) 74020083
– www.angelusrestaurant.co.uk
– Closed 24-25 December and 1 January
Menu £ 28/41 – Carte £ 39/54
• French • Brasserie • Neighbourhood •
The hospitable owner has created an attractive French brasserie within a 19C former pub, with a warm and inclusive feel. Satisfying and honest French cooking uses seasonal British ingredients.

Pomona's

X ♿ AC

47 Hereford Rd ✉ W2 5AH
Plan: **C2**
– Ⓜ Bayswater – ✆ (020) 7229 1503
– www.pomonas.co.uk
– Closed 25-26 December
Carte £ 23/51
• World cuisine • Neighbourhood • Fashionable •
A large neighbourhood restaurant with bright décor, an airy, open feel and a fun, laid-back Californian vibe. All-day menus offer soulful, colourful cooking with breakfast, smoothies, salads, house specials and small plates.

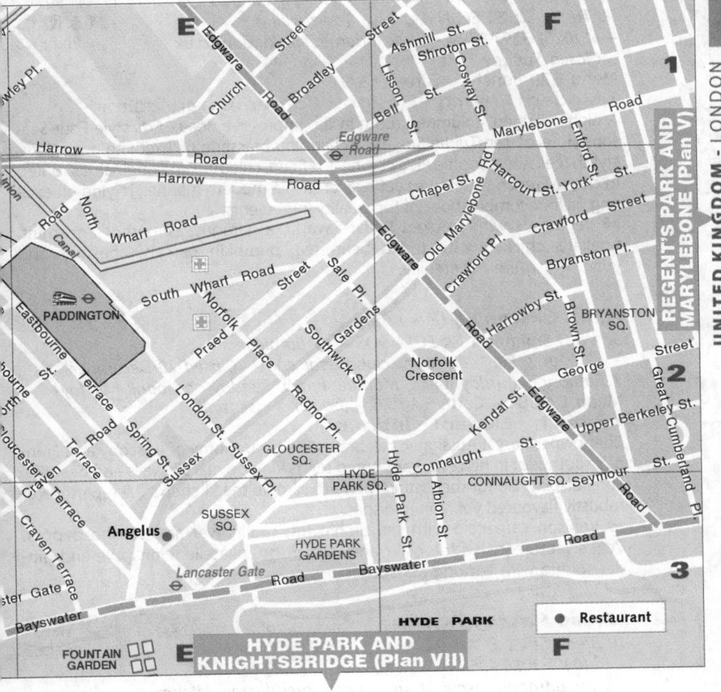

CITY OF LONDON – SOUTHWARK

PLAN IX

City of London

City Social

Plan: **M3**

Tower 42 (24th floor), 25 Old Broad St ✉ EC2N 1HQ
– Ⓜ Liverpool Street
– ✆ (020) 78777703
– www.citysociallondon.com
– Closed Sunday and bank holidays

Carte £ 47/90

• Modern cuisine • Elegant • Design •

Jason Atherton's dark and moody restaurant with an art deco twist, set on the 24th floor of Tower 42; the City views are impressive, especially from tables 10 and 15. The flexible menu is largely European and the cooking manages to be both refined and robust at the same time.

➜ Brixham crab with pickled kohlrabi, nashi pear and pink grapefruit. Isle of Gigha halibut with Wye Valley asparagus and tomato consommé. Hazelnut plaisir sucré, chocolate syrup, biscuit and milk ice cream.

✿

La Dame de Pic – Four Seasons Hotel London at Ten Trinity Square

10 Trinity Sq ✉ EC3N 4AJ – Ⓜ Tower Hill
– ✆ (020) 3297 3799 – www.ladamedepiclondon.co.uk
– Closed Sunday

XX ♿ AC ⛶ Plan: **N3**

Menu £ 39 (lunch) – Carte £ 69/91

• Modern French • Design • Contemporary décor •

A high-ceilinged, columned room in the impressive Beaux-Arts style Four Seasons Hotel at Ten Trinity Square; a charming brasserie deluxe with a spacious, stylish feel. Anne-Sophie Pic's cuisine is refined, colourful and original; it's rooted in classic French techniques yet delivered in a modern manner, relying on exciting flavour combinations of top quality ingredients.

→ Berlingots with smoked Brillat-Savarin, asparagus, bergamot and mint. Challans chicken with tonka bean tea, pumpkin parcels, chestnut and yuzu. The white millefeuille.

✿

Club Gascon (Pascal Aussignac)

XX ❀ AC

57 West Smithfield ✉ EC1A 9DS – Ⓜ Barbican
– ✆ (020) 76006144 – www.clubgascon.com – Closed 22 December-7 January, Saturday lunch, Monday lunch, Sunday and bank holidays

Plan: **L2**

Menu £ 40/84 – Carte £ 46/76 – *(booking essential)*

• French • Elegant • Intimate •

Chef-owner Pascal Aussignac celebrates the gastronomy of Gascony and France's southwest in his restaurant noted for its vintage marble walls and beautiful floral display. Go for the tasting menu to sample the kitchen's full repertoire of robustly flavoured yet refined dishes.

→ Venison carpaccio with sea urchin jus, cauliflower and sansho pepper. Veal sweetbreads with lobster and cuttlefish tagliatelle. Pineapple and ginger soufflé with lemongrass sorbet.

IO

Bread Street Kitchen

XX AC

10 Bread St ✉ EC4M 9AJ – Ⓜ St Paul's
– ✆ (020) 3030 4050
– www.gordonramsayrestaurants.com/bread-street-kitchen

Plan: **L3**

Carte £ 32/62

• Modern cuisine • Trendy • Brasserie •

Gordon Ramsay's take on NY loft-style dining comes with a large bar, thumping music, an open kitchen and enough zinc ducting to kit out a small industrial estate. For the food, think modern bistro dishes with an element of refinement.

IO

Brigadiers

XX ⛱ ♿ AC ⛶

1-5 Bloomberg Arcade ✉ EC4N 8AR – Ⓜ Bank
– ✆ (020) 3319 8140 – www.brigadierslondon.com – Closed Christmas

Plan: **M3**

Menu £ 25 (lunch) – Carte £ 27/45 – *(booking essential)*

• Indian • Exotic décor • Vintage •

The army mess clubs of India provide the theme for this large restaurant on the ground floor of the Bloomberg building. BBQ and street food from around India is the focus; with 'Feast' menus for larger parties. Beer and whisky are also a feature. The atmosphere is predictably loud and lively.

IO

Cigalon

XX AC ⛶

115 Chancery Ln ✉ WC2A 1PP – Ⓜ Chancery Lane
– ✆ (020) 7242 8373 – www.cigalon.co.uk – Closed Christmas, New Year, Saturday, Sunday and bank holidays

Plan: **K3**

Menu £ 23/37 – Carte lunch £ 31/46

• French • Elegant • Romantic •

Hidden away among the lawyers' offices on Chancery Lane, this bright, high-ceilinged restaurant pays homage to the food and wine of Provence. Expect flavoursome French classics like salade niçoise and bouillabaisse.

Fenchurch

Level 37, Sky Garden, 20 Fenchurch St EC3M 3BY – Monument – (0333) 772 0020 – www.skygarden.london – Closed 25-27 December

Plan: **M3**

Menu £ 35 (weekday lunch) – Carte £ 53/68

• Modern cuisine • Design •

Arrive at the 'Walkie Talkie' early so you can first wander round the Sky Garden and take in the views. The smartly dressed restaurant is housed in a glass box within the atrium. Dishes are largely British and the accomplished cooking uses modern techniques.

Vanilla Black

17-18 Tooks Ct. EC4A 1LB – Chancery Lane – (020) 72422622 – www.vanillablack.co.uk – Closed 2 weeks Christmas and bank holidays

Plan: **K2**

Menu £ 22 (weekday lunch)/55 – *(booking essential)*

• Vegetarian • Intimate • Romantic •

A vegetarian restaurant where real thought has gone into the creation of dishes, which deliver an array of interesting texture and flavour contrasts. Modern techniques are subtly incorporated and while there are some original combinations, they are well-judged.

Yauatcha City

Broadgate Circle EC2M 2QS – Liverpool Street – (020) 38179880 – www.yauatcha.com – Closed 24 December-3 January and bank holidays

Plan: **M2**

Menu £ 35/48 – Carte £ 32/77

• Chinese • Fashionable •

A more corporate version of the stylish Soho original, with a couple of bars and a terrace at both ends. All the dim sum greatest hits are on the menu but the chefs have some work to do to match the high standard found in Broadwick Street.

Cabotte

48 Gresham St EC2V 7AY – Bank – (020) 7600 1616 – www.cabotte.co.uk – Closed Saturday, Sunday and bank holidays

Plan: **M3**

Carte £ 35/51 – *(booking essential)*

• French • Wine bar • Intimate •

A bistro de luxe with a stunning wine list – owned by two master sommeliers who share a passion for the wines of Burgundy. Cooking comes with the same regional bias and the accomplished classics are simple in style and rich in flavour.

José Pizarro

36 Broadgate Circle EC2M 1QS – Liverpool Street – (020) 72565333 – www.josepizarro.com – Closed Sunday

Plan: **M2**

Carte £ 17/56

• Spanish • Tapas bar • Friendly •

The eponymous chef's third operation is a good fit here: it's well run, flexible and fairly priced – and that includes the wine list. The Spanish menu is nicely balanced, with the seafood dishes being the standouts.

Keep up with the arrow! ➜
We list typical dishes for every Starred restaurant.
These may not always be on the menu but you're sure to find similar, seasonal dishes - do try them.

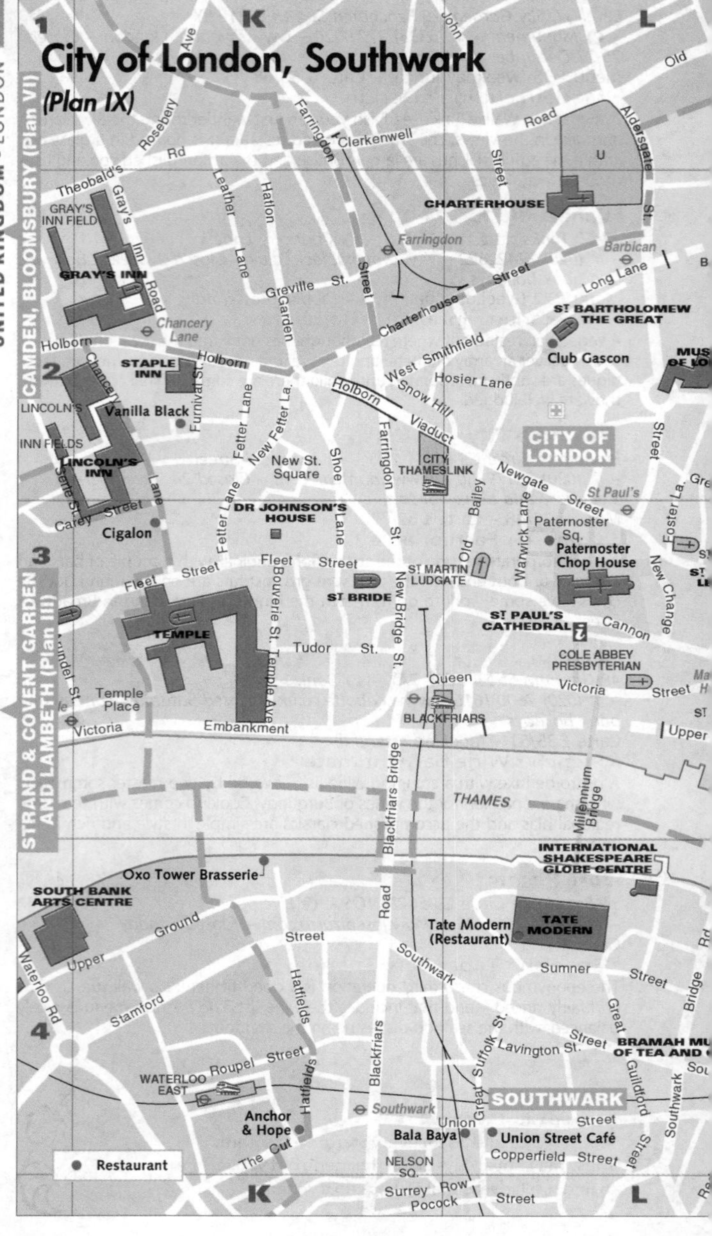
City of London, Southwark
(Plan IX)
CAMDEN, BLOOMSBURY (Plan VI)
STRAND & COVENT GARDEN AND LAMBETH (Plan III)
K
L
1
2
3
4
CHARTERHOUSE
GRAY'S INN FIELD
GRAY'S INN
STAPLE INN
LINCOLN'S INN FIELDS
LINCOLN'S INN
Vanilla Black
Cigalon
DR JOHNSON'S HOUSE
ST BRIDE
TEMPLE
ST MARTIN LUDGATE
CITY THAMESLINK
ST BARTHOLOMEW THE GREAT
Club Gascon
CITY OF LONDON
Paternoster Chop House
ST PAUL'S CATHEDRAL
COLE ABBEY PRESBYTERIAN
BLACKFRIARS
THAMES
Millennium Bridge
INTERNATIONAL SHAKESPEARE GLOBE CENTRE
Oxo Tower Brasserie
SOUTH BANK ARTS CENTRE
Tate Modern (Restaurant)
TATE MODERN
WATERLOO EAST
Anchor & Hope
Bala Baya
Union Street Café
SOUTHWARK
NELSON SQ.
BRAMAH MU OF TEA AND
Farringdon
Barbican
Chancery Lane
St Paul's
Southwark
Clerkenwell Road
Farringdon Street
Charterhouse Street
Long Lane
Aldersgate St.
Holborn
Holborn Viaduct
West Smithfield
Hosier Lane
Snow Hill
Newgate Street
Fleet Street
Victoria Embankment
Queen Victoria Street
Blackfriars Bridge
Blackfriars Road
Southwark Street
Upper Ground
Stamford Street
The Cut
Union Street
Restaurant

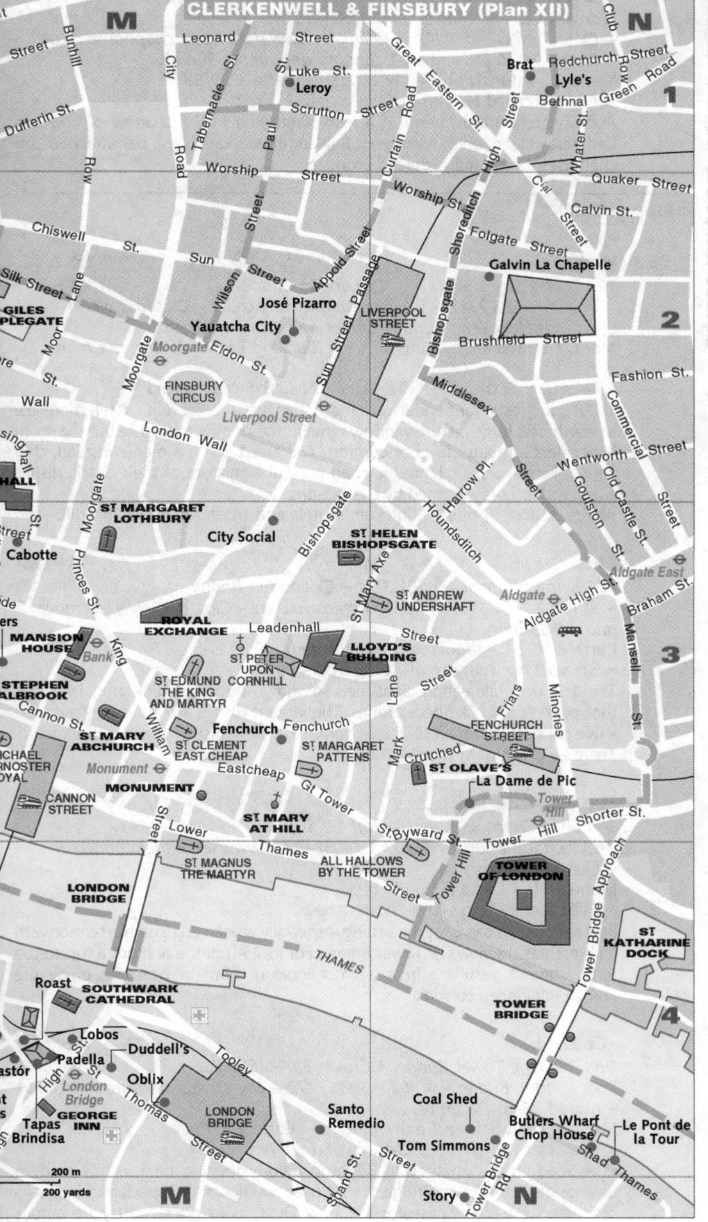
CLERKENWELL & FINSBURY (Plan XII)
M
N
1
2
3
4
Brat
Lyle's
Leroy
Galvin La Chapelle
José Pizarro
Yauatcha City
LIVERPOOL STREET
FINSBURY CIRCUS
City Social
Cabotte
ST MARGARET LOTHBURY
ST HELEN BISHOPSGATE
ST ANDREW UNDERSHAFT
ROYAL EXCHANGE
MANSION HOUSE
LLOYD'S BUILDING
ST PETER UPON CORNHILL
ST EDMUND THE KING AND MARTYR
STEPHEN WALBROOK
ST MARY ABCHURCH
ST CLEMENT EAST CHEAP
Fenchurch
ST MARGARET PATTENS
FENCHURCH STREET
ST OLAVE'S
La Dame de Pic
MONUMENT
CANNON STREET
ST MARY AT HILL
ST MAGNUS THE MARTYR
ALL HALLOWS BY THE TOWER
TOWER OF LONDON
LONDON BRIDGE
ST KATHARINE DOCK
THAMES
TOWER BRIDGE
Roast
SOUTHWARK CATHEDRAL
Lobos
Duddell's
Padella
Oblix
GEORGE INN
Tapas Brindisa
LONDON BRIDGE
Santo Remedio
Coal Shed
Butlers Wharf Chop House
Le Pont de la Tour
Tom Simmons
Story
Moorgate
Liverpool Street
Bank
Monument
Aldgate
Aldgate East
Tower Hill
London Bridge
200 m
200 yards
Leonard Street
Great Eastern St.
Redchurch Street
Bethnal Green Road
Luke St.
Scrutton Street
Worship Street
Chiswell St.
Sun Street
Silk Street
Appold Street
Sun Street Passage
Folgate Street
Brushfield Street
Bishopsgate
Middlesex Street
Commercial Street
Wentworth Street
London Wall
Eldon St.
Leadenhall Street
Fenchurch Street
Eastcheap
Cannon St.
Lower Thames Street
Tooley Street
Shad Thames
Tower Bridge Approach
Tower Bridge Rd
Houndsditch
Minories
Aldgate High St.
Shorter St.
Byward St.

Paternoster Chop House

Warwick Ct., Paternoster Sq. ✉ EC4M 7DX Plan: **L3**
– Ⓜ St Paul's – ✆ (020) 70299400 – www.paternosterchophouse.co.uk
– Closed 26-30 December, 1 January and dinner Sunday
Menu £ 24 (lunch and early dinner) – Carte £ 29/58
• Traditional British • Brasserie • Trendy •
Appropriately British menu in a restaurant lying in the shadow of St Paul's Cathedral. Large, open room with full-length windows; busy bar attached. Kitchen uses thoughtfully sourced produce.

Bermondsey

Story (Tom Sellers)

199 Tooley St ✉ SE1 2JX – Ⓜ London Bridge Plan: **N5**
– ✆ (020) 7183 2117 – www.restaurantstory.co.uk – Closed 2 weeks Christmas-New Year, Sunday dinner and Monday lunch
Menu £ 80 (weekday lunch)/145 – *(booking essential) (surprise menu only)*
• Modern cuisine • Design • Neighbourhood •
In 2018 the restaurant underwent more than just a major refit – it felt more like a rebirth. The huge picture window remains the dominant feature but the room now offers a greater level of comfort. You aren't given a menu; instead, chef Tom Sellers and his talented kitchen present a mixture of their classic dishes along with others informed by the seasons.
→ Bread and 'dripping'. Chicken, morels and truffle. Almond and dill.

José

104 Bermondsey St ✉ SE1 3UB – Ⓜ London Bridge Plan: **D2**
– ✆ (020) 7403 4902 – www.josepizarro.com – Closed 25-27 December and 1-2 January
Carte £ 16/34 – *(bookings not accepted)*
• Spanish • Minimalist • Tapas bar •
Standing up while eating tapas feels so right, especially at this snug, lively bar that packs 'em in like boquerones. The vibrant dishes are intensely flavoured – five per person should suffice; go for the daily fish dishes from the blackboard. There's a great list of sherries too.

Le Pont de la Tour

36d Shad Thames, Butlers Wharf ✉ SE1 2YE Plan: **N4**
– Ⓜ London Bridge – ✆ (020) 74038403 – www.lepontdelatour.co.uk
– Closed 1 January
Menu £ 30 – Carte £ 35/75
• French • Elegant • Intimate •
Few restaurants can beat the setting, especially when you're on the terrace with its breathtaking views of Tower Bridge. For its 25th birthday it got a top-to-toe refurbishment, resulting in a warmer looking room in which to enjoy the French-influenced cooking.

Coal Shed

Unit 3.1, One Tower Bridge, 4 Crown Sq ✉ SE1 2SE Plan: **N4**
– Ⓜ London Bridge – ✆ (020) 3384 7272 – www.coalshed-restaurant.co.uk
– Closed 25-26 December
Menu £ 20 (lunch and early dinner) – Carte £ 27/54
• Meats and grills • Design • Friendly •
Coal Shed was established in Brighton before opening here in this modern development by Tower Bridge. It's set over two floors and specialises in steaks but there's also plenty of seafood on offer. Desserts are good too; try the various 'sweets'.

Duddell's

XX Plan: **M4**

9A St. Thomas St ✉ SE1 9RY – Ⓜ London Bridge – ✆ (020) 3957 9932 – www.duddells.co/london – Closed 25 December and 1 January

Menu £ 25 (weekday lunch) – Carte £ 36/69

• Chinese • Historic • Design •

A former church, dating from 1703, seems an unlikely setting for a Cantonese restaurant but this striking conversion is the London branch of the Hong Kong original. Lunchtime dim sum is a highlight but be sure to order the Peking duck which comes with 8 condiments in two servings.

Londrino

XX A/C Plan: **D2**

36 Snowsfields ✉ SE1 3SU – Ⓜ London Bridge – ✆ (020) 3911 4949 – www.londrino.co.uk – Closed Christmas-New Year, Sunday dinner and Monday

Menu £ 22 (weekday lunch) – Carte £ 29/58

• Portuguese • Design • Neighbourhood •

The chef-owner takes his influences from his home country of Portugal, from the various London restaurants in which he has worked and from his own extensive travels. The modern dishes are meant for sharing and the bright, open space has an easy-going feel.

Oblix

XX A/C Plan: **M4**

Level 32, The Shard, 31 St Thomas St. ✉ SE1 9RY – Ⓜ London Bridge – ✆ (020) 72686700 – www.oblixrestaurant.com

Menu £ 38 (weekday lunch) – Carte £ 33/111

• Meats and grills • Trendy • Design •

A New York grill restaurant on the 32nd floor of The Shard; window tables for two are highly prized. Meats and fish from the rotisserie, grill and Josper oven are the stars of the show; brunch is served in the lounge bar at weekends.

Butlers Wharf Chop House

X A/C Plan: **N4**

36e Shad Thames, Butlers Wharf ✉ SE1 2YE – Ⓜ London Bridge – ✆ (020) 7403 3403 – www.chophouse-restaurant.co.uk – Closed 1 January

Menu £ 30 – Carte £ 29/58

• Traditional British • Brasserie • Simple •

Grab a table on the terrace in summer and dine in the shadow of Tower Bridge. Rustic feel to the interior; noisy and fun. The menu focuses on traditional English ingredients and dishes; grilled meats a speciality.

Casse Croûte

X Plan: **D2**

109 Bermondsey St ✉ SE1 3XB – Ⓜ London Bridge – ✆ (020) 7407 2140 – www.cassecroute.co.uk – Closed Sunday dinner

Carte £ 31/37 – *(booking essential)*

• French • Bistro • Friendly •

Squeeze into this tiny bistro and you'll find yourself transported to rural France. A blackboard menu offers three choices for each course but new dishes are added as others run out. The cooking is rustic, authentic and heartening.

Flour & Grape

X A/C Plan: **D2**

214 Bermondsey St ✉ SE1 3TQ – Ⓜ London Bridge – ✆ (020) 7407 4682 – www.flourandgrape.com – Closed Christmas and Monday lunch

Carte £ 15/28 – *(bookings not accepted)*

• Italian • Simple • Cosy •

The clue's in the name – pasta and wine. A choice of 7 or 8 antipasti are followed by the same number of homemade pasta dishes, with a dessert menu largely centred around gelato. Add in a well-chosen wine list with some pretty low mark-ups and it's no wonder this place is busy.

Pique-Nique

Tanner St. Park ✉ SE1 3LD – Ⓜ London Bridge Plan: **D2**
– ✆ (020) 7403 9549 – www.pique-nique.co.uk – Closed Sunday dinner
Carte £ 24/44 – *(booking essential)*
• French • Bistro • Friendly •
Set in a converted 1920s park shelter is this fun French restaurant with a focus on rotisserie-cooked Bresse chicken. Concise menu of French classics; go for the 6 course 'Menu autour du poulet de Bresse' which uses every part of the bird.

Pizarro

194 Bermondsey St ✉ SE1 3TQ – Ⓜ London Bridge Plan: **D2**
– ✆ (020) 73789455 – www.josepizarro.com – Closed 25-27 December and 1-2 January
Carte £ 19/50
• Mediterranean cuisine • Neighbourhood • Simple •
José Pizarro has a refreshingly simple way of naming his establishments: after José, his tapas bar, comes Pizarro, a larger restaurant a few doors down. Go for the small plates, like prawns with piquillo peppers and jamón.

Santo Remedio

152 Tooley St ✉ SE1 2TU – Ⓜ London Bridge Plan: **M4**
– ✆ (020) 7403 3021 – www.santoremedio.co.uk – Closed Christmas and Sunday dinner
Menu £ 20 (weekday lunch) – Carte £ 23/35
• Mexican • Colourful • Simple •
The cooking inspiration comes from the owner's time spent in Mexico City, the Yucatan and Oaxaca. Ingredients are a mix of imported – like grasshoppers to liven up the guacamole – and home-grown like Hertfordshire pork. Spread over two floors, the rooms are as colourful as the food.

Tom Simmons

2 Still Walk ✉ SE1 2RA – Ⓜ London Bridge Plan: **N4**
– ✆ (020) 3848 2100 – www.tom-simmons.co.uk – Closed Monday
Menu £ 24/27 – Carte £ 29/54
• Modern cuisine • Simple • Friendly •
The eponymous chef went from being a contestant on 'MasterChef: The Professionals' to having his name above the door of his own restaurant here in this modern development near Tower Bridge. His Welsh heritage comes through on the modern menu, with its use of Welsh lamb and beef.

Garrison

99-101 Bermondsey St ✉ SE1 3XB – Ⓜ London Bridge. Plan: **D2**
– ✆ (020) 70899355 – www.thegarrison.co.uk – Closed 25 December
Carte £ 26/40 – *(booking essential at dinner)*
• Mediterranean cuisine • Pub • Friendly •
Known for its charming vintage look, booths and sweet-natured service, The Garrison boasts a warm, relaxed vibe. Open from breakfast until dinner, when a Mediterranean-led menu pulls in the crowds.

Southwark

Padella

6 Southwark St, Borough Market ✉ SE1 1TQ Plan: **M4**
– Ⓜ London Bridge – www.padella.co – Closed 25-26 December and bank holidays
Carte £ 12/22 – *(bookings not accepted)*
• Italian • Bistro • Simple •
This lively little sister to Trullo offers a short, seasonal menu where hand-rolled pasta is the star of the show. Sauces and fillings are inspired by the owners' trips to Italy and prices are extremely pleasing to the pocket. Sit at the ground floor counter overlooking the open kitchen.

Roast

The Floral Hall, Borough Market ✉ SE1 1TL Plan: **M4**
– Ⓜ London Bridge – ✆ (020) 30066111 – www.roast-restaurant.com
– Closed 25-26 December, 1 January and Sunday dinner
Carte £ 35/63 – *(booking essential)*
• Modern British • Friendly • Fashionable •
Known for its British food and for promoting UK producers – not surprising considering the restaurant's in the heart of Borough Market. The 'dish of the day' is often a highlight; service is affable and there's live music at night.

Union Street Café

47-51 Great Suffolk St ✉ SE1 0BS – Ⓜ London Bridge Plan: **L4**
– ✆ (020) 7592 7977 – www.gordonramsayrestaurants.com
Menu £ 26 – Carte £ 22/49
• Italian • Trendy • Design •
Occupying a former warehouse, this Gordon Ramsay restaurant has been busy since day one and comes with a New York feel, a faux industrial look and a basement bar. The Italian menu keeps things simple and stays true to the classics.

Bala Baya

Arch 25, Old Union Yard Arches, 229 Union St Plan: **L4**
✉ SE1 0LR – Ⓜ Southwark – ✆ (020) 8001 7015 – www.balabaya.co.uk
– Closed 25-26 December and Sunday dinner
Menu £ 19 (lunch) – Carte £ 31/45
• Middle Eastern • Design • Friendly •
A friendly, lively restaurant which celebrates the Middle Eastern heritage of its passionate owner. Dishes are fresh, vibrant and designed for sharing and the bright, modern interior is inspired by the Bauhaus architecture of Tel Aviv.

El Pastór

7a Stoney St, Borough Market ✉ SE1 9AA Plan: **M4**
– Ⓜ London Bridge – ✆ (020) 7440 1461 – www.tacoselpastor.co.uk
– Closed 25-26 December, 1 January, Sunday dinner and bank holidays
Carte £ 14/32 – *(bookings not accepted)*
• Mexican • Trendy • Simple •
A lively, informal restaurant under the railway arches at London Bridge; inspired by the taquerias of Mexico City. Flavours are beautifully fresh, fragrant and spicy; don't miss the Taco Al Pastór after which the restaurant is named.

Elliot's

12 Stoney St, Borough Market ✉ SE1 9AD Plan: **L4**
– Ⓜ London Bridge – ✆ (020) 74037436 – www.elliotscafe.com – Closed Sunday and bank holidays
Carte £ 21/41
• Modern cuisine • Rustic • Friendly •
A lively, unpretentious café which sources its ingredients from Borough Market, in which it stands. The appealing menu is concise and the cooking is earthy, pleasingly uncomplicated and very satisfying. Try one of the sharing dishes.

Lobos

14 Borough High St ✉ SE1 9QG – Ⓜ London Bridge Plan: **M4**
– ✆ (020) 74075361 – www.lobostapas.co.uk – Closed 25-26 December and 1 January
Carte £ 15/48
• Spanish • Tapas bar • Rustic •
A dimly lit, decidedly compact tapas bar under the railway arches – sit upstairs to enjoy the theatre of the open kitchen. Go for one of the speciality meat dishes like the leg of slow-roasted milk-fed Castilian lamb.

Oxo Tower Brasserie

Plan: **K4**

Oxo Tower Wharf (8th floor), Barge House St
SE1 9PH – Southwark
– (020) 7803 3888 – www.oxotower.co.uk
– Closed 25 December
Menu £ 30 (lunch) – Carte £ 27/49
• Modern cuisine • Design •
Less formal but more fun than the next-door restaurant. The open-plan kitchen produces modern, colourful and easy-to-eat dishes with influences from the Med. Great views too from the bar.

Tapas Brindisa

Plan: **M4**

18-20 Southwark St, Borough Market SE1 1TJ
– London Bridge – (020) 73578880
– www.brindisatapaskitchens.com
Carte £ 14/38 – *(bookings not accepted)*
• Spanish • Tapas bar •
A blueprint for many of the tapas bars that subsequently sprung up over London. It has an infectious energy and the well-priced, robust dishes include Galician-style octopus and black rice with squid; try the hand-carved Ibérico hams.

Tate Modern (Restaurant)

Plan: **L4**

Switch House (9th floor), Tate Modern, Bankside
SE1 9TG – Southwark
– (020) 7401 5621 – www.tate.org.uk
– Closed 24-26 December
Menu £ 25 – Carte £ 26/36 – *(lunch only and dinner Friday-Saturday)*
• Modern British • Design • Brasserie •
A contemporary, faux-industrial style restaurant on the ninth floor of the striking Switch House extension. Modern menus champion British ingredients; desserts are a highlight and the wine list interesting and well-priced.

Wright Brothers

Plan: **L4**

11 Stoney St, Borough Market SE1 9AD
– London Bridge
– (020) 74039554 – www.thewrightbrothers.co.uk
– Closed 25-26 December and 1 January
Carte £ 29/40
• Seafood • Cosy • Traditional décor •
Originally an oyster wholesaler; now offers a wide range of oysters along with porter, as well as fruits de mer, daily specials and assorted pies. It fills quickly and an air of contentment reigns.

Anchor & Hope

Plan: **K4**

36 The Cut SE1 8LP – Southwark.
– (020) 79289898
– www.anchorandhopepub.co.uk
– Closed Christmas-New Year, Sunday dinner, Monday lunch and bank holidays
Menu £ 17 (weekday lunch) – Carte £ 19/46 – *(bookings not accepted)*
• Modern British • Pub • Rustic •
As popular as ever thanks to its congenial feel and lived-in looks but mostly because of the appealingly seasonal menu and the gutsy, bold cooking that delivers on flavour. No reservations so be prepared to wait at the bar.

Chelsea

✿✿✿ Gordon Ramsay

XXXX ✿ AC ⌚ Plan: F7

68-69 Royal Hospital Rd. ✉ SW3 4HP – Ⓜ Sloane Square – ☎ (020) 73524441 – www.gordonramsayrestaurants.com – Closed 21-28 December, Sunday and Monday

Menu £ 70/120 – *(booking essential)*

• French • Elegant • Intimate •

A kitchen redesign in 2018 proved that Gordon Ramsay's flagship restaurant is not one to ever rest on its laurels. The large kitchen team create dishes that are classical in make-up but never backward-looking. Dishes are executed with great confidence and the component parts marry perfectly. Service is polished and professional but also has personality.

➜ Ravioli of lobster, langoustine and salmon with oxalis and sorrel. Herdwick lamb with spring vegetable 'navarin'. Lemonade parfait with honey, bergamot and sheep's milk yoghurt.

✿✿ Claude Bosi at Bibendum

XXX ✿ AC Plan: E6

Michelin House, 81 Fulham Rd ✉ SW3 6RD – Ⓜ South Kensington – ☎ (020) 7581 5817 – www.bibendum.co.uk – Closed 24-26 December, 31 December-7 January, 26 August-5 September, Monday, lunch Tuesday-Wednesday and bank holidays

Menu £ 110 (dinner)/130 – Carte £ 53/109 – *(booking essential)*

• French • Elegant • Historic •

Bibendum – on the first floor of the historic art deco building which was built as Michelin's London HQ in 1911 –sports a clean, contemporary look, and its handsome interior cannot fail to impress – sports Bosi's cooking shows a man proud of his French heritage and confident of his abilities. His dishes are poised and assured.

➜ Duck jelly, Oscietra caviar, spring onion and smoked sturgeon. My mum's tripe and cuttlefish gratin with pig's ear and ham cake. Cep vacherin, banana and crème fraîche.

✿ Five Fields (Taylor Bonnyman)

XXX ✿ ♿ AC ⛶ Plan: F6

8-9 Blacklands Terr ✉ SW3 2SP – Ⓜ Sloane Square – ☎ (020) 7838 1082 – www.fivefieldsrestaurant.com – Closed Christmas-mid-January, 2 weeks August, Saturday, Sunday and bank holidays

Menu £ 65/90 – *(dinner only) (booking essential)*

• Modern cuisine • Neighbourhood • Intimate •

A formally run yet intimate restaurant, with a discreet atmosphere and a warm, comfortable feel. Modern dishes are skilfully conceived, quite elaborate constructions; attractively presented and packed with flavour. Produce is top-notch and often comes from the restaurant's own kitchen garden in East Sussex.

➜ Foie gras with shimeji mushrooms and beetroot. Roe deer, morels, celeriac and sorrel. Apple with green shiso and jasmine.

✿ Elystan Street (Philip Howard)

XX ♿ AC ⛶ Plan: E6

43 Elystan St ✉ SW3 3NT – Ⓜ South Kensington – ☎ (020) 7628 5005 – www.elystanstreet.com – Closed 25-26 December and 1 January

Menu £ 43 (lunch) – Carte dinner £ 57/88 – *(booking essential)*

• Modern British • Elegant • Friendly •

This elegant, understated restaurant is a joint venture between chef Philip Howard and experienced restaurateur Rebecca Mascarenhas. Cooking has a classical base yet displays a healthy lightness of touch; there's also a vigour and energy to it which suggests that it comes from the heart.

➜ Ravioli of Orkney scallops and Cornish crab with spring onions, radish and chives. Fillet of cod with parmesan gnocchi, garlic leaf pesto and morels. Lemon tart with yoghurt ice cream.

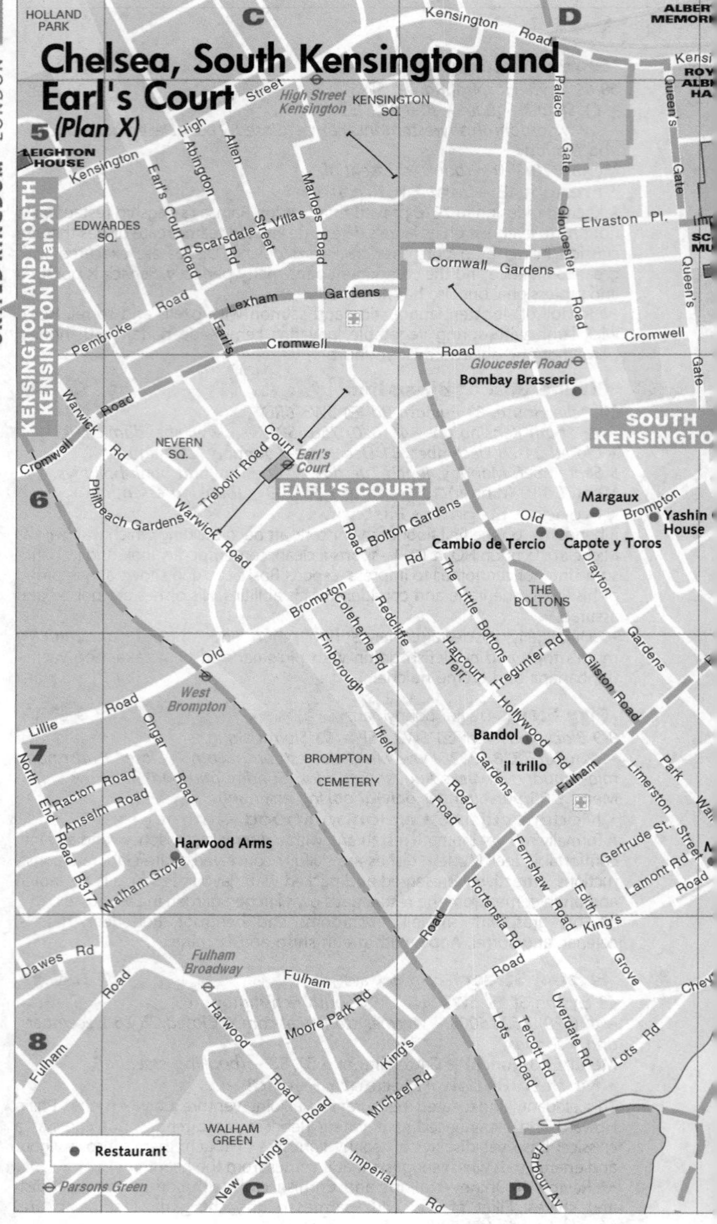

Chelsea, South Kensington and Earl's Court
(Plan X)
HOLLAND PARK
C
D
5
6
7
8
ALBERT MEMORI
Kensington Road
LEIGHTON HOUSE
KENSINGTON AND NORTH KENSINGTON (Plan XI)
High Street Kensington
KENSINGTON SQ.
Kensington High Street
Abingdon
Allen
Earl's Court Road
Marloes Road
EDWARDES SQ.
Scarsdale Villas
Street
Rd
Palace Gate
Gloucester Road
Queen's Gate
Elvaston Pl.
Cornwall Gardens
Lexham Gardens
Pembroke Road
Earl's
Cromwell Road
Gloucester Road
Bombay Brasserie
SOUTH KENSINGTON
Warwick Road
NEVERN SQ.
Earl's Court
Trebovir Road
Court
EARL'S COURT
Philbeach Gardens
Warwick Road
Margaux
Old Brompton
Yashin House
Bolton Gardens
Road
Rd
Cambio de Tercio
Capote y Toros
Drayton Gardens
THE BOLTONS
The Little Boltons
Brompton
Coleherne Rd
Redcliffe
Finborough
Harcourt Terr.
Tregunter Rd
Gilston Road
Hollywood Rd
Old
West Brompton
Lillie Road
Ongar Road
North End Road B317
Racton Road
Anselm Road
BROMPTON CEMETERY
Ifield
Bandol
il trillo
Gardens
Road
Road
Fulham
Limerston Street
Park
Gertrude St.
Lamont Rd
Road
Harwood Arms
Walham Grove
Fernshaw Road
Hortensia Rd
Edith Grove
King's Road
Road
Dawes Rd
Fulham Broadway
Fulham
Road
Harwood Road
Moore Park Rd
King's
Lots Road
Tetcott Rd
Uverdate Rd
Lots Rd
Fulham
Michael Rd
King's Road
WALHAM GREEN
Restaurant
Imperial Rd
New King's
Parsons Green
Harbour Av

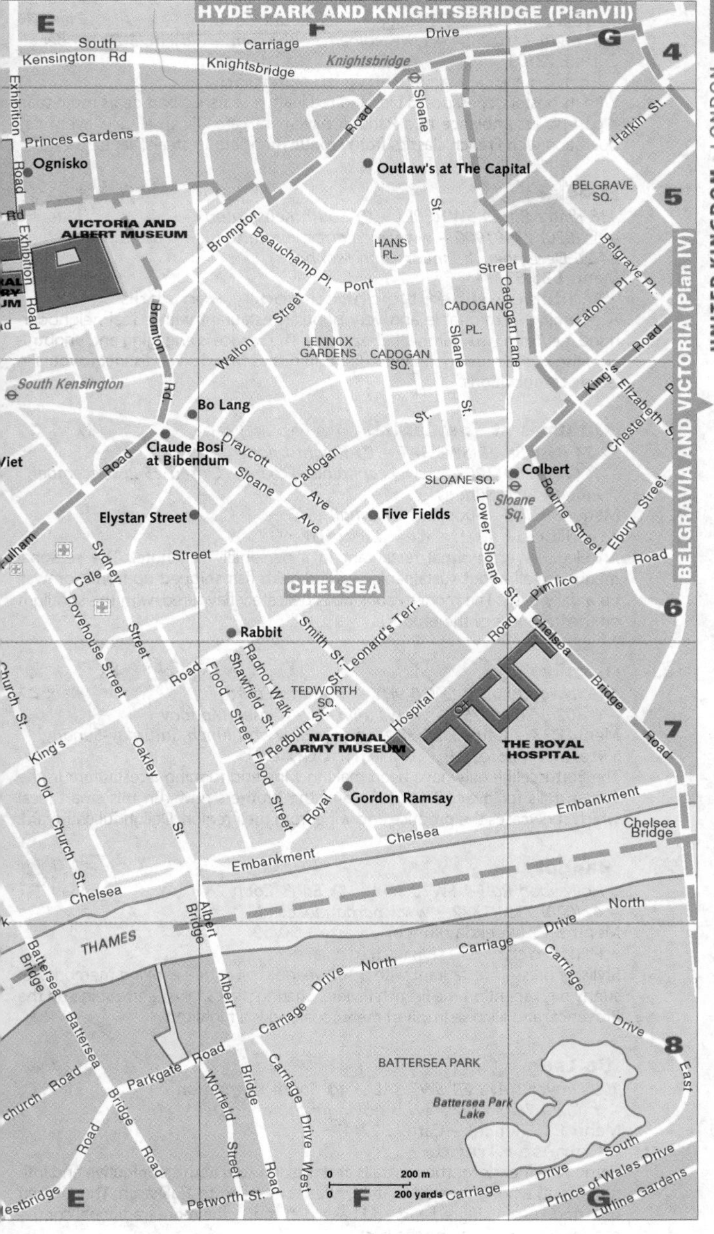
HYDE PARK AND KNIGHTSBRIDGE (PlanVII)
BELGRAVIA AND VICTORIA (Plan IV)
Ognisko
Outlaw's at The Capital
VICTORIA AND ALBERT MUSEUM
BELGRAVE SQ.
HANS PL.
LENNOX GARDENS
CADOGAN SQ.
CADOGAN PL.
Bo Lang
Claude Bosi at Bibendum
Colbert
SLOANE SQ.
Elystan Street
Five Fields
CHELSEA
Rabbit
TEDWORTH SQ.
NATIONAL ARMY MUSEUM
THE ROYAL HOSPITAL
Gordon Ramsay
THAMES
BATTERSEA PARK
Battersea Park Lake
Chelsea Bridge
Albert Bridge
Battersea Bridge
South Kensington
Knightsbridge
Sloane Sq.
200 m
200 yards

Colbert

XX

50-52 Sloane Sq ✉ SW1W 8AX – Ⓜ Sloane Square Plan: **G6**
– ✆ (020) 7730 2804 – www.colbertchelsea.com – Closed 25 December
Carte £ 23/63

• French • Brasserie • Neighbourhood •

With its posters, chessboard tiles and red leather seats, Colbert bears more than a passing resemblance to a Parisian pavement café. It's an all-day, every day operation with French classics from croque monsieur to steak Diane.

Medlar

XX

438 King's Rd ✉ SW10 0LJ – Ⓜ South Kensington Plan: **E7**
– ✆ (020) 73491900 – www.medlarrestaurant.co.uk – Closed 24-26 December, 1 January and Monday
Menu £ 35/53

• Modern cuisine • Neighbourhood • Romantic •

A charming, comfortable and very popular restaurant with a real neighbourhood feel, from two alumni of Chez Bruce. The service is engaging and unobtrusive; the kitchen uses good ingredients in dishes that deliver distinct flavours in classic combinations.

Outlaw's at The Capital – The Capital Hotel

XX

22-24 Basil St. ✉ SW3 1AT – Ⓜ Knightsbridge Plan: **F5**
– ✆ (020) 75911202 – www.capitalhotel.co.uk – Closed 25-26 December, 1 January and Sunday
Menu £ 33/69 – *(booking essential)*

• Seafood • Intimate • Elegant •

An elegant yet informal restaurant in a personally run hotel. The seasonal menus are all about sustainable seafood, with fish shipped up from Cornwall on a daily basis. The modern cooking is delicately flavoured, with the spotlight on the freshness of the produce.

il trillo

XX

4 Hollywood Rd ✉ SW10 9HY – Ⓜ Earl's Court Plan: **D7**
– ✆ (020) 3602 1759 – www.iltrillo.net – Closed Monday
Menu £ 33 – Carte £ 35/58 – *(dinner only and lunch Saturday-Sunday)*

• Italian • Friendly • Neighbourhood •

The Bertuccelli family have been making wine and running a restaurant in the Tuscan Hills for over 30 years. Two of the brothers now run this smart local which showcases the produce and wine from their region. Delightful courtyard.

Bandol

X

6 Hollywood Rd ✉ SW10 9HY – Ⓜ Earl's Court Plan: **D7**
– ✆ (020) 7351 1322 – www.barbandol.co.uk
Menu £ 15 (weekday lunch) – Carte £ 30/59

• Provençal • Design • Intimate •

Stylishly dressed restaurant with a 100 year old olive tree evoking memories of sunny days spent on the French Riviera. Sharing plates take centre stage on the Provençal and Niçoise inspired menu; seafood is a highlight.

Bo Lang

X

100 Draycott Ave ✉ SW3 3AD – Ⓜ South Kensington Plan: **E6**
– ✆ (020) 7823 7887 – www.bolangrestaurant.co.uk
Menu £ 15 (lunch) – Carte £ 27/47

• Chinese • Trendy •

Come with friends for the cocktails and the dim sum at this diminutive and intimate spot, whose decorative style owes something to Hakkasan. The kitchen uses good quality ingredients and has a deft touch; the more traditional combinations often prove to be the best.

Rabbit

Plan: F6

172 King's Rd ✉ SW3 4UP – Ⓜ Sloane Square – ✆ (020) 3750 0172 – www.rabbit-restaurant.com – Closed 22 December-2 January

Menu £ 15 (weekday lunch)/42 – Carte £ 26/40

• Modern British • Rustic • Friendly •

The Gladwin brothers followed the success of The Shed with another similarly rustic and warmly run restaurant. Share satisfying, robustly flavoured plates; game is a real highlight, particularly the rabbit dishes.

South Kensington

Bombay Brasserie

Plan: D6

Courtfield Rd. ✉ SW7 4QH – Ⓜ Gloucester Road – ✆ (020) 73704040 – www.bombayb.co.uk – Closed 25 December

Menu £ 27 (weekday lunch) – Carte £ 32/53

• Indian • Exotic décor • Chic •

A well-run, well-established and comfortable Indian restaurant, featuring a very smart bar and conservatory. Creative dishes sit alongside more traditional choices on the various menus and vegetarians are well-catered for.

Cambio de Tercio

Plan: D6

163 Old Brompton Rd. ✉ SW5 0LJ – Ⓜ Gloucester Road – ✆ (020) 72448970 – www.cambiodetercio.co.uk – Closed 2 weeks December and 2 weeks August

Menu £ 24 (weekday lunch) – Carte £ 33/55

• Spanish • Cosy • Family •

A long-standing, ever-improving Spanish restaurant. Start with small dishes like the excellent El Bulli inspired omelette, then have the popular Pluma Iberica. There are super sherries and a wine list to prove there is life beyond Rioja.

Ognisko

Plan: E5

55 Prince's Gate, Exhibition Rd ✉ SW7 2PN – Ⓜ South Kensington – ✆ (020) 7589 0101 – www.ogniskorestaurant.co.uk – Closed 24-26 December and 1 January

Menu £ 22 (lunch and early dinner) – Carte £ 27/37

• Polish • Elegant • Historic •

Ognisko Polskie – The Polish Hearth Club – was founded in 1940 in this magnificent townhouse; its elegant restaurant serves traditional dishes from across Eastern Europe and the cooking is without pretence and truly from the heart.

Yashin Ocean House

Plan: D6

117-119 Old Brompton Rd ✉ SW7 3RN – Ⓜ Gloucester Road – ✆ (020) 7373 3990 – www.yashinocean.com – Closed Christmas

Carte £ 20/55

• Japanese • Chic • Elegant •

The USP of this chic Japanese restaurant is 'head to tail' eating, although, as there's nothing for carnivores, 'fin to scale' would be more precise. Stick with specialities like the whole dry-aged sea bream for the full umami hit.

Capote y Toros

Plan: D6

157 Old Brompton Road ✉ SW5 0LJ – Ⓜ Gloucester Road – ✆ (020) 73730567 – www.cambiodetercio.co.uk – Closed 2 weeks Christmas, Sunday and Monday

Carte £ 23/61 – *(dinner only)*

• Spanish • Tapas bar • Cosy •

Expect to queue at this compact and vividly coloured spot which celebrates sherry, tapas, ham... and bullfighting. Sherry is the star; those as yet unmoved by this most underappreciated of wines will be dazzled by the variety.

Go-Viet

53 Old Brompton Rd ✉ SW7 3JS – Ⓜ South Kensington Plan: **E6**
– ✆ (020) 7589 6432 – www.vietnamfood.co.uk – Closed 24-26 December
Carte £ 22/51

• Vietnamese • Contemporary décor •

A Vietnamese restaurant from experienced chef Jeff Tan. Lunch concentrates on classics like pho and bun, while dinner provides a more sophisticated experience, offering interesting flavourful dishes with a distinct modern edge.

Margaux

152 Old Brompton Rd ✉ SW5 0BE Plan: **D6**
– Ⓜ Gloucester Road – ✆ (020) 7373 5753 – www.barmargaux.co.uk
– Closed 24-26 December, 1 January and lunch August
Menu £ 15 (weekday lunch) – Carte £ 28/58

• Mediterranean cuisine • Neighbourhood • Bistro •

An earnestly run modern bistro with an ersatz industrial look.The classically trained kitchen looks to France and Italy for its primary influences and dishes are flavoursome and satisfying. The accompanying wine list has been thoughtfully compiled.

KENSINGTON – NORTH KENSINGTON – NOTTING HILL — PLAN XI

Kensington

Kitchen W8

11-13 Abingdon Rd ✉ W8 6AH Plan: **C5**
– Ⓜ High Street Kensington – ✆ (020) 79370120 – www.kitchenw8.com
– Closed 24-26 December and bank holidays
Menu £ 28/30 (weekdays) – Carte £ 41/54

• Modern cuisine • Neighbourhood • Brasserie •

A joint venture between Rebecca Mascarenhas and Philip Howard. Not as informal as the name suggests but still refreshingly free of pomp. The cooking has depth and personality and prices are quite restrained considering the quality of the produce and the kitchen's skill.

→ Smoked eel with grilled mackerel, golden beetroot and sweet mustard. Caramelised lamb shoulder with Pink Fir potatoes, pickles, Calçot onions and thyme. Poached Comice pear with spiced financier and honey ice cream.

Launceston Place

1a Launceston Pl ✉ W8 5RL – Ⓜ Gloucester Road Plan: **D5**
– ✆ (020) 7937 6912 – www.launcestonplace-restaurant.co.uk – Closed 25-26 December, Monday and lunch Tuesday
Menu £ 28/60

• Modern cuisine • Neighbourhood • Fashionable •

A favourite of many thanks to its palpable sense of neighbourhood, pretty façade and its nooks and crannies which make it ideal for trysts or tête-à-têtes. The menu is fashionably terse and the cooking is quite elaborate, with dishes big on originality and artfully presented.

Clarke's

124 Kensington Church St ✉ W8 4BH Plan: **C4**
– Ⓜ Notting Hill Gate – ✆ (020) 72219225 – www.sallyclarke.com
– Closed 1 week August, Christmas-New Year and bank holidays
Menu £ 33/39 – Carte £ 42/64

• Modern cuisine • Neighbourhood •

Its unhurried atmosphere, enthusiastic service and dedication to its regulars are just a few reasons why Sally Clarke's eponymous restaurant has instilled such unwavering loyalty for over 30 years. Her kitchen has a light touch and understands the less-is-more principle.

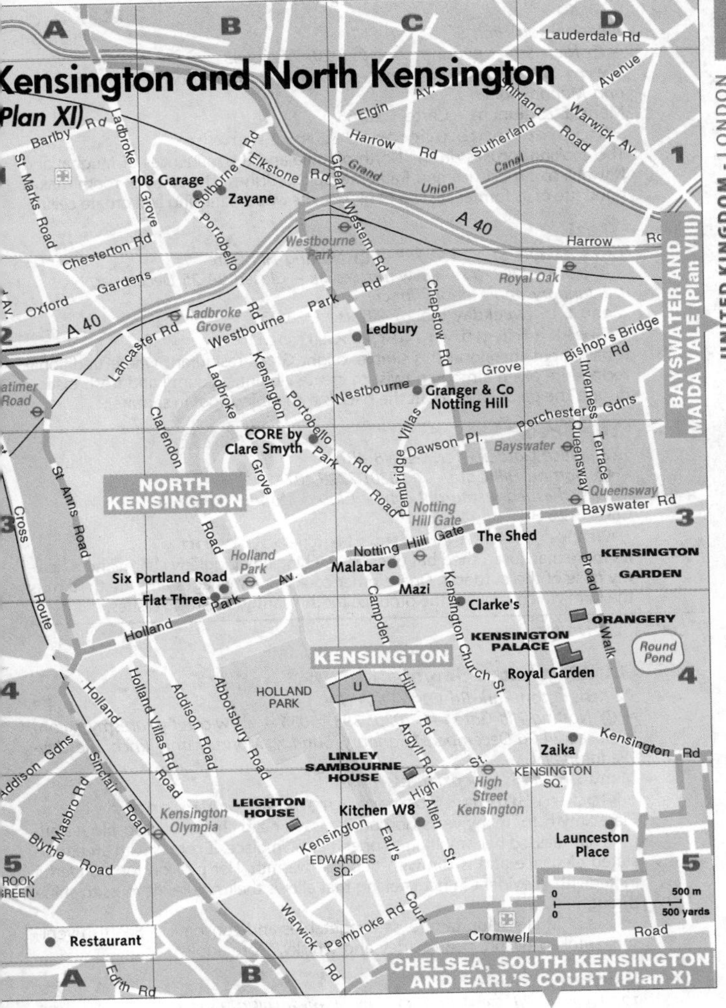

Malabar

XX A/C

27 Uxbridge St. ✉ W8 7TQ – Ⓜ Notting Hill Gate – ✆ (020) 77278800 – www.malabar-restaurant.co.uk – Closed 1 week Christmas

Plan: C3

Carte £ 18/38 – *(dinner only and lunch Saturday-Sunday)*

• Indian • Neighbourhood •

Still going strong in this smart residential Notting Hill street, having opened back in 1983. Refreshingly, the menu is a single page – order a curry and something charcoal-grilled. The buffet lunch on Sunday is a veritable institution in these parts.

Zaika

XX

1 Kensington High St. ✉ W8 5NP – Ⓜ High Street Kensington – ☎ (020) 77956533 – www.zaikaofkensington.com – Closed 25-26 December, 1 January and Monday lunch

Plan: **D4**

Menu £ 23 (lunch) – Carte £ 28/65

• Indian • Contemporary décor • Friendly •

The cooking focuses on the North of India and the influences of Mughal and Nawabi, so expect rich and fragrantly spiced dishes. The softly-lit room makes good use of its former life as a bank, with its wood-panelling and ornate ceiling.

Mazi

X

12-14 Hillgate St ✉ W8 7SR – Ⓜ Notting Hill Gate – ☎ (020) 72293794 – www.mazi.co.uk – Closed 24-25 December, 1-2 January and Monday lunch

Plan: **C3**

Menu £ 15 (weekday lunch) – Carte £ 28/43

• Greek • Friendly • Neighbourhood •

It's all about sharing at this simple, bright Greek restaurant where traditional recipes are given a modern twist to create vibrant, colourful and fresh tasting dishes. The garden terrace at the back is a charming spot in summer.

The Shed

X

122 Palace Gardens Ter. ✉ W8 4RT – Ⓜ Notting Hill Gate – ☎ (020) 7229 4024 – www.theshed-restaurant.com – Closed Monday lunch and Sunday

Plan: **C3**

Carte £ 26/38

• Modern British • Rustic • Neighbourhood •

It's more than just a shed but does have a higgledy-piggledy charm and a healthy dose of the outdoors. One brother cooks, one manages and the third runs the farm which supplies the produce for the earthy, satisfying dishes.

North Kensington

CORE by Clare Smyth (Clare Smyth)

XXX

92 Kensington Park Rd ✉ W11 2PN – Ⓜ Notting Hill Gate – ☎ (020) 3937 5086 – www.corebyclaresmyth.com – Closed 24-26 December, 1 January, Sunday, Monday and lunch Tuesday-Wednesday

Plan: **B3**

Menu £ 65/105 – *(booking essential)*

• Modern British • Contemporary décor • Friendly •

Clare Smyth, for many years Gordon Ramsay's head chef in his flagship restaurant, has realised her ambition to open her own place. It comes with an understated elegance and is run with genuine warmth. Her passion for wonderful ingredients is evident in her cooking that allows their natural flavours to shine through.

→ Isle of Mull scallop tartare, sea vegetables and consommé. Scottish venison, smoked bacon, pearl barley and whisky. 'Core apple'.

Ledbury (Brett Graham)

XXX

127 Ledbury Rd. ✉ W11 2AQ – Ⓜ Notting Hill Gate – ☎ (020) 7792 9090 – www.theledbury.com – Closed 25-26 December, August bank holiday and lunch Monday-Tuesday

Plan: **C2**

Menu £ 80/150

• Modern cuisine • Neighbourhood • Contemporary décor •

Brett Graham's husbandry skills and close relationship with his suppliers ensure the quality of the produce shines through and flavour combinations linger long in the memory. Game is always a highlight; Sika deer is raised on their own small estate. This smart yet unshowy restaurant comes with smooth and engaging service.

→ White beetroot baked in clay with English caviar and dried eel. Sika deer with smoked bone marrow, rhubarb, red leaves and vegetables. Brown sugar tart with stem ginger ice cream.

Flat Three

Plan: **B3/4**

120-122 Holland Park Ave ✉ W11 4UA – Ⓜ Holland Park – ✆ (020) 7792 8987 – www.flatthree.london – Closed 24 December-7 January, 20 August-3 September, Sunday and Monday

Menu £ 35/59 – *(dinner only and lunch Friday-Saturday)*

• Creative • Design • Minimalist •

The open kitchen is the main feature of this roomy, basement restaurant. The flavours of Korea and Japan feature heavily in the elaborately constructed, original and creative dishes which deliver plenty of flavour. Service can be rather formal.

Granger and Co. Notting Hill

Plan: **C2**

175 Westbourne Grove ✉ W11 2SB – Ⓜ Bayswater – ✆ (020) 7229 9111 – www.grangerandco.com – Closed August bank holiday weekend and 25 December

Carte £ 20/42 – *(bookings not accepted)*

• Modern cuisine • Friendly • Fashionable •

When Bill Granger moved from sunny Sydney to cool Notting Hill he opened a local restaurant too. He brought with him that delightful 'matey' service that only Aussies do, his breakfast time ricotta hotcakes and a fresh, zesty menu.

Six Portland Road

Plan: **B3**

6 Portland Rd ✉ W11 4LA – Ⓜ Holland Park – ✆ (020) 7229 3130 – www.sixportlandroad.com – Closed Christmas-New Year, last 2 weeks August, Sunday dinner and Monday

Menu £ 17 (weekday lunch) – Carte £ 32/55

• French • Neighbourhood • Cosy •

An intimate and personally run neighbourhood restaurant owned by Oli Barker, previously of Terroirs. The menu changes frequently and has a strong French accent; dishes are reassuringly recognisable, skilfully constructed and very tasty.

Zayane

Plan: **B1**

91 Golborne Rd ✉ W10 5NL – Ⓜ Westbourne Park – ✆ (020) 8960 1137 – www.zayanerestaurant.com – Closed 10 days January, 26 August-3 September, Sunday and Monday

Carte £ 25/42

• Moroccan • Neighbourhood • Friendly •

An intimate neighbourhood restaurant owned by Casablanca-born Meryem Mortell and evoking the sights and scents of North Africa. Carefully conceived dishes have authentic Moroccan flavours but are cooked with modern techniques.

108 Garage

Plan: **B1**

108 Golborne Rd ✉ W10 5PS – Ⓜ Westbourne Park – ✆ (020) 8969 3769 – www.108garage.com – Closed 2 weeks August, 2 weeks Christmas, Sunday and Monday

Menu £ 60 (dinner) – Carte £ 43/57 – *(booking essential)*

• Modern British • Neighbourhood • Intimate •

A daily changing 6 course menu is offered, with a choice of main course; the modern dishes offer plenty of contrasts and originality. This former garage has a utilitarian look that's all bare brick, exposed ducting and polished concrete. Sit at the counter if you want to chat with the chefs.

Clerkenwell

St John

26 St John St ✉ EC1M 4AY – Ⓜ Farringdon — Plan: L2
– ✆ (020) 7251 0848 – www.stjohnrestaurant.com
– Closed 25-26 December, 1 January, Saturday lunch and Sunday dinner
Carte £ 26/63 – *(booking essential)*

• Traditional British • Simple • Friendly •

A glorious celebration of British fare and a champion of 'nose to tail' eating. Utilitarian surroundings and a refreshing lack of ceremony ensure the food is the focus; it's appealingly simple, full of flavour and very satisfying.

→ Roast bone marrow with parsley salad. Grilled ox heart with beetroot, red cabbage and pickled walnut. Ginger loaf with butterscotch sauce.

Comptoir Gascon

61-63 Charterhouse St. ✉ EC1M 6HJ – Ⓜ Farringdon — Plan: K2
– ✆ (020) 7608 0851 – www.comptoirgascon.com
– Closed Christmas-New Year, Saturday lunch, Sunday, Monday and bank holidays
Carte £ 18/34 – *(booking essential)*

• French • Bistro • Rustic •

A buzzy, well-priced restaurant; sister to Club Gascon. Rustic and satisfying specialities from the SW of France include wine, bread, cheese and plenty of duck, with cassoulet and duck rillettes perennial favourites and the duck burger popular at lunch. There's also produce on display to take home.

Luca

88 St. John St ✉ EC1M 4EH – Ⓜ Farringdon — Plan: L1
– ✆ (020) 3859 3000 – www.luca.restaurant
– Closed Sunday
Menu £ 19 (lunch and early dinner) – Carte £ 35/79 – *(booking essential)*

• Italian • Design • Fashionable •

Owned by the people behind The Clove Club, but less a little sister, more a distant cousin. There's a cheery atmosphere, a bar for small plates and a frequently changing menu of Italian dishes made with quality British ingredients.

Foxlow

69-73 St John St ✉ EC1M 4AN – Ⓜ Farringdon — Plan: L2
– ✆ (020) 7680 2702 – www.foxlow.co.uk – Closed 24 December-1 January and bank holidays
Menu £ 18 (weekdays) – Carte £ 22/39

• Meats and grills • Neighbourhood •

From the clever Hawksmoor people comes this fun and funky place where the staff ensure everyone's having a good time. There are steaks available but plenty of other choices too, with influences from Italy, Asia and the Middle East.

Palatino

71 Central St ✉ EC1V 8AB – Ⓜ Old Street — Plan: L1
– ✆ (020) 3481 5300 – www.palatino.london
– Closed 23 December-3 January, Sunday and bank holidays
Menu £ 16 (lunch and early dinner) – Carte £ 16/38

• Italian • Design • Minimalist •

Stevie Parle's airy, canteen-like, all-day restaurant has an open kitchen, yellow booths and an industrial feel. The seasonal Italian menu has a strong emphasis on Rome, with dishes like rigatoni with veal pajata.

Finsbury

Angler – South Place Hotel

Plan: **M2**

3 South Pl ✉ EC2M 2AF – Ⓜ Moorgate – ✆ (020) 32151260 – www.anglerrestaurant.com – Closed 26-30 December, Saturday lunch and Sunday

Menu £ 34 (weekday lunch) – Carte £ 50/72

• Seafood • Elegant • Design •

As the name suggests, fish is the mainstay of the menu – mostly from Scotland and Cornwall. The kitchen has a light yet assured touch and understands that when fish is this good it doesn't need too much adornment. The ornate mirrored ceiling adds to the brightness of the room.

➜ Roast octopus with taramasalata, potatoes and red wine bagna càuda. Cod with garlic, morels and squid. Rhubarb, Brillat-Savarin cream and stem ginger ice cream.

Morito

Plan: **K1**

32 Exmouth Mkt ✉ EC1R 4QE – Ⓜ Farringdon – ✆ (020) 72787007 – www.morito.co.uk – Closed 24 December-2 January

Carte £ 14/29

• Spanish • Tapas bar • Rustic •

From the owners of next door Moro comes this authentic and appealingly down to earth little tapas bar. Seven or eight dishes between two should suffice but over-ordering is easy and won't break the bank.

The Drunken Butler

Plan: **K1**

20 Rosebery Ave ✉ EC1R 4SX – Ⓜ Farringdon – ✆ (020) 7101 4020 – www.thedrunkenbutler.com – Closed 1 week August, Saturday lunch, Sunday and Monday

Menu £ 24/49 – *(booking essential)*

• French • Regional décor • Family •

The chef-owner's quiet enthusiasm pervades every aspect of this small but bright restaurant. The cooking is classical French at heart but also informed by his travels and Persian heritage; dishes provide plenty of colour, texture and flavour.

Nuala

Plan: **M1**

70-74 City Rd ✉ EC1Y 2BJ – Ⓜ Old Street – ✆ (020) 3904 0462 – www.nualalondon.com – Closed Christmas-New Year, Sunday and Monday

Menu £ 20 (lunch) – Carte £ 20/44

• Modern British • Rustic • Fashionable •

The infectiously enthusiastic Northern Irish chef-owner trained as a butcher and much of the produce comes from the family farm. The main ingredients are cooked over an open flame with a mix of oak, apple, birch, ash and beech. The open kitchen allows the aromas to whet the appetite.

Quality Chop House

Plan: **K1**

92-94 Farringdon Rd ✉ EC1R 3EA – Ⓜ Farringdon – ✆ (020) 7278 1452 – www.thequalitychophouse.com – Closed 24-31 December, Sunday dinner and bank holidays

Menu £ 25 (weekday lunch) – Carte £ 23/51 – *(booking essential)*

• Traditional British • Cosy • Bistro •

In the hands of owners who respect its history, this 'progressive working class caterer' does a fine job of championing gutsy British grub; game is best but steaks from the butcher next door are also worth ordering. The terrific little wine list has lots of gems. The Grade II listed room, with its trademark booths, has been an eating house since 1869.

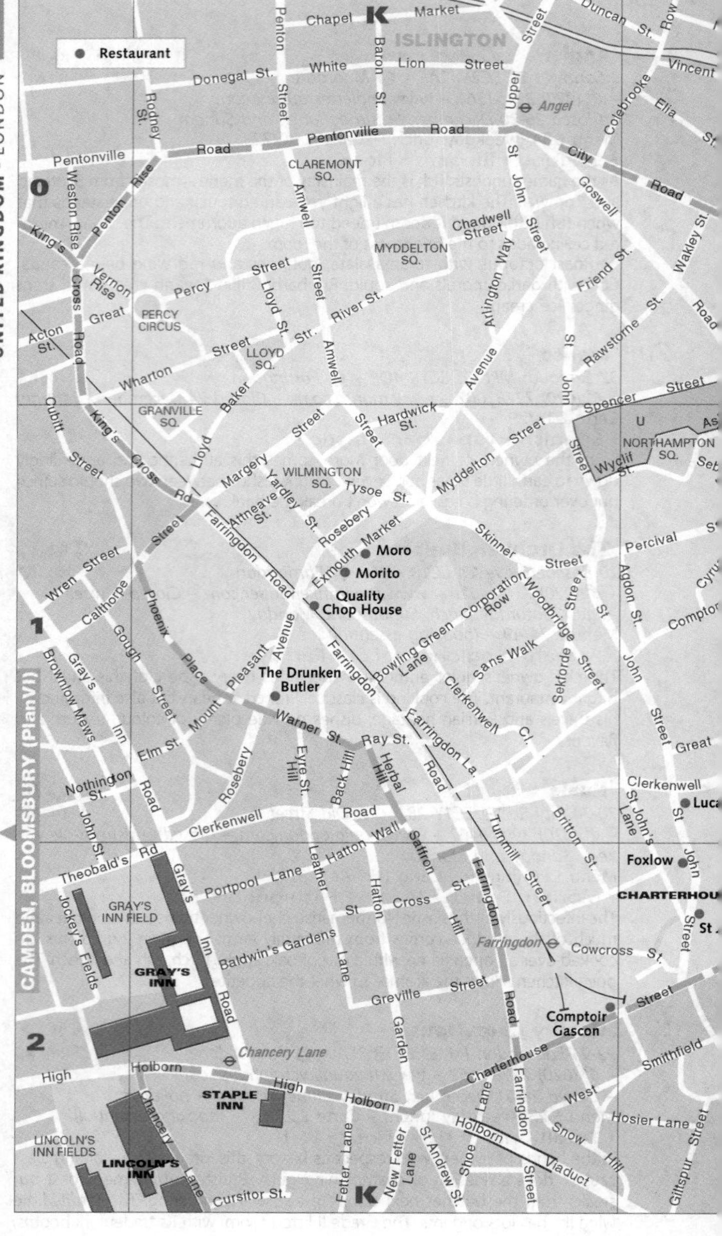
Restaurant
ISLINGTON
K
U
0
1
2
Angel
Farringdon
Chancery Lane
CLAREMONT SQ.
MYDDELTON SQ.
PERCY CIRCUS
LLOYD SQ.
GRANVILLE SQ.
WILMINGTON SQ.
NORTHAMPTON SQ.
GRAY'S INN FIELD
GRAY'S INN
STAPLE INN
LINCOLN'S INN FIELDS
LINCOLN'S INN
CHARTERHOU
Moro
Morito
Quality Chop House
The Drunken Butler
Luca
Foxlow
Comptoir Gascon
St .
CAMDEN, BLOOMSBURY (PlanVI)
Chapel Market
Donegal St.
White Lion Street
Penton Street
Baron St.
Upper Street
Duncan St.
Row
Vincent
Colebrooke
Elia St.
Pentonville Road
City Road
Goswell Road
Rodney St.
Pentonville Rise
Weston Rise
Penton Rise
King's Cross Road
Vernon Rise
Great Percy Street
Acton St.
Amwell Street
Chadwell Street
Arlington Way
St John Street
Friend St.
Wakley St.
Lloyd St.
River St.
Rawstorne St.
Lloyd Baker Street
Wharton Street
Cubitt Street
Hardwick St.
Spencer Street
Wyclif St.
Seb
Margery Street
Yardley St.
Attneave St.
Tysoe St.
Myddelton Street
Rosebery Avenue
Exmouth Market
Skinner Street
Percival St
Farringdon Road
Wren Street
Calthorpe
Phoenix Place
Gough Street
Corporation Row
Woodbridge Street
Agdon St.
Cyru
Compton
Gray's Inn Road
Brownlow Mews
Mount Pleasant
Bowling Green Lane
Sans Walk
Sekforde Street
Clerkenwell Cl.
Warner St.
Ray St.
Herbal Hill
Eyre St. Hill
Back Hill
Farringdon La.
Great Clerkenwell
Elm St.
Nothington St.
John St.
Clerkenwell Road
Britton St.
St John's Lane
Theobald's Rd
Saffron Hill
Hatton Wall
Leather Lane
Turnmill Street
Portpool Lane
Hatton Garden
Cross St
Jockey's Fields
Baldwin's Gardens
Cowcross St.
Greville Street
Charterhouse Street
Smithfield
High Holborn
West
Hosier Lane
Giltspur Street
Shoe Lane
Holborn Viaduct
Snow Hill
Chancery Lane
Fetter Lane
New Fetter Lane
St Andrew St.
Cursitor St.

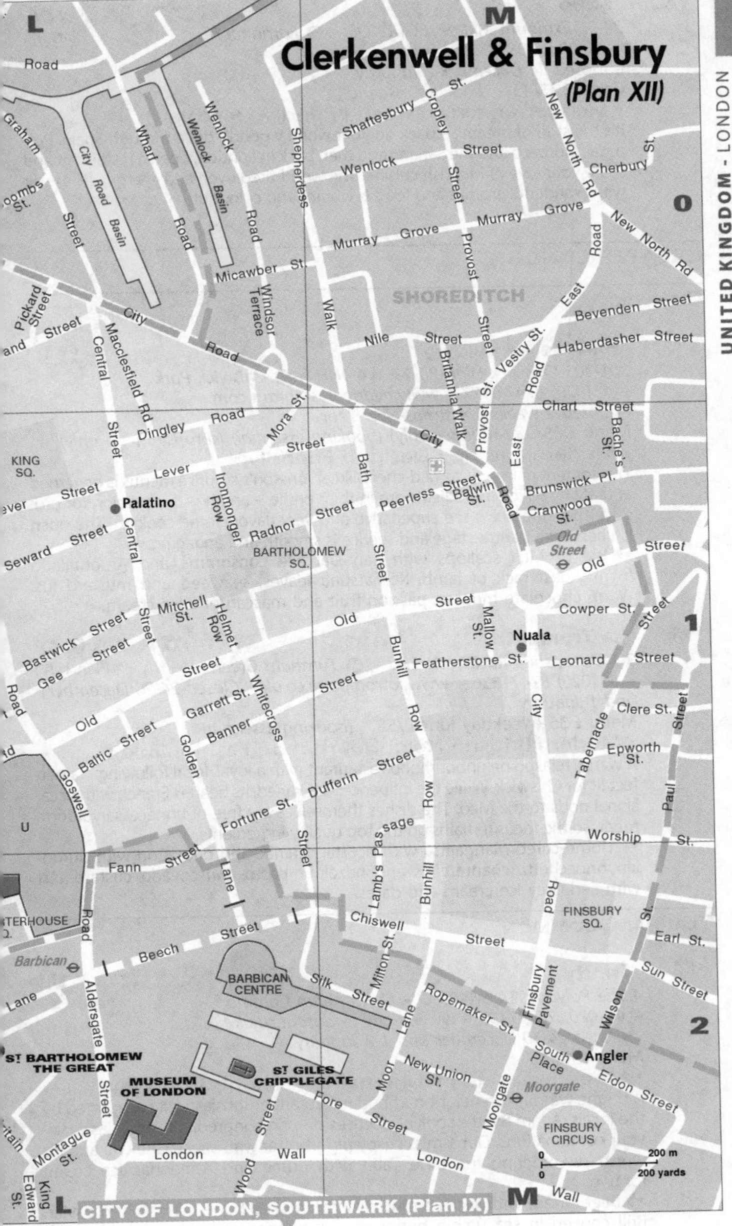
Clerkenwell & Finsbury
(Plan XII)
SHOREDITCH
KING SQ.
BARTHOLOMEW SQ.
FINSBURY SQ.
FINSBURY CIRCUS
BARBICAN CENTRE
MUSEUM OF LONDON
ST GILES CRIPPLEGATE
ST BARTHOLOMEW THE GREAT
Palatino
Nuala
Angler
Old Street
Barbican
Moorgate
City Road
Old Street
Goswell Road
Aldersgate Street
London Wall
Chiswell Street
Beech Street
Whitecross Street
Bunhill Row
Featherstone St.
Moorgate
Finsbury Pavement
Eldon Street
Ropemaker St.
Moor Lane
Fore Street
Wood Street
Silk Street
Golden Lane
Central Street
Wenlock Basin
City Road Basin
New North Rd
East Road
Provost Street
Shepherdess Walk
Murray Grove
Wenlock Street
Nile Street
Bath Street
Lever Street
Seward Street
Leonard Street
Tabernacle Street
Paul Street
Worship St.
Sun Street
Wilson St.
Earl St.
Fann Street
Fortune St.
Dufferin Street
Banner Street
Baltic Street
Garrett St.
Bastwick Street
Gee Street
Mitchell St.
Helmet Row
Radnor Street
Peerless Street
Ironmonger Row
Dingley Road
Macclesfield Rd
Mora St.
Micawber St.
Windsor Terrace
Wharf Road
Graham Street
Pickard Street
Haberdasher Street
Bevenden Street
Chart Street
Brunswick Pl.
Cranwood St.
Cowper St.
Mallow St.
Clere St.
Epworth St.
Lamb's Passage
Milton St.
New Union St.
South Place
Montague St.
King Edward St.
Lane
200 m
200 yards
L
M
O
1
2
U
CITY OF LONDON, SOUTHWARK (Plan IX)

Moro

34-36 Exmouth Mkt ✉ EC1R 4QE – Ⓜ Farringdon Plan: **K1**
– ✆ (020) 78338336 – www.moro.co.uk
– Closed 24 December-2 January
Carte £ 33/45 – *(booking essential)*
• Mediterranean cuisine • Friendly • Simple •
It's the stuff of dreams – pack up your worldly goods, drive through Spain, Portugal, Morocco and the Sahara, and then back in London, open a restaurant and share your love of Moorish cuisine. The wood-fired oven and chargrill fill the air with wonderful aromas and food is vibrant and colourful.

GREATER LONDON

Chiswick

Hedone (Mikael Jonsson)

301-303 Chiswick High Rd ✉ W4 4HH – Ⓜ Chiswick Park
– ✆ (020) 8747 0377 – www.hedonerestaurant.com
– Closed 2 weeks Christmas-New Year
Menu £ 65/95 – *(dinner only) (booking essential) (surprise menu only)*
• Modern cuisine • Design • Friendly •
The content of lawyer-turned-chef Mikael Jonsson's surprise menus is governed entirely by which ingredients are in their prime – and it is this passion for produce that underpins the superlative and very flavoursome cooking. The open kitchen takes centre-stage and service is smooth and engaging.
→ Isle of Mull scallops with San Danielle consommé and Amontillado foam. Roast rack of lamb, Komatsuna leaves, seaweed and mustard jus. Warm chocolate mousse, passion fruit and mascarpone ice cream.

La Trompette

3-7 Devonshire Rd ✉ W4 2EU – Ⓜ Turnham Green Plan I: **A3**
– ✆ (020) 87471836 – www.latrompette.co.uk – Closed 24-26 December and 1 January
Menu £ 35 (weekday lunch)/55 – *(booking essential)*
• Modern British • Neighbourhood • Fashionable •
A warm, relaxed neighbourhood restaurant with a loyal, local following – a perfect fit for Chiswick. While the influences are varied, its heart is French with occasional nods to the Med. The dishes themselves are free of unnecessary adornment, so the focus remains on the top quality ingredients.
→ Home-cured Mangalitsa with ricotta, celeriac and pear. Cod with pumpkin gnocchetti, chanterelles and hazelnut pesto. Muscovado custard tart with Earl Grey ice cream and dates.

Clapham Common

Trinity

4 The Polygon ✉ SW4 0JG – Ⓜ Clapham Common Plan I: **C3**
– ✆ (020) 76221199 – www.trinityrestaurant.co.uk
– Closed 24-30 December and 1-2 January
Menu £ 40/68
• Modern cuisine • Fashionable • Neighbourhood •
A bright, warmly run neighbourhood restaurant enthusiastically supported by the locals. Adam Byatt's cooking focuses on prime ingredients and classic flavour combinations. Don't miss crispy pig's trotter with sauce Gribiche and it's worth pre-ordering the tarte Tatin with prune and Armagnac ice cream for two.
→ Beef tartare with pickled mushrooms, smoked bone marrow and caviar. Brill cooked in sea urchin butter with asparagus and sauce Maltaise. Salt caramel custard tart with salt caramel ice cream.

Fulham

✿ Harwood Arms

Plan X: C7

Walham Grove ✉ SW6 1QP – Ⓜ Fulham Broadway. – ✆ (020) 73861847 – www.harwoodarms.com – Closed 24-26 December, lunch 27 December and 1 January and Monday lunch except bank holidays

Menu £ 33 (weekday lunch)/50 – *(booking essential)*

• Modern British • Pub • Neighbourhood •

Its reputation may have spread like wildfire but this remains a proper, down-to-earth pub that just happens to serve really good food. The cooking is very seasonal, proudly British, full of flavour and doesn't seem out of place in this environment. Service is suitably relaxed and friendly.

→ Wood pigeon and prune faggots with onion cream and thyme. Roast fallow deer with baked crapaudine beetroot, smoked bone marrow and walnut. Rhubarb and sherry trifle.

Hammersmith

✿ River Café (Ruth Rogers)

Plan I: A3

Thames Wharf, Rainville Rd ✉ W6 9HA – Ⓜ Barons Court – ✆ (020) 73864200 – www.rivercafe.co.uk – Closed Christmas-New Year and Sunday dinner

Carte £ 64/70 – *(booking essential)*

• Italian • Fashionable • Design •

It's more than 30 years since this iconic restaurant opened, and superlative ingredients are still at the centre of everything they do. Dishes come in hearty portions and are bursting with authentic Italian flavours. The on-view kitchen with its wood-fired oven dominates the stylish and buzzing riverside room.

→ Asparagus with anchovy butter and parmesan. Anjou pigeon with Allegrini Valpolicella and green beans 'in umido'. Nespole and almond tart.

Kew

✿ The Glasshouse

14 Station Par. ✉ TW9 3PZ – Ⓜ Kew Gardens – ✆ (020) 89406777 – www.glasshouserestaurant.co.uk – Closed 24-26 December, 1 January, Sunday dinner and Monday except bank holidays

Menu £ 38/58

• Modern cuisine • Fashionable • Neighbourhood •

2019 sees the 20th birthday of this very model of a modern neighbourhood restaurant. The quirkily-shaped room comes with textured walls and vibrant artwork and, as the name implies, it's a bright spot. The unfussy, natural style of cooking focuses on seasonal flavours that complement one another.

→ Salmon sashimi, with pickled rhubarb, ginger and white soy. Venison haunch and pie with smoked creamed potato, rainbow chard and pickled walnuts. Chocolate and hazelnut pavé with milk ice cream.

Shoreditch

✿ Brat (Tomos Parry)

Plan IX : N1

4 Redchurch St (1st Floor) ✉ E1 6JL – Ⓜ Shoreditch High Street – www.bratrestaurant.com – Closed 24-26 December, Easter, Sunday dinner and Monday

Carte £ 23/40 – *(booking essential)*

• Traditional British • Neighbourhood • Fashionable •

In this room on the first floor of a pub, it's all about cooking over fire – the stove, grill and oven were all hand-built to chef-owner Tomos Parry's own specification. Whole turbot, grilled in a handmade basket over lump wood charcoal, is a speciality but there are plenty of other dishes to enjoy, some inspired by his Welsh heritage.

→ Soused red mullet. Herdwick lamb. Burnt cheesecake with rhubarb.

The Clove Club (Isaac McHale) Plan I: **D2**

380 Old St ✉ EC1V 9LT – Ⓜ Old Street – ✆ (020) 77296496 – www.thecloveclub.com – Closed 2 weeks Christmas-New Year, August bank holiday, Monday lunch and Sunday

Menu £ 75/110 – *(booking essential)*

• Modern cuisine • Trendy •

The smart, blue-tiled open kitchen takes centre stage in this sparse room at Shoreditch Town Hall. Menus showcase expertly sourced produce in dishes that are full of originality, verve and flair – but where flavours are expertly judged and complementary; seafood is a highlight.

➜ Hot-smoked wild Irish trout with almond milk sauce and Oscietra caviar. Aylesbury duck with red cabbage, blackcurrant purée and beetroot. Loquat sorbet, loquat kernel mousse, amaranth and popcorn.

Leroy (Sam Kamienko) Plan IX : **M1**

18 Phipp St ✉ EC2A 4NU – Ⓜ Old Street – ✆ (020) 7739 4443 – www.leroyshoreditch.com – Closed 24-30 December, Monday lunch and Sunday

Menu £ 20 (weekday lunch) – Carte £ 29/48

• Modern British • Neighbourhood • Design •

How can you not fall for a place where the first thing you see is a couple of shelves of vinyl? Putting all their experience to bear, the owners have created a restaurant with a relaxed, easy vibe and great food. The core ingredient shines through in every unshowy dish; there's little division between starters and main courses – just order a few dishes to share.

➜ Peas, lardo, mint and slow-cooked egg yolk. Brill, beurre blanc, borage and sorrel. Sauternes crème caramel.

Lyle's (James Lowe) Plan IX : **N1**

Tea Building, 56 Shoreditch High St ✉ E1 6JJ – Ⓜ Shoreditch High Street – ✆ (020) 30115911 – www.lyleslondon.com – Closed Sunday and bank holidays

Menu £ 59 (dinner) – Carte lunch £ 34/48

• Modern British • Simple •

The young chef-owner is an acolyte of Fergus Henderson and delivers similarly unadulterated flavours from seasonal British produce, albeit from a set menu at dinner. This pared-down approach extends to a room that's high on functionality, but considerable warmth comes from the keen young service team.

➜ Peas with Ticklemore cheese. Dexter rib, broccoli leaf and anchovy. Caramel ice cream with espresso meringue.

Spitalfields

Galvin La Chapelle (Jeff Galvin) Plan IX : **N2**

35 Spital Sq ✉ E1 6DY – Ⓜ Liverpool Street – ✆ (020) 7299 0400 – www.galvinrestaurants.com – Closed 25-26 December and 1 January

Menu £ 34 (lunch and early dinner) – Carte £ 53/78

• French • Elegant •

With its vaulted ceiling, arched windows and marble pillars, this restaurant remains as impressive now as when it first opened nearly a decade ago. Service is professional and the atmosphere, relaxed and unstuffy. Cooking is assured, with a classical French foundation and a sophisticated modern edge.

➜ Lasagne of Dorset crab with beurre Nantais & pea shoots. Roast loin and slow-cooked venison with butternut, chestnuts and sauce grand veneur. Banoffee cheesecake with chocolate ice cream.

Wandsworth

Chez Bruce (Bruce Poole)

2 Bellevue Rd ✉ SW17 7EG – Ⓜ Tooting Bec – ✆ (020) 86720114 – www.chezbruce.co.uk – Closed 24-26 December and 1 January
Menu £ 38/58 – *(booking essential)*

• French • Brasserie • Neighbourhood •

The longevity of this neighbourhood restaurant is no accident. Cooking techniques are kept unapologetically traditional; the base is largely classical French but with a pronounced Mediterranean influence and the food is all about flavour and balance. The atmosphere is clubby and the service sprightly.

➜ Grilled tuna with lemon dressing, aioli and aubergine. Pig's cheek and pork belly with boudin noir, celeriac and mustard. Buttermilk pudding with rhubarb, lemon and pistachio.

EDINBURGH

EDINBURGH

walencienne/iStock

EDINBURGH IN...

→ **ONE DAY**
Calton Hill, Royal Mile, Edinburgh Castle, New Town café, Old Town pub.

→ **TWO DAYS**
Water of Leith, Scottish National Gallery of Modern Art, Leith.

→ **THREE DAYS**
Arthur's Seat, National Museum of Scotland, Holyrood Park, Pentland Hills.

The beautiful Scottish capital is laid out on seven, formerly volcanic, hills – a contrast to the modern city, which is elegant, cool and sophisticated. It's essentially two cities in one: the medieval Old Town, huddled around and beneath the crags and battlements of the castle, and the smart Georgian terraces of the New Town, overseen by the 18C architect Robert Adam. You could also say there's now a third element to the equation: the revamped port of Leith, just two miles away.

This is a city that's been attracting tourists since the 19C; and since 1999 it's been the home of the Scottish Parliament, adding

a new dimension to its worldwide reputation. It accepts its plaudits with the same ease that it accepts an extra half million visitors at the height of summer, and its status as a UNESCO World Heritage site confirms it as a city that knows how to be both ancient and modern. In the middle is the castle, to the south is the Old Town and to the north is the New Town. There's a natural boundary to the north at the Firth of Forth, while to the south lie the rolling Pentland Hills. Unless you've had a few too many drams, it's just about impossible to get lost here, as prominent landmarks like the Castle, Arthur's Seat and Calton Hill access all areas. Bisecting the town is Princes Street, one side of which invites you to shop, the other, to sit and relax in your own space.

EATING OUT

Edinburgh enjoys a varied and interesting restaurant culture so, whatever the occasion, you should find somewhere that fits the bill. The city is said to have more restaurants per head than anywhere in the UK and they vary from lavish establishments in grand hotels to cosy little bistros; you can dine with ghosts in a basement eatery or admire the city from a rooftop table. Scotland's great larder provides much of the produce, and cooking styles range from the innovative and contemporary to the simple and traditional. There are also some good pubs to explore in the old town, and drinking dens also abound in Cowgate and Grassmarket. Further away, in West End, you'll find enticing late-night bars, while the stylish variety, serving cocktails, are more in order in the George Street area of the new town. If you'd rather drink something a little more special then try the 19C Cadenhead's on the Royal Mile – it's the place to go for whiskies and it sells a mindboggling range of rare distillations. The peaty flavoured Laphroaig is a highly recommended dram.

Number One – Balmoral Hotel

1 Princes St ✉ EH2 2EQ – ☎ (0131) 5576727 Plan: **G2**
– www.roccofortehotels.com – Closed first 2 weeks January
Menu £ 80 – *(dinner only)*

• Modern cuisine • Intimate • Elegant •

A stylish, long-standing restaurant with a chic cocktail bar, set in the basement of a grand hotel. Richly upholstered banquettes and red lacquered walls give it a plush, luxurious feel. Cooking is modern and intricate and prime Scottish ingredients are key. Service is professional and has personality.

→ Hand-dived scallop, 'Cullen Skink' with smoked haddock and baby leeks. Guinea fowl with coco bean cassoulet, hispi cabbage and girolles. Raspberry soufflé, with white chocolate and crème fraîche ice cream.

21212 (Paul Kitching)

3 Royal Terr ✉ EH7 5AB – ☎ (0345) 222 1212 Plan: **H1**
– www.21212restaurant.co.uk – Closed 10 days January, 10 days September, Sunday and Monday
Menu £ 28/85 – *(booking essential)*

• Creative • Elegant • Design •

Stunningly refurbished Georgian townhouse designed by William Playfair. The glass-fronted kitchen is the focal point of the stylish, high-ceilinged dining room. Cooking is skilful and innovative and features quirky combinations; '21212' reflects the number of dishes per course at lunch – at dinner it's '31313'. Some of the luxurious bedrooms overlook the Firth of Forth.

→ Haggis risotto with caramelised onion and aubergine sauce. Chicken with fig, black garlic and smoked cheese. Chocolate & rhubarb.

Galvin Brasserie De Luxe – Waldorf Astoria Edinburgh The Caledonian Hotel

Princes St ✉ EH1 2AB – ☎ (0131) 222 8988 Plan: **F2**
– www.galvinrestaurants.com
Menu £ 25 (lunch and early dinner) – Carte £ 30/46

• French • Brasserie • Chic •

It's accurately described by its name: a simply styled restaurant which looks like a brasserie of old, but with the addition of a smart shellfish counter and formal service. There's an appealing à la carte and a good value two-choice daily set selection; dishes are refined, flavoursome and of a good size.

The Scran & Scallie

1 Comely Bank Rd, Stockbridge ✉ EH4 1DT – ☎ (0131) 332 6281 – www.scranandscallie.com – Closed 25 December Plan: **E1**
Menu £ 18 (weekday lunch) – Carte £ 24/46

• Traditional British • Neighbourhood • Family •

The more casual venture from Tom Kitchin, located in a smart, village-like suburb. It has a wood-furnished bar and a dining room which blends rustic and contemporary décor. Extensive menus follow a 'Nature to Plate' philosophy and focus on the classical and the local.

The Pompadour by Galvin – Waldorf Astoria Edinburgh The Caledonian Hotel

Princes St ✉ EH1 2AB – ☎ (0131) 222 8975 Plan: **F2**
– www.galvinrestaurants.com –
Closed 1-15 January, Monday and Tuesday
Menu £ 35 (early dinner)/65 – *(dinner only and Sunday lunch)*

• French • Elegant • Intimate •

A grand hotel restaurant which opened in the 1920s and is modelled on a French salon. Classic Gallic dishes showcase Scottish produce, using techniques introduced by Escoffier, and are executed with a lightness of touch.

Angels with Bagpipes

343 High St, Royal Mile ✉ EH1 1PW – ✆ (0131) 220 1111 – www.angelswithbagpipes.co.uk – Closed 6-22 January and 24-27 December Plan: **G2**

Menu £ 18 (lunch) – Carte £ 34/56

• Modern cuisine • Bistro • Design •

Small, stylish restaurant named after the wooden sculpture in St Giles Cathedral, opposite. Dishes are more elaborate than the menu implies; modern interpretations of Scottish classics could include 'haggis, neeps and tattiesgine'.

Castle Terrace

33-35 Castle Terr ✉ EH1 2EL – ✆ (0131) 2291222 – www.castleterracerestaurant.com – Closed Christmas, New Year, 1 week April, 1 week July, 1 week October, Sunday and Monday Plan: **F2**

Menu £ 33 (lunch)/70

• Modern cuisine • Intimate • Elegant •

Set in the shadow of the castle is this bright, contemporary restaurant with hand-painted wallpapers and a mural depicting the Edinburgh skyline. Cooking is ambitious with a playful element and combines many different textures and flavours. The wine list also offers plenty of interest.

The Honours

58A North Castle St ✉ EH2 3LU – ✆ (0131) 220 2513 – www.thehonours.co.uk – Closed 25-26 December, 1-2 January, Sunday and Monday Plan: **F2**

Menu £ 23 (lunch and early dinner) – Carte £ 33/63

• Classic cuisine • Brasserie • Fashionable •

Bustling brasserie with a smart, stylish interior and a pleasingly informal atmosphere. Classical brasserie menus have French leanings but always offer some Scottish dishes too; meats cooked on the Josper grill are popular.

Ondine

2 George IV Bridge (1st floor) ✉ EH1 1AD – ✆ (0131) 2261888 – www.ondinerestaurant.co.uk – Closed 1 week early January and 24-26 December Plan: **G2**

Menu £ 19 (lunch and early dinner) – Carte £ 35/78

• Seafood • Brasserie • Elegant •

Smart, lively restaurant dominated by an impressive horseshoe bar and a crustacean counter. Classic menus showcase prime Scottish seafood in tasty, straightforward dishes which let the ingredients shine. Service is well-structured.

Timberyard

10 Lady Lawson St ✉ EH3 9DS – ✆ (0131) 221 1222 – www.timberyard.co – Closed 1-7 January,1 week April, 1 week October, Christmas, Sunday and Monday Plan: **F2**

Menu £ 25 (lunch and early dinner)/55 – *(booking essential at dinner)*

• Modern cuisine • Rustic • Simple •

Trendy warehouse restaurant; its spacious, rustic interior incorporating wood-burning stoves. The Scandic-influenced menu offers 'bites', 'small' and 'large' sizes, with some home-smoked ingredients and an emphasis on distinct, punchy flavours. Cocktails are made with vegetable purées and foraged herbs.

Aizle

107-109 St Leonard's St ✉ EH8 9QY – ✆ (0131) 662 9349 – www.aizle.co.uk – Closed 22 December-23 January, 7-23 July, Sunday except August and December, Monday and Tuesday Plan: **H3**

Menu £ 55 – *(dinner only) (tasting menu only)*

• Modern cuisine • Simple • Neighbourhood •

Modest little suburban restaurant whose name means 'ember' or 'spark'. Well-balanced, skilfully prepared dishes are, in effect, a surprise, as the set menu is presented as a long list of ingredients – the latest 'harvest'.

Edinburgh Centre

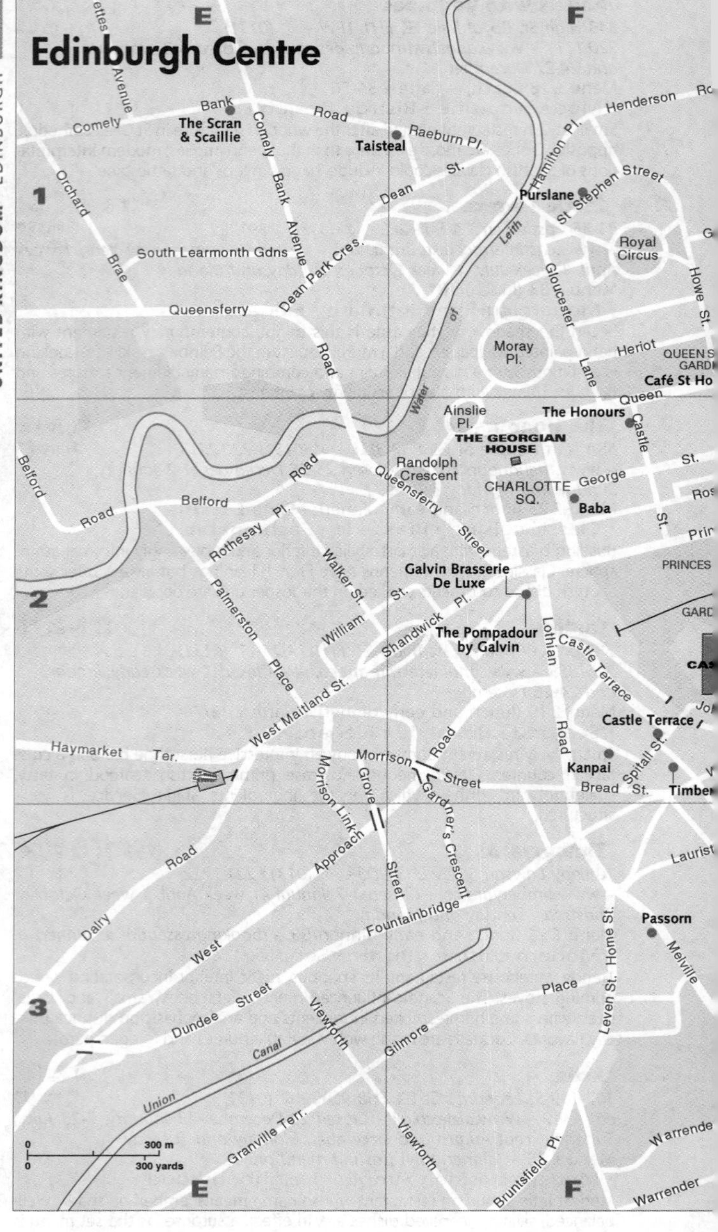

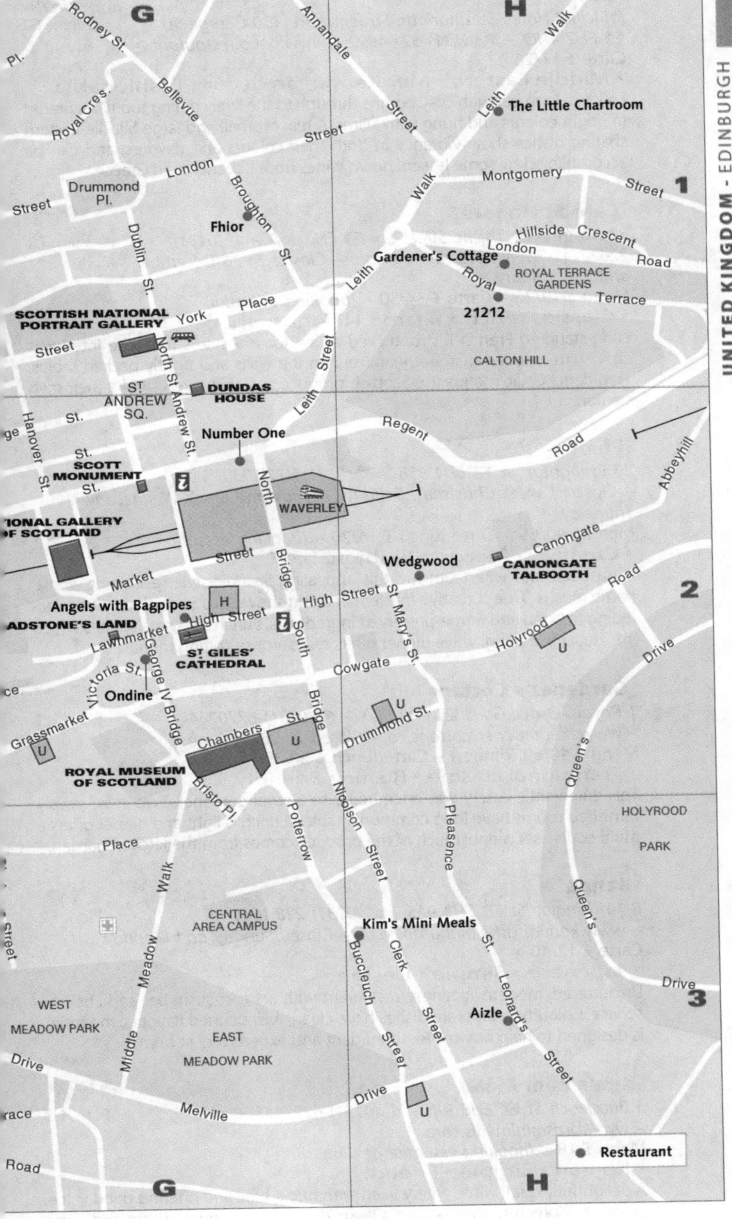
G
H
Rodney St.
Annandale Street
Leith Walk
The Little Chartroom
Royal Cres.
Bellevue
London Street
Montgomery Street
Drummond Pl.
Broughton St.
Fhior
Dublin St.
Hillside Crescent
London Road
Gardener's Cottage
Royal Terrace
ROYAL TERRACE GARDENS
21212
SCOTTISH NATIONAL PORTRAIT GALLERY
York Place
Leith Street
CALTON HILL
DUNDAS HOUSE
ST ANDREW SQ.
North St Andrew St.
Hanover St.
Number One
Regent Road
SCOTT MONUMENT
North Bridge
WAVERLEY
Abbeyhill
NATIONAL GALLERY OF SCOTLAND
Market Street
Wedgwood
Canongate
CANONGATE TALBOOTH
High Street
Angels with Bagpipes
GLADSTONE'S LAND
Lawnmarket
ST GILES' CATHEDRAL
South Bridge
St Mary's St.
Holyrood Road
Cowgate
Victoria St.
George IV Bridge
Ondine
Grassmarket
Chambers St.
Drummond St.
Queen's Drive
ROYAL MUSEUM OF SCOTLAND
Bristo Pl.
Potterrow
Nicolson Street
Pleasence
HOLYROOD PARK
Place
Walk
CENTRAL AREA CAMPUS
Kim's Mini Meals
Buccleuch Street
Clerk Street
St. Leonard's Street
Aizle
WEST MEADOW PARK
Middle Meadow Walk
EAST MEADOW PARK
Drive
Melville Drive
Road
Restaurant
1
2
3

Baba

Principal Hotel, 38 Charlotte Sq (entrance 130 George St) — Plan: F2
EH2 4HQ – (0131) 527 4999 – www.baba.restaurant
Carte £ 17/26

• Middle Eastern • Mediterranean décor • Fashionable •

Follow a long bar with cosy booths through to the lively dining room decorated in bright colours and hung with kilims. A mix of small and large Middle-Eastern sharing dishes show vibrancy in both their colours and flavours, and can be accompanied by some lesser-known wines from Lebanon and Greece.

Café St Honoré

34 North West Thistle Street Ln. EH2 1EA – (0131) 2262211 – www.cafesthonore.com – Closed 24-26 December and 1-2 January — Plan: F1
Menu £ 19/26 – Carte £ 34/50 – *(booking essential)*

• Classic French • Bistro • Neighbourhood •

Long-standing French bistro, tucked away down a side street. The interior is cosy, with wooden marquetry, mirrors on the walls and tightly packed tables. Traditional Gallic menus use Scottish produce and they even smoke their own salmon.

Fhior

36 Broughton St EH1 3SB – (0131) 477 5000 – Closed 1 week Christmas, Sunday-Tuesday and lunch Wednesday-Thursday — Plan: G1
Menu £ 40/65 – Carte lunch £ 14/20 – *(booking essential)*

• Creative • Design • Fashionable •

A husband and wife team run this appealing Scandic-style restaurant whose name means 'True'. Creative modern cooking showcases Scottish produce, including foraged and home-preserved ingredients. Lunch sees small plates which are ideal for sharing, while dinner offers two surprise tasting menus.

Gardener's Cottage

1 Royal Terrace Gdns EH7 5DX – (0131) 6770244 – www.thegardenerscottage.co – Closed 25-26 December — Plan: H1
Menu £ 40/60 (dinner) – Carte lunch £ 20/39

• Traditional cuisine • Rustic • Friendly •

This quirky little eatery was once home to a royal gardener. Two cosy, simply furnished rooms have long communal tables. Lunch is light and dinner offers a multi-course set menu; much of the produce comes from the kitchen garden.

Kanpai

8-10 Grindlay St EH3 9AS – (0131) 228 1602 – www.kanpaisushiedinburgh.co.uk – Closed Sunday and Monday — Plan: F2
Carte £ 12/40

• Japanese • Simple • Design •

Uncluttered, modern Japanese restaurant with a smart sushi bar and cheerful service. Colourful, elaborate dishes have clean, well-defined flavours; the menu is designed to help novices feel confident and experts feel at home.

Kim's Mini Meals

5 Buccleuch St EH8 9JN – (0131) 6297951 – www.kimsminimeals.com — Plan: H3
Menu £ 18 – *(booking essential at dinner)*

• Korean • Simple • Friendly •

A delightfully quirky little eatery filled with bric-a-brac and offering good value, authentic Korean home cooking. Classic dishes like bulgogi, dolsot and jjigae come with your choice of meat or vegetables as the main ingredient.

The Little Chartroom

Plan: **H1**

30-31 Albert Pl ✉ EH7 5HN
– ✆ (0131) 556 6600
– www.thelittlechartroom.com
– Closed first 2 weeks January, 1 week March, 1 week June, 1 week October, Monday and Tuesday
Carte £ 20/37 – *(booking essential)*

• Modern British • Simple • Bistro •

There's a lively buzz to this laid-back little restaurant on Leith Walk, which is run by an experienced young couple and filled with nautical charts. Cooking is fresh and flavoursome. Simple small plates and sharing dishes are followed by a modern menu with a Scottish edge; at weekends they serve brunch.

Passorn

Plan: **F3**

23-23a Brougham Pl ✉ EH3 9JU
– ✆ (0131) 229 1537 – www.passornthai.com
– Closed 25-26 December, 1-2 January, Sunday and lunch Monday
Menu £ 16 (lunch and early dinner) – Carte £ 23/38 –
(booking essential)

• Thai • Friendly • Neighbourhood •

The staff are super-friendly at this popular neighbourhood restaurant whose name means 'Angel'. Authentic menus feature Thai classics and old family recipes; the seafood dishes are a highlight and everything is attractively presented. Spices and other ingredients are flown in from Thailand.

Purslane

Plan: **F1**

33a St Stephen St ✉ EH3 5AH
– ✆ (0131) 226 3500 – www.purslanerestaurant.co.uk
– Closed 25-26 December, 1 January and Monday
Menu £ 15/35 – *(booking essential)*

• Modern cuisine • Neighbourhood • Rustic •

A cosy, atmospheric basement restaurant made up of just 9 tables. The young chef-owner creates ambitious modern dishes which mix tried-and-tested flavours with modern techniques. Lunch is particularly good value.

Taisteal

Plan: **F1**

1-3 Raeburn Pl, Stockbridge ✉ EH4 1HU
– ✆ (0131) 332 9977 – www.taisteal.co.uk
– Closed first 2 weeks September, 1 week January, Sunday and Monday
Menu £ 16 (lunch and early dinner) – Carte £ 27/39

• Modern British • Neighbourhood • Friendly •

Taisteal is Irish Gaelic for 'journey' and is the perfect name: photos from the chef's travels line the walls and dishes have global influences, with Asian flavours to the fore. The wine list even has a sake section.

Wedgwood

Plan: **H2**

267 Canongate ✉ EH8 8BQ
– ✆ (0131) 5588737 – www.wedgwoodtherestaurant.co.uk
– Closed 1-24 January and 25-26 December
Menu £ 20 (lunch) – Carte dinner £ 36/52

• Modern cuisine • Friendly • Intimate •

Atmospheric bistro hidden away at the bottom of the Royal Mile. Well-presented dishes showcase produce foraged from the surrounding countryside and feature some original, modern combinations. It's personally run by a friendly team.

Martin Wishart

54 The Shore (via Bernard St) ✉ EH6 6RA – ✆ (0131) 5533557 – www.martin-wishart.co.uk – Closed one week July, 25-26 December, 2 weeks in January, Sunday and Monday
Menu £ 32 (weekday lunch)/95 – *(booking essential)*
• Modern cuisine • Elegant • Intimate •

This elegant, modern restaurant is becoming something of an Edinburgh institution. Choose between three 6 course menus – Classic, Seafood and Vegetarian – and a concise à la carte. Top ingredients are used in well-judged, flavourful combinations; dishes are classically based but have elaborate, original touches.

➜ Scallop, Jerusalem artichoke, hazelnut and truffle pesto. Wild sea bass, cauliflower and shrimp gratin, caviar and champagne velouté. Buttermilk mousse, fennel sorbet and sorrel parfait.

Kitchin (Tom Kitchin)

78 Commercial Quay (via Bernard St and Commercial St) ✉ EH6 6LX – ✆ (0131) 5551755 – www.thekitchin.com – Closed 25 December-14 January, 2-6 April, 16-20 August, 15-19 October, Sunday and Monday
Menu £ 33 (lunch)/75 – *(booking essential)*
• Modern cuisine • Design • Fashionable •

A smartly converted whisky warehouse provides the perfect setting for this patriotic restaurant, where the windswept highlands are brought indoors courtesy of tartan tweed, tree bark, whisky barrels and dry stone walls. Menus mix boldly flavoured classics with fresh modern dishes. Each ingredient has a purpose and is allowed to shine; vegetables are the chef's passion.

➜ Seafood with sea vegetables, ginger and shellfish consommé. Roasted loin and braised haunch of roe deer with root vegetable mash and a red wine sauce. Warm apple tart, vanilla ice cream and calvados sauce.

Daniel Tomlinson/iStock

662

Europe in maps and numbers

Eurozone : €

 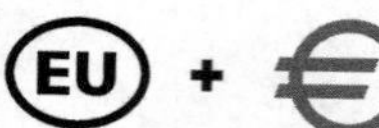

 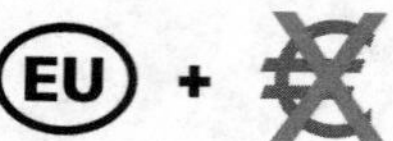

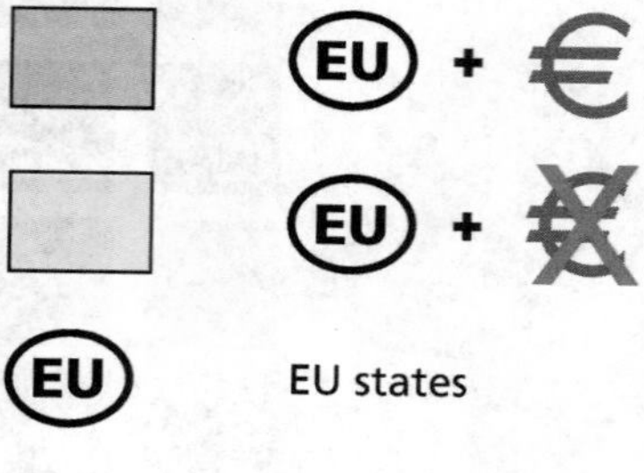

EU states

Schengen Countries

Area of free movement between member states

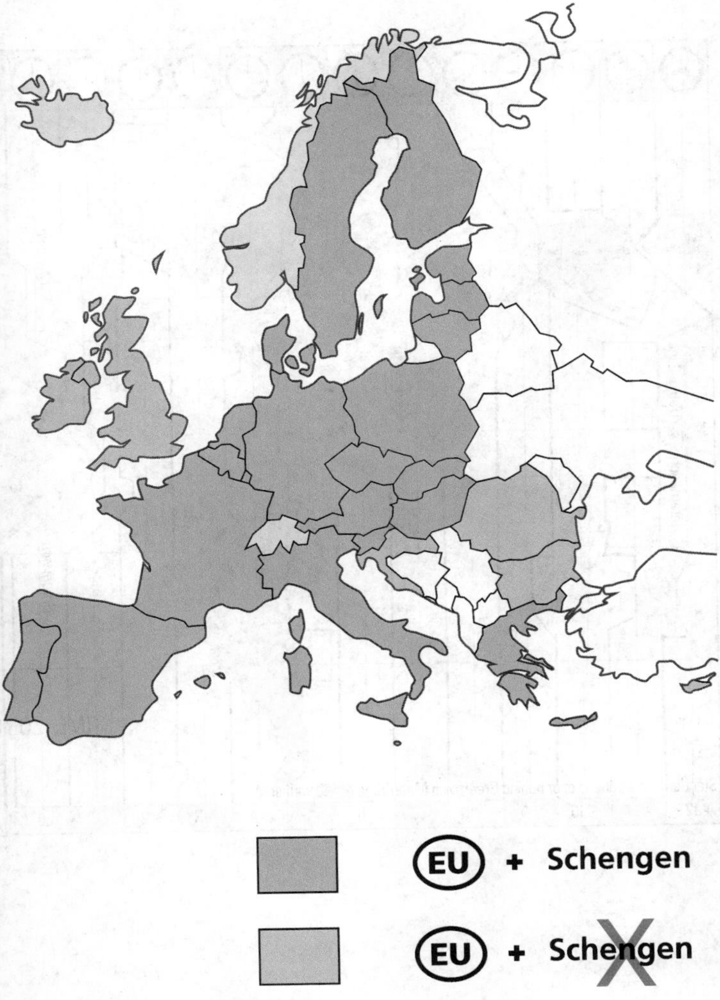

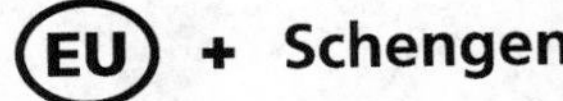

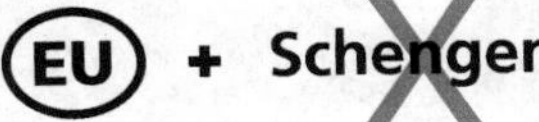

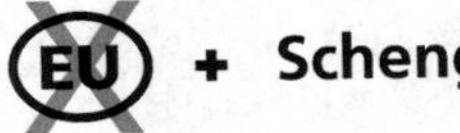

Time zones

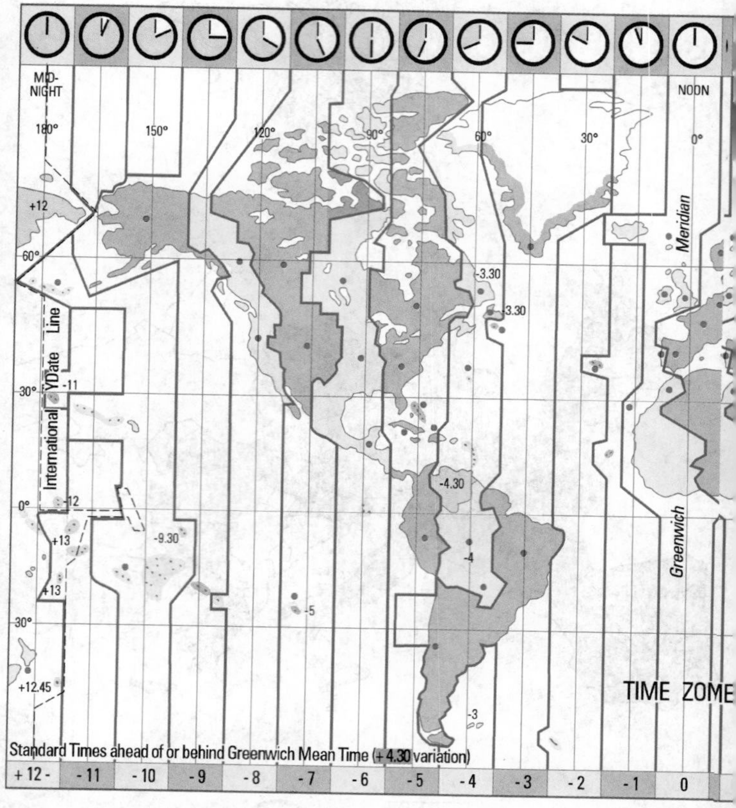

MID-
NIGHT
NOON
180°
150°
120°
90°
60°
30°
0°
+12
60°
30°
0°
30°
International Date Line
-11
-12
+13
+13
+12.45
-9.30
-5
-3.30
-3.30
-4.30
-4
-3
Meridian
Greenwich
TIME ZONE
Standard Times ahead of or behind Greenwich Mean Time (+ 4.30 variation)
+ 12 -
- 11
- 10
- 9
- 8
- 7
- 6
- 5
- 4
- 3
- 2
- 1
0

Time zones

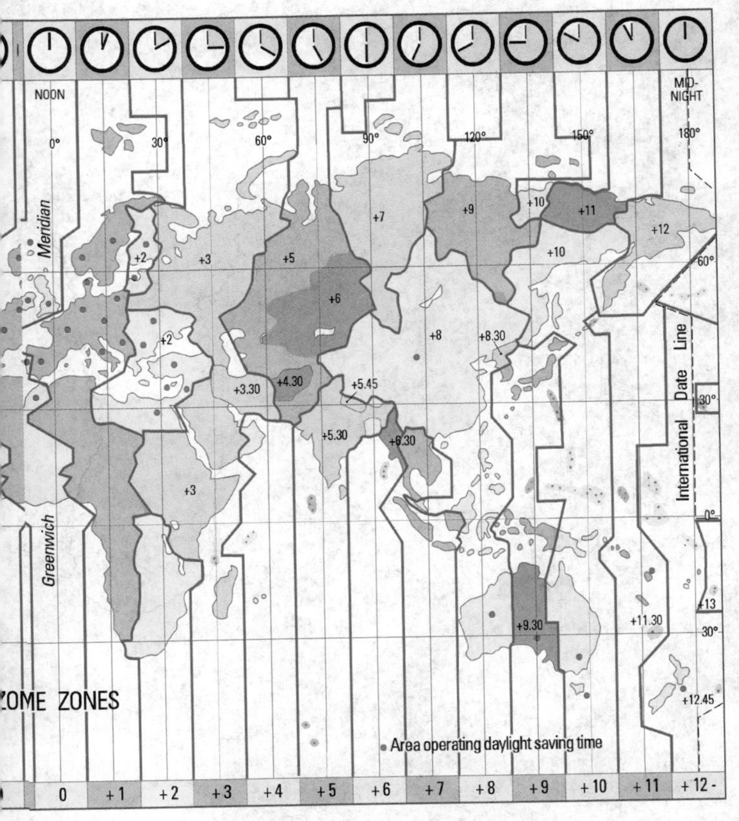

NOON
MID-
NIGHT
0°
30°
60°
90°
120°
150°
180°
Meridian
Greenwich
+2
+3
+5
+6
+7
+9
+10
+11
+12
+10
60°
+2
+8
+8.30
+3.30
+4.30
+5.45
+5.30
+6.30
+3
Line
Date
International
30°
0°
+13
+9.30
+11.30
30°
+12.45
ZOME ZONES
Area operating daylight saving time
0
+ 1
+ 2
+ 3
+ 4
+ 5
+ 6
+ 7
+ 8
+ 9
+ 10
+ 11
+ 12 -

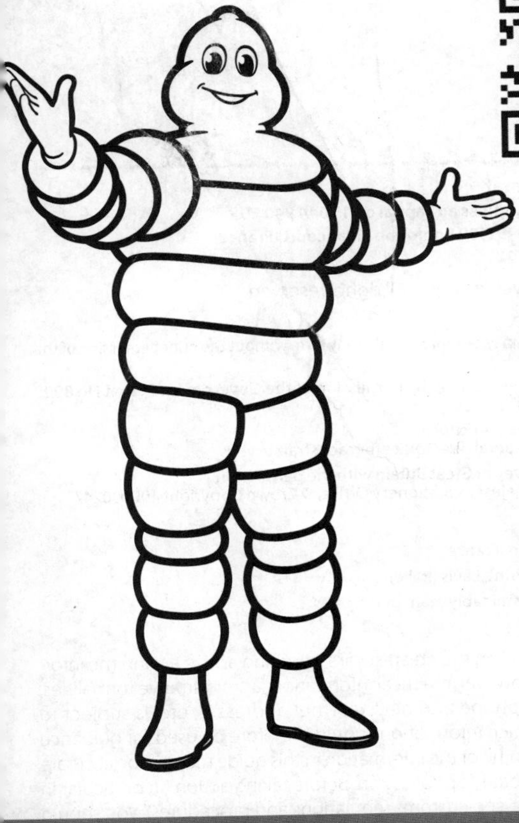

Michelin Travel Partner
Société par actions simplifiées au capital de 15 044 940 EUR
27 Cours de l'Île Seguin - 92100 Boulogne Billancourt (France)
R.C.S. Nanterre 433 677 721

Legal deposit: 02-2019

Printed in Italy: 02-2019

Typesetting: JOUVE, Saran (France)

Printing-binding: LEGO Print, Lavis (Italie)

Printed on paper from sustainably managed forests

Our editorial team has taken the greatest care in writing and checking the information in this guide. However, practical information (administrative formalities, prices, addresses, telephone numbers, Internet addresses, etc) is subject to frequent change and such information should therefore be used for guidance only. It is possible that some of the information in this guide may not be accurate or exhaustive as of the date of publication. Before taking action (in particular in regard to administrative and customs regulations and procedures), you should contact the appropriate official administration. We hereby accept no liability in regard to such information.